Dear Rio Salado College Student:

The high cost of college textbooks has long been an issue for students across the nation. Rio Salado College shares this concern. In an effort to control costs for our students, Rio Salado is pleased to announce an innovative solution: the Rio Salado Textbook Savings Program that reduces your up-front costs. Rio Salado students can now purchase new customized textbooks for their courses for a savings up to 50%. The result of this savings program is that the cost of a new textbook will be much less than the cost of most used books.

Rio Salado has partnered with Pearson Custom Publishing to produce its own streamlined versions of textbooks, starting with the Spring 2008 term–and the savings will be passed on to you. During the next three years, most textbooks used by the college will be revised and published under the Textbook Saving Program. In addition to lower out-of-pocket costs, you will benefit by learning from a textbook containing exactly the material Rio Salado's faculty have determined you need to master the course.

We know this price cut occurs just when you need it the most–at the start of your class.

Best wishes for this and all future Rio courses!

Dr. Linda M. Thor
President

HUM 250

ARTS AND CULTURE
An Introduction to the Humanities
Volume 1

Taken from:

Arts and Culture: An Introduction to the Humanities Volume One,
Third Edition
by Janetta Rebold Benton and Robert DiYanni

Custom Publishing

New York   Boston   San Francisco
London   Toronto   Sydney   Tokyo   Singapore   Madrid
Mexico City   Munich   Paris   Cape Town   Hong Kong   Montreal

Cover Art: Courtesy of PhotoDisc/Getty Images.

Taken from:

Arts and Culture: An Introduction to the Humanities Volume One, Third Edition
by Janetta Rebold Benton and Robert DiYanni
Copyright © 2008, 2005, 1998 by Pearson Education, Inc.
Published by Prentice Hall
Upper Saddle River, New Jersey 07458

Printed in the United States of America

10 9 8 7 6 5 4

2007420232

LR

**Pearson
Custom Publishing**
is a division of

www.pearsonhighered.com

ISBN 10: 0-536-08795-4
ISBN 13: 978-0-536-08795-9

CONTENTS OVERVIEW

CONTENTS

CHAPTER 6

Islamic Civilization   235

CHAPTER 7

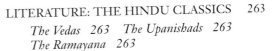

Indian Civilization   259

CHAPTER 12

Gothic and Late Middle Ages   405

CHAPTER 13

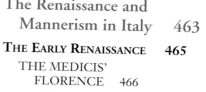

The Renaissance and Mannerism in Italy   463

As in our first two editions of *Arts and Culture*, we provide in this Third Edition an introduction to the world's major civilizations—to their artistic achievements, their history, and their cultures. Through an integrated approach to the humanities, *Arts and Culture* offers an opportunity to view works of art, read literature, and listen to music in historical and cultural contexts.

Works of art from different cultures reveal common human experiences of birth and death, love and loss, pleasure and pain, hope and frustration, elation and despair. Study of the humanities—literature, philosophy, history, religion, and the arts—reveals what others value and believe, inviting each of us to consider our personal, social, and cultural values in relation to those of others.

In studying the humanities, we focus our attention on works of art that reflect and embody the central values and beliefs of particular cultures and specific historical moments. In our approach we consider the following questions:

1. *What kind of artwork is it? To what artistic category does it belong?* These questions lead us to consider a work's type.

2. *Why was the artwork made? What was its function, purpose, or use? Who was responsible for producing it? Who paid for or commissioned it?* These questions lead us to consider the context of a work.

3. *What does the work express or convey? What does it reveal about its creator? What does it reveal about its historical and social context?* These questions lead us to considerations of a work's meaning.

4. *How was the artwork made or constructed?* This question leads us to consider materials and techniques.

5. *What are the parts or elements of a work of art? How are these parts related to create a unified artwork?* These questions lead us to considerations of formal analysis, understanding the ways the artwork satisfies aesthetically.

6. *What social, cultural, and moral values does the work express, reflect, or embody?* This question leads us to consider the social, cultural, and moral values of an artwork.

In *Arts and Culture*, we highlight the individual artistic qualities of numerous works, always in view of the cultural worlds in which they were created. We discuss each work's significance in conjunction with the social attitudes and cultural values it embodies, without losing sight of its individual expression and artistic achievement.

Two important questions underlie our choice of works in *Arts and Culture*: (1) What makes a work a masterpiece of its type? (2) What qualities of a work of art enable it to be appreciated over time? These questions imply that certain qualities appeal to something fundamental and universal in all of us, no matter where or when we may live. These are the aesthetic principles and predilections that link all of us together.

MAKING CONNECTIONS

We believe that a study of the humanities involves more than an examination of the artistic monuments of civilizations past and present. In our view, it also involves a consideration of how forms of human achievement in many times and places echo and reinforce, as well as alter and modify each other. An important aspect of humanities study involves seeing connections among the arts and ideas of a given culture and discovering relationships between the arts and ideas of different cultures. We have highlighted three forms of connections that are especially important:

1. *Interdisciplinary connections* among artworks of an individual culture
2. *Cross currents* among artworks of different cultures
3. Transhistorical links between past and present, *then and now*
4. The *cultural impact* or influence of one culture on later cultures

These forms of connection invite our readers to locate relationships among various humanities disciplines and to identify links between the achievements of diverse cultures. Discovering such connections can be intellectually stimulating and emotionally stirring since the forms of human experience reflected in the works of art of many cultures resonate with common human concerns. These artworks address social questions about who we are, philosophical questions about why we exist at all, and religious questions concerning what awaits us after death. These and other perennial questions and the varying perspectives taken on them have been central to many cultures, and find expression in their arts. To highlight these questions, we have included the following features throughout the text.

INTERDISCIPLINARY CONNECTIONS

For example, one type of interdisciplinary connection appears in the ways the music and architecture of Renaissance Florence were influenced by mathematical proportion and ancient notions of "harmony." Mathematics played a crucial role in all the arts of the Renaissance. Architects were guided in the design of their buildings by mathematical ratios and proportions; composers likewise wrote music that reflected mathematical ratios in both its melody and harmony.

CULTURAL **CROSS CURRENTS**

These reflect the ways artistic ideals, literary movements, and historical events influence the arts of other cultures. For example, Turkish military music found its way into the symphonies and piano compositions of Viennese composers, such as Mozart and Beethoven. Japanese woodblock prints influenced the art of the Impressionist painter Claude Monet and the Post-Impressionist painter Vincent van Gogh. And the dynamic cybernetic sculpture of contemporary artist Wen-Ying Tsai weds Western technology with ancient Chinese aesthetic principles.

THEN & NOW

Also considered are connections between the past and present. *Then & Now* offers discussions of a wide range of subjects that form various types of historical bridges.

CULTURAL IMPACT

This feature appears at the end of the end of each chapter. It explains the influence of one culture or civilization on later ones, showing how the essential, broad themes explored in the chapter continue to impact today's world.

GLOBAL COVERAGE

Arts and Culture includes a wide-ranging overview of the world's civilizations. In addition to Western culture, we examine the civilizations of Africa, China, India, Japan, Latin America, and Mesoamerica. We emphasize the contributions of women, from the eleventh-century writings of the Japanese Murasaki Shikibu, the twelfth-century music of the German Hildegard of Bingen, and the fourteenth-century writings of the Italian Christine de Pizan, to the Renaissance painting of the Italian Properzia de'Rossi, or the Baroque still lives by the Flemish Clara Peeters, to the Rococo art of the French painter Marie-Louise-Elisabeth Vigée-Le Brun and the numerous women writers, painters, sculptors, architects, and photographers of the nineteenth and twentieth centuries from many parts of our world. In the final chapter of *Arts and Culture* we bring together a broad spectrum of styles, voices, and perspectives, which, although focusing on contemporary multicultural America, reflects trends and influences from around the globe. We highlight a number of current issues in the arts including how technology has globalized the arts. The numerous and varied contributions of artists and writers include works by Native American painters such as Lisa Fifield and Jaune Quick-to-See

Smith, Latina/Latino writers such as Sandra Cisneros and Oscar Hijuelos, and Australian Aborigine artists.

Throughout the book, we have tried to present the arts and cultures of the world to suggest their richness, variety, and humanity. As a reader of *Arts and Culture* you can find in these pages the background necessary to understand not only the artistic achievements of many civilizations but also the representation of human experience in all its complexity. In a time of rapid social change when the world's cultures are becoming increasingly globalized, it has become necessary to understand the values of human beings around the world. The common humanity we share has been recorded, inscribed, and celebrated in arts and achievements of all cultures.

LEARNING TOOLS FOR STUDENTS

Arts and Culture offers a number of learning tools for students. A helpful starter kit appears at the beginning of the book, giving readers a brief introduction to the study of the visual arts, literature, music, history, and philosophy. Each chapter begins with a full-page timeline and Chapter Overview to introduce the chapter's content. Maps and tables appear within each chapter to further illustrate and organize important information. Each chapter ends with a list of key terms as well as suggested websites for further study. A glossary appears at the end of the book; terms in the glossary are highlighted in boldface in the text.

BOOK FORMAT

For flexibility in teaching, *Arts and Culture* is available in three volumes: Volume I contains chapters 1-13, Volume II contains chapters 13-24, and the Combined Volume contains chapters 1-24. Chapter 13 on The Renaissance and Mannerism in Italy appears in both Volumes I and II, so instructors have the flexibility to cover the Renaissance while using either volume. Additionally, reading selections appear at the end of each chapter in Volumes I and II, but not in the Combined Volume; instructors preferring a single volume text without readings may select the Combined Volume.

NEW IN THE THIRD EDITION

In this Third Edition of *Arts and Culture*, we have preserved the book's key features but have made important adjustments and necessary corrections of fact and perspective throughout. We have also expanded and contracted various discussions to create a better balance among the arts and humanities and to improve the historical contexts. In doing so, we have added many new photographs to accompany new discussions, in addition to replacing numerous photographs from the previous edition with images that better reflect the original artwork.

EXPANDED COVERAGE OF HUMANITIES FROM AROUND THE GLOBE

We have responded to requests to expand coverage of humanities from around the globe. Chapter 7 on Indian Civilization has been revised and expanded with new material. Former chapter 9 on Early Chinese and Japanese Civilizations has been expanded into two new chapters, Chapter 8 on Early Chinese Civilization and Chapter 9 on Early Japanese Civilization, each with extensive new material. Chapter 10 has been augmented with new material on early African civilization, along with coverage of the early Americas. In the second half of the book, we have revised our coverage of China and Japan, expanding the material in chapter 19 on Chinese Civilization and in chapter 20 on Japanese Civilization. Chapter 22 on Modern Africa and Latin America has also been revised and expanded with new material.

INCREASED FOCUS ON WOMEN ARTISTS

Twenty-four women painters, sculptors, and photographers, from the sixteenth to the twentieth century, active in various parts of the globe, have been added. The Third Edition of *Arts and Culture* places greater emphasis on the accomplishments of women than is found in any other book on global humanities.

CRITICAL THINKING

In addition to retaining the popular boxed features from the first two editions, we have added a new feature in each chapter. This Critical Thinking boxed feature invites students to do just that—think critically about an aspect of culture relevant to each chapter.

NEW TOPICS FOR CONNECTIONS, CROSS CURRENTS, AND THEN & NOW BOXES

We have updated several of the boxed features. New topics have been provided for all of the special boxed features: Then & Now, Connections, and Cross Currents.

NEW READINGS

Many of the reading selections at the end of each chapter in Volumes I and II are new. Some longer works have been scaled back to make space for a greater variety of selections.

NEW ORGANIZATION OF INFORMATION

Highlights of our new content include a new organization of the chapters, combining Prehistoric, Mesopotamian, and Egyptian Civilizations, a separate chapter for Early Chinese and for Early Japanese Civilizations, and major restructuring of the chapters on the twentieth century.

FACULTY AND STUDENT RESOURCES TO ACCOMPANY *ARTS AND CULTURE*

Music for the Humanities CD—This music CD is included with each new copy of the text. Musical selections represent important works from a broad variety of time periods and styles.

Humanities Notes—This tool is designed to help students organize their course notes. For each chapter of the book, it includes key illustrations and short extracts from the text with a space next to each where students may take notes. *Humanities Notes* can be packaged at a substantial discount with the book upon request.

OneKey—OneKey is Prentice Hall's exclusive course management system that delivers all student and instructor resources in one place. Powered by Blackboard and WebCT, OneKey offers an abundance of online study and research tools for students and a variety of teaching and presentation resources for instructors, including an easy-to-use gradebook and access to an image library. For more information, go to www.prenhall.com/onekey

Companion WebsiteTM—With the *Arts and Culture* Companion Website, students have access to this extensive online study resource, which includes quizzes, web links, chapter objectives, and more. Please visit the Companion Website at www.prenhall.com/benton.

Instructor's Manual with Tests—An invaluable professional resource and reference for new and experienced instructors, providing chapter summaries, further topics for discussion, activities, and hundreds of sample test questions, these resources are carefully organized to make preparation, classroom instruction, and student testing smoother and more effective. ISBN: 978-0-13-228392-2.

TestGen—This computerized test management program allows instructors to select items from the test bank and design their own exams. ISBN: 978-0-13-228393-9.

Fine Art Slides and Videos—For qualified adopters, slides and videos are available. Contact your local Prentice Hall representative for more information.

The Prentice Hall *Atlas of the Humanities*—Prentice Hall collaborates with Dorling Kindersley, the world's most innovative producer of maps and atlases. This atlas features mulit-dimensional maps that include global, thematic, regional, and chronological perspectives showing political, economic, and cultural changes over time. It is available at a significant discount when packaged with the text. ISBN: 978-0-13-238628-9.

ACKNOWLEDGMENTS

Arts and Culture represents the cooperative efforts of many people. The book originated with a suggestion fifteen years ago by Tony English, then of Macmillan Publishing. Work on the project began with Tony and his Macmillan colleagues and continued with Prentice Hall when Simon & Schuster acquired Macmillan in 1993. At Prentice Hall we had the good fortune to work with Bud Therien, Publisher, who oversaw the book's development in every respect, and Clare Payton, Development Editor, who helped shape the first edition.

Also deserving of particular mention for their work on the first edition are Sylvia Moore for her contribution to the introductory materials, Jenny Moss for her work on the timelines and glossary, and Ailsa Heritage and Andrea Fairbrass for their imaginative work on the maps.

We owe thanks to Henry Sayre, without whom we could not have completed the first edition of *Arts and Culture* on schedule. Professor Sayre helped us shape the drafts of our chapters, melding our styles and recommending organizational changes that have resulted, we believe, in an integrated and compelling overview of the humanities.

For the Third Edition, we owe a special debt of gratitude to Amber Mackey, Acquisitions Editor, who ably shepherded *Arts and Culture* through the revision process. Our thanks also go to Sarah Touborg, Editor-in-Chief; Melissa Feliberty, Executive Marketing Manager; Leslie Osher, Creative Director; Bruce Hobart, Production Editor; and Carla Worner, Editorial Assistant.

We would like to thank the following reviewers, who offered us wise counsel: Jane Anderson Jones, Manatee Community College; Richard Mahon, Riverside Community College; Brian A. Pavlac, King's College; Danney Ursery, St. Edward's University; Richard A. Voeltz, Cameron University; and Katherine Wyly, Hillsborough Community College.

We want to thank Margaret Manos for her excellent work on early versions of the manuscript, and for her wise and extremely helpful advice in making decisions on what to cut and what to add for the previous edition. In addition, we would like to extend our appreciation to A. Daniel Frankforter of Pennsylvania State University, for his many helpful corrections and suggestions on the history portions; to Jane Pyle of Miami Dade College for expanding our music coverage; to Stephen Addiss of the University of Richmond for his work revising and expanding our Asian chapters; to Jonathan T. Reynolds of Northern Kentucky University for his expansion of the African chapters; and, finally, to Bill Christy of Ohio University for his work on the timelines, key terms, and web links.

We also wish to thank our reviewers for this third edition. Their comments and suggestions helped us in many ways. Thanks to: Lynn Spencer, Brevard Community College; Richard A. Voeltz, Cameron University; Scott H. Boyd, College of DuPage; Richard Mahon, Riverside Community College; and Jane Anderson Jones, Manatee Community College.

We would also like to thank each other for offering mutual support, encouragement, advice, and help throughout a long and sometimes arduous process of writing, revising, and editing. Our families, too, deserve our thanks, for without their patience and understanding we could not have completed our work with equanimity and good humor. In particular, the encouragement and loving support of our spouses, Elliot Benton and Mary DiYanni, enabled us to do our work on *Arts and Culture* with a minimum of anxiety and a maximum of pleasure.

INTRODUCTION

Arts and Culture is an introduction to the humanities, from the earliest times to the present day. The goal of the book is to familiarize readers with a fundamental body of art, history, and ideas as a basis for understanding Western and non-Western cultures. In demonstrating the interrelationships between the creators of art and the historical and social forces at work in various cultures, the text fosters an understanding of the creative process and the uses of the arts.

THE HUMANITIES AND THE ARTS

The humanities are those areas of thought and creation whose subject is human experience. They include history, philosophy, religion, and the arts. Broadly speaking, the arts are objects or experiences created by human beings. The role of the human creator, therefore, is central to any study of the arts since, ultimately, the arts and humanities are a record of human experience and concerns. The arts convey information—a lyric poem or a water-color can describe or portray a summer's day, for example—yet this is not their primary function. More importantly, the arts give form to what is imagined, express human beliefs and emotions, create beauty, move, persuade, and entertain their audiences.

The arts include visual art and architecture, drama, music, and literature, and photography and film. Seeing the arts within their historical and social context is necessary for understanding their development. For example, the figure of the biblical giant-killer, David, was popular during the Renaissance in the Italian city-state of Florence. Michelangelo's *David* was commissioned by the Florentine city officials (see fig. 13.27). Florence had recently fought off an attempt at annexation by the much larger city-state of Milan. Thus, the biblical David slaying the giant, Goliath, became a symbol of Florentine cleverness and courage in defense of independence. It is a theme particular to its time and place, yet one that has been used throughout history to express the success of the "little" person against powerful exploiters.

RECORDS OF CULTURE

We study what survives, which is not necessarily all that once existed. Not all arts survive the passage of time. Art can be divided into the durable and the ephemeral, or short-lived. Surviving objects tend to be large (the Pyramids) or hidden (the contents of tombs). Until human beings created the means of capturing moving images and sounds, the ephemeral arts such as music and dance could be described but not reexperienced. Therefore, some of the oldest arts—music and dance of the ancient world, for example—are lost. With the development of writing, humans began the long process of liberating themselves from the tyranny of time. They began to communicate across space and time, leaving a record of their lives. In our own century, we have seen our recording abilities explode from sound recording and silent movies at the turn of the century into the digitized world of the CD-ROM and the Internet today. The result has been an unprecedented expansion in the humanities.

THE ROLE OF THE ARTIST

The functions of the artist and the artwork have varied widely during the past five thousand years. In our time, the artist is seen as an independent worker, dedicated to the expression of a unique subjective experience. Often the artist's role is that of the outsider, a critical or rebellious figure. He or she is a specialist who has usually undergone advanced training in a university department of art or theater, or a school with a particular focus, such as a music conservatory. In our societies, works of art are presented in specialized settings: theaters, concert halls, performance spaces, galleries, and museums. There is usually a sharp division between the artist and her or his audience of nonartists. We also associate works of art with money: art auctions in which paintings sell for millions of dollars, ticket sales to the ballet, or fundraising for the local symphony.

In other societies and in parts of our own society, now and in the past, the arts are closer to the lives of ordinary people. For the majority of their history, artists have expressed the dominant beliefs of a culture, rather than rebelling against them. In place of our emphasis on the development of a personal or original style, artists were trained to conform to the conventions of their art form. Nor have artists always been specialists; in some societies and periods, all members of a society participated in art. The modern Western economic mode, which treats art as a commodity for sale, is not universal. In societies such as that of the Navajo, the concept of selling or creating a salable version of a sand painting would be completely incomprehensible. Selling Navajo sand paintings created as part of a ritual would profane a sacred experience.

Artists' identities are rarely known before the Renaissance, with the exception of the period of Classical Greece, when artists were highly regarded for their individual talents and styles. Among artists who were known, there were fewer women than men. In the twentieth century, many female artists in all the disciplines have been recognized.

Their absence in prior centuries does not indicate lack of talent, but reflects lack of opportunity. The necessary social, educational, and economic conditions to create art rarely existed for women in the past.

Artists of color have also been recognized in the West only recently. The reasons for this absence range from the simple—there were few Asians in America and Europe prior to the middle of the nineteenth century—to the complexities surrounding the African diaspora. The art of indigenous peoples, while far older than that of the West, did not share the same expressive methods or aims as Western art. Until recently, such art was ignored or dismissed in Western society by the dominant cultural gatekeepers.

CONTEXTS AND AESTHETICS

Our understanding of the arts depends in part on our knowledge of the historical and social context surrounding a work. For instance, for whom was a particular work intended—a private or a public audience? What was or is its setting—public, private, accessible, or hidden? How is the work related to the economic workings of its time: for example, was it commissioned by a ruler, a religious organization, a group of guildspeople, a corporation? Was it created by nuns or monks, by peasants, or by specially-trained craftspersons? Each of these considerations expands our understanding of a given work, even when we cannot know all the answers.

The branch of philosophy devoted to thinking about the arts is called "aesthetics." Aesthetic knowledge is both intuitive and intellectual; that is, we can grasp a work of art on an emotional level while at the same time analyzing it. There is no single, unquestionable body of aesthetic knowledge, although philosophers have tried to create universal systems. Each culture has its own aesthetic preferences. In addition, different disciplines and different styles within a culture reflect different aesthetic values.

FORM AND CONTENT

When discussing works of art, it is useful to distinguish between the form of the artwork and its content. The form of a work of art is its structural or organizing principle—the shape of its content. A work's content is what it is about—its subject matter. At its most basic, formal analysis provides a description of the apparent properties of an artwork. Artists use these properties to engineer our perception and response. In music, for example, a formal analysis would discuss the melody, the harmony, and the structure. In visual art, comparable elements would be line, color, and composition. The goal of formal analysis is to understand how an artwork's form expresses its content.

Contextual approaches to the arts seek to situate artworks within the circumstances of their creation. Histori-

ans of the arts conduct research aimed at recreating the context of a given work. Armed with this information, the historian interprets the work in light of that context. Knowing, for example, that *Guernica* (see fig. 21.20), Pablo Picasso's anti-war painting, depicts an aerial bombing of a small village of unarmed civilians in the Spanish Civil War, drives its brutal images of pain and death home to viewers. Picasso chose black, white, and grey for this painting because he learned of the attack through the black and white photojournalism of the newspapers. Knowing the reason for this choice, which may otherwise have seemed arbitrary to modern viewers of the work, adds to the meaning of the image. Picasso's choice of black and white also intensifies the horrors he depicts.

CRITICAL THINKING

Among the most important purposes of any study of the arts and humanities is to develop habits of mind, including critical thinking. By critical thinking, we do not mean "being critical" of something in the ordinary sense. Rather, we mean developing a capacity to analyze and synthesize, compare and contrast, understand causes and effects, understand, appreciate, and evaluate the cultural productions—the architecture, sculpture, painting, photography, film, literature, music, philosophy, and other arts of all civilizations, whether ancient or modern, and whether similar to or radically different from our own.

Critical Thinking in this sense involves asking questions, making observations and connections, drawing inferences and provisional interpretive conclusions about the meaning of artworks and considering their importance to the civilizations in which they were created. It also involves considering basic issues, such as: what does it mean to live in a society as an individual human being? To what extent does living in one kind of society, in a particular civilization at a particular historical moment, affect one's thoughts, perceptions, attitudes, and feelings? How does the world view of ancient Africans, Babylonians, Chinese, Egyptians, Greeks, Romans, Sumerians, and others compare and contrast with one another and with those of people living in different cultures around the world today?

Each chapter of *Arts and Culture* contains much information and analysis that invites such considerations. And, although the book does not contain study questions or review assignments (those can be found in supplements to *Arts and Culture*), it does contain, in each chapter, a highlighted brief discussion labeled "Critical Thinking." You are invited to think about the issues raised in each of those discussions, as for example, why cows are considered sacred in India, a Hindu civilization, along with the effects of treating cows as sacred animals, as well as considering what "sacred cows," in a metaphorical sense, exist in your own culture.

An additional thought about such critical thinking questions is that when we study civilizations of the past, we are not just studying cultural artifacts and learning about historical events. Additionally, we are learning about people, human beings, who, like us, experience joy and sorrow, frustration and elation, pleasure and pain. And, finally, here we will use the word "critical" in still another sense, for the study of the humanities disciplines through history is critical to understanding ourselves in today's world. We put before you for critical consideration the notion that studying the humanities not only adds to your stock of knowledge, while enriching your own life and imaginatively extending its possibilities but also deepens your appreciation of other peoples and their values.

STARTER KIT

THE HUMANITIES

This Starter Kit provides you with a brief reference guide to key terms and concepts for studying the humanities. The following section will give you a basis for analyzing, understanding, and describing art forms.

COMMONALITIES

We refer to the different branches of humanities—art and architecture, music, literature, philosophy, history—as **disciplines.** The various humanistic disciplines have many key terms in common. However, each discipline has defining characteristics, a distinct vocabulary, and its own conventions, so that the same word may mean different things in different disciplines.

Every work of art has two core components: form and content. **Form** refers to the arrangement, pattern, or structure of a work, how a work is presented to our senses. **Content** is what a work is about its meaning or substance. The form might be a Tang Dynasty painting; the content might be the beauty of nature in a particular place. To comprehend how the form expresses the content is one of the keys to understanding a work of art, music or literature.

The term **artist** is used for the producer of artworks in any discipline. All artworks have a **composition,** the arrangement of its constituent parts. **Technique** refers to the process or method that produced the art. The **medium** is the physical material that makes up the work, such as oil paint on canvas.

STYLE

We use the term **style** to mean several different things. Most simply, style refers to the manner in which something is done. Many elements form a style. Artists working at the same time and place are often trained in the same style. When mentioned in a text, historical styles are usually capitalized, as in *Classical Greek* art, referring to the arts of that particular time and place, which shared distinct characteristics. If used with lowercase letters, such as *classical* style, the term refers to works which, although not from Classical Greece, are similar in character to Classical Greek art, or to Roman art, which was largely derived from Greek forms.

Conventions are accepted practices, such as the use of a frontal eye in a profile face, found in the art of the ancient Egyptians, or the use of the sonnet form by Shakespeare and his contemporaries.

FUNCTIONS AND GENRES

In the most general terms, the functions of the arts can be divided into religious and secular art. **Religious** or liturgical art, music, or drama is used as part of the ritual of a given religion. Art that is not religious art is termed **secular** art. Secular art is primarily used to provide pleasure and entertainment, but among other functions has been its use in the service of political or propaganda ends.

Each discipline has subsets, called **genres.** In music, for example, we have the symphony, a large, complex work for orchestra, in contrast to a quartet, written for only four instruments. In literature we might contrast the novel, with its extended narrative and complexities of character, with the compression of a short story. From the seventeenth to the nineteenth centuries, certain subjects were assigned higher or lower rank by the academies that controlled the arts in most European countries. Portrait painting, for example, was considered lower than history painting. That practice has been abandoned; today the genres are usually accorded equal respect and valued for their distinctive qualities.

THE VISUAL ARTS

The visual arts are first experienced by sight, yet they often evoke other senses such as touch or smell. Because human beings are such visual creatures, our world is saturated with visual art, in advertising, on objects from CD covers to billboards, on TV and the Internet. The visual arts occur in many varieties of two-dimensional and three-dimensional forms, from painting, printmaking, and photography, to sculpture and architecture.

As is the case with other arts, the origins of the visual arts are now lost. However, their development represents a milestone in human civilization. Drawing, the representation of three-dimensional forms (real or imagined) on a two-dimensional surface, is an inherent human ability, and failure to draw by a certain stage in a child's growth is a sign of serious trouble. The creation and manipulation of images was and is a first step toward mastery of the physical world itself.

The visual arts use different methods. **Representation** is an ancient function of visual art, in which a likeness of an object or life form is produced. Artists use different methods to represent a subject (what is actually depicted, such as a portrait of a person, a still life, a landscape, a historical event, etc.). If the work is realistic, the subject is accurately depicted and readily recognizable. If the work is abstracted, the subject, although not photographically

Visual Arts

Line: A mark on a surface. Lines may be continuous or broken. They are used to create patterns and textures, to imply three dimensions, and to direct visual movement.

Shape: An area with identifiable boundaries. Shapes may be **organic,** based on natural forms and thus rounded or irregular, or they may be **geometric,** based on measured forms.

Mass: The solid parts of a three-dimensional object. An area of space devoid of mass is called **negative space;** while **positive space** is an area occupied by mass.

Form: The shape and structure of something. In discussion of art, form refers to visual aspects such as line, shape, color, texture, and composition.

Color: The sensation produced by various wavelengths of light. Also called **hue.** Red, blue, and yellow are the **primary colors,** which cannot be made from mixing other colors. **Secondary colors** (orange, green, and purple) are hues produced by mixing two primary colors.

Value: The lightness or darkness of an area of color, or as measured between black and white. The lighter, the higher in value it is; the **darker,** the lower in value.

Texture: The appearance or feel of a surface, basically smooth or rough. Texture may be actual, as the surface of a polished steel sculpture, or implied, as in a painting of human flesh or the fur of an animal.

Composition: The arrangement of the formal components of a work, most frequently used to describe the organization of elements in a drawing or painting.

One-point perspective

Two-point perspective

Perspective: A system of portraying three-dimensional space on a two-dimensional surface. In **one-point** linear perspective, lines recede toward a single **vanishing point** on the horizon line. In **two-point** perspective there are two vanishing points. **Atmospheric** or **aerial** perspective uses properties of light and air, in which objects become less distinct and cooler in color as they recede into distance.

recorded, is nevertheless identifiable. If the work is nonobjective there is no longer a recognizable subject.

Realistic paintings, drawings, and prints often create an illusion of pictorial space (an illusion of three dimensions on a two-dimensional surface) by using perspective. There are two types: 1) atmospheric perspective, and 2) linear perspective, both defined in the box above. These are characteristic of Western art, whereas Eastern art tends to Emphasize the picture plane. Landscapes, as Zho Jan's *Seeking the Tao in the Autumn Mountains* (Figure 8.8), does not employ Western methods of creating illusions of space. Inscriptions, as in Shitao's *Searching for the Past* (Figure 19.5), by stressing the picture plane, further compress the sense of space. Abstract and nonobjective art, arising in the twentieth century, are more concerned with the elements on the picture plane (the surface of the paper or canvas) rather than in creating an illusion of depth.

FORMAL ANALYSIS

To analyze a work of visual art formally, its visual elements are considered without reference to the content, whereas moving to more sophisticated levels involves the content as well. At its simplest, the content is what is represented, the subject matter, whether a person, an orange, or a flag. However, the image may not stop with the representation; there may be a symbolic element. It is useful to distinguish between signs and symbols. **Signs** convey visual information

FIGURE 0.1   Edvard Munch, *The Scream*, 1893, tempera and casein on cardboard, 36 × 29″ (91.3 × 73.7 cm), Nasjonal-galleriet, Oslo. © 2003 The Munch Museum/The Munch-Ellingson Group/Artists Rights Society (ARS), New York/ADAGP, Paris. J. Lathion/© Nasjionalgalleriet 02.

economically by means of images or words. **Symbols** are images that have resonance, or additional meaning. Works of visual art may use both signs and symbols. Artists use symbolic systems, part of the visual language of their time. Like all languages, these must be learned. Sometimes artists create their own symbols.

Iconography is the language of symbols. The **iconography** of a work of art is often religious in nature. For example, different representations of Jesus derive from incidents in his life. To understand the deeper levels of the work, it is necessary to understand the iconography. The use of personal iconography by an artist is a relatively recent development of the past few centuries.

The following analysis of *The Scream* by Edvard Munch (fig. 0.1) will serve as an example of this process. Viewed formally, the major visual elements used by Munch in this painting are line and color. There are two kinds of lines: the geometric lines that form the sharply receding bridge contrast with the swirling organic lines of the main figure and the landscape, sea, and sky. There is little or no modelling or shading. The colors contrast bright red and yellow with rich blue, offset by neutral tones. *The Scream* is a painting executed on cardboard with rapid, loose brush-

strokes. The composition is dynamic; the artist has used exaggerated diagonals to suggest a dramatic perspective for the bridge. The figure at the front is the focal point. The craft is secondary to the expressive purpose of the work.

It should be obvious that in *The Scream* more is going on than the preceding analysis indicates. Three people are on a bridge at sunset. Two are walking away; one stands transfixed with his hands over his ears. The expression on his face functions as a sign to convey shock or horror. To understand the significance of his expression, we turn to the historical context and the artist's life. Munch, a Norwegian artist who worked in the late-nineteenth and early-twentieth centuries, was one of the artists who rejected conventions and created personal symbolic systems, based largely on his experience. *The Scream* is usually interpreted as representing a screaming person. This is not correct. As we know from the artist's diary, the work refers to the "scream of nature." The image captured is a powerful evocation of a sensitive man overwhelmed by nature's power, which his companions cannot sense. The swirling lines suggest the impact of screaming nature on this person. The blood-red sky resonates as a symbol of savage nature oblivious to the puny humans below.

COMPONENTS OF THE VISUAL ARTS

The basic elements used to construct a work of visual art are line, shape, mass, form, color, value, texture, and composition. While many drawings are executed in black mediums, such as pencil and charcoal, on a white ground, color is a vital ingredient of art, especially important in conveying information as well as emotion to the viewer. Color affects us both physically and psychologically and has significance to us both in our personal lives and in our cultural traditions.

There can be no color without light. In the seventeenth century, Sir Isaac Newton observed that when sunlight passed through a glass prism it was broken up, or **refracted,** into rainbow colors. Our perception of color depends upon reflected light rays of various wavelengths. Theorists have arranged colors on a **color wheel** (fig 0.2) that is well-known to students of painting and even young schoolchildren. On it are the **primary colors**—red, yellow, and blue—and **secondary colors**—orange, green, and purple. Some wheels show **tertiary colors** such as yellow-green and red-purple. The primary colors cannot be created by mixing other colors, but secondary and tertiary colors are made, respectively, by mixing two primaries, or primaries and secondaries, together. **Complementary** colors are those opposite each other on the wheel, so that red is opposite from green, orange from blue, and yellow from purple. Many artists have studied and worked with the **optical effects** of color, especially the French Impressionist Claude Monet and the Post-Impressionist Georges Seurat.

FIGURE 0.2 Color wheel.

SCULPTURE

A sculpture is a three-dimensional form made by carving, modeling, or assembling. Unlike paintings, drawings, and prints, which have two dimensions (height and width), sculptures have three dimensions (height, width, and depth).

Subtractive Sculpture. Using materials that have natural solid mass, such as stone, wood, or ivory, the sculptor shapes the work of art by removing material, cutting it away, usually with a hammer and chisel. The finished work must fit within the dimensions of, for example, the block of marble. Obviously, the work must be planned carefully in advance, for if a major error is made in carving, such as breaking off an extremity of a figure, correction is virtually impossible.

Physical strength may be required to carve in stone, as the *Seated Buddha* (Figure 7.6) of schist. However, greater control is required to carve in wood, as the Yoruba mask from the Republic of Benin (Figure 22.1), due to the varying resistance offered by the wood, depending upon whether the sculptor cuts with or against the grain.

Marble is the traditional medium for sculpture. Marble, limestone, and sandstone are all essentially calcium carbonate, the difference being the size and density of the crystalline structure of the stone. Limestone and sandstone are grainier, softer, and more easily worked than marble. They have a mat surface, whereas marble can be polished to a shine.

Additive Sculpture. Using materials that have no natural mass, shape, or dimensions, such as plaster, clay, or wax, the sculptor gradually builds up the desired form by modeling it. The scale of the sculpture is not limited, as it would be by the size of a block of stone or piece of wood. Because the material is soft, an **armature** (a rigid structure, usually of metal) may be needed for support. The artist can continually revise the form while working, and can easily make changes. For this reason, wax and clay are often used to make small studies for sculpture to be carved on a larger scale in stone.

Alternatively, a work modeled in clay or wax, which are rather impermanent materials, may be cast in metal—traditionally, bronze is used. A small **statuette** can be cast solid, as the tiny bronze horse shown in Figure 2.15, but a large piece, as the huge statue of Marcus Aurelius shown in Figure 4.19, must be hollow. This is not only because of the expense and weight, but because, were it solid, the bronze, which must be heated to make it molten for the casting process, would crack as it gradually cooled.

The material selected by the sculptor affects the form of the finished work, or, conversely, the sculptor selects the material according to the form he or she wishes to create. For example, bronze is very strong—a figure made of bronze could be posed as if balancing on one toe, whereas the same figure, if carved of stone, would be likely to break.

Assembled Sculpture. A modern type of sculpture is the **mobile,** invented by the American **Alexander Calder.** As the name suggests, the sculpture, which is usually suspended from the ceiling, actually moves with every breeze. As Figure 23.11 shows, the colored shapes are linked together, and a delicate balance carefully achieved. Calder also created **stabiles,** which used the same brightly colored metal shapes, but rest on the ground and do not move.

Another modern form of sculpture is the **assemblage** made of **found objects,** sometimes called **ready-mades.** As the term "assemblage" suggests, the mixed-media sculpture is created by assembling or compiling various bits, pieces, and objects, as was done by **Robert Rauschenberg** in Figure 23.13.

ARCHITECTURE

Architecture is a branch of the visual arts that combines practical function and artistic expression; it is art to inhabit. The function served by a building usually determines its form. In addition to the purely useful purpose of providing shelter, architecture answers prevailing social needs. The use of architects to design and erect public and religious structures has given rise to many innovative forms throughout history. Architecture reflects the society in which it is built. Structural systems depend upon the available building materials, technological advancements, the intended function of the building, and aesthetics of the culture. The relationship between a building and its **site,** or location, is integral to architecture. The Greek Parthenon (fig. 0.3), for example, crowns a hill overlooking Athens. The elevated location indicates its importance, and the pathway one must ascend to reach the Parthenon is part of the experience. A striking example of the adaptation of architecture to the natural environment is seen in homes of the Anasazi culture at Mesa Verde, Colorado, built into the cliff (Fig. 10.14).

LITERATURE

SPEECH, WRITING, AND LITERATURE

Literature differs from the visual arts since it is not built from physical elements, such as paint and stone; nor is it composed of sound as is music, but from words, the basic elements of language. Paint and sound have no intrinsic meaning; words do. Speech depends on meaningful units of sound—words, which are the building blocks of communication in language. Literature presupposes language, with its multitudes of meaning (content), its **grammar** (rules for construction), and its **syntax,** the arrangement of words.

Language, essentially communicative, has many functions. We use language to make emotional contact with others: for example, a parent using baby talk to a child too young to understand the meaning of words. Through language we convey information to each other, as in the classroom, where a dialogue between teacher and student is part of the educational process. All literature is language, but not all language is literature. Distinguishing between literature and other forms of language is sometimes difficult, but refinement in language and careful structure or form typically characterize literature.

FIGURE 0.3 Ictinus and Callicrates, Parthenon, Acropolis, Athens, 448–432 B.C.E.

Literature, in the broadest sense, is widely apparent in everyday life. Popular songs, magazine essays, greeting card verse, hymns and prayers are all forms of literature. One meaning of the word *literature,* in fact, is what is written. Generally, however, the term "literature" is reserved for those works that exhibit "the best that has been thought and said," works that represent a culture's highest literary achievements.

LITERACY AND LITERATURE

The Development of Literature. Literature predates literacy. Ancient literature was **oral**—spoken—rather than written. To make it easier to remember and recite, much of this was in the form of song or poetry. The invention of writing enabled people to communicate across space and time. It was with this invention that recorded history was born. The earliest writings of the ancient world are businesslike records of laws, prayers, and commerce—informative but not expressive. When mechanical methods of printing were developed, literacy spread. Today, universal literacy is a goal in all civilized countries.

The Functions of Literature. Literature serves a variety of social functions. One of its most ancient functions is as **religious literature,** the prayers and mythology of a given culture. The myths of the Greeks and Romans have exerted a powerful influence on Western culture; their origins lie deep in the history of Egypt and Mesopotamia. **Epic literature,** such as the African Epic of Son Jara, or the sagas from Norway and Iceland, were passed down by oral tradition. Literature distinct from liturgical or epic forms was invented by the ancient Greeks, and, broadly speaking included history, philosophy, drama, and poetry. Novels and short stories as we know them today were a much later development. The novel in its modern form was named for tales popular in Italy in the late-thirteenth century, though the novel is generally identified with prose narratives that developed in the eighteenth century in Europe.

Since literature is a communicative act, it is important to consider the audience and setting. Silent reading is a recent development, alien to the oral roots of literature. Most literature through the ages was meant to be recited, sung, or read aloud in groups ranging from general public gatherings to the intimate setting of the private home. Authors today may give readings from their work in libraries, bookstores, and educational institutions.

FORMS OF LITERATURE

Literature can be divided into fiction and nonfiction, poetry and prose.

Poetry is distinguished by its concentrated and precise language, "the best words in the best order," as one poet defined it. **Diction** is the poet's selection of words, and

Architecture

Architect: One who designs and supervises the construction of buildings. Ideally, the architect is part builder with a sound knowledge of engineering principles, materials, structural systems, and other such practical necessities, as well as part artist who works with form, space, scale, light, and other aesthetic properties.

Scale: The relative size of one thing compared to another. The relationship of a building to another element, often the height of a human being.

Site: The location of an object or building. Care must be taken to choose a solid, attractive, and appropriate building site.

Structural System: The engineering principles used to create a structure. Two basic kinds of structural system are the **shell** system, where one or more building materials such as stone or brick provide both support and covering, and the **skeleton and skin** system, as in modern skyscrapers with steel skeletons and glass skin.

Column: A supporting pillar consisting of a base, a cylindrical shaft, and a decorative capital at the top. Three Classical orders, established in ancient Greece, are the **Doric, Ionic,** or **Corinthian,** identified by the capital.

Post and Lintel: A basic structural system dating from ancient times that uses paired vertical elements (posts) to support a horizontal element (lintel).

Arch, Dome, and Vault: An arch consists of a series of wedged-shaped stones, called **voussoirs,** locked in place by a **keystone** at the top center. In principle, an arch rotated 180 degrees creates a **dome.** A series of arches forms a **barrel** or **tunnel vault.** When two such vaults are constructed so that they intersect at right angles, a **cross** or **groin vault** is created. Roman and Romanesque masons used semi-circular arches, whereas Gothic masons built with pointed arches to create vaults that were reinforced with **ribs,** permitting large openings in the walls. The true arch, dome, and vault are dynamic systems—the lateral thrust that they exert must be buttressed externally to prevent collapse.

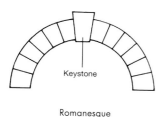

Romanesque

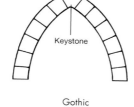

Gothic

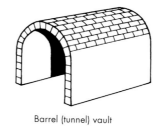

Barrel (tunnel) vault

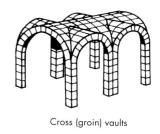

Cross (groin) vaults

syntax the ordering of those words in sentences. Other poetic elements include images—details that evoke sense perception—along with metaphor and other forms of comparison. With its roots in song, poetry of many eras and places exhibits rhyme and other types of sound play as well as rhythm and meter, the measured pattern of accent in poetic lines. Drama, plays intended for performance, are sometimes written in verse, rhymed or unrhymed, as, for example, in **blank verse.**

Language that is not poetry is **prose.** Not all prose is literature; some, such as journalism or technical writing, is purely descriptive or informative, as some visual art is purely representational. Literature can be fiction or nonfiction, or a combination of both. Fiction is a work of the imagination. Fictional forms can be long and complex, as

in a novel or play, or short and concise, as in a novella or short story. Nonfiction, which deals with actual events or persons, includes expressions of opinion, such as political essays. Functions of nonfiction include explanation, persuasion, commentary, exposition, or any blend of these. Sometimes philosophic essays and works of history are included in the category of literature.

Fiction and drama, and much nonfiction as well, create their effects through elements such as the plot, or story line, characters, description of the setting, dialogue between the characters, and exposition, or explanation. The latter is presented in the voice of a narrator, who may represent the author using the third-person perspective, or may instead be a character expressing a first-person point of view.

Literature

Fiction: Literature that is imaginative, rather than descriptive of actual events. Typical fictional forms are the short story and the novel, which has greater length and complexity.

Nonfiction: An account of actual events and people. Forms of nonfiction include essays, biography and autobiography, and journalistic writing, as for newspapers and magazines.

Narrative: The telling of a story; a structured account of events.

Narrator: The storyteller from whose **point of view** the story is told. The point of view can be **first-person** or **third-person,** and may shift within the work. The narrator can be **omniscient,** knowing everything, or limited to what she or he can know personally or be told by others.

Plot: The plan or story line. To plot a story is to conceive and arrange the action of the characters and the sequence of events. Plots typically involve **rising action,** events that complicate the plot and move it forward to a **climax,** the moment of greatest intensity. This is followed by the **denouement,** the resolution of the plot.

Characters: The people in a literary work. The leading character is known as the **protagonist,** a word stemming from ancient Greek drama in which the protagonist was opposed by an **antagonist.**

Dialogue: Conversation between two or more characters. Drama is mainly rendered through dialogue; it is used in fiction to a lesser extent.

Setting: Where the events take place; includes location, time, and situation. In theatrical productions, a **set** is the scenery, sometimes very elaborate, constructed for a stage performance. In films the set is the sound stage or the enclosure where a scene is filmed.

Exposition: Explanatory material, which, especially in drama, often lays out the current situation as it arises from the past.

In common with visual art and music, literature has **themes,** or overarching ideas that are expressed by all the elements working together. The structure of a work of literature is analogous to the composition of a symphony or a painting. Writers use symbolism, much as visual artists do. A successful work of literature will likely establish a mood, hold the reader's interest through a variety of incidents or ideas with evident focus, yet possess an overall sense of unity.

Autobiography, as a separate literary and historical endeavor, began with the *Confessions* of St. Augustine (354–430 C.E.), in which he told the story of his life and the progress of his religious convictions. Autobiography is history written from a subjective point of view. The memoir, so popular in recent years, is descended from this first, spiritual autobiography.

Biography is a branch of both literature and history. The author's role is complicated because a biographer must check the facts of the subject's life, usually by interviewing both the subject and many other people. Deciding the major theme of a person's life, the relationship between that person and his or her time, and considering what is true as well as what is germane are the biographer's responsibility. Different biographers may offer quite different interpretations of a subject's life.

History is a powerful force that shapes the humanities as a whole. The writing of history varies across cultures, and as cultures change, history itself is continuously under revision. The leaders of some societies would never allow the publication of versions of history that vary from their orthodox beliefs, no matter what the facts might be. Because history is an interpretative discipline, several versions of events may coexist, with scholars arguing and defending the merits of each. This is particularly true in our multicultural and pluralist era.

MUSIC

We are surrounded by sounds at all times. The art that derives from our sense of hearing is music, order given to sounds by human intent. A temporal art, one that exists in time, music is the least material of the arts, its basic elements being sound and silence. Silence in music is analogous to a painter's, sculptor's, or architect's use of negative space: unoccupied but important, so that the intervals between the notes are necessary parts of a musical piece. Music permeates our daily lives—in the movies, on radio and television, in elevators and stores. The success of the Sony Walkman and the recently developed MP3 players reflects our human desire to surround ourselves with music.

Until the development of sound recording, music was one of the **ephemeral** arts, like dance and live theater, which exist only for the duration of their performances. Until the late Middle Ages, music in the West was not written down, or **notated.** It was taught by ear, passed on from one generation to the next.

SOCIAL AND RITUAL ROLES

Music has many different functions. It has been and remains a major element in religious ritual. It is also used frequently in collective labor; the regular rhythm that characterizes work songs keeps the pace steady and makes the work more fun. For example, aerobics classes and workout tapes depend on music to motivate exercisers and help them keep the pace. On the other hand, parents use lullabies to lull their babies to sleep.

Since the late Middle Ages, Western music has developed many conventional types. These genres vary with the audience, the instruments, and the musical structures. **Liturgical** music was designed for churches, used sacred texts, and took advantage of church acoustics. The soaring vaults of Gothic cathedrals were perfect for the music of the Middle Ages. Music known as **chant** or **plainsong** is simply the human voice singing a religious text without instrumental accompaniment. When the voice is unaccompanied, it is known as **a cappella.** When the sound is made by specialized devices, called **instruments,** the music is termed **instrumental.**

Secular, that is nonreligious, music brought about other forms. **Chamber music,** instrumental music that was originally played in palaces for royalty and nobility, calls for more intimate spaces, a small ensemble of players, and small audiences. **Orchestral music** is the most public and complex form, involving a full orchestra and a concert hall, where the acoustics, or quality of sound, is very important. **Popular music,** often shortened to **pop,** appeals to a wide audience. It includes rock, folk, country, rap, and other types of music. **Jazz** is an improvisational form that arose in the United States from blues and ragtime. **Musical theater,** as the name implies, is a combination of drama and music. Its songs often enter the pop repertoire as **show tunes. Opera,** a narrative in which both dialogue and exposition is sung, combines music with literature and drama.

INSTRUMENTS

Musical instruments, which vary widely across cultures, can nevertheless be grouped in families. Probably most ancient are the **percussion** instruments, which make noise as they are struck. Drums, blocks, cymbals, and tambourines are percussion instruments. **Stringed** instruments, deriving from the hunting bow, have strings stretched between two points; sounds are produced when they are plucked, strummed, bowed, or struck. **Woodwinds** are hollow instruments that were originally made of wood, such as the flute, recorder, and panpipes. **Reed** instruments, such as the oboe, are woodwinds that use a mouthpiece created from a compressed reed. **Brasses** are metal horns like the tuba, trumpet, and cornet. In addition to their musical function, brasses were long used by the military to communicate over distances in battle or in camp. Using a prearranged trumpet call, the commander could sound "retreat" or "charge."

MUSICAL QUALITIES AND STRUCTURE

Musical structure ranges from a simple tune or rhythm to the intricacy of a symphony or an opera. The tone, or sound of a specific quality, is the basis of all music, using varieties of high or low pitches and timbres with varying intensity and tempos. Music appeals to our emotions through tempo, musical color or timbre, and harmonic structure. We associate different emotions with different timbres. The harp, for example, evokes gentleness or calm, whereas brasses evoke more stirring emotions.

Musical structure can be simple, such as Ravel's *Bolero*, which uses the repetition of a single melody with increased tempo and volume to build to a climax. Increases in tempo generate excitement, literally increasing the listener's heart rate and breathing speed. These qualities were used to good advantage in Blake Edwards's film *10*. Composers of movie music manipulate our emotions expertly, heightening the appeal of the action.

The comparatively uncomplicated pop songs we sing are based on melodies, a succession of notes, with accompanying words. We are also familiar with the 32-bar structure of most pop and rock music, in which **verses** alternate with repeated **choruses.** To appreciate and enjoy more complex music, some understanding of structure is important. The simple song "Row, Row, Row Your Boat," familiar to many of us from childhood, is a **round** or **canon;** the same melody is sung by each voice, but voices enter one after the other, creating overlapping notes, or **chords.** More elaborate forms stemming from such simple structures are found in **classical** music, beginning with European music of the eighteenth and nineteenth centuries.

Harmonic structure is a complex topic. Western music is written in **keys,** a system of notes based on one central note, such as the key of C Major. The different keys have their own emotional connotations. A **minor key** is often associated with sadness; a **major key** seems happier or more forceful. Notes that seem to fit together are consonant, while clashing notes are dissonant. Generally, consonance seems peaceful or happy to most people, while dissonance may be unsettling.

Music

Acoustics: The qualities of sound, often used to describe the relationship between sound and architecture, as in a concert hall.

Vibrations: Trembling or oscillating motions that produce sound. When singers or stringed instruments produce a wavering sound, causing a fluctuation in pitch, it is termed **vibrato.**

Pitch: The sound produced by vibrations. The speed of vibrations controls the pitch: slow vibrations produce low pitches; fast vibrations produce high pitches.

Tempo: The speed at which music is played or sung. This is shown on sheet music, usually in Italian terms, by **tempo marks** that indicate the desired speed. A device called a **metronome** can indicate tempo with precision.

Timbre: The characteristic sound or tonal quality of an instrument or voice. Also termed **color,** it can refer to the combination produced by more than one instrument's timbres, as **orchestral color.**

Tone: A sound of specific pitch and quality, the basic building material of music. Its properties are pitch, timbre, duration, and intensity.

Note: The written symbol for a tone, shown as **whole notes, half notes,** etc. These indicate the time a note is held, with a corresponding **rest** sign. **Notation** is the use of a set of symbols to record music in written form.

Melody: The succession of notes or pitches played or sung. Music with a single melodic line is called **monophony,** while music with more than one melodic line is **polyphony.**

Texture: In music, this refers to the number of diffent melodic lines; the greater the number, the thicker the texture.

Harmony: The combination of notes sung or played at one time, or **chords;** applies to homophonic music. **Consonance** refers to the sound of notes that are agreeable together; **dissonance** to the sound of notes that are discordant.

NON-WESTERN MUSIC

Music of the non-Western world shares with Western music a tradition of early oral transmission and an affiliation with the values and beliefs of its originating culture. Like Western music, too, music of non-Western traditions has undergone change and reflects the influence of musical traditions with which it has had contact over the centuries.

Nonetheless, there are distinctive differences among the world's many and varied musical traditions, and a number of differences between Western and non-Western musical forms, textures, and harmonic, melodic, and rhythmic systems. Pentatonic scales, for example (the 5-note scales illustrated by the black piano keys), are of non-Western origin. Micro-tones, pitches that exist between the half-tone steps of traditional Western musical scales, are another non-Western influence. So too are the intricate rhythmic patterns of Indian music, as performed by tabla players as they accompany master musicians performing on the sitar, an instrument that produces sounds, pitches, and harmonies beyond the scope of those common to Western music.

The best way to learn about and listen to music from other times, places, and traditions, is to understand it within its cultural context and to approach differences with an open mind and an attentive ear. Whether you are listening to Japanese shakuhachi music, which has a ceremonial quality, or to Indonesian gamelan music, with its uniquely orchestral combination of xylophone, bronze bowls, gongs, flutes, percussive and plucked instruments, or to African Mbira music, with its repetitive melodies and strong dance connections, the route to understanding and enjoyment is to be willing to entertain new sounds, new combinations of instruments, and new musical experiences.

HISTORY, RELIGION, AND PHILOSOPHY

History, the recording and explanation of events, and philosophy, the search for truth, have both influenced the arts. These subjects have themselves evolved as humanistic disciplines. **Aesthetics,** the branch of philosophy concerned with the functions, practice, and appreciation of the arts, along with their role in society, is an important part of this book and of cultural studies in general.

HISTORY

Unlike expressive literature, or fiction, history is an inquiry into and report upon real events and people. Until the Greek historian Herodotus, traveling in the Mediterranean lands of the sixth century B.C.E., turned his questioning and skeptical eye on the received beliefs and tales of peoples he met, history was inseparable from religious faith and folk memory. Herodotus began as a kind of cultural anthropologist, and he deliberately distinguished his historical writing from the epic tradition by writing prose. Historians have since developed methods of inquiry, questioning the likelihood of stories and delving into the motives of their informants. They learned to consider nonhistorical accounts and records as checks on the official versions of events. They began to consider the psychological motives of the people they chronicled. The artistry of their presentation became a part of the discipline.

RELIGION AND PHILOSOPHY

Religion has played a crucial role in the development of the arts, which provide images, sounds, and words for use in worship, prayers, and religious stories. **Theology,** study of the nature of the divine, prescribes religious practices, moral beliefs, and rules for social behavior. The dominant religion in a culture often controls the art, either directly by training artists and commissioning art, or indirectly. The medieval Catholic belief in the efficacy of **relics** to heal or give aid, for example, led to the practice of pilgrimage, and from that to the creation of churches and cathedrals. As religious orders acquired holy relics, they housed them in shrines within the churches. Problems arose when the many pilgrims who came to be healed and blessed disrupted services. Romanesque architects then developed the **ambulatory,** or walkway, that allowed pilgrims to see the relics without interrupting worshipers at a service, thereby altering religious architecture. Different religions hold different aesthetic beliefs. Nudity was acceptable in the temple statues of Classical Greece and Hindu India. Islam prohibits any figurative images in places of worship, and some Native Americans believe a permanent house of worship is itself inappropriate.

In many cultures, philosophy and religion are intertwined. Confucianism, Taoism, Hinduism, and Buddhism are all based on intricate philosophical systems that become allied with various social and religious beliefs and practices. Like religion, philosophy is concerned with the basic truths and principles of the universe. Both are also concerned with human perception and understanding of these truths, and with the development of moral and ethical principles for living.

ARTS AND CULTURE

AN INTRODUCTION TO THE HUMANITIES

CHAPTER 1

HISTORY

ca. 35,000–10,000 B.C.E.	*Homo sapiens* begins supplanting Neanderthal in Europe
ca. 8000–3000 B.C.E.	Farming replaces hunting
ca. 3000 B.C.E.	Bronze Age begins in Mesopotamia and Egypt
ca. 2700 B.C.E.	King Gilgamesh reigns in Sumer
ca. 2332–2279 B.C.E.	King Sargon I rules Akkad
1792–1750 B.C.E.	King Hammurabi reigns in Babylon unites Sumer and Akkad
ca. 3100 B.C.E.	King Narmer unites Upper and Lower Egypt
1674 B.C.E.	Hyksos invade northern Egypt
1478–1458 B.C.E.	Queen Hatshepsut rules
1479–1425 B.C.E.	King Thutmose III, first pharaoh, rules
1352–1336 B.C.E.	King Amenhotep IV (Akhenaten) rules
ca. 1336–1327 B.C.E.	King Tutankhamen rules
689 B.C.E., 648 B.C.E.	Assyrians sack Babylon
669–627 B.C.E.	Ashurbanipal reigns in Assyria
525 B.C.E.	Persia conquers Egypt

ART AND ARCHITECTURE

ca. 25,000–20,000 B.C.E.	*Woman of Willendorf*
ca. 15,000–10,000 B.C.E.	Wall paintings at Lascaux
ca. 8000–3000 B.C.E.	Wall paintings in the Valtorta Gorge
ca. 2530–2470 B.C.E.	Great Pyramids at Giza
ca. 2500 B.C.E.	Great Sphinx
ca. 2500–2050 B.C.E.	Ziggurat of King Urnammu
ca. 2300–2200 B.C.E.	*Victory Stele of Naram-Sin*
ca. 2000 B.C.E.	Stonehenge
ca. 3100 B.C.E.	*Palette of Narmer*
ca. 2600 B.C.E.	Stepped Pyramid of Zoser
ca. 2470 B.C.E.	Statue of Mycernius and Khamerernebty
ca. 1478–1458 B.C.E.	Temple of Queen Hatshepsut *Nobleman Hunting in the Marshes*
1352–1336 B.C.E.	Queen Nefertiti sculpture
1260 B.C.E.	Temple of Amen-Mut-Khonsu
	Temple of Ramesses II
ca. 650 B.C.E.	Limestone relief of *Sack of the City of Hamanu by Ashurbanipal*

LITERATURE AND PHILOSOPHY

ca. 100,000 B.C.E.	Evidence of religious practice
ca. 3300 B.C.E.	Earliest preserved tablets with pictographs
ca. 3000 B.C.E.	Writing begins in Mesopotamia
ca. 2500 B.C.E.	Papyrus in use in Egypt
2040–1786 B.C.E.	Hieratic (cursive) writing develops during the Middle Kingdom
ca. 1900–1600 B.C.E.	*The Epic of Gilgamesh,* first written down by Akkadians
ca. 1760 B.C.E.	Stele inscribed with the Law Code of Hammurabi
196 B.C.E.	Rosetta Stone

Prehistoric, Mesopotamian, and Egyptian Civilizations

Great Pyramids, Giza, built for Old Kingdom pharaohs Cheops, ca. 2530 B.C.E., Chefren, ca. 2500 B.C.E., and Mycerinus, ca. 2470 B.C.E., Fourth Dynasty, limestone and granite.

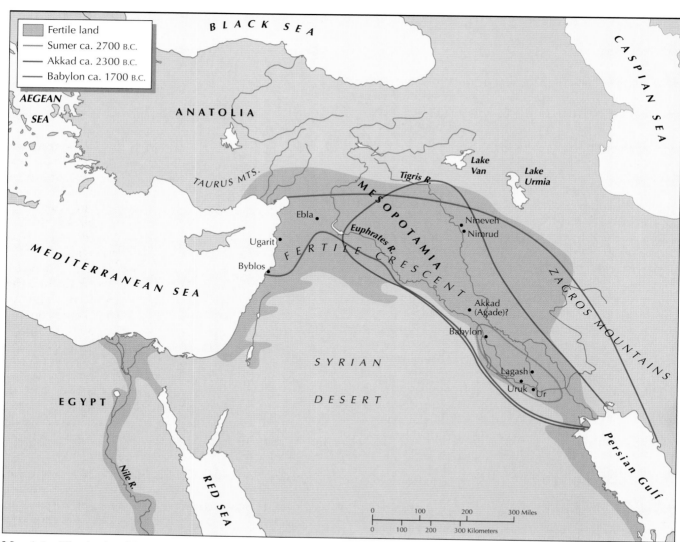

MAP 1.1   The Ancient Near East and the Fertile Crescent.

CHAPTER OVERVIEW

THE EARLIEST CULTURES
Prehistoric society and the birth of the visual arts

MESOPOTAMIA: THE CRADLE OF CIVILIZATION
The expansion of agrarian peoples' borders and ideas in the ancient Near East

THE CIVILIZATION OF THE NILE
A divided Egypt comes together through a shared culture and religion

THE OLD KINGDOM
Dynasties 3–6: The rise of the pyramids, sculpture, and relief painting

THE MIDDLE KINGDOM
Dynasties 11–14: Egypt prospers

THE NEW KINGDOM
Dynasties 18–20: A mature and powerful Egypt rules in art and world politics

THE EARLIEST CULTURES

A CULTURE IS A WAY OF THINKING AND living established by a group of people and transmitted from one generation to the next. It is, in other words, the basis of communal life. A culture's collective values are expressed in its arts, writings, customs, and intellectual pursuits. The ability of a culture to express itself well, especially in writing, and to organize itself thoroughly, as a social, economic, and political entity, distinguishes it as a civilization. It is important to note, however, that some aspects of civilizations predate writing—monumental architecture and urban organization, for example. Further, an occasional civilization, such as that of the Inca, never developed writing.

Just when the earliest cultures took form, and then subsequently transformed themselves into civilizations, is a matter of some conjecture among anthropologists, scientists who study humankind's institutions and beliefs from the earliest times. The first historical evidence of a culture coming into being can be found in the artifacts of the earliest *homo sapiens*, or "the one who knows." About 35,000 years ago, the hominid species *homo sapiens*, which had come into being about 200,000 B.C.E., probably in Africa, began to assert itself in the forests and plains of Europe, gradually supplanting the Neanderthal *homo erectus* who had roamed the same areas for the previous hundred thousand years.

Both *homo sapiens* and *homo erectus* were tool makers, as even our earliest ancestors seem to have been. *Kenya pithecus* (the "Kenya ape"), for instance, which lived in the Olduvai Gorge in east-central Africa between nineteen and fourteen million years ago, made crude stone weapons or tools. *Homo sapiens* and the Neanderthals both cooked with fire, wore skins as clothing, and used tools. They evidently buried their dead in ritual ceremonies, which provide the earliest indications of religious beliefs and practices. These activities suggest the transmission of knowledge and patterns of social behavior from one generation to the next. But between 35,000 and 10,000 B.C.E.—the last part of the period known as the **Paleolithic,** or Old Stone Age, when *homo sapiens* became more and more dominant and the Neanderthal line died out—the first objects that can be considered works of art began to appear, objects that seem to express the values and beliefs of the Paleolithic people. The Paleolithic period thus represents the very earliest cultural era.

THE PALEOLITHIC PERIOD

The Paleolithic period corresponds to the geological Pleistocene era, or Ice Age. Periodically, glaciers moved south over the European and Asian continents, forcing the inhabitants of the areas to move south, around the Mediterranean and into Africa. These people lived nomadic lives, following animal herds (bison, mammoths, reindeer, and wild horses were abundant), on which they depended for food.

Wall Paintings. What is known of Paleolithic life derives largely from paintings found in caves, particularly in the Franco-Cantabrian area of southern France and northern Spain. The most famous prehistoric wall paintings are those in the cave at Lascaux, France (fig. 1.1), which were created between ca. 15,000 and 10,000 B.C.E. The Lascaux paintings are quite naturalistic. Many of the animals—bison, mammoths, reindeer, boars, wolves, and horses—gracefully jump, run, and romp, conveying a remarkable sense of animation. Painting is done in blacks, browns, reds, and yellows, with most of the pigments used of mineral oxides, with deeper black from burned bones.

How and why were these paintings created? The paintings at Lascaux and at Vallon-Pont-d'Arc, in the Ardèche region of southern France, are located deep within the caves and are often very hard to reach. There is no evidence of human habitation where the paintings are located—instead, people seem to have lived at or near the entrances to the caves, where natural light was available. It is thought that the artists worked by the light of oil lamps. One theory holds that by creating these animals in paint, deep within the caves, the artists may have hoped that more animals would actually be born. Associated with this theory is the possibility that the superimposing, or layering, of animals was intended to show them mating.

Ritual and Religion. Unlike much of the art created in later eras, prehistoric art is thought to be related to ritual, linked with prayer to placate the powers of nature. In a form of sympathetic magic, power could be gained over elements of nature. For example, the theory that hunting rituals were performed in the caves to gain control over the animals depicted there is strongly supported not only by the painting of spears on the animals, but also by actual spearheads found driven into some of the painted animals, which are shown to bleed as a result of their injuries. Thus, in order to ensure a successful hunt, the animal may have been killed in effigy before the hunt.

Art, religion, and ritual were bound together as images, words, and physical movement were combined to achieve success in the hunt. Religion and ritual were critically important for prehistoric cultures in which some measure of control over nature was necessary for survival.

Sculpture. Only a fraction of the sculpture made in prehistoric times of durable materials such as ivory, bone, horn, stone, and clay is known today, and still fewer sculptures made of a perishable material, such as wood, remain.

Depictions of the human figure are rare in Paleolithic sculpture, and the few known are mostly female figures. The most famous example of prehistoric sculpture is the so-called *Woman* (or *Venus*) *of Willendorf* (fig. 1.2), a stone figure small enough to be held in a hand, dated to about 25,000–20,000 B.C.E., and named for the place where it was found in western Austria near the Danube River.

FIGURE 1.1   *Overview of the Hall of the Bulls, Lascaux, Dordogne, France, ca. 15,000–10,000 B.C.E., cave painting.* Prehistoric artists depicted with notable realism the animals on which they depended for food. With very few exceptions, the animals represented in such paintings are identifiable.

The *Woman of Willendorf* is highly stylized. The greatly enlarged breasts and abdomen—which suggest pregnancy—indicate the work's possible connection to human fertility. In fact, prior to the Neolithic period, almost no other human types are known. Perhaps such figures were a type of idol and were intended to promote human fertility, much as the cave paintings of animals might have been intended to "create" animals for the hunters.

THE NEOLITHIC PERIOD

By 8000 B.C.E., possibly the most important transformation in the history of human civilization took place: Around the world, in the Near East, in South and Central America, and in Southeast Asia, human beings ceased to hunt and began instead to farm, plowing and planting seeds, growing crops, and domesticating animals, using them not only as a reliable source of food and clothing but also as beasts of burden, inaugurating what is known as the **Neolithic** period, or New Stone Age. Hunters and gatherers became herders and farmers, and more permanent societies began to develop.

This transformation from a nomadic life of hunting to a more settled life of herding and agriculture revolutionized life for prehistoric peoples. One historian has characterized the Neolithic era as the matrix from which civilization appears and provides the preconditions on which it rests. These preconditions include the ability to grow wheat, maize, rice, and barley, along with the capability of domesticating formerly wild pigs, goats, sheep, and cattle. These developments radically altered the conditions of human existence.

Wall Paintings.   In the Valtorta Gorge (fig. 1.3) on the southeast coast of Spain, paintings that date from sometime after 8000 B.C.E. and possibly as late as 3000 B.C.E. suggest that hunting remained the chief preoccupation of these peoples. But changes and advances are evident. Unlike the paintings of the Franco-Cantabrian area that are located deep in caves, the Valtorta Gorge paintings are on the smooth limestone walls in rock shelters and beneath cliff overhangs. The subjects portrayed differ significantly also, for here the human figure is given prominence, with people shown hunting animals, fighting, and dancing together, as a group or community.

A degree of narrative is evident in the Valtorta wall paintings as the hunters, running from the left, attack the herd crossing a stream from the right. The composition is organized with a definite flow to the chase, a sense of action and movement conveyed by the lively postures of the figures—indeed, this appears to be a record of an actual event. A superb document of early hunting techniques, the scene shows hunters using the bow and arrow, a weapon not seen in Franco-Cantabrian art.

Architecture.   Prehistoric architecture survives only from the Neolithic period, and very little survives at all. Structures made of wood, other plant material, or mud brick decayed and disappeared long ago.

The most famous example of prehistoric architecture is surely the **cromlech,** or circle of stones having a religious purpose, known as Stonehenge (fig. 1.4), located on the Salisbury Plain in Wiltshire, England, and completed ca. 2000 B.C.E. A **henge** is a circle of stones or posts. Stonehenge is not the only prehistoric cromlech to have sur-

FIGURE 1.3   Herd crossing river, hunters with bows and arrows, Valtorta Gorge, Levant, Spain, ca. 8000–3000 B.C.E., rock painting. Because humans are prominently depicted, are shown using weapons, and because this scene has a definite composition, the Valtorta Gorge paintings are believed to date later than those at Lascaux.

nected with several "correspondences." If you stand in the center of Stonehenge and look to the so-called heelstone, you see that the top aligns with the horizon. The sun rises directly over the heelstone at the summer solstice, the longest day of the year. On each of the four mounds were other stones at horizon level—the one to the southwest is

FIGURE 1.2   *Woman of Willendorf,* found at Willendorf, Austria, ca. 25,000–20,000 B.C.E., limestone, height $4\frac{3}{8}''$ (11 cm), Naturhistorisches Museum, Vienna. The so-called *Venus of Willendorf* is the most famous (but not the most physically distorted) of several extant female figurines thought to be associated with prehistoric beliefs about human fertility, or, alternatively, fat as a sign of physical beauty in an era when food was scarce.

FIGURE 1.4   Stonehenge, Salisbury Plain, Wiltshire, England, completed ca. 2000 B.C.E., bluestone and sarsen, height of stones of outer circle 20′ (6.09 m). This enigmatic remnant of prehistoric architecture is believed to have been a monumental clock, laid out so the stones relate to the position of the sun at the summer and winter solstices.

vived, but it is the most impressive and best preserved. The outer trench is approximately 150 feet in diameter, and the individual stones approximately 20 feet high. There is a definite entranceway, as well as four mounds evenly placed on the outer trench, and a central stone referred to as the altar stone. The huge upright stones form an outer circle and two inner circles or U shapes. Some of the stones are shaped into rectangles, and some also have patterns cut into them. Stonehenge is constructed using the **post and lintel** system—in its simplest form, two vertical posts support a horizontal lintel. At Stonehenge, the vertical posts have dowel pins carved into their uppermost end, which fit into circular depressions carved on the underside of the lintels at both ends, thereby locking the posts and lintels together.

What can the purpose or function of so monumental an undertaking have been? The answer seems to be con-

at the point of the setting sun at the winter solstice, the shortest day of the year. Stonehenge, therefore, seems to be an enormous sun clock or calendar, based on the rising and setting sun at the summer and winter solstices.

MESOPOTAMIA: THE CRADLE OF CIVILIZATION

Even before Stonehenge was built in England, two far more advanced civilizations were developing in the Near East: that of Mesopotamia and that of Egypt. Mesopotamian civilization developed in the valley between the Tigris and Euphrates Rivers: Mesopotamia is a Greek word meaning literally "the land between two rivers." Consisting of the eastern part of what is known as the Fertile Crescent, which extends northward along the eastern coast of the Mediterranean through what is today Israel and Lebanon, eastward into present-day Syria and Iraq, and south down the Tigris and Euphrates valleys to the Persian Gulf, Mesopotamia was the most fertile and arable land in the Near East, and perhaps, at the dawn of the Neolithic Age, the most fertile in the world. It was here, at any rate, that around 9000 B.C.E. agriculture—literally, from the Latin *cultura*, or cultivation, of the *ager*, land—was first fully developed.

By about 3000 B.C.E., two further developments had taken place that had a decisive influence on the course of civilization. Sometime after 6000 B.C.E. people learned to mine and use copper; by 3000 B.C.E., they had discovered that by combining tin with copper they could produce a much stronger alloy, bronze, which allowed tremendous innovations in the production of weapons, tools, and jewelry. This marked the beginning of the Bronze Age.

The second development marks the move from prehistory into the first historical period—that is, a period for which written records exist. By about 3000 B.C.E., the people of ancient Mesopotamia were using written language, known today largely from clay tablets that were first unearthed in the mid-nineteenth century. Chiefly the province of the upper class and priests, this writing was accomplished in wedge-shaped **cuneiform** characters (from the Latin *cuneus*, meaning "wedge") made with a stylus that was itself wedge shaped and that was pressed into wet clay tablets. The original purpose of this writing seems to have been to keep agricultural records. Among the oldest examples of cuneiform writing, for instance, is a tablet from a temple complex at Uruk that lists sacks of grains and heads of cattle. Cuneiform writing began as a **pictographic** system. In its earliest form, the symbol for "cow" was an abstract "picture" of a cow's head:

But the pictographs were quickly abstracted even further, presumably in no small part because it was difficult

to draw a curve with a reed stylus in wet clay. Between 2500 and 1800 B.C.E., the sign for "cow" was first turned ninety degrees sideways and then converted into a series of quickly imprinted wedges:

By combining pictograms, more complex ideas—or **ideograms**—and even abstract ideas could be represented. A bird next to an egg meant "fertility." Two crossed lines meant "hatred" or "enmity," and parallel lines signified "friendship":

Sometime around 2000 B.C.E., another important development occurred, when pictograms began to represent not only objects but sounds—the birth of phonetic writing.

Assisted by these technical advances, three successive civilizations—those of Sumer, Akkad, and Babylon—blossomed in Mesopotamia over the following 1500 years.

Table 1–1   DEVELOPMENT OF WRITING
Cuneiform (Mesopotamian): wedge-shaped images incised in clay
Pictographic: pictures of objects as "words"—cow = ⟨
Ideographic: combinations of pictures as ideograms— hatred = ✕
Hieroglyphic (Egyptian): pictures and sounds together
Phonetic (Phoenician): sounds as syllables
Alphabetic (Greek): letters as sounds

SUMER

The Sumerians, who lived at the southern end of the Tigris and Euphrates Rivers, founded the Mesopotamian cvilization between 3500 and 3000 B.C.E., contemporary with the beginning of Egyptian civilization. Sumerian culture reached its zenith by approximately 2800–2700 B.C.E. It was at this time that Sumer's most famous king, GILGAMESH [GIL-gah-mesh] (ca. 2700 B.C.E.), ruled Uruk, one of the many independent city-states that grew up in Mesopotamia.

Each Sumerian city-state had its own local god and its own local ruler. The kings were not thought of as gods—rather, the god was considered the owner of the city-state, with the king as an intermediary between the god and the people. In each city-state, the buildings were clustered around the temple of the city's god. Religion focused on seasonal fertility. Agricultural mythology included the Bull of Heaven, whose fiery breath could burn crops, and Imdugud, a lion-headed eagle whose wings covered the heavens in dark clouds, a good creature who brought rain and ended droughts brought on by the Bull of Heaven.

Like most early religions, Sumerian and later Mesopotamian religions were **polytheistic**—that is, there were many gods and goddesses, who often competed with one another for the attention of the worshipers. The gods were human in form, and possessed human personalities and foibles—that is, they were **anthropomorphic.** The four chief gods were Anu, the heaven god; Ninhursag, the mother goddess; Enlil, the god of air; and Enki, the god of water. As human as the behavior of these gods might be, they were nonetheless clearly superior to humans, particularly by their immortality. The cuneiform sign for god is a star, which also means "on high," or "elevated," as well as "in the heavens."

Architecture.   Sumerian domestic architecture seems to have consisted largely of houses that were square or rectangular in plan and built of mud brick. Archaeologists have not been able to work out the precise layouts of Mesopotamian cities, but it seems certain that at the heart of the settlement would have been the temple. Sumerian temples were built on raised platforms known as **ziggurats,** an example of which is the Ziggurat of King Urnammu at Ur, in Iraq (fig. 1.5), constructed ca. 2500–2050 B.C.E. of sun-baked mud brick and, consequently, now greatly disintegrated. The lowest level is fifty feet high. The walls are **battered,** that is, sloping, making them stronger than vertical walls because they are self-buttressing. The walls are constructed with **weeper holes** to allow water that collects in the masonry to run out through these small,

regularly placed openings. The ziggurat at Ur demonstrates the use of specific orientation in architecture, for the corners point north, south, east, and west.

The actual temple was atop the ziggurat. Within the temple, a statue of the god stood in the sanctuary, a long room running the entire length of the temple. The lower levels of the ziggurat were covered with dirt and planted with trees, thus creating the effect of a mountain with a temple on top. This practice is explained by the belief that the gods lived on the mountain tops, so ziggurats brought worshippers closer to heaven.

Sculpture.   Although Sumerian sculpture includes occasional secular subjects, most examples appear to be religious or commemorative in purpose, and to have been made for temples. The human figure is represented in a distinctive manner unique to Sumerian sculpture. The style is one of formal simplification, geometric and symmetrical. The figure type is squat in proportions, with broad hips and heavy legs.

A statue formerly thought to represent Abu (Abu means "father" in Arabic languages), the god of vegetation (fig. 1.6), comes from a group of similar statues dated ca. 2600 B.C.E., carved of white gypsum, with black limestone and white shell insets, found in the Abu temple at Tell Asmar. Some of these statues may represent gods. Others may represent worshippers. Curiously, it appears that Sumerian people might have a statue carved to represent themselves and do their worshipping for them—in their place, as a stand-in. An inscription on one such statue translates, "It offers prayers." Another inscription says, "Statue, say unto my king (god) . . ."

FIGURE 1.5   Ziggurat of King Urnammu (Nanna), Ur (El Muqeiyar), Iraq, ca. 2500–2050 B.C.E., sun-baked mud brick. The Sumerians built their temples atop ziggurats—rectangular mountains constructed of mud brick, with battered (sloping) walls.

FIGURE 1.6   Standing man, formerly thought to represent Abu, the god of vegetation. From Tell Asmar, ca. 2600 B.C.E. White gypsum, insets of black limestone and white shell, height ca. $11\frac{3}{4}''$ (29.8 cm), Fletcher Fund, 1940, Metropolitan Museum of Modern Art, New York. Sumerian statues are easily recognized by their large eyes, single eyebrow, and seemingly astonished facial expression.

Although little Sumerian painting remains, decorative objects have survived. A noteworthy example is an inlaid standard (fig. 1.7), from Ur, dated ca. 2700–2600 B.C.E. The figures on this double-sided panel are made of shell or mother-of-pearl inlaid in bitumen, with the background formed from pieces of the blue stone, lapis lazuli, and additional bits of red limestone. The standard, on which scenes of war are portrayed, is commemorative with events arranged in horizontal rows. On one side, on the top row, the king steps out of his chariot to inspect his captives. The king is shown to be taller than anyone else—his head breaks through the border. On the two lower rows are scenes of battle, with fighters wearing metal helmets, cloaks, fleece kilts, and riding in four-wheeled chariots. On the other side, on the top row, the victory feast is shown. The king and his officers sit in chairs and drink.

The king is, again, largest. On the two lower rows, booty taken in battle is paraded in front of them, including cows and animals of unidentifiable species.

Literature.   The oldest known major literary work in the world is *The Epic of Gilgamesh*, the earliest elements of which date from about 1900 B.C.E., when Gilgamesh reigned in the Euphrates city-state of Uruk. Legends about Gilgamesh were told but not recorded until hundreds of years after his death. Before about 2000 B.C.E., these stories were recorded on cuneiform tablets. From around 1900–1600 B.C.E. onward, the Gilgamesh stories were written down by the Akkadians, a people who spoke an early Semitic language related to both Hebrew and Arabic. The earliest known version of the epic was discovered in the seventh century B.C.E. in the library of the Assyrian king Ashurbanipal (669–627 B.C.E.).

Like other ancient epics such as those of Homer (see Chapter 2), *The Epic of Gilgamesh* includes elements of folklore, legend, and myth that accrued over time. The work is compiled of originally separate stories concerning Gilgamesh; Enkidu, a primeval human figure; Utnapishtim [OOT-nah-PISH-tim], a Babylonian counterpart of Noah; and a number of other figures.

The epic begins with a kind of prologue that emphasizes Gilgamesh's wisdom as a ruler and his importance to recorded history. The prologue also characterizes him as a semidivine figure, who, though not immortal, is courageous, strong, and beautiful. He is also described as an arrogant and oppressive ruler. When his people cry out for help to their gods for assistance, the god Anu creates Enkidu, a primitive combination of man and wild animal, a figure related to those depicted on the lyre from the tomb of Queen Puabi in Ur.

The story of the mutually positive influences Gilgamesh and Enkidu exert upon each other, of their developing friendship, and their heroic adventures occupies the bulk of the epic. An additional segment concerning Gilgamesh in the Underworld forms a kind of epilogue. In their first adventure, Gilgamesh and Enkidu confront and kill the giant Humbaba. When the goddess Ishtar proposes that Gilgamesh become her lover, he refuses, which precipitates the goddess sending the Bull of Heaven to destroy the city of Uruk by famine.

The second adventure of Gilgamesh and Enkidu involves the slaying of the destructive Bull, the punishment for which is Enkidu's death through illness. After losing his companion, Gilgamesh journeys to visit Utnapishtim, the only human ever granted immortality, but fails to learn the secret of everlasting life, though he does return home having gleaned much else from the wisdom of Utnapishtim. With this knowledge he rules as a wise king. Gilgamesh's adventures are occasions for writers to explore questions that will be raised again in later epics. What is the relationship between human beings and their deities? How are human beings linked with the world of nature

Cross Currents

SUMERIAN MYTH AND THE BIBLE

There are strong parallels between Sumerian mythology and the stories in the biblical book of Genesis. For instance, surviving Sumerian texts parallel the story of Noah and the flood, including an episode in The Epic of Gilgamesh—a huge flood did indeed inundate Mesopotamia about 2900 B.C.E. In another Sumerian myth, the story of Enki and Ninhursag, which is some three hundred verses long, Enki, the great Sumerian god of water, creates a garden paradise in Dilmun by bringing water up from the earth. In Genesis 2:6, a similar event occurs: "But there went up a mist from the earth, and watered the whole face of the ground." Ninhursag,

the mother-goddess of the Sumerians, causes eight plants to sprout in this proto-Garden of Eden, and Enki, wanting to taste the plants, has another lesser god pick them. Ninhursag is furious and pronounces the curse of death upon Enki. This is a moment in the story that anticipates the biblical God's fury at Adam and Eve for eating the apple that Satan has tempted them with and their expulsion from the garden into a fallen world in which they must confront their mortality. Unlike Adam and Eve, however, Enki is eventually restored to immortality by Ninhursag, but the parallels between the two stories are striking.

Also close in spirit to the biblical Creation story is the *Poem of the Supersage*, an Akkadian text written down about

1700 B.C.E. Like most Akkadian texts, it is probably based on Sumerian legend. The story begins in a divine society where the gods, in order to satisfy their material needs, had to work. Some gods, the leaders, called Anunnaki, were pure consumers, but the rest were laborers. These last, called Igigu, finally revolted, creating the prospect of famine among the Anunnaki. It was Enki who resolved the crisis by proposing that the gods create a substitute labor force out of the clay of the earth, whose destiny it would be to work and whose life would have a limited duration. Thus, as in Genesis, humankind is created out of clay, must labor, and is mortal.

and animals? What are the obligations of friendship, family, and public duty? How should we live in the face of mortality?

The earliest known poet, from Mesopotamia, is the poet-priestess Enheduanna, who wrote in the Sumerian language.

Daughter of the Akkadian kiing Sargon, Enheduanna wrote works that in part assisted her father in his attempt to unite Akkadia and Sumeria. Her best known poems are hymns to Akkadian and Sumerian gods and goddesses, most notably to Inanna, the Sumerian goddess of love.

FIGURE 1.7   Inlaid standard, from the "royal cemetery" at Ur, ca. 2700–2600 B.C.E., double-sided panel, shell or mother-of-pearl, lapis lazuli, and red limestone, inlaid in bitumen, ca. 8″ × 19″ (20.3 × 48.3 cm), British Museum, London. Much like today's comic strips, a series of scenes are arranged in chronological sequence to tell a tale—in this case, that of a successful battle, the victory feast, and the taking of war spoils.

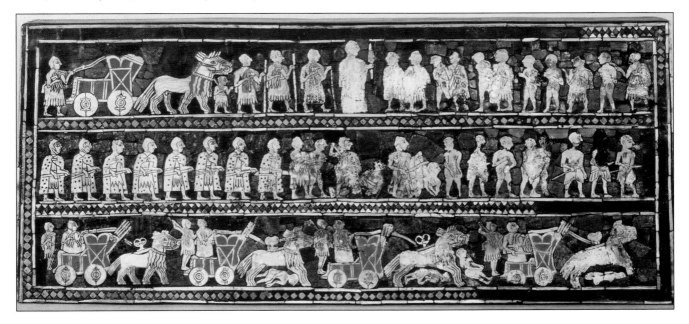

Then & Now

AKKAD

Under the leadership of King SARGON I, who ruled ca. 2332–2279 B.C.E., and his grandson and successor NARAM-SIN [NA-ram-sin], the Semitic people of Akkad conquered all of the city-states of Sumer. Subsequently, the governors of these cities were 'slaves" to the king of Akkad, and he himself was a god to them.

The most celebrated example of Akkadian art is the *Victory Stele of Naram-Sin* (fig. 1.8), ca. 2300–2200 B.C.E. A **stele** is a vertical slab of stone that serves as a marker. The *Victory Stele of Naram-Sin*, which is six and a half feet high, is carved on one side only. At the top of the scene is a set of stars—the sign for Naram-Sin's protecting gods—and below, Naram-Sin and his army victoriously climb a mountain, as if to place themselves in closer proximity to the gods, the defeated lying slaughtered or begging for mercy at their feet. Naram-Sin himself, taller than the rest, as is always the case in Akkadian depictions of royalty, wearing the horned helmet used to identify the gods, and, standing at the very top of the battle, on the bodies of two victims, strides confidently to his place as the leader of all Mesopotamia.

BABYLON

However powerful Sargon I and Naram-Sin might have been, the Akkad kingdom lasted under two hundred years. For the next three hundred years, until about 1900 B.C.E., Mesopotamia was subject to constant division and conflict among its various city-states. Then a tribe of nomads, originally known as the Amorites, invaded the region from the Arab peninsula and established a royal city in Babylon. In 1792 B.C.E., when HAMMURABI [hamooh-RAH-bee] (r. 1792–1750 B.C.E.), the first great king of Babylon, took power, the Sumerian and Akkadian city-states were unified as a single kingdom under his rule.

Sculpture. One of Hammurabi's great accomplishments was to codify the laws of the region. The stele inscribed with the Law Code of Hammurabi (fig. 1.9), carved of basalt ca. 1760 B.C.E., which stands seven feet high, is both a work of art and a historic legal document. Hammurabi's law code is the earliest known written body of laws. The code consists of 282 laws arranged in six chapters: 1. Personal property; 2. Land; 3. Trade and commerce (this

FIGURE 1.8 *Victory Stele of Naram-Sin*, ca. 2300–2200 B.C.E., limestone, height 6′ 6″ (1.98 m), Musée du Louvre, Paris. This stone slab carved in relief served as a public monument to commemorate the military accomplishments of Naram-Sin. In this, it deserves comparison to the palette of the Egyptian pharaoh Narmer (see fig. 1.17).

FIGURE 1.9 Stele inscribed with the Law Code of Hammurabi, ca. 1760 B.C.E., basalt, height of stele ca. 7′ (2.13 m), height of relief ca. 28″ (71.1 cm), Musée du Louvre, Paris. The significance of this legal document was made clear to the Babylonian people by the relief at the top of the stele that depicts the sun god Shamash giving these laws directly to Hammurabi, king of Babylon.

chapter seems strikingly modern, for it includes fixing of prices, contracts, rates of interest, promissory notes, and credit); 4. Family; 5. Maltreatment; and 6. Labor (including the fixing of wages). The penalties, which included death, varied according to the social class of the harmed person and were based on an eye-for-an-eye, tooth-for-a-tooth approach to law.

The relief at the top of the Law Code of Hammurabi shows Shamash, the sun god who controlled plant life and weather, dispelled evil spirits of disease, and personified righteousness and justice—the appropriate god for a law code. (Shamash is also represented in the *Stele of Naram-Sin* as one of the stars overlooking the scene.) Hammurabi appears to converse with Shamash, from whom he receives the laws. The difference in importance between the two figures is made clear, the king standing while Shamash is shown larger, elevated, and enthroned.

ASSYRIA

Babylon fell to the nomadic Kassite people in about 1550 B.C.E. This was followed by a period of relative cultural decline, before the great ancient Mesopotamian civilization was developed by the Assyrians. The Assyrian culture began in the middle of the second millennium B.C.E., achieved significant power around 900 B.C.E., and lasted until 612 B.C.E. when Nineveh and Syria fell. The ideals of an imperialistic culture mobilized for conquest are reflected in the emphasis on fortifications and military subjects in art.

Sculpture. Stone was abundant in the northern region of the Tigris and Euphrates valleys where the Assyrians originated, permitting them to produce large scale sculpture. Between the ninth and seventh centuries B.C.E., stone guardian monsters were placed at gateways and defined an Assyrian style; several examples survive, including those from the palace of ASHURNASIRPAL II [ash-er-na-SEER-pal] (r. 883–859 B.C.E.) at Nimrud (fig. 1.10). The headdress is peculiar to Mesopotamian deities and is similar to that worn by Shamash on the Babylonian stele with the Law Code of Hammurabi. With the body of a lion, wings of a bird, and head of a human, such guardian figures were perhaps intended to combine human intelligence with animal strength. Perhaps they were intended to be frightening as well or to impress people with the king's power. Alternatively, they have been said to represent the Assyrian god Nergal, whose emblem is a winged lion.

Seen from the front, only the two front legs of these creatures are visible. Seen from the side, four legs are visible and the creature appears to be walking. To make this monster appear correct both from the front and the side, the sculptor has generously given him five legs!

Other than gateway guardians, Assyrian sculpture consists mostly of **reliefs**—figures cut from a flat, two-dimensional background. **Statues in the round**—sculptures that are freestanding and can be seen from all sides—are extremely rare. Assyrian reliefs were part of the architecture; the carved panels were set into the walls of the palaces.

One such relief, the depiction of *Ashurnasirpal II Killing Lions* (fig. 1.11), carved ca. 850 B.C.E., from Nimrud, portrays a militaristic subject commonly used to glorify the king. In fact, this event was more a ceremony than an actual lion hunt, since soldiers lined up to form a square, and the lion was released from a cage into the square. The artist has not tried to duplicate observed reality. Three horses are shown, but each receives only two legs. Although figures overlap, there is no sense of space, no setting, and everything takes place on the same ground line. The result is more a decorative surface than a realistic three-dimensional depiction.

FIGURE 1.10 *Human-Headed Winged Lion* (lamassu), from the northwest palace of Ashurnasirpal II at Numrud (Calah), ca. 883–859 B.C.E., limestone, height 10′ 2½″ (3.11 m), length 9′ 1½″ (2.78 m), Metropolitan Museum of Art, New York. Part human and part animal, the five-legged Assyrian gate monsters are among a vast population of early imaginary composite creatures. Later artists, in various cultures, created generations of descendants with a remarkable range of implausible physiognomies.

The limestone relief depicting the *Sack of the City of Hamanu by Ashurbanipal* (fig. 1.12), from the palace of ASHURBANIPAL [ash-er-BAN-ee-pul] (r. 669–ca. 627 B.C.E.) at Nineveh, was carved two hundred years after the Nimrud relief, in approximately 650 B.C.E. The carving illustrated is one of a series of historical reliefs that records the defeat of the Elamites by Ashurbanipal. Here, the story of the Assyrian sack of Hamanu is clearly told. Buildings are burned; Ashurbanipal's soldiers tear down buildings with pickaxes; pieces of the structures fall through the air; soldiers carry contraband down the hill. This matter-of-fact record was no doubt intended to glorify Ashurbanipal's military achievements and to intimidate enemies wanting to challenge his authority. It should be added that the Assyrians had a reputation for ferocity, which they earned, in part, by their practice of impaling the heads of their enemies on spikes.

NEBUCHADNEZZAR'S BABYLON

The description of Rome in the book of Revelation in the New Testament of the Bible includes the following description of the great sixth-century B.C.E. Mesopotamian city of Babylon: "What city is like unto this great city . . . that great city that was clothed in fine linen and purple and scarlet and decked with gold and precious stones and pearls! . . . Babylon, the Great, the Mother of Harlots and of the Abominations of the Earth." The biblical prophet tells us as much about his own Judeo-Christian morality as he does about Babylon's decadence, but of Babylon's great wealth and position in the sixth century B.C.E. there can be no doubt.

The Assyrians undertook a major rebuilding of the original city that Hammurabi had built a thousand years ear-

FIGURE 1.11 *Ashurnasirpal II Killing Lions*, from the palace of Ashurnasirpal II at Nimrud (Calah), Iraq, ca. 850 B.C.E., limestone relief, 3′ 3″ × 8′ 4″ (0.99 × 2.54 m), British Museum, London. This precisely carved relief records a ceremony used to emphasize the power of the Assyrian king—he is shown overcoming a lion, long regarded as "king of beasts."

Connections

THE FUNDAMENTALS OF CIVILIZATION

Civilization requires many different components to function. The study of early cultures indicates what some of these things are: technology, or tools and special technical skills that give rise to trade; laws, for the regulation of society; governmental structures; cities, or permanent settlements; and writing, through which culture is transmitted.

One Sumerian text outlines the knowledge necessary to live as civilized people. An extraordinary tale, narrated by Berossos, a Babylonian scholar who, around 300 B.C.E., recorded in Greek the history and traditions of his country, it recalls a time when the people of Chaldea, on the Persian Gulf, in Lower Mesopotamia, "lived an irreligious life, similar to that of animals":

In the first year an extraordinary monster appeared . . . on the shore of the Red Sea, and its name was Oannes. Its entire body was that of a fish, and underneath his head was a second one, as well as feet similar to those of a man—an image that is still remembered and that is still depicted up to today. This being lived among the people without eating anything and taught them writing, science, and technology of all types, the foundation of cities, the building of temples, jurisprudence, and geometry. He also revealed to them [how to cultivate] grains and how to harvest fruits. In short, he revealed to them all that constitutes civilized life. He did it so well that ever since one has found nothing exceptional in it. When the sun set, the monster Oannes plunged back into the sea to pass the night in the water, because he was amphibious. Later similar creatures appeared . . .

The story is not meant to be interpreted literally. Like many of the adventures in *The Epic of Gilgamesh*, it is a **myth**, a story involving legendary heroes, gods, and creatures that explains important cultural practices or beliefs. However "true" or otherwise the story may be, the lesson is clear: No one thing guarantees civilization. It is the combination of science, technology, agriculture, mathematics, law, literature, architecture, and the arts that constitutes civilized life.

FIGURE 1.12 *Sack of the City of Hamanu by Ashurbanipal*, from the palace of Ashurbanipal Nineveh (Kuyunjik), Iraq, ca. 650 B.C.E., limestone relief, 36″ × 24½″ (92.7 × 62.2 cm), British Museum, London. Assyrian emphasis on narration and documentation permitted disregard for relative scale and spatial logic. Realistic representation of a military campaign in stone relief first appears on the Column of Trajan (see figs. 4.17 and 4.18) in the second century C.E.

lier, after sacking and destroying it in 689 B.C.E. Only forty years later in 648 B.C.E., its population had once again become sufficiently irritating to the Assyrian kings to cause Ashurbanipal to attack it again, killing all those who opposed him. "I fed their corpses to the dogs, pigs, *zibu*-birds, vultures, the birds of the sky and the fish of the ocean," Ashurbanipal bragged.

After the death of Ashurbanipal, when Assyrian dominance in the region collapsed, the city again rose to prominence. Referred to by scholars as Neo-Babylon, to distinguish it from the Babylon of Hammurabi, and sometimes called Chaldea as well, it was rebuilt by the architects of NEBUCHADNEZZAR II [ney-book-ad-NEZ-zahr] (r. 604–562 B.C.E.) to become the greatest city in the Near East. It was graced by its famous Hanging Gardens, one of the so-called Seven Wonders of the World. Rising high above the flat plain of the valley floor was its Marduk ziggurat—sometimes believed to be the biblical Tower of Babel, since Bab-il was an early form of the city's name.

The richness of the city is embodied in the most remarkable of its surviving parts, the Ishtar Gate (fig. 1.13), built ca. 575 B.C.E. by Nebuchadnezzar himself and today housed in the Berlin State Museum. Ishtar is the Sumerian goddess of love and war. Her gate is ornamented with bulls, lions, and dragons—all emblematic of her power—arranged in tiers, on a blue background, in brown, yellow, and white. The gate rose over the Processional Way, known in Babylonian as *Aibur-shabu*, the place "the enemy shall never pass." Leading up to the gate was a broad paved road lined with high walls that were decorated with the

FIGURE 1.13 Ishtar Gate, from Babylon, ca. 575 B.C.E., glazed brick, Staatliche Museen zu Berlin, Preussischer Kulturbesitz, Vorderasiatisches Museum, Berlin. The appeal of animals as architectural ornaments to the Babylonians is evident on this gate to Nebuchadnezzar's sacred precinct.

figures of 120 lions, symbols of Ishtar. The animals on both the Ishtar Gate and the wall of the Processional Way are made in relief of **glazed** (painted and fired) **brick,** the technique for making them probably invented in Mesopotamia during Nebuchadnezzar's reign. The glaze made the mud bricks waterproof, which accounts for their survival.

PERSIA

In 539 B.C.E., the King of Persia, CYRUS II [SI-rus] (r. 559–530 B.C.E.), entered Babylon without significant resistance and took over the city, forbidding looting and appointing a Persian governor. Cyrus offered peace and friendship to the Babylonians, and he allowed them to continue worshipping their own gods. In fact, legend quickly had it that as he advanced on the city, the Babylonian god Marduk was at his side.

The Persians originated from Elam, in modern-day western Iran. Although some sites date back to around 5000 B.C.E., the Persians had begun to rise to power by the sixth century B.C.E. and by 480 B.C.E. their empire extended from the Indus River in the east to the Danube in the north. Moreover, in the same period that Cyrus overran Mesopotamia, the other great Near Eastern civilization, Egypt, lost its independence to the Persians. Persian art is found across this large geographical area.

Religion. Perhaps the most lasting innovation made by Persian culture was in religion. The prophet Zoroaster, or Zarathustra, who lived around 600 B.C.E., rejected the polytheism of earlier Mesopotamian cultures and instead developed a **dualistic religion,** in which the universe is divided between two forces, one good and one evil. According to Zoroaster, Ahuramazda, the god of light, was caught up in an eternal struggle with Ahriman, the god of darkness. As noted earlier, the Christian Bible may have been influenced in some of its stories by *The Epic of Gilgamesh*. Similarly, some ideas in Zoroastrianism may have influenced later religions, such as the idea of a "Prince of Darkness" (Satan) and a Last Judgment.

FIGURE 1.14 Palace of Darius and Xerxes, Persepolis, Iran, 518–ca. 460 B.C.E., overview. Constructed on a raised platform and impressive in its enormous scale, the palace includes large rooms filled with forests of columns. The plan—axial, formal, and repetitious—appears to have been laid out on a grid.

Then & Now

BEER

The beer people drink today is an alcoholic beverage made by fermenting grains and usually incorporating hops, but the process of making it was discovered nearly 8000 years ago, around 6000 B.C.E., in Sumeria. The Sumerians made beer out of *bappir*, or half-baked, crusty loaves of bread, which they crumbled into water, fermented, and then filtered through a basket. Surviving records indicate that as much as fifty per cent of each grain harvest went into the production of beer and that in Ur, around 3000 B.C.E., needy persons were allotted one gallon of beer each day as part of a general social welfare program.

Literally hundreds of surviving cuneiform tablets contain recipes for beer, including *kassi* (a black beer), *kassag* (fine black beer), and *kassagsaan* (the finest premium beer). There were wheat beers, white beers, and red beers as well. One surviving tablet, which is rather reminiscent of modern advertising slogans, reads "Drink Ebla—the beer with the heart of a lion." Kings were buried with elaborate straws made of gold and lapis lazuli, designed for sipping beer. There was even a goddess, Ninkasi—"she who fills the mouth"—who looked over the production and distribution of the drink. "I feel wonderful, drinking beer," wrote one poet, about 3000 B.C.E., "in a blissful mood with joy in my heart

and a happy liver." But the Law Code of Hammurabi specifically banned the selling of beer for money. It could be bartered only for barley: "If a beer seller do not receive barley as the price for beer, but if she receive money or make the beer a measure smaller than the barley measure received, they shall throw her into the water."

Today there are over six hundred breweries making beer in the United States alone, each with its own unique process, producing perhaps ten times that many beers, each with its own unique flavor and color. The tradition, clearly, is as long and venerable as civilization itself.

Architecture. Because the ancient Persian religion centered on fire altars in the open air, no religious architecture was needed. However, huge palaces with many rooms, halls, and courts were constructed. The visitor to the palace at Persepolis (fig. 1.14), built 518–ca. 460 B.C.E. by DARIUS [DAR-ee-uss] (r. 521–486 B.C.E.) and XERXES I (r. 485–465 B.C.E.) who were the successors of Cyrus, is met by huge guardian monsters at the entrance towers of the Porch of Xerxes, reminiscent of the Assyrian guardian monsters. The palace of Persepolis is also similar to Assyrian palaces in being set on a raised platform. At Persepolis the palace stands on a rock-cut terrace, 545 by 330 yards, approached by a broad stairway of 106 shallow steps. Beyond were the main courtyards and the Throne Hall of Xerxes, known as the Hall of One Hundred Columns. This room was a forest of pillars, filled by ten rows of ten columns, each column rising forty feet. This was a new style for Mesopotamia, based on the use of tall columns.

Sculpture. The earliest extant Persian art consists of portable objects characteristic of nomadic peoples. Objects buried with the dead have survived—weapons, decorative items including jewelry, containers such as jugs, bowls, and cups, and other objects. Their style is referred to as an "animal style" because the objects are characterized by the decorative use of animal motifs. Small forms are used in ornamental jewel-like concentration. Popular motifs derive from the ibex, serpent, bird, bull, and sheep; the human figure plays a minor role.

A later example of this animal style, and a high point in technical accomplishment, is the winged ibex (fig. 1.15), a

FIGURE 1.15 Vase handle in the form of a winged ibex, from Persia, fourth century B.C.E., silver, partly gilded, height ca. $10\frac{1}{2}''$ (26.7 cm), Musée du Louvre, Paris. The skill of Persian metalsmiths is clearly evident in this exquisitely crafted wild mountain goat. Embellished by the addition of wings, two of nature's creatures have been combined to create a new species.

Critical Thinking

THE CONCEPT OF "CIVILIZATION"

The words "civil," "civilization," and "civilized" denote the elements of an organized society with a structured set of behaviors. These words are often set off against the words "barbaric," "barbarous," and "barbarian," which suggest the absence of civilized elements. Consider the extent to which civilized societies can exhibit barbaric qualities and the extent to which groups characterized as barbarians might exhibit aspects of civilized behavior. To what extent do these words continue to identify useful and valid distinctions? To what extent have they lost that function?

wild mountain goat made of silver, partly gilded, and intended to serve as a handle to a vase, dating from the fourth century B.C.E. This ibex has been magically graced with wings. Striking a lively pose, it seems also to have been given life. Despite its supernatural characteristics, the care with which it has been crafted underscores the Persian fascination with, and love of, animals. In fact, the Persians built gardens and "paradises"—enclosed sanctuaries where birds and animals were protected.

Relief Sculpture.   The palace at Persepolis was decorated with stone reliefs, including that of *Tribute Bearers Bringing Offerings* (fig. 1.16), flanking the stairway and carved ca. 490 B.C.E. Such ceremonial sculpture is concentrated almost exclusively along the staircases, giving a decorative emphasis to the main approaches. Three to six figures are used to represent each of twenty-three different nations of the empire. The repetition of stylized figures—in attendance, as servants, and in processions—may be said to become monotonous. These figures are stiff, if not frozen; representations of animals in Persian art have greater life and personality than representations of humans.

THE CIVILIZATION OF THE NILE

LIKE ITS MESOPOTAMIAN COUNTERPART, ancient Egyptian civilization developed slowly from about 5000 B.C.E. to approximately 3100 B.C.E. with no united or central government. There were in essence two independent Egypts: Upper Egypt and Lower Egypt ("Lower" Egypt actually lies north of "Upper" Egypt). Upper Egypt was a narrow strip of land on either side of the Nile River, extending seven hundred miles from the first cataract, or waterfall, in the south to the Nile Delta. Lower Egypt was situated in

FIGURE 1.16   *Tribute Bearers Bringing Offerings,* flanking stairway, Palace of Darius and Xerxes, Persepolis, Iran, ca. 490 B.C.E., limestone relief, height 8′ 4″ (2.54 m). Courtesy of the Oriental Institute of the University of Chicago. The message conveyed by these stiff, formal, and generous gift-bearing figures, passed by the visitor when entering the palace, is hardly subtle.

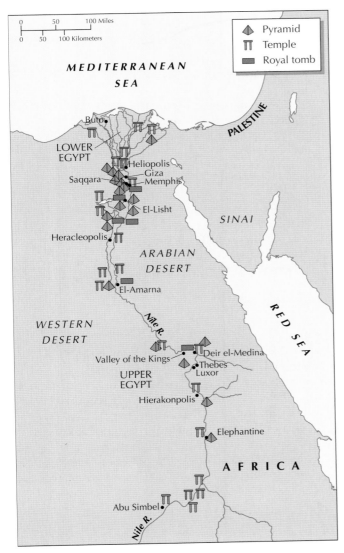

MAP 1.2   Ancient Egypt

mediate" periods of relative instability intervened between each of the "Kingdoms," and the last, "New" Kingdom was followed by a Late Period that concludes around 525 B.C.E. when Egypt finally lost its independence and was absorbed into the Persian Empire.

Despite times of relative disruption, life was unusually secure in ancient Egypt. The fertility of the Nile Valley, which was due to the huge amounts of topsoil swept each summer into the Nile River delta from far upstream in the African lake region and the Ethiopian plateau, supported the establishment of a permanent agricultural society. Moreover, the surrounding deserts largely eliminated the fear of invasion. The king, later called "pharaoh," which means "great house," was the absolute ruler and considered divine. Beneath him was a large class of priests and government bureaucrats. The permanence and stability of life and the highly centralized organization of ancient Egyptian society is reflected in the monumental and essentially permanent architecture of the pyramids. In fact, with few exceptions the art of Egypt remained remarkably consistent in style over three millennia. The unquestioning acceptance of convention is a major characteristic of ancient Egyptian culture. As a result, a sense of order and continuity pervades the history of ancient Egyptian life and art.

HIEROGLYPHICS

The Egyptians had developed a calendar, used irrigation systems, discovered the use of basic metals, and started using **hieroglyphics,** their writing system, all before 3000 B.C.E. For centuries scholars thought that the "glyphs" or characters used in hieroglyphics all represented complete ideas rather than individual units of sound. Indeed, until 1822 the actual meaning of the hieroglyphics was unknown. In that year, however, a Frenchman, Jean François Champollion, deciphered the Rosetta Stone (fig. 1.18). This was a large fragment of basalt that had been found during Napoleon's military campaign in Egypt near the town of Rosetta in the Nile Delta. When it became apparent that the three languages on the Rosetta Stone expressed almost the same thing—a decree in honor of Ptolemy V (196 B.C.E.), Champollion was able to establish that the corresponding Egyptian symbols were meant, as in Sumerian, to be read not just symbolically but phonetically as well. Thus, although a pictograph of a fish did indeed represent a "fish," combined with other pictographs it represented the sound of the word "fish," which is pronounced "nar." For instance, the name of the king of a united Egypt, Narmer, consists of the sign for a fish, "nar," and the sign for a chisel, which is pronounced "mer."

RELIGIOUS BELIEFS

Ancient Egyptian religion was polytheistic, involving belief in a profusion of gods. Among the most important gods in Egypt were the cosmic forces, including the sun,

the northern lands of the fertile Nile Delta where the river branches out and runs into the Mediterranean. Then, around 3100 B.C.E., the two Egypts were united by the king of Upper Egypt, NARMER, also known as MENES [ME-neez], and it is with this event that Egyptian history is usually said to begin. The event is celebrated in one of the earliest surviving Egyptian stone sculptures, the so-called *Palette of Narmer* (fig. 1.17).

Egyptian history is traditionally divided into about thirty dynasties. We know very little of the first two **dynasties,** but beginning with the third, the Egyptian dynasties are grouped into several major periods distinguished by their stability and achievement: the Old Kingdom (2686–2181 B.C.E., consisting of dynasties 3–6), the Middle Kingdom (2040–1786 B.C.E., consisting of dynasties 11–14), and the New Kingdom, or Empire (1552–1069 B.C.E., consisting of dynasties 18–20). So-called "Inter-

FIGURE 1.17   *Palette of Narmer,* front and back, from Hierakonpolis, ca. 3100 B.C.E., First Dynasty, slate, height 25″ (63.5 cm), Egyptian Museum, Cairo. This celebrated work is simultaneously a functional palette, an exquisite relief carving, and an historical document of the uniting of Lower and Upper Egypt by Narmer, the first pharaoh of the first Egyptian dynasty.

FIGURE 1.18   Rosetta Stone, 196 B.C.E., basalt, British Museum, London. The same information is inscribed in three languages: (1) Greek; (2) demotic script, a simplified form of hieroglyphic (the common language of Egypt); and (3) hieroglyphic, a pictographic script. By comparing the languages, hieroglyphics were finally translated in the early nineteenth century.

earth, sky, air, and water. The Nile was also worshipped as a deity, not surprisingly given its importance to Egyptian life. These forces and aspects of nature were depicted in various forms, often as animals, humans, or as hybrids. For example, the sun was sometimes pictured as a falcon, other times as a falcon-headed man wearing a sun disk as a crown. The animal attributes of the gods were often a shorthand for their qualities. For example, Hathor, who was the goddess of joy and love—attributes which the Egyptians viewed the cow as possessing—was depicted as a cow.

Among the most important of the Egyptian gods was Osiris, originally a local god of Lower Egypt, whose worship eventually spread throughout the country. The legend of Osiris's death at the hands of his brother Set, and the search for the corpse by Isis, Osiris's wife, plays an important part in Egyptian mythology, and is connected with Egyptian belief in the afterlife. According to the myth, after Isis discovered her husband's dead body in Phoenicia, she brought it back to Egypt and buried it there. Set came upon the buried body and, enraged, tore the dead Osiris

Table 1–2   MAJOR ANCIENT EGYPTIAN GODS AND GODDESSES

Amen/Amon	creation deity; linked to the god Ra as Amen-Ra/Amon-Ra
Anubis	god of embalming, of preserving the dead
Apis	god of fertility
Aten	sun god
Bast	a cat goddess; protects cats as well as people who care for cats
Bes	helps women in childbirth; protects children
Hapi/Hapy	god of the Nile River flood
Hathor	goddess of fertility; goddess of the sky; protectress of the dead and of the royal palace; Ra's mother, wife, and daughter
Horus	originally the god of the sky; associated with the pharaoh; son of Osiris and Isis
Imhotep	architect of the stepped pyramid of the pharaoh Zoser; deified as the god of medicine and patron of scribes
Isis	the divine mother goddess; guardian of the dead; healed the sick; a skilled magician; sister and wife of Osiris and mother of Horus
Khons	god of the moon
Maat	goddess of truth, right, and proper behavior; the ostrich feather in her hair was weighed against the heart of the dead person to determine whether they had led a pure life
Min	god of virility; consort of Qetesh
Mut	"mother"; wife/consort of Amon
Neith	goddess of war and of wisdom
Nephthys	with her sister Isis, a protectress of the dead
Nut	goddess of the sky
Osiris	god of the dead, of the afterlife, of the underworld
Ptah	patron god of craftsmen; creator of the universe
Qetesh	goddess of love and beauty; consort of Min
Ra/Re	the sun god
Selket	a goddess whose scorpion killed wicked people; aided women in childbirth
Set/Seth	god of storms and violence; brother and murderer of Osiris; rival of Horus
Shu	god of air and wind
Tefnut	goddess of mist and clouds
Thoth	god of writing; of wisdom; messenger of the gods
Thoueris	goddess of fertility; protected women in childbirth

limb from limb, scattering the pieces throughout the country. Again Isis found her dead husband's body parts and buried each where it lay.

The son of Isis and Osiris avenged his father's death by engaging Set in battle and defeating him. However, when Set was brought to Isis, instead of killing him, she set him free. According to some versions of the myth, Osiris was restored to life and became king of the underworld. This myth of Osiris's resurrection later became an important element of the cult of Isis, the most important mother goddess in Egyptian religion, and a significant influence on Egyptian belief in life after death.

The Afterlife. Much of Egyptian life appears to have been oriented toward preparing for the hereafter. The Old Kingdom Egyptians believed that the body of the deceased must be preserved if the **ka,** the indestructible essence or vital principle of each person, roughly equivalent to the Christian concept of a soul, were to live on. This is why the Egyptians embalmed and bound their dead. This process of mummification was a complex procedure that involved emptying the bodily cavities of their organs, refilling them with spices and Arabic gums, and then wrapping the body in layers of bandages. This took seventy days to complete, after which the mummified body was ready for the hereafter, where it would rejoin its *ka.* To be doubly sure of the survival of the *ka,* a likeness of the dead person was made in a hard stone, intended to serve as a backup, should anything happen to the mummy. One Egyptian word for sculptor translates literally as "he who keeps alive." Members of the noble class were mummified and accompanied by their personal likeness; common people were merely buried in holes, though Egyptian religion does appear to have offered them the hope of life in an afterworld, too. The belief

Then & Now

THE NILE

"Egypt," the Greek historian Herodotus wrote, "is a gift of the Nile." In ancient Egypt, the Nile flooded every summer, from July to October. The floods began when the rain in the central Sudan raised the level of the White Nile, one of its tributaries, followed by the summer monsoon in the Ethiopian highlands raising the level of the Blue Nile, another of its tributaries. By August, these waters reached Egypt proper, flooding the entire basin except for the highest ground, where villages and temples were built, and depositing a deep layer of silt over the fields.

If rainfall came short of expectations, the next season's crops could be dramatically affected; and, sometimes just as disastrous, if rainfall was excessive, villages and farms had to be evacuated. To combat this, gauges, or "Nilometers," were placed upstream on the Nile, and river levels could be compared with records kept over the centuries, so those downstream might know what to expect each August. In fact, annual taxes were levied according to the height of the river in any particular year.

In 1899, in order to gain greater control over the Nile and help local agriculture, the British financed a dam project on the Nile at Aswan, 550 miles upstream from Cairo. At Aswan, the Nile pours rapidly through steep cliffs and gorges, and it seemed a perfect spot for a dam. When the dam was finished in 1902, it regulated the flow of the river and allowed for an extra 10 to 15 percent of land to be farmed.

Originally 98 feet high, the dam was raised to 138 feet in 1933. By then a giant lake, 140 miles long, stretched behind it, submerging Nubian villages and a large number of monuments for part of the year, most famously the Temple of Isis.

In the 1950s, President Nasser proposed another dam, the Aswan High Dam. The endangered Temples of Isis and Hathor were removed to higher ground for safety.

Designed to provide Egypt with predictable and sufficient water resources, as well as providing for the country's electrical needs, the Aswan High Dam has had foreseeable negative impacts as well as beneficial ones. Even the early British dam had stopped the natural flow of silt down the Nile, forcing farmers to rely on chemical fertilizers instead. But worse, perhaps, is the fact that Lake Nasser, behind the Aswan High Dam, has changed rainfall patterns in the region and significantly raised the level of the underground water table far downstream, threatening even the temples of Luxor 133 miles to the north. The Nile today never floods, but this victory has had its costs.

---

in the necessity of housing the dead in a tomb that would endure forever, for the benefit of the *ka* of the deceased, gave rise to Egypt's monumental conception of architecture, exemplified most spectacularly in the pyramids.

THE OLD KINGDOM

The Old Kingdom (2686–2181 B.C.E.) was a time of political and social stability in Egypt, a stability reflected in its grandest achievements, the great pyramids. Although tradition long held that slaves built these giant funerary monuments to the kings, it now seems clear that an entire class of artisans, sculptors, and builders was responsible for them. That a culture could organize such mammoth undertakings and accomplish them with what appears to be the willing cooperation of its people emphasizes the unity of the society as a whole.

ARCHITECTURE

The ancient Egyptian architecture extant today is made of stone. Many kinds of stone were abundantly available, and this availability must in part explain the giant proportions of these surviving buildings. Limestone and sandstone were easily quarried in nearby locations along the Nile cliffs. Harder stones, such as granite, basalt, and quartzite, were obtained from more remote regions.

Although Egypt lacked timber, other plant materials could be employed instead. For instance, lotus and papyrus reeds, bundled together and matted with clay, were used as building materials. Mud brick, made by mixing mud from the Nile River with straw, shaping the resulting substance into bricks, and then allowing them to dry in the sun, was also used. Mud-brick buildings were cool in the summer, warm in the winter, and, because Egypt has little rainfall, lasted quite well. Homes of peasants were made in this way. The pharaoh's home was also made of mud brick, but was larger, lime washed, and painted.

Mastabas.   The earliest burial places of the Old Kingdom Egyptian nobility were **mastabas,** flat-topped one-story rectangular buildings with slanted walls. Faced with brick or stone, the *mastabas* were oriented very specifically, with the four sides facing north, south, east, and west. Surviving *mastabas* vary in length from 15 to 170 feet, and vary in height from 10 to 30 feet. The interiors have different layouts, but all include the following: (1) a chapel or offering room, used to make offerings to the spirit of the dead person (there are two doors to this room, one real, the other false—to be used by the spirit to collect what was offered); (2) the **serdab** or cellar, a tiny secret room in the center of the *mastaba*, containing a statue of the dead person (the *ka* statue) and treasure; and (3) a shaft running from the mastaba down through the earth, and into the actual burial chamber located perhaps over a hundred feet below ground level. The plan of the *mastaba* is believed to be an adaptation of a house plan, for the tomb was regarded as the house of the soul.

The Stepped Pyramid of Zoser.   The stepped pyramid of King Zoser [ZHO-suh] (Third Dynasty, ca. 2600 B.C.E.), built on the west bank of the Nile at Saqqara (fig. 1.19), makes clear how the true pyramid developed from the *mastaba*. The stepped pyramid is essentially a stack of *mastabas;* if the steps were filled in, the pure pyramidal form would be achieved. The stepped pyramid was built by IMHOTEP [EE-moh-tep], King Zoser's architect. Imhotep is the first artist/architect in history whose name has been recorded for posterity (his name appears on Zoser's *ka* statue in the *serdab* of the pyramid). Imhotep was also an astronomer, writer, sage, priest, and, above all,

a physician who came to be deified as the god of medicine and science.

The six levels of this stepped pyramid rise over two hundred feet high, making it the oldest sizable stone structure in the world. It was once surrounded by courts and buildings, the whole complex enclosed by a wall over thirty feet high. Zoser's *ka* statue was oriented to peer out toward an adjacent funerary temple through two peep-holes in the *serdab*, so that, in the afterlife, he could continue to observe the rituals in his honor.

The Great Pyramids.   The Great Pyramids at Giza (fig. 1.20) on the west bank of the Nile were built in the Fourth Dynasty of the Old Kingdom. The three pyramids were built by the pharaohs CHEOPS [KEE-ops], ca. 2530 B.C.E.; CHEFREN [KEF-run], ca. 2500 B.C.E.; and MYCERINUS [MIK-ur-EE-nus], ca. 2470 B.C.E. Because the pharaoh was considered divine and would consequently return to the gods when he died, the pyramids were designed to soar to heaven. Inscribed on the walls of later

FIGURE 1.19   Imhotep, Stepped Pyramid of Zoser, Saqqara, ca. 2600 B.C.E., Third Dynasty. This stepped pyramid was transitional between the rectangular *mastabas* (here seemingly placed one on top of another) and the true pyramidal form.

FIGURE 1.20 Great Pyramids, Giza, built for the Old Kingdom pharaohs Cheops, ca. 2530 B.C.E., Chefren, ca. 2500 B.C.E., and Mycerinus, ca. 2470 B.C.E., Fourth Dynasty, limestone and granite. The permanence of the pyramids, built to last forever, was related to the Egyptian concept of an afterlife and the mummification of their dead.

pyramids are descriptions of kings climbing the sides of the pyramids to join the sun god Ra, and the triangular shape may itself symbolize the falling rays of the sun.

The Great Pyramids are extraordinary accomplishments of engineering. Satisfying the Egyptian craving for permanence, the pyramid is one of the most stable geometric forms. The Great Pyramids are built of solid limestone masonry. The blocks were cut with metal tools in the eastern Nile cliffs, marked by the stone masons with red ink to indicate their eventual location, floated across the river during the seasonal floods, and then dragged up temporary ramps and moved into their final position. The largest and oldest pyramid, that of Cheops, covers thirteen acres and is made up of approximately 2.3 million blocks, each averaging 2.5 tons in weight. When the polished, pearly white limestone encasement stones were still intact, it is believed to have soared skyward approximately 480 feet.

With characteristic Egyptian mathematical precision, the three Great Pyramids are aligned, their corners ori-

ented north, south, east, and west. The proportions of the base width to the height of the pyramids are eleven to seven, a proportion that modern research has shown is inherently pleasing to many people. Inside, the pyramids have systems of corridors that lead to the burial chamber, where the mummified body of the pharaoh was placed, along with the rich possessions that were to accompany him to the afterlife.

THE BOOK OF THE DEAD

The expectation of life after death colored all aspects of Egyptian culture. Among the objects found in the coffins of the dead were papyrus scrolls containing prayers and incantations, or spells, to guide the soul in the afterlife. *The Book of the Dead*, which the Egyptians referred to as *The Book of Coming Forth by Day*, spells out the procedures through which the deceased had to pass before being admitted to the Field of Reeds, the eternal realm of the god

Osiris. There the deceased soul's heart was weighed against how well he or she had treated others and respected the gods. A favorable judgment could be rendered for those able to recite a confession like the following[1]:

I have not inflicted pain. I have not caused anyone to go hungry. I have not made any man to weep. I have not committed murder. I have not given the order for murder to be committed. I have not caused calamities to befall men and women. I have not plundered the offerings in the temples. I have not defrauded the gods of their cake-offerings. I have not carried off the fenkhu cakes [offered] to Spirits. I have not committed fornication. . . . I have not filched [land from my neighbor's estate] or added it to my own acre. I have not encroached upon the fields [of others].

I have not committed sin. . . . I have not committed robbery with violence . . . I have not stolen. . . . I have not slain men and women. . . . I have not stolen grain. . . . I have not purloined offerings. . . . I have not uttered lies. . . . I have not uttered curses. . . . I have not committed adultery. . . . I have not attacked any man. . . . I have not blasphemed. . . . I have wronged none, I have done no evil.

A favorable judgment meant the soul would join other living souls in a realm of peace and joy. An unfavorable judgment meant the soul's heart would be devoured by the monster Ament. For those who could not claim to have led a good life, *The Book of the Dead* contained incantations that might protect against an unfavorable judgment.

SCULPTURE

The Great Sphinx.
Most extant Egyptian sculpture is religious or political in purpose, and either reflects the characteristic Egyptian desire for immortality and belief in an afterlife or demonstrates the pharaoh's power and divinity. The Great **Sphinx** (fig. 1.21), which guards the

FIGURE 1.21   Great Sphinx, Giza, ca. 2500 B.C.E., Fourth Dynasty, sandstone, height 65′ (19.81 m). Although similar to the Assyrian guardian monsters in combining a human head and an animal body (see fig. 1.10), here the facial features are those of the pharaoh, and the monumental dimensions are intended to impress the viewer with his power.

[1]Adapted from *The Book of the Dead*, ed. E. A. Wallis Budge (New York: Gramercy/Random House, 1999), 574–579.

pyramid of Chefren at Giza, is a majestic and monumental symbol of the king's strength created by combining a human head (probably an idealized portrait of Chefren himself, the face of which is now damaged) with the body of a lion. The Great Sphinx is 65 feet high, the scale indicative not only of the power of the pharaoh, but also of the Egyptian love of enormous proportions. The Sphinx reappears in Classical Greek mythology, in particular in the story of Oedipus (see Chapter 3).

Mycerinus and Khamerernebty.
Egyptian sculptors depicted the human figure in a very limited number of poses: sitting on a block, standing with one foot forward, sitting cross-legged on the floor (a less common pose), or kneeling on both knees (quite rare). Further, each of these poses is shown in a specific way and according to certain conventions. These standard poses were established in the Old Kingdom and continued largely unchanged through the three millennia of ancient Egyptian culture. To be original and innovative was not a goal for ancient Egyptian artists.

The double statue of the royal couple Mycerinus and his wife, Queen Khamerernebty (fig. 1.22), carved of slate, ca. 2470 B.C.E., demonstrates the conventions of representing the standing figure. This is believed to have been the first double statue of its kind; it set a fashion for showing the pharaoh embraced by, or supported by, the queen. The queen's revealing dress clings to her contours. The king, in addition to a wrapped linen skirt, wears a ceremonial false beard and headdress, both symbols of rank.

Certain features seen here are characteristic of all Egyptian standing figures: the frontality, the erect stance with the left foot forward and the arms rigidly against the body, and the sense of vigor and dignity. In spite of both having a foot forward, these stiff figures do not appear to be walking, for weight is equally distributed on both feet. This is not a natural stance; people normally stand with their weight equally on both feet, only when side by side, or, more frequently, stand with their weight supported on one foot.

Because such sculpture was funerary in purpose and was placed in the tomb as a precaution against having no home for the *ka* if the mummy were destroyed, permanence was of great importance—the web of stone between the queen and king is intended to prevent breakage. (This statue was actually buried with Mycerinus in his pyramid at Giza.)

RELIEF SCULPTURE AND PAINTING

Relief sculpture and painting were closely linked in ancient Egyptian art, and reliefs were often painted. Clarity in storytelling seems to have been more important to the artist than naturalistic representation. The style, which includes few nonessentials, is condensed and abbreviated. Figures are shown predominantly from the side, although the eye and shoulders are shown from the front. Clearly, these

FIGURE 1.22 *King Menkaure (Mycerinus) and Queen.* Egypt, Giza, Menkaure Valley Temple. Greywacke. Egyptian, Old Kingdom, Dynasty 4. Reign of Menkaure ca. 2490–2472 B.C.E. Height 56″ × 22$\frac{1}{2}$″ × 21$\frac{3}{4}$″ (142.2 × 57.1 × 56.2 cm). Harvard University/Boston Museum of Fine Arts. In common pose the figure stands, one leg forward, yet rigidly erect, weight equally distributed on both feet, and therefore seemingly immobile.

nonanatomical figures are not drawn directly from models but are instead memory images of a composite view of the human body, each part of the body shown from its most characteristic point of view. Egyptian art does not portray what the eye sees, but what the mind knows is there.

Ti Watching a Hippopotamus Hunt.

An engaging depiction known as *Ti Watching a Hippopotamus Hunt* (fig. 1.23) was painted on the wall of Ti's tomb in Saqqara, dated ca. 2500–2400 B.C.E. in the Fifth Dynasty. Ti does not actually participate in the killing; instead, he stands on a small boat and directs his servants, who hold harpoons.

As is traditional, Ti is distinguished from his social inferiors by being made bigger, and his pose combines both frontal and profile views. The water of the Nile River is shown as wavy lines, with fish, hippopotami, and a crocodile shown in profile. The ribbed background represents the papyrus plants along the banks of the Nile. At the top of the painting, where Egyptian artists often put background detail, there are buds and flowers, and birds of various kinds, some of which are being stalked by foxes.

A tomb painting such as this was meant to be seen only by the *ka* of the deceased—in this case the *ka* of Ti, whose position was that of "Curator of Monuments." His own final monument, like those of other high-ranking Egyptians, was painted with murals showing him in the afterlife. However, because the afterlife was believed to be a more blissful continuation of real life, it may be assumed that such tomb paintings documented daily life in ancient Egypt—at least in its more pleasant aspects.

FIGURE 1.23 *Ti Watching a Hippopotamus Hunt,* Tomb of Ti, Saqqara, ca. 2500–2400 B.C.E., Fifth Dynasty, painted limestone wall relief, height ca. 3 9″ (1.14 m). Standard conventions of mixed perspective in ancient Egyptian art include depiction of the eye from the front, though the head is shown in profile, and the shoulders from the front, though the legs are shown from the side.

THE MIDDLE KINGDOM

After the collapse of the Old Kingdom, a period of political and social turmoil ensued—the first of the so-called intermediate periods of Egyptian history. For over 150 years no single dynasty could reunite the country as Narmer had done a thousand years earlier. Finally, in about 2040 B.C.E., a prince by the name of Mentuhotep II, from Thebes, managed to subdue both upper and lower parts, inaugurating the Middle Kingdom. The subsequent government was far less centralized than that of the Old Kingdom, with only affairs of national import being left to the king, while much more authority was given to regional governors. Under these new conditions, the country prospered as never before. Largescale waterworks were undertaken to irrigate higher ground in the Nile basin, and farming yields, which were already higher than anywhere else in the world, increased dramatically.

ARCHITECTURE

Few monuments of the Middle Kingdom can be seen today, for they were replaced by grander structures during the New Kingdom or were built of mud brick and, consequently, have largely disappeared. A few traces of pyramids remain—they appear to have been similar to those of the Old Kingdom but smaller, and a number of rock-cut tombs, burial places hollowed out of the faces of cliffs, survive. These are to be found at Beni Hasan, located 125 miles up the river from Giza, and were built ca. 2100–1800 B.C.E., during the Eleventh Dynasty.

The basic plan of these tombs is believed to be similar to that of an Egyptian home of the time. Each tomb consists of a vestibule or portico, a hall with pillars, a private sacred chamber, and a small room at the rear to contain a statue of the dead person. The interior has certain elements that appear to be stone versions of structures originally made of other materials. Thus, although the columns are of stone, the form is that of a bundle of reeds tied together. The ceiling is painted with a diapered and checkered pattern that looks much like the woven matting used to cover houses. The walls are also often painted, though there is a change from Old Kingdom subjects discernible here. Instead of military exploits, the paintings now feature depictions of domestic and farm life.

THE NEW KINGDOM

After the Middle Kingdom collapsed and a second intermediate period had begun, an eastern Mediterranean tribe called the Hyksos invaded northern Egypt in 1674 B.C.E., bringing with them bronze weapons and horsedrawn chariots. For over two hundred years, Egypt was again divided. But beginning in 1552 B.C.E., the old order was reestablished, perhaps by means of the new technology that the Hyksos tribes had introduced to their unwilling hosts. Certainly, it was through contact with the Hyksos that Egypt entered the Bronze Age. The New Kingdom or Empire that resulted was the most brilliant period in Egyptian history. It was a Theban king, AHMOSE I [AR-mohz], who first pushed back the Hyksos into Palestine, conquering foreign peoples along the way and bringing into being the first Egyptian empire. During the reign of THUTMOSE III [thoot-MOS-uh], (r. 1479–1425 B.C.E.), the first Egyptian king to be called "pharaoh," Egypt controlled not only the entire Nile basin but the entire eastern Mediterranean coast as far as present-day Syria. The great empire only fell into decline after about 1200 B.C.E., when it came under the successive influence of Assyria and Libya, and finally lost its independence to Persia in about 525 B.C.E.

ARCHITECTURE

The New Kingdom established its capital at Thebes, and a great amount of building was done there as well as up and down the length of the Nile. Much art was produced in an exuberant display of wealth and sophistication. Burial was still carried out with great care during the New Kingdom, but the futility of pyramids as places of safe preservation was now fully recognized, Pyramids, monumental advertisements of the treasures contained within, were irresistibly attractive to robbers and looters. Consequently, nobility and royalty were now buried in chambers hollowed deep into the cliffs on the west bank of the Nile River in the Valley of the Kings at Thebes. Here, rock-cut tombs were approached by corridors up to 500 feet long hollowed straight into the hillside. The entrances were carefully hidden, and rocks were arranged over the entrances to look as if they had fallen there. Many clever tricks and precautions were used by the ancient Egyptians to protect their tombs. In one case, their success lasted until 1922, when the shaft tomb of Tutankhamen (sometimes referred to popularly today as King Tut) was found nearly intact. All other known tombs were looted in antiquity.

Temple of Queen Hatshepsut. The Old Kingdom has been called the period of the pyramids; the New Kingdom is the time of the temples. The concern for concealment brought about the end of monumental memorial architecture. A mortuary temple of the queen or king would now be built far from the actual tomb. The funerary Temple of Queen Hatshepsut (fig. 1.24), for instance, was built against a cliff at Deir el-Bahari, Thebes, ca. 1478–1458 B.C.E., early in the Eighteenth Dynasty, by the architect SENMUT [SEN-mut].

In a culture dominated by male kings, HATSHEPSUT [hat-SHEP-sut] (r. 1478–1458 B.C.E.) is a figure of some significance. At the death of her husband, Thutmose II, she became regent of Thutmose III, her son-in-law. For the next twenty years, Thutmose III, who would later

FIGURE 1.24 Senmut, Funerary Temple of Queen Hatshepsut, Deir el-Bahari, Thebes, ca. 1478–1458 B.C.E., early Eighteenth Dynasty. In the New Kingdom, the body of the queen or pharaoh was buried in a different location from the mortuary temple. That of Queen Hatshepsut was built with terraces, ramps, sculptures, and hanging gardens.

conquer so much of the Mediterranean, was at best something like her prime minister, carrying out her will. The size and magnificence of her temple reflect her political importance.

The huge temple is constructed of repeated elements—colonnaded terraces with columnar porticoes (covered walkways), halls, and private chambers. The three terraces are connected by ramps to the cliff, and chambers are cut into the cliff. These chambers are chapels to the god Amen; to the cow-headed goddess Hathor, who protects the city of the dead; to Anubis, the god of embalming, who protects the dead; and to the queen herself.

Typical of Egyptian buildings, the Temple of Hatshepsut was roofed with stone. As a result, the rooms are dense forests of statues and square or sixteen-sided support columns—the distance between these supports had to be small enough to span with a stone lintel. Sculpture was used lavishly; there were perhaps two hundred statues in Hatshepsut's funerary temple. The walls were covered with brightly painted low relief. The terraces, now bare, were once filled with gardens.

Temple of Amen-Mut-Khonsu.   In the New Kingdom, many temples dedicated to the gods were built, and the

FIGURE 1.25   Temple of Amen-Mut-Khonsu, Luxor, major construction under Amenhotep III, ca. 1390 B.C.E., and Ramesses II, ca. 1260 B.C.E. Like all ancient Egyptian temples, this is constructed on the post and lintel system. Columns and capitals look like plant stalks and buds—perishable forms have been made permanent in stone.

priesthood remained powerful. The Temple of Amen-Mut-Khonsu (the god Amen, and his wife Mut, the goddess of heaven, were the parents of Khonsu) at Luxor (fig. 1.25) is one of the largest Egyptian temples. It was built over a long time period, with major construction under Amenhotep III (r. 1390–1352 B.C.E.), and under Ramesses II (r. ca. 1279–1212 B.C.E.). The temple, which was considered the home of the god, was based on house plans, but made larger and more permanent. The entire temple complex, like many other Egyptian temple complexes, is organized around a longitudinal axis and is essentially symmetrical.

Family Homes.   Much of what is known today about the ancient Egyptians derives from the study of royal tombs; consequently, knowledge of Egyptian life is largely limited to the uppermost levels of society. But at a few sites the homes of everyday people have been unearthed, and much

can be learned about the lifestyle of average Egyptians from these excavations.

One such site is Deir el-Medina, a village that first came into being in the Eighteenth Dynasty as the permanent residence of the tomb builders and artisans who worked across the Nile at Luxor. The city existed for nearly four centuries, through the Twentieth Dynasty, and grew to contain about seventy homes within its walls and fifty outside. The interior layout of each of the houses is relatively uniform. The entrance room, which opened onto the street, was the household chapel, with niches for offerings and an image of the god Bes, a family deity associated with childbirth. Behind this was the main room, with a high roof supported by one or more columns. A raised platform on one wall served as both an eating area and bed. Beneath this was a cellar. One or two smaller rooms for sleeping or storage led off the main room. At the back of the house was a walled garden, which also served as the kitchen, with an oven in one corner and, nearby, a grain silo and grinding equipment. A staircase led from this courtyard to the roof of the house, where the cool evening breezes of the Nile could be enjoyed. Furniture might have included stools, tables, wooden beds, and lamps made of pottery, containing oil and a wick.

More lavish homes, with large gardens and pools, were built by Egyptians of higher standing. A painting of the home and garden of the royal scribe Nakte (fig. 1.26), from the Eighteenth Dynasty, shows him with his wife, standing before their home, giving praise to the king and queen. Their garden pool is surrounded by trees, including a grape arbor. The house is whitewashed to reflect the heat. High up on the wall are windows into the main room, and on the roof are two triangular vents designed to catch the evening breezes. The house is elevated on a platform to protect its mud brick from moisture and flood.

SCULPTURE

Temple of Ramesses II.   The perpetuation of Old Kingdom types into the New Kingdom is demonstrated at the Temple of Ramesses II at Abu Simbel (fig. 1.27), built ca. 1260 B.C.E., during the Nineteenth Dynasty. The facade and inner rooms are cut into the sandstone on the west bank of the Nile. In theory, the temple was built in honor of the sun; there is a statue of the sun god in a niche in the center of the facade. At the top of this facade is a row of dog-headed apes, sacred to the worship of the rising sun. Reliefs and hieroglyphs on the facade also have to do with the pharaoh

Ramesses II's respect for the sun god. But all this is overshadowed by the four enormous statues of Ramesses II, each 65 feet high. (The much smaller figures around and between the legs of these statues are members of his family.)

Despite their giant scale, however, these four statues look very much like statues carved more than a millennium earlier during the Old Kingdom in the pose, physical type, and attire. When they are compared closely, differences between sculpture of the Old, Middle, and New Kingdoms do become apparent: Old Kingdom sculpture is relatively realistic; New Kingdom sculpture is more elegant. But, in view of the enormous time span, the differences are minor. Once again, Egyptian art is seen to be characterized by remarkable uniformity.

RELIEF SCULPTURE AND PAINTING

As in the Old and Middle Kingdoms, New Kingdom temples and tombs were decorated with reliefs and paintings. There were some innovations, however. For instance, greater freedom of pose, wider variety of movement, more complex figure groupings, and a more flowing line are seen in the New Kingdom than in the Old Kingdom. But the basic conventions endure, such as the profile head with frontal eye, the impossible poses, and the arrangement of figures in zones of the register system.

Nobleman Hunting in the Marshes.   Painted around 1400 B.C.E., in the Eighteenth Dynasty, in a tomb at Thebes, the *Nobleman Hunting in the Marshes* (fig. 1.28) illustrates this new freedom, as well as the perpetuation of long-established

FIGURE **1.26**   *House and Garden of the Scribe Nakte*, from Nakte's *Book of the Dead*, Eighteenth Dynasty, British Museum, London. In the New Kingdom, papyrus scrolls that would assist the dead in successfully passing their last test before Osiris prior to enjoying the afterlife were often placed among the wrappings of mummified bodies. Called *Books of the Dead*, these scrolls were often beautifully decorated.

FIGURE 1.27   *Four Seated Figures of Ramesses II*, Temple of Ramesses II, Abu Simbel, facade, ca. 1260 B.C.E., Nineteenth Dynasty. So completely governed by tradition and convention was Egyptian art and culture that, more than 1,200 years after Chefren was carved, these figures of Ramesses II demonstrate that the seated figure continued to be depicted in almost exactly the same way.

FIGURE 1.28   *Nobleman Hunting in the Marshes*, from a tomb at Thebes, ca. 1400 B.C.E., Eighteenth Dynasty, wall painting on dry plaster, British Museum, London. Created a millennium after the painting of *Ti Watching a Hippopotamus Hunt*, (fig. 1.23) the painting *Nobleman Hunting in the Marshes* demonstrates the remarkable consistency of ancient Egyptian style. Emphasis continued to be placed on the clarity with which information was conveyed rather than on realistic representation.

tradition in New Kingdom painting. Active and agile, the nobleman holds three birds in one hand and a wand in the other. Equally impressive is the acrobatic accomplishment of the cat sitting on the bending lotus stems, for she catches one bird with her teeth, another with her claws, and a third with her tail. One bird is catching a butterfly. All people, birds, animals, and fish are shown in profile. The birds neatly form a series of overlapping profiles.

Nobleman Hunting in the Marshes deserves comparison with *Ti Watching a Hippopotamus Hunt* (see fig. 1.23), painted a thousand years earlier in the Fifth Dynasty. The similarities are striking. Both men are longhaired and wear white skirts. Both stand *on* their boats, rather than *in*. Both of their boats are *on* rather than *in* the water. In both, people are drawn with the heads and legs seen from the sides, but eyes and chest from the front. The continued use of relative size to indicate importance is shown by the small figure between the nobleman's legs; she cannot be interpreted as being in the distant background, for she grasps his shin.

AKHENATEN AND TUTANKHAMEN

The sole significant challenge—and it proved only a temporary deviation—to Egypt's consistency of attitude and approach to representation and design came in the

Connections

DANCE AND MUSIC IN ANCIENT EGYPT

What we know of music and dance in ancient Egypt depends on two very different kinds of evidence: the visual record of dancers and musicians we find in surviving reliefs and paintings; and, more problematic, present musical and dance forms that appear to have survived since ancient times. Of the first, we have, for instance, a detail of a wall painting from the tomb of Nebamun at Thebes, dating from about 1400 B.C.E. (fig. 1.29). It shows four seated women, three of whom are watching and apparently clapping along with music played on a double oboe by the fourth. Two nude figures dance to the music. So relaxed is the scene that most of the conventions of traditional Egyptian representation have been abandoned.

In addition to the double oboe seen here, Egyptian music made special use of harps, lutes, and lyres. Surviving paintings often show a blind man playing the harp, but lutes and lyres were apparently played predominantly by women. Single oboes, flutes, and clarinets were also popular, and trumpets were used in military and religious ceremonies. Religious festivals appear to have been primarily musical occasions, and participants routinely danced throughout the celebration.

Many modern Egyptians, as well as scholars, believe contemporary belly dancing derives from dances such as that seen in the wall painting on the tomb of Nebamun. The belly dance, called the *baladi*, probably originated in Egypt as part of both fertility and funeral rituals. Like the contemporary belly dance, the original dances may well have been designed to create a sense of physical and emotional rhapsody, and they probably utilized many of the same musical effects, particularly ever-increasing rhythmic pace and provocative physical movement.

FIGURE 1.29 *Musicians and Dancers,* detail of a wall painting from the tomb of Nebamun, Thebes, ca. 1400 B.C.E., fragment, $11\frac{3}{4} \times 27\frac{1}{4}''$ (29.9 × 69.2 cm), British Museum, London. The two central figures, the one playing the reeds and the seated figure next to her, are remarkable in the way that they face the viewer, a point of view rarely seen in Egyptian painting.

Eighteenth Dynasty under Amenhotep IV [am-EN-oh-TEP] (r. 1352–1336 B.C.E.). He closed the Amen temples, displaced the sun god Amen-Ra, officially dispensed with the pantheon of other Egyptian gods, and replaced them all with a monotheistic system, worshiping the single god Aten, the sun disk. He moved the capital from Thebes to a new city far to the north that he called Akhetaten, "the horizon of Aten," modernday Tell el-Amarna. He then changed his name to Akhenaten [AK-uhn-AH-tan], too, which means "He who is effective on behalf of Aten." Just as significantly he transformed the art of Egypt, liberating it from convention.

Akhenaten, Nefertiti, and Their Children Worshiping the Sun. This painted limestone relief (fig. 1.30), dated

ca. 1348–1336 B.C.E., represents an extraordinary change from traditional Egyptian art. Akhenaten and his Queen, Nefertiti, play with their three daughters, who are shown as miniature adults. Akhenaten even kisses one of his children, a rare display of affection in Egyptian art. These people are shown in casual poses. More notable, however, are their physical distortions—long necks and skulls, protruding abdomens, and large hips, presumably shown to create a likeness. Although royalty, Akhenaten and his family are not idealized, perfect physical types. Royalty is now depicted in domestic situations, casually, intimately. Rather than stressing dignity, this art is playful and informal.

Queen Nefertiti. Akhenaten's wife, the beautiful Queen Nefertiti (fig. 1.31), was recorded in a life-size portrait in

FIGURE 1.30 *Akhenaten, Nefertiti, and Their Children Worshiping the Sun,* ca. 1348–1336 B.C.E., Eighteenth Dynasty, painted limestone relief, $12\frac{1}{4}'' \times 15\frac{1}{4}''$ (31.1 × 8.7 cm), Staatliche Museen zu Berlin, Preussischer Kulturbesitz, Agyptisches Museum. The only notable break in the continuity of Egyptian life were the changes—political, religious, and artistic—instituted by the pharaoh Akhenaten in the Eighteenth Dynasty.

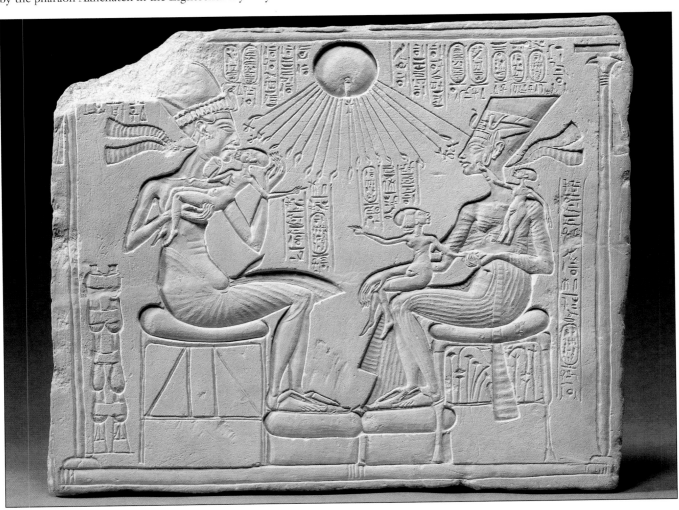

FIGURE 1.31 *Queen Nefertiti*, ca. 1348–1336 B.C.E., Eighteenth Dynasty, painted limestone, rock crystal eyes, height 20 (50.8 cm), Staatliche Museen zu Berlin, Preussischer Kulturbesitz, Agyptisches Museum. Although ideals of beauty have changed greatly throughout time, the appeal of Nefertiti, elegant wife of Akhenaten, endures.

FIGURE 1.32 Inner coffin of Tutankhamen's sarcophagus, ca. 1336–1327 B.C.E., polished gold, inlaid with enamel and semiprecious stones, height 6′ 1″ (1.85 m), weight 250 lbs., Egyptian Museum, Cairo/Hirmer Fotoarchiv, Munich, Germany. Akhenaten's successor, popularly known today as King Tut, was a minor ruler who died young. Yet the splendor of his burial indicates the care lavished on the burial of royalty, as well as the reason why tombs were plundered by grave robbers.

Cross Currents

NUBIA

Far up the Nile river, near Khartoum, Nubia was the first complex hierarchical society south of the Sahara desert. Egypt maintained extended contact with Nubia, which was famed for its reserves of iron, copper, and gold. Nubia, in fact, means "gold" in the Egyptian language. In exchange for these valued metals, Egypt sent pottery, wine, honey, and finely woven textiles to Nubia.

By about 2500 B.C.E., Nubian leaders had established the kingdom of Kush, a wealthy state that came to dominate the upper reaches of the Nile. Around 2300 B.C.E., the Egyptian pharaohs sent a prince of Aswam named Harkuf on three journeys to Nubia to trade and to recruit Nubian mercenaries to fight in Egypt's armies.

During the Middle Kingdom, Nubia came under Egyptian rule, but during the ninth century BCE, the Nubian kingdom of Kush ruled southern Egypt. By the eighth century B.C.E., Kush had five of its kings reign as Egyptian pharaohs, known as the twenty-fifth or "Ethiopian" dynasty.

ca. 1348–1336 B.C.E., carved of limestone and painted, the eyes inlaid with rock crystal. Discovered in 1912 in the studio of Thutmosis, Akhenaten's chief sculptor, this individualized portrait is characteristic of the more informal, relaxed style of Akhenaten's reign. The carving of this charming portrait is sensitive and refined, and its beauty is probably not exaggerated. Surviving texts refer to the Queen as "Fair of Face," "Great of Love," and "Endowed with Favors."

Tomb of Tutankhamen.   Akhenaten's successor was TUTANKHAMEN [too-tan-KAH-moon] (r. ca. 1336–1327 B.C.E.), at the end of the Eighteenth Dynasty. Tutankhamen was married to one of the daughters of Akhenaten and Nefertiti. However, as king, Tutankhamen disavowed his parents-in-law and returned to the worship of Amen, reestablishing the capital at Thebes. Tutankhamen's fame today derives from the discovery of his tomb, nearly intact and containing an extraordinary treasure, in the early 1920s by the British archaeologist Howard Carter. Tutankhamen's tomb, which was uncovered in the Valley of the Kings near Thebes, consisted of a corridorlike shaft leading to four decorated rooms.

From this tomb comes the inner coffin of Tutankhamen's sarcophagus (fig. 1.32), made of polished gold about a quarter of an inch thick, inlaid with enamel and semiprecious stones, 73″ inches long, and weighing 250 pounds. This alone makes clear why tombs were sacked. Tutankhamen was probably between eighteen and twenty years old when he died from a blow to the head. Despite the brevity of his reign, this minor ruler was buried in a sarcophagus that contained three coffins, one inside another, the outer two of wood covered with gold sheets, and the innermost one made of solid gold.

EGYPTIAN MUSIC

Because historians have found no Egyptian musical notation to speak of, we can only speculate about the sound of the music itself; however, thanks to the pictorial characteristics of hieroglyphics, we do know of the widespread use of music in Egyptian culture. Drawings of both secular and sacred rituals, plus actual instruments found in tombs, suggest that music formed an important part of life for the ancient Egyptians. Like so many of the arts of this ancient time, music was spread by the aural tradition, passed down from generation to generation. Although vocal music was probably the most prominent musical genre, because it is the most natural means of expression, instrumental music accompanied Egyptian poems, making them into songs of celebration, mourning, or declarations of love. Small ensembles performed at the many rituals of harvest, birth, and death.

A closer look at music instruments gives us the best clue as to the importance and function of music in this era.

The harp seems to be the most prominent Egyptian instrument. It consisted of a bent piece of wood much like the bow of a bow and arrow, but with many gut strings of varying lengths producing a variety of pitches. Pictures showing several strings being plucked at the same time indicate there was probably harmony in the music, which contradicts the common historical claim that one melody was the only texture of music for the ancients. A melody with harmony might have been possible, or even two different melodies played simultaneously. Modes or scales were obviously used imitating melodic lines because the structures of string instruments indicate a gradation from low pitches to high.

Cross Currents

ANCIENT EGYPT IN THE EUROPEAN IMAGINATION

Of the "Seven Wonders of the World" first listed by Greek authors in the second century B.C.E., only the pyramids at Giza survive. Perhaps because of this, they have come to symbolize in Western consciousness what is perhaps the closest thing to eternity on earth. As a twelfth-century Arab historian put it: "All things fear time, but time fears the pyramids." When Napoleon Bonaparte attacked Egypt in 1798, in order to cut off England's lifeline to India, he inspired his troops on the day of one of the most famous battles in history, the Battle of the Pyramids, with the words: "Soldiers, forty centuries look down upon you."

The Frenchman Hubert Robert's 1760 painting *The Pyramid* (fig. 1.33) captures another of its aspects: Not only was it eternal, it was colossal. Robert's painting overstates its scale: The figures that approach it are minuscule and the pyramid itself disappears off the canvas into the clouds and airy mists, like a Himalayan peak, as if the painting cannot contain it. But Robert does capture something of its emotional power. Unable to perceive its bounds, we realize we are in the presence of something that approaches, imaginatively at least, the infinite—what eighteenth-century writers would call the "sublime."

The sublime is both spiritual—an earthly manifestation of God—and terrifying, because it makes our own being seem so insignificant and ephemeral. Probably no writer in the nineteenth century summed up the ability of Egyptian art to so move us better than the English poet Percy Bysshe Shelley, whose poem "Ozymandias" is based on a statue in the mortuary temple of Ramesses II:

> I met a traveler from an antique land,
> Who said: Two vast and trunkless legs of
>   stone
> Stand in the desert . . . Near them, on the
>   sand,
> Half sunk, a shattered visage lies, whose
>   frown,
> And wrinkled lip, and sneer of cold com-
>   mand,
> Tell that its sculptor well those passions read
> Which yet survive, stamped on these lifeless
>   things,
> The hand that mocked them, and the heart
>   that fed,
> And on the pedestal these words appear:
> "My name is Ozymandias, king of kings:
> Look on my works, ye Mighty, and despair!"
> Nothing beside remains, Round the decay
> Of that colossal wreck, boundless and bare
> The lone and level sands stretch far away.

FIGURE 1.33 Hubert Robert, *The Pyramid*, 1760, oil on wood, $4' \times 4' \times 2\frac{1}{4}''$ (1.22 × 1.28 m), Smith College Museum of Art, Northampton, Massachusetts. Robert's work was painted amidst a general revival in France of monumental Egyptian architecture, particularly of funerary monuments, many of which were proposed in competitions organized by the French government, but none of which was ever built.

Cultural Impact

Ideas seen in prehistoric art reappear in later eras, evidence of a continuum of human creativity and concerns through the ages. Certain depictions of animals, as seen in the cave paintings at Lascaux and the sculptures at Le Tuc d'Audoubert, suggest that the ability to recreate an image has a long history. The greater realism in the depictions of animals than of humans, evidenced by the *Woman of Willendorf*, indicates that artistic distortion was already a conscious choice in prehistoric times. Intentional deviation from absolute visual reality is evident as early as the steles that record the victory of Naram-Sin and the laws of Hammurabi. Indeed, the entire history of art may be regarded as a series of fluctuations between degrees of realism and abstraction.

Early cultures developed at very different times in various parts of the globe. Certain cultures regarded as prehistoric, due to absence of extant documentation, actually postdate other cultures. For example, prehistoric Stonehenge was constructed ca. 2000 B.C.E., making it a relatively new structure when compared to the great pyramids of Egypt, built between ca. 2530 and ca. 2470 B.C.E. The simple static post and lintel seen at Stonehenge was used as a basic construction method throughout the centuries—it is seen in buildings as disparate as the Parthenon, a temple of the fifth century B.C.E. (fig. 3.3), and Le Corbusier's Savoye House, a private home of 1929–30 (fig. 23.9).

Ancient Egypt, one of the most structured societies of all times, created art of correspondingly extreme stylistic consistency over thousands of years. Nowhere else is the apparent avoidance of innovation and disinterest in experimentation found. Yet we may wonder if the same qualities were characteristic of art produced for people other than royalty, and for purposes other than political or funereal.

The appeal of ancient Egypt's pyramids persists, the form perpetuated in our own time most notably by the architect I. M. Pei in his 1988 design for the entry to the Louvre Museum in Paris. Although the pyramidal form is repeated, rather than emphasizing its permanence by building in stone like the ancient Egyptians, Pei's pyramid, constructed of glass, assumes a sense of fragility. The ancient Egyptian pyramid functioned as a tomb to protect the remains of the pharaoh and the accompanying treasure from the public, whereas its Parisian descendant serves to promote public access to the Louvre's artistic treasures.

Use of large-scale sculpture both to immortalize and to glorify political leaders seen in the images of the pharaoh and his family, as of Ramesses II on the facade of his temple at Abu Simbel, begins in ancient Egypt. We see how very effectively art was employed to convey a political message in later cultures, for example, in the sculpture of the ancient Roman emperor Augustus of ca. 20 B.C.E. (fig. 4.15) and in Jean-Antoine Houdon's portrait of George Washington of 1788–92 (fig. 16.16).

Pictures of percussion instruments also indicate that music was used for walking, chanting, and dancing. Such evidence of a beat suggests the music had a more complicated rhythm and was much more musically advanced than that of the early Western church (see Chapter 5). The Egyptians' poetic language itself would have influenced the rhythm and as a means of expression, inflections in the voice would have had an automatic transference into the rhythm. Pictures of metal instruments being struck by dancing girls or actual wood and brass instruments preserved in tombs give us an idea of the tone color of Egyptian music.

Certainly, wind instruments evolved from an ample supply of reeds and other water plants growing beside the Nile River. Wind blowing through these vibrating sources would have produced sounds of nature that were copied and adapted to a mode of expression for this culture so closely connected to the land. Instruments similar to the shofar (ram's horn) of the Hebrew people were abundant and used as a means of communication.

Performances were given by professionals. There was a variety of social levels with the highest belonging to those musicians of the temple that were both male and female. Lower on the social scale were musicians who acted as entertainers for various festivals or who accompanied dancers or workers in action.

LITERATURE: LYRIC POETRY

The literature of the ancient Egyptians is not readily available: Most of what remains exists only in scattered fragments. The oldest Egyptian poems, dating from ca. 2650 to 2050 B.C.E., are religious. Most are incantations and invocations to the gods to aid the departed Egyptian kings. But one of the most important Egyptian religious poems is the pharaoh Akhenaten's "Hymn to the Sun." In this poem, Akhenaten presents himself as the son of Aten, and then describes the sun's rising: "At dawn you rise shining in the horizon, you shine as Aten in the sky and drive away darkness by sending forth your rays. The Two Lands [Lower and Upper Egypt] awake in festivity, and people stand on their feet, for you have raised them up. They wash their bodies, they take their garments, and their arms are raised to praise your rising. The whole world does its work."

Other ancient Egyptian poems of interest include "The Song of the Harper" (ca. 1160 B.C.E.) and a series of lyrics composed between ca. 2000 and 1000 B.C.E., especially the love poems written during the late Rameside period (ca. 1300–1100 B.C.E.). The harper's song differs from Egypt-ian religious poetry in emphasizing the joys and pleasures of life. The spirit of the poem anticipates later Roman poetry that emphasizes the enjoyment of life's pleasures in an attitude of carpe diem ("seize the day"). As with later Greek and Roman love poetry, and the nearly equally ancient love poetry of the Hebrews (the biblical Song of Songs), ancient Egyptian love poems display a wide range of mood and feeling. Written on limestone as well as on papyrus, these ancient love poems reflect attitudes that appear strikingly modern.

KEY TERMS

culture
Paleolithic
Neolithic
cromlech
henge
post and lintel
cuneiform

pictographic
ideograms
polytheism
anthropomorphism
ziggurat
battered
weeper holes

stele
relief sculpture
statues in the round
myth
glazed
dualistic religion
dynasties

hieroglyphics
ka
mastaba
serdab
sphinx

WWW. WEBSITES FOR FURTHER STUDY

http://www.culture.gouv.fr/culture/arcnat/chauvet/en/
(explores the cave at Chauvet)

http://www.greatbuildings.com/buildings/Stonehenge.html
(excellent images and commentary concerning Stonehenge)

http://www.usc.edu/schools/annenberg/asc/projects/comm544/library/images/828.html
(takes a look at the Victory Stele of Naram-Sin)

http://oi.uchicago.edu/OI/MUS/HIGH/OI_Museum_Assyria.html
(Assyrian art museum)

http://www.metmuseum.org/works_of_art/department.asp?dep-3
(Metropolitan Museum of Art, Ancient Near East collection)

http://logos.uoregon.edu/explore/orthography/egypt.html
(examines Egyptian hieroglyphs)

http://greatpyramid.org/aip/index.htm
(The American Institute of Pyramidology)

http://touregypt.net/egyptantiquities/
(site on Egyptian antiquities)

http://academic.memphis.edu/egypt/index.html
(Institute of Egyptian Art and Archeology)

http://touregypt.net/museum/index.htm
(a virtual museum concerning the dynasties)

READINGS

THE EPIC OF GILGAMESH

Selected Episodes

The Epic of Gilgamesh *is more than likely the oldest literary work in the world, parts of it dating from as early as 1900* B.C.E. *It describes the friendship and heroic adventures of the Sumerian ruler Gilgamesh and Enkidu, a primeval human figure. When Enkidu dies, Gilgamesh journeys to see Utnapishtim, the only human ever granted immortality. Gilgamesh learns that immortality is a gift of the gods. The sage tells him, however, about an herb that grows deep beneath the sea that can restore his youth. Tying stones to his feet, Gilgamesh dives to the bottom of the sea to find this youth-restoring plant. When he finds the plant, however, a snake makes off with it, casting off its old skin and returning to youth. Gilgamesh weeps and understands that no human being can escape the inevitability of aging and death. Ready to accept the common fate he shares with all men, Gilgamesh returns to his homeland, where he dies.*

The following extract includes the story of the flood. Comparison with the biblical account of a flood in Genesis suggests that the author of one of these works borrowed from the other, or that both drew from an earlier common source.

THE DREAM AND DEATH OF ENKIDU

As Enkidu slept alone in his sickness, in bitterness of spirit he poured out his heart to his friend. "It was I who cut down the cedar, I who levelled the forest, I who slew Humbaba and now see what has become of me. Listen, my friend, this is the dream I dreamed last night. The heavens roared, and earth rumbled back an answer; between them stood I before an awful being, the sombre-faced man-bird; he had directed on me his purpose. His was a vampire face, his foot was a lion's foot, his hand was an eagle's talon. He fell on me and his claws were in my hair, he held me fast and I smothered; then he transformed me so that my arms became wings covered with feathers. He turned his stare towards me, and he led me away to the palace of Irkalla, the Queen of Darkness,[1] to the house from which none who enters ever returns, down the road from which there is no coming back.

"There is the house whose people sit in darkness; dust is their food and clay their meat. They are clothed like birds with wings for covering, they see no light, they sit in darkness. I entered the house of dust and I saw the kings of the earth, their crowns put away for ever; rulers and princes, all those who once wore kingly crowns and ruled the world in the days of old. They who had stood in the place of the gods like Anu and Enlil, stood now like servants to fetch baked meats in the house of dust, to carry cooked meat and cold water from the water-skin. In the house of dust which I entered were high priests and acolytes, priests of the incantation and of ecstasy; there were servers of the temple, and there was Etana, that king of Kish whom the eagle carried to heaven in the days of old. I saw also Samuqan, god of cattle, and there was Ereshki-

gal the Queen of the Underworld; and Belit-Sheri squatted in front of her, she who is recorder of the gods and keeps the book of death. She held a tablet from which she read. She raised her head, she saw me and spoke: 'Who has brought this one here?' Then I awoke like a man drained of blood who wanders alone in a waste of rushes; like one whom the bailiff has seized and his heart pounds with terror."

Gilgamesh had peeled off his clothes, he listened to his words and wept quick tears, Gilgamesh listened and his tears flowed. He opened his mouth and spoke to Enkidu: "Who is there in strong-walled Uruk who has wisdom like this? Strange things have been spoken, why does your heart speak strangely? The dream was marvellous but the terror was great; we must treasure the dream whatever the terror; for the dream has shown that misery comes at last to the healthy man, the end of life is sorrow." And Gilgamesh lamented, "Now I will pray to the great gods, for my friend had an ominous dream."

This day on which Enkidu dreamed came to an end and he lay stricken with sickness. One whole day he lay on his bed and his suffering increased. He said to Gilgamesh, the friend on whose account he had left the wilderness, "Once I ran for you, for the water of life, and I now have nothing." A second day he lay on his bed and Gilgamesh watched over him but the sickness increased. A third day he lay on his bed, he called out to Gilgamesh, rousing him up. Now he was weak and his eyes were blind with weeping. Ten days he lay and his suffering increased, eleven and twelve days he lay on his bed of pain. Then he called to Gilgamesh, "My friend, the great goddess cursed me and I must die in shame. I shall not die like a man who fallen in the battle; I feared to fall, but happy is the man who falls in the battle, for I must die in shame." And Gilgamesh wept over Enkidu. With the first light of dawn he raised his voice and said to the counsellors of Uruk:

Hear me, great ones of Uruk,
I weep for Enkidu, my friend,
Bitterly moaning like a woman mourning
I weep for my brother.
O Enkidu, my brother,   5
You were the axe at my side.
My hand's strength, the sword in my belt,
The shield before me,
A glorious robe, my fairest ornament;
An evil Fate has robbed me.   10
The wild ass and the gazelle
That were father and mother,
All long-tailed creatures that nourished you
Weep for you,
All the wild things of the plain and pastures;   15
The paths that you loved in the forest of cedars
Night and day murmur.
Let the great ones of strong-walled Uruk
Weep for you;
Let the finger of blessing   20
Be stretched out in mourning;
Enkidu, young brother. Hark,
There is an echo through all the country
Like a mother mourning.
Weep all the paths where we walked together;   25
And the beasts we hunted, the bear and hyena,
Tiger and panther, leopard and lion,

---

[1]Also Ereshkigal, queen of the underworld.

The stag and the ibex, the bull and the doe.
The river along whose banks we used to walk,
Weeps for you,   *30*
Ula of Elam and dear Euphrates
Where once we drew water for the water-skins.
The mountain we climbed where we slew the Watchman,
Weeps for you.
The warriors of strong-walled Uruk   *35*
Where the Bull of Heaven was killed,
Weep for you.
All the people of Eridu
Weep for you Enkidu.
Those who brought grain for your eating   *40*
Mourn for you now;
Who rubbed oil on your back
Mourn for you now;
Who poured beer for your drinking
Mourn for you now.   *45*
The harlot who anointed you with fragrant ointment
Laments for you now;
The women of the palace, who brought you a wife,
A chosen ring of good advice,
Lament for you now.   *50*
And the young men your brothers
As though they were women
Go long-haired in mourning.
What is this sleep which holds you now?
You are lost in the dark and cannot hear me.   *55*

He touched his heart but it did not beat, nor did he lift his eyes again. When Gilgamesh touched his heart it did not beat. So Gilgamesh laid a veil, as one veils the bride, over his friend. He began to rage like a lion, like a lioness robbed of her whelps. This way and that he paced round the bed, he tore out his hair and strewed it around. He dragged off his splendid robes and flung them down as though they were abominations.

In the first light of dawn Gilgamesh cried out, "I made you rest on a royal bed, you reclined on a couch at my left hand, the princes of the earth kissed your feet. I will cause all the people of Uruk to weep over you and raise the dirge of the dead. The joyful people will stoop with sorrow; and when you have gone to the earth I will let my hair grow long for your sake, I will wander through the wilderness in the skin of a lion." The next day also, in the first light, Gilgamesh lamented; seven days and seven nights he wept for Enkidu, until the worm fastened on him. Only then he gave him up to the earth, for the Anunnaki, the judges, had seized him.

Then Gilgamesh issued a proclamation through the land, he summoned them all, the coppersmiths, the goldsmiths, the stone-workers, and commanded them, "Make a statue of my friend." The statue was fashioned with a great weight of lapis lazuli for the breast and of gold for the body. A table of hard-wood was set out, and on it a bowl of carnelian filled with honey, and a bowl of lapis lazuli filled with butter. These he exposed and offered to the Sun; and weeping he went away.

THE STORY OF THE FLOOD

"You know the city Shurrupak, it stands on the banks of Euphrates? That city grew old and the gods that were in it were old. There was Anu, lord of the firmament, their father, and

warrior Enlil their counsellor, Ninurta the helper, and Ennugi watcher over canals; and with them also was Ea. In those days the world teemed, the people multiplied, the world bellowed like a wild bull, and the great god was aroused by the clamour. Enlil heard the clamour and he said to the gods in council, 'The uproar of mankind is intolerable and sleep is no longer possible by reason of the babel.' So the gods agreed to exterminate mankind. Enlil did this, but Ea because of his oath warned me in a dream. He whispered their words to my house of reeds, 'Reed-house, reed-house! Wall, O wall, hearken reed-house, wall reflect; O man of Shurrupak, son of Ubara-Tutu; tear down your house and build a boat, abandon possessions and look for life, despise worldly goods and save your soul alive. Tear down your house, I say, and build a boat. These are the measurements of the barque as you shall build her: let her beam equal her length, let her deck be roofed like the vault that covers the abyss; then take up into the boat the seed of all living creatures.'

"When I had understood I said to my lord, 'Behold what you have commanded I will honour and perform, but how shall I answer the people, the city, the elders?' Then Ea opened his mouth and said to me, his servant, 'Tell them this: I have learnt that Enlil is wrathful against me, I dare no longer walk in his land nor live in his city; I will go down to the Gulf to dwell with Ea my lord. But on you he will rain down abundance, rare fish and shy wild-fowl, a rich harvest-tide. In the evening the rider of the storm will bring you wheat in torrents.'

"In the first light of dawn all my household gathered round me, the children brought pitch and the men whatever was necessary. On the fifth day I laid the keel and the ribs, then I made fast the planking. The groundspace was one acre, each side of the deck measured one hundred and twenty cubits, making a square. I built six decks below, seven in all, I divided them into nine sections with bulkheads between. I drove in wedges where needed, I saw to the punt-poles, and laid in supplies. The carriers brought oil in baskets, I poured pitch into the furnace and asphalt and oil; more oil was consumed in caulking, and more again the master of the boat took into his stores. I slaughtered bullocks for the people and every day I killed sheep. I gave the shipwrights wine to drink as though it were river water, raw wine and red wine and oil and white wine. There was feasting then as there is at the time of the New Year's festival; I myself anointed my head. On the eleventh day the boat was complete.

"Then was the launching full of difficulty; there was shifting of ballast above and below till two thirds was submerged. I loaded into her all that I had of gold and of living things, my family, my kin, the beast of the field both wild and tame, and all the craftsmen. I sent them on board, for the time that Shamash had ordained was already fulfilled when he said, 'In the evening, when the rider of the storm sends down the destroying rain, enter the boat and batten her down.' The time was fulfilled, the evening came, the rider of the storm sent down the rain. I looked out at the weather and it was terrible, so I too boarded the boat and battened her down. All was now complete, the battening and the caulking; so I handed the tiller to Puzur-Amurri the steersman, with the navigation and the care of the whole boat.

"With the first light of dawn a black cloud came from the horizon; it thundered within where Adad, lord of the storm was riding. In front over hill and plain Shullat and Hanish, heralds of the storm, led on. Then the gods of the abyss rose up; Nergal pulled out the dams of the nether waters, Ninurta the war-lord threw down the dykes, and the seven judges of hell, the Annunaki, raised their torches, lighting the land with their livid flame. A stupor of despair went up to heaven when the god of the storm turned daylight to darkness, when he smashed the land like a cup. One whole day the tempest raged, gathering fury as it went, it poured over the people like the tides of battle; a man could not see his brother nor the people be seen from heaven. Even the gods were terrified at the flood, they fled to the highest heaven, the firmament of Anu; they crouched against the walls, cowering like curs. Then Ishtar the sweet-voiced Queen of Heaven cried out like a woman in travail: 'Alas the days of old are turned to dust because I commanded evil; why did I command this evil in the council of all the gods? I commanded wars to destroy the people, but are they not my people, for I brought them forth? Now like the spawn of fish they float in the ocean.' The great gods of heaven and of hell wept, they covered their mouths.

"For six days and six nights the winds blew, torrent and tempest and flood overwhelmed the world, tempest and flood raged together like warring hosts. When the seventh day dawned the storm from the south subsided, the sea grew calm, the flood was stilled; I looked at the face of the world and there was silence, all mankind was turned to clay. The surface of the sea stretched as flat as a roof-top; I opened a hatch and the light fell on my face. Then I bowed low, I sat down and I wept, the tears streamed down my face, for on every side was the waste of water. I looked for land in vain, for fourteen leagues distant there appeared a mountain, and there the boat grounded; on the mountain of Nisir the boat held fast, she held fast and did not budge. One day she held, and a second day on the mountain of Nisir she held fast and did not budge. A third day, and a fourth day she held fast on the mountain and did not budge; a fifth day and a sixth day she held fast on the mountain. When the seventh day dawned I loosed a dove and let her go. She flew away, but finding no resting-place she returned. Then I loosed a swallow, and she flew away but finding no resting-place she returned. I loosed a raven, she saw that the waters had retreated, she ate, she flew around, she cawed, and she did not come back. Then I threw everything open to the four winds, I made a sacrifice and poured out a libation on the mountain top. Seven and again seven cauldrons I set up on their stands, I heaped up wood and cane and cedar and myrtle. When the gods smelled the sweet savour, they gathered like flies over the sacrifice. Then, at last, Ishtar also came, she lifted her necklace with the jewels of heaven that once Anu had made to please her. 'O you gods here present, by the lapis lazuli round my neck I shall remember these days as I remember the jewels of my throat; these last days I shall not forget. Let all the gods gather round the sacrifice, except Enlil. He shall not approach this offering, for without reflection he brought the flood; he consigned my people to destruction."

"When Enlil had come, when he saw the boat, he was wrath and swelled with anger at the gods, the host of heaven, 'Has any of these mortals escaped? Not one was to have survived the destruction.' Then the god of the wells and canals Ninurta opened his mouth and said to the warrior Enlil, 'Who is there of the gods that can devise without Ea? It is Ea, alone who knows all things.' Then Ea opened his mouth and spoke to warrior Enlil, 'Wisest of gods, hero Enlil, how could you so senselessly bring down the flood?

Lay upon the sinner his sin,
Lay upon the transgressor his transgression,
Punish him a little when he breaks loose,
Do not drive him too hard or he perishes;
Would that a lion had ravaged mankind
Rather than the flood,
Would that a wolf had ravaged mankind
Rather than the flood,
Would that famine had wasted the world
Rather than the flood,
Would that pestilence had wasted mankind
Rather than the flood.

It was not I that revealed the secret of the gods; the wise man learned it in a dream. Now take your counsel what shall be done with him.'

"Then Enlil went up into the boat, he took me by the hand and my wife and made us enter the boat and kneel down on either side, he standing between us. He touched our foreheads to bless us saying, 'In time past Utnapishtim was a mortal man; henceforth he and his wife shall live in the distance at the mouth of the rivers.' Thus it was that the gods took me and placed me here to live in the distance, at the mouth of the rivers."

THE RETURN

Utnapishtim said, "As for you, Gilgamesh, who will assemble the gods for your sake, so that you may find that life for which you are searching? But if you wish, come and put it to the test: only prevail against sleep for six days and seven nights." But while Gilgamesh sat there resting on his haunches, a mist of sleep like soft wool teased from the fleece drifted over him, and Utnapishtim said to his wife, "Look at him now, the strong man who would have everlasting life, even now the mists of sleep are drifting over him." His wife replied, "Touch the man to wake him, so that he may return to his own land in peace, going back through the gate by which he came." Utnapishtim said to his wife, "All men are deceivers, even you he will attempt to deceive; therefore bake loaves of bread, each day one loaf, and put it beside his head; and make a mark on the wall to number the days he has slept."

Then Utnapishtim spoke to Urshanabi the ferryman: "Woe to you Urshanabi, now and for ever more you have become hateful to this harbourage; it s not for you, nor for you are the crossings of this sea. Go now, banished from the shore. But this man before whom you walked, bringing him here, whose body is covered with foulness and the grace of whose limbs has been spoiled by wild skins, take him to the washing-place. There he shall wash his long hair clean as snow in the water, he shall throw off his skins and let the sea carry them away, the beauty of his body shall be shown, the fillet on his forehead shall be renewed, and he shall be given clothes to cover his nakedness. Till he reaches his own city and his journey is accomplished, these clothes will show no sign of age, they will wear like a new garment." So Urshanabi took Gilgamesh and led him to the washing-place, he washed his long hair as clean as snow in the water, he threw off his skins, which the sea carried away, and showed the beauty of his body. He renewed the fillet on his forehead, and to cover his naked-ness gave him clothes which would show no sign of age, but would wear like a new garment til he reached his own city, and his journey was accomplished.

Then Gilgamesh and Urshanabi launched the boat on to the water and boarded it, and they made ready to sail away; but the wife of Utnapishtim the Faraway said to him, "Gilgamesh came here wearied out, he is worn out; what will you give him to carry him back to his own country?" So Utnapishtim spoke, and Gilgamesh took a pole and brought the boat in to the bank. "Gilgamesh, you came here a man wearied out, you have worn yourself out; what shall I give you to carry you back to your own country? Gilgamesh, I shall reveal a secret thing, it is a mystery of the gods that I am telling you. There is a plant that grows under the water, it has a prickle like a thorn, like a rose; it will wound your hands, but if you succeed in taking it, then your hands will hold that which restores his lost youth to a man."

When Gilgamesh heard this he opened the sluices so that a sweet-water current might carry him out to the deepest channel; he tied heavy stones to his feet and they dragged him down to the water-bed. There he saw the plant growing; although it pricked him he took it in his hands; then he cut the heavy stones from his feet, and the sea carried him and threw him on to the shore. Gilgamesh said to Urshanabi the ferryman, "Come here, and see this marvellous plant. By its virtue a man may win back all his former strength. I will take it to Uruk of the strong walls; there I will give it to the old men to eat. Its name shall be 'The Old Men Are Young Again'; and at last I shall eat it myself and have back all my lost youth." So Gilgamesh returned by the gate through which he had come, Gilgamesh and Urshanabi went together. They travelled their twenty leagues and then they broke their fast; after thirty leagues they stopped for the night.

Gilgamesh saw a well of cool water and he went down and bathed; but deep in the pool there was lying a serpent, and the serpent sensed the sweetness of the flower. It rose out of the water and snatched it away, and immediately it sloughed its skin and returned to the well. Then Gilgamesh sat down and wept, the tears ran down his face, and he took the hand of Urshanabi; "O Urshanabi, was it for this that I toiled with my hands, is it for this I have wrung out my heart's blood? For myself I have gained nothing; not I, but the beast of the earth has joy of it now. Already the stream has carried it twenty leagues back to the channels where I found it. I found a sign and now I have lost it. Let us leave the boat on the bank and go."

After twenty leagues they broke their fast, after thirty leagues they stopped for the night; in three days they had walked as much as a journey of a month and fifteen days. When the journey was accomplished they arrived at Uruk, the strong-walled city. Gilgamesh spoke to him, to Urshanabi the ferryman, "Urshanabi, climb up on to the wall of Uruk, inspect its foundation terrace, and examine well the brickwork; see if it is not of burnt bricks; and did not the seven wise men lay these foundations? One third of the whole is city, one third is garden, and one third is field, with the precinct of the goddess Ishtar. These parts and the precinct are all Uruk."

This too was the work of Gilgamesh, the king, who knew the countries of the world. He was wise, he saw mysteries and knew secret things, he brought us a tale of the days before the flood. He went a long journey, was weary, worn out with labour, and returning engraved on a stone the whole story.

THE DEATH OF GILGAMESH

The destiny was fulfilled which the father of the gods, Enlil of the mountain, had decreed for Gilgamesh: "In nether-earth the darkness will show him a light: of mankind, all that are known, none will leave a monument for generations to come to compare with his. The heroes, the wise men, like the new moon have their waxing and waning. Men will say, 'Who has ever ruled with might and with power like him?' As in the dark month, the month of shadows, so without him there is no light. O Gilgamesh, this was the meaning of your dream. You were given the kingship, such was your destiny, everlasting life was not your destiny. Because of this do not be sad at heart, do not be grieved or oppressed; he has given you power to bind and to loose, to be the darkness and the light of mankind. He has given unexampled supremacy over the people, victory in battle from which no fugitive returns, in forays and assaults from which there is no going back. But do not abuse this power, deal justly with your servants in the palace, deal justly before the face of the Sun."

> The king has laid himself down and will not rise again,
> The Lord of Kullab will not rise again;
> He overcame evil, he will not come again;
> Though he was strong of arm he will not rise again;
>
> He had wisdom and a comely face, he will not come again;
> He is gone into the mountain, he will not come again;
> On the bed of fate he lies, he will not rise again,
> From the couch of many colours he will not come again.

The people of the city, great and small, are not silent; they lift up the lament, all men of flesh and blood lift up the lament. Fate has spoken; like a hooked fish he lies stretched on the bed, like a gazelle that is caught in a noose. Inhuman Namtar is heavy upon him, Namtar that has neither hand nor foot, that drinks no water and eats no meat.

For Gilgamesh, son of Ninsun, they weighed out their offerings; his dear wife, his son, his concubine, his musicians, his jester, and all his household; his servants, his stewards, all who lived in the palace weighed out their offerings for Gilgamesh the son of Ninsun, the heart of Uruk. They weighed out their offerings to Ereshkigal, the Queen of Death, and to all the gods of the dead. To Namtar, who is fate, they weighed out the offering. Bread for Neti the Keeper of the Gate, bread for Ningizzida the god of the serpent, the lord of the Tree of Life; for Dumuzi also, the young shepherd, for Enki and Ninki, for Endukugga and Nindukugga, for Enmul and Ninmul, all the ancestral gods, forbears of Enlil. A feast for Shulpae the god of feasting. For Samuqan, god of the herds, for the mother Ninhursag, and the gods of creation in the place of creation, for the host of heaven, priest and priestess weighed out the offering of the dead.

Gilgamesh, the son of Ninsun, lies in the tomb. At the place of offerings he weighed the bread-offering, at the place of libation he poured out the wine. In those days the lord Gilgamesh departed, the son of Ninsun, the king, peerless, without an equal among men, who did not neglect Enlil his master. O Gilgamesh, lord of Kullab, great is thy praise.

ENHEDUANNA[3]

from the "Hymn to Inanna"

The earliest identified author in world literature, Enheduanna was the daughter of the Sumerian king Sargon and a high priestess in the service of the moon-god, Nanna, and the moon goddess, Inanna. The portion of the "Hymn to Inanna" excerpted here describes the fierce female energy of Inanna and the goddess's exalted position among Sumerian deities.

Lady of all powers,
In whom light appears,
Radiant one
Beloved of Heaven and Earth,
Tiara-crowned
Priestess of the Highest God,
My Lady, you are the guardian
Of all greatness.
Your hand holds the seven powers:
You lift the powers of being,
You have hung them over your fingers,
You have gathered the many powers,
You have clasped them now
Like necklaces onto your breast.

Like a dragon,
You poisoned the land—
When you roared at the earth
In your thunder,
Nothing green could live.
A flood fell from the mountain:
You, Inanna,
Foremost in Heaven and Earth.
Lady riding a beast,
You rained fire on the heads of men.
Taking your power from the Highest,
Following the commands of the Highest,
Lady of all the great rites,
Who can understand all that is yours?

In the toretront
Of the battle,
All is struck down by you—
O winged Lady,
Like a bird
You scavenge the land.
Like a charging storm
You charge,
Like a roaring storm
You roar,
You thunder in thunder,
Snort in rampaging winds.
Your feet are continually restless.

Carrying your harp of sighs,
You breathe out the music of mourning.

It was in your service
That I first entered
The holy temple,
I, Enheduanna,
The highest priestess.
I carried the ritual basket,
I chanted your praise.
Now I have been cast out
To the place of lepers.
Day comes,
And the brightness
Is hidden around me.
Shadows cover the light,
Drape it in sandstorms.
My beautiful mouth knows only confusion.
Even my sex is dust.

What once was chanted of Nanna,
Let it now be yours—
That you are as lofty as Heaven,
Let it be known!
That you are as wide as the Earth,
Let it be known!
That you devastate the rebellious,
Let it be known!
That you roar at the land,
Let it be known!
That you rain your blows on their heads,
Let it be known!
That you feast on corpses like a dog,
Let it be known!
That your glance is lifting toward them,
Let it be known!
That your glance is like striking lightning,
Let it be known!
That you are victorious,
Let it be known!
That this is not said of Nanna,
It is said of you—
This is your greatness.
You alone are the High One.

O my Lady,
Beloved of Heaven,
I have told your fury truly.
Now that her priestess
Has returned to her place,
Inanna's heart is restored.
The day is auspicious,
The priestess is clothed
In beautiful robes,
In womanly beauty,
As it in the light of the rising moon.
The gods have appeared
In their rightful places,
The doorsill of Heaven cries "Hail!"
Praise to the destroyer endowed with power,

---

[3]Jane Hirshfied, translator. *Women in Praise of the Sacred,* HarperCollins New York, 2005. Based on translation of William W. Hallo and J.J.A. Van Dijk, *The Exhalation of Inanna,* Yale University Press, New Haven, 2003.

To my Lady enfolded in beauty.
Praise to Inanna.

EGYPTIAN BOOK OF THE DEAD

The Book of the Dead is a collection of texts composed by the ancient Egyptian scribes for the benefit of the dead. They include spells and incantations, hymns and litanies, magical formulas and names, words of power and prayer. These were carved or painted on walls of pyramids and tombs, and painted on coffins, sarcophagi, and rolls of papyri. The following excerpt describes a soul declaring his innocence of wrong doing.

THE DECLARATION OF INNOCENCE BEFORE THE GODS OF THE TRIBUNAL

O Wide-strider who came forth from Heliopolis, I have not done wrong.

O Fire-embracer who came forth from Kheraha, I have not robbed.

O Nosey who came forth from Hermopolis, I have not stolen.

O Swallower of Shades who came forth from Kernet, I have not slain people.

O Terrible of Face who came forth from Rosetjau, I have not destroyed the food offerings.

O Double Lion who came forth from the sky, I have not reduced measures.

O He-whose-Eyes-are-in-Flames who came forth from Asyut, I have not stolen the god's property.

O Burning One who came forth backwards, I have not told lies.

O Breaker of Bones who came forth from Heracleopolis, I have not stolen food.

O Orderer of Flame who came forth from Memphis, I was not sullen.

O He-of-the-Cavern who came forth from the West, I have not fornicated with the fornicator.

O He-whose-Face-is-behind-him who came forth from his hole, I have not caused (anyone) to weep.

O Anointed One who came forth from the chapel, I have not dissembled.

O Hot-Legs who came forth at twilight, I have not transgressed.

O He-who-is-Blood who came forth from the place of slaughter, I have not done grain-profiteering.

O Eater of Entrails who came forth from the Council of Thirty, I have not robbed a parcel of land.

O Lord of Truth who came forth from Hall of Two Truths, I have not discussed (secrets).

O Strayer who came forth from Bubastis, I have brought no lawsuits.

O Planter(?) who came forth from Heliopolis, I have not disputed at all about property.

O Doubly Evil One who came forth from the Busirite Nome, I have not had intercourse with a married woman.

O Wammety-serpent who came forth from the place of execution, I have not had intercourse with a married woman.

O He-who-Sees-what-he-has-brought who came forth from the House of Min, I have not (wrongly) copulated.

O He-who-is-over-the-Great-Ones who came forth from -?-, I have not struck terror.

O Demolisher who came forth from -?-, I have not transgressed.

O Proclaimer of Speech who came forth from Weryt, I have not been hot(-tempered).

O Youth who came forth from the Double Scepter Nome, I have not been neglectful of truthful words.

O Dark One who came forth from darkness, I have not cursed.

O He-who-Brings-his-Offering who comes forth from Asyut, I have not been violent.

O Proclaimer of Voice who came forth from Wenis, I have not confounded (truth).

O Possessor of Faces who came forth from Nedjefet, I have not been impatient.

O Captain who came forth from Weten, I have not discussed.

O Possessor of Two Horns who came forth from Asyut, I have not been garrulous about matters.

O Nefertum who came forth from Memphis, I have not done wrong, I have not done evil.

O He-who-does-not-(allow)-Survivors who came forth from Busiris, I have not disputed the King.

O He-who-Acts-as-he-Wishes who came forth from Antinaiopolis, I have not waded in the water.

O Ihy who came forth from the Primordial Waters, my voice was not loud.

O He-who-Prospers-the-Common-People who came forth from Asyut, I have not cursed a god.

O Uniter of Attributes who came forth from the Cavern, I have not made extollings(?).

O Uniter of Good who came forth from the Cavern, I have not harmed the bread-ration of the Gods.

O Upraised of Head who came forth from the shrine, I have not stolen the Khenef-cakes from the Blessed.

O He-who-Brings-his-Portion who came forth from the Hall of the Two Truths, I have not stolen Hefnu-cakes of a youth, (nor) have I fettered the god of my town.

O He-who-Brightens-the-Land who came forth from Faiyum(?), I have not slain sacred cattle.

EGYPTIAN LYRIC POETRY

The very earliest Egyptian poems, dating from 2650 to 2050 B.C.E., are religious. However, it is the secular poems from the next millennium, 2000–1000 B.C.E., that are of greater interest. The "Song of the Harper" emphasizes the pleasures of life, anticipating the spirit of carpe diem *of Roman poetry. A series of love lyrics from the Rameside period (ca. 1300–1100 B.C.E.) also survives. These ancient love poems display a wide variety of feeling and mood.*

SONG OF THE HARPER

I

All who come into being as flesh
    pass on, and have since God walked the earth;
      and young blood mounts to their places.

The busy fluttering souls and bright transfigured spirits
   who people the world below   5
      and those who shine in the stars with Orion,
They built their mansions, they built their tombs—
   and all men rest in the grave.

So set your home well in the sacred land
   that your good name last because of it;   10
Care for your works in the realm under God
   that your seat in the West be splendid.

The waters flow north, the wind blows south,
   and each man goes to his hour.

II

So, seize the day! hold holiday!   15
   Be unwearied, unceasing, alive,
      you and your own true love;
Let not your heart be troubled during your sojourn on
         earth,
   but seize the day as it passes!

Put incense and sweet oil upon you,   20
   garlanded flowers at your breast,
While the lady alive in your heart forever
   delights, as she sits beside you.

Grieve not your heart, whatever comes;
   let sweet music play before you;   25
Recall not the evil, loathsome to God,
   but have joy, joy, joy, and pleasure!

O upright man, man just and true,
   patient and kind, content with your lot,
      rejoicing, not speaking evil:—
Let your heart be drunk on the gift of Day   31
   until that day comes when you anchor.

LOVE, HOW I'D LOVE
TO SLIP DOWN TO THE POND

Love, how I'd love to slip down to the pond,
   bathe with you close by on the bank.
Just for you I'd wear my new Memphis swimsuit,
   made of sheer linen, fit for a queen—
Come see how it looks in the water!   5

Couldn't I coax you to wade in with me?
   Let the cool creep slowly around us?
Then I'd dive deep down
   and come up for you dripping,
Let you fill your eyes   10
   with the little red fish that I'd catch.

And I'd say, standing there tall in the shallows:
Look at my fish, love,
   how it lies in my hand,
How my fingers caress it,   15
   slip down its sides . . .

But then I'd say softer,
   eyes bright with your seeing:
      A gift, love, No words.
Come closer and   20
   look, it's all me.

LOVE POEMS FROM ANCIENT EGYPT

The following love poems date from the thirteenth to the eleventh centuries B.C.E. They reveal a range of characters, situations, and feelings, and show how universal the theme of love is, having changed so little over the millennia.

LOVE OF YOU IS MIXED DEEP IN MY VITALS

Love of you is mixed deep in my vitals,
   like water stirred into flour for bread,
Like simples compound in a sweet-tasting drug,
   like pastry and honey mixed to perfection.
Oh, hurry to look at your love!
   Be like horses charging in battle,
Like a gardener up with the sun
   burning to watch his prize bud open.
High heaven causes a girl's lovelonging.
   It is like being too far from the light,   10
Far from the hearth of familiar arms.
   It is this being so tangled in you.

MY LOVE IS ONE AND ONLY, WITHOUT PEER

My love is one and only, without peer,
   lovely above all Egypt's lovely girls.
On the horizon of my seeing,
   see her, rising,
Glistening goddess of the sunrise star   5
   bright in the forehead of a lucky year.
So there she stands, epitome
   of shining, shedding light,
Her eyebrows, gleaming darkly, marking
   eyes which dance and wander.   10
Sweet are those lips, which chatter
   (but never a word too much),
And the line of the long neck lovely, dropping
   (since song's notes slide that way)
To young breasts firm in the bouncing light   15
   which shimmers that blueshadowed sidefall of hair.
And slim are those arms, overtoned with gold,
   those fingers which touch like a brush of lotus.
And (ah) how the curve of her back slips gently
   by a whisper of waist to god's plenty below.   20
(Such thighs as hers pass knowledge
   of loveliness known in the old days.)
Dressed in the perfect flesh of woman
   (heart would run captive to such slim arms),
      she ladies it over the earth,   25
Schooling the neck of each schoolboy male
   to swing on a swivel to see her move.
(He who could hold that body tight
   would know at last
      perfection of delight—   30

Best of the bullyboys,
     first among lovers.)
Look you, all men, at that golden going,
     like Our Lady of Love,
                    without peer.   *35*

WHY, JUST NOW, MUST
YOU QUESTION YOUR HEART?

Why, just now, must you question your heart?
     Is it really the time for discussion?
To her, say I,
     take her tight in your arms!
For god's sake, sweet man,
     it's me coming at you,
My tunic
     loose at the shoulder!

I LOVE YOU THROUGH THE DAYTIMES

I love you through the daytimes,
          in the dark,
Through all the long divisions of the night,
          those hours
I, spendthrift, waste away alone,
          and lie, and turn, awake 'til whitened dawn.
And with the shape of you I people night,
          and thoughts of hot desire grow live within me.
What magic was it in that voice of yours
          to bring such singing vigor to my flesh,
To limbs which now lie listless on my bed without you?

Thus I beseech the darkness:
          Where gone, O loving man?
Why gone from her whose love
          can pace you, step by step, to your desire?

          No loving voice replies.
And I (too well) perceive
               how much I am alone.

SPELL FOR CAUSING THE BELOVED
TO FOLLOW AFTER

Hear me, O Rê, Falcon of Twin Horizons,
                    father of gods!
Hear me, you seven Hathors
               who weave fate with a scarlet thread!
O Hear, all you gods of heaven and earth!—
               Grant

That this girl, true child of her mother,
               pursue me with undying passion,
Follow close on my heels
          like a cow seeking pasture,
     like a nursemaid minding her charge,
               like a guardian after his herd!

For if you will not cause her to love me,
     I must surely abandon the day
          consumed to dust in the fire of my burning.

AKHENATEN HYMN TO THE SUN

The text of the "Hymn to the Sun" was found inscribed on the walls of a tomb prepared for a courtier. It was probably chanted at fertility rituals and celebrations honoring Egypt's rulers. However, it is also something of a revolutionary statement of belief. The poem was written by the pharaoh Akhenaten himself and is regarded as the fullest expression of Atenism, the monotheistic religious system with which Akhenaten replaced earlier Egyptian polytheism and that seems to have anticipated the ideas of the later Hebrew and Christian religions.

I

When in splendor you first took your throne
          high in the precinct of heaven,
     O living God,
          life truly began!
Now from eastern horizon risen and streaming,   *5*
     you have flooded the world with your beauty.
You are majestic, awesome, bedazzling, exalted,
          overlord over all earth,
     yet your rays, they touch lightly, compass the
          lands
     to the limits of all your creation.
There in the Sun, you reach to the farthest of those   *11*
     you would gather in for your Son,° whom you love;
Though you are far, your light is wide upon earth;
     and you shine in the faces of all   *15*
          who turn to follow your journeying.

II

When you sink to rest below western horizon
     earth lies in darkness like death,
Sleepers are still in bedchambers, heads veiled,
     eye cannot spy a companion;   *20*
All their goods could be stolen away,
     heads heavy there, and they never knowing!
Lions come out from the deeps of their caves,
     snakes bite and sting;
Darkness muffles, and earth is silent: *25*
     he who created all things lies low in his tomb.

III

Earth-dawning mounts the horizon,
     glows in the sun-disk as day:
You drive away darkness, offer your arrows of shining,
     and the Two Lands° are lively with morningsong.
Sun's children awaken and stand,   *31*
     for you, golden light, have upraised the sleepers;
Bathed are their bodies, who dress in clean linen,
     their arms held high to praise your Return.
Across the face of the earth   *35*
     they go to their crafts and professions.

---

[12] *your Son:* Akhenaten.
[30] *Two Lands:* Upper and Lower Egypt.

IV

The herds are at peace in their pastures,
 trees and the vegetation grow green;
Birds start from their nests,
 wings wide spread to worship your Person;   *40*
Small beasts frisk and gambol, and all
 who mount into flight or settle to rest
  live, once you have shone upon them;
Ships float downstream or sail for the south,
 each path lies open because of your rising;   *45*
Fish in the River leap in your sight,
 and your rays strike deep in the Great Green Sea.°

V

It is you create the new creature in Woman,
 shape the life-giving drops into Man,
Foster the son in the womb of his mother,   *50*
 soothe him, ending his tears;
Nurse through the long generations of women
 to those given Air,° you ensure that your handiwork
 prosper.
When the new one descends from the womb   *55*
 to draw breath the day of its birth,
You open his mouth,
 make him aware of life newly given,
  for you determine his destiny.

VI

Hark to the chick in the egg,   *60*
 he who speaks in the shell!
 You give him air within
  to save and prosper him;
And you have allotted to him his set time
 before the shell shall be broken;   *65*
Then out from the egg he comes,
 from the egg to peep at his natal hour!
 and up on his own two feet goes he
  when at last he struts forth therefrom.

VII

How various is the world you have created,   *70*
 each thing mysterious, sacred to sight,
O sole God,
 beside whom is no other!
You fashioned earth to your heart's desire,
 while you were still alone,   *75*
Filled it with man and the family of creatures,
 each kind on the ground, those who go upon feet,
  he on high soaring on wings,
The far lands of Khor and Kush,°
 and the rich Black Land of Egypt.   *80*

VIII

And you place each one in his proper station,
 where you minister to his needs;
Each has his portion of food,
 and the years of life are reckoned him.
Tongues are divided by words,   *85*
 natures made diverse as well,
Even men's skins are different
 that you might distinguish the nations.

IX

You make Hapy,° the Nile, stream through the
  underworld,
 and bring him, with whatever fullness you will, *90*
To preserve and nourish the People
 in the same skilled way you fashion them.
You are Lord of each one,
 who wearies himself in their service,
Yet Lord of all earth, who shines for them all,   *95*
 Sun-disk of day, Great Lightener!
All of the far foreign countries—
 you are the cause they live,
For you have put a Nile in the sky
 that the might descend upon them in rain—   *100*
He makes waves on the very mountains
 like waves on the Great Green Sea
 to water their fields and their villages.

X

How splendidly ordered are they,   *104*
 your purposes for this world,
 O Lord of eternity, Hapy in heaven!
Although you belong to the distant peoples,
 to the small shy beasts
  who travel the deserts and uplands,
 Yet Hapy, he comes from Below   *110*
  for the dear Land of Egypt as well.
And your Sunlight nurses each field and meadow:
 when you shine, they live,
  they grow sturdy and prosper through you.
You set seasons to let the world flower and flourish—
 winter to rest and refresh it,
  the hot blast of summer to ripen;   *116*
And you have made heaven far off
 in order to shine down therefrom,   *119*
  in order to watch over all your creation.

XI

You are the one God,
 shining forth from your possible incarnations
  as Aten, the Living Sun,
Revealed like a king in glory, risen in light,
 now distant, now bending nearby.   *125*
You create the numberless things of this world

---

[47] *Great Green Sea:* the Mediterranean.
[53] *Air:* life.
[79] *Khor and Kush:* Kush is in the Nubian region in the Sudan, which is to the south. Khor is Syro-Palestine in the northeast.

---

[89] *Hapy:* God of the Nile's flooding.

from yourself, who are One alone—
    cities, towns, fields, the roadway, the River;
And each eye looks back and beholds you
    to learn from the day's light perfection.   *130*
O God, you are in the Sun-disk of Day,
    Over-Seer of all creation—your legacy
        passed on to all who shall ever be;
For you fashioned their sight, who perceive your
    universe,   *135*
    that they praise with one voice
        all your labors.

XII

And you are in my heart;
    there is no other who truly knows you
        but for your son, Akhenaten.   *140*
May you make him wise with your inmost counsels,
    wise with your power,

that earth may aspire to your godhead,
    its creatures fine as the day you made them.
Once you rose into shining, they lived;   *145*
    when you sink to rest, they shall die.
For it is you who are Time itself,
    the span of the world;
        life is by means of you.

Eyes are filled with Beauty   *150*
    until you go to your rest;
All work is laid aside
    as you sink down the western horizon.
Then, Shine reborn! Rise splendidly!
    my Lord, let life thrive for the King!   *155*
For I have kept pace with your every footstep
    since you first measured ground for the world.
Lift up the creatures of earth for your Son
    who came forth from your Body of Fire!

CHAPTER 2

HISTORY

ca. 1800 B.C.E.	Mycenaeans arrive on Greek peninsula
1623 B.C.E.	Volcanic eruption on the island of Thera
ca. 1460 B.C.E.	Mycenaeans conquer Crete
ca. 1400 B.C.E.	Knossos destroyed by Greeks
ca. 1250 B.C.E.	Trojan War; Mycenaean sack of Troy
ca. 1100 B.C.E.	Dorian invasions
776 B.C.E.	Olympic games begin
594–593 B.C.E.	Solon reforms Athenian government
507 B.C.E.	Cleisthenes divides Athens into demes
490 B.C.E.	Battle of Marathon

ART AND ARCHITECTURE

third millennium B.C.E.	Statuette of a woman
ca. 1800 B.C.E.	Kamares Ware pithos
ca. 1700–1500 B.C.E.	The *Snake Goddess*
1700–1300 B.C.E.	Palace of Minos, built and modified
1630–1500 B.C.E.	Landscape, wall painting
ca. 1550–1450 B.C.E.	*Toreador Fresco*
ca. 1550–1500 B.C.E.	Gold mask from tomb V
ca. 1400 B.C.E.	Palace Style amphora
ca. 1300–1200 B.C.E.	Lion Gate
	Treasury of Atreus
ca. 1200 B.C.E.	*Warrior Vase*
750 B.C.E.	Geometric style Dipylon krater
ca. 650 B.C.E.	Levy Oinochoe
ca. 600 B.C.E.	Kouros
560–550 B.C.E.	Temple of Hera I
550–525 B.C.E.	Exekias, amphora
ca. 515 B.C.E.	Euxitheos and Euphronios calyx krater
ca. 510 B.C.E.	Temple of Aphaia

LITERATURE AND PHILOSOPHY

ca. 800 B.C.E.	Homer, *Iliad and Odyssey*
mid-7th century B.C.E.	Alphabetic writing derived from Phoenicians, begins
621 B.C.E.	Draco publishes Athenian code of laws
(ca. 610–580 B.C.E.)	Sappho, *He Is More than a Hero*
7th century B.C.E.	Hesiod's *Theogony*
6th and 5th century B.C.E.	Herakleitos' materialist philosophy
560–550 B.C.E.	Democritus' atomist philosophy
550–525 B.C.E.	Pythagoras' number philosophy

Aegean Culture and Early Greece

Funerary Krater, attributed to the Hirschfeld Workshop. Geometric style from the Dipylon Cemetery, Athens, ca. 750 B.C.E. Terracotta, height $42\frac{5}{8}''$ (108.3 cm.), dia. at mount $28\frac{1}{2}''$ (72.4) cm.). The Metropolitan Museum of Art, Rogers Fund, 1914 (14.130.14). Photograph © 1996, The Metropolitan Museum of Art.

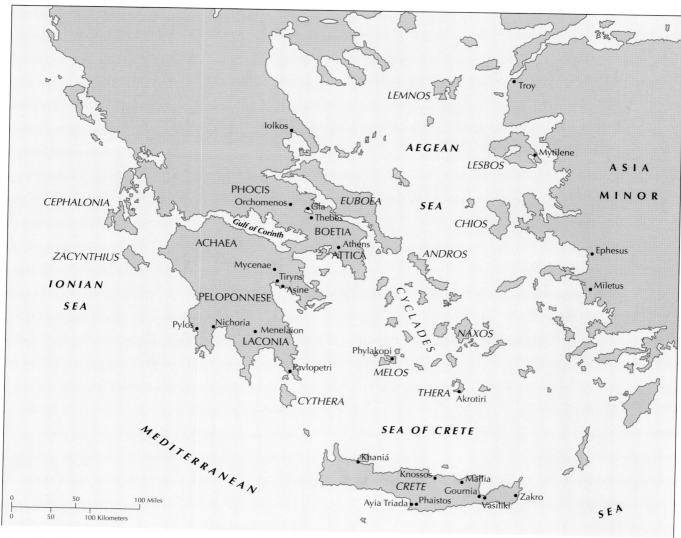

MAP 2.1 The Aegean world.

CHAPTER OVERVIEW

AEGEAN CULTURES
Early Mediterranean people, mythology, and the arts

THE RISE OF ANCIENT GREECE
Western civilization takes root

AEGEAN CULTURES

WE NOW KNOW THAT BETWEEN approximately 3000 and 1100 B.C.E., prior to the rise of the Greek city-states, a number of cultures flourished along the coasts of the eastern Mediterranean and on the islands in the Aegean Sea. However, until about 1870,

the existence of these cultures—Troy in Anatolia, Mycenae on mainland Greece, and Knossos on Crete—was considered more likely than not the creation of one poet's imagination. For the principal evidence for these great early cultures was to be found in Homer's Greek epics, *The Iliad* and *The Odyssey*. But when the archaeologist HEINRICH SCHLIEMANN [SHLEE-man] (1822–1890) first uncovered Helen's Troy and, subsequently, Agamemnon's Mycenae, and then, in 1899, when SIR ARTHUR EVANS (1851–1941) uncovered the labyrinth of Knossos on Crete, it became clear that the world of Homer's *Iliad* and *Odyssey* had really existed. More important still, it seemed that the stories and myths from these Bronze Age civilizations were, at some deep and important level, the basis of later Greek traditions and beliefs. Three civilizations rose to dominance in quick succession in this early Aegean period: the Cycladic culture on the Cyclades islands, the Minoan culture centered on the island of Crete, and the Mycenaean or Helladic culture on the Greek mainland.

Early Aegean culture was dominated by one important geographical factor, the Aegean Sea itself, which was dotted with over a thousand islands and could be sailed with confidence long before the development of sophisticated navigational equipment. What appears to have been a rich maritime culture developed. The Minoans certainly traded with mainland Greece, especially with the city of Mycenae. There is also evidence of commerce with Egypt. Surviving tablets found at Knossos on Crete are written in two different scripts known as Linear A and Linear B. The first of these remains undeciphered, although there are indications it may have originated in Phoenicia, present-day Lebanon. Such linguistic influence again suggests trade contacts. The second script, Linear B, which has been dated to before 1460 B.C.E., was deciphered in 1952 by an English scholar, who discovered it to be an early version of Greek. It has also been found on similar tablets across Greece and at Mycenae itself. Two important conclusions can be drawn from this. In the first place, Mycenaeans must have occupied Crete by 1460 B.C.E. Second, and more important, is the suggestion that by around this date the Aegean cultures shared a common, Greek language.

CYCLADIC CULTURE

The most ancient of the Aegean civilizations developed in the Cyclades in the second half of the third millennium B.C.E. (2500–2000 B.C.E.). It continued to thrive, probably under the influence of the Minoan civilization in Crete, to the south, until the middle of the second millennium B.C.E.

Many statuettes found in tombs in the Cyclades were carved of marble in workshops there during the third and second millennia B.C.E. They range in size from a few inches to lifesize. The marble statuette of a nude female with her arms crossed over her body (fig. 2.1) is characteristic of most extant examples of Cycladic art. The only indication of attire or jewelry are lines incised at the neck. Although the legs are together and straight, the figure was not made to stand up. These Cycladic figures are presumed in general to represent the Mother Goddess, bringer of fertility and the major deity in the ancient Aegean. Since they were often buried with people, they are also presumed to have had a part in the funeral ritual.

FIGURE 2.1 Statuette of a woman, third millennium B.C.E., marble, height $24\frac{3}{4}''$ (62.9 cm), Gift of Cristas–G. Bastis. The Metropolitan Museum of Art, New York. This flattened physique forms a striking contrast to the bulbous body of the prehistoric *Woman of Willendorf* (see fig. 1.2). Yet this Cycladic figure, and others like it, are also thought to have been connected with early beliefs about human fertility.

The non-naturalistic anatomy of the carving is characteristically Cycladic. An angular torso is flattened and two dimensional; a cylindrical neck supports an oval head, flattened on top, with receding forehead. The eyes would probably have been painted on, and lips and ears may have been carved in relief. But the most notable facial feature is the particularly prominent nose. The proportions of the Cycladic figures vary somewhat—some are rounder, others more angular, the shoulders and hips broader or narrower. The pose, however, is almost unvarying.

A number of wall paintings recently discovered at Akrotiri on Thera include a landscape unlike any other known to have survived from antiquity (fig. 2.2). Swallows fly above a landscape consisting of a series of jagged peaks, with giant plumes of red lilies erupting from their tops and sides. It is thought that the art of wall painting was probably brought to the Cyclades from Crete soon

FIGURE 2.2   *Landscape*, from Akrotiri, Thera, Cyclades, before 1630–1500 B.C.E., wall painting with areas of modern reconstruction, Archaeological Museum of Herakleion/Museum of Prehistoric Thera, Crete, Greece. Recently discovered, these murals show an affection for nature, though the subjects are by no means copied literally. Rather, nature's forms have been translated by the painters into a colorful, rhythmic decoration. The result is quite unlike anything else known from antiquity.

after 1700 B.C.E., but nothing like this work is found in Minoan culture.

MINOAN CULTURE

According to later Greek myth, the Minoan civilization on the island of Crete was created by an offspring of Zeus, the chief deity in the Greek pantheon of the gods. Zeus's main characteristics include his ability to change his physical form and his attraction to mortal women. On one occasion, Zeus is said to have fallen in love with Europa, a Phoenician princess. He, therefore, transformed himself into a beautiful white bull and approached Europa who, entranced by the creature, climbed onto its back. Zeus immediately flew up into the sky with his prey. According to the myth, the product of their union was King Minos, the founder of the civilization on Crete. It was after this king that the archaeologist Sir Arthur Evans later named Minoan civilization. Evans's archaeological work established that life had flourished on the island between around 2800 B.C.E. and 1400 B.C.E., a period that Evans subdivided into three main phases—Early Minoan, Middle Minoan, and

Late Minoan. It was with the beginning of the Middle Minoan phase, ca. 2000 B.C.E., that the civilization appeared to have developed significantly, at which time a series of large urban centers grew up on the island at Knossos, Phaistos, Mallia, and Zakro.

The Minoans were sailors and traders. Crete, which is the largest of the Aegean islands, nearly 150 miles in length, was provided with natural protection by the sea; life was secure on this idyllic island. Consequently military subjects are rarely found in Minoan painting and sculpture, and Minoan architecture is not fortified. Moreover, the extant Minoan architecture is largely domestic and secular, for although religion appears to have played an important cultural role, temples do not seem to have been a part of it. The most significant architectural remains are generally referred to as palaces, although they appear to have served a wide variety of functions beyond simply housing the ruling families.

The Palace of Minos.   The major surviving Minoan architectural monument is the so-called Palace of Minos at Knossos (fig. 2.3), built between 1700 and 1300 B.C.E. The

FIGURE 2.3 Palace of Minos, Knossos, Crete, ca. 1700–1300 B.C.E. Built on a site that receives cool sea breezes even in midsummer, the palace is decorated with delicate and colorful wallpaintings that feature aquatic motifs.

palace was continually modified—parts were added, demolished, and reconstructed, until the arrangement seemed to be without a plan. It was also enormous, once covering six acres and including 1,300 rooms. Built around a central courtyard and several smaller courtyards, the palace is a seemingly arbitrary accumulation of rooms linked together by corridors, highly irregular and confused in layout (fig. 2.4). The Greeks later referred to it as the "Labyrinth," meaning literally the House of the Double Axes (from the Greek *labyrs*, "double ax"). Over time, however, the word **labyrinth** has taken on the meaning of "maze."

Open and airy, the palace was constructed with many porticoes, staircases, airshafts, and lightwells (uncovered vertical shafts in buildings allowing light into the lower stories), and built on several levels and in several stories—up to five stories in some areas. But the room ceilings were low and, consequently, the palace never rose very high. The wall surfaces were stuccoed and covered with **murals.**

The Minoans built with an unusual and distinctive type of column. The Minoan column is referred to as an "in-

verted" column because, unlike the later Greek column, it tapers downward, the diameter being smaller at the bottom than at the top. The columns were made of wood rather than stone and were painted bright red. They stood on simple stone bases and were topped by bulging cushion-shaped capitals (fig. 2.5). Replicas now line the Great Staircase of the palace at Knossos. This impressive staircase once served as a lightwell and gave access to all five stories of the palace.

The basement of the palace was the storage area for food, supplies, and valuables. Some of the earthenware storage vases remain in place. These huge **pithoi** (singular, **pithos**) were used to store oil, grain, dried fish, beans, and olives. The palace was a self-sufficient unit that included oil and wine presses as well as grain mills. Highly valued items, such as those made of gold and other precious materials, were stored beneath the floor of the basement. These objects were placed in carefully cut holes lined with stone slabs.

Because of today's tendency to judge other cultures on the basis of their plumbing and level of sanitation, it may

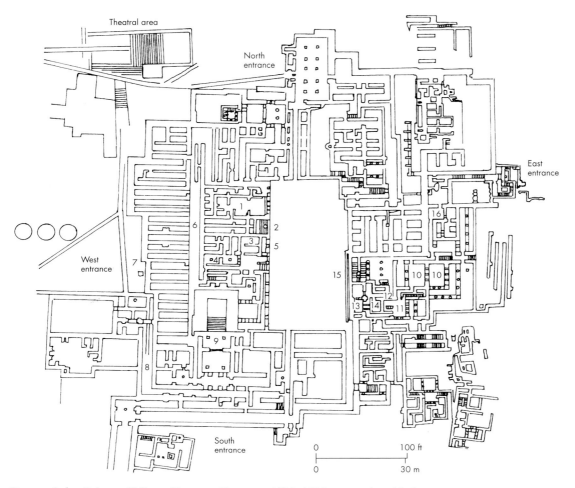

FIGURE 2.4   Palace of Minos, Knossos, Crete, ca. 1700–1300 B.C.E., plan: (1) throne room; (2) staircase; (3) temple repositories; (4) pillar crypt; (5) main shrine; (6) corridor access to magazines; (7) altars; (8) corridor of the processions; (9) staircase; (10) Hall of the Double Axes; (11) Queen's Hall; (12) bathroom; (13) lavatory; (14) storeroom; (15) Great Staircase; (16) lapidary workshop.

FIGURE 2.5   Palace of Minos, Knossos, Crete, ca. 1700–1300 B.C.E., staircase in east wing with inverted columns. Structurally as sound as the usual column shape that tapers to the top (compare the columns on the ancient Greek Parthenon, fig. 3.3), this inverted shape, which tapers toward the bottom, is a characteristic of Minoan architecture.

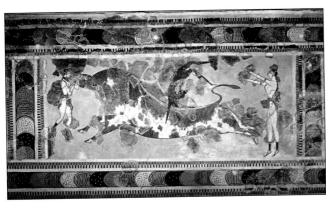

FIGURE 2.6 *Toreador Fresco*, from the Palace of Minos at Knossos, Crete, ca. 1550–1450 B.C.E., wall painting, height with border ca. 24½″ (62.2 cm), Archaeological Museum, Herakleion (Iraklion), Crete. The importance of the bull in Minoan culture is evidenced by this display of bull vaulting. In spite of extensive restoration, the delicacy and lively animation typical of Minoan wall painting remains evident.

FIGURE 2.7 Kamares Ware, spouted three-handled pithos, with fish, from Phaistos, Crete, ca. 1800 B.C.E., terra cotta, height 19⅞″ (50 cm), Archaeological Museum, Herakleion (Iraklion), Crete. Kamares Ware, identified by its color, was often decorated with aquatic motifs in accord with the artists' island home.

also be worth mentioning that the palace had fine bathrooms with decorated **terra cotta** bathtubs, as well as good plumbing and an effective sewage system.

The Toreador Fresco. The Minoans made lavish use of wall paintings. The most famous example features the bull, known to have been a sacred animal on Crete. Known as the *Toreador Fresco* (fig. 2.6), it was painted around 1550–1450 B.C.E. in the Palace of Minos at Knossos. The dark areas are original; the rest is restoration. The activity depicted here is bull-vaulting, in which a person jumps over a running bull's back. As the painting illustrates, when the bull charges, the jumper must "take the bull by the horns," so to speak, vault onto its back, and hope to land standing up like the figure on the far right of this painting. Despite the fact that there are other representations of this activity, the purpose of bull-vaulting remains unclear. It may have been a means of sacrificing people or it may have been an early form of bullfighting; whether this was a ritual or a sport remains uncertain. It has even been questioned if the acrobatic feat depicted is actually possible, but no one has come forward with an offer to prove it one way or the other.

Ceramics. Painting, in several distinctive styles, was also done on Minoan ceramic objects. The most important styles of Minoan ceramic painting are known as **Kamares Ware** and the **Palace Style.** A spouted three-handled pithos (fig. 2.7), decorated with fish and made ca. 1800 B.C.E., is an example of Kamares Ware, which is distinguished by its color: a dark purplish brown background is painted with chalk white and touches of orange red. Dynamic and decorative swirls, spirals, and S-shapes are

typical motifs on Kamares Ware ceramics. The forms flow—wave patterns were popular with the seafaring Minoans, as were other marine and plant forms. Kamares Ware pieces are heavy, with thick walls and asymmetrical shapes.

The Palace Style, which dates from approximately 1600 to 1300 B.C.E., is represented by a three-handled vase, with naturalistic lilies and papyrus (fig. 2.8), made ca. 1400 B.C.E., from Knossos. Like Kamares Ware, the Palace Style is characterized by graceful forms that derive from nature. But unlike Kamares Ware decoration, the forms do not flow over the surface of the vase. Instead, the plants seem to grow up the side of the vase. Palace Style decoration is more delicate than that of Kamares Ware. The color, too, is different, for Palace Style decoration is painted with dark colors on a light background.

The Snake Goddess. Although the Minoans produced no large-scale sculpture in the round, they did create

FIGURE 2.8 Palace Style three-handled vase, with lilies and papyrus, from Knossos, Crete, ca. 1400 B.C.E., terra cotta, Archaeological Museum, Herakleion (Iraklion), Crete. In Palace Style, as in Kamares Ware, forms of nature are used as inspiration for decorations. However, rather than swirling over the surface, in Palace Style the decoration appears to grow up the vase.

MYCENAEAN CULTURE

Beginning about 2000 B.C.E., Greek-speaking peoples began to invade the Greek mainland, inaugurating the Mycenaean or Helladic Age (*Hellas* is the Greek word for "Greece"). After about 1500 B.C.E., when Minoan culture began to decline, these mainland peoples started to have increasing influence throughout the region. As opposed to the islanders, who relied on the sea for protection and whose palaces were, as a result, open and airy, the mainland Greeks built strong fortresses and, under continual threat of invasion from the north, were evidently much more concerned with things military. Most of these strongholds—such as Mycenae and Tiryns—were in southern Greece, the Peloponnese, although there were also settlements in the north, in particular at Athens and Thebes. Among these, Mycenae was the most powerful and richest center; as a result, the entire culture takes its name from this city.

In Homer's *Iliad*, the Trojan War begins when the king of Mycenae, Agamemnon, leads the Greeks against the city of Troy. In legend, the battle was said to have been precipitated when the Trojan prince Paris abducted Helen, the wife of Agamemnon's brother. Homer's story seems to have had a basis in history, although it is more plausible that the Greeks were prompted in their aggression by their predilection for plunder. The Mycenaeans also conquered other territories in the Mediterranean area, including Cyprus, Rhodes, and Crete, assimilating many aspects of the defeated people's art, especially that of the Minoan civilization.

The Palace at Mycenae. The main gateway to the fortified hilltop city of Mycenae was the famous Lion Gate (fig. 2.10), built ca. 1300–1200 B.C.E. The Lion Gate is constructed of huge stones, with the horizontal **lintel** above the doorway estimated to weigh twenty tons. Above the lintel is a **relieving triangle,** an opening that serves to relieve the weight on the lintel. The relieving triangle is filled by a relatively thin slab of limestone on which lions are carved in relief. Symmetrical rampant guardian lions, muscular and powerful, flank a Minoan column—an "inverted" column that tapers downward and has a cushion-like capital. This relief is the oldest piece of monumental sculpture in Europe.

The Lion Gate leads to, among other structures extant at Mycenae, the so-called Treasury of Atreus (fig. 2.11), built ca. 1300–1200 B.C.E. Atreus was the father of Agamemnon. The building was given its name by the archaeologist Heinrich Schliemann, who had a fanatical interest in Homer's heroes. It is, however, a little misleading, since it was neither a treasury nor was it associated with Atreus. It was actually a tomb.

The **dromos,** or entranceway, was cut into the hillside, and the walls were lined with **ashlar masonry,** in which each stone is carefully cut with right-angle corners. At the end of the dromos, the doorway to the tomb is surmounted

small-scale figures. The best known example of Minoan sculpture is the *Snake Goddess*, or *Snake Priestess*, a statuette made of **faience,** a lustrous glazed ceramic, ca. 1700–1500 B.C.E. (fig. 2.9). The physical type of the statuette, with its rounded limbs and body and pinched waist, is typically Minoan. The chief deities of the Minoan religion were female—mother or fertility goddesses. The goddess portrayed here holds a snake in each hand. In many religions snakes were associated with earth deities and with male fertility. Snakes were believed to be in direct contact with the gods of the lower world and therefore supposed to be able to cure disease and restore life. The snakes, combined with the goddess's frankly female form and bared breasts, suggest fertility.

Then & Now

THE SNAKE GODDESS

The efforts of the Feminist movement in the United States and Europe in the late 1960s and early 1970s gave rise not only to a vast array of social and political reforms but to revisions of historical interpretation as well. Most art history texts before the early 1970s, reflecting the social balance within the society that produced them, paid little or no attention to art by women, and most works of art were viewed from a particularly male perspective. Attempting to redress the balance, Feminist historians became especially interested in the art of Aegean civilizations because it seemed that artifacts such as the Minoan *Snake Goddess* (see fig. 2.9) were the products of a matriarchal culture in which women, rather than men, played the dominant roles.

Key to this theory is a 1976 book by Merlin Stone entitled *When God Was a Woman*. "It was quite apparent," Stone wrote, describing her research into Aegean culture, "that the myths and legends that grew from, and were propagated by, a religion in which the deity was female, and revered as wise, valiant, powerful and just, provided very different images from those which are offered by the male-oriented religions of today." If it were a male, King Minos, for example, who exercised governmental authority, it was perhaps the female goddess who exercised spiritual and moral authority in Crete.

The demonization of woman has had a long tradition in Western culture dating from the Ancient Sumerian epic of Gilgamesh with its snakes and dangerously seductive women. This demonization is reflected in the Greek transformation of the Minoan Snake Goddess into the mythic figure of the Medusa, whose hair is a nest of vipers and whose gaze turns men into stone, as well as in the Christian story of Eve's seduction by the Devil, who, significantly, takes the form of a snake, bringing about humankind's expulsion from Paradise.

FIGURE 2.9 *Snake Goddess*, ca. 1700–1500 B.C.E., faience, height $11\frac{5}{8}''$ (29.5 cm), Archaeological Museum, Herakleion (Iraklion), Crete. Minoan religion focused on female deities. In Minoan art, both women and men were depicted with unusually tiny waists and long flowing hair.

FIGURE 2.10 Lion Gate, entrance to Mycenae, Greece, ca. 1300–1200 B.C.E., limestone, height of relief ca. 9′ 6″ (2.89 m). The lion, the animal most frequently depicted throughout the history of art, was often used as a guardian figure.

by a lintel and a relieving triangle. Originally the doorway facade was elaborately decorated with carved reliefs of various colored stones, and the doorway was flanked by slender columns carved with ornamental relief, the columns tapering downward in the Minoan manner. The tomb itself is a **tholos** (plural, **tholoi**), the term for any round building, in this case a domed circular tomb shaped like a beehive about 43 feet high. The technical name for this kind of structure is a **corbeled dome.** Such a building is constructed by first digging a circular pit in the earth. Courses of ashlar masonry are then laid in a circle around the circumference of this space, each successive course slightly overhanging the one below, gradually diminishing the diameter of the circle, until a single stone, the "capstone," covers the small remaining opening. The projecting corners of the masonry blocks are then cut off and smoothed to create a continuous curving surface.

Just inside the Lion Gate at Mycenae is Royal Grave Circle A (there is also a second—Grave Circle B), dated

FIGURE 2.12 Gold mask, from tomb V of Grave Circle A, Mycenae, Greece, ca. 1550–1500 B.C.E., gold, height ca. 12″ (30.5 cm), National Archeological Museum, Athens/Hirmer Fotoarchiv, Munich, Germany. The rich burials of Mycenaean nobility included a variety of sheet gold objects. Homer described Mycenae as "rich in gold."

FIGURE 2.11 Interior, Treasury of Atreus, Mycenae, Greece, ca. 1300–1200 B.C.E., stone, height of vault ca. 43′ (13.11 m), diameter 47′6″ (14.48 m). The final step in the construction of a corbeled dome was to cut off all projecting edges and smooth the stone surface into a continuous curve.

1600–1500 B.C.E., which was excavated by Schliemann in 1876. Schliemann found that this double circle of stone slabs enclosed six shaft graves. In these graves Schliemann found golden treasure. Many of the bodies buried here had been literally laden with gold. Two children were found wrapped in sheets of gold. Among the objects unearthed here were a magnificent gold diadem embossed with geometric patterns, small individual ornaments of gold plate sewn or stuck onto the clothing, a **rhyton** (drinking vessel) in the shape of a lion's head, gold cups, bronze dagger blades inlaid with gold, silver, and copper, a gold breast plate, and gold masks (fig. 2.12), some of which were found placed over the faces of the dead. These last were made of thin sheet gold and hammered into shape over a wooden core.

The objects found in the excavations of Grave Circle A make it easy to understand why Homer referred to the city of Mycenae as *polychrysos*—"rich in gold." These are the graves of the nobility—the Mycenaean ruling system was one of family dynasties—but they are not the graves of Atreus and Agamemnon, even though the mask illustrated here is often referred to as the "mask of Agamemnon." In fact, the mask predates any possible Mycenaean invasion of Troy by nearly three hundred years (the Trojan War is now dated to ca. 1250 B.C.E.).

Then & Now

HEINRICH SCHLIEMANN AND THE MODERN DISCOVERY OF TROY

Born into a poor German family, Heinrich Schliemann (d. 1890) was a linguistic genius who learned Russian in six weeks, became involved in the indigo trade in Moscow, cornered the market, and became very rich while still a young man. He amassed more wealth by establishing a banking and loan business in California. He divorced his first wife because she was not interested in archaeology; among his second wife's attractions was the fact that she knew *The Iliad* in Greek by heart—the new couple entertained themselves by reciting passages in turn.

Schliemann was convinced Homer's *Iliad* was factual and the location of Troy could be determined from descriptions in the story. Excavation began in 1870. In 1873, Schliemann found walls and believed he had discovered ancient Troy. However, he was having difficulty obtaining permission to excavate from the Turkish government, which feared Schliemann would steal any treasure he might find. These fears were well founded, for when Schliemann came upon a few gold objects, he dismissed the workmen and dug out these objects with the aid of his wife. The Schliemanns concealed their finds, probably hiding them in Greece.

The city of Troy was in nine levels. Although Schliemann believed Homer's Troy was at the second level from the bottom, Troy Two, it was, in fact, Troy Six or Seven; Homer's Troy was about a millennium more recent than Schliemann thought. Yet Schliemann did prove the Trojan War was fact, and his finds provided great impetus to the study of archaeology, a new field in the 1870s. Considered the founder of modern archaeology, Heinrich Schliemann excavated at Troy, Mycenae, Tiryns, and Orchomenos.

FIGURE 2.13 *Warrior Vase*, from Mycenae, Greece, ca. 1200 B.C.E., terra cotta, height ca. 16″ (40.6 cm), National Archaeological Museum, Athens. Differing from the characteristic flora-and-fauna decoration of the Minoans, whose safety was ensured by their island location, the war motifs of this vase reflect the more military aspect of Mycenaean life. Although not realistically drawn, the decoration of the Warrior Vase provides a document of early defensive arms and armor.

The Warrior Vase. Probably no surviving artifact better embodies the warlike character of the Mycenaeans than the famed Warrior Vase (fig. 2.13), made ca. 1200 B.C.E. Between bands of decoration, soldiers march, seemingly in single file. At the far left, a woman raises her arm to bid farewell to the troops. The execution of the painting is careless, the figures are caricatures, and the vase itself is crudely constructed. The base is significantly smaller than the opening, making the shape unstable and impractical. The *Warrior Vase* dates from the end of the Mycenaean civilization and, in its unrefined execution and decoration, can be seen to portend the destruction of social order in Mycenae. Around 1100 B.C.E. the Aegean civilization died out, resulting in a period of decline in which writing seems to have disappeared, and art-making ground to a halt. Faced with Dorian invaders from the north, whose weapons were made of iron instead of bronze—perhaps the very invaders the soldiers depicted on the Warrior Vase are marching to meet—Mycenaean civilization collapsed.

THE RISE OF ANCIENT GREECE

Mycenaean civilization, and with it the Bronze Age in the Aegean, came to an abrupt end around 1100 B.C.E. During the following century, many of the accomplishments of the previous millennia appear to have been forgotten. Not until around 1000 B.C.E. did the Greeks of the mainland begin to forge a new civilization that would culminate in the fifth century B.C.E. in the achievements of Classical Athens. The history of Greece in the intervening centuries is usually subdivided into several phases: the Geometric period, ca. 1000–700 B.C.E.; the Orientalizing period, a period of Greek colonization and contact with the East, ca. 700–600 B.C.E.; and the Archaic period, ca. 600–480 B.C.E. It was owing to the achievements of these five hundred years that Greek culture was able to flourish so spectacularly after 480 B.C.E. and that the artistic, cultural, and political foundations of modern Western civilization were laid.

THE PANTHEON OF GREEK GODS

According to Greek **mythology,** before the world was created, before the division into earth, water, and sky, there was Chaos. From this Chaos there emerged a god named URANOS [YOOR-ah-noss], representing the heavens, and a goddess named GAEA [JEE-ah], representing the earth. Their union produced a race of giants called the Titans. One of these, KRONOS [KROH-nos], overthrew his father, Uranos, and married his sister RHEA [REE-ah]. Their offspring were the Olympian gods. However, there was a prophecy that Kronos himself would be overthrown by one of his own children, and so to forestall this he decided to eat all his own progency. Only ZEUS [ZOOSS] survived, saved by Rhea. When Zeus ultimately and inevitably revolted against his father, Kronos regurgitated all the other children—DEMETER [du-MEE-ter], the goddess of agriculture and fertility; HERA [HEAR-ah], goddess of marriage and stability; HADES [HAY-deez], god of the underworld; POSEIDON [pu-SIGH-dun], god of the sea; and HESTIA [HESS-tiah], goddess of the hearth and home. Zeus married Hera, and from them emerged a second order of gods and goddesses: APOLLO [a-POLL-oh], who as god of the sun and light represents intellectual beauty; DIONYSOS [die-oh-KNEE-see-us], god of wine and revelry; APHRODITE [ah-fro-DI-tee], goddess of love, who represents physical beauty; ARES [AIR-ease], god of war; and ARTEMIS [AR-tum-iss], goddess of the moon and the hunt. ATHENA [a-THEE-nuh], goddess of wisdom, and of the arts and crafts, and patron goddess of Athens, sprang full grown from the brow of Zeus himself—a pure idea.

It was Prometheus, a Titan, who first took earth, mixed it with water, and fashioned human beings out of the resulting mud, forming them in the image of the gods. His brother fashioned the animals, bestowing on them the various gifts of courage, strength, swiftness, and wisdom, together with the claws, shells, and wings that distinguish them from one another. The first woman was Pandora, a joint creation of all the gods. According to one version of the story, each of the gods gave her something—Aphrodite gave her beauty, Hermes the gift of persuasion, Apollo musical skill. Zeus presented her to Prometheus's brother, and she brought with her a box containing all her marriage presents. When she opened the box, all the blessings escaped—except hope! In another, darker version, Pandora was given to humankind as a punishment, and the jar she carried contained curses that plague humans.

Unlike the gods of the ancient Hebrews and of India, those of ancient Greece could rarely be counted on for help. Exceptions are Prometheus, who gave humans fire, and Athena, who helped Odysseus in many ways. Traditionally inhabiting the top of Mount Olympus, in northeastern Greece, the Greek pantheon, the family headed by Zeus, supervises human society. Unlike the Christian system, there is no god who represents complete good or complete evil. Zeus is a patriarch, a father, in some sense a model for the tyrant of the Greek polis, but frequently an adulterous husband. His wife, Hera, is often jealous with good cause. Their marital relationship reflects the weakness of human relationships, and their monumental jealousies and rages were reflected not only in the devastating wars that disrupted Greek life but also in the petty animosities that spoiled civic harmony.

Fate, however, was a reality that transcended the power of the gods. And although there was no single "God" with absolute power, there was a coherence to the Greek mythological universe that set limits to the power of the gods. The ancient Greek attitude toward their gods embodied their skeptical view of human nature, and many of the more famous Greek myths reflect this. However, unlike Christianity and Judaism, Greek culture never developed a single unified account of these myths, which exist instead in many varying forms.

Mystery Cults. As with other cultural traditions, Greek myths served as the basis for religious cults, which created a sense of community among disparate groups that comprised the Greek populace. Cults, such as the Eleusinian mystery cult, conducted special rituals open only to initiates or cult members. The Eleusinians emphasized strong moral standards, and they held a ritual meal. Other cults, such as the fertility cult of the goddess Demeter, admitted only women. Such cults provided women, who were excluded from political life, with roles outside the home. Demeter cult members would gather on a hill for three days, offer sacrifices to the goddess, and hold a communal feast of celebration.

Perhaps the best known of the Greek cults was the cult of Dionysus, the god of wine and revelry, whose mysteries were celebrated in the spring. Dionysian revelers would stream into the mountains to dance and sing to frenzied music, which drove the celebrants to rip apart sacrificial victims, usually a goat, but on occasion a human being.

Oracles. Oracles were religious professionals who interpreted the will of the gods. The most famous of the Greek oracles was the oracle of Apollo at Delphi. This oracle was a woman who was reputed to receive cryptic messages from the god while she was in a trance. Messages relayed to the oracles typically took the form of riddles, which demanded careful analysis and interpretation. One inquiry of the Delphic oracle was made by King Croesus of Lydia, who asked whether he should wage war against the Persians. The oracle's answer was that if Croesus did war against Persia, a mighty empire would be destroyed. Croesus thought that the prophecy referred to the destruction of Persia; however, it was his own empire that fell at the hands of the Persian king Cyrus. Another famous inquiry was brought by Oedipus, who sought the oracle's help in identifying the murderer of King Laius, who, unbeknown to Oedipus, was his biological father. What the oracle said, how it was interpreted, and what consequences resulted are described in Sophocles's play *Oedipus the King*.

Cross Currents

HESIOD'S THEOGONY AND MESOPOTAMIAN CREATION MYTHS

In his *Theogony*, HESIOD [HEH-see-ud] (ca. seventh century B.C.E.) presents a poetic account of the origins of the Greek gods. The *Theogony* identifies Gaia as the original divine being. Gaia is both the physical earth and a giant humanlike deity who produces her own mate, Uranos, the sky. This primal couple then spawns the first beings, the Titans, whom Uranos tries to eliminate by stuffing them back into the recesses of their mother. One of these children, the Titan Kronos, slays his father and replaces him as Gaia's consort.

Like his father Uranos, Kronos disposes of his offspring. However, one child, Zeus, is saved by Gaia and grows in safety until he can liberate the other devoured children, battle with the Titans, and displace his father as the chief male deity.

The Greek account of the origin of the gods is indebted to various Mesopotamian creation accounts. From Mesopotamia, Greece derived the idea of projecting a magnified version of human power onto the divine realm. Greece also borrowed the idea of the universe as a city governed by a succession of rulers, each displaced by the next in a power struggle. Moreover, with its lists of succeeding gods, Hesiod's *Theogony* echoes Mesopotamian lists of kings, which are traced back genealogically to the gods. Both Mesopotamian and ancient Greek poetry account for the order and hierarchy of the universe.

Like Homer's epics, Hesiod's works had a profound effect on succeeding generations of Greek culture. Hesiod's poems were considered repositories of wisdom and technical knowledge about a host of matters, including farming and war. The works of both Homer and Hesiod went on to form the foundation of classical Athenian education in the fifth century B.C.E.

THE GEOMETRIC PERIOD

The geometric period (ca. 1000–700 B.C.E.) is sometimes referred to as the Heroic Age, since it was during this time that Homer created his poetic epics, the *Iliad* and *Odyssey*, centered on the figures of the great heroes Achilles and Odysseus. The other arts are less well preserved for us now. There is very little trace of architecture and not much sculpture. Most of the evidence for the visual art of the period is derived from pottery.

Cultural development in this period appears to have been slow. After the destruction of the Mycenaean empire, mainland Greece lacked a political center. When communities began to emerge, as at Athens in Attica and at Sparta in Laconia, they took the form of independent city-states, **poleis** (singular, **polis**).

The development of the Greek polis, which provided the focus for political, artistic, and religious activities in the region, is central to the later Western ideal of democracy. However, in this early period, each polis was ruled by a council of aristocrats. It is also important to note that the polis, with its tradition of fierce independence, meant that even at its artistic and cultural height in the fifth century B.C.E., Greece remained politically fragmented and always on the verge of violent self-destruction. Athens and Sparta, for instance, remained hostile neighbors. Their temporary alliance in the early fifth century B.C.E. managed to beat off Persian invaders, but Greek civilization was delivered a fatal blow later in the same century by the Peloponnesian War between these same two city-states.

Ceramics.   There was undoubtedly some cultural continuity between Mycenaean Greece and the civilization that reemerged after 1000 B.C.E. However, the distinctive style of art that appears around the latter date was probably influenced by the Dorian invaders. Known as the **Geometric style** and characterized by geometric forms, it soon dominated the art of the Greek mainland.

Geometric pottery is distinguished by decoration in bands that cover the entire surface, the decoration adapted to the zones or divisions of the vase. In contrast, the decoration on earlier Aegean pottery flows over the entire surface of the object.

A characteristic example of the Geometric style is the eighth-century B.C.E. terra cotta **krater,** a large vase with a wide mouth, seen in fig. 2.14. The subject depicted on this vase, used to mark a burial, is a common one: mourners lamenting the deceased, who is shown lying on a funeral bier. Funerary processions are pictured going from the home of the deceased to the cemetery. Other Dipylon vases include depictions of funeral processions, horse-drawn chariots, animals to be eaten at the funeral banquet, and funeral games—it was customary to have games at funerals in honor of the deceased. Significant to the future course of vase painting is the beginning of narrative. Greek potters would increasingly decorate a greater percentage of the surface with larger and more representational figures that relate a tale.

Sculpture.   Prior to the mid–seventh century B.C.E., Greek sculptors restricted their work to small-scale pieces in wood, clay, ivory, and bronze (bronze casting of sculpture seems to have started in Greece in the ninth century B.C.E.). All work in perishable materials has been lost, but there are a few extant ivory pieces and many fine bronzes.

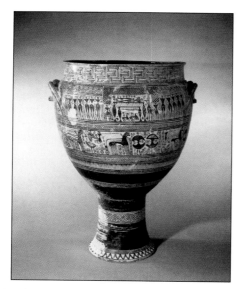

FIGURE 2.14   *Funerary Crater,* attributed to the Hirschfeld Workshop. Terracotta, height $42\frac{5}{8}''$ (108.3 cm.), dia. at mount $28\frac{1}{2}''$ (72.4 cm). The Metropolitan Museum of Art, Rogers Fund, 1914 (14.130.14). Photograph © 1996 The Metropolitan Museum of Art. Geometric-style vases are, as the term indicates, decorated with precisely drawn, simple geometric forms. Each of the several shapes of Greek vases has a name and was used for a specific purpose; this very large krater was used as a burial marker.

FIGURE 2.15   Horse, second half of the eighth century B.C.E., bronze, height ca. $6\frac{3}{8}''$ (16 cm), Staatliche Museum, Berlin. In the Geometric Period, forms of nature were simplified and made literally geometric; torsos of horses and humans (as on the Geometric vase in fig. 2.14) turned into triangles.

The surviving examples, found in tombs and sanctuaries, are statuettes of humans and animals. Bronze cows and rams were used as votive offerings to the gods in place of actual sacrificial animals. Because horses were associated with certain goddesses and gods, they received special attention and may have been used as votive offerings to the deities. The example shown here (fig. 2.15) dates to the second half of the eighth century B.C.E. This late Geometric horse is simplified, abstracted, and highly sophisticated. It is representative of a physical type found in sculpture and in painting—the horse looks like those on contemporary Geometric vases. The pinched waist, moreover, is common to both horses and humans in Geometric art, be it in sculpture or in painting.

Homer's Iliad *and* Odyssey.   Greek poetry in written form begins with the two most famous epics in Western literature, *The Iliad* and *The Odyssey.* Tradition credits the authorship of these poems to Homer, about whom nothing is known with certainty except his name. Early Greeks believed Homer to have been blind, and many scholars think he lived in Ionia, in Asia Minor, but none of this is sure. Both *The Iliad* and *The Odyssey* were first put in writing during the seventh century B.C.E., although they are based on a long oral tradition predating their written versions by hundreds of years. Despite their long genesis, each epic bears the stylistic imprint and imaginative vision of a single resourceful poet.

Both *The Iliad* and *The Odyssey* reflect their social context, a warring aristocratic society in which honor, courage, heroism, and cunning are the prime human virtues. The gods and goddesses of the Greek pantheon figure prominently in the Homeric epics. Each of the poems centers on a single heroic figure. *The Iliad* describes the wrath of Achilles and its consequences for himself and his comrades. *The Odyssey* tells the story of Odysseus, who, after long years spent wandering, returns to reclaim what is his own from a group of Greek princes who have more or less laid siege to his wife and home. Homer's *Iliad* and *Odyssey* have been enormously influential in the history of Western poetry. The Roman poet Virgil's *Aeneid* (see Chapter 4) and John Milton's *Paradise Lost* (see Chapter 14) both imitate Homer's epics in their different ways, to cite only two famous examples.

The Iliad describes a short period toward the end of the Trojan War (ca. 1250 B.C.E.), the ten-year siege that a band of ancient Greek military adventures laid against the city of Troy. The work focuses on the anger and exploits of its hero, Achilles, renowned as the greatest of all soldiers. The epic begins with a quarrel between Achilles and the Greek king and military commander, Agamemnon, over the beautiful Trojan woman, Briseis. Agamemnon had taken Briseis as his royal right, even though Achilles believed he had earned her as his share of the battle spoils. Achilles expresses his disgust with Agamemnon by withdrawing sulkily and refusing to do battle with the enemy. Without Achilles' help, the Greeks are repeatedly defeated by the Trojans. Achilles returns to battle only after his friend Patroclus is killed. He kills Hector, the son of the Trojan king Priam, and abuses his corpse out of frustration and guilt at having let his friend Patroclus die through his anger. The source of the quarrel, the reason for Achilles' return to battle, and the military exploits Homer describes in vivid detail all reflect the warrior world *The Iliad* celebrates. Though the gods are present throughout to comment on the action, at the center of Homer's world are his human actors. The poet is concerned with human responsibility and motivation, and for these reasons his work stands at the very beginning of the Western literary tradition.

Although *The Iliad* glorifies great deeds performed on the battlefield, the poem also conveys a sense of war's terrible consequences. Homer vividly describes battles, with armies arrayed against one another in deadly combat. He describes with equal drama the conflicting loyalties of heroes on both sides as they take leave of their wives and families to kill one another in defense of honor and in pursuit of military glory. These heroic values are honored consistently throughout the epic, though *The Iliad*'s worldview is occasionally tempered by scenes that portray other, less military virtues. For example, kindheartedness and forgiveness are exemplified in the scenes between the Trojan warrior Hector and his family, and in the scene describing Achilles' meeting with the old Trojan king Priam, who comes to ask Achilles for the body of his son Hector.

Perhaps the most famous adventure story in Western literature, Homer's *Odyssey* contains a number of memorable episodes. Two of the most famous concern dangerous escapes. In one episode, Odysseus is captured by the giant one-eyed Cyclops. Odysseus gets the Cyclops drunk, blinds him with a stake, and escapes from the monster's cave by clinging to the belly of a sheep so the Cyclops cannot feel him. In a second adventure, Odysseus and his men have to sail through the dangerous seas inhabited by the Sirens, whose enchanting singing causes sailors to crash their boats on the rocky shores of their island. To avoid this fate, Odysseus plugs his men's ears with wax and then has them tie him to the mast of their ship.

These and other exotic events make *The Odyssey* different in spirit from *The Iliad*. Other differences concern *The Odyssey*'s hero, Odysseus, who after a twenty-year absence from home, returns to his wife, Penelope, and his son, Telemachos. Whereas Achilles' strength in *The Iliad* is purely physical, Odysseus also has mental fortitude. Odysseus's cunning and wit enable him to escape numerous dangerous predicaments, and he also pursues self-knowledge. Odysseus seems much more modern than Achilles, and his journeys toward understanding and toward "home" and all that means take place in a world much closer to our own than the more primitive world of *The Iliad*. Moreover, where the focus of *The Iliad* is narrowly trained on the military world, the vision of *The Odyssey* is much wider. Its values are those of home and hearth, of patience and fidelity, of filial piety, of the wisdom gained through suffering. The range and depth of its depiction of women far surpasses *The Iliad*'s image of women as the mere property of men. In addition to the clever and faithful Penelope, *The Odyssey*'s female characters include the intelligent and beautiful princess Nausicaa; the dangerously seductive witch Circe; the goddess Calypso, who offers Odysseus immortality; Athena, who serves as Odysseus's guide and protector; and Odysseus's nurse, Euryclea. Moreover, when Odysseus visits the Land of the Dead, he sees not only his mother, Anticleia, who had died in his absence, but other famous women of heroic times.

Odysseus's journey home is interrupted by his one-year stay with Circe and by the eight years he remains on Calypso's island. In total, he is absent from Penelope and home for twenty years, ten for the long siege of Troy and ten for his voyage. This long delay is due partly to Odysseus's unalterable fate and partly to his temperament. Warring within him are two contrary impulses: a wish to return to the peaceful kingdom of Ithaca, where he reigns as prince, and a desire to experience adventure and test himself against dangerous challenges. This split is echoed by the clash between Odysseus's temptation to forget his identity as husband, father, and king in his adventures, and his responsibility to resume these less exotic and more stable roles.

The Odyssey makes reference at a number of points to characters and events of *The Iliad*, most notably to the death of Achilles. In an important scene near the middle of *The Odyssey*, Homer has his hero descend to the underworld, where he meets the spirit of Achilles. Odysseus also encounters the shade of Agamemnon, whose murder by his wife serves as a warning of the fate that could befall a man who has been away too long. Homer uses the tragic story of the house of Atreus in thematic counterpoint to the duties and responsibilities of husband, wife, and son that *The Odyssey* endorses.

Insofar as they reflect an entire culture's values, the Homeric poems became the basis of Greek education. The human characters in *The Iliad* and *The Odyssey* served as models of conduct—of heroism and pride, of cunning and loyalty—for later generations. The Homeric gods, however, were less models of ideal behavior than influences on human events. Homer gives them a secondary importance, choosing instead to emphasize men and women living out mysterious destinies. Moreover, Homer reveals the gods as subject to the same implacable fate as humans. Although they are honored and worshipped by the characters, the gods are also portrayed as worthy of blame as well as praise, of laughter as well as fear.

Sappho and the Lyric Poem. As with epic poetry, there was an oral tradition of lyric poetry long before the first

Critical Thinking

THE ODYSSEY ON FILM

The Odyssey of Homer was made into a television film in 1997. Directed by Andrei Konchalovsky, it was later released in theaters and is now available on DVD. Whether or not you have seen the film version of Homer's epic, you can consider the following questions, if you have read it.

1. What do you think the director should emphasize in filming the story? Why?
2. To what extent do you think the director should include references to the Trojan War? Why?
3. What actors would you cast in the following roles: Odysseus, Penelope, Athena, Telemachus, Circe (Kirke), Calypso, Cyclops?
4. How might the gods on Mount Olympus be portrayed? Explain.

---

verse was written down. Unlike epic, which was chanted, lyric poetry was originally sung, accompanied by the lyre, the stringed instrument from which the name *lyric* derives. Also unlike epic, which flourished in Ionia, lyric flourished on the island of Lesbos, especially in the sixth century B.C.E. with the lyric poetry of Sappho [SAFF-oh] (ca. 610–580 B.C.E.). Where epic provides a somewhat distant and communal perspective on human experience in narrative, lyric offers a poetic, personal voice, an intimate expression of subjective feeling and sensation.

Sappho's fame as a poet was acclaimed by Plato, who described her as "the tenth Muse." The Early Christian Church, however, did not appreciate the sensuality of the poems, nor the lesbian subject matter of many of them. Much of Sappho's work was destroyed during the Middle Ages, with manuscripts of her poetry consigned to fires during the fourth century C.E. in Constantinople and during the eleventh century in Rome. Only a few poems remain in their entirety along with a series of fragments of others.

Little is known of Sappho's life, except she was married and had a daughter, Cleis. Even from what little survives of Sappho's works, readers can appreciate the intensity of emotion they express and the direct and graceful way they celebrate female experience.

THE ORIENTALIZING PERIOD

In the Orientalizing period, ca. 700–600 B.C.E., the Greek city-states began to foster trade links, particularly across the Aegean Sea, and many built up large merchant fleets. For the first time in three hundred years, Greece made contact with the civilizations of the Near East, in particular Egypt, Persia, and Phoenicia, and began to import objects as well as ideas. It is from the mid–seventh century B.C.E. that the earliest Greek stone sculptures of the human figure date, and it seems certain that the Greek sculptors were inspired by the example of the Egyptians. It is also around this time that Greece began to be unified linguistically through the introduction of a new alphabet, seemingly derived from that of the Phoenicians.

Ceramics.   Between 700 and 600 B.C.E., the style of Greek pottery was influenced by trade with the Near East, Asia Minor, and Egypt. An example is the seventh-century *Levy Oinochoe* (fig. 2.16) (an **oinochoe** is a wine jug with a pinched lip). Although the design appears to be stenciled, in fact the outlines and details are incised. Oriental motifs appear—lotuses, palmettes, rosettes, winged animals, and sphinxes.

FIGURE 2.16   *Levy Oinochoe*, Orientalizing style, east Greek, ca. 650 B.C.E., terra cotta, height $15\frac{1}{2}''$ (39.4 cm), Musée du Louvre, Paris. Reunion des Musées National/Art Resource, N.Y. The importance of figures in vase painting was gradually increased. Contact with the East resulted in the use of Oriental motifs.

By 600 B.C.E., this Orientalizing style influenced Corinth, a port city with close ties to the cultures of the East. From 600 to 550 B.C.E., Corinth was the leading vase-producing city in Greece. The color of Corinthian ware is distinctive: purplish brown, reddish brown, red, and black are painted on a lighter background. The origin of a vase may be determined by the color of the clay from which it was made; the clay of Corinth is beige whereas that of Athens is orange.

An example of Corinthian ware is the **olpe,** or pitcher, dating from about 600 B.C.E., seen in fig. 2.17. Animals are popular motifs on Corinthian ware, some real, as goats, panthers, lions, stags, bulls, and birds; others imaginary, as sirens and sphinxes.

THE ARCHAIC PERIOD

The Archaic period, ca. 600–480 B.C.E., saw the emergence of the two most important types of Greek vase painting, known as black-figure and red-figure, both focusing in

FIGURE 2.17   Pitcher (olpe), from Corinth, ca. 600 B.C.E., terra cotta, height $11\frac{1}{2}''$ (29.2 cm), British Museum, London. Corinthian ware was made in the city of Corinth, where the clay is beige in color, differing from the orange clay found in Athens. Corinth and Athens competed in the production of vases.

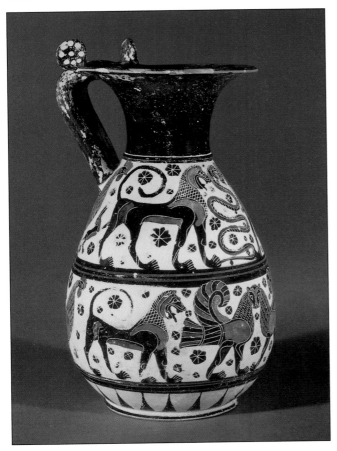

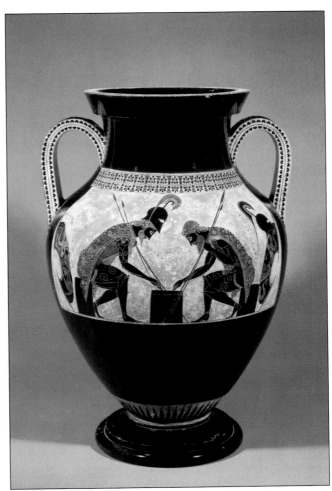

FIGURE 2.18   Exekias, *Ajax and Achilles,* amphora, black-figure style, 550–525 B.C.E., terra cotta, height $26\frac{3}{8}''$ (67 cm), Vatican Museums, Rome. Narrative became progressively more popular on vases, the subjects often taken from mythology. Exekias, master of the black-figure style, is especially noted for his carefully composed scenes.

Athens, which took the lead in vase manufacturing from Corinth.

Black-Figure Vases.   The black-figure style was refined in the second half of the seventh century B.C.E. and reached its peak between 600 and 500 B.C.E. In the **black-figure style,** painting is done with a black glaze on a natural orange clay background. The artist draws the outlines and then fills in the color. Details are created by scraping through the black glaze to reveal the orange clay beneath. Because the artist must exert considerable pressure to make these details, the lines do not tend to flow readily.

The **amphora,** a two-handled vessel, by EXEKIAS [egg-ZEEK-yas] dated 550–525 B.C.E. (fig. 2.18) is a mature example of the black-figure style. On it are depicted Achilles and Ajax from Homer's epic *The Iliad.*

The figures stand on a baseline, suggesting some concept of a three-dimensional space. The composition is a perfect balance of verticals, horizontals, and diagonals, the figures' poses conforming to the shape of the vase. Exekias paints perfect profile portraits yet the eye is seen from the front in the Egyptian manner; not until around 470 B.C.E. would artists depict the eye in profile.

Narratives dominate vase decoration over the next centuries, the subjects frequently derived from mythology as well as daily life. A special type of vase that recorded a specific aspect of ancient Greek life were the amphoras representing the Pan-Athenaic Games, which were held every summer in Athens in honor of Athena. Almost always done in the black-figure technique, the type is represented here by an example (fig. 2.19) signed by NIKIAS [NEEK-i-as],

FIGURE 2.19   Signed by Nikias as potter, Pan-Athenaic amphora, black-figure style, ca. 560–555 B.C.E., terra cotta, height 24$\frac{1}{3}$" (61.7 cm), "Athena Polias" View #2. Purchase Fund 1978. Metropolitan Museum of Art, New York. A special type of vase, routinely painted in black-figure even after the introduction of red-figure, Pan-Athenaic amphoras were given as prizes. The specific competition for which the vase was awarded is shown on the other side of the vase.

ca. 560–555 B.C.E. The scenes on Pan-Athenaic amphoras are always much the same. Depicted on the vase is Athena, patron goddess of Athens, armed with shield and spear. On the other side the activity for which the vase was awarded is shown.

Red-Figure Vases.   Around 530 B.C.E., under pressure from the Persians, a flood of Ionian Greek refugees came to Greece from Asia Minor, introducing Oriental and Ionic influences to mainland art. At the same time, **red-figure style** vase painting started in Athens. As this style took hold, the black-figure style gradually disappeared. Red-figure finally replaced black-figure around 500 B.C.E.

The red-figure technique is essentially an inversion of the black-figure technique, for now the figures are left the color of the clay and the background is painted black. Details within the contours of the figures are painted with a brush and are consequently more fluid than when incised in the black-figure technique.

Signed by EUXITHEOS [yoog-SITH-ios] as potter and EUPHRONIOS [yoo-FRO-nios] as painter is a **calyx krater** (fig. 2.20), dating from about 515 B.C.E., on which is depicted the *Death of Sarpedon* from the story of the Trojan War. In this scene, Sarpedon is lifted by the twin brothers Sleep and Death in the presence of Hermes and two Trojans. The narrative element is highly developed, as is the refined style. Sarpedon is shown from the front, the anatomy realistically rendered, details of the muscles, tendons, and beards finely depicted.

The Greek Temple.   The monumental structures erected by ancient Greek architects have influenced much of Western architecture. Even today, the principles and vocabulary of the ancient Greeks continue to be an extremely significant source of inspiration for architects. Because buildings constructed of impermanent materials—wood, for instance—no longer exist, virtually nothing remains of domestic architecture. However, many structures built of stone survive. Because the functions of these buildings tend to be limited to religious purposes, the history of ancient Greek architecture focuses largely on Greek temples.

The Temple of Hera I at Paestum.   The earliest style of Greek temples is known as the **Doric** (see Fig. 3.2), after the tribes that invaded Mycenae from the north after about 1100 B.C.E. The Doric style is simple, severe, powerful in appearance, with little decorative embellishment.

Dated 560–550 B.C.E., the Temple of Hera I (fig. 2.21), so called to distinguish it from the later Temple of Hera built at the same site in southern Italy, was constructed of local limestone. Its closely spaced columns support a high and heavy entablature that makes them appear squat. Thick heavy columns taper noticeably to the top, with an abrupt transition from shaft to capital, which projects widely beyond the shaft. Little **entasis**—a subtle convex bulge in the middle of a column shaft—is seen in these

Connections

LANDSCAPE AND ARCHITECTURE

According to Vincent Scully, an architectural historian, the great Greek temples can best be understood by exploring their relation to the landscape around them. Characteristically, the Greek landscape is formed by mountains of moderate size, which surround very clearly defined areas of valley and plain, and by islands, clearly demarcated land surfaces surrounded by flat blue sea. Unlike the deserts of Asia Minor and northern Africa or the Alps of central Europe, the Greek landscape is of a scale and clarity that can be contained, so to speak, by the human eye.

With this in mind, Scully notes that each of the Minoan palaces possesses the same relation to the landscape. The palace is set in an enclosed valley on a north–south axis; there is, nearby, a gently mounded or conical hill; beyond this, on the same axis, is a higher, double-peaked or cleft mountain.

The two temples of Hera at Paestum have an analogous relation to the landscape. Hera is not only the wife of Zeus, and thus the goddess of marriage and domestic stability, but also the earth mother. The temples at Paestum were built side by side, on the same axis, oriented toward a conical notched mountain to the east. Standing beside them, at their western end, the direction from which the viewer would naturally approach them, the perspective created by their sides points toward the mountain itself. "Once seen together," Scully writes, "both landscape and temple will seem forever incomplete without the other. Each ennobles its opposite, and their relationship brings the universe of nature and man into a new stable order."

FIGURE 2.20 Euxitheos and Euphronios, *Death of Sarpedon*, calyx krater, red-figure style, ca. 515 B.C.E., terra cotta, height 18″ (45.7 cm), Purchase, Bequest of Joseph H. Durkee, Gift of Darius Ogden Mills and Gift of C. Raston Love, by exchange, 1972. Metropolitan Museum of Art, New York. Whereas in the black-figure technique details must be scraped through the black glaze, in the red-figure technique details are painted on with a tiny brush. Details are therefore achieved more easily, and greater fluidity of line is possible.

early columns. The entire effect, although monumental, appears somewhat disproportionate and awkward.

Sculpture.   The history of ancient Greek sculpture is dominated by images of the human figure, particularly the **kouros** (plural, **kouroi**) [COO-ross; COO-roy] (fig. 2.22), a lifesize representation of a nude male youth, seen standing with one foot forward and arms to his sides, and the **kore** (plural, **korai**) [CO-ray], the female equivalent, but clothed.

Strictly speaking, the first large-scale sculptures of the human figure date from the Orientalizing period, although the form developed so rapidly in the Archaic period that we concentrate on sixth-century B.C.E. examples. The early Near Eastern influence appears to have been decisive. The characteristic pose of the kouros is believed to have derived from Egyptian sculpture. The marble kouros (fig. 2.22), carved ca. 600 B.C.E., shares many of its features with Egyptian figures (see fig. 1.22): the rigid frontality, erect stance, and pose with left foot forward. However, the Greek figure is nude and has been carved to be freestanding. There are thus no webs of stone between the arms and body and between the legs, and no supporting back pillars.

Table 2–1	TIME PERIODS IN ANCIENT GREEK CULTURE
Geometric	ca. 1000–ca. 700 B.C.E.
Orientalizing	ca. 700–ca. 600 B.C.E.
Archaic	ca. 600–ca. 480 B.C.E.
Classical	ca. 480 B.C.E.–323 B.C.E. (death of Alexander the Great)
Hellenistic	323 B.C.E.–30 B.C.E. (death of Cleopatra)

FIGURE 2.21   Temple of Hera I, Paestum, Italy, 560–550 B.C.E., limestone. The sixth century B.C.E. was a time of architectural experimentation. The proportions used here are not entirely harmonious, and the two temples built later at Paestum have thinner columns and less overhang to the capitals.

The kouros reproduced here was originally painted—sculpture was customarily colored with reds, yellows, blues, and greens. Some pieces still retain some of their original color; touches of red pigment remain on this kouros's hair and elsewhere.

Early kouros figures are highly stylized and characteristically have an enigmatic expression, which is often referred to as an **Archaic smile.** The eyes are abnormally large, and the hair forms a decorative beadlike pattern. The anatomy is arranged for design rather than in strict imitation of nature; thus the abdominal muscles and kneecaps become surface decoration. The figures are not portraits of individuals and there is no evidence that they were done from models.

Over time, kouros and kore figures become less stylized and more naturalistic and the poses more relaxed. They remain slender, but the waist gradually expands. Proportions of the various body parts become more natural and are no longer indicated by lines on the surface but rather by the sculpting of the material itself. It is possible to assign approximate dates to examples on the basis of these changes.

The changes that were gradually taking place are demonstrated by a late Archaic kore (fig. 2.23), carved ca. 520 B.C.E. Made of marble, this particular kore was elab-orately painted. Figures like this with one hand extended may represent a goddess or donor.

Exquisitely sculpted, this delicate and dainty figure appears soft and sensual. The face still has an "archaic smile," but the eyes are smaller than they were before, and the slanting eyes, hairstyle, and decorative treatment of the costume suggest an Eastern origin for this figure in the Ionian islands—perhaps the island of Chios.

The figure is dressed in a chiton, a belted single-piece garment for women with buttoned sleeves, which was imported to Athens from eastern Ionia just before the middle of the sixth century B.C.E. The sculptor gives much attention to this costume. The fabric is thin and clings to the body, the folds and draping are complex, the cut of the garment is asymmetrical, and the hemlines are emphasized with colored bands. The cloak, worn over the chiton, ties on one shoulder, creating diagonal patterns and curved lines. The simplicity of earlier sculpture has given way to more sophisticated, subtle modeling, even as Greek culture was becoming more sophisticated itself.

Philosophy.   Perhaps nothing distinguishes the rise of ancient Greece as a civilization more than its love of pure thought. The Greeks were the first to practice **philosophy,** literally the "love of wisdom," in a systematic way, cate-

FIGURE 2.23 Kore, wearing an Ionic chiton, ca. 520 B.C.E., marble, height $22\frac{1}{8}''$ (56.3 cm), Acropolis Museum, Athens. The decorative chiton, made of soft thin fabric, clings to the body. The Archaic smile is still evident here.

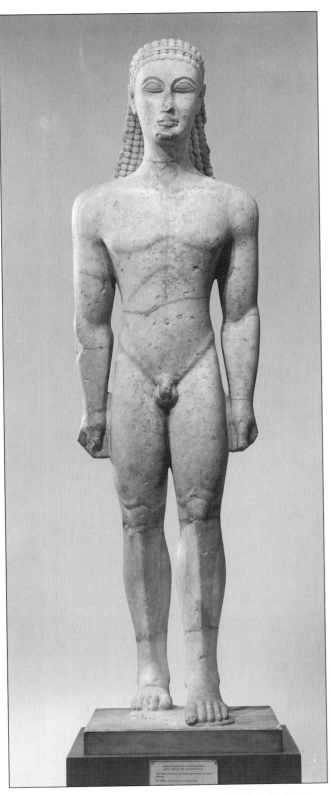

FIGURE 2.22 Kouros, ca. 600 B.C.E., marble, height 6′4″ (1.93 m), Fletcher Fund, 1932, Metropolitan Museum of Art, New York. A Greek kouros is a statue of a standing nude male. Details of the anatomy form a decorative surface pattern. The pose, with one foot forward yet the weight of the body equally distributed on both feet, comes from Egypt.

gorizing the various aspects of the world and their relation to it in terms that were based not on faith or emotion but on logic and reasoning.

Before the ascendancy of Socrates and his pupil Plato in the late fifth century B.C.E. a group of early Greek thinkers, called the Presocratics, hotly debated the nature of the world and their place in it. The Presocratic philosophers located near the Ionian city of Miletus in Asia Minor changed the way the world can be understood. Instead of an approach based on mythological tradition, Milesian thinkers such as THALES [THAY-lees] (624–526 B.C.E.) and HERACLITUS [hair-a-CLITE-us] (ca. 537–475 B.C.E.) offered more abstract conceptual explanations based on their observations and their sense that the universe was governed by impersonal and uniform laws. These forces and laws the earliest Greek philosophers attempted to identify and explain. For Thales, the source of the universe and its primal material was water, which, he reasoned, could explain both the changing and the more stable qualities of the universe. Thales brings to his

Cultural Impact

Ideals of physical beauty—male and female—vary greatly from one culture and time period to another. That of the slender Cycladic woman (Fig. 2.1) contrasts strikingly with the curves of the Greek feminine ideal seen in the kore of ca. 520 B.C.E. These early female figures may be compared with later versions of female beauty as seen in Botticelli's sensuously fluid Venus (fig. 13.18), Rubens' fleshy mermaids (fig. 15.20), Ingres's languidly linear *Odalisque*, and Rodin's solidly and realistically sculpted woman in *The Kiss* (fig. 18.15). Curiously, the angular, segmented, two-dimensional body of the Cycladic female figure has less in common with these substantial feminine images than with

more modern figures, such as the faceted females in Picasso's 1907 *Demoiselles d'Avignon*, (Fig. 21.3) and more recently, with contemporary fashion models, whose slim bodies and angular features adorn the covers of popular women's magazines.

Ancient Greece has also had a significant influence on the literature of subsequent civilizations. Homeric epic continued in a line through Virgil's first-century *Aeneid*, to Dante's fourteenth-century *Commedia* and Milton's seventeenth-century *Paradise Lost*. And although epic is no longer a popular literary genre, the epic similes or extended comparisons found in *The Iliad* and *The Odyssey* remain a staple of contemporary

poetry. One literary genre, however, that has flourished from ancient Greek times until today is the lyric poem, the earliest major recorded exemplar of which is Sappho, whose passionate love lyrics directly influenced the Roman poet Catullus and numerous Renaissance poets, including Shakespeare's contemporary, Ben Jonson. Love poems, which trace their lineage to Sappho, are among the most popular literary genres, as evidenced by new editions of love poems by earlier authors, such as Shakespeare, and by numerous anthologies of love poems in the twenty-first century, one of which, *To Woo and to Wed*, was edited by Robert Pinsky, an American poet laureate.

---

thinking a more naturalistic, even empirical outlook than had been in evidence previously.

For Heraclitus, the primary material of the universe was fire, which also exists in constantly fluctuating forms. Heraclitus saw the world as being in a state of constant flux, and especially in a state of strife, in which opposites constantly conflict. Nothing *is*, he claimed; rather all is in a constant state of *becoming*. One can never step in the same river twice, he wrote. And perhaps equally enigmatically, he suggested that human beings should seek to understand the order of the universe, which he called its Logos, and live their lives in conjunction with its spirit.

Another group of thinkers, the **atomists,** led by DEMOCRITUS [dih-MAH-crih-tus] (ca. 460 B.C.E.), conceived of the world as being made up of two basic elements: atoms—small, invisible particles that cannot be divided into smaller units—and the void, the empty space between atoms. Atomism survived in a changed form in the later

philosophy of the Epicureans (see Chapter 3) and had a dramatic influence on the thinking of the scientists who evolved modern atomic theory and quantum mechanics.

But perhaps the most important of these Presocratic thinkers was PYTHAGORAS [pih-THAY-guh-rus] (582–507 B.C.E.). For him, "number" was at the heart of all things. Today he is most often remembered for his theorem in geometry—in right-angle triangles, the square of the hypotenuse is equal to the sum of the square of the other two sides. These triangles are unified by number. Pythagoras extended this principle to music. He discovered that a string of a certain length, when plucked, made a certain sound; divided in half, it played the same note, only an octave higher. Mathematical ratios, he reasoned, determined musical sound relationships. The entire natural world, including the movement of the planets, depended on these same ratios, he believed. There was, underlying all things, a "harmony of the spheres."

KEY TERMS

mural
labyrinth
pithos
terra cotta
Kamares Ware
Palace Style
faience
lintel

relieving triangle
dromos
ashlar masonry
tholos
corbeled dome
rhyton
mythology
polis (pl. poleis)

Geometric style
krater
oinochoe
olpe
black-figure style
amphora
red-figure style
calyx krater

Doric
entasis
kouros (pl. kouroi)
kore (pl. korai)
Archaic smile
philosophy
atomist

WWW. WEBSITES FOR FURTHER STUDY

http://www.getty.edu/art/collections/objects/o15054.html
(This site contains a brief description and image of Cycladic sculpture.)

http://www.perseus.tufts.edu/cache/perscoll Greco-Roman.html
(A good general site on all things Greek and Roman, including ancient written works.)

http://www.varchive.org/schorr/warvase.htm
(An excellent discussion of the Warrior Vase can be found here.)

http://lib.haifa.ac.il/www/art/mythology westart.html
(A collection of images concerning classical mythology of all the gods, and many links.)

http://faculty.etsu.edu/kortumr/06archaicgreece/htmdescriptionpages/23architecture.htm
(The basic elements of a typical Greek temple facade.)

READINGS

HESIOD

WORKS AND DAYS, EXCERPT

Hesiod is one of the oldest known Greek poets. He lived in central Greece in the late eighth century B.C.E. The earlier of his two surviving poems, the Theogony, *contains a genealogy of the gods. The excerpt from the work that follows,* The Works and Days, *is a compendium of moral and practical instruction for a life of honest husbandry, which throws a unique and fascinating light on archaic Greek society. Hesiod is the first known personality in Western literature. In the excerpt that follows from his* Works and Days, *he offers advice on hospitality, morality, and practical living.*

Make sacrifice to the immortal gods according to your means in holy purity, and burn gleaming thighbones; and at other times propitiate them with libations and oblations, both when you go to bed and when the divine light returns, so that they may have a propitious heart and mind towards you, that you may negotiate for others' allotments, not another man for yours.

Invite to dinner him who is friendly, and leave your enemy be; and invite above all him who lives near you. For if something untoward happens at your place, neighbours come ungirt, but relations have to gird themselves. A bad neighbour is as big a bane as a good one is a boon: he has got good value who has got a good neighbour. Nor would a cow be lost, but for a bad neighbour. Get good measure from your neighbour, and give good measure back, with the measure itself and better if you can, so that when in need another time you may find something to rely on. Seek no evil gains: evil gains are no better than losses.

> *Be a friend to him who is your friend,*
> *and give your company to him that seeks it.*
> *Give whoso gives, and give not whoso gives not:*
> *to a giver one gives, to an ungiver none gives.*
> *Give is good, Snatch bad, a giver of death.*

For if a man gives voluntarily, even a big gift, he is glad at the giving and rejoices in his heart; but if a man takes of his own accord, trusting in shamelessness, even something little, that puts a frost on the heart.

For if you lay down even a little on a little, and do this often, even that may well grow big. He who adds to what is there, wards off burning hunger. What is stored up at home is not a source of worry; better for things to be in the house, for what is outside is at risk. It is good to take from what is available, but sorrow to the heart to be wanting what is not available. I suggest you reflect on this.

At the start of a cask or the end of it, take your fill, in the middle be sparing: parsimony at the bottom is mean. Let the agreed wage for a man of good will be assured; and even with your brother, smile but bring in a witness. Trust and mistrust alike have ruined men. No arse-rigged woman must deceive your wits with her wily twitterings when she pokes into your granary; he who believes a woman, believes cheaters. Hope for

an only son to nourish his father's house, for this is how wealth waxes in the halls; and to die in old age leaving another child within. Yet Zeus can easy provide great prosperity for more: more hands, more work, and greater surplus.

If your spirit in your breast yearns for riches, do as follows, and work, work upon work.

> *When the Pleiades born off Atlas rise before the sun,*
> *begin the reaping; the ploughing, when they set.*

For forty nights and days they are hidden, and again as the year goes round they make their first appearance at the time of iron-sharpening. This is the rule of the land, both for those who live near the sea and for those who live in the winding glens far from the swelling sea, a rich terrain: naked sow and naked drive the oxen, and naked reap, if you want to bring in Demeter's works all in due season, so that you have each crop grow in season. Otherwise you may find yourself later in want, and beg at others' houses and achieve nothing—as even now you have come to me; but I will give you nothing extra or measure out more. Work, foolish Perses, do the work that the gods have marked out for men, lest one day with children and wife, sick at heart, you look for livelihood around the neighbours and they pay no heed. Twice, three times you may be successful, but if you harass them further, you will achieve nothing, all your speeches will be in vain, and however wide your words range it will be no use.

No, I suggest you reflect on the clearing of your debts and the avoidance of famine. First, a household, a woman, and a ploughing ox—a chattel woman, not wedded, one who could follow the herds. The utilities in the house must all be got ready, lest you ask another, and he refuse, and you be lacking, and the right time go past, and your cultivation suffer. Do not put things off till tomorrow and the next day. A man of ineffectual labour, a postponer, does not fill his granary: it is application that promotes your cultivation, whereas a postponer of labour is constantly wrestling with Blights.

When the keen sun's strength stops scorching and sweltering, after mighty Zeus begins the autumn rain, and human skin feels the change with relief—for then the star Sirius goes but briefly by day above the heads of men who are born to die, having a larger share of the night—then timber is freest from the worm when hewn by the iron, when it sheds its leaves to the ground and stops putting out shoots. Then do your woodcutting, do not neglect it, a job in season. Cut a mortar to three feet, a pestle to three cubits, an axle to seven feet, that will do very well; or if to eight feet, you may cut a mallet off it too. Cut a three-span wheel for a ten-palm cart. Many timbers are bent: take a plough-tree home when you find one, searching on the mountain or on the ploughland—one of holm-oak, for that is the firmest for ploughing with oxen when Athene's servant has fixed it in the stock with dowels and brought it up and fastened it to the pole. Take the trouble to provide yourself with two ploughs at home, a self-treed one and a joined one, for it is much better so: if you should break one, you can set the other to the oxen. Bay or elm make the most worm-free poles, oak the stock, and holm-oak the plough-tree.

As for the pair of oxen, have nine-year-old males in their prime: their strength will not be feeble. They are the best for working. They are not likely to quarrel in the furrow and break the plough and leave the job there undone. Behind them I would have there go a sturdy man of forty years who has made his meal of a quarterloaf, an eight-section one; a man who would attend to the work and drive a straight furrow, not still peering about after his fellows but with his mind on the work. And no younger man is better beside him to distribute the seed and avoid oversowing. A younger man is a-flutter after his fellows.

Take heed when you hear the voice of the crane from high in the clouds, making its annual clamour; it brings the signal for ploughing, and indicates the season of winter rains, and it stings the heart of the man with no ox. Then be feeding up the oxen under your roof. For while it is easy to say 'Give me a pair of oxen and a cart', it is easy too to refuse: 'But the oxen have work to do'. A man rich in fancy thinks to construct a cart—the fool, he does not know there are a hundred planks to a cart. Attend to laying them up at home beforehand.

As soon as the ploughing-time reveals itsef to mortals, then go at it, yourself and your labourers, ploughing dry or wet in ploughing season, getting on with it good and early so that your fields may be full. Go over it first in spring; if it is turned in summer too it will not let you down; and sow the fallow while it is still light soil. Fallow is defence against ruin, the soother of Aïdoneus. Pray to Zeus of the earth and pure Demeter for Demeter's holy grain to ripen heavy, at the beginning of ploughing when you take the end of the stilt in your hand and come down with a stick on the oxen's back as they pull the yoke-peg by the strapping. And the labourer just behind with the mattock should make it hard work for the birds by covering up the seed. Good order is best for mortal men, and bad order is worst.

In this way the ears may nod towards the earth with thickness, should Olympian Zeus himself grant a successful outcome later, and you may banish the cobwebs from the storage-jars. And I am confident that you will be happy as you draw on the stores under your roof; you will reach the bright spring in prosperity, and not look towards others, rather will another man be in need of you. But if you do not plough the divine earth until the solstice period, you will reap sitting down, gathering little in the crook of your arm; binding opposite ways, dust-blown, none too cheerful; you will carry it away in a basket, and few will be impressed. Yet the mind of Zeus the aegis-bearer is different at different times, and hard for mortal men to recognize, and if you do plough late, this may be your remedy: when cuckoo first cuckoos in leaves of oak, gladdening mortals on the boundless earth, then hope that Zeus may rain on the third day without intermission, not rising above an ox's hoof nor falling short. So may late-plougher rival early-plougher. But be alert for everything, and do not miss either the coming of bright spring or the seasonal rain.

Pass by the smith's bench and the cosy parlour in wintertime when the cold keeps men from the fields—then an industrious man may do much for his household—lest in severe weather Helplessness overtakes you together with Poverty, and you squeeze a swollen foot with emaciated hand. Many are the ills that a workshy man, waiting on empty hope, in want of livelihood, complains of to his heart. Hope is no good provider for a needy man sitting in the parlour without substance to depend on. Point out to your labourers while it is still midsummer: 'It will not always be summer. Build your huts.'

HOMER

from The Iliad

The first of the following passages from The Iliad *describes the altercation between Achilles and Agamemnon. The second passage describes Achilles' slaying of the Trojan hero Hector, followed by the grief expressed by Hector's wife, Hecuba, and his father, Priam. The passages reveal the heroic code at work in the poem.*

THE ILIAD[1]

From BOOK I

[THE RAGE OF ACHILLES]

Rage—Goddess,[2] sing the rage of Peleus' son Achilles,
murderous, doomed, that cost the Achaeans[3]
    countless losses,
hurling down to the House of Death so many sturdy
    souls,
great fighters' souls, but made their bodies carrion,
feasts for the dogs and birds,   *5*
and the will of Zeus was moving toward its end,
Begin, Muse, when the two first broke and clashed,
Agamemnon lord of men and brilliant Achilles.

What god drove them to fight with such a fury?
Apollo the son of Zeus and Leto, Incensed at
    the king   *10*
he swept a fatal plague through the army—men were
    dying
and all because Agamemnon spurned Apollo's priest.
Yes, Chryses[4] approached the Achaeans' fast ships
to win his daughter back, bringing a priceless ransom
and bearing high in hand, wound on a golden staff, *15*
the wreaths of the god, the distant deadly Archer.
He begged the whole Achaean army but most of all
the two supreme commanders, Atreus' two sons,
"Agamemnon, Menelaus—all Argives geared for war!
May the gods who hold the halls of Olympus give you *20*
Priam's[5] city to plunder, then safe passage home.
Just set my daughter free, my dear one . . . here,
accept these gifts, this ransom. Honor the god
who strikes from worlds away—the son of Zeus,
    Apollo!"

And all ranks of Achaeans cried out their assent: *25*
"Respect the priest, accept the shining ransom!"
But it brought no joy to the heart of Agamemnon.
The king dismissed the priest with a brutal order
ringing in his ears: "Never again, old man,
let me catch sight of you by the hollow ships!   *30*
Not loitering now, not slinking back tomorrow.
The staff and the wreaths of god will never save you then.

---

[1]Translated by Robert Fagles.
[2]The Muse, inspiration for epic poetry.
[3]The Greeks. Homer also calls them Danaans and Argives.
[4]His daughter is called Chryseis, and the place where he lives, Chryse.
[5]King of Troy. Olympus is the mountain in northern Greece that was supposed to be the home of the gods.

The girl—I won't give up the girl. Long before that,
old age will overtake her in *my* house, in Argos,
far from her fatherland, slaving back and forth   35
at the loom, forced to share my bed!
                    Now go,
don't tempt my wrath—and you may depart alive."

     The old man was terrified. He obeyed the order,
trailing away in silence down the shore
where the battle lines of breakers crash and drag.   40
And moving off to a safe distance, over and over
the old priest prayed to the son of sleek-haired Leto,
lord Apollo, "Hear me, Apollo: God of the silver bow
who strides the walls of Chryse and Cilla sacrosanct—
lord in power of Tenedos—Smintheus,[6] god
          of the plague!   45
If I ever roofed a shrine to please your heart,
ever burned the long rich bones of bulls and goats
on your holy altar, now, now bring my prayer to pass.
Pay the Danaans back—your arrows for my tears!"

     His prayer went up and Phoebus Apollo heard him.   50
Down he strode from Olympus' peaks, storming at heart
with his bow and hooded quiver slung across his shoulders.
The arrows clanged at his back as the god quaked with
          rage,
the god himself on the march and down he came like
          night.
Over against the ships he dropped to a knee, let fly a
          shaft   55
and a terrifying clash rang out from the great silver bow.
First he went for the mules and circling dogs but then,
launching a piercing shaft at the men themselves,
he cut them down in droves—
and the corpse-fires burned on, night and day, no end
          in sight.   60

     Nine days the arrows of god swept through the army.
On the tenth Achilles called all ranks to muster—
the impulse seized him, sent by white-armed Hera[7]
grieving to see Achaean fighters drop and die.
Once they'd gathered, crowding the meeting grounds, 65
the swift runner Achilles rose and spoke among them:
"Son of Atreus, now we are beaten back, I fear,
the long campaign is lost. So home we sail . . .
if we can escape our death—if war and plauge
are joining forces now to crush the Argives.   70
But wait: let us question a holy man,
a prophet, even a man skilled with dreams—
dreams as well can come our way from Zeus—
come, someone to tell us why Apollo rages so;
whether he blames us for a vow we failed, or sacrifice. 75
If only the god would share the smoky savor of lambs.
and full-grown goats, Apollo might be willing, still,
somehow, to save us from this plague."
                    So he proposed

and down he sat again as Calchas rose among them,
Thestor's son, the clearest by far of all the seers   80
who scan the flight of birds. He knew all things that are,
all things that are past and all that are to come,
the seer who had led the Argive ships to Troy
with the second sight that god Apollo gave him.
For the armies' good the seer began to speak: 85
"Achilles, dear to Zeus . . .
you order me to explain Apollo's anger,
the distant deadly Archer? I will tell it all
But strike a pact with me, swear you will defend me
with all your heart, with words and strength of hand.   90
For there is a man I will enrage—I see it now—
a powerful man who lords it over all the Argives,
one the Achaeans must obey . . . A mighty king,
raging against an inferior, is too strong.
Even if he can swallow down his wrath today,   95
still he will nurse the burning in his chest
until, sooner or later, he sends it bursting forth.
Consider it closely, Achilles. Will you save me?"

     And the matchless runner reassured him: "Courage!
Out with it now, Calchas. Reveal the will of god,   100
whatever you may know. And I swear by Apollo
dear to Zeus, the power you pray to, Calchas,
when you reveal god's will to the Argives—no one,
not while I am alive and see the light on earth, no one
will lay his heavy hands on you by the hollow ships.   105
None among all the armies. Not even if you mean
Agamemnon here who now claims to be, by far,
the best of the Achaeans."
                    The seer took heart
and this time he spoke out, bravely. "Beware—
he casts no blame for a vow we failed, a sacrifice.   110
The god's enraged because Agamemnon spurned his
          priest,
he refused to free his daughter, he refused the ransom.
That's why the Archer sends us pains and he will send us
          more
and never drive this shameful destruction from the
          Argives,
not till we give back the girl with sparkling eyes   115
to her loving father—no price, no ransom paid—
and carry a sacred hundred bulls to Chryse town.
Then we can calm the god, and only then appease him."

     So he declared and sat down. But among them rose
the fighting son of Atreus, lord of the far-flung
          kingdoms,   120
Agamemnon—furious, his dark heart filled to the brim,
blazing with anger now, his eyes like searing fire.
With a sudden, killing look he wheeled on Calchas first:
"Seer of misery! Never a word that works to my
          advantage!
Always misery warms your heart, your prophecies— 125
never a word of profit said or brought to pass.
Now, again, you divine god's will for the armies,
bruit it out, as fact, why the deadly Archer
multiplies our pains: because I, I refused
that glittering price for the young girl Chryseis.   130
Indeed, I prefer *her* by far, the girl herself,
I want her mine in my own house! I rank her higher

---

[6]A cult name of Apollo, probably a reference to his role as the destroyer
of field mice. The Greek *sminthos* means "mouse." Chryse and Chilla are
cities near Troy. Tenedos is an island off the Trojan coast.
[7]Sister and wife of Zeus (the father of the gods); she was hostile to the
Trojans.

than Clytemnestra, my wedded wife—she's nothing less
in build or breeding, in mind or works of hand.
But I am willing to give her back, even so,   135
if that is best for all. What I really want
is to keep my people safe, not see them dying.
But fetch me another prize, and straight off too,
else I alone of the Argives go without my honor.
That would be a disgrace. You are all witness,   140
look—*my* prize is snatched away!"
                    But the swift runner
Achilles answered him at once, "Just how, Agamemnon,
great field marshal . . . most grasping man alive,
how can the generous Argives give you prizes now?
I know of no troves of treasure, piled, lying idle.   145
anywhere. Whatever we dragged from towns we
          plundered,
all's been portioned out. But collect it, call it back
from the rank and file? *That* would be the disgrace.
So return the girl to the god, at least for now.
We Achaeans will pay you back, three, four times
          over,   150
if Zeus will grant us the gift, somehow, someday,
to raze Troy's massive ramparts to the ground."

     But King Agamemnon countered, "Not so quickly,
brave as you are, godlike Achilles—trying to cheat *me*.
Oh no, you won't get past me, take me in that way!   155
What do you want? To cling to your own prize
while I sit calmly by—empty-handed here?
Is that why you order me to give her back?
No—if our generous Argives *will* give me a prize,
a match for my desires, equal to what I've lost,   160
well and good. But if they give me nothing
I will take a prize myself—your own, or Ajax'
or Odysseus'[8] prize—I'll commandeer her myself
and let that man I go to visit choke with rage!
Enough. We'll deal with all this later, in due time.   165
Now come, we haul a black ship down to the
          bright sea,
gather a decent number of oarsmen along her locks
and put aboard a sacrifice, and Chryseis herself,
in all her beauty . . . we embark her too.
Let one of the leading captains take command.   170
Ajax, Idomeneus, trusty Odysseus or you, Achilles,
you—the most violent man alive—so you can perform
the rites for us and calm the god yourself."
                    A dark glance
and the headstrong runner answered him in kind:
     "Shameless—
armored in shamelessness—always shrewd with
          greed!   175
How could any Argive soldier obey your orders,
freely and gladly do your sailing for you
or fight your enemies, full force? Not I, no.
It wasn't Trojan spearmen who brought me here to
          fight.
The Trojans never did *me* damage, not in the least,   180
they never stole my cattle or my horses, never

in Phthia[9] where the rich soil breeds strong men
did they lay waste my crops. How could they?
Look at the endless miles that lie between us . . .
shadowy mountain ranges, seas that surge and
          thunder.   185
No, you colossal, shameless—we all followed you,
to please you, to fight for you, to win your honor
back from the Trojans—Menelaus[10] and you, you dog-
          face!
What do *you* care? Nothing. You don't look right or left.
And now you threaten to strip me of my prize in
          person—   190
the one I fought for long and hard, and sons of Achaea
handed her to me.
                    My honors never equal yours,
whenever we sack some wealthy Trojan stronghold—
my arms bear the brunt of the raw, savage fighting,
true, but when it comes to dividing up the plunder   195
the lion's share is yours, and back I go to my ships,
clutching some scrap, some pittance that I love,
when I have fought to exhaustion.
                    No more now—
back I go to Phthia. Better that way by far,
to journey home in the beaked ships of war.   200
I have no mind to linger here disgraced,
brimming your cup and piling up your plunder."

     But the lord of men Agamemnon shot back,
"*Desert*, by all means—if the spirit drives you home!
I will never beg you to stay, not on *my* account.   205
Never—others will take my side and do me honor,
Zeus above all, whose wisdom rules the world.
You—I hate you most of all the warlords
loved by the gods. Always dear to your heart,
strife, yes, and battles, the bloody grind of war.   210
What if you are a great soldier? That's just a gift of god.
Go home with your ships and comrades, lord it over
          your Myrmidons![11]
You *are* nothing to me—you and your overweening
          anger!
But let this be my warning on your way:
since Apollo insists on taking my Chryseis,   215
I'll send her back in my own ships with my crew.
But I, I will be there in person at your tents
to take Briseis in all her beauty, your own prize—
so you can learn just how much greater I am than you
and the next man up may shrink from matching words
          with me,   220
from hoping to rival Agamemnon strength for
          strength!"

From BOOK XXII

Bright as that star amid the stars in the night sky,
star of the evening, brightest star that rides the heavens,
so fire flared from the sharp point of the spear Achilles

---

[8]The most subtle and crafty of the Greeks. Ajax was the bravest of the
Greeks after Achilles.

[9]Achilles' home in northern Greece.
[10]The aim of the expedition was to recapture Menelaus's wife Helen, who
had run off to Troy with Priam's son Paris.
[11]The name of Achilles' people.

brandished high in his right hand, bent on Hector's
    death,
scanning his splendid body—where to pierce it best?
The rest of his flesh seemed all encased in armor,
burnished, brazen—*Achilles*' armor that Hector
    stripped   *380*
from strong Patroclus when he killed him—true,
but one spot lay exposed,
where collarbones lift the neckbone off the shoulders,
the open throat, where the end of life comes
    quickest—there
as Hector charged in fury brilliant Achilles drove his
    spear   *385*
and the point went stabbing clean through the tender
    neck
but the heavy bronze weapon failed to slash the
    windpipe—
Hector could still gasp out some words, some last reply . . .
he crashed in the dust—
             godlike Achilles gloried over him:
"Hector—surely you thought when you stripped
    Patroclus' armor   *390*
that you, you would be safe! Never a fear of me—
far from the fighting as I was—you fool!
Left behind there, down by the beaked ships
his great avenger waited, a greater man by far—
that man was I, and I smashed your strength!
    And you—   *395*
the dogs and birds will maul you, shame your corpse
while Achaeans bury my dear friend in glory!"

Struggling for breath, Hector, his helmet flashing,
said, "I beg you, beg you by your life, your parents—
don't let the dogs devour me by the Argive ships!   *400*
Wait, take the princely ransom of bronze and gold,
the gifts my father and noble mother will give you—
but give my body to friends to carry home again,
so Trojan men and Trojan women can do me honor
with fitting rites of fire once I am dead."   *405*

Staring grimly, the proud runner Achilles answered,
"Beg no more, you fawning dog—begging me by my
    parents!
Would to god my rage, my fury would drive me now
to hack your flesh away and eat you raw—
such agonies you have caused me! Ransom?   *410*
No man alive could keep the dog-packs off you,
not if they haul in ten, twenty times that ransom
and pile it here before me and promise fortunes more—
no, not even if Dardan Priam should offer to weigh out
your bulk in gold! Not even then will your noble
    mother   *415*
lay you on your deathbed, mourn the son she bore . . .
The dogs and birds will rend you—blood and bone!"

At the point of death, Hector, his helmet flashing,
said, "I know you well—I see my fate before me.
Never a chance that I could win you over . . .   *420*
Iron inside your chest, that heart of yours.
But now beware, or my curse will draw god's wrath
upon your head, that day when Paris and lord Apollo—
for all your fighting heart—destroy you at the Scaean
    Gates!"

Death cut him short. The end closed in around
    him.   *425*
Flying free of his limbs
his soul went winging down to the House of Death,
wailing his fate, leaving his manhood far behind,
his young and supple strength. But brilliant Achilles
taunted Hector's body, dead as he was, "Die, die!   *430*
For my own death, I'll meet it freely—whenever Zeus
and the other deathless gods would like to bring it on!"

With that he wrenched his bronze spear from the
    corpse,
laid it aside and ripped the bloody armor off the back.
And the other sons of Achaea, running up around
    him,   *435*
crowded closer, all of them gazing wonder-struck
at the build and marvelous, lithe beauty of Hector.
And not a man came forward who did not stab his body,
glancing toward a comrade, laughing: "Ah, look here—
how much softer he is to handle now, this Hector,   *440*
than when he gutted our ships with roaring fire!"

Standing over him, so they'd gloat and stab his body.
But once he had stripped the corpse the proud runner
    Achilles
took his stand in the midst of all the Argive troops
and urged them on with a flight of winging orders: *445*
"Friends—lords of the Argives, O my captains!
Now that the gods have let me kill this man
who caused us agonies, loss on crushing loss—
more than the rest of all their men combined—
come, let us ring their walls in armor, test them,   *450*
see what recourse the Trojans still may have in mind.
Will they abandon the city heights with this man fallen?
Or brace for a last, dying stand though Hector's gone?
But wait—what am I saying? Why this deep debate?
Down by the ships a body lies unwept, unburied—   *455*
Patroclus . . . I will never forget him,
not as long as I'm still among the living
and my springing knees will lift and drive me on.
Though the dead forget their dead in the House of
    Death,
I will remember, even there, my dear companion.
    Now,   *460*
come, you sons of Achaea, raise a song of triumph!
Down to the ships we march and bear this corpse on
    high—
we have won ourselves great glory. We have brought
magnificent Hector down, that man the Trojans
glorified in their city like a god!"   *465*
             So he triumphed
and now he was bent on outrage, on shaming noble
    Hector.
Piercing the tendons, ankle to heel behind both feet,
he knotted straps of rawhide through them both,
lashed them to his chariot, left the head to drag
and mounting the car, hoisting the famous arms
    aboard,   *470*
he whipped his team to a run and breakneck on they
    flew,
holding nothing back. And a thick cloud of dust rose up
from the man they dragged, his dark hair swirling round

that head so handsome once, all tumbled low in the
      dust—
since Zeus had given him over to his enemies now   475
to be defiled in the land of his own fathers.

      So his whole head was dragged down in the dust.
And now his mother began to tear her hair . . .
she flung her shining veil to the ground and raised
a high, shattering scream, looking down at her son.   480
Pitifully his loving father groaned and round the king
his people cried with grief and wailing seized the city—
for all the world as if all Troy were torched and
      smoldering
down from the looming brows of the citadel to her
      roots.
Priam's people could hardly hold the old man back,
frantic, mad to go rushing out the Dardan Gates.
He begged them all, groveling in the filth,
crying out to them, calling each man by name,
"Let go, my friends! Much as you care for me,
let me hurry out of the city, make my way,   490
all on my own, to Achaea's waiting ships!
I must implore that terrible, violent man . . .
Perhaps—who knows?—he may respect my age,
may pity an old man. He has a father too,
as old as I am—Peleus sired him once,   495
Peleus reared him to be the scourge of Troy
but most of all to me—he made my life a hell.
So many sons he slaughtered, just coming into bloom . . .
but grieving for all the rest, one breaks my heart the
      most
and stabbing grief for him will take me down
      to Death—   500
my Hector—would to god he had perished in my arms!
Then his mother who bore him—oh so doomed,
she and I could glut ourselves with grief."

      So the voice of the king rang out in tears,
the citizens wailed in answer, and noble Hecuba   505
led the wives of Troy in a throbbing chant of sorrow:
"O my child—my desolation! How can I go on living?
What agonies must I suffer now, now *you* are dead and
      gone?
You were my pride throughout the city night and day—
a blessing to us all, the men and women of Troy: 510
throughout the city they saluted you like a god.
You, you were their greatest glory while you lived—
now death and fate have seized you, dragged you down!"

      Her voice rang out in tears, but the wife of Hector
had not heard a thing. No messenger brought the
      truth   515
of how her husband made his stand outside the gates.
She was weaving at her loom, deep in the high halls,
working flowered braiding into a dark red folding robe.
And she called her well-kempt women through the house
to set a large three-legged cauldron over the fire   520
so Hector could have his steaming hot bath
when he came home from battle—poor woman,
she never dreamed how far he was from bathing,
struck down at Achilles' hands by blazing-eyed Athena.
But she heard the groans and wails of grief from the
      rampart now   525

and her body shook, her shuttle dropped to the ground,
she called out to her lovely waiting women, "Quickly—
two of you follow me—I must see what's happened.
That cry—that was Hector's honored mother I heard!
My heart's pounding, leaping up in my throat,   530
the knees beneath me paralyzed—Oh I know it . . .
something terrible's coming down on Priam's children.
Pray god the news will never reach my ears!
Yes but I dread it so—what if great Achilles
has cut my Hector off from the city, daring Hector,   535
and driven him out across the plain, and all alone?—
He may have put an end to that fatal headstrong pride
that always seized my Hector—never hanging back
with the main force of men, always charging ahead,
giving ground to no man in his fury!"
      So she cried,   540
dashing out of the royal halls like a madwoman,
her heart racing hard, her women close behind her.
But once she reached the tower where soldiers massed
she stopped on the rampart, looked down and saw it
      all—
saw him dragged before the city, stallions galloping,   545
dragging Hector back to Achaea's beaked warships—
ruthless work. The world went black as night
before her eyes, she fainted, falling backward,
gasping away her life breath . . .
She flung to the winds her glittering headdress,   550
the cap and the coronet, braided band and veil,
all the regalia golden Aphrodite gave her once,
the day that Hector, helmet aflash in sunlight,
led her home to Troy from her father's house
with countless wedding gifts to win her heart.   555
But crowding round her now her husband's sisters
and brothers' wives supported her in their midst,
and she, terrified, stunned to the point of death,
struggling for breath now and coming back to life,
burst out in grief among the Trojan women: "O
      Hector—   560
I am destroyed! Both born to the same fate after all!
You, you at Troy in the halls of King Priam—
I at Thebes, under the timberline of Placos,
Eetion's house . . . He raised me as a child,
that man of doom, his daughter just as doomed—   565
would to god he'd never fathered me!
      Now you go down
to the House of Death, the dark depths of the earth,
and leave me here to waste away in grief, a widow
lost in the royal halls—and the boy only a baby,
the son we bore together, you and I so doomed.   570
Hector, what help are you to him, now you are dead?—
what help is he to you? Think, even if he escapes
the wrenching horrors of war against the Argives,
pain and labor will plague him all his days to come.
Strangers will mark his lands off, stealing his estates. 575
The day that orphans a youngster cuts him off from
      friends.
And he hangs his head low, humiliated in every way . . .
his cheeks stained with tears, and pressed by hunger
the boy goes up to his father's old companions,
tugging at one man's cloak, another's tunic,   580
and some will pity him, true,

and one will give him a little cup to drink,
enough to wet his lips, not quench his thirst.
But then some bully with both his parents living
beats him from the banquet, fists and abuses flying: *585*
'You, get out—you've got no father feasting with us
    here!'
And the boy, sobbing, trails home to his widowed
    mother . . .
Astyanax!
          And years ago, propped on his father's knee,
he would only eat the marrow, the richest cuts of
    lamb,   *590*
and when sleep came on him and he had quit his play,
cradled warm in his nurse's arms he'd drowse off,
snug in a soft bed, his heart brimmed with joy.
Now what suffering, now he's lost his father—
          Astyanax!   *595*
The Lord of the City, so the Trojans called him,
because it was you, Hector, you and you alone
who shielded the gates and the long walls of Troy.
But now by the beaked ships, far from your parents,
glistening worms will wriggle through your flesh,   *600*
once the dogs have had their fill of your naked corpse—
though we have such stores of clothing laid up in the
    halls,
fine things, a joy to the eye, the work of women's hands.
Now, by god, I'll burn them all, blazing to the skies!
No use to you now, they'll never shroud your body—*605*
but they will be your glory
burned by the Trojan men and women in your honor!"

    Her voice rang out in tears and the women
wailed in answer.

HOMER

from The Odyssey

The following passage from near the end of The Odyssey *describes Odysseus's reunion, after twenty years, with his wife, Penelope. Homer creates interest by having Penelope refuse to acknowledge Odysseus until he can offer incontrovertible proof that he is indeed her husband.*

FROM BOOK XXIII

The old nurse went upstairs exulting,
with knees toiling, and patter of slapping feet,
to tell the mistress of her lord's return,
and cried out by the lady's pillow:
          "Wake,
wake up, dear child! Penélopê, come down,   *5*
see with your own eyes what all these years you longed for!
Odysseus is here! Oh, in the end, he came!
And he has killed your suitors, killed them all
who made his house a bordel and ate his cattle
and raised their hands against his son!"

Penélopê said: *10*
"Dear nurse . . . the gods have touched you.
They can put chaos into the clearest head
or bring a lunatic down to earth. Good sense

you always had. They've touched you. What is this
mockery you wake me up to tell me,   *15*
breaking in on my sweet spell of sleep?
I had not dozed away so tranquilly
since my lord went to war, on that ill wind to Ilion.
        Oh, leave me! Back down stairs!
If any other of my women came in babbling   *20*
things like these to startle me, I'd see her
flogged out of the house! Your old age spares you that."

Eur'ykleia said:

"Would I play such a trick on you, dear child?
It is true, true, as I tell you, he has come!   *25*
That stranger they were baiting was Odysseus.
Telémakhos knew it days ago—
cool head, never to give his father away,
till he paid off those swollen dogs!"

The lady in her heart's joy now sprang up   *30*
with sudden dazzling tears, and hugged the old one,
crying out:

        "But try to make it clear!
If he came home in secret, as you say,
could he engage them singlehanded? How?
They were all down there, still in the same crowd."   *35*

To this Eur'ykleia said:

        "I did not see it,
I knew nothing; only I heard the groans
of men dying. We sat still in the inner rooms
holding our breath, and marvelling, shut in,
until Telémakhos came to the door and called me—   *40*
your own dear son, sent this time by his father!
So I went out, and found Odysseus
erect, with dead men littering the floor
this way and that. If you had only seen him!
It would have made your heart glow hot!—a lion   *45*
splashed with mire and blood.
           But now the cold
corpses are all gathered at the gate,
and he has cleansed his hall with fire and brimstone,
a great blaze. Then he sent me here to you.
Come with me: you may both embark this time   *50*
for happiness together, after pain,
after long years. Here is your prayer, your passion,
granted: your own lord lives, he is at home,
he found you safe, he found his son. The suitors
abused his house, but he has brought them down."   *55*
The attentive lady said:
          "Do not lose yourself
in this rejoicing: wait: you know
how splendid that return would be for us,
how dear to me, dear to his son and mine;
but no, it is not possible, your notion   *60*
must be wrong.
        Some god has killed the suitors,
a god, sick of their arrogance and brutal
malice—for they honored no one living,

good or bad, who ever came their way.
Blind young fools, they've tasted death for it. 65
But the true person of Odysseus?
He lost his home, he died far from Akhaia."
The old nurse sighed:
                    "How queer, the way you talk!
Here he is, large as life, by his own fire,
and you deny he ever will get home! 70
Child, you always were mistrustful!
But there is one sure mark that I can tell you:
that scar left by the boar's tusk long ago.
I recognized it when I bathed his feet
and would have told you, but he stopped my mouth, 75
forbade me, in his craftiness.
                    Come down,
I stake my life on it, he's here!
Let me die in agony if I lie!"

                    Penélopê said:

"Nurse dear, though you have your wits about you,
still it is hard not to be taken in 80
by the immortals. Let us join my son, though,
and see the dead and that strange one who killed them."

She turned then to descend the stair, her heart
in tumult. Had she better keep her distance
and question him, her husband? Should she run 85
up to him, take his hands, kiss him now?
Crossing the door sill she sat down at once
in firelight, against the nearest wall,
across the room from the lord Odysseus.
                    There
leaning against a pillar, sat the man 90
and never lifted up his eyes, but only waited
for what his wife would say when she had seen him.
And she, for a long time, sat deathly still
in wonderment—for sometimes as she gazed
she found him—yes, clearly—like her husband, 95
but sometimes blood and rags were all she saw.
Telémakhos' voice came to her ears:
                    "Mother,
cruel mother, do you feel nothing,
drawing yourself apart this way from Father?
Will you not sit with him and talk and question
          him? 100
What other woman could remain so cold?
Who shuns her lord, and he come back to her
from wars and wandering, after twenty years?
Your heart is hard as flint and never changes!"

                    Penélopê answered:

                    "I am stunned, child. 105
I cannot speak to him. I cannot question him.
I cannot keep my eyes upon his face.
If really he is Odysseus, truly home,
beyond all doubt we two shall know each other
better than you or anyone. There are 110
secret signs we know, we two."
                    A smile

came now to the lips of the patient hero, Odysseus,
who turned to Telémakhos and said:

Peace: let your mother test me at her leisure.
Before long she will see and know me best. 115
These tatters, dirt—all that I'm caked with now—
make her look hard at me and doubt me still.
As to this massacre, we must see the end.
Whoever kills one citizen, you know,
and has no force of armed men at his back, 120
had better take himself abroad by night
and leave his kin. Well, we cut down the flower of
          Ithaka,
the mainstay of the town. Consider that."

Telémakhos replied respectfully:

                    "Dear Father,
enough that you yourself study the danger, 125
foresighted in combat as you are,
they say you have no rival.
                    We three stand
ready to follow you and fight. I say
for what our strength avails, we have the courage."

And the great tactician, Odysseus, answered:

                    "Good. 130
Here is our best maneuver, as I see it:
bathe, you three, and put fresh clothing on,
order the women to adorn themselves,
and let our admirable harper choose a tune
for dancing, some lighthearted air, and strum it. 135
Anyone going by, or any neighbor,
will think it is a wedding feast he hears.
These deaths must not be cried about the town
till we can slip away to our own woods. We'll see
what weapon, then, Zeus puts into our hands." 140

They listened attentively, and did his bidding,
bathed and dressed afresh; and all the maids
adorned themselves. Then Phêmios the harper
took his polished shell and plucked the strings,
moving the company to desire 145
for singing, for the sway and beat of dancing,
until they made the manor hall resound
with gaiety of men and grace of women.
Anyone passing on the road would say:

"Married at last, I see—the queen so many courted. 150
Sly, cattish wife! She would not keep—not she!—
the lord's estate until he came."
                    So travellers'
thoughts might run—but no one guessed the truth.
Greathearted Odysseus, home at last,
was being bathed now by Eurýnomê 155
and rubbed with golden oil, and clothed again
in a fresh tunic and a cloak. Athena
lent him beauty, head to foot. She made him
taller, and massive, too, with crisping hair
in curls like petals of wild hyacinth 160

but all red-golden. Think of gold infused
on silver by a craftsman, whose fine art
Hephaistos taught him, or Athena: one
whose work moves to delight: just so she lavished
beauty over Odysseus' head and shoulders.   165
He sat then in the same chair by the pillar,
facing his silent wife, and said:

                              "Strange woman,
the immortals of Olympos made you hard,
harder than any. Who else in the world
would keep aloof as you do from her husband   170
if he returned to her from years of trouble,
cast on his own land in the twentieth year?

Nurse, make up a bed for me to sleep on.
Her heart is iron in her breast."

                    Penélopê
spoke to Odysseus now. She said:

                              "Strange man,   175
if man you are . . . This is no pride on my part
nor scorn for you—not even wonder, merely.
I know so well how you—how he—appeared
boarding the ship for Troy. But all the same . . .
Make up his bed for him, Euríkleia.   180
Place it outside the bedchamber my lord
built with his own hands. Pile the big bed
with fleeces, rugs, and sheets of purest linen."

With this she tried him to the breaking point,
and he turned on her in a flash raging: 185

"Woman, by heaven you've stung me now!
Who dared to move my bed?
No builder had the skill for that—unless
a god came down to turn the trick. No mortal
in his best days could budge it with a crowbar.   190
There is our pact and pledge, our secret sign,
built into that bed—my handiwork
and no one else's!

                    An old trunk of olive
grew like a pillar on the building plot,
and I laid out our bedroom round that tree,   195
lined up the stone walls, built the walls and roof,
gave it a doorway and smooth-fitting doors.
Then I lopped off the silvery leaves and branches,
hewed and shaped that stump from the roots up
into a bedpost, drilled it, let it serve   200
as model for the rest. I planed them all,
inlaid them all with silver, gold and ivory,
and stretched a bed between—a pliant web
of oxhide thongs dyed crimson.
                    There's our sign!
I know no more. Could someone's else's hand   205
have sawn that trunk and dragged the frame away?"

Their secret! as she heard it told, her knees
grew tremulous and weak, her heart failed her.
With eyes brimming tears she ran to him,
throwing her arms around his neck, and kissed him,
murmuring: 210

"Do not rage at me, Odysseus!
No one ever matched your caution! Think
what difficulty the gods gave: they denied us
life together in our prime and flowering years,
kept us from crossing into age together.   215
Forgive me, don't be angry. I could not
welcome you with love on sight! I armed myself
long ago against the frauds of men,
impostors who might come—and all those many
whose underhanded ways bring evil on!   220
Helen of Argos, daughter of Zeus and Leda,
would she have joined the stranger, lain with him,
if she had known her destiny? known the Akhaians
in arms would bring her back to her own country?
Surely a goddess moved her to adultery,   225
her blood unchilled by war and evil coming,
the years, the desolation; ours, too.
But here and now, what sign could be so clear
as this of our own bed?
No other man has ever laid eyes on it—   230
only my own slave, Aktoris, that my father
sent with me as a gift—she kept our door.
You make my stiff heart know that I am yours."

Now from his breast into his eyes the ache
of longing mounted, and he wept at last,
his dear wife, clear and faithful, in his arms,   235
longed for
          as the sunwarmed earth is longed for by a
          swimmer
spent in rough water where his ship went down
under Poseidon's blows, gale winds and tons of sea.
Few men can keep alive through a big surf   240
to crawl, clotted with brine, on kindly beaches
in joy, in joy, knowing the abyss behind:
and so she too rejoiced, her gaze upon her husband,
her white arms round him pressed as though forever.

The rose Dawn might have found them weeping
          still   245
had not grey-eyed Athena slowed the night
when night was most profound, and held the Dawn
under the Ocean of the East. That glossy team,
Firebright and Daybright, the Dawn's horses
that draw her heavenward for men—Athena   250
stayed their harnessing.

                    Then said Odysseus:

"My dear, we have not won through to the end.
One trial—I do not know how long—is left for me
to see fulfilled. Teirêsias' ghost forewarned me
the night I stood upon the shore of Death, asking   255
about my friends' homecoming and my own.

But now the hour grows late, it is bed time,
rest will be sweet for us; let us lie down."

To this Penélopê replied:

                    "That bed,
that rest is yours whenever desire moves you,   260

now the kind powers have brought you home at last.
But as your thought has dwelt upon it, tell me:
what is the trial you face? I must know soon;
what does it mater if I learn tonight?"

The teller of many stories said:

           "My strange one,   *265*
must you again, and even now,
urge me to talk? Here is a plodding tale;
no charm in it, no relish in the telling.
Teirêsias told me I must take an oar
and trudge the mainland, going from town to town,   *270*
until I discover men who have never known
the salt blue sea, nor flavor of salt meat—
strangers to painted prows, to watercraft
and oars like wings, dipping across the water.
The moment of revelation he foretold   *275*
was this, for you may share the prophecy:
some traveller falling in with me will say:
'A winnowing fan, that on your shoulder, sir?'
There I must plant my oar, on the very spot,
with burnt offerings to Poseidon of the Waters: *280*
a ram, a bull, a great buck boar. Thereafter
when I come home again, I am to slay
full hekatombs to the gods who own broad heaven,
one by one.
        Then death will drift upon me
from seaward, mild as air, mild as your hand,   *285*
in my well-tended weariness of age,
contented folk around me on our island.
He said all this must come."
           Penélopê said:
"If by the gods' grace age at least is kind,
we have that promise—trials will end in peace."   *290*

So he confided in her, and she answered.
Meanwhile Eurýnomê and the nurse together
laid soft coverlets on the master's bed,
working in haste by torchlight. Eurýkleia
retired to her quarters for the night,   *295*
and then Eurýnomê, as maid-in-waiting,
lighted her lord and lady to their chamber
with bright bands.

          She vanished.
          So they came
into that bed so steadfast, loved of old,
opening glad arms to one another.   *300*
Telémakhos by now had hushed the dancing,
hushed the women. In the darkened hall
he and the cowherd and the swineherd slept.

The royal pair mingled in love again
and afterward lay revelling in stories: *305*
hers of the siege her beauty stood at home
from arrogant suitors, crowding on his sight,
and how they fed their courtship on his cattle,
oxen and fat sheep, and drank up rivers
of wine out of the vats.
         Odysseus told   *310*
of what hard blows he had dealt out to others

and of what blows he had taken—all that story.
She could not close her eyes till all was told.

His raid on the Kikonês, first of all,
then how he visited the Lotos Eaters,   *315*
and what the Kyklops did, and how those shipmates,
pitilessly devoured, were avenged.
Then of his touching Aiolos's isle
and how that king refitted him for sailing
to Ithaka; all vain: gales blew him back   *320*
groaning over the fishcold sea. Then how
he reached the Laistrygonians' distant bay
and how they smashed his ships and his
        companions.
Kirkê, then: of her deceits and magic,
then of his voyage to the wide underworld   *325*
of dark, the house of Death, and questioning
Teirêsias, Theban spirit.
          Dead companions,
many, he saw there, and his mother, too.
Of this he told his wife, and told how later
he heard the choir of maddening Seirênês,   *330*
coasted the Wandering Rocks, Kharybdis' pool
and the fiend Skylla who takes toll of men.
then how his shipmates killed Lord Hêlios' cattle
and how Zeus thundering in towering heaven
split their fast ship with his fuming bolt,   *335*
so all hands perished.
         He alone survived,
cast away on Kalypso's isle, Ogýgia.
He told, then, how that nymph detained him there
in her smooth caves, craving him for her husband,
and how in her devoted lust she swore   *340*
he should not die nor grow old, all his days,
but he held out against her.
          Last of all
what sea-toil brought him to the Phaiákians;
their welcome; how they took him to their hearts
and gave him passage to his own dear island   *345*
with gifts of garments, gold and bronze . . .
          Remembering,
he drowsed over the story's end. Sweet sleep
relaxed his limbs and his care-burdened breast.

Other affairs were in Athena's keeping.
Waiting until Odysseus had his pleasure   *350*
of love and sleep, the grey-eyed one bestirred
the fresh Dawn from her bed of paling Ocean
to bring up daylight to her golden chair,
and from his fleecy bed Odysseus
arose. He said to Penélopê:

          "My lady,   *355*
what ordeals have we not endured! Here, waiting
you had your grief, while my return dragged out—
my hard adventures, pitting myself against
the gods' will, and Zeus, who pinned me down
far from home. But now our life resumes: *360*
we've come together to our longed-for bed.
Take care of what is left me in our house;
as to the flocks that pack of wolves laid waste
they'll be replenished: scores I'll get on raids

and other scores our island friends will give me   *365*
till all the folds are full again.
                    This day
I'm off up country to the orchards. I must see
my noble father, for he missed me sorely.
And here is my command for you—a strict one,
though you may need none, clever as you are.   *370*
Word will get about as the sun goes higher
of how I killed those lads. Go to your rooms
on the upper floor, and take your women. Stay there
with never a glance outside or a word to anyone."

Fitting cuirass and swordbelt to his shoulders,   *375*
he woke his herdsmen, woke Telémakhos,
ordering all in arms. They dressed quickly,
and all in war gear sallied from the gate,
led by Odysseus.
                    Now it was broad day
but these three men Athena hid in darkness   *380*
going before them swiftly from the town.

SAPPHO

Selected Poems

Lyric poetry, which offers a personal expression of human experience and subjective feeling, flourished in the sixth century B.C.E. with the female poet Sappho. It is relatively unusual to have such direct celebrations of female experience as we find in her lyrics. In "Alone" the speaker evokes feelings of passionate solitude, and in "Seizure" the speaker describes what it is like to experience attraction to another.

ALONE

The moon and Pleiades
are set. Midnight,
and time spins away.
I lie in bed, alone.

SEIZURE

To me he seems like a god
as he sits facing you and
hears you near as you speak
softly and laugh

in a sweet echo that jolts   *5*
the heart in my ribs. For now
as I look at you my voice
is empty and

can say nothing as my tongue
cracks and slender fire is quick   *10*
under my skin. My eyes are dead
to light, my ears

pound, and sweat pours over me.
I convulse, paler than grass,
and feel my mind slip as I   *15*
go close to death.

ARCHAIC LYRIC POETRY

Along with epic, lyric poetry flourished in ancient Greece, typically accompanied by a stringed instrument, such as the lyre, form which the word "lyric" derives. Among Greek lyric poets, Arkhilokhos stands opposed to the idealizing tendencies of Homeric epic. Another ancient Greek lyric poet, Alkaios, a contemporary of Sappho and like her from the island of Lesbos, also used Homeric epic as a source for his poems. Both poets lived in the seventh century sixth century B.C.E.

ARKHILOKHOS

THE FOX AND THE HEDGEHOG[1]

The fox knows lots of tricks,
the hedgehog only one—but it's a winner.

ELEGIES[1]

I am a servant of the lord god of war,
and one versed in the Muses' lovely gifts.
On my spear's my daily bread,
  on my spear my wine
from Ismaros; and drinking it,
  it's on my spear I recline.

There won't be many bows drawn, nor much slingshot,
when on the plain the War-god brings the fight
together; it will be an agony
of swords—that is the warfare that the doughty
barons of Euboea are expert at . . .

But come now, take the cup and pass along
the clipper's benches, open up the casks
and draw the red wine off the lees—we too
shall need some drink to get us through this watch.

Some Saian sports my splendid shield:
  I had to leave it in a wood,
but saved my skin. Well, I don't care—
  I'll get another just as good.

ALKAIOS

AND FLUTTERED ARGIVE HELEN'S HEART[1]

and fluttered Argive Helen's heart
  within her breast. She, crazy for
the Trojan cheat-host, sailed away with him,

abandoning her daughter dear
  and her rich husband's bed: the child
of Zeus and Leda heard the call of love.

[Now Paris has his due.] The earth
  full many of his brothers keeps,
felled in the Trojan plain because of her.

---

[1]Translated by M. C. West.

Many the chariots that hit
  the dust, many the bright-eyed lads
trampled, as prince Achilles gleed in blood.

HERAKLEITOS

Maxims and Sayings

Herakleitos was known in antiquity as "the obscure" because his writings were so difficult to interpret. His extant work consists of sharply pointed and provocative maxims and sayings. Their style is compact and cryptic, partly because of Herakleitos's belief that his meaning goes beyond the limits of ordinary language. Among the most interesting sayings are those about the unity of opposites.

God is day and night, winter and summer, war and peace, satiety and hunger; but he assumes different forms, just as when incense is mingled with incense; everyone gives him the name he pleases.

If all things should become smoke, then perception would be by the nostrils.

Cool things become warm, the warm grows cool; the wet dries, the parched becomes wet.

It scatters and brings together; it approaches and departs.

You could not step twice in the same river; for other and yet other waters are ever flowing on.

War is father of all and king of all; and some he made gods and some men, some slaves and some free.

Men do not understand how that which draws apart agrees with itself; harmony lies in the bending back, as for instance of the bow and the lyre.

Opposition unites. From what draws apart results the most beautiful harmony. All things take place by strife.

Men who desire wisdom must be learners of very many things.

For woolcarders the straight and the crooked path are one and the same.

Good and bad are the same.

Thou shouldst unite things whole and things not whole, that which tends to unite and that which tends to separate, the harmonious and the discordant; from all things arises the one, and from the one all things.

All the things we see when awake are death, and all the things we see when asleep are sleep.

The name of the bow is life, but its work is death.

For to souls it is death to become water, and for water it is death to become earth; but water is formed from earth, and from water, soul.

Upward, downward, the way is one and the same.

The limits of the soul you could not discover, though traversing every path.

Life and death, and waking and sleeping, and youth and old age, are the same; for the latter change and are the former, and the former change back to the latter.

I inquired of myself.

CHAPTER 3

HISTORY

480 B.C.E.	Athens destroyed by Persians
479 B.C.E.	Athenians defeat Persians
461–429 B.C.E.	Perikles rules Athens
431–404 B.C.E.	Peloponnesian War
430–429 B.C.E.	Plague kills Perikles
404 B.C.E.	Athens falls to Sparta
359–336 B.C.E.	Philip of Macedon reigns
338 B.C.E.	Philip of Macedon conquers Greece
336–323 B.C.E.	Alexander the Great reigns

ART AND ARCHITECTURE

480 B.C.E.	*Kritios Boy*
ca. 450–440 B.C.E.	Polykleitos, *Doryphoros*
448/447–438/432 B.C.E.	Iktinos and Kallikrates, Parthenon
ca. 445–430 B.C.E.	Achilles Painter, *Muse and Maiden*
437–432 B.C.E.	Mnesikles, Propylaia
431–404 B.C.E.	Polykleitos the Younger, theatre Epidauros
ca. 350–300 B.C.E.	Praxiteles, *Aphrodite of Knidos*
ca. 330 B.C.E.	Lysippos, *Apoxyomenos*
ca. 200–190 B.C.E.	*Nike of Samothrace*
ca. 180–160 B.C.E.	Altar of Zeus
begun 175 B.C.E., finished C.E. 132	Temple of the Olympian Zeus
ca. 150 B.C.E.– first century C.E.	Hagesandros, Athanodoros, Polydoros of Rhodes, *Laocoön and His Sons*

LITERATURE AND PHILOSOPHY

458 B.C.E.	Aeschylus, the *Oresteia*
ca. 441 B.C.E.	Sophocles, *Antigone*
430–429 B.C.E.	Sophocles, *Oedipus the King*
415 B.C.E.	Euripides, *The Trojan Women*
411 B.C.E.	Aristophanes, *Lysistrata*
407 B.C.E.	Plato becomes Socrates' student
387 B.C.E.	Plato founds Academy at Athens
367–347 B.C.E.	Aristotle studies at Academy under Plato
360 B.C.E.	Plato, *The Republic*
ca. 350–300 B.C.E.	Aristotle, *The Poetics*
343–336 B.C.E.	Aristotle serves as tutor to Alexander the Great
335 B.C.E.	Aristotle founds Lyceum in Athens

Classical and Hellenistic Greece

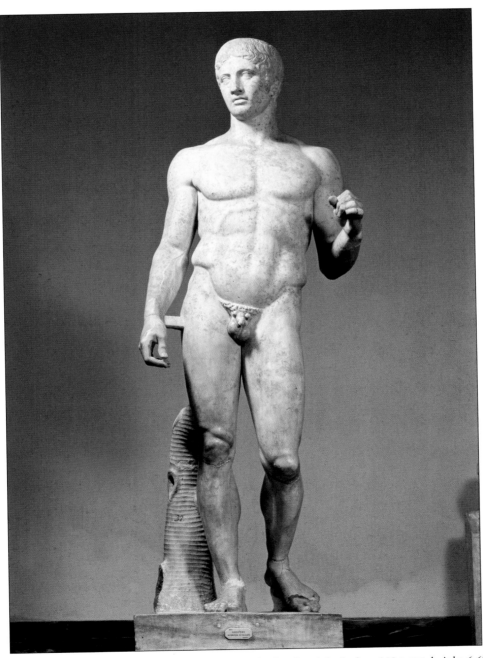

Doryphoros (Spear-Bearer), Roman marble copy of a Greek original of ca. 440 B.C.E. height 6 6″ (1.98 m), Museo Archeologico Nazionale, Naples, Italy. Scala/Art Resource, NY.

MAP 3.1   Classical Greece

Legend:
- Delian League ca 470 B.C.
- Athenian allies 460 - 446 B.C.
- Persian Empire
- Sparta 446 B.C.
- Sparta's allies 446 B.C.

CHAPTER OVERVIEW

CLASSICAL GREECE
The golden age of the arts

HELLENISTIC GREECE
A geographic expansion of the empire and a scholarly exploration of the past

CLASSICAL GREECE

In the decade between 490 and 480 B.C.E., something remarkable happened in Greece, and in Athens in particular, that resulted in one of the most culturally productive eras in the history of humankind. Before 490 B.C.E., as we explored in the last chapter, the Greeks had developed a highly sophisticated culture, but it pales by comparison to developments in the so-called Athenian Golden Age, a period of unsurpassed cultural achievement that can be said to begin with the Athenian defeat of the Persians in 479 B.C.E. and end nearly eighty years later, in 404 B.C.E., when Athens fell to Sparta. But the cultural achievement of the era was by no means exhausted with Athens's fall. This Golden Age had sparked a **Classical** period in Greece—"classical" because it forms the very basis of Western tradition down to this day—that would extend nearly another century until the death of Alexander the Great in 323 B.C.E. Even as the political power of Greece waned, its cultural preeminence carried on, through a **Hellenistic** period (from the verb "to Hellenize," or spread the influence of Greek culture), in which the basic tenets of Greek thought were perpetuated by the three dynasties that emerged after Alexander's death—the Ptolemies in Egypt, the Seleucids in Syria and Mesopotamia, and the Antigonids in Macedon—despite the competition for political dominance among them. Only after Rome captured Corinth in 146 B.C.E., making Greece into a province of the Roman Empire, did Greek culture begin to be absorbed into the new "Romanized" world. Even then the Hellenistic period was not truly at an end, continuing in Egypt until the death of Queen Cleopatra in 30 B.C.E.

FROM ARCHAIC TO CLASSICAL

Political Reform. Many things contributed to the astonishing rise of Athens as the cultural center of the world in the fifth century B.C.E. Chief among them is the century of political reform that preceded the Golden Age. As early as 621 B.C.E., the benevolent ruler DRACO [DRAY-koh] published what is thought to be the first comprehensive code of laws in Athens. This offered a single standard of justice to all Athenians, whether the landed aristocracy, the growing commercial class, or poor farmers.

Just as important to this process of change was SOLON [SOH-lon] (ca. 640–558 B.C.E.), who reformed the civil administration of Athens. He divided the citizens into four classes, all of whom had the right to take part in the debates in the political Assembly. Though Solon limited the highest offices to members of the nobility, he did allow the lower classes to sit on juries, and jury duty became a civic responsibility. He ended debt slavery (the practice of paying off a debt by becoming the creditor's slave), employed large numbers of artisans, and promoted trade, particularly trade in pottery. PISIS-TRATOS [pi-SIS-truh-tus] (ca. 605–527 B.C.E.) went even further, redistributing the large estates of some nobility to landless farmers, who, as a result of their improved economic status, suddenly found themselves able to vote. Like Solon, Pisistratos also championed the arts, commissioning the first editions of *The Iliad* and *The Odyssey* for students and scholars, and encouraging the development of Greek theater.

Shortly prior to 508 B.C.E., CLEISTHENES [KLICE-thuh-nees] (d. 508 B.C.E.) divided Athens into **demes** (neighborhoods), representing what he had labeled the ten "tribes" of Athens. Each "tribe" was allotted fifty seats on a Council of Five Hundred. The fifty representatives for each neighborhood were selected at random from a list of nominees. The Council elected ten generals yearly to run the city, and at the head of them was a commander in chief, also elected yearly. Thus, out of the demes of Athens, developed the first democracy.

The Persian Threat. This democracy was put to the test beginning in 490 B.C.E. when the same Darius who built the palace at Persepolis in Persia (see fig. 1.14) invaded the Greek mainland. On the plain of Marathon, north of Athens, Darius's mighty army was confronted by a mere ten thousand Greeks, led by General MILTI-ADES [mil-TIE-uh-dees]. In a surprise dawn attack, Miltiades' troops crushed the Persians, killing an estimated six thousand; the Greeks suffered only minimal losses. Victory was announced to the waiting citizens of Athens by a messenger who ran many miles from Marathon to Athens with the news, an early form of what would, centuries later, become a marathon run.

But the Persian giant was not yet tamed. A rebellion in Egypt and the death of Darius in 486 B.C.E., following which his son Xerxes ascended the throne, preoccupied the Persians temporarily. But all the while the Athenian general THEMISTOCLES [thih-MIS-tu-klees] was preparing for what he believed to be the inevitable return of the Persian army. And come Xerxes did, in 480 B.C.E., with an army so large that reports had it drinking rivers dry.

It is to HERODOTUS [heh-ROD-ut-us] (484–420 B.C.E.), the first writer to devote himself solely to history and who is therefore known as the Father of History, that we are indebted for much of our knowledge of the Persian Wars. He estimated the Persian army at five million men, surely an exaggeration, but certainly the Persians far outnumbered the Greeks. Although a Greek allied army fought most of the battle, a small force of three hundred Spartan soldiers has gone down in history. Led by LEONIDES [lee-ON-ih-dees], they went north from Athens to Thermopylai [thur-MOP-uh-lye], a narrow pass between the sea and the mountains, where they held off the Persian advance for days, buying time for the Greek army to retreat and set up a second line of defense. Betrayed by a local guide, who showed Xerxes a path around the pass, the Spartans were finally surrounded, but continued fighting until all were dead. Athens was destroyed by the Persians, and Themistocles retreated to the island of Salamis

[SAL-ah-miss]. This was a trick, however, for when the Persians sailed after him, they were unable to maneuver in the narrow bay, and the Persian fleet was entirely destroyed. Within a year, the Persian land forces were also driven from the mainland, and Greece was free.

THE GOLDEN AGE OF ATHENS

Over the centuries Athens had grown and prospered, a city within strong stone walls, protected by a vast citadel on an **acropolis** (literally, the high point of the city, from *akros*, meaning "high," and *polis*, "city"). There, temples were erected, law courts and shrines were built, and a forum for the Pan-Athenaic Games was constructed. The Persians destroyed all this and more in 480 B.C.E. The whole of Athens had to be rebuilt.

The entire population was put to work restoring the city's walls. When the walls were completed, the Athenians turned their attention to the **agora,** or marketplace, in which shopkeepers and craftspeople made, displayed, and sold their wares. Here, at the foot of the Acropolis, they built a council chamber, a court house, several long **stoas,** or roofed colonnades, to house shops, and a smaller

royal stoa in which the "Laws of Solon" were carved on stone and could be viewed by all citizens.

No attempt was made to rebuild the temples on the Acropolis. Their foundations were left bare as a reminder of the Persian aggression. But by mid-century, the restoration of the site seemed a matter of civic responsibility, an act of homage to Athena who had helped the Greeks defeat the Persians, and it was taken on by the great Athenian leader PERIKLES [PAIR-ih-klees] (ca. 500–429 B.C.E.). Perikles was first elected general-in-chief in 461 B.C.E., and, except for two years when he was voted out of office, remained in command until his death in 429 B.C.E. Under the artistic and administrative supervision of PHIDIAS [FI-dee-us], the best artists and artisans were hired, over 22,000 tons of marble were transported from quarries ten miles away, and vast numbers of workers were employed in a construction project that lasted until the end of the century. The acropolis embodied, for Perikles, the Athenians' "love of beauty," as he put it in an oration delivered in 430 B.C.E. at a state funeral for Athenian citizens who had died in battle. Its buildings were "things of the mind," he said, embodiments of the greatness of Athens itself (fig. 3.1). And it is true that when work on

FIGURE 3.1   General view of the Acropolis. Even in relative ruin, the Athenian Acropolis remains a breathtaking sight and a poignant reminder of past accomplishments.

the citadel was completed, the Acropolis at Athens was, with the possible exception of the Egyptian pyramids, probably the most impressive visual spectacle in the world.

It is often said that the Greeks' characteristic pursuit of balance and order in their art was a reaction to the extreme disorder of the world around them. Two major disasters struck Athens in the late fifth century B.C.E. The first, a devastating plague, occurred in 430–429 B.C.E., its most important victim being Perikles himself. The Greek historian THUCYDIDES [thyou-SID-id-ease] (ca. 460–ca. 400 B.C.E.) described how the "bodies of the dying were heaped upon one another" as "half-dead creatures" were "staggering about in the streets or flocking around the fountains in their desire for water." A year earlier, the long-standing Spartan resentment of Athenian power had erupted in the Peloponnesian War, which ended with Athens's defeat at the hands of the Spartans in 404 B.C.E. The war brought an end to Athenian supremacy and to the Greek golden age. It also signaled the breakdown in the city-state structure that had prevailed for centuries.

ARCHITECTURE AND ARCHITECTURAL SCULPTURE ON THE ACROPOLIS

The Greek Orders.   The ancient Greeks developed the three **orders** or arrangements of architecture—the Doric order, the Ionic order, and the Corinthian order (fig. 3.2). Although there are differences in the entablature, shaft, and base, the column capital is the easiest way to deter-mine whether the order used in the construction of a building is Doric, Ionic, or Corinthian.

As noted in Chapter 2, the **Doric** is the oldest and simplest of the three orders and was the order most frequently employed by the ancient Greek architects. By the Golden Age it had been perfected. Its capital is characterized by the square block of the **abacus** and the cushion-shaped **echinus,** usually cut from the same piece of stone. There is no base beneath the Doric column, whereas there is a base beneath the Ionic and Corinthian columns. The Doric **frieze** consists of alternating **triglyphs,** so called because they have three sections, and **metopes,** square or rectangular areas that may be decorated.

The **Ionic** order is characterized by the scroll/volute capital—graceful and curling. The Ionic was Eastern in origin and was especially popular in Asia Minor and the Greek islands. The **entablature** has a frieze of continous decoration.

The **Corinthian** order, a development of the Hellenistic age, is characterized by the large curling acanthus leaves that ornament the capital. The Corinthian is the most ornamental and delicate of the three orders. It was the order least used by the Greeks but most favored later by the Romans.

The Parthenon.   Built by Perikles with funds intended for the defense of Athens, the Parthenon [PAR-theeh-none] (fig. 3.3) is the only Acropolis building that was actually finished—construction of the rest was halted by the Peloponnesian War. The Parthenon is considered the ultimate

FIGURE 3.2   Diagram of the Doric, Ionic, and Corinthian orders. The three orders of Greek architecture were developed in antiquity and continue to be used even today.

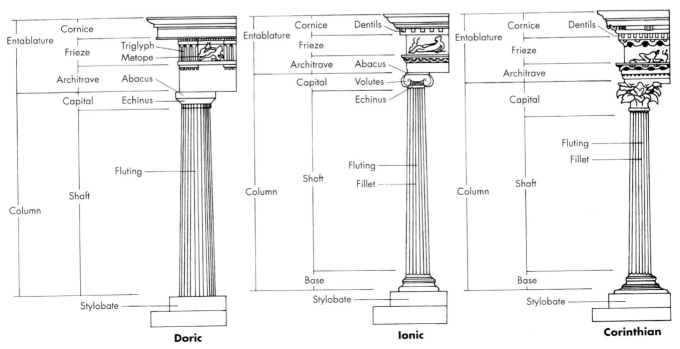

FIGURE 3.3   Iktinos and Kallikrates seen from the northwest, Parthenon, Acropolis, Athens, 448–432 B.C.E., marble. The epitome of Classical Greek architecture, the Parthenon is a regular Doric temple. All major lines actually curve slightly. Such refinements are now believed to have been intended to add to the beauty of the building rather than to correct for optical distortion.

example of ancient Greek architecture, the paradigm of perfection. Dated by inscriptions to between 448/447 and 438 or 432 B.C.E., it is the perfect example of the Classical Doric temple and is dedicated to the goddess Athena. Located at the highest point on the Acropolis, the Parthenon is the largest building there and is also the largest Doric building on the Greek mainland. The architects were IKTINOS [ik-TIE-nus] and KALLIKRATES [ka-LIK-kratees]. Phidias took on the task of its sculptural decoration, and he made a gold and ivory cult image of Athena Parthenos, dedicated in 437 B.C.E.

The beauty of the Parthenon derives largely from the perfection of its proportions. The facade is based on the so-called **Golden Section:** the width of the building is 1.618 times the height, a ratio of approximately 8:5. Plato regarded this ratio as the key to understanding the cosmos. Additionally the Parthenon possesses all of the "refinements"—the deviations from absolute regularity and rigidity—used by ancient Greek architects. Despite appearances, there are no straight lines to the Parthenon. The steps and the entablature both form convex curves. Each block of marble is a rectangular prism with precisely

Table 3–1	BUILDINGS ON THE ACROPOLIS, ATHENS, GREECE	
Building	**Architect**	**Date of Construction**
Propylaia	Mnesikles	437–432 B.C.E.
Parthenon	Iktinos and Kallikrates	448–432 B.C.E.
Erechtheion	Mnesikles	437 or 421–406/405 B.C.E.
Temple of Athena Nike	probably Kallikrates or Mnesikles	427–424 B.C.E.

FIGURE 3.4   Lapith and centaur, metope, Parthenon, ca. 440 B.C.E., marble, height 4′5″ (1.34 m), British Museum, London. The struggle of the Lapiths against the centaurs served the Greeks as a metaphor for the conflict between the civilized and the barbaric.

cut right-angle corners, but when the courses were laid, the blocks were positioned so as to be faceted in relation to one another. The columns have **entasis,** the slight bulge in the column shaft, and they taper to the top—that is, their diameter is less at the top than at the bottom. Further, the columns at the corners are wider and are placed closer together than elsewhere.

Parthenon Sculpture.   There are three categories of surviving Parthenon sculpture: ninety-two squarish metopes on the entablature, carved in high relief—most of those that survive have as their subject the mythological battle between the Lapiths and centaurs (fig. 3.4); the frieze on the upper wall of the cella, carved in low relief; and the huge figures that filled the east and west pediments, carved in the round.

The west pediment depicts the competition between Athena and Poseidon for the land of Attica. The east pediment depicts the birth of Athena from the head of Zeus. The figures are badly damaged, but nonetheless demonstrate the Classical balance between idealism and naturalism. Perfectly and powerfully proportioned bodies are revealed by naturalistic drapery folds (fig. 3.5).

The frieze (fig. 3.6) was carved ca. 440 B.C.E. of marble. The background of the frieze was painted and so were details of the horses' bridles and reins. Other accessories were made of bronze and riveted on. A recent interpretation suggests that the Parthenon frieze is a version of one of the foundation myths of Athens, that of King Erechtheus and his daughters.

FIGURE 3.5   Three seated goddesses, east pediment, Parthenon, 438–432 B.C.E., marble. Far from their stiff ancestors, the movements of these casual figures seem to flow easily. The drapery is contrived to reveal the body and appears almost wet.

FIGURE 3.6   *Procession of Women*, relief, from the Parthenon, Acropolis, Athens, ca. 440 B.C.E., marble, height of relief frieze 3′6″ (1.07 m), Musée du Louvre, Paris. Herve Lewandowski/ Reunion des Musées National/Art Resource, NY. The aesthetic principle of unity and variety is demonstrated here: The figures have enough in common to appear unified, yet sufficient variety to avoid monotony. The physical type favored in the Classical Period was strong and young, idealized rather than individualized.

The Propylaia.   The visitor to the Acropolis entered through the Propylaia [PROP-uh-LIE-yuh] (fig. 3.7), the front gates, constructed at the only natural access point to the Acropolis. The architect was MNESIKLES [mee-NES-ih-klees]. A porch with six Doric columns leads into

FIGURE 3.7   Mnesikles, Propylaia, Acropolis, Athens seen from the west, 437–432 B.C.E., marble. To gain access to the Acropolis ("high city"), the visitor ascended the many stairs of the Propylaia ("front gates").

a hall, from which the wings of the Propylaia extend. Ascending several levels, passing between Ionic columns, the visitor emerged on the east side, exiting through another porch with six Doric columns. The Parthenon and the Propylaia both combine Doric exteriors with Ionic interiors.

The Erechtheion.   The most architecturally complex building on the Acropolis, the Erechtheion [er-EK-thee-on] (fig. 3.8), was begun either in 437 B.C.E., the same year as the Propylaia, or in 421 B.C.E., after the death of Perikles. Work continued until 406/405 B.C.E., but the building was never finished. The architect may have been Mnesikles, the architect of the Propylaia.

The most famous part of the Erechtheion is the Porch of the Maidens on the south side. Here are six **caryatids**—female figures used as architectural supports (male figures that function in the same way are called **atlantes**). The structural use of sculpture in architecture is a rarity in ancient Greece. These statues blend with the building, the curls of their hair flowing into the capitals. They stand in the *contrapposto* pose (see next section), the supporting leg hidden by the drapery of their dress that falls in folds simulating the fluting of a column, emphasizing their architectural role. The figures form an obvious group, yet each of the six is slightly different—an example of the Greek aesthetic principle of "unity and variety."

FIGURE 3.8   Mnesikles, Erechtheion, Acropolis, Athens, 437 or 421–406/405 B.C.E., marble. The most complex of the Acropolis buildings, the highly irregular plan of the Erechtheion covers several areas sacred to the early history of Athens. On the Porch of the Maidens, female figures (caryatids) perform the structural role of columns.

The Temple of Athena Nike.   The Temple of Athena Nike (fig. 3.9), dated between 427 and 424 B.C.E., was probably built from a plan by either Kallikrates or Mnesikles. This miniature temple has four Ionic columns on the front and four on the back. The continuous sculpted frieze on the entablature is also an Ionic feature. Between 410 and 407 B.C.E. a surrounding wall covered with low-relief sculpted panels depicting Athena as she prepared for her victory celebration was added—*Nike* is the Greek for "victory."

SCULPTURE

The chief subject of the sculpture on the Acropolis, characteristically Greek, is the human figure. Just as the design of the temples was determined by carefully conceived orders as well as mathematically precise notions of proper

proportion and scale, the human figure was portrayed according to equally formalized ideal standards.

The Kritios Boy.   The kouros called the "Kritios Boy" (fig 3.10) was executed in a style associated with that of the sculptor KRITIOS [CRIT-i-os] of Athens, whose work is otherwise known only from Roman copies. The *Kritios Boy* differs from earlier kouroi significantly in terms of pose. The spine forms a gentle S curve; one hip is raised slightly in apparent response to the displacement of weight onto one leg. This is the **contrapposto** (counterpoise) pose, introduced by the ancient Greeks at the beginning of the transition to the Classical period. The head is turned slightly to the side, the pose is relaxed and natural. The body is carved with accurate anatomical detail, and the Archaic smile has gone. A new sense of movement appears, in large part a result of his weight falling on a single leg. Although the arms are broken off, it is apparent that they

FIGURE 3.9   Probably Kallikrates or Mnesikles, Temple of Athena Nike, Acropolis, Athens, 427–424 B.C.E., marble. Dedicated to Nike, the winged goddess of victory, this tiny Ionic temple was largely dismantled and has now been reconstructed.

were not placed rigidly at the sides as in earlier figures. The *Kritios Boy* indicates a growing anatomical understanding of bone, muscles, tendons, fat, flesh, and skin, and the way in which they work together.

Polykleitos.   The sense of naturalness and perfection hinted at in the *Kritios Boy* is fully realized in the *Doryphoros (Spear-Bearer)* (fig. 3.11). This was originally made in bronze, ca. 450–440 B.C.E., by POLYKLEITOS [pohl-ee-KLYE-tus], but now survives only in a marble Roman copy. At about the same time as he was working on *The Spear-Bearer*, Polykleitos developed a set of written rules for sculpting the ideal human form. By careful study of copies of Polykleitos's work, the basics of *The Canon* can be discerned. All parts of the body were considered. The height of the head was used as the unit of measurement for determining the overall height of the body—*The Spear-Bearer* is eight heads tall. This statue was viewed in antiquity as the definitive word on perfect proportions and was copied many times.

The *Spear-Bearer* stands in a fully developed *contrapposto* pose. Because only one leg is weight-bearing, the two sides are not identical. The pelvis and shoulders are tilted in opposite directions. The spine forms a gentle S shape. The pose is natural, relaxed, and perfectly balanced. With complete understanding of the human body, Polykleitos recorded everything—down to the veins in the backs of the hands.

Praxiteles.   The sculptor PRAXITELES [prac-SIT-el-ease] is known especially for Aphrodite (Venus) figures, represented by the *Aphrodite of Knidos* (fig. 3.12), another

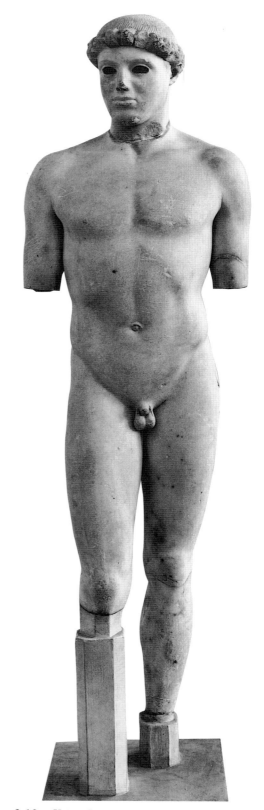

FIGURE 3.10   *Kritios Boy*, ca. 480 B.C.E., marble, height 3′ 10″ (1.17 m), Acropolis Museum, Athens. This work is transitional between the Archaic and Classical periods. The rigid frontality of the Archaic era is broken by the gentle turn of the head and the slight movement in the torso.

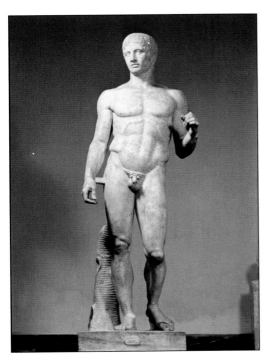

FIGURE 3.11 Polykleitos of Argos, *Doryphoros (Spear-Bearer)*, Roman copy of a Greek original ca. 440 B.C.E. Height 6′6″ (1.98 m). Museo Archeologico Nazionale, Naples, Italy, Scala/Art Resource, NY. In the Classical period, the relaxed and natural *contrapposto* (counterpoise) pose, with the weight on one leg, hips and shoulders no longer parallel, and spine in a gentle S curve, became the norm.

Roman copy after an original of ca. 350–300 B.C.E. Aphrodite is the goddess of love, born from the sea. In the sixth and fifth centuries B.C.E., male nudes were commonplace, as we have seen, but the female nude was a rarity. However, due to the influence of Praxiteles, whose work was highly praised in ancient times, the female nude became a major subject for late Classical and Hellenistic artists. The subject here is the modest Aphrodite—she covers herself—yet sensuality is not suppressed in the slightest. She stands in a slight S curve, weight on one foot, turning her head, in a relaxed and easy pose.

Lysippos. Sculpture continued to flourish in the late Classical period between the end of the Peloponnesian War in 404 B.C.E. and the death of Alexander the Great in 323 B.C.E. The sculptor LYSIPPOS [lee-SI-pus] was active by 370 B.C.E. and still working ca. 310 B.C.E., a longevity that earned him the name "Lysippos the old man." During these many years, Lysippos is said to have produced two thousand works of art, but he is known today only through a few Roman copies. From 328 to 325 B.C.E., Lysippos held the position of court sculptor to Alexander the Great.

We know Lysippos's *Apoxyomenos* (*The Scraper*) (fig. 3.14) from a Roman marble copy of the bronze original of ca. 330 B.C.E. that was found in the Trastevere section of Rome. In this sculpture, an athlete is shown using a *strigil*, or scraper, to clean the dirt and sweat off his body

FIGURE 3.12 Praxiteles, *Aphrodite of Knidos*, Roman marble copy of a Greek original of ca. 350–300 B.C.E., height 6′8″ (2.03 m), Museo Pio Clementino, Musei Vaticani, Rome, Scala/Art Resource, NY. The female nude became a popular subject in the Hellenistic Period. An illusion of warm soft flesh is created from cold hard stone.

after exercising on the *palaestra*—the school where young men learned to wrestle and box under the guidance of a master. The figure's pose is relaxed and spontaneous; it looks as if he has just shifted or is just about to shift his weight from one leg to the other. Moreover, he is not only moving from left to right but is also advancing out toward the viewer as he stretches his arms forward. Thus, Lysippos makes his subject move in three dimensions.

The Scraper is a slender figure with a small head. The body is rounded, with long, loose, lithe legs. The proportions are different from those of Polykleitos's *Spear-Bearer* of 450–440 B.C.E. (see fig. 3.11). Indeed, Lysippos, working

Then & Now

THE OLYMPIAD

The ancient Greeks had a prescription for good living that is still popular today: "*mens sana in corpore sano*," as the Romans translated it, "A sound mind in a sound body." The Greeks celebrated the human body and physical accomplishment as no other culture had before, particularly in sporting contests. These events were an important part of the Pan-Athenaic festival in Athens, but the most enduring of all sporting contests was the Olympiad, begun in 776 B.C.E. at Olympia on the Greek Peloponnese. These Olympic Games were held every four years until 394 C.E., when the Roman Emperor Theodosius abolished all non-Christian events in the empire.

From the outset, the short foot race, or *stade*, was the most important event. Held in honor of Zeus, the course was six hundred feet in length (the length of the *stadium* at Olympia), about equivalent to a modern-day two-hundred meter race. Legend has it that at the first Olympics, Herakles paced off the length himself by placing one foot in front of the other six hundred times.

The first thirteen Olympic Games consisted solely of this race, but soon the *diaulos* was added, consisting of two lengths of the stadium (or about one time around a modern track), as well as the *dolichos*, a long-distance race consisting of either twenty or twenty-four lengths of the stadium, perhaps two and a half miles. An athlete who won all three races was known as a *triastes*, or "tripler." The greatest tripler of them all was Leonidas

of Rhodes, who won all three events in four successive Olympiads between 164 and 152 B.C.E.

Over the years, other events were added, including, in 708 B.C.E., the *pentathlon*, consisting of five events—discus, long-jump, javelin, running, and wrestling—all contested in the course of a single afternoon. Only two measurements of the early long-jumps survive, from the mid–fifth century B.C.E., both of which are over sixteen meters in length. Since the current world long-jump record is just under nine meters, it is probable that the Greek long-jump was a multiple jump event, comparable to the modern triple-jump (the modern record of which is just over seventeen meters). By the mid–fifth century B.C.E. the games had become a five-day event and had been expanded to include a chariot race and even sculpture exhibitions.

Centuries after their suppression by Theodosius, the Olympic Games were reinitiated in Athens in 1896. At this first modern Olympiad, the organizers celebrated the return of the games by introducing a new running event, the "marathon," to celebrate Phidippides's legendary run in 490 B.C.E. from the plain of Marathon to Athens with news of the stunning Greek defeat of the Persians.

Today the Olympic Games have become more than just an athletic contest. They are big business. The United States Olympic Committee has an annual operating budget of $388 million for funding the training and preparation

of U.S. athletes. They are also usually a major economic boon to the community that hosts the games. When Atlanta hosted the 1996 Summer Games, for instance, 73,000 hotel rooms were filled within a ninety-minute radius of the Olympic Center, pumping over $5.1 billion into the local economy. After more than a century of being held outside Greece, the Olympics returned to Athens in the Summer of 2004.

FIGURE 3.13 Myron of Athens, *Discobolus* (*Discus Thrower*), Roman marble copy after a bronze original of ca. 450 B.C.E., lifesize, Museo Nazionale Romano delle Terme, Rome, Italy. Scala/Art Resource NY.

---

about a century later, created a new canon of ideal proportions for the human body. According to the Roman historian Pliny, the height ratio of head to overall figure size in Lysippos's sculpture was 1:9, whereas Polykleitos's was 1:8. This new physique was to gain favor and dominate through the end of the Hellenistic era.

The expressive face of *The Scraper*, sensitively rendered, appears somewhat nervous as he glances to the side. This individualized face may be a portrait of the noted wrestler Cheilon of Patrai, who died in 322 B.C.E., of whom Lysippos is known to have made a statue after his death. This is

another important development after the idealized figures and faces of the Classical period. Anonymity has been abandoned, and a new interest in individualization has arrived (see also fig. 3.17).

VASE PAINTING

White-Ground Ceramics.   In the first half of the fifth century B.C.E., a new technique was introduced into Greek ceramic production. In this **white-ground technique,** the vase is made of the same reddish Attic clay that was used

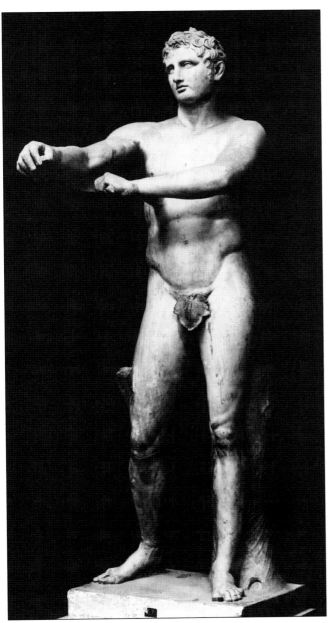

FIGURE 3.14   Lysippos, *Apoxyomenos* (*The Scraper*), Roman copy after the original bronze of ca. 330 B.C.E., marble, height 6′ 9″ (2.06 m), Gabinetto dell'Apoxymenos, Museo Pio Clementino, Musei Vaticani, Rome. Anderson–Roma, Art Resource, NY. A little more than a century after the *Spear-Bearer*, the ideal male nude has slenderer proportions and moves freely in space. No longer to be seen solely from the front, *The Scraper* is of interest from all sides.

for earlier black- and red-figure pottery. However, here a white slip is painted over the surface of the vase. The figures are not then filled in, as they were in the black-figure technique, nor is the background filled in, as in the red-figure technique. Instead, the central picture and surrounding decorative patterns are painted on with a fine brush. The style is characterized by free and spontaneous

lines. The white-ground technique presents the painter with no more technical problems than working on the equivalent of a white piece of paper—except that the surface of the vase curves.

The white-ground technique is associated in particular with **lekythoi** (singular, **lekythos**), small cylindrical oil jugs with a single handle, used as funerary monuments and offerings. A lekythos (fig. 3.15) by the Achilles Painter, painted ca. 445–430 B.C.E. in a mature Classical style, shows a muse and maiden on Mount Helikon playing a kithara, a stringed musical instrument. Mount Helikon is the mountain of the muses; muses, goddesses of the arts, excelled in song.

THE EMERGENCE OF DRAMA

Aeschylus.   Greek drama developed from choral celebrations honoring Dionysos, the Greek god of wine and fertility. These celebrations included dancing as part of the religious ritual. Legend has it that the poet Thespis

FIGURE 3.15   Achilles Painter, *Muse and Maiden*, lekythos, white-ground style, ca. 445–430 B.C.E., terra cotta, height 16″ (40.7 cm), Staatliche Antikensammlungen, Munich. Alinari, Art Resource, NY. One of the great advantages of working in the white-ground technique is that technical restrictions are reduced to a minimum. Neither the figures (as in the black-figure style) nor the background (as in the red-figure style) need to be filled in.

introduced a speaker who was separate from the chorus but who engaged in dialogue with the chorus. From this dialogue drama emerged. A second actor was then added to this first speaker and the chorus by AESCHYLUS [ESS-kuh-luss] (ca. 524–456 B.C.E.), who is today acknowledged as the "creator of tragedy."

Greek plays were performed in huge outdoor amphitheaters capable of seating upward of fifteen thousand people. The theater at Epidauros, for example, accommodated sixteen thousand (fig. 3.16). The audience sat in tiers of seats built into the slope of the hillside. The hills echoed the sound of the actors' voices, which were projected through large masks that further amplified them. The words appear to have been mostly sung to music, and music accompanied the dances performed by the chorus.

Ancient Greek plays were performed on an elevated platform. Behind the acting area was a building (*skene*) that functioned as both dressing room and scenic background. Below the stage was the orchestra, or dancing place for the chorus. Standing between the actors and the audience,

FIGURE 3.16   Polykleitos the Younger, theater, Epidauros, ca. 350 B.C.E., later modified. Alinari, Art Resource, NY. Ancient Greek theaters were built into a hillside that provided support for the tiers of seats. Ancient Roman theaters, in contrast, were built freestanding.

the chorus had an important part in the drama, often representing the communal perspective. One of the chorus's principal functions was to mark the divisions between the scenes of a play, by dancing and chanting poetry. These lyrical choral interludes typically comment on the action and interpret it while providing the author's perspective on the mythic sources of the plays.

Aeschylus is the earliest dramatist whose works have survived. Seven of his ninetten plays are still extant. His plays, like those of his successors Sophocles and Euripides, were all written for the twice-annual festivals for Dionysos held at Athens. Each dramatist had to submit three tragedies and a lighthearted "satyr" play for performance together at the festival. The work for which Aeschylus is best known—the trilogy called the *Oresteia* [oar-es-TIE-uh], after the central character, Orestes [oar-ES-tees]—won first prize in the festival at Athens of 458 B.C.E. The first play in the trilogy, *Agamemnon*, dramatizes the story of the murder of the Greek king, Agamemnon, who upon returning from the Trojan War is slain by his wife, Clytemnestra [clie-tem-NES-tra], and her lover Aegisthus [aye-GISS-this]. The second play, *The Libation Bearers*, describes the return of Agamemnon and Clytemnestra's son, Orestes, who kills his mother and her lover to avenge the death of his father. The concluding play, *The Eumenides* [you-MEN-ih-dees], describes the pursuit of Orestes by the Furies for his act of vengeance and Orestes' ultimate exoneration in an Athenian court of law.

Taken together, the three plays dramatize the growth of Greek civilization—the movement from a Homeric tribal society system, in which vengeance was the rule and individuals felt obligated to exact private vengeance, to a modern society ruled by law. The third play of the trilogy describes the establishment in Athens, under the jurisdiction of the goddess Athena, the city's patron, of a court of law to decide Orestes' case. Athena herself must render the verdict as the jury of citizens is unable to decide Orestes' guilt or innocence. Symbolically, with the establishment of the court of law in the last part of the trilogy, the old order passes and a new order emerges. Communal justice rather than the pursuit of individual vengeance comes to regulate civil society.

Sophocles. Of the Greek tragic dramatists, SOPHOCLES [SAH-fuh-clees] (496–406 B.C.E.) is perhaps the most widely read and performed today. Unlike those of his forebear Aeschylus, Sophocles' plays focus on individual human, rather than broad civil and religious, concerns. His most famous plays—*Oedipus the King* and *Antigone*—center on private crises and portray characters under extreme duress. *Antigone*, which takes place in Thebes, a city prostrated by war, turns on the difficult decisions that Antigone, Oedipus's daughter, and King Creon, his brother-in-law, must make. In *Oedipus the King*, set against a background of a plague-stricken city, Sophocles examines the behavior of Oedipus, who has been destined before birth to murder his father and marry his mother.

Athenian audiences watching performances of *Oedipus the King* would have been familiar with Oedipus's story from sources such as Homer's *Odyssey*. Oedipus's parents, King Laius and Queen Jocasta of Thebes, had been foretold of their son's terrible fate and therefore left him as a baby in the wilderness to die. This plan went awry when the child was taken by a shepherd to Corinth, where he was adopted by a childless couple, King Polybus and Queen Merope. Upon hearing an oracle pronounce his fate, and believing Polybus and Merope to be his natural parents, Oedipus then left Corinth to get far away from the king and queen. Ironically, however, en route to his true birthplace, Thebes, Oedipus kills an old man who gets in his way. This old man, Oedipus only much later discovers, was his true father, Laius.

Sophocles' version of the story, *Oedipus the King*, begins at the point when Thebes has been suffering a series of catastrophes, the most terrible of which is a devastating plague. Oedipus had previously saved Thebes from the Sphinx, a winged creature with the body of a lion and the head of a woman. The Sphinx had terrorized the city by devouring anyone who crossed its path and was unable to answer its riddle correctly—"What goes on four legs in the morning, two legs in the afternoon, and three legs in the evening?" Oedipus solved the riddle by answering "Man." After slaying the Sphinx, Oedipus was given the kingship of Thebes and the hand of its recently widowed queen, Jocasta, in reward. Unknown to Oedipus, but known to the Athenian audience, was the fact that Jocasta was his mother and her recently slain husband, Laius, had been killed by Oedipus himself. All this and more Oedipus soon discovers as he comes to self-knowledge.

Sophocles' *Oedipus the King* is one of the greatest tragedies in theatrical history—one of the definitions of **tragedy** is the representation of the downfall of a great hero. It also provides one of the best examples of **dramatic irony,** where speeches have different meanings for the audience and the speaker: The audience knows much more than the speaker. Thematically, the play raises questions about fate and human responsibility, particularly the extent to which Oedipus is responsible for his own tragic destiny. Sophocles portrays his tragic protagonists heroically. These tragic heroes suffer the consequences of their actions nobly and with grandeur.

In the twentieth century, Sigmund Freud used the Oedipus story as the basis for his theory of the **Oedipus complex.** According to Freud's theory, a boy grows up competing with his father for his mother's attention and affection, so much so that the boy at times hates his rival father enough to wish him dead. Conversely, his feelings for his mother are rooted in his unresolved desire for sexual gratification with her.

Euripides. One of the greatest and most disturbing of Greek tragic dramatists is EURIPIDES [you-RIP-ideas] (ca. 480–406 B.C.E.). As Aristotle put it, where Sophocles depicts people as they ought to be, Euripides depicts them as they really are. His plays were written under the shadow of the Peloponnesian War, and they spare no one, showing humankind at its worst. Although ostensibly about the enslavement of the female survivors of Troy, *The Trojan Women*, first staged in 415 B.C.E., is a barely disguised indictment of the women of Melos after the Athenian defeat of that city. In *The Bacchae*, Euripides depicts a civilization gone mad, as followers of Dionysos kill the king of Thebes under the drunken belief that he is a wild animal. Dionysos's followers, perhaps in part a portrait of the Athenian people, are unwilling to think for themselves and hence liable to be led blindly into the most senseless of acts.

In *Electra*, a play that somewhat parallels *Oedipus the King*, Euripides creates a female counterpart to Sophocles' tragic hero. With the help of her brother, Orestes, Electra murders her mother, Clytemnestra, thus avenging the death of her father, Agamemnon, at the hands of Clytemnestra and her lover. Euripides emphasizes Electra's haunted mind after her just but morally horrifying act.

Aristophanes.   All was not tragedy on the Greek stage, however. Comedy was very popular, and the master of the medium was ARISTOPHANES [air-ihs-TOF-fannees] (ca. 445–388 B.C.E.). His plays satirized contemporary politics and political personalities, poking fun at Greek society and ridiculing the rich in particular. Aristophanes even took on Socrates, depicting him as a hopeless dreamer. In *Lysistrata*, produced in 411 B.C.E. in the midst of the same Peloponnesian War that so outraged Euripides, Aristophanes' title character persuades her fellow Athenian women to withhold sexual favors from their husbands until peace is declared. They carry out their plans with merriment, teasing their husbands and even occupying the Acropolis. The women win the day, judging their husbands' priorities acutely, and at the end of the play Spartans and Athenians are reconciled and dance together in joy.

Socrates.   SOCRATES [SOC-ra-tees] (469–399 B.C.E.), the most famous of Western philosophers, is known primarily through his characterization in Plato's dialogues. In Plato's writings, Socrates (fig. 3.17) appears as a figure whose goal is self-knowledge and truth. Best known for questioning others' beliefs and eliciting their assumptions in a form of dialectical inquiry known as the "Socratic method," Socrates is a model of intellectual honesty. He was sentenced to death in 399 B.C.E. after being put on trial for impiety and corruption of the young. The authorities offered Socrates the chance to escape, but the philosopher chose death over exile.

Known as the "Father of Ethics," Socrates pursued wisdom so as to know the good, the just, and the beautiful. His pursuit of right living was governed by his famous maxim "Know thyself." Socrates urged self-examination and questioning of one's own and others' ideas and assumptions. Socrates believed that such discourse was necessary for the moral life and happiness.

Socrates was active at a time when **Sophists** taught philosophy for practical and opportunistic ends. Although Sophist philosophers shared Socrates' emphasis on the concerns of life in the world, their aims and practices differed from his. In place of eternal truths, the Sophists believed that morals and ethics were matters of convention

FIGURE 3.17   Lysippos, Portrait bust of Socrates, Roman copy of an original bronze of ca. 350 B.C.E., marble, lifesize, Museo Nazionale Romano, Rome. At his trial in 399 B.C.E. for impropriety toward the gods and corruption of the young, Socrates cheerfully admitted to causing unrest and insisted it was his duty to seek the truth.

ATHENS AND SPARTA

Athens	Sparta
Literate society; poetry and drama	Militaristic society; no poetry and no drama
Democracy	Oligarchy
Scientific/philosophical	No science or philosophy
Girls not educated	Girls educated
Women excluded from athletic contests	Women competed in athletic contests
Women prevented from owning property	Women allowed to own property

PHILOSOPHY

Of all the legacies of Greece, its philosophical tradition is one of the most enduring. The Greeks believed that what distinguished human beings was their ability to reason, and thus the philosopher held a special place in their society.

and that no such thing as truth existed. Knowledge, the Sophists said, was relative, based on individual experience, and hence could be reduced to opinion. Unlike Socrates, the Sophists would argue either side of an issue with the sole goal of being persuasive. The phrase "mere rhetoric" and the term "sophistry" to mean specious reasoning refer to the practices of the Greek Sophists.

For Socrates, as expressed in his maxim "The unexamined life is not worth living," self-awareness through reason determines how to master passion and appetite. Living a virtuous life directed by a reasoned pursuit of moral perfection leads to happiness.

Socrates provided Western thought with a new philosophical direction. By living according to his principles, by making philosophy a lifelong process, Socrates also provided a model and ideal of one who loves wisdom, the literal meaning, in Greek, of the word "philosopher."

Plato PLATO [PLAY-toh] (427–347 B.C.E.), a pupil of Socrates, and Socrates are frequently spoken of in the same breath because so many of Plato's dialogues present Socrates as a character and speaker. As a result, it is not easy to determine where Socrates leaves off and Plato begins. It is perhaps best to consider Plato's idealist philosophy as extending key elements of Socratic thought. In dialogues such as *The Symposium* and *The Republic*, Plato (fig. 3.18) developed the perspective implicit in his mentor's life and teaching.

Plato believed that truth could be found in mathematical perfection. Plato argued, for instance, that the *idea* of a circle, rather than any actual example of one, was true and perfect. Any example of a circle only approximated the perfect idea which existed in a special realm that transcended all particular manifestations. Plato identified this realm as the realm of Perfect Forms or Ideas. Virtues such as courage and kindness similarly transcended their everyday exemplary manifestations.

Plato postulated that ideal Goodness, Truth, and Beauty were all One, in the realm of Ideal Forms. Thus all actions can be measured against an ideal, and that ideal standard can be used as a goal toward which human beings might strive. According to Plato, human beings should be less concerned with the material world of impermanence and change and more concerned with the spiritual realm of Perfect Forms. Thus the highest spiritual principle, reason, should be used to control the lower human aspects of energy and desire.

Both ideas are advanced in Plato's best known work, *The Republic*, a complex and ambitious book concerned primarily with justice and how to achieve a just society. Plato proposes the division of society into three layers, each of which reflects one of the three aspects of the soul. Plato argues that people whose impulse is toward satisfying their desires are not capable of making judgments in accordance with reason and should therefore occupy the lowest position in society, that of servitude. Above these workers are the soldiers, whose primary force is that of energy or spirit-

FIGURE 3.18 Silanion (?), Portrait bust of Plato, 350–340 B.C.E., Roman copy of an original bronze of ca. 427–347 B.C.E., marble, Staatliche Antikensammlungen und Glyptothek, Munich. Although his real name was Arsitocles, Plato went by his nickname, which means "the broad one," a physical trait evident even in this portrait bust.

edness. The soldiers and the workers in Plato's republic work together at their allotted tasks under the directorship of the highest social group, the philosophers, whose decisions govern the republic by reason.

In Book 7 of *The Republic*, Plato uses two analogies to explain his idea about different levels of knowledge or understanding. One, the analogy of the Divided Line, presents a vertical line divided into four segments, with the upper two representing the intellectual world and the lower two the visible world. The lowest part represents shadows and reflections (explained below in the Allegory of the Cave); the one above that represents material and natural things. The two lower parts are complemented by the upper segments, which represent reasoning about the world and its objects (the lower segment of the upper line), and philosophical principles arrived at without reference to objects (abstract thought, the uppermost portion of the line).

Plato supplements this image about the nature of knowledge with his famous Allegory of the Cave. In this, he describes a cave in which human beings are chained to

Connections

LITERARY ELEMENTS OF PLATO'S DIALOGUES

Plato's *Philosophical Dialogues* have long been regarded as a literary as well as a philosophic masterpiece. In addition to their engaging conversational style, Plato's writings exhibit the following characteristics:

- The *Dialogues* individually are cast as intellectual dramas. They dramatize a conflict of ideas, typically represented by Socrates and one or more other speakers.

- The *Dialogues* collectively present a quest or epic journey in search of wisdom. An additional epic dimension is evident in the character of Socrates, who is unafraid of the unjust death to which he is condemned by the Athenian authorities. The neoclassical French painter, David, portrayed Socrates as he was preparing to drink the hemlock that would kill him.

- The *Dialogues* employ various forms of metaphorical thinking and analogy, the most famous of which is Plato's Allegory of the Cave in Book 7 of the *Republic*.

- The *Dialogues* contain various repeating images, the most important of which, light, symbolizes the highest form of knowledge, a form of divinely intuited illumination.

---

a wall. The only light visible is that reflected from a fire behind and above them. When objects are cast as shadows on the wall, the cave inhabitants take these shadows for reality. Only the one freed from the cave can see that what he had previously considered real are simply shadowy reflections of their actual counterparts. Instead of being a prisoner of illusion like those still chained in the cave, the escapee has a true knowledge of reality.

For Plato, such a revelation reflects the difference between ignorance and knowledge of truth, between the world of material objects and the realm of Ideal Essences, the true forms of those things. This division between the higher spiritual forms and the lower material world is echoed by other dualisms in Plato's philosophy. Foremost among the divisions are those between the philosopher and the common people, the perfect and the imperfect, and the spiritual life and the physical life.

Aristotle. Born in Stageira, in Thrace, ARISTOTLE [air-iss-TOT-ul] (384–322 B.C.E.) studied in Plato's school, the Academy, in Athens. He remained there for twenty years until Plato's death in 347 B.C.E., when he left to establish his own school, first in Assos and later in Lesbos. Aristotle's most famous pupil was Alexander the Great, whom the philosopher served as private tutor from 343 until 336 B.C.E., when Alexander succeeded to the Macedonian throne.

In 335 B.C.E. Aristotle, known as the "Father of Science," returned to Athens to establish his own school at the Lyceum, where lectures and discussions took place under a covered walkway. Lecturers moved about among their audiences, thereby acquiring the designation "Peripatetics" (walkers). Like Socrates, Aristotle was charged with impiety and condemned by the Athenian tribunal of judges. Upon leaving Athens before a sentence of death could be

carried out, Aristotle is reputed to have remarked that he would not allow Athens to commit a second crime against philosophy.

Aristotle's logic provides a framework for scientific and philosophical thinking still in use today. The basis of Aristotle's logic is an analysis of argument. Its central feature is the **syllogism.** In syllogistic reasoning, one proposition or statement follows from another by necessity, when the premises are true. In such a case the syllogism is considered valid, as in the following example:

All philosophers are mortal.
Aristotle is a philosopher.
Aristotle is moral.

In the next example, the syllogism is invalid even though the conclusion is true, because one of the propositions—the first—is untrue:

All philosophers are men.
Aristotle was a philosopher.
Aristotle was a man.

Aristotle's logic also includes an analysis of the basic categories used to describe the natural world. According to Aristotle, things possess substance (their primary reality) and incidental qualities. A dog, for example, possesses something—this is its substance—that distinguishes it from other animals, making it a dog and not a cat or a horse. At the same time, the dog may be large and brown with long shaggy hair—these are incidental qualities and secondary compared to the dog's substantial reality. Another dog, which is small and white with short fine hair, nonetheless possesses the same substance as the first larger darker dog.

Aristotle disagreed with his teacher Plato on a number of important issues. For Aristotle, an object's matter and form are inseparable. Even though we can think of the "white-ness" of a dog and its "dogness," those concepts do not have independent existence outside of the things they embody. Unlike Plato, who posited a realm where the perfect idea of a dog exists independent of actual dogs, for Aristotle the idea of a dog can only exist in relation to an actual canine quadruped. By insisting on the link between form and matter, Aristotle brought Platonic ideas down to earth.

Similarly, Aristotle emphasized the way the substance of a thing becomes itself in a *process* of growth and development. With his early study of biology as an influence, Aristotle's thinking takes account of development and process in ways that Plato's more mathematically influenced philosophy does not. For example, Aristotle describes the *potential* of a seed to become a flower or a fruit, of an embryo to become a living human or animal.

Aristotle's philosophy is grounded in the notion of teleology, which views the end or goal of an object or being as more important than its starting point or beginning. His teleological mind explains the way all material things are designed to achieve their purpose and attain their end. This end or goal of each thing is the fulfillment of the potential it embodies from the beginning of its existence.

Aristotle arrives at a conviction about the nature of God from logic rather than from ethics or religious faith. In his *Physics*, Aristotle argues that everything is in motion toward realizing its potential. Because everything is in motion, there must be something that provided the first impulse (the prime mover) and that itself is not in motion. For to be in motion is to be in a potential state, and the prime mover must be in a state of completeness and thus not in motion. The prime mover must be immaterial as well as unchanging.

Finally, Aristotle differed from his Greek predecessors significantly in his approach to ethics. For Aristotle, there were no absolutely unchanging ethical norms to guide behavior and determine conduct. Instead, there were only approximations based on the principle of the mean between extremes. Courage thus exists as a balance between cowardice and rash behavior, and temperance as a balance between deprivation and overindulgence. Virtue consists of negotiating between extremes, the balance point changing according to circumstances.

Aristotle's ethics is grounded in the realities and contingencies of this world. Aristotle consistently emphasized concrete, tangible, everyday experience and thus provided a necessary empirical counterpoint to the idealism espoused by his teacher and predecessor, Plato. Together their complementary philosophies have spurred theological and philosophical speculation for more than two thousand years. If, as one modern philosopher put it, "All philosophy is but a footnote to Plato," Aristotle's has been the richest, most complex, and most influential "footnote" of all.

Of his many achievements, Aristotle's work as the first Western literary theorist has been among his most influential. Aristotle's literary ideas are developed in his *Poetics*, a treatise on the nature of literature, focusing particularly on Sophocles' *Oedipus the King*. *The Poetics* offers a provocative and enduring set of ideas about the literary experience. Aristotle, in fact, is concerned in *The Poetics* not only with literature but with art in general.

An important idea derived from *The Poetics* concerns Aristotle's notion of "catharsis." Aristotle explains catharsis as a purging of the passions of pity and fear aroused in an audience during the tragic action of a play. Aristotle considers this catharsis the goal or end of tragedy. Aristotle's reasoning reverses conventional wisdom, suggesting that an audience's experience of pity and fear at, for example, Oedipus's tragic fate, would provide pleasure and not pain. The reason is that the emotions built up during the course of the tragic dramatic action are "purged" by the end of the performance. In Aristotle's view, the purging includes both physical purging through the excitement generated and released, and a spiritual purgation analogous to the release or cleansing of the soul for religious purposes. Such purging thus contributes to the health of the society beyond the theater.

Aristotle's insights into literary language and dramatic structure have remained influential for more than two thousand years. Throughout the Renaissance, and well into the eighteenth and nineteenth centuries, Aristotle was recognized as having set the standards for literary appreciation. At the end of the second millennium, nearly 2,500 years after Aristotle wrote *The Poetics*, literary historians and critics continue to employ Aristotle's categories and terminology.

PLATO AND ARISTOTLE CONTRASTED

1. Plato separated Ideal Forms from material things. Aristotle insisted on the inseparability of form and matter.
2. Plato made universals primary and particulars secondary. Aristotle made particulars primary and universals secondary.
3. Plato emphasized Being over Becoming. Aristotle emphasized Becoming over Being.
4. Plato celebrated mathematics as the model of pure thought. Aristotle grounded his philosophical system in biology.
5. Plato's philosophy emphasized stasis. Aristotle's philosophy emphasized growth and development.
6. For Plato the highest form of knowledge was knowledge of the pure Forms or Ideals—Platonic Idealism. For Aristotle, knowledge was grounded in empirical reality—Aristotelian Empiricism.
7. Plato's philosophy tended toward the transcendental. Aristotle's philosophy was directed toward the immanent.
8. Plato favored intuition over logic. Aristotle made logic the basis of his philosophy.
9. Plato used reason to overcome the physical world. Aristotle used reason to discover the order of the world.
10. Plato's philosophy influenced Augustine's theology. Aristotle's philosophy influenced Aquinas's theology.

Connections

MUSIC AND MATHEMATICS IN ANCIENT GREECE

Music, for the ancient Greeks, was not an isolated art. The basic elements of Greek music derived from mathematics, which served as the foundation of ancient Greek philosophy and astronomy. Music thus became associated with these other Hellenic achievements, largely through ideas about number, especially numerical relationships expressed as ratios. The most important early Greek theorist of music was PYTHAGORAS [Pi-THA-go-rus] (ca. 580–507 B.C.E.). Pythagoras's influence extended into the Middle Ages and beyond, largely through the *De Musica* of BOETHIUS [BEE-thee-us] (ca. 480–524 C.E.), a Christian philosopher who once described music as "number made audible." Pythagoras and Boethius believed all things beautiful are subject to number, an idea Boethius expressed in his formulation that "music demonstrates in sound the pure world of number and derives its beauty from that world."

More is known about Greek musical theory than about its practice, largely because few music manuscripts have survived. Treatises such as *The Section of the Canon*, attributed to Euclid (fl. ca. 300 B.C.E.), the Greek mathematician who invented geometry, provide the earliest full account of Pythagoras's acoustical theory.

For Pythagoras, numbers provided the key to understanding the universe. He believed music and arithmetic function as a single unit, with the system of musical sounds governed by mathematical laws. Pythagoras argued that because music embodies number in ratios and proportions, music exemplifies the harmony of the universe.

Pythagoras studied the relationships between two or more given notes and represented them in numerical equations. (The ratios 12:6, 9:6, 12:9, and 9:8 represent the proportions between musical intervals, and these ratios have remained the basis of the tonal system of Western music since ca. 500–1500 C.E.). Pythagoras's concern with beautiful numerical ratios is echoed not only in the sounds described in ancient Greek musical treatises but also in the proportions Greek architects used to design buildings and Greek sculptors employed in modeling the human figure. It finds further expression in ancient Greek astronomy.

Although musical analysis has undergone considerable change since Pythagoras's time, his basic ideas about tonal relationships remain an important element of music theory today. Moreover, his connection between music and mathematics and its later adaptations in philosophy and astronomy reveal his continued influence well beyond the bounds of his famous geometrical theorem. To take only one example, the medieval quadrivium's inclusion of music, along with arithmetic, geometry, and astronomy, suggests both the importance of music in the medieval curriculum and its close relationship with mathematics. Finally, Pythagoras's belief in the fundamental unity of the world, grounded in number, has served as a powerful influence for scientists, mathematicians, and philosophers seeking to understand the laws of the universe.

MUSIC AND GREEK SOCIETY

Music is mentioned in ancient Greece as early as Homer's *Iliad*, which includes a reference to Achilles playing a lyre in his tent. It was not uncommon for a warrior to soothe his spirits with the charms of music, much as in ancient Israel David played the harp to assuage the anxieties of King Saul.

An integral part of Greek life, music was associated with festivals and banquets, religion and social ritual, including marriages, funerals, and harvest rites. It was associated with Greek drama, for which a special place, the orchestra, was set aside for dancers. Music was an essential part of the Homeric epics, which were chanted to the accompaniment of the lyre. In addition, music formed a significant part of the Olympic athletic contests. At the festivals, the ancient Greeks held contests for musicians equal to those of the athletes, awarding prizes and honors of similar measure.

The **lyre** appears on numerous Greek vases. Its tortoise-shell bowl provided the resonance, much as the body of an acoustic guitar does today. The strings were plucked with the fingers or with a plectrum (the quill of a feather). The aulos was a double-piped wind instrument with a double reed that vibrated with an aggressive and strident tone much like that of a modern oboe. It was probably the aulos that supported choruses of Greek plays by duplicating the melodic line.

Music was so important to the ancient Greeks that all philosophers, including Plato and Aristotle, made a point of discussing it. Plato, for example, believed music could influence human emotion and character. He argued that only music that encouraged bravery and emotional stability should be taught to the young. Aristotle also believed in the importance of music for building character. Like Plato, Aristotle wrote about music's power to affect the development of the inner person, particularly music's power to affect the soul. Other ancient philosophers commented on music's ethical influence. Like Plato and Aristotle, they associated certain musical modes with virtue and vice, spiritual development and spiritual danger.

The Musical Modes. Greek music was primarily a music of melody, with little concern for harmony. For the ancient Greeks, musical scales, or **modes,** on which melodies were based, had particular ethical effects associated with them. Each mode used a particular sequence of intervals that established its modality. The Greek system, still in use today, divides the octave into twelve equal-sounding smaller intervals, each called a **half step.** In a musical mode or scale, there are eight tones with seven intervals between them, five of which are half steps and two **whole steps.** The position of the whole and half steps in the scale or mode affects the specific character or quality of the scale or mode. Some scales or modes sound "happy" or "bright"; others sound "mournful" or "dark." Strings on lyres were often tuned to one of the "calming scales" as dictated by the doctrine of *ethos.*

Each of the Greek musical modes was considered to have a specific ethical effect on hearers, thus resulting in the various strictures placed on them by Plato and Aristotle. The best of the modes, the one most conducive to virtue, was thought to be the Dorian mode, which, for Aristotle, represented the golden mean of music, comparable to the golden mean of his ethics.

Although ancient Greek instruments, such as the lyre, can be recognized from their depiction in painting and sculpture, the melodies played on them are virtually extinct. The scraps of melody inscribed on papyrus or incised in stone do not provide much help in understanding what ancient Greek music sounded like. The best available examples of ancient Greek musical manuscripts date from the second century B.C.E. and are tributes to the god Apollo.

HELLENISTIC GREECE

After the fall of Athens in 404 B.C.E., Sparta controlled the Greek mainland, until Thebes ended Spartan hegemony. In 359 B.C.E., Macedonia, a minor Greek state on the northern end of the Aegean, beyond Mount Olympus, began to assert itself when Philip II became ruler. In 338 B.C.E., Macedonia defeated the Greeks decisively at Chaeronea. Ambassadors were dispatched to Athens and Thebes with terms for peace. Among the ambassadors to Athens was Philip's eighteen-year-old son, Alexander—Alexander the Great (356–323 B.C.E.), as he would come to be known (fig. 3.19). Raised to rule, Alexander came to enjoy the enthusiastic support of almost all Greek intellectuals. When Philip II was assassinated in 336 B.C.E.—possibly at Alexander's behest, since Philip had divorced his mother and removed his son from substantive roles in the government—Alexander took control.

On his accession, he crushed a rebellion in Thebes, destroying the city and selling the entire population into slavery. He then set out to expand the Macedonian empire and control the world. By 334 B.C.E., he had defeated the Persians. Prior to entering Egypt, Alexander controlled only the coast of the eastern Mediterranean. By 332 B.C.E., he had conquered Egypt, where he founded the great port city of Alexandria in the Nile Delta. Marching back into Mesopotamia, he entered Babylon and made a sacrifice to the local god, Marduk. Then he marched on Persepolis and burned it. Convinced India was small, and that beyond it lay Ocean, as he called it, by which route he could return to Europe by sea, he set out to conquer present-day Pakistan. However, his troops were exhausted and met unexpected resistance in the form of war elephants; Alexander was thus

FIGURE 3.19 Portrait bust of Alexander the Great, Roman copy of a Greek original of ca. 330 B.C.E., marble, Staatliche Kuntsammlungen, Dresden Museum, Germany. Although a womanizer, an excessive drinker, and perhaps a megalomaniac, Alexander was nevertheless a great general who astonished the world with his stunning succession of military triumphs, which gave the word "empire" a new meaning.

forced to sail down the Indus River to the Indian Ocean. Along this route he founded present-day Karachi—at the time named Alexandria after himself. Returning finally to Babylon, in 323 B.C.E., Alexander caught a fever and died.

The Hellenistic era begins with Alexander's death at the age of thirty-three. Alexander had brought about a mingling of Eastern and Western cultures through his policies and conquests. For instance, he encouraged marriages between his soldiers and Middle Eastern women by providing large wedding gifts and by marrying two Persian women himself. But culturally the Greek army had a greater impact on the Middle East than the Middle East had on it. In fact, the term "Hellenistic," first used in 1833 by the historian Johann Gustav Droysen, was coined to describe the impact of Greece on the Middle East—its "Hellenization"—after Alexander's death. The generals Alexander had installed as governors of the different territories in his empire set themselves up as kings. Political, artistic, social, and economic dominance shifted from the mainland of Greece to the new Hellenistic kingdoms such as those of the Seleucids in Syria and the Ptolemies in Egypt. The cities of Pergamon

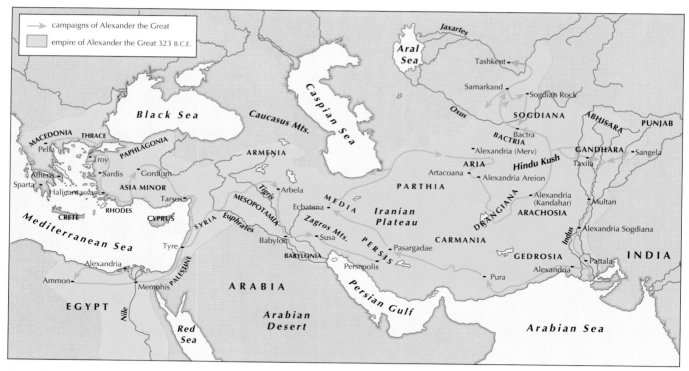

MAP 3.2   Alexander's empire

in Turkey and Alexandria in Egypt in particular were great centers of learning. The massive library at Alexandria contained over 700,000 papyri and scrolls, and Pergamon's library rivaled it. As if inspired by the dramatic successes of Alexander himself, the art such Hellenistic cities spawned was itself highly dramatic. Where Classical Greek art was concerned with balance and order and idealized its subjects, Hellenistic art focused on the individual, in all the individual's unidealized particularity, and on emotional states. Even the dominant philosophies of the day reflect this tendency.

More important for the future of Western thought were the acts of preservation and dispersion performed by Hellenistic scholars as they collected, edited, analyzed, and interpreted the philosophical works of the past. This work of humanistic scholarship included preserving not only the works of ancient Greek philosophy and literature, especially those of Plato and Homer, for example, but the Greek translation of the Hebrew Bible as well. Moreover, the emergence of humanistic scholarship was accompanied by educational institutions established for its continued development. In the spectacular libraries at Alexandria and Pergamon, and in Athens, which was home to a great academy of its own, Greek intellectual achievements endured.

ARCHITECTURE

The Temple of the Olympian Zeus.

The popularity of the Corinthian order in the Hellenistic era is demonstrated by the Temple of the Olympian Zeus in Athens (fig. 3.20). This temple was originally built in the Doric order in the sixth

century B.C.E., but was reconstructed in Hellenistic times, beginning in the second century B.C.E., with work continuing into the second century C.E. in Roman times under the Emperor Hadrian. The Corinthian capital was given greater prominence here than it ever was in Classical Greek architecture. This extraordinary structure once was an eight-by-twenty temple, the columns in the peristyle formed with double rows of twenty columns on the sides and three rows of eight columns on the ends. Today, although little remains of this monumental undertaking, there is enough to make it obvious that the Corinthian order is the most ornamental and the most luxurious of the three orders.

Pergamon's Altar of Zeus.

Perhaps nothing better embodies the extravagant Hellenistic attitude to architecture and the visual arts in general than the upper city of Pergamon in Asia Minor, built by KING ATTALOS [ah-TAL-us] (r. 241–197 B.C.E.) and almost finished by EUMENES II [you-MEN-ease] (197–159 B.C.E.). This Hellenistic city was grand in vision, designed on a large scale and embellished with a profusion of ornament. Essentially a large complex of architecture and sculpture built in the slope of a hill, Pergamon appears as if nature has been sculpted into several terraces occupied by splendid structures. The upper city included the celebrated Altar of Zeus (fig. 3.21), built 180–160 B.C.E. under Eumenes II, a demonstration of the dramatic theatricality and large scale favored in the Hellenistic era. In 278 B.C.E., the Gauls came sweeping into Asia Minor, to be conquered by Attalos I of Pergamon in 241 B.C.E. This monument was erected to com-

FIGURE 3.20   Temple of the Olympian Zeus, Athens, second century B.C.E.–second century C.E. This once enormous temple was the first large-scale use of the Corinthian order on the exterior of a building. The Romans would favor the ornate Corinthian order.

FIGURE 3.21   Altar of Zeus, from Pergamon, west front, restored, built ca. 180–160 B.C.E., under Eumenes II, base 100′ square (30.5 m. sq.), Staatliche Museen, Berlin. The subject depicted on the frieze on the Pergamon altar is highly emotional, its rendering charged with the dramatic action and expression characteristic of Hellenistic art.

FIGURE 3.22   *Battle of the Gods and the Giants*, Altar of Zeus, Pergamon, ca. 180–160 B.C.E., height 7′ 6″ (2.34 m), Staatliche Museen, Berlin. Here Athena has grabbed the hair of a winged monster who writhes in agony. His mother, identifiable by her "monstrous" curled locks, rises to help him.

memorate the victory over the Gauls. The Altar of Zeus occupied a terrace all its own on the hill at Pergamon.

SCULPTURE

The Battle of the Gods and the Giants.   The Altar of Zeus at Pergamon was much celebrated in antiquity. On the sides of the podium of the altar was the relief frieze of the *Battle of the Gods and the Giants* (fig. 3.22), four hundred feet in length. The relief carving is very deep; the figures are almost carved in the round.

Known as **gigantomachy,** the subject of the revolt of the giants—the Titans of Greek mythology—against the gods was popular with Hellenistic artists. On the Altar of Zeus its treatment can be interpreted symbolically. Here the gods' triumph over the giants symbolizes the victories of Attalos I—art and politics working together for propagandistic ends. The style of this work—its action, violence, display of emotion, and windblown drapery—also defines the Hellenistic age in the arts. All restraint is gone, much as Alexander had abandoned it politically at the era's outset.

Cross Currents

THE HELLENIZATION OF INDIA

By 326 B.C.E., Alexander the Great's forces had pushed as far east as the Punjab in northwest India. It was there that they confronted, for the first time, war elephants, two hundred strong. Although Alexander's troops defeated the Indian troops, it was rumored that the army of the Ganges, further east, was equipped with five thousand such beasts, and thus the Greek troops refused to go on. But the connection between the Greek world and India had been established.

Remnants of Alexander's forces settled in Bactria, between the Oxus River and the Hindu Kush mountains. Excavations at the Bactrian Greek city of Al Khanum have revealed Corinthian capitals and fragments of statues of various gods and goddesses. Coins with images of Herakles, Apollo, and Zeus were produced. There were portraits of the Bactrian kings on the other sides: Euthydemus, Demetrius, and Menander. However, it was not always Greek ideas that triumphed over Indian cultural traditions. Around 150 B.C.E., King Menander was converted to Buddhism by the monk Nagasena. The monk's conversation with the king is preserved as *The Questions of Melinda* (Melinda was the Indian version of Menander's name).

At Gandhara, on the north end of the Indus River, across the Khyber Pass from Bactria, Greek influence was especially strong. Although Gandharan art is mostly Buddhist in content, it has a Hellenistic style. In Taxila, a temple resembling the Parthenon in structure was constructed between 50 B.C.E. and 65 C.E. There is even evidence that the Homeric legend of the Trojan horse was known here (fig. 3.23).

FIGURE 3.23   Trojan horse frieze, Gandhara, second to third century C.E. Although the style shows local influences, the subject matter here is most definitely Greek as the Trojan prophetess Cassandra and the priest Laocoön (see fig. 3.25) attempt to block the entry of the Greek gift-horse into Troy.

The Nike of Samothrace.   The splendid Hellenistic *Nike of Samothrace* (fig. 3.24), also known as the *Winged Victory*, is related to the figures in the Pergamon frieze in the great sweeping gesture of the body, in the suggestion of movement through space, and in the revealing treatment of the drapery. The date of the Nike of Samothrace is debated, but it was probably created between 200 and 190 B.C.E. The statue was originally placed on the prow of a stone ship located in a niche cut into the mountainside above the Sanctuary of the Great Gods at Samothrace. The head was turned to face the sea. The composition was designed to give the impression that the goddess had just descended to the prow of the ship, her garments still responding to her movement through space.

Laocoön and His Sons.   An expenditure of still greater energy, induced by agony, is seen in the *Laocoön* group (fig. 3.25), sculpted by Hagesandros, Athanodoros, and Polydoros of Rhodes according to ancient sources. The date of this statue is debated, the possibilities ranging from 150 B.C.E. to the first century C.E. It was rediscovered only in 1506 in Rome.

The subject of the sculpture is taken from Homer's *Iliad*. Laocoön was a priest of Apollo of Troy. He and his sons were strangled by snakes sent from the sea by Apollo when Laocoön tried to warn the Trojans against accepting the wooden horse, seemingly left as a gift to them by the retreating Greeks. In the sculpture the figures writhe violently, but all in one plane, like a relief. Laocoön and his two sons try to move apart, but are bound together by the serpent's coils, creating an extraordinary dynamism.

PHILOSOPHY

The English words "stoic," "skeptic," "epicurean," and "cynic" derive from schools of Greek philosophy—Stoicism, Skepticism, Epicureanism, and Cynicism. Although none of these philosophical systems has had the long-term impact of Platonism or Aristotelianism, Stoicism and

FIGURE 3.24 *Nike of Samothrace*, ca. 200–190 B.C.E., marble, height 8′ (2.44 m), Musée du Louvre, Paris. Stone seemingly brought to life, this dynamic figure of Victory moves through space, the drapery blown against her body by her rapid movement.

Epicureanism dominated Greek philosophy during the Hellenistic period. In addition, all four philosophies were embraced by the Romans, with Stoicism also later finding a home in Christian philosophy.

Stoicism. **Stoicism** was less concerned with formulating a systematic philosophy than with providing an approach to everyday living. Primarily ethical in impulse, it offered a basis for conduct in responding to life's misfortunes. According to the Stoic view, an intelligent spiritual force resembling reason, the *Logos*, pervades the universe. Human beings can achieve happiness only by bringing their wills into harmony with this pervasive universal reason. The individual must accept whatever fortune brings; all the individual can do is exercise control over her or his own will. Characteristic Stoic virtues are serenity, self-discipline, and courage in the face of suffering and affliction.

FIGURE 3.25 *Laocoön and His Sons*, perhaps a Roman marble copy after a Greek original by Hagesandros, Athanodoros, and Polydoros of Rhodes, variously dated between the second century B.C.E. and the first century C.E., height 7′ (2.10 m), Museo Pio Clementino, Musei Vaticani, Rome. Reunion de Musées Nationaux (RMN), Art Resource, NY. In the Hellenistic period, drama replaced the emotional restraint of the Classical period. Laocoön and his sons, attacked by serpents, make obvious their torment through straining poses and agonized facial expressions.

Epicureanism. **Epicureanism** is frequently thought of as a philosophy of self-indulgence and pleasure seeking. Its primary practical impulse, however, is to escape fear and pain. The founder, EPICURUS [ep-ee-CURE-us] (341–271 B.C.E.), taught that fear, especially the fear of death and punishment after death, is responsible for human misery. As an antidote to what he considered religious and mythological superstition, Epicurus argued that the gods lack interest in the affairs of human beings, and death utterly extinguishes pain. Thus, according to Epicurus, human beings have nothing to fear from it.

A materialist, Epicurus believed the soul, like the body, was a physical substance, composed of tiny particles in motion. As such, for Epicurus the only path to knowledge was through physical sensation; consequently, the way to achieve happiness was to enhance physical pleasure and to limit physical pain. Epicurus argued that the way to achieve lasting pleasure was to avoid what he called "kinetic" pleasure in favor of "static" pleasure, which creates a state of equilibrium. For example, Epicurus recommended rejecting the pleasure of indulging in spicy or rich food for a simpler diet that prevented the pain of hunger while avoiding the dangers of indigestion. Similarly, Epicurus preferred the stability of friendship over the shifting pleasure and pain afforded by romantic passion.

Skepticism. The English word "skeptic" derives from the Greek *skeptikos*, which means "inquirer." **Skepticism** is not necessarily a negative perspective; rather it requires an attitude of questioning. Two early and important exponents of Skepticism were SEXTUS EMPIRICUS [em-PIR-i-cuss], who lived in the mid–second century B.C.E., and his intellectual ancestor, PYRRHO [PIE-roh] (ca. 360–270 B.C.E.). As with Stoicism and Epicureanism, Skepticism was less a philosophical system than a perspective on experience anchored in practical advice about how to live an unperturbed life. The aim of the Skeptic, like that of the Stoic and the Epicurean, was to establish and preserve a state of physical and mental composure, a condition of psychological stability and emotional equilibrium.

What distinguishes Skepticism from Stoicism and Epicureanism is its emphasis on achieving this state of unperturbed equilibrium through suspending judgment about nearly everything. The reason for this suspension of judgment is that we cannot know anything with certainty, because for every assertion there can be a counterassertion, and all evidence is inconclusive in itself. The conflict between opposing assertions—for example, "the gods exist" and "the gods do not exist"—can only be settled by an appeal to an additional criterion, in this case, a belief. But because the criterion can be similarly called into question, there is nothing on which finally to base knowledge. Thus, according to the Skeptics, peace of mind can only be achieved by abandoning the search for knowledge and accepting uncertainty.

Cynicism. **Cynicism** was a school of thought founded by ANTISTHENES [An-TIS-the-nees] (ca. 455–360 B.C.E.), a pupil of Socrates. Anticipating the Epicurean thinkers, Antisthenes argued that happiness can be attained only by freeing oneself from desires. (This notion is also central to classical Buddhism.) Perhaps the best known exemplar of the philosophy of Cynicism was Diogenes (ca. 404–323 B.C.E.), who influenced later Stoic thinkers. Little is known of Diogenes beyond some anecdotes, including one about how he wished hunger could be as easily gratified and satisfied as masturbation satisfied the need for sex.

The Cynics, however, are important largely for their sense of detachment from desire. Like the Stoics, who came after and were influenced by them, the Cynics advocated the absence of desire rather than a lust for life. The Cynics' rule, as it were, was to pursue the more laborious path of virtue rather than the easier road of pleasure. Although the meaning of the term "cynic" is allied with "one who lives a dog's life," shamelessly and without a secure sense of humor, the philosophical overtones of the Cynics' writings suggest one who distrusts all easy claims to altruism and comfort.

Critical Thinking

BLACK ATHENA

In his book *Black Athena: The Afroasiatic Roots of Classical Civilization*, Martin Bernal argues that ancient Greek culture derived from Egypt and Phoenicia. Bernal contends, moreover, that European scholars have consistently failed to acknowledge the African and Asian roots of Classical civilization. In response, Mary Lefkowitz has rebutted Bernal's arguments in her book *Not Out of Africa*. Two questions underscore the disagreement: (1) whether the Egyptians were a black African people; (2) whether the Greeks were indebted to Egyptian learning. How would you go about deciding with whom to agree on these issues? What steps would you take in evaluating Bernal's claims and Lefkowitz's counterarguments?

Cultural Impact

Classical Greek civilization, especially that of Golden Age Athens, was crucial to the development of Western civilization as we know it today. The Greeks of antiquity developed a rich and vibrant culture, whose achievements consisted of preeminent masterpieces of pottery, sculpture, and architecture, poetry and drama. Their achievements also included expertise in the practical arts of commerce and seafaring; metalwork, coining, and engraving, medicine and athletics; and philosophy, education, and government—many of which continue to exert a significant influence on the contemporary Western world.

PROTAGORAS [proh-TA-go-rus] (ca. 485–415 B.C.E.) wrote, "People are the measure of all things," a phrase that heralded the enterprise first undertaken in Classical Greece but has been central to Western culture ever since. Classical Greek civilization thoroughly explored the human condition, recognizing the realities and constraints of human life, yet constantly striving to realize ideals. The Greeks invented democracy and left it as a legacy for nations to emulate two millennia after Athens's decline. The Greek ideal of political freedom also served as the basis for the pursuit of other ideals, such as justice, truth, and beauty. Political freedom was one aspect of the culture's belief in individual expression.

Another important legacy left by Classical Greece was its system of *paideia*, or learning, which was grounded in respect for individual thought and emphasized logic, dialectic, debate, and elegance of expression. The philosophy of Plato and Aristotle continued to be influential through the Middle Ages and into the Renaissance. In some areas of thought—logic, poetics, and rhetoric—Aristotelian principles remain influential today, as for example in the rhetoric of Stephen Toulmin. The Greek philosophical tradition continues as contemporary philosophers, such as Robert Nozick and Marth Nussbaum, analyze intellectual problems. Greek educational ideals are reflected in the contemporary university.

The impact of Classical and Hellenistic Greek civilization has been so pervasive and so extensive that the public buildings of many cities in Europe and America reflect Greek architectural style. The influence of Greek sculpture can be seen in grand public buildings and in palatial private residences. Above all, against the backdrop of a warring mainland Greece in the fifth century B.C.E., the Greeks provided the Western world with a sense of the value of harmony and balance in all things—in art and architecture, literature and philosophy, politics and everyday life.

KEY TERMS

Classical
Hellenistic
demes
acropolis
agora
stoa
orders
Doric
abacus
echinus

frieze
triglyphs
metopes
Ionic
entablature
Corinthian
Golden Section
entasis
caryatids
atlantes

contrapposto
white-ground technique
lekythos (pl., lekythoi)
tragedy
dramatic irony
Oedipus complex
Sophists
syllogism
lyre
modes

half step
whole step
gigantomachy
Stoicism
Epicureanism
Skepticism
Cynicism

WWW. WEBSITES FOR FURTHER STUDY

http://www.hyperhistory.com/online_n2/maptext_n2/greece_pers.html
(A basic map of the Persian wars, including links to the wars themselves.)

http://www.culture.gr/2/21/211/21101a/e211aa01.html
(A good discussion of the architecture of the Acropolis.)

http://www.arwhead.com/Greeks/
(A basic general site on all things Greek, including architecture, theatre, war, and pottery.)

http://lib.haifa.ac.il//www/art/gr_menu.html
(An excellent collection of 220 images of Greek painting and sculpture.)

http://classics.mit.edu/Browse/browse-Sophocles.html
(A good site devoted to the works of Sophocles with discussion boards.)

READINGS

HERODOTUS

from the *History of the Persian Wars*

Herodotus (484–420 B.C.E.) was the first Greek historian. His History of the Persian Wars describes the end of the Greek Archaic period. An outstanding storyteller, Herodotus inaugurates in Western writing a tradition of narrative history with an emphasis on action and character. In examining the ramifications of the Persian War Herodotus also initiated historical study, with war as its primary topic.

The story he tells of the Greek battle with the Persians bears both religious and political implications. For the ancient Greeks the Persian defeat could be attributed to their excessive hubris, *or pride. For others it conveys the social and political value of Greek unity in the face of a common enemy at a time when Greek city-states constantly warred against one another.*

The following passage describes the Persian advance into Greece under Xerxes in 480 B.C.E., and the small contingent of Greek soldiers who attempted to block the passage of the Persian army at the narrow pass at Thermopylae. Herodotus's skill as a writer is evident in both his vivid use of detail and in his building of suspense as he describes the outcome of this famous episode in Greek history.

The Persian army was now close to the pass, and the Greeks, suddenly doubting their power to resist, held a conference to consider the advisability of retreat. It was proposed by the Peloponnesians generally that the army should fall back upon the Peloponnese and hold the Isthmus; but when the Phocians and Locrians expressed their indignation at this suggestion, Leonidas gave his voice for staying where they were and sending, at the same time, an appeal for reinforcements to the various states of the confederacy, as their numbers were inadequate to cope with the Persians.

During the conference Xerxes sent a man on horseback to ascertain the strength of the Greek force and to observe what the troops were doing. He had heard before he left Thessaly that a small force was concentrated here, led by the Lacedaemonians under Leonidas of the house of Heracles. The Persian rider approached the camp and took a thorough survey of all he could see—which was not, however, the whole Greek army; for the men on the further side of the wall which, after its reconstruction, was now guarded, were out of sight. He did, nonetheless, carefully observe the troops who were stationed on the outside of the wall. At that moment these happened to be the Spartans, and some of them were stripped for exercise, while others were combing their hair. The Persian spy watched them in astonishment; nevertheless he made sure of their numbers, and of everything else he needed to know, as accurately as he could, and then rode quietly off. No one attempted to catch him, or took the least notice of him.

Back in his own camp he told Xerxes what he had seen. Xerxes was bewildered; the truth, namely that the Spartans were preparing themselves to kill and to be killed according to their strength, was beyond his comprehension, and what

they were doing seemed to him merely absurd. Accordingly he sent for Demaratus, the son of Ariston, who had come with the army, and questioned him about the spy's report, in the hope of finding out what the unaccountable behaviour of the Spartans might mean. "Once before," Demaratus said, "when we began our march against Greece, you heard me speak of these men. I told you then how I saw this enterprise would turn out, and you laughed at me. I strive for nothing, my lord, more earnestly than to observe the truth in your presence; so hear me once more. These men have come to fight us for possession of the pass, and for that struggle they are preparing. It is the common practice of the Spartans to pay careful attention to their hair when they are about to risk their lives. But I assure you that if you can defeat these men and the rest of the Spartans who are still at home, there is no other people in the world who will dare to stand firm or lift a hand against you. You have now to deal with the finest kingdom in Greece, and with the bravest men."

Xerxes, unable to believe what Demaratus said, asked further how it was possible that so small a force could fight with his army. "My lord," Demaratus replied, "treat me as a liar, if what I have foretold does not take place." But still Xerxes was unconvinced.

For four days Xerxes waited, in constant expectation that the Greeks would make good their escape; then, on the fifth, when still they had made no move and their continued presence seemed mere impudent and reckless folly, he was seized with rage and sent forward the Medes and Cissians with orders to take them alive and bring them into his presence. The Medes charged, and in the struggle which ensued many fell; but others took their places, and in spite of terrible losses refused to be beaten off. They made it plain enough to anyone, and not least to the king himself, that he had in his army many men, indeed, but few soldiers. All day the battle continued; the Medes, after their rough handling, were at length withdrawn and their place was taken by Hydarnes and his picked Persian troops—the King's Immortals—who advanced to the attack in full confidence of bringing the business to a quick and easy end. But, once engaged, they were no more successful than the Medes had been; all went as before, the two armies fighting in a confined space, the Persians using shorter spears than the Greeks and having no advantage from their numbers.

On the Spartan side it was a memorable fight; they were men who understood war pitted against an inexperienced enemy, and amongst the feints they employed was to turn their backs in a body and pretend to be retreating in confusion, whereupon the enemy would come on with a great clatter and roar, supposing the battle won; but the Spartans, just as the Persians were on them, would wheel and face them and inflict in the new struggle innumerable casualties. The Spartans had their losses too, but not many. At last the Persians, finding that their assaults upon the pass, whether by divisions or by any other way they could think of, were all useless, broke off the engagement and withdrew. Xerxes was watching the battle from where he sat; and it is said that in the course of the attacks three times, in terror for his army, he leapt to his feet.

Next day the fighting began again, but with no better success for the Persians, who renewed their onslaught in the hope that the Greeks, being so few in number, might be badly enough disabled by wounds to prevent further resistance. But the Greeks never slackened; their troops were ordered in divisions corresponding to the states from which they came, and each division took its turn in the line except the Phocian, which had been posted to guard the track over the mountains. So when the Persians found that things were no better for them than on the previous day, they once more withdrew.

How to deal with the situation Xerxes had no idea; but while he was still wondering what his next move should be, a man from Malis got himself admitted to his presence. This was Ephialtes, the son of Eurydemus, and he had come, in hope of a rich reward, to tell the king about the track which led over the hills to Thermopylae—and the information he gave was to prove the death of the Greeks who held the pass.

Later on, Ephialtes, in fear of the Spartans, fled to Thessaly, and during his exile there a price was put upon his head at an assembly of the Amphictyons at Pylae. Some time afterwards he returned to Anticyra, where he was killed by Athenades of Trachis. In point of fact, Athenades killed him not for his treachery but for another reason, which I will explain further on; but the Spartans honoured him none the less on that account. According to another story, which I do not at all believe, it was Onetes, the son of Phanagoras, a native of Carystus, and Corydallus of Anticyra who spoke to Xerxes and showed the Persians the way round by the mountain track; but one may judge which account is the true one, first by the fact that the Amphictyons, who must surely have known everything about it, set a price not upon Onetes and Corydallus but upon Ephialtes of Trachis, and, secondly, by the fact that there is no doubt that the accusation of treachery was the reason for Ephialtes' flight. Certainly Onetes, even though he was not a native of Malis, might have known about the track, if he had spent much time in the neighbourhood—but it was Ephialtes, and no one else, who showed the Persians the way, and I leave his name on record as the guilty one.

Xerxes found Ephialtes' offer most satisfactory. He was delighted with it, and promptly gave orders to Hydarnes to carry out the movement with the troops under his command. They left camp about the time the lamps are lit.

The track was originally discovered by the Malians of the neighbourhood; they afterwards used it to help the Thessalians, taking them over it to attack Phocis at the time when the Phocians were protected from invasion by the wall which they had built across the pass. That was a long time ago, and no good ever came of it since. The track begins at the Asopus, the stream which flows through the narrow gorge, and, running along the ridge of the mountain—which, like the track itself, is called Anopaea—ends at Alpenus, the first Locrian settlement as one comes from Malis, near the track known as Black-Buttocks' Stone and the seats of the Cercopes. Just here is the narrowest part of the pass.

This then, was the mountain track which the Persians took, after crossing the Asopus. They marched throughout the night, with the mountains of Oeta on their right hand and those of Trachis on their left. By early dawn they were at the summit of the ridge, near the spot where the Phocians, as I mentioned before, stood on guard with a thousand men, to watch the track and protect their country. The Phocians were ready enough to undertake this service, and had, indeed, volunteered for it to Leonidas, knowing that the pass at Thermopylae was held as I have already described.

The ascent of the Persians had been concealed by the oakwoods which cover this part of the mountain range, and it was only when they reached the top that the Phocians became aware of their approach; for there was not a breath of wind, and the marching feet made a loud swishing and rustling in the fallen leaves. Leaping to their feet, the Phocians were in the act of arming themselves when the enemy was upon them. The Persians were surprised at the sight of troops preparing to resist; they had not expected any opposition—yet here was a body of men barring their way. Hydarnes asked Ephialtes who they were, for his first uncomfortable thought was that they might be Spartans; but on learning the truth he prepared to engage them. The Persian arrows flew thick and fast, and the Phocians, supposing themselves to be the main object of the attack, hurriedly withdrew to the highest point of the mountain, where they made ready to face destruction. The Persians, however, with Ephialtes and Hydarnes paid no further attention to them, but passed on along the descending track with all possible speed.

The Greeks at Thermopylae had their first warning of the death that was coming with the dawn from the seer Megistias, who read their doom in the victims of sacrifice; deserters, too, had begun to come in during the night with news of the Persian movement to take them in the rear, and, just as day was breaking, the look-out men had come running from the hills. At once a conference was held, and opinion was divided, some urging that they must on no account abandon their post, others taking the opposite view. The result was that the army split; some dispersed, the men returning to their various homes, and others made ready to stand by Leonidas.

There is another account which says that Leonidas himself dismissed a part of his force, to spare their lives, but thought it unbecoming for the Spartans under his command to desert the post which they had originally come to guard. I myself am inclined to think that he dismissed them when he realized that they had no heart for the fight and were unwilling to take their share of the danger; at the same time honour forbade that he himself should go. And indeed by remaining at his post he left a great name behind him, and Sparta did not lose her prosperity, as might otherwise have happened; for right at the outset of the war the Spartans had been told by the oracle, when they asked for advice, that either their city must be laid waste by the foreigner or one of their kings be killed. The prophecy was in hexameter verse and ran as follows:

> *Hear your fate, O dwellers in Sparta of the wide spaces:*
> *Either your famed, great town must be sacked by Perseus' sons,*
> *Or, if that be not, the whole land of Lacedaemon*
> *Shall mourn the death of a king of the house of Heracles,*
> *For not the strength of lions or of bulls shall hold him,*
> *Strength against strength: for he has the power of Zeus,*
> *And will not be checked till one of these two he has consumed.*

I believe it was the thought of this oracle, combined with his wish to lay up for the Spartans a treasure of fame in which no other city should share, that made Leonidas dismiss those troops; I do not think that they deserted, or went off without orders, because of a difference of opinion. Moreover, I am strongly supported in this view by the case of Megistias, the seer from Acarnania who foretold the coming doom by his inspection of the sacrificial victims: this man—he was said to be descended from Melampus—was with the army, and quite plainly received orders from Leonidas to quit Thermopylae, to save him from sharing the army's fate. But he refused to go, sending away instead an only son of his, who was serving with the forces.

Thus it was that the confederate troops, by Leonidas' orders, abandoned their posts and left the pass, all except the Thespians and the Thebans who remained with the Spartans. The Thebans were detained by Leonidas as hostages very much against their will—unlike the loyal Thespians, who refused to desert Leonidas and his men, but stayed, and died with them. They were under the command of Demophilus the son of Diadromes.

In the morning Xerxes poured a libation to the rising sun, and then waited till about the time of the filling of the marketplace, when he began to move forward. This was according to Ephialtes' instructions, for the way down from the ridge is much shorter and more direct than the long and circuitous ascent. As the Persian army advanced to the assault, the Greeks under Leonidas, knowing that the fight would be their last, pressed forward into the wider part of the pass much further than they had done before; in the previous days' fighting they had been holding the wall and making sorties from behind it into the narrow neck, but now they left the confined space and battle was joined on more open ground. Many of the invaders fell; behind them the company commanders plied their whips, driving the men remorselessly on. Many fell into the sea and were drowned, and still more were trampled to death by their friends. No one could count the number of the dead. The Greeks, who knew that the enemy were on their way round by the mountain track and that death was inevitable, fought with reckless desperation, exerting every ounce of strength that was in them against the invader. By this time most of their spears were broken, and they were killing Persians with their swords.

In the course of that fight Leonidas fell, having fought like a man indeed. Many distinguished Spartans were killed at his side—their names, like the names of all the three hundred, I have made myself acquainted with, because they deserve to be remembered. Amongst the Persian dead, too, were many men of high distinction—for instance, two brothers of Xerxes, Habrocomes and Hyperanthes, both of them sons of Darius by Artanes' daughter Phratagune.

There was a bitter struggle over the body of Leonidas; four times the Greeks drove the enemy off, and at last by their valour succeeded in dragging it away. So it went on, until the fresh troops with Ephialtes were close at hand; and then, when the Greeks knew that they had come, the character of the fighting changed. They withdrew again into the narrow neck of the pass, behind the walls, and took up a position in a single compact body—all except the Thebans—on the little hill at the entrance to the pass, where the stone lion in memory of Leonidas stands today. Here they resisted to the last, with their swords, if they had them, and, if not, with their hands and teeth, until the Persians, coming on from the front over the ruins of the wall and closing in from behind, finally overwhelmed them.

Of all the Spartans and Thespians who fought so valiantly on that day, the most signal proof of courage was given by the Spartan Dieneces. It is said that before the battle he was told by a native of Trachis that, when the Persians shot their arrows, there were so many of them that they hid the sun. Dieneces, however, quite unmoved by the thought of the terrible strength of the Persian army, merely remarked: "This is pleasant news that the stranger from Trachis brings us: for if the Persians hide the sun, we shall have our battle in the shade." He is said to have left on record other sayings, too, of a similar kind, by which he will be remembered. After Dieneces the greatest distinction was won by the two Spartan brothers, Alpheus and Maron, the sons of Orsiphantus; and of the Thespians the man to gain the highest glory was a certain Dithyrambus, the son of Harmatides.

The dead were buried where they fell, and with them the men who had been killed before those dismissed by Leonidas left the pass. Over them is this inscription, in honour of the whole force:

Four thousand here from Pelops' land
Against three million once did stand.

The Spartans have a special epitaph; it runs:

Go tell the Spartans, you who read
We took their orders, and are dead.

For the seer Megistias there is the following:

I was Megistias once, who died
When the Mede passed Spercheius' tide.
I knew death near; yet would not save
Myself, but share the Spartans' grave.

THUCYDIDES

from the *History of the Peloponnesian War*

With Herodotus, Thucydides (ca. 460–400 B.C.E.) is recognized as the greatest of ancient Greek historians. Exiled by Athens for failing as a military commander while defending a Macedonian town, Thucydides traveled widely and wrote his History of the Peloponnesian War, *during which Athens suffered defeat in 404 B.C.E. at the hands of the Spartans. Like Herodotus, Thucydides makes war his central subject. Thucydides disagrees with Herodotus, however, in claiming that the Peloponnesian War rather than the Persian War was the greatest and most important conflict of the time. For him, the war signaled the breakdown of the city-state structure that had prevailed for centuries and reached its culmination during the Classical period, which ended with Athens's defeat.*

In the following passage, Thucydides presents the famous funeral oration given by Perikles over the bodies of the Greek heroes who died defending Athens. He clearly admires Perikles' integrity and ideals. Yet the historian is aware of the suffering Periclean Athens created.

In the same winter the Athenians, in accordance with their traditional institution, held a public funeral of those who had been the first to die in the war. The practice is this. Two days before the funeral they set up a tent and lay out in it the bones of the deceased, for each man to bring what offerings he wishes to his own kin. On the day of the procession, cypress-wood coffins are carried on wagons, one for each tribe, with each man's bones in his own tribe's coffin. In addition there is one empty bier carried, laid out for the missing, that is, for those whose bodies could not be found and recovered. Every man who wishes joins the procession, whether citizen or foreigner, and the women of the families are present to lament at the grave. In this way the dead are placed in the public tomb, which is situated in the most beautiful suburb of the city. Those who die in war are always buried there, apart from those who fell at Marathon, whose virtue was judged outstanding and who were given a tomb on the spot.

When they have been covered with earth, appropriate words of praise are spoken over them by a man chosen by the state for the intelligence of his mind and his outstanding reputation, and after that the people depart. That is how the funeral is conducted: this institution was followed throughout the war when occasion arose. Over these first casualties, then, Perikles son of Xanthippus was chosen to make the speech. When the time arrived, he came forward from the grave on to a high platform which had been erected so that he should be as clearly audible as possible to the crowd; and he spoke these lines.

"The majority of those who have spoken here before have praised the man who included this speech in our institution, and have claimed that it is good that they should make a speech over those who are buried in consequence of war. However, I should have thought that when men have been good in action it is sufficient for our honors of them to be made evident in action, as you see we have done in providing for this public funeral, and that the virtues of many ought not to be put at risk by being entrusted to one man, who speak well or ill. It is hard to speak appropriately in circumstances where even the appearance of truth can only with difficulty be confirmed. The listener who knows what has happened and is favorably disposed can easily think that the account given falls short of his wishes and knowledge, while the man lacking in experience may through jealousy think some claims exaggerated if he hears of things beyond his own capacity. Praise spoken of others is bearable up to the point where each man believes himself capable of doing the things he hears of: anything which goes beyond that arouses envy and so disbelief. Nevertheless, since in the past this has been approved as a good practice, I too must comply with our institution, and try as far as I can to coincide with the wishes and opinions of each of you.

"I shall begin first of all with our ancestors. It is right, and on an occasion like this it is appropriate, that this honor should be paid to their memory, for the same race of men has always occupied this land, as one generation has succeeded another, and by their valor they have handed it on as a free land until the present day. They are worthy of praise; and particularly worthy are our own fathers, who by their efforts gained the great empire which we now possess, in addition to what they had received, and left this too to us of the present generation. We ourselves, who are still alive and have reached the settled stage of life, have enlarged most parts of this empire, and we have made our city's resources most ample in all respects both for war and for peace. The deeds in war by which each acquisition was won, the enthusiastic responses of ourselves or our fathers to the attacks of the barbarians or our Greek enemies, I do not wish to recount at length to those who already know of them, so I shall pass them over. What I shall expound first, before I proceed to praise these men, is the way of life which has enabled us to pursue these objectives, and the form of government and the habits which made our great achievements possible. I think in the present circumstances it is not unfitting for these things to be mentioned, and it is advantageous for this whole assemblage of citizens and foreigners to hear of them.

"We have a constitution which does not seek to copy the laws of our neighbors: we are an example to others rather than imitators of them. The name given to this constitution is democracy, because it is based not on a few but on a larger number. For the settlement of private disputes all are on an equal footing in accordance with the laws, while in public life men gain preferment because of their deserts, when anybody has a good reputation for anything: what matters is not rotation but merit. As for poverty, if a man is able to confer some benefit on the city, he is not prevented by the obscurity of his position. With regard to public life, we live as free men; and, as for the suspicion of one another which can arise from daily habits, if our neighbor behaves with a view to his own pleasure, we do not react with anger or put on those expressions of disgust which, though not actually harmful, are nevertheless distressing. In our private dealings with one another we avoid offense, and in the public realm what particularly restrains us from wrongdoing is fear; we are obedient to the officials currently in office, and to the laws, especially those which have been enacted for the protection of people who are wronged, and those which have not been written down but which bring acknowledged disgrace on those who break them.

"Moreover, we have provided the greatest number of relaxations from toil for the spirit, by holding contests and sacrifices throughout the year, and by tasteful private provisions, whose daily delight drives away sorrow. Because of the size of our city, everything can be imported from all over the earth, with the result that we have no more special enjoyment of our native goods than of the goods of the rest of mankind.

"In military practices we differ from our enemy in this way. We maintain an open city, and do not from time to time stage expulsions of foreigners to prevent them from learning or seeing things, when the sight of what we have not troubled to conceal might benefit an enemy, since we trust not so much in our preparations and deceit as in our own inborn spirit for action. In education, they start right from their youth to pursue manliness by arduous training, while we live a relaxed life but nonetheless go to confront the dangers to which we are equal. Here is a sign of it. Even the Spartans do not invade our territory on their own, but with all their allies; and we attack our neighbors' territory, and for the most part have no difficulty in winning battles on their land against men defending their own property. No enemy has yet encountered our whole force together, because we simultaneously maintain our fleet and send out detachments of our men in many directions by land. If they come into conflict with a part of our forces, either they boast that they have repelled all of us when they have defeated only some, or if beaten they claim that it was all of us who defeated them. Yet if we are prepared to face danger, though we live relaxed lives rather than making a practice of toil, and rely on courageous habits rather than legal compulsion, we have the advantage of not suffering in advance for future pain, and when we come to meet it we are shown to be no less daring than those committed to perpetual endurance. In this respect as well as in others our city can be seen to be worthy of admiration.

"We are lovers of beauty without extravagance, and of wisdom without softness. We treat wealth as an opportunity for action rather than a matter for boastful words, and poverty as a thing which it is not shameful for anyone to admit to, but rather is shameful not to act to escape from. The same men accept responsibility both for their own affairs and for the state's, and although different men are active in different fields they are not lacking in understanding of the state's concerns: we alone regard the man who refuses to take part in these not as noninterfering but as useless.

"We have the ability to judge or plan rightly in our affairs, since we think it is not speech which is an obstacle to action but failure to expound policy in speech before action has to be taken. We are different also in that we particularly combine boldness with reasoning about the business we are to take in hand, whereas for other people it is ignorance that produces courage and reasoning produces hesitation. When people have the clearest understanding of what is fearful and what is pleasant, and on that basis do not flinch from danger, they would rightly be judged to have the best spirit.

"With regard to displays of goodness, we are the opposite of most people, since we acquire our friends not by receiving good from them but by doing good to them. If you do good, you are in a better position to keep the other party's favor, as something owed in gratitude by the recipient: if you owe a return, you are less alert, knowing that when you do good it will not be as a favor but as the payment of a debt. We alone are fearless in helping others, not calculating the advantage so much as confident in our freedom.

"To sum up, I maintain that our city as a whole is an education to Greece; and I reckon that each individual man among us can keep his person ready to profit from the greatest variety in life and the maximum of graceful adaptability. That this is not just a momentary verbal boast but actual truth is demonstrated by the very strength of our city, which we have built up as a result of these habits. Athens alone when brought to the test proves greater than its current reputation; Athens alone does not give an enemy attacker the right to be indignant at the kind of people at whose hands he suffers, or a subject the right to complain that his rulers are unworthy of their position. Our power does not lack witnesses, but we provide mighty proof of it, to earn the admiration both of our contemporaries and of posterity. We do not need the praise of a Homer, or of anyone whose poetry gives immediate pleasure but whose impression of the facts is undermined by the truth. We have compelled the whole of sea and land to make itself accessible to our daring, and have joined in setting up everywhere undying memorials both of our failures and of our successes. Such is our city. These men fought and died, nobly judging that it would be wrong to be deprived of it; and it is right that every single one of those who are left should be willing to struggle for it."

SOPHOCLES

OEDIPUS THE KING

Oedipus the King begins at the point when Thebes is undergoing a series of catastrophes, most important of which is a devastating plague. Prior to this series of events, Oedipus had saved Thebes from the Sphinx, a winged creature with the body of a lion and the head *of a woman. In return for slaying the creature, Oedipus is given the kingship of Thebes and the hand of its recently widowed queen, Jocasta (Iocastê). Unknown to Oedipus, but known to the Athenian audience, was the fact that Jocasta was his mother and that her recently slain husband, Laïos, had been killed by Oedipus himself. All this and more Oedipus soon discovers.*

Aristotle chose Oedipus the King *to illustrate the elements of tragedy in his* Poetics. *In that first work of Western literary criticism, Aristotle described the perfect tragedy as having a plot that focused on a single conflict centered in a character who possesses a "tragic flaw" that precipitates the tragic action.*

Oedipus the King *raises questions about fate and human responsibility, particularly the extent to which Oedipus is responsible for his own tragic destiny. Sophocles portrays his tragic protagonists heroically, Oedipus the greatest among them. They suffer the consequences of their actions nobly and with grandeur, serving as models not only of fatal attitudes but also of courage and determination.*

SCENE I

OEDIPUS   Is this your prayer? It may be answered. Come,
 Listen to me, act as the crisis demands,
 And you shall have relief from all these evils.

    Until now I was a stranger to this tale,
As I had been a stranger to the crime.   5
Could I track down the murderer without a clue?
But now, friends,
As one who became a citizen after the murder,
I make this proclamation to all Thebans:
If any man knows by whose hand Laïos, son of
 Labdakos,   10
Met his death, I direct that man to tell me everything,
No matter what he fears for having so long withheld it.
Let it stand as promised that no further trouble
Will come to him, but he may leave the land in safety.
Moreover: If anyone knows the murderer to be
 foreign,   15
Let him not keep silent: he shall have his reward
 from me.
However, if he does conceal it; if any man
Fearing for his friend or for himself disobeys this
 edict,
Hear what I propose to do:

I solemnly forbid the people of this country,   20
Where power and throne are mine, ever to receive
 that man
Or speak to him, no matter who he is, or let him
Join in sacrifice, lustration, or in prayer.
I decree that he be driven from every house,

Being, as he is, corruption itself to us: the Delphic   25
Voice of Zeus has pronounced this revelation.
Thus I associate myself with the oracle
and take the side of the murdered king.

As for the criminal, I pray to God—
Whether it be a lurking thief, or one of a number—
I pray that that man's life be consumed in evil and
 wretchedness.   31

And as for me, this curse applies no less
If it should turn out that the culprit is my guest here,
Sharing my hearth.
                              You have heard the penalty.
I lay it on you now to attend to this   *35*
For my sake, for Apollo's, for the sick
Sterile city that heaven has abandoned.
Suppose the oracle had given you no command:
Should this defilement go uncleansed for ever?
You should have found the murderer: your king,   *40*
A noble king, had been destroyed!
                              Now I,
Having the power that he held before me,
Having his bed, begetting children there
Upon his wife, as he would have, had he lived—
Their son would have been my children's brother,   *45*
If Laïos had had luck in fatherhood!
(But surely ill luck rushed upon his reign)—
I say I take the son's part, just as though
I were his son, to press the fight for him
And see it won! I'll find the hand that brought   *50*
Death to Labdakos' and Polydoros' child,
Heir of Kadmos' and Agenor's line.
And as for those who fail me,
May the gods deny them the fruit of the earth,
Fruit of the womb, and may they rot utterly!   *55*
Let them be wretched as we are wretched, and worse!

For you, for loyal Thebans, and for all
Who find my actions right, I pray the favor
Of justice, and of all the immortal gods.

CHORAGOS   Since I am under oath, my lord, I swear   *60*
         I did not do the murder, I cannot name
         The murderer. Might not the oracle
         That has ordained the search tell where to find him?
OEDIPUS   An honest question. But no man in the world
         Can make the gods do more than the gods will.   *65*
CHORAGOS   There is one last expedient—
OEDIPUS   Tell me what it is.
         Though it seem slight, you must not hold it back.
CHORAGOS   A lord clairvoyant to the lord Apollo,
         As we all know, is the skilled Teiresias.
         One might learn much about this from him,
            Oedipus.   *70*
OEDIPUS   I am not wasting time:
         Creon spoke of this, and I have sent for him—
         Twice, in fact; it is strange that he is not here.
CHORAGOS   The other matter—that old report—seems
            useless.
OEDIPUS   Tell me. I am interested in all reports.   *75*
CHORAGOS   The King was said to have been killed by
            highwaymen.
OEDIPUS   I know. But we have no witnesses to that.
CHORAGOS   If the killer can feel a particle of dread,
         Your curse will bring him out of hiding!
OEDIPUS   No.
         The man who dared that act will fear no curse.   *80*

Enter the blind seer Teiresias, led by a Page

CHORAGOS   But there is one man who may detect the
         criminal.

This is Teiresias, this is the holy prophet
In whom, alone of all men, truth was born.
OEDIPUS   Teiresias: seer: student of mysteries,
         Of all that's taught and all that no man tells,   *85*
         Secrets of Heaven and secrets of the earth:
         Blind though you are, you know the city lies
         Sick with plague; and from this plague, my lord,
         We find that you alone can guard or save us.

         Possibly you did not hear the messengers?   *90*
         Apollo, when we sent to him,
         Sent us back word that this great pestilence
         Would lift, but only if we established clearly
         The identity of those who murdered Laïos.
         They must be killed or exiled.
                              Can you use   *95*
         Birdflight or any art of divination
         To purify yourself, and Thebes, and me
         From this contagion? We are in your hands.
         There is no fairer duty
         Than that of helping others in distress.   *100*
TEIRESIAS   How dreadful knowledge of the truth can be
         When there's no help in truth! I knew this well,
         But did not act on it: else I should not have come.
OEDIPUS   What is troubling you? Why are your eyes so
            cold?
TEIRESIAS   Let me go home. Bear your own fate, and I'll
         Bear mine. It is better so: trust what I say.   *106*
OEDIPUS   What you say is ungracious and unhelpful
         To your native country. Do not refuse to speak.
TEIRESIAS   When it comes to speech, your own is
            neither temperate
         Nor opportune. I wish to be more prudent.   *110*
OEDIPUS   In God's name, we all beg you—
TEIRESIAS   You are all ignorant.
         No; I will never tell you what I know.
         Now it is my misery; then, it would be yours.
OEDIPUS   What! You do know something, and will not tell
            us?
         You would betray us all and wreck the State?   *115*
TEIRESIAS   I do not intend to torture myself, or you.
         Why persist in asking? You will not persuade me.
OEDIPUS   What a wicked old man you are! You'd try a stone's
         Patience! Out with it! Have you no feeling at all?
TEIRESIAS   You call me unfeeling. If you could only see
         The nature of your own feelings . . .   *121*
OEDIPUS   Why,
         Who would not feel as I do? Who could endure
         Your arrogance toward the city?
TEIRESIAS   What does it matter!
         Whether I speak or not, it is bound to come.
OEDIPUS   Then, if "it" is bound to come, you are bound
            to tell me.   *125*
TEIRESIAS   No, I will not go on. Rage as you please.
OEDIPUS   Rage? Why not!
                              And I'll tell you what I think:
         You planned it, you had it done, you all but
         Killed him with your own hands: if you had eyes,
         I'd say the crime was yours, and yours alone.   *130*
TEIRESIAS   So? I charge you, then,
         Abide by the proclamation you have made:

From this day forth
Never speak again to these men or to me;
You yourself are the pollution of this country.   135

OEDIPUS   You dare say that! Can you possibly think you have
Some way of going free, after such insolence?

TEIRESIAS   I have gone free. It is the truth sustains me.

OEDIPUS   Who taught you shamelessness? It was not your craft.

TEIRESIAS   You did. You made me speak. I did not want to.   140

OEDIPUS   Speak what? Let me hear it again more clearly.

TEIRESIAS   Was it not clear before? Are you tempting me?

OEDIPUS   I did not understand it. Say it again.

TEIRESIAS   I say that you are the murderer whom you seek.

OEDIPUS   Now twice you have spat out infamy. You'll pay for it!   145

TEIRESIAS   Would you care for more? do you wish to be really angry?

OEDIPUS   Say what you will. Whatever you say is worthless.

TEIRESIAS   I say you live in hideous shame with those
Most dear to you. You cannot see the evil.

OEDIPUS   It seems you can go on mouthing like this for ever.   150

TEIRESIAS   I can, if there is power in truth.

OEDIPUS   There is:
But not for you, not for you,
You sightless, witless, senseless, mad old man!

TEIRESIAS   You are the madman. There is no one here
Who will not curse you soon, as you curse me.   155

OEDIPUS   You child of endless night! You cannot hurt me
Or any other man who sees the sun.

TEIRESIAS   True: it is not from me your fate will come.
That lies within Apollo's competence,
As it is his concern.

OEDIPUS   Tell me: 160
Are you speaking for Creon, or for yourself?

TEIRESIAS   Creon is no threat. You weave your own doom.

OEDIPUS   Wealth, power, craft of statesmanship!
Kingly position, everywhere admired!
What savage envy is stored up against these,   165
If Creon, whom I trusted, Creon my friend,
For this great office which the city once
Put in my hands unsought—if for this power
Creon desires in secret to destroy me!

He has brought this decrepit fortune-teller, this   170
Collector of dirty pennies, this prophet fraud—
Why, he is no more clairvoyant than I am!

Tell us:
Has your mystic mummery ever approached the truth?
When that hellcat the Sphinx was performing here,
What help were you to these people?   175
Her magic was not for the first man who came along:
It demanded a real exorcist. Your birds—
What good were they? or the gods, for the matter of that?
But I came by,
Oedipus, the simple man, who knows nothing—   180
I thought it out for myself, no birds helped me!
And this is the man you think you can destroy,

That you may be close to Creon when he's king!
Well, you and your friend Creon, it seems to me,
Will suffer most. If you were not an old man,   185
You would have paid already for your plot.

CHORAGOS   We cannot see that his words or yours
Have been spoken except in anger, Oedipus,
And of anger we have no need. How can God's will
Be accomplished best? That is what most concerns us.   190

TEIRESIAS   You are a king. But where argument's concerned
I am your man, as much a king as you.
I am not your servant, but Apollo's.
I have no need of Creon to speak for me.

Listen to me. You mock my blindness, do you?   195
But I say that you, with both your eyes, are blind:
You cannot see the wretchedness of your life,
Nor in whose house you live, no, nor with whom.
Who are your father and mother? Can you tell me?
You do not even know the blind wrongs   200
That you have done them, on earth and in the world below.
But the double lash of your parents' curse will whip you
Out of this land some day, with only night
Upon your precious eyes.
Your cries then—where will they not be heard?   205
What fastness of Kithairon will not echo them?
And that bridal-descant of yours—you'll know it then,
The song they sang when you came here to Thebes
And found your misguided berthing.
All this, and more, that you cannot guess at now,   210
Will bring you to yourself among your children.
Be angry, then. Curse Creon. Curse my words.
I tell you, no man that walks upon the earth
Shall be rooted out more horribly than you.

OEDIPUS   Am I to bear this from him?—Damnation   215
Take you! Out of this place! Out of my sight!

TEIRESIAS   I would not have come at all if you had not asked me.

OEDIPUS   Could I have told that you'd talk nonsense, that
You'd come here to make a fool of yourself, and of me?

TEIRESIAS   A fool? Your parents thought me sane enough.

OEDIPUS   My parents again!—Wait: who were my parents?   221

TEIRESIAS   This day will give you a father, and break your heart.

OEDIPUS   Your infantile riddles! Your damned abracadabra!

TEIRESIAS   You were a great man once at solving riddles.

OEDIPUS   Mock me with that if you like; you will find it true.   225

TEIRESIAS   It was true enough. It brought about your ruin.

OEDIPUS   But if it saved this town?

TEIRESIAS   (to the Page). Boy, give me your hand.

OEDIPUS   Yes, boy; lead him away.
—While you are here
We can do nothing. Go; leave us in peace.

TEIRESIAS   I will go when I have said what I have to say.   230

How can you hurt me? And I tell you again:
The man you have been looking for all this time,
The damned man, the murderer of Laïos,
That man is in Thebes. To your mind he is
    foreignborn,
But it will soon be shown that he is a Theban,   *235*
A revelation that will fail to please.
                   A blind man,
Who has his eyes now; a penniless man, who is rich
    now;
And he will go tapping the strange earth with his
    staff;
To the children with whom he lives now he will be
Brother and father—the very same; to her   *240*
Who bore him, son and husband—the very same
Who came to his father's bed, wet with his father's
    blood.

Enough. Go think that over.
If later you find error in what I have said,
You may say that I have no skill in prophecy.   *245*
Exit Teiresias, led by his Page. Oedipus goes into the
    palace.

ODE I[1]

Strophe 1

CHORUS   The Delphic stone of prophecies
Remembers ancient regicide
And a still bloody hand.
That killer's hour of flight has come.
He must be stronger than riderless   *5*
Coursers of untiring wind,
For the son of Zeus[2] armed with his father's thunder
Leaps in lightning after him;
And the Furies[3] follow him, the sad Furies.

Antistrophe 1

Holy Parnossos' peak of snow   *10*
Flashes and blinds that secret man,
That all shall hunt him down:
Though he may roam the forest shade
Like a bull gone wild from pasture
To rage through glooms of stone.   *15*
Doom comes down on him; flight will not avail him;
For the world's heart calls him desolate,
And the immortal Furies follow, for ever follow.

Strophe 2

But now a wilder thing is heard
From the old man skilled at hearing Fate in the
    wingbeat of a bird.   *20*
Bewildered as a blown bird, my soul hovers and
    cannot find

Foothold in this debate, or any reason or rest of mind.
But no man ever brought—none can bring
Proof of strife between Thebes' royal house,
Labdakos' line,[4] and the son of Polybos;[5]   *25*
And never until now has any man brought word
Of Laïos' dark death staining Oedipus the King.

Antistrophe 2

Divine Zeus and Apollo hold
Perfect intelligence alone of all tales ever told;
And well though this diviner works, he works in his
    own night;   *30*
No man can judge that rough unknown or trust in
    second sight,
For wisdom changes hands among the wise.
Shall I believe my great lord criminal
At a raging word that a blind old man let fall?
I saw him, when the carrion woman faced him of
    old,   *35*
Prove his heroic mind! These evil words are lies.

AESCHYLUS

AGAMEMNON

Agamemnon, the first play in a trilogy, the Oresteia, *derives from a legend about the house of Atreus, a story riddled with murders and retribution that occupy three generations of a royal family. The following excerpt describes the homecoming of Agamemnon, the Greek military leader, from the Trojan War. As he arrives, he is murdered by his wife Clytemnestra and her lover Aegisthus. Clytemnestra justifies her act as retribution for Agamemnon's sacrificing their daughter Iphigenia in exchange for military assistance from the goddess Athena during a difficult time in the war. Aegisthus justifies his participation as retaliation for the murder of his brothers by Agamemnon's father, Atreus.*

    The issue at stake is one of justice. How should murder be punished, and by whom?

AGAMEMNON   Aagh!
    Struck deep—the death-blow, deep—
LEADER   Quiet. Cries,
    but who? Someone's stabbed—
AGAMEMNON   Aaagh, again . . .   *1370*
    second blow—struck home.
LEADER   The work is done,
    you can feel it. The king, and the great cries—
    Close ranks now, find the right way out.

    [*But the old men scatter, each speaks singly.*]

CHORUS   —I say send out heralds, muster the guard,
    they'll save the house.

               —And I say rush in now,   *1375*

    catch them red-handed—butchery running on
    their blades.

---

[1]*Ode:* a poetic song sung by the chorus.
[2]*son of Zeus:* Apollo.
[3]*the Furies:* three women spirits who punished evildoers.

---

[4]*Labdakos' line:* his descendants.
[5]*Polybos:* King of Corinth who adopted Oedipus as an infant.

—Right with you, do something—now or never!

—Look at them, beating the drum for insurrection.

—Yes,
we're wasting time. They rape the name of caution,
their hands will never sleep.

—Not a plan in sight.   *1380*
Let men of action do the planning, too.

—I'm helpless. Who can raise the dead with words?

—What, drag out our lives? bow down to the tyrants,
the ruin of the house?

—Never, better to die
on your feet than live on your knees.

—Wait,   *1385*
do we take the cries for signs, prophesy like seers
and give him up for dead?

—No more suspicions,
not another word till we have proof.

—Confusion
on all sides—one thing to do. See how it stands
with Agamemnon, once and for all we'll see—   *1390*

[*He rushes at the doors. They open and reveal a silver cauldron that holds the body of* AGAMEMNON *shrouded in bloody robes, with the body of* CASSANDRA *to his left and* CLYTAEMNESTRA *standing to his right, sword in hand. She strides towards the* CHORUS.]

CLYTAEMNESTRA   Words, endless words I've said to serve
the moment—
Now it makes me proud to tell the truth.
How else to prepare a death for deadly men
who seem to love you? How to rig the nets
of pain so high no man can overleap them?   *1395*

I brooded on this trial, this ancient blood feud
year by year. At last my hour came.
Here I stand and here I struck
and here my work is done.
I did it all. I don't deny it, no.   *1400*
He had no way to flee or fight his destiny—

[*Unwinding the robes from* AGAMEMNON's *body, spreading there before the altar where the old men cluster around them, unified as a chorus once again.*]

our never-ending, all embracing net, I cast it
wide for the royal haul, I coil him round and round
in the wealth, the robes of doom, and then I strike him
once, twice, and at each stroke he cries in
agony—   *1405*
he buckles at the knees and crashes here!
And when he's down I add the third, last blow,
to the Zeus who saves the dead beneath the ground
I send that third blow home in homage like a prayer.[6]

So he goes down, and the life is bursting out of
him—   *1410*

great sprays of blood, and the murderous shower
wounds me, dyes me black and I, I revel
like the Earth when the spring rains come down,
the blessed gifts of god, and the new green spear
splits the sheath and rips to birth in glory!   *1415*

So it stands, elders of Argos gathered here.
Rejoice if you can rejoice—I glory.
And if I'd pour upon his body the libation
it deserves, what wine could match my words?
It is right and more than right. He flooded   *1420*
the vessel of our proud house with misery,
with the vintage of the curse and now
he drains the dregs. My lord is home at last.

LEADER   You appall me, you, your brazen words—
exulting over your fallen king.

CLYTAEMNESTRA   And you,   *1425*
you try me like some desperate woman.
My heart is steel, well you know. Praise me,
blame me as you choose. It's all one.
Here is Agamemnon, my husband made a corpse
by this right hand—a masterpiece of Justice.   *1430*
Done is done.

CHORUS   Woman!—what poison cropped from the soil
or strained from the heaving sea, what nursed you,
drove you insane? You brave the curse of Greece.
You have cut away and flung away and now
the people cast you off to exile,   *1435*
broken with our hate.

CLYTAEMNESTRA   And now you sentence me?—
you banish *me* from the city, curses breathing
down my neck? But *he*—
name one charge you brought against him then.
He thought no more of it than killing a beast,   *1440*
and his flocks were rich, teeming in their fleece,
but he sacrificed his own child, our daughter,
the agony I labored into love,
to charm away the savage winds of Thrace.[7]

Didn't the law demand you banish him?—   *1445*
hunt him from the land for all his guilt?
But now you witness what I've done
and you are ruthless judges.

Threaten away!
I'll meet you blow for blow. And if I fall
the throne is yours. If god decrees the reverse,   *1450*
late as it is, old men, you'll learn your place.

CHORUS   Mad with ambition,
shrilling pride!—some Fury
crazed with the carnage rages through your brain—
I can see the flecks of blood inflame your
eyes!   *1455*
But vengeance comes—you'll lose your loved ones,
stroke for painful stroke.

CLYTAEMNESTRA   Then learn this, too, the power of my
oaths.
By the child's Rights I brought to birth,
by Ruin, by Fury—the three gods to whom   *1460*
I sacrificed this man—I swear my hopes

---

[6]Like the third libation to Zeus.

[7]Winds from the North (at Aulis).

will never walk the halls of fear so long
as Aegisthus lights the fire on my hearth.
Loyal to me as always, no small shield
to buttress my defiance.
                     Here he lies.   *1465*
He brutalized me. The darling of all
the golden girls[8] who spread the gates of Troy.
And here his spearprize . . . what wonders she beheld!—
the seer of Apollo shared my husband's bed,
his faithful mate who knelt at the
    rowing-benches,   *1470*
worked by every hand.
                    They have their rewards.
He as you know. And she, the swan of the gods
who lived to sing her latest, dying song—
his lover lies beside him.
She brings a fresh, voluptuous relish to my bed! *1475*

CHORUS   Oh quickly, let me die—
no bed of labor, no, no wasting illness . . .
bear me off in the sleep that never ends,
    now that he has fallen,
now that our dearest shield lies battered—   *1480*
Woman made him suffer,
    woman struck him down.
Helen the wild, maddening Helen,
one for the many, the thousand lives
you murdered under Troy. Now you are
crowned   *1485*
with this consummate wreath, the blood
that lives in memory, glistens age to age.
Once in the halls she walked and she was war,
angel of war, angel of agony, lighting men to death.

CLYTAEMNESTRA   Pray no more for death, broken *1490*
as you are. And never turn
    your wrath on her, call her
the scourge of men, the one alone
who destroyed a myriad Greek lives—
Helen the grief that never heals.   *1495*

CHORUS   The *spirit!*—you who tread
the house and the twinborn sons of Tantalus[9]—
you empower the sisters, Fury's twins
    whose power tears the heart!
Perched on the corpse your carrion raven   *1500*
    glories in her hymn,
        her screaming hymn of pride.

CLYTAEMNESTRA   Now you set your judgment straight,
you summon *him!* Three generations
    feed the spirit in the race.   *1505*
Deep in the veins he feeds our bloodlust—
aye, before the old wound dies
it ripens in another flow of blood.

CHORUS   The great curse of the house, the spirit,
dead weight wrath—and you can praise it!   *1510*
Praise the insatiate doom that feeds

relentless on our future and our sons.
Oh all through the will of Zeus,
the cause of all, the one who works it all.
    What comes to birth that is not Zeus?   *1515*
Our lives are pain, what part not come from god?

    Oh, my king, my captain,
    how to salute you, how to mourn you?
    What can I say with all my warmth and love?
    Here in the black widow's web you lie,   *1520*
    gasping out your life
    in a sacrilegious death, dear god,
    reduced to a slave's bed,
    my king of men, yoked by stealth and Fate,
    by the wife's hand that thrust the two-edged
    sword.   *1525*

CLYTAEMNESTRA   You claim the work is mine, call me
    Agamemnon's wife—you are so wrong.
Fleshed in the wife of this dead man,
    the spirit lives within me,
our savage ancient spirit of revenge.   *1530*
In return for Atreus' brutal feast
he kills his perfect son—for every
murdered child, a crowning sacrifice.

CHORUS   And *you*, innocent of his murder?
    And who could swear to that? and how? . . . *1535*
and still an avenger could arise,
bred by the fathers' crimes, and lend a hand.
He wades in the blood of brothers,
stream on mounting stream—black war erupts
    and where he strides revenge will stride,   *1540*
clots will mass for the young who were devoured.

    Oh my king, my captain,
    how to salute you, how to mourn you?
    What can I say with all my warmth and love?
    Here in the black widow's web you lie,   *1545*
    gasping out your life
    in a sacrilegious death, dear god,
    reduced to a slave's bed,
    my king of men, yoked by stealth and Fate,
    by the wife's hand that thrust the two-edged
    sword.   *1550*

CLYTAEMNESTRA   No slave's death, I think—
    no stealthier than the death he dealt
our house and the offspring of our loins,
    Iphigeneia, girl of tears.
Act for act, wound for wound!   *1555*
Never exult in Hades, swordsman,
here you are repaid. By the sword
you did your work and by the sword you die.

CHORUS   The mind reels—
           where to turn?
    All plans dashed, all hope! I cannot think . . . *1560*
the roofs are toppling, I dread the drumbeat
    thunder
    the heavy rains of blood will crush the house
    the first light rains are over—
    Justice brings new acts of agony, yes,
on new grindstones Fate is grinding sharp the

---

[8]In Greek *chryseidon*, which recalls the girl in the first book of the *Iliad* (1.130–33). Chryseis, whom Agamemnon said he preferred to Clytaemnestra.

[9]Father of Pelops, grandfather of Atreus. *Sons:* descendants—that is, Agamemnon and Menelaus.

sword of Justice.   *1565*
Earth, dear Earth,
if only you'd drawn me under
long before I saw him huddled
in the beaten silver bath.
Who will bury him, lift his dirge?   *1570*

[*Turning to* CLYTAEMNESTRA.]

You, can you dare *this?*
To kill your lord with your own hand
then mourn his soul with tributes, terrible tributes—
do his enormous works a great dishonor.
This godlike man, this hero. Who at the grave   *1575*
will sing his praises, pour the wine of tears?
Who will labor there with truth of heart?

CLYTAEMNESTRA   This is no concern of yours.
The hand that bore and cut him down
will hand him down to Mother Earth.   *1580*
This house will never mourn for him.
    Only our daughter Iphigeneia,
    by all rights, will rush to meet him
    first at the churning straits,[10]
the ferry over tears—   *1585*
she'll fling her arms around her father,
pierce him with her love.

CHORUS   Each charge meets counter-charge.
None can judge between them. Justice.
The plunderer plundered, the killer pays the
        price.   *1590*
The truth still holds while Zeus still holds the
        throne:
the one who acts must suffer—
that is law. Who, who can tear from the veins
the bad seed, the curse? The race is welded to its
        ruin.

CLYTAEMNESTRA   At last you see the future and the
        truth!   *1595*
But I will swear a pact with the spirit
born within us. I embrace his works,
cruel as they are but done at last,
    if he will leave our house
in the future, bleed another line   *1600*
with kinsmen murdering kinsmen.
Whatever he may ask. A few things
are all I need, once I have purged
our fury to destroy each other—
    purged it from our halls.

[AEGISTHUS *has emerged from the palace with his bodyguard
and stands triumphant over the body of* AGAMEMNON.]

AEGISTHUS   O what a brilliant day   *1605*
it is for vengeance! Now I can say once more
there are gods in heaven avenging men,
blazing down on all the crimes of earth.
Now at last I see this man brought down
in the Furies' tangling robes. It feasts my eyes—   *1610*
he pays for the plot his father's hand contrived.

---

[10]The river of the underworld over which the dead were ferried.

EURIPIDES

MEDEA

*Medea was produced in 431 B.C.E., the year in which the Pelopon-
nesian War began. It is an iconoclastic play, one that departs from
the traditional subject and the familiar tone of most Greek plays of
the time. For one thing, Euripides' protagonist is a woman, not a
man, as was customary. The myth elaborated in the play is erotic
and the taboo violated disturbing. Without the rights of male citizens, and with even fewer rights than foreign men, Medea is driven
to desperate measures to redress what she considers society's injustice.*

*The excerpt here describes the action just after Medea has mur-
dered her children. She explains her reasons for having done so and
engages in a raging argument with her husband, Jason, over its justification. This part of the play and the work overall are meant to
shake up the prejudices of the original audience, which favored
Greek masculine ideals, to shock the audience out of its complacency,
and to provoke discussion about the limits of violence.*

[*Enter* MEDEA, *from the spectators' right.*]

MEDEA   Friends, I can tell you that for long I have
        waited   *1090*
For the event. I stare towards the place from where
The news will come. And now, see one of Jason's
        servants
Is on his way here, and that labored breath of his
Shows he has tidings for us, and evil tidings.

[*Enter, also from the right, the* MESSENGER.]

MESSENGER   Medea, you who have done such a dreadful
        thing,   *1095*
So outrageous, run for your life, take what you can,
A ship to bear you hence or chariot on land.
MEDEA   And what is the reason deserves such flight as this?
MESSENGER   She is dead, only just now, the royal princess,
And Kreon dead too, her father, by your poisons.   *1100*
MEDEA   The finest words you have spoken. Now and
        hereafter
I shall count you among my benefactors and friends.
MESSENGER   What! Are you right in the mind? Are you
        not mad,
Woman? The house of the king is outraged by you.
Do you enjoy it? Not afraid of such doings?   *1105*
MEDEA   To what you say I on my side have something too
To say in answer. Do not be in a hurry, friend,
But speak. How did they die? You will delight me
        twice
As much again if you say they died in agony.
MESSENGER   When those two children, born of you, had
        entered in,   *1110*
Their father with them, and passed into the bride's
        house,
We were pleased, we slaves who were distressed by
        your wrongs.
All through the house we were talking of but one thing,
How you and your husband had made up your quarrel.
Some kissed the children's hands and some their
        yellow hair,   *1115*
And I myself was so full of my joy that I
Followed the children into the women's quarters.
Our mistress, whom we honor now instead of you,

Before she noticed that your two children were there,
Was keeping her eye fixed eagerly on Jason.   *1120*
Afterwards however she covered up her eyes,
Her cheek paled and she turned herself away from him,
So disgusted was she at the children's coming there.
But your husband tried to end the girl's bad temper,
And said "You must not look unkindly on your
          friends.   *1125*
Cease to be angry. Turn your head to me again.
Have as your friends the same ones as your husband
          has.
And take these gifts, and beg your father to reprieve
These children from their exile. Do it for my sake."
She, when she saw the dress, could not restrain
          herself.   *1130*
She agreed with all her husband said, and before
He and the children had gone far from the palace,
She took the gorgeous robe and dressed herself in it,
And put the golden crown around her curly locks,
And arranged the set of the hair in a shining
          mirror,   *1135*
And smiled at the lifeless image of herself in it.
Then she rose from her chair and walked about the
          room,
With her gleaming feet stepping most soft and delicate,
All overjoyed with the present. Often and often
She would stretch her foot out straight and look
          along it.   *1140*
But after that it was a fearful thing to see.
The color of her face changed, and she staggered back,
She ran, and her legs trembled, and she only just
Managed to reach a chair without falling flat down.
An aged woman servant who, I take it, thought   *1145*
This was some seizure of Pan[11] or another god,
Cried out "God bless us," but that was before she saw
The white foam breaking through her lips and her
          rolling
The pupils of her eyes and her face all bloodless.
Then she raised a different cry from that "God
          bless us,"   *1150*
A huge shriek, and the women ran, one to the king,
One to the newly wedded husband to tell him
What had happened to his bride; and with frequent
          sound
The whole of the palace rang as they went running.
One walking quickly round the course of a
          race-track   *1155*
Would now have turned the bend and be close to the
          goal,
When she, poor girl, opened her shut and speechless
          eye,
And with a terrible groan she came to herself.
For a two-fold pain was moving up against her.
The wreath of gold that was resting around her
          head   *1160*
Let forth a fearful stream of all-devouring fire,

And the finely-woven dress your children gave to her,
Was fastening on the unhappy girl's fine flesh.
She leapt up from the chair, and all on fire she ran,
Shaking her hair now this way and now that,
          trying   *1165*
To hurl the diadem away; but fixedly
The gold preserved its grip, and, when she shook her
          hair,
Then more and twice as fiercely the fire blazed out.
Till, beaten by her fate, she fell down to the ground,
Hard to be recognized except by a parent.   *1170*
Neither the setting of her eyes was plain to see,
Nor the shapeliness of her face. From the top of
Her head there oozed out blood and fire mixed
          together.
Like the drops on pine-bark, so the flesh from her
          bones
Dropped away, torn by the hidden fang of the
          poison.   *1175*
It was a fearful sight; and terror held us all
From touching the corpse. We had learned from
          what had happened.
But her wretched father, knowing nothing of the event,
Came suddenly to the house, and fell upon the corpse,
And at once cried out and folded his arms about
          her,   *1180*
And kissed her and spoke to her, saying, "O my
          poor child,
What heavenly power has so shamefully destroyed you?
And who has set me here like an ancient sepulchre,
Deprived of you? O let me die with you, my child!"
And when he had made an end of his wailing and
          crying,   *1185*
Then the old man wished to raise himself to his feet;
But, as the ivy clings to the twigs of the laurel,
So he stuck to the fine dress, and he struggled fearfully.
For he was trying to lift himself to his knee,
And she was pulling him down, and when he
          tugged hard   *1190*
He would be ripping his aged flesh from his bones.
At last his life was quenched and the unhappy man
Gave up the ghost, no longer could hold up his head.
There they lie close, the daughter and the old father,
Dead bodies, an event he prayed for in his
          tears.   *1195*
As for your interests, I will say nothing of them,
For you will find your own escape from punishment.
Our human life I think and have thought a shadow,
And I do not fear to say that those who are held
Wise amongst men and who search the reasons of
          things   *1200*
Are those who bring the most sorrow on themselves.
For of mortals there is no one who is happy.
If wealth flows in upon one, one may be perhaps
Luckier than one's neighbor, but still not happy.

[*Exit.*]

CHORUS   Heaven, it seems, on this day has fastened
          many   *1205*
          Evils on Jason, and Jason has deserved them.
          Poor girl, the daughter of Kreon, how I pity you

---

[11]As the god of wild nature he was supposed to be the source of the sudden, apparently causeless terror that solitude in wild surroundings may produce and hence of all kinds of sudden madness (compare the English word *panic*).

And your misfortunes, you who have gone quite away
To the house of Hades because of marrying Jason.
MEDEA   Women, my task is fixed: as quickly as I may   *1210*
    To kill my children, and start away from this land,
    And not, by wasting time, to suffer my children
    To be slain by another hand less kindly to them.
    Force every way will have it they must die, and since
    This must be so, then I, their mother, shall kill
        them.   *1215*
    O arm yourself in steel, my heart! Do not hang
        back
    From doing this fearful and necessary wrong.
    O come, my hand, poor wretched hand, and take the
        sword,
    Take it, step forward to this bitter starting point,
    And do not be a coward, do not think of them,   *1220*
    How sweet they are, and how you are their mother.
        Just for
    This one short day be forgetful of your children,
    Afterwards weep; for even though you will kill them,
    They were very dear,—O, I am an unhappy woman!

[*With a cry she rushes into the house.*]

CHORUS   O Earth, and the far shining   *1225*
    Ray of the sun, look down, look down upon
    This poor lost woman, look, before she raises
    The hand of murder against her flesh and blood.
    Yours was the golden birth from which
    She sprang, and now I fear divine   *1230*
    Blood may be shed by men.
    O heavenly light, hold back her hand,
    Check her, and drive from out the house

    The bloody Fury raised by fiends of Hell.
    Vain waste, your care of children;   *1235*
    Was it in vain you bore the babes you loved,
    After you passed the inhospitable strait
    Between the dark blue rocks, Symplegades?
    O wretched one, how has it come,
    This heavry anger on your heart,   *1240*
    This cruel bloody mind?
    For God from mortals asks a stern
    Price for the stain of kindred blood
    In like disaster falling on their homes.

[*A cry from one of the* CHILDREN *is heard.*]

CHORUS   Do you hear the cry, do you hear the children's
        cry?   *1245*
    O you hard heart, O woman fated for evil!
ONE OF THE CHILDREN   [*From within.*] What can I do and
        how escape
        my mother's hands?
ONE OF THE CHILDREN   [*Front within.*] O my dear broth-
        er, I cannot tell.
    We are lost.
CHORUS   Shall I enter the house? O surely I should   *1250*
    Defend the children from murder.
A CHILD   [*From within.*] O help us, in God's name, for
        now we need your help.
    Now, now we are close to it. We are trapped by the
        sword.
CHORUS   O your heart must have been made of rock or
        steel,

You who can kill   *1255*
With your own hand the fruit of your own womb.
Of one alone I have heard, one woman alone
Of those of old who laid her hands on her children,
Ino, sent mad by heaven when the wife of Zeus
Drove her out from her home and made her
    wander;   *1260*
And because of the wicked shedding of blood
Of her own children she threw
Herself, poor wretch, into the sea and stepped away
Over the sea-cliff to die with her two children.
What horror more can be? O women's love,   *1265*
So full of trouble,
How many evils have you caused already!

[*Enter* JASON, *with attendants.*]

JASON   You women, standing close in front of this dwelling,
    Is she, Medea, she who did this dreadful deed,
    Still in the house, or has she run away in flight?   *1270*
    For she will have to hide herself beneath the earth,
    Or raise herself on wings into the height of air,
    If she wishes to escape the royal vengeance.
    Does she imagine that, having killed our rulers,
    She will herself escape uninjured from this house?*1275*
    But I am thinking not so much of her as for
    The children,—her the king's friends will make to
        suffer
    For what she did. So I have come to save the lives
    Of my boys, in case the royal house should harm them
    While taking vengeance for their mother's wicked
        deed   *1280*
CHORUS   Jason, if you but knew how deeply you are
    Involved in sorrow, you would not have spoken so.
JASON   What is it? That she is planning to kill me also?
CHORUS   Your children are dead, and by their own
        mother's hand.
JASON   What! This is it? O woman, you have destroyed
        me.   *1285*
CHORUS   You must make up your mind your children are
        no more.
JASON   Where did she kill them? Was it here or in the
        house?
CHORUS   Open the gates and there you will see them
        murdered.
JASON   Quick as you can unlock the doors, men, and undo
    The fastenings and let me see this double evil,   *1290*
    My children dead and her,—O her I will repay.

[*His attendants rush to the door.* MEDEA *appears above the
house in a chariot drawn by dragons. She has the dead bodies
of the* CHILDREN *with her.*]

MEDEA   Why do you batter these gates and try to unbar
        them,
    Seeking the corpses and for me who did the deed?
    You may cease your trouble, and, if you have need of
        me,
    Speak, if you wish. You will never touch me with your
        hand,   *1295*
    Such a chariot has Helios, my father's father,
    Given me to defend me from my enemies.
JASON   You hateful thing, you woman most utterly loathed
    By the gods and me and by all the race of mankind,

You who have had the heart to raise a sword against   *1300*
Your children, you, their mother, and left me childless,—
You have done this, and do you still look at the sun
And at the earth, after these most fearful doings?
I wish you dead. Now I see it plain, though at that time
I did not, when I took you from your foreign home   *1305*
And brought you to a Greek house, you, an evil thing,
A traitress to your father and your native land.
The gods hurled the avenging curse of yours on me.
For your own brother you slew at your own hearthside,
And then came aboard that beautiful ship, the Argo.   *1310*
And that was your beginning. When you were married
To me, your husband, and had borne children to me,
For the sake of pleasure in the bed you killed them.
There is no Greek woman who would have dared such deeds,
Out of all those whom I passed over and chose you   *1315*
To marry instead, a bitter destructive match,
A monster not a woman, having a nature
Wilder than that of Scylla[12] in the Tuscan sea.
Ah! no, not if I had ten thousand words of shame
Could I sting you. You are naturally so brazen.   *1320*
Go, worker in evil, stained with your children's blood.
For me remains to cry aloud upon my fate,
Who will get no pleasure from my newly-wedded love,
And the boys whom I begot and brought up, never
Shall I speak to them alive. Oh, my life is over!   *1325*

MEDEA   Long would be the answer which I might have made to
These words of yours, if Zeus the father did not know
How I have treated you and what you did to me.
No, it was not to be that you should scorn my love,
And pleasantly live your life through, laughing at me;   *1330*
Nor would the princess, nor he who offered the match,
Kreon, drive me away without paying for it,
So now you may call me a monster, if you wish,
Or Scylla housed in the caves of the Tuscan sea
I too, as I had to, have taken hold of your heart.   *1335*

JASON   You feel the pain yourself. You share in my sorrow.

MEDEA   Yes, and my grief is gain when you cannot mock it.

JASON   O children, what a wicked mother she was to you!

MEDEA   They died from a disease they caught from their father.

JASON   I tell you it was not my hand that destroyed them.   *1340*

MEDEA   But it was your insolence, and your virgin wedding.

JASON   And just for the sake of that you chose to kill them.

MEDEA   Is love so small a pain, do you think, for a woman?

JASON   For a wise one, certainly. But you are wholly evil.

MEDEA   The children are dead. I say this to make you suffer.   *1345*

JASON   The children, I think, will bring down curses on you.

MEDEA   The gods know who was the author of this sorrow.

JASON   Yes, the gods know indeed, they know your loathsome heart.

MEDEA   Hate me. But I tire of your barking bitterness.

JASON   And I of yours. It is easier to leave you.   *1350*

MEDEA   How then? What shall I do? I long to leave you too.

JASON   Give me the bodies to bury and to mourn them.

MEDEA   No, that I will not. I will bury them myself,
Bearing them to Hera's temple on the promontory;
So that no enemy may evilly treat them   *1355*
By tearing up their grave. In this land of Corinth
I shall establish a holy feast and sacrifice[13]
Each year for ever to atone for the blood guilt.
And I myself go to the land of Erechtheus
To dwell in Aigeus' house, the son of Pandion.   *1360*
While you, as is right, will die without distinction,
Struck on the head by a piece of the Argo's timber,
And you will have seen the bitter end of my love.

JASON   May a Fury for the children's sake destroy you,
And justice, requitor of blood.   *1365*

MEDEA   What heavenly power lends an ear
To a breaker of oaths, a deceiver?

JASON   O, I hate you, murderess of children.

MEDEA   Go to your palace. Bury your bride.

JASON   I go, with two children to mourn for.   *1370*

MEDEA   Not yet do you feel it. Wait for the future.

JASON   Oh, children I loved!

MEDEA   I loved them, you did not.

JASON   You loved them, and killed them.

MEDEA   To make you feel pain.

JASON   Oh, wretch that I am, how I long
To kiss the dear lips of my children!   *1375*

MEDEA   Now you would speak to them, now you would kiss them.
Then you rejected them.

JASON   Let me, I beg you,
Touch my boys' delicate flesh.

MEDEA   I will not. Your words are all wasted.

JASON   O God, do you hear it, this persecution,   *1380*
These my sufferings from this hateful
Woman, this monster, murderess of children?
Still what I can do that I will do:
I will lament and cry upon heaven,
Calling the gods to bear me witness   *1385*
How you have killed my boys and prevent me from
Touching their bodies or giving them burial.
I wish I had never begot them to see them
Afterwards slaughtered by you.

CHORUS   Zeus in Olympus is the overseer   *1390*
Of many doings. Many things the gods
Achieve beyond our judgment. What we thought
Is not confirmed and what we thought not god
Contrives. And so it happens in this story.

---

[12]A monster located in the straits between Italy and Sicily, who snatched sailors off passing ships and devoured them. See *Odyssey* 12.

[13]Some such ceremony was still performed at Corinth in Euripides' time.

PLATO

from *The Apology*

In The Apology, *Socrates offers a defense against the charge that he corrupted the youth of Athens. The word apology here does not indicate Socrates' expression of regret or remorse, but refers to his explanation of his behavior, which is, in fact, a repudiation of the charges brought against him. This excerpt concludes Socrates' speech and includes his famous idea that the unexamined life is not worth living. In the speech, Socrates challenges his accusers and criticizes them for the kind of unreflective and immoral lives they lead. He warns them that in condemning him to death, they are condemning themselves in the court of history.*

There are a great many reasons, gentlemen, why I am not distressed by this result—I mean your condemnation of me—but the chief reason is that the result was not unexpected. What does surprise me is the number of votes cast on the two sides. I should never have believed that it would be such a close thing; but now it seems that if a mere thirty votes had gone the other way, I should have been acquitted. Even as it is, I feel that so far as Meletus's part is concerned I have been acquitted; and not only that, but anyone can see that if Anytus and Lycon had not come forward to accuse me, Meletus would actually have lost a thousand drachmae for not having obtained one fifth of the votes.

However, we must face the fact that he demands the death penalty. Very good. What alternative penalty shall I propose to you, gentlemen? Obviously it must be what's deserved. Well, what penalty do I deserve to pay or suffer, in view of what I have done?

I have never lived an ordinary quiet life. I did not care for the things that most people care about: making money, having a comfortable home, high military or civil rank, and all the other activities—political appointments, secret societies, party organizations—which go on in our city; I thought that I was really too fair-minded to survive if I went in for this sort of thing. So instead of taking a course which would have done no good either to you or to me, I set myself to do you individually in private what I hold to be the greatest possible service: I tried to persuade each one of you not to think more of practical advantages than of his mental and moral well-being, or in general to think more of advantage than of well-being, in the case of the State or of anything else. What do I deserve for behaving in this way? Some reward, gentlemen, if I am bound to suggest what I really deserve; and what is more, a reward which would be appropriate for myself. Well, what is appropriate for a poor man who is a public benefactor and who requires leisure for the purpose of giving you moral encouragement? Nothing could be more appropriate for such a person than free dining in the Prytaneum. He deserves it much more than any victor in the races at Olympia, whether he wins with a single horse or a pair or a team of four. These people give you the semblance of success, but I give you the reality; they do not need maintenance, but I do. So if I am to suggest an appropriate penalty which is strictly in accordance with justice, I suggest free maintenance by the State.

Perhaps when I say this I may give you the impression, as I did in my remarks about exciting sympathy and making passionate appeals, that I am showing a stubborn perversity. That is not so, gentlemen; the real position is this. I am convinced that I never wrong anyone intentionally, but I cannot convince you of this, because we have had so little time for discussion. If it was your practice, as it is with other nations, to give not one day but several to the hearing of capital trials, I believe that you might have been convinced; but under present conditions it is not easy to dispose of grave allegations in a short space of time. So being convinced that I do no wrong to anybody, I can hardly be expected to wrong myself by asserting that I deserve something bad, or by proposing a corresponding penalty. Why should I? For fear of suffering this penalty proposed by Meletus, when, as I said, I do not know whether it is a good thing or a bad? Do you expect me to choose something which I know very well is bad by making my counter-proposal? Imprisonment? Why should I spend my days in prison, in subjection to whichever Eleven hold office? A fine, with imprisonment until it is paid? In my case the effect would be just the same, because I have no money to pay a fine. Or shall I suggest banishment? You would very likely accept the suggestion.

I should have to be desperately in love with life to do that, gentlemen. I am not so blind that I cannot see that you, my fellow-citizens, have come to the end of your patience with my discussions and conversations; you have found them too irksome and irritating, and now you are trying to get rid of them. Will any other people find them easy to put up with? That is most unlikely, gentlemen. A fine life I should have if I left this country at my age and spent the rest of my days trying one city after another and being turned out every time! I know very well that wherever I go the young people will listen to my conversation just as they do here; and if I try to keep them off, they themselves will prevail upon their elders and have me thrown out, while if I do not, the fathers and other relatives will drive me out of their own accord for the sake of the young.

Perhaps someone may say, 'But surely, Socrates, after you have left us you can spend the rest of your life in quietly minding your own business.' This is the hardest thing of all to make some of you understand. If I say that this would be disobedience to God, and that is why I cannot 'mind my own business', you will not believe me — you'll think I'm pulling your leg. If on the other hand I tell you that to let no day pass without discussing goodness and all the other subjects about which you hear me talking and examining both myself and others is really the very best thing that a man can do, and that life without this sort of examination is not worth living, you will be even less inclined to believe me. Nevertheless that is how it is, gentlemen, as I maintain; though it is not easy to convince you of it. Besides, I am not accustomed to think of myself as deserving punishment. If I had money, I would have suggested a fine that I could afford, because that would not have done me any harm. As it is, I cannot, because I have none; unless of course you like to fix the penalty at what I could pay. I suppose I could probably afford a hundred drachmae and I suggest a fine of that amount.

One moment, gentlemen. Plato here, and Crito and Critobulus and Apollodorus, want me to propose three thousand drachmae on their security. Very well, I agree to this sum, and you can rely upon these gentlemen for its payment.

Translated by Hugh Tarrant. From *Plato: The Last Days of Socrates*, Penguin. London, 2003

The penalty is death. Socrates converses with the jurymen after being sentenced by an increased majority of jurors (over two-thirds) to death rather than a fine.

Well, gentlemen, for the sake of a very small gain in time you are going to earn the reputation — and the blame from those who wish to disparage our city — of having put Socrates to death, 'that wise man', because they will say I am wise even if I am not, these people who want to find fault with you. If you had waited just a little while, you would have had your way in the course of nature. You can see that I am well on in life and near to death. I am saying this not to all of you but to those who voted for my execution, and I have something else to say to them as well.

No doubt you think, gentlemen, that I have been condemned for lack of the arguments which I could have used if I had thought it right to leave nothing unsaid or undone to secure my acquittal. But that is very far from the truth. It is not a lack of arguments that has caused my condemnation, but a lack of effrontery and impudence, and the fact that I have refused to address you in the way which would give you most pleasure. You would have liked to hear me weep and wail, doing and saying all sorts of things which I declare to be unworthy of myself, but which you are used to hearing from other people. But I did not think then that I ought to stoop to servility because I was in danger, and I do not regret now the way in which I pleaded my case; I would much rather die as the result of this defence than live as the result of the other sort. In a court of law, just as in warfare, neither I nor any other ought to use his wits to escape death by any means. In battle it is often obvious that you could escape being killed by giving up your arms and throwing yourself upon the mercy of your pursuers; and in every kind of danger there are plenty of devices for avoiding death if you are unscrupulous enough to stop at nothing. But I suggest, gentlemen, that the difficulty is not so much to escape death; the real difficulty is to escape from wickedness, which is far more fleet of foot. In this present instance I, the slow old man, have been overtaken by the slower of the two, but my accusers, who are clever and quick, have been overtaken by the faster: by iniquity. When I leave this court I shall go away condemned by you to death, but they will go away convicted by Truth herself of depravity and injustice. And they accept their sentence even as I accept mine. No doubt it was bound to be so, and I think that the result is fair enough.

Having said so much, I feel moved to prophesy to you who have given your vote against me; for I am now at that point where the gift of prophecy comes most readily to men: at the point of death. I tell you, my executioners, that as soon as I am dead, vengeance shall fall upon you with a punishment far more painful than your killing of me. You have brought about my death in the belief that through it you will be delivered from submitting the conduct of your lives to criticism; but I say that the result will be just the opposite. You will have more critics, whom up till now I have restrained without your knowing it; and being younger they will be harsher to you and will cause you more annoyance.

If you expect to stop denunciation of your wrong way of life by putting people to death, there is something amiss with your reasoning. This way of escape is neither possible nor creditable; the best and easiest way is not to stop the mouths of others, but to make yourselves as well behaved as possible.

This is my last message to you who voted for my condemnation.

As for you who voted for my acquittal, I should very much like to say a few words to reconcile you to this result, while the officials are busy and I am not yet on my way to the place where I must die. I ask you, gentlemen, to spare me these few moments; there is no reason why we should not exchange a few words while the law permits. I look upon you as my friends, and I want to show you the meaning of what has now happened to me.

Gentlemen of the jury — for you deserve to be so called — I have had a remarkable experience. In the past the prophetic voice to which I have become accustomed has always been my constant companion, opposing me even in quite trivial things if I was going to take the wrong course. Now something has happened to me, as you can see, which might be thought and is commonly considered to be a supreme calamity; yet neither when I left home this morning, nor when I was taking my place here in the court, nor at any point in any part of my speech, did the divine sign oppose me. In other discussions it has often checked me in the middle of a sentence; but this time it has never opposed me in any part of this business in anything that I have said or done. What do I suppose to be the explanation? I will tell you. I suspect that this thing that has happened to me is a blessing, and we are quite mistaken in supposing death to be an evil. I have good grounds for thinking this, because my accustomed sign could not have failed to oppose me if what I was doing had not been sure to bring some good result.

We should reflect that there is much reason to hope for a good result on other grounds as well. Death is one of two things. Either it is annihilation, and the dead have no consciousness of anything; or, as we are told, it is really a change: a migration of the soul from this place to another. Now if there is no consciousness but only a dreamless sleep, death must be a marvellous gain. I suppose that if anyone were told to pick out the night on which he slept so soundly as not even to dream, and then to compare it with all the other nights and days of his life, and then were told to say, after due consideration, how many better and happier days and nights than this he had spent in the course of his life — well, I think that the Great King himself, to say nothing of any private person, would find these days and nights easy to count in comparison with the rest. If death is like this, then, I call it gain; because the whole of time, if you look at it in this way, can be regarded as no more than one single night. If on the other hand death is a removal from here to some other place, and if what we are told is true, that all the dead are there, what greater blessing could there be than this, gentlemen of the jury? If on arrival in the other world, beyond the reach of these so-called jurors here, one will find there the true jurors who are said to preside in those courts, Minos and Rhadamanthys and Aeacus and Triptolemus and all those other demigods who were upright in their earthly life, would that be an unrewarding place to settle? Put it in this way: how much would one of you give to meet Orpheus and Musaeus, Hesiod and Homer? I am willing to die ten times over if this account is true. For me at least it would be a wonderful personal experience to join them there, to meet Palamedes and Ajax the son of Telamon and any other heroes of the old days who met their death through an unjust trial, and to compare my fortunes with theirs — it would be rather amusing, I think — and above all I should like to spend my time there, as here, in examining and searching people's minds, to find out who is really wise among them, and who only thinks that he is. What would one not give, gentlemen, to be able to scrutinize the leader of that great host against Troy, or Odysseus, or Sisyphus, or the thousands of other men and women whom one could mention? Their company and conversation — like the chance to examine them — would be unimaginable happiness. At any rate I presume that they do not put one to death there for such conduct; because apart from the other happiness in which their world surpasses ours, they are now immortal for the rest of time, if what we are told is true.

You too, gentlemen of the jury, must look forward to death with confidence, and fix your minds on this one belief, which is certain: that nothing can harm a good man either in life or after death, and his fortunes are not a matter of indifference to the gods. This present experience of mine does not result from mere earthly causes; I am quite clear that the time had come when it was better for me to die and be released from my distractions. That is why my sign never turned me back. For my own part I bear no grudge at all against those who condemned me and accused me, although it was not with this kind intention that they did so, but because they thought that they were hurting me; and that is culpable of them. However, I ask them to grant me one favour. When my sons grow up, gentlemen, if you think that they are putting money or anything else before goodness, take your revenge by plaguing them as I plagued you; and if they fancy themselves for no reason, you must scold them just as I scolded you, for neglecting the important things and thinking that they are good for something when they are good for nothing. If you do this, I shall have had justice at your hands — I *and* my children.

Well, now it is time to be off, I to die and you to live; but which of us has the happier prospect is unknown to anyone but God.

PLATO

from *The Republic, "Allegory of the Cave"*

The Republic *is Plato's longest and most complex book. In presenting his version of the ideal society, Plato explains the importance of true knowledge, which he distinguishes from false knowledge, really a form of ignorance. To convey the difference between true and false knowledge, Plato introduces an extended metaphor, the Allegory of the Cave. People chained to the floor of an underground cave imagine that the shadows cast on the cave's walls by the light of a fire behind them are real. The cave's inhabitants know only such shadows, which for them become the only reality they know. Their ignorance can only be dispelled by someone not limited to the shadowy notions of reality believed by the cave dwellers. Only the philosopher, who knows the true, the good, and the beautiful as they really exist in their pure ideal forms, can free humankind from its limited knowledge of material reality. Here Socrates is speaking to Glaucon.*

And now, I said, let me show in a figure how far our nature is enlightened or unenlightened:—Behold! human beings living in an underground den, which has a mouth open towards the light and reaching all along the den; here they have been from their childhood, and have their legs and necks chained so that they cannot move, and can only see before them, being prevented by the chains from turning round their heads. Above and behind them a fire is blazing at a distance, and between the fire and the prisoners there is a raised way; and you will see, if you look, a low wall built along the way, like the screen which marionette players have in front of them, over which they show the puppets.

I see.

And do you see, I said, men passing along the wall carrying all sorts of vessels, and statues and figures of animals made of wood and stone and various materials, which appear over the wall? Some of them are talking, others silent.

You have shown me a strange image, and they are strange prisoners.

Like ourselves, I replied; and they see only their own shadows, or the shadows of one another, which the fire throws on the opposite wall of the cave?

True, he said; how could they see anything but the shadows if they were never allowed to move their heads?

And of the objects which are being carried in like manner they would only see the shadows?

Yes, he said.

And if they were able to converse with one another, would they not suppose that they were naming what was actually before them?

Very true.

And suppose further that the prison had an echo which came from the other side, would they not be sure to fancy when one of the passers-by spoke that the voice which they heard came from the passing shadow?

No question, he replied.

To them, I said, the truth would be literally nothing but the shadows of the images.

That is certain.

And now look again, and see what will naturally follow if the prisoners are released and disabused of their error. At first, when any of them is liberated and compelled suddenly to stand up and turn his neck round and walk and look towards the light, he will suffer sharp pains; the glare will distress him, and he will be unable to see the realities of which in his former state he had seen the shadows; and then conceive someone saying to him, that what he saw before was an illusion, but that now, when he is approaching nearer to being and his eye is turned towards more real existence, he has a clearer vision—what will be his reply? And you may further imagine that his instructor is pointing to the objects as they pass and requiring him to name them—will he not be perplexed? Will he not fancy that the shadows which he formerly saw are truer than the objects which are now shown to him?

Far truer.

And if he is compelled to look straight at the light, will he not have a pain in his eyes which will make him turn away to take refuge in the objects of vision which he can see, and which he will conceive to be in reality clearer than the things which are now being shown to him?

True, he said.

And suppose once more, that he is reluctantly dragged up a steep and rugged ascent, and held fast until he is forced into the presence of the sun himself, is he not likely to be pained and irritated? When he approaches the light his eyes will be dazzled, and he will not be able to see anything at all of what are now called realities.

Not all in a moment, he said.

He will require to grow accustomed to the sight of the upper world. And first he will see the shadows best, next the reflections of men and other objects in the water, and then the objects themselves; then he will gaze upon the light of the moon and the stars and the spangled heaven; and he will see the sky and the stars by night better than the sun or the light of the sun by day?

Certainly.

Last of all he will be able to see the sun, and not mere reflections of him in the water, but he will see him in his own proper place, and not in another; and he will contemplate him as he is.

Certainly.

He will then proceed to argue that this is he who gives the season and the years, and is the guardian of all that is in the visible world, and in a certain way the cause of all things which he and his fellows have been accustomed to behold?

Clearly, he said, he would first see the sun and then reason about him.

And when he remembered his old habitation, and the wisdom of the den and his fellow-prisoners, do you not suppose that he would felicitate himself on the change, and pity them?

Certainly, he would.

And if they were in the habit of conferring honours among themselves on those who were quickest to observe the passing shadows and to remark which of them went before, and which followed after, and which were together; and who were therefore best able to draw conclusions as to the future, do you think that he would care for such honours and glories, or envy the possessors of them? Would he not say with Homer,

BETTER TO BE THE POOR SERVANT OF A POOR MASTER,

and to endure anything, rather than think as they do and live after their manner?

Yes, he said, I think that he would rather suffer anything than entertain these false notions and live in this miserable manner.

Imagine once more, I said, such an one coming suddenly out of the sun to be replaced in his old situation; would he not be certain to have his eyes full of darkness?

To be sure, he said.

And if there were a contest, and he had to compete in measuring the shadows with the prisoners who had never moved out of the den, while his sight was still weak, and before his eyes had become steady (and the time which would be needed to acquire this new habit of sight might be very considerable), would he not be ridiculous? Men would say of him that up he went and down he came without his eyes; and that it was better not even to think of ascending; and if any one tried to loose another and lead him up to the light, let them only catch the offender, and they would put him to death.

No question, he said.

This entire allegory, I said, you may now append, dear Glaucon, to the previous argument; the prison-house is the world of sight, the light of the fire is the sun, and you will not misapprehend me if you interpret the journey upwards to be the ascent of the soul into the intellectual world according to my poor belief, which, at your desire, I have expressed—whether rightly or wrongly God knows. But, whether true or false, my opinion is that in the world of knowledge the idea of good appears last of all, and is seen only with an effort; and, when seen, is also inferred to be the universal author of all things beautiful and right, parent of light and of the lord of light in this visible world, and the immediate source of reason and truth in the intellectual; and that this is the power upon which he who would act rationally either in public or private life must have his eye fixed.

I agree, he said, as far as I am able to understand you.

Moreover, I said, you must not wonder that those who attain to this beatific vision are unwilling to descend to human affairs; for their souls are ever hastening into the upper world where they desire to dwell; which desire of theirs is very natural, if our allegory may be trusted.

Yes, very natural.

And is there anything surprising in one who passes from divine contemplations to the evil state of man, misbehaving himself in a ridiculous manner; if, while his eyes are blinking and before he has become accustomed to the surrounding darkness, he is compelled to fight in courts of law, or in other places, about the images or the shadows of images of justice, and is endeavouring to meet the conceptions of those who have never yet seen absolute justice?

Anything but surprising, he replied.

Any one who has common sense will remember that the bewilderments of the eyes are of two kinds, and arise from two causes, either from coming out of the light or from going into the light, which is true of the mind's eye, quite as much as of the bodily eye; and he who remembers this when he sees any one whose vision is perplexed and weak, will not be too ready to laugh; he will first ask whether that soul of man has come out of the brighter life, and is unable to see because unaccustomed to the dark, or having turned from darkness to the day is dazzled by excess of light. And he will count the one happy in his condition and state of being, and he will pity the other; or, if he have a mind to laugh at the soul which comes from below into the light, there will be more reason in this than in the laugh which greets him who returns from above out of the light into the den.

That, he said, is a very just distinction.

But then, if I am right, certain professors of education must be wrong when they say that they can put a knowledge into the soul which was not there before, like sight into blind eyes.

They undoubtedly say this, he replied.

Whereas, our argument shows that the power and capacity of learning exists in the soul already; and that just as the eye was unable to turn from darkness to light without the whole body, so too the instrument of knowledge can only by the movement of the whole soul be turned from the world of becoming into that of being, and learn by degrees to endure the sight of being, and of the brightest and best of being, or in other words, of the good.

Very true.

And must there not be some art which will effect conversion in the easiest and quickest manner; not implanting the faculty of sight, for that exists already, but has been turned in the wrong direction, and is looking away from the truth?

Yes, he said, such an art may be presumed.

And whereas the other so-called virtues of the soul seem to be akin to bodily qualities, for even when they are not originally innate they can be implanted later by habit and exercise, the virtue of wisdom more than anything else contains a divine element which always remains, and by this conversion is rendered useful and profitable; or, on the other hand, hurtful and useless. Did you never observe the narrow intelligence flashing from the keen eye of a clever rogue—how eager he is, how clearly his paltry soul sees the way to his end; he is the reverse of blind, but his keen eye-sight is forced into the service of evil, and he is mischievous in proportion to his cleverness?

Very true, he said.

But what if there had been a circumcision of such natures in the days of their youth; and they had been severed from those sensual pleasures, such as eating and drinking, which, like leaden weights, were attached to them at their birth, and which drag them down and turn the vision of their souls upon the things that are below—if, I say, they had been released from these impediments and turned in the opposite direction, the very same faculty in them would have seen the truth as keenly as they see what their eyes are turned to now.

Very likely.

Yes, I said; and there is another thing which is likely, or rather a necessary inference from what has preceded, that neither the uneducated and uninformed of the truth, or yet those who never make an end of their education, will be able ministers of State; not the former, because they have no single aim of duty which is the role of all their actions, private as well as public, nor the latter, because they will not act at all except upon compulsion, fancying that they are already dwelling apart in the islands of the blest.

Very true, he replied.

Then, I said, the business of us who are the founders of the State will be to compel the best minds to attain that knowledge which we have already shown to be the greatest of all—they must continue to ascend until they arrive at the good; but when they have ascended and seen enough we must not allow them to do as they do now.

What do you mean?

I mean that they remain in the upper world: but this must not be allowed; they must be made to descend again among the prisoners in the den, and partake of their labours and honours, whether they are worth having or not.

But is not this unjust? he said; ought we to give them a worse life, when they might have a better?

You have again forgotten, my friend, I said, the intention of the legislator, who did not aim at making any one class in the State happy above the rest; the happiness was to be in the whole State, and he held the citizens together by persuasion and necessity, making them benefactors of the State, and therefore benefactors of one another; to this end he created them, not to please themselves, but to be his instruments in binding up the State.

True, he said, I had forgotten.

Observe, Glaucon, that there will be no injustice in compelling our philosophers to have a care and providence of others; we shall explain to them that in other States, men of their class are not obliged to share in the toils of politics: and this is reasonable, for they grow up at their own sweet will, and the government would rather not have them. Being self-taught, they cannot be expected to show any gratitude for a culture which they have never received. But we have brought you into the world to be rulers of the hive, kings of yourselves and of the other citizens, and have educated you far better and more perfectly than they have been educated, and you are better able to share in the double duty. Wherefore each of you, when his turn comes, must go down to the general underground abode, and get the habit of seeing in the dark. When you have acquired the habit, you will see ten thousand times better than the inhabitants of the den, and you will know what the several images are, and what they represent, because you have seen the beautiful and just and good in their truth. And thus our State which is also yours will be a reality, and not a dream only, and will be administered in a spirit unlike that of other States, in which men fight with one another about shadows only and are distracted in the struggle for power, which in their eyes is a great good. Whereas the truth is that the State in which the rulers are most reluctant to govern is always the best and most quietly governed, and the State in which they are most eager, the worst.

Quite true, he replied.

And will our pupils, when they hear this, refuse to take their turn at the toils of State, when they are allowed to spend the greater part of their time with one another in the heavenly light?

Impossible, he answered; for they are just men, and the commands which we impose upon them are just; there can be no doubt that every one of them will take office as a stern necessity, and not after the fashion of our present rulers of State.

Yes, my friend, I said; and there lies the point. You must contrive for your future rulers another and a better life than that of a ruler, and then you may have a well-ordered State; for only in the State which offers this, will they rule who are truly rich, not in silver and gold, but in virtue and wisdom, which are the true blessings of life. Whereas if they go to the administration of public affairs, poor and hungering after their own private advantage, thinking that hence they are to snatch the chief good, order there can never be; for they will be fighting about office, and the civil and domestic broils which thus arise will be the ruin of the rulers themselves and of the whole State.

Most true, he replied.

And the only life which looks down upon the life of political ambition is that of true philosophy. Do you know of any other?

Indeed, I do not, he said.

ARISTOTLE

from *The Nicomachean Ethics*

In the following passage from his Nicomachean Ethics, *Aristotle describes his principle of the mean between extremes. Although Aristotle emphasizes the acquisition of moral virtue, he also refers to how the doctrine of the mean applies to works of art. Moderation is a critical element in Aristotle's doctrine of the mean, as is the notion that the ideal mean of any feeling, impulse, or attitude is rel-*

ative, varying from one person to another. In this section, also, Aristotle explains why achieving the balance of the mean is difficult.

VIRTUE DEFINED: THE DIFFERENTIA

It is not sufficient, however, merely to define virtue in general terms as a characteristic: we must also specify what kind of characteristic it is. It must, then, be remarked that every virtue or excellence (1) renders good the thing itself of which it is the excellence, and (2) causes it to perform its function well. For example, the excellence of the eye makes both the eye and its function good, for good sight is due to the excellence of the eye. Likewise, the excellence of a horse makes it both good as a horse and good at running, at carrying its rider, and at facing the enemy. Now, if this is true of all things, the virtue or excellence of man, too, will be a characteristic which makes him a good man, and which causes him to perform his own function well. To some extent we have already stated how this will be true; the rest will become clear if we study what the nature of virtue is.

Of every continuous entity that is divisible into parts it is possible to take the larger, the smaller, or an equal part, and these parts may be larger, smaller, or equal either in relation to the entity itself, or in relation to us. The "equal" part is something median between excess and deficiency. By the median of an entity I understand a point equidistant from both extremes, and this point is one and the same for everybody. To take an example: if ten is many and two is few, six is taken as the median in relation to the entity, for it exceeds and is exceeded by the same amount, and is thus the median in terms of arithmetical proportion. But the median relative to us cannot be determined in this manner: if ten pounds of food is much for a man to eat and two pounds little, it does not follow that the trainer will prescribe six pounds, for this may in turn be much or little for him to eat; it may be little for Milo [the wrestler] and much for someone who has just begun to take up athletics. The same applies to running and wrestling. Thus we see that an expert in any field avoids excess and deficiency, but seeks the median and chooses it—not the median of the object but the median relative to us.

If this, then, is the way in which every science perfects its work, by looking to the median and by bringing its work up to that point—and this is the reason why it is usually said of a successful piece of work that it is impossible to detract from it or to add to it, the implication being that excess and deficiency destroy success while the mean safeguards it (good craftsmen, we say, look toward this standard in the performance of their work)—and if virtue, like nature, is more precise and better than any art, we must conclude that virtue aims at the median. I am referring to moral virtue: for it is moral virtue that is concerned with emotions and actions, and it is in emotions and actions that excess, deficiency, and median are found. Thus we can experience fear, confidence, desire, anger, pity, and generally any kind of pleasure and pain either too much or too little, and in either case not properly. But to experience all this at the right time, toward the right objects, toward the right people, for the right reason, and in the right manner—that is the median and the best course, the course that is a mark of virtue.

Similarly, excess, deficiency, and the median can also be found in actions. Now virtue is concerned with emotions and actions; and in emotions and actions excess and deficiency miss the mark, whereas the median is praised and constitutes success. But both praise and success are signs of virtue or excellence. Consequently, virtue is a mean in the sense that it aims at the median. This is corroborated by the fact that there are many ways of going wrong, but only one way which is right—for evil belongs to the indeterminate, as the Pythagoreans imagined, but good to the determinate. This, by the way, is also the reason why the one is easy and the other hard: it is easy to miss the target but hard to hit it. Here, then, is an additional proof that excess and deficiency characterize vice, while the mean characterizes virtue: for "bad men have many ways, good men but one."

We may thus conclude that virtue or excellence is a characteristic involving choice, and that it consists in observing the mean relative to us, a mean which is defined by a rational principle, such as a man of practical wisdom would use to determine it. It is the mean by reference to two vices: the one of excess and the other of deficiency. It is, moreover, a mean because some vices exceed and others fall short of what is required in emotion and in action, whereas virtue finds and chooses the median. Hence, in respect of its essence and the definition of its essential nature virtue is a mean, but in regard to goodness and excellence it is an extreme.

Not every action nor every emotion admits of a mean. There are some actions and emotions whose very names connote baseness, e.g., spite, shamelessness, envy; and among actions, adultery, theft, and murder. These and similar emotions and actions imply by their very names that they are bad; it is not their excess nor their deficiency which is called bad. It is, therefore, impossible ever to do right in performing them: to perform them is always to do wrong. In cases of this sort, let us say adultery, rightness and wrongness do not depend on committing it with the right woman at the right time and in the right manner, but the mere fact of committing such an action at all is to do wrong. It would be just as absurd to suppose that there is a mean, an excess, and a deficiency in an unjust or a cowardly or a self-indulgent act. For if there were, we would have a mean of excess and a mean of deficiency, and an excess of excess and a deficiency of deficiency. Just as there cannot be an excess and a deficiency of self-control and courage—because the intermediate is, in a sense, an extreme—so there cannot be a mean, excess, and deficiency in their respective opposites: their opposites are wrong regardless of how they are performed; for, in general, there is no such thing as the mean of an excess of a deficiency, or the excess and deficiency of a mean.

HOW TO ATTAIN THE MEAN

Our discussion has sufficiently established (1) that moral virtue is a mean and in what sense it is a mean; (2) that it is a mean between two vices, one of which is marked by excess and the other by deficiency; and (3) that it is a mean in the sense that it aims at the median in the emotions and in actions. That is why it is a hard task to be good; in every case it is a task to find the median: for instance, not everyone can find the middle of a circle, but only a man who has the proper knowledge. Similarly, anyone can get angry—that is easy—or can give away money or spend it; but to do all this to the right person, to the right extent, at the right time, for the right reason, and in the right way is no longer something easy that anyone can do. It is for this reason that good conduct is rare, praiseworthy, and noble.

The first concern of a man who aims at the median should, therefore, be to avoid the extreme which is more opposed to it, as Calypso advises: "Keep clear your ship of yonder spray and surf." For one of the two extremes is more in error than the other, and since it is extremely difficult to hit the mean, we must, as the saying has it, sail in the second best way and take the lesser evil; and we can best do that in the manner we have described.

Moreover we must watch the errors which have the greatest attraction for us personally. For the natural inclination of one man differs from that of another, and we each come to recognize our own by observing the pleasure and pain produced in us [by the different extremes]. We must then draw ourselves away in the opposite direction, for by pulling away from error we shall reach the middle, as men do when they straighten warped timber. In every case we must be especially on our guard against pleasure and what is pleasant, for when it comes to pleasure we cannot act as unbiased judges. Our attitude toward pleasure should be the same as that of the Trojan elders was toward Helen, and we should repeat on every occasion the words they addressed to her. For if we dismiss pleasure as they dismissed her, we shall make fewer mistakes.

ARISTOTLE

from *The Poetics*

In the following passage from The Poetics, *Aristotle defines tragedy and identifies its elements or parts. The section focuses on plot, which, for Aristotle, is intimately and intricately related to character. Aristotle's comments about these two elements of drama have powerfully influenced literary criticism for nearly 2,500 years.*

Thus, Tragedy is an imitation of an action that is serious, complete, and possessing magnitude; in embellished language, each kind of which is used separately in the different parts; in the mode of action and not narrated; and effecting through pity and fear the *catharsis* of such emotions. By "embellished language" I mean language having rhythm and melody, and by "separately in different parts" I mean that some parts of a play are carried on solely in metrical speech while others again are sung.

THE CONSTITUENT PARTS OF TRAGEDY

Since the imitation is carried out in the dramatic mode by the personages themselves, it necessarily follows, first, that the arrangement of Spectacle will be a part of tragedy, and next, that Melody and Language will be parts, since these are the media in which they effect the imitation. By "language" I mean precisely the composition of the verses, by "melody" only that which is perfectly obvious. And since tragedy is the imitation of an action and is enacted by men in action, these persons must necessarily possess certain qualities of Character and Thought, since these are the basis for our ascribing qualities to the actions themselves—character and thought are two natural causes of actions—and it is in their actions that men universally meet with success or failure. The imitation of the action is the Plot. By plot I here mean the combination of the events; Character is that in virtue of which we say that the personages are of such and such a quality; and Thought is present in everything in their utterances that aims to prove a point or that expresses an opinion. Necessarily, therefore, there are in tragedy as a whole, considered as a special form, six constituent elements, viz. Plot, Characters, Language, Thought, Spectacle, and Melody. Of these elements, two are the *media* in which they effect the imitation, one is the *manner*, and three are the *objects* they imitate; and besides these there are no other parts. So then they employ these six forms, not just some of them, so to speak; for every drama has spectacle, character, plot, language, melody, and thought in the same sense, but the most important of them is the organization of the events [the plot].

PLOT AND CHARACTER

For tragedy is not an imitation of men but of actions and of life. It is in action that happiness and unhappiness are found, and the end we aim at is a kind of activity, not a quality; in accordance with their characters men are of such and such a quality, in accordance with their actions they are fortunate or the reverse. Consequently, it is not for the purpose of presenting their characters that the agents engage in action, but rather it is for the sake of their actions that they take on the characters they have. Thus, what happens—that is, the plot—is the end for which a tragedy exists, and the end of purpose is the most important thing of all. What is more, without action there could not be a tragedy, but there could be without characterization.

Now that the parts are established, let us next discuss what qualities the plot should have, since plot is the primary and most important part of tragedy. I have posited that tragedy is an imitation of an action that is a whole and complete in itself and of a certain magnitude—for a thing may be a whole, and yet have no magnitude to speak of. Now a thing is a whole if it has a beginning, a middle, and an end. A beginning is that which does not come necessarily after something else, either as its necessary sequel or as its usual sequel, but itself has nothing after it. A middle is that which both comes after something else and has another thing following it. A well-constructed plot, therefore, will neither begin at some chance point nor end at some chance point, but will observe the principles here stated.

Contrary to what some people think, a plot is not ipso facto a unity if it revolves about one man. Many things, indeed an endless number of things, happened to any one man some of which do not go together to form a unity, and similarly among the action one man performs there are many that do not go together to produce a single unified action. Those poets seem all to have erred, therefore, who have composed a *Heracleid*, a *Theseid*, and other such poems, it being their idea evidently that since Heracles was one man, their plot was bound to be unified.

From what has already been said, it will be evident that the poet's function is not to report things that have happened, but rather to tell of such things as might happen, things that are possibilities by virtue of being in themselves inevitable or probable. Thus the difference between the historian and the poet is not that the historian employs prose and poet verse—the work of Herodotus could be put into verse, and it be no less a history with verses than without them; rather the difference is that the one tells of things that have been and the other such things as might be. Poetry, therefore, is a more philosophical and a higher thing than history, in that poetry tends rather to express the universal, history rather the particular fact. A universal is: The sort of thing that (in the circumstances) a certain kind of person will say or do either probably or necessarily, which in fact is the universal that poetry aims for (with the addition of names for the persons); a particular, on the other hand, is: What Alcibiades did or had done to him.

Among plots and actions of the simple type, the episodic form is the worst. I call episodic a plot in which the episodes follow one another in no probable or inevitable sequence. Plots of this kind are constructed by bad poets on their own account, and by good poets on account of the actors; since they are composing entries for a competitive exhibition, they stretch the plot beyond what it can bear and are often compelled, therefore, to dislocate the natural order.

Some plots are simple, others complex; indeed the actions of which the plots are imitation are at once so differentiated to begin with. Assuming the action to be continuous and unified, as already defined, I call that action simple in which the change of fortune takes place without a reversal or recognition, and that action complex in which the change of fortune involves a recognition or a reversal or both. These events ought to be so rooted in the very structure of the plot that they follow from the preceding events as their inevitable or probable outcome; for there is a vast difference between following from and merely following after.

Reversal (Peripety) is, as aforesaid, a change from one state of affairs to its exact opposite, and this, too, as I say, should be in conformance with probability or necessity. For example, in *Oedipus*, the messenger comes to cheer Oedipus by relieving him of fear with regard to his mother, but by revealing his true identity, does just the opposite of this.

Recognition, as the word itself indicates, is a change from ignorance to knowledge, leading either to friendship or hostility on the part of those persons who are marked for good fortune or bad. The best form of recognition is that which is accompanied by a reversal, as in the example from *Oedipus*.

Next in order after the points I have just dealt with, it would seem necessary to specify what one should aim at and what avoid in the construction of plots, and what it is that will produce the effect proper to tragedy.

Now since in the finest kind of tragedy the structure should be complex and not simple, and since it should also be a representation of terrible and piteous events (that being the special mark of this type of imitation), in the first place,

it is evident that good men ought not to be shown passing from prosperity to misfortune, for this does not inspire either pity or fear, but only revulsion; nor evil men rising from ill fortune to prosperity, for this is the most untragic plot of all—it lacks every requirement, in that it neither elicits human sympathy nor stirs pity or fear. And again, neither should an extremely wicked man be seen falling from prosperity into misfortune, for a plot so constructed might indeed call forth human sympathy, but would not excite pity or fear, since the first is felt for a person whose misfortune is undeserved and the second for someone like ourselves—pity for the man suffering undeservedly, fear for the man like ourselves—and hence neither pity nor fear would be aroused in this case. We are left with the man whose place is between these extremes. Such is the man who on the one hand does not fall into misfortune through vice or depravity, but falls because of some mistake; one among the number of the highly renowned and prosperous, such as Oedipus and Thyestes and other famous men from families like theirs.

It follows that the plot which achieves excellence will necessarily be single in outcome and not, as some contend, double, and will consist in a change of fortune, not from misfortune to prosperity, but the opposite from prosperity to misfortune, occasioned not by depravity, but by some great mistake on the part of one who is either such as I have described or better than this rather than worse. (What actually has taken place confirms this; for though at first the poets accepted whatever myths came to hand, today the finest tragedies are founded upon the stories of only a few houses, being concerned, for example, with Alcmeon, Oedipus, Orestes, Meleager, Thyestes, Telephus, and such others as have chanced to suffer terrible things or to do them.) So, then, tragedy having this construction is the finest kind of tragedy from an artistic point of view. And consequently, those persons fall into the same error who bring it as a charge against Euripides that this is what he does in his tragedies and that most of his plays have unhappy endings. For this is in fact the right procedure, as I have said; and the best proof is that on the stage and in the dramatic contests, plays of this kind seem the most tragic, provided they are successfully worked out, and Euripides, even if in everything else his management is faulty, seems at any rate the most tragic of the poets.

In the characters and the plot construction alike, one must strive for that which is either necessary or probable, so that whatever a character of any kind says or does may be the sort of thing such a character will inevitably or probably say or do and the events of the plot may follow one after another either inevitably or with probability.

CHAPTER 4

Roman Civilization

Roman man holding busts of his ancestors. Late first century B.C.E., marble, lifesize, Musei Capitolini, Rome, Italy. Photograph © Scala/Art Resource, NY.

MAP 4.1 The expansion of Roman rule to 200 B.C.E.

CHAPTER OVERVIEW

ETRUSCAN CIVILIZATION
Rome's ancestors set the stage for greatness

THE ROMAN REPUBLIC
Conquest, feats of engineering, and portrait sculpture

THE EMPIRE
All roads lead to Rome—Augustus builds, Constantine converts to Christianity

THE GREEK LEGACY
AND THE ROMAN IDEAL

IN MANY WAYS, ROME INHERITED ITS culture—its art, its literature, its philosophical and religious life—from Greece. By the seventh century B.C.E., and along with the Latins, Etruscans, and Celts, the Greeks occupied parts of the Italian peninsula. This ensured the influence of Greek ways on the developing Italian culture. However, it was the later Roman determination to control and rule the entire Western world that consolidated the Hellenization of the West and much of the Eastern world. Even more effectively than Alexander the Great, the Romans spread Greek art and literature as far as Britain in the north, Africa in the south, the Euphrates River in the east, and Spain in the west. Apart from disseminating Greek culture, Roman civilization produced remarkable achievements of its own, in the fields of politics, law, and engineering.

ETRUSCAN CIVILIZATION

While the Greeks were settling in southern Italy and Sicily, another people—the Etruscans—inhabited the central Italian mainland. Little is known about the Etruscans. Their alphabet is derived from Greek, but their language seems unique, insofar as can be judged from the small amount of undeciphered literature and the few inscriptions on works of art that survive. Herodotus, the fifth-century B.C.E. Greek historian, said that the Etruscans came to Italy from Lydia (Turkey) in Asia Minor around 800 B.C.E. Dionysius of Halicarnassus, however, claims they were an indigenous Italian people, which appears more likely.

Etruscan civilization proper dates from about 700 B.C.E. and was at its peak in the seventh and sixth centuries B.C.E.—the same time as the Archaic period in Greece. While Etruscan civilization was at its height, the future imperial capital of Rome remained little more than a cluster of mud huts inhabited by shepherds and farmers known as Latins. Why Rome would eventually be transformed into the most powerful city in the world is difficult to say, except that, positioned on the south bank of the Tiber River in central Italy, it was midway between the Etruscan settlements to the north and the Greek colonies in the south of the peninsula. Rome thus lay on the trade route between the two civilizations. The Etruscans were influenced by the Greeks and came to know them literally "through" Rome. They sent skillfully manufactured bronze household utensils down the Tiber through Rome and on to the Greeks in the south in return for Greek vases, many of which have been found in Etruscan tombs. Greek heroes and deities were incorporated into the Etruscan pantheon, and their temples reflected Greek influence. In turn, the Etruscans exerted an important civilizing influence over the Latins in Rome.

FIGURE 4.1 Reconstruction of an Etruscan temple according to Vitruvius, Instituto di Etruscologia e Antichità Italiche, University of Rome. To a great extent, the Etruscan temple form was a modification of the Greek. Different from the Greek, however, are the high flight of stairs on one side only, deeper porch, and wider cella.

ARCHITECTURE

Temples. Only the stone foundations of Etruscan temples have survived. Fortunately, the ancient Roman author and architect VITRUVIUS [vi-TROO-vee-us] (fl. first century C.E.) described an Etruscan temple, on the basis of which it has been possible to create a reconstruction (fig. 4.1).

The Etruscan temple was similar to the Greek temple in its rectangular plan, raised podium, and peaked roof. Some temples were built with columns of the **Tuscan order,** which is the Doric order modified by the addition of a base. Nonetheless, the Etruscan temple differs from the Greek temple in several significant ways. For instance, the Etruscan temple has steps on only one side, whereas the Greek temple has steps on all four sides. The Etruscan temple has a deep front porch, occupying much more of the platform than is occupied by the porch of a Greek temple. And the cella (enclosed part) of the Etruscan temple is divided into three rooms, further differing from the Greek temple plan.

Tombs. Although Etruscan temples have disappeared, a significant number of tombs remain. Etruscan tombs were rich with weapons, gold work, and vases. As a result, like their Egyptian and Mycenaean counterparts, they were the targets of grave robbers. Scientific excavation of Etruscan tombs began only in the mid—nineteenth century.

The tombs are of two types: corbeled domes covered with mounds of earth, and rock-cut chambers with rectangular rooms. The most famous and most impressive of the rock-cut tombs at the ancient site of Cerveteri is the so-called Tomb of the Reliefs (fig. 4.2), of the third century B.C.E. The tomb is made of **tufa,** a type of stone that is soft when cut, but hardens when exposed to the air and tends to remain white. Such tombs were used for families; this one has places for over forty bodies. The interior of the

FIGURE 4.2   Tomb of the Reliefs, Cerveteri, third century B.C.E., interior. This exceptional tomb is believed to duplicate an actual Etruscan home in stone, even including pillows and pets. An entire family was buried here.

Tomb of the Reliefs replicates a home and provides a document of Etruscan life. The beds even have stone pillows! Roof beams are carved, and on the walls are depictions of weapons, armor, household items, and busts of the dead. The column capitals are similar to an early Ionic type brought to Greece from Asia Minor, which supports Herodotus's theory that the Etruscans originated in Lydia.

Other tombs were painted with scenes from everyday life. Particularly fine examples have been found at Tarquinia, where the subjects include scenes of hunting and fishing, banquets, musicians, dancers, athletic competitions, and religious ceremonies. The paintings in the Tomb of Hunting and Fishing (fig. 4.3), of ca. 520 B.C.E., in which fish jump out of the water in front of a man who attempts to catch them, and birds fly around a man who attempts to shoot one with a sling shot, convey a sense of energy and even humor.

This wall painting is presumably a view of the afterlife. Its optimism is also seen in Etruscan sculpture. An early example is offered by a wife and husband sarcophagus, from Cerveteri (fig. 4.4), ca. 520 B.C.E. The sarcophagus, mod-

eled in clay and once brightly painted, is shaped like a couch, with the deceased couple shown to recline on top; women and men were social equals. Like contemporary Greek statues, the pair have Archaic smiles (see Chapter 2). They are shown as if alive, comfortable, healthy, and happy, although they do not seem to be individualized portraits.

SCULPTURE

The Etruscans were celebrated in antiquity for their ability to work in metal. Their homeland of Tuscany (which is named for the Etruscans) is rich in copper and iron and provided ample raw materials. From 600 B.C.E. onward, the Etruscans produced many bronze statuettes and utensils, some of which they exported. The most famous Etruscan bronze sculpture is the so-called *Capitoline She-Wolf* (fig. 4.5), of ca. 500 B.C.E. The two suckling babes, the legendary twin founders of the city, Romulus and Remus, were added in the Renaissance. However, the she-wolf is authentic and has the energy and vitality characteristic of

FIGURE 4.3   Tomb of Hunting and Fishing, Tarquinia, wall painting, ca. 520 B.C.E. This and other tomb paintings record the good life when Etruria prospered in the sixth century B.C.E. Later, as the economic situation declined, the outlook on the afterlife was less optimistic.

FIGURE 4.4   Wife and Husband Sarcophagus, from Cerveteri, ca. 520 B.C.E., terra cotta, length 6'7" (2.01 m), Museo Nazionale di Villa Giulia, Rome. The deceased couple is shown as if alive, healthy, and enjoying themselves. The rounded forms are readily achieved in malleable terra cotta, unlike hard stone.

FIGURE 4.5   *Capitoline She-Wolf*, ca. 500 B.C.E., bronze, height 33½" (85.1 cm), Museo Capitolino, Rome. The Etruscans were famed in antiquity for their fine metalwork. With the twin infants, added in the Renaissance, this Etruscan bronze has become the symbol of Rome.

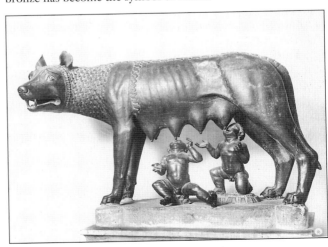

Etruscan art. A beautiful decorative surface is achieved by contrasting the crisp, curving patterns of the neck fur with the wolf's sleek, smooth body.

THE ROMAN REPUBLIC

Beginning with Romulus, Rome was ruled first by a succession of kings and then, in 509 B.C.E., constituted itself a republic, which lasted until 27 B.C.E. Romulus himself is said to have established the traditional Roman distinction between the **patricians,** the land-owning aristocrats who served as priests and magistrates, lawyers and judges, and the **plebeians,** the poorer class who tilled the land, herded livestock, and worked for wages as craftspeople, tradespeople, and laborers. To complicate this traditional distinction, however, there is evidence of wealthy plebeian families and poor patricians. In fact, the distinction between these Roman social strata may very well have been one of "first" families versus later immigrants.

Initially, the plebeians depended on the patricians for support. According to one ancient historian, each plebeian in Romulus's Rome could choose for himself any patrician as a patron, initiating the system known as **patronage.**

The essentially paternalistic relationship of patrician to plebeian reflects the family's central role in Roman society. At the head of the family was the *pater*, the father, and it was his duty to protect not only his wife and children, but also his clients, those who had submitted to his patronage. In return for the *pater*'s protection, his family and his clients were obligated to give him their total obedience and to defer to him in all things—an attitude the Romans referred to as *pietas.* The patrician males led the state as they led the family, contributing to the state's well-being in return for the people's gratitude and veneration. So fundamental was this attitude that by imperial times, the Roman emperor was referred to as the *pater patriae*, "the father of the fatherland."

From the outset, the republic was plagued by conflict between the patricians and the plebeians. There was obvious political inequality. The Senate, the political assembly responsible for formulating new law, was almost exclusively patrician. Thus the plebeians formed their own legislative assembly, the Consilium Plebis, electing their own officers, called tribunes, to protect them from the patrician magistrates. Initially, patricians were not subject to legislation passed by the plebeian assembly—the plebiscite. Finally, in 287 B.C.E., however, the plebiscite became binding legislation on all citizens, whether plebeian or patrician, and something resembling equal citizenship was established for all.

At about the same time, Rome began a series of military campaigns that would, eventually, result in its control of the largest and most powerful empire ever created. By the middle of the third century B.C.E., Rome had established dominion over the Italian peninsula. Beginning in 264 B.C.E., the city inaugurated a series of campaigns against Carthage, a Phoenician state in North Africa. The Punic Wars ensued (from the Latin *poeni*, meaning "Phoenician"). When they ended, in 146 B.C.E., Carthage had been razed, and Rome had established an overseas empire, with control over the islands of Sicily, Corsica, and Sardinia.

The Roman army had traditionally been made up of citizen property owners, but in about 107 B.C.E., a general named Gaius Marius began to enroll men in the army who did not meet the property or citizenship qualification. These men saw military service as a career, and a professional army was soon in place. Each soldier served for twenty years and, when not involved in combat, was occupied by the construction of roads, bridges, and aqueducts. At the end of their service, they were given land in the province where they had served, as well as Roman citizenship.

The financial opportunities afforded by imperial conquest stimulated the growth of a new "class" of Roman citizen. Born into families that could pursue senatorial status, these men instead chose careers in business and finance. They called themselves *equites* ("equestrians"), probably because they served in the cavalry in the military—only the wealthy could afford horses—and they embraced a commercial world that their patrician brothers (sometimes quite literally their brothers) found crass and demeaning. By the first century B.C.E., these *equites* were openly in conflict with the Senate, pressing for greater and greater rights for both themselves and the plebeians.

Civil war among Roman political factions soon erupted. The general LUCIUS CORNELIUS SULLA [SOO-lah] ruled as dictator from 82 to 79 B.C.E., murdering thousands of his opponents and introducing a new constitution, that placed power firmly in the hands of the Senate. But all he finally succeeded in doing was exacerbating the situation. Struggles for power between Gaeus Pompeius Magnus—Pompey the Great—and GAIUS JULIUS CAESAR [SEE-zar] (fig. 4.6) finally ended in 48 B.C.E. with Caesar's defeat of Pompey. Caesar became dictator of an empire that included Italy, Spain, Greece, Syria, Egypt, and North Africa. In 45 B.C.E., on the Ides of March—March 15—Caesar himself was assassinated. The civil wars that followed brought the republic to a definitive end, and Caesar's adopted grand-nephew and heir, Octavian, became the sole power in Rome, the *pater patriae*, "father of the fatherland." Renaming himself Augustus, "the revered one," Caesar Augustus reigned as emperor from 27 B.C.E. until 14 C.E.

ART OF THE ROMAN REPUBLIC

Although the Romans conquered the Greeks militarily and politically, the Greeks conquered the Romans artistically and culturally. As the first-century B.C.E. poet Horace put it, "*Graecia capta ferum victorem cepit*" ("Captive Greece conquered her wild conqueror"). Roman writers rarely make reference to Roman artists. Instead, they write about

Cross Currents

THE ROMAN PANTHEON

The major gods of the Romans were essentially the same as those of the Greeks. In adopting the Greek gods, the Romans demonstrated in yet another way how the great military conquerors were themselves conquered by Greek culture. The accompanying chart identifies the deities of Rome with their Greek counterparts and their corresponding roles and responsibilities:

Greek	Roman	Role/Function
Zeus	Jupiter/Jove	chief god/sky
Hera	Juno	wife of Zeus/Jove
Eros	Cupid	god of love
Dionysos	Bacchus	god of wine/revelry
Demeter	Ceres	earth goddess/grain

Greek	Roman	Role/Function
Persephone	Proserpina	queen of the underworld
Aphrodite	Venus	goddess of love and beauty
Ares	Mars	god of war
Apollo	Apollo	god of sun, music, and the arts
Artemis	Diana	goddess of the hunt
Hermes	Mercury	messenger of the gods
Poseidon	Neptune	god of the sea
Hades	Pluto	god of the underworld
Athena	Minerva	goddess of wisdom
Hephaistos	Vulcan	god of metalwork

There were, nonetheless, some important differences in the way the Romans viewed their gods. The Roman pantheon reflected the culture's political rather than spiritual values, and Roman gods tended to be less embodiments of various human virtues and foibles and more personifications of abstract ideas—love, war, and fortune, for instance.

The Romans also had a vast array of other, local gods. Every place, tree, stream, meadow, and wood had its own spirit. Unlike the gods of Greek origin, anthropomorphic, or human, characteristics were rarely attributed to these spirits. However, it was essential for, say, a farmer to keep on good terms with the spirit of his fields. Because so much depended on annual water flow, the sources of rivers were especially venerated spots and often decorated with numerous shrines.

the Greek masters—Polykleitos, Phidias, Praxiteles, Lysippos. Roman authors refer to the Greeks as the "ancients"; Greek art already had the authority of antiquity for the Romans. The Romans not only imported Greek vases, marbles, and bronzes, but Greek artists as well, many of whom they then put to work copying Greek originals.

Yet Roman art is not solely a continuation of Greek art. The Romans were very different from the Greeks, and their art is accordingly different in emphasis and focus. The Romans were impressed with great size—the size of their empire, of their buildings, of their sculptures. Above all, the Romans were a practical people. They were superb engineers. Their sculpture and painting is realistic, with an emphasis on particulars—specific people, places, and times—a trend that continued until the second century C.E., when Christianity began to foster a more abstract and mystical direction.

Architecture The Romans adopted the Greek orders—the Doric, Ionic, and Corinthian—but made modifications. Directly influenced by the Tuscan order of Etruscan architecture, the Romans made Doric columns taller and slimmer and gave them a base. The acanthus leaves of the Corinthian order were combined with the volutes of the Ionic order to create the **composite order.** The Romans used the orders with greater freedom than the Greeks, often taking elements from each for use on a single building. The Romans used the Corinthian order most, the Doric least—the opposite of the Greeks. Unlike Greek architects, Roman architects often used **engaged columns** (columns that are attached to the wall) on the inside and outside of buildings.

Much Roman building, like Greek building, was done with ashlar masonry, using carefully cut stone blocks laid in horizontal courses. But in the late second century B.C.E., the Romans developed a type of wall made by setting small broken stones in cement. Such walls were very strong and could be faced with different types of patterned stonework. This construction method opened new directions in architecture, including construction using **concrete,** which consists of cement mixed with small pieces of stone. Concrete is strong, can be cast into any shape, and is far less costly than stone construction. Although the Romans did not invent concrete, they developed its potential.

The rectangular Ionic Temple of "Fortuna Virilis" in Rome (fig. 4.7) was built late second to mid–first century B.C.E. and was probably dedicated to Portunus, the Roman god of harbors and rivers. Etruscan elements include the raised platform or podium, the entry on one end only by ascending a flight of stairs, a front porch that takes up

FIGURE 4.6   Portrait bust of Julius Caesar, first century B.C.E., marble, height 38″ (96.5 cm), Museo Archeologico Nazionale, Naples. Like all Roman portrait sculpture of the time, the bust is stunningly realistic. Every anomaly of the facial terrain has been observed and recorded.

FIGURE 4.7   Temple of "Fortuna Virilis," Rome, late second to mid-first century B.C.E. The rectangular Roman temple form is essentially a combination of the Greek and Etruscan temple forms—compare to the Greek Parthenon (see fig. 3.3) and the Etruscan temple (see fig. 4.1).

about one-third of the whole podium area, and a cella nearly as wide as the podium.

The Romans, however, unlike the Greeks, favored circular temples, an example being the Temple of Vesta in Rome (fig. 4.8), built ca. 80 B.C.E. Vesta was the goddess of the hearth and of fire. The temple is simple in plan and small in scale. Circular Roman temples were made of concrete and faced with brick or stone. The Corinthian columns here are tall and slender. The entablature is much reduced and the roof rests almost directly on the columns.

Aqueducts.   The Romans constructed an extensive network of **aqueducts** throughout their territories. Some of the aqueducts were many miles long, crossing valleys, spanning rivers, going over mountains and even passing underground. In Rome itself, beginning in 144 B.C.E., a system of aqueducts brought water to all seven of the city's hills, paid for by spoils from the victory in Carthage.

The most famous and best preserved of the ancient Roman aqueducts is the Pont du Gard (bridge over the Gard River) at Nîmes, in southern France (fig. 4.9), built first century B.C.E.–first century C.E. The Pont du Gard is based on a series of arches, each arch buttressed by the arches on either side of it. The water channel is at the very

top and is lined with cement. Flat stone slabs were placed over the top to keep out leaves and debris.

Sculpture.   The ancient Romans made extensive use of sculpture—on both the inside and outside of public and private buildings, on columns, arches, tombs, and elsewhere.

The Romans imported and copied Greek statues, and they modeled their own sculpture on that of the Greeks. But whereas the Greeks made statues of deities and idealized heroes, Roman sculpture focused on individual people, particularly political figures.

A Roman Patrician with Busts of His Ancestors (fig. 4.10), from the late first century B.C.E., also makes clear the great emphasis placed on lineage by the ancient Romans. The high level of realism may have been assisted by the custom of making deathmasks, called *imagines* by the Romans. Shortly after death, a wax mask was modeled on the face of the deceased and was then sometimes transferred to stone. Masks of the ancestors of the deceased were carried or worn in funeral processions, and portrait busts and *imagines* of ancestors were generally displayed in homes. This man wears the toga, a garment fashionable in the Republican era.

FIGURE 4.8 Temple of Vesta, ca. 80 B.C.E., Rome. In addition to perpetuating the Greek and Etruscan rectangular temple, the Romans made significant use of the circular temple. Among the orders, Greeks used the simple Doric most, whereas the Romans preferred the ornate Corinthian order, seen here.

FIGURE 4.9 Pont du Gard, Nîmes, France, late first century B.C.E.—early first century C.E., height 180′ (54.9 m), current length approx. 900′ (275 m). Between 8,000 and 12,000 gallons of water were delivered to Nîmes per day through this aqueduct, which extended for thirty-one miles.

LITERATURE

Like their counterparts in the visual arts, Roman writers owe an immense debt to the Greeks. For the most part, Roman poets used Greek genres, although satire appears to have been a Roman invention. Roman playwrights sometimes adapted Greek plays, with varying degrees of ingenuity.

Catullus Like the Greek lyric poet Sappho, CATULLUS [ka-TUL-us] (84–54 B.C.E.) wrote passionate love poems, one of which is, in fact, a translation into Latin of one of Sappho's most celebrated lyrics, "Seizure."

Reflecting daily life in first-century B.C.E. Rome, many of Catullus's poems are written in a racy colloquial style. Catullus also wrote twenty-five poems about his love affair with Lesbia. These demonstrate his range and show him at his passionate best. Catullus can also be moving in expressing grief, as his lament for the death of his brother demonstrates.

Roman Drama: Plautus and Terence Although Greek theater excelled in the grandeur of tragedy, the theatrical glory of Rome is its comedy. The two most important

Roman comic dramatists are PLAUTUS [PLOW-tus] (ca. 254–184 B.C.E.) and Terence (195–159 B.C.E.). Terence's plays were aimed at an aristocratic audience, by whom he was subsidized; Plautus wrote for the common people. Not surprisingly, Plautus is the more robust and ribald of the two. Although the plays of both dramatists are humorous, Terence's wit is more cerebral than Plautus's, which more often elicits a belly laugh. Despite these differences, the works of both playwrights are adaptations of Greek comedy.

Terence offers subtlety of plot for Plautus's farce; he provides character development and interplay for Plautus's stock figures; and he presents economical dialogue in place of Plautus's colorful wordplay. Terence more obviously exhibits tolerance for his characters and appreciation for their mixed motives and muddled but often good intentions. He is more sympathetic toward the elderly, particularly the old fathers that Plautus ridicules. Terence is also more interested in women than Plautus, generally making them more complex and interesting characters.

Plautus's chief characters, those who run the dramatic engine of his plots, are typically slaves and parasites who turn the tables on their masters. With a notable lack of respect for authority, Plautus's characters flout social regulations, especially by undermining figures of authority—masters, fathers, and husbands. In Plautine comedy, slaves outwit their masters, sons fool their fathers, and wives dupe their husbands.

FIGURE 4.10 A Roman man holding busts of his ancestors. Late first century B.C.E., marble, lifesize, Museo Capitolino, Rome, Italy. Photograph © Scala/Art Resource, NY. The great importance Romans attached to family and lineage, exemplified here in this austere sculpture, is one of the motivating forces in the development of highly realistic portraiture during the Republican era.

THE EMPIRE

When Octavian, Caesar Augustus (63 B.C.E.–14 C.E.), as he was soon known, assumed power in 27 B.C.E., he claimed to have restored the Republic. In reality, however, he had complete authority over not only the Senate but over all of Roman life. By 12 C.E. he had been given the title *Pontifex Maximus,* or "High Priest," and when he died, two years later, the Senate ordered that he be venerated henceforth as a god. Together with his wife Livia, who was herself a skilled administrator, he created the conditions for a period of peace and stability in the empire that lasted for two hundred years. Known as the *Pax Romana,* the "Roman Peace," it was made possible in large part by Augustus's sensitivity to the people that Rome had conquered. Augustus dispatched governors to all the provinces with armies to maintain law and order. But these armies, freed of the need to conduct wars, turned to building great public works—aqueducts, theaters, libraries, marketplaces, and roads. Trade was greatly facilitated, and economic prosperity spread throughout the empire. Rome, however, remained at the heart of this trade network. After nearly a century of political turmoil, Augustus's rule ushered in a new Golden Age. The art and literature of the Augustan period are regarded as the pinnacle of Roman cultural accomplishment.

The empire was so strong by the end of Augustus's reign that even a series of debauched and decadent emperors, such as CALIGULA [cal-IG-you-lah] (12–41 C.E.) and NERO [NEAR-oh] (37–68 C.E.), could not destroy it.

There were also some very able emperors, including the so-called "Five Good Emperors"—NERVA [NER-vah] (r. 96–98 C.E.), TRAJAN [TRA-jan] (r. 98–117 C.E.), HADRIAN [HAY-dree-an] (r. 117–138 C.E.), ANTONINUS PIUS [PIE-us] (r. 138–161 C.E.), and MARCUS AURELIUS [OW-REE-lee-us] (r. 161–180 C.E.). These five ruled for eighty-four consecutive years, during which Rome flourished as never before. By 180 C.E. the Roman empire had grown to enormous proportions, extending from Spain in the west to the Persian Gulf in the Middle East, and from Britain and the Rhine River in the north to Egypt and the Sahara Desert in the south. It encompassed some 1,750,000 square miles and about fifty million people.

However, beginning with the rule of Marcus Aurelius's son COMMODUS [coh-MODE-us] (r. 180–192 C.E.), the empire started to flounder. His murder inaugurated a series of civil wars. Of the twenty-six emperors to rule between 235 and 284 C.E., twenty-five were murdered, as various military factions vied for power. In addition, plague ravaged Rome—between 251 and 266 C.E. many thousands of Romans died from it. And, perhaps most ominously, the empire's borders began to be seriously threatened by barbarian hordes.

In 284 C.E., DIOCLETIAN [DI-oh-CLEE-shun] briefly restored order by dividing the empire into four portions—the **tetrarchy**—and assumed personal control of Asia Minor, Syria, and Egypt. His counterpart in the West, also designated "Augustus," was MAXIMIAN [mac-SIM-ee-an].

Then & Now

PLAUTUS AND THE CONTEMPORARY BROADWAY THEATER

Plautus has been called "the father of musical comedy." This designation applies not only because his plays include numerous and extensive song passages, but also because of his enormous influence on subsequent drama, including the contemporary Broadway stage. Unfortunately, the music for the songs in Plautus's plays has long been lost. Only the lyrics remain.

Nevertheless, Plautus is alive and well in modern American theater. In the 1930s, and again in the 1990s, his popular *Menaechmi (The Menaechmi Twins)* was turned into an American musical entitled *The Boys from Syracuse* (the Italian, not the New York, city). The *Menaechmi* had earlier been transformed by Shakespeare into *The Comedy of Errors*, which, like Plautus's original, revolves around the mistaken identities of identical twins. In the mid-1990s, Broadway was home to a revival of *A Funny Thing Happened on the Way to the Forum*, which had an original Broadway run in 1962. This modern adaptation of Plautus mines the vein of comic gold found in three of Plautus's plays.

Why does Plautus's dramatic and comic genius speak to a contemporary American audience? Essentially for the same reasons it spoke to his Roman contemporaries: It pokes fun at sober pieties; it mocks conventional wisdom; and it expresses an irreverent attitude toward what is fashionable and important. It makes people laugh both at themselves and at their society, even while they remain obliged to live within it.

After the abdication of Diocletian and Maximian in 305 C.E., the tetrarchy briefly continued until CONSTANTINE [CON-stan-tine] seized control of the entire empire in 324, ruling until his death in 337. In 330, Constantine moved the seat of government from Rome to the port city of Byzantium, which he renamed Constantinople after himself—humility was not part of the job description of the Roman emperor (today the city, known as Istanbul, is in Turkey). Rome's long ascendancy as the cultural center of the Western world was at an end (see Chapter 6).

One invaluable source for our knowledge of the Roman empire was provided by a natural disaster. In 79, the volcano Vesuvius, located about 150 miles south of Rome near the bay of Naples, erupted, engulfing a number of small Roman towns, including the fashionable suburban residences of Herculaneum and Pompeii. Most inhabitants escaped—but with only their lives. Everything else was left in place, food literally still on the tables. Vesuvius buried Herculaneum in hot mud and lava that hardened like stone thirty-five to eighty feet deep. Pompeii was covered in twenty to thirty feet of pumice stone and ash. Excavation was begun at both sites in the mid-eighteenth century—a process that has been far easier at Pompeii, but which today is still not complete at either site and has provided a great deal of information on first-century C.E. life in the Roman empire. Our knowledge of Roman painting, for instance, would be immeasurably poorer without the evidence of these towns.

MUSIC

Our knowledge of Roman music is based on what we can learn from mosaics, sculpture, and the remains of brass instruments found on ancient battlefields. Just as Romans adopted much of Greek architecture, sculpture, poetry, and philosophy, so too Greek music was absorbed. Roman music differed, however. Whereas Greek music was basically contemplative and served as a background to plays and poetry, Roman music was loud and aggressive and featured in open-air games, festival parades, and military attacks.

Brass instruments such as the cornu (a "G"-shaped instrument) and the tuba (a long straight trumpet) played accompaniment through raging wars. These instruments were also used to communicate field orders and to announce important visitors. Applying their engineering skills, the Romans used the flow of water to power an organ that could be heard for miles. This instrument, called the hydraulos, was used in the Circus Maximus and the Colosseum to rouse the crowd, much like the organ at today's baseball games. This instrumental music, a painful reminder of Christians killed for sport, was banned from the early Christian church.

Roman pipers played a flutelike instrument at funerals and between acts at plays. Guests at a dinner party might be entertained by vocal and instrumental dinner music. Theater music evolved from interludes between acts to longer pieces that frequently appealed to the audience as much as the drama itself.

ARCHITECTURE

An active builder, Augustus once claimed to have restored eighty-two temples in a single year. Suetonius's *Lives of the Caesars* says that Augustus boasted, "I found Rome a city of brick, and left it a city of marble," although he did so largely by putting a marble veneer over the brick.

The Roman Forum.   One of Augustus's most ambitious projects was his forum, dedicated in 2 B.C.E. Augustus, a skilled manipulator of public opinion, gave political

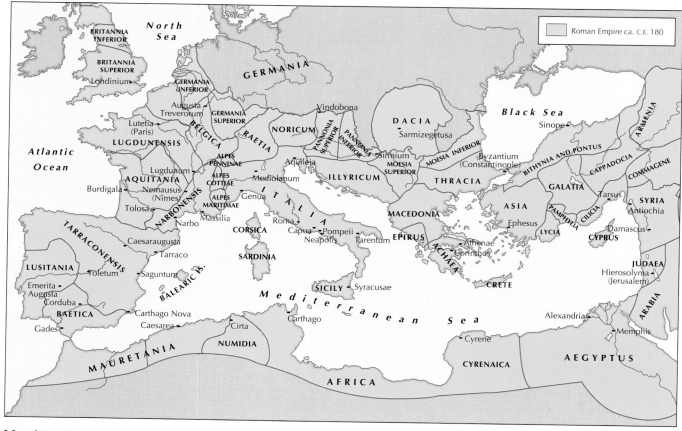

MAP 4.2 The Roman Empire at its greatest extent, ca. 180 C.E.

significance to this forum by dedicating its temple to Mars the Avenger. It was intended to serve as a reminder of the revenge he had taken on the murderers of his uncle, Julius Caesar, and the temple, with eight columns across its front, was one of the largest in the city, rivaling the Athenian Parthenon in size. The Forum of Augustus is actually one of many fora traditionally referred to collectively in the singular as "the forum." The Roman forum consists of nineteen fora—those of Julius Caesar, Augustus, Trajan, Nerva, a forum of peace, and so on—all abutting one another (fig. 4.11). The original use of the forum was similar to that of the Greek agora. The forum was the center of city life, the public area where assemblies were held, justice was administered, and markets were located. There were also a number of temples, such as two dedicated to Vesta, the Temple of Saturn, the Temple of Castor and Pollux, and the Temple of Antoninus Pius and Faustina. Although each forum was symmetrical in plan, the different fora were combined chaotically. The Romans, more cosmopolitan and materialistic than the ancient Greeks, built on a larger scale, using a greater variety of building materials, and paid less attention to minute details. The Roman predilection was for combining diverse elements to achieve a grand overall effect.

The Colosseum. Another form of public architecture was the theater. The celebrated Flavian Colosseum in Rome (fig. 4.12), so called because of its association with a colossal statue of the emperor Nero, was dedicated in 80 C.E. The Colosseum is an **amphitheater,** a type of building developed by the Romans. The word "theater" refers to the semicircular form. The prefix "amphi" means "both"; an amphitheater is a theater at both ends and therefore circular or oval in plan. The seating area of the Colosseum accommodated over fifty thousand people, each of whom had a clear view of the arena. To protect the audience from the brilliant Roman sunshine, an awning could be stretched over part of the Colosseum.

The supporting structure of the Colosseum is made of concrete, but the exterior was covered with a stone facing of **travertine** (a form of limestone) and tufa. Holes can now be seen in the stone where people dug to get at the bronze clamps that held the facing in place. These stones hide the supporting structure. This is fundamentally different from the Greek approach to architecture, where the structure was not hidden but, rather, emphasized.

On the exterior, entablatures separate the stories and engaged columns separate the arches. The three architectural orders are combined. On the lowest level is the Tuscan variation on the Doric order; above is the Ionic; and

FIGURE 4.11 Forum, Rome. A forum, a public area with markets, meeting places, and temples, was roughly the Roman equivalent of the Greek agora. The area of the forum in Rome was expanded over many years.

FIGURE 4.12 Colosseum, Rome, dedicated 80 C.E. The freestanding amphitheater, developed by the Romans, was made possible by the use of concrete and the arch principle. Compare this to the Greek theater of Epidauros where support for the seats is provided by the hillside (see fig. 3.16).

the third level is Corinthian. These columns, engaged to the wall, have no structural function; their only purpose is as surface decoration.

The practical Roman designers combined the use of concrete with another extremely important architectural development—the arch. The visitor to the Colosseum can enter or exit through any of eighty arches around the Colosseum at street level. Each of these arches is buttressed by its neighbors and buttresses its neighbors in turn, as is true of the Pont du Gard. The interior is constructed with vaulted corridors and many staircases to permit the free movement of a large number of people.

A tremendous number of amphitheaters were built throughout the empire because it was official policy that the state should provide entertainment for the public. This entertainment included several categories of bloody combat: human versus human; human versus animal; animal versus animal; and naval battles—the Colosseum could be flooded to accommodate warships. The quality of this "entertainment" soon turned into a political issue, but the displays nonetheless became progressively more extravagant.

The Pantheon. Built between 118 and 125 C.E. during the reign of Emperor Hadrian and designed by the architect Apollodorus of Damascus, the magnificent Roman Pantheon (fig. 4.13) is a large circular temple dedicated to

"all the gods" (the literal meaning of the word *pantheon*). Originally, steps led up to the entrance, but over the centuries the level of the street has been raised, and once there was also more to the porch. Otherwise, the Pantheon is very well preserved. In contrast to the Greek emphasis on the exterior of temples, the most important part of the Pantheon is the interior. Inside, the enormous dome that crowns this building is the focus of attention. The space is not interrupted by interior supports, creating a feeling of vast spaciousness (fig. 4.14). The Pantheon was considered the most harmonious interior of antiquity.

The dome, based upon the arch principle, is another of the great innovations of Roman architecture. A series of arches forms a **vault.** An arch rotated 180 degrees forms a **dome.**

The Pantheon's dome is raised on a high base, making the height and diameter of the dome the same—144 feet. The Pantheon was the largest dome until the twentieth century. The dome is made of concrete, the weight of which is concentrated on eight pillars distributed around its circumference. The **oculus,** the "eye" or opening in

FIGURE 4.13   Apollodorus of Damascus, Pantheon, Rome, 118–25 C.E., exterior. A superb display of Roman engineering skill, the Pantheon includes a variety of ingenious devices to deal with the lateral thrust exerted by the dome. The paradigm of circular temples, the Pantheon would prove to be the model for many buildings in the following centuries.

FIGURE 4.14   Giovanni Paolo Panini (Roman, 1691–1765), *Interior of the Pantheon, Rome,* ca. 1734, oil on canvas $50\frac{1}{2}'' \times 39''$ $(1.28 \times .99\,\mathrm{m})$, Samuel H. Kress Collection. Photograph © 2001 Board of Trustees, National Gallery of Art, Washington, DC, 1939. 124(135)/pA. Photo by Richard Carafelli.

the center of the ceiling, is thirty feet across and the sole source of light in the building. The squarish indentations in the dome, called **coffers,** were once plated with gold and each had a bronze rosette fastened in the center. The effect, with the brilliant sunlight of Rome coming from the central oculus above, must have been dazzling.

SCULPTURE

With Augustus's rise to power in 27 B.C.E., sculpture changed its style. Depictions of realistically rendered aging Republicans were jettisoned in favor of more idealized versions of youth and an increased taste for things Greek. This change in taste was in part the result of Augustus's efforts to import Greek craftspeople and artists. In the new Augustan style, Greek idealism was combined with Roman realism.

Augustus of Primaporta.   The statue the *Augustus of Primaporta* (fig. 4.15), of ca. 20 B.C.E., is a slightly over-lifesize marble figure that was intended to glorify the emperor and Roman peace under his rule. The face of the statue is recognizably that of Augustus; the same features are seen on other portraits of the emperor, although here they are somewhat idealized. Augustus is shown to be heroic, aloof, self-contained. A prototype is seen in figures such as the *Doryphoros* (*Spear-Bearer*) of Polykleitos (see fig. 3.11); indeed, Augustus probably held a spear in his left hand originally, but it has since been restored as a scepter. There is perhaps even a concession to traditional Greek nudity in showing the emperor barefoot. The grand gesture with one arm extended—as if addressing his troops—was a common pose. The cupid riding on a dolphin beside Augustus's right leg is an allusion to Aeneas's mother, Venus, in Virgil's heroic poem, *The Aeneid*, suggesting Augustus's own supposed divine heritage. The relief on Augustus's cuirass (breastplate) is symbolic and refers to the *Pax Romana*, the peace and harmony that prevailed under his reign.

The Ara Pacis.   At times the distinction between architecture and sculpture is blurred, for a building that is totally covered with relief sculpture, as is the *Ara Pacis* (*Altar of Peace*), built 13–9 B.C.E. by Augustus. Whether it is sculpture or architecture, however, it is undoubtedly the greatest artistic work of the Augustan age. Augustus billed himself as the "Prince of Peace," and this altar is an example of art used as political propaganda.

The *Ara Pacis* is a small rectangular building. Among the extensive reliefs that adorn its sides is an imperial procession including Augustus and Livia (fig. 4.16). Accompanying them is the imperial household, including children, priests, and dignitaries. These figures move along both of the side walls of the altar, converging toward the entrance. The degree of naturalism achieved in this marble relief is striking. The depictions of people are varied— some stand still, others talk with their neighbors, or form

FIGURE 4.15   *Augustus of Primaporta*, ca. 20 B.C.E., marble, height 6′ 8″ (2.03 m), Braccio Nuovo, Musei Vaticani, Rome. Although this statue does record the appearance of Emperor Augustus, under his reign harsh Roman republican realism was somewhat softened by Greek idealism.

groups, or look off in different directions; figures are seen from the front, from the side, and in three-quarter views. Drapery is skillfully rendered so that fabric falls naturalistically, yet also forms a pleasing rhythmic pattern of loops and curves across the whole relief.

An illusion of spatial recession has been created in stone relief. Figures in the front are a little larger than those in the back and are carved in higher relief. Because the different levels of relief create an illusion of space, blank areas between the figures no longer look like a solid wall but

FIGURE 4.16   *Ara Pacis*, relief of procession of figures, 13–9 B.C.E., height ca. 5′3″ (1.6 m). Augustus, now older, is depicted with his wife, Livia. Unlike the timeless, generalized, idealized Greek relief from the Parthenon (see fig. 3.6), the Roman relief shows specific people at a specific event.

rather read as actual space into and from which figures recede and emerge. A particularly clever illusionistic touch is the positioning of toes so they protrude over the ledge on which the figures stand. It is as if the figures are genuinely three dimensional and capable of stepping out of their space and into ours, adding to the immediacy of the work.

The Column of Trajan.   Columns, usually erected to celebrate a military victory, are another distinctively Roman form of movement. The emperor Trajan (r. 98–117 C.E.) erected the Column of Trajan (fig. 4.17) in the Forum of Trajan in Rome in 106–113 C.E. The creator of the Pantheon, Apollodorus of Damascus, designed the column.

The base is made of huge blocks with a square stairway inside, while a circular stairway consisting of 182 steps winds around the interior of the actual column. The surface of the column is covered with a continuous band of relief 656 feet long that makes twenty-three turns as it spirals upward like a twisting tapestry. The relief consists of about 150 scenes and 2,500 figures.

The reliefs (fig. 4.18), reading from the bottom to the top, document an actual event—the military campaign of 101–03 C.E. to subdue the forces of Decebalus, prince of Dacia, present-day Romania. This was the first of Rome's wars against the Dacians. In the second, in 105–07 C.E., Trajan completely destroyed his enemy.

The Equestrian Statue of Marcus Aurelius.   The overlifesize equestrian statue of Emperor Marcus Aurelius (fig. 4.19), of 164–66 C.E., became a favorite type of commemorative sculpture. This statue has survived to the present only because it was long mistaken for a portrait of Constantine, the first Christian emperor, and was thus spared the fate of being melted down as so many other "pagan" Roman bronzes were (for instance, the statue of Trajan on top of his column—see fig. 4.17). A philosopher-emperor, gentle and wise, who held Stoic beliefs, Marcus Aurelius

FIGURE 4.17   Apollodorus of Damascus, Column of Trajan, Rome, 106–13 C.E., marble, height with base 125′ (38.1 m). In spite of the obvious difficulty the viewer encounters in following a story told in a relief that spirals around a column rising high above, this was not the only such commemorative column erected by the Romans.

is garbed in the traditional robes of the Republican philosophers. He subdues his enemies without weapons or armor—originally, a barbarian lay beneath the horse's upraised hoof—and in victory brings with him the promise of peace.

Connections

THE *ARA PACIS* AND THE POLITICS OF FAMILY LIFE

Three generations of Augustus's family appear in the section of the *Ara Pacis* illustrated in fig. 4.16. On the left, his head covered by his robe, is Marcus Agrippa. At the time of the carving he was married to Augustus's daughter Julia and was next in line to be emperor after Augustus, but he died in 12 C.E., two years before Augustus himself. Next to him in the relief is his eldest son, Gaius Caesar, who clings to Agrippa's robe. Augustus was particularly fond of Gaius and his younger brother Lucius. The two boys often traveled with the emperor, and he took on important aspects of their education, teaching them to swim, to read, and to imitate his own handwriting. The proud grandmother, Augustus's wife Livia, stands beside Marcus Agrippa and Gaius Caesar. Behind her is her own son Tiberius, who would in fact succeed Augustus as emperor. Behind Tiberius is Antonia, Augustus's niece and the wife of Tiberius's brother Drusus, at whom she is looking. Antonia holds the hand of her and Drusus's son, Germanicus. Drusus's nephew Gnaeus clings to his uncle's robe.

In the period before the *Ara Pacis*, there are very few examples of depictions of children in Roman public sculpture, a fact that raises an important question: What moved Augustus to include children so conspicuously in this monument? By the time Augustus took control of Rome, slaves and freed slaves threatened to outnumber Roman citizens in Rome itself, and they clearly outnumbered the Roman nobility. Augustus took this seriously and saw it as the result of a crisis in Roman family life. Adultery and divorce had become commonplace. Furthermore, the cost of maintaining a family was increasing. Consequently Roman families were becoming smaller and smaller.

Augustus introduced a series of measures to combat this decline in the traditional Roman family. He criminalized adultery and passed a number of laws designed to promote marriage as an institution and encourage larger families. Men between the ages of twenty-five and sixty and women between the ages of twenty and fifty were required to marry. A divorced woman was required to remarry within six months, a widow within a year. A childless woman, married or not, was required to pay large taxes on her property. A childless man was denied any inheritance. And the nobility were granted political advantages in line with the size of their families.

The *Ara Pacis* can be seen as part of Augustus's general program to revitalize the institution of marriage in Roman life. His own family, so prominently displayed in the frieze, was intended to serve as a model for all Roman families.

FIGURE 4.19 *Equestrian Statue of Marcus Aurelius*, 164–66 C.E., gilded bronze, height 11′6″ (3.51 m), Piazza del Campidoglio, Rome. This equestrian image became a model for future representations of military leaders.

FIGURE 4.18 Apollodorus of Damascus, Column of Trajan, Rome, 106–13 C.E., relief, detail of fig. 4.17. The long band of reliefs records Trajan's victories over the Dacians with documentary accuracy. Details of setting, armor, weapons, and even military tactics are included.

Portrait Head of Caracalla. A time of political revolution and social change, the violence of the third century in Rome is embodied in the portrait head of Caracalla (fig. 4.20). The emperor's real name was Antoninus; his *Constitutio Antoniniana* gave everyone living in the Roman empire civil rights.

Yet he was also a brutal soldier who consolidated his hold on the throne by murdering his brother, and it is this aspect of his character that is portrayed in sculpture. How has the sculptor accomplished this? His facial expression is stressed, the eyes emphasized by carving out the pupils and engraving the irises. Caracalla gazes into the distance, seemingly focusing on a definite point. His forehead is furrowed, his brow contracted, as if in anxiety.

Many copies of the bust survive—Caracalla must have approved of this image himself. It is as if brutality has become the very sign of power and authority. The portrait set a style for the third century, which emphasizes such animated facial expression. The skillful carving, creating a vivid contrast between flesh and hair, is descriptive rather than decorative.

Head of Constantine. The eyes of this head of Constantine the Great (fig. 4.21), the first Christian emperor, who ruled 306–37, gaze out into the distance like Caracalla's, but Constantine no longer seems to focus on anything in particular. Instead, in keeping with the spirituality of the times, he appears to be in a kind of trance. The head itself, over eight feet high, was originally part of an enor-

FIGURE 4.21 *Constantine the Great*, head from a huge statue, 325–26 C.E., marble, height 8′5″ (2.58 m), Palazzo dei Conservatori, Rome. This image of Constantine, the first Christian emperor, impresses through enormous scale rather than photographic realism. With the spread of Christianity came a turn away from the factual and toward the spiritual.

FIGURE 4.20 *Caracalla*, ca. 215 C.E., marble, lifesize. Samuel D. Lee Fund. Metropolitan Museum of Art, New York. This bust records Emperor Caracalla's physical appearance, but goes beyond the superficial representation of the subject's facial terrain to reveal his personality—which was described as often angry.

mous thirty-foot-high seated sculpture of the emperor, of which only a few marble fragments survive, among them a giant hand that points heavenward. Placed behind the altar of the Basilica Nova in Rome, it dominated the interior space. Constantine is both mystical and majestic. He is shown to be calm, capable, and composed by an image that is self-glorifying and self-exalting.

The Arch of Constantine. Constantine had come to power after defeating the emperor Maxentius. To celebrate his victory, the Senate erected a giant triple arch next to the Colosseum in Rome (fig. 4.22). Much of the decoration was taken from second-century C.E. monuments, and the figures changed to look like Constantine (fig. 4.23). The medallions decorating the arch were carved 128–38 C.E. during

Table 4–1   EMPERORS OF ANCIENT ROME

The most significant Roman emperors and the dates they reigned:

Augustus	27 B.C.E.–14 C.E.	Septimius Severus	193–211
Tiberius	14–37	Caracalla	211–217
Caligula	37–41	Alexander Severus	222–235
Claudius	41–54	Maximinus Thrax	235–238
Nero	54–68	Philip the Arab	244–249
Vespasion	69–79	Gallienus	253–268
Titus	79–81	Aurelian	270–275
Domitian	81–96	Diocletian	284–305
Nerva	96–98	Maximian	286–305
Trajan	98–117	Constantius Chlorus	305–306
Hadrian	117–138	Galerius	305–311
Antonius Pius	138–161	Maxentius	306–312
Lucius Verus	161–169	Licinius	311–324
Marcus Aurelius	161–180	Constantine the Great	307–337
Commodus	180–193		

FIGURE 4.22   Arch of Constantine, 312–15 C.E., Rome. The simple type of ancient Roman triumphal arch has a single opening; the more complex type like the Arch of Constantine has three openings. Typically Roman is the nonstructural use of columns as surface decoration.

FIGURE 4.23   Arch of Constantine, north side, medallions carved 128–38 C.E., frieze carved early fourth century C.E., Rome. The contrast between the naturalism of the medallions and the simplified distortions and absence of interest in spatial illusionism in the frieze reveals major changes in Roman art.

the time of Hadrian. In the medallion showing Emperor Hadrian hunting a boar, a variety of levels of relief create a sense of depth. Horses move on diagonals. Figures twist, turn, and bend in space. By way of contrast, the frieze below, carved in the early fourth century, had Constantine in the center, but he was later replaced by a figure of Jesus, and now the head is gone. A complete disgregard for the Classical tradition is evident here. No attempt is made to create space—there are no diagonals, no foreshortening, and all the carving is done to the same depth. The figures are not united in a common action. Instead, each figure is isolated. Rather than being depicted in the *contrapposto* pose, the figures stand with their weight equally distributed on both feet. Figures are indicated as being behind others by rows of heads above. The proportions of the figures are stocky and doll-like, very different from Classical Greek proportions.

PAINTING

Only a fraction of the paintings produced by ancient Roman artists remain. The small-scale portable paintings on ivory, stone, and wood are now almost entirely gone, al-though it is known that such paintings sold for high prices. Almost the only Roman painting to survive is found on walls in the form of **murals.**

The walls of private homes were frequently painted. The best extant examples of ancient Roman wall painting are those that were preserved in Pompeii and Hercula-neum by the eruption of the volcano Vesuvius in 79 C.E. A few later examples have survived in Rome, Ostia, and the provinces.

The German historian August Mau classified ancient Roman wall painting into four styles in 1882. Although Mau's system continues to be used today, there is dis-agreement among art historians as to precisely when one style ends and the next begins.

First Style.   The First Style starts in the second century B.C.E. and continues until ca. 80 B.C.E. It is referred to as the "incrustation" or "masonry" style, since the paintings of this period attempt to imitate the appearance of col-ored marble slabs. The wall surface from the Casa di Sal-lustio at Pompeii (fig. 4.24), of the mid-second century B.C.E., is divided into squares and rectangles which are painted to look like costly marble wall-facing. There are no figures and no attempt to create the illusion of three-dimensional space—the only illusion is that of marble created in paint.

Second Style. The Second Style begins about 80 B.C.E. and lasts until 30 or 20 B.C.E. it is often referred to as the "architectonic," "architectural," or "illusionistic" style. In this period actual architectural structures, which were themselves colored, were copied in paint. The Villa of the Mysteries, outside Pompeii (fig. 4.25), dates to the mid-first century B.C.E. One room here is especially famous, partly for the puzzle it presents. Many theories have been suggested to explain the activities depicted on the four walls of this room—the subject may have to do with a bridal initiation into the mystery cult of Dionysos. The figures are solid and substantial, and almost all female. They move in a shallow space with green floors and red walls, which are divided up into sections. A novel feature is that the figures act and react across the corners of the room, animating and activating the space.

A more characteristic example of the Second Style is the *cubiculum* (fig. 4.26) from the Villa at Boscoreale, a mile north of Pompeii, built shortly after the mid-first century B.C.E. The bedroom of a wealthy Roman by the name of Publius Fannius Synistor, this room was at the northwest corner of a colonnaded court of the house. It was buried by the eruption of Mount Vesuvius in 79 C.E. and was only rediscovered in the late nineteenth century.

The walls of the room are painted with illusionistic architecture that creates open vistas into space. The painter has extended the dimensions of the room; the solid wall is obliterated. It has been suggested that this was inspired by

FIGURE 4.25 Scenes of Dionysiac mystery cult, Villa of the Mysteries, outside Pompeii, ca. 50 B.C.E. Although the exact subject depicted in this room remains unclear, it seems to be connected with the cult of Dionysos, god of wine. Clever use is made of space, for the figures interact with one another on adjoining walls across the corners of the room.

stage painting—there are theater masks at the top of the wall, and Vitruvius refers to the use of stage scenery as house decoration. Or perhaps this reflects actual contemporary architecture. Might this be a portrayal of an ideal villa? Could this be a visual retreat—the idea of escaping from daily cares into this fantastic architectural realm?

The painter uses perspective, but not scientifically or consistently. It is not possible to make a logical ground-plan of this cityscape. What do the buildings stand on? Yet the light falls as if from an actual window in the back wall.

Both the First and Second Styles evidence the Roman delight in fooling the viewer's eyes. Such realism was admired in antiquity. In his *Natural History*, Pliny says a certain painted decoration was praised "because some crows, deceived by a painted representation of roof-tiles, tried to alight on them." With different textures, with marble columns that appear round, with painted colonnades on a projecting base, a fairly convincing illusion of three dimensions is created on a two-dimensional surface. The Boscoreale *cubiculum* is intended to trick the eye on a grand scale. The murals may be indicative of the villa owner's desire to amuse, to entertain, and, especially, to impress his guests.

Third Style. The Third Style dates from the late first century B.C.E. to the mid–first century C.E. The Third Style is variously known as the "ornamental/ornamented,"

FIGURE 4.24 Casa di Sallustio, Pompeii, second century B.C.E. The first of the four styles of ancient Roman wall painting (a system of classification developed not by the ancient Romans but by a nineteenth-century historian) is readily recognizable. Also known as the "incrustation" style, the First Style consists of painted imitations of marble slabs.

FIGURE 4.26   Roman paintings. Pompeian, Villa at Boscoreale. Bedroom (*cubiculum, nocturnum*) overview, first century B.C.E. Rogers Fund, 1903 Metropolitan Museum of Art, New York. In this example of the Second Style, also known as the "architectonic" style, an entire bedroom is painted with illusionistic architecture and distant cityscapes.

"capricious," "ornate," "candelabra," or "classic" style. There is a new concern with decorative detail. The abrupt shift evident in the Third Style coincides with the reign of Augustus.

The Third Style places an emphasis on the wall surface rather than on illusions of depth (fig. 4.27). Walls are now often almost monochromatic, the range of colors restricted to red, black, or white. These large areas of monochrome emphasize the wall's two-dimensionality. Landscapes are no longer spread over the wall to create spatial illusions, but are instead treated as framed pictures on the wall, as vignettes, not located in depth behind the wall surface but on the surface. The surrounding flat fields of colors are painted with elaborate details of architecture, plant forms, and figures, delicate and decorative. The massive columns and architectural framework of the Second Style have given way to spindly nonstructural columns.

Fourth Style.   The Fourth, and final, Style largely dates from the mid–first century C.E. or from the earthquake in 62 C.E. until the eruption of the volcano Vesuvius in 79 C.E., although extant examples postdate the eruption of Vesuvius. The Fourth Style is the most elaborate of all and is known as the "composite," "fantasy," or "intricate" style. The painting technique is somewhat freer, sketchier, more impressionistic than in the First, Second, or Third Styles. There is greater use of still life, mythological, and landscape subjects.

The Ixion Room of the House of the Vettii in Pompeii (fig. 4.28), painted 63–79 C.E., is typical. Within the Fourth Style are returns to "false" earlier styles. This example combines the simulated marble inlay of the First Style on the lower wall, the illusionistic architecture of the Second Style on the upper wall, and the framed vignette surrounded by a flat area of solid color of the Third Style. A

FIGURE 4.27   House of M. Lucretius Fronto, Pompeii, mid–first century C.E. In the Third Style, also known as the "ornamental" style, there is a return to a flatter effect with large areas of solid color and scenes treated as framed pictures hanging on the wall.

completely painted fantasy is achieved. Figures and architecture are combined. What more could possibly be added to this playful and decorative ornament?

PHILOSOPHY

Stoicism.   Like so much else in the artistic and philosophical traditions of Greece, Stoicism migrated to Rome (see Chapter 3). From the second century B.C.E. through the period of the Roman empire, Stoicism was the dominant Roman philosophy. The great Roman orator MARCUS TULLIUS CICERO [SIS-ur-oh] (106–43 B.C.E.) commented on it, but Stoicism's two best known adherents and practitioners were EPICTETUS [eh-pic-TEE-tus] (ca. 60–110 C.E.), a Greek slave and secretary in the imperial administration, and Epictetus's student Marcus Aurelius, who reigned as emperor some years after Nero.

Like the Greek philosophers who came after Aristotle, Epictetus was a practical philosopher. His interest lay less in elaborating a metaphysical system than in providing guidance for living a life of virtue and equanimity. Epictetus exemplified the Stoic ideal in his own life, living simply and avoiding the temptations and distractions of the

world as much as possible. He urged his followers, in his *Discourses*, to control what elements of their lives they could and to avoid worrying about those they could not. Epictetus accepted, for example, that he could not change the fact he was a slave. What he could control, however, was his attitude toward his situation. It was this attitude, according to Epictetus, that determined one's moral worth, not one's external circumstances.

Unlike Epictetus, Marcus Aurelius was born into a wealthy Roman family. He succeeded his uncle, Antoninus Pius, to the imperial throne in 161 C.E. This was a time of great difficulty for Rome, which had suffered a devastating plague as well as incursions into its territories by barbarians. As emperor, Marcus Aurelius spent nearly half his life on military campaigns. It was during his military duties that he composed his *Meditations*, a series of reflections on the proper conduct of life.

The Meditations are more attentive to religious questions than Epictetus's *Discourses*. Like his Greek Stoic predecessors, Marcus Aurelius described the divine less in terms of a personal god in the Judeo-Christian tradition and more as an indwelling spirit of rationality. Marcus Aurelius considered the entire universe to be governed by reason, and

FIGURE 4.28 Ixion Room, House of the Vettii, Pompeii, 63–79 C.E., The Fourth Style, also known as the "composite" style, combines aspects of the earlier styles: imitation marble incrustation; illustionistic architecture; and areas of flat color with small framed scenes.

he accepted the world as fundamentally good. It is the ethical dimension of *The Meditations*, however, that has determined their popularity and influence. In preaching a doctrine of acceptance, Marcus Aurelius recommended that a person not return evil for evil, but rather ignore the evil that others did to one, since what happened to an individual's person and possessions was insignificant. According to Marcus Aurelius, only the soul, the inner self, counted.

ROMAN HISTORIANS

Gaius Sallustus Crispis, Sallust (ca. 86–34 B.C.E.), began writing about 43 B.C.E. Sallust's birth during a time of civil war, and his maturation during a period of foreign war and political strife, likely contributed to his preoccupation with violence and political conflict. Sallust's historical writing deals with corruption in Roman politics, the origins of party struggles, and the history of Rome from 78 to 67 B.C.E.

Titus Livius, or Livy (59 B.C.E.–17 C.E.), wrote an extensive history of Rome, from the mythological founding of the city to the year 9 C.E. Livy's history was written in 142 books, of which only about 36 have been preserved. His work differs from Sallust's in its emphasis on individual historical figures and their influence, rather than on conflicting political forces. Livy wrote history to provide his countrymen with a panoramic account of their past, to celebrate its glories, and to encourage them to abandon decadent behavior. His varied and flexible writing style, although sometimes factually inaccurate, is particularly well suited to the analysis of historical characters and to recreating the rhetorical brilliance of their speeches.

Like Livy, much of the work of GAIUS CORNELIUS TACITUS [TASS-i-tus] (ca. 56–120 C.E.) has been lost. About a third of his important works, the *Histories* and the *Annals*, have survived. The *Histories* provide an account of Tacitus's own time, from 69 to 96 C.E., whereas the *Annals* cover an earlier period from the death of Augustus and the succession of Tiberius in 14 C.E. to the end of Nero's reign in 68 C.E. Tacitus's work analyzes the decline of political freedom in Rome and criticizes dynastic power. Tacitus found Tiberius false, Claudius weak, Nero unstable, and the imperial wives dangerous.

Just how false, weak, unstable, and dangerous the Roman emperors were is taken up in considerable detail in the *Lives of the Caesars* by GAIUS SUETONIUS [Sway-TONE-ee-us] (ca. 69–122 C.E.). A biographer as well as a historian, Suetonius's *Of Famous Men* includes short biographies of Roman orators, rhetoricians, philosophers, and poets, including lives of Horace, Terence, and Virgil. His *Lives of the Caesars*, which covers the first twelve emperors from Julius Caesar to Domitian, presents a vivid picture of Roman society, particularly the political corruption and moral decadence of its leaders.

LITERATURE

Poetry in the Roman empire flourished as never before under the rule of Augustus. Augustus himself appears to have been a significant patron of the literary arts and he encouraged writers to glorify the themes of his reign—peace and the imperial destiny of Rome.

Virgil. Latin poets celebrated Roman culture while emulating the cultural achievements of their Greek predecessors. The poet who best harmonized these two cultural and literary strains was Publius Vergilius Maro, known simply as VIRGIL [VER-jil] (70–19 B.C.E.), whose poem *The Aeneid* [ee-NEE-id] rivals the Homeric epics in literary splendor and cultural significance.

Virgil was almost certainly commissioned by the emperor himself to write his great epic. Much in the poem is Augustan in theme.

The Aeneid is a heroic account of the events that led to the founding of the city of Rome and the Roman empire, especially the misfortunes and deprivations that accompany heroic deeds. The poem concerns the Trojan prince AENEAS [ee-NEE-as], who flees his home as it is being destroyed at the end of the Trojan War and sails away to found a new city in Italy—the successor to the great Trojan civilization. Clearly Aeneas's new city is the forerunner of Rome, and the person of Aeneas in the poem is obvi-

Then & Now

GRAFFITI

The urge to write on walls is apparently as old as civilization itself. Before the invention of writing, for instance, prehistoric people outlined their hands on cave walls, as if to say, "I was here." In contemporary society, our national parks and monuments are plagued by this apparently basic human need to announce our presence, as generation after generation have inscribed their names and dates of visit on canyon walls and giant redwoods. One of the earliest records of the Spanish conquest of the American Southwest is preserved on Inscription Rock at El Morro National Monument in New Mexico. It reads, "Passed by here the Adelantado Don Juan de Oñate, from the discovery of the Sea of the South, the 16th April of 1605." It is the first of a long legacy of such inscriptions, culminating in the graffiti that today "decorates" so much of the local landscape—the so-called "tags," or names, of graffiti "writers" that vie for prominence on many walls of urban America.

The Romans, it seems, were themselves great practitioners of the "art" of graffiti. In Pompeii alone over 3,500 graffiti have been found. Among them is the normal fare: "Successus was here;" "Publius Comicius Restitutus stood here with his brother;" "We are here, two dear friends, comrades forever. If you want to know our names, they are Gaius and Aulus;" and "Gaius Julius Primigenius was here. Why are you late?" But the Romans were also adept at the kind of graffiti we normally associate today with "bathroom humor": One wit apparently paraphrases Julius Caesar's famous boast "I came, I saw, I conquered," transforming it into "I came here, I screwed, I returned home." There are as well many graffiti of the "Marcus loves Spendusa" and "Serena hates Isidore" variety. But one writer sums up the feelings of future generations of graffiti readers: "I am amazed, O wall, that you have not collapsed and fallen, since you must bear the tedious stupidities of so many scrawlers."

---

ously in some degree intended to honor Augustus himself—the links between Augustus and Aeneas were alluded to by other artists (see p. 184).

The first of the *Aeneid*'s twelve books begins *in mediasres* (in the middle of things), as Aeneas and his men are caught in a storm and shipwrecked at Carthage on the north African coast. Dido, the Carthaginian queen, provides food and shelter, and Aeneas describes the destruction of Troy at the hands of the Greeks (Book II) and his journey to Carthage (Book III). Enamored of Aeneas, Dido urges him to remain at her court rather than travel to Italy to establish a new home for his people. When Aeneas instead leaves her to fulfill his destiny, the queen commits suicide by throwing herself on a funeral pyre, the spiking flames of which are visible to Aeneas as he sails away (Book IV). Books V and VI describe Aeneas's arrival in Italy and his journey to the underworld—a characteristic feature of epic poems. In the second half of the poem (Books VII-XII), Virgil describes Aeneas's arrival at the Tiber River, which will be the site of the future city of Rome, and the Battle of the Trojans with the Latin people who live there, a battle ultimately won by the Trojans.

Aeneas struggles with both his destiny and his conscience. He experiences danger and suffering in his arduous journeys and battles; and he experiences anguish over his harsh treatment of Queen Dido. While celebrating Aeneas's victory and heroism and highlighting his courage and filial piety, Virgil also expresses sympathy and compassion for all human beings, whose existence is characterized by suffering and sorrow, an experience beautifully captured in Virgil's words from Book II, *lacrimae rerum*, "the tears of things."

It is probable that Augustus felt that his great empire should have a literary work to rival Homer. Like Homer's *Iliad*, Virgil's epic depicts the horrors and the glories of war. Like Homer's *Odyssey*, Virgil's poem describes its hero's adventures, both dangerous and amorous. In spite of Virgil's debt to Greek epic, however, *The Aeneid* is a thoroughly Roman poem. It is saturated in Roman traditions and marked at every turn by its respect for family and country, characterized by *pietas*, or piety, a devotion to duty, especially love and honor of one's family and country.

Roman Satire.   Although Latin literature, like much Roman art and architecture, was based closely on Greek models, the Romans developed one literary genre almost exclusively as their own—**satire.** It is true that a few Greek poets wrote satirical verse, most notably, Arkilokhos in the seventh century B.C.E., but the Greeks did not have a name for satire and did not recognize it as a distinct literary genre. Arkilokhos's poems were called *elegies*, not satires. It was left to the imagination of Gaius Lucillius (ca. 180–102 BCE) to devise a poetic form and manner called *satura*, or *satira*, and to write more than thirty books of satires, in which he laments the triviality of the world and the greed and stupidity of people. What would become popular and typical targets of satire first appear in his poems: bores, cuckolds, gluttons, misers, politicians, thieves, and whores, among others.

Horace.   The most important writer of **odes**—lyric poems on particular subjects made up of lines of varying lengths—was Quintus Horatius Flaccus, known simply as Horace (65–8 B.C.E.). Of humble origins, Horace was freed from economic worry when he was befriended by Virgil, who

Cultural Impact

The Roman genius for organization and problem solving is among its most significant cultural legacies. The Romans were superb engineers.

Their roads, bridges, baths, aqueducts, theaters, forums, walls, palaces, and monuments can be found in more than thirty modern nations. These numerous feats of engineering are massive in scale, technically sophisticated, extraordinarily practical, and built with a meticulous attention to the craft of surveying.

The road system they put in place across Europe is, in part, still in use today. The Romans built bridges and aqueducts that crossed rivers and valleys and carried fresh water to houses and public baths. Roman town architecture was also eminently practical. Great amphitheaters like the Colosseum in Rome were designed to accommodate vast crowds and to let them enter and exit quickly and efficiently. Today's sports fans attend football games and soccer matches at similarly sized stadiums that owe much to their Roman antecedents.

Romans' love for the efficient and practical is also seen in their political structure. The Romans invented the field of civil law—the branch of law that deals with property rights—which became the foundation of legal systems in many Western countries. The Romans were also responsible for the idea of natural law, which emerged from the philosophy of Stoicism. Natural law postulated a set of rights beyond those described in civil (or property) law and became the basis for the "inalienable rights" promised by the framers of the American Declaration of Independence many centuries later (see Chapter 17).

The idea of civility in social conduct and civilized discourse in public life is another of Rome's cultural legacies (although we must remember that Rome had slaves, and women had few rights). But perhaps the Romans' greatest impact was in their language, Latin, which is the ancestor language for the Romance languages—Italian, Spanish, French, and Romansh all descend from it. And although English is Germanic in root, it nonetheless contains thousands of Latin loan words, so much so that studying Latin in school provides the basis for developing an extensive English vocabulary. And finally, the Romans, who inherited their alphabet from the Greeks through the Phoeneicians, but who also made changes in it, left in the Roman alphabet an even more pervasive cultural legacy.

---

helped him secure the support of Maecenas, a wealthy patron of the arts. Like Virgil, Horace was also encouraged to write poetry by Augustus. Horace's odes espouse a philosophy of moderation, which derives from earlier Greek culture. Horace's influence on English poetry was perhaps greatest from the sixteenth to eighteenth centuries. One of his most famous poems, "Ars Poetica" ("The Art of Poetry"), was especially valued as a guide to poetic practice during the Renaissance and the eighteenth century.

Horace was fully aware of his genius, boasting that "not all of me shall die," and "I have raised a monument more lasting than bronze." His odes celebrate wine, women, and song, while also recounting the glories of Roman history. And though Horace's fame rests most squarely on his four books of Odes, he is also recognized as a consummate satirist, inspired by Lucillus, but more urbane in style and tone and more tempered in his satirical indictments. Unlike Lucillus, Horace satirized general types rather than specific individuals, thus becoming a major influence on the satirical traditions that developed in seventeenth century Europe, especially in England and France.

Ovid.   Augustan Rome's successor to Catullus, OVID [O-vid] (43 B.C.E.–17 C.E.) wrote witty and ironic poems. The titles of Ovid's books reveal his persistent interest in the erotic—the *Amores* (*Loves*) and the *Ars Amatoria* (*The Art of Love*). His most famous work, the *Metamorphoses* [meh-tah-MOR-foh-sees], is based on a series of stories about transformation, many derived from Greek mythology. These are often related with an erotic twist. Ovid's poetry combines skillful narrative with elegance and grace. In addition, Ovid is generally recognized as a subtle analyst of the human heart. Though ironic, Ovid's poetry is not cruel or sarcastic; rather, Ovid seems almost compassionate toward the characters whose experiences he describes.

Catullus.   Although the Greeks had their love poetry, most notably the poems of Sappho, it was the Roman poet Catullus who gave the Western world its first body of love poetry, a suite of poems in which the complexities of love were presented in detail across a span of love's phases from a highly subjective point of view. Catullus depicted love as a way of living and not just as a mad aberration or as simple lust. Like other love poets who succeeded him in the Renaissance, Catullus based his poems on and dedicated them to a particular woman to whom he gave the name Lesbia, as echo of the Greek island of Lesbos, home of Sappho, his Greek amatory poetric predecessor. In fact some of Catullus's love poems are Latin translations of poems by Sappho, though Catullus wrote many others that were original love poems, which alternate between praise of and scorn for the Lesbia that inspired them. Catullus's legacy remains not so much any of his individual poetic masterpieces, but rather an overall strategy of recounting the story of a love affair in all its emotional and psychological complexity.

Seneca.   LUCIUS ANNAEUS SENECA [SEN-uh-kuh] (4 B.C.E.–65 C.E.) was a Stoic thinker, a statesman, and a

Critical Thinking

ANCIENT ROME IN THE MOVIES: *GLADIATOR*

Many films have been made in which Rome has been depicted at different historical stages. Among the most popular is the recent movie *Gladiator*, starring Russell Crowe, a film that won a number of major film awards, including the Oscars for best actor and best film of 2000.

Why do you think *Gladiator* became a hit? What accounts for its popularity?

To what extent is the film historically accurate? And how would you go about evaluating its historical accuracy?

Would it matter greatly if the plot were fiction while the general spirit of the times was accurately depicted? Explain.

How would you characterize the film's treatment of Commodus, marcus Aurelius, Maximus, and Lucilla? To what extent have they been portrayed with reasonable historical accuracy?

---

dramatist. Seneca was the tutor to the Roman emperor Nero and, when the young prince ascended to the throne, he served as a trusted adviser. Eventually he fell out of favor, however, and after being implicated in a conspiracy to assassinate the emperor, he was ordered to kill himself. Stoic to the end, Seneca opened his veins and bled to death.

Seneca's plays, written more to be recited than performed, are deeply indebted to his Greek precursors: Sophocles, Aeschylus, and Euripides. In fact, the titles of a number of his plays are identical to those of the Greek dramatists—*Medea*, *Agamemnon*, and *Oedipus*, for example. Characterized by violence and bloodshed, Seneca's plays had an important influence on Renaissance drama, particularly on the development of revenge tragedy in Elizabethan England, including Shakespeare's *Hamlet*.

Petronius.   First-century C.E. Rome was saturated in material rather than spiritual values. The Roman emperor Nero set the tone with elaborate banquets, orgiastic feastings, and bloody entertainments. During Nero's reign, the satirist PETRONIUS [peh-TROHN-ee-us] provided a sharply realistic picture of the manners, luxuries, and vices of the age. The *Satyricon* [sah-TIR-ih-con], usually attributed to Petronius, depicts the pragmatic materialism of first-century C.E. Rome. Although only fragments of the work survive, the *Satyricon* nonetheless vividly conveys early Rome's veneration of material wealth and infatuation with physical pleasure.

In the longest extant section of the work, "Dinner with Trimalchio," an aristocratic narrator describes a meal he and his friends share with the slave-turned-millionaire, Trimalchio. The dinner conversation reflects the temper of early Roman civilization in the characters' selfishness, their anti-intellectualism, and their obsession with cheating one another. The satire is enhanced by numerous echoes of the Greek heroic traditions with references to Homer's *Iliad* and *Odyssey*. The ironic references reflect the Roman characters' distance from the heroic ideal—they live only for themselves and only for the moment. Already the idealism of Augustan Rome seems very distant.

KEY TERMS

Tuscan order	*pietas*	tetrarchy	oculus
tufa	composite order	amphitheater	coffer
patrician	engaged column	travertine	ode
plebian	concrete	vault	satire
patronage	aqueduct	dome	

www. WEBSITES FOR FURTHER STUDY

http://www.initaly.com/regions/classic/etruscan.html
(An introductory site on Etruscan art, culture, and architecture with links.)

http://classics.mit.edu/Carus/nature_things.html
(This site discusses Lucretius's On the Nature of Things, including commentary.)

http://www.alnpete.co.uk/lepcis/plans/tour.html
(This is a tour of the major sights of the site of Lepcis Magna.)

http://harpy.uccs.edu/roman/html/romptg.html
(The Four Pompeiian painting styles are presented in various Roman villas.)

R E A D I N G S

VIRGIL

from *The Aeneid*

*The first excerpt printed here represents the very first lines of Vir-
gil's epic poem in which the destiny of his hero Aeneas is described:
"so hard and huge / A task it was to found the Roman people." In
the passage that follows from Book II, Aeneas has escaped from Troy
after it has been devastated by the Greeks and has landed in
Carthage, where he has met the queen, Dido. Here he relates to
Dido the story of the fall of Troy, how the Greeks entered the city
walls inside the infamous Trojan horse. There are Homeric references to Agamemnon's slaying of Iphigenia and to the fate of Priam,
father of the slain Trojan hero Hector. The conclusion of Book II
shows Aeneas separated from his wife Creusa, leading his father
and son out of Troy.*

FROM BOOK I

I sing of warfare and a man at war.[1]

From the sea-coast of Troy in early days
He came to Italy by destiny.
To our Lavinian[2] western shore,
A fugitive, this captain, buffeted   5
Cruelly on land as on the sea
By blows from powers of the air—behind them
Baleful Juno[3] in her sleepless rage.
And cruel losses were his lot in war.
Till he could found a city and bring home   10
His gods to Latium, land of the Latin race.
The Alban[4] lords, and the high walls of Rome.
Tell me the causes now. O Muse, how galled
In her divine pride, and how sore at heart
From her old wound, the queen of gods compelled
      him—   15
A man apart, devoted to his mission—
To undergo so many perilous days
And enter on so many trials. Can anger
Black as this prey on the minds of heaven?
Tyrian[5] settlers in that ancient time   20
Held Carthage,[6] on the far shore of the sea.

Set against Italy and Tiber's[7] mouth,
A rich new town, warlike and trained for war.
And Juno, we are told, cared more for Carthage
Than for any walled city of the earth,   25
More than for Samos,[8] even. There her armor
And chariot were kept, and, fate permitting,
Carthage would be the ruler of the world.
So she intended, and so nursed that power.
But she had heard long since   30
That generations born of Trojan blood
Would one day overthrow her Tyrian walls,
And from that blood a race would come in time
With ample kingdoms, arrogant in war,
For Libya's ruin: so the Parcae[9] spun.   35
In fear of this, and holding in memory
The old war she had carried on at Troy
For Argos'[10] sake (the origins of that anger,
That suffering, still rankled: deep within her,
Hidden away, the judgment Paris[11] gave,   40
Snubbing her loveliness: the race she hated;
The honors given ravished Ganymede).
Saturnian Juno,[12] burning for it all,
Buffeted on the waste of sea those Trojans
Left by the Greeks and pitiless Achilles,   45
Keeping them far from Latium. For years
They wandered as their destiny drove them on
From one sea to the next: so hard and huge
A task it was to found the Roman people.

BOOK II

The room fell silent, and all eyes were on him,
As Father Aeneas from his high couch began:
"Sorrow too deep to tell, your majesty,
You order me to feel and tell once more:
How the Danaans[13] leveled in the dust   5
The splendor of our mourned-forever kingdom—
Heartbreaking things I saw with my own eyes
And was myself a part of. Who could tell them,
Even a Myrmidon or Dolopian
Or ruffian of Ulysses,[14] without tears?   10
Now, too, the night is well along, with dewfall

---

[1]*a man at war:* Aeneas, a Trojan champion in the fight for Troy, son of
Venus and Anchises, and a member of the royal house of Troy.
[2]*Lavinian:* Near Rome, named after the city of Lavinium. After the fall
of Troy, Aeneas went in search of a new home, eventually settling here.
[3]*Juno:* Wife of the ruler of the gods (Hera in Greek). As in the *Iliad*, she
is a bitter enemy of the Trojans.
[4]*Alban:* The city of Alba Longa was founded by Aeneas's son Ascanius.
Romulus and Remus, the builders of Rome, were also from Alba. Latium
is the coastal plain on which Rome is situated.
[5]*Tyrian:* From Tyre, on the coast of Palestine, the principal city of the
Phoenicians, a seafaring people.
[6]*Carthage:* On the coast of North Africa, opposite Sicily. Originally a
Tyrian colony, it became a rich commercial center, controlling traffic in
the western Mediterranean.

[7]*Tiber's:* The river that flows through Rome.
[8]*Samos:* A large island off the coast of Asia Minor, famous for its cult of
Hera (Juno).
[9]*Parcae:* The Fates, who were imagined as female divinities who spun
human destinies. Rome captured and destroyed Carthage in 146 B.C.E.
Libya is used as an inclusive name for the North African coast.
[10]*Argos':* Home city of the Achaean (Greek) kings Agamemnon and
Menelaus. Juno was on their side when they went to Troy to retrieve
Helen, Menelaus' wife.
[11]*Paris:* Son of King Priam of Troy. He was asked to judge which goddess—Venus, Juno, or Minerva (Athena)—was most beautiful. All three
offered bribes, but Venus's promise (of Helen's love) prevailed, and Paris
awarded her the prize.
[12]*Saturnian Juno:* Her father was Saturn, a Titan. Ganymede was a Trojan boy of extreme beauty who was taken up into heaven by Jupiter (Zeus),
ruler of the gods.
[13]*Danaans:* Greeks.
[14]*Ulysses:* Odysseus in Greek. Myrmidons and Dolopians were Achilles'
soldiers.

Out of heaven, and setting stars weigh down
Our heads toward sleep. But if so great desire
Moves you to hear the tale of our disasters,
Briefly recalled, the final throes of Troy,   15
However I may shudder at the memory
And shrink again in grief, let me begin.

Knowing their strength broken in warfare, turned
Back by the fates, and years—so many years—
Already slipped away, the Danaan captains   20
By the divine handicraft of Pallas built
A horse of timber, tall as a hill,
And sheathed its ribs with planking of cut pine.
This they gave out to be an offering
For a safe return by sea, and the word went round.   25
But on the sly they shut inside a company
Chosen from their picked soldiery by lot,
Crowding the vaulted caverns in the dark—
The horse's belly—with men fully armed.

Offshore there's a long island, Tenedos,   30
Famous and rich while Priam's kingdom lasted,
A treacherous anchorage now, and nothing more.
They crossed to this and hid their ships behind it
On the bare shore beyond. We thought they'd gone,
Sailing home to Mycenae before the wind,   35
So Teucer's town is freed of her long anguish,
Gates thrown wide! And out we go in joy
To see the Dorian[15] campsites, all deserted,
The beach they left behind. Here the Dolopians
Pitched their tents, here cruel Achilles lodged,   40
There lay the ships, and there, formed up in ranks,
They came inland to fight us. Of our men
One group stood marveling, gaping up to see
The dire gift of the cold unbedded goddess,[16]
The sheer mass of the horse.
                          Thymoetes shouts   45
It should be hauled inside the walls and moored
High on the citadel—whether by treason
Or just because Troy's fate went that way now.
Capys opposed him; so did the wiser heads:
'Into the sea with it,' they said, 'or burn it,   50
Build up a bonfire under it,
This trick of the Greeks, a gift no one can trust,
Or cut it open, search the hollow belly!'

Contrary notions pulled the crowd apart.
Next thing we knew, in front of everyone,   55
Laocoön with a great company
Came furiously running from the Height,[17]
And still far off cried out: 'O my poor people,
Men of Troy, what madness has come over you?
Can you believe the enemy truly gone?   60
A gift from the Danaans, and no ruse?
Is that Ulysses' way, as you have known him?
Achaeans must be hiding in this timber,

Or it was built to butt against our walls,
Peer over them into our houses, pelt   65
The city from the sky. Some crookedness
Is in this thing. Have no faith in the horse!
Whatever it is, even when Greeks bring gifts
I fear them, gifts and all.'
                  He broke off then
And rifled his big spear with all his might   70
Against the horse's flank, the curve of belly.
It stuck there trembling, and the rounded hull
Reverberated groaning at the blow.
If the gods' will had not been sinister,
If our own minds had not been crazed,   75
He would have made us foul that Argive den
With bloody steel, and Troy would stand today—
O citadel of Priam, towering still!

But now look: hillmen, shepherds of Dardania,
Raising a shout, dragged in before the king   80
An unknown fellow with hands tied behind—
This all as he himself had planned,
Volunteering, letting them come across him,
So he could open Troy to the Achaeans.
Sure of himself this man was, braced for it   85
Either way, to work his trick or die.
From every quarter Trojans run to see him,
Ring the prisoner round, and make a game
Of jeering at him. Be instructed now
In Greek deceptive arts: one barefaced deed   90
Can tell you of them all.
As the man stood there, shaken and defenceless,
Looking around at ranks of Phrygians,
'Oh god,' he said, 'what land on earth, what seas
Can take me in? What's left me in the end,   95
Outcast that I am from the Danaans,
Now the Dardanians will have my blood?'

The whimpering speech brought us up short; we felt
A twinge for him. Let him speak up, we said,
Tell us where he was born, what news he brought,   100
What he could hope for as a prisoner.
Taking his time, slow to discard his fright,
He said:
            'I'll tell you the whole truth, my lord,
No matter what may come of it. Argive
I am by birth, and will not say I'm not.   105
That first of all: Fortune has made a derelict
Of Sinon, but the bitch
Won't make an empty liar of him, too.
Report of Palamedes[18] may have reached you,
Scion of Belus' line, a famous man   110
Who gave commands against the war. For this,
On a trumped-up charge, on perjured testimony,
The Greeks put him to death—but now they mourn him,
Now he has lost the light. Being kin to him,
In my first years I joined him as companion,   115
Sent by my poor old father on this campaign,

---

[15]*Dorian:* Greek.
[16]*unbedded goddess:* Athena.
[17]*the Height:* the citadel.

---

[18]*Palamedes:* A Greek warrior who advised Agamemnon to abandon the war against Troy; his downfall was engineered by Ulysses.

And while he held high rank and influence
In royal councils, we did well, with honor.
Then by the guile and envy of Ulysses—
Nothing unheard of there!—he left this world,   *120*
And I lived on, but under a cloud, in sorrow,
Raging for my blameless friend's downfall.
Demented, too, I could not hold my peace
But said if I had luck, if I won through
Again to Argos, I'd avenge him there.   *125*
And I roused hatred with my talk; I fell
Afoul now of that man. From that time on,
Day in, day out, Ulysses
Found new ways to bait and terrify me,
Putting out shady rumors among the troops,   *130*
Looking for weapons he could use against me.
He could not rest till Calchas[19] served his turn—
But why go on? The tale's unwelcome, useless,
If Achaeans are all one,
And it's enough I'm called Achaean, then   *135*
Exact the punishment, long overdue;
The Ithacan[20] desires it; the Atridae
Would pay well for it.'
           Burning with curiosity,
We questioned him, called on him to explain—
Unable to conceive such a performance,   *140*
The art of the Pelasgian. He went on,
Atremble, as though he feared us:
           'Many times
The Danaans wished to organize retreat,
To leave Troy and the long war, tired out.
If only they had done it! Heavy weather   *145*
At sea closed down on them, or a fresh gale
From the Southwest would keep them from embarking,
Most of all after this figure here,
This horse they put together with maple beams,
Reached its full height. Then wind and thunderstorms *150*
Rumbled in heaven. So in our quandary
We sent Eurypylus to Phoebus'[21] oracle,
And he brought back this grim reply:

'Blood and a virgin slain[22]
You gave to appease the winds, for your first voyage   *155*
Troyward, O Danaans. Blood again
And Argive blood, one life, wins your return.'

When this got round among the soldiers, gloom
Came over them, and a cold chill that ran
To the very marrow. Who had death in store?   *160*
Whom did Apollo call for? Now the man
Of Ithaca haled Calchas out among us
In tumult, calling on the seer to tell
The true will of the gods. Ah, there were many
Able to divine the crookedness   *165*

And cruelty afoot for me, but they
Looked on in silence. For ten days the seer
Kept still, kept under cover, would not speak
Of anyone, or name a man for death,
Till driven to it at last by Ulysses' cries—   *170*
By prearrangement—he broke silence, barely
Enough to designate me for the altar.[23]
Every last man agreed. The torments each
Had feared for himself, now shifted to another,
All could endure. And the infamous day came,   *175*
The ritual, the salted meal, the fillets[24]. . .
I broke free, I confess it, broke my chains,
Hid myself all night in a muddy marsh,
Concealed by reeds, waiting for them to sail
If they were going to.
           Now no hope is left me   *180*
Of seeing my home country ever again,
My sweet children, my father, missed for years.
Perhaps the army will demand they pay
For my escape, my crime here, and their death,
Poor things, will be my punishment. Ah, sir,   *185*
I beg you by the gods above, the powers
In whom truth lives, and by what faith remains
Uncontaminated to men, take pity
On pain so great and so unmerited!'

For tears we gave him life, and pity, too.   *190*
Priam himself ordered the gyves removed
And the tight chain between. In kindness then
He said to him:
           'Whoever you may be,
The Greeks are gone; forget them from now on;
You shall be ours. And answer me these questions: *195*
Who put this huge thing up, this horse?
Who designed it? What do they want with it?
Is it religious or a means of war?'

These were his questions. Then the captive,
    trained
In trickery, in the stagecraft of Achaea,   *200*
Lifted his hands unfettered to the stars.
'Eternal fires of heaven,' he began,
'Powers inviolable, I swear by thee,
As by the altars and blaspheming swords
I got away from, and the gods' white bands[25]   *205*
I wore as one chosen for sacrifice,
This is justice, I am justified
In dropping all allegiance to the Greeks—
As I had cause to hate them; I may bring
Into the open what they would keep dark.   *210*
No laws of my own country bind me now.
Only be sure you keep your promises
And keep faith, Troy, as you are kept from harm

---

[19]*Calchas:* the prophet of the Greek army.
[20]*The Ithacan:* Ulysses.
[21]*Phoebus':* Apollo. Eurypylus was a minor Greek chieftain.
[22]*a virgin slain:* Iphigenia, Agamemnon's daughter.

[23]*the altar:* of sacrifice.
[24]*fillets:* Tufts of wool attached to the victim.
[25]*bands:* The fillets.

If what I say proves true, if what I give
Is great and valuable.
        The whole hope   *215*
Of the Danaans, and their confidence
In the war they started, rested all along
In help from Pallas. Then the night came
When Diomedes and that criminal,
Ulysses, dared to raid her holy shrine.   *220*
They killed the guards on the high citadel
And ripped away the statue, the Palladium,[26]
Desecrating with bloody hands the virginal
Chaplets of the goddess. After that,
Danaan hopes waned and were undermined,   *225*
Ebbing away, their strength in battle broken,
The goddess now against them. This she made
Evident to them all with signs and portents.
Just as they set her statue up in camp,
The eyes, cast upward, glowed with crackling flames,
And salty sweat ran down the body. Then—   *231*
I say it in awe—three times, up from the ground,
The apparition of the goddess rose
In a lightning flash, with shield and spear atremble.
Calchas divined at once that the sea crossing   *235*
Must be attempted in retreat—that Pergamum
Cannot be torn apart by Argive swords
Unless at Argos first they beg new omens,
Carrying homeward the divine power
Brought overseas in ships. Now they are gone   *240*
Before the wind to the fatherland, Mycenae,
Gone to enlist new troops and gods. They'll cross
The water again and be here, unforeseen.
So Calchas read the portents. Warned by him,
They set this figure up in reparation   *245*
For the Palladium stolen, to appease
The offended power and expiate the crime.
Enormous, though, he made them build the thing
With timber braces, towering to the sky,
Too big for the gates, not to be hauled inside   *250*
And give the people back their ancient guardian.
If any hand here violates this gift
To great Minerva,[27] then extinction waits,
Not for one only—would god it were so—
But for the realm of Priam and all Phrygians.   *255*
If this proud offering, drawn by your hands,
Should mount into your city, then so far
As the walls of Pelops' town[28] the tide of Asia
Surges in war: that doom awaits our children.'

This fraud of Sinon, his accomplished lying,   *260*
Won us over; a tall tale and fake tears
Had captured us, whom neither Diomedes
Nor Larisaean[29] Achilles overpowered,
Nor ten long years, nor all their thousand ships.

And now another sign, more fearful still,   *265*
Broke on our blind miserable people,
Filling us all with dread. Laocoön,
Acting as Neptune's priest that day by lot,
Was on the point of putting to the knife
A massive bull before the appointed altar,   *270*
When ah—look there!
From Tenedos, on the calm sea, twin snakes—
I shiver to recall it—endlessly
Coiling, uncoiling, swam abreast for shore,
Their underbellies showing as their crests   *275*
Reared red as blood above the swell; behind
They glided with great undulating backs.
Now came the sound of thrashed seawater foaming;
Now they were on dry land, and we could see
Their burning eyes, fiery and suffused with blood,   *280*
Their tongues a-flicker out of hissing maws.
We scattered, pale with fright. But straight ahead
They slid until they reached Laocoön.
Each snake enveloped one of his two boys,
Twining about and feeding on the body.   *285*
Next they ensnared the man as he ran up
With weapons: coils like cables looped and bound him
Twice round the middle; twice about his throat
They whipped their back-scales, and their heads
    towered,
While with both hands he fought to break the
    knots,   *290*
Drenched in slime, his head-bands black with venom,
Sending to heaven his appalling cries
Like a slashed bull escaping from an altar,
The fumbled axe shrugged off. The pair of snakes
Now flowed away and made for the highest shrines,   *295*
The citadel of pitiless Minerva,
Where coiling they took cover at her feet
Under the rondure of her shield. New terrors
Ran in the shaken crowd; the word went round
Laocoön had paid, and rightfully,   *300*
For profanation of the sacred hulk
With his offending spear hurled at its flank.

'The offering must be hauled to its true home,'
They clamored. 'Votive prayers to the goddess
Must be said there!'
        So we breached the walls   *305*
And laid the city open. Everyone
Pitched in to get the figure underpinned
With rollers, hempen lines around the neck.
Deadly, pregnant with enemies, the horse
Crawled upward to the breach. And boys and girls   *310*
Sang hymns around the towrope as for joy
They touched it. Rolling on, it cast a shadow
Over the city's heart. O Fatherland,
O Ilium, home of gods! Defensive wall
Renowned in war for Dardanus's people!   *315*
There on the very threshold of the breach
It jarred to a halt four times, four times the arms
In the belly thrown together made a sound—
Yet on we strove unmindful, deaf and blind,
To place the monster on our blessed height.   *320*

---

[26]*the Palladium:* the statue of Pallas Athena.
[27]*Minerva:* Athena.
[28]*Pelops' town:* Argos. Pelops was Atreus' father.
[29]*Larisaean:* After Larissa, a town in Achilles' homeland.

Then, even then, Cassandra's[30] lips unsealed
The doom to come: lips by a god's command
Never believed or heeded by the Trojans.
So pitiably we, for whom that day
Would be the last, made all our temples green   325
With leafy festal boughs throughout the city.

As heaven turned, Night from the Ocean stream
Came on, profound in gloom on earth and sky
And Myrmidons in hiding. In their homes
The Teucrians lay silent, wearied out,   330
And sleep enfolded them. The Argive fleet,
Drawn up in line abreast, left Tenedos
Through the aloof moon's friendly stillnesses
and made for the familiar shore. Flame signals
Shone from the command ship. Sinon, favored   335
By what the gods unjustly had decreed,
Stole out to tap the pine walls and set free
The Danaans in the belly. Opened wide,
The horse emitted men; gladly they dropped
Out of the cavern, captains first, Thessandrus,   340
Sthenelus and the man of iron, Ulysses;
Hand over hand upon the rope, Acamas, Thoas,
Neoptolemus[31] and Prince Machaon,
Menelaus and then the master builder,
Epeos, who designed the horse decoy.   345
Into the darkened city, buried deep
In sleep and wine, they made their way,
Cut the few sentries down,
Let in their fellow soldiers at the gate,
And joined their combat companies as planned.   350

That time of night it was when the first sleep,
Gift of the gods, begins for all mankind,
Arriving gradually, delicious rest.
In sleep, in dream, Hector appeared to me,
Gaunt with sorrow, streaming tears, all torn—   355
As by the violent car on his death day—
And black with bloody dust,
His puffed-out feet cut by the rawhide thongs.
Ah god, the look of him! How changed
From that proud Hector who returned to Troy   360
Wearing Achilles' armor,[32] or that one
Who pitched the torches on Danaan ships;
His beard all filth, his hair matted with blood,
Showing the wounds, the many wounds, received
Outside his father's city walls. I seemed   365
Myself to weep and call upon the man
In grieving speech, brought from the depth of me:

'Light of Dardania, best hope of Troy,
What kept you from us for so long, and where?
From what far place, O Hector, have you come,   370

Long, long awaited? After so many deaths
Of friends and brothers, after a world of pain
For all our folk and all our town, at last,
Boneweary, we behold you! What has happened
To ravage your serene face? Why these wounds?'   375
He wasted no reply on my poor questions
But heaved a great sigh from his chest and said:
'Ai! Give up and go, child of the goddess,
Save yourself, out of these flames. The enemy
Holds the city walls, and from her height   380
Troy falls in ruin. Fatherland and Priam
Have their due; if by one hand our towers
Could be defended, by this hand, my own,
They would have been. Her holy things, her gods
Of hearth and household[33] Troy commends to you.   385
Accept them as companions of your days;
Go find for them the great walls that one day
You'll dedicate, when you have roamed the sea.'
As he said this, he brought out from the sanctuary
Chaplets and Vesta,[34] Lady of the Hearth,   390
With her eternal fire.

                    While I dreamed,
The turmoil rose, with anguish, in the city.
More and more, although Anchises' house
Lay in seclusion, muffled among trees,
The din at the grim onset grew; and now   395
I shook off sleep, I climbed to the roof top
To cup my ears and listen. And the sound
Was like the sound a grassfire makes in grain,
Whipped by a Southwind, or a torrent foaming
Out of a mountainside to strew in ruin   400
Fields, happy crops, the yield of plowing teams,
Or woodlands borne off in the flood; in wonder
The shepherd listens on a rocky peak.
I knew then what our trust had won for us,
Knew the Danaan fraud: Deïphobus'[35]   405
Great house in flames, already caving in
Under the overpowering god of fire;
Ucalegon's already caught nearby;
The glare lighting the straits beyond Sigeum;[36]
The cries of men, the wild calls of the trumpets.   410

To arm was my first maddened impulse—not
That anyone had a fighting chance in arms;
Only I burned to gather up some force
For combat, and to man some high redoubt.
So fury drove me, and it came to me   415
That meeting death was beautiful in arms.
Then here, eluding the Achaean spears,
Came Panthus, Orthrys' son, priest of Apollo,
Carrying holy things, our conquered gods,

---

[30]*Cassandra:* Daughter of King Priam of Troy. She was able to foretell the future correctly, but because of a curse, no one believed her.
[31]*Neoptolemus:* Son of Achilles.
[32]*Achilles' armor:* Hector stripped it from the corpse of Patroclus, whom Hector killed in battle. Achilles avenged Patroclus by killing Hector.

[33]*Of hearth and household:* The Romans kept images of household gods, the Penatës, in a shrine in their homes; the custom is here transferred, unhistorically, to Troy.
[34]*Vesta:* the goddess of the hearth and fire.
[35]*Deïphobus':* A son of Priam.
[36]*Sigeum:* A promontory overlooking the strait that connects the Aegean with the Black Sea.

and pulling a small grandchild along: he ran   420
Despairing to my doorway.
                        'Where's the crux,
Panthus,' I said. 'What strongpoint shall we hold?'

Before I could say more, he groaned and answered:
'The last day for Dardania has come,
The hour not to be fought off any longer.   425
Trojans we have been; Ilium has been;
The glory of the Teucrians is no more;
Black Jupiter has passed it on to Argos.
Greeks are the masters in our burning city.
Tall as a cliff, set in the heart of town,   430
Their horse pours out armed men. The conqueror,
Gloating Sinon, brews new conflagrations.
Troops hold the gates—as many thousand men
As ever came from great Mycenae; others
Block the lanes with crossed spears; glittering   435
In a combat line, swordblades are drawn for slaughter.
Even the first guards at the gates can barely
Offer battle, or blindly make a stand.'
Impelled by these words, by the powers of heaven,
Into the flames I go, into the fight,   440
Where the harsh Fury, and the din and shouting,
Skyward rising, calls. Crossing my path
In moonlight, five fell in with me, companions:
Ripheus, and Epytus, a great soldier,
Hypanis, Dymas, cleaving to my side   445
With young Coroebus, Mygdon's son. It happened
That in those very days this man had come
To Troy, aflame with passion for Cassandra,
Bringing to Priam and the Phrygians
A son-in-law's right hand. Unlucky one,   450
To have been deaf to what his bride foretold!
Now when I saw them grouped, on edge for battle,
I took it all in and said briefly,
                        'Soldiers,
Brave as you are to no end, if you crave
To face the last fight with me, and no doubt of it,   455
How matters stand for us each one can see.
The gods by whom this kingdom stood are gone,
Gone from the shrines and altars. You defend
A city lost in flames. Come, let us die,
We'll make a rush into the thick of it.   460
The conquered have one safety: hope for none.'

The desperate odds doubled their fighting spirit:
From that time on, like predatory wolves
In fog and darkness, when a savage hunger
Drives them blindly on, and cubs in lairs   465
Lie waiting with dry famished jaws—just so
Through arrow flights and enemies we ran
Toward our sure death, straight for the city's heart,
Cavernous black night over and around us.
Who can describe the havoc of that night   470
Or tell the deaths, or tally wounds with tears?
The ancient city falls, after dominion
Many long years. In windows, on the streets,
In homes, on solemn porches of the gods,
Dead bodies lie. And not alone the Trojans   475

Pay the price with their heart's blood; at times
Manhood returns to fire even the conquered
And Danaan conquerors fall. Grief everywhere,
Everywhere terror, and all shapes of death.

Androgeos was the first to cross our path   480
Leading a crowd of Greeks; he took for granted
That we were friends, and hailed us cheerfully:
'Men, get a move on! Are you made of lead
To be so late and slow? The rest are busy
Carrying plunder from the fires and towers.   485
Are you just landed from the ships?'
                        His words
Were barely out, and no reply forthcoming
Credible to him, when he knew himself
Fallen among enemies. Thunderstruck,
He halted, foot and voice, and then recoiled   490
Like one who steps down on a lurking snake
In a briar patch and jerks back, terrified,
As the angry thing rears up, all puffed and blue.
So backward went Androgeos in panic.
We were all over them in a moment, cut   495
And thrust, and as they fought on unknown ground,
Startled, unnerved, we killed them everywhere.
So Fortune filled our sails at first. Coroebus,
Elated at our feat and his own courage,
Said:
        'Friends, come follow Fortune. She has shown 500
The way to safety, shown she's on our side.
We'll take their shields and put on their insignia!
Trickery, bravery: who asks, in war?
The enemy will arm us.'
                        He put on
The plumed helm of Androgeos, took the shield   505
With blazon and the Greek sword to his side.
Ripheus, Dymas—all were pleased to do it,
Making the still fresh trophies our equipment.
Then we went on, passing among the Greeks,
Protected by our own gods now no longer;   510
Many a combat, hand to hand, we fought
In the black night, and many a Greek we sent
To Orcus.[37] There were some who turned and ran
Back to the ships and shore; some shamefully
Clambered again into the horse, to hide   515
In the familiar paunch.
                        When gods are contrary
They stand by no one. Here before us came
Cassandra, Priam's virgin daughter, dragged
By her long hair out of Minerva's shrine,
Lifting her brilliant eyes in vain to heaven—   520
Her eyes alone, as her white hands were bound.
Coroebus, infuriated, could not bear it,
But plunged into the midst to find his death.
We all went after him, our swords at play,
But here, here first, from the temple gable's height,   525
We met a hail of missiles from our friends,

---

[37] *Orcus:* The abode of the dead.

Pitiful execution, by their error,
Who thought us Greek from our Greek plumes and
   shields.
Then with a groan of anger, seeing the virgin
Wrested from them, Danaans from all sides   530
Rallied and attacked us: fiery Ajax,[38]
Atreus' sons, Dolopians in a mass—
As, when a cyclone breaks, conflicting winds
Will come together, Westwind, Southwind, Eastwind
Riding high out of the Dawnland; forests   535
Bend and roar, and raging all in spume
Nereus[39] with his trident churns the deep.
Then some whom we had taken by surprise
Under cover of night throughout the city
And driven off, came back again: they knew   540
Our shields and arms for liars now, our speech
Alien to their own. They overwhelmed us.
Coroebus fell at the warrior goddess' altar,
Killed by Peneleus; and Ripheus fell,
A man uniquely just among the Trojans,   545
The soul of equity; but the gods would have it
Differently. Hypanis, Dymas died,
Shot down by friends; nor did your piety,
Panthus, nor Apollo's fillets shield you
As you went down.
                    Ashes of Ilium!   550
Flames that consumed my people! Here I swear
That in your downfall I did not avoid
One weapon, one exchange with the Danaans,
And if it had been fated, my own hand
Had earned my death. But we were torn away   555
From that place—Iphitus and Pelias too,
One slow with age, one wounded by Ulysses,
Called by a clamor at the hall of Priam.
Truly we found here a prodigious fight,
As though there were none elsewhere, not a death   560
In the whole city: Mars[40] gone berserk, Danaans
In a rush to scale the roof; the gate besieged
By a tortoise shell of overlapping shields.[41]
Ladders clung to the wall, and men strove upward
Before the very doorposts, on the rungs,   565
Left hand putting the shield up, and the right
Reaching for the cornice. The defenders
Wrenched out upperworks and rooftiles: these
For missiles, as they saw the end, preparing
To fight back even on the edge of death.   570
And gilded beams, ancestral ornaments,
They rolled down on the heads below. In hall
Others with swords drawn held the entrance way,

Packed there, waiting. Now we plucked up heart
To help the royal house, to give our men   575
A respite, and to add our strength to theirs,
Though all were beaten. And we had for entrance
A rear door, secret, giving on a passage
Between the palace halls; in other days
Andromachë, poor lady, often used it,   580
Going alone to see her husband's parents
Or taking Astyanax[42] to his grandfather.
I climbed high on the roof, where hopeless men
Were picking up and throwing futile missiles.
Here was a tower like a promontory   585
Rising toward the stars above the roof:
All Troy, the Danaan ships, the Achaean camp,
Were visible from this. Now close beside it
With crowbars, where the flooring made loose joints,
We pried it from its bed and pushed it over.   590
Down with a rending crash in sudden ruin
Wide over the Danaan lines it fell;
But fresh troops moved up, and the rain of stones
With every kind of missile never ceased.

Just at the outer doors of the vestibule   595
Sprang Pyrrhus,[43] all in bronze and glittering,
As a serpent, hidden swollen underground
By a cold winter, writhes into the light,
On vile grass fed, his old skin cast away,
Renewed and glossy, rolling slippery coils,   600
With lifted underbelly rearing sunward
And triple tongue a-flicker. Close beside him
Giant Periphas and Automedon,
His armor-bearer, once Achilles' driver,
Besieged the place with all the young of Scyros,[44] 605
Hurling their torches at the palace roof.
Pyrrhus shouldering forward with an axe
Broke down the stony threshold, forced apart
Hinges and brazen door-jambs, and chopped through
One panel of the door, splitting the oak,   610
To make a window, a great breach. And there
Before their eyes the inner halls lay open,
The courts of Priam and the ancient kings,
With men-at-arms ranked in the vestibule.
From the interior came sounds of weeping,   615
Pitiful commotion, wails of women
High-pitched, rising in the formal chambers
To ring against the silent golden stars;
And, through the palace, mothers wild with fright
Ran to and fro or clung to doors and kissed them. 620
Pyrrhus with his father's brawn stormed on,
No bolts or bars or men availed to stop him:
Under his battering the double doors
Were torn out of their sockets and fell inward.
Sheer force cleared the way: the Greeks broke through 625
Into the vestibule, cut down the guards,
And made the wide hall seethe with men-at-arms—

---

[38]*Ajax:* The lesser Ajax, son of Oileus, who raped Cassandra after dragging her away from the shrine; as punishment, he was drowned on his way
back to Greece. This is not the great Greek warrior Ajax; he had committed suicide before Troy fell.
[39]*Nereus:* An old sea god and the father of the Nereids, the sea nymphs.
[40]*Mars:* The war god (Ares in Greek).
[41]*overlapping shields:* When attacking a walled position, Roman soldiers
protected themselves from overhead missiles by holding their shields
above their heads, forming a "roof," which looked like the plates of a
tortoiseshell.

[42]*Astyanax:* Son of Andromachë and Hector.
[43]*Pyrrhus:* Neoptolemus.
[44]*Scyros:* The island in the north Aegean where Neoptolemus grew up.

A tumult greater than when dykes are burst
And a foaming river, swirling out in flood,
Whelms every parapet and races on   630
Through fields and over all the lowland plains,
Bearing off pens and cattle. I myself
Saw Neoptolemus furious with blood
In the entrance way, and saw the two Atridae;
Hecuba[45] I saw, and her hundred daughters,   635
Priam before the altars, with his blood
Drenching the fires that he himself had blessed.
Those fifty bridal chambers, hope of a line
So flourishing; those doorways high and proud,
Adorned with takings of barbaric gold,   640
Were all brought low: fire had them, or the Greeks.

What was the fate of Priam, you may ask.
Seeing his city captive, seeing his own
Royal portals rent apart, his enemies
In the inner rooms, the old man uselessly   645
Put on his shoulders, shaking with old age,
Armor unused for years, belted a sword on,
And made for the massed enemy to die.
Under the open sky in a central court
Stood a big altar; near it, a laurel tree   650
Of great age, leaning over, in deep shade
Embowered the Penatës. At this altar
Hecuba and her daughters, like white doves
Blown down in a black storm, clung together,
Enfolding holy images in their arms.   655
Now, seeing Priam in a young man's gear,
She called out:
              'My poor husband, what mad thought
Drove you to buckle on these weapons?
Where are you trying to go? The time is past   660
For help like this, for this kind of defending,
Even if my own Hector could be here.
Come to me now: the altar will protect us,
Or else you'll die with us.'
                    She drew him close,
Heavy with years, and made a place for him
To rest on the consecrated stone.
                    Now see   665
Politës, one of Priam's sons, escaped
From Pyrrhus' butchery and on the run
Through enemies and spears, down colonnades,
Through empty courtyards, wounded. Close behind
Comes Pyrrhus burning for the death-stroke: has him, 670
Catches him now, and lunges with the spear.
The boy has reached his parents, and before them
Goes down, pouring out his life with blood.
Now Priam, in the very midst of death,
Would neither hold his peace nor spare his anger.   675
'For what you've done, for what you've dared,' he said,
'If there is care in heaven for atrocity,
May the gods render fitting thanks, reward you
As you deserve. You forced me to look on

At the destruction of my son: defiled   680
A father's eyes with death. That great Achilles
You claim to be the son of—and you lie—
Was not like you to Priam, his enemy;
To me who threw myself upon his mercy
He showed compunction, gave me back for burial   685
The bloodless corpse of Hector, and returned me
To my own realm.'
              The old man threw his spear
With feeble impact; blocked by the ringing bronze,
It hung there harmless from the jutting boss.
Then Pyrrhus answered:
                  'You'll report the news   690
To Pelidës,[46] my father; don't forget
My sad behavior, the degeneracy
Of Neoptolemus. Now die.'
                  With this,
To the altar step itself he dragged him trembling,
Slipping in the pooled blood of his son,   695
And took him by the hair with his left hand.
The sword flashed in his right; up to the hilt
He thrust it in his body.
                  That was the end
Of Priam's age, the doom that took him off,
With Troy in flames before his eyes, his towers   700
Headlong fallen—he that in other days
Had ruled in pride so many lands and peoples,
The power of Asia.
                  On the distant shore
The vast trunk headless lies without a name.
For the first time that night, inhuman shuddering   705
Took me, head to foot. I stood unmanned,
And my dear father's image came to mind
As our king, just his age, mortally wounded,
Gasped his life away before my eyes.
Creusa[47] came to mind, too, left alone;   710
The house plundered; danger to little Iulus.
I looked around to take stock of my men,
But all had left me, utterly played out,
Giving their beaten bodies to the fire
Or plunging from the roof.
                  It came to this,   715
That I stood there alone. And then I saw
Lurking beyond the doorsill of the Vesta,
In hiding, silent, in that place reserved,
The daughter of Tyndareus.[48] Glare of fires
Lighted my steps this way and that, my eyes   720
Glancing over the whole scene, everywhere.
That woman, terrified of the Trojans' hate
For the city overthrown, terrified too
Of Danaan vengeance, her abandoned husband's
Anger after years—Helen, that Fury   725
Both to her own homeland and Troy, had gone
To earth, a hated thing, before the altars.

---

[45]*Hecuba:* Mother of Hector.

[46]*Pelidës:* Achilles, son of Peleus.
[47]*Creusa:* Aeneas's wife.
[48]*daughter of Tyndareus:* Helen.

Now fires blazed up in my own spirit—
A passion to avenge my fallen town
And punish Helen's whorishness.
        'Shall this one   730
Look untouched on Sparta and Mycenae
After her triumph, going like a queen,
And see her home and husband, kin and children,
With Trojan girls for escort, Phrygian slaves?
Must Priam perish by the sword for this?   735
Troy burn, for this? Dardania's littoral
Be soaked in blood, so many times, for this?
Not by my leave. I know
No glory comes of punishing a woman,
The feat can bring no honor. Still, I'll be   740
Approved for snuffing out a monstrous life,
For a just sentence carried out. My heart
Will teem with joy in this avenging fire,
And the ashes of my kin will be appeased.'

So ran my thoughts, I turned wildly upon her,   745
But at that moment, clear, before my eyes—
Never before so clear—in a pure light
Stepping before me, radiant through the night,
My loving mother came: immortal, tall,
And lovely as the lords of heaven know her.   750
Catching me by the hand, she held me back,
Then with her rose-red mouth reproved me:
                           'Son,
Why let such suffering goad you on to fury
Past control? Where is your thoughtfulness
For me, for us? Will you not first revisit   755
The place you left your father, worn and old,
Or find out if your wife, Creusa, lives,
And the young boy, Ascanius—all these
Cut off by Greek troops foraging everywhere?
Had I not cared for them, fire would by now   760
Have taken them, their blood glutted the sword.
You must not hold the woman of Laconia,[49]
That hated face, the cause of this, nor Paris.
The harsh will of the gods it is, the gods,
That overthrows the splendor of this place   765
And brings Troy from her height into the dust.
Look over there: I'll tear away the cloud
That curtains you, and films your mortal sight,
The fog around you.—Have no fear of doing
Your mother's will, or balk at obeying her.—   770
Look: where you see high masonry thrown down,
Stone torn from stone, with billowing smoke and dust,
Neptune is shaking from their beds the walls
That his great trident pried up, undermining,
Toppling the whole city down. And look: 775
Juno in all her savagery holds
The Scaean Gates,[50] and raging in steel armor
Calls her allied army from the ships.
Up on the citadel—turn, look—Pallas Tritonia

Couched in a stormcloud, lightening, with her
    Gorgon![51]   780
The Father himself empowers the Danaans,
Urges assaulting gods on the defenders.
Away, child; put an end to toiling so.
I shall be near, to see you safely home.'

She hid herself in the deep gloom of night,   785
And now the dire forms appeared to me
Of great immortals, enemies of Troy.
I knew the end then: Ilium was going down
In fire, the Troy of Neptune[52] going down,
As in high mountains when the countrymen   790
Have notched an ancient ash, then make their axes
Ring with might and main, chopping away
To fell the tree—ever on the point of falling,
Shaken through all its foliage, and the treetop
Nodding; bit by bit the strokes prevail   795
Until it gives a final groan at last
And crashes down in ruin from the height.

Now I descended where the goddess guided,
Clear of the flames, and clear of enemies,
For both retired; so gained my father's door,   800
My ancient home. I looked for him at once,
My first wish being to help him to the mountains;
But with Troy gone he set his face against it,
Not to prolong his life, or suffer exile.

'The rest of you, all in your prime,' he said,   805
'Make your escape; you are still hale and strong.
If heaven's lords had wished me a longer span
They would have saved this home for me. I call it
More than enough that once before I saw
My city taken and wrecked,[53] and went on living.   810
Here is my death bed, here. Take leave of me.
Depart now. I'll find death with my sword arm.
The enemy will oblige; they'll come for spoils.
Burial can be dispensed with. All these years
I've lingered in my impotence, at odds   815
With heaven, since the Father of gods and men
Breathed high winds of thunderbolt upon me
And touched me with his fire.'[54]
                  He spoke on
In the same vein, inflexible. The rest of us,
Creusa and Ascanius and the servants,   820
Begged him in tears not to pull down with him
Our lives as well, adding his own dead weight
To the fates' pressure. But he would not budge,
He held to his resolve and to his chair.
I felt swept off again to fight, in misery   825

---

[49]*woman of Laconia:* Helen.
[50]*Scaean Gates:* One of the principal entrances to Troy.

---

[51]*Gorgon:* Monster whose appearance turned people to stone; Athena had
a Gorgon face on her shield.
[52]Neptune was hostile to Troy.
[53]*My city taken and wrecked:* By the hero Heracles.
[54]Anchisës was struck by a thunderbolt and crippled as punishment by
Jupiter.

Longing for death. What choices now were open,
What chance had I?
           'Did you suppose, my father,
That I could tear myself away and leave you?
Unthinkable; how could a father say it?
Now if it please the powers above that nothing   *830*
Stand of this great city; if your heart
Is set on adding your own death and ours
To that of Troy, the door's wide open for it:
Pyrrhus will be here, splashed with Priam's blood;
He kills the son before his father's eyes,   *835*
The father at the altars.
             My dear mother,
Was it for this, through spears and fire, you brought me,
To see the enemy deep in my house,
To see my son, Ascanius, my father,
And near them both, Creusa,   *840*
Butchered in one another's blood? My gear,
Men, bring my gear. The last night calls the conquered.
Give me back to the Greeks. Let me take up
The combat once again. We shall not all
Die this day unavenged.'
             I buckled on   *845*
Swordbelt and blade and slid my left forearm
Into the shield-strap, turning to go out,
But at the door Creusa hugged my knees,
Then held up little Iulus to his father.

'If you are going out to die, take us   *850*
To face the whole thing with you. If experience
Leads you to put some hope in weaponry
Such as you now take, guard your own house here.
When you have gone, to whom is Iulus left?
Your father. Wife?—one called that long ago.'   *855*

She went on, and her wailing filled the house,
But then a sudden portent came, a marvel:
Amid his parents' hands and their sad faces
A point on Iulus' head seemed to cast light,
A tongue of flame that touched but did not burn him,   *860*
Licking his fine hair, playing round his temples.
We, in panic, beat at the flaming hair
And put the sacred fire out with water;
Father Anchises lifted his eyes to heaven
And lifted up his hands, his voice, in joy: *865*

'Omnipotent Jupiter, if prayers affect you,
Look down upon us, that is all I ask,
If by devotion to the gods we earn it,
Grant us a new sign, and confirm this portent!'
The old man barely finished when it thundered   *870*
A loud crack on the left. Out of the sky
Through depths of night a star fell trailing flame
And glided on, turning the night to day.
We watched it pass above the roof and go
To hide its glare, its trace, in Ida's[55] wood;   *875*

But still, behind, the luminous furrow shone
And wide zones fumed with sulphur.
            Now indeed
My father, overcome, addressed the gods,
And rose in worship of the blessed star.

'Now, now, no more delay. I'll follow you.   *880*
Where you conduct me, there I'll be.
           Gods of my fathers,
Preserve this house, preserve my grandson. Yours
This portent was. Troy's life is in your power.
I yield. I go as your companion, son.'
Then he was still. We heard the blazing town   *885*
Crackle more loudly, felt the scorching heat.

'Then come, dear father. Arms around my neck:
I'll take you on my shoulders, no great weight.
Whatever happens, both will face one danger,
Find one safety. Iulus will come with me,   *890*
My wife at a good interval behind.
Servants, give your attention to what I say.
At the gate inland there's a funeral mound
And an old shrine of Ceres the Bereft;[56]
Near it an ancient cypress, kept alive   *895*
For many years by our fathers' piety.
By various routes we'll come to that one place.
Father, carry our hearthgods, our Penatës.
It would be wrong for me to handle them—
Just come from such hard fighting, bloody work—   *900*
Until I wash myself in running water.'

When I had said this, over my breadth of shoulder
And bent neck, I spread out a lion skin
For tawny cloak and stooped to take his weight.
Then little Iulus put his hand in mine   *905*
And came with shorter steps beside his father.
My wife fell in behind. Through shadowed places
On we went, and I, lately unmoved
By any spears thrown, any squads of Greeks,
Felt terror now at every eddy of wind,   *910*
Alarm at every sound, alert and worried
Alike for my companion and my burden.
I had got near the gate, and now I thought
We had made it all the way, when suddenly
A noise of running feet came near at hand,   *915*
And peering through the gloom ahead, my father
Cried out:
           'Run, boy: here they come; I see
Flame light on shields, bronze shining.'
            I took fright,
And some unfriendly power, I know not what,
Stole all my addled wits—for as I turned   *920*
Aside from the known way, entering a maze
Of pathless places on the run—
           Alas,
Creusa, taken from us by grim fate, did she

---

[55]*Ida:* The mountain range near Troy.

[56]*Ceres the Bereft:* So-called because she mourns the loss of her daughter.

Linger, or stray, or sink in weariness?
There is no telling. Never would she be   925
Restored to us. Never did I look back
Or think to look for her, lost as she was,
Until we reached the funeral mound and shrine
Of venerable Ceres. Here at last
All came together, but she was not there;   930
She alone failed[57] her friends, her child, her husband.
Out of my mind, whom did I not accuse,
What man or god? What crueller loss had I
Beheld, that night the city fell? Ascanius,
My father, and the Teucrian Penatës,   935
I left in my friends' charge, and hid them well
In a hollow valley.
        I turned back alone
Into the city, cinching my bright harness.
Nothing for it but to run the risks
Again, go back again, comb all of Troy,   940
And put my life in danger as before:
First by the town wall, then the gate, all gloom,
Through which I had come out—and so on backward,
Tracing my own footsteps through the night;
And everywhere my heart misgave me: even   945
Stillness had its terror. Then to our house,
Thinking she might, just might, have wandered there.
Danaans had got in and filled the place,
And at that instant fire they had set,
Consuming it, went roofward in a blast;   950
Flames leaped and seethed in heat to the night sky.
I pressed on, to see Priam's hall and tower.
In the bare colonnades of Juno's shrine
Two chosen guards, Phoenix and hard Ulysses,
Kept watch over the plunder. Piled up here   955
Were treasures of old Troy from every quarter,
Torn out of burning temples: altar tables,
Robes, and golden bowls. Drawn up around them,
Boys and frightened mothers stood in line.
I even dared to call out in the night;   960
I filled the streets with calling; in my grief
Time after time I groaned and called Creusa,
Frantic, in endless quest from door to door.
Then to my vision her sad wraith appeared—
Creusa's ghost, larger than life, before me.   965
Chilled to the marrow, I could feel the hair
On my head rise, the voice clot in my throat;
But she spoke out to ease me of my fear:

'What's to be gained by giving way to grief
So madly, my sweet husband? Nothing here   970
Has come to pass except as heaven willed.
You may not take Creusa with you now;
It was not so ordained, nor does the lord
Of high Olympus give you leave. For you
Long exile waits, and long sea miles to plough.   975
You shall make landfall on Hesperia
Where Lydian Tiber flows, with gentle pace,

Between rich farmlands, and the years will bear
Glad peace, a kingdom, and a queen for you.
Dismiss these tears for your beloved Creusa.   980
I shall not see the proud homelands of Myrmidons
Or of Dolopians, or go to serve
Greek ladies, Dardan lady that I am
And daughter-in-law of Venus the divine.
No: the great mother of the gods detains me   985
Here on these shores. Farewell now; cherish still
Your son and mine.'
        With this she left me weeping,
Wishing that I could say so many things,
And faded on the tenuous air. Three times
I tried to put my arms around her neck,   990
Three times enfolded nothing, as the wraith
Slipped through my fingers, bodiless as wind,
Or like a flitting dream.
        So in the end
As night waned I rejoined my company.
And there to my astonishment I found   995
New refugees in a great crowd: men and women
Gathered for exile, young—pitiful people
Coming from every quarter, minds made up,
With their belongings, for whatever lands
I'd lead them to by sea.
        The morning star   1000
Now rose on Ida's ridges, bringing day.
Greeks had secured the city gates. No help
Or hope of help existed.
So I resigned myself, picked up my father,
And turned my face toward the mountain range."

CATULLUS

SELECTED POEMS

Catullus is the author of one of the best-known series of love poems ever written, which has provided a model for many poets since in their own amorous writings. Catullus addressed twenty-five pieces of verse to a mistress, Lesbia, in which he demonstrates a magnificent range of moods. Three examples are printed here, beginning with "We should live, my Lesbia, and love," which was translated and reworked by, among others, the English poets Ben Jonson and Andrew Marvell in the seventeenth century.

WE SHOULD LIVE, MY LESBIA, AND LOVE

We should live, my Lesbia, and love
And value all the talk of stricter
Old men at a single penny.
Suns can set and rise again,
For us, once our brief light has set,   5
There's one unending night for sleeping.
Give me a thousand kisses, then a hundred,
Then another thousand, then a second hundred;
Then still another thousand, then a hundred;
Then, when we've made many thousands,   10
We'll muddle them so as not to know
Or lest some villain overlook us
Knowing the total of our kisses.

---

[57]*failed*: The original Latin does not imply fault and is better read "was not to be found" (literally, "was lacking to").

THAT MAN IS SEEN BY ME AS A GOD'S EQUAL

That man is seen by me as a God's equal
Or (if it may be said) the God's superior,
Who sitting opposite again and again
Watches and hears *you*

Sweetly laughing—which dispossesses poor me   *5*
Of all my senses, for no sooner, Lesbia,
Do I look at you than there's no power left me
(Of speech in my mouth,)

But my tongue's paralysed, invisible flame
Courses down through my limbs, with din of their own *10*
My ears are ringing and twin darkness covers
The light of my eyes.

Leisure, Catullus, does not agree with you.
At leisure you're restless, too excitable.
Leisure in the past has ruined rulers and   *15*
Prosperous cities.

I HATE AND LOVE

I hate and love. Perhaps you're asking why I do that?
I don't know, but I feel it happening, and am racked.

MARTIAL

SELECTED POEMS

Marcus Valerius Martialis, called Martial (ca. 42–102 C.E.), is best known for his epigrammatic poems, which paint a graphic picture of life in first-century Rome. The poems are characterized by wit and elegance and by a satiric tone. Through the centuries, his many admirers have paid him the compliment of quotation, translation, and imitation. The samples included here illustrate Martial's sense of what is to be valued and what avoided in life.

MY FRIEND, THE THINGS THAT DO ATTAIN

Translated by Henry Howard, Earl of Surrey

*My friend, the things that do attain
The happy life be these, I find:
The riches left, not got with pain;
The fruitful ground; the quiet mind;*

*The equal friend; no grudge, no strife;
No charge of rule, nor governance;
Without disease, the healthy life;
The household of continuance;*

*The mean diet, no dainty fare;
Wisdom joined with simpleness;
The night dischargéd of all care,
Where wine the wit may not oppress;*

*The faithful wife, without debate;
Such sleeps as may beguile the night;
Content thyself with thine estate,
Neither wish death, nor fear his might.*

TO A SCHOOLMASTER

Translated by F. A. Wright

*Good schoolmaster, pray give your classes a rest,
If you do, I will ask that next term you be pressed
By curly-haired boys flocking next to your table,
And no short-hand clerk or quick counter be able
To boast that he has a more studious crew
Of pupils and fonder of teacher than you.
The hot sunny days are upon us again,
And blazing July burns the ripening grain,
So let your grim rod and your whip, put to sleep,
Till the Ides of October a holiday keep.
In summer if children can only stay well,
They learn quite enough and can rest for a spell.*

OVID

SELECTED POEMS

Publis Ovidius Naso, or Ovid (ca. 43 B.C.E.–17 C.E.), was a highly regarded poet of his time. His Ars Amatoria (The Art of Love) was an instant success. His Amores (Loves) describes the phases of a love affair. The excerpt here describes a sultry summer love tryst. Ovid's most important work was his Metamorphoses, a book of legends from the beginning of the world to the time of Julius Caesar. Its theme is transformation: A woman is transformed into a bird, stones become people, a girl becomes a laurel tree. The excerpt included here describes the transformation of Icarus into a boy who can fly using the wax wings his father, Daedalus, made. When Icarus flies too high and too close to the sun, his wax wings melt, and he plunges to his death in the sea.

SIESTA TIME IN SULTRY SUMMER

Translated by Guy Lee

*Siesta time in sultry summer.
I lay relaxed on the divan.*

*One shutter closed, the other ajar,
made sylvan semi-darkness,*

*a glimmering dusk, as after sunset,
or between night's end and day's beginning—*

*the half light shy girls need
to hide their hesitation.*

*At last—Corinna. On the loose in a short dress,
long hair parted and tumbling past the pale neck—*

*lovely as Lais of the many lovers,
Queen Semiramis gliding in.*

*Breasts in high relief above the smooth belly.
Long and slender waist. Thighs of a girl.*

*Why list perfection?
I hugged her tight.*

The rest can be imagined—we fell asleep.
Such afternoons are rare.

I grabbed the dress; it didn't hide much,
but she fought to keep it,

only half-heartedly though.
Victory was easy, a self-betrayal.

There she stood, faultless beauty
in front of me, naked.

Shoulders and arms challenging eyes and fingers.
Nipples firmly demanding attention.

THE STORY OF DAEDALUS AND ICARUS

Translated by Rolfe Humphries

Homesick for homeland, Daedalus hated Crete
And his long exile there, but the sea held him.
"Though Minos blocks escape by land or water,"
Daedalus said, "surely the sky is open,
And that's the way we'll go. Minos' dominion   5
Does not include the air." He turned his thinking
Toward unknown arts, changing the laws of nature.
He laid out feathers in order, first the smallest,
A little larger next it, and so continued,
The way that pan-pipes rise in gradual sequence.   10
He fastened them with twine and wax, at middle,
At bottom, so, and bent them, gently curving,
So that they looked like wings of birds, most surely.
And Icarus, his son, stood by and watched him,
Not knowing he was dealing with his downfall,   15
Stood by and watched, and raised his shiny face
To let a feather, light as down, fall on it,
Or stuck his thumb into the yellow wax,
Fooling around, the way a boy will, always,
Whenever a father tries to get some work done.   20
Still, it was done at last, and the father hovered,
Poised, in the moving air, and taught his son:
"I warn you, Icarus, fly a middle course:
Don't go too low, or water will weigh the wings down;
Don't go too high, or the sun's fire will burn them. 25
Keep to the middle way. And one more thing,
No fancy steering by star or constellation,
Follow my lead!" That was the flying lesson,
And now to fit the wings to the boy's shoulders.
Between the work and warning the father found   30
His cheeks were wet with tears, and his hands trembled.
He kissed his son (*Good-bye*, if he had known it),
Rose on his wings, flew on ahead, as fearful
As any bird launching the little nestlings
Out of high nest into thin air. *Keep on*,   35
Keep on, he signals, *follow me!* He guides him
In flight—O fatal art!—and the wings move
And the father looks back to see the son's wings
      moving.
Far off, far down, some fisherman is watching
As the rod dips and trembles over the water,
Some shepherd rests his weight upon his crook,   40

Some ploughman on the handles of the ploughshare,
And all look up, in absolute amazement,
At those air-borne above. They must be gods!
They were over Samos, Juno's sacred island,   45
Delos and Paros toward the left, Lebinthus
Visible to the right, and another island,
Calymne, rich in honey. And the boy
Thought *This is wonderful!* and left his father,
Soared higher, higher, drawn to the vast heaven,   50
Nearer the sun, and the wax that held the wings
Melted in that fierce heat, and the bare arms
Beat up and down in air, and lacking oarage
Took hold of nothing. *Father!* he cried, and *Father!* 55
Until the blue sea hushed him, the dark water
Men call the Icarian now. And Daedalus,
Father no more, called "Icarus, where are you!
Where are you, Icarus? Tell me where to find you!" 60
And saw the wings on the waves, and cursed his talents,
Buried the body in a tomb, and the land
Was named for Icarus.
                During the burial
A noisy partridge, from a muddy ditch,   65
Looked out, drummed with her wings in loud approval.
No other bird, those days, was like the partridge,
Newcomer to the ranks of birds; the story
Reflects no credit on Daedalus. His sister,
Ignorant of the fates, had sent her son   70
To Daedalus as apprentice, only a youngster,
Hardly much more than twelve years old, but clever,
With an inventive turn of mind. For instance,
Studying a fish's backbone for a model,
He had notched a row of teeth in a strip of iron, 75
Thus making the first saw, and he had bound
Two arms of iron together with a joint
To keep them both together and apart,
One standing still, the other traversing
In a circle, so men came to have the compass.   80
And Daedalus, in envy, hurled the boy
Headlong from the high temple of Minerva,
And lied about it, saying he had fallen
Through accident, but Minerva, kind protectress
Of all inventive wits, stayed him in air,   85
Clothed him with plumage; he still retained his aptness
In feet and wings, and kept his old name, Perdix,
But in the new bird-form, Perdix, the partridge,
Never flies high, nor nests in trees, but flutters
Close to the ground, and the eggs are laid in
      hedgerows.   90
The bird, it seems, remembers, and is fearful
Of all high places.

HORACE

AH GOD HOW THEY RACE

Horace wrote poems in many different forms, including satire and the ode, the genre for which he is best known. In the following poem, Horace treats a common theme—the inevitability of death ending the lives of everyone—in an unusual way. While addressing the lines directly to his friend, Postumus, Horace widens their application to all of us—the "we" mentioned in the poem's final stanzas.

Ah god how they race, Postumus, Postumus,
how the years run out, and doing what is right
will not delay wrinkles and age's
onslaught and death who cannot be beaten;

no, dear friend, not even if every day   *5*
you tried with three hundred bulls to please Pluto,
who has no tears, who holds in prison
three-bodied Geryon and Tityos

by the sorrowful river whose crossing is
certain for those who live by the gifts of the earth,   *10*
a must for all, the high and mighty
and the poverty-stricken small farmers.

It will do no good to escape bloody Mars
and breaking waves on the rough Adriatic,
it will do no good to spend autumn   *15*
in terror of sirocco and sickness:

we must see the dark waters of Cocytos
winding slowly, and the infamous daughters
of Danaus, and Sisyphus, son of
Aeolus, condemned to endless labor.   *20*

We must leave behind us earth and home and dear
wife, and of all the trees that you care for now,
not one will follow you, so briefly
its master, only the loathsome cypress.

An heir who deserves it will drink Caecuban   *25*
you kept safe with a hundred keys, and he will
soak the floor with magnificent wine,
finer than the priests drink at their festivals.

*Juvenal (ca. 60–130 C.E.), was among the severest critics of Rome
in his time. Among his sixteen* Satires *are the following passages
that attack, respectively, the city of Rome and its people, and in particular, the behavior of women, who are castigated for their laziness,
love of luxury, and licentiousness.*

from "Against the city of Rome"

Translated by Rolfe Humphries

"Rome, good-bye! Let the rest stay in the town if they
          want to,   *1*
Fellows like A, B, and C, who make black white at their
          pleasure,
Finding it easy to grab contracts for rivers and harbors,
Putting up temples, or cleaning out sewers, or hauling
          off corpses,
Or, if it comes to that, auctioning slaves in the market. *5*
Once they used to be hornblowers, working the cameys;
Every wide place in the road knew their puffed-out
          cheeks and their squealing.
Now they give shows of their own. Thumbs up!
          Thumbs down![60] And the killers

Spare or slay, and then go back to concessions for
          private privies.
Nothing they won't take on. Why not?—since the
          kindness of Fortune   *10*
(Fortune is out for laughs) has exalted them out of the
          gutter.

"If you're poor, you're a joke, on each and every
          occasion.
What a laugh, if your cloak is dirty or torn, if your
          toga
Seems a little bit soiled, if your shoe has a crack in the
          leather,
Or if more than one patch attests to more than one
          mending!   *15*
Poverty's greatest curse, much worse than the fact of it,
          is that
It makes men objects of mirth, ridiculed, humbled,
          embarrassed.
'Out of the front-row seats!' they cry when you're out
          of money,
Yield your place to the sons of some pimp, the spawn
          of some cathouse,
Some slick auctioneer's brat, or the louts some trainer
          has fathered   *20*
Or the well-groomed boys whose sire is a gladiator.

"Here in town the sick die from insomnia mostly.
Undigested food, on a stomach burning with ulcers,
Brings on listlessness, but who can sleep in a
          flophouse?
Who but the rich can afford sleep and a garden
          apartment?   *25*
That's the source of infection. The wheels creak by on
          the narrow
Streets of the wards, the drivers squabble and brawl
          when they're stopped,
More than enough to frustrate the drowsiest son of a sea
          cow.
When his business calls, the crowd makes way, as the
          rich man,
Carried high in his car, rides over them, reading or
          writing,   *30*
Even taking a snooze, perhaps, for the motion's
          composing.
Still, he gets where he wants before we do; for all of our
          hurry
Traffic gets in our way, in front, around and behind us.
Somebody gives me a shove with an elbow, or two-
          by-four scantling.[61]
One clunks my head with a beam, another cracks down
          with a beer keg.   *35*
Mud is thick on my shins, I am trampled by somebody's
          big feet.
Now what?—a soldier grinds his hobnails into my
          toes."

---

[60]To turn the thumb down was the signal to kill a wounded gladiator; to
turn it up signaled that he should be spared.

[61]A piece of lumber.

from Juvenal's "Against Women" (ca. 110–127)

Where, you ask, do they come from, such monsters as
    these? In the old days   *1*
Latin women were chaste by dint of their lowly fortunes.
Toil and short hours for sleep kept cottages free from
    contagion,
Hands were hard from working the wood, and husbands
    were watching,
Standing to arms at the Colline Gate, and the shadow of
    Hannibal's looming.[62]   *5*
Now we suffer the evils of long peace. Luxury hatches
Terrors worse than the wars, avenging a world beaten
    down.
Every crime is here, and every lust, as they have been
Since the day, long since, when Roman poverty per-
    ished.
Over our seven hills,[63] from that day on, they came
    pouring.   *10*
The rabble and rout of the East, Sybaris, Rhodes, Mile-
    tus,
Yes, and Tarentum[64] too, garlanded, drunken, shameless.
Dirty money it was that first imported among us
Foreign vice and our times broke down with overindul-
    gence.
Riches are flabby, soft. And what does Venus care for   *15*
When she is drunk? She can't tell one end of a thing
    from another,
Gulping big oysters down at midnight, making the
    unguents
Foam in the unmixed wine, and drinking out of a conch-
    horn
While the walls spin round, and the table starts in danc-
    ing,
And the glow of the lamps is blurred by double their
    number.   *20*

There's nothing a woman won't do, nothing she thinks is
    disgraceful
With the green gems at her neck, or pearls distending
    her ear lobes.
Nothing is worse to endure than your Mrs. Richbitch,
    whose visage
Is padded and plastered with dough, in the most ridicu-
    lous manner.
Furthermore, she reeks of unguents, so God help her
    husband   *25*
With his wretched face stunk up with these, smeared by
    her lipstick.
To her lovers she comes with her skin washed clean. But
    at home
Why does she need to look pretty? Nard[65] is assumed
    for the lover,
For the lover she buys all the Arabian perfumes.

It takes her some time to strip down to her face, remov-
    ing the layers   *30*
One by one, till at last she is recognizable, almost,
Then she uses a lotion, she-asses' milk; she'd need herds
Of these creatures to keep her supplied on her northern-
    most journeys.
But when she's given herself the treatment in full, from
    the ground base
Through the last layer of mud pack, from the first wash
    to a poultice,   *35*
What lies under all this—a human face, or an ulcer?

MARCUS AURELIUS

from The Meditations

The Meditations *of the Roman emperor Marcus Aurelius reflect the philosophical idea of Stoicism. Marcus Aurelius jotted his meditations in odd moments between his imperial duties at court and his many months and years in the field with his Roman troops defending the city against enemy incursions. Book II is characteristic of the emperor's method, which is to record his reflections on a variety of topics in no special order. What holds* The Meditations *together in Book II and overall is the tone of unswerving endurance in the face of pain and suffering and the recognition that the human spirit can withstand any difficulty life puts in its path.*

1. Say to yourself in the morning: I shall meet people who are interfering, ungracious, insolent, full of guile, deceitful and antisocial; they have all become like that because they have no understanding of good and evil. But I who have contemplated the essential beauty of good and the essential ugliness of evil, who know that the nature of the wrongdoer is of one kin with mine—not indeed of the same blood or seed but sharing the same mind, the same portion of the divine—I cannot be harmed by any one of them, and no one can involve me in shame. I cannot feel anger against him who is of my kin, nor hate him. We were born to labor together, like the feet, the hands, the eyes, and the rows of upper and lower teeth. To work against one another is therefore contrary to nature, and to be angry against a man or turn one's back on him is to work against him.

2. Whatever it is which I am, it is flesh, breath of life, and directing mind. The flesh you should despise: blood, bones and a network woven of nerves, veins and arteries. Consider too the nature of the life-breath: wind, never the same, but disgorged and then again gulped in, continually. The third part is the directing mind. Throw away your books, be no longer anxious: that was not your given role. Rather reflect thus as if death were now before you: "You are an old man, let this third part be enslaved no longer, nor be a mere puppet on the strings of selfish desire; no longer let it be vexed by your past or present lot, or peer suspiciously into the future."

3. The works of the gods are full of Providence. The works of Chance are not divorced from Nature or from the spinning and weaving together of those things which are governed by Providence. Thence everything flows. There is also Necessity and what is beneficial to the whole ordered universe of which you are a part. That which is brought by the nature of the Whole, and preserves it, is good for every part. As do changes in the elements, so changes in their compounds

---

[62]In 213 B.C.E. the Carthaginian general, Hannibal, Rome's most formidable enemy, was camped only a few miles outside Rome, poised to attack (see Livy, xxvi:10).
[63]The hills surrounding the city of Rome.
[64]Greek cities associated with luxury and vice.
[65]Spikenard, a fragrant ointment.

preserve the ordered universe. That should be enough for you, these should ever be your beliefs. Cast out the thirst for books that you may not die growling, but with true graciousness, and grateful to the gods from the heart.

4. Remember how long you have delayed, how often the gods have appointed the day of your redemption and you have let it pass. Now, if ever, you must realize of what kind of ordered universe you are a part, of what kind of governor of that universe you are an emanation, that a time limit has now been set for you and that if you do not use it to come out into the light, it will be lost, and you will be lost, and there will be no further opportunity.

5. Firmly, as a Roman and a man should, think at all times how you can perform the task at hand with precise and genuine dignity, sympathy, independence, and justice, making yourself free from all other preoccupations. This you will achieve if you perform every action as if it was the last of your life, if you rid yourself of all aimless thoughts, of all emotional opposition to the dictates of reason, of all pretence, selfishness and displeasure with your lot. You see how few are the things a man must overcome to enable him to live a smoothly flowing and godly life; for even the gods will require nothing further from the man who keeps to these beliefs.

6. You shame yourself, my soul, you shame yourself, and you will have no further opportunity to respect yourself; the life of every man is short and yours is almost finished while you do not respect yourself but allow your happiness to depend upon the souls of others.

7. Do external circumstances to some extent distract you? Give yourself leisure to acquire some further good knowledge and cease to wander aimlessly. Then one must guard against another kind of wandering, for those who are exhausted by life, and have no aim at which to direct every impulse and generally every impression, are foolish in their deeds as well as in their words.

8. A man is not easily found to be unhappy because he takes no thought for what happens in the soul of another; it is those who do not attend to the disturbances of their own soul who are inevitably in a state of unhappiness.

9. Always keep this thought in mind: what is the essential nature of the universe and what is my own essential nature? How is the one related to the other, being so small a part of so great a Whole? And remember that no one can prevent your deeds and your words being in accord with nature.

10. Theophrastus speaks as a philosopher when, in comparing sins as a man commonly might, he states that offences due to desire are worse than those due to anger, for the angry man appears to be in the grip of pain and hidden pangs when he discards Reason, whereas he who sins through desire, being overcome by pleasure, seems more licentious and more effeminate in his wrongdoing. So Theophrastus is right, and speaks in a manner worthy of philosophy, when he says that one who sins through pleasure deserves more blame than one who sins through pain. The latter is more like a man who was wronged first and compelled by pain to anger; the former starts on the path to sin of his own accord, driven to action by desire.

11. It is possible to depart from life at this moment. Have this thought in mind whenever you act, speak, or think. There is nothing terrible in leaving the company of men, if the gods exist, for they would not involve you in evil. If, on the other hand, they do not exist or do not concern themselves with human affairs, then what is life to me in a universe devoid of gods or of Providence? But they do exist and do care for humanity, and have put it altogether within a man's power not to fall into real evils. And if anything else were evil they would have seen to it that it be in every man's power not to fall into it. As for that which does not make man worse, how could it make the life of man worse?

Neither through ignorance nor with knowledge could the nature of the Whole have neglected to guard against this or correct it; nor through lack of power or skill could it have committed so great a wrong, namely that good and evil should come to the good and the evil alike, and at random, True, death and life, good and ill repute, toil and pleasure, wealth and poverty, being neither good nor bad, come to the good and the bad equally. They are therefore neither blessings nor evils.

12. How swiftly all things vanish; in the universe the bodies themselves, and in time the memories of them. Of what kind are all the objects of sense, especially those which entice us by means of pleasure, frighten us by means of pain, or are shouted about in vainglory; how cheap they are, how contemptible, sordid, corruptible and dead—upon this our intellectual faculty should fix its attention. Who are these men whose voice and judgment make or break reputations? What is the nature of death? When a man examines it in itself, and with his share of intelligence dissolves the imaginings which cling to it, he conceives it to be no other than a function of nature, and to fear a natural function is to be only a child. Death is not only a function of nature but beneficial to it.

How does man reach god, with what part of himself, and in what condition must that part be?

13. Nothing is more wretched than the man who runs around in circles busying himself with all kinds of things—investigating things below the earth, as the saying goes—always looking for signs of what his neighbors are feeling and thinking. He does not realize that it is enough to be concerned with the spirit within oneself and genuinely to serve it. This service consists in keeping it free from passions, aimlessness, and discontent with its fate at the hands of gods and men. What comes from the gods must be revered because of their goodness; what comes from men must be welcomed because of our kinship, although sometimes these things are also pitiful in a sense, because of men's ignorance of good and evil, which is no less a disability than to be unable to distinguish between black and white.

14. Even if you were to live three thousand years or three times ten thousand, remember nevertheless that no one can shed another life than this which he is living, nor live another life than this which he is shedding, so that the longest and the shortest life come to the same thing. The present is equal for all, and that which is being lost is equal, and that which is being shed is thus shown to be but a moment. No one can shed that which is past, nor what is still to come; for how could he be deprived of what he does not possess?

Therefore remember these two things always: first, that all things as they come round again have been the same from eternity, and it makes no difference whether you see the same things for a hundred years, or for two hundred years, or for an infinite time; second, that the longest-lived or the shortest-lived sheds the same thing at death, for it is the present moment only of which he will be deprived, if indeed only the present moment is his, and no man can discard what he does not have.

15. "All is but thinking so." The retort to the saying of Monimus the Cynic is obvious, but the usefulness of the saying is also obvious, if one accepts the essential meaning of it insofar as it is true.

16. The human soul violates itself most of all when it becomes, as far as it can, a separate tumor or growth upon the universe; for to be discontented with anything that happens is to rebel against that Nature which embraces, in some part of itself, all other natures. The soul violates itself also whenever it turns away from a man and opposes him to do him harm, as do the souls of angry men; thirdly, whenever it is overcome by pleasure or pain; fourthly, whenever it acts a part and does or says anything falsely and hypocritically; fifthly, when it fails to direct any action or impulse to a goal, but acts at random, without purpose, whereas even the most trifling actions must be directed toward the end; and this end, for reasonable creatures, is to follow the reason and the law of the most honored commonwealth and constitution.

17. In human life time is but a point, reality a flux, perception indistinct, the composition of the body subject to easy corruption, the soul a spinning top, fortune hard to make out, fame confused. To put it briefly: physical things are but a flowing stream, things of the soul dreams and vanity; life is but a struggle and the visit to a strange land, posthumous fame but a forgetting.

What then can help us on our way? One thing only: philosophy. This consists in guarding our inner spirit inviolate and unharmed, stronger than pleasures and pains, never acting aimlessly, falsely or hypocritically, independent of the actions or inaction of others, accepting all that happens or is given as coming from hence one came oneself, and at all times awaiting death with contented mind as being only the release of the elements of which every creature is composed. It is nothing fearful for the elements themselves that one should continually change into another. Why should anyone look with suspicion upon the change and dissolution of all things? For this is in accord with nature and nothing evil is in accord with nature.

SUETONIUS

LIVES OF THE CAESARS

In the following excerpt from his Lives of the Caesars, Gaius Suetonius Tranquillus (ca. 69–after 122 C.E.) describes the excessive cruelties of the Roman emperors Tiberius and Caligula. Although Suetonius cannot be counted on for complete historical accuracy, the general gist of his characterization of these and the other Roman emperors is apt, if horrifying. Although some of the Caesars whose lives be chronicles, such as Julius Caesar and Augustus Caesar, are not characterized as bloodthirsty, diabolical, and psychopathic, his descriptions of the vices of Tiberius and Caligula certainly make for entertaining reading.

24. Tiberius did not hesitate to exercise imperial power immediately by calling on the Praetorians to provide him with a bodyguard; which was to be Emperor in fact and in appearance. Yet a long time elapsed before he assumed the position of Emperor. When his friends urged him to accept it he went through the farce of scolding them for the suggestion, saying that they did not realize what a monstrous beast the monarchy was; and kept the Senate guessing by his carefully evasive answers and hesitations, even when they threw themselves at his feet imploring him to change his mind. This made some of them lose patience, and in the confusion a voice was heard shouting: 'Oh, let him either take it or leave it!' And another senator openly taunted him with: 'Some people are slow to do what they promise; you are slow to promise what you have already done.' Finally, with a great show of reluctance, and complaints that they were forcing him to become a miserable and overworked slave, Tiberius accepted the title of Emperor; but hinted that he might later resign it. His actual words were: 'Until I grow so old that you may be good enough to grant me a respite.' . . .

41. On his return to Capreae he let all affairs of state slide: neither filling vacancies that occurred in the Equestrian Order, nor making new appointments to senior military posts, or the governorships of any province. Spain and Syria were left without their governors of consular rank for several years. He allowed the Parthians to overrun Armenia; the Dacians and Sarmatians to ravage Moesia; and the Germans to invade Gaul—a negligence as dangerous to the Empire as it was dishonourable.

42. But having found seclusion at last, and no longer feeling himself under public scrutiny, he rapidly succumbed to all the vicious passions which he had for a long time tried, not very successfully, to disguise. I shall give a faithful account of these from the start. Even as a young officer he was such a hard drinker that his name, Tiberius Claudius Nero, was displaced by the nickname 'Biberius Caldius Mero'—meaning: 'Drinker of hot wine with no water added'. When already Emperor and busily engaged on the reform of public morals, he spent two whole days and the intervening night in an orgy of food and drink with Pomponius Flaccus and Lucius Piso—at the conclusion of which he made Flaccus Governor of Syria; and Piso, City Prefect—actually eulogizing them in their commissions as 'good fellows at all hours of the day or night'. Being invited to dinner by Cestius Gallus, a lecherous old spendthrift whom Augustus had ignominiously removed from the Senate and whom he had himself reprimanded only a few days previously, Tiberius accepted on condition that the dinner should follow Gallus' usual routine; and that the waitresses should be naked. At another banquet a very obscure candidate for the quaestorship drained a huge two-handled tankard of wine at Tiberius' challenge, whereupon he was preferred to rival candidates from the noblest families. Tiberius also paid Asellius Sabinus 2,000 gold pieces, to show his appreciation of a dialogue in which a mushroom, a fig-picker, an oyster, and a thrush took part in a competition; and established a new office, Comptroller of Pleasures, first held by a knight named Titus Caesonius Priscus.

43. On retiring to Capreae he made himself a private sportinghouse, where sexual extravagances were practised for his secret pleasure. Bevies of girls and young men, whom he had collected from all over the Empire as adepts in unnatural practices, and known as *spintriae*, would copulate before him in groups of three, to excite his waning passions. A number of small rooms were furnished with the most indecent

pictures and statuary obtainable, also certain erotic manuals from Elephantis in Egypt; the inmates of the establishment would know from these exactly what was expected of them. He furthermore devised little nooks of lechery in the woods and glades of the island, and had boys and girls dressed up as Pans and nymphs prostituting themselves in front of caverns or grottoes; so that the island was now openly and generally called 'Caprineum'.[1]

44. Some aspects of his criminal obscenity are almost too vile to discuss, much less believe. Imagine training little boys, whom he called his 'minnows', to chase him while he went swimming and get between his legs to lick and nibble him. Or letting babies not yet weaned from their mother's breast suck at his breast or groin—such a filthy old man he had become! Then there was a painting by Parrhasius, which had been bequeathed him on condition that, if he did not like the subject, he could have 10,000 gold pieces instead. Tiberius not only preferred to keep the picture but hung it in his bedroom. It showed Atalanta performing fellatio with Meleager.

The story goes that once, while sacrificing, he took an erotic fancy to the acolyte who carried the incense casket, and could hardly wait for the ceremony to end before hurrying him and his brother, the sacred trumpeter, out of the temple and indecently assaulting them both. When they jointly protested at this disgusting behaviour he had their legs broken.

45. What nasty tricks he used to play on women, even those of high rank, is clearly seen in the case of Mallonia whom he summoned to his bed. She showed such an invincible repugnance to complying with his lusts that he set informers on her track and during her very trial continued to shout: 'Are you sorry?' Finally she left the court and went home; there she stabbed herself to death after a violent tirade against 'that filthy-mouthed, hairy, stinking old man'. So a joke at his expense, slipped into the next Atellan farce, won a loud laugh and went the rounds at once:

THE OLD GOAT GOES

FOR THE DOES

WITH HIS TONGUE.

61. Soon Tiberius broke out in every sort of cruelty and never lacked for victims: these were, first, his mother's friends and even acquaintances; then those of his grandsons and daughter-in-law; finally, those of Sejanus. With Sejanus out of the way his savageries increased; which proved that Sejanus had not, as some thought, been inciting him to commit them, but merely providing the opportunities that he demanded. Nevertheless, in Tiberius' brief and sketchy autobiography we find him daring to assert that Sejanus had been killed because he had found him persecuting Nero and Drusus, the sons of Germanicus; the fact being that he had himself put Nero to death when Sejanus was already an object of suspicion, and Drusus after he had fallen from power. A detailed list of Tiberius' barbarities would take a long time to compile; I shall content myself with a few samples. Not a day, however holy, passed without an execution; he even desecrated New Year's Day. Many of his men victims were accused and punished with their children—some actually by

their children—and the relatives forbidden to go into mourning. Special awards were voted to the informers who had denounced them and, in certain circumstances, to the witnesses too. An informer's word was always believed. Every crime beame a capital one, even the utterance of a few careless words. A poet found himself accused of slander—he had written a tragedy which presented King Agamemnon in a bad light—and a historian had made the mistake of describing Caesar's assassins, Brutus and Cassius, as 'the last of the Romans'. Both these authors were executed without delay, and their works—though once publicly read before Augustus, and accorded general praise—were called in and destroyed. Tiberius denied those who escaped a prison sentence not only the solace of reading books, but the privilege of talking to their fellow-prisoners. Some of the accused, on being warned to appear in court, felt sure that the verdict would be 'guilty' and, to avoid the trouble and humiliation of a trial, stayed at home and severed an artery; yet Tiberius' men bandaged their wounds and hurried them, half-dead, to prison. Others obeyed their summons and then drank poison in full view of the Senate. The bodies of all executed persons were flung on the Stairs of Mourning, and dragged to the Tiber with hooks—as many as twenty a day, including women and children. Tradition forbade the strangling of virgins; so, when little girls had been condemned to die in this way, the executioner began by violating them. Tiberius used to punish with life those who wished to die. He regarded death as a comparatively light affliction, and on hearing that a man named Carnulus had forestalled his execution by suicide, exclaimed: 'Carnulus has got away!' Once, during a gaol inspection, a prisoner begged to be put out of his misery; Tiberius replied: 'No, we are not yet friends again.' An ex-consul has recorded in his memoirs that he attended a banquet at which Tiberius was suddenly asked loudly by a dwarf, standing among a group of jesters near the table: 'What of Paconius? Why is he still alive after being charged with treason?' Tiberius told him to hold his saucy tongue; but a few days later requested the Senate to make a quick decision about Paconius' execution.

62. On eventually discovering that his own son Drusus the Younger had after all died, not as a result of his debauched habits, but from poison administered by his wife Livilla in partnership with Sejanus, Tiberius grew enraged and redoubled his cruelties until nobody was safe from torture and death. He spent whole days investigating the Drusus affair, which obsessed him to such a degree that when a man whose guest he had been at Rhodes arrived in response to his own friendly invitation, he mistook him for an important witness in the case and had him put to the torture at once. When the truth came out he actually executed the man to avoid publicizing the scandal.

In Capreae they still show the place at the cliff top where Tiberius used to watch his victims being thrown into the sea after prolonged and exquisite tortures. A party of marines were stationed below, and when the bodies came hurtling down they whacked at them with oars and boat-hooks, to make sure that they were completely dead. An ingenious torture of Tiberius' devising was to trick men into drinking huge draughts of wine, and then suddenly to knot a cord tightly round their genitals, which not only cut into the flesh but prevented them from urinating. Even more people would have died, it is thought, had Thrasyllus the astrologer not

---

[1] A play on the word *caper* (goat).

persuaded him, deliberately it is said, to postpone his designs by an assurance that he still had many years of life in hand. These victims would have included his remaining grandsons, Gaius whom he suspected, and Tiberius Gemellus whom he hated as having been born from adultery. The story is credible, because he sometimes used to express envy of Priam for having outlived his entire family.

24. It was his habit to commit incest with each of his three sisters and, at large banquets, when his wife reclined above him, placed them all in turn below him. They say that he ravished his sister Drusilla before he came of age: their grandmother Antonia, at whose house they were both staying, caught them in bed together. Later, he took Drusilla from her husband, the former Consul Lucius Cassius Longinus, openly treating her as his lawfully married wife; and when he fell dangerously ill left Drusilla all his property, and the Empire too. At her death he made it a capital offence to laugh, to bathe, or to dine with one's parents, wives, or children while the period of public mourning lasted; and was so crazed with grief that he suddenly rushed from Rome by night, drove through Campania, took ship to Syracuse, and returned just as impetuously without having shaved or cut his hair in the meantime. Afterwards, whenever he had to take an important oath, he swore by Drusilla's divinity, even at a public assembly or an army parade. He showed no such extreme love or respect for the two surviving sisters, and often, indeed, let his boy friends sleep with them; and at Aemilius Lepidus' trial, felt no compunction about denouncing them as adulteresses who were party to plots against him—openly producing letters in their handwriting (acquired by trickery and seduction) and dedicating to Mars the Avenger the three swords with which, the accompanying placard alleged, they had meant to kill him.

25. It would be hard to say whether the way he got married, the way he dissolved his marriages, or the way he behaved as a husband was the most disgraceful. He attended the wedding ceremony of Gaius Piso and Livia Orestilla, but had the bride carried off to his own home. After a few days, however, he divorced her, and two years later banished her, suspecting that she had returned to Piso in the interval. According to one account he told Piso, who was reclining opposite him at the wedding feast: 'Hands off my wife!' and abducted her from the table at once; and announced the next day that he had taken a wife in the style of Romulus and Augustus.[1] Then he suddenly sent for Lollia Paulina, wife of Gaius Memmius, a Governor of consular rank, from his province, because somebody had remarked that her grandmother was once a famous beauty; but soon discarded her, forbidding her ever again to sleep with another man. Caesonia was neither young nor beautiful, and had three daughters by a former husband, besides being recklessly extravagant and utterly promiscuous; yet he loved her with a passionate faithfulness and often, when reviewing the troops, used to take her out riding in helmet, cloak, and shield. For his friends he even paraded her naked; but would not allow her the dignified title of 'wife' until she had borne him a child, whereupon he announced the marriage and the birth simultaneously. He

named the child Julia Drusilla; and carried her around the temples of all the goddesses in turn before finally entrusting her to the lap of Minerva, whom he called upon to supervise his daughter's growth and education. What finally convinced him of his own paternity was her violent temper; while still an infant she would try to scratch her little playmates' faces and eyes.

26. It would be trivial and pointless to record how Gaius treated such relatives and friends as his cousin King Ptolemy of Mauretania (the son of King Juba and grandson of Antony by his daughter Cleopatra Selene), or Macro the Guards Commander, with his wife Ennia, by whose help he had become Emperor. Their very nearness and services to him earned them cruel deaths.

Nor was he any more respectful or considerate in his dealings with the Senate, but made some of the highest officials run for miles beside his chariot, dressed in their togas; or wait in short linen tunics at the head or foot of his dining couch. Often he would send for men whom he had secretly killed, as though they were still alive, and remark off-handedly a few days later that they must have committed suicide. When two Consuls forgot to announce his birthday, he dismissed them and left the country for three days without officers of state. One of his quaestors was charged with conspiracy; Gaius had his clothes stripped off and spread on the ground, to give the soldiers who flogged him a firmer foothold.

He behaved just as arrogantly and violently towards the other orders of society. A crowd bursting into the Circus about midnight to secure free seats angered him so much that he had them driven away with clubs; more than a score of knights, as many married women, and numerous others were crushed to death in the ensuing panic. Gaius liked to stir up trouble in the Theatre by scattering gift vouchers before the seats were occupied, thus tempting commoners to invade the rows reserved for knights. During gladiatorial shows he would have the canopies removed at the hottest time of the day and forbid anyone to leave; or take away the usual equipment, and pit feeble old fighters against decrepit wild animals; or stage comic duels between respectable householders who happened to be physically disabled in some way or other. More than once he closed down the granaries and let the people go hungry.

27. The following instances will illustrate his blood-thirstiness. Having collected wild animals for one of his shows, he found butcher's meat too expensive and decided to feed them with criminals instead. He paid no attention to the charge-sheets, but simply stood in the middle of a colonnade, glanced at the prisoners lined up before him, and gave the order: 'Kill every man between that bald head and the other one over there!' Someone had sworn to fight in the arena if Gaius recovered from his illness; Gaius forced him to fulfil this oath, and watched his swordplay closely, not letting him go until he had won the match and begged abjectly to be released. Another fellow had pledged himself, on the same occasion, to commit suicide; Gaius, finding that he was still alive, ordered him to be dressed in wreaths and fillets, and driven through Rome by the imperial slaves—who kept harping on his pledge and finally flung him over the embankment into the river. Many men of decent family were branded at his command, and sent down the mines, or put to work on the roads, or thrown to the wild beasts. Others were confined in narrow cages, where they had to crouch on all fours like animals; or

---

[1] See Augustus 69.

were sawn in half—and not necessarily for major offences, but merely for criticizing his shows, or failing to swear by his Genius.

Gaius made parents attend their sons' executions, and when one father excused himself on the ground of ill-health, provided a litter for him. Having invited another father to dinner just after the son's execution, he overflowed with good-fellowship in an attempt to make him laugh and joke. He watched the manager of his gladiatorial and wild-beast shows being flogged with chains for several days running, and had him killed only when the smell of suppurating brains became insupportable. A writer of Atellan farces was burned alive in the amphitheatre, because of a line which had an amusing *double-entendre*. One knight, on the point of being thrown to the wild beasts, shouted that he was innocent; Gaius brought him back, removed his tongue, and then ordered the sentence to be carried out.

28. Once he asked a returned exile how he had been spending his time. To flatter him the man answered: 'I prayed continuously to the gods for Tiberius' death, and your accession; and my prayer was granted.' Gaius therefore concluded that the new batch of exiles must be praying for his own death; so he sent agents from island to island and had them all killed. Being anxious that one particular senator should be torn in pieces he persuaded some of his colleagues to challenge him as a public enemy when he entered the House, stab him with their pens, and then hand him over for lynching to the rest of the Senate; and was not satisfied until the victim's limbs, organs, and guts had been dragged through the streets and heaped up at his feet.

29. Gaius' savage crimes were made worse by his brutal language. He claimed that no personal trait made him feel prouder than his 'inflexibility'—by which he must have meant 'brazen impudence'. As though mere deafness to his grandmother Antonia's good advice were not enough, he told her: 'Bear in mind that I can treat anyone exactly as I please!' Suspecting that young Tiberius Gemellus had taken drugs as prophylactics to the poison he intended to administer, he scoffed: 'Can there really be an antidote against Caesar?' And, on banishing his sisters, he remarked: 'I have swords as well as islands.' One ex-praetor, taking a cure at Anticyra, made frequent requests for an extension of his sick leave; Gaius had him put to death, suggesting that if hellebore had been of so little benefit over so long a period, he must need to be bled. When signing the execution list he used to say: 'I am clearing my accounts.' And one day, after sentencing a number of Gauls and Greeks to die in the same batch, he boasted of having 'subdued Gallo-Graecia'.

CHAPTER 5

HISTORY

ca. 2000 B.C.E.	Abraham is called from Mesopotamia to Canaan
ca. 1600 B.C.E.	Hebrews leave Canaan for Egypt
ca. 1250 B.C.E.	Moses and Hebrews wander in Sinai desert, reach Canaan
ca. 1000 B.C.E.	Israelites establish monarchy
ca. 1000–961 B.C.E.	David reigns
ca. 961–922 B.C.E.	Solomon reigns
ca. 922 B.C.E.	Monarchy split into kingdoms of Israel and Judah
722 B.C.E.	Israel falls to Assyrians and its people scatter
587 B.C.E.	Judah falls to Nebuchadnezzar II; hostages sent to Babylon
539 B.C.E.	Babylonian Captivity ends when Persians defeat Babylon
34 C.E.	Stephen, first martyr, is stoned to death
35 C.E.	Paul converts to Christianity
200 C.E.	Rome is center of Christianity
313 C.E.	Constantine the Great legalizes Christianity
325 C.E.	First Council of Nicaea develops Nicene Creed
330 C.E.	Constantine names Constantinople new capital of Roman Empire
391 C.E.	Theodosius I declares Christianity the official religion of the Roman Empire
395 C.E.	Roman Empire split into East and West
527–65 C.E.	Justinian reigns
1054 C.E.	Schism between Eastern and Western Churches
1071 C.E.	Conquest of eastern Byzantine provinces by Seljuk Turks
1204 C.E.	Crusaders pillage Constantinople
1453 C.E.	Constantinople falls to Turks

ARTS AND ARCHITECTURE

mid-third century C.E.	*Jesus the Good Shepherd*
ca. 333 C.E.	Old St. Peter's
391 C.E.	Sarcophagus of Junius Bassus
fourth century C.E.	Catacomb of Santi
	Pietro e Marcellino, Dome of Heaven
526–47 C.E.	San Vitale
532–37 C.E.	Anthemius of Tralles and Isidorus of Miletus, Hagia Saphia
ca. 547 C.E.	Mosaics of Emperor Justinian and Empress Theodora
begun 1063 C.E.	Saint Mark's, Venice
ca. 1200 C.E.	Creation Dome mosaic
late thirteenth century C.E.	*Madonna and Child Enthroned*

LITERATURE AND PHILOSOPHY

ca. 3000 B.C.E.	Portions from book of Genesis circulated orally
ca. twelfth–tenth centuries B.C.E.	Book of Genesis recorded
early first century C.E.	Books of Ezra and Nehemiah written
ca. 70–100 C.E.	Gospels written
75–95 C.E.	Book of Revelation written
397 C.E.	Augustine, *Confessions*

Judaism, Early Christianity, and Byzantine Civilization

Theodora and her Attendants, San Vitale, Ravenna, ca. 547, mosaic.

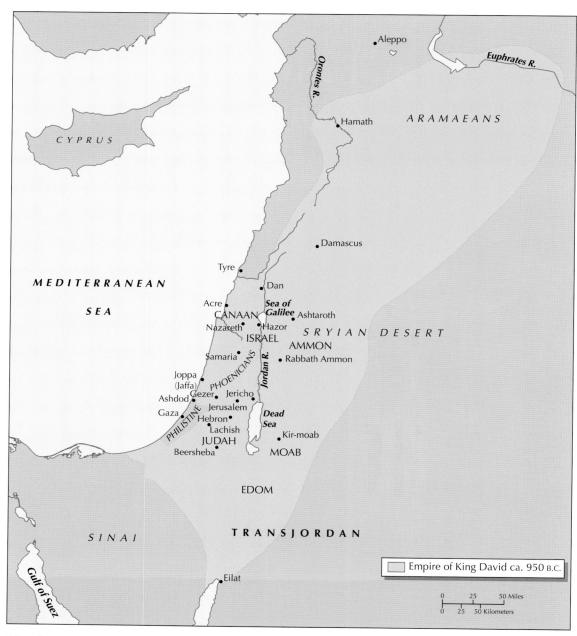

MAP 5.1 Ancient Israel.

CHAPTER OVERVIEW

JUDAISM
The Hebraic faith establishes its history and tradition with the Bible

EARLY CHRISTIANITY
The arts nurture and transmit the beliefs of the Christian faith

BYZANTINE CIVILIZATION
The schism of the church forges the way for Byzantium in the East

JUDAISM

THE GREEKS AND THE ROMANS dominated the ancient world politically and socially, but another tradition, although not as significant artistically or politically, came to influence Western civilization as well. The founders of this tradition called themselves the "Children of Israel," the Israelites, or Hebrews (from *Habiru*, meaning "nomad" or "outcast"). Later they became known as Jews, a name derived from their place of habitation, the area around Jerusalem known as Judaea.

Whereas the Greco-Roman tradition was rational, practical, and dedicated to the arts, the Hebrew tradition was spiritual, mystical, and founded on faith. The Jews produced a "religion of the book," what Christians regard as the Old Testament portion of the Bible, providing a spiritual and moral foundation for Western culture. Judaism itself sought no converts—the Hebrew scriptures represented God's words to his "Chosen People." These scriptures emphasized a special national destiny, privilege, and responsibility. Christianity, which grew out of Judaism, did seek converts, and was from its earliest days in the first century C.E. a missionary religion, seeking to attract as many followers as possible. It spread the word of God through **evangelists,** from the Greek *euangelos,* meaning "bearer of good news"—*eu* means "good" and *angelos* "messenger." The missionary zeal of the Early Christians ultimately united the Greco-Roman and biblical traditions. In 313 C.E., the Roman emperor Constantine granted toleration to Christians, and then received Christian baptism on his deathbed in 337 himself.

The nomadic Hebrew people were forced out of the Mesopotamian basin about 2000 B.C.E. by the warlike Akkadians and the ascendancy of the Babylonians. Led by the patriarch Abraham, the Hebrews settled in Canaan, the hilly country between the Jordan River and the eastern Mediterranean coast. Canaan became their homeland and was, the Hebrews believed, promised to them by their god. **Monotheistic** (meaning the belief in only one God), as opposed to the polytheistic religions of Greece, Rome, and other Near Eastern peoples, the Hebrew religion had but one God—Yahweh, a name so sacred that the pious never speak or write it.

In contrast, other Near Eastern tribes worshiped the multiple divine beings. The Babylonians, for instance, paid homage to, among others, a storm god and a rain god. Where the gods of Egypt and Mesopotamia were immanent, or present in nature, Yahweh was transcendent, apart from nature, which he also controlled. Thus the sun, which the Egyptians worshiped as a god, was for the Hebrews subject to the power of their god, who had created it. Moreover, they considered the figures of other religions subordinate to the God of Israel.

HISTORY AND RELIGION

The history and religion of the Hebrews are essentially one and the same, and that history and religion are recorded in the Bible. The Hebrew Bible can be read as the history of the Hebrews' relationship with their god. For the Israelites, God's power was made manifest in particular events, such as the creation of the world and its destruction in the great flood.

Creation. The Hebrews believed that God created heaven and earth. The Bible describes both the world and the human beings that originally populated it as "good." Human kind no longer lives in the original paradise, however, because, as related in Genesis, Adam and Eve disobey God's word in the Garden of Eden and eat the forbidden fruit. Adam and Eve's expulsion inaugurates a pattern of exile that continues in the wanderings of the patriarchs.

Patriarchs. The early patriarchs of ancient Israel believed they were favored by God and consequently led lives that honored God. The first of the patriarchs was Abraham, regarded as the ancestor of the Jews. When God called Abraham out of the land of Ur to Canaan, Abraham's response was an immediate and total acceptance of God's will.

To Abraham and his followers and descendants God made the solemn promise of the **covenant.** An agreement between God and his people, it was passed down to the patriarchs who followed Abraham—to his son Isaac and his grandson Jacob, or Israel. In the covenant, God agrees to be the Hebrew deity if the Hebrews agree, in turn, to be his people and to follow his will. With each patriarch, God renews the covenant originally made with Abraham. This covenant is referred to many times in the first five books of the Bible, which are called the Law, or the *Torah* (Hebrew for "instruction" or "teaching").

Seven hundred years after the time of Abraham, a renewal of the covenant took place while the Hebrews were living in Egypt. Why they had left Canaan for Egypt in about 1600 B.C.E., we do not know, but they prospered there until the Egyptians enslaved them. In about 1250 B.C.E., the patriarch Moses defied the pharaoh, and led his people out of Egypt (the Exodus) into the Sinai desert, which lies on the peninsula between Egypt and Canaan. There, on top of Mt. Sinai, God is said to have given Moses the Decalogue, or Ten Commandments.

1. You shall have no other gods before me.
2. You shall not make for yourself a graven image, or any likeness of any thing that is in heaven above, or that is on the earth beneath, or that is in the water under the earth.
3. You shall not take the name of the Lord your God in vain.

4. Observe the sabbath day, to keep it holy, as the Lord your God commanded you.
5. Honor your father and your mother.
6. You shall not kill.
7. Neither shall you commit adultery.
8. Neither shall you steal.
9. Neither shall you bear false witness against your neighbor.
10. Neither shall you covet your neighbor's wife, or anything that is your neighbor's.

The Hebrews carried the Decalogue with them, carved into stone tablets kept in a sacred chest called the Ark of the Covenant (fig. 5.1). Other sacred objects were also kept in the Ark such as the menorahs (seven-branched candelabra), which had been described by God to Moses, and which originally lit the Ark in its portable tabernacle. Although they do not cover every aspect of the wide-ranging ethical thinking of the Biblical authors, the Ten Commandments contain the essence of the religious law of the ancient Judeo-Christian world. Their influence has been enormous. Beginning with the six hundred and more laws recorded in the book of Leviticus, and continuing with the exploration of morality in the time of Jesus, the Commandments provide a basis for moral reflection and analysis.

For the ancient Hebrews, divine acts like the conferring of the Ten Commandments were acknowledgements of their status as God's Chosen People. And though the Hebrews wandered for forty years "in the wilderness" of the Sinai, they were delivered to the Promised Land, the land of "milk and honey," by the patriarch Joshua, who led them across the Jordan River and into Canaan once again. Over the next two hundred years, they gained control of the entire region, calling themselves Israelites, after the patriarch Jacob, who had named himself Israel.

Prophets.   Despite the imperative of God's covenant, the ancient Hebrews believed human beings were ultimately responsible for their own actions and for doing whatever was necessary to improve their lot. When something was wrong in the social order, the onus was on believers to correct it. This would become the central message of the biblical prophets from the eighth through the sixth century B.C.E.

The Israelite prophets spoke for God. They were not "prophetic" in the sense that they foretold the future. Instead they functioned as mouthpieces, preaching what they had been instructed by God in vision or through ecstasy. They taught the importance of living according to the Ten Commandments. In many cases, the prophets operated as voices of conscience, confronting the Israelite kings with their wrongdoings. The most important biblical prophets were Isaiah, Jeremiah, and Ezekiel, although there were another twelve whose books are included in the Old Testament.

Isaiah called for social justice and for an end to war. A verse from the book of Isaiah adorns the United Nations building in New York City: "And they shall beat their swords into ploughshares, and their spears into pruning hooks; nation shall not lift up sword against nation, neither shall they learn war any more" (Isa. 2:4).

FIGURE 5.1   *Menorahs and Ark of the Covenant,* wall painting in a Jewish catacomb, third century C.E., 3′11″ × 5′9″ (1.19 × 1.8 m), Villa Torlonia, Rome. The form of the menorah probably derives from the Tree of Life, an ancient Mesopotamian symbol.

Then & Now

THE BIBLE

The books of the Hebrew Bible were composed over a period of nearly fifteen hundred years, from approximately 3000 B.C.E., from the earliest Genesis materials until near the beginning of the second century B.C.E. when the book of Daniel was written. Original manuscripts of the biblical books have not survived. The earliest extant passages are those found in caves in Qumran—the "Dead Sea Scrolls"—which include parchment scrolls of the prophetic book of Isaiah (fig. 5.2).

Originally written in Hebrew, with brief sections in Aramaic, a Near Eastern Semitic language, the present-day Bible in English has been influenced by a series of different translations: Greek (the Septuagint); Latin (the Vulgate—translated by St. Jerome); and Renaissance English, initially translated by John Wycliffe and William Tyndale. The most important early English translation, however, was that undertaken by a committee established by King James I. Known as the "King James translation" or the "Authorized Version" or "AV," this rendering has exerted profound influence on English and American literature for nearly four hundred years.

During the 1940s and 1950s, the King James translation was updated and corrected, taking account of archaeological discoveries made in the late nineteenth and early twentieth centuries, and reflecting developments in historical and linguistic scholarship. The resulting Revised Standard Version (RSV) was revised once more and published as the New Revised Standard Version (NRSV) in the 1990s.

FIGURE 5.2   The Dead Sea Isaiah Scroll (detail), first-century B.C.E.-first-century C.E. The Scrolls are copies of the Hebrew Bible made by a radical Jewish sect that disavowed the leadership of Jerusalem. The Scroll contains all sixty-six chapters of the Bible's longest book.

Kings.   By 1000 B.C.E., the kingdom of Israel was established, with SAUL (r. ca. 1040–1000 B.C.E.) as its first king. The first book of Samuel describes Saul's kingship and the arrival of David, who saves the Israelites from their enemy, the Philistines, by slaying the giant Goliath with a stone from a slingshot.

DAVID (r. ca. 1000–961 B.C.E.) was Israel's greatest king. His reign lasted about forty years and was a time of military success, a period that included the capture of Jerusalem, which David made the capital of his kingdom. David's rule did not prevent him from composing poetry and music, including, as is traditionally held, though doubted by some scholars, some of the biblical Psalms. Perhaps the most interesting aspect of David, however, is his imperfection, for the Bible depicts him as a person who was both a sinner and a penitent. His transgressions include having one of his soldiers, Uriah, dispatched to the front line where he would undoubtedly be killed, so David could marry his widow, Bathsheba. Yet David was also to suffer the death of his son Absalom, who mounted a military rebellion against

Cross Currents

THE BIBLE AND ASIAN RELIGIONS

When Jesus said, "You shall love your neighbor as yourself" (Mark 12:29–31), he was expanding on a text from the book of Deuteronomy in the Old Testament, where the biblical writer presents what Jesus called the first great commandment: to "love the Lord your God with all your heart, with all your mind, and with all your strength" (Deut. 6:4–5). Allied with this statement is a version of it that has come to be known as the Golden Rule: "Do unto others as you would have them do unto you" (Matt. 7:12).

More than five hundred years before Christ, however, Confucius had said something similar: "What you do not wish done to yourself, do not do to others" (*Analects*). Another version of this teaching was voiced by the Jewish rabbi Hillel, around the time of Christ as: "What you yourself hate, don't do to your neighbor. This is the whole Law; the rest is commentary."

The essence of this message is also anticipated in Taoist and Buddhist texts. Here are Lao-Tzu and Buddha offering still other versions of the command to love all beings:

> To those who are good to me, I am good; and to those who are not good to me, I am also good, and thus all get to be good.

Lao-Tzu, *Tao Te Ching*, 49

> Hatred is never appeased by hatred in this world; it is appeased by love. This is an eternal Law.

Buddha, *Dhammapada*, 5

Islamic and Hindu traditions record similar advice:

> Hindu: Do naught unto others which would cause pain if done to you.

Mahābhārata XIII:14

> Islamic: No one of you is a believer until he desires for his brother that which he desires for himself.

Mohammed/Koran

---

him. The books of Samuel reveal political intrigues and complex familial dynamics with great subtlety and literary artistry.

The last important Israelite king was David's son, SOLOMON [SOL-oh-mun] (r. ca. 961–922 B.C.E.). Famous for his wisdom, Solomon is also associated with the Temple he had built in Jerusalem. Like his father, Solomon was a poet. He is the reputed author of the biblical Song of Songs, a sensual love poem that has been read by later critics as a metaphor for the love between God and his people.

Following the death of Solomon, the kingdom of Israel was split in two. The Northern Kingdom retained the name Israel; the Southern Kingdom was called Judah. The Northern Kingdom fell to the Assyrians in 722 B.C.E.; the Southern Kingdom was overrun in 587 B.C.E. by the Babylonians under the command of NEBUCHADNEZ-ZAR [ne-BYUK-ad-NEZ-ah], who destroyed Solomon's magnificent temple. The Southern Kingdom Hebrews were carried off into exile, which inaugurated a period known as the Babylonian Captivity.

Jerusalem in the Time of David and Solomon.

King David chose Jerusalem as the seat of political power. In neutral territory, midway between the northern and southern kingdom power centers, Jerusalem straddles the crest of a mountain range, between the sea and the river Jordan.

During David's reign, the city defenses were strengthened, largely through the extension of the city's walls and the erection of defensive towers. A royal palace was constructed and houses were built for David's wives and concubines, for his many court officials, and for his bodyguards and mercenary soldiers. In addition, after plan-

ning an elaborate temple that could be constructed later, during the reign of David's successor, his son, Solomon, David arranged to have the Ark of the Covenant brought to Jerusalem and housed in a special tent.

From his newly established capital, David extended his control over the neighboring tribes, conquering territory ranging from the Red Sea north to Damascus and from the Mediterranean into the desert beyond the Jordan River. David failed, however, to unite the kingdoms of Judah in the north and Israel in the south, and after having his rule challenged by his son Absalom, David eventually turned over his kingdoms and his capital city to Solomon, son of David and Bathsheba.

Politically astute, Solomon aligned himself with neighboring territories by taking wives from competing tribes. Also an astute businessman, he increased his country's foreign trade and exploited its natural resources of copper and iron. He used slave labor to fortify the city and then to build a magnificent palace and an elaborate temple to house the Ark of the Covenant.

Solomon's reign was peaceful; riches accumulated but morals began to decay. Solomon's many foreign wives brought their foreign gods with them to Jerusalem, introducing idolatry. With Solomon's death, the country split, and the Babylonian king, Nebuchadnezzar, captured the city, inaugurating a period known as the Babylonian captivity. The golden age of Israel ended.

Return from Exile.

The Hebrews remained in exile for over sixty years. Those returning to their homeland around 539 B.C.E., rebuilt their Temple. The period from the rebuilding of the Temple to 70 C.E. was one of almost continuous foreign occupation. The Roman destruction of

Jerusalem marked the end of Jewish power in the region until the middle of the twentieth century.

However, after rebuilding the Temple, the Jews established a theocracy (a religiously governed state). Although many exiles returned to Judah, many others remained dispersed outside Judah and were known as Jews of the Diaspora, or Dispersion. During the post-exilic period, Jewish beliefs began to include new features, very likely influenced by the Persian religion of Zoroastrianism, especially the idea that the world was divided into two competing and contrasting forces of Good and Evil, imaged as forces of Light and Darkness, respectively. From this period also derive a number of concepts that would later prove of importance to Christianity—an apocalyptic day of judgment and a Messiah, or Anointed One, who would create a time of peace.

THE BIBLE AS LITERATURE

The Hebrew Bible (from the Greek name for the city of Byblos, the major exporter of papyrus, the material used for making books in the ancient world) consists of the canon of books accepted and officially sanctioned by Judaism. These include three major groupings: the Law, the Prophets, and the Writings. The Law comprises the first five books: Genesis, Exodus, Leviticus, Numbers, and Deuteronomy. (Authorship of these books is ascribed to Moses.) The Prophets include those just mentioned and, in addition, the books of Joel, Obadiah, Jonah, Micah, Nahum, Habakkuk, Zephaniah, Haggai, Zechariah, and Malachi, as well as six historical books: Joshua, Judges, Samuel (two books), and Kings (two books). The remaining books, known as the Writings, include the narrative books of Ruth, Esther, and Daniel; the poetic books of Psalms and the Song of Songs; and the wisdom books of Proverbs, Job, and Ecclesiastes. Also part of the Writings are Chronicles, Lamentations, Ezra, and Nehemiah.

Some of the biblical books ascribed to the time of Solomon are actually products of the Hellenic age. Ecclesiastes and The Song of Songs, for example, include concepts such as philosophy, chance, and wisdom that would have been foreign to Jews in Solomon's time. These ideas, however, were eventually assimilated into Jewish thought.

The stories about David in the book of Samuel, and those of Daniel and Jonah, the poetry of the Song of Songs and the Psalms, and the wisdom of Ecclesiastes are significant literary achievements. Two books of the Hebrew Bible, however, tower above the rest: Genesis and Job—Genesis for its fascinating narratives, and Job for its sublime philosophical poetry. Both Genesis and Job, moreover, reflect the ideals of ancient Israel.

History and Fiction.   The narratives in the book of Genesis can be read as being literally true. However, if they are looked at from a literary perspective, they may be divided into two categories: prehistoric myths and historicized fiction. The stories of the Creation and the Fall, of the Great Flood, and of the Tower of Babel are myths explaining the origin of the universe and its creatures, the reason human beings suffer pain and death, and the emergence of the world's languages. These **etiological stories,** or stories about the origins and causes of things, occupy the first eleven chapters of Genesis.

The second category of narrative—historicized fiction—includes the stories of the patriarchs Abraham, Isaac, and Jacob. These stories passed down through oral tradition, and achieved written form around the twelfth to the tenth centuries B.C.E. The patriarchal stories have the character of history, as accounts of deeds performed by particular individuals. However, they differ from later biblical narratives, such as the books of Samuel, which have been termed "fictionalized history."

The stories about David in the book of Samuel use techniques of fiction and take liberties with the historical facts on which they are based. The earlier patriarchal stories describe characters and situations to convey theological ideas and to account for events, such as how the Hebrews found themselves in Egypt (which is explained in the stories about Joseph and his brothers [Gen. 37–50]).

Table 5–1	BOOKS OF THE BIBLE	
Hebrew Scriptures (Old Testament) In order of appearance		
Genesis	2 Chronicles	Daniel
Exodus	Ezra	Hosea
Leviticus	Nehemiah	Joel
Numbers	Esther	Amos
Deuteronomy	Job	Obadiah
Joshua	Psalms	Jonah
Judges	Proverbs	Micah
Ruth	Ecclesiastes	Nahum
1 Samuel	Song of Solomon	Habakkuk
2 Samuel	Isaiah	Zephaniah
1 Kings	Jeremiah	Haggai
2 Kings	Lamentations	Zechariah
1 Chronicles	Ezekiel	Malachi
Greek Scriptures (New Testament) In order of appearance		
Matthew	Ephesians	Hebrews
Mark	Phillipians	James
Luke	Collosians	1 Peter
John	1 Thessalonians	2 Peter
Acts	2 Thessalonians	1 John
Romans	1 Timothy	2 John
1 Corinthians	2 Timothy	3 John
2 Corinthians	Titus	Jude
Galatians	Philemon	Revelation

Biblical Poetry.   As with other ancient civilizations, Hebraic poetry was bound up with the religious, social, and military life of the Hebrews. War victories were celebrated in verse, as were other achievements, such as the liberation of the Hebrew slaves from their Egyptian masters. Indeed, the two oldest recorded Hebrew poems are celebrations of great accomplishments. The Bible's oldest poem, the Song of Deborah (Judges 5:1–31) describes how its heroine, Jael, saves the Hebrew people by killing the Canaanite military leader Sisera. Better known is the "Song of the Sea," which celebrates the destruction of the Egyptian pharaoh's army, along with his chariots and horsemen, in the Red Sea.

Religious faith is the consistent concern of ancient Hebrew poetry, such as the poetry of the Psalms, the prophecies of Isaiah, and the wisdom of Job. Complementing these religious works are other biblical poems in a more secular vein (although they, too, have been interpreted allegorically as religious). The most beautiful of these are the Song of Songs (also known as the Song of Solomon) and the book of Ecclesiastes.

EARLY CHRISTIANITY

With its belief that a Messiah would come into the world to save humankind, thereby fulfilling God's promises, Judaism was fundamental to the emergence of Christianity and to the formulation of the new religion's central tenets. Many apocalyptic Hebrew writings, including chapters 7–10 of the book of Daniel, predicted the coming of a Savior. John the Baptist further prepared the way for Jesus's ministry by preaching that a Messiah was at hand. Those who believed Jesus when he preached the Kingdom of God was imminent, and who saw that Kingdom as represented in Jesus, became the first Christians.

Just as Jews believe they are God's Chosen People and Muslims their holy book, the Quran, is the word of God, Christians believe Jesus is God and Savior. Moreover, they maintain that by accepting Jesus as their Savior, they will share eternal life with him in heaven. One element of their faith is the belief that Jesus rose from the dead after being crucified by the Romans. Their faith gave rise to a revision of the Messianic prophecy, which converted a hope for an earthly king into a belief in a divine king, whose coming to earth signaled new hope in human redemption. Jesus's kingdom would be a kingdom of the next world, the afterlife, to which the redeemed Christian soul would be taken after death.

JESUS AND HIS MESSAGE

Jesus was Jewish. His followers, who identified him as the Christ—which means "Messiah" or "Anointed One"—were the first Christians. Jesus was born in Judaea, a land under the political control of the Romans, during the reign of the emperor Augustus.

The public ministry of Jesus began when he was thirty years old, with the performance of his first miracle, the changing of water into wine, at the marriage feast of Cana, a small village north of Nazareth, where Jesus was born. This first miracle is recorded in the New Testament Gospel of John.

Yet it is Jesus's teaching, rather than his miracles, that is central to Christian beliefs and values. He delivered his message in simple and direct language that common people could understand: Believe in him and be saved; beware of false prophets; don't get lost in the intricacies of religious ritual observance; stick to the essentials of faith in God, love of humanity, and hope for the future. He taught through stories, or **parables,** such as that of the Good Samaritan. Parables illustrate an essential Christian principle: in the case of the Good Samaritan, that believing Christians should love their "neighbors"—and that their neighbors include all human beings.

Jesus's teaching can be reduced to two essentials: to love God above all, and to love others as one loves oneself. Jesus's ideals are summed up in the Sermon on the Mount, the fullest version of which is in the Gospel of Matthew.

CHRISTIAN ANTECEDENTS

The antecedents of Christianity take three basic forms: cult antecedents, philosophical antecedents, and Jewish antecedents. Christian cult antecedents involve specific symbolic rituals that influenced later Christian practices; Christian philosophical antecedents involve particular ideas that came to influence Christian beliefs. Jewish antecedents of Christianity were largely scriptural, although common bonds linked Jewish and Christian rituals as well.

Cult Antecedents.   Christianity did not spring fully formed from the teachings of Jesus, or from the writings of Paul. The special form of individualized immortality associated with Christianity had been a feature of the mystery cults that flourished in Egypt, Persia, and Greece. Besides postulating a form of personal immortality, many mystery cults performed symbolic rituals to enact the birth, death, and rebirth of deities. The Isis cult of Egypt, for example, as well as the cults of Mithra in Persia and Dionysius in Greece, included such symbolic reenactments. As the god of wine and revelry, Dionysus inspired initiates to partake of wine, symbolizing the blood of the deity. Cult members were typically initiated into the mysteries or secrets of the cult by participating in symbolic rituals that included fasting, on the one hand, and eating a symbolic meal, on the other. Such symbolic rituals would influence later Christian rituals.

Another background to and source from which early Christianity derived rituals and borrowed traditions was that of Roman paganism, itself a blend of local and borrowed traditions and religious practices. Among these was the recognition of Roman gods and goddesses as protectors with specialized functions. The household gods, for example, protected the home; Vesta protected the hearth; the locus genii protected the outside areas of a place. Among the specialized functions of Mars, god of war, was the protection of soldiers. It is not far from these Roman beliefs and practices to later Christian traditions that honor saints, as it is not far from the Near Eastern cult practices to later Christian symbolic communal celebrations of a shared communion meal and an emphasis on spiritual purification through fasting.

Philosophical Antecedents. Additional background to and influences on early Christianity include Greek philosophical ideas, especially those of Stoicism and Neoplatonism. Stoicism emphasized self-control and human brotherhood, both of which became hallmarks of Christian thinking. Neo-Platonism emphasized the refined spiritual nature of reality, with a special emphasis on the spiritual union of the individual soul with the "One" or ultimate reality that underlay physical appearances. The Neoplatonist philosopher Plotinus was perhaps the most significant influence, especially his notion of a soul's ascent through ever higher levels of spiritual purification and perfection, an idea found in Christian mysticism and one that found expression in Dante's *Paradiso*.

Jewish Influences. In addition to Roman, Greek, and Near Eastern influences on the development of Christianity, there was also a strong Jewish influence. As a religion that would share a large part of its scriptures with Judaism, Christianity leaned heavily on Jewish traditions and beliefs. Most important among these were a shared vision of a personal universal deity, a God who made moral demands on his subjects. Also central were the strong ethical standards at the heart of Judaism and Christianity. In addition, Christian rhetorical and literary practice was influenced by Jewish prophetic and apocalyptic writings.

Strong bonds linked Jewish and Christian ritualistic traditions, most notably perhaps the connection between Jewish Passover and Christian Easter, which celebrates Jesus's resurrection from the dead, a ritual and belief influenced as well by death and resurrection elements in the mystery cults. On a smaller scale, both religions embrace the idea of a weekly holy day, the Jewish Sabbath (observed on Saturday) and the later Christian day devoted to churchgoing and worship of God on Sunday.

EARLY CHRISTIAN HISTORY

Christianity spread throughout the Mediterranean due to the efforts of martyrs and missionaries. Stephen, the first Christian martyr, was stoned to death in 34 C.E. for preaching blasphemy against the Jewish god; Sebastian was tied to a tree and shot full of arrows, martyred for refusing to acknowledge the Roman gods.

Paul was the most important of the first-century Christian missionaries. Born Saul, at first he was strongly opposed to Christianity until he underwent conversion on the road to Damascus in 35 C.E. (the so-called Damascene conversion). From then until his execution ca. 62 C.E., he proselytized tirelessly for Christianity, formulating doctrine,

MAP 5.2   The Spread of Christianity by 600 C.E.

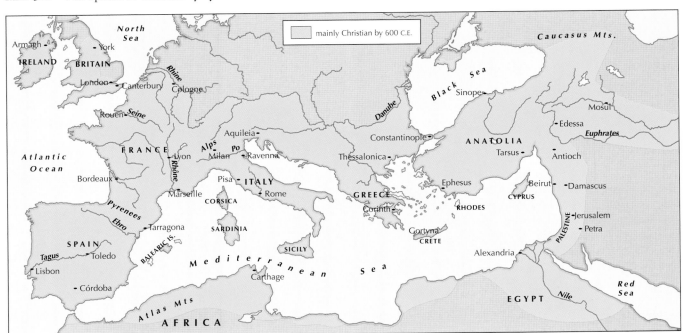

writing to other Christian communities, and traveling at least as far west as Rome.

The next centuries were a period of slow growth for Christianity and of continual persecution at the hands of the Romans. For instance, in 64 C.E. Nero blamed the Christians for a fire that burned down the imperial capital. Two hundred years later, the emperor Decius expelled the Christians from Rome. Such persecution was unusual in the Roman empire, where other sects and religions were usually tolerated. The problem for the Roman authorities appears to have been the Christians' refusal to worship the Roman gods alongside their own God. The first great turning point came in 313 C.E., when the emperor Constantine issued the Edict of Milan, which granted Christianity toleration as a religion. Constantine convened councils concerned with matters of faith, such as the trinitarian nature of the godhead. The First Council of Nicaea developed the Nicene Creed, the conventional recitation of Christian belief in Jesus as both the son of God and as God incarnate. After Constantine's death, Julian attempted to restore paganism, but in 391 Theodosius I declared Christianity the Roman state religion, banning all pagan cults.

The Christian church, however, united in name only. In spreading across the Mediterranean from Jerusalem, Christianity encompassed varying practices and factions, resulting in separate Christian churches in the Roman and Greek worlds. Finally, the Christian church split into two branches in the Great Schism of 1054. The Eastern Church, with a patriarchal leader in Constantinople, formerly Byzantium (currently Istanbul), challenged the supremacy of the Roman leader, the bishop of Rome, the pope. Each leader excommunicated the other. The different languages of the two churches and their differing perspectives on issues, including the legitimacy of a married clergy, led to the development of widely differing institutions.

EARLY CHRISTIAN ART

There is no such thing as an "Early Christian style" of art. In fact, at first Christianity was averse to art because it served the worship of idols. However, Christians recognized that art could help illustrate the Bible's teachings to illiterate followers. No longer the object of worship but a means to worship, art became an important instrument of theology.

Architecture. When Christianity was made an official state religion, the need for churches arose. Derived from the Roman basilica, the Early Christian basilica was well established by the fourth century. Old St. Peter's in Rome (fig. 5.3) is the quintessential example. Erected by Constantine over the tomb of St. Peter, it was destroyed in the fifteenth century to make way for the present St. Peter's (see Chapter 13).

When entering an Early Christian basilica like Old St. Peter's (fig. 5.4), the visitor first came into the **atrium,** a

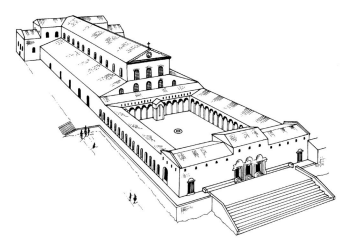

FIGURE 5.3   Old St. Peter's, Rome, begun ca. 333 C.E., reconstruction drawing. Based on the Roman basilica, which would house, in the apse, a statue of the emperor, the new Christian church placed a *cathedra* or "chair of the bishop" in the emperor's place—hence the origin of the word "cathedral."

rectangular forecourt, open in the center to the sky, surrounded on all four sides by columnar arcades. The atrium was the area for people not yet baptized. Next, the visitor passed through the **narthex,** an entrance hall or vestibule. Having now reached the actual church, the visitor entered

FIGURE 5.4   Old St. Peter's, Rome, begun ca. 333 C.E., plan. The type of church established here, known as the early Christian basilica, would be the basis for later churches built with a longitudinal axis—the Latin-cross plan.

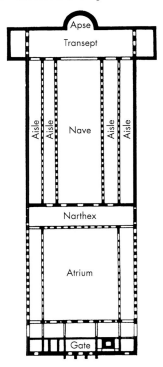

the **nave,** a large rectangular space for the masses of people, and flanked on both sides by one or two **aisles,** separated from the nave by colonnades. The **transept** provided additional space. The **apse** is a semicircular space at the end of the church. The visitor had to walk from one end of the church to the other to reach the altar located just in front of the apse.

The reconstruction drawing of the exterior (fig. 5.3) shows the nave with **clerestory** windows, that is, a row of windows on an upper story. Because the nave ceiling was of lightweight wood, it was easy to support, windows could be made in the walls, and sunlight admitted. The disadvantage of wood was the danger of fire.

A surviving example of an Early Christian basilica, but one that has now been expanded and modified, is Santa Maria Maggiore in Rome (fig. 5.5), originally built ca. 430. Early Christian basilicas had drab exteriors—the outside of the building was not the part intended to be admired. But the interiors, as demonstrated by Santa Maria Maggiore, were very elaborate, with patterned marble floors, marble columns, and mosaics of colored stone, glass, and gold on the walls and ceilings.

In addition to the basilica plan with its longitudinal axis, as used in Old St. Peter's and Santa Maria Maggiore, round or polygonal buildings with domed roofs were also built in the Early Christian era. The finest example is Santa

FIGURE 5.5   Santa Maria Maggiore, Rome, ca. 430 C.E., later modified, view of nave looking toward altar. An advantage of the longitudinal axis of the Early Christian basilica is that, upon entering, the visitor's eyes are automatically directed toward the altar. But a disadvantage of its post and lintel construction is the limited open space, and fire was a constant threat to a building in which candles burned below a wooden ceiling.

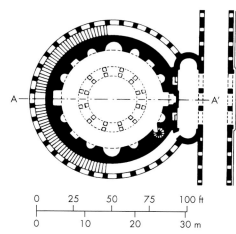

FIGURE 5.6   Santa Costanza, Rome, ca. 350 C.E., plan. A central plan (circular or polygonal) building, when roofed with a dome, as here, offers an uninterrupted interior space.

Costanza in Rome (fig. 5.6 and fig. 5.7), built ca. 350 C.E. This mausoleum, constructed for the emperor Constantine's daughter Constantia, was once part of a larger church.

The exterior, made of unadorned brick, is plain and simple, but the interior is ornate with rich materials, textures, colors, and designs. Light comes in through the clerestory windows. The surrounding circular aisle, or **ambulatory,** is covered with a barrel vault, which is ornamented with mosaics (fig. 5.8).

These mosaics consist of a vine pattern with small scenes along the sides. Laborers are shown picking grapes, putting them into carts, and transporting the grapes to a press, where three men crush them underfoot. This subject, common on tavern floor mosaics, may seem out of place here. But because wine plays an important part in the Christian liturgy, it was possible to adopt and adapt a pagan subject to Christian needs.

Sculpture.   In the Early Christian era, due to Christianity's disdain for idol worship, sculpture was secondary to painting and mosaic. One of the rare examples of Early Christian figure sculpture is the statue of *Jesus the Good Shepherd* (fig. 5.9), which dates from the mid–third century C.E., and depicts Jesus carrying a sheep across his shoulders. The subject was common in catacomb painting (see fig. 5.11). There are several versions of this statue, this being one of the earliest and the best. Jesus is portrayed in the Classical tradition. The pose is free, natural, and relaxed, with the weight on one foot and the head turned to the side, the *contrapposto* stance similar to that of the ancient Greek *Spear-Bearer* (see fig. 3.11). Young and idealized, Jesus gazes into the distance.

For the most part, sculptors turned to small-scale relief work on stone **sarcophagi** (coffins) and ivory panels. Marble sarcophagi, the fronts and occasionally the lids of which were carved with figures in high relief, are among the ear-

liest works of Christian sculptors, with examples dating from the early third century C.E. onward. The *Sarcophagus of Junius Bassus*, a prefect of Rome (a high position similar to that of a governor or administrator), is among the most notable of these (fig. 5.10). Bassus converted to Christianity shortly before his death in 359. The front of his sarcophagus is divided by two tiers of columns into ten areas. The subjects depicted in these panels are drawn from the Old and New Testaments of the Bible. The upper row, left to right, shows the sacrifice of Isaac; St. Peter taken prisoner; Jesus enthroned with Saints Peter and Paul; and, in two separate sections, Jesus before Pontius Pilate. The lower row, left to right, shows the misery of Job; Adam and Eve after eating from the Tree of Knowledge; Jesus entering Jerusalem; Daniel in the lions' den; and St. Paul being led to his death. The proportions of the figures are far from Classical and reflect a late Roman style, as also seen in the fourth-century reliefs on the Arch of Constantine in Rome (see fig. 4.23). Large heads are supported on doll-like bodies. Background setting is almost entirely eliminated in these crowded scenes, action or drama kept to a minimum, and the figures, even when the story suggests they should be animated, are passive and calm. These little vignettes are not intended to provide the viewer with a detailed narrative, for they are only required to bring to mind a story that the viewer is expected to know already.

Painting.   The earliest Christian art is found in the **catacombs**—the underground cemeteries of the Christians in and around Rome. The catacombs were practically underground towns of sepulchers and funeral chapels, miles of subterranean passageways cut into the rock.

A painted ceiling in the Catacomb of Santi Pietro e Marcellino in Rome (fig. 5.11), from the fourth century, is a well-preserved example. The walls of catacombs were decorated with **frescoes,** paintings made quickly on freshly applied lime plaster. The subjects depicted were generally related to the soul's future life. Especially common was the subject of *Jesus the Good Shepherd*, seen also in sculpture (see fig. 5.9). Filling the center of the ceiling, the painting embodies the idea that the Christian people make up Jesus's flock and, as the Good Shepherd, Jesus watches over and cares for them. The arrangement painted here represents the dome of heaven, with the decoration positioned to form a cross. The story of Jonah is shown in the surrounding semicircles. Jonah is thrown overboard into the mouth of the waiting whale (the curly serpent-dog makes clear that whales were not known from firsthand experience in fourth-century Rome). Jonah emerges from the whale and then relaxes in safety under the vines. The figures that stand between the semicircles have assumed a common early prayer pose—the *orans* (from the Latin word for "praying"), with hands raised to heaven.

Popular Old Testament subjects for catacomb paintings were Noah and the Ark, Moses, Jonah and the whale, Daniel in the lions' den, and the story of Susanna. Popu-

FIGURE 5.7 Santa Costanza, Rome, ca. 350 C.E., interior. The basic scheme of Santa Costanza would later be used by Byzantine architects and would also serve as the model for the baptisteries connected to Christian churches.

FIGURE 5.8   *Wine-Making Scene,* ambulatory vault of Santa Costanza, Rome, ca. 350 C.E., mosaic. Demonstrating the Christian adaptation of pagan subjects, the vine here represents the words of Jesus, "I am the true vine." The grapes came to symbolize the eucharistic wine and, therefore, the blood of Jesus.

lar New Testament themes were taken from the life of Jesus, especially the miracles, such as the healing of the paralytic and the resurrection of Lazarus. These subjects illustrate how God is merciful and will intervene to save the faithful. The rewards of prayer are emphasized. Depictions of Jesus's passion (his suffering at the end of his life) are entirely omitted; the earliest known representations of the passion are fifth-century carvings. The catacomb paintings do not treat the subject of Jesus's death and resurrection, which was a popular subject in the Renaissance (see Chapters 13 and 14).

THE NEW TESTAMENT AS LITERATURE

The New Testament is for Christianity what the Hebrew scriptures are for Judaism and the Quran is for Islam: the repository of revealed religious truth. The New Testament, written in Greek, records and interprets the acts and words of the Christian Savior, Jesus Christ. The New Testament contains four distinct types of writing: the gospels, or accounts of Jesus's life and ministry; the epistles, or letters to the early Christian churches; the Acts of the Apostles, a history of the spread of Christianity during the thirty years after Jesus's death and resurrection; and Revelation, or the Apocalypse, the last biblical book, which is concerned with the end of the world.

Gospels.   Apart from Paul's letters, the gospels are the earliest books of the New Testament. Written from about

FIGURE 5.9   *Jesus the Good Shepherd,* mid–third century C.E., marble, height 39″ (99 cm), Vatican Museums, Rome. Large-scale sculptures such as this are extremely rare in Early Christian art. The lamb represents Jesus's followers, whom he guards and guides.

FIGURE 5.10   *Sarcophagus of Junius Bassus*, ca. 359 C.E. marble, 3'10½" × 8' (1.18 × 2.44 m), Museo Petriano, St. Peter's, Rome. Early Christian sculpture consists primarily of reliefs carved on sarcophagi and small ivory plaques. Greater importance was attached to the recognition of the subjects than to realistic representation of the human body.

forty to around one hundred years after the death of Jesus, the New Testament is far closer in time of composition to the events it describes than is the Old Testament to the events it describes. None, however, is an eyewitness account of Jesus's life and work.

Of the surviving gospels, the Gospel of Mark is the earliest, composed around 70 C.E. It portrays Jesus as a miracle worker as well as a dynamic and vibrant social reformer. The Gospel of Mark is action centered, moving quickly from one event to the next, describing Jesus's life, ministry, passion, and death.

The Gospel of Matthew, written ten to twenty years after that of Mark, emphasizes Jesus as the Messiah referred to in Old Testament prophecies, the one who would complete the Jewish community's destiny. Luke's gospel is the only one that describes Jesus's birth in a manger in Bethlehem. Luke's gospel also focuses more on women—from Mary the mother of Jesus, to Mary Magdalene, a sinner Jesus forgives, to Jainus's daughter whose illness he cures, to the sinful woman who washes and anoints Jesus's feet.

The Gospel of John differs radically from the three synoptic gospels, even as those three gospels differ from one another in focus, emphasis, and degree of sophistication. John's is the most theological of the gospels, the one most attuned to the religious and philosophical implications of Jesus's work and words.

John's gospel begins, for example, with an idea inherited from Greek thought. Jesus is the *Logos*, the divine word that came into the world as a light into darkness. Another image that pervades John's gospel is that of water. John describes Jesus as the living water who quenches the spiritual thirst of those unable to find satisfaction in their lives. This image is closely tied to Jesus's emphasis on being reborn into the kingdom of heaven through the agency of baptism in water and a spiritual and methaphorical baptism of the spirit.

Epistles.   The New Testament contains twenty-one epistles addressed to Early Christian communities. Fourteen of these letters are traditionally ascribed to the apostle Paul. The titles of the Pauline epistles are derived from their recipients: Romans, Corinthians, Ephesians, and so on. They were written as a means of explaining points of doctrine, clarifying misunderstandings, and exhorting various communities to remain committed to their faith in Jesus. The importance of Paul to the spread of Christianity in the first century C.E. and his influence in formulating Christian doctrine can hardly be exaggerated. Along with his travels, Paul's epistles served his missionary

FIGURE 5.11 *Dome of Heaven*, painted ceiling in the catacomb of Santi Pietro e Marcellino, Rome, fourth century C.E. Catacombs, the underground burial areas of the Early Christians, were painted with symbolic subjects. Jesus was repeatedly shown as the good shepherd with his flock of followers.

vocation, to spread Christianity throughout the Greco-Roman world.

Paul's epistles expound the Christian doctrines of the Incarnation and the Atonement, or Redemption. The Incarnation refers to the birth of God in human form as Jesus. As a co-equal member of the Holy Trinity (the union of Father, Son, and Holy Ghost in a single godhead), Jesus is divine. In taking on a human form, in the flesh and living and dying like any mortal, Jesus revealed his love for humankind. Paul also wrote that Jesus became human so he could suffer and die for the sins of humankind; his suffering atones for human beings' sins and redeems humankind.

The theology in the Pauline epistles is intricate and complex. In developing theories to explain Christian beliefs, such as the resurrection of the body and the immortality of the soul, Paul relied both on Greek philosophical ideas and on the Old Testament, which he interpreted in light of the new teaching. Paul's ideas have influenced Christian teaching for nearly two thousand years and are reflected in many works of Western literature, including Chaucer's *Canterbury Tales*, Dante's *Divine Comedy*, Shakespeare's plays, and Milton's *Paradise Lost*.

Revelation. Also known as "The Apocalypse," the Greek word for "unveiling," Revelation presents a visionary ac-

Cross Currents

CHRISTIAN AND PAGAN GODS

From the beginning, Christianity was at odds with pagan religions and their multiple deities. From the standpoint of Christian monotheism, the pagan gods were false idols, and the myths associated with them, fictions.

And yet, as different as Christianity was, it nonetheless absorbed elements of pagan myths and belief. Pagan elements had counterparts in a number of features of Christianity. These similarities included belief in a god who died and was reborn; communal worship; celebration of ritual ceremonies commemorating the deity; pilgrimages, processions, fasting; and initiates taking new names upon entrance into the religious community.

This connection was most evident, however, with regard to the pagan and Christian deities. The accommodation of the pagan gods into Christianity was one of reinterpretation. For although the characteristics of the pagan deities were retained, their qualities were given a new Christian meaning. The Greek god Apollo, for example, became a precursor of the Son of God; Apollo's prophetic power affiliated him with the Holy Spirit. Similarly, Prometheus's sacrificial effort to liberate humanity was seen in light of Christ's sacrifice; Prometheus's transgression—his exceeding his human state by interfering with the gods— linked him with Lucifer, the angel who rebelled against God, and when hurled into hell, became known as Satan.

In the same way that pagan deities such as Apollo, Prometheus, and Orpheus were reinterpreted in connection with Christ, God the Father subsumed elements and characteristics associated with pagan deities such as Zeus and Kronos. The Virgin Mary assumed qualities linked with those of Aphrodite, Persephone, and Artemis. This absorption of the pagan deities into Christianity, moreover, extended to the Christian saints. Saint Michael, for example, absorbed the militant qualities of Mars. And Saint Christopher, who as legend has it, bore the Christ child on his shoulders to ford a stream, was linked with Atlas, who bore the world on his shoulders.

count of the Last Judgment and the end of the world. Written sometime near the end of the first century C.E., ca. 75–95, this final book of the Bible presents a symbolic vision of the future. The symbols used include the seven seals, the seven lamps, the Great Beast, the seven bowls, and the woman, child, and dragon. The meaning of this symbolism has spawned numerous conflicting interpretations through the centuries.

EARLY CHRISTIAN MUSIC

The music of the Early Christian church had its roots in Jewish worship. Jewish religious rites were accompanied by chanting of sacred texts, with an instrumental doubling on the harp or lyre. Essentially, two different kinds of singing developed in Christian services: **responsorial** and **antiphonal**. In Christian services, the congregation sang simple responses to cantors and choirs, which sang the more complex parts. In singing a psalm, for example, the cantor or choir would sing the verses and the congregation the standard response of "Amen" or "Alleluia."

This responsorial type of chanting was complemented by antiphonal singing, in which either a cantor and the congregation or different parts of the congregation alternated in singing verses of the psalm. In some cases the congregation would be divided into parts, usually positioned on opposite sides of the church, to enhance the effectiveness of this alternation of the chant.

Early Christianity, unlike Judaism, prohibited instrumental accompaniment of any kind, which was considered pagan. Up until the fourth century, early Christian **liturgical** music (music used in religious ritual) was based exclusively on sacred texts. Starting in the fifth century, some nonscriptural hymns supplemented these scripture-based chants.

Musical practice differed somewhat in churches that followed the Byzantine liturgy rather than that of St. Ambrose. The Western liturgy of Ambrose made accommodations for active musical participation by the congregation. This required the music to be kept relatively simple, with a single note sung to each syllable. In contrast, Byzantine liturgical music was more complex, with many notes sung to a syllable in a florid style. These sixth-century Byzantine liturgical musical practices were modified, however, by the seventh-century reforms toward less complex chant melodies.

PHILOSOPHY: AUGUSTINE AND THE NEOPLATONIC INHERITANCE

The spread of Christianity during the early centuries was accompanied by a need to explain and systematize Christian thought. After Paul, the single most important expounder of Christian doctrine was Augustine (354–430) from Hippo (near present-day Algeria), in northern Africa.

Augustine achieved a synthesis of the Platonic philosophical tradition and the Judeo-Christian emphasis on divine revelation. For Augustine, human beings can only know true ideas when they are illuminated in the soul by

Connections

GREEK AND ROMAN INFLUENCES ON CHRISTIANITY

Inclusion in the Roman empire was not limited by ethnic identity; Roman citizenship was available to conquered people in other lands. This universalist tendency paralleled Christianity's missionary impulse to spread the Christian message throughout the world.

The *Pax Romana*, or Roman peace, that extended throughout the Roman empire made possible the rapid spread of Christianity.

Aspects of Platonism harmonized with Christian thought and were absorbed during the early history of the church. The major Platonic tenets taken over include the following:

1. the existence of a perfect transcendental reality outside of the world of materiality and time;

2. the immortality of the soul;
3. the priority of spirit over matter;
4. an emphasis on self-knowledge;
5. the subjection of the passions to reason;
6. a view of death as a release from the bonds of the body;
7. an emphasis on goodness, beauty, and truth.

These elements of Platonic thought were synthesized with the Judeo-Christian emphasis on a personal god acting with providential design in effecting the divine plan for history.

Yet however much early Christianity absorbed elements of Greek philosophy differences remained. Most important among these differences are these:

1. Judaism and Christianity imagined divinity to be singular, unique, and historically present.
2. The Judeo-Christian concept of history was progressive and linear, moving forward to the grand culmination of the Messianic kingdom (Judaism) and the Parousia (Presence and Return of Christ at the end of the world—Christianity).

Ironically, Rome, which had been the great persecutor of early Christianity, became the center of Christianity in the West. The administration of Roman law was displaced by the Catholic Church with its institutional hierarchy and its spreading empire. Rome became Christianized; Christianity became Romanized.

Critical Thinking

CHRISTIANITY'S INFLUENCES

Although Christianity was a new and different religion from the religions that predated and preceded it, it also has been associated with beliefs and practices of Hebraic Roman religious traditions as well as Greek philosophical traditions. Why do you think these earlier religious and philosophical traditions impacted Christianity so strongly? What do you think the early leaders of Christianity thought of those influences? To what extent do you think the theologians of the early Christian Church would have found such influences congenial and to what extent dangerous? Why?

God. Augustine dismissed knowledge derived from sense experience as unreliable. Such empirical knowledge was suspect due to humanity's fall from grace. To Plato's emphasis on pure ideas, Augustine added divinely revealed truth as recorded in scripture and interpreted by church tradition.

In his early adulthood, Augustine had lived a life of self-indulgence and debauchery. His *Confessions* describe his dissatisfaction with this way of life, his search for spiritual fulfillment, and, finally, his conversion to Christianity.

As the first Western autobiography, Augustine's *Confessions* was enormously influential. Throughout the Middle Ages the book was read, copied, and imitated. The book's image of the spiritual journey influenced medieval poems of pilgrimage, such as William Langland's *Piers Ploughman* and Dante's *Divine Comedy*. As well as providing a framework for these and other forms of spiritual autobiography, the *Confessions* paved the way for the Renaissance rediscovery of the self.

In addition to his *Confessions*, Augustine wrote *On Christian Doctrine*, which analyzes and explains the central tenets of Christian teaching, and the *City of God*, in which he explores the relationship between faith and reason, and the cause of history as a movement toward the clash of two opposite visions of life, represented by two contrasting cities, an earthly city and a heavenly one, the city of God.

Connections

GNOSTICISM AND CHRISTIANITY

Alternative, suppressed forms of quasi-Christian belief existed alongside orthodox Christianity in the early church. One influential form of early Christianity was Gnosticism, central to which was a belief that redemption could be achieved through possessing special secret knowledge. Gnostics believed they had access to secret wisdom (*gnosis* is the Greek word for "knowledge"). This special knowledge was restricted to small groups of Gnostic adherents who pursued lives of asceticism and who observed strict dietary practices, refraining from sensual indulgence and removing themselves from temptation.

Gnosticism was a dualist philosophy, which, like Zoroastrianism and Manicheism, divided the world into good and evil. The evil part, which was material rather than spiritual, was created by a demonic spirit. It was this demonic spirit that was said to be responsible for the fall of humanity. Second century C.E. Gnostics believed humankind predates the fall and that, before that event, all human beings contained a spark of divinity within them.

Gnosticism shocked the followers of early orthodox Christianity, who were dismayed by Gnostic beliefs in reincarnation and equality for women. Gnosticism nonetheless managed to establish itself as an alternative form of Christianity. Suppressed Gnostic texts coexisted with the canonical Christian scriptures, the Gospel of Thomas, dating from the second century perhaps being the best known and most widely disseminated, and the Gospel of Judas Iscariot, the betrayer of Jesus, the latest to stir controversy among christians.

One of Augustine's central ideas is that evil does not possess reality in the same sense that good does. According to Augustine, evil is a deficiency in good rather than something that exists in its own right. God did not create evil; rather, evil entered the world through incorrect choices made by human beings, as when Adam chose to disobey God's injunction not to eat the forbidden fruit (Genesis 1). Regardless of the source of sin, however, Augustine follows St. Paul in explaining how Christ redeemed humanity, and how life is a spiritual pilgrimage toward God, in whom human beings find their salvation and their eternal rest.

Like Paul, whose epistles he echoes frequently, Augustine distrusted the fleshly body, which he held accountable for humankind's fall from grace. Augustine, in fact, described the original sin as "concupiscence," or lust, to which he had himself succumbed during his early adulthood. This distrust of the physical body and his subordination of it to the faculties of the spiritual soul were to affect church teaching for many centuries.

Another influential Augustinian idea was that of humankind's inability to obtain salvation on its own. Augustine argued that only God could freely grant this grace. Because human beings were unable to save themselves, their only hope for salvation lay in accepting God's truth as revealed in sacred scripture, including the New Testament. Furthermore, since human beings were prone to error, misunderstanding, and sin due to the corruption they inherited from Adam and Eve's original sin, they were not in a position to understand the complexities of divine revelation on their own. For that, they needed the authoritative teaching of the church.

Augustine wrote voluminously in support of church authority and unity in matters of doctrine. He made vigorous attacks on the doctrines that circulated around the church in the early centuries. He also defended Christianity against charges that the new religion was responsible for the decline of Roman civilization. Instead, Augustine saw the fall of Rome as part of God's providential plan for the progressive development of human history toward its fulfillment in the Parousia—the return of Jesus to earth at the end of the world.

BYZANTINE CIVILIZATION

In 330 C.E., with the Roman empire in severe economic and political decline, the emperor Constantine established the trading city of Byzantium as his new Eastern capital, renaming it Constantinople in the process.

From this time on, power and influence increasingly deserted Rome, which became a favorite target for invading barbarian hordes from the north. In 410, a barbarian tribe from Germany, the Visigoths, laid siege to the former capital and, when the Senate refused to pay the invaders tribute, Rome was sacked for the first time in eight hundred years. Another group, the Vandals, sacked the city again in 455.

Meanwhile, the Western empire was crumbling. Successive waves of Saxons, Angles, and Jutes attacked and occupied Britain; Burgundians wrested large parts of France from the Romans, and the Vandals came to control North Africa and Spain. By the end of the fifth century, Roman power had disintegrated, and the empire had been replaced by a patchwork of barbarian kingdoms.

FIGURE 5.12 San Vitale, Ravenna, 526–47. A central-planned building is either circular, like Santa Costanza (see figs. 5.6–5.7), or polygonal, like San Vitale. An advantage of the central dome is the large space covered; a potential disadvantage is that the visitor's eyes tend to be attracted up into the dome rather than toward the altar.

FIGURE 5.13 San Vitale, Ravenna, 526–47, interior. This view only begins to indicate the complexity of San Vitale's interior space. Light enters on three levels, playing over the polished marble surfaces and glittering glass mosaics.

In the east, however, imperial life flourished in the capital of Constantinople. There, a new and influential Christian civilization took root, usually known as BYZANTIUM [bi-ZAN-tee-um] after Constantinople's original name. Christian Byzantium continued to thrive for hundreds of years, although after the seventh century it had to compete with the rising civilization of Islam for control of the Mediterranean basin. Finally, in the fifteenth century, Constantinople itself was occupied by Muslim forces.

Of the early Byzantine emperors, JUSTINIAN [jus-TIN-ee-an] (r. 527–565) exerted the greatest cultural and political influence. His armies defeated Germanic tribes in Italy, Spain, and North Africa. Most important, however, was his rebuilding program in Constantinople itself. It was Justinian's wife and empress, THEODORA [THEE-oh-DOOR-ah], who persuaded her husband not to abandon Constantinople. Together, Justinian and Theodora sought to restore the grandeur of the empire and of their capital, Constantinople.

BYZANTINE ART

So generously did Justinian patronize the arts that his reign is referred to as the First Golden Age of Byzantine art, with Constantinople as its artistic capital. However, much of the art created during this First Golden Age survives only outside Constantinople, in particular in the city of Ravenna and in the monastery of St. Catherine built by Justinian at Mount Sinai.

San Vitale, Ravenna. The architecture and mosaics of the church of San Vitale in Ravenna (fig. 5.12), dated 526–47, are especially important accomplishments of the First Golden Age. Though begun by Bishop Maximian in 526, San Vitale bears the imprint of the influence of Constantinople and Justinian. It is octagonal in plan, a shape favored in Constantinople. Light is admitted to the interior by windows on the lower levels. However, this light is filtered through the aisles, which are two stories high, before reaching the nave. The only direct light, and therefore the strongest and most dramatic, enters the nave from the third-story clerestory above.

Like the circular church of Santa Costanza in Rome (see figs. 5.6–5.7) the polygonal San Vitale has no longitudinal axis and is therefore referred to as having a central plan. Unlike the Early Christian churches of the basilica type that have a longitudinal axis (see figs. 5.3–5.5), such structures have no need of rows of columns to hold up their roofs and are capped with domes, which are supported by the walls and external buttresses instead. The result is that the interior feels light and spacious. However, two focal points compete for the visitor's attention. Whereas on entering a church with a longitudinal axis, the worshipper is naturally directed toward the altar, the cen-

ter of the ritual, this is less obviously the case at San Vitale, where the worshipper's eyes are also drawn up to the dome.

In striking contrast to its drab exterior, the interior of San Vitale (fig. 5.13) is opulent in its ornament, made colorful by mosaics that cover all the upper portions (the angels on clouds are later additions), by thin slabs of marble veneer, and by marble columns with carved and painted capitals (fig. 5.14). Seemingly insubstantial, the lacy delicacy of the surface decoration belies the underlying strength of the structure.

Flanking the altar at San Vitale and drawing the worshiper's gaze down from the dome are the celebrated mosaics of the emperor Justinian and the empress Theodora

FIGURE 5.14 San Vitale, Ravenna, 526–47, capital. The surfaces of the capital and impost block above are carved to appear lacelike, which both masks and contradicts the stone's solidity and strength.

FIGURE 5.15   *Theodora and her Attendants*, San Vitale, Ravenna, ca. 547, mosaic. The typical Byzantine face is shown to have large eyes, a long nose, and a tiny mouth. The body is characteristically slender and weightless—or so we might hope, since the figures appear to step on one another's feet.

(fig. 5.15) of ca. 547. Justinian and Theodora, each accompanied by attendants, are shown as good Christian rulers, ever to be in attendance at the religious service. The figures are not necessarily intended to be recognizable portraits of specific individuals. Instead, everyone looks much alike, with big dark eyes, curved eyebrows, long noses, and small mouths—the characteristic Byzantine facial type. Their drapery gives no suggestion of a body beneath; the only indication that these people have legs is the appearance of feet below the hem of their garments. Their elongated bodies seem insubstantial, ethereal and immaterial, motionless, their gestures frozen.

The flat frontal figures form a rhythmic pattern across the surface of the mosaic. Three-quarter views, which suggest a degree of movement and dimension, are avoided. The Byzantine lack of concern for realistic or even consistent representation of space is illustrated by the doorway on the left, the top and bottom of which are seen from two different vantage points. The ancient Roman interests in specific details and spatial illusion are gone. Yet whatever this architectural decoration may lose in realism, it gains in splendor. Realism is not the goal here. Glittering mosaic is an ideal medium with which to enhance the image of divine power promoted by the Byzantine emperor and empress while simultaneously increasing the splendor of San Vitale.

THE GOLDEN AGE OF CONSTANTINOPLE

Constantinople (known as Istanbul after 1930) lies on the straits of Bosphorus, at the confluence of the Black Sea and the Sea of Marmara. The city has a fine harbor, controlling the land route from Europe to Asia and the waterways that lead to the ports on the Black Sea, the Aegean, and the Mediterranean. Fortified by walls on three sides and the straits on the other, it withstood attacks for a thousand years, until the Turks captured it in 1453, after which it became a Muslim city.

Life in Constantinople at the time of Justinian was rich in pleasures. The well-to-do enjoyed a level of hygiene

FIGURE 5.16   Anthemius of Tralles and Isidorus of Miletus, Hagia Sophia, Istanbul, 532–37. The towers surrounding Hagia Sophia are a later, Ottoman addition. The central dome is buttressed by smaller half domes, in turn buttressed by smaller half domes, creating a structurally sound and visually striking church.

and health unknown in Europe at the time. Entertainments included chariot races at the amphitheater and theatrical productions notorious for their indecency. The empress Theodora had been an actress before marrying Justinian and had a somewhat unsavory reputation as a result. This, however, was only one aspect of the city. Constantinople was also a place of elegance and splendor, with one of the most magnificent religious buildings ever constructed, the Church of the Holy Wisdom, or Hagia Sophia, built by Justinian and Theodora after the revolt in 532. The great domed structure stands as testimony to their ambitions (fig. 5.16).

Well into the ninth and tenth centuries Constantinople remained the largest, richest, and most sophisticated city in the world. The immense city walls with their 37 gates and 486 towers—not to mention Constantinople's hundreds of churches and chapels and the monumental Hagia Sophia, which sailors could use as a landmark twenty miles out at sea—gave the impression of indomitable power.

The wealth of Constantinople was legendary. The city produced manuscripts and jewelry of every description, as well as rich fabrics in cotton, linen, and silk, embroidered with gold. Valuable metals, ivory, and precious stones were abundant, as were spices, including ginger and cloves, pepper, and saffron. So too were medicinal drugs and ingredients for dyeing fabric.

As the world's richest and largest market, Constantinople was tightly controlled; its customs duties were high and restrictive. Demand for its goods was maintained by limiting their supply and by keeping prices high. Although commerce with cities throughout western Europe developed, only Venice was given privileged trading status.

By virtue of its easy access to land and sea trade routes, Constantinople was well situated to transport goods between East and West. Yet despite this abundant mercantile exchange, there was still mutual mistrust between Constantinople and the West.

Most important of all were the deep-rooted differences between the Christian churches of the West and East. Latin was the language of the Roman church, Greek that of the Byzantine church. In Rome, the early church was ruled by local bishops, one of whom was elevated by Rome's lay Christians. In Constantinople, the church was controlled by a patriarch who was appointed, and often disposed of, by the emperor. In the West, priests were encouraged to be celibate and in 1139 celibacy became compulsory; in the East, priests could and often did marry. These differences were exacerbated when the Eastern patriarch refused to submit to the authority of the Roman pope in 1054, precipitating a final and permanent **schism,** or split, between the Eastern and Western churches.

Hagia Sophia.   Hagia Sophia, the Church of the Holy Wisdom in Constantinople (fig. 5.16), was built for Justinian and Theodora between 532 and 537 by the architects Anthemius of Tralles and Isidorus of Miletus. There is little exterior decoration (the four minarets, or towers, are later Ottoman additions). Seen from the outside, Hagia Sophia appears to be a solid structure, building up by waves to the huge central dome.

The plan (fig. 5.17) shows the arrangement around the central dome, with half domes on opposite sides, which are in turn flanked by smaller half domes. Thus Hagia Sophia, although domed, is not a pure central-plan church like San Vitale, because a longitudinal axis is created by the oval nave. Hagia Sophia's ingenious plan has a single focus of attention as well as a great open space, combining the advantages of the longitudinal basilica plan with those of the domed central plan.

Unlike the dome of the Roman Pantheon (see fig. 4.13), which rests on a circular base, the dome of Hagia Sophia is supported by a square base formed by four huge piers. Transition from circle to square is achieved through the use of four **pendentives,** pieces of triangular supporting masonry. In effect, the dome rests on a larger dome from which segments have been removed. Hagia Sophia is one of the earliest examples of a dome on pendentives.

The interior (fig. 5.18) is an extremely lofty, light-filled, unobstructed space. From the inside, the dome seems to billow or to float—as if it were suspended from above rather than supported from below. Because the dome is made of lightweight tiles, it was possible for the architects to puncture the base of the dome with a band of forty windows. The light that streams through these windows is used as an artistic element, for it is reflected in the mosaics and the marbles. A rich polychromatic scheme is created by the red and green porphyry columns, the polished marble slabs on the lower walls, and the mosaics on the upper walls. Like San Vitale, the elaborate surface decoration conceals the strength of the underlying structure.

St. Mark's, Venice.   The First Golden Age of Byzantine art ended with the "iconoclastic controversy." Yet when in 843 the **iconophiles**—the lovers of artistic images—triumphed over the iconoclasts, a Second Golden Age of Byzantine art began, lasting until the beginning of the thirteenth century. The biggest and most elaborate church of the Second Golden Age is St. Mark's in Venice, begun in 1063. Its location on one side of a large **piazza** (open public area) is particularly impressive. The original facade has since been modified.

The plan is a **Greek cross**—that is, a cross with four arms of equal length. There is a dome over the center, plus

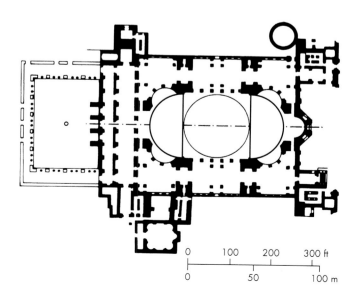

FIGURE 5.17   Anthemius of Tralles and Isidorus of Miletus, Hagia Sophia, Istanbul, 532–37, plan. Hagia Sophia demonstrates that the advantages of the longitudinal axis of the basilica plan can be combined with those of the dome of the central plan. Here the central dome is flanked and buttressed by half domes, thereby creating a longitudinal axis.

FIGURE 5.18 Anthemius of Tralles and Isidorus of Miletus, Hagia Sophia, Istanbul, 532–37, interior. Triangular pendentives provide the transition between the circular dome and the square base on which it rests. The closely spaced windows at the base of the dome create a ring of light that makes the dome appear to float.

a dome over each arm (fig. 5.19). All five domes are covered with wood and gilt copper, making them very striking and giving St. Mark's a distinctive silhouette.

The interior of St. Mark's (fig. 5.20) offers the visitor an experience in ultimate splendor. The vast space is quite dark, originally illuminated only by windows in the bases of the domes and by the flickering light of countless candles. Yet all the surfaces glitter, for they are covered with mosaics, many of which are made with gold **tesserae** (the small cubes of color material that are pressed into wet plaster to make a mosaic).

Among the celebrated mosaics of St. Mark's, the most famous is the Creation Dome in the narthex, made about 1200. The story of Genesis is told in a series of scenes arranged in three concentric circles. The narrative begins in the innermost circle with the creation of heaven and earth. The story of Adam and Eve occupies part of the second circle and the outermost circle (fig. 5.21). In the scene shown here, God is pictured creating Eve from Adam's rib. Among the other memorable scenes is that in which God is shown giving Adam his soul, usually represented by a tiny winged figure entering Adam's mouth.

These mosaic figures hardly appear to have been taken from live models. Instead, the figures—doll-like and stocky with big heads—are intended to express the superhuman nature of the subject portrayed. The setting is symbolic only and represented in the simplest manner possible to convey the ideas. To elucidate the narrative, aids, such as bands of lettering and symbols, are employed. Emphasis is on design, decoration, and on the didactic message.

Madonna and Child Enthroned. Characteristic of this Byzantine style is the *Madonna and Child Enthroned* (fig. 5.22), a late-thirteenth-century egg tempera painting on a

FIGURE 5.19 St. Mark's, Venice, begun 1063, exterior. A dramatic silhouette is created by the five domes. St Mark's Greek-cross plan, with four equal arms, differs from the Latin-cross plan with one dominant axis, represented by Old St. Peter's (see fig. 5.4).

wooden panel. Egg tempera (pigment mixed with egg yolk) was the standard medium used to paint on wood throughout the Middle Ages.

Madonna and Child Enthroned represents a type repeated over and over according to strict rules. It is an **icon,** a painted image of a religious figure or religious scene used in worship. In this *Madonna and Child Enthroned,* Mary's typically Byzantine face has a somewhat wistful or melancholy expression. She is gentle and graceful, her bodily proportions elongated. Jesus's proportions are those of a tiny adult. Moreover, he acts as an adult, holding the scroll of law in one hand and blessing with the other.

Mary is traditionally shown wearing garments of red and blue—both primary colors. Jesus wears orange and green—two secondary colors. Byzantine drapery is characterized by elaborate and unrealistic folds, seemingly having a life of their own, independent of the body beneath. The hard ornamental highlights contrast with the soft skin of the figures.

These figures, barely of our species, do not inhabit our earthly realm. Compression of space is emphasized by the flat decorative designs. The throne, which has been compared to the Colosseum in Rome, is drawn in such a way that the interior and exterior do not correspond. Similarly, the footstool does not obey the rules of **linear perspective,** which require objects to diminish in scale as they recede into space. The artist does not seek to portray our earthly world; instead, this is God's heavenly domain.

FIGURE 5.20 St. Mark's, Venice, begun 1063, interior. Glittering gold mosaics covering the walls and vaults successfully transport the visitor from the crowded streets of the island city of Venice to an extraordinary otherworldly environment.

FIGURE 5.21   *God Creates Eve*, detail of the Creation Dome, narthex of St. Mark's, Venice, ca. 1200, mosaic. Engaging narrative is more important than realism in these mosaics. The intended audience was assumed to be familiar with the biblical stories told here, which, therefore, could be depicted in summary rather than in detail.

Floating in this golden realm are two half angels. Each carries a staff, a symbol of Jesus's passion, and an orb or globe with a cross, which signifies Jesus's domination over the world. These are examples of **iconography,** the language of symbols, which was especially useful in an era when few people were literate. It was intended that the audience would be able to recognize the subject immediately. Consistency in the use of symbols, therefore, was important. The quest for innovation, for the novel, for things unique, had no place in Byzantine religious art.

FIGURE 5.22   *Madonna and Child Enthroned*, ca. 1270. Tempera on panel, $38\frac{1}{8}''\times 19\frac{1}{2}''$ (.970 × .495 m). Framed: $40\frac{1}{4}''\times 22\frac{3}{4}''$ (1.022 × .578 m). Samuel H. Kress Collection. Margarite d'Arezzo, Photograph © Board of Trustees, National Gallery of Art, Washington, D.C. The characteristic Byzantine figure type is slender and delicate. The drapery that forms angular folds is typically Byzantine.

Cultural Impact

Judaism's legacy centers on ethics and social justice. From the beginning, the ancient Hebrews emphasized the importance of ethical principles, which they read in the Ten Commandments, the book of Deuteronomy, and the teachings of the Hebrew prophets. To this day, the Jewish concern for social justice is expressed in countless Jewish philanthropic programs. Like their Jewish predecessors, Christians, too, have a long tradition of social service, running schools, shelters, hospices, and hospitals.

A powerful missionary impulse spread Christianity throughout the world, disseminating the philosophical thought of the early church fathers. Like their Jewish counterparts, Christian thinkers developed elaborate interpretations of the Bible; finely discriminating textual analysis characterizes both traditions and persists to this day.

Painting, sculpture, and architecture in medieval western Europe were almost exclusively Christian in inspiration. Medieval music, philosophy, and literature also reveal a strong Christian influence. And though the modern and contemporary worlds have become decidedly more secular, the influence of Judaism and Christianity persists in Jewish and Christian religious beliefs and practices of peoples around the world.

Byzantine civilization has also left a legacy. Throughout the Middle Ages, the Code of Justinian was the standard legal text in universities. Byzantine trade enabled the patronage of the arts in Renaissance Italian cities. Like their Western monastic predecessors, Byzantine scholars preserved ancient Greek texts, which were ultimately disseminated throughout Europe in the fifteenth century. Moreover, Orthodox Eastern Christianity continues to be practiced today in both Greece and Russia.

KEY TERMS

evangelist	nave	catacomb	iconophiles
monotheistic	aisles	fresco	piazza
covenant	transept	responsorial	Greek cross
etiological stories	apse	antiphonal	tesserae
parables	clerestory	liturgical	icon
atrium	ambulatory	schism	linear perspective
narthex	sarcophagus	pendentives	iconography

www. Websites for Further Study

http://www.ibiblio.org/expo/deadsea.scrolls.exhibit/intro.html
(The exhibition of Scrolls from the Dead Sea at the Ancient Library of Qumran and Modern Scholarship exhibit at the Library of Congress, Washington, D.C.)

http://www.religioustolerance.org/chr_otb4.htm
(The books of the Hebrew Scriptures [Old Testament] of the major prophets.)

http://www.ntcanon.org/places.shtml
(This table summarizes a few of the important places, and their important witnesses, in the development of the canon of the New Testament and links to some early images of various figures.)

http://www.metmuseum.org/explore/Byzantium/byz_1.html
(A Brief Summary of Byzantine History—this is a full site of many links and images, sponsored by the Metropolitan Museum of New York.)

READINGS

Genesis

The Creation to the Tower of Babel

In the following selections from the book of Genesis, the biblical writers describe the creation of the world and the first human beings, as well as the story of their temptation and fall. The origin of human evil, including the first murder, is also described. Among the world's best known stories, these oldest of biblical narratives continue to engage readers of diverse backgrounds and faiths.

The Creation

1 In the beginning God created the heaven and the earth.

2 And the earth was without form, and void; and darkness was upon the face of the deep. And the Spirit of God moved upon the face of the waters.

3 And God said, Let there be light: and there was light.

4 And God saw the light, that it was good: and God divided the light from the darkness.

5 And God called the light Day, and the darkness he called Night. And the evening and the morning were the first day.

6 And God said, Let there be a firmament in the midst of the waters, and let it divide the waters from the waters.

7 And God made the firmament, and divided the waters which were under the firmament from the waters which were above the firmament: and it was so.

8 And God called the firmament Heaven. And the evening and the morning were the second day.

9 And God said, Let the waters under the heaven be gathered together unto one place, and let the dry land appear: and it was so.

10 And God called the dry land earth; and the gathering together of the waters called he Seas: and God saw that it was good.

11 And God said, Let the earth bring forth grass, the herb yielding seed, and the fruit tree yielding fruit after his kind, whose seed is in itself, upon the earth: and it was so.

12 And the earth brought forth grass, and herb yielding seed after his kind, and the tree yielding fruit, whose seed was in itself, after his kind: and God saw that it was good.

13 And the evening and the morning were the third day.

14 And God said, Let there be lights in the firmament of the heaven to divide the day from the night; and let them be for signs, and for seasons, and for days, and years:

15 And let them be for lights in the firmament of the heaven to give light upon the earth: and it was so.

16 And God made two great lights; the greater light to rule the day, and the lesser light to rule the night: he made the stars also.

17 And God set them in the firmament of the heaven to give light upon the earth,

18 And to rule over the day and over the night, and to divide the light from the darkness: and God saw that it was good.

19 And the evening and the morning were the fourth day.

20 And God said, Let the waters bring forth abundantly the moving creature that hath life, and fowl that may fly above the earth in the open firmament of heaven.

21 And God created great whales, and every living creature that moveth, which the waters brought forth abundantly, after their kind, and every winged fowl after his kind: and God saw that it was good.

22 And God blessed them, saying, Be fruitful, and multiply, and fill the waters in the seas, and let fowl multiply in the earth.

23 And the evening and the morning were the fifth day.

24 And God said, Let the earth bring forth the living creature after his kind, cattle, and creeping thing, and beast of the earth after his kind: and it was so.

25 And God made the beast of the earth after his kind, and cattle after their kind, and every thing that creepeth upon the earth after his kind: and God saw that it was good.

26 And God said, Let us make man in our image, after our likeness: and let them have dominion over the fish of the sea, and over the fowl of the air, and over the cattle, and over all the earth, and over every creeping thing that creepeth upon the earth.

27 So God created man in his own image, in the image of God created he him; male and female created he them.

28 And God blessed them, and God said unto them, Be fruitful, and multiply, and replenish the earth, and subdue it: and have dominion over the fish of the sea, and over the fowl of the air, and over every living thing that moveth upon the earth.

29 And God said, Behold, I have given you every herb bearing seed, which is upon the face of all the earth, and every tree, in the which is the fruit of a tree yielding seed; to you it shall be for meat.

30 And to every beast of the earth, and to every fowl of the air, and to every thing that creepeth upon the earth, wherein there is life, I have given every green herb for meat: and it was so.

31 And God saw every thing that he had made, and, behold, it was very good. And the evening and the morning were the sixth day.

2 Thus the heavens and the earth were finished, and all the host of them.

2 And on the seventh day God ended his work which he had made; and he rested on the seventh day from all his work which he had made.

3 And God blessed the seventh day, and sanctified it: because that in it he had rested from all his work which God created and made.

4 These are the generations of the heavens and of the earth when they were created, in the day that the LORD God made the earth and the heavens,

5 And every plant of the field before it was in the earth, and every herb of the field before it grew: for the LORD God had not caused it to rain upon the earth, and there was not a man to till the ground.

6 But there went up a mist from the earth, and watered the whole face of the ground.

7 And the LORD God formed man of the dust of the ground, and breathed into his nostrils the breath of life; and man became a living soul.

8   And the LORD God planted a garden eastward in Eden; and there he put the man whom he had formed.

9   And out of the ground made the LORD God to grow every tree that is pleasant to the sight, and good for food; the tree of life also in the midst of the garden, and the tree of knowledge of good and evil.

10   And a river went out of Eden to water the garden; and from thence it was parted, and became into four heads.

11   The name of the first is Pison: that is it which compasseth the whole land of Havilah, where there is gold;

12   And the gold of that land is good: there is bdellium and the onyx stone.

13   And the name of the second river is Gihon: the same is it that compasseth the whole land of Ethiopia.

14   And the name of the third river is Hiddekel: that is it which goeth toward the east of Assyria. And the fourth river is Euphrates.

15   And the LORD God took the man, and put him into the garden of Eden to dress it and to keep it.

16   And the LORD God commanded the man, saying, Of every tree of the garden thou mayest freely eat:

17   But of the tree of the knowledge of good and evil, thou shalt not eat of it: for in the day that thou eatest thereof thou shalt surely die.

18   And the LORD God said, It is not good that the man should be alone; I will make him an help meet for him.

19   And out of the ground the LORD God formed every beast of the field, and every fowl of the air; and brought them unto Adam to see what he would call them: and whatsoever Adam called every living creature, that was the name thereof.

20   And Adam gave names to all cattle, and to the fowl of the air, and to every beast of the field; but for Adam there was not found an help meet for him.

21   And the LORD God caused a deep sleep to fall upon Adam, and he slept: and he took one of his ribs, and closed up the flesh instead thereof;

22   And the rib, which the LORD God had taken from man, made he a woman, and brought her unto the man.

23   And Adam said, This is now bone of my bones, and flesh of my flesh: she shall be called Woman, because she was taken out of Man.

24   Therefore shall a man leave his father and his mother, and shall cleave unto his wife: and they shall be one flesh.

25   And they were both naked, the man and his wife, and were not ashamed.

3   Now the serpent was more subtil than any beast of the field which the LORD God had made. And he said unto the woman, Yea, hath God said, Ye shall not eat of every tree of the garden?

2   And the woman said unto the serpent, We may eat of the fruit of the trees of the garden:

3   But of the fruit of the tree which is in the midst of the garden, God hath said, Ye shall not eat of it, neither shall ye touch it, lest ye die.

4   And the serpent said unto the woman, Ye shall not surely die:

5   For God doth know that in the day ye eat thereof, then your eyes shall be opened, and ye shall be as gods, knowing good and evil.

6   And when the woman saw that the tree was good for food, and that it was pleasant to the eyes, and a tree to be de-

sired to make one wise, she took of the fruit thereof, and did eat, and gave also unto her husband with her; and he did eat.

7   And the eyes of them both were opened, and they knew that they were naked; and they sewed fig leaves together, and made themselves aprons.

8   And they heard the voice of the LORD God walking in the garden in the cool of the day: and Adam and his wife hid themselves from the presence of the LORD God amongst the trees of the garden.

9   And the LORD God called unto Adam, and said unto him, Where art thou?

10   And he said, I heard thy voice in the garden, and I was afraid, because I was naked; and I hid myself.

11   And he said, Who told thee that thou wast naked? Hast thou eaten of the tree, whereof I commanded thee that thou shouldest not eat?

12   And the man said, The woman whom thou gavest to be with me, she gave me of the tree, and I did eat.

13   And the LORD God said unto the woman, What is this that thou hast done? And the woman said, The serpent beguiled me, and I did eat.

14   And the LORD God said unto the serpent, Because thou hast done this, thou art cursed above all cattle, and above every beast of the field; upon thy belly shalt thou go, and dust shalt thou eat all the days of thy life:

15   And I will put enmity between thee and the woman, and between thy seed and her seed; it shall bruise thy head, and thou shalt bruise his heel.

16   Unto the woman he said, I will greatly multiply thy sorrow and thy conception; in sorrow thou shalt bring forth children; and thy desire shall be to thy husband, and he shall rule over thee.

17   And unto Adam he said, Because thou hast hearkened unto the voice of thy wife, and hast eaten of the tree, of which I commanded thee, saying, Thou shalt not eat of it; cursed is the ground for thy sake; in sorrow shalt thou eat of it all the days of thy life;

18   Thorns also and thistles shall it bring forth to thee; and thou shalt eat the herb of the field;

19   In the sweat of thy face shalt thou eat bread, till thou return unto the ground; for out of it wast thou taken: for dust thou art, and unto dust shalt thou return.

20   And Adam called his wife's name Eve; because she was the mother of all living.

21   Unto Adam also and to his wife did the LORD God make coats of skins, and clothed them.

22   And the LORD God said, Behold, the man is become as one of us, to know good and evil: and now, lest he put forth his hand, and take also of the tree of life, and eat, and live for ever:

23   Therefore the LORD God sent him forth from the garden of Eden, to till the ground from whence he was taken.

24   So he drove out the man; and he placed at the east of the garden of Eden Cherubims, and a flaming sword which turned every way, to keep the way of the tree of life.

4   And Adam knew Eve his wife; and she conceived, and bare Cain, and said, I have gotten a man from the LORD.

2   And she again bare his brother Abel. And Abel was a keeper of sheep, but Cain was a tiller of the ground.

3   And in process of time it came to pass, that Cain brought of the fruit of the ground an offering unto the LORD.

4   And Abel, he also brought of the firstlings of his flock and of the fat thereof. And the LORD had respect unto Abel and to his offering:

5   But unto Cain and to his offering he had not respect. and Cain was very wroth, and his countenance fell.

6   And the LORD said unto Cain, Why art thou wroth? and why is thy countenance fallen?

7   If thou doest well, shalt thou not be accepted? and if thou doest not well, sin lieth at the door. And unto thee shall be his desire, and thou shalt rule over him.

8   And Cain talked with Abel his brother: and it came to pass, when they were in the field, that Cain rose up against Abel his brother, and slew him.

9   And the LORD said unto Cain, Where is Abel thy brother? And he said, I know not: Am I my brother's keeper?

10   And he said, What hast thou done? the voice of thy brother's blood crieth unto me from the ground.

11   And now art thou cursed from the earth, which hath opened her mouth to receive thy brother's blood from thy hand;

12   When thou tillest the ground, it shall not henceforth yield unto thee her strength; a fugitive and a vagabond shalt thou be in the earth.

13   And Cain said unto the LORD, My punishment is greater than I can bear.

14   Behold, thou hast driven me out this day from the face of the earth; and from thy face shall I be hid; and I shall be a fugitive and a vagabond in the earth; and it shall come to pass, that every one that findeth me shall slay me.

15   And the LORD said unto him, Therefore whosoever slayeth Cain, vengeance shall be taken on him sevenfold. And the LORD set a mark upon Cain, lest any finding him should kill him.

16   And Cain went out from the presence of the LORD, and dwelt in the land of Nod, on the east of Eden.

The Book of Job

Chapters 1–3, 38–42

The poetry contained in the book of Job is among the most sublime in the Bible. The book of Job includes a frame story, a narrative legend that describes a wager between God and Satan that God's faithful servant Job would curse God if Job were made to suffer. When God grants Satan power to kill Job's flocks, servants, and children, Job responds by praising God rather than cursing him. However, before God restores Job's fortune, Job raises important theological and philosophical questions, such as why the good suffer and the wicked prosper. Job challenges his friends and then God to provide answers to some of his questions.

1   There was a man in the land of Uz, whose name was Job; and that man was perfect and upright, and one that feared God, and eschewed evil.

2   And there were born unto him seven sons and three daughters.

3   His substance also was seven thousand sheep, and three thousand camels, and five hundred yoke of oxen, and five hundred she asses, and a very great household; so that this man was the greatest of all the men of the east.

4   And his sons went and feasted in their houses, every one his day; and sent and called for their three sisters to eat and to drink with them.

5   And it was so, when the days of their feasting were gone about, that Job sent and sanctified them, and rose up early in the morning, and offered burnt offerings according to the number of them all: for Job said, It may be that my sons have sinned, and cursed God in their hearts. Thus did Job continually.

6   Now there was a day when the sons of God came to present themselves before the LORD, and Satan came also among them.

7   And the LORD said unto Satan, Whence comest thou? Then Satan answered the LORD and said, From going to and fro in the earth, and from walking up and down in it.

8   And the LORD said unto Satan, Hast thou considered my servant Job, that there is none like him in the earth, a perfect and an upright man, one that feareth God, and escheweth evil?

9   Then Satan answered the LORD and said, Doth Job fear God for nought?

10   Hast not thou made an hedge about him, and about his house, and about all that he hath on every side? thou hast blessed the work of his hands, and his substance is increased in the land.

11   But put forth thine hand now, and touch all that he hath, and he will curse thee to thy face.

12   And the LORD said unto Satan, Behold, all that he hath is in thy power; only upon himself put not forth thine hand. So Satan went forth from the presence of the LORD.

13   And there was a day when his sons and his daughters were eating and drinking wine in their eldest brother's house:

14   And there came a messenger unto Job, and said, The oxen were plowing, and the asses feeding beside them:

15   And the Sabeans fell upon them, and took them away; yea, they have slain the servants with the edge of the sword; and I only am escaped alone to tell thee.

16   While he was yet speaking, there came also another, and said, The fire of God is fallen from heaven, and hath burned up the sheep, and the servants, and consumed them; and I only am escaped alone to tell thee.

17   While he was yet speaking, there came also another, and said, The Chaldeans made out three bands, and fell upon the camels, and have carried them away, yea, and slain the servants with the edge of the sword; and I only am escaped alone to tell thee.

18   While he was yet speaking, there came also another, and said, Thy sons and thy daughters were eating and drinking wine in their eldest brother's house:

19   And, behold, there came a great wind from the wilderness, and smote the four corners of the house, and it fell upon the young men, and they are dead; and I only am escaped alone to tell thee.

20   Then Job arose, and rent his mantle, and shaved his head, and fell down upon the ground, and worshipped,

21   And said, Naked came I out of my mother's womb, and naked shall I return thither: the LORD gave, and the LORD hath taken away; blessed be the name of the LORD.

22   In all this Job sinned not, nor charged God foolishly.

2   Again there was a day when the sons of God came to present themselves before the LORD, and Satan came also among them to present himself before the LORD.

2   And the LORD said unto Satan, From whence comest thou? And Satan answered the LORD, and said, From going to and fro in the earth, and from walking up and down in it.

3   And the LORD said unto Satan, Hast thou considered my servant Job, that there is none like him in the earth, a perfect and an upright man, one that feareth God, and escheweth evil? and still he holdeth fast his integrity, although thou movedst me against him, to destroy him without cause.

4   And Satan answered the LORD, and said, Skin for skin, yea, all that a man hath will he give for his life.

5   But put forth thine hand now, and touch his bone and his flesh, and he will curse thee to thy face.

6   And the LORD said unto Satan, Behold, he is in thine hand; but save his life.

7   So went Satan forth from the presence of the LORD, and smote Job with sore boils from the sole of his foot unto his crown.

8   And he took him a potsherd to scrape himself withal; and he sat down among the ashes.

9   Then said his wife unto him, Dost thou still retain thine integrity? curse God, and die.

10   But he said unto her, Thou speakest as one of the foolish women speaketh. What? shall we receive good at the hand of God, and shall we not receive evil? In all this did not Job sin with his lips.

11   Now when Job's three friends heard of all this evil that was come upon him, they came every one from his own place; Eliphaz the Temanite, and Bildad the Shuhite, and Zophar the Naamathite: for they had made an appointment together to come to mourn with him and to comfort him.

12   And when they lifed up their eyes afar off, and knew him not, they lifted up their voice, and wept; and they rent every one his mantle, and sprinkled dust upon their heads toward heaven.

13   So they sat down with him upon the ground seven days and seven nights, and none spake a word unto him: for they saw that his grief was very great.

3   After this opened Job his mouth, and cursed his day.

2   And Job spake, and said,

3   Let the day perish wherein I was born, and the night in which it was said, There is a man child conceived.

4   Let that day be darkness; let not God regard it from above, neither let the light shine upon it.

5   Let darkness and the shadow of death stain it; let a cloud dwell upon it; let the blackness of the day terrify it.

6   As for that night, let darkness seize upon it; let it not be joined unto the days of the year, let it not come into the number of the months.

7   Lo, let that night be solitary; let no joyful voice come therein.

8   Let them curse it that curse the day, who are ready to raise up their mourning.

9   Let the stars of the twilight thereof be dark; let it look for light, but have none; neither let it see the dawning of the day:

10   Because it shut not up the doors of my mother's womb, nor hid sorrow from mine eyes.

11   Why died I not from the womb? why did I not give up the ghost when I came out of the belly?

12   Why did the knees prevent me? or why the breasts that I should suck?

13   For now should I have lain still and been quiet, I should have slept: then had I been at rest,

14   With kings and counsellors of the earth, which built desolate places for themselves;

15   Or with princes that had gold, who filled their houses with silver:

16   Or as an hidden untimely birth I had not been; as infants which never saw light.

17   There the wicked cease from troubling; and there the weary be at rest.

18   There the prisoners rest together; they hear not the voice of the oppressor.

19   The small and great are there; and the servant is free from his master.

20   Wherefore is light given to him that is in misery, and life unto the bitter in soul;

21   Which long for death, but it cometh not; and dig for it more than for hid treasures;

22   Which rejoice exceedingly, and are glad, when they can find the grave?

23   Why is light given to a man whose way is hid, and whom God hath hedged in?

24   For my sighing cometh before I eat, and my roarings are poured out like the waters.

25   For the thing which I greatly feared is come upon me, and that which I was afraid of is come unto me.

26   I was not in safety, neither had I rest, neither was I quiet; yet trouble came.

38   Then the LORD answered Job out of the whirlwind, and said,

2   Who is this that darkeneth counsel by words without knowledge?

3   Gird up now thy loins like a man; for I will demand of thee, and answer thou me.

4   Where wast thou when I laid the foundations of the earth? declare, if thou hast understanding.

5   Who hath laid the measures thereof, if thou knowest? or who hath stretched the line upon it?

6   Whereupon are the foundations thereof fastened? or who laid the corner stone thereof;

7   When the morning stars sang together, and all the sons of God shouted for joy?

8   Or who shut up the sea with doors, when it brake forth, as if it had issued out of the womb?

9   When I made the cloud the garment thereof, and thick darkness a swaddlingband for it,

10   And brake up for it my decreed place, and set bars and doors,

11   And said, Hitherto shalt thou come, but no further: and here thy proud waves be stayed?

12   Hast thou commanded the morning since thy days; and caused the dayspring to know his place;

13   That it might take hold of the ends of the earth, that the wicked might be shaken out of it?

14   It is turned as clay to the seal; and they stand as a garment.

15   And from the wicked their light is withholden, and the high arm shall be broken.

16   Hast thou entered into the springs of the sea? or hast thou walked in the search of the depth?

17   Have the gates of death been opened unto thee? or hast thou seen the doors of the shadow of death?

18   Hast thou perceived the breadth of the earth? declare if thou knowest it all.

19   Where is the way where light dwelleth? and as for darkness, where is the place thereof,

20   That thou shouldest take it to the bound thereof, and that thou shouldest know the paths to the house thereof?

21   Knowest thou it, because thou wast then born? or because the number of thy days is great?

22   Hast thou entered into the treasures of the snow? or hast thou seen the treasures of the hail,

23   Which I have reserved against the time of trouble, against the day of battle and war?

24   By what way is the light parted, which scattereth the east wind upon the earth?

25   Who hath divided a watercourse for the overflowing of waters, or a way for the lightning of thunder;

26   To cause it to rain on the earth, where no man is; on the wilderness, wherein there is no man;

27   To satisfy the desolate and waste ground; and to cause the bud of the tender herb to spring forth?

28   Hath the rain a father? or who hath begotten the drops of dew?

29   Out of whose womb came the ice? and the hoary frost of heaven, who hath gendered it?

30   The waters are hid as with a stone, and the face of the deep is frozen.

31   Canst thou bind the sweet influences of Pleiades, or loose the bands of Orion?

32   Canst thou bring forth Mazzaroth in his season? or canst thou guide Arcturus with his sons?

33   Knowest thou the ordinances of heaven? canst thou set the dominion thereof in the earth?

34   Canst thou lift up thy voice to the clouds, that abundance of waters may cover thee?

35   Canst thou send lightnings, that they may go, and say unto thee, Here we are?

36   Who hath put wisdom in the inward parts? or who hath given understanding to the heart?

37   Who can number the clouds in wisdom? or who can stay the bottles of heaven,

38   When the dust groweth into hardness, and the clods cleave fast together?

39   Wilt thou hunt the prey for the lion? or fill the appetite of the young lions,

40   When they couch in their dens, and abide in the covert to lie in wait?

41   Who provideth for the raven his food? when his young ones cry unto God, they wander for lack of meat.

39

Knowest thou the time when the wild goats of the rock bring forth? or canst thou mark when the hinds do calve?

2   Canst thou number the months that they fulfil? or knowest thou the time when they bring forth?

3   They bow themselves, they bring forth their young ones, they cast out their sorrows.

4   Their young ones are in good liking, they grow up with corn; they go forth, and return not unto them.

5   Who hath sent out the wild ass free? or who hath loosed the bands of the wild ass?

6   Whose house I have made the wilderness, and the barren land his dwellings.

7   He scorneth the multitude of the city, neither regardeth he the crying of the driver.

8   The range of the mountains is his pasture, and he searcheth after every green thing.

9   Will the unicorn be willing to serve thee, or abide by thy crib?

10   Canst thou bind the unicorn with his band in the furrow? or will he harrow the valleys after thee?

11   Wilt thou trust him, because his strength is great? or wilt thou leave thy labour to him?

12   Wilt thou believe him, that he will bring home thy seed, and gather it into thy barn?

13   Gavest thou the goodly wings unto the peacocks? or wings and feathers unto the ostrich?

14   Which leaveth her eggs in the earth, and warmeth them in the dust,

15   And forgetteth that the foot may crush them, or that the wild beast may break them.

16   She is hardened against her young ones, as though they were not her's: her labour is in vain without fear;

17   Because God hath deprived her of wisdom, neither hath he imparted to her understanding.

18   What time she lifteth up herself on high, she scorneth the horse and his rider.

19   Hast thou given the horse strength? hast thou clothed his neck with thunder?

20   Canst thou make him afraid as a grasshopper? the glory of his nostrils is terrible.

21   He paweth in the valley, and rejoiceth in his strength: he goeth on to meet the armed men.

22   He mocketh at fear, and is not affrighted; neither turneth he back from the sword.

23   The quiver rattleth against him, the glittering spear and the shield.

24   He swalloweth the ground with fierceness and rage: neither believeth he that it is the sound of the trumpet.

25   He saith among the trumpets, Ha, ha; and he smelleth the battle afar off, the thunder of the captains, and the shouting.

26   Doth the hawk fly by thy wisdom, and stretch her wings toward the south?

27   Doth the eagle mount up at thy command, and make her nest on high?

28   She dwelleth and abideth on the rock, upon the crag of the rock, and the strong place.

29   From thence she seeketh the prey, and her eyes behold afar off.

30   Her young ones also suck up blood: and where the slain are, there is she.

40

Moreover the LORD answered Job, and said,

2   Shall he that contendeth with the Almighty instruct him? he that reproveth God, let him answer it.

3   Then Job answered the LORD, and said,

4   Behold, I am vile; what shall I answer thee? I will lay mine hand upon my mouth.

5   Once have I spoken; but I will not answer: yea, twice; but I will proceed no further.

6   Then answered the LORD unto Job out of the whirlwind, and said,

7   Gird up thy loins now like a man: I will demand of thee, and declare thou unto me.

8   Wilt thou also disannul my judgment? wilt thou condemn me, that thou mayest be righteous?

9   Hast thou an arm like God? or canst thou thunder with a voice like him?

10   Deck thyself now with majesty and excellency; and array thyself with glory and beauty.

11   Cast abroad the rage of thy wrath: and behold every one that is proud, and abase him.

12   Look on every one that is proud, and bring him low; and tread down the wicked in their place.

13   Hide them in the dust together; and bind their faces in secret.

14   Then will I also confess unto thee that thine own right hand can save thee.

15   Behold now behemoth, which I made with thee; he eateth grass as an ox.

16   Lo now, his strength is in his loins, and his force is in the navel of his belly.

17   He moveth his tail like a cedar: the sinews of his stones are wrapped together.

18   His bones are as strong pieces of brass; his bones are like bars of iron.

19   He is the chief of the ways of God: he that made him can make his sword to approach unto him.

20   Surely the mountains bring him forth food, where all the beasts of the field play.

21   He lieth under the shady trees, in the covert of the reed, and fens.

22   The shady trees cover him with their shadow; the willows of the brook compass him about.

23   Behold, he drinketh up a river, and hasteth not: he trusteth that he can draw up Jordan into his mouth.

24   He taketh it with his eyes: his nose pierceth through snares.

41 CANST thou draw out leviathan with an hook? or his tongue with a cord which thou lettest down?

2   Canst thou put an hook into his nose? or bore his jaw through with a thorn?

3   Will he make many supplications unto thee? will he speak soft words unto thee?

4   Will he make a covenant with thee? wilt thou take him for a servant for ever?

5   Wilt thou play with him as with a bird? or wilt thou bind him for thy maidens?

6   Shall the companions make a banquet of him? shall they part him among the merchants?

7   Canst thou fill his skin with barbed irons? or his head with fish spears?

8   Lay thine hand upon him, remember the battle, do no more.

9   Behold, the hope of him is in vain: shall not one be cast down even at the sight of him?

10   None is so fierce that dare stir him up: who then is able to stand before me?

11   Who hath prevented me, that I should repay him? whatsoever is under the whole heaven is mine.

12   I will not conceal his parts, nor his power, nor his comely proportion.

13   Who can discover the face of his garment? or who can come to him with his double bridle?

14   Who can open the doors of his face? his teeth are terrible round about.

15   His scales are his pride, shut up together as with a close seal.

16   One is so near to another, that no air can come between them.

17   They are joined one to another, they stick together, that they cannot be sundered.

18   By his neesings a light doth shine, and his eyes are like the eyelids of the morning.

19   Out of his mouth go burning lamps, and sparks of fire leap out.

20   Out of his nostrils goeth smoke, as out of a seething pot or caldron.

21   His breath kindleth coals, and a flame goeth out of his mouth.

22   In his neck remaineth strength, and sorrow is turned into joy before him.

23   The flakes of his flesh are joined together: they are firm in themselves; they cannot be moved.

24   His heart is as firm as a stone; yea, as hard as a piece of the nether millstone.

25   When he raiseth up himself, the mighty are afraid: by reason of breakings they purify themselves.

26   The sword of him that layeth at him cannot hold: the spear, the dart, nor the habergeon.

27   He esteemeth iron as straw, and brass as rotten wood.

28   The arrow cannot make him flee: slingstones are turned with him into stubble.

29   Darts are counted as stubble: he laugheth at the shaking of a spear.

30   Sharp stones are under him: he spreadeth sharp pointed things upon the mire.

31   He maketh the deep to boil like a pot: he maketh the sea like a pot of ointment.

32   He maketh a path to shine after him; one would think the deep to be hoary.

33   Upon earth there is not his like, who is made without fear.

34   He beholdeth all high things: he is a king over all the children of pride.

42 THEN Job answered the LORD, and said, I know that thou canst do every thing, and that no thought can be withholden from thee.

3   Who is he that hideth counsel without knowledge? therefore have I uttered that I understood not; things too wonderful for me, which I knew not.

4   Hear, I beseech thee, and I will speak: I will demand of thee, and declare thou unto me.

5   I have heard of thee by the hearing of the ear: but now mine eye seeth thee.

6   Wherefore I abhor myself, and repent in dust and ashes.

7   And it was so, that after the LORD had spoken these words unto Job, the LORD said to Eliphaz the Temanite, My wrath is kindled against thee, and against thy two friends: for ye have not spoken of me the thing that is right, as my servant Job hath.

8   Therefore take unto you now seven bullocks and seven rams, and go to my servant Job, and offer up for yourselves a burnt offering; and my servant Job shall pray for you: for him will I accept: lest I deal with you after your folly, in that ye have not spoken of me the thing which is right, like my servant Job.

9   So Eliphaz the Temanite and Bildad the Shuhite and Zophar the Naamathite went, and did according as the LORD commanded them: the LORD also accepted Job.

10   And the LORD turned the captivity of Job, when he prayed for his friends: also the LORD gave Job twice as much as he had before.

11   Then came there unto him all his brethren, and all his sisters, and all they that had been of his acquaintance before, and did eat bread with him in his house: and they bemoaned him, and comforted him over all the evil that the LORD had brought upon him: every man also gave him a piece of money, and every one an earring of gold.

12   So the LORD blessed the latter end of Job more than his beginning: for he had fourteen thousand sheep, and six thousand camels, and a thousand yoke of oxen, and a thousand she asses.

13   He had also seven sons and three daughters.

14   And he called the name of the first, Jemima; and the name of the second, Kezia; and the name of the third, Keren-happuch.

15   And in the land were no women found so fair as the daughters of Job: and their father gave them inheritance among their brethren.

16   After this lived Job an hundred and forty years, and saw his sons, and his sons' sons, even four generations.

17   So Job died, being old and full of days.

Gospel of Matthew

Chapters 5–7

So much of early Christian teaching is concentrated in the Sermon on the Mount that some scholars have suggested it is less a single sermon than a collection of Jesus's sayings from many different occasions. Whatever the historical circumstances of their utterance, the arrangement of the sermon in its present form conveys its message powerfully. One of Jesus's most pervasive and powerful rhetorical techniques is his use of contrast, which takes a variety of forms in the Sermon on the Mount, such as "You have heard it said, but I say to you" and "Don't do that, do this." In addition, Jesus enriches his carefully balanced utterances with metaphors, such as the wide gate and road that lead to destruction and the narrow gate and path that lead to salvation, which identify the moral and spiritual ideals he encouraged his listeners to embrace.

The Sermon on the Mount

5   AND seeing the multitudes, he went up into a mountain: and when he was set, his disciples came unto him:

2   And he opened his mouth, and taught them, saying,

3   Blessed are the poor in spirit: for their's is the kingdom of heaven.

4   Blessed are they that mourn: for they shall be comforted.

5   Blessed are the meek: for they shall inherit the earth.

6   Blessed are they which do hunger and thirst after righteousness: for they shall be filled.

7   Blessed are the merciful: for they shall obtain mercy.

8   Blessed are the pure in heart: for they shall see God.

9   Blessed are the peacemakers: for they shall be called the children of God.

10   Blessed are they which are persecuted for righteousness' sake: for their's is the kingdom of heaven.

11   Blessed are ye, when men shall revile you, and persecute you, and shall say all manner of evil against you falsely, for my sake.

12   Rejoice, and be exceeding glad: for great is your reward in heaven: for so persecuted they the prophets which were before you.

13   Ye are the salt of the earth: but if the salt have lost his savour, wherewith shall it be salted? it is thenceforth good for nothing, but to be cast out, and to be trodden under foot of men.

14   Ye are the light of the world. A city that is set on an hill cannot be hid.

15   Neither do men light a candle, and put it under a bushel, but on a candlestick; and it giveth light unto all that are in the house.

16   Let your light so shine before men, that they may see your good works, and glorify your Father which is in heaven.

17   Think not that I am come to destroy the law, or the prophets: I am not come to destroy, but to fulfil.

18   For verily I say unto you, Till heaven and earth pass, one jot or one tittle shall in no wise pass from the law, till all be fulfilled.

19   Whosoever therefore shall break one of these least commandments, and shall teach men so, he shall be called the least in the kingdom of heaven: but whosoever shall do and teach them, the same shall be called great in the kingdom of heaven.

20   For I say unto you, That except your righteousness shall exceed the righteousness of the scribes and Pharisees, ye shall in no case enter the kingdom of heaven.

21   Ye have heard that it was said by them of old time, Thou shalt not kill; and whosoever shall kill shall be in danger of the judgment:

22   But I say unto you, That whosoever is angry with his brother without a cause shall be in danger of the judgment: and whosoever shall say to his brother, Raca, shall be in danger of the council: but whosoever shall say, Thou fool, shall be in danger of hell fire.

23   Therefore if thou bring thy gift to the altar, and there rememberest that thy brother hath ought against thee;

24   Leave there thy gift before the altar, and go thy way; first be reconciled to thy brother, and then come and offer thy gift.

25   Agree with thine adversary quickly, whiles thou art in the way with him; lest at any time the adversary deliver thee to the judge, and the judge deliver thee to the officer, and thou be cast into prison.

26   Verily I say unto thee, Thou shalt by no means come out thence, till thou hast paid the uttermost farthing.

27   Ye have heard that it was said by them of old time, THOU SHALT NOT COMMIT ADULTERY:

28   But I say unto you, That whosoever looketh on a woman to lust after her hath committed adultery with her already in his heart.

29   And if thy right eye offend thee, pluck it out, and cast it from thee: for it is profitable for thee that one of thy members should perish, and not that thy whole body should be cast into hell.

30   And if thy right hand offend thee, cut it off, and cast it from thee: for it is profitable for thee that one of thy members should perish, and not that thy whole body should be cast into hell.

31   It hath been said, WHOSOEVER SHALL PUT AWAY HIS WIFE, LET HIM GIVE HER A WRITING OF DIVORCEMENT:

32   But I say unto you, That whosoever shall put away his wife, saving for the cause of fornication, causeth her to com-

mit adultery: and whosoever shall marry her that is divorced committeth adultery.

33   Again, ye have heard that it hath been said by them of old time, Thou shalt not forswear thyself, but shalt perform unto the Lord thine oaths:

34   But I say unto you, Swear not at all; neither by heaven; for it is God's throne:

35   Nor by the earth; for it is his footstool: neither by Jerusalem; for it is the city of the great King.

36   Neither shalt thou swear by thy head, because thou canst not make one hair white or black.

37   But let your communication be, Yea, yea; Nay, nay: for whatsoever is more than these cometh of evil.

38   Ye have heard that it hath been said, AN EYE FOR AN EYE, AND A TOOTH FOR A TOOTH:

39   But I say unto you, That ye resist not evil: but whosoever shall smite thee on thy right cheek, turn to him the other also.

40   And if any man will sue thee at the law, and take away thy coat, let him have thy cloke also.

41   And whosoever shall compel thee to go a mile, go with him twain.

42   Give to him that asketh thee, and from him that would borrow of thee turn not thou away.

43   Ye have heard that it hath been said, THOU SHALT LOVE THY NEIGHBOUR, AND HATE THINE ENEMY.

44   But I say unto you, Love your enemies, bless them that curse you, do good to them that hate you, and pray for them which despitefully use you, and persecute you;

45   That ye may be the children of your Father which is in heaven: for he maketh his sun to rise on the evil and on the good, and sendeth rain on the just and on the unjust.

46   For if ye love them which love you, what reward have ye? do not even the publicans the same?

47   And if ye salute your brethren only, what do ye more than others? do not even the publicans so?

48   Be ye therefore perfect, even as your Father which is in heaven is perfect.

6   TAKE heed that ye do not your alms before men, to be seen of them: otherwise ye have no reward of your Father which is in heaven.

2   Therefore when thou doest thine alms, do not sound a trumpet before thee, as the hypocrites do in the synagogues and in the streets, that they may have glory of men. Verily I say unto you, They have their reward.

3   But when thou doest alms, let not thy left hand know what thy right hand doeth:

4   That thine alms may be in secret: and thy Father which seeth in secret himself shall reward thee openly.

5   And when thou prayest, thou shalt not be as the hypocrites are: for they love to pray standing in the synagogues and in the corners of the streets, that they may be seen of men. Verily I say unto you, They have their reward.

6   But thou, when thou prayest, enter into thy closet, and when thou hast shut thy door, pray to thy Father which is in secret; and thy Father which seeth in secret shall reward thee openly.

7   But when ye pray, use not vain repetitions, as the heathen do: for they think that they shall be heard for their much speaking.

8   Be not ye therefore like unto them: for your Father knoweth what things ye have need of, before ye ask him.

9   After this manner therefore pray ye: Our Father which art in heaven, Hallowed be thy name.

10   Thy kingdom come. Thy will be done in earth, as it is in heaven.

11   Give us this day our daily bread.

12   And forgive us our debts, as we forgive our debtors.

13   And lead us not into temptation, but deliver us from evil: For thine is the kingdom, and the power, and the glory, for ever. Amen.

14   For if ye forgive men their trespasses, your heavenly Father will also forgive you:

15   But if ye forgive not men their trespasses, neither will your Father forgive your trespasses.

16   Moreover when ye fast, be not, as the hypocrites, of a sad countenance: for they disfigure their faces, that they may appear unto men to fast. Verily I say unto you, They have their reward.

17   But thou, when thou fastest, anoint thine head, and wash thy face;

18   That thou appear not unto men to fast, but unto my Father which is in secret: and thy Father, which seeth in secret, shall reward thee openly.

19   Lay not up for yourselves treasures upon earth, where moth and rust doth corrupt, and where thieves break through and steal:

20   But lay up for yourselves treasures in heaven, where neither moth nor rust doth corrupt, and where thieves do not break through nor steal:

21   For where your treasure is, there will your heart be also.

22   The light of the body is the eye: if therefore thine eye be single, thy whole body shall be full of light.

23   But if thine eye be evil, thy whole body shall be full of darkness. If therefore the light that is in thee be darkness, how great is that darkness!

24   No man can serve two masters: for either he will hate the one, and love the other; or else he will hold to the one, and despise the other. Ye cannot serve God and mammon.

25   Therefore I say unto you, Take no thought for your life, what ye shall eat, or what ye shall drink; nor yet for your body, what ye shall put on. Is not the life more than meat, and the body than raiment?

26   Behold the fowls of the air: for they sow not, neither do they reap, nor gather into barns; yet your heavenly Father feedeth them. Are ye not much better than they?

27   Which of you by taking thought can add one cubit unto his stature?

28   And why take ye thought for raiment? Consider the lilies of the field, how they grow; they toil not, neither do they spin:

29   And yet I say unto you, That even Solomon in all his glory was not arrayed like one of these.

30   Wherefore, if God so clothe the grass of the field, which to day is, and to morrow is cast into the oven, shall he not much more clothe you, O ye of little faith?

31   Therefore take no thought, saying, What shall we eat? or, What shall we drink? or, Wherewithal shall we be clothed?

32   (For after all these things do the Gentiles seek:) for your heavenly Father knoweth that ye have need of all these things.

33   But seek ye first the kingdom of God, and his righteousness; and all these things shall be added unto you.

34 Take therefore no thought for the morrow: for the morrow shall take thought for the things of itself. Sufficient unto the day is the evil thereof.

7 JUDGE not, that ye be not judged.

2 For with what judgment ye judge, ye shall be judged: and with what measure ye mete, it shall be measured to you again.

3 And why beholdest thou the mote that is in thy brother's eye, but considerest not the beam that is in thine own eye?

4 Or how wilt thou say to thy brother, Let me pull out the mote out of thine eye; and, behold, a beam is in thine own eye?

5 Thou hypocrite, first cast out the beam out of thine own eye; and then shalt thou see clearly to cast out the mote out of thy brother's eye.

6 Give not that which is holy unto the dogs, neither cast ye your pearls before swine, lest they trample them under their feet, and turn again and rend you.

7 Ask, and it shall be given you; seek, and ye shall find; knock, and it shall be opened unto you:

8 For every one that asketh receiveth; and he that seeketh findeth; and to him that knocketh it shall be opened.

9 Or what man is there of you, whom if his son ask bread, will he give him a stone?

10 Or if he ask a fish, will he give him a serpent?

11 If ye then, being evil, know how to give good gifts unto your children, how much more shall your Father which is in heaven give good things to them that ask him?

12 Therefore all things whatsoever ye would that men should do to you, do ye even so to them: for this is the law and the prophets.

13 Enter ye in at the strait gate: for wide is the gate, and broad is the way, that leadeth to destruction, and many there be which go in thereat:

14 Because strait is the gate, and narrow is the way, which leadeth unto life, and few there be that find it.

15 Beware of false prophets, which come to you in sheep's clothing, but inwardly they are ravening wolves.

16 Ye shall know them by their fruits. Do men gather grapes of thorns, or figs of thistles?

17 Even so every good tree bringeth forth good fruit; but a corrupt tree bringeth forth evil fruit.

18 A good tree cannot bring forth evil fruit, neither can a corrupt tree bring forth good fruit.

19 Every tree that bringeth not forth good fruit is hewn down, and cast into the fire.

20 Wherefore by their fruits ye shall know them.

21 Not every one that saith unto me, Lord, Lord, shall enter into the kingdom of heaven; but he that doeth the will of my Father which is in heaven.

22 Many will say to me in that day, Lord, Lord, have we not prophesied in thy name? and in thy name have cast out devils? and in thy name done many wonderful works?

23 And then will I profess unto them, I never knew you: depart from me, ye that work iniquity.

24 Therefore whosoever heareth these sayings of mine, and doeth them, I will liken him unto a wise man, which built his house upon a rock:

25 And the rain descended, and the floods came, and the winds blew, and beat upon that house; and it fell not: for it was founded upon a rock.

26 And every one that heareth these sayings of mine, and doeth them not, shall be likened unto a foolish man, which built his house upon the sand:

27 And the rain descended, and the floods came, and the winds blew, and beat upon that house; and it fell: and great was the fall of it.

28 And it came to pass, when Jesus had ended these sayings, the people were astonished at his doctrine:

29 For he taught them as one having authority, and not as the scribes.

Gospel of Luke

Chapter 15

One of the most eloquent and elegant features of Luke's writing is the way he presents Jesus's teaching through parables. Chapter 15 of Luke's gospel contains three related parables, the most famous of these being the parable of the prodigal son, which has inspired numerous artists throughout the ages.

Three Parables

15 THEN drew near unto him all the publicans and sinners for to hear him.

2 And the Pharisees and scribes murmured, saying, This man receiveth sinners, and eateth with them.

3 And he spake this parable unto them, saying,

4 What man of you, having an hundred sheep, if he lose one of them, doth not leave the ninety and nine in the wilderness, and go after that which is lost, until he find it?

5 And when he hath found it, he layeth it on his shoulders, rejoicing.

6 And when he cometh home, he calleth together his friends and neighbours, saying unto them, Rejoice with me; for I have found my sheep which was lost.

7 I say unto you, that likewise joy shall be in heaven over one sinner that repenteth, more than over ninety and nine just persons, which need no repentance.

8 Either what woman having ten pieces of silver, if she lose one piece, doth not light a candle, and sweep the house, and seek diligently till she find it?

9 And when she hath found it, she calleth her friends and her neighbours together, saying, Rejoice with me; for I have found the piece which I had lost.

10 Likewise, I say unto you, there is joy in the presence of the angels of God over one sinner that repenteth.

11 And he said, A certain man had two sons:

12 And the younger of them said to his father, Father, give me the portion of goods that falleth to me. And he divided unto them his living.

13 And not many days after the younger son gathered all together, and took his journey into a far country, and there wasted his substance with riotous living.

14 And when he had spent all, there arose a mighty famine in that land; and he began to be in want.

15 And he went and joined himself to a citizen of that country; and he sent him into his fields to feed swine.

16   And he would fain have filled his belly with the husks that the swine did eat: and no man gave unto him.

17   And when he came to himself, he said, How many hired servants of my father's have bread enough and to spare, and I perish with hunger!

18   I will arise and go to my father, and will say unto him, Father, I have sinned against heaven, and before thee,

19   And am no more worthy to be called thy son: make me as one of thy hired servants.

20   And he arose, and came to his father. But when he was yet a great way off, his father saw him, and had compassion, and ran, and fell on his neck, and kissed him.

21   And the son said unto him, Father, I have sinned against heaven, and in thy sight, and am no more worthy to be called thy son.

22   But the father said to his servants, Bring forth the best robe, and put it on him; and put a ring on his hand, and shoes on his feet:

23   And bring hither the fatted calf, and kill it; and let us eat, and be merry:

24   For this my son was dead, and is alive again; he was lost, and is found. And they began to be merry.

25   Now his elder son was in the field: and as he came and drew nigh to the house, he heard musick and dancing.

26   And he called one of the servants, and asked what these things meant.

27   And he said unto him, Thy brother is come; and thy father hath killed the fatted calf, because he hath received him safe and sound.

28   And he was angry, and would not go in: therefore came his father out, and intreated him.

29   And he answering said to his father, Lo, these many years do I serve thee, neither transgressed I at any time thy commandment: and yet thou never gavest me a kid, that I might make merry with my friends:

30   But as soon as this thy son was come, which hath devoured thy living with harlots, thou hast killed for him the fatted calf.

31   And he said unto him, Son, thou art ever with me, and all that I have is thine.

32   It was meet that we should make merry, and be glad: for this thy brother was dead, and is alive again; and was lost, and is found.

Gnostic Gospel of Thomas

Sayings of Jesus

The following passage from the Gnostic Gospel of Thomas includes a series of Jesus's sayings. The sayings, which are described as "secret," include paradoxes and parables, as do the canonical or officially accepted gospels. They are also rich in comparisons and images, and are presented with Jesus's canonical concreteness and directness. Their gnosticism is evident in their emphasis on enlightenment.

Prologue

These are the secret sayings that the living Jesus spoke and Judas Thomas the Twin recorded.

Saying 1   He said, "Whoever finds the interpretation of these sayings will not taste death."

Saying 2   Jesus said, "Let one who seeks not stop seeking until one finds.

When one finds, one will be disturbed.

When one is disturbed, one will be amazed, and will reign over all."

Saying 3   Jesus said, "If your leaders say to you, 'Behold, the kingdom is in the sky,' then the birds in the sky will get there before you. If they say to you, 'It is in the sea,' then the fish will get there before you.

"Rather, the kingdom is inside you and outside you. When you know yourselves, then you will be known, and will understand that you are children of the living Father. But if you do not know yourselves, then you live in poverty, and embody poverty."

Saying 4   Jesus said, "The older person many days old will not hesitate to ask a little child seven days old about the realm of life, and this person will live. For many of the first will be last, and will become a single one."

Saying 5   Jesus said, "Know what is within your sight, and what is hidden from you will become clear to you. For there is nothing hidden that will not be revealed."

Saying 6   His disciples asked him and said,

Do you want us to fast?

How shall we pray?

Shall we give to charity?

What food may we eat?

Jesus said, "Do not lie or do what you dislike, since all things are clear before heaven. For there is nothing hidden that will not be revealed, and nothing covered that will not be uncovered."

Saying 7   Jesus said,

"Blessed is the lion that the human eats,
    so that the lion becomes human.

Cursed is the human that the lion eats,
so that the lion becomes human."

Saying 8   He said, "A person is like a wise fisher who cast a net into the sea, and drew it up from the sea full of little fish. Among them the wise fisher discovered a fine big fish. So the fisher threw all the little fish back into the sea, and with no hesitation kept the big fish. Whoever has ears to hear ought to listen."

Saying 9   Jesus said, "Behold, the sower went out, took a handful of seeds, and scattered them. Some fell on the road, and the birds came and ate them. Others fell on rock, and they did not take root in the soil or produce any heads of grain. Others fell among thorns, and the thorns choked the seeds and worms consumed them. Still others fell on good soil, and brought forth a good crop: it yielded sixty per measure and one hundred twenty per measure."

Saying 10   Jesus said, "I have thrown fire on the world and, behold, I am guarding it until it is ablaze."

Saying 11   Jesus said,

"This heaven will pass away,
    and the heaven above it will pass away.

The dead are not alive,
    and the living will not die.

During the days when you ate what is dead,
    you made it alive.

When you become enlightened,
    what will you do?

On the day when you were one,
   you became two.
But when you become two,
   what will you do?"

Saying 12   The disciples said to Jesus, "We know you will leave us. Who is going to be our leader then?"

Jesus said to them, "No matter where you reside, you are to go to James the Just, for whose sake heaven and earth came into being."

Saying 13   Jesus said to his disciples, "Compare me with someone, and tell me whom I am like."

Simon Peter said to him, "You are like a just angel."

Matthew said to him, "You are like a wise philosopher."

Thomas said to him, "Teacher, my mouth is utterly unable to say whom you are like."

Jesus said, "I am not your teacher. You have become intoxicated because you have drunk from the bubbling spring that I have tended." And he took Thomas and withdrew, and told him three things.

When Thomas came back to his friends, they asked him, "What did Jesus tell you?"

Thomas said to them, "If I tell you even one of the things he told me, you will pick up rocks and stone me. Then fire will come forth from the rocks and devour you."

Saying 14   Jesus said to them,

"If you fast, you will bring sin upon yourselves.

If you pray, you will be condemned.

If you give to charity, you will harm your spirits.

"When you go into any country and wander from place to place, and the people receive you, eat what they serve you and heal their sick. For what goes into your mouth will not contaminate you; rather, what comes out of your mouth will contaminate you."

Saying 15   Jesus said, "When you see one who was not born of a woman, bow down and worship. That is your Father."

Saying 16   Jesus said, "Perhaps people think that I have come to bring peace to the world. They do not know that I have come to bring conflict to the earth: fire, sword, war. For five people will be in a house:

      It will be three against two
      and two against three,
      father against son
      and son against father,
      and they will stand alone."

Saying 17   Jesus said, "I shall give you
      what no eye has seen
      what no ear has heard
      what no hand has touched,
      and what has never arisen
      in a human mind."

Saying 18   The disciples said to Jesus, "Tell us about the end."

Jesus said, "Have you already discovered the beginning, that now you can seek after the end? For where the beginning is, the end will be.

Blessed is one who stands at the beginning: that one will know the end, and will not taste death."

Saying 19   Jesus said,

"Blessed is one who came to life before coming to life.

"If you become my disciples and hearken to my sayings, these stones will serve you.

"For there are five trees in Paradise for you. They do not change, summer or winter, and their leaves do not drop. Whoever knows about them will not taste death."

Augustine

from The Confessions

Augustine's Confessions *is both an autobiography and an allegory of the journey of a soul toward salvation. In the course of describing his life, Augustine illustrates and explains a process of scriptural interpretation that was to become influential for hundreds of years. According to Augustine's typological interpretation, the Old Testament prefigures or anticipates the New Testament, with Old Testament characters and events serving as types or prefigurations of those in the New Testament. Christ, for example, is the second Adam. Augustine himself serves as a type for the lost soul who finds salvation in an acceptance of Christian revelation.*

As the first Western autobiography, Augustine's Confessions *was enormously influential. Besides providing an influence and framework for other spiritual autobiographies, the* Confessions *paved the way for the Renaissance rediscovery of the self. In the following excerpt from this spiritual autobiography Augustine describes his early wickedness and his conversion.*

The Pear Tree

I propose now to set down my past wickedness and the carnal corruptions of my soul, not for love of them but that I may love Thee, O my God. I do it for love of Thy love, passing again in the bitterness of remembrance over my most evil ways that Thou mayest thereby grow ever lovelier to me, O Loveliness that dost not deceive, Loveliness happy and abiding: and I collect my self out of that broken state in which my very being was torn asunder because I was turned away from Thee, the One, and wasted myself upon the many.

Arrived now at adolescence I burned for all the satisfactions of hell, and I sank to the animal in a succession of dark lusts: my beauty consumed away, and I stank in Thine. eyes, yet was pleasing in my own and anxious to please the eyes of men.

My one delight was to love and to be loved. But in this I did not keep the measure of mind to mind, which is the luminous line of friendship; but from the muddy concupiscence of the flesh and the hot imagination of puberty mists steamed up to becloud and darken my heart so that I could not distinguish the white light of love from the fog of lust. Both love and lust boiled within me, and swept my youthful immaturity over the precipice of evil desires to leave me half drowned in a whirlpool of abominable sins. Your wrath had grown mighty against me and I knew it not. I had grown deaf from the clanking of the chain of my mortality, the punishment for the pride of my soul: and I departed further from You, and You left me to myself: and I was tossed about and wasted and poured out and boiling over in my fornications: and You were silent, O my late-won Joy. You were silent, and I, arrogant and depressed, weary and restless, wandered further and further from You into more and more sins which could bear no fruit save sorrows . . .

Where then was I, and how far from the delights of Your house, in that sixteenth year of my life in this world, when the madness of lust—needing no licence from human shamelessness, receiving no licence from Your laws—took complete control of me, and I surrendered wholly to it? My family took no care to save me from this moral destruction by marriage: their only concern was that I should learn to make as fine and persuasive speeches as possible . . .

Your law, O Lord, punishes theft; and this law is so written in the hearts of men that not even the breaking of it blots it out: for no thief bears calmly being stolen from—not even if he is rich and the other steals through want. Yet I chose to steal, and not because want drove me to it—unless a want of justice and contempt for it and an excess for iniquity. For I stole things which I already had in plenty and of better quality. Nor had I any desire to enjoy the things I stole, but only the stealing of them and the sin. There was a pear tree near our vineyard, heavy with fruit, but fruit that was not particularly tempting either to look at or to taste. A group of young blackguards, and I among them, went out to knock down the pears and carry them off late one night, for it was our bad habit to carry on our games in the streets till very late. We carried off an immense load of pears, not to eat—for we barely tasted them before throwing them to the hogs. Our only pleasure in doing it was that it was forbidden. Such was my heart, O God, such was my heart: yet in the depth of the abyss You had pity on it. Let that heart now tell You what it sought when I was thus evil for no object, having no cause for wrong-doing save my wrongness. The malice of the act was base and I loved it—that is to say I loved my own undoing, I loved the evil in me—not the thing for which I did the evil, simply the evil: my soul was depraved, and hurled itself down from security in You into utter destruction, seeking no profit from wickedness but only to be wicked . . .

Student at Carthage

I came to Carthage where a cauldron of illicit loves leapt and boiled about me. I was not yet in love, but I was in love with love, and from the very depth of my need hated myself for not more keenly feeling the need. I sought some object to love, since I was thus in love with loving; and I hated security and a life with no snares for my feet. For within I was hungry, all for the want of that spiritual food which is Thyself, my God; yet [though I was hungry for want of it] I did not hunger for it: I had no desire whatever for incorruptible food, not because I had it in abundance but the emptier I was, the more I hated the thought of it. Because of all this my soul was sick, and broke out in sores, whose itch I agonized to scratch with the rub of carnal things—carnal, yet if there were no soul in them, they would not be objects of love. My longing then was to love and to be loved, but most when I obtained the enjoyment of the body of the person who loved me.

Thus I polluted the stream of friendship with the filth of unclean desire and sullied its limpidity with the hell of lust. And vile and unclean as I was, so great was my vanity that I was bent upon passing for clean and courtly. And I did fall in love, simply from wanting to. O my God, my Mercy, with how much bitterness didst Thou in Thy goodness sprinkle the delights of that time! I was loved, and our love came to the bond of consummation: I wore my chains with bliss but with torment too, for I was scourged with the red hot rods of jealousy, with suspicions and fears and tempers and quarrels.

I developed a passion for stage plays, with the mirror they held up to my own miseries and the fuel they poured on my flame. How is it that a man wants to be made sad by the sight of tragic sufferings that he could not bear in his own person? Yet the spectator does want to feel sorrow, and it is actually his feeling of sorrow that he enjoys. Surely this is the most wretched lunacy? For the more a man feels such sufferings in himself, the more he is moved by the sight of them on the stage. Now when a man suffers himself, it is called misery; when he suffers in the suffering of another, it is called pity. But how can the unreal sufferings of the stage possibly move pity? The spectator is not moved to aid the sufferer but merely to be sorry for him; and the more the author of these fictions makes the audience grieve, the better they like him. If the tragic sorrows of the characters—whether historical or entirely fictitious—be so poorly represented that the spectator is not moved to tears, he leaves the theatre unsatisfied and full of complaints; if he is moved to tears, he stays to the end, fascinated and revelling in it . . .

Those of my occupations at that time which were held as reputable were directed towards the study of the law, in which I meant to excel—and the less honest I was, the more famous I should be. The very limit of human blindness is to glory in being blind. By this time I was a leader in the School of Rhetoric and I enjoyed this high station and was arrogant and swollen with importance: though You know, O Lord, that I was far quieter in my behavior and had no share in the riotousness of the eversores—the Overturners—for this blackguardly diabolical name they wore as the very badge of sophistication. Yet I was much in their company and much ashamed of the sense of shame that kept me from being like them. I was with them and I did for the most part enjoy their companionship, though I abominated the acts that were their specialty—as when they made a butt of some hapless newcomer, assailing him with really cruel mockery for no reason whatever, save the malicious pleasure they got from it. There was something very like the action of devils in their behavior. They were rightly called Overturners, since they had themselves been first overturned and perverted, tricked by those same devils who were secretly mocking them in the very acts by which they amused themselves in mocking and making fools of others.

With these men as companions of my immaturity, I was studying the books of eloquence; for in eloquence it was my ambition to shine, all from a damnable vaingloriousness and for the satisfaction of human vanity. Following the normal order of study I had come to a book of one Cicero, whose tongue practically everyone admires, though not his heart. That particular book is called *Hortensius* and contains an exhortation to philosophy. Quite definitely it changed the direction of my mind, altered my prayers to You, O Lord, and gave me a new purpose and ambition. Suddenly all the vanity I had hoped in I saw as worthless, and with an incredible intensity of desire I longed after immortal wisdom. I had begun that journey upwards by which I was to return to You. My father was now dead two years; I was eighteen and was receiving money from my mother for the continuance of my study of eloquence. But I used that book not for the sharpening of my tongue; what won me in it was what it said, not the excellence of its phrasing . . .

So I resolved to make some study of the Sacred Scriptures and find what kind of books they were. But what I came upon was something not grasped by the proud, not revealed either to children, something utterly humble in the hearing but sublime in the doing, and shrouded deep in mystery. And I was not of the nature to enter into it or bend my neck to follow it. When I first read those Scriptures, I did not feel in the least what I have just said; they seemed to me unworthy to be compared with the majesty of Cicero. My conceit was repelled by their simplicity, and I had not the mind to penetrate into their depths. They were indeed of a nature to grow in Your little ones. But I could not bear to be a little one; I was only swollen with pride, but to myself I seemed a very big man . . .

Worldly Ambitions

By this time my mother had come to me, following me over sea and land with the courage of piety and relying upon You in all perils. For they were in danger from a storm, and she reassured even the sailors—by whom travelers newly ventured upon the deep are ordinarily reassured—promising them safe arrival because thus You had promised her in a vision. She found me in a perilous state through my deep despair of ever discovering the truth. But even when I told her that if I was not yet a Catholic Christian, I was no longer a Manichean, she was not greatly exultant as at some unlooked-for good news, because she had already received assurance upon that part of my misery; she bewailed me as one dead certainly, but certainly to be raised again by You, offering me in her mind as one stretched out dead, that You might say to the widow's son: "*Young man, I say to thee arise*"[1]: and he should sit up and begin to speak and You should give him to his mother . . .

Nor did I then groan in prayer for Your help. My mind was intent upon inquiry and unquiet for argumentation. I regarded Ambrose as a lucky man by worldly standards to be held in honor by such important people: only his celibacy seemed to me a heavy burden. I had no means of guessing, and no experience of my own to learn from, what hope he bore within him, what struggles he might have against the temptations that went with his high place, what was his consolation in adversity, and on what joys of Your bread the hidden mouth of his heart fed. Nor did he know how I was inflamed nor the depth of my peril. I could not ask of him what I wished as I wished, for I was kept from any face to face conversation with him by the throng of men with their own troubles, whose infirmities he served. The very little time he was not with these he was refreshing either his body with necessary food or his mind with reading. When he read, his eyes traveled across the page and his heart sought into the sense, but voice and tongue were silent. No one was forbidden to approach him nor was it his custom to require that visitors should be announced; but when we came into him we often saw him reading and always to himself; and after we had sat long in silence, unwilling to interrupt a work on which he was so intent, we would depart again. We guessed that in the small time he could find for the refreshment of his mind, he would wish to be free from the distraction of other men's affairs and not called away from what he was doing. Perhaps he was on his guard lest [if he read loud] someone listening should be troubled and want an explanation if the author he was reading expressed some idea over-obscurely, and it might be necessary to expound or discuss some of the more difficult questions. And if he had to spend time on this, he would get through less reading than he wished. Or it may be that his real reason for reading to himself was to preserve his voice, which did in fact readily grow tired. But whatever his reason for doing it, that man certainly had a good reason . . .

I was all hot for honors, money, marriage: and You made mock of my hotness. In my pursuit of these, I suffered most bitter disappointments, but in this You were good to me since I was thus prevented from taking delight in anything not Yourself. Look now into my heart, Lord, by whose will I remember all this and confess it to You. Let my soul cleave to You now that You have freed it from the tenacious hold of death. At that time my soul was in misery, and You pricked the soreness of its wound, that leaving all things it might turn to You, who are over all and without whom all would return to nothing, that it might turn to You and be healed. I was in utter misery and there was one day especially on which You acted to bring home to me the realization of my misery. I was preparing an oration in praise of the Emperor in which I was to utter any number of lies to win the applause of people who knew they were lies. My heart was much wrought upon by the shame of this and inflamed with the fever of the thoughts that consumed it. I was passing along a certain street in Milan when I noticed a beggar. He was jesting and laughing and I imagine more than a little drunk. I fell into gloom and spoke to the friends who were with me about the endless sorrows that our own insanity brings us: for here was I striving away, dragging the load of my unhappiness under the spurring of my desires, and making it worse by dragging it: and with all our striving, our one aim was to arrive at some sort of happiness without care: the beggar had reached the same goal before us, and we might quite well never reach it at all. The very thing that he had attained by means of a few pennies begged from passers-by—namely the pleasure of a temporary happiness—I was plotting for with so many a weary twist and turn.

Certainly his joy was no true joy; but the joy I sought in my ambition was emptier still. In any event he was cheerful and I worried, he had no cares and I nothing but cares. Now if anyone had asked me whether I would rather be cheerful or fearful, I would answer: "Cheerful"; but if he had gone on to ask whether I would rather be like that beggar or as I actually was, I would certainly have chosen my own state though so troubled and anxious. Now this was surely absurd. It could not be for any true reason. I ought not to have preferred my own state rather than his merely because I was the more learned, since I got no joy from my learning, but sought only to please men by it—not even to teach them, only to please them. Therefore did You break my bones with the rod of Your discipline. . . .

Great effort was made to get me married. I proposed, the girl was promised me. My mother played a great part in the matter for she wanted to have me married and then cleansed with the saving waters of baptism, rejoicing to see me grow every day more fitted for baptism and feeling that her prayers and Your promises were to be fulfilled in my faith. By my request and her own desire she begged You daily with the uttermost intensity of her heart to show her in a vision something of my future marriage, but You would never do it. She did indeed see certain vain fantasies, under the pressure of her mind's preoccupation with the matter; and she told

---

[1]Throughout the *Confessions* Augustine quotes liberally from the Bible; the quotations are set off in italics.

them to me, not, however, with the confidence she always had when You had shown things to her, but as if she set small store by them; for she said that there was a certain unanalyzable savor, not to be expressed in words, by which she could distinguish between what You revealed and the dreams of her own spirit. Still she pushed on with the matter of my marriage, and the girl was asked for. She was still two years short of the age for marriage but I liked her and agreed to wait.

There was a group of us friends who had much serious discussion together, concerning the cares and troubles of human life which we found so hard to ensure. We had almost decided to seek a life of peace, away from the throng of men. This peace we hoped to attain by putting together whatever we could manage to get, and making one common household for all of us: so that in the clear trust of friendship, things should not belong to this or that individual, but one thing should be made of all our possessions, and belong wholly to each one of us, and everybody own everything. It seemed that there might be perhaps ten men in this fellowship. Among us there were some very rich men, especially Romanianus, our fellow townsman, who had been a close friend of mine from childhood and had been brought to the court in Milan by the press of some very urgent business. He was strongest of all for the idea and he had considerable influence in persuasion because his wealth was much greater than anyone else's. We agreed that two officers should be chosen every year to handle the details of our life together, leaving the rest undisturbed. But then we began to wonder whether our wives would agree, for some of us already had wives and I meant to have one. So the whole plan, which we had built up so neatly, fell to pieces in our hands and was simply dropped. We returned to our old sighing and groaning and treading of this world's broad and beaten ways: for many thoughts were in our hearts, but *Thy counsel standeth forever*. And out of Thy counsel didst Thou deride ours and didst prepare Thine own things for us, meaning to *give us meat in due season and to open Thy hands and fill our souls with Thy blessing*.

Meanwhile my sins were multiplied. She with whom I had lived so long was torn from my side as a hindrance to my forthcoming marriage. My heart which had held her very dear was broken and wounded and shed blood. She went back to Africa, swearing that she would never know another man, and left with me the natural son I had had of her. But I in my unhappiness could not, for all my manhood, imitate her resolve. I was unable to bear the delay of two years which must pass before I was to get the girl I had asked for in marriage. In fact it was not really marriage that I wanted. I was simply a slave to lust. So I took another woman, not of course as a wife; and thus my soul's disease was nourished and kept alive as vigorously as ever, indeed worse than ever, that it might reach the realm of matrimony in the company of its ancient habit. Nor was the wound healed that had been made by the cutting off of my former mistress. For there was first burning and bitter grief; and after that it festered, and as the pain grew duller it only grew more hopeless . . .

Conversion

Thus I was sick at heart and in torment, accusing myself with a new intensity of bitterness, twisting and turning in my chain in the hope that it might be utterly broken, for what held me

was so small a thing! But it still held me. And You stood in the secret places of my soul, O Lord, in the harshness of Your mercy redoubling the scourges of fear and shame lest I should give way again and that small slight tie which remained should not be broken but should grow again to full strength and bind me closer even than before. For I kept saying within myself: "Let it be now, let it be now," and by the mere words I had begun to move toward the resolution. I almost made it, yet I did not quite make it. But I did not fall back into my original state, but as it were stood near to get my breath. And I tried again and I was almost there, and now I could all but touch it and hold it: yet I was not quite there, I did not touch it or hold it. I still shrank from dying unto death and living unto life. The lower condition which had grown habitual was more powerful than the better condition which I had not tried. The nearer the point of time came in which I was to become different, the more it struck me with horror; but it did not force me utterly back nor turn me utterly away, but held me there between the two.

Those trifles of all trifles, and vanities of vanities, my one-time mistresses, held me back, plucking at my garment of flesh and murmuring softly: "Are you sending us away?" And "From this moment shall we not be with you, now or forever?" And "From this moment shall this or that not be allowed you, now or forever?" What were they suggesting to me in the phrase I have written "this or that," what were they suggesting to me, O my God? Do you in your mercy keep from the soul of Your servant the vileness and uncleanness they were suggesting. And now I began to hear them not half so loud; they no longer stood against me face to face, but they were there as I tried to depart, plucking stealthily at me to make me look behind. Yet even that was enough, so hesitating was I, to keep me from snatching myself free, from shaking them off and leaping upwards on the way I was called: for the strong force of habit said to me: "Do you think you can live without them?"

But by this time its voice was growing fainter. In the direction toward which I had turned my face and was quivering in fear of going, I could see the austere beauty of Continence, serene and indeed joyous but not evilly, honorably soliciting me to come to her and not linger, stretching forth loving hands to receive and embrace me, hands full of multitudes of good examples. With her I saw such hosts of young men and maidens, a multitude of youth and of every age, gray widows and women grown old in virginity, and in them all Continence herself, not barren but the fruitful mother of children, her joys, by You, Lord, her Spouse. And she smiled upon me and her smile gave courage as if she were saying: "Can you not do what these men have done, what these women have done? Or could men or women have done such in themselves, and not in the Lord their God? The Lord their God gave me to them. Why do you stand upon yourself and so not stand at all? Cast yourself upon Him and be not afraid; He will not draw away and let you fall. Cast yourself without fear, He will receive you and heal you."

Yet I was still ashamed, for I could still hear the murmuring of those vanities, and I still hung hesitant. And again it was as if she said: "Stop your ears against your unclean members, that they may be mortified. They tell you of delights, but not of such delights as the law of the Lord your God tells." This was the controversy raging in my heart, a controversy about myself against myself. And Alypius stayed by my side and awaited in silence the issue of such agitation as he had never seen in me.

When my most searching scrutiny had drawn up all my vileness from the secret depths of my soul and heaped it in my heart's sight, a mighty storm arose in me, bringing a mighty rain of tears. That I might give way to my tears and lamentations, I rose from Alypius: for it struck me that solitude was more suited to the business of weeping. I went far enough from him to prevent his presence from being an embarrassment to me. So I felt, and he realized it. I suppose I had said something and the sound of my voice was heavy with tears. I arose, but he remained where we had been sitting, still in utter amazement. I flung myself down somehow under a certain fig tree and no longer tried to check my tears, which poured forth from my eyes in a flood, *an acceptable sacrifice to Thee.* And much I said not in these words but to this effect: *"And Thou, O Lord, how long? How long, Lord; wilt Thou be angry forever? Remember not our former iniquities."* For I felt that I was still bound by them. And I continued my miserable complaining: "How long, how long shall I go on saying tomorrow and again tomorrow? Why not now, why not have an end to my uncleanness this very hour?"

Such things I said, weeping in the most bitter sorrow of my heart. And suddenly I heard a voice from some nearby house, a boy's voice or a girl's voice, I do not know: but it was a sort of singsong, repeated again and again. "Take and read, take and read." I ceased weeping and immediately began to search my mind most carefully as to whether children were accustomed to chant these words in any kind of game, and I could not remember that I had ever heard any such thing. Damming back the flood of my tears I arose, interpreting the incident as quite certainly a divine command to open my book of Scripture and read the passage at which I should open. For it was part of what I had been told about Anthony, that from the Gospel which he happened to be reading he had felt that he was being admonished as though what he read was spoken directly to himself: *Go, sell what thou hast and give to the poor and thou shalt have treasure in heaven; and come follow Me.* By this experience he had been in that instant converted to You. So I was moved to return to the place where Alypius was sitting, for I had put down the Apostle's book there when I arose. I snatched it up, opened it and in silence read the passage upon which my eyes first fell: *Not in rioting and drunkenness, not in chambering and impurities, not in contention and envy, but put ye on the Lord Jesus Christ and make not provision for the flesh in its concupiscences.* [Romans 13.13.] I had no wish to read further, and no need. For in that instant, with the very ending of the sentence, it was as though a light of utter confidence shone in all my heart, and all the darkness of uncertainty vanished away. Then leaving my finger in the place or marking it by some other sign, I closed the book and in complete calm told the whole thing to Alypius and he similarly told me what had been going on in himself, of which I knew nothing. He asked to see what I had read. I showed him, and he looked further than I had read. I had not known what followed. And this is what followed: *"Now him that is weak in faith, take unto you."* He applied this to himself and told me so. And he was confirmed by this message, and with no troubled wavering gave himself to God's goodwill and purpose—a purpose indeed most suited to his character, for in these matters he had been immeasurably better than I.

Then we went in to my mother and told her, to her great joy. We related how it had come about: she was filled with triumphant exultation, and praised You who are mighty beyond what we ask or conceive: for she saw that You had given her more than with all her pitiful weeping she had ever asked. For You converted me to Yourself so that I no longer sought a wife nor any of this world's promises, but stood upon that same rule of faith in which You had shown me to her so many years before. Thus You changed her mourning into joy, a joy far richer than she had thought to wish, a joy much dearer and purer than she had thought to find in grandchildren of my flesh.

Jewish Rabbinic Stories

Instead of writing theology, history, geography, or autobiography, the rabbis of antiquity told stories. Their stories convey their understanding of their religion, their responsibilities, and their world. Composed between 200 and 600 C.E., the stories that follow represent the collective wisdom of a community: they are not attributable to a named individual storyteller. The stories here all involve marriage, wives, and husbands. They are colorful, imaginative, picturesque, and fantastic.

Chapter 21

God as Marriage-Maker (Leviticus Rabbah 8:1)

Just as God brought Eve to Adam and thus served as the marriage-maker for the first human couple, so the rabbis believed that God played a role in forging every marital union. Finding a "soulmate" and the love between men and women were understood as products of the divine element in all marriages. This understanding of God's activity also responds to the theological question of the nature of God's participation in the world since creation. If God finished creating the world in six days, as the Bible reports, then how does he continue to be involved? In what way does God still participate in the creation of life? Or does God now remain apart from the world and indifferent to his creations?

The following story addresses these issues with a lighthearted description of an encounter between a sage and an aristocratic Roman woman. When the marriages she arranges among her slaves soon deteriorate into violence, she recognizes how great an accomplishment it is to bring about a successful marriage and praises the wisdom of the Torah. The sage's equation of the difficulty of marriage with that of splitting the Reed Sea suggests that the rabbis considered a loving union to be a near miracle. While this lesson is ostensibly for the benefit of the Gentile, it implies that the rabbinic storytellers were well acqainted with unhappy marriages in their society as well (see chapter 22 herein).

Rabbinic literature contains five or six similar stories of a Roman matron asking questions of various rabbis about troubling theological concepts. These encounters are probably literary fictions; to attribute difficult theological questions to a Gentile allows the rabbinic storytellers to confront the issues in a less threatening manner than were the rabbis to articulate the problems themselves.

   a. A Roman matron questioned R. Yose b. Halfuta. She said to him, "In how many days did God create his world?" He said to her, "In six days, as is written, *For in six days the Lord made Heaven and earth* (Exod

31:17)." She said to him, "What does he sit and do now?" He said to her, "He sits and arranges marriages: Mr. So-and-so's daughter is for Mr. So-and-so, the wife of So-and-so [who died] is for Mr. So-and-so, the estate of Mr. So-and-so is for Mr. So-and-so."

b. She said to him, "How many slaves and bondmaidens do I have, and in a moment or two I can marry them off!" He said to her, "Although it is a small thing in your eyes, it is as difficult before God as the parting of the Reed Sea, as is written, *God restores the lonely to their homes, [sets free the imprisoned, safe and sound, while the rebellious must live in a parched land]* (Ps 68:7)." R. Yose b. Halfuta went home.

c. What did she do? She sent [word] and they brought one thousand slaves and one thousand bondwomen and she lined them up in rows. She said to them, "So-and-so will marry So-and-so, and So-and-so will marry So-and-so."

d. That night they came to her. This one's head was disheveled. That one's eye was blinded. This one's hand was broken. That one's leg was broken. This one said, "I don't want her." That one said, "I don't want him."

e. She sent word to him [R. Yose] and said to him, "Your Torah is good, beautiful and praiseworthy." He said to her, "Did I not say to you that 'Although it is a small thing in your eyes, it is as difficult before God as the parting of the Red Sea'?"

Chapter 22

Rabbis, Husbands and Wives

Oaths were much more common in ancient society than they are today. While some swore oaths to inspire themselves to greater spiritual goals, others swore out of anger and impulsiveness, and for no higher purpose at all. Having argued with a friend, a man might become irate and rashly swear that his friend should never derive benefit from him. The friend was then forbidden to eat his food or enter his house or profit from him in any way. Needless to say, many subsequently cooled down and felt deep remorse for making such reckless oaths.

Many rabbinic stories tell of husbands becoming angry with their wives and swearing oaths forbidding their wives to benefit from them unless certain conditions should be met. These oaths constituted dire threats to the marriage; if the stipulations could not be fulfilled then the couple had no choice but to divorce. In this way a rash oath could cause the wife—and sometimes the husband too—terrible suffering.

In the following stories rabbis help wives to satisfy the conditions of their husbands' oaths to allow for the lawful endurance of the marriage. In story A, R. Meir endures public humiliation by encouraging a woman to spit in his face. Interestingly, the husband becomes angry at his wife because she attends synagogue and listens to R. Meir's sermon. In contrast to chapter 20, where men neglect their wives because of their devotion to Torah study, here the wife's love of Torah and absence from the home annoy the husband. In story B, a rabbi uses his cleverness and ingenuity to satisfy the conditions of the husband's oath. Rabbis were not only students of Torah, judges, lawyers, holy men and political leaders, but also, in some respects, marriage counselors.

The Pious Wife

(Yerushalmi Sotah 1:4, 16b)

a. R. Meir used to preach in the synagogue of Hammat every Sabbath eve, and a certain woman there used to listen to his voice. One day he preached for a long time. She went and tried to enter her house but found that the lamp had gone out. Her husband said to her, "Where have you been?" She said to him, "I was listening to the preacher." He said to her, "I swear that you will never enter this house until you go and spit in the face of the preacher."

b. R. Meir saw [what had happened] by means of the holy spirit and pretended that he had a pain in his eye. He said, "Any woman who knows how to whisper [a charm] for the eye should come and whisper it." Her neighbors said to her. "Here is your chance to return to your house. Pretend that you are whispering [a charm] and spit in his eye."

c. She went to him. He said to her, "Do you know how to whisper [a charm] for the eye?" She took fright and said, "No." He said to her, "If one spits in it seven times it feels better." After she spit he said to her, "Go and say to your husband, 'You told me once, but behold, I have spit seven times.'"

d. His students said to him, "Master. Does one degrade the Torah in this way? Had you told us, would we not have brought him and whipped him upon a bench and made him reconcile with his wife?" He said to them, "Should not the honor of Meir be like the honor of his Creator? If scripture instructs to erase the Holy Name, which was written in a state of holiness, in order to restore peace between a man and his wife, how much the more so should the honor of Meir [be debased]?"

CHAPTER 6

Islamic Civilization

Mosque, Cordova, begun 786, interior.

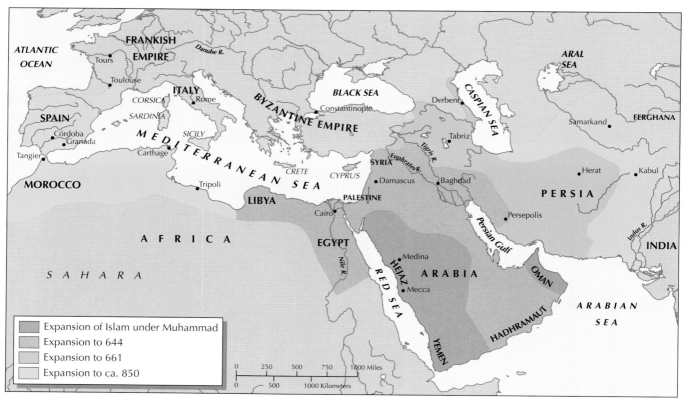

MAP 6.1 The expansion of Islam to ca. 850 C.E.

Map legend:
- Expansion of Islam under Muhammad
- Expansion to 644
- Expansion to 661
- Expansion to ca. 850

CHAPTER OVERVIEW

ISLAMIC CIVILIZATION
A New Religion Emerges from the Middle East

ISLAMIC CIVILIZATION

Islam is the youngest of the world's major religions. It was first proclaimed by MUHAMMAD (ca. 570–632) in the town of Mecca, in Arabia, in about the year 610. The followers of Islam, Muslims, consider their faith to be the third and final revelation of God's truth—the first and second manifestations being Judaism and Christianity. Islam, from the Muslim perspective, is seen as a fulfillment of Judaism and Christianity, and thus Muslims accept the sanctity of significant portions of Hebrew and Christian scripture. All three religions share a belief in a single God and are thus monotheistic. In Islam, God is called "Allah."

Islam absorbed foreign influences from both East and West, and served as a bridge between them. Initially, after its founding by Muhammed, Islam provided a unifying function, bringing together under one spiritual banner, a multitude of Arabic tribes with varied customs, speaking different languages. As Islam grew, it absorbed aspects of the cultures it conquered. Islam today is the religion of a billion and a half people spread around the globe, one testimony among many to its continued importance spiritually and culturally.

What accounts for the rapid spread of Islam? One explanation is the simplicity of its basic teachings—its five pillars of faith, prayer, charity, fasting, and pilgrimage. Another is the convergence of its religious, political, and military objectives in a messianic mission. And once conquered by Islam, foreign populations were offered economic opportunities, which won as many converts to Islam as did militarism. It spread in part through spiritual appeal, in part through commercial magnetism, and in part through military subjugation. Thus, Islam grew rapidly throughout the world—through Arabia, Egypt, Syria, Iraq, and North Africa, and then on to southern Spain and east Asia to the borders of China.

RELIGION

Muhammad. Muhammad is revered as a prophet. Muslims consider him the "seal," or final culmination, of the prophetic tradition that extends from the biblical patriarch Abraham through Moses and on to Jesus, whom Muslims also revere as a prophet but do not consider a divinity. The word *Muslim* literally means "one who surrenders"; *Islam* means "submission to God." In the first place, Muslims surrender themselves to the prophet Muhammad and through him to Allah, by obeying Muhammad's instructions for living.

A merchant by profession, Muhammad received, at about the age of forty, what he described as a call to become God's messenger and prophet. According to Islamic tradition, Muhammad heard a voice enjoining him to "recite," to which he responded, "What shall I recite?" The answer came to him in the form of a series of revelations from Allah that lasted more than twenty years, beginning at Mecca and continuing in Medina, a city north of Mecca, to which Muhammad fled in 622 because of hostility to his religious message. He died in Medina ten years later. Muhammad's flight to Medina is known as the *Hijrah* or *Hegira*, and marks the beginning of the Muslim calendar (622 C.E. = 1 for Muslims).

Upon Muhammad's death, a succession of caliphs took his place, which led to a division among the Islamic faithful. In 656 C.E., those who favored choosing only a member of Muhammad's family as caliph, rallied around ALI [AH-lee], Muhammad's cousin. They called themselves SHI'ITES [SHE-ites]. But when Ali was chosen caliph, civil war broke out, Ali was murdered, and the UMAYYAD [OO-MY-ad] dynasty, which bore no family relation to Muhammad, took control. The ninety-year Umayyad rule was marked by prosperity, but Shi'ite resentment remained. In 750, led by the great-grandson of a cousin of Muhammad, Abu-1 Abbas, the Shi'ites overthrew the Umayyad caliphs, and the capital of Islam was moved east from Damascus to Baghdad, under the ABASSID [a-BAA-sid] dynasty.

The consequences of this transfer of power and change in capital city were significant, shifting the center of gravity from the Mediterranean to Mesopotamia, where many trade routes intersected. Culturally, it meant a transfer of power from a Byzantine world to a Middle Eastern one, in which traditional influences were important. The Caliphate was also transformed, becoming the seat of divine authority with a military force and a salaried bureaucracy to sustain and support it. The Abbasids created significant economic changes as well, improving commerce and banking systems and developing a vast network of trade that encompassed India, China, Ceylon, the East Indies, and reaching to the Baltic via the Caspian and Baltic Seas. It extended on to Russia and then to Africa, the chief trade commodities being gold and slaves.

ISLAM, THE OTTOMAN EMPIRE, AND EUROPE

In the thirteenth century, a group of Asiatic nomads, later called Ottoman Turks, converted to Islam and brought an increased energy to Muslim expansion. Under a series of powerful rulers, called sultans, the Ottomans conquered the Byzantine city of Constantinople in 1453. A century later, under Sultan Suleyman I (the Magnificent), the Ottoman Empire was at the height of its power. However, by 1700, the Ottoman sultans had lost control over Egypt and Lebanon, and by the early nineteenth century had lost control of Serbia and Greece. Fueled by the fires of nationalism, other Eastern European states, including the Balkans, swept themselves out from under Ottoman control.

The seeds of destruction of Ottoman rule, however, had been sown centuries before. First came a deterioration in the quality of imperial leadership, with the two immediate successors to Suleyman the Magnificent—Selim the Sot and Ibrahim the Crazy—notoriously weak and ineffectual rulers. Secondly, religious tensions and political factions exacerbated the problem.

Equally important was a military decline occasioned in part by the high cost of maintaining increasingly expensive land and naval forces. In addition, unproductive wars fought against European enemies sapped Ottoman economic strength. And, finally, the advances in science and technology that were fueled by capitalist expansion in Europe did not occur at a similar rate and to the same degree in the Ottoman Empire. As a result, European Christendom increased, Turkish Islam decreased, and the center of economic and military power shifted westward in the mid-nineteenth century.

Nevertheless, the influence of Islam on the west remained considerable, especially on the art, music, and architecture of the Iberian Peninsula. But perhaps the Ottoman empire's greatest achievement was less its influence on the west or its military conquests than its unification of Arab peoples under the banner of Islam and its continuing spread as the world's fastest growing religion.

The Quran. Despite this political strife, Islam remained strong. At the center of the religion is the Quran (or Koran), the scripture of Islam. The word *Quran* means "recitation" and reflects the Muslim belief that the book is a recitation of God's words to Muhammad. Muhammad, who was illiterate, memorized the messages he received and dictated them to various scribes. Unlike the Hebrew scriptures, which were composed over a period of more than twelve hundred years and which for a long time remained in many different versions, the text of the Quran was definitively established after Muhammad's death by the third caliph, Uthman, around 650.

Slightly shorter than the New Testament, the Quran is divided into 114 **Surahs,** or chapters, which become

Cross Currents

THE SILK TRADE

As early as the first century B.C.E., silk from China began to reach Rome, where it was received with astonishment and admiration. Here was the lightest and most beautiful cloth ever seen, but the secrets of its production remained closely guarded by the Chinese.

The trade route that linked China to the West, and most importantly to Rome, was called the "Silk Road." Less a direct land route than a shifting network of caravan trails between remote kingdoms and trading posts, the Silk Road traversed China from the Han capital of Xi'an, north and west across the Taklamakan Desert, and on to the oasis city of Kashgar. From there, caravans carrying Chinese silk proceeded across the mountain passes of northern India, and on into the ancient Persian cities of Samarkand and Bukhara. Eventually the land route would come to an end at Constantinople, or at the Mediterranean ports of Antioch or Tyre, after which ships would complete the journey to Rome.

Although silk was the primary commodity traded with the West, eastern merchants also loaded camels with ceramics, fur, and lacquered goods. In exchange, they received gold, wool, ivory, amber, and glass from the West. It was Chinese silk, however, that captured the imagination of Rome, so much so that the Romans, who had learned about the Chinese from the Greeks, called the material *serica*, from the Greek word for the Chinese, *Seres*. For the Romans, China was synonymous with silk.

Until the sixth century A.D., silk was regularly supplied to the Romans by the Persians, who monopolized the silk trade and charged high prices. It was the Byzantine emperor Justinian who eventually broke this monopoly in the sixth century. According to the historian Procopius (died A.D. 562), "certain monks from India, knowing with what zeal the emperor Justinian endeavored to prevent the Romans from buying silk from the Persians (who were his enemy), came to visit the emperor and promised him that they would undertake the manufacture of silk." These monks explained to Justinian that silk was made by silkworms fed on mulberry leaves; Justinian promised them "great favors" if they would smuggle the requisite worms and mulberry trees back to Constantinople and begin to cultivate them there for him. This they did, and Justinian initiated a flourishing silk trade that was to become one of the chief sources of his vast wealth.

---

shorter as the Quran progresses. The first Surah contains 287 **ayas,** or verses; the last contains only three. Each Surah begins with the words, "In the name of Allah, the Beneficent, the Merciful."

The words of the Quran are the first Muslims hear when they are born and the last many hear before death. The Quran forms the core of Muslim education and serves as a textbook for the study of Arabic. Moreover, verses from it are inscribed on the walls of Muslim homes and mosques as decoration and as a reminder of their faith.

An additional important source of Islamic teaching, the **hadith** ("narrative" or "report"), consists of the sayings of Muhammad and anecdotes about him, which were initially passed on orally, but in the ninth century were collected and written down by scholars. Six canonical collections of hadith are used to determine points of Islamic theology and doctrine.

Basic Tenets and the Five Pillars of Islam. The basic tenets of Islam concern the nature of God, creation, humankind, and the afterlife. According to Islam, God is one, immaterial, invisible, and omnipotent. This single God dominates the entire universe with his power and his mercy. He is also the creator of the universe, which, because it is his creation, is also beautiful and good.

The supreme creation of Allah, however, is humankind. As in the Judeo-Christian scriptures, human beings, made in the image of God, are viewed as the culmination of creation. Women and men possess distinct, individual souls, which are immortal, and can live eternally with God—provided individuals live their earthly lives according to Islamic teaching.

To achieve heaven, Muslims must accept belief in Allah as the supreme being and the only God. They must also practice their religion by fulfilling the obligations characterized as the "five pillars" of Islam. These are repetition of the creed, daily prayer, almsgiving, fasting during Ramadan, and pilgrimage to Mecca.

The Islamic creed (*shahadah*) consists of a single sentence: *La ilaha illa Allah; Muhammad rasul Allah* ("There is no God but Allah; Muhammad is the messenger of Allah"). All Muslims must say this creed slowly, thoughtfully, and with conviction at least once during their lives, though many practicing Muslims recite it several times each day.

Daily prayer (*salat*) is recited five times: at dawn, midday, midafternoon, sunset, and nightfall. In Muslim communities, *muezzins* call the faithful to prayer from mosque towers. Whether the people pray where they are or go to the mosque, they must cleanse themselves of impurities before praying. During prayer, Muslims face Mecca and perform a series of ritual gestures that includes bowing and prostration.

Charity or almsgiving (*zakat*) is the third pillar of Islam. In addition to ad hoc giving to the poor, Islam instructs its followers to contribute one-fortieth of their income and assets to the needy. Originally a form of tax, today the *zakat* is a respected form of holy offering.

The fourth pillar is the fast (*sawm*) during the holy month of Ramadan, the ninth month of the Muslim lunar calendar. The fast includes abstaining from food, drink, medicine, tobacco, and sexual intercourse from sunrise to sundown. Moreover, during the month of fasting, Muslims are expected to recite the entire Quran at least once. Ramadan is considered the Islamic holy month because it was during Ramadan that Muhammad received his initial call as a prophet and during Ramadan that he made his historic flight from Mecca to Medina ten years later.

The final pillar of Islam is the pilgrimage (*hajj*) to Mecca, which all healthy adult Muslims are expected to complete at least once (fig 6.1).

Islamic Mysticism: The Sufis.

Like all other major religions, Islam has its mystics. Because it developed in Byzantium, where there was a strong Jewish and Christian mystical tradition, and also in India, which had its own ascetic tradition, Islam was influenced to find its own mystical path. This path was followed most powerfully by the **Sufis.** The word *sufi* means "woolen" and refers to the coarse woolen clothing the Sufis wear as a sign of their rejection of worldly comforts.

Although the Sufis trace their lineage back to the seventh century, it is more likely the movement began in earnest in the ninth century, when there was an increase in materialism; the Sufis' choice of austerity was a direct

FIGURE 6.1   *Jesus Watching Muhammad Leave Mecca*, from a medieval Persian manuscript, from Al-Biruni, "Chronicle of Ancient Nations." ORMS. 161.f.10v. Courtesy of Edinburgh University Library. Muhammad leaves Mecca on camelback in the *hijrah* or emigration in the year 622 that became the founding moment of Islam, escaping the wrath of the polytheistic Meccans who rejected his message of faith in the one true God. Regarded in Islam as one of Muhammad's prophetic predecessors, Jesus is shown looking on approvingly, in an image that both suggests continuity and also shows Muhammad about to go beyond the religious understandings of his day (Edinburgh University Library.)

Table 6-1   FIVE PILLARS OF ISLAM
1. Repetition of the creed (**shahadah**): There is no God but Allah; Muhammad is the messenger of Allah.
2. Daily prayer (**salat**): Dawn, mid-day, mid-afternoon, sunset, nightfall
3. Almsgiving (charity): One-fortieth of income and assets (**zakat**)
4. Fasting during Ramadan (**sawm**): Abstention from food, drink, medicine, tobacco, sex from sunrise to sundown
5. Pilgrimage (**hajj**): Once in a lifetime pilgrimage to Mecca, the Muslim holy city

response to this. During the twelfth century, the Sufis organized themselves into monastic orders, much like the monks of medieval Christendom. A convert to a Sufi order was called a *fakir* ("poor man") or *dervish* ("beggar"), terms intended to indicate the monk's experience of poverty and begging. Although the monastic practices of the Sufis varied, they generally included strict discipline along with abstinence, poverty, and sometimes celibacy.

One of the more notable features of Sufism in early Islam is that it recognized women as fully equal to men. A woman could become a Sufi leader or *shaykh* (feminine *shaykha*). Among the most prominent of *shaykhas* was RABIA AL-ADAWIYYA [RAA-be-ah] (d. 801), who preached an intensely devotional love of God with a corresponding withdrawal from the ordinary world. Her emphasis on worshiping God out of pure love, rather than for either temporal or eternal reward, served as both an inspiration and a model for other Sufis.

Prominent among Sufi ideas is the soul's yearning and perpetual search for God, since God is the ultimate source

Table 6-2   ISLAMIC AND CHRISTIAN BELIEFS
Although Islam shares many beliefs with Christianity, there are important differences between the doctrines of these Western faiths. The table lists some of the fundamental ones.

Muslims	Christians
Revere Jesus as a great prophet.	Worship Jesus as God.
Believe Jesus ascended into heaven but did not die on the cross.	Believe in the resurrection and ascension of Jesus.
Believe in the sin of Adam and Eve, but not the idea of inherited sin for all.	Believe all humanity inherited the original sin of Adam and Eve.
Accept the Torah, Psalms, and Gospels as sacred scripture, but do not accept the rest of the Hebrew or Christian scriptures.	Accept as sacred scripture a larger biblical canon than Muslims, one that includes historical and prophetic books as well as poetic and wisdom literature.

of all life. This notion is expressed in the poetry of the thirteenth-century Persian mystic JALALODDIN RUMI [ROO-me] (1207–73), whose poems often feature a lover seeking his beloved as a metaphor for the soul's seeking of God.

PHILOSOPHY

Avicenna and Averroes. If the Quran expresses Islamic theology and the Sufis the mystical element of Islamic thought, Islam's philosophical bent is best figured by AVICENNA [ah-vee-SEN-ah] (980–1037) and AVER-ROES [a-VER-o-ease] (1126–1198).

Better known as a doctor than as a philosopher, Avicenna articulated the beliefs of Islam in terms drawn from Aristotle and Plato, wedding two divergent Greek philosophical traditions as well as linking Greek philosophy with Islamic beliefs. Following Aristotle, Avicenna argued that God was the creator, or Prime Cause, of all that exists, a necessary being whose existence and essence were one and the same.

The second major voice of Islamic philosophy was raised not in Arabia but in Spain by Averroes, another physician-philosopher. Like Avicenna, Averroes attempted to build a bridge between the philosophy of Aristotle and the more Neoplatonically based theology of Islamic thinkers.

By following Aristotle's lead in paying renewed attention to the natural world, Averroes paved the way for Thomas Aquinas (see Chapter 12) to develop his scholastic philosophical system, which was also indebted to Aristotle and which, like the philosophy of Averroes, privileged reason above faith. Both Aquinas and Averroes, for example, argue that the existence of God can be proved by reason without the aid of revelation.

Averroes and Avicenna helped preserve the Western intellectual tradition through their reverence for education, books, and philosophy. The libraries acquired by Islamic rulers and philosophers continued the philosophic tradition that began in the West with the Greeks and found renewed expression in the religious thought of the Middle Ages and the scientific spirit of later centuries.

MATH, SCIENCE, AND SCHOLARSHIP

Among the most important contributions of Islamic culture to the west was Arabic numbers and the concept of zero, a discovery of Al-Khwaizmi (780–850), arguably the greatest of Muslim scholars. Among his achievements was the invention of algebra. Before his introduction of the nine numbers we know today and the placeholder, zero, the west made do with Roman numerals, a cumbersome system, far inferior to the elegance of the Arabic numeric system. A further numerical refinement was made by Al Uglidisi in the next century—the concept of decimal fractions, as for example, in the value of Pi: 3.1416.

Critical Thinking

SCHOLARLY CROSS FERTILIZATION

During the early Middle Ages, when Islam was born in the seventh century, there was little contact between Europe and the Arab world. While Arab power consolidated and Islam spread over the next centuries, Arab scholars picked up where the Greeks had left off. Arab mathematicians, for example, became masters of algebra and trigonometry, adding to the Greek invention of geometry. Translation was the crux, as Arabic scholars translated Greek and Indian texts into Arabic, and then translated these and other Arabic works into Latin and Hebrew. Medieval Arab scholars, thus, served as a bridge linking ancient and medieval scholarship of the world, centuries before the European Renaissance.

Why do you think that such scholarly cross-fertilization has been on the decline for the last half century? To what extent do you think religious and political factors influenced this decline?

In addition to their mathematical inventions, Muslim scholars made a number of key scientific discoveries and contributions. Muslim chemists invented the process of distillation and created the distillate, alkuhl (alcohol), which is forbidden to Muslims. Islamic astronomers made more precise instruments such as the astrolabe, which is used to measure the altitude of stars above the horizon. The Egyptian Muslim scientist, Al Hazen (d. 1038) advanced the field of optics and improved the technology for making and grinding lenses. Muslim physicians wrote books on diseases such as rabies, measles, and smallpox, among them Rhazes (d. 932), director of a Baghdad hospital. Moreover, the famous Jewish doctor, Moses Maimonides, was trained in Arabic medicine. Maimonides and other Arabic-trained Jewish physicians were consulted by the sultan of Baghdad and by the Pope in their respective centuries.

In addition to such practical mathematical and scientific contributions to knowledge, Islamic scholars, following the admonition of Muhammad to "seek knowledge," preserved numerous Greek manuscripts of Plato, Aristotle, Gales, Ptolemy, and others. These scholars copied, edited, and translated the Greek texts into Arabic. They also provided commentaries on Aristotle's works and preserved much knowledge of botany, astrology, and medicine among Greek-influenced Mediterranean peoples. All of this scholarship and practical knowledge became enormously influential in the development of medieval European universities.

ISLAMIC ART AND ARCHITECTURE

Islamic art is not the art of one particular group of people, nor that of one country. Rather, it is the art associated with the life of one person, Muhammad, and the teachings of one book, the Quran. It is therefore a fusion of many different cultures, the most influential of which are Turkish, Persian, and, particularly and originally, Arabic.

The Mosque. There is little evidence of art in Arabia before Islam and, at first, Islam did not encourage art. Islam opposes idol worship—Muhammad had all pagan idols destroyed. Furthermore, a Muslim could pray anywhere without the need of religious architecture. Nonetheless, in the late seventh century, Muslim rulers started to build palaces and **mosques**—the buildings in which Muslims assemble for religious purposes. In an attempt to compete with Byzantium, the caliphs built with materials and on a scale to rival Christian churches. Typically, a mosque is rectangular in plan, with an open court, and a fountain in the center used for purification. Covered walkways, with flat roofs supported on columns and arches, lead to the side, on which is located the **mihrab,** a small niche indicating the side facing Mecca. All mosques are oriented toward Mecca, Muhammad's place of birth, and it is the direction in which Muslims turn when praying. **Minarets** are towers beside mosques from which the faithful are called to prayer by the **muezzin,** the person who ascends a spiral staircase to a platform at the top.

Construction of the mosque at Cordova in Spain (fig. 6.2) was started in 786. The plan (fig. 6.3) is simple, making it easy to enlarge the mosque by adding more aisles, as was done on several occasions. The interior (fig. 6.5) contains hundreds of columns. A visitor must follow the aisles through this forest to reach the mihrab side. There are two tiers of arches, which create a light and airy interior, an impression enhanced by the contrasting stripes of the **voussoirs**—the wedge-shaped stones that make up the arches. The individual arches are the characteristically Muslim horseshoe shape. The result is a fluid, almost mystical space.

The Mosque of Sultan Sulayman (Suleiman) (fig. 6.6), built 1550–57, is the main mosque of Istanbul, an enormous complex including tombs, hospitals, and facilities for traveling merchants that symbolizes the city's importance as the center of Western Islamic civilization. The architect of the mosque was SINAN [sin-AHN], the greatest master

FIGURE 6.2   Mosque, Cordova, begun 786, exterior. This mosque, a masterpiece of Islamic architecture, was started by Abd-al Rahman I. It is an example of the work of the Umayyad dynasty in Spain.

FIGURE 6.3   Mosque, Cordova, begun 786, plan. Although the original structure was enlarged four times, the traditional plan continued to be organized and precise, as if laid out on a grid. The mosque includes a court, prayer hall, and arcades.

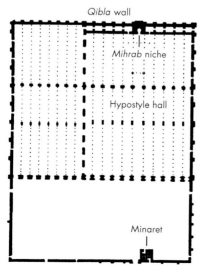

of his day. The mosque appears to build up in waves, as does Hagia Sophia (see Chapter 5), which was built a thousand years earlier in the same city: The Muslims were clearly attempting to rival the Byzantines. The very tall minarets give emphasis to the vertical; those at Hagia Sophia are later Muslim additions. The similarity between the buildings continues with the domes for, like Hagia Sophia, the mosque has a large dome, two big half domes, and several smaller ones. The surface decoration of the facade is so light and lacy that it makes the building appear delicate and fragile. The courtyard is constructed with columns and arches but, rather than a flat roof, there is a series of domes—the same roofing system employed in the mosque itself, creating a sense of unity between inside and out.

The interior of the mosque (fig. 6.7) has a ring of windows at the base of the dome, which makes the dome appear weightless and floating, and a large number of windows in the walls, turning them into airy screens. The shimmering tile decoration has the effect of separating the surface from its underlying structural function. Ornamental patterns and inscriptions are found everywhere.

Then & Now

JERUSALEM

The possession of the city of Jerusalem has historically been contested by three major world faiths: Judaism, Christianity, and Islam. The city's history is one of warring religious factions, all claiming its holy ground for themselves. Today, within a space of five hundred yards, sometimes in peaceful coexistence, sometimes not, lie the western wall of ancient Israel's Temple of Solomon, the rock marking the place of Jesus' tomb, and the Muslim shrine designating the site where Muhammad is believed to have ascended to heaven.

Archaeological evidence indicates that Jerusalem began in the Bronze Age as a mere nine-acre settlement at the edge of the Judaean desert. The Hebrew king David made Jerusalem the capital of the unified country of ancient Israel during the early tenth century B.C.E. He extended the city limits, building towers and battlements throughout. The city's most glorious years, however, occurred during the reign of King Solomon, David's successor. Solomon built a magnificent temple to house the holy Ark of the Covenant. To this temple he attached an equally magnificent palace while also extending the city walls and further enlarging its defenses.

Numerous times in its history, Jerusalem has been captured or destroyed. Alexander the Great took the city without resistance in 332 B.C.E. In 250 B.C.E., Ptolemy the Great destroyed the city walls. In 168 B.C.E., the Syrian king Antiochus Epiphanes enslaved Jerusalem's inhabitants. The Roman leader Pompey captured the city in the first century B.C.E., and the Roman general Titus crushed a rebellion a century later, leveling the city in the process. A thousand years later, the Crusaders conquered the city, taking it from the Muslims, and leaving it little more than a military outpost, dispersing those citizens who were spared from death.

Muslims, Jews, and Christians all lay claim to the Temple Mount, the site of Solomon's Temple. For Muslims, the Temple Mount and the magnificent mosque constructed on it, the Dome of the Rock (fig. 6.4), are second only to Mecca and Medina as holy sites. For Jews and Christians, this was the site of the patriarch Abraham's aborted sacrifice of his son Isaac. For members of all three faiths, Solomon's Temple was the site of Jesus's debate with the rabbis and a place where he preached.

The city of Jerusalem is constructed out of the history and cultures of many peoples. Roman vaults are coupled with Christian convents; an Arab arch cannot be separated from a Jewish wall. This complex mix of religions and cultures makes Jerusalem a truly multicultural city, whose bedrock is a faith in God, albeit a God called by various names, and conceived under a variety of identities.

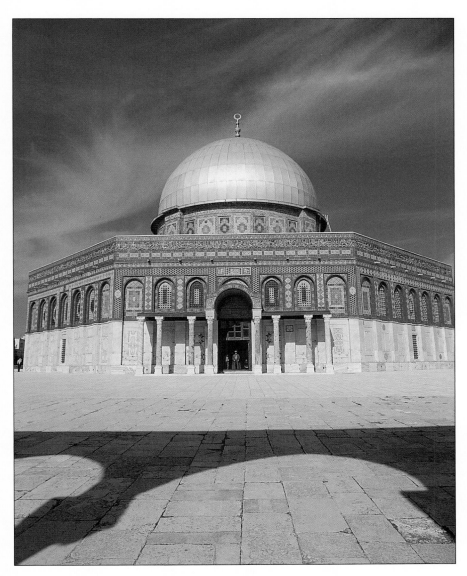

FIGURE 6.4   Dome of the Rock, Jerusalem, late 680s–692.

FIGURE 6.5 Mosque, Cordova, begun 786, interior. Decoration in plaster and marble creates an effect of delicacy and lightness, of the material made immaterial. Walls have not one plane but many, and the layers of space overlap, becoming meshlike.

The tiles are often floral and polychromatic; ceramicists and architects worked together to create an effect whereby visitors feel surrounded by gardens of luxurious flowers.

The Alhambra Palace. The Alhambra Palace in Granada, Spain, is one of the finest examples of Islamic architecture. A palace fortress, the Alhambra is the most remarkable legacy of the Nasirid dynasty, which ruled southern Spain from 1232 until the united armies of Catholic Spain under the leadership of Ferdinand and Isabella chased the last Muslim rulers out of the country in 1492.

The Alhambra is built on top of a hill overlooking the city of Granada, providing spectacular views and a cool respite from the heat of southern Spain. Surrounded by gardens built in terraces, the palace is irregular in plan, with several courts and a number of towers added by successive rulers.

Here, architectural function is obscured. Walls become lacelike webs. Surfaces are decorated with intricate patterns that disguise and seem to dissolve material substance. The solidity of stone is eclipsed as domes filled with designs seem to become floating lace canopies. The dissolution of matter is a fundamental principle of Islamic art. This style is unlike any other in the history of art.

Decoration is made of tile and stucco, which is either modeled in low relief or is built up in layers that are then cut away to create the effect of stalactites. Surfaces are cov-

FIGURE 6.6   Sinan, Mosque of Sultan Sulayman, Istanbul, 1550–57, exterior. Like Hagia
Sophia, built in the same city by the Christian Byzantines a millennium earlier (see fig. 5.16),
this Islamic mosque consists of a large central dome with abutting half domes and smaller semi
domes.

ered with a seemingly infinite variety of complex geometric patterns. Decoration is exquisite, achieving the height
of sophistication, refinement, and richness. Ornament is
profuse, yet the whole is controlled by a predilection for
symmetry and repeated rhythms. Much use is made of cal-

ligraphic designs, including decorative Cufic writing, floral patterns, and purely abstract linear elements. Arabic
calligraphy—fine handwriting—pervades Islamic art, appearing not only in manuscripts, but also on buildings, textiles, pottery, and elsewhere. The popularity of calligraphy

FIGURE 6.7   Sinan, Mosque of Sultan Sulayman, Istanbul, 1550–57, interior. The interior of this Islamic mosque, with a ring of windows at the base of the dome, is worthy of comparison with the interiors of the Byzantine churches of Hagia Sophia and St. Mark's (see figs. 5.18 and 5.20).

is in part a result of traditional Muslim iconoclasm. Because the figurative arts were discouraged, artists elaborated the abstract beauty of handwriting.

The Court of the Lions (fig. 6.8), built 1354–91 by Mohammed V, is probably the most famous part of the Alhambra. It is named for the stone lions that form the base

of a fountain in the middle of the court. The Court of the Lions is considered the quintessence of the Moorish style. Slender columns surround the courtyard, arranged singly or in pairs, and support a series of arches of fantastic shapes.

Ceramics and Miniature Painting.   Islamic pictorial arts were curtailed by Muhammad's opposition to idolatry. The Quran's view that statues are the work of the devil largely eliminated sculpture. The lions in the Court of the Lions at the Alhambra Palace are rare examples, and, moreover, they serve a functional purpose, acting as supports for the water basin of the fountain. Although the Quran does not mention painting or any other artistic medium, the argument against the portrayal of human figures or animals—or, indeed, anything living—is that only God can create life and the artist must not try to imitate God. Thus mosques contain no figurative representations; geometric and plant designs were preferred. Nonetheless, Islamic art does include some images of living things, but they are not large scale, nor made for public display. Instead, such images are usually restricted to small-scale paintings or functional objects, such as textiles and vessels (fig. 6.9). Thus, despite this ban on figurative images, a rich tradition of figurative miniature painting extends from the thirteenth to the late seventeenth century, depicting the **hadith,** or traditional leg-

FIGURE 6.8   Court of the Lions, Alhambra Palace, Granada, 1354–91. Rather than stressing the supporting structure, emphasis is on the decorative surfaces, the slender columns, and the extreme sophistication with which all surfaces are ornamented.

Cross Currents

PAPER: ISLAM'S GIFT TO THE WEST

The paper on which the words you are reading are printed owes a great deal to Islamic civilization. Although paper was invented in China during the first century C.E., it was Muslim merchants traveling the Silk Road routes in the eighth century who first brought it to the west. More-over, it was through Islamic culture in North Africa that paper found its way to Europe during the early Middle Ages. Islamic civilization thus provides the link between the invention of paper in ancient China and its extensive distribution after the invention of printing in fifteenth-century Germany. In both Islamic and European civilizations, paper became an effective medium for conveying religious beliefs—through many beautifully cal-ligraphied versions of the Quran and handsomely printed versions of the Bible, both of which reached a vast audience of readers. And though digital images and electronic transmission of information comprise the most recent mass commu-nications technology, paper remains a vital medium for communicating ideas and ex-pressing artistic visions.

ends appended to the Quran, as well as the poetry of reli-gious mystics. For example, *A Sheik Meditating in a Pavil-ion* (fig. 6.10) illustrates a scene from the poem *Haft Aurang* (*The Seven Thrones*), written by the Persian poet JAMI [JAR-me] (1414–1492).

LITERATURE

Arabic and Persian Poetry. Like English poetry, Ara-bic poetry appeared in written form around 700 as Arab lexicographers and philologists began to collect and

FIGURE 6.9 Bowl, from Iran, twelfth or thirteenth century, ceramic, diameter $8\frac{1}{2}''$ (21.7 cm), Khalili Collection, London. The Naser D. Khalili Collection of Islamic Art (POT 12), Photograph © NOUR Foundation. © Copyright The British Museum. The figurative design showing a couple in a garden was popular in the period. The decorative bands of script that are around the rim of the plate repeat two words: "Glory" and "Piety."

FIGURE 6.10 *A Sheik Meditating in a Pavilion*, illustrating the poem *Haft Aurang* (*The Seven Thrones*), by Jami, 1556–65, $13\frac{1}{2}'' \times 9\frac{1}{8}''$ (34.3 × 23.9 cm). Courtesy of the Freer Gallery of Art, Smithsonian Institution, Washington, D.C. The delicacy of the technique and the decoratively pat-terned two-dimensional quality of Islamic painting is similar to Chinese painting (see Chapter 8).

record poems that had survived orally in various Arab tribal traditions. These poems had long been chanted by *rawi*, professional reciters, who kept the verse alive.

One of the oldest forms of Arabic poetry is the *qasidah*, a highly formalized ode. The *qasidah* has three parts: (1) a visit to an abandoned encampment to find the beloved, whose departure the poet laments; (2) the poet's journey to find her, replete with descriptions of flowers and animals, especially his camel, which he eulogizes; and (3) a eulogy on a neighbor or tribe that often includes a tribute to the poet's own ancestry. The *qasidah* ranges from 30 to 120 lines in length, each line ending with the same rhyme. Central to any *qasidah* is the image, or rather a series of juxtaposed images, that vividly expresses what the poet has observed.

When Arabs invaded and conquered Persia in 637 C.E., they brought with them Islam and their Arabic script, which the Persians adopted in place of their complicated ideograms. Many Arabic words passed into Persian and some literary forms underwent modification. With the adoption of the Arabic script came an explosion of Persian poetry, including work by the early Persian poet FIRDAWSI [fear-DOW-see] (late tenth–early eleventh century). Like other Persian poets of his time and later, Firdawsi wrote in both Arabic and Persian, translating poems readily from one language to the other. The first major Persian poet and one of the greatest, Firdawsi wrote the epic *Shahnamah* (*Book of Kings*), a work of sixty thousand couplets (fig. 6.11).

One consequence of translating Persian poems into Arabic was the introduction into Arabic poetry of the quatrain (*ruba'i*, plural *ruba'iyat*), a Persian form of four lines with rhyming pattern of AABA. The *ruba'i* is familiar to readers of English through Edward Fitzgerald's translation of *The Ruba'iyat of Omar Khayyam*. The influence of the two poetic traditions, however, was reciprocal, and the Arabic *qasidah* was taken into Persian. The exchange of forms also includes the *ghazal*, a short Arabic love lyric of five to fifteen couplets believed to be of Persian origin.

Persian poetry is almost always lyrical, and its most frequent subject is love. Common features include the distraught lover, who, anguished over imagined slights, is completely at the mercy of a haughty and indifferent beloved. Some scholars have suggested the relationship of sorrowful lover to paramour is a metaphor for the relationship between the believer and God. In fact, there is a school of Persian poetry, influenced by the mystical ideas of Sufism, that uses many of the same images as love poetry. The ambiguity of subject found in some Persian love poetry can also be found in the biblical Song of Songs. In addition, the technique of using the language of physical love to describe the love of divinity is analogous to that of certain Western poets, such as John Donne and Emily Dickinson. Persian writers, moreover, have a long history of using mysticism and symbolism to veil meaning in politically perilous times.

FIGURE 6.11　Persian, Safavid, page from a manuscript of the *Shahnama of Firdawsi*, Shiraz, Iran. 1562–83, opaque watercolor, ink, and gold on paper, 13″ × 18$\frac{11}{16}$ (3 × 43 cm). Francis Bartlett Donation and Picture Fund (14.692). Reproduced with permission. © 2005 Museum of Fine Arts, Boston. All Rights Reserved. Until recent times, every Muslim text began with the phrase "In the name of Allah." Called the *bismillah*, the phrase opens the Quran. Here it is at the top righthand corner (Arabic texts read right to left). To write the *bismillah* as beautifully as possible is the highest form of Islamic art.

A further characteristic of Persian poetry is its celebration of spring, a time of renewal and hope. Seasonal celebration has a prominence in Persian poetry for a number of reasons. One reason has to do with the climate and topography of Persia, an area that is largely desert, in which the blossoming of flowers in the spring is an especially welcome sight. Another is that, since Persians celebrate their solar New Year on March 21, the first day of spring, the season is associated with gift-giving and a renewal of hope. In addition, Persian poets often celebrate the transience of the flowers of spring as emblems of the transience of earthly joy.

Connections

SUFISM, DANCING, AND MUSIC

Sufism attempted to achieve direct contact with God through mystical trance. One method of achieving trance and thus connection with the divine was through dance, especially the spinning circular form of dance that became associated with the "whirling dervishes." Dance provided the Sufi with an outlet for emotion and an opportunity to achieve ecstasy through psychic illumination in trance.

The music that accompanied such dancing would probably have been primarily percussive, for example, a drum beat, that pounded out a steady rhythm, or would perhaps have included wooden flutes, tambourines, or even a stringed instrument, such as an *ud*, or Arabic lute.

The painting reproduced here (fig. 6.12) appears in a Turkish manuscript dating from the sixteenth century. The dancers in the center raise their hands in ecstatic celebration, while the figures in the foreground may have succumbed to dizziness. Music and dancing were disapproved of by some Muslims, but they were nonetheless practiced by many Sufi orders, for whom the dance may be seen as representing the soul's movement toward God.

FIGURE 6.12 Turkish miniature of dervishes dancing, from a copy of the *Sessions of the Lovers*, sixteenth century, illuminated manuscript, ca. 9'6" (25.0 15.0 cm), Bodleian Library, Oxford.

Arabic Prose: The Thousand and One Nights. One of the most famous of all Arabic works of literature is *The Thousand and One Nights*, better known in the West as *The Arabian Nights*. Of Indo-Persian origin, the stories recounted in *The Thousand and One Nights* were introduced into written Arabic some time during the tenth century and subsequently embellished, polished, and expanded. Different as their ethnic origins may be—Persian, Indian, Arabic—the stories of *The Thousand and One Nights* became assimilated to reflect the cultural and artistic history of the Arabic Islamic tradition.

The stories cast a romantic glow of Eastern enchantment, and, although they do not chronicle the adventures of a single hero as do medieval narratives such as the *Song of Roland* or the *Divine Comedy*, they are linked by the device of a single narrator, Shahrazad, the wife of the Persian king Shahrayar, who is entertained night after night by her storytelling, which prolongs her life and cures his hatred of women. The stories are remarkable for their blending of the marvelous with the everyday.

MUSIC

During the period of the four orthodox caliphs, or representatives of Muhammad, who reigned from the prophet's death in 632 until 661, music was classed as one of the *malahi*, or forbidden pleasures. Associated with frivolity, sensuality, and luxury, it was deemed to be at odds with the religious values of Islam. With the advent of the Umayyad dynasty (661–750), however, music began to find a favorable audience throughout the Islamic world. The Umayyads held a lively court in Damascus, one that encouraged the development of the arts and sciences.

Persian music had an influence on Arabic music, and vice versa. Moreover, in the same way that Islam influenced poetry in southern Spain, so the Cordovan Islamic community supported the development of a new and distinctive musical style in Andalusian Spain. Music, especially Arabic music, flourished most, however, during the Abbasid dynasty (750–1258), the period immediately following the

Cultural Impact

During the two centuries following Muhammad's death, Arab conquerors introduced Islam throughout Asia and North Africa, India, southern Spain, and the Mediterranean islands. Diplomats, merchants, and other travelers exchanged news and goods, and an extensive trade and communications network emerged. As Islam spread, it encountered Hinduism, Judaism, and Christianity, as well as with Greek philosophy, science, and political thought. Absorbing and adapting these and other traditions, the Muslim empire prospered.

One important legacy of Islamic civilization is its architecture, particularly in southern Spain in Andalusia. Examples of Moorish-style architecture can be found in southern Europe and in the southern United States, especially in Florida and Texas, where Spanish influence is strong. Muslim artists also introduced the institution of courtly love poetry and music, in which poets sang to their mistresses, accompanied by a lute, tambourine, or guitar.

Islamic civilization also left us the tradition of the prayer rug, a small carpet or portion of a carpet used by devout Muslims when they pray. Each small rug or section of a larger carpet is just the right size for an individual supplicant.

Finally, the tales in *The Thousand and One Nights* captured the imagination of European readers from their first publication. Although these tales did not reach the West until after Chaucer and Boccaccio had written their comic masterpieces, Chaucer's "Squire's Tale" from his *Canterbury Tales* and some of the tales from Boccaccio's *Decameron* were of Arabian origin. The exotic tales of *The Thousand and One Nights* continue to delight today, both in their written form and in their cinematic transformations.

reign of the Umayyads. During the reign of the Abbasids, music became an obligatory accomplishment for every educated person, much as it did later at the courts of Renaissance Europe. Yet with the collapse of the Abbasid dynasty and the destruction of Baghdad by the Mongol armies in 1258, music declined during a period of general intellectual and cultural stagnation.

Medieval Arabic music was influenced to a significant degree by ancient Greek musical theory, which reached Near Eastern scholars in the ninth century when the works of Ptolemy, Pythagoras, and other Greek theorists were translated into Arabic. One Arabic theorist in particular who was influenced by Greek musical theory was AL-KINDI [al-KIN-dee] (790–874), who, like his Greek precursors, was interested in the effects of music on people's feelings and behavior.

Although much Islamic music was court music, which served either as vocal entertainment or as an accompaniment for dancing by professional dancers in palaces and private residences, religion also made use of music. Music was, and still is, used in calling Muslims to prayer, in chanting verses of the Quran, in hymns for special occasions and holy days, and in the *dhikr*, in which music accompanies the solemn repetition of the name of God.

KEY TERMS

Surah

ayas

hadith

Sufi

mosque

mihrab

minaret

muezzin

voussoirs

calligraphy

www. WEBSITES FOR FURTHER STUDY

http://www.fordham.edu/halsall/source/arab-y67s11.html
(Islamic political philosophy: Al-Farabi, Avicenna, Averroes—good information for comparison.)

http://archnet.org/library/sites/one-site.tcl?site_id=3005
(Sinan, Mosque of Sultan Sulayman, Instanbul, 1550–57. Click on thumbnail image to select from five views of the mosque: interior, exterior, and detail.)

http://www.4literature.net/Firdawsi/Book_of_Kings_Epic_of_Kings_/
(Isfandiyar passing through the snowstorm Shah-nama [Firdawsi's Book of Kings] and other illustrated texts from Firdawsi's Book of Kings.)

READINGS

THE QURAN

Selected Passages

The following passages, excerpted from the Quran, describe the contrasting positions of women and men in ancient (and modern) Islamic society. Women's subservience to men is strongly accentuated in the first passage. The second emphasizes man's responsibilities to God, revealing the material and spiritual rewards he will reap due to the beneficence of the Almighty. And the third accentuater emphasizes the distinction between believers and unbelievers.

CHAPTER 4

WOMEN

In the Name of God, the Compassionate, the Merciful

Men, have fear of your Lord, who created you from a single soul. From that soul He created its mate, and through them He bestrewed the earth with countless men and women.

Fear God, in whose name you plead with one another, and honour the mothers who bore you. God is ever watching over you.

Give orphans the property which belongs to them. Do not exchange their valuables for worthless things or cheat them of their possessions: for this would surely be a great sin. If you fear that you cannot treat orphans with fairness, then you may marry other women who seem good to you: two, three, or four of them. But if you fear that you cannot maintain equality among them, marry one only or any slavegirls you may own. This will make it easier for you to avoid injustice.

Give women their dowry as a free gift; but if they choose to make over to you a part of it, you may regard it as lawfully yours.

Do not give the feeble-minded the property with which God has entrusted you for their support; but maintain and clothe them with its proceeds, and give them good advice.

Put orphans to the test until they reach a marriageable age. If you find them capable of sound judgement, hand over to them their property, and do not deprive them of it by squandering it before they come of age.

Let not the rich guardian touch the property of his orphan ward; and let him who is poor use no more than a fair proportion of it for his own advantage.

When you hand over to them their property, call in some witnesses; sufficient is God's accounting of your actions.

Men shall have a share in what their parents and kinsmen leave; and women shall have a share in what their parents and kinsmen leave: whether it be little or much, they shall be legally entitled to their share.

If relatives, orphans, or needy men are present at the division of an inheritance, give them, too, a share of it, and speak to them kind words.

Let those who are solicitous about the welfare of their young children after their own death take care not to wrong orphans. Let them fear God and speak for justice.

Those that devour the property of orphans unjustly, swallow fire into their bellies; they shall burn in a mighty conflagration.

God has thus enjoined you concerning your children:

A male shall inherit twice as much as a female. If there be more than two girls, they shall have two-thirds of the inheritance; but if there be one only, she shall inherit the half. Parents shall inherit a sixth each, if the deceased have a child; but if he leave no child and his parents be his heirs, his mother shall have a third. If he have brothers, his mother shall have a sixth after payment of any legacy he may have bequeathed or any debt he may have owed.

You may wonder whether your parents or your children are more beneficial to you. But this is the law of God; God is all-knowing and wise.

You shall inherit the half of your wives' estate if they die childless. If they leave children, a quarter of their estate shall be yours after payment of any legacies they may have bequeathed or any debt they may have owed.

Your wives shall inherit one quarter of your estate if you die childless. If you leave children, they shall inherit one-eighth, after payment of any legacies you may have bequeathed or any debts you may have owed.

If a man or a woman leave neither children nor parents and have a brother or sister, they shall each inherit one-sixth. If there be more they shall equally share the third of the estate, after payment of any legacy that he may have bequeathed or any debt he may have owed, without prejudice to the rights of the heirs. That is a commandment from God. God is all-knowing and gracious.

Such are the bounds set by God. He that obeys God and His apostle shall dwell for ever in gardens watered by running streams. That is the supreme triumph. But he that defies God and His apostle and transgresses His bounds, shall be cast into a fire wherein he will abide for ever. A shameful punishment awaits him.

If any of your women commit fornication, call in four witnesses from among yourselves against them; if they testify to their guilt confine them to their houses till death overtakes them or till God finds another way for them.

If two men among you commit indecency punish them both. If they repent and mend their ways, let them be. God is forgiving and merciful.

God forgives those who commit evil in ignorance and then quickly turn to Him in repentance. God will pardon them. God is wise and all-knowing. But He will not forgive those who do evil and, when death comes to them, say: 'Now we repent!' Nor those who die unbelievers: for them We have prepared a woeful scourge.

Believers, it is unlawful for you to inherit the women of your deceased kinsmen against their will, or to bar them from re-marrying, in order that you may force them to give up a part of what you have given them, unless they be guilty of a proven crime. Treat them with kindness; for even if you dislike them, it may well be that you may dislike a thing which God has meant for your own abundant good.

If you wish to (replace a wife with) another, do not take from her the dowry you have given her even if it be a talent of gold. That would be improper and grossly unjust; for how can you take it back when you have lain with each other and entered into a firm contract?

CHAPTER 76

MAN

In the Name of God, the Compassionate, the Merciful

Does there not pass over man a space of time when his life is a blank?

We have created man from the union of the two sexes so that We may put him to the proof. We have endowed him with hearing and sight and, be he thankful or oblivious of Our favours, We have shown him the right path.

For the unbelievers We have prepared fetters and chains, and a blazing Fire. But the righteous shall drink of a cup tempered at the Camphor Fountain, a gushing spring at which the servants of God will refresh themselves: they who keep their vows and dread the far-spread terrors of Judgementday; who, though they hold it dear, give sustenance to the poor man, the orphan, and the captive, saying: "We feed you for God's sake only; we seek of you neither recompense nor thanks: for we fear from God a day of anguish and of woe."

God will deliver them from the evil of that day and make their faces shine with joy. He will reward them for their steadfastness with robes of silk and the delights of Paradise. Reclining there upon soft couches, they shall feel neither the scorching heat nor the biting cold. Trees will spread their shade around them, and fruits will hang in clusters over them.

They shall be served with silver dishes, and beakers as large as goblets; silver goblets which they themselves shall measure: and cups brim-full with ginger-flavoured water from the Fount of Salsabil. They shall be attended by boys graced with eternal youth, who to the beholder's eyes will seem like sprinkled pearls. When you gaze upon that scene you will behold a kingdom blissful and glorious.

They shall be arrayed in garments of fine green silk and rich brocade, and adorned with bracelets of silver. Their Lord will give them pure nectar to drink.

Thus you shall be rewarded; your high endeavours are gratifying to God.

We have made known to you the Quran by gradual revelation; therefore wait with patience the judgement of your Lord and do not yield to the wicked and the unbelieving. Remember the name of your Lord morning and evening; in the nighttime worship Him: praise Him all night long.

The unbelievers love this fleeting life too well, and thus prepare for themselves a heavy day of doom. *We* created them, and endowed their limbs and joints with strength; but if We please We can replace them by other men.

This is indeed an admonition. Let him that will, take the right path to his Lord. Yet you cannot will, except by the will of God. God is wise and all-knowing.

He is merciful to whom He will: but for the wrongdoers He has prepared a woeful punishment.

CHAPTER 67

MUHAMMAD

In the Name of God, the Compassionate, the Merciful

God will bring to nothing the deeds of those who disbelieve and debar others from His path. As for the faithful who do good works and believe in what has been revealed to Muham-

mad—which is the Truth from their Lord—He will forgive them their sins and ennoble their state.

This, because the unbelievers follow falsehood, while the faithful follow the truth from their Lord. Thus God lays down for mankind their rules of conduct.

When you meet the unbelievers in the battlefield strike off their heads and, when you have laid them low, bind your captives firmly. Then grant them their freedom or take a ransom from them, until War shall lay down her burdens.

Thus shall you do. Had God willed, He could Himself have punished them; [but He has ordained it thus] that He may test you, the one by the other.

As for those who are slain in the cause of God, He will not allow their works to perish. He will vouchsafe them guidance and ennoble their state; He will admit them to the Paradise He has made known to them.

Believers, if you help God, God will help you and make you strong. But the unbelievers shall be consigned to perdition. He will bring their deeds to nothing. Because they have abhorred His revelations, He will frustrate their works.

Have they never journeyed through the land and seen what was the end of those who have gone before them? God destroyed them utterly. A similar fate awaits the unbelievers, because God is the protector of the faithful: because the unbelievers have no protector.

God will admit those who embrace the true Faith and do good works to gardens watered by running streams. The unbelievers take their fill of pleasure and eat as cattle eat: but the Fire shall be their home.

How many cities were mightier than your own city, which has cast you out! We destroyed them all, and there was none to help them.

Can he who follows the guidance of his Lord be compared to him who is led by his desires and whose foul deeds seem fair to him?

Such is the Paradise which the righteous have been promised: Therein shall flow rivers of water undefiled, and rivers of milk for ever fresh; rivers of wine delectable to those that drink it, and rivers of clarified honey. There shall they eat of every fruit, and receive forgiveness from their Lord. Are they to be compared to those who shall abide in Hell for ever, and drink scalding water which will tear their bowels?

THE THOUSAND AND ONE NIGHTS

The Tale of the Merchant

The following selection from The Thousand and One Nights *(also known as* The Arabian Nights*) is taken from near the beginning of the series of linked stories. These are the first stories told by Shahrazad to her royal husband. Their high level of narrative interest, coupled with the narrator's postponed revelation of the outcome, ensures both the reader's interest and her survival to tell a tale another day.*

THE FIRST NIGHT

It is said, O wise and happy King, that once there was a prosperous merchant who had abundant wealth and investments and commitments in every country. He had many women and children and kept many servants and slaves. One day, having resolved to visit another country, he took provisions, filling his saddlebag with loaves of bread and with dates, mounted his horse, and set out on his journey. For many days and nights, he journeyed under God's care until he reached his destination. When he finished his business, he turned back to his home and family. He journeyed for three days, and on the fourth day, chancing to come to an orchard, went in to avoid the heat and shade himself from the sun of the open country. He came to a spring under a walnut tree and, tying his horse, sat by the spring, pulled out from the saddlebag some loaves of bread and a handful of dates, and began to eat, throwing the date pits right and left until he had had enough. Then he got up, performed his ablutions, and performed his prayers.

But hardly had he finished when he saw an old demon, with sword in hand, standing with his feet on the ground and his head in the clouds. The demon approached until he stood before him and screamed, saying, "Get up, so that I may kill you with this sword, just as you have killed my son." When the merchant saw and heard the demon, he was terrified and awestricken. He asked, "Master, for what crime do you wish to kill me?" The demon replied, "I wish to kill you because you have killed my son." The merchant asked, "Who has killed your son?" The demon replied, "You have killed my son." The merchant said, "By God, I did not kill your son. When and how could that have been?" The demon said, "Didn't you sit down, take out some dates from your saddlebag, and eat, throwing the pits right and left?" The merchant replied, "Yes, I did." The demon said, "You killed my son, for as you were throwing the stones right and left, my son happened to be walking by and was struck and killed by one of them, and I must now kill you." The merchant said, "O my lord, please don't kill me." The demon replied, "I must kill you as you killed him—blood for blood." The merchant said, "To God we belong and to God we turn. There is no power or strength, save in God the Almighty, the Magnificent. If I killed him, I did it by mistake. Please forgive me." The demon replied, "By God, I must kill you, as you killed my son." Then he seized him and, throwing him to the ground, raised the sword to strike him. The merchant began to weep and mourn his family and his wife and children. Again, the demon raised his sword to strike, while the merchant cried until he was drenched with tears, saying, "There is no power or strength, save in God the Almighty, the Magnificent." Then he began to recite the following verses:

> "Life has two days: one peace, one wariness,
> And has two sides: worry and happiness.
> Ask him who taunts us with adversity,
> "Does fate, save those worthy of note, oppress?
> Don't you see that the blowing, raging storms
> Only the tallest of the trees beset,
> And of earth's many green and barren lots,
> Only the ones with fruits with stones are hit,
> And of the countless stars in heaven's vault
> None is eclipsed except the moon and sun?
> You thought well of the days, when they were good,
> Oblivious to the ills destined for one.
> You were deluded by the peaceful nights,
> Yet in the peace of night does sorrow stun."

When the merchant finished and stopped weeping, the demon said, "By God, I must kill you, as you killed my son, even if you weep blood." The merchant asked, "Must you?" The demon replied, "I must," and raised his sword to strike.

But morning overtook Shahrazad, and she lapsed into silence, leaving King Shahrayar burning with curiosity to hear the rest of the story. Then Dinarzad said to her sister Shahrazad, "What a strange and lovely story!" Shahrazad replied, "What is this compared with what I shall tell you tomorrow night if the king spares me and lets me live? It will be even better and more entertaining." The king thought to himself, "I will spare her until I hear the rest of the story; then I will have her put to death the next day." When morning broke, the day dawned, and the sun rose; the king left to attend to the affairs of the kingdom, and the vizier, Shahrazad's father, was amazed and delighted. King Shahrayar governed all day and returned home at night to his quarters and got into bed with Shahrazad. Then Dinarzad said to her sister Shahrazad, "Please, sister, if you are not sleepy, tell us one of your lovely little tales to while away the night." The king added, "Let it be the conclusion of the story of the demon and the merchant, for I would like to hear it." Shahrazad replied: "With the greatest pleasure, dear, happy King":

THE SECOND NIGHT

It is related, O wise and happy King, that when the demon raised his sword, the merchant asked the demon again, "Must you kill me?" and the demon replied, "Yes." Then the merchant said, "Please give me time to say goodbye to my family and my wife and children, divide my property among them, and appoint guardians. Then I shall come back, so that you may kill me." The demon replied, "I am afraid that if I release you and grant you time, you will go and do what you wish, but will not come back." The merchant said, "I swear to keep my pledge to come back, as the God of heaven and earth is my witness." The demon asked, "How much time do you need?" The merchant replied, "One year, so that I may see enough of my children, and bid my wife good-bye, discharge my obligations to people, and come back on New Year's Day." The demon asked, "Do you swear to God that if I let you go, you will come back on New Year's Day?" The merchant replied, "Yes, I swear to God."

After the merchant swore, the demon released him, and he mounted his horse sadly and went on his way. He journeyed until he reached his home and came to his wife and children. When he saw them, he wept bitterly, and when his family saw his sorrow and grief, they began to reproach him for his behavior, and his wife said, "Husband, what is the matter with you? Why do you mourn, when we are happy, celebrating you return?" He replied, "Why not mourn when I have only one year to live?" Then told her of his encounter with the demon and informed her that he had sworn to return on New Year's Day, so that the demon might kill him.

When they heard what he said, everyone began to cry. His wife struck her face in lamentation and cut her hair, his daughters wailed, and his little children cried. It was a day of mourning, as all the children gathered around their father to weep and exchange goodbyes. The next day he wrote his will, dividing his property, discharged his obligations to people, left bequests and gifts, distributed alms, and engaged reciters to read portions of the Quran in his house. Then he summoned legal witnesses and in their presence freed his slaves and slave-girls, divided among his elder children their shares of the property, appointed guardians for his little ones, and gave his wife her share, according to her marriage contract.

He spent the rest of the time with his family, and when the year came to an end, save for the time needed for the journey, he performed his ablutions, performed his prayers, and, carrying his burial shroud, began to bid his family good-bye. His sons hung around his neck, his daughters wept, and his wife wailed. Their mourning scared him, and he began to weep, as he embraced and kissed his children good-bye. He said to them, "Children, this is God's will and decree, for man was created to die." Then he turned away and, mounting his horse, journeyed day and night until he reached the orchard on New Year's Day.

He sat at the place where he had eaten the dates, waiting for the demon, with a heavy heart and tearful eyes. As he waited, an old man, leading a deer on a leash, approached and greeted him, and he returned the greeting. The old man inquired, "Friend, why do you sit here in this place of demons and devils? For in this haunted orchard none come to good." The merchant replied by telling him what had happened to him and the demon, from beginning to end. The old man was amazed at the merchant's fidelity and said, "Yours is a magnificent pledge," adding, "By God, I shall not leave until I see what will happen to you with the demon." Then he sat down beside him and chatted with him. As they talked . . .

But morning overtook Shahrazad, and she lapsed into silence. As the day dawned, and it was light, her sister Dinarzad said, "What a strange and wonderful story!" Shahrazad replied, "Tomorrow night I shall tell something even stranger and more wonderful than this."

THE THIRD NIGHT

When it was night and Shahrazad was in bed with the king, Dinarzad said to her sister Shahrazad, "Please, if you are not sleepy, tell us one of your lovely little tales to while away the night." The king added, "Let it be the conclusion of the merchant's story." Shahrazad replied, "As you wish":

I heard, O happy King, that as the merchant and the man with the deer sat talking, another old man approached, with two black hounds, and when he reached them, he greeted them, and they returned his greeting. Then he asked them about themselves, and the man with the deer told him the story of the merchant and the demon, how the merchant had sworn to return on New Year's Day, and how the demon was waiting to kill him. He added that when he himself heard the story, he swore never to leave until he saw what would happen between the merchant and the demon. When the man with the two dogs heard the story, he was amazed, and he too swore never to leave them until he saw what would happen between them. Then he questioned the merchant, and the merchant repeated to him what had happened to him with the demon.

While they were engaged in conversation, a third old man approached and greeted them, and they returned his greeting. He asked, "Why do I see the two of you sitting here, with this merchant between you, looking abject, sad, and dejected?" They told him the merchant's story and explained that they were sitting and waiting to see what would happen to him with the demon. When he heard the story, he sat down with them, saying, "By God, I too like you will not leave, until I see what happens to this man with the demon." As they sat, conversing with one another, they suddenly saw the dust ris-

ing from the open country, and when it cleared, they saw the demon approaching, with a drawn steel sword in his hand. He stood before them without greeting them, yanked the merchant with his left hand, and, holding him fast before him, said, "Get ready to die." The merchant and the three old men began to weep and wail.

But dawn broke and morning overtook Shahrazad, and she lapsed into silence. Then Dinarzad said, "Sister, what a lovely story!" Shahrazad replied, "What is this compared with what I shall tell you tomorrow night? It will be even better; it will be more wonderful, delightful, entertaining, and delectable if the king spares me and lets me live." The king was all curiosity to hear the rest of the story and said to himself, "By God, I will not have her put to death until I hear the rest of the story and find out what happened to the merchant with the demon. Then I will have her put to death the next morning, as I did with the others." Then he went out to attend to the affairs of his kingdom, and when he saw Shahrazad's father, he treated him kindly and showed him favors, and the vizier was amazed. When night came, the king went home, and when he was in bed with Shahrazad, Dinarzad said, "Sister, if you are not sleepy, tell us one of your lovely little tales to while away the night." Shahrazad replied, "With the greatest pleasure."

JALALODDIN RUMI

The Questions

Jalaloddin Rumi is the best known and the most influential of Persian poets. His deeply mystical works reflect the spirituality of the Sufis, emphasizing their withdrawal from the material world and their desire to achieve union with the divine. In the following poem two visions of the divine are described—a fire and a stream. Each is reflected by a voice that calls out to come and enter it. The contrasting images and voices of the fire and the water, however, are presented in a paradoxical relationship in which what appears to be one thing is its opposite.

One dervish to another, *What was your vision of God's presence?*
I haven't seen anything.
But for the sake of conversation, I'll tell you a story.

God's presence is there in front of me, a fire on the left,
a lovely stream on the right.   5
One group walks toward the fire, *into* the fire, another
toward the sweet flowing water.
No one knows which are blessed and which not.
Whoever walks into the fire appears suddenly in the
     stream.
A head goes under on the water surface, that head
pokes out of the fire.   10
Most people guard against going into the fire;
and so end up in it.
Those who love the water of pleasure and make it their
     devotion
are cheated with this reversal.   15

The trickery goes further.
The voice of the fire tells the *truth*, saying *I am not fire.*
I am fountainhead. Come to me and don't mind the sparks.

If you are a friend of God, fire is your water.
You should wish to have a hundred thousand sets of
    mothwings,   20
so you could burn them away, one set a night.
The moth sees light and goes into fire. You should see fire
and go toward light. Fire is what of God is world-
    consuming.
Water, world-protecting.
Somehow each gives the appearance of the other. To
    these eyes you have now   25
what looks like water burns. What looks like
fire is a great relief to be inside.
You've seen a magician make a bowl of rice
seem a dish full of tiny, live worms.
Before an assembly with one breath he made the floor
    swarm   30
with scorpions that weren't there.
How much more amazing God's tricks.
Generation after generation lies down, defeated, they
    think,
but they're like a woman underneath a man, circling him,
One molecule-mote-second thinking of God's reversal
    of comfort and pain   35
is better than any attending ritual. That splinter
of intelligence is substance.
The fire and water themselves:
Accidental, done with mirrors.

THREE ANCIENT TALES OF THE DERVISHES

The following tales were popular among the Sufi dervishes, who passed them down orally through the centuries. They were recorded over the past thousand years and served primarily as teaching material. Like other ancient folktales and parables from the Hindu, Buddhist, and Judeo-Christian traditions, these stories are valued for their ethical as well as their entertainment value.

THE TALE OF THE SANDS

A stream, from its source in far-off mountains, passing through every kind and description of countryside, at last reached the sands of the desert. Just as it had crossed every other barrier, the stream tried to cross this one, but it found that as fast as it ran into the sand, its waters disappeared.

It was convinced, however, that its destiny was to cross this desert, and yet there was no way. Now a hidden voice, coming from the desert itself, whispered: 'The Wind crosses the desert, and so can the stream.'

The stream objected that it was dashing itself against the sand, and only getting absorbed: that the wind could fly, and this was why it could cross a desert.

'By hurtling in your own accustomed way you cannot get across. You will either disappear or become a marsh. You must allow the wind to carry you over, to your destination.'

But how could this happen? 'By allowing yourself to be absorbed in the wind.'

This idea was not acceptable to the stream. After all, it had never been absorbed before. It did not want to lose its individuality. And, once having lost it, how was one to know that it could ever be regained?

'The wind', said the sand, 'performs this function. It takes up water, carries it over the desert, and then lets it fall again. Falling as rain, the water again becomes a river.'

'How can I know that this is true?'

'It is so, and if you do not believe it, you cannot become more than a quagmire, and even that could take many, many years; and it certainly is not the same as a stream.'

'But can I not remain the same stream that I am today?'

'You cannot in either case remain so,' the whisper said. 'Your essential part is carried away and forms a stream again. You are called what you are even today because you do not know which part of you is the essential one.'

When he heard this, certain echoes began to arise in the thoughts of the stream. Dimly, he remembered a state in which he—or some part of him, was it?—had been held in the arms of a wind. He also remembered—or did he?—that this was the real thing, not necessarily the obvious thing, to do.

And the stream raised his vapour into the welcoming arms of the wind, which gently and easily bore it upwards and along, letting it fall softly as soon as they reached the roof of a mountain, many, many miles away. And because he had had his doubts, the stream was able to remember and record more strongly in his mind the details of the experience. He reflected, 'Yes, now I have learned my true identity.'

The stream was learning. But the sands whispered: 'We know, because we see it happen day after day: and because we, the sands, extend from the riverside all the way to the mountain.'

And that is why it is said that the way in which the Stream of Life is to continue on its journey is written in the Sands.

THE BLIND ONES AND THE MATTER OF THE ELEPHANT

Beyond Ghor there was a city. All its inhabitants were blind. A king with his entourage arrived near by; he brought his army and camped in the desert. He had a mighty elephant, which he used in attack and to increase the people's awe.

The populace became anxious to see the elephant, and some sightless from among this blind community ran like fools to find it.

As they did not even know the form or shape of the elephant they groped sightlessly, gathering information by touching some part of it.

Each thought that he knew something, because he could feel a part.

When they returned to their fellow-citizens eager groups clustered around them. Each of these was anxious, misguidedly, to learn the truth from those who were themselves astray.

They asked about the form, the shape of the elephant: and listened to all that they were told.

The man whose hand had reached an ear was asked about the elephant's nature. He said: 'It is a large, rough thing, wide and broad, like a rug.'

And the one who had felt the trunk said: 'I have the real facts about it. It is like a straight and hollow pipe, awful and destructive.'

The one who had felt its feet and legs said: 'It is mighty and firm, like a pillar.'

Each had felt one part out of many. Each had perceived it wrongly. No mind knew all: knowledge is not the companion of the blind. All imagined something, something incorrect.

The created is not informed about divinity. There is no Way in this science by means of the ordinary intellect.

THE ANCIENT COFFER OF NURI BEY

Nuri Bey was a reflective and respected Albanian, who had married a wife much younger than himself.

One evening when he had returned home earlier than usual, a faithful servant came to him and said:

'Your wife, our mistress, is acting suspiciously.'

'She is in her apartments with a huge chest, large enough to hold a man, which belonged to your grandmother.'

'It should contain only a few ancient embroideries.'

'I believe that there may now be much more in it.'

'She will not allow me, your oldest retainer, to look inside.'

Nuri went to his wife's room, and found her sitting disconsolately beside the massive wooden box.

'Will you show me what is in the chest?' he asked.

'Because of the suspicion of a servant, or because you do not trust me?'

'Would it not be easier just to open it, without thinking about the undertones?' asked Nuri.

'I do not think it possible.'

'Is it locked?'

'Yes.'

'Where is the key?'

She held it up, 'Dismiss the servant and I will give it to you.'

The servant was dismissed. The woman handed over the key and herself withdrew, obviously troubled in mind.

Nuri Bey thought for a long time. Then he called four gardeners from his estate. Together they carried the chest by night unopened to a distant part of the grounds, and buried it.

The matter was never referred to again.

RABI'A THE MYSTIC

Rabi'a al-'Adawiyya, known as Rabi'a the Mystic (712–801), was born in Basra (now in Iraq). She was a celibate and an ascetic who lived in seclusion in the desert; she was later canonized as an Islamic saint. Fire was a central symbol in both her poems and her spiritual life.

[O My Lord, If I Worship You from Fear of Hell]
O my Lord, if I worship you from fear of Hell
Burn me in Hell.

If I worship you from hope of Paradise,
Exclude me from that place.
But if I worship you for your own sake,
Do not withhold from me your eternal beauty.

[O My Lord, The Stars Glitter and Eyes of Men Are Closed]
O my Lord, the stars glitter and eyes of men are closed,
Kings have shut their doors
And each lover is alone with his love.
Here, I am alone with you.

AL-KHANSA

Al-Khansa (575–646), an Arabic poet, belonged to a rich and powerful family. Her full name was Tumadir bint Amkir ibn al Harith ibn al Sharid. Almost all of her poems deal with the death of her two brothers, whom she laments after they have been killed in a tribal battle. Her poems, earthy and imaginative, employ desert and tribal details.

ON HER BROTHER SAKHR

No day was sad as the day Sakhr
left me. Sweet and forever bitter.

Sakhr was our lord, our chief.
In the winter Sakhr made a feast

and led us when we rode.
Sakhr killed when we were hungry.

Sakhr was our guide
like a mountain whose top is fire.

Firm, perfect face, and pious,
he kindled wars on the morning of fear.

He bore flags, saved our blood, was
witness for assemblies, an army for armies.

Sacrificer of camels, a refuge for the oppressed,
liberator of prisoners, mender of bones.

I say there was no one like him in the world.

CHAPTER 7

HISTORY

ca. 326 B.C.E.	Alexander the Great invades north India
324–301 B.C.E.	Chandragupta Maurya reigns
ca. 250 B.C.E.	Sarnath Capital
269–232 B.C.E.	Ashoka reigns
375–415 C.E.	Chandra Gupta II reigns
710 C.E.	First Muslim invasion of India
ca. 12th century C.E.	Mahadeviyakka active
1192 C.E.	Delhi Sultanate, first Muslim kingdom Buddhism declines
1526	Mogul empire established

ARTS AND ARCHITECTURE

ca. 530 B.C.E.	Vishnu Narayana on the Cosmic Waters
3rd B.C.E.–1st century C.E.	Great Stupa at Sanchi
4th–5th century C.E.	Standing Buddha
5th century C.E.	Ajanta cave paintings
1025–50 C.E.	Kandariya Mahadeo temple
11th–12th century C.E.	Shiva Nataraja
1630–48 C.E.	Taj Mahal

LITERATURE AND PHILOSOPHY

1500 B.C.E.	Hinduism evolves from Aryan religious beliefs
1500–1000 B.C.E.	*Vedas* first recorded by Aryans
ca. 550 B.C.E.	Valmiki's *Ramayana* first recorded
ca. 4th century B.C.E.	*Jataka* tales
ca. 260 B.C.E.	Ashoka establishes Buddhism as state religion
ca. 1st century B.C.E.	*Bhagavad Gita*

Indian Civilization

Taj Mahal, Agra, 1630–48.

MAP 7.1 Muslim India under the Delhi Sultanate.

CHAPTER OVERVIEW

THE VEDIC PERIOD
Hinduism takes root

THE MAURYA PERIOD
Buddhism rises in political and religious prominence

THE KUSHAN ERA
Greco-Roman artistic influences meet Buddhism

THE GUPTA ERA
Flourishing culture and commerce

THE HINDU DYNASTIES
Southern Indian arts prosper despite constant war

THE VEDIC PERIOD

India, as we know it today, is a distinct subcontinent bordered on the north by the Himalayan mountains, on the east by the Bay of Bengal, and on the west by the Arabian Sea. The only land routes into or out of the country are the northwestern passes through the Hindu Kush, the mountains separating India from Iran, and eastward past the mouth of the Ganges River, through Burma into China.

But despite its relative geographic isolation, India has long been the center of trade between East and West, on both land and sea. In his *Geography*, the ancient author Ptolemy records the visits of Western traders to stations on the Silk Road in the second century C.E. Between the fifth and ninth centuries C.E., the Chinese regularly traveled along Indian trade routes. In addition, maritime trade routes up and down the Indian coast connected China to the West long after Mongol hordes had laid waste the Silk Road itself in the thirteenth century.

The first known indigenous people, from the Indus Valley civilization (2500 B.C.E.–1500 B.C.E.), were known as the Dasas, or Pre-Aryan culture of India. The Indus Valley people developed an extremely advanced and sophisticated culture that covered a region roughly the size of western Europe. The major Indus cities discovered so far are Mohenjo-daro on the Indus River and Harappa in the Punjab.

Mohenjo-daro had an estimated population of 35,000 to 40,000 people, larger than Pompei, which had 25,000. Excavations of the site reveal a civilization of great organization and centralization; cities were laid out in grid patterns, reflecting a high degree of civil planning. Moreover, a centralized drainage system ran through the city, and seven hundred wells supplied water to its inhabitants. Workshops for dyeing, pottery, and metalwork have also been found.

Of the artifacts found, the most interesting are the more than four thousand seals carved in **intaglio** (negative relief). These seals are about 1.5 inches square and reveal a variety of animal, vegetable, and human designs (fig. 7.1). But more significantly, they reveal a written language that has yet to be deciphered.

Sometime around 1500 B.C.E. light-skinned **nomadic** Aryan tribes from the Russian steppes and Central Asia brought horses and chariots and settled in northern India. In many ways they were much less advanced—technologically and intellectually—than the native Indian population; however, they brought with them early forms of a language—**Sanskrit**—and of a religion—Hinduism—that would evolve to become very important to Indian cultural life. This era is referred to as the vedic period (1500 B.C.E.–300 B.C.E.), named after the oldest surviving sacred Indian writings, the **Vedas,** and represents a time of cultural assimilation that proved critical to India's subsequent development.

FIGURE 7.1   Indus Valley Seal with an image of a two-horned bull, India, Indus Valley period, 3000–1500 B.C.E. Steatite, $1\frac{1}{4} \times 1\frac{1}{4}''$ 3.2 × 3.2 cm. The Cleveland Museum of Art, Purchase from the J.H. Wade Fund, 1973. 160.

It would take over a thousand years for the Aryans and Dasas to become fully integrated. During this period, in response to the growing complexity and social rigidity of Hinduism, various alternative religions emerged—most notably Buddhism and Jainism, both of which challenged the Hindu hereditary class structure.

HINDUISM

The origins of Hinduism are unknown, although they are believed to date to around the sixth century B.C.E., perhaps even as early as 1500 B.C.E. The word **Hindu** derives from *Sindhu*, the Sanskrit name for the Indus River. Like the Ganges, another important Indian river, the Indus was used for religious ceremonies, especially for rites of purification.

Hindu worship focuses on a pantheon of gods who personify natural forces, not on a historical teacher or prophet. In Hinduism the ideal life has four basic goals: (1) *dharma:* the pursuit of human righteousness, duty, and cosmic order; (2) *artha:* the accumulation of worldly success; (3) *kama:* pursuit of spiritual love; and (4) *moksha:* release from empty pleasures and suffering in the world. Moksha is the most important goal; by breaking bonds with daily existence and focusing on integrating the self with the universal truth (Absolute Reality), one can escape the cycle of birth and death.

Hindu Gods. At the center of Hindu religious thought is the idea of BRAHMAN [BRAH-man], the indivisible essence of all spiritual reality, the divine source of all being. In ancient Hinduism (sometimes called Brahmanism), **Brahman** is the essence of the universe, manifesting itself in creation, preservation, and destruction. In later Hinduism, Brahman's three functions are divided among three gods: BRAHMA [BRAH-mah], the creator (as distinct from Brahman, the ubiquitous spirit of the universe); VISHNU [VISH-noo], the preserver; and SHIVA [SHE-vah], the destroyer.

The most popular of the three gods, **Vishnu,** is the god of benevolence, forgiveness, and love. He enjoys games and pranks. His consort, or companion, is **LAKSHMI** [LACK-shmee], with whom he is often depicted. Because of his great love for humankind, Vishnu is said to have appeared on earth many times in various forms, including that of a man. Among his **avatars,** or appearances in earthly form, is his incarnation as KRISHNA [KRISH-nah], a charioteer who advises the warrior Arjuna about his military responsibilities. **Krishna** is also believed by some Hindus to have been reincarnated as the Buddha.

Shiva represents and reflects life's processes and paradoxes. He is both the creative and destructive flow of life: motion and calm, male and female, dark and light, everything and its opposite. Shiva is an ambivalent god who embodies, defies, and reconciles himself with all aspects of life. He is also the god of dance, an extremely important aspect of Indian culture and expression. His most frequent consort is Paravati, with whom he has several sons; the most popular is Ganesha, the elephant-headed deity who bestows prosperity. Paravati's fierce, destructive manifestation is KALI [KAH-lee], often depicted with a necklace of human skulls. Because for Hindus, death is a prelude to rebirth, Shiva and Kali are also gods of sexuality and reproduction. According to one tradition, there are 330 million Hindu gods, and a single god can be worshipped under a variety of manifestations. Hindus accept and worship numerous gods because they are able to accept many varying perspectives on existence. Gods and goddesses often are depicted with multiple heads and arms as a way of conveying their immense power and ability to be all seeing.

Ganesha (fig. 7.2) is one of the more lovable of the Hindu gods. The son of Shiva and Paravati, he is associated with playfulness and prosperity. According to one legend, his mother Paravati was taking a bath and created a boy from the dirt of her own body. She then asked the boy to stand guard while she finished bathing. In the meantime, Shiva returned home to find a stranger blocking the door to his wife's room. Shiva became angry and cut off the boy's head. Paravati, learning of this, was grief stricken. In order to console her, Shiva ordered his troops to fetch the head of anyone found sleeping with his head pointing north. The troops found an elephant sleeping and brought back its head. Shiva attached the elephant head to the body of the boy and revived him.

FIGURE 7.2 *Ganesha*, Southern Deccan Karnataka, Hoyshala Period, ca. early 12th century. Gray chloritic schist. 33″ × 20¼″ × 10″ (83.8 × 51.4 × 25.4 cm). The Nasli and Alice Heeramaneck Collection, gift of Paul Mellon. Katherine Wetzel/Virginia Museum of Fine Arts, Richmond. Ganesha, god of properity, is among the most popular of Hindu gods.

Table 7–1 MAJOR HINDU GODS AND THEIR FUNCTIONS	
God	**Role or Function**
Brahma	Creator: source of being
Vishnu	Preserver: benevolence, forgiveness, love
Shiva	Destroyer: disease and death
Lakshmi	Consort of Vishnu: sexuality and reproduction
Kali	Consort of Shiva: sexuality and reproduction

Ganesha is usually shown with his favorite round sweets in his hand that represent the seeds of the universe and are offered by other gods and devotees. He wears a snake tied around his middle because when riding on his rat vehicle one day, the rat tripped on a snake and Ganesha tumbled to the ground. His belly ripped open in the process, and the sweets he had already eaten fell out. The sweets were put back into his belly, which was then tied closed with the snake.

Samsara. Both Hinduism and Buddhism, the two major religions that emerged in India, revolve around the idea of **samsara,** the transmigration of the soul, or reincarnation. The goal of both religions is to escape the continuous cycle of death and rebirth through enlightenment (*nirvana* in Buddhism, or *moksha* in Hinduism).

Karma. The idea of **karma** is central to Hindu thought. *Karma* (which means "action") involves a kind of moral cause and effect, in which people's actions affect their moral development. An individual's actions and the accumulation of merit through these actions determine the form in which he or she will be reincarnated; it places responsibility for one's thoughts and actions on oneself. The law of karma suggests that the present condition of a person's life has been determined by actions in previous existences.

Hindu Class Structure. The social structure of ancient Indian society derives from and reflects these religious concepts and beliefs, and it is based on the division of society into four distinct classes, or castes.

At the top of the social order, the Brahmins serve as Hindu society's priests, leaders, seers, and religious authorities. Next in rank are the Kshatriyas, who in ancient times were Hindu society's kings and aristocratic warriors, but more recently have been its administrators, politicians, and civil authorities. Beneath the Kshatriyas are the Vaishyas, the society's entrepreneurs: in ancient times merchants and traders, in more recent times also its professionals, such as doctors, lawyers, and teachers. The Shudras are Hindu society's laborers, its servant class. **Outcastes,** who fall outside the four main castes, are considered "untouchable" and therefore avoided by members of other castes. Outcastes are either non-Aryan by birth or were originally members of the other castes but violated caste laws, such as those regarding work or marriage.

This hierarchical model of society was later challenged by certain communities that were based on different religious ideals, such as the Jains and the Buddhists. The caste system, however, has continued to be the governing principle of Indian society for two thousand years.

LITERATURE: THE HINDU CLASSICS

The Vedas. The earliest Indian literature was composed by the Aryans, the nomads who migrated to India around 1500 B.C.E. Composed between 1500 and 1000 B.C.E. in Sanskrit it consists of a set of hymns known as *The Vedas,* which praise the Hindu gods. All later works ultimately derive from these Vedic songs, and most are a commentary on them. Transmitted orally at first, *The Vedas* were chanted during religious rituals, accompanied by various instruments. The Vedic religion and text emphasized social hierarchy and ritual sacrifice to obtain the favor of the gods.

The Upanishads. *The Upanishads,* an anthology of philosophical poems and discourses, were later added to *The Vedas.* Although not as popular with ordinary people as the hymns and prayers of *The Vedas, The Upanishads* have been influential in Indian philosophy. They contain discussion and teachings that, although at odds with the polytheism of Vedic myth and legend, explain key Hindu ideas such as **maya** (illusion) and karma (action). The Upanishads were largely a reaction against the ritualistic, sacrificial religious practices of the Vedics as well as the increasingly powerful priest group.

According to *The Upanishads,* human beings do not realize that what appears real to the senses is entirely illusory, and that what counts eternally is the spiritual essence of life (Brahman), of which they are a part. The idea of unity and oneness with the universe becomes central to Upanishad thought.

The Upanishads typically illustrate the idea of maya and ignorance with a story about a tiger that had been orphaned as a cub and raised among goats. Believing itself to be a goat, the cub ate grass and made goat noises. One day, another tiger came upon it and took the confused tiger to a pool in which his tiger image was reflected. It was then that the cub realized his true nature. In the same way, human beings need to realize their true nature, the divinity that resides within all.

The Ramayana. The oldest of Hindu epics, *The Ramayana (The Way of Rama)* by VALMIKI [val-MIH-kee] (sixth century B.C.E.) is also the most popular work of Indian literature, and arguably among the most influential literary works in the world. The story of Prince Rama and his queen, Sita, has its narrative origins in Indian folk traditions that go back to as early as the seventh century B.C.E. *The Ramayana* itself is dated approximately 550 B.C.E., when Valmiki, much like Homer in ancient Greece, gathered the various strands of the story into a cohesive work of literature organized in seven **kanda,** or books.

Blending historical sagas, myths, legends, and moral tales with religious and social teaching, *The Ramayana* has long been the single most important repository of Indian social, moral, and ethical values.

Devout Hindus believe Rama is one of the two most important avatars, or incarnations, of the god Vishnu, who assumed human form to save humankind. Reading or witnessing a performance of episodes from *The Ramayana* is thus considered a religious exercise, as is repeating the name of Rama.

Connections

THE LOGIC OF JAINISM

Jainism, which arose at the same time as Buddhism, was also a reaction to Hinduism, particularly the caste system and the claims of the Brahmins to social superiority. Its founder was MAHAVIRA [ma-ha-VEE-rah] (599–527 B.C.E.), which means "Great Man." His early life resembles that of Sakyamuni, the founder of Buddhism. Born a prince, who, as legend has it, was attended by five nurses, "a wet-nurse, a nurse to bathe him, one to dress him, one to play with him, and one to carry him," Mahavira was raised in the lap of luxury. But as he grew older, he tired of this life, and at the age of thirty he joined a band of monks who practiced an ascetic existence. But even the monks had too indulgent a lifestyle for his taste, and so Mahavira set out on his own, wandering the Indian countryside entirely naked, maintaining that salvation is possible only through severe deprivation of the pleasures of life and the practice of *ahimsa*, not causing harm to any living thing.

The ultimate goal in Jainism is also release from the cycle of samsara, but more than any other Indian religion, it emphasizes self-reliance and responsibility for one's own fate. The individual must control personal passions in order to purify and perfect the soul. The soul is hindered by karma, which to the Jains is not actions, but imperceptible particles of matter that fill the whole cosmos. These bits of karma penetrate the soul through one's actions of the mind, body, and speech and wrap themselves around the soul, which must be released from this mass of particles by annihilating both old and new karma. The individual can prevent the penetration of karma particles through total isolation, fasting, meditation, self-control, and renunciation of the ego. Once free of karma particles, the soul is released from the cycle of rebirth. Jainism is a profoundly ethical faith emphasizing virtue, self-control, and nonviolence against all life-forms.

Jainism has gained a wide following in India, and today the Jains number about two million, with an especially large community in Bombay, where MAHATMA GANDHI [GAHN-dee] (1869–1948), the great twentieth-century pacifist leader, was influenced by its tenets. One of the most distinctive features of the Jain philosophy is a special sensitivity to the relativity of all things. A favorite Jain parable is the story of the six blind men, each of whom puts his hands on a different part of an elephant and describes what he feels in totally different terms—it is like a fan, a wall, a snake, a rope, and so on. In Jainist thought, each description is satisfactory given each person's limited knowledge of the whole of the elephant. In one sense, an elephant is like a snake, but only in a very limited way. By extension, all knowledge is, from one point of view, true, and, from another, false or incomplete.

The Ramayana stands, moreover, as an enduring monument and a living guide to political, social, and family life in Vedic India. The behavior of its hero, Prince Rama, serves as a model for the behavior of the ideal son, brother, husband, warrior, and king. Rama's respect for his father and love for his wife, along with his regal bearing and self-control, represent the paradigm for Indian males to emulate. Rama's behavior is also closely linked to the religious values embodied in the epic. His wife Sita loves, honors, and serves her husband with absolute fidelity. In being governed by dharma ("truth" or "law") rather than self-interest, Rama and Sita stand as models for Hindu life.

The story of *The Ramayana* is complex and intricate. One of its central motifs concerns Rama's disinheritance, which is instigated by the jealous queen, Rama's stepmother Kaikeyi, who wants her own son, Bharatha, to become king instead of Rama. The king, Rama's father, reluctantly has his son exiled, but thereafter soon dies, desolate over Rama's departure. With his wife, Sita, and his brother, Lakshmana, Rama lives in the wilderness of central India. After fourteen years of living in the jungle, Sita is abducted by the king of the demons, Ravana, who holds Sita captive for several years before she is rescued by Rama with the help of Hanamun and his monkey army. However, because Sita has dwelled in another man's house, Rama must reject her. Once her innocence is proven, however, Sita is hailed as the embodiment of chasity and fidelity. She represents the ideal Indian female beauty, and Rama goes on to rule as a wise and compassionate king.

The Mahabharata. The second great Indian epic is *The Mahabharata*, which was composed over a period of more than eight hundred years, between 400 B.C.E. and 400 C.E. Unlike *The Ramayana*, which focuses on the adventures of one central hero, *The Mahabharata* chronicles the story of a pair of rival warring families, the Pandavas and the Kauravas. The warlike world of *The Mahabharata* is more akin to that of *The Iliad*, whereas the adventure-filled quest of *The Ramayana* has more of the character of Homer's other great epic, *The Odyssey*. With its hundred thousand verses, *The Mahabharata* is four times the length of *The Ramayana*, and more than eight times that of *The Iliad* and *The Odyssey* combined. What *The Mahabharata* lacks in unity and focus, however, it makes up for in multiplicity of incident, breadth of social panorama, and philosophical discursiveness.

Forming part of the sixth book of *The Mahabharata* is the *Bhagavad Gita*, the section most familiar to Western readers. It is also the epic's most important source of spiritual teaching. Written early in the first century B.C.E., the *Bhagavad Gita* centers on the moral conflict experienced by Arjuna, a warrior who struggles with his duty to kill his kinsmen during the war between the Pandavas and Kauravas, a great battle that ends in the destruction of both armies.

When Arjuna sees his relatives ready to do battle against one another, he puts down his weapons and refuses to fight. His charioteer, Krishna, an avatar of the god Vishnu, explains it is Arjuna's duty to fight: Even though the Hindu religion generally prohibits killing, the sanction is lifted for members of Arjuna's warrior class, the Kshatriyas. He also tells Arjuna that fighting can break the karmic cycle of samsara, the endless cycle of birth, death, and reincarnation to which mortal beings are subject, and move him toward spiritual liberation. Arjuna learns that the spirit in which an act is performed counts more than the act itself. Because Arjuna is not fighting to achieve any particular goal but only to fulfill his duty, his behavior is irreproachable.

THE MAURYA PERIOD

In ancient India, each region was politically autonomous. These regions were governed by small dynasties that remained relatively immune from outside influences and challenges. From time to time, however, the governments of individual regions would join together in loose federations to create empires. One of the earliest and most important of these was the empire of the Maurya, which emerged in response to a power vacuum created by Alexander the Great's conquest of northern India around 326 B.C.E.

CHANDRAGUPTA MAURYA [MOW-ya], effectively the first emperor of India, reigned from 324 to 301 B.C.E. His empire extended from the Ganges River to the Indus and into the northern mountains. After Chandragupta's death, and following the reign of his son Bindusara, came the most important of Mauryan emperors, ASHOKA [a-SHOW-ka], who assumed the throne in 269 B.C.E. Lasting nearly forty years (269–232 B.C.E.), Ashoka's reign marked a critical turning point in Indian history—the emergence of Buddhism as a political force in India. Regretting the terrible destruction his armies had wrought in a victorious battle with the armies of a neighboring region, Ashoka became a champion of nonviolence and embraced **Buddhism,** which had begun to displace the more worldly Hinduism three centuries earlier.

The connection between political power and religious idealism continued throughout Ashoka's life and for half a century after his death. The emperor sent missionaries, including his daughter and son, throughout India to spread the Buddhist faith. He also had sites marked that were of religious and historical significance to Buddhists, and monuments to house the possessions and remains of the Buddha.

BUDDHISM

The historical Buddha was born Siddhartha Gautama Sakya (ca. 563–483 B.C.E.), a prince in a kingdom in the foothills of the Himalayas, in present-day Nepal. He is also known as Sakyamuni, meaning "the sage or silent one of the Sakya." At his birth, it was prophesied that Sakyamuni would be either a king or a world redeemer. He was raised in a princely household, and so as a young man was sheltered from pain and suffering. Wanting to experience the world beyond the palace walls, he asked his father to allow him to see the city. His father arranged an excursion befitting the young prince. The king ordered that all commoners and those afflicted with ailments be kept out of sight so as not to distress the prince. The sick, old, and maimed were also cleared from the prince's path.

Seeing that the city was joyful and the people content, the prince was delighted. But the gods, in an attempt to incite the prince's renunciation of the world, led him to an old man, then a sick man, and then a corpse. Encountering all these conditions of human existence caused the prince to meditate on his experiences. As he pondered what he had seen, a mendicant monk appeared and explained his life as an ascetic. Sakyamuni's experiences with old age, disease, death, and the monk are referred to as the Four Encounters. The prince decided he would leave his father's palace and live the life of an ascetic, searching for a way to relieve human suffering.

Upon leaving the palace, Sakyamuni wandered the countryside and meditated with a group of ascetics for six years. When he realized asceticism would not lead to salvation, he rejected this path. Instead, he determined there must be some path to enlightenment that would not exhaust one's body and mind. He sat under a pipal tree (known as the Bodhi tree or tree of wisdom) where he vowed not to move until he attained enlightenment. Sakyamuni mediated for forty-nine days and nights and was subject to numerous distractions by Mara the Tempter, who sought to destroy Sakyamuni's concentration and resolve.

Finally, on the night of the full moon, Sakyamuni achieved enlightenment. He then set out to help and educate others in this path. He gave his first sermon at Deer Park in India, setting into motion the dharma (religious truth or law) represented in the Four Noble Truths and the Eightfold Path (listed later).

The Buddha also reiterated the importance of the **Middle Path,** rejecting the extremes of both asceticism, which only weakens the body and mind, and indulgence, which obstructs wisdom. After forty-five years of preaching and dedicating himself to others, the Buddha (a word derived from the name of the tree under which he first achieved enlightenment—the Bo tree, short for **Bodhi,** meaning "wisdom" or "enlightenment") died at the age of eighty.

Buddhism versus Hinduism. Unlike Hinduism, which developed over many centuries, Buddhism seemed to arise overnight, even if it took many centuries for a political leader to adopt it. Buddhists challenged Hindu religious practice in a number of ways. Sakyamuni's followers argued that the caste of Brahmins was granted too much power and given too many privileges. The forms of ritual had become, they believed, devoid of meaning, and were debased by being linked with commercial transactions. Hindu philosophical thought had become excessively intricate and arcane, and consequently increasingly disconnected from everyday spiritual life. Religious mystery had degenerated into mystification and magic. Superstition and divination had replaced miracle and true mysticism. Perhaps worst of all, too many people had come to believe their actions did not matter, that whatever they believed they would be caught up in samsara, the endless cycle of rebirth, from which escape was impossible.

Buddhists responded to this by providing an alternative religious practice in which each individual had to find her or his own way to enlightenment. So devoid of the notion of higher authority is Buddhism that it was originally a religion without a god. There is only enlightenment. Furthermore, ritual is an irrelevant diversion from the real work of achieving enlightenment. The Buddha taught that it need not take hundreds of lifetimes or thousands of reincarnations to break out of the round of existence. A determined individual could achieve enlightenment in a single lifetime and so attain **nirvana,** that is, liberation from the limitations of existence and rebirth in the cycle of samsara.

As a result of these new objectives, early Buddhism had few of the characteristics of traditional religions. It posited no creation or last judgment. It presented no revelation from a god. Instead, it emphasized the here and now.

The Four Noble Truths and the Eightfold Path. Buddhist thought is based on an analysis of the human condition founded on four basic axioms or truths. These principles have come to be known as the Four Noble Truths:

1. Life consists of suffering, impermanence, imperfection, incompleteness.
2. The cause of life's suffering is selfishness.
3. Suffering and selfishness can be brought to an end.
4. The answer to life's problems of suffering is the Eightfold Path.

The Eightfold Path itself consists of knowledge of these Four Noble Truths, the first step on the path, followed by seven other steps: right aspiration toward the goal of enlightenment; right speech that is honest and charitable; right conduct—no drinking, killing, lying, or lust; right

living according to the goals of Buddhism; right effort; right thinking with an emphasis on self-awareness; and the right use of meditation to achieve enlightenment.

MAURYA ART

The earliest large and significant body of Indian art extant today dates from the Maurya period, chiefly from the reign of the emperor Ashoka. Much of this work was created to celebrate Ashoka's conversion to Buddhism. Ashoka ordered the construction of numerous **stupas,** or memorial buildings, that enshrined relics of the Buddha, marking sites sacred to his memory. Many of the eighty thousand or more stupas erected during Ashoka's reign were dedicated to the Buddha and his miracles. Later, stupas were used for burial of the remains of sacred monks.

The Sarnath Capital. Ashoka also had a large number of stone columns built to memorialize significant events in the Buddha's life. Carved into many of these, as well as into rocks and caves, were edicts that promoted various aspects of the Buddhist creed. The stone pillars usually had capitals, often carved in the forms of animals, usually lions. One of the most magnificent of these is a beautifully preserved lion capital (fig. 7.3) from a pillar at Sarnath that dates from about 250 B.C.E.

The Sarnath capital consists of three elements. On top of a Persian-style fluted bell are four animals, bull, horse, elephant, and lion, walking around in a clockwise direction, and four wheels carved in relief. The animals may have directional significance, and they appear to be keeping the wheels in motion, turning around the pillar. Above these elements are four lions carved back to back all the way around the capital. The stylization of the lions' facial features and claws, along with the decorative handling of their manes and upper torsos, is similar to that of the lion sculptures at Persepolis, a city destroyed by Alexander the Great before his invasion of northern India. As described in Chapter 3, Alexander's forces made an enduring cultural impression on the region. It is highly likely therefore that either Persian sculptors or Persian-trained Greek sculptors created this capital, which marks a dramatic growth in the style, complexity, and beauty of Indian sculpture.

The seven-foot sculpture was originally surmounted by a large stone wheel on the lions' shoulders. This capital (now used as the emblem of the modern Republic of India) is highly symbolic. Hailing from a period during which Buddhist art avoided representing the Buddha directly, the Sarnath lion capital suggests his presence in other ways. The wheel symbolizes the wheel of the law (the dharma) and the Buddha's sermon at Deer Park in Sarnath where this capital was located. The wheel is also a symbol of cosmic order in Upanishad thought, representing the flow of life and all that is possible. The lion itself is the Persian symbol of royalty and may have been borrowed in this context to represent Ashoka. The lion is also a symbol of Sakyamuni's clan, and the Buddha is often referred to as having a "lion's roar." Thus Ashoka's edicts carved on the pillars, and the lions roaring, proclaim the Buddha's words concretely and symbolically.

FIGURE 7.3 Lion capital of a pillar erected by Ashoka at Sarnath, Mauryan, ca. 250 B.C.E., Chunar sandstone, height 7'$\frac{1}{2}$" (2.15 m), Archaeological Museum, Sarnath, India. This lion capital reveres the lion as king of the animal world while honoring the Buddha as king lion among religious teachers.

The Great Stupa at Sanchi. Many of the stupas (burial mounds containing the relics of the Buddha) erected by Ashoka were enlarged by subsequent dynasties in the second and first centuries B.C.E. For instance, at Sanchi in central India, Ashoka had built a stupa sixty feet in diameter and twenty-five feet high. The Andhras, who ruled in the region toward the end of the first century B.C.E., doubled its size (fig. 7.4). They replaced Ashoka's wooden railings with new stone ones nine feet high. A sixteen-foot-high passage encircling the stupa was also added. At the very top of the stupa are three umbrellas (**chattras**) that symbolize protection of the objects below. The umbrellas are positioned on a central axis (**yasti**), which is the most important symbol of the stupa because it represents the world axis, a concept similar to Ashoka's pillars.

However, the architectural glories of the Sanchi stupa are four carved stone gates, each of which is more than thirty feet high (fig. 7.5). Begun during the first century B.C.E., but only completed during the first century C.E., the gates are adorned with symbols associated with the Buddha, including the wheel of the law, stories from his life, and tales of his animal incarnations. Additional figures include elephants, peacocks, and **yakshis,** or protective female earth spirits.

The Sanchi stupa symbolizes the cosmos, its four gates representing the four corners of the universe. Its umbrella points toward the sky, linking heaven with earth and a life of bliss with that of pain and suffering below. Entering the eastern gate of the stupa, a visitor would move clockwise in a circle around it on a path especially constructed for that purpose. Even though the stupa can not be entered directly, like Hindu temples it invites worshipers to enter into a spiritual state of mind.

MAURYAN TO BACTRIAN TO KUSHAN

During its decline, the Mauryan empire suffered from acute economic difficulties attributable to its large and salaried core of administrators. By about 185 B.C.E., the Mauryan empire had disappeared, and yet India's local rulers maintained order in various large regions of the Indian subcontinent. Among the most important of these was the Bactrian kingdom of northwest India, which came under the rule of the imperial heirs of Alexander of Macedon, who had blended with local populations and who had invaded northern India in the early second century B.C.E. Bactria was a vibrant center of trade that had commercial links with China to the east and the Mediterranean to the west. The northern region of Gandhara became a center of both commercial and cultural exchange, promoting cross-cultural East–West interaction.

FIGURE 7.4 Great Stupa, Sanchi, from the east, third century B.C.E.–early first century C.E. For the increasing numbers of Buddhist faithful, the stupa became a central symbol of religious faith.

FIGURE 7.5 Gate of the Great Stupa, Sanchi, inner facade of the north gate, third century B.C.E.– early first century C.E., stone, height 34′ (10.35 m), Depicted on the columns and cross beams of this large stone gate are events in the life of the Buddha and stories from the *Jataka* tales.

By the end of the first century B.C.E., nomadic conquerors from central Asia defeated the Indo-Greek kingdom in Bactria. Rule was established by the Kushan emperors, whose kingdom spread from modern-day Pakistan and Afghanistan, across northern India to Gujurat and the central part of the Ganges River valley. Like their Bactrian predecessors, the Kushan rulers contributed to the silk road commercial network, in large part by ensuring peace in the region between Persia and China.

As nomads, the Kushan had no artistic legacy of their own, so once they were settled in the northern frontier of Afghanistan they adopted foreign traditions, most notably Greco-Roman forms of sculpture. As they gained power, they entered Northwest India and adopted Buddhism, building monasteries and stupas. Most significantly, however, they applied the Greco-Roman sculptural aesthetic to Buddhist imagery and they are often credited with commissioning the first iconic (anthropomorphic) images of the Buddha (fig. 7.6).

Instead of a spiritually inspirational mortal never depicted artistically in human form, the Buddha was now a deity on which followers could focus their devotion. These iconographic images appear as translations of Greco-Roman sculpture, their traditional monks' robes resembling Roman togas with deep ridges and their faces revealing Apollo-like features. However, these early artists made sure these figures could be clearly identified as the Buddha. He can be distinguished by thirty-two physical characteristics (**laksana**), the three most identifiable being:

Ushnishna: the cranial protuberance signifying symbolic omniscient power.
Urna: the round mark in the center of his forehead symbolizing the power to illuminate the world.
Elongated ears: the result of the heavy earrings worn during his princely days. The removal of the earrings symbolizes his renunciation of the material world.

The Kushan are also credited with the creation of the first bodhisattva figures. **Bodhisattvas** are regal, elegant beings with princely bearing who have attained enlightenment but who choose to remain in this world in order to help others on their path to enlightenment. Bodhisattvas represent fully compassionate beings. Popular mainly in northern India, this new Mahayana form of Buddhism spread rapidly to China, Japan, and Korea, along the trade routes that ran through India's mountain passes.

THE GUPTA ERA

Of the ancient Indian empires that developed from this period, the most important was that of the Gupta, which lasted from the fourth to the sixth century C.E. During the reign of the Guptas, India flourished culturally and commercially. Significant scientific discoveries were made; important developments occurred in literature, music, sculpture, and painting. In terms of Indian cultural achievements, the Gupta era is comparable to Periklean Athens, Han China, and Augustan Rome. It was during the reign of Chandra Gupta II (r. 375–415 C.E.), for example, that the cave paintings at Ajanta were undertaken.

The Gupta empire eventually collapsed under repeated onslaughts by the Huns, who had previously invaded and conquered the Roman world. Regional autonomy was reestablished as the empire became increasingly fractured. From early in the eighth century, Islamic influences began to appear in India, culminating five hundred years later when northern India and the Ganges area fell directly under Turkish Islamic control. Buddhism was eclipsed to a large extent, and as Hinduism gradually reasserted itself, it became mixed with Muslim influences.

GUPTA ART

Gupta art has become associated with the deeply spiritual figure of the Buddha, standing with equanimity, eyes half closed in meditation. Whether standing or seated, Buddhas sculpted in the Gupta Buddhist style appear calm, their worldly cares replaced by an inner tranquillity that suggests otherworldliness. Purely Indian ideals

FIGURE 7.6 *Seated Buddha*, from Gandhara, Peshawar District (Pakistan), Kushan, second–third century C.E., dark gray schist. 55 1/4" × 27 3/8" × 6 1/4" (89.53 × 68.67 × 15.88 cm). The Adolph D. and Wilkins C. Williams Fund. Katherine Wetzel/Virginia Museum of Fine Arts, Richmond. This Buddha figure exhibits grace, calm, and elegance.

of spirituality were never more fully expressed than in Gupta sculpture. India was no longer under the aesthetic influence of the Roman empire, and native artists were free to develop forms featuring native aesthetics and spiritual richness. Gupta-period sculpture is described as "classical" in terms of its perfection of beauty and expression. The spiritual ideals of the Buddha are now fully balanced and harmonized with the physical manifestations of the Buddha figure.

In the "Standing Buddha" (fig. 7.7), the heavy Greco-Roman-style robe of the Kushan period piece, with its deeply carved drapery folds, is replaced by a sheer robe with drapery abstracted into thin strings cascading rhythmically down the body. The face is softer, more serene, and the compassion of the figure shows through with a lightness and spiritual dignity indicative of Gupta sculpture. There is also an emphasis on the body beneath the robe, which is a very Indian aesthetic, creating a sense of life breath (**prana**) that is important in Indian culture.

As in all sculptural representations of the Buddha, the hands are highly symbolic. Different hand gestures (**mudra**) are used to convey different messages to the viewer. This figure reaches forward with his right hand (now missing) in the *abhaya* mudra, a sign of reassurance, blessing, and protection. His left hand drops to his side in the *varada* mudra, signifying charity and the fulfillment of all wishes. Other mudra include the *dharmachakra* mudra, a sign of teaching in which the hands make a circle with the thumb and forefinger, a reference to the wheel of dharma and the Buddha's first sermon at Deer Park. The mudra most familiar to Westerners is the *dhyana* mudra, in which the hands rest on the Buddha's lap, palms facing upward. A gesture of meditation and harmony, it symbolizes the path to enlightenment.

The political and cultural unity of the Gupta era gave rise to a luxurious aristocratic culture that culminated in the rich aesthetic at Ajanta, where a series of about thirty caves were cut into the side of a 80-meter cliff running from east to west for 600 meters. At Ajanta, the sensuous physical beauty associated with Indian art now symbolizes spiritual beauty as well. The main cave was originally covered with paintings, including the ceiling. The paintings describe the various lives and incarnations of the Buddha as narrated in the **Jataka** tales. The central Buddha sculpture is flanked by two painted bodhisattva figures forming a trinity. The facial features of the bodhisattvas Padmapani and Avalokitesvera are serene, reflecting the embodiment of compassion. Padmapani is shown holding a blue lotus and standing in the classic **tribhanga** sculptural pose (fig. 7.8), in which the figure stands, his body in a slight S-curve, with his weight on one leg. Gupta-period Buddhist images were to influence the development of Buddhist art throughout Southeast Asia and the Far East.

FIGURE 7.7 *Standing Buddha*, from Mathura, Gupta, late fourth-early fifth century C.E., red sandstone, height $7'\frac{3}{8}''$ (2.17 m), National Museum, New Delhi. The elegance of this standing figure, especially its calm serenity, characterizes the Gupta Buddhist style of sculpture.

FIGURE 7.8 *Bodhisattva Padmapani,* Ajanta caves, Gupta, late fifth century C.E., wall painting. Oblivious to the figures that surround him, this bodhisattva is encircled in an other-worldly light, created by the burnishing of the painting's outer coating with a smooth stone.

THE *JATAKA* AND THE *PANCATANTRA*

Ancient Indian literature contains many folktales and animal stories. One of the most important collections of early stories is the *Jataka,* which means "the story of a birth," consisting of 547 tales that describe the lives the Buddha passed through before achieving enlightenment. The **Pancatantra** is a group of didactic stories, designed with the practical aim of providing advice about getting on in the world.

One of the most famous tales of the fourth-century B.C.E., *Jataka* describes a hare who sacrifices itself to feed a hungry brahmin. The tale's action reveals the hare to be a bodhisattva in the form of an animal. Like another *Jataka* hero, a monkey who gives up his life for others, the hare displays the perfection of spiritual being in a completely selfless act.

This is quite different from the spirit and flavor of the *Pancatantra,* in which the behavior of its animal heroes is more self-serving and pragmatic. *Pancatantra,* which means "the five strategies," suggests the book's pragmatic inclination. Composed during the second or third century C.E., the stories are linked so one story is joined to another in a continuous chain. This is similar to the connected stories of *The Thousand and One Nights* (see Chapter 6), which may have been influenced by the *Pancatantra.* The authors of the *Jataka* and the *Pancatantra* provide fast-moving action, witty dialogue, and memorable counsel in stories that entertain as they instruct, be that in Buddhist spirituality or in more worldly wisdom.

THE HINDU DYNASTIES

Although Buddhism flourished during the Gupta era, the Gupta monarchs themselves were increasingly attracted to Hinduism. Temples and sculptures of Hindu gods began to appear, and they continued to proliferate well into the fifteenth and sixteenth centuries, when Muslim kings from Persia took control of most of the subcontinent. Particularly in the south, where the warring Hindu dynasties of the Pallavas and the Cholas vied for power, a long period of great artistic production was set in motion, marked both by decorated temples, rich in stone sculpture, and by the rise of bronze as a favored medium for sculpture.

THE HINDU TEMPLE

The structures and designs of Hindu temples were established in the series of ancient texts called **shastras.** These function as guides to many different activities, not just temple building, and include advice on cooking, warfare, love-making, poetry, and music. The guides to architecture, especially those concerning temple architecture, do not always concur in every detail with actual temple construction.

Temples in the south are better preserved than northern temples, since the Muslim incursion into India was most destructive in the north. One of the most magnificent and largest of medieval Hindu temples and one in an exceptional state of preservation is the Kandariya Mahadeo temple at Khajuraho, dating from the eleventh century (fig. 7.9). As with many temples of that period, it forms part of a cluster of temples in the area.

The Kandariya Mahadeo temple is situated on a high masonry platform that emphasizes height and verticality; the **sikhara** (tower) rises over thirty meters from the base of the temple. The temple's profile reveals its symbolism as a mountain with intricate domelike roofs that rise in a crescendo of grandeur. Equally compelling is the vibrancy and richness of their surface ornamentation. The richly decorated walls include over six hundred sculptures on the

FIGURE 7.9   Kandariya Mahadeo temple, Khajuraho, Chandella, ca. 1025–50. This temple's tower soars more than a hundred feet into the air, its eighty-four subordinate towers providing a visual display of majestic grandeur.

exterior and two hundred on the interior, dominating the overall aesthetic. Niches and screens, pillars and openings, pavilions and courtyards enhance the splendor of the edifice. Adorning the temple is a wealth of sculpture that depicts historical and mythological subjects, such as the monarchs who reigned during the temple's construction; the **Surasun-daris,** or divine nymphs, in amatory poses; figures of dancers and musicians; mothers with children; lovers; women adjusting their hair; and a vast array of other images.

SCULPTURE

Bronze was the medium most favored by the southern Indian Chola dynasties from the tenth to the twelfth centuries. Chola sculptors employed the **cire perdue,** or **lost-wax process.** In this technique, a model of the subject was first made in wax, which is easy to mold. The wax model was then encased in clay and heated; the wax melted but the clay did not. Holes were made in the clay surround before it was heated, however, to permit the wax to run out. The hollow clay case was then filled with molten bronze. When the bronze cooled and hardened, the clay was broken away, leaving a finished bronze cast.

The *Shiva Nataraja* (*Lord of the Dance*) (fig. 7.11) is perhaps the most famous of Hindu icons. Numerous examples

of this icon exist—strict rules governing its production have resulted in a remarkable consistency across individual instances—and it continues to be produced in southern India to this day. The icon depicts the dancing Shiva as creator and destroyer of the universe, symbolized by the ring of flames around him. With his hair flying out in two directions, and his arms and legs seemingly in motion, the dancing Shiva crushes Apasmarapurusha, the demon of ignorance, promising relief from life's illusoriness, and also offering reassurance and blessing in the *abhaya* mudra of his front right hand. This dance is said to herald the last night of the world, when all the stars fall from the sky and the universe is reduced to ashes. But the dance promises the renewal of creation itself.

HINDU LYRIC POETRY

The poetry of the twelfth-century mystic MAHADE-VIYAKKA [ma-ha-de-VEE-ha-ka], the foremost Indian woman poet before the modern era, represents the quintessential medieval genre of **bhakti,** or devotional religious poetry. Bhakti poetry was part of a larger movement in which the poets were recognized as saints and celebrated as models of religious devotion. Their poems honored the chief Hindu gods Shiva and Vishnu, especially the latter's major avatars Krishna and Rama.

Then & Now

MUSLIM INDIA

Islam arrived in India as early as the eighth century, but it was not until the twelfth century that it began to have a powerful impact on the subcontinent. In 1192, the Afghan king Muhammad of Ghur, invading from the north by land, defeated the Hindus. After initial fighting, a spirit of peaceful coexistence lasted for several centuries. But no two religions could be more different than Hinduism and Islam. Hinduism is sufficiently loose in its religious structure to allow great divergences in spiritual beliefs and practices, whereas Islam controls almost every aspect of daily life. But where Hinduism is intellectually liberal and Islam conservative, the opposite is true socially. The social restrictions of Hinduism's caste system, in contrast to the possibilities of social mobility and equality offered by Islam, may have led many Indians to adopt the Islamic faith. Especially around Delhi and Agra, where the Muslim rulers held sway, Islam took firm hold and was responsible for creating some of the greatest monuments of Indian culture.

The most famous building in India is the Taj Mahal (fig. 7.10), in Agra, built 1630–48 by the Muslim Shah Jahan as a mausoleum for his wife, Mumtaz Mahal. Some 20,000 workers took nearly twenty years to build the Taj, including transporting thousands of white marble blocks 120 miles.

The Taj Mahal's white marble walls are deeply cut with arched recesses that catch shadows, creating a three-dimensional facade. The building appears to be weightless, the dome floating like a balloon. Decoration includes floral relief carving and gray stone inlay. Jade and crystal from China, lapis lazuli from Afghanistan, and coral and mother of pearl from the Indian Ocean were used in its lavish detail. The landscape setting continues the formal concern with symmetry: The building is reflected in a long pool flanked by rows of small trees and shrubs. The Taj Mahal is celebrated for its exquisite refinement and enchanting elegance.

By the twentieth century, relations between India's Hindus and Muslims had reached crisis point, and in 1947, after a violent and bloody partition, the independent Muslim state of Pakistan was born, consisting of two separate areas: West Pakistan, with its capital at Islamabad near the Khyber Pass on the Indus River, and East Pakistan (which seceded from the union in 1971 to become Bangladesh), with its capital at Dacca. The fifty million Muslims who were left in India became an official minority with the right to be represented in the Indian parliament.

FIGURE 7.10   Taj Mahal, Agra, 1630–48. This mausoleum was built by Shah Jahan for his wife, Mumtaz Mahal. The white marble domes seem to reach heavenward while they are reflected in the long pool of water.

FIGURE 7.11   *Shiva Nataraja (Lord of the Dance),* Chola, eleventh-twelfth centuries, bronze, height $32\frac{1}{2}''$ (82 cm), Von der Heydt Collection, Museum Rietherg, Zurich. The most famous of Hindu icons, the dancing Shiva is both the creator and destroyer of the universe.

Bhakti devotional poetry is rooted in deeply felt emotion. As with the mystical and devotional poetry of other cultures, it uses colloquial language and draws on imagery from everyday experience in an attempt to convey a sense of earthly longing for the divine. Like the poems of the English Renaissance poet John Donne (see Chapter 14), those of Mahadeviyakka employ images of physical love and experience to convey a sense of spirituality. Mahadeviyakka's poetry also exhibits a carefree, daredevil attitude that is, perhaps surprisingly, not at odds with a deep longing for communion with the godhead.

INDIAN DRAMA: KALIDASA'S SAKUNTALA

Kalidasa (fourth to fifth centuries C.E.) is best known as the author of *Sakuntala and the Ring of Recollection,* usually referred to by its short title, *Sakuntala.* Kalidasa flourished during the classical era of the Guptas, between 390 and 470. The plot of this most beloved of Indian plays was adapted from the *Mahabharata.* The play tells the story of the beautiful maiden Sakuntala, who is first seen in the woodland hermitage of the King Dusyanta, who falls in love with her. The ring of the title figures in the plot as it

is first lost, then found, and serves, with the aid of gods and sages, to reunite the lovers in a happy ending.

Like all Sanskrit plays, *Sakuntala* ends happily because that is what the dramatic tradition requires. Ancient Sanskrit drama thus differs strongly from ancient Greek drama, which often ends tragically. Tragedy, however, is alien to the Hindu conception of the universe, in which history is cyclical and in which human action is based on karma rather than on character and destiny, as in Greek drama.

MUSIC

Indian music is essentially melodic. Harmony is present only as a backdrop, in the form of the continuous sounding of a single tone; the complex melody is elaborated over the top. Indian music is rarely written out formally as a score. This independence from notation offers performers great interpretive latitude, allowing them the opportunity to improvise creatively and develop the mood of the pieces they play. The music is typically performed by a soloist, who plays or sings the melody; a drummer, who supplies the rhythm; and a third player, who provides the drone chord, which is a single three-note chord sounded continuously throughout the piece, usually on the lutelike **tambura.**

Although also serving a purpose as entertainment, Indian music is rich in religious associations. Hindu deities, for example, are frequently evoked in classical dance and songs. Moreover, it is not uncommon for musicians to consider their performance an act of religious devotion.

The most important instrument in the performance of Indian music is the human voice. With its great flexibility and expressiveness, the voice provides a model for other instruments. As in the Western classical tradition, singers of Indian music are trained to perform an extensive range of vocal intricacies. These vocal acrobatics include modulations of pitch involving many more tones than those of standard Western musical scales.

The **sitar** is a lute-shaped instrument with an extended neck and movable frets that enable performers to produce an enormous number of tones. The standard sitar has five melody strings, two drone strings, and a dozen or more sympathetic strings beneath them. These lower strings are not struck with the fingers or a plectrum like the others. Instead, they vibrate in sympathy with those actually played, lending the music an enriched shimmering sound.

The sitar is the chief instrument used in playing **ragas,** musical compositions based on one of the eight primary **rasas**—moods or flavors—of Indian aesthetics: love, courage, hatred, anger, mirth, terror, pity, and surprise, all of which are balanced in tranquility. Ragas can also be expressed in painting and poetry. A raga, then, is a work of art that conveys a distinct impression (the word *raga* means "passion" or "feeling"). Because of their highly specific

Cross Currents

RAVI SHANKAR AND PHILIP GLASS

Born in Baltimore in 1937, American composer Philip Glass was trained at the Julliard School of Music in New York. He was frustrated with the state of contemporary music until, in the 1960s, he was hired to work on the soundtrack for *Chappaqua*, a now-forgotten alternative film. His job was to take the improvised Indian ragas of Indian musician RAVI SHANKAR [SHAN-kah] (b. 1920) (fig. 7.12) and transcribe them into Western musical notation, so Western musicians could perform them on the soundtrack. Glass was particularly impressed with the background drone chord of the raga. He thought it was made up of units of two and three notes that formed long chains of modular rhythmic patterns. He was in fact entirely wrong in terms of musicology, but it led him, as misreadings so often can, to invent his own distinct musical style. He traveled to India many times and gradually developed an almost hypnotic rhythmic style of his own. The music he began to compose consisted of the rhythmic units he had heard in Shankar's work, with simple and apparently arbitrarily chosen notes or pitches strung together in cyclical groups. The repetitiveness of the musical form suggests the drone chord of the raga.

The culmination of the Indian connection in Glass's music was his opera *Satyagraha*, first performed in Rotterdam, Holland, in 1980. The work consists of several stories from the life of the young Mahatma Gandhi, the great pacifist and political and spiritual leader who led the campaign to free India from British rule. The work's title, *Satyagraha*, means "holding fast to the truth" and refers to Gandhi's nonviolent method of noncooperation and civil disobedience. Slow and meditative in its rhythm, the music evokes the image of Gandhi sitting in protest as he fasted and meditated, in full confidence that India would eventually triumph.

FIGURE 7.12   Ravi Shankar playing the sitar, *Life* magazine, 1958. The sitar is a lute-shaped instrument with an extended neck and moveable frets that enable performers to produce a wide range of scale tones.

Critical Thinking

SACRED COWS

According to Hinduism, cows are sacred and thus not to be killed for their meat. Cows wander the streets of Indian towns and villages unharmed. The expression "a sacred cow" has come to refer to an idea or concept in a culture that is not permitted to be harmed or tampered with. In the United States, for example, the concept of social security, a system in which workers make monetary contributions during their working lives so that they can collect a modest monthly stipend when they retire, is considered a metaphorical sacred cow. In France, the idea of a guaranteed job from which it is almost impossible to be fired is another example of such a conceptual sacred cow. Politicians in both countries are reluctant to change these policies. What are some other sacred cows? You might think of social, political, economic, religious, or other cultural beliefs and behaviors that through tradition have become solidified such that it is difficult if not impossible to challenge or change them. What are some benefits and drawbacks of such sacred cows?

Cultural Impact

Unlike the Chinese Tang and Song dynasties and the Islamic Umayyad and Abbasid dynasties, India's political organization was not centralized. India's traditions, although centered on Hinduism, found room for other religious developments such as Buddhism. Like other societies, India experienced cultural change, with Indian traditions influencing and being influenced by cultural and religious developments in other lands.

Like Islam, Hinduism emerged as an important popular religious faith within the Indian subcontinent. In addition, Indian merchants helped establish not only Hinduism, but Buddhism and Islam as well in Southeast Asia.

The most significant legacy of ancient India is its Hindu religious heritage. The *Bhagavad Gita*, for example, has become famous well beyond the borders of India. This ancient text had a decisive influence on the American transcendentalist writer Henry David Thoreau, who alludes to it in his book *Walden*. The *Bhagavad Gita*, moreover, has also served as inspiration for political and social action as well as a stimulus for the practice of nonviolent resistance, made famous in the twentieth century by Mahatma Gandhi in India and by Martin Luther King, Jr., in the United States during the civil rights struggle in the 1960's.

character, ragas are typically associated with a particular Hindu deity, a particular time of day or season of the year, or a particular religious festival.

A standard musical raga form includes an improvised prelude or introductory section called an **alap,** played in a free tempo. The purpose of the alap is to introduce the spirit and mood of the raga. The alap is followed by a formally composed musical section for a solo instrument with a percussion accompaniment. The final section is an improvisation on the composed music with many returns of the theme, in a form loosely comparable to the rondo (or returning theme) of Western music. Toward the end of a raga performance, the emphasis shifts from melodic elaboration to a display of the performer's own virtuosity.

KEY TERMS

intaglio
nomad
Sanskrit
Vedas
Hindu
Brahman
Vishnu
Lakshmi
avatar
Krishna
Shiva

samsara
karma
Outcastes
maya
kanda
Jainism
Buddhism
Middle Path
Bodhi
nirvana
stupa

chattras
yasti
yakshis
laksana
ushnishna
urna
bodhisattva
prana
mudra
Jataka
tribhanga

Pancatantra
shastras
sikhara
Surasun-daris
cire perdue/lost-wax process
bhakti
tambura
sitar
ragas
rasas
alap

WWW. WEBSITES FOR FURTHER STUDY

http://www.gosai.com/links/india-links.html
(This is a good source for the Vedic culture, with many links.)

http://mcel.pacificu.edu/as/students/cgono/siddhartha.html
(This site has an excellent history of Buddhism.)

http://www.indiantravelportal.com/temples//index.html
(This site covers many general topics of all things Indian.)

READINGS

Bhagavad Gita

From The First Teaching[1]

[Arjuna's[2] Dejection]

20 Arjuna, his war flag a rampant monkey,
saw Dhritarashtra's[3] sons assembled
as weapons were ready to clash,
and he lifted his bow.

21 He told his charioteer:
    "Krishna,[4]
    halt my chariot
    between the armies!

22   Far enough for me to see
    these men who lust for war,
    ready to fight with me
    in the strain of battle.

23   I see men gathered here,
    eager to fight,
    bent on serving the folly
    of Dhritarashtra's son."[5]

24 When Arjuna had spoken,
Krishna halted
their splendid chariot
between the armies.

25 Facing Bhishma and Drona[6]
and all the great kings,
he said, "Arjuna, see
the Kuru men,[7] assembled here!"

26 Arjuna saw them standing there:
fathers, grandfathers, teachers,
uncles, brothers, sons,
grandsons, and friends.

27 He surveyed his elders
and companions in both armies,
all his kinsmen
assembled together.

28 Dejected, filled with strange pity,
he said this:
    "Krishna, I see my kinsmen
    gathered here, wanting war.

29 My limbs sink,
    my mouth is parched,
    my body trembles,
    the hair bristles on my flesh.

30 The magic bow[8] slips
from my hand, my skin burns,
I cannot stand still,
my mind reels.

31 I see omens of chaos,
Krishna; I see no good
in killing my kinsmen
in battle.

32 Krishna, I see no victory,
or kingship or pleasures.
What use to us are kingship,
delights, or life itself?

33 We sought kingship, delights,
and pleasures for the sake of those
assembled to abandon their lives
and fortunes in battle.

34 They are teachers, fathers, sons,
and grandfathers, uncles, grandsons,
fathers and brothers of wives,
and other men of our family.

35 I do not want to kill them
even if I am killed, Krishna;
not for kingship of all three worlds,
much less for the earth!

36 What joy is there for us, Krishna,
in killing Dhritarashtra's sons?
    Evil will haunt us if we kill them,
    though their bows are drawn to kill.

37 Honor forbids us to kill
our cousins, Dhritarashtra's sons;
how can we know happiness
if we kill our own kinsmen?

38 The greed that distorts their reason
blinds them to the sin they commit
in ruining the family, blinds them
to the crime of betraying friends.

39 How can we ignore the wisdom
of turning from this evil
when we see the sin
of family destruction, Krishna?

40 When the family is ruined,
the timeless laws of family duty
perish; and when duty is lost,
chaos overwhelms the family.

41 In overwhelming chaos, Krishna,
women of the family are corrupted:
and when women are corrupted,
disorder[9] is born in society.

---

[1] Translated by Barbara Stoler Miller.
[2] The third of the five Pāndava brothers.
[3] The blind king of the Hāstinapura and father of the Kauravas.
[4] Incarnation of Visnu, the preserver god.
[5] Here Duryodhana.
[6] Preceptor of the Kauravas and the Pāndavas. Bhishma is their granduncle.
[7] The Kauravas.

---

[8] Gāndīva, which he won from the fire god.
[9] Specifically, disruption of the proper ordering of the four principal social classes: brahman, warrior, merchant, and laborer.

42 This discord drags the violators
    and the family itself to hell;
    for ancestors fall when rites
    of offering rice and water lapse.[1]

43 The sins of men who violate
    the family create disorder in society
    that undermines the constant laws
    of caste and family duty.

44 Krishna, we have heard
    that a place in hell
    is reserved for men
    who undermine family duties.

45 I lament the great sin
    we commit when our greed
    for kingship and pleasures
    drives us to kill our kinsmen.

46 If Dhritarashtra's armed sons
    kill me in battle when I am unarmed
    and offer no resistance,
    it will be my reward."

47 Saying this in the time of war,
    Arjuna slumped into the chariot
    and laid down his bow and arrows,
    his mind tormented by grief.

From The Second Teaching

[Philosophy and Spiritual Discipline]

LORD KRISHNA:

11 You grieve for those beyond grief,
    and you speak words of insight;
    but learned men do not grieve
    for the dead or the living.

12 Never have I not existed,
    nor you, nor these kings:
    and never in the future
    shall we cease to exist.

13 Just as the embodied self
    enters childhood, youth, and old age,
    so does it enter another body:
    this does not confound a steadfast man.[2]

14 Contacts with matter make us feel
    heat and cold, pleasure and pain.
    Arjuna, you must learn to endure
    fleeting things—they come and go!

15 When these cannot torment a man,
    when suffering and joy are equal
    for him and he has courage,
    he is fit for immortality.

16 Nothing of nonbeing comes to be,
    nor does being cease to exist;
    the boundary between these two
    is seen by men who see reality.

17 Indestructible is the presence
    that pervades all this;
    no one can destroy
    this unchanging reality.

18 Our bodies are known to end,
    but the embodied self is enduring,
    indestructible, and immeasurable;
    therefore, Arjuna, fight the battle!

19 He who thinks this self a killer
    and he who thinks it killed,
    both fail to understand;
    it does not kill, nor is it killed.

20 It is not born,
    it does not die;
    having been,
    it will never not be;
    unborn, enduring,
    constant, and primordial,
    it is not killed
    when the body is killed.

21 Arjuna, when a man knows the self
    to be indestructible, enduring, unborn,
    unchanging, how does he kill
    or cause anyone to kill?

22 As a man discards
    worn-out clothes
    to put on new
    and different ones,
    so the embodied self
    discards
    its worn-out bodies
    to take on other new ones.

23 Weapons do not cut it,
    fire does not burn it,
    waters do not wet it,
    wind does not wither it.

24 It cannot be cut or burned;
    it cannot be wet or withered;
    it is enduring, all-pervasive,
    fixed, immovable, and timeless.

25 It is called unmanifest,
    inconceivable, and immutable;
    since you know that to be so,
    you should not grieve!

26 If you think of its birth
    and death as ever-recurring,
    then too, Great Warrior,
    you have no cause to grieve!

27 Death is certain for anyone born,
    and birth is certain for the dead;
    since the cycle is inevitable,
    you have no cause to grieve!

---

[1]Hindus are required to make these ritual offerings to their ancestors.
[2]Here Krishna begins to explain the implications of reincarnation, emphasizing the identity of the seemingly finite embodied soul with the infinite and imperishable universal spirit (Brahman).

28   Creatures are unmanifest in origin,
     manifest in the midst of life,
     and unmanifest again in the end.
     Since this is so, why do you lament?

29   Rarely someone
     sees it,
     rarely another
     speaks it,
     rarely anyone
     hears it—
     even hearing it,
     no one really knows it.

30   The self embodied in the body
     of every being is indestructible;
     you have no cause to grieve
     for all these creatures, Arjuna!

31   Look to your own duty;[3]
     do not tremble before it;
     nothing is better for a warrior
     than a battle of sacred duty.

32   The doors of heaven open
     for warriors who rejoice
     to have a battle like this
     thrust on them by chance.

33   If you fail to wage this war
     of sacred duty,
     you will abandon your own duty
     and fame only to gain evil.

34   People will tell
     of your undying shame,
     and for a man of honor
     shame is worse than death.

                    * * *

47   Be intent on action,
     not on the fruits of action;
     avoid attraction to the fruits
     and attachment to inaction!

48   Perform actions, firm in discipline,
     relinquishing attachment;
     be impartial to failure and success—
     this equanimity is called discipline.

49   Arjuna, action is far inferior
     to the discipline of understanding,[4]
     so seek refuge in understanding—pitiful
     are men drawn by fruits of action.

50   Disciplined by understanding,
     one abandons both good and evil deeds;
     so arm yourself for discipline—
     discipline is skill in actions.

51   Wise men disciplined by understanding
     relinquish the fruit born of action;
     freed from these bonds of rebirth,
     they reach a place beyond decay.

52   When your understanding passes beyond
     the swamp of delusion,
     You will be indifferent to all
     that is heard in sacred lore.[5]

53   When your understanding turns
     from sacred lore to stand fixed,
     immovable in contemplation,
     then you will reach discipline.[6]

54   ARJUNA:
     Krishna, what defines a man
     deep in contemplation whose insight
     and thought are sure? How would he speak?
     How would he sit? How would he move?

55   LORD KRISHNA:
     When he gives up desires in his mind,
     is content with the self within himself,[7]
     then he is said to be a man
     whose insight is sure, Arjuna.

56   When suffering does not disturb his mind,
     when his craving for pleasures has vanished,
     when attraction, fear, and anger are gone,
     he is called a sage whose thought is sure.

57   When he shows no preference
     in fortune or misfortune
     and neither exults nor hates,
     his insight is sure.

58   When, like a tortoise retracting
     its limbs, he withdraws his senses
     completely from sensuous objects,
     his insight is sure.

From The Third Teaching

[Discipline of Action]

ARJUNA:

1   If you think understanding
    is more powerful than action,
    why, Krishna, do you urge me
    to this horrific act?

2   You confuse my understanding
    with a maze of words:
    speak one certain truth
    so I may achieve what is good.

---

[3]*Dharma*, which for Arjuna is that of his class (warrior) and stage of life (householder).
[4]The rational facilities, including intuitive intelligence, in contrast to the mind, or discursive intellect.

---

[5]The *Vedas* and their ritualistic doctrine. Krishna says that the older ritualistic learning is useless for the emancipation of the soul from *karma*.
[6]Used in its broadest sense.
[7]A play on the word *ātman*, which means both "the self" (soul) and "oneself." Only one who has realized the true (immutable) nature of the self can be *content with the self within himself*. Krishna now begins to describe the techniques and effects of withdrawing one's senses from the outside and focusing them on the interior self, the infinite soul.

LORD KRISHNA:

3 Earlier I taught the twofold
basis of good in this world—
for philosophers, disciplined knowledge;
for men of discipline, action.

4 A man cannot escape the force
of action by abstaining from actions;
he does not attain success
just by renunciation.

5 No one exists for even an instant
without performing action;
however unwilling, every being is forced
to act by the qualities of nature.[8]

6 When his senses are controlled
but he keeps recalling
sense objects with his mind,
he is a self-deluded hypocrite.

7 When he controls his senses
with his mind and engages in the discipline
of action with his faculties of action,
detachment sets him apart.

8 Perform necessary action;
it is more powerful than inaction;
without action you even fail
to sustain your own body.

9 Action imprisons the world
unless it is done as sacrifice;
freed from attachment, Arjuna,
perform action as sacrifice!

10 When creating living beings and sacrifice,
Prajapati, the primordial creator, said:
"By sacrifice will you procreate!
Let it be your wish-granting cow![9]

11 Foster the gods with this,
and may they foster you;
by enriching one another,
you will achieve a higher good.

12 Enriched by sacrifice, the gods
will give you the delights you desire;
he is a thief who enjoys their gifts
without giving to them in return."

13 Good men eating the remnants
of sacrifice are free of any guilt,
but evil men who cook for themselves
eat the food of sin.

14 Creatures depend on food,
food comes from rain,
rain depends on sacrifice,
and sacrifice comes from action.

15 Action comes from the spirit of prayer,
whose source is OM,[1] sound of the imperishable;
so the pervading infinite spirit
is ever present in rites of sacrifice.

16 He who fails to keep turning
the wheel here set in motion
wastes his life in sin,
addicted to the senses, Arjuna.

17 But when a man finds delight
within himself and feels inner joy
and pure contentment in himself,
there is nothing more to be done.

18 He has no stake here
in deeds done or undone,
nor does his purpose
depend on other creatures.

19 Always perform with detachment
any action you must do;
performing action with detachment,
one achieves supreme good.

20 Janaka[2] and other ancient kings
attained perfection by action alone;
seeing the way to preserve
the world, you should act.

21 Whatever a leader does,
the ordinary people also do.
He sets the standard
for the world to follow.

22 In the three worlds,[3]
there is nothing I must do,
nothing unattained to be attained,
yet I engage in action.

23 What if I did not engage
relentlessly in action?
Men retrace my path
at every turn, Arjuna.

24 These worlds would collapse
if I did not perform action;
I would create disorder in society,
living beings would be destroyed.

25 As the ignorant act with attachment
to actions, Arjuna,
so wise men should act with detachment
to preserve the world.

Buddhist Sermons

In the following selections from Buddhist texts, key Buddhist concepts are elaborated. The first selection, "Setting in Motion the Wheel of Truth," describes the Four Noble Truths of Buddhism.

---

[8]That is, sublimity, dynamism (passion), and inertia.
[9]This image derives from the importance of cattle in Vedic society and religion. Prajapati is a god of the *Vedas*. In the Vedic worldview the preservation of the universe depended on sacrifices made to the gods, and such ritual was at the center of the religion.

---

[1]Beginning with the *Upanishads*, the primeval sound, representing the infinite spirit that underlies the universe.
[2]Celebrated character in the dialogues of the *Bṛhadāraṇyaka Upaniṣad*; an exemplar of the warrior-king who is also a man of discipline (a *yogī*).
[3]Heaven, earth, and the underworld.

The second selection, "The Fire Sermon," describes how the burning flame of desire and sensation is at the root and heart of life's dissatisfactions, disappointments, and disenchantments.

Setting in Motion the Wheel of Truth

(Dhammacakkappavattana-sutta)

(The First Sermon of the Buddha)

Thus have I heard. The Blessed One was once living in the Deer Park at Isipatana (the Resort of Seers) near Bārānasi (Benares). There he addressed the group of five bhikkhus:

'Bhikkhus, these two extremes ought not to be practised by one who has gone forth from the household life. What are the two? There is devotion to the indulgence of sense-pleasures, which is low, common, the way of ordinary people, unworthy and unprofitable; and there is devotion to self-mortification, which is painful, unworthy and unprofitable.

'Avoiding both these extremes, the Tathāgata has realized the Middle Path: it gives vision, it gives knowledge, and it leads to calm, to insight, to enlightenment, to Nibbāna. And what is that Middle Path . . . ? It is simply the Noble Eightfold Path, namely, right view, right thought, right speech, right action, right livelihood, right effort, right mindfulness, right concentration. This is the Middle Path realized by the Tathāgata, which gives vision, which gives knowledge, and which leads to calm, to insight, to enlightenment, to Nibbāna.

'The Noble Truth of suffering (*Dukkha*) is this: Birth is suffering; aging is suffering; sickness is suffering; death is suffering; sorrow and lamentation, pain, grief and despair are suffering; association with the unpleasant is suffering; dissociation from the pleasant is suffering; not to get what one wants is suffering—in brief, the five aggregates of attachment are suffering.

'The Noble Truth of the origin of suffering is this: It is this thirst (craving) which produces re-existence and rebe-coming, bound up with passionate greed. It finds fresh delight now here and now there, namely, thirst for sense-pleasures; thirst for existence and becoming; and thirst for non-existence (self-annihilation).

'The Noble Truth of the Cessation of suffering is this: It is the complete cessation of that very thirst, giving it up, renouncing it, emancipating oneself from it, detaching oneself from it.

'The Noble Truth of the Path leading to the Cessation of suffering is this: It is simply the Noble Eightfold Path, namely right view; right thought; right speech, right action, right livelihood; right effort; right mindfulness; right concentration.

'"This is the Noble Truth of Suffering (Dukkha)": such was the vision, the knowledge, the wisdom, the science, the light, that arose in me with regard to things not heard before. "This suffering, as a noble truth, should be fully understood": such was the vision, the knowledge, the wisdom, the science, the light, that arose in me with regard to things not heard before. "This suffering, as a noble truth, has been fully understood": such was the vision, the knowledge, the wisdom, the science, the light, that arose in me with regard to things not heard before.

'"This is the Noble Truth of the Origin of suffering": such was the vision . . . "This Origin of suffering, as a noble truth,

should be abandoned": such was the vision, . . . "This Origin of suffering, as a noble truth, has been abandoned": such was the vision, . . . with regard to things not heard before.

'"This is the Noble Truth of the Cessation of suffering": such was the vision . . . "This Cessation of suffering, as a noble truth, should be realized": such was the vision, . . . "This Cessation of suffering, as a noble truth, has been realized": such was the vision, . . . with regard to things not heard before.

'"This is the Noble Truth of the Path leading to the Cessation of suffering": such was the vision, . . . "This Path leading to the Cessation of suffering, as a noble truth, should be followed (cultivated)": such was the vision, . . . "This Path leading to the Cessation of suffering, as a noble truth, has been followed (cultivated)": such was the vision, the knowledge, the wisdom, the science, the light, that arose in me with regard to things not heard before.

'As long as my vision of true knowledge was not fully clear in these three aspects, in these twelve ways, regarding the Four Noble Truths,[1] I did not claim to have realized the perfect Enlightenment that is supreme in the world with its gods, with its Māras and Brahmas, in this world with its recluses and brāhmanas, with its princes and men. But when my vision of true knowledge was fully clear in these three aspects, in these twelve ways, regarding the Four Noble Truths, then I claimed to have realized the perfect Enlightenment that is supreme in the world with its gods, its Māras and Brahmas, in this world with its recluses and brāhmanas, with its princes and men. And a vision of true knowledge arose in me thus: My heart's deliverance is unassailable. This is the last birth. Now there is no more rebecoming (rebirth).

This the Blessed One said. The group of five bhikkhus was glad, and they rejoiced at his words.

(*SAMYUTTA-NIKĀYA*, LVI, II)

The Fire Sermon[1]

(Adittapariyāya-sutta)

Thus have I heard. The Blessed One was once living at Gayāsīsa in Gayā with a thousand bhikkhus. There he addressed the bhikkhus:

---

[1]As may be seen from the four preceding paragraphs, with regard to each of the Four Noble Truths there are three aspects of knowledge: 1. The knowledge that it is the Truth (sacca-nāna) 2. The knowledge that a certain function or action with regard to this Truth should be performed (kicca-nāna), and 3. The knowledge that that function or action with regard to this Truth has been performed (kata-nāna). When these three aspects are applied to each of the Four Noble Truths, twelve ways are obtained.

[1]It is interesting to note here that Section III of *The Waste Land* by T. S. Eliot is called *The Fire Sermon*. In the note to line 308: 'Burning burning burning burning,' Eliot writes: "The complete text of the Buddha's Fire Sermon (which corresponds in importance to the Sermon on the Mount) from which these words are taken, will be found translated in the late Henry Clarke Warren's *Buddhism in Translation* (Harvard Oriental Series). Mr. Warren was one of the great pioneers of Buddhist studies in the Occident."

The translation of the *Sutta* given here, made by the present author specially for this edition, is from the original Pali of the *Samyutta-nikā-ya* of the *Sutta-pitaka*. Warrens translation was of the narrative as found in the *Mahāvagga* of the *Vinayapitaka*.

'Bhikkhus, all is burning. And what is the all that is burning?

'Bhikkhus, the eye is burning, visible forms are burning, visual consciousness is burning, visual impression is burning, also whatever sensation, pleasant or painful or neither-painful-nor-pleasant, arises on account of the visual impression, that too is burning. Burning with what? Burning with the fire of lust, with the fire of hate, with the fire of delusion; I say it is burning with birth, aging and death, with sorrows, with lamentations, with pains, with griefs, with despairs.

'The ear is burning, sounds are burning, auditory consciousness is burning, auditory impression is burning, also whatever sensation, pleasant or painful or neither-painful-nor-pleasant, arises on account of the auditory impression, that too is burning. Burning with what? Burning with the fire of lust. . . .

'The nose is burning, odours are burning, olfactory consciousness is burning, olfactory impression is burning, also whatever sensation, pleasant or painful or neither-painful-nor-pleasant, arises on account of the olfactory impression, that too is burning. Burning with what? Burning with the fire of lust. . . .

'The tongue is burning, flavours are burning, gustative consciousness is burning, gustative impression is burning, also whatever sensation, pleasant or painful or neither-painful-nor-pleasant, arises on account of the gustative impression, that too is burning. Burning with what? Burning with the fire of lust. . . .

'The body is burning, tangible things are burning, tactile consciousness is burning, tactile impression is burning, also whatever sensation, pleasant or painful or neither-painful-nor-pleasant, arises on account of the tactile sensation, that too is burning. Burning with what? Burning with the fire of lust. . . .

'The mind is burning, mental objects (ideas, etc.) are burning, mental consciousness is burning, mental impression is burning, also whatever sensation, pleasant or painful or neither-painful-nor-pleasant, arises on account of the mental impression, that too is burning. Burning with what? Burning with the fire of lust, with the fire of hate, with the fire of delusion; I say it is burning with birth, aging and death, with sorrows, with lamentations, with pains, with griefs, with despairs.

'Bhikkhus, a learned and noble disciple, who sees (things) thus, becomes dispassionate with regard to the eye, becomes dispassionate with regard to visible forms, becomes dispassionate with regard to the visual consciousness, becomes dispassionate with regard to the visual impression, also whatever sensation, pleasant or painful or neither-painful-nor-pleasant, arises on account of the visual impression, with regard to that too he becomes dispassionate. He becomes dispassionate with regard to the ear, with regard to sounds . . . He becomes dispassionate with regard to the nose . . . with regard to odours . . . He becomes dispassionate with regard to the tongue . . . with regard to flavours . . . He becomes dispassionate with regard to the body . . . with regard to tangible things . . . He becomes dispassionate with regard to the mind, becomes dispassionate with regard to mental objects (ideas, etc.), becomes dispassionate with regard to mental consciousness, becomes dispassionate with regard to mental impression, also whatever sensation, pleasant or painful or neither-painful-nor-pleasant, arises on account of mental impression, with regard to that too he becomes dispassionate.

'Being dispassionate, be becomes detached; through detachment he is liberated. When liberated there is knowledge that he is liberated. And he knows: Birth is exhausted, the holy life has been lived, what has to be done is done, there is no more left to be done on this account.'

This the Blessed One said. The bhikkhus were glad, and they rejoiced at his words.

While this exposition was being delivered, the minds of those thousand bhikkhus were liberated from impurities, without attachment.

(SAMYUTTA-NIKĀYA, XXXV, 28)

Universal Love

(Metta-sutta)

He who is skilled in good and who wishes to attain that state of Calm should act (thus):

He should be able, upright, perfectly upright, compliant, gentle, and humble.

Contented, easily supported, with few duties, of simple livelihood, controlled in senses, discreet, not impudent, he should not be greedily attached to families.

He should not commit any slight wrong such that other wise men might censure him. (Then he should cultivate his thoughts thus:)

May all beings be happy and secure; may their minds be contented.

Whatever living beings there may be—feeble or strong, long (or tall), stout, or medium, short, small, or large, seen or unseen, those dwelling far or near, those who are born and those who are yet to be born—may all beings, without exception, be happy-minded!

Let not one deceive another nor despise any person whatever in any place. In anger or illwill let not one wish any harm to another.

Just as a mother would protect her only child even at the risk of her own life, even so let one cultivate a boundless heart towards all beings.

Let one's thoughts of boundless love pervade the whole world—above, below and across—without any obstruction, without any hatred, without any enmity.

Valmiki

from *The Ramayana*

The following excerpt is taken from near the end of the Ramayana, *when, after fourteen years in exile, the rightful king, Rama, returns to his kingdom and is reconciled with his stepmother Kaikeyi, who had caused his disinheritance in the first place.*

Rama explained that he had to adopt this trial in order to demonstrate Sita's purity beyond a shadow of doubt to the whole world. This seemed a rather strange inconsistency on the part of one who had brought back to life and restored to her husband a person like Ahalya, who had avowedly committed a moral lapse; and then there was Sugreeva's wife, who had been forced to live with Vali, and whom Rama commended as worthy of being taken back by Sugreeva after Vali's death. In Sita's case Ravana, in spite of repeated and desperate attempts, could not approach her. She had remained inviolable. And the fiery quality of her essential being burnt out the God of fire himself, as he had admitted after Sita's ordeal. Under these circumstances, it was very strange that Rama should have spoken harshly as he had done at the first sight of Sita, and subjected her to a dreadful trial.

The gods, who had watched this in suspense, were now profoundly relieved but also had an uneasy feeling that Rama had, perhaps, lost sight of his own identity. Again and again this seemed to happen. Rama displayed the tribulations and the limitations of the human frame and it was necessary from time to time to remind him of his divinity. Now Brahma, the Creator, came forward to speak and addressed Rama thus: "Of the Trinity, I am the Creator. Shiva is the Destroyer and Vishnu is the Protector. All three of us derive our existence from the Supreme God and we are subject to dissolution and rebirth. But the Supreme God who creates us is without a beginning or an end. There is neither birth nor growth nor death for the Supreme God. He is the origin of everything and in him everything is assimilated at the end. That God is yourself, and Sita at your side now is a part of that Divinity. Please remember that this is your real identity and let not the fear and doubts that assail an ordinary mortal ever move you. You are beyond everything; and we are all blessed indeed to be in your presence."

In the high heavens, Shiva encouraged Dasaratha to go down to the earth and meet Rama. He said, "Rama needs your benediction after having carried out your commands, and having gone through so much privation for fourteen years in order to safeguard the integrity of your promises." Dasaratha descended in his true form into the midst of his family. Rama was overjoyed to see him again and prostrated himself at his feet.

Dasaratha said, "This moment is one of supreme joy for me. For the first time in all these years, my heart is lighter. The memory of the evil use that Kaikeyi had made of my promise to her had stuck in my heart like a splinter and had stayed there. Although I had shed my physical body, the pain had remained unmitigated—until this minute. It is now gone. You with Sita are the primordial being and I was indeed blessed to have begotten you as my son. This is a moment of fulfilment for me. I have nothing more to say and I will go back to my world and repose there in eternal peace. But before I go I want you to ask of me something, anything, any wish I could fulfil for you."

Rama said, "Your arrival here is the greatest boon for me, and I have nothing more to seek. All along, my only desire has been to see you again, and that is fulfilled." Dasaratha still insisted that Rama should state a wish that he could grant. Rama said, "If that is so, please find a place in your heart for both Kaikeyi and Bharatha, and take back your vow by which you cut off their blood connection with you. I cannot think of her except as a mother and Bharatha as a brother."

Dasaratha at once replied, "Bharatha is different. He has proved his greatness. Yes, I will accept him. But Kaikeyi— she ruined us all. She prevented your being crowned at the last moment. I can never forgive her."

Rama explained, "It was not her mistake. I committed an unforgivable blunder in straightway accepting the kingship when you offered it, without pausing to consider the consequences. I should have had more forethought. It was not her mistake." Rama continued his plea for Kaikeyi so earnestly that Dasaratha finally acceded to it. A burden was lifted from Rama's mind, and he felt completely at peace with the world again. Dasaratha offered him his blessings and a few words of guidance, and bade farewell to him. Then he took leave of Sita and Lakshmana separately, and returned to his place in heaven.

When this was over, the gods counselled Rama, "Tomorrow, the fifth day of the full moon, you will be completing the fourteenth year of your exile and it is imperative that you reappear in Ayodhya on completion of this term. Bharatha waits for you at Nandigram single-mindedly. If you do not appear there at the precise hour we dread to think what he may do to himself."

Rama realized the urgency and turning to Vibishana asked, "Is there any means by which you can help me return to Ayodhya within a day?"

Vibishana said, "I will give you the Pushpak Vimana. It was Kubera's at one time; later Ravana appropriated it for his own use. It will take you back to Ayodhya within any time you may wish." He immediately summoned the Vimana to be brought.

Rama ascended this vehicle, taking with him an entire army and all his supporters, such as Vibishana, Sugreeva, and others, who were unwilling to part from him, and started back in the direction of Ayodhya. As they flew along, he pointed out to Sita various landmarks that he had crossed during his campaign, and when they crossed the northern portals of Lanka he pointed out to her the spot far below where Ravana had finally fallen. They flew over mountains and forests; every inch of ground had a meaning for Rama. He made a brief descent at Kiskinda, where Sita had expressed a desire to gather a company of women to escort her when she re-entered Ayodhya. His next halt was at the ashram of Sage Bharadwaj, who had been hospitable to him once. At this point, Rama dispatched Hanuman to go forward in advance to Nandigram and inform Bharatha of his coming.

At Nandigram, Bharatha had been counting the hours and realized that the fourteenth year was nearly over. There was no sign of Rama yet; nor any news. It seemed as though all his austerities and penances of all these years were fruitless. He looked forlorn. He had kept Rama's sandals enthroned on a pedestal and was reigning as a regent. He summoned his brother Sathrugna and said, "My time is up. I cannot imagine where Rama is gone or what fate has overtaken him. I gave my word to wait for fourteen years and in a few moments I will have passed it. I have no right to live beyond that. Now I pass on my responsibilities to you. You will go back to Ayodhya and continue to rule as a regent." He made preparations to immolate himself in fire.

Sathrugna argued and tried to dissuade Bharatha in various ways, but Bharatha was adamant. Luckily, just at this moment, Hanuman arrived in the form of a brahmin youth, and the first thing he did was to put out the fire. Bharatha asked, "Who are you? What right have you to extinguish a fire I have raised?"

Hanuman explained, "I have brought you a message from Rama. He will be here presently."

Bharatha would not believe him, whereupon Hanuman assumed for a moment his gigantic form, explaining who he was, and then narrated to Bharatha all the incidents that had taken place these fourteen years. "Now make a public announcement of Rama's coming," he concluded, "and let all the streets and buildings be decorated to receive him."

This changed the whole atmosphere. Bharatha immediately dispatched messengers to the city and made preparations to receive Rama and lead him to his rightful place back in Ayodhya.

Shortly, Rama's Vimana arrived. Rama's mothers including Kaikeyi, had assembled at Nandigram to receive him. The reunion was a happy one. The first thing that Rama did was to discard his austere garments. He groomed and clothed himself as befitting a King, and he advised Sita to do likewise. Vasishtha received the new King and Queen and fixed the hour for the coronation, interrupted fourteen year, before.

Pancatantra

Selected Tales

The Pancatantra *is a delightful, worldly collection of stories which offer a pragmatic perspective on life. The tales are linked together in a continuous chain—a structure that may have influenced the later* Thousand and One Nights *(see Chapter 6).*

The Monk Who Left His Body Behind

In the Koshala country is a city called Unassailable. In it ruled a king named Fine-Chariot, over whose footstool rippled rays of light from the diadems of uncounted vassal princes.

One day a forest ranger came with this report: "Master, all the forest kings have become turbulent, and in their midst is the forest chief named Vindhyaka. It is the king's affair to teach him modest manners." On hearing this report, the king summoned Counselor Strong, and dispatched him with orders to chastise the forest chieftains.

Now in the absence of the counselor, a naked monk arrived in the city at the end of the hot season. He was master of the astronomical specialties, such as problems and etymologies, rising of the zodiacal signs, augury, ecliptic intersection, and the decanate; also stellar mansions divided into nine parts, twelve parts, thirty parts; the shadow of the gnomon, eclipses, and numerous other mysteries. With these the fellow in a few days won the entire population, as if he had bought and paid for them.

Finally, as the matter went from mouth to mouth, the king heard a report of its character, and had the curiosity to summon the monk to his palace. There he offered him a seat and asked: "Is it true, Professor, as they say, that you read the thoughts of others?" "That will be demonstrated in the sequel," replied the monk, and by discourses adapted to the occasion he brought the poor king to the extreme pitch of curiosity.

One day he failed to appear at the regular hour, but the following day, on entering the palace, he announced: "O King, I bring you the best of good tidings. At dawn today I flung this body aside within my cell, assumed a body fit for the world of the gods, and, inspired with the knowledge that all the im-

mortals thought of me with longing, I went to heaven and have just returned. While there, I was requested by the gods to inquire in their name after the king's welfare."

When he heard this, the king said, his extreme curiosity begetting a feeling of amazement: "What, Professor! You go to heaven?" "O mighty King," replied the fellow, "I go to heaven every day." This the king believed—poor dullard!—so that he grew negligent of all royal business and all duties toward the ladies, concentrating his attention on the monk.

While matters were in this state, Strong entered the king's presence, after settling all disturbances in the forest domain. He found the master wholly indifferent to every one of his counselors, withdrawn in private conference with that naked monk, discussing what seemed to be some miraculous occurrence, his lotus-face ablossom. And on learning the facts, Strong bowed low and said: "Victory, O King! May the gods give you wit!"

Thereupon the king inquired concerning the counselor's health, and said: "Sir, do you know this professor?" To which the counselor replied: "How could there be ignorance of one who is lord and creator of a whole school of professors? Moreover, I have heard that this professor goes to heaven. Is it a fact?" "Everything that you have heard," answered the king, "is beyond the shadow of doubt."

Thereupon the monk said: "If this counselor feels any curiosity, he may see for himself." With this he entered his cell, barred the door from within, and waited there. After the lapse of a mere moment, the counselor spoke: "O King," he said, "how soon will he return?" And the king replied: "Why this impatience? You must know that he leaves his lifeless body within this cell, and returns with another, a heavenly body."

"If this is indeed the case," said Strong, "then bring a great quantity of firewood, so that I may set fire to this cell." "For what purpose?" asked the king. And the counselor continued: "So that, when this lifeless body has been burned, the gentleman may stand before the king in that other body which visits heaven. In this connection I will tell you the story of

The Girl Who Married a Snake

In Palace City lived a Brahman named Godly, whose childless wife wept bitterly when she saw the neighbors' youngsters. But one day the Brahman said: "Forget your sorrow, mother dear. See! When I was offering the sacrifice for birth of children, an invisible being said to me in the clearest words: "Brahman, you shall have a son surpassing all mankind in beauty, character, and charm.""

When she heard this, the wife felt her heart swell with supreme delight. "I only hope his promises come true," she said. Presently she conceived, and in course of time gave birth to a snake. When she saw him, she paid no attention to her companions, who all advised her to throw him away. Instead, she took him and bathed him, laid him with motherly tenderness in a large, clean box, and pampered him with milk, fresh butter, and other good things, so that before many days had passed, he grew to maturity.

But one day the Brahman's wife was watching the marriage festival of a neighbor's son, and the tears streamed down her face as she said to her husband: "I know that you despise me, because you do nothing about a marriage festival for my boy." "My good wife," answered he, "am I to go to the depths of the underworld and beseech Vasuki the serpent-king? Who else, you foolish woman, would give his own daughter to this snake?"

But when he had spoken, he was disturbed at seeing the utter woe in his wife's countenance. He therefore packed provisions for a long journey, and undertook foreign travel from love of his wife. In the course of some months he arrived at a spot called Kutkuta City in a distant land. There in the house of a kinsman whom he could visit with pleasure since each respected the other's character, he was hospitably received, was given a bath, food, and the like, and there he spent the night.

Now at dawn, when he paid his respects to his Brahman host and made ready to depart, the other asked him: "What was your purpose in coming hither? And where will your errand lead you?"

To this he replied: "I have come in search of a fit wife for my son." "In that case," said his host, "I have a very beautiful daughter, and my own person is yours to command. Pray take her for your son." So the Brahman took the girl with her attendants and returned to his own place.

But when the people of the country beheld her incomparable opulence of beauty, her supreme loveliness and superhuman graces, their eyes popped out with pleasure, and they said to her attendants: "How can right-thinking persons bestow such a pearl of a girl upon a snake?" On hearing this, all her elderly relatives without exception were troubled at heart, and they said: "Let her be taken from this imp-ridden creature." But the girl said: "No more of this mockery! Remember the text:

Do once, once only, these three things:
Once spoken, stands the word of kings;
The speech of saints has no miscarriage;
A maid is given once in marriage.

And again:

All fated happenings, derived
From any former state,
Must changeless stand: the very gods
Endured poor Blossom's fate."

Whereupon they all asked in chorus: "Who was this Blossom person?" And the girl told the story of

Poor Blossom

God Indra once had a parrot named Blossom. He enjoyed supreme beauty, loveliness, and various graces, while his intelligence was not blunted by his extensive scientific attainments.

One day he was resting on the palm of great Indra's hand, his body thrilling with delight at that contact, and was reciting a variety of authoritative formulas, when he caught sight of Yama, lord of death, who had come to pay his respects at the time appointed. Seeing the god, the parrot edged away. And all the thronging immortals asked him: "Why did you move away, sir, upon beholding that personage?" "But," said the parrot, "he brings harm to all living creatures. Why not move away from him?"

Upon hearing this, they all desired to calm his fears, so said to Yama: "As a favor to us, you must please not kill this

parrot." And Yama replied: "I do not know about that. It is Time who determines these matters."

They therefore took Blossom with them, paid a visit to Time, and made the same request. To which Time replied: "It is Death who is posted in these affairs. Pray speak to him."

But when they did so, the parrot died at the mere sight of Death. And they were all distressed at seeing the occurrence, so that they said to Yama: "What does this mean?" And Yama said: "It was simply fated that he should die at the mere sight of Death." With this reply they went back to heaven.

"And that is why I say:
All fated happenings, . . .

and the rest of it. Furthermore, I do not want my father reproached for double dealing on the part of his daughter." When she had said this, she married the snake, with the permission of her companions, and at once began devoted attendance upon him by offering milk to drink and performing other services.

One night the serpent issued from the generous chest which had been set for him in her chamber, and entered her bed. "Who is this?" she cried. "He has the form of a man." And thinking him a strange man, she started up, trembling in every limb, unlocked the door, and was about to dart away when she heard him say: "Stay, my dear wife. I am your husband." Then, in order to convince her, he re-entered the body which he had left behind in the chest, issued from it again, and came to her.

When she beheld him flashing with lofty diadem, with earrings, bracelets, armbands, and rings, she fell at his feet, and then they sank into a glad embrace.

Now his father, the Brahman, rose betimes and discovered how matters stood. He therefore seized the serpent's skin that lay in the chest, and consumed it with fire, for he thought: "I do not want him to enter that again." And in the morning he and his wife, with the greatest possible joy, introduced to everybody as their own an extraordinarily handsome son, quite wrapped up in his love affair.

Bhartrhari

Bhartrhari, a fifth-century philosopher, is reputed to be the author of the Satakatraya, *a collection of lyrics devoted separately to three topics: political wisdom, erotic passion, and renunciation. Believed to have been a court poet, Bhartrhari wrote poems that reflect both the sensuousness of sexual intimacy and the intensity of love's pain. Pride and bitterness, wisdom and honesty pervade the poems.*

34

Like clusters of blossoms,
wise men have two destinies:
to grace the summit of the world
or wither in the forest.

35

When silent, the courtier is branded dumb;
when eloquent, pretentious or a prating fool;
when intimate, presumptuous;
when distant, diffident;
when patient, pusillanimous;

when impetuous, ill-bred.
The rules of service are a mystery
inscrutable even to masters of wisdom.

70

Knowledge is man's crowning mark,
a treasure secretly buried,
the source of luxury, fame, and bliss,
a guru most venerable, a friend on foreign journeys,
the pinnacle of divinity.
Knowledge is valued by kings beyond wealth—when
he lacks it, a man is a brute.

76

Armlets do not adorn a person,
or necklaces luminous as the moon;
or ablutions, or ointments,
or blossoms, or beautiful hair.
Eloquent speech that is polished well
really adorns a person—
When other ornaments are ruined,
the ornament of speech is an enduring jewel.

85

Why all these words and empty prattle?
Only two worlds are worth a man's devotion:
the youth of beautiful women wearied by heavy breasts
and full of fresh wine's excitement,
or the forest.

Amaru

A slightly later poet than Bhartrhari, Amaru's seventh-century verse collection, Amarusatuku, anthologizes more than a hundred lyrics. Amaru's poems evoke the moods, emotional and psychological, experienced by lovers. Although Amaru's love poems comply strictly with the conventions of erotic verse of his times, they display a remarkable range of tone as well as a gift for dramatic immediacy.

23

Lying on the same bed,
backs to each other,
without any answers,
holding their breaths,

even though making up
each to the other
was in their hearts,
each guarded their pride,
but slowly,
each looked sideways,
glances mingled
and the quarrel
exploded in laughter;
in enfolding embraces.

34

She's just a kid,
but I'm the one who's fainthearted.
She's the woman,
but I'm the coward.
She bears that high, swollen set of breasts,
but I'm the one who's burdened.
The heavy hips are hers,
but I'm unable to move.

It's a wonder
how clumsy I've become
because of flaws
that shelter themselves
in another.

38

When anger
was a crease in the brow
and silence
a catastrophe,
When making up
was a mutual smile
and a glance
a gift,
now just look at this mess
that you've made of that love.

You grovel at my feet
and I berate you
and can't let my anger go.

101

When my lover came to bed,
the knot came untied
all by itself.

My dress,
held up by the strings of a loosened belt,
barely stayed on my hips.
Friend,
that's as much as I know now.

When he touched my body,
I couldn't at all remember
who he was,
who I was,
or how It was.

Mahadeviyakka

Selected Poems

Mahadeviyakka, who wrote in the twelfth century, was the foremost woman poet in India before the modern period. She writes in the most characteristic medieval genre of bhakti, *or devotional religious poetry. The poems are addressed to the Hindu gods, but the language is colloquial, and the speaker's carefree—though still devout—attitude gives the poems a very appealing flavor:*

What's to Come Tomorrow

What's to come tomorrow
let it come today.
What's to come today
let it come right now.

Lord white as jasmine,   5
don't give us your nows and thens!

You Can Confiscate

You can confiscate
money in hand;
can you confiscate
the body glory?

Or peel away every strip   5
you wear,

But can you peel
the Nothing, the Nakedness
that covers and veils?

To the shameless girl   10
wearing the White Jasmine Lord's
light of morning,
you fool,
where's the need for cover and jewel?

I Love the Handsome One

I love the Handsome One:
    he has no death
    decay nor form
    no place or side
    no end nor birthmarks.   5
    I love him O mother. Listen.

I love the Beautiful One
    with no bond nor fear
    no clan no land
    no landmarks   10
    for his beauty.

So my lord, white as jasmine, is my husband.

    Take these husbands who die,
    decay, and feed them
    to your kitchen fires!

KALIDASA

Śakuntalā and the Ring of Recollection[1]

Kalidasa's Śakuntalā is among the most popular of Indian plays. Its goal is to recreate emotional harmony among the spectators by revealing the hidden correspondences that unify the apparent contradictions of life. In Act One, which follows, the two primary characters are introduced. As is typical for classical Indian drama, these characters represent generic types, in this case the beautiful maiden and the good and noble king.

Characters

Players in the prologue:

DIRECTOR: Director of the players and manager of the theater.
ACTRESS: The lead actress.

Principal roles:

KING: Duṣyanta, the hero; ruler of Hastināpura; a royal sage of the lunar dynasty of Puru.
ŚAKUNTALĀ: The heroine; daughter of the royal sage Viśvāmitra and the celestial nymph Menakā; adoptive daughter of the ascetic Kaṇva.
BUFFOON: Mādhavya, the king's comical brahman companion.

Members of Kaṇva's hermitage:

ANASŪYĀ AND PRIYAMVADĀ: Two young female ascetics; friends of Śakuntalā.
KAṆVA: Foster father of Śakuntalā and master of the hermitage; a sage belonging to the lineage of the divine creator Marīci, and thus related to Mārīca.
GAUTAMĪ: The senior female ascetic.
ŚĀRṄGARAVA AND ŚĀRADVATA: Kaṇva's disciples.
Various inhabitants of the hermitage: a monk with his two pupils, two boy ascetics (named Gautama and Nārada), a young disciple of Kaṇva, a trio of female ascetics.

Members of the king's forest retinue:

CHARIOTEER: Driver of the king's chariot.
GUARD: Raivataka, guardian of the entrance to the king's quarters.
GENERAL: Commander of the king's army.
KARABHAKA: Royal messenger.
Various attendants, including Greco-Bactrian bow-bearers.

Members of the king's palace retinue:

CHAMBERLAIN: Vātāyana, chief officer of the king's household.
PRIEST: Somarāta, the king's religious preceptor and household priest.
DOORKEEPER: Vetravatī, the female attendant who ushers in visitors and presents messages.
PARABHṚTIKĀ AND MADHUKARIKĀ: Two maids assigned to the king's garden.
CATURIKĀ: A maidservant.

City dwellers:

MAGISTRATE: The king's low-caste brother-in-law; chief of the city's policemen.
POLICEMEN: Sūcaka and Jānuka.
FISHERMAN: An outcaste.

---

[1]Translated by Barbara Stoler Miller.

Celestials:

MĀRĪCA: A divine sage; master of the celestial hermitage in which Śakuntalā gives birth to her son; father of Indra, king of the gods, whose armies Duṣyanta leads.

ADITI: Wife of Mārīca.

MĀTALI: Indra's charioteer.

SĀNUMATĪ: A nymph; friend of Śakuntalā's mother Menakā.

Various members of Mārīca's hermitage: two female ascetics, Mārīca's disciple Gālava.

BOY: Sarvadamana, son of Śakuntalā and Duṣyanta; later known as Bharata.

Offstage voices:

VOICES OFFSTAGE: From the backstage area or dressing room; behind the curtain, out of view of the audience. The voice belongs to various players before they enter the stage, such as the monk, Śakuntalā's friends, the buffoon, Mātali; also to figures who never enter the stage, such as the angry sage Durvāsas, the two bards who chant royal panegyrics (*vaitālikau*).

VOICE IN THE AIR: A voice chanting in the air from somewhere offstage: the bodiless voice of Speech quoted in Sanskrit by Priyaṁvadā; the voice of a cuckoo who represents the trees of the forest blessing Śakuntalā in Sanskrit; the voice of Haṁsapadikā singing a Prakrit love song.

The setting of the play shifts from the forest hermitage (Acts I–IV) to the palace (Acts V–VI) to the celestial hermitage (Act VII). The season is early summer when the play begins and spring during the sixth act; the passage of time is otherwise indicated by the birth and boyhood of Śakuntalā's son.

Act I

The water that was first created,
the sacrifice-bearing fire, the priest,
the time-setting sun and moon,
audible space that fills the universe,
what men call nature,[2] the source of all seeds,   5
the air that living creatures breathe—
through his eight embodied forms,
may Lord Śiva come to bless you![3]

Prologue

DIRECTOR: [*Looking backstage.*] If you are in costume now, madam, please come on stage!   10
ACTRESS: I'm here, sir.[4]

---

[2]Here, earth.

[3]This verse is a *nāndī* ("benedictory verse") recited at the beginning of a Sanskrit play, immediately after the preparatory rituals performed before a dramatic performance in ancient India. The benedictory verses of Sanskrit plays usually invoke the blessings of Śiva, dancer of the cosmic dance of creation and destruction as well as patron god of the drama. In this verse, Kālidāsa praises Śiva as the cosmic divinity pervading the universe in his eight manifest forms—the five elements (ether, air, fire, water, and earth), the sun and moon, and the sacrificing priest.

[4]The prologues to many plays present the actress as the director's wife.

DIRECTOR: Our audience is learned. We shall play Kālidāsa's new drama called *Śakuntalā and the Ring of Recollection*. Let the players take their parts to heart!
ACTRESS: With you directing, sir, nothing will be lost.   15
DIRECTOR: Madam, the truth is:

I find no performance perfect
until the critics are pleased;
the better trained we are
the more we doubt ourselves.   20

ACTRESS: So true . . . now tell me what to do first!
DIRECTOR: What captures an audience better than a song? Sing about the new summer season and its pleasures:

To plunge in fresh waters
swept by scented forest winds   25
and dream in soft shadows
of the day's ripened charms.

ACTRESS: [*Singing.*]

Sensuous women
in summer love
weave   30
flower earrings
from fragile petals
of mimosa
while wild bees
kiss them gently.[5]   35

DIRECTOR: Well sung, madam! Your melody enchants the audience. The silent theater is like a painting. What drama should we play to please it?
ACTRESS: But didn't you just direct us to perform a new play called *Śakuntalā and the Ring of Recollection*?   40
DIRECTOR: Madam, I'm conscious again! For a moment I forgot.

The mood of your song's melody
carried me off by force,
just as the swift dark antelope
enchanted King Dusyanta.   45

[*They both exit; the prologue ends. Then the* KING *enters with his* CHARIOTEER, *in a chariot, a bow and arrow in his hand, hunting an antelope.*]

CHARIOTEER: [*Watching the* KING *and the antelope.*]

I see this black buck move
as you draw your bow
and I see the wild bowman Śiva,
hunting the dark antelope.[6]

KING: Driver, this antelope has drawn us far into the forest. There he is again: 50

---

[5]Such verses are sung by women in Prakrit and set to a melody, whereas the Sanskrit *kāvya* verses of the play are recited or sung to a simple tune that follows the rhythmic pattern of the verse quarter. The women's songs generally feature nature descriptions or the nuances of love in natural settings.

[6]The comparison is based on an ancient myth of Śiva's pursuit of the creator god Prajāpati, who had taken the form of an antelope. The verse flatters the king.

The graceful turn of his neck
as he glances back at our speeding car,
the haunches folded into his chest
in fear of my speeding arrow,   55
the open mouth dropping
half-chewed grass on our path—
watch how he leaps, bounding on air,
barely touching the earth.

[He shows surprise.]
Why is it so hard to keep him in sight?   60
CHARIOTEER: Sir, the ground was rough. I tightened the
    reins to slow the chariot and the buck raced ahead.
    Now that the path is smooth, he won't be hard to
    catch.
KING: Slacken the reins!
CHARIOTEER: As you command, sir. [He mimes the speeding
    chariot.] Look!   65

Their legs extend as I slacken the reins,
plumes and manes set in the wind, ears angle
    back;
our horses outrun their own clouds of dust,
straining to match the antelope's speed.   70

KING: These horses would outrace the steeds of the sun.[7]

What is small suddenly looms large,
split forms seem to reunite,
bent shapes straighten before my eyes—
from the chariot's speed   75
nothing ever stays distant or near.

CHARIOTEER: The antelope is an easy target now. [He mimes
    the fixing of an arrow.]
VOICE OFFSTAGE: Stop! Stop, king! This antelope belongs
    to our hermitage! Don't kill him!
CHARIOTEER: [Listening and watching.] Sir, two ascetics are pro-
    tecting the black buck from your arrow's deadly aim.   80
KING: [Showing confusion.] Rein in the horses!
CHARIOTEER: It is done!
    [He mimes the chariot's halt. Then a MONK enters
    with TWO PUPILS, his hand raised.]
MONK: King, this antelope belongs to our hermitage.
    Withdraw your well-aimed arrow! Your weapon should
        rescue victims, not destroy the innocent!   85
KING: I withdraw it. [He does as he says.]
MONK: An act worthy of the Puru dynasty's shining light!

Your birth honors
the dynasty of the moon![8]   90
May you beget a son
to turn the wheel of your empire![9]

THE TWO PUPILS: [Raising their arms.] May you beget a son
    to turn the wheel of your empire!
KING: [Bowing.] I welcome your blessing.   95

MONK: King, we were going to gather firewood.[1] From
    here you can see the hermitage[2] of our master Kaṇva
    on the bank of the Mālinī river. If your work permits,
    enter and accept our hospitality.

When you see the peaceful rites of devoted ascetics,
you will know how well your scarred arm protects us.[3] 100

KING: Is the master of the community there now?
MONK: He went to Somatīrtha,[4] the holy shrine of the
    moon, and put his daughter Śakuntalā in charge of
    receiving guests. Some evil threatens her, it seems.
KING: Then I shall see her. She will know my devotion and
    commend me to the great sage.   105
MONK: We shall leave you now.
    [He exits with his pupils.]
KING: Driver, urge the horses on! The sight of this holy
    hermitage will purify us.
CHARIOTEER: As you command, sir. [He mimes the chariot's
    speed.]   110
KING: [Looking around.] Without being told one can see that
    this is a grove where ascetics live.
CHARIOTEER: How?
KING: Don't you see—

Wild rice grains under trees   115
where parrots nest in hollow trunks,
stones stained by the dark oil
of crushed iṅgudī nuts[5]
trusting deer who hear human voices
yet don't break their gait,   120
and paths from ponds streaked
by water from wet bark cloth.[6]

CHARIOTEER: It is perfect.
KING: [Having gone a little inside.] We should not disturb the
    grove! Stop the chariot and let me get down!   125
CHARIOTEER: I'm holding the reins. You can dismount now,
    sir.
KING: [Dismounting.] One should not enter an ascetics'
    grove in hunting gear. Take these! [He gives up his or-
    naments and his bow.] Driver, rub down the horses
    while I pay my respects to the residents of the her-
    mitage!   130
CHARIOTEER: Yes, sir! [He exits.]
KING: This gateway marks the sacred ground. I will enter.
    [He enters, indicating he feels an omen.]

The hermitage is a tranquil place,
yet my arm is quivering . . .
do I feel a false omen of love   135
or does fate have doors everywhere?

VOICE OFFSTAGE: This way, friends!

---

[7]The seven horses that draw the sun god's chariot.
[8]Known as the "lunar dynasty," because it traces its descent to the moon
god.
[9]Any ancient Indian emperor is a *cakravartin*, a turner of the wheel of
empire.

[1]For the fire rituals and Vedic sacrifices performed at the hermitage.
[2]It includes men and women and is organized like an extended family.
[3]One of a king's chief duties is to protect hermits and ascetics.
[4]A place of pilgrimage in western India.
[5]These nuts are pressed by forest dwellers for oil.
[6]Forest dwellers wear a cloth made of tree bark.

KING: [*Straining to listen.*] I think I hear voices to the right of the grove. I'll find out.
   [*Walking around and looking.*]
   Young female ascetics with watering pots cradled on their hips are coming to water the saplings. [*He mimes it in precise detail.*] This view of them is sweet.   140

> These forest women have beauty
> rarely seen inside royal palaces—
> the wild forest vines far surpass   145
> creepers in my pleasure garden.

I'll hide in the shadows and wait.

ŚAKUNTALĀ *and her two friends enter, acting as described.*]

ŚAKUNTALĀ: This way, friends!

ANASŪYĀ: I think Father Kaṇva cares more about the trees in the hermitage than he cares about you. You're as delicate as a jasmine, yet he orders you to water the trees.   150

ŚAKUNTALĀ: Anasūyā, it's more than Father Kaṇva's order. I feel a sister's love for them. [*She mimes the watering of trees.*]

KING: [*To himself.*] Is this Kaṇva's daughter? The sage does show poor judgment in imposing the rules of the hermitage on her.   155

> The sage who hopes to subdue
> her sensuous body by penances
> is trying to cut firewood
> with a blade of blue-lotus leaf.

Let it be! I can watch her closely from here in the trees.   160
   [*He does so.*]

ŚAKUNTALĀ: Anasūyā, I can't breathe! Our friend Priyaṁvadā tied my bark dress too tightly! Loosen it a bit!

ANASŪYĀ: As you say. [*She loosens it.*]

PRIYAṀVADĀ: [*Laughing.*] Blame your youth for swelling your breasts. Why blame me?   165

KING: This bark dress fits her body badly, but it ornaments her beauty . . .

> A tangle of duckweed adorns a lotus,
> a dark spot heightens the moon's glow,
> the bark dress increases her charm—   170
> beauty finds its ornaments anywhere.

ŚAKUNTALĀ: [*Looking in front of her.*] The new branches on this mimosa tree are like fingers moving in the wind, calling to me. I must go to it! [*Saying this, she walks around.*]

PRIYAṀVADĀ: Wait, Śakuntalā! Stay there a minute! When you stand by this mimosa tree, it seems to be guarding a creeper.   175

ŚAKUNTALĀ: That's why your name means "Sweet-talk."[7]

KING: "Sweet-talk" yes, but Priyaṁvadā speaks the truth about Śakuntalā:

> Her lips are fresh red buds,   180
> her arms are tendrils,
> impatient youth is poised
> to blossom in her limbs.

ANASŪYĀ: Śakuntalā, this is the jasmine creeper who chose the mango tree in marriage,[8] the one you named "Forestlight." Have you forgotten her?   185

ŚAKUNTALĀ: I would be forgetting myself? [*She approaches the creeper and examines it.*] The creeper and the tree and twined together in perfect harmony. Forestlight has just flowered and the new mango shoots are made for her pleasure.   190

PRIYAṀVADĀ: [*Smiling.*] Anasūyā, don't you know why Śakuntalā looks so lovingly at Forestlight?

ANASŪYĀ: I can't guess.

PRIYAṀVADĀ: The marriage of Forestlight to her tree makes her long to have a husband too.   195

ŚAKUNTALĀ: You're just speaking your own secret wish. [*Saying this, she pours water from the jar.*]

KING: Could her social class be different from her father's?[9] There's no doubt!

> She was born to be a warrior's bride,
> for my noble heart desires her—   200
> when good men face doubt,
> inner feelings are truth's only measure.

Still, I must learn everything about her.

ŚAKUNTALĀ: [*Flustered.*] The splashing water has alarmed a bee. He is flying from the jasmine to my face. [*She dances to show the bee's attack.*]   205

KING: [*Looking longingly.*]

> Bee, you touch the quivering
> corners of her frightened eyes,
> you hover softly near
> to whisper secrets in her ear;
> a hand brushes you away,   210
> but you drink her lips' treasure—
> while the truth we seek defeats us,
> you are truly blessed.

ŚAKUNTALĀ: This dreadful bee won't stop. I must escape. [*She steps to one side, glancing about.*] Oh! He's pursuing me. . . . Save me! Please save me! This mad bee is chasing me!   215

BOTH FRIENDS: [*Laughing.*] How can we save you? Call King Dusyanta. The grove is under his protection.

KING: Here's my chance. Have no fear . . . [*With this half-spoken, he stops and speaks to himself.*] Then she will know that I am the king. . . . Still, I shall speak.   220

ŚAKUNTALĀ: [*Stopping after a few steps.*] Why is he still following me?

---

[7]The characters of the two friends correspond to their names: Anasūyā (Without Envy) is a serious, straightforward, decisive young woman, while Priyamvadā (Sweet Talker) loves to tease and laugh and has a way with words. As noted above, the women speak Prakrit, whereas the king and other upper-class male characters speak Sanskrit.

[8]In calling the jasmine creeper *svayamvara-vadhū* ("bride by her own choice"), Anasūyā refers to the public ceremony called *svayamvara* ("choosing one's own bridegroom") in which women of the warrior class chose their own husbands, thus foreshadowing Śakuntalā's own action later in the play.

[9]Marrying outside one's class in the fourfold Hindu scheme of classes (*varṇa*) is forbidden. As the sage Kaṇva's daughter. Śakuntalā would be a brahman, and the king, being of the *kṣatriya* (warrior) class, would not be allowed to marry her.

KING: [*Approaching quickly.*]

> While a Puru king rules the earth
> to punish evildoers,   225
> who dares to molest
> these innocent young ascetics?

[*Seeing the* KING, *all act flustered.*]

ANASŪYĀ: Sir, there's no real danger. Our friend was frightened when a bee attacked her. [*She points to* ŚAKUNT-
ALĀ.]

KING: [*Approaching* ŚAKUNTALĀ.] Does your ascetic practice
go well? [ŚAKUNTALĀ *stands speechless.*]

ANASŪYĀ: It does now that we have a special guest. Śakuntalā, go to our hut and bring the ripe fruits. We'll use
this water to bathe his feet.[1]   230

KING: Your kind speech is hospitality enough.

PRIYAMVADĀ: Please sit in the cool shadows of this shade
tree and rest, sir.   235

KING: You must also be tired from your work.

ANASŪYĀ: Śakuntalā, we should respect our guest. Let's sit
down. [*All sit.*]

ŚAKUNTALĀ: [*To herself.*] When I see him, why do I feel an
emotion that the forest seems to forbid?

KING: [*Looking at each of the girls.*] Youth and beauty complement your friendship.   240

PRIYAMVADĀ: [*In a stage whisper.*] Anasūyā, who is he? He's
so polite, fine looking, and pleasing to hear. He has
the marks of royalty.

ANASŪYĀ: I'm curious too, friend. I'll just ask him. [*Aloud.*]
Sir, your kind speech inspires trust. What family of
royal sages do you adorn? What country mourns
your absence? Why does a man of refinement subject
himself to the discomfort of visiting an ascetics'
grove?[2]   245

ŚAKUNTALĀ: [*To herself.*] Heart, don't faint! Anasūyā speaks
your thoughts.   250

KING: [*To himself.*] Should I reveal myself now or conceal
who I am? I'll say it this way: [*Aloud.*] Lady, I have
been appointed by the Puru king as the officer in
charge of religious matters. I have come to this sacred
forest to assure that your holy rites proceed unhin-
dered.

ANASŪYĀ: Our religious life has a guardian now.   255
[ŚAKUNTALĀ *mimes the embarrassment of erotic emotion.*]

BOTH FRIENDS: [*Observing the behavior of* ŚAKUNTALĀ *and the*
KING; *in a stage whisper.*] Śakuntalā, if only your father
were here now!

ŚAKUNTALĀ: [*Angrily.*] What if he were?

BOTH FRIENDS: He would honor this distinguished guest
with what he values most in life.

ŚAKUNTALĀ: Quiet! Such words hint at your hearts' conspiracy. I won't listen.   260

KING: Ladies, I want to ask about your friend.

BOTH FRIENDS: Your request honors us, sir.

KING: Sage Kaṇva has always been celibate, but you call
your friend his daughter. How can this be?   265

---

[1]A traditionally mandated rite of hospitality.
[2]Anasūyā uses the formal, florid style of courtly conversation.

ANASŪYĀ: Please listen, sir. There was a powerful royal
sage[3] of the Kauśika clan . . .

KING: I am listening.

ANASŪYĀ: He begot our friend, but Kaṇva is her father because he cared for her when she was abandoned.   270

KING: "Abandoned"? The word makes me curious. I want
to hear her story from the beginning.

ANASŪYĀ: Please listen, sir. Once when this great sage was
practicing terrible austerities on the bank of the
Gautamī river, he became so powerful that the jealous gods sent a nymph named Menakā to break his
self-control.[4]   275

KING: The gods dread men who meditate.

ANASŪYĀ: When springtime came to the forest with all its
charm, the sage saw her intoxicating beauty . . .

KING: I understand what happened then. She is the nymph's
daughter.   280

ANASŪYĀ: Yes.

KING: It had to be!

> No mortal woman could give birth to such beauty—
> lightning does not flash out of the earth.

[ŚAKUNTALĀ *stands with her face bowed. The* KING *continues
speaking to himself.*]
My desire is not hopeless. Yet, when I hear her friends
teasing her about a bridegroom, a new fear divides my
heart.   285

PRIYAMVADĀ: [*Smiling, looking at* ŚAKUNTALĀ, *then turning to
the* KING.] Sir, you seem to want to say more.

[ŚAKUNTALĀ *makes a threatening gesture with her finger.*]

KING: You judge correctly. In my eagerness to learn more
about your pious lives, I have another question.

PRIYAMVADĀ: Don't hesitate! Ascetics can be questioned
frankly.   292

KING: I want to know this about your friend:

> Will she keep the vow of hermit life
> only until she marries . . .
> or will she always exchange
> loving looks with deer in the forest?   295

PRIYAMVADĀ: Sir, even in her religious life, she is subject to
her father, but he does intend to give her to a suitable
husband.

KING: [*To himself.*] His wish is not hard to fulfill.

> Heart, indulge your desire—
> now that doubt is dispelled,   300
> the fire you feared to touch
> is a jewel in your hands.

ŚAKUNTALĀ: [*Showing anger.*] Anasūyā, I'm leaving!

ANASŪYĀ: Why?

---

[3]Viśvāmitra, who was born in the warrior class but acquired the spiritual
powers of a brahman sage.
[4]A standard theme in classical Indian mythology, appearing in the narratives of the life of the Buddha as well. The gods feel threatened by the
supernatural powers that ascetics amass through self-denial.

ŚAKUNTALĀ: I'm going to tell Mother Gautamī that
    Priyaṁvadā is talking nonsense.   *305*
ANASŪYĀ: Friend, it's wrong to neglect a distinguished guest
    and leave as you like.[5]
    [ŚAKUNTALĀ *starts to go without answering.*]
KING: [*Wanting to seize her, but holding back, he speaks to himself.*] A lover dare not act on his impulsive thoughts!

> I wanted to follow the sage's daughter,   *310*
> but decorum abruptly pulled me back;
> I set out and returned again
> without moving my feet from this spot.

PRIYAṀVADĀ: [*Stopping* ŚAKUNTALĀ.] It's wrong of you
    to go!
ŚAKUNTALĀ: [*Bending her brow into a frown.*] Give me a rea-
    son why!   *315*
PRIYAṀVADĀ: You promised to water two trees for me.
    Come here and pay your debt before you go! [*She
    stops her by force.*]
KING: But she seems exhausted from watering the trees:

> Her shoulders droop, her palms
> are red from the watering pot—   *320*
> even now, breathless sighs
> make her breasts shake;
> beads of sweat on her face
> wilt the flower at her ear;
> her hand holds back   *325*
> disheveled locks of hair.

Here, I'll pay her debt!

> [*He offers his ring. Both friends recite the syllables of the
> name on the seal and stare at each other.*][6]

Don't mistake me for what I am not! This is a gift from
the king to identify me as his royal official.
PRIYAṀVADĀ: Then the ring should never leave your finger.
    Your word has already paid her debt. [*She laughs a
    little.*] Śakuntalā, you are freed by this kind man . . .
    or perhaps by the king. Go now!   *330*
ŚAKUNTALĀ: [*To herself.*] If I am able to . . . [*Aloud.*] Who are
    you to keep me or release me?
KING: [*Watching* ŚAKUNTALĀ.] Can she feel toward me what
    I feel toward her? Or is my desire fulfilled?   *335*

> She won't respond directly to my words,
> but she listens when I speak;
> she won't turn to look at me,
> but her eyes can't rest anywhere else.   *340*

VOICE OFFSTAGE: Ascetics, be prepared to protect the crea-
    tures of our forest grove! King Duṣyanta is hunting
    nearby!

> Dust raised by his horses' hooves
> falls like a cloud of locusts swarming
> at sunset over branches of trees   *345*
> where wet bark garments hang.

> In terror of the chariots, an elephant
> charged into the hermitage
> and scattered the herd of black antelope,
> like a demon foe of our penances—   *350*
> his tusks garlanded with branches
> from a tree crushed by his weight,
> his feet tangled in vines
> that tether him like chains.

    [*Hearing this, all the girls are agitated.*]
KING: [*To himself.*] Oh! My palace men are searching for me
    and wrecking the grove. I'll have to go back.   *355*
BOTH FRIENDS: Sir, we're all upset by this news. Please let
    us go to our hut.
KING: [*Showing confusion.*] Go, please. We will try to protect
    the hermitage.   *360*

    [*They all stand to go.*]
BOTH FRIENDS: Sir, we're ashamed that our bad hospitality
    is our only excuse to invite you back.
KING: Not at all. I am honored to have seen you.
    [ŚAKUNTALĀ *exits with her two friends, looking back
    at the* KING, *lingering artfully.*]
I have little desire to return to the city. I'll join my men
and have them camp near the grove. I can't control my
feelings for Śakuntalā.   *365*

> My body turns to go,
> my heart pulls me back,
> like a silk banner
> buffeted by the wind.   *370*

    [*All exit.*]

---

[5]Śakuntalā's failure here foreshadows her neglect of this duty and its consequences later in the play.
[6]A clear indication that women were part of the literate courtly culture
of classical India.

CHAPTER 8

HISTORY

ca. 1050–221 B.C.E.	Zhou dynasty
604 B.C.E.	Laozi born
551–479 B.C.E.	Confucius lives
221 B.C.E.	Qin dynasty (221–206 B.C.E.) first unites China
206–220 C.E.	Han dynasty
ca. 220–590 C.E.	Buddhism spreads
ca. 350 C.E.	Six Dynasties
460–70 C.E.	Buddha of Yun Kang
6th century C.E.	Buddhism introduced to Japan from China
618–907 C.E.	Tang dynasty
907–60 C.E.	Civil war
960–1279	Song dynasty
1271 C.E.	Marco Polo arrives in Hangzhou
1274 C.E., 1281 C.E.	Mongol attacks under Kublai Khan

ARTS AND ARCHITECTURE

12th century B.C.E.	*Fang ding*
433 B.C.E.	Bronze bells
ca. 970 C.E.	Zhu Jan, *Seeking the Tao in the Autumn Mountains*
1072 C.E.	Guo Xi, *Early Spring*

LITERATURE AND PHILOSOPHY

604 B.C.E.	*Tao Te Ching* composed
551–479 B.C.E.	*Analects* composed
6th century B.C.E.	*Book of Songs* compiled
ca. 220–590 C.E.	Midnight Songs composed
365–427 ca.	Tao Qian lives and writes poems
699–761 ca.	Wang Wei lives and writes poems
701–762 ca.	Li Bai lives and writes poems
712–770 ca.	Du Fu lives and writes poems

Early Chinese Civilization

Li Song, *The Red Cliff*, Southern Song dynasty (1127–1279). Album leaf mounted as a hanging scroll, ink and color on silk, ivory roller. $9\frac{3}{4} \times 10\frac{1}{4}''$ (25 × 26 cm), Robert Newcombe/The Nelson-Atkins Museum of Art. Kansas City, Missouri.

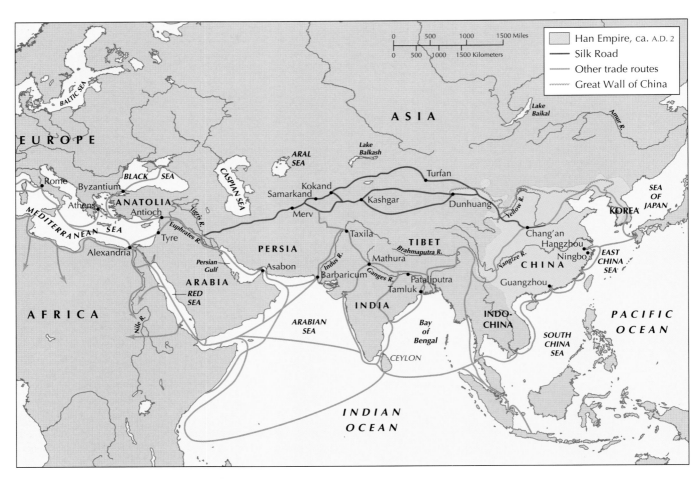

MAP 8.1 Han China and the Silk Road.

CHAPTER OVERVIEW

THE EARLY DYNASTIES

THE EARLY DYNASTIES

THE SHANG AND ZHOU DYNASTIES

CHINA IS THE WORLD'S OLDEST CIVILIZATION, tracing its roots back as far as the fifth millennium B.C.E., although the earliest of the Chinese eras for which archaeological evidence has been found is that of the Shang dynasty, dating from ca. 1600 B.C.E. The Shang dynasty itself was long believed to be only legend and myth, until its existence was verified through twentieth-century excavations. These have yielded not only ancient artifacts but also the oldest examples of Chinese writing, utilizing a separate graph (character) for each word. This written language has remained virtually unchanged for centuries, uniting a country about the size of the United States, where the spoken form of the language has varied so much that it cannot be understood from region to region.

The ancient Shang people inhabited the central Yellow River Valley area of China and developed the most advanced technology of the Chinese Bronze Age. The ruler of the Shang state had a quasi-divine status, which was honored by the people in ritual ceremonies and through serving the ruler in war. The talents of Shang craftworkers were also deployed in honoring their god-king rulers.

Although the oldest Shang cities discovered so far were at Erlitou (2000 B.C.E.) and ZHENGZHOU [Zheng-JOE] (1600 B.C.E.), it is the later city site of Anyang (ca. 1384–1111 B.C.E.) that has yielded the majority of Shang artifacts. At Anyang, archaeologists have found rich burial sites, but no city walls or dwellings, leading them to believe Anyang may have been a royal burial site for another city.

The Shang kings ruled until about eleventh century B.C.E., when the Zhou people came from the northwest and conquered them. The new Zhou dynasty (ca. eleventh century–221 B.C.E.) then introduced organized agriculture, which replaced the Shang emphasis on hunting. The Zhou established a feudal society—in which land was granted to someone by the king or an overlord in return for support in war and loyalty—with the Zhou king ruling as a "T'ien," or "Son of Heaven." The principles of societal relationships that the Zhou formulated were to influence later Chinese civilization, and they can be found in such Chinese classics as the *Book of Odes* and the *Book of Ritual.* Yet although the Zhou modified the social and religious practices of the Shang, they adopted other aspects of Shang culture, in particular the Shang use of bronze casting and their decorative techniques.

Shang and Zhou Bronzes. Although jade and glazed pottery artifacts dating from the Shang dynasty have been found, by far the most numerous and important Shang artifacts are made of bronze. These, buried with the dead, were presumably meant to serve the king or nobleman in his future life. The *fang ding* (fig. 8.1) was used for storing food and wine for social and religious ceremonial functions. The emphasis on animal motifs, which is typical of the intricate ornamental design found in Shang bronze artifacts, suggests the importance of hunting in Shang culture. The most important and numerous of these mysterious motifs is the T'ao-t'ieh mask, which can be

FIGURE 8.1 *Fang ding,* Tomb 1004, Houjiazhang, Anyang, Henan, Shang dynasty, bronze, twelfth century B.C.E., © The British Museum. The ornate design on this square vessel was typical for Shang bronze artifacts, suggesting both animals and more mysterious forms of life.

found hidden within the surface patterns of most Shang and Zhou period bronzes. The creature can most easily be found by locating its two eyes, then deciphering the rest of its facial features.

Such bronze objects remained of great importance throughout the Zhou period that followed. In addition to being buried in graves, bronzes were now also used to honor the living, as inscriptions carved in their bases indicate. One indication of the great wealth of the Zhou rulers is the monumental carillon, consisting of sixty-five bronze bells, discovered in the tomb of Marquis Yi of Zheng (fig. 8.2). Each of the bells, believed to have been used in rituals to communicate with the supernatural, produces two quite distinct tones when struck near the center or at the rim.

CHINESE PHILOSOPHY

CONFUCIANISM

Toward the middle of the Zhou dynasty, the two great philosophical and religious traditions indigenous to China took hold: Confucianism and Taoism. Like Buddhism (see Chapter 7), which would later have its own impact on China, **Confucianism** is based on the teachings of one man. CONFUCIUS [con-FYOU-shus] (551–479 B.C.E.) was the son of aristocratic parents who had lost their wealth during the decline of feudalism in China. Confucius's father died before he was born, and he was raised by his mother in poverty. He received an education from the village tutor, studying poetry, history, music, hunting, fishing, and archery, the traditional educational disciplines of the time. After a brief stint as a government official, Confucius embarked on a career as a teacher. He wandered from place to place, offering his services as an adviser on human conduct and on government. After many years as a successful and famous teacher, Confucius spent the last part of his life quietly teaching at home.

After his death, Confucius's sayings, along with those of his followers, were collected together during the fifth century in a volume called *The Analects.* Drawing on cultural values anchored in ancient Chinese tradition, these eminently practical sayings focus on this world rather than the next. Although Confucius deeply respected the Chinese cultural heritage, valuing its best aspects, he adapted ancient traditions to the circumstances of his own time. Living in a period of political chaos and moral confusion, Confucius emphasized the importance of the traditional values of self-control, propriety, and filial piety to maintain a productive and good society. It was through such virtues that Confucius believed anarchy could be overcome and social cohesion restored.

Confucius's point of departure was the individual rather than society. He believed that if each individual could be virtuous, the family would live in harmony. Similarly, if each family lived according to certain moral principles,

FIGURE 8.2   Bronze bells, Zhou dynasty, 433 B.C.E., frame height 9′ (2.74 m), length 25′ (7.62 m), Hubei Provincial Museum, Wuhan. Not only a major feat of bronze casting, these bells are also a musical marvel, with two different notes available from each bell.

the village would be harmonious. Village harmony, in turn, would lead to a country focused on moral values, coupled with an aesthetic sensibility that would allow life to be lived to its fullest creative potential.

Four qualities in particular—*li, jen, te,* and **wen**—were valued in Confucian teaching. *Li* equates to propriety, ceremony, and civility, and it requires the development of proper attitudes and a due respect for established forms of conduct. At its heart are the four basic social rules of human relationships: courtesy, politeness, good manners, and respect, especially a reverence for age. These are supplemented by a fifth rule or concept, that of *yi*, or duty, a sense of the obligation one has to others. These five key rules strongly underpin the centrality of the family in Chinese life. Children's duty to their parents is the root from which moral and social virtues grow. In talking to an older person, for example, the younger person responds only after the elder has spoken. The younger person also listens with due deference and does not interrupt or contradict.

Jen, sometimes translated as benevolence, refers to the ideal relationship that should exist between people. Based on respect for oneself, *jen* extends this respect to others and manifests itself in acts of charity and courtesy. According to the Confucian ideal, *jen* and *li* together make for a superior human being.

Te refers to virtue. Originally it referred to the quality of greatness that enabled an individual to subdue enemies, inspire respect, and influence others. However, in Confucian teaching it came to signify a different kind of power—that of moral example rather than that of physical strength or might. A strong leader who guides by example exhibits *te*. So do the forces of nature, as the following saying from *The Analects* illustrates:

Asked by the ruler whether the lawless should be executed, Confucius answered: "What need is there of the death penalty in government? If you showed a sincere desire to be good, your people would likewise be good. The virtue of the prince is like the wind; the virtue of the people is like grass. It is the nature of grass to bend when the wind blows upon it."

The final characteristic of Confucian tradition, *wen*, refers to the arts of peace, that is, to music, poetry, art, and other cultural activities. Confucius considered the arts a form of moral education. He saw music as especially conducive to order and harmony, and he believed the greatest painting and poetry function in the same way as an excellent leader, since they provide a model of excellence.

Ultimately, Confucius was an empiricist, justifying the value of his moral prescriptions by an appeal to experience. His teachings were designed to help his followers live a better individual and communal life in the present rather than to achieve an eternal reward after death. Morality, moreover, depended on context. There was no inflexible "thou shalt not." Instead, any moral decision was guided by the circumstances of a particular problem.

TAOISM

Like Confucianism, TAOISM [DOW-ism] is principally concerned with morality and ethical behavior insofar as they benefit people in the present world. Thus it is often considered a philosophy rather than a religion. Its founder was LAOZI [LOW-ZEE] (b. 604 B.C.E.), whose name means "the Old Master." Little is known about him, although a number of legends exist to explain how he came to write the *Tao Te Ching (The Way and Its Power)*, which summarizes Taoist teaching. In the most popular of these legends, Laozi, having retired from court life, was journeying out of China when a guard at a mountain pass recognized him and insisted he write down the sum of his wisdom before leaving the country.

The Tao (or Dao) is the ultimate reality behind existence, a transcendent and eternal spiritual essence. Mysterious and mystical, it is finally impossible to define in words. As the *Tao Te Ching* states, "Tao called Tao is not Tao, names can name no lasting name. . . . Tao is the mysterious center of all things."

At the same time, however, the Tao is immanent, existing in nature and manifesting its ordering principle in the cycle of the seasons, the flowing of rivers, and the singing of birds. In this sense, Tao is the governing order of life represented by the rhythm and force of nature. "Tao in action: vague and intangible, shadowy and obscure, but within it there is life, life so real that within it there is trust. Look—you won't see it; listen—you won't hear it; use it— you will never use it up."

Taoism is also a way of ordering one's life so as to achieve peace and harmony with the rest of creation.

"The ancients who followed Tao were dark, wondrous, profound, penetrating, deep beyond knowing. Because they cannot be known, they can only be described: cautious, like crossing a winter stream; hesitant, like re-

specting one's neighbors; polite, like a guest; yielding, like ice about to melt; blank, like uncarved wood; open, like a valley; mixing freely, like muddy water. Calm the muddy water, it becomes clear; move the inert, it comes to life.

Like Confucianism, Taoism values *te*, or power: "Great *te* appears flowing from Tao." In Taoism, however, *te* is the sense of essential identity and integrity. The characteristic nature of each thing is its *te*; for a person it is integrity or genuineness—one's authentic self at its best. Instead of competition, *te* proposes cooperation; instead of insistent willfulness, patient attentiveness. "Knowing others is intelligent, knowing oneself is profound; therefore the sage desires no desires, prizes no prizes, but helps all beings find their own nature."

Along with *te*, Taoists encourage **wu-wei** (nonaction), a kind of creative calm without excessive purposefulness, involving relaxing the conscious mind. Like the Buddhist and Hindu ascetic ideals, *wu-wei* seeks the denial of the personal and the dissolution of the conscious individual self. "Those highest in *te* take no action, and don't need to act. Those lowest in *te* take action, and do need to act. . . . Tao bears them and *te* nurses them, rears them, supports them, shelters them, nurtures them, supports them, protects them."

Taoism further illustrates the concept of *wu-wei* with examples from nature, especially water. Supple yet strong, water adapts itself to its surroundings, flowing over or filling what it encounters. "Best to be like water, which benefits the ten thousand things and does not contend. It pools where humans disdain to dwell, close to the Tao."

The Taoist ideal of **p'u**, which literally means "unpainted wood," stresses simplicity. The Taoist prefers unvarnished wood, and thus Taoist architecture employs wood in its natural state, leaving gilt and lacquer to the Confucians, along with ceremonialism and the intricate forms and formulas of civilized life. Taoist painting uses only simple lines, suggesting much in little. Human figures in such paintings are kept small in relation to the vastness of nature.

Taoism and Confucianism together represent the yin and yang of Chinese religious philosophy. They are complementary sides of a complex and intricate system of belief and behavior. The table below identifies the contrasting yet complementary features of these two systems of thought.

CONFUCIANISM AND TAOISM

Confucianism represents the classical; Taoism represents the romantic.

Confucianism stresses social responsibility; Taoism stresses responsibility toward nature.

Confucianism emphasizes humans; Taoism emphasizes nature.

Confucianism is practical; Taoism is mystical.

The Chinese say that Confucius roams with society, whereas Laozi roams beyond it. They also tell a story about a Confucian and a Taoist that reflects the difference in tone and style between the two approaches to life.

The Taoist Zhuangzi and the Confucianist Huizi were walking together over a bridge when Zhuangzi said, "Look how the minnows dart here and there at will. Such is the pleasure fish enjoy." "You are not a fish," retorted Huizi. "How do you know what pleasures fish experience?" "You are not I," responded Zhuangzi. "How do you know I do not know what gives pleasure to fish?"

Yin and Yang.   One of the best known of all Chinese images is that of the yin and yang (fig. 8.3). **Yin and yang** represent contrasting but complementary principles that sum up life's basic opposing elements—pain and pleasure, good and evil, light and dark, male and female, and so on. Instead of seeing these contrasting elements as contradictory, the Chinese emphasize the way in which they interact with and complement one another.

Illustrating the philosophical ideal of harmonious integration, the two forms, yin and yang, coexist peacefully within a larger circle. Each form provides the border for its opposite, partly defining it. In the very center of each form, there is the defining aspect of the complementary form: The dark teardrop contains a spot of white; the white teardrop includes a small dark circle. One cannot exist without the other.

Yin is the negative form, associated with earth, darkness, and passivity. Conversely, the yang form is positive and associated with heaven, light, and the constructive impulse. Yin and yang represent the perpetual interplay and mutual relation of all things.

Lyric Poetry.   Unlike most national literatures, which typically have their origins in prose tales, epic poetry, or other narrative forms, the earliest known Chinese literature is lyric poetry. Lyrics are usually written to be set to music and are personal in nature. Educated Chinese were expected not only to understand and appreciate poetry, but also to compose it.

The Book of Songs, which contains material passed down orally from as far back as the tenth century B.C.E., was first

FIGURE 8.3   The yin/yang symbol. Yin and yang represent the complementary negative and positive principles of the universe.

written down in the sixth century B.C.E. in Confucius's time. It is one of the five ancient Confucian classics, and some scholars have suggested that Confucius himself edited the collection. The poems are variously concerned with love and war, lamentation and celebration, and reflect the perspectives of all strata of ancient Chinese society, from peasants to kings.

As suggested by its title, *The Book of Songs* contains poems meant to be accompanied by music. More than half of the 305 poems are classified as folk songs; the remainder were either written for performance at court or as part of a ritual. The individualism and occasional rebelliousness of the speakers in the poems sometimes make them seem at odds with the Confucian ideal. However, the depth of feeling they express and the richness of the experience they draw on have ensured that *The Book of Songs* remains not only popular but also essential reading for educated Chinese to the present day.

Music.   During the time of Confucius and Laozi, music was categorized according to its social functions. Particular types of music played on certain instruments in specified tonalities were designated for use in accompanying the chanting of poetry, the worship of ancestors, as well as at court banquets, country feasts, archery contests, military parades, and the like. Confucius, like Plato, believed music should be used to educate. Music was meant to display the qualities of moderation and harmony, mirroring the emphasis that Confucius placed on those virtues in social and political life. Certain dangerous aspects of music were to be avoided, such as its ability to induce excited states of emotion.

EMPIRE: THE QIN AND HAN DYNASTIES

Both Confucianism and Taoism developed in response to the political instability of the Zhou dynasty, which began to be undermined by invasions from the west in 771 B.C.E. Political fragmentation continued until the QIN [CHIN—the origin of the name China] dynasty (221–206 B.C.E.) unified the country for the first time.

Although the Qin dynasty's rule was brief, it introduced many measures to ensure that the empire could be ruled efficiently and would remain unified, which indeed it has been almost always to the present day. The Qin rulers established a central bureaucracy, divided the country into administrative units, and standardized the writing system, as well as the currency, weights, and measures. All citizens were made subject to Qin laws, and everyone had to pay taxes to the Qin emperor.

The Qin initiated major building projects—networks of roads and canals that would link the different parts of the empire. It was also the Qin who created most of the 1,400-mile-long Great Wall as a defense for their empire against invaders from the northwest. The Great Wall was made in part by joining together the border walls of the formerly independent regions, and it remains one of the world's most remarkable structures, visible from high in space.

There was a downside to this great imperial ambition, however. In order to maintain control, the Qin suppressed free speech, persecuting scholars and destroying classical literary and philosophical texts, which were only preserved by the ingenuity of those who memorized and later reconstructed them. Confucianism was temporarily supplanted with a new philosophical system called *Legalism* created by Qin intellectuals. Reflecting a belief in the absolute power of the emperor, Qin rule proved so harsh that rebellions soon broke out and the dynasty was overthrown after only fifteen years in power.

Some idea of the aspirations of grandeur of the Qin dynasty can be gained from viewing the tomb of the first Qin emperor, QIN SHI HUANG DI [CHIN-SHEE-HUANG-DI] (r. 221–206 B.C.E.) (fig. 8.4). Excavators working in Shaanxi province inadvertently uncovered thousands of lifesize terra cotta figures, that had been buried in the emperor's tomb to accompany and serve him in the afterlife. The emperor's burial ground was also richly stocked with furniture, as well as with wooden chariots, and even

contained a model of the Qin universe, with representations of rivers and constellations of stars and planets.

With the advent of the Han dynasty (206 B.C.E.–220 C.E.), Chinese culture found its most characteristic and defining forms. Han emperors restored Confucianism to favor, making it the state philosophy, established a national academy to train civil servants, and reinvigorated classical learning by honoring scholars and employing them in the national bureaucracy.

It was under the Han dynasty that the Silk Road trade route was established. It was along this route that goods traveled from China to India, and on to Greece and finally Rome. It was also on the Silk Road that religious missionaries from the West brought Christianity to India and Persia, and even more significantly, that Buddhism spread from India into China, where it soon flourished.

THE SIX DYNASTIES

Intrigue and rebellion led to political and social disunity during the period of the "Six Dynasties" (220–589 C.E.), which followed the Han dynasty. Warring factions fought for control of the country, with six successive dynasties

FIGURE 8.4 Tomb figures, from the mausoleum of the first Qin emperor, Lintong, Shaanxi. Qin dynasty, ca. 210 B.C.E., terra cotta, lifesize. This army of soldiers, found buried near the mausoleum of the first Qin emperor, was meant to serve him in the afterlife.

Then & Now

EAST/WEST TRADE

Trade between Asia and the West has an ancient history, with the Silk Road its earliest and most important route. In the early twenty-first century, trade between East and West continues to flourish. Now, however, the goods travel by boat and plane rather than by camel. Communication occurs via phone, fax, and computer. And the international language of communication is, for the most part, English.

The northwest coast of the United States trades vigorously with the Asian countries of the Pacific Rim. These include but are not limited to China, Korea, Indonesia, and Japan. Western Europe has long carried on significant trade with Japan, and now with China's membership in the World Trade Organization, with China as well. Throughout the United States, trade with Southeast Asia, especially Vietnam, has increased dramatically with the normalization of U.S.–Vietnamese relations

twenty years after the end of the Vietnam War.

Many U.S. and Western European companies anticipate a long and financially rewarding relationship as countries such as China and Vietnam enter the world of telecommunications and computing. One thing is virtually certain. As long as political stability exists in Asia, and as long as Asian governments are receptive to open markets, trade between East and West will increase dramatically in the twenty-first century.

---

gaining power for a brief time. From this period of political turmoil there survives a series of monumental stone sculptures cut into caves at Yun Kang (Yungang, Shanxi), testifying to the fervor with which many Chinese accepted Buddhism. The most colossal of these is a forty-five-foot-high image of the Buddha (fig. 8.5), made around 460–470 C.E. The statue is carved directly into the rock cave, in the manner of Indian monumental sculpture, from which the figure clearly derives (compare fig. 7.6). This earliest of Buddhist styles of sculpture in China has been termed "archaic," and, as in ancient Greece (see fig. 2.22), the figures characteristically wear what has been called an "archaic smile."

THE TANG DYNASTY

At the end of the Six Dynasties period, the Sui rulers (581–618 C.E.) reunited China. The Sui, the last of the six dynasties, were quickly overcome, however, by the Tang dynasty, who went on to reestablish China as a world power during nearly three hundred years of prosperity and cultural enrichment (618–907 C.E.).

The Tang emperors restored the Silk Road, which had fallen into disuse during the Six Dynasties period, forging trade and cultural links with other countries, especially Persia, India, and, by sea, Japan. During the Tang dynastic period, literature and the other arts were held in high esteem, with civil servants and gentry required to master calligraphy, as well as the Confucian classics, and to compose poetry of their own.

Li Bai and Du Fu.   Much early Chinese poetry was composed according to ancient folk-song models. These poems were called **shih.** Two of the great practitioners of shih were Li Bai, previously known as Li Po (701–762) and DU FU [DOO FOO] (712–770). Both poets have long been

associated with Confucianism and Taoism. Du Fu is often described as a Confucian poet, since his poems stress the importance of love of family and of harmonious social relationships. They also celebrate the Confucian ideals of self-discipline and serenity.

The poems of Li Bai are written in a more open style and take greater liberties with the formal poetic conventions of the time than the poems of Du Fu. Li Bai (fig. 8.6) has been described as a poetic individualist and a precursor of the Western Romantic poets (see Chapter 18). His verse has been profoundly influential in China and also in Japan, where he is known as Rihaku. Through the translations of Ezra Pound and the sinologist Arthur Waley, he has also had a strong impact on modern American poetry.

THE SONG DYNASTY

When the Tang dynasty came to an end in 907, China was thrown into a half century of civil war. The empire was reunified in 960 under the Song rulers, who inaugurated a period of great technological advancement. During the Song dynasty (960–1279), China saw within its borders the invention of the navigational compass, paper currency, gunpowder, and printing, well before Gutenberg's invention of movable type in fifteenth-century Germany. The rule of the Song emperors created two conditions necessary for artistic development: first, an abundance of leisure time, which allowed for intellectual pursuits, including a reformulation of Confucian ideals; second, the availability of patronage, which helped bring about a resurgence in the art of painting and, with it, elaborations of art theory.

Painting.   The art of painting flourished during the Song period. *Seeking the Tao in the Autumn Mountains* (fig. 8.8),

FIGURE 8.5   Colossal Buddha, cave 20, Yungang, Shaanxi, 460–470 C.E., stone, height 45′ (13.72 m). Carved out of living rock, this huge image demonstrates the importance of Buddhism in China during a time of nearly incessant warfare.

by ZHU JAN [JOO JAN] (active. ca. 960–980), is, as its title suggests, representative of the Taoist-influenced artistic tradition. Huge mountains evoke a sense of the remote and the eternal; rising dramatically and powerfully in the center of the painting, they suggest the modest position of humanity in the grand scale of the natural world.

Neo-Confucianism, which developed during the Song dynasty, unified Taoism and Buddhism into a single system of thought. *Early Spring* (fig. 8.9), by GUO XI [GOO-OH SEE] (after 1000–ca. 1090), embodies the Confucian ideal of *li*, which is the principle at the heart of nature. As in Zhu Jan's painting, the human presence in this landscape

passes almost unnoticed, so vast is the scale of the central mountain. Small figures can be identified in the lower foreground on both the left and right, and in the middle distance on the right a village is tucked between the hills. The mountain, representing nature, is a powerful symbol of eternity that dwarfs human existence.

A court painter during the reign of Emperor Shenzong (r. 1068–1085), Guo Xi was given the task of painting all the murals in the Forbidden City, the imperial compound in Beijing that foreigners were prohibited from entering. His ideas about painting were recorded by his son in a book entitled *The Lofty Message of the Forests and Streams.*

Connections

THE SEVEN SAGES OF THE BAMBOO GROVE

According to semi-legendary tradition, early in the Six Dynasties period seven Taoist poet-philosophers, seeking relief from the formalities of Confucianism, began to hold meetings in a bamboo grove. There, these "Seven Sages" gathered to consider the spiritual side of their life, write and discuss poetry, play musical instruments, play chess, contemplate nature, and, perhaps above all, drink wine. The latter, they felt, released the spirit from all constraint. As one famous saying of the Sages had it,

> Brief indeed is a man's life!
> So, let's sing over our wine.

Ruan Ji was said to have given up a high official post in order to live near a brewery. In one of his famous poems, entitled "Singing from My Heart," he remembers his seriousness as a youth and comments that now "I mock myself for my past gloom." Liu Ling, another sage, wrote the "Hymn to the Virtue of Wine" and is notorious for having tricked his teetotaling wife by telling her he too had decided to give up alcohol and having her prepare a feast for the gods, and then drinking all the wine intended for the gods himself.

The Seven Sages inaugurated a tradition that would last for many centuries in China. During the Tang dynasty, the poet Li Bai took his followers on a similar retreat to a garden of peach and plum trees on a moonlit spring night. There, they too drank wine and, having liberated themselves from the constraints of their everyday lives, composed their poems. Both the gathering of the Seven Sages in the bamboo grove and Li Bai's conclave in the orchard would be a subject for painters for generations to come (fig. 8.6).

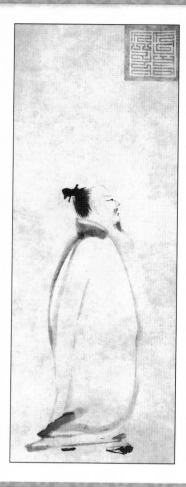

FIGURE 8.6　Liang Kai, *The Poet Li Bai Walking and Chanting a Poem*, Southern Song dynasty, ca. 1200, hanging scroll, ink on paper, 31″ × 11⅞″ (80.6 × 30.2 cm), Tokyo National Museum, Japan. This depiction of Li Bai, considered Zen in style, juxtaposes the quick brushstrokes used to describe the robe with the precise and detailed work on his face.

Critical Thinking

MARCO POLO

The most famous medieval Westerner believed to have contact with medieval China is Marco Polo (1254–1324) of Venice. His *Travels* describes his journey through China, Burma, and Tibet, and include his description of the city of Hangzhou, famed for its bridges and canals, as well as of the palace and kingdom of Kublai Khan in Mongolia. Some scholars, however, have cast doubt on the authenticity of Marco Polo's descriptions. They argue, for example, that he exaggerated what he saw to attract readers, and that his not mentioning perhaps one of the greatest and most awesome of sights—the Great Wall of China—indicates that he may not have actually been in China at all. Suspicion about his book has arisen also because Polo himself is absent from his *Travels*. His book, some say, is more of a medieval bestiary that describes strange (and wildly imaginary) creatures. Others contend that much of the geography, history, and anthropology included in Polo's book are authentic.

How would you go about deciding which of these scholars to believe? What kinds of evidence would you look for to confirm, refute, or qualify Marco Polo's descriptions of what he saw on his travels through medieval China? And how might you explain his absence from the *Travels* and his neglect of the Great Wall?

FIGURE 8.7 Liang King, *Scholar of the Eastern Fence*, China, ca. thirteenth century. © National Palace Museum, Taiwan, Republic of China. This portrait of the poet and scholar Tao Qian identifies him with the eastern fence of his property, against which his beloved chrysanthemums thrived. The poet-recluse is framed by pines, emblematic of consistency and integrity, and by red-leaved trees suggesting autumnal decline and old age.

FIGURE 8.8 Zhu Jan, *Seeking the Tao in the Autumn Mountains*, ca. 970, ink on silk, 61 × 30″ (156.2 × 78.1 cm), National Palace Museum, Taipei, Taiwan. Long sweeping brushstrokes complemented by carefully placed dots of dark ink accentuate the mountain's grandeur as they guide the viewer's gaze upward.

FIGURE 8.9 Guo Xi, *Early Spring*, Northern Song dynasty, 1072, hanging scroll, ink and slight color on silk, height 5' (1.52 m), National Palace Museum, Taipei, Taiwan. This landscape represents the integration of three different forms of perspective: high distance (looking up at the main peak), deep distance (looking down into valleys), and level distance (looking across marshes).

According to this interpretation, the central peak in *Early Spring* symbolizes the emperor himself, its tall pines the gentlemanly ideals of the court. Here Guo Xi has painted the ideal Confucian and Buddhist world; the emperor, like the Buddha surrounded by his bodhisattvas, gathers all around him, just as in *Early Spring* the mountain, the trees, and the hills suggest the proper order and rhythm of the universe.

Another form of painting also began in the Song dynasty, practiced by and for the scholar-poet-artists who served as officials, and therefore could practice their art as amateurs. This became known as the literati school, and was to become the single most important tradition in Chinese art in succeeding dynasties. One of the leading figures in this movement was the poet-calligrapher Su Shi (1036–1101), who wrote that painting merely to depict outer reality was like the work of a child, and true painters became so totally immersed that their art came from within

themselves. For example, he wrote that his friend Wen Tong (1018–1079), when he painted bamboo, "forgot himself and became a bamboo."

In his two prose poems written in 1082 on the "Red Cliff" (fig. 8.10) where a famous battle had been fought centuries earlier, Su Shi gave voice to fundamental literati views of humans and nature, with a Buddhist sense of human impermanence. He has been out boating with a companion, and soon his friend becomes melancholy at the fleeting nature of life and fame, saying, "we are no more than the flies of summer, grains of millet on the ocean vastness—it grieves me that life is so short." Su replies that the river flows and the moon waxes and wanes, but they are always the same river and moon. "If we look at things from the eyes of change, there's not an instant of stillness in the universe. But if we observe the changelessness of things, then we, and all beings, have no end. . . . The clear breeze over the river, the bright moon over the hills, these we may enjoy and they will never be exhausted."

Ceramics. Among the most important of China's contributions is the development of a highly-refined art of ceramics. For over 3000 years, Chinese potters have produced masterpieces of ceramics in an amazing variety of shapes, colors, and decorative styles. Among the best known and most appreciated in the west are Tang porcelain pieces—tomb figures, horses, camels, soldiers, and courtesans, among others. Equally prized are the fine de-

FIGURE 8.10 Li Song, *The Red Cliff*, Southern Song dynasty (1127–1279). Album leaf mounted as a hanging scroll, ink and color on silk, ivory roller. $9\frac{3}{4} \times 10\frac{1}{4}"$ (24.76 × 26.03 cm). Robert Neucombe/The Nelson-Atkins Museum of Art, Kansas City, Missouri. The small but nevertheless significant figures, viewing the cliff from the boat, are a visualization of the prose poetry of Su Shi, in which feelings of unity with nature can dispel human unhappiness.

Cross Currents

MARCO POLO'S HANGZHOU

Little was known about China and the Far East in the West before the nineteenth century. One of the most important sources was the account written by the Venetian traveler Marco Polo (ca. 1254–1324). His description of the Song capital, Hangzhou, is particularly vivid.

Hangzhou, formerly called Kinsai, or the "City of Heaven," might also have been called the "City of Bridges," since twelve thousand wood and stone bridges cross its wide waterways. Described by Polo, who arrived in the city in 1271, as, "without doubt the finest and most splendid city in the world," Hangzhou in the Song dynasty was an important commercial center as well as the imperial capital of China. Its population—of more than a million people—was then the largest in the world. Thirty-foot-high crenelated walls, studded with tow-ers, protected the city against enemy attack. Guards stationed strategically at the bridges to repulse invaders also served as timekeepers, striking a gong and drum to mark the passing of the hours.

On the city's streets, porters carried goods suspended from long poles in baskets and jars. On its canals, boats and ships of many sizes transported food and building materials. Its markets, open three days a week in the city's squares, were crammed with food and spices, books and flowers, cloth and gemstones, in addition to a huge variety of meats and game. Dress, as in the West, was a mark of social and financial status for both women and men. The rank of **mandarins** (government officials) was indicated by robes and headgear. On special occasions, these mandarins wore silk robes embroidered with flowers, animals, and symbols. Their belt buckles were made of jade or rhinoceros horn, and their caps were adorned with buttons, again signaling the officials' importance.

Among the places people congregated were parks and lakes, especially the great West Lake, often filled with boats, barges, and floating teahouses, from which passengers could view the numerous palaces, temples, pagodas, and pavilions that dotted the surrounding landscape. On land, the wealthy congregated in clubs and centers to read poems, enjoy plays, song, and dance, as well as to practice calligraphy and painting. It was especially important for young men with the ambition to become scholar officials to become well versed in the Chinese classics in preparation for the civil service examinations. Young women were also expected to take lessons, with classes in music, dancing, spinning, embroidery, and social etiquette preparing them for the good marriages they hoped to contract.

---

signs of flowers and animals enlivened by special effects of "partridge feather," "hare's fur," and "oil spot," used on white, ivory, willow, celadon and shades of blue porcelain produced during the Song dynasty. The Chinese were able to create such astonishing ceramic and porcelain works due to their understanding of how to control kiln temperatures and to their extensive knowledge of glazes, including how to mix them to create unusual effects of color.

Song ceramics are valued for their superb integration of shape, glaze, and decoration, evidencing an outstanding command of the technical aspects of potting, firing, and glazing techniques by Song ceramics masters. The shape of Song ceramic ware tends toward the simple and elegant (fig. 8.11). Unlike Tang dynasty ceramic pieces, in which a clear distinction is evident among the neck, body, and foot, Song ceramic ware blends these three parts in a unified and flowing harmony. The glazes of Song ceramics tend to be monochromatic and also done in a flat or matte finish rather than polished to a high glaze shine. When decoration is used (and it is used sparingly in Song ceramics), it serves to enhance the form of the piece rather than to attract attention to itself.

Calligraphy and Writing. Unlike the West, where calligraphy, or beautiful writing, is considered a minor art, in China the art of calligraphy has long enjoyed a high status among the arts. At the heart of the higher forms of Chinese culture and one of the three perfections or gentlemanly arts, calligraphy is linked with its companion arts of poetry and painting. All three—poetry, painting, and calligraphy—were considered aspects of the same aesthetic expression since poems were written in calligraphy and paintings were typically accompanied by such calligraphied poems. An example by Su Shih (1036–1101) is seen in figure 8.12.

Because writing and calligraphy were held in such high esteem, the brushes used in their creation were highly valued, some considered works of art in their own right, much as a violin bow might be so considered. In recording the movements of hand, wrist, and arm, the calligraphy brush acts like a kind of seismograph, through which a person's calligraphy conveys something essential about the calligrapher. In producing calligraphy according to the ancient rules and guidelines, the writer reveals his character and spirit as well as his or her intentions.

Finally, it should be remembered that Chinese art forms a continuum with religion, politics, philosophy, and everyday life. Just as painting, poetry, and calligraphy are aspects of a single harmonious artistic whole, so too are the related aspects of creating art, collecting it, studying it, and writing about its history and philosophy.

Cultural Impact

Among the many legacies left by ancient Chinese culture has been the influence of its Tang dynasty poets, especially Li Bai (Li Po). The American modernist poet Ezra Pound, with the help of the Asian scholar Ernest Fenellosa, made a series of translations or adaptations of Li Bai's poems, the most famous of these is *The River-Merchant's Wife: A Letter.* More important than any single poem, however, was the adoption of a modernist literary aesthetic that emphasizes the importance of the image to convey a poem's meaning and feeling. This Pound and other modernist poets derived from their reading of Li Bai and Tang dynasty poets.

The ethical and philosophical legacy of Confucianism remains a major influence, particularly in its Neo-Confucianist form, which incorporates Buddhist thought within a Confucian value system. Neo-Confucianism has influenced East Asian thought over a long period of time, and remains today a dominant factor in Korea. Vietnam, and Japan, where it has shaped moral thought and traditional cultural values. In addition, Chinese commodities such as silk, porcelain, and lacquerware remain highly prized. And, of course, the Chinese inventions of gunpowder, paper, and the magnetic compass have had an enormous impact throughout history.

FIGURE 8.11 Celadon vase. Height 11″ (28 cm). China. Song dynasty. Song ceramics pieces were often glazed with various shades of green.

FIGURE 8.12 Fragment of calligraphy by Su Shih (1036–1101) of his poem "Cold Provisions Day." Su Shih was a fine scholar, poet, and calligrapher, and a noted painter of bamboo.

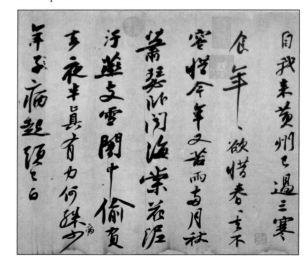

KEY TERMS

Confucianism	*te*	*p'u*	Neo-Confucianism
li	*wen*	yin and yang	mandarins
yi	Taoism	*shih*	
jen	*wu-wei*		

WWW. **WEBSITES FOR FURTHER STUDY**

http://www.friesian.com/confuci.htm
(This is a worthwhile site on Confucian philosophy.)

http://www.wsu.edu/~dee/CHIINRES.HTM #Philosophy
(Visit this site for a thorough explanation of yin and yang and Chinese philosophy.)

http://www.chinavista.com/experience/shijing/shijing.html
(Shijing [The Book of Songs] is the earliest collection of Chinese poems including 305 poems of the Zhou dynasty (1122–256 B.C.E.). The page has one of the poems in translation, but the whole page can be converted to two forms of Chinese.)

READINGS

The Book of Songs

Selected Poems

The following lyrics from the ancient Chinese Book of Songs *reflect the importance of appropriate social behavior. They also reveal the way ancient Chinese poets used imagery, particularly images from nature to convey emotion.*

She Threw a Quince to Me

She threw a quince to me;
In requital I gave a bright girdle-gem.
No, not just as requital;
But meaning I would love her for ever.

She threw a tree-peach to me;   *5*
As requital I gave her a bright greenstone.
No, not just as requital;
But meaning I would love her for ever.

She threw a tree-plum to me;
In requital I gave her a bright jet-stone.   *10*
No, not just as requital,
But meaning I would love her for ever.

I Beg of You, Chung Tzu

I beg of you, Chung Tzu,
Do not climb into our homestead,
Do not break the willows we have planted.
Not that I mind about the willows,
But I am afraid of my father and mother.   *5*
Chung Tzu I dearly love;
But of what my father and mother say
Indeed I am afraid.

I beg of you, Chung Tzu,
Do not climb over our wall,   *10*
Do not break the mulberry-trees we have planted.
Not that I mind about the mulberry-trees,
But I am afraid of my brothers.
Chung Tzu I dearly love;
But of what my brothers say   *15*
Indeed I am afraid.

I beg of you, Chung Tzu,
Do not climb into our garden,
Do not break the hard-wood we have planted.
Not that I mind about the hard-wood,   *20*

But I am afraid of what people will say.
Chung Tzu I dearly love;
But of all that people will say
Indeed I am afraid.

If Along the Highroad

If along the highroad
I caught hold of your sleeve,
Do not hate me;
Old ways take time to overcome.

If along the highroad   *5*
I caught hold of your hand,
Do not be angry with me;
Friendship takes time to overcome.

By the Willows of the Eastern Gate

By the willows of the Eastern Gate,
Whose leaves are so thick,
At dusk we were to meet;
And now the morning star is bright.

By the willows of the Eastern Gate,   *5*
Whose leaves are so close,
At dusk we were to meet;
And now the morning star is pale.

Midnight Songs[1]

1

The sun sinks low. I
go to my front gate,
and look long, and see
you passing by.

Seductive face,
so many charms,
such hair!
—and sweet perfume
that spills
in from the road.

2

My perfume?
No more

---

[1]Translated by Jeanne Larsen. Most likely the work of many female entertainers writing lyrics to the same plaintive melody in the late 4th century, these are attributed to one well-known singer named Midnight.

than incense leaves.
Seductive face?
You really think I'd dare?

But heaven doesn't rob us
of desires:
that's why it's sent me
here, why I've
seen you.

3

Night after night, I do not
comb my hair. Silky
tangles hang
across my shoulders.

I stretch my limbs
around that young man's
hips. Is there any
place on him
I could not
love?

7

When I started wanting
to know that man,
I hoped our coupled hearts
would be like one.

Silk thoughts threaded[2]
on a broken loom—
who'd have known
the tangled snarls to come?

9

So soon. Today, love, we
part. And our re-
union—when
will that time come?

A bright lamp
shines on an empty place,
in sorrow and longing:
not yet, not yet, not
yet.

12

Through the front gate,
my morning thoughts

take off; from river-
isles out back,
at twilight, they return.

Talk and
laughter—who
shall I share them with?
Deep in my belly, dark and
damp, I think of you.

16

Seize the moment!—
while you're still young.
Miss your chance—
one day, and you've grown old.

If you don't
believe my words, just look
out at those grasses
underneath the frost.

CONFUCIUS

from *The Analects*

Soon after Confucius's death, his sayings and those of his followers were gathered together in a collection called The Analects. *Not surprisingly, especially since Confucius lived in a period of great social unrest in China, these emphasize the duties and obligations of the individual and proper forms of human conduct. Confucius is referred to as the "Master:"*

Book I

1. The Master said, "Is it not a pleasure, having learned something, to try it out at due intervals? Is it not a joy to have friends come from afar? Is it not gentlemanly not to take offence when others fail to appreciate your abilities?"
11. The Master said, "Observe what a man has in mind to do when his father is living, and then observe what he does when his father is dead. If, for three years, he makes no changes to his father's ways, he can be said to be a good son."

Book II

1. The Master said, "The rule of virtue can be compared to the Pole Star which commands the homage of the multitude of stars without leaving its place."
2. The Master said, "*The Odes* [*The Book of Songs*] are three hundred in number. They can be summed up in one phrase,

SWERVING NOT FROM THE RIGHT PATH."

3. The Master said, "Guide them by edicts, keep them in line with punishments, and the common people will stay out

---

[2]In some of the several puns throughout this series, the word "silk" resembles the word for "thoughts [of love]," and "mate" resembles "length of cloth."

of trouble but will have no sense of shame. Guide them by virtue, keep them in line with the rites, and they will, besides having a sense of shame, reform themselves."

4.   The Master said, "At fifteen I set my heart on learning; at thirty I took my stand; at forty I came to be free from doubts; at fifty I understood the Decree of Heaven; at sixty my ear was atuned; at seventy I followed my heart's desire without overstepping the line."

7.   The Master said, "There is no contention between gentlemen. The nearest to it is, perhaps, archery. In archery they bow and make way for one another as they go up and on coming down they drink together. Even the way they contend is gentlemanly."

19. Duke Ai asked, "What must I do before the common people will look up to me?"

Confucius answered, "Raise the straight and set them over the crooked and the common people will look up to you. Raise the crooked and set them over the straight and the common people will not look up to you."

21. Duke Ai asked Tsai Wo about the altar to the god of earth. Tsai Wo replied, "The Hsia used the pine, the Yin used the cedar, and the men of Chou used the chestnut (li), saying that it made the common people tremble (li)."

The Master, on hearing of this reply, commented, "One does not explain away what is already done, one does not argue against what is already accomplished, and one does not condemn what has already gone by."

The Tao Te Ching

Among the eighty-one lyric poems that constitute the philosophical Tao Te Ching are some that offer direct advice to the reader. Others are more indirect using paradox and analogy to invite thoughtful reflection.

from *The Tao Te Ching*

Translated by Stephen Addiss

8

The supreme good is like water,
which nourishes all things without trying to.
It is content with the low places that people disdain.
Thus it is like the Tao.

In dwelling, live close to the ground.
In thinking, keep to the simple.
In conflict, be fair and generous.
In governing, don't try to control.
In work, do what you enjoy.
In family life, be completely present.

When you are content to be simply yourself
and don't compare or compete,
everybody will respect you.

9

Fill your bowl to the brim
and it will spill.
Keep sharpening your knife
and it will blunt.
Chase after money and security
and your heart will never unclench.
Care about people's approval
and you will be their prisoner.

Do your work, then step back.
The only path to serenity.

11

We join spokes together in a wheel,
but it is the center hole
that makes the wagon move.

We shape clay into a pot,
but it is the emptiness inside
that holds whatever we want.

We hammer wood for a house,
but it is the inner space
that makes it livable.

We work with being,
but non-being is what we use.

51

Every being in the universe
is an expression of the Tao.
It springs into existence,
unconscious, perfect, free,
takes on a physical body,
lets circumstances complete it.
That is why every being
spontaneously honors the Tao.

The Tao gives birth to all beings,
nourishes them, maintains them,
cares for them, comforts them, protects them,
takes them back to itself,
creating without possessing,
acting without expecting,
guiding without interfering.
That is why love of the Tao
is in the very nature of things.

52

In the beginning was the Tao.
All things issue from it;
all things return to it.

To find the origin,
trace back the manifestations.
When you recognize the children
and find the mother,
you will be free of sorrow.

If you close your mind in judgments
and traffic with desires,
your heart will be troubled.
If you keep your mind from judging
and aren't led by the senses,
your heart will find peace.

Seeing into darkness is clarity.
Knowing how to yield is strength.
Use your own light
and return to the source of light.
This is called practicing eternity.

TAO QIAN

Tao Qian (365–427), also known as Tao Yuanming, was one of the most influential of pre-Tang dynasty poets. More than one hundred of his poems survive, including the following poem with a prose preface describing a man returning to his village following a long absence.

The Return[1]

I was poor, and what I got from farming was not enough to support my family. The house was full of children, the rice-jar was empty, and I could not see any way to supply the necessities of life. Friends and relatives kept urging me to become a magistrate, and I had at last come to think I should do it, but there was no way for me to get such a position. At the time I happened to have business abroad and made a good impression on the grandees as a conciliatory and humane sort of person. Because of my poverty an uncle offered me a job in a small town, but the region was still unquiet and I trembled at the thought of going away from home. However, P'eng-tse was only thirty miles from my native place, and the yield of the fields assigned the magistrate was sufficient to keep me in wine, so I applied for the office. Before many days had passed, I longed to give it up and go back home. Why, you may ask. Because my instinct is all for freedom, and will not brook discipline or restraint. Hunger and cold may be sharp, but this going against myself really sickens me. Whenever I have been involved in official life I was mortgaging myself to my mouth and belly, and the realization of this greatly upset me. I was deeply ashamed that I had so compromised my principles, but I was still going to wait out the year, after which I might pack up my clothes and slip away at night. Then my sister who had married into the Ch'eng family died in Wuch'ang, and my only desire was to go there as quickly as possible. I gave up my office and left of my own accord. From mid-autumn to winter I was altogether some eighty days in office, when events made it possible for me to do what I wished. I have entitled my piece "The Return"; my preface is dated the eleventh moon of the year *i-ssu* (405).

To get out of this and go back home!
My fields and garden will be overgrown with weeds—I
    must go back.
It was my own doing that made my mind my body's
    slave
Why should I go on in melancholy and lonely grief?
I realize that there's no remedying the past   *5*
But I know that there's hope in the future.
After all I have not gone far on the wrong road
And I am aware that what I do today is right, yesterday
    wrong.
My boat rocks in the gentle breeze
Flap, flap, the wind blows my gown;   *10*
I ask a passerby about the road ahead,
Grudging the dimness of the light at dawn.
Then I catch sight of my cottage—
Filled with joy I run.
The servant boy comes to welcome me   *15*
My little son waits at the door.
The three paths are almost obliterated[2]
But pines and chrysanthemums are still here.
Leading the children by the hand I enter my house
    Where there is a bottle filled with wine.   *20*
I draw the bottle to me and pour myself a cup;
Seeing the trees in the courtyard brings joy to
    my face.
I lean on the south window and let my pride expand,
I consider how easy it is to be content with a little
    space.
Every day I stroll in the garden for pleasure,   *25*
There is a gate there, but it is always shut.
Cane in hand I walk and rest
Occasionally raising my head to gaze into the distance.
The clouds aimlessly rise from the peaks,
The birds, weary of flying, know it is time to
    come home.   *30*
As the sun's rays grow dim and disappear from view
I walk around a lonely pine tree, stroking it.

---

[1]Translated by James Robert Hightower. Introduced by a prose preface, this is an example of a *fu* or rhymeprose, a hybrid form usually directed toward descriptive or elegiac purposes but employed by Tao Qian here for more personal ends.

[2]The "three paths" on which a famous earlier hermit walked with two friends had become part of the vocabulary of reclusion.

Back home again!
May my friendships be broken off and my wanderings
    come to an end.
The world and I shall have nothing more to do with
    one another.   *35*
If I were again to go abroad, what should I seek?
Here I enjoy honest conversation with my family
And take pleasure in books and cither to dispel my
    worries.
The farmers tell me that now spring is here
There will be work to do in the west fields.   *40*
Sometimes I call for a covered cart
Sometimes I row a lonely boat
Following a deep gully through the still water
Or crossing the hill on a rugged path.
The trees put forth luxuriant foliage,   *45*
The spring begins to flow in a trickle.
I admire the seasonableness of nature
And am moved to think that my life will come to its
    close.
It is all over—
So little time are we granted human form in the
    world!   *50*
Let us then follow the inclinations of the heart:
Where would we go that we are so agitated?
I have no desire for riches
And no expectation of Heaven.
Rather on some fine morning to walk alone   *55*
Now planting my staff to take up a hoe,
Or climbing the east hill and whistling long
Or composing verses beside the clear stream:
So I manage to accept my lot until the ultimate
    homecoming.
Rejoicing in Heaven's command, what is there
    to doubt?   *60*

WANG-WEI

Wang Wei (ca. 699–761) was a favorite of the Tang princes. Like other court poets, he produced graceful poems for public occasions. But he could also write less formal poems with a more personal dimension in a spare style. His poems combine a respect for a love of nature with a Buddhist understanding of the illusory nature of appearances.

Villa on Chung-nan Mountain

*In my middle years I came to love the Way
and made my home late by South Mountain's edge.*

*When the mood came upon me, I went off alone,
and had moments of splendor all to myself.*

*I would walk to the point where a stream ends,
and sitting, would watch when the clouds rise.*

*By chance I would meet old men in the woods;
we would laugh and chat, no fixed time to turn home.*

Answering Magistrate Chang

*Now late in life I love only stillness,
all the world's troubles touch not my heart.*

*I look within and find there no great plans,
know only to return to the woods of my home.*

*There wind through pines blows my sash untied,
moon of the hills shines on playing a harp.*

*You ask the pattern of failure and success?—
the fisherman's song reaches deep over the shore.*

LI BAI

Li Bai, also known as Li Po (701–762), invented himself as an eccentric personality and as a poet. During the period of the Tang dynasty, a poet of importance either had to have family connections or had to pass a rigorous series of civil service examinations. Li Bai, however, had neither of these credentials, and so he had to enter the poetic fraternity through the back door. His poems can be extravagant, even brash, when compared with the more austere control of Wang Wei. But his poems, in addition to looking closely at everyday life, also evoke the worlds of history and of legend.

Dialogue in the Mountains

*You ask me why I lodge in these emerald hills;
I laugh, don't answer—my heart is at peace.
Peach blossoms and flowing waters
    go off to mysterious dark,
And there is another world,
    not of mortal men.*

Drinking Alone by Moonlight

*Here among flowers a single jug of wine,
No close friends here, I pour alone
And lift cup to bright moon, ask it to join me,
Then face my shadow and we become three.
The moon never has known how to drink,
All my shadow does is follow my body,
But with moon and shadow as companions a while,
This joy I find must catch spring while it's here.
I sing, the moon just lingers on,
I dance, and my shadow scatters wildly.
When still sober we share friendship and pleasure,
Then entirely drunk each goes his own way—*

Let us join in travels beyond human feelings
And plan to meet far in the river of stars.

The Jewel Stairs' Grievance[1]

The jewelled steps are already quite white with dew,
It is so late that the dew soaks my gauze stockings,
And I let down the crystal curtain
And watch the moon through the clear autumn.

The River Merchant's Wife: A Letter[1]

While my hair was still cut straight across my forehead
I played about the front gate, pulling flowers.
You came by on bamboo stilts, playing horse,
You walked about my seat, playing with blue plums.
And we went on living in the village of Chokan: 5
Two small people, without dislike or suspicion.

At fourteen I married My Lord you.
I never laughed, being bashful.
Lowering my head, I looked at the wall.
Called to, a thousand times, I never looked back.   10

At fifteen I stopped scowling,
I desired my dust to be mingled with yours
Forever and forever and forever.
Why should I climb the look out?

At sixteen you departed,   15
You went into far Ku-to-yen, by the river of swirling
   eddies,
And you have been gone five months.
The monkeys make sorrowful noise overhead.

You dragged your feet when you went out.
By the gate now, the moss is grown, the different
   mosses,   20
Too deep to clear them away!
The leaves fall early this autumn, in wind.
The paired butterflies are already yellow with August
Over the grass in the West garden;
They hurt me. I grow older.   25
If you are coming down through the narrows of the river
   Kiang,
Please let me know beforehand,
And I will come out to meet you
                                   As far as Cho-fu-Sa.

----
[1]Translated by Ezra Pound. Pound didn't know classical Chinese, but he worked from the notes to poems of Ernest Fenellosa, a scholar of Japanese culture. With his first volume of these translations, *Cathay* (1915). Pound was said by T. S. Eliot to have become "the inventor of Chinese poetry for our time."
[1]Translated by Ezra Pound.

DU FU

Du Fu (or Tu Fu, 712–770) is associated with Confucian ideals as his compatriot contemporary Li Bai is associated with Taoism. Du Fu's poems center on issues of political commitment, social concern, and a love of family. His poems reveal a character that has suffered, endured much, and changed. At the same time, the poems highlight significant moments of Chinese history.

Spending the Night in a Tower by the River

A visible darkness grows up mountain paths,
I lodge by river gate high in a study,
Frail cloud on cliff edge passing the night,
The lonely moon topples amid the waves.
Steady, one after another, a line of cranes in flight,
Howling over the kill, wild dogs and wolves.
No sleep for me. I worry over battles.
I have no strength to right the universe.

A Guest Comes

North of my cottage, south of my cottage,
   spring waters everywhere,
And all that I see are the flocks of gulls
   coming here day after day,
My path through the flowers has never yet
   been swept for a visitor,
But today this wicker gate of mine
   stands open just for you.
The market is far, so for dinner
   there'll be no wide range of tastes,
Our home is poor, and for wine
   we have only an older vintage.
Are you willing to sit here and drink
   with the old man who lives next door?
I'll call to him over the hedge,
   and we'll finish the last of the cups.

Ballad of the Army Carts[1]

Carts rattle and squeak,
   Horses snort and neigh—
Bows and arrows at their waists, the conscripts march
   away.
Fathers, mothers, children, wives run to say goodbye.
The Xianyang Bridge in clouds of dust is hidden from   5
   the eye.
They tug at them and stamp their feet, weep, and
   obstruct their way.

----
[1]Translated by Vikram Seth.

The weeping rises to the sky.
Along the road a passer-by
Questions the conscripts. They reply:

They mobilize us constantly. Sent northwards at fifteen *10*
To guard the River, we were forced once more to
      volunteer,
Though we are forty now, to man the western front this
      year.
The headman tied our headcloths for us when we first
      left here.
We came back white-haired—to be sent again to the
      frontier.
Those frontier posts could fill the sea with the blood
      of those who've died,   *15*
But still the Martial Emperor's aims remain unsatisfied.
In county after county to the east, Sir, don't you know,
In village after village only thorns and brambles grow.
Even if there's a sturdy wife to wield the plough and hoe,
The borders of the fields have merged, you can't
      tell east from west.   *20*
It's worse still for the men from Qin, as fighters they're
      the best—
And so, like chickens or like dogs, they're driven to and
      fro.

Though you are kind enough to ask,
Dare we complain about our task?
Take, Sir, this winter. In Guanxi   *25*
The troops have not yet been set free.
The district officers come to press
The land tax from us nonetheless.
But, Sir, how can we possibly pay?
Having a son's a curse today.   *30*
Far better to have daughters, get them married—
A son will lie lost in the grass, unburied.
Why, Sir, on distant Qinghai shore
The bleached ungathered bones lie year on year.
New ghosts complain, and those who died before   *35*
Weep in the wet gray sky and haunt the ear.

Moonlit Night[1]

In Fuzhou, far away, my wife is watching
The moon alone tonight, and my thoughts fill
With sadness for my children, who can't think
Of me here in Changan; they're too young still.
Her cloud-soft hair is moist with fragrant mist.   *5*
In the clear light her white arms sense the chill.
When will we feel the moonlight dry our tears,
Leaning together on our window-sill?

LI CH'ING-CHAO (LI QINGZHAO)

*Li Ch'ing-chao (Li Qingzhao, 1084–ca. 1151) is considered the
finest woman lyric poet ever to have written in Chinese. During her
time, poets created lyrics for popular songs with irregular melodies.
These poems, which were often about love and evoked feeling with
great delicacy, were called* tz'u, *or "song lyrics." Li Chi'ing-chao's
characteristic tone is reflected in the following poems.*

To "Southern Song"

*Up in heaven the star-river turns,
curtains are drawn in man's world below.
A chill comes to pallet and pillow,
      damp with marks of tears.
I rise to take off my gossamer dress
and just happen to ask, "How late is it now?"
The tiny lotus pods,
      kingfisher feathers sewn on;
as the gilt flakes away
      the lotus leaves grow few.
Same weather as in times before,
      the same old dress—
only the feelings in the heart
are not as they were before.*

To the Tune "Wuling chun"[1]

The wind has ceased, dust is fragrant, flowers all have
      fallen.
Late is the day—too tired to comb my hair.
Things remain but he has gone. Everything has ended.
I wish to speak: tears flow first.

I've heard it said at Twin Stream, spring's still fine.
I too would like to float there in a light boat.
Only I fear that Twin Stream's tiny "locust" boat
Could not carry so much grief.

To the Tune "Sheng sheng man"[1]

Seeking, seeking, searching, searching,
Cold, cold, chill, chill,
Sad, sad, grieved, grieved, mournful, mournful.
This season of sudden warmth, then cold again:
Hardest of all is finding rest.   *5*
Two or three cups of watery wine—
How can they fend off that late wind's sharpness?
Geese pass by;

---

[1]Translated by Vikram Seth.

[1]Translated by Pauline Yu.
[1]Translated by Pauline Yu.

Just then I grieve,
Yet I recognize them from before.   10

Yellow flowers cover the ground in heaps,
Withered and spoiled:
Now who can bear to pluck them?

Keeping the window,
How can I live alone til dark?   15
On the *wutong* tree still a fine rain
Until dusk goes drip, drip, drop, drop.
At this moment—
How can one word "sorrow" say it all?

CHAPTER 9

HISTORY

330–352 C.E.	Yomoto rule (Warlords)
6th century C.E.	Buddhism introduced into Japan from China
552–646 C.E.	Asuka born and dies
712 C.E.	Kojiki, record of ancient matters
794–1185	Heian Period
1147–99	Minamoto Yoritomo born and dies
1185–1392	Kamakura Period
1192	Minomoto Yoritomo declared 1st Shogun
1392–1523	Ashikaga Period

ARTS AND ARCHITECTURE

623 C.E.	Tori Busshi, *Shaka Triad*
670 C.E.	Horyu-ji, temple compound
1120	Hand scrolls
15th century	Tea ceremony

LITERATURE AND PHILOSOPHY

8th century	Manyoshu, poetry collection
689–700	Kokinoto no Hitomoro, poet active
834–?	Ono no Komachi lives and writes poems
966–1017	Sei Shonogan, *Pillow Book*
ca. 1021	Murasaki Shikibu, *The Tale of Genji*
1283–1350	Yoshida Kenko, *Essays in Idleness*

Early Japanese Civilization

Handscroll illustration for the *Tale of Genji*, late Heian period, ink and color on paper, height
8′ (21.6 cm), Tokugawa Art Museum, Nagoya.

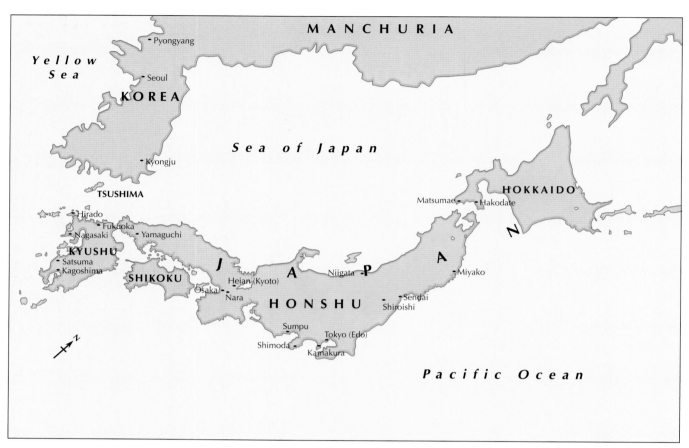

MAP 9.1 Japan Before the Fifteenth Century.

C H A P T E R   O V E R V I E W

JAPAN BEFORE THE TWELFTH CENTURY

JAPAN FROM THE TWELFTH TO THE FIFTEENTH CENTURY

JAPAN BEFORE THE TWELFTH CENTURY

PREHISTORIC JAPAN

In 1960, the field of archaeology was given a shock when scientific carbon dating showed that the world's first pottery was created in Japan. Recent tests have pushed back the dating to 10,000 B.C.E., well before any other cultures developed their own ceramic traditions. Because it has generally been believed Japan followed the lead of China in cultural development, scholars at first doubted

the tests, and since then they have debated how Japan could have led the world in creating pottery.

The general theory is that human societies can be grouped into the few basic divisions of hunting-gathering, agricultural, and urban. These are most easily understood by knowing where people obtain their food; they hunt or find it, they grow it, or they buy it at the store. Pottery, being heavy and cumbersome, was not developed by hunting-gathering peoples, who moved from place to place over the course of a year and did not store food for very long. When cultures developed to agricultural phases, however, people tended to stay in one place, needed to store food

320

from one harvest to the next, and also required vessels to cook the different forms of grains they were growing.

This has been the theory, but the early inhabitants of Japan created pottery twelve thousand years ago while still in a hunting-gathering phase. How could this be? One explanation is that from the traces of foodstuffs still remaining in archaeological sites, it can be determined that the early peoples had sufficient supplies of fish, seafood, and plants to live year round in certain areas, rather than migrating, and therefore they were able to make use of pottery in their daily lives.

The early pots in Japan were simply constructed from clay into various forms, especially large cooking and storage vessels, and then fired in trenches, since kilns had not been developed yet. In order to add strength to the pottery as well as create attractive patterns on the surface, many vessel walls were impressed with ropes or cords, and so the era itself became known as **Jomon,** meaning "cord patterned." Over the course of centuries, these Jomon vessels developed, were further embellished with coils and geometric patterns, and eventually emerged as some of the most spectacular pottery ever created, with rim designs that went well beyond practicality and can only be described as flamboyantly artistic. Because there are no written records from this period, much of what we know about early Japan comes from Jomon pottery (fig. 9.1), which exhibits a great variety of both shape and decoration, suggesting a society that was bold and confident in its way of life.

Around the year 300 C.E. a new wave of people came from the Korean peninsula, bringing elements of culture that led to great changes in Japan. Agriculture, which had begun in a rudimentary way during the Jomon period, now was greatly advanced, particularly rice cultivation, which meant that larger-scale groupings of people were now possible, leading to Japan's first emperors. The Jomon people, who were racially Caucasian, were gradually pushed to the north and formed the basis of the Ainu peoples, who still live on the island of Hokkaido.

The new peoples, racially the same as present-day Japanese, built huge graves for their leaders, some with artificial hills surrounded by moats. Upon these graves they began to erect ceramic tubes, perhaps to help the earth stay in place. Before long these cylinders, called *haniwa* [hah-nee-wah], were decorated with models of boats, houses, and animals. The final forms to emerge were human figures (fig. 9.2), who were shown in many different guises and activities.

There is some debate as to the purpose of these ceramic *haniwa.* In China as in other early cultures, sculptures were placed inside tombs to assist the dead in their next lives, but in Japan they were placed on top of the graves. Were these figures meant to be guardians? If so, why are there birds and animals, mothers nursing babies, falconers, shamans, and people doing ordinary everyday tasks? Again, without written records, we can only speculate, but it seems these *haniwa* formed some kind of link between the

FIGURE 9.1   *Storage Vessel, Earthenware.* Japan, Middle Jomon period, ca. 2000 B.C.E. Height: 2′ (61 cm). © The Cleveland Museum of Art, John L. Severenance Fund, 1984. 68. The geometric decorative patterns on the body resemble plates of armor; the raised designs on the rim have a more organic expression, testifying to the dramatic artistic imagination of the prehistoric potter.

living, who could view them atop the grave mounds from across the moats, and the dead, over whom they stood.

The next major change in Japan took place beginning in the fifth and sixth centuries, when a new wave of influence came over from Korea and China. This brought many things that were to become vital parts of Japanese culture, including a writing system, Buddhism, advances in medicine, more complex governmental systems, new forms of poetry, music and architecture, and the arts of brush painting and calligraphy.

RELIGION

Buddhism and Shinto.   Of the influences Japan received from China and Korea, perhaps the most significant was Buddhism, which China had itself imported from India. After an initial reluctance, Japan embraced the new religion with great fervor, copying sacred texts (which was also a way to practice the written language that was now learned from China), building temples, and ordaining monastics—the first of whom were three women.

Japan, however, already had its own religious practices, later designated as **Shinto** to distinguish them from the imported forms of Buddhism. Over many centuries, Shinto developed from a kind of nature worship into a state religion of patriotic appreciation of the Japanese land. Shinto came to require a commemoration of Japanese heroes and

FIGURE 9.2 *Smiling Earthenware Haniwa Figure,* from the Akabori Site, Gumma Prefecture, Japan, fourth–fifth centuries B.C.E. $36\frac{1}{4}''$ (92 cm) tall, Tokyo National Museum. TNM Image Archives. Source: http://TnmArchives.jp/. This figure is believed to represent a farmer holding a plow blade on his shoulder, evidence of the agricultural society that had developed by this time in central Japan.

Table 9–1 EARLY JAPANESE HISTORICAL PERIODS AND THEIR MAJOR ACHIEVEMENTS	
Kofun (300–552)	Yamoto rule (warlords)
Asuka (552–646)	Shaka Triad (ca. 623)
Nara (646–794)	Horyi-ji temple (ca. 670), oldest wooden temple in the world
Heian (794–1185)	*The Tale of Genji* (ca. 1000)
Kamakura (1185–1392)	Hand scrolls (twelfth century)
Ashikaga (1392–1523)	Tea ceremony

COURTLY JAPAN: ASUKA AND NARA PERIODS

Art and Architecture. The earliest surviving wooden Japanese sculptures and architecture, those of the Asuka period, 552–646 C.E., are closely identified with Buddhism. One of the best preserved and most important Japanese temples is Horyu-ji, the oldest wooden temple in the world (ca. 670) (fig. 9.3). Horyu-ji's architectural design reveals how Buddhist-inspired Chinese architecture influenced early Japanese temple building, although its asymmetrical relationship of structures is a typically Japanese aesthetic trait.

Among the many treasures housed in the buildings of Horyu-ji is a sculpture known as the *Shaka Triad* (fig. 9.4). This triple image shows the Buddha, whose Japanese name is Shaka or Shakyamuni, with attending bodhisattvas on either side. The large figures, especially the Buddha sitting

FIGURE 9.3 Horyu-ji compound, with pagoda and Golden Hall, Nara, Japan, ca. 670 C.E., aerial view. Visitors entering this temple compound move through the first building and then must take a turn to the right or the left rather than moving in a straight line from one building to the next. This favoring of lateral over linear movement is a characteristic of Japanese artistic style.

significant events from the nation's history. Later Shinto could also include earlier aspects of animism, nature worship, and ancestor worship, and Shinto rituals could be carried out in private homes as well as in Shinto temples.

To some extent, the formal development of Shinto was a reaction against Chinese religious and cultural influence. In addition, during the seventh and eighth centuries, the Japanese collected their native myths in the **Kojiki,** "Chronicles of Ancient Events." In explaining the origin of Japanese culture, the *Kojiki* describe the creation of the Japanese islands by two Shinto **kami,** or gods, Izanagi and his consort Izanami. All other gods descend from these two, of whom the most important is Ameterasu, the sun goddess, who is considered the ancestor of the Japanese emperors.

in the center, reveal the sculptor TORI BUSSHI's [BOOSH-yi] awareness of the Chinese sculptural tradition from the pre-Tang period, including the focus of attention on the large head and hands. The expert use of gilt bronze demonstrates how quickly and successfully the international sculptural tradition was adopted in Japan.

From the late seventh century on, Japanese rulers were true monarchs, no longer merely aristocratic warlords. Around the same time, Nara became Japan's first true capital. Although the rulers of ancient Japan are often referred to as emperors, these rulers are best thought of as sovereigns. The distinction is important because it signals a shift from the military authority of the earlier warlords to a genuine pursuit of political and cultural cohesion. The patronage of Buddhism became one of the most important facets of court life, and many temples were built within and without the city of Nara that were much larger than Horyu-ji and featured outpouring of sculptures and paintings of Buddhist dieties.

Kojiki and Nihongi.   Kojiki, or the Records of Ancient Matters, is the oldest volume of Japanese ancient history. It begins with the creation of the world by the Kami, or

FIGURE 9.4   Tori Busshi, *Shaka Triad*, Nara Prefecture, Asuka period, 623, bronze, height 5′ 9′ (1.76 m), Horyu-ji. The Buddha, flanked by attendant bodhisattvas, sits on a simple throne against a decorative background that testifies to his sacred status.

deities, Izanagi and Izanami; it concludes with the period of Empress Suiko, Japan's first empress, who reigned from 592–628 C.E.

Divided into three major parts, the Kojiki contains songs and poems along with myths and historical records. The myths and records are written in a mixture of Chinese and Japanese, whereas the songs are written strictly in Chinese characters.

The first part of the Kojiki, the Kamitsumaki or "upper roll," focuses on the creation of the world and of various deities. The second part, the Nakatsumaki, or "middle roll," covers the period between the first Japanese Emperor, Jimmu, and the 15th, Emperor Ojin. The third part, the Shimosutsumaki, or "lower roll," covers the period from the 16th to the 33rd Emperors.

The Nihongi, or Nihonshoki, or the "Chronicles of Japan," picks up where the Kojiki leaves off and catalogs the descent of the Yamato rulers through the end of the seventh century. In combination with the Kojiki, the Nihongi has been an influential document in Japan, including its naming of the country "Nippon."

COURTLY JAPAN: THE HEIAN PERIOD

In 794, the Japanese capital was moved to Heian (now Kyoto), which became one of the most densely populated cities in the world. The Heian period was a period of rich productivity and peace, with the Japanese sovereign strongly supported by aristocratic families. Court culture during the Heian era became extremely refined and elegant, and the secular as well as sacred arts flourished.

Courtiers of both sexes, if they wanted to inspire respect among their peers, were expected to be able to write poetry in the classical five-line ***waka*** form, with syllables of 5-7-5-7-7 (the haiku was later to develop from the first three lines of a *waka*). Featuring *mono no aware* ("the emotion of things" or "the sadness of things"), court poetry expressed the feelings that lay under the surface of elegant court life. For example, Lady Akazome Emon (eleventh century) wrote this verse after her lover failed to appear:

> I should not have waited—
> it would have been wiser
> to sleep and dream
> than to see the night pass
> and watch this moon slowly sink

Many *waka* were about romantic love, but one poem by the ninth-century courtier Narihira might apply to any of us at crucial moments of our lives:

> I have always known
> someday I must take this road—
> but just yesterday
> I did not realize that
> it would be today

Although both men and women wrote classical poetry, it was women who wrote most of the prose fiction of the time, including the world's first novel, *The Tale of Genji*

(Genji Monogatari). The most enduring and influential of all works of Japanese literature, *The Tale of Genji* is a sprawling narrative of court life, spanning many generations and featuring the hero, Prince Genji, among a host of other characters. This novel was written by MURASAKI SHIKIBU [moo-rah-sah-key] (ca. 976–ca. 1026), a member of the Japanese aristocracy. Her work is highly regarded for its psychological sublety and its rich portrayal of character, and it tells us a great deal about the exquisite refinement of court life during Japan's most elegant era.

The Heian era was a time of cultural sophistication, during which Japanese painters and poets broke away from the Chinese aesthetic influence of previous periods. To some extent, the novel romanticizes courtly life as the author experienced it, although without idealizing the characters so much that they lose their credibility. According to an eighteenth-century Japanese scholar, Matoori Noringa, the greatness of *The Tale of Genji* lies in the way it conveys the sorrow of human existence as reflected in the behavior of its hero, Genji. Although he sometimes violates the injunctions of Confucianism and Buddhism, Genji nonetheless "combines in himself all good things." Like the author who created him, Genji exhibits great sensitivity to the people who cross his path, especially the many women who share his love.

Heian Hand Scrolls. The art of the Heian period includes both religious and secular subjects, all done with great refinement. The works of this era also reflect the development of more distinctively indigenous Japanese styles. Landscape painting, for example, began to depart from Chinese depictions of majestic mountains, replacing them with representations of softer rolling hills, maple trees, and cherry blossoms. In general, Japanese landscapes of this period are utilized as the backgrounds to narrative tales, which often evoke the sense of transience and poignant sadness also found in Japanese poetry.

One of the most distinctive of secular Japanese painting style is exhibited in the painting of narrative hand scrolls, or ***emaki-mano,*** associated with religions or court life. Some of the most celebrated hand scrolls depict *The Tale of Genji* (fig. 9.5). The oldest illustrations of this work, dating from ca. 1120, survive only in self-contained sections, along with short pieces of the handwritten text.

The highly decorative *Genji* illustrations emphasize the placement of figures, their costumes, and the use of color. The artist breaks up the composition by using screens, walls, and the sliding panels found in traditional Japanese palaces. Figures are usually shown at an angle, with the viewpoint from above. Women are depicted in broadly draped garments that hide their figures, leaving only their heads and hands visible. They are engaged in calm activity, one combing another's hair while others read and look at picture scrolls. The overall effect is to convey a sense of court life quietly, with little overt dramatic action, but the figures placed in strong assymetrical compositions convey a sense of deep emotion.

Noh Theatre. Masked dance forms came into use in Japan during the sixth century C.E., functioning as religious and secular ritual and as entertainment. Noh masks

FIGURE 9.5   Illustration to the Azumaya chapter of *The Tale of Genji*, late Heian period, twelfth century, hand scroll, ink and color on paper, height 8′ (21.6 cm), Tokugawa Art Museum, Nagoya. This hand scroll section illustrates a scene in which Prince Genji holds the baby he knows is not his while his wife looks down in sadness. Despite their lofty positions, they are unable to find happiness, as shown by the way they huddle into a corner of the painting.

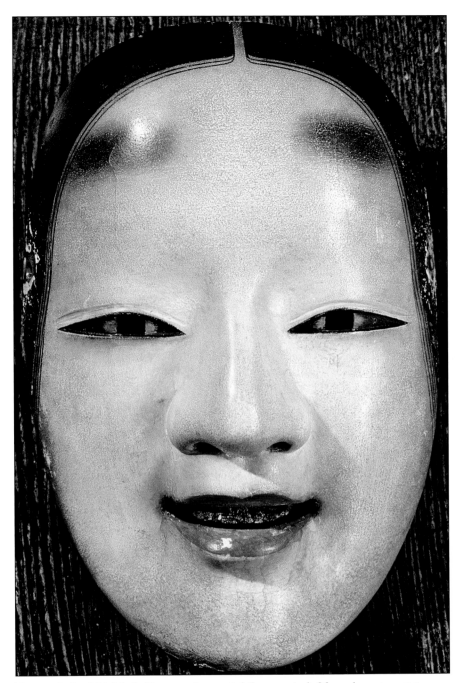

FIGURE 9.6   *Noh Mask: Ko-omote.* Japan. Ashikaga period, fifteenth century C.E. Painted wood, height about 10″ (25.4 cm). Kongo Family Collection, Tokyo. Mask used in Noh dramas.

(fig 9.6) are smaller than those used for Bugaku, which reached its peak during the Heian period, and which was performed initially at court and later at local shrines. Each Bugaku dance had a mask associated with it.

Noh plays are virtuoso performances that combine chant, mime, and dance. They are accompanied by music, masks, and elaborate costumes. Influenced by Buddhist spirituality, the Noh play's subjects are taken from history, legend, and magic. Traditionally performed in sets of five plays—a play each for a god, warrior, woman, and demon followed by a contemporary or other miscellaneous play, Noh dramas are performed with minimal props and scenery. As with classical Greek tragedy, the audience for Noh plays usually already knows the plot. Costumes and masks make the actors heroic and heighten the force of their gestures and words—much as in ancient Greek

Connections

COURTS, CULTURE, AND WOMEN

One of the most unusual aspects of medieval Japanese court culture was the importance and position it accorded women writers. The most renowned works of early Japanese literature were written by women: *The Tale of Genji, The Pillowbook, The Sarashina Diary,* and many poems of the *Manyoshu,* an eighth-century collection of Japanese poems. The women who wrote these important literary works were either situated at the imperial court or were closely associated with it.

Two major reasons account for the prominence of women writers in Japan at this time. The first relates to the Japanese writing system. Fujiwara leaders engaged in competition to have their daughters married to the emperor. They thus educated them well in Japanese script although writing in Chinese was mostly reserved for men. When successful, these women became the emperor's consorts or his empresses. Even when not quite this successful, women like Sei Shonogan and Murasaki Shikibu became ladies in waiting to aristocratic royalty and wrote works that were highly valued in circles of power and influence.

---

drama. The Noh actors' anonymity contributes to the play's mystery and power.

WARRIOR JAPAN: THE KAMAKURA PERIOD

During the later Heian era, rulers began to see their power diminish at the hands of the **samurai,** regional warriors in the service of the governing nobility. Because these warriors were at the disposal of families competing for power, they were instrumental in the change during the twelfth century from court rule to that of military leaders who effectively controlled Japan while the court retained only its cultural and symbolic meaning.

The era from 1185 to 1333 is known as the Kamakura period because the capital was now moved to Kamakura, in part to escape the effete influence of the court. In a tradition inaugurated by MINAMOTO YORITOMO [MIna-MO-to] (1147–99), these warriors began to give themselves the title of **shogun** (general in chief) of the samurai. They continued to pay lip service to the official sovereign, but it was the shogun who exercised authority until 1868, when imperial rule was restored. The shogun and his samurai prided themselves on their self-reliance, and they were particularly attracted to Zen, a form of Buddhism that promoted self-sufficiency.

Zen Buddhism. By the ninth century, Buddhism and Shinto had converged, to a certain extent, with the boundaries between the two religions becoming blurred. Shinto kami and Buddhist deities, for example, gradually became conflated, Buddhist priests used Shinto temples for meditation and worship, and Shinto temples assumed elements of the Buddhist architectural style. New forms of Buddhism, however, began to assume prominence, including esoteric sects with a galaxy of deities and complex ceremonies that appealed to courtiers, and in response, the Pure Land sect, which became popular with everyday people. In **Pure Land Buddhism,** the believer had only to repeat the mantra "Namu Amida Butsu" (NAH-MOO-AH-MEE-DAH-BOOT-TZU, Praise to Amida Buddha), to be reborn in Amida's Western Paradise.

In the Kamakura period, however, a new form of Buddhism arrived from China that especially appealed to warriors for its focus on self-discipline and inner strength. That form, known as **Chan** (Meditation) in China, in Japan became **Zen Buddhism.** Although it had always been a form of counterculture in China, for those who did not feel satisfied with Confucian society, in Japan it became a major religious and cultural force, with a strong

FIGURE 9.7   *Minamoto no Yoritomo* by Fujiwara Takanobu (1142–1205). Twelfth century. Hanging scroll; ink, colour on silk. The portrait of the Shogun Minamoto no Yoritomo is still tinged with some Heian opacity and formality.

Cross Currents

JAPAN AND CHINA

Many main elements of Japanese culture derive from China, as do the central elements of other East Asian countries, including Korea and Vietnam. China has served for East Asian countries as cultural stimulus, source, and inspiration. From China, Japan inherited a major religion, Buddhism, which had come to China from India. Japan also borrowed Chinese characters for writing until developing its own vernacular writing system, Kana, in the ninth century.

Prior to using the Kana system, Japanese literature and history were recorded using Chinese characters to represent the sounds of Japanese (the Kojiki, for example), or Chinese characters for the Chinese language (the Nihonji, for example). Yet while these and other areas of Japanese culture, such as the tea ceremony and landscape painting, owe much to Chinese influence, the Japanese people over the centuries have made them their own, putting their distinctive cultural stamp upon them.

---

influence on the aesthetics of various arts from ink painting to the tea ceremony.

Zen has been defined as "the art of seeing into the nature of one's own being." It is less a religion or a philosophy than a way of life, an attitude, an active stance toward everyday experience. A unique combination of Taoism and Buddhism, Zen emphasizes meditation to discover the Buddha within each one of us. Nor is Zen concerned with the afterlife—with heaven or hell—or with the immortality of the soul. Its focus instead is on living in the world around us. When a Zen master was asked about life after death, he replied, "Leave that to Buddha, it is no business of ours."

When another Zen master was questioned as to how one could escape the reality of cold and heat, the pangs of hunger and the parching of thirst, he answered, "In winter you shiver, in summer you sweat. When you are hungry eat, and drink when you are thirsty." One does not try to escape physical reality. In Zen, one accepts it for what it is. Life is to be lived right here and now, attentively and appreciatively, and so Zen meditation can permeate everything from getting dressed and eating, to reading, working, and relaxing.

LATER WARRIOR JAPAN: THE ASHIKAGA PERIOD

One great problem with warrior culture was that the samurai were in the service of feudal lords, rather than a central government. The Kamakura period ended in civil war in 1333, and insurrections of one kind or another continued to plague Japan almost continuously until 1573. During this era, known as the Ashikaga period, Japan was ruled by shoguns and their samurai warriors, and as a result Zen influence dominated Japanese culture.

Although started earlier, the tea ceremony rose to prominence in the 1470s when the Ashikaga ruler Yoshimasa retreated from the conflicts that dominated urban life to collect Chinese paintings and ceramics at his villa on the island of Higashiyama. The Zen monk Murata Juko suggested to him that by drinking tea in a small hut like that illustrated here, in the Katsura Palace gardens (fig. 9.8), with only a few companions, he could experience *wabi*, "lonely seclusion." This requires a heightened sense of awareness, in which the practitioner experiences, for instance, "the cold winter wind on his skin." Murata also insisted in selflessness, writing that "nothing holds back the way of tea more than attachment to oneself and feelings of self-satisfaction; we must always be aware of our own shortcomings."

In the tea ceremony proper, the iron kettle, the pottery tea bowls made in China or, later, in local Japanese kilns, the small jars for holding powdered tea, and even the bamboo tea scoops were objects to be contemplated and appreciated for their humble practicality. In time, the most celebrated of these items came to be worth astonishing amounts of money and prestige, and were used as major gifts between feudal lords, but they generally expressed a spirit of natural simplicity. The tea hut was decorated with a hanging scroll of a painting or calligraphy, preferably by a Chinese or Japanese Zen monk, and a flower arrangement appropriate for the time of year might also be displayed. The hut itself was built of natural materials in a carefully designed garden through which visitors would arrive and later depart, clearing their minds of worldy concerns. As Rikyu stated, in the act of drinking tea together, "here the Buddha-mind reveals itself."

In most cultures, there has been a trend over the centuries toward ever more refined and technically complex forms of art. In Japan this can be seen in the developments from the Asuka and Nara eras to the Heian period, as court culture favored increasingly richly decorative styles and techniques in calligraphy, painting, architecture, and other arts. The tea ceremony, strongly influenced by Zen, turned these aesthetics upside-down. Rikyu taught that in the tearoom it is best if every object is less than perfect, and he saw the beauty of utensils that had been broken or otherwise damaged. Therefore in the *wabi* sensibility of Rikyu and his followers, a rough pot from the Japanese countryside or a mended Korean bowl could be as highly admired as a

Then & Now

SUMO WRESTLING

One of Japan's most distinctive sports is *sumo*, or Japanese wrestling, which originated during the Heian period, when it became a popular spectator sport. Sumo differs from Western-style wrestling, which originated in Greece. Unlike Western wrestling, where the object is to pin one's opponent to the mat by his shoulders, in sumo the object is to push one's opponent out of the competition ring or to throw him down within it. Sumo wrestlers confront each other much like two football linemen trying to block each other or knock each other off balance. One similarity between Western wrestling and sumo is the ritual in which the wrestlers parade into the ring wearing, in the case of sumo wrestlers, long decorated skirts, and Western wrestlers, a kind of robe that bears the wrestler's name. Both Western and sumo wrestlers then strip down to a more basic attire, trunks or trunks and tank top for the Western wrestler and loin cloth for their sumo counterparts. Sumo involves more ritual, including the wrestlers tossing salt to purify the ring, squatting across from and glaring at each other, and performing a series of standardized gestures. Today some of these rituals have been reduced, though they continue in attenuated form to link Japanese sumo past and present.

---

delicate Chinese porcelain, and unglazed ceramics were often preferred to, or mixed with, elaborately decorated ones. There were exceptions to this rule of modesty and sparseness; one Shogun even commissioned a tea hut covered with gold leaf. Nevertheless, the virtues of natural rusticity and unpretentious functionality as seen in the tea ceremony have continued to influence Japanese design and taste to this day.

Tea Ceremony. One of the major cultural institutions founded on Zen thinking is the ***cha-no-yu,*** or the "tea ceremony," which developed during the Ashikaga period and not only has survived but flourishes to this day. According to Rikyu, one of its founders, "The tea ceremony is nothing more than boiling water, making tea, and drinking it." But it has usually been a much more elaborate ceremony than Rikyu suggests, one that the Portuguese Jesuit priest Joâo Rodrigues (1562–1633) described after thirty years of life in Japan as a ritual designed "to produce courtesy, politeness, modesty, moderation, calmness, peace of body and soul, without pride or arrogance, fleeing from all ostentation, pomp, external grandeur and magnificence."

Cultural Impact

The influence of early Japanese civilization on later periods and in countries in both Asia and the West has been considerable. Among the cultural legacies of ancient and medieval Japan are swordsmanship, flower arranging, and the tea ceremony. Associated with the warrior culture of the Japanese samurai, swordsmanship and swordcraft, or the making of swords, have continued well into the twentieth century, but exist today mostly as relics of a bygone era. Japanese flower arranging and the tea ceremony, also of medieval origin, retain their cultural significance not only in Japan, but in countries in which Japan has had cultural contact.

The impact of Zen on modern Japanese culture has been noted, but not to be overlooked is the influence of the books by D.T. Suzuki, one of the world's most renowned scholar/practitioners of Zen. His book *Zen and Japanese Culture* reveals the extent to which Zen continues to pervade everyday life in Japan. Suzuki's works have influenced and inspired others who have written their own accounts that reveal Zen's influence in Germany through the art of *Zen in the Art of Archery* by Eugene Herrigel and in the United States with *Zen and the Art of Motorcycle Maintenance* by Robert Pirsig.

Herrigel's book describes his attempt to learn archery Zen style while in Japan. Herrigel learned the Zen lessons of replacing fear of failure with an expectation of fulfillment. He also learned how "not to shoot," but to "let the shot fall from him," like ripe fruit falling naturally from a tree. Pirsig's book applies Zen principles to the author's life as a teacher and as a father who is developing a relationship with his teen-age son. Like Herrigel, Pirsig uses the skills associated with a mechanical art, in his case, motorcycle maintenance, to develop Zen values and ideals by which to live.

Critical Thinking

ZEN AND EVERYDAY LIFE

Although Zen is firmly linked with Japanese culture, it has become a deeply entrenched U.S. cultural import. Among the numerous contemporary books about Zen one might find in a de-

cent-sized bookstore are the following: *Zen Miracles: Find Peace in an Insane World; Zen Training; Zen Living; Zen Commitments; Voices of Insight; Song of Mind; Waking Up to What You Do; The Companion of Zen;* and *Zen 24/7.*

Why do you think Zen continues to exert such an influence today—not only in Japan, but in other countries, especially in the United States? What aspects of the Zen approach to living do you think are particularly influential? Why?

FIGURE 9.8   Shokintei (Pavilion of the Pine Lute), Katsura Palace gardens, near Kyoto, early 1660s. Named after the sound of wind in the pines that surround it, the pavilion is larger than many tea huts, but its setting conveys the harmony with nature that is such an important feature of Japanese aesthetics.

KEY TERMS

Jomon	*kami*	shogun	*cha-no-yu*
haniwa	*waka*	Pure Land Buddhism	*wabi*
Shinto	*emaki-mano*	Chan	
Kojiki	samurai	Zen Buddhism	

WWW. WEBSITES FOR FURTHER STUDY

http://www.japan-guide.com/e/e2055.html
(General information about Buddhism and its importation and development in Japan. Important dates and names are hyperlinked to other sections.)

http://www.city.kasugai.aichi.jp/world/english/tofu.html
(Tofu Ono [894–966] is one of the most best-known calligraphers in Japan. During the Heian period there was a movement to create culture indigenous to the Japanese people and not the prevailing influence of Chinese culture.)

READINGS

KAKINOMOTO NO HITOMARO

Kakinomoto no Hitomaro is generally considered the greatest poet of the Manyoshu, an eighth-century collection. His poems mostly consist of choka *(long poems) accompanied by envoys in the* tanka *(short poem) form. The following choka and tanka describe the poet/speaker's grief over the death of his wife.*

A poem by Kakinomoto no Hitomaro as he shed tears of blood in his grief following the death of his wife, with short poems.[1]

On the Karu Road
is the village of my wife,
and I desired to meet her intimately,
but if I went there too much
the eyes of others would cluster around us,   *5*
and if I went there too often
others would find us out.
And so I hoped
that later we would meet like
tangling vines,   *10*
trusted that we would
as I would trust a great ship,[2]
and hid my love:
faint as jewel's light,
a pool walled in by cliffs.   *15*
Then came the messenger,
his letter tied
to a jewelled catalpa twig,
to tell me,
in a voice   *20*
like the sound
of a catalpa bow,
that my girl,
who had swayed to me in sleep
like seaweed of the offing,   *25*
was gone
like the coursing sun
gliding into dusk,
like the radiant moon
secluding itself behind the clouds,   *30*
gone like the scarlet leaves of autumn.
I did not know what to say.
what to do,

but simply could not listen
and so, perhaps to solace   *35*
a single thousandth
of my thousand-folded longing,
I stood at the Karu market
where often she had gone,
and listened,   *40*
but could not even hear
the voices of the birds
that cry on Unebi Mountain,
where the maidens
wear strands of jewels,   *45*
and of the ones who passed me
on that road
straight as a jade spear,[3]
not one resembled her.
I could do nothing   *50*
but call my wife's name
and wave my sleeves.

Envoys

Too dense the yellowed leaves
on the autumn mountain:
my wife is lost   *55*
and I do not know the path
to find her by.

With the falling away
of the yellowed leaves,
I see the messenger   *60*
with his jeweled catalpa staff,
and I recall the days I met her.

ONO NO KOMACHI

Ono no Komachi (ca. 834–?) was a Japanese court lady who served at the imperial court in what is now Kyoto. Her intricate and passionate poems helped direct Japanese poetry toward a more subjective and personal style.

552

Did you come to me
because I dropped off to sleep
tormented by love?
If I had known I dreamed,
I would not have awakened.

---

[1]Translated by Ian Levy.
[2]A pillow phrase for "trust."

---

[3]A pillow-phrase for "road."

553

Since encountering
my beloved as I dozed,
I have come to feel
that it is dreams, not real life,
on which I can pin my hopes.

797

So much I have learned:
the blossom that fades away,
its color unseen,
is the flower in the heart
of one who lives in this world.

938

In this forlorn state
I find life dreary indeed:
if a stream beckoned,
I would gladly cut my roots
and float away like duckweed.

SEI SHŌNAGAN

Sei Shōnagan (ca. 966–1017) was one of a gifted coterie of women writers who served as ladies-in-waiting to the Japanese empresses of the late tenth and early eleventh centuries. Shōnagon's Pillow Book *(ca. 1002) is one of the two most popular and important books of its time; the other was Murasaki's* Tale of Genji. *Unlike* Genji, *which is a long, intricate work of fiction,* The Pillow Book *is an informal, unstructured work of personal observation and experience.*

Hateful Things

One is in a hurry to leave, but one's visitor keeps chattering away. If it is someone of no importance, one can get rid of him by saying, "You must tell me all about it next time"; but, should it be the sort of visitor whose presence commands one's best behaviour, the situation is hateful indeed.

One finds that a hair has got caught in the stone on which one is rubbing one's inkstick, or again that gravel is lodged in the inkstick, making a nasty, grating sound.

Someone has suddenly fallen ill and one summons the exorcist. Since he is not at home, one has to send messengers to look for him. After one has had a long fretful wait, the exorcist finally arrives, and with a sigh of relief one asks him to start his incantations. But perhaps he has been exorcizing too many evil spirits recently; for hardly has he installed himself and begun praying when his voice becomes drowsy. Oh, how hateful!

A man who has nothing in particular to recommend him discusses all sorts of subjects at random as though he knew everything.

An elderly person warms the palms of his hands over a brazier and stretches out the wrinkles. No young man would dream of behaving in such a fashion; old people can really be quite shameless. I have seen some dreary old creatures actually resting their feet on the brazier and rubbing them against the edge while they speak. These are the kind of people who in visiting someone's house first use their fans to wipe away the dust from the mat and, when they finally sit on it, cannot stay still but are forever spreading out the front of their hunting costume or even tucking it up under their knees. One might suppose that such behaviour was restricted to people of humble station; but I have observed it in quite well-bred people, including a Senior Secretary of the Fifth Rank[1] in the Ministry of Ceremonial and a former Governor of Suruga.

I hate the sight of men in their cups who shout, poke their fingers in their mouths, stroke their beards, and pass on the wine to their neighbours with great cries of "Have some more! Drink up!" They tremble; shake their heads, twist their faces, and gesticulate like children who are singing, "We're off to see the Governor." I have seen really well-bred people behave like this and I find it most distasteful.

To envy others and to complain about one's own lot; to speak badly about people; to be inquisitive about the most trivial matters and to resent and abuse people for not telling one, or, if one does manage to worm out some facts, to inform everyone in the most detailed fashion as if one had known all from the beginning—oh, how hateful!

One is just about to be told some interesting piece of news when a baby starts crying.

A flight of crows circle about with loud caws.

An admirer has come on a clandestine visit, but a dog catches sight of him and starts barking. One feels like killing the beast.

One has been foolish enough to invite a man to spend the night in an unsuitable place—and then he starts snoring.

A gentleman has visited one secretly. Though he is wearing a tall, lacquered hat,[2] he nevertheless wants no one to see him. He is so flurried, in fact, that upon leaving he bangs into something with his hat. Most hateful! It is annoying too when

---

[1]A codified system of court ranks designated various levels of preferment in descending order from Senior First Rank to Junior Eighth Rank, Lower Grade. The real cutoff point came after the Fifth Rank, because, in most cases, those of the first five ranks were the only ones eligible to be named *tenjōbito*, or "hall men." Their names were inscribed on a special roster, and they enjoyed the privilege of entering the Courtiers' Hall of the emperor's private quarters within the palace compound. The cream of society, numbering anywhere from twenty-five to one hundred, hall men were the courtiers who came into constant contact with the emperor and his entourage, including ladies-in-waiting like Sei Shōnagon and Murasaki Shikibu. These women, the chroniclers of court life, wrote about the men they saw every day: hall men of the Fifth Rank or above.
[2]Worn by noblemen; a bit too conspicuous for a clandestine visit.

he lifts up the Iyo blind[3] that hangs at the entrance of the room, then lets it fall with a great rattle. If it is a head-blind,[4] things are still worse, for being more solid it makes a terrible noise when it is dropped. There is a no excuse for such carelessness. Even a head-blind does not make any noise if one lifts it up gently on entering and leaving the room; the same applies to sliding-doors. If one's movements are rough, even a paper door will bend and resonate when opened; but, if one lifts the door a little while pushing it, there need be no sound.

One has gone to bed and is about to doze off when a mosquito appears, announcing himself in a reedy voice. One can actually feel the wind made by his wings and, slight though it is, one finds it hateful in the extreme.

A carriage passes with a nasty, creaking noise. Annoying to think that the passengers may not even be aware of this! If I am travelling in someone's carriage and I hear it creaking, I dislike not only the noise but also the owner of the carriage.

One is in the middle of a story when someone butts in and tries to show that he is the only clever person in the room. Such a person is hateful, and so, indeed, is anyone, child or adult, who tries to push himself forward.

One is telling a story about old times when someone breaks in with a little detail that he happens to know, implying that one's own version is inaccurate—disgusting behaviour!

Very hateful is a mouse that scurries all over the place.

Some children have called at one's house. One makes a great fuss of them and gives them toys to play with. The children become accustomed to this treatment and start to come regularly, forcing their way into one's inner rooms and scattering one's furnishings and possessions. Hateful!

A certain gentleman whom one does not want to see visits one at home or in the Palace, and one pretends to be asleep. But a maid comes to tell one and shakes one awake, with a look on her face that says, "What a sleepyhead!" Very hateful.

A newcomer pushes ahead of the other members in a group; with a knowing look, this person starts laying down the law and forcing advice upon everyone—most hateful.

A man with whom one is having an affair keeps singing the praises of some woman he used to know. Even if it is a thing of the past, this can be very annoying. How much more so if he is still seeing the woman! (Yet sometimes I find that it is not as unpleasant as all that.)

A person who recites a spell himself after sneezing.[5] In fact I detest anyone who sneezes, except the master of the house.

Fleas, too, are very hateful. When they dance about under someone's clothes, they really seem to be lifting them up.

The sound of dogs when they bark for a long time in chorus is ominous and hateful.

I cannot stand people who leave without closing the panel[6] behind them.

How I detest the husbands of nurse-maids! It is not so bad if the child in the maid's charge is a girl, because then the man will keep his distance. But; if it is a boy, he will behave as though he were the father. Never letting the boy out of his sight, he insists on managing everything. He regards the other attendants in the house as less than human, and, if anyone tries to scold the child, he slanders him to the master. Despite this disgraceful behaviour, no one dare accuse the husband; so he strides about the house with a proud, self-important look, giving all the orders.

I hate people whose letters show that they lack respect for wordly civilities, whether by discourtesy in the phrasing or by extreme politeness to someone who does not deserve it. This sort of thing is, of course, most odious if the letter is for oneself, but it is bad enough even if it is addressed to someone else.

As a matter of fact, most people are too casual, not only in their letters but in their direct conversation. Sometimes I am quite disgusted at noting how little decorum people observe when talking to each other. It is particularly unpleasant to hear some foolish man or woman omit the proper marks of respect when addressing a person of quality; and, when servants fail to use honorific forms of speech in referring to their masters, it is very bad indeed. No less odious, however, are those masters who, in addressing their servants, use such phrases as "When you were good enough to do such-and-such" or "As you so kindly remarked." No doubt there are some masters who, in describing their own actions to a servant, say, "I presumed to do so-and-so!"[7]

Sometimes a person who is utterly devoid of charm will try to create a good impression by using very elegant language; yet he only succeeds in being ridiculous. No doubt he believes this refined language is to be just what the occasion demands, but, when it goes so far that everyone bursts out laughing, surely something must be wrong.

---

[3]A rough type of reed blind made in the province of Iyo.
[4]An elegant type of blind whose top and edges were decorated with silk strips; it had thin strips of bamboo along the edges and thus was heavier than ordinary blinds.

[5]Sneezing, a bad omen, was counteracted by reciting an auspicious formula, such as wishing long life to the person who had sneezed.
[6]A sliding door.
[7]Shaky command of the various levels of honorific language was an anathema in this hierarchic society.

It is most improper to address high-ranking courtiers, Imperial Advisers, and the like simply by using their names without any titles or marks of respect; but such mistakes are fortunately rare.

If one refers to the maid who is in attendance on some lady-in-waiting as "Madam" or "that lady," she will be surprised, delighted, and lavish in her praise.

When speaking to young noblemen and courtiers of high rank, one should always (unless Their Majesties are present) refer to them by their official post. Incidentally, I have been very shocked to hear important people use the word "I" while conversing in Their Majesties' presence.[8] Such a breach of etiquette is really distressing, and I fail to see why people cannot avoid it.

A man who has nothing in particular to recommend him but who speaks in an affected tone and poses as being elegant.

An inkstone with such a hard, smooth surface that the stick glides over it without leaving any deposit of ink.

Ladies-in-waiting who want to know everything that is going on.

Sometimes one greatly dislikes a person for no particular reason—and then that person goes and does something hateful.

A gentleman who travels alone in his carriage to see a procession or some other spectacle. What sort of a man is he? Even though he may not be a person of the greatest quality, surely he should have taken along a few of the many young men who are anxious to see the sights. But no, there he sits by himself (one can see his silhouette through the blinds), with a proud look on his face, keeping all his impressions to himself.

A lover who is leaving at dawn announces that he has to find his fan and his paper.[9] "I know I put them somewhere last night," he says. Since it is pitch dark, he gropes about the room, bumping into the furniture and muttering, "Strange! Where on earth can they be?" Finally he discovers the objects. He thrusts the paper into the breast of his robe with a great rustling sound; then he snaps open his fan and busily fans away with it. Only now is he ready to take his leave. What charmless behaviour! "Hateful" is an understatement.

---

[8]Court etiquette demanded that in the presence of the emperor or empress one referred to oneself by one's name rather than by the first-person singular.

[9]Paper squares (often colored) that courtiers carried in the folds of their clothes; they were used to write notes or poems and also as a kind of elegant tissue.

Equally disagreeable is the man who, when leaving in the middle of the night, takes care to fasten the cord of his headdress. This is quite unnecessary; he could perfectly well put it gently on his head without tying the cord. And why must he spend time adjusting his cloak or hunting costume? Does he really think someone may see him at this time of night and criticize him for not being impeccably dressed?

A good lover will behave as elegantly at dawn as at any other time. He drags himself out of bed with a look of dismay on his face. The lady urges him on: "Come, my friend, it's getting light. You don't want anyone to find you here." He gives a deep sigh, as if to say that the night has not been nearly long enough and that it is agony to leave. Once up, he does not instantly pull on his trousers. Instead he comes close to the lady and whispers whatever was left unsaid during the night. Even when he is dressed, he still lingers, vaguely pretending to be fastening his sash.

Presently he raises the lattice, and the two lovers stand together by the side door while he tells her how he dreads the coming day, which will keep them apart; then he slips away. The lady watches him go, and this moment of parting will remain among her most charming memories.

Indeed, one's attachment to a man depends largely on the elegance of his leave-taking. When he jumps out of bed, scurries about the room, tightly fastens his trouser-sash, rolls up the sleeves of his Court cloak, over-robe, or hunting costume, stuffs his belongings into the breast of his robe and then briskly secures the outer sash—one really begins to hate him.

MURASAKI SHIKIBU

from *The Tale of Genji*

One modern critic has suggested that The Tale of Genji *is "a study of the distinctive features of love—its language, forms, and conventions" and that its author is "really interested in the dynamic of love at the emotional and psychological level." These qualities are well illustrated in the following excerpt.*

The Shell of the Locust

Genji lay sleepless.

"I am not used to such treatment. Tonight I have for the first time seen how a woman can treat a man. The shock and the shame are such that I do not know how I can go on living."

The boy was in tears, which made him even more charming. The slight form, the not too long hair—was it Genji's imagination that he was much like his sister? The resemblance was very affecting, even if imagined. It would be undignified to make an issue of the matter and seek the woman out, and so Genji passed the night in puzzled resentment. The boy found him less friendly than usual.

Genji left before daylight. Very sad, thought the boy, lonely without him.

The lady too passed a difficult night. There was no further word from Genji. It seemed that he had had enough of her. She would not be happy if he had in fact given her up, but with half her mind she dreaded another visit. It would be as well to have an end of the affair. Yet she went on grieving.

For Genji there was gnawing dissatisfaction. He could not forget her, and he feared he was making a fool of himself.

"I am in a sad state," he said to the boy. "I try to forget her, and I cannot. Do you suppose you might contrive another meeting?"

It would be difficult, but the boy was delighted even at this sort of attention. With childish eagerness he watched for an opportunity. Presently the governor of Kii had to go off to his province. The lady had nothing to do through the long twilight hours. Under cover of darkness, the boy took Genji to the governor's mansion in his own carriage. Genji had certain misgivings. His guide was after all a mere child. But this was no time for hesitation. Dressed inconspicuously, he urged the boy on, lest they arrive after the gates were barred. The carriage was brought in through a back gate and Genji dismounted.

So young a boy attracted little attention and indeed little deference from the guards. He left Genji at an east door to the main hall. He pounded on the south shutters and went inside.

"Shut it, shut it!" shrieked the women. "The whole world can see us."

"But why do you have them closed on such a warm evening?"

"The lady from the west wing has been here since noon. They have been at Go."

Hoping to see them at the Go board, Genji slipped from his hiding place and made his way through the door and the blinds. The shutter through which the boy had gone was still raised. Genji could see through to the west. One panel of a screen just inside had been folded back, and the curtains, which should have shielded off the space beyond, had been thrown over their frames, perhaps because of the heat. The view was unobstructed.

There was a lamp near the women. The one in silhouette with her back against a pillar—would she be the one on whom his heart was set? He looked first at her. She seemed to have on a purple singlet with a woven pattern, and over it a cloak of which the color and material were not easy to determine. She was a small, rather ordinary lady with delicate features. She evidently wanted to conceal her face even from the girl opposite, and she kept her thin little hands tucked in her sleeves. Her opponent was facing east, and Genji had a full view of her face. Over a singlet of white gossamer she had thrown a purplish cloak, and both garments were somewhat carelessly open all the way to the band of the red trousers. She was very handsome, tall and plump and of a fair complexion, and the lines of her head and forehead were strong and pleas-

ing. It was a sunny face, with a beguiling cheerfulness about the eyes and mouth. Though not particularly long, the hair was rich and thick, and very beautiful where it fell about her shoulders. He could detect no marked flaws, and saw why her father, the governor of Iyo, so cherished her. It might help, to be sure, if she were just a little quieter. Yet she did not seem to be merely silly. She brimmed with good spirits as she placed a stone upon a dead spot to signal the end of the game.

"Just a minute, if you please," said the other very calmly. "It is not quite over. You will see that we have a *ko to get out of the way first.*"

"I've lost, I've lost. Let's just see what I have in the corners." She counted up on her fingers. "Ten, twenty, thirty, forty." She would have had no trouble, he thought, taking the full count of the baths of Iyo—though her manner might have been just a touch inelegant.

The other woman, a model of demureness, kept her face hidden. Gazing at her, Genji was able to make out the details of the profile. The eyelids seemed a trifle swollen, the lines of the nose were somewhat erratic, and there was a weariness, a want of luster, about the face. It was, one had to admit, a little on the plain side. Yet she clearly paid attention to her appearance, and there were details likely to draw the eye to a subtler sensibility than was evident in her lively companion. The latter, very engaging indeed, laughed ever more happily. There was no denying the bright gaiety, and in her way she was interesting enough. A shallow, superficial thing, no doubt, but to his less than pure heart she seemed a prize not to be flung away. All the ladies he knew were so prim and proper. This was the first time he had seen one so completely at her ease. He felt a little guilty, but not so guilty that he would have turned away had he not heard the boy coming back. He slipped outside.

Apologetic that his master should still be at the beginning, the boy said that the unexpected guest had interfered with his plans.

"You mean to send me off frustrated once more? It is really too much."

"No, sir. But I must ask you to wait until the other lady has gone. I'll arrange everything then, I promise you."

Things seemed to be arranging themselves. The boy was very young, but he was calmly self-possessed and had a good eye for the significant things.

The game of Go was apparently over. There was a stir inside, and a sound as of withdrawing.

"Where will that boy have gone?" Now there was a banging of shutters. "Let's get the place closed up."

"No one seems to be stirring." said Genji after a time. "Go and do your best."

The boy knew well enough that it was not his sister's nature to encourage frivolity. He must admit Genji when there was almost no one with her.

"Is the guest still here?" asked Genji. "I would like a glimpse of her."

"Quite impossible. There are curtains inside the shutters."

Genji was amused, but thought it would be bad manners to let the boy know that he had already seen the lady. "How slowly time does go by."

This time the boy knocked on the corner door and was admitted.

"I'll just make myself comfortable here," he said, spreading bedclothes where one or two of the sliding doors had been left open. "Come in, breezes."

Numbers of older women seemed to be sleeping out near the veranda. The girl who had opened the door seemed to have joined them. The boy feigned sleep for a time. Then, spreading a screen to block the light, he motioned Genji inside.

Genji was suddenly shy, fearing he would be defeated once more. He followed the boy all the same. Raising a curtain, he slipped into the main room. It was very quiet, and his robes rustled alarmingly.

With one part of her mind the woman was pleased that he had not given up. But the nightmare of the earlier evening had not left her. Brooding days, sleepless nights—it was summer, and yet it was 'budless spring.'

Her companion at Go, meanwhile, was as cheerful as could be. "I shall stay with you tonight," she announced. It was not likely that she would have trouble sleeping.

The lady herself sensed that something was amiss. Detecting an unusual perfume, she raised her head. It was dark where the curtain had been thrown over the frame, but she could see a form creeping toward her. In a panic, she got up. Pulling a singlet of raw silk over her shoulders, she slipped from the room.

Genji was delighted to see that there was only one lady asleep behind the curtains. There seemed to be two people asleep out toward the veranda. As he pulled aside the bedclothes it seemed to him that the lady was somewhat larger than he would have expected. He became aware of one odd detail after another in the sleeping figure, and guessed what had happened. How very stupid! And how ridiculous he would seem if the sleeper were to awaken and see that she was the victim of a silly mistake. It would be equally silly to pursue the lady he had come for, now that she had made her feelings so clear. A new thought came to him: might this be the girl who had so interested him in the lamplight? If so, what had he to lose? It will be observed that a certain fickleness was at work.

The girl was now awake, and very surprised. Genji felt a little sorry for her. But though inexperienced in the ways of love, she was bright and modern, and she had not entirely lost her composure. He was at first reluctant to identify himself. She would presently guess, however, and what did it matter if she did? As for the unfriendly one who had fled him and who was so concerned about appearances—he did have to think of her reputation, and so he said to the girl that he had taken advantage of directional taboos to visit her. A more experienced lady would have had no trouble guessing the truth, but this one did not sense that his explanation was a little forced. He was not displeased with her, nor was he strongly drawn to her. His heart was resentfully on the other. No doubt she would be off in some hidden chamber gloating over her victory. She had shown a most extraordinary firmness of purpose. In a curious way, her hostility made her memorable. The girl beside him had a certain young charm of her own, and presently he was deep in vows of love.

"The ancients used to say that a secret love runs deeper than an open one." He was most persuasive. "Think well of me. I must worry about appearances, and it is not as if I could go where my desires take me. And you: there are people who would not at all approve. That is sad. But you must not forget me."

"I'm afraid." Clearly she was afraid. "I won't be able to write to you."

"You are right that we would not want people to know. But there is the little man I brought with me tonight. We can exchange notes through him. Meanwhile you must behave as if nothing has happened." He took as a keepsake a summer robe the other lady seemed to have thrown off.

The boy was sleeping nearby. The adventure was on his mind, however, and Genji had no trouble arousing him. As he opened the door an elderly serving woman called out in surprise.

"Who's there?"

"Just me," replied the boy in some confusion.

"Wherever are you going at this time of the night?" The woman came out, wishing to be helpful.

"Nowhere," said the boy gruffly. "Nowhere at all."

He pushed Genji through the door. Dawn was approaching. The woman caught sight of another figure in the moonlight.

"And who is with you? Oh, Mimbu, of course. Only Mimbu reaches such splendid heights." Mimbu was a lady who was the victim of much humor because of her unusual stature. So he was out walking with Mimbu, muttered the old woman. "One of these days you'll be as tall as Mimbu yourself." Chattering away, she followed after them. Genji was horrified, but could not very well shove her inside. He pulled back into the darkness of a gallery.

Still she followed. "You've been with our lady, have you? I've been having a bad time with my stomach these last few days and I've kept to my room. But she called me last night and said she wanted more people around. I'm still having a terrible time. Terrible," she muttered again, getting no answer. "Well, goodbye, then."

She moved on, and Genji made his escape. He saw more than ever how dangerous these adventures can be.

The boy went with him to Nijō. Genji recounted the happenings of the night. The boy had not done very well, he said, shrugging his shoulders in annoyance at the thought of the woman's coldness. The boy could find no answer.

"I am rejected, and there is nothing to be done for me. But why could she not have sent a pleasant answer? I'm no match for that husband of hers. That's where the trouble lies." But when he went to bed he had her cloak beneath his own. He kept the boy beside him, audience for his laments.

"It's not that you aren't a nice enough boy; and it's not that I'm not fond of you. But because of your family I must have doubts about the durability of our relationship."

A remark which plunged the boy into the darkest melancholy.

Genji was still unable to sleep. He said that he required an inkstone. On a fold of paper he jotted down a verse as if for practice:

'Beneath a tree, a locust's empty shell.
Sadly I muse upon the shell of a lady.'

He wondered what the other one, the stepdaughter, would be thinking of him; but though he felt rather sorry for her and though he turned the matter over in his mind, he sent no message. The lady's fragrance lingered in the robe he had taken. He kept it with him, gazing fondly at it.

The boy, when he went to his sister's house, was crushed by the scolding he received. "This is the sort of thing a person cannot be expected to put up with. I may try to explain what has happened, but can you imagine that people will not come to their own conclusions? Does it not occur to you that even your good master might wish to see an end to this childishness?"

Badgered from the left and badgered from the right, the poor boy did not know where to turn. He took out Genji's letter. In spite of herself his sister opened and read it. That reference to the shell of the locust: he had taken her robe, then. How very embarrassing. A sodden rag, like the one discarded by the fisherman of Ise.

The other lady, her stepdaughter, returned in some disorder to her own west wing. She had her sad thoughts all to herself, for no one knew what had happened. She watched the boy's comings and goings, thinking that there might be some word; but in the end there was none. She did not have the imagination to guess that she had been a victim of mistaken identity. She was a lighthearted and inattentive creature, but now she was lost in sad thoughts.

The lady in the main hall kept herself under tight control. She could see that his feelings were not to be described as shallow, and she longed for what would not return, her maiden days. Besides his poem she jotted down a poem by Lady Ise:

THE DEW UPON THE FRAGILE LOCUST WING
IS LOST AMONG THE LEAVES. LOST ARE MY TEARS.

YOSHIDA KENKO

Yoshida Kenko (ca. 1283–1350) was a Buddhist monk who wrote during the Muromachi and the Kamakura periods. He is best known for his Tsurezuregusa, *usually translated as* Essays in Idleness, *but sometimes as* Leisure Notes. *His collection of brief essays is one of the most studied of Japanese literary works, and it remains today a staple of the Japanese high school curriculum.*

Essay 75

I wonder what feelings inspire a man to complain of "having nothing to do." I am happiest when I have nothing to distract me and I am completely alone.

If a man conforms to society, his mind will be captured by the filth of the outside world, and he is easily led astray; if he mingles in society, he must be careful that his words do not offend others, and what he says will not at all be what he feels

in his heart. He will joke with others only to quarrel with them, now resentful, now happy, his feelings in constant turmoil. Calculations of advantage will wantonly intrude, and not a moment will be free from considerations of profit and loss. Intoxication is added to delusion, and in a state of inebriation the man dreams. People are all alike: they spend their days running about frantically, oblivious to their insanity.

Even if a man has not yet discovered the path of enlightenment, as long as he removes himself from his worldly ties, leads a quiet life, and maintains his peace of mind by avoiding entanglements, he may be said to be happy, at least for the time being.

It is written in *Maka Shikan*, "Break your ties with your daily activities, with personal affairs, with your arts, and with learning."

Essay 189

You may intend to do something today, only for pressing business to come up unexpectedly and take up all of your attention the rest of the day. Or a person you have been expecting is prevented from coming, or someone you hadn't expected comes calling. The thing you have counted on goes amiss, and the thing you had no hopes for is the only one to succeed. A matter which promised to be a nuisance passes off smoothly, and a matter which should have been easy proves a great hardship. Our daily experiences bear no resemblance to what we had anticipated. This is true throughout the year, and equally true for our entire lives. But if we decide that everything is bound to go contrary to our anticipations, we discover that naturally there are also some things which do not contradict expectations. This makes it all the harder to be definite about anything. The one thing you can be certain of is the truth that all is uncertainty.

Essay 108

Nobody begrudges wasting a little time. Does this represent a reasoned judgement or merely foolishness, I wonder. If I were to address myself to those who are lazy out of foolishness, I should point that a single copper coin is of trifling value, but an accumulation of these coins will make a rich man of a poor man. That is why a merchant so jealously hoards each coin. We may not be aware of the passing instants, but as we go on ceaselessly spending them, suddenly the term of life is on us. For this reason, the man who practices the Way should not begrudge the passage of distant time to come, but the wasting of a single present moment.

If some man came and informed you that you would certainly lose your life the following day, what would you have to look forward to, what would you do to occupy yourself while waiting for this day to end? In what does the day we are now living differ from our last day? Much of our time during any day is wasted in eating and drinking, at stool, in sleeping, talking and walking. To engage in useless activities, to talk about useless things, and to think about useless things during the brief moments of free time left us is not only to waste this time, but to blot out days that extend into months and eventually into a whole lifetime. This is most foolish of all.

Hsieh Ling-yun edited the translation of the Lotus Sutra, but his mind was constantly preoccupied with his hopes for advancement; Hui-yuan therefore denied his admission to the White Lotus society.

A man who fails even for a short time to keep in mind the preciousness of time is no different from a corpse. If you wish to know why each instant must be guarded so jealously, it is so that a man inwardly will have no confusing thoughts and outwardly no concern with worldly matters; that if he wishes to rest at that point, he may rest, but if he wishes to follow the Way, he may follow it.

CHAPTER 10

HISTORY

5000 B.C.E.	Sedentary agriculture in West African savannahs
3000 B.C.E.	Bantu Migration
700 B.C.E.	Iron working in northern Tanzania
500 B.C.E.	Iron working in West Africa
3rd century B.C.E.	Jenne-Jeno and Gao settled in fertile inland delta of Niger river
1st century B.C.E.	Traders from Mediterranean and India sail to East African coast
early centuries C.E.	Romans unify Mediterranean region, including North Africa; Christianity spreads throughout region
219–38 C.E.	Yax Moch Xoc rules over Tikal
431 C.E.	Bahlum Kuk founds Palenque
650–700 C.E.	Earthquake in Andes
651 C.E.	Defeat of Muslim forces by Christian Nubians at the battle of Dongala
ca. 750 C.E.	Teotihuacán sacked and burned
8th century C.E.	Islamic state firmly entrenched in North Africa
9th century C.E.	Igbo-Ukwu developed in forest region of Southeastern Nigeria
1000 C.E.	Introduction of bananas from the Indian Ocean
13th century C.E.	Benin, one of the largest and longest-lived forest states strengthens
ca. 1325 C.E.	Aztecs build city of Tenochtitlán
15th century C.E.	Portuguese establish trading posts at El Mina (modern day Ghana) and with Kongo Kingdom at Luenda
ca. 1502–20 C.E.	Moctezuma II reigns as Aztec emperor
1519 C.E.	Cortés arrives in Mexico
1532 C.E.	Pizarro encounters and overthrows Inca empire
18th century C.E.	Slave trade peaks at ca. 100,000 per year

ARTS AND ARCHITECTURE

70,000 B.C.E.	Cave artifacts at Blombos in South Africa
4800 B.C.E.	Rock paintings in Sahara and South Africa regions
ca. 900–500 B.C.E.	Colossal Head
ca. 100 B.C.E.–500 C.E.	*Moche Lord with a Feline*
ca. 150 C.E.	Pyramid of the Sun
451 C.E.	Coptic (Egyptian) and Nestorian (Middle Eastern) Christian churches break with Roman church
ca. 500 C.E.	Huaca del Sol (Pyramid of the Sun)
7th century C.E.	Temple of Inscriptions
13th century C.E.	Benin region develops sophisticated state-sponsored art program built around the casting of bronze sculptures using "lost wax" casting
15th century C.E.	Coatlicue
ca. 1450 C.E.	Machu Picchu built

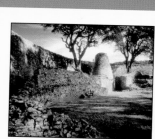

LITERATURE AND PHILOSOPHY

16th century C.E.	*Popol Vuh* Cantares Mexicanes

Early Civilizations
of the Americas and Africa

Machu Picchu, Inca culture, Peru, ca. 1450.

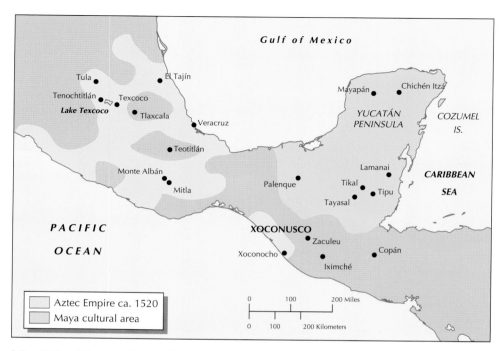

MAP 10.1 Mesoamerica on the Eve of the Spanish Conquest.

CHAPTER OVERVIEW

MESOAMERICA
"Middle America" Establishes Itself as a Cultural Mecca

THE CULTURES OF PERU
Geographical Constraints Fail to Hinder Civilizations Unique to the World

NORTH AMERICA
Vast Lands and Opportunities Provide the Basis for Rich Cultural Heritages from Coast to Coast

CIVILIZATION OF EARLY AFRICA
Multiple Cultures Thrive and Evolve

Sometime between 30,000 and 12,000 years ago, at the height of the Ice Age, tribal hunters began to migrate from Asia into the Americas across a land bridge that extended for perhaps a thousand miles south of the present-day Bering Straits. This giant plain was rich in grass and animal life, and the tribes were naturally drawn on further across it, and then on southward, in pursuit of game. By 11,000 B.C.E., they had reached the tip of South America and the Atlantic coast of North America.

As the ice melted and the oceans rose at the close of the Ice Age, the tribes in the Americas were cut off from Asia and Europe. This isolation lasted until October 12, 1492, when Christopher Columbus landed on San Salvador in the Bahamas. Thinking he was on the east coast of Asia, near India, Columbus called the people who met him "Indios," Indians. These Native Americans seemed simple and uncivilized to Columbus, but they were in fact the descendants of ancient and often quite magnificent civilizations, some of which dated back to the first millennium B.C.E.

MESOAMERICA

Mesoamerica is a cultural area extending from central Mexico to Honduras, and includes Belize and Guatemala. The ancient Mesoamerican cultures include those of the Olmecs (1300–600 B.C.E.), the Maya (250 B.C.E.–900 C.E.), and the Toltecs (900–1200), precursors of the Aztecs (1350–1521), along with the civilization of Teotihuacán (100–800). The Mesoamericans spoke many languages. Among these was the Nahua family of languages, which includes the language of the Aztecs and the Maya, dialects of which survive to this day in southern Mexico and Guatemala. The diverse early Mesoamerican civilizations shared other cultural features, including hieroglyphic writing, an applied knowledge of astronomy, early cultivation of maize, the use of calendars, and a form of monarchical government intimately linked with religious ideas and practices.

Prior to the arrival of Europeans in Mesoamerica, the various complex civilizations that sprouted and withered influenced one another and were interconnected. The high level of interaction among these ancient Mesoamerican societies included trading in raw materials, such as obsidian, and products such as carved jade. Over the roughly 2,500 years from the rise of the Olmecs to the decline of the Aztecs, ideas and inventions, such as writing and the calendar, were exchanged along with the trade in goods.

THE OLMECS

The earliest Mesoamerican art dates from about 1300 B.C.E. when the Olmecs inhabited the southern coast of the Gulf of Mexico, especially the area between Veracruz and Tabasco. There is some question whether the Olmecs were a distinct people and culture or whether the term "Olmec," which derives from a word for rubber, refers to an artistic style that prevailed throughout ancient Central America.

Whoever they were, the Olmecs were outstanding stone carvers. The most remarkable carvings that have survived to the present day are a series of sixteen colossal stone heads up to twelve feet high (fig. 10.1). Eight of these heads were found in San Lorenzo, Veracruz, where they were placed facing outward on the circumference of a ceremonial area. They are carved of basalt. Because the nearest basalt quarry is fifty miles away in the Tuxtla Mountains, the enormous stones from which the heads were carved had, apparently, to be dragged down from the mountains, loaded onto rafts, floated down to the Gulf of Mexico, then up river to San Lorenzo, and finally dragged up and positioned on the ceremonial plateau.

Believed to be portraits of Olmec rulers, the heads share similar facial features, including flattened noses, thick lips, and puffy cheeks. They all are capped with headgear similar to old-style American football helmets. This is believed to have served as protection in war and in a type of

FIGURE 10.1 Colossal Head, from La Venta, Mexico, Olmec culture, ca. 900–500 B.C.E., basalt, height 7′ 5″ (2.26 m), La Venta Park, Villahermosa, Tabasco, Mexico. This example of a giant carved stone head represents the height of sculptural achievement among the ancient Olmecs.

ceremonial ball game played throughout Mesoamerica. Among other discoveries at San Lorenzo are stone figurines of ball players and a ball court. (See Then & Now p. 348 and Figure 10.2.)

TEOTIHUACÁN

Among the most splendid of all Mesoamerican sites must be the ancient city of TEOTIHUÁCAN [te-oh-te-wu-KAN], which means "where one becomes a god." **Teotihuacán** (fig. 10.3) grew to dominance after 300 B.C.E. By the time it reached the height of its political and cultural influence, between ca. 350–650 C.E., its population numbered between 100,000 and 200,000, making it one of the largest cities on earth at the time.

Critical Thinking

WHAT IS A CITY?

Scholars have debated the issue of what constitutes a "city," or an urban center, in the ancient world. Much of the debate has centered on whether writing is an essential characteristic. Other potential characteristics include formal organization, diverse populations, and interdependence. Which of these traits do you think is most important in deciding on whether a place might be defined as a city? Why? And what other traits could or should be considered as elements that would qualify a site as a city?

The people of Teotihuacán were great pyramid builders. The city is laid out in a grid pattern with a giant avenue (the Avenue of the Dead) at its center. This central artery links two great pyramids, the Pyramids of the Moon and of the Sun, which are the focal points of six hundred smaller pyramids, five hundred workshop areas, nearly two thousand apartment compounds, numerous plazas, and a giant market area. Built in about 150 C.E. over a natural cave (but only rediscovered in 1971), the Pyramid of the Sun is oriented to mark the passage of the sun from east to west and the rising of the stellar constellation the Pleiades on the days of the equinox. Thus it links the underworld to the heavens, the forces of life and death.

Along the Avenue of the Dead are a series of ziggurat-like structures with numerous steps leading to an elevated platform, which originally supported a temple. After the Pyramids of the Sun and the Moon, the most important structure in Teotihuacán was the Temple of Quetzalcoatl, the god of priestly wisdom. This temple contains elaborate relief carvings, which include the heads of feathered serpents and fire serpents.

The overall design and layout of Teotihuacán suggests its role as an astronomical and ritualistic center. The relation of the Pyramid of the Sun to the others suggests the order of the universe, a cosmological order that influenced all aspects of life, including political organization, social behavior, and religious ritual. Even time was represented. Each of the two staircases of the Pyramid of the Sun, for example, contains 182 steps, which, when the platform at the apex is added, together total 365. This spatial representation of the solar calendar is echoed in the Temple of Quetzalcoatl, which has 364 serpent fangs.

By about 700, Teotihuacán's influence had waned, and the city was sacked and burned in about 750. We can only speculate about what finally led to its demise, but an ecological explanation is possible. The surrounding countryside had been pillaged to provide lime for the mortar used to build Teotihuacán. As the city's population grew, adequate provision of food became a problem. Coupled with the effects of drought, the environmental catastrophe wreaked on the countryside probably made it impossible to maintain a stable civilization.

FIGURE 10.2   An ancient ball court at Monte Alban in the Mexican valley of Oaxaca. © Danny Lehman/CORBIS, NY. All Rights Reserved. Various types of ball games were played in Mexico for more than two thousand years.

Then & Now

Chocolate

Chocolate has long been a popular food in the Americas and in Europe, especially in Belgium, France, Spain, and Switzerland. The origins of chocolate go deep into ancient Mesoamerica. Centuries before the Maya used chocolate as currency and the Aztecs consumed it in unsweetened liquid form, chocolate seeds of the *Theobroma* cacao tree were transformed into an edible treat. The Aztecs declared *xocaltl*, or chocolate, to be a gift from their god Quetzalcoatl and served it as a drink to members of the court. The Toltecs staged rituals in which chocolate-colored dogs were sacrificed. According to Hernando Cortez's account of Aztec life, Montezuma's court drank two thousand pitchers of chocolate a day. And when the conquistadors searched his palace, looking for gold and silver, they found enormous quantities of cocoa beans instead.

The Maya were also chocolate lovers and served a spicy, bittersweet fermented drink made from the seeds of cocoa beans and mixed with maize and chili peppers. With the Spanish conquest of the Maya in central America, chocolate was introduced into Europe, where its bitterness was tempered by mixing in sugar and vanilla, and where it became the stimulating drink of kings and aristocrats, and later, a popular dessert treat for the masses (the Hershey bar), prior to its more recent status as a luxury item (the truffles of Godiva). Its popularity today remains unabated as a component of "sinful" desserts (what restaurant omits chocolate from its desserts?), as a hot drink for adults when mixed with coffee in café mocha, as a cold sweetened drink for children, as a supposed aphrodisiac, as a stimulus with purported medical benefits, and, of course, as the main ingredient in the most decadent of desserts, including the chocolate bombe and a mousse called Chocolate Suicide offered by a restaurant in St. Louis.

FIGURE 10.3   Teotihuacán, Mexico, Teotihuacán culture, 350–650 C.E. The city of Teotihuacán covered an area nine miles square and contained between 100,000 and 200,000 people, an enormous scale and population for a culture of its time.

Connections

Recently, archaeologists have made a number of stunning discoveries amidst ancient ruins in San Barto, Guatemala. Among the most important of these finds is the earliest known Mayan writing, a column of hieroglyphs that pushes back the date of a developed writing system hundreds of years. One problem, however, is that the archaeologists have had great difficulty translating these newly discovered hieroglyphs. They are expected to be helped, though, by another discovery nearby of murals in vivid colors depicting the Mayan myth of creation and kingship. Scholars will analyze the murals seeking clues to breaking the code of the ancient pre-classical period writing. They will also use Mayan writing of a millennium later to find connections with the earlier hieroglyphs. In addition, the discovery of additional examples of the ancient writing at other sites is also expected to aid in their decoding efforts.

MAYAN CULTURE

The ancient Maya inhabited the Yucatán peninsula, which extends into Belize and Guatemala, parts of the Mexican states of Chiapas and Tabasco, and the western part of Honduras and El Salvador. The culture appears to have lasted from about 250 B.C.E. to 900 C.E. Although the Maya possessed their own form of hieroglyphic writing, they shared with other Mesoamerican peoples the use of books made of fig-bark paper or deerskin that unfolded into screens.

The ancient Maya are set apart from their ancient Mesoamerican neighbors, however, in their arithmetical and astronomical knowledge, which rivaled that of the ancient Babylonians. The Maya possessed a profound understanding of the regularity and continuity of the heavenly bodies, which they saw as a metaphor for the ruler's consistent safeguarding of his people.

Mayan writing is the most expressive and complex in the Native American world. Mayan writing survived in part because it was carved into stone and thus was able to withstand destruction and decay. Mayan writing falls into two main categories: (1) dynastic records, including the genealogies of rulers and records of their victories, sacrifices, and communion with their ancestors; (2) astronomical records and priestly timekeeping records. Interestingly and paradoxically, the Mayan writing system was designed less to communicate than to keep information secret, one reason that its esoteric code took so long for scholars to crack and interpret.

The Mayan Universe. For the Maya, the universe consisted of three layers—the Upperworld of the heavens, the Middleworld of human civilization, and the Underworld below—linked by a great tree, the **Wacan Chan** which grew from the center of the Middleworld and from which the cardinal directions flowed. Each direction possessed its own symbolic significance and was represented by its own color, bird, and gods. East was the principal direction, since the sun rose there, and its color was red. North was the direction of the dead, and its color was white. The king was the personification of the Wacah Chan. When he stood at the top of a pyramid in ritual activity, he was seen to link the three layers of the universe in his own person. During such rituals, the king would let his own blood in order to give sustenance to the spiritual world. Although ritual bloodletting seems to many people to be a barbaric or at least an exotic practice, we should remember that Christians symbolically drink the blood of Jesus when they celebrate Holy Communion. The role of blood in Mayan ritual is similar.

To the Maya, time was not linear, as we conceive it, but cyclical. They used two calendars. The first was a 365-day farming calendar that consisted of eighteen "months" of twenty days each and one short month of just five days. The second was a sacred calendar of 260 days, which probably relates to the average length of human gestation from the first missed menstrual flow to birth (actually 266 days). It is clear that this second calendar possesses a close connection to Mayan bloodletting rituals. The Mayans combined the two calendars to create a long cycle of fifty-two years, or 18,980 days (a particular day in one calendar will fall on the same day in the other calendar every fifty-two years), at the end of which time repeated itself.

Mayan Literature and Myth. The great work of Mayan myth and literature is the *Popol Vuh*, an epic narrative that describes the creation of the world. Written in the Quiche language around 1500, but regarded as extant during the Mayan classic era, the *Popol Vuh* outlines traditional Mayan views on human beings as well as the origins of the world. According to the story, the gods wished to create intelligent beings who would praise them. They made three unsuccessful attempts, using mud, wood, and animals as materials, before they decided to use water and maize, critically important substances in Mesoamerican culture. Like the Homeric epics for ancient Greece and the Mahabharata of ancient India, the *Popol Vuh* serves Mesoamerica as a repository of its cultural ideals and values.

Tikal. Among the most important sites of classic Mayan culture is that of TIKAL [te-KAL], in present-day Guatemala. There, one of the great "ancestors" of Mayan civilization, Yax Moch Xoc (r. 219–38 C.E.), ruled over a city that contained in an area of just over six square miles six giant temple-pyramids used for the celebration of religious rituals of the kind just described.

The meticulously ordered layout of Teotihuacán is not characteristic of Mayan cities. Tikal and other Mayan urban centers seem instead to have grown by accretion, undergoing rebuilding and modification over centuries. Most striking among the remains of Tikal's buildings are six enormous temple-pyramids (fig. 10.4). Two of these are unusually steep, rising to a height of nearly 230 feet, and face each other across a large grassy square. Each is topped by an extension that resembles the comb of a rooster, called a **roof comb,** and gives the impression of an elevated throne on an enormously high dais.

War dominated Tikal life. For two hundred years after 300 C.E., Tikal exercised power over the southeastern region of Mesoamerica. Its patron and protector was the Jaguar God, whose strength and hunting ability were likened to the power of the king himself and the warlike ferocity of the Tikal people. Like the king, the jaguar can adapt to every environment, hunting with equal facility on land, in water, and even in the Upperworld of the trees. That it hunts at night, with eyesight that penetrates the darkness, suggests its magical powers.

The Jaguar Kings of Palenque. The Jaguar God is common to all Mesoamerican cultures, from the Olmecs to the Aztecs. At Palenque, the Mayan kings called themselves Bahlum, "Jaguar," and their history is recorded on the Temple of Inscriptions (fig. 10.5). According to king lists carved in the temple's corridors, the first king was Bahlum Kuk ("Jaguar Quetzal"), who founded the city on March 11, 431 C.E.

These king lists, which record a dynasty of some twelve kings, were commissioned by two rulers: Pacal ("Shield") and his oldest son Chan **Bahlum** ("Snake Jaguar"). Pacal ruled for sixty-seven years, beginning in 615, and the Temple of Inscriptions was erected as his tomb. In 1952, the Mexican archaeologist Alberto Ruz discovered a hidden staircase at the heart of the temple, and at its bottom Pacal's body, adorned with a jade collar and green headband, lying in a red-painted stone sarcophagus. The outside of the sarcophagus is decorated with a magnificent stone relief carving (fig. 10.6), which depicts Pacal's fall down the Wacah Chan, the great tree at the center of the world. Pacal lands at the bottom on an altarlike image that represents the setting sun.

FIGURE 10.4 Tikal, Guatemala, Mayan culture, ca. 700 C.E. University of Pennsylvania Museum. Because Mayan rituals were conducted in the open air, temple architecture atop pyramids emphasized external features.

FIGURE 10.5 Temple of Inscriptions, Palenque, Mexico, Mayan culture, seventh century C.E. Rising in nine steps, like the temples at Tikal, the temple is inscribed with the history of the Palenque kings and rests over the grave of Pacal, one of its greatest leaders.

FIGURE 10.6 Sarcophagus lid, tomb of Pacal, Temple of Inscriptions, Palenque, Mexico, Mayan culture, ca. 683 C.E., limestone, ca. 12′ 6″ × 7′(3.80 × 2.14 m). The lid represents Pacal's fall in death from the sacred tree of the Maya, whose roots are in the earth and whose branches are in the heavens.

THE TOLTECS AND AZTECS

Among the best known of the Mesoamerican civilizations is that of the Aztecs (or Mexica, as they referred to themselves). This civilization flourished relatively late, after approximately 1350, and continued until it was overcome by the Spaniards in 1521.

The greatest Aztec families claimed descent from the Toltecs, who were said to have invented the calendar and who were the mightiest of warriors. The Toltecs came to power in Tula in Hidalgo Province around 900 C.E. after Teotihuacán's power had diminished. In the twelfth century, the militaristic Toltecs carne to a violent end, when Tula was burned and its inhabitants scattered. Among the escaping tribes were the Mexica, who wandered into the Valley of Mexico around 1325 and built a village on the shores of Lake Texcoco. There they dug canals, draining high areas of the lake and converting them into fertile fields, and also built the magnificent city of Tenochtitlán. By 1440, when MOCTEZUMA ILHUICAMINA [muck-tay-ZOO-mah] (r. 1440–86) assumed power, they considered themselves masters of the entire world.

Perhaps the most frequently cited aspect of Aztec culture is human sacrifice, which was linked with religious ritual. As in Mayan culture, the shedding of human blood was seen as necessary for the continuance of the earth's fertility. The sun, moon, earth, and vegetation gods required human blood for their sustenance and the continuance of human life. During the reign of Moctezuma Ilhuicamina's successor, Ahuitzotl (r. 1486–1501), no fewer than twenty thousand captives were sacrificed in the city.

The central activity of the Aztec state was war, with the primary goal to secure enough captives for sacrifice. Young

Then & Now

THE MAYA

Like Pacal himself, Palenque and the other Mayan states would eventually fall. Some time in the ninth century, the Maya abandoned their cities and returned to the countryside to farm, where their descendants work the fields to this day. Scattered across the southern Mexican state of Chiapas and throughout Guatemala, the contemporary Mayans speak twenty different dialects of their original language and engage in distinctly different cultural practices, sometimes in villages separated by no more than ten or twelve miles. In Chiapas, for instance, the Mayan inhabitants of the village of Zinacantán characteristically dress in bright red and purple and celebrate fiestas with loud bands and fireworks; in nearby Chamula the men wear white or black wool serapes, carry large, intimidating sticks, and practice a stern, mystical brand of Catholicism that blends Mayan interest in the spirit world of animals with a part-Christian, part-Mayan sense of self-sacrifice.

Many traditional Mayan practices survive in contemporary culture. Not only do the beautiful embroidery and weaving of the contemporary Mayans contain references to ancient Mayan hieroglyphics, but Mayan women still associate giving birth with the ancient 260-day calendar. In fact, children born on particular days are still esteemed by contemporary Mayans as **daykeepers,** persons able to receive messages from the external world, both natural and supernatural, through their bodies. These daykeepers describe a sensation in their bodies as if air were rapidly moving over it in a flickering manner, similar to sheet lightning moving over a lake at night. The daykeepers learn to interpret these tremblings and eventually become the head **mother-fathers,** or priest-shamans, of their respective families.

Blood also continues to play a significant role in contemporary Mayan culture. Throughout Guatemala and Chiapas, blood is still considered an animate object, capable of speaking. Shamans can receive messages from a patient's blood by "pulsing," or touching a patient's body at various pressure points. An ancient poem, which continues to be recited among contemporary Mayan peoples who no longer practice the ritual, describes the dance of the bowman, who sharpens his arrows and dances around the victims in preparation for their sacrifice. The song recalls and memorializes the staging of the sacrificial action, and testifies to the importance of memory as an aspect of Mayan culture.

---

men were prepared for war from their birth. A newborn male was greeted with war cries by his midwife, who took him from the mother and dedicated him to the sun and to battle. His umbilical cord was buried by a veteran warrior in a place of battle. Following soon upon birth was the naming ceremony, during which the baby boy's hand was closed around a tiny bow, arrows, and shield. Shortly after this ceremony, priests fitted the child with the decorative lip plug worn by Aztec warriors.

At puberty most commoner (i.e., nonroyal) boys, with the exception of those destined to become priests, were placed under the jurisdiction of the youth house, which was associated with a local warrior house. Although young boys were trained for war, they were also taught various horticultural, mercantile, hunting, and fishing skills. Nonetheless, the way a young man secured prestige and fame was in war rather than in the pursuit of a vocation, with success measured in the number of enemy captured alive for later ritual killing on ceremonial occasions.

For Aztec men, dying in battle was considered a great honor, as is evident in the following Nahuatl song:

> There is nothing like death in war,
> nothing like the flowery death
> so precious to Him who gives life:
> far off I see it: my heart yearns for it!

Aztec art typically reflects the fierceness of the culture. A colossal statue of Coatlicue, the "Serpent Skirt" (fig. 10.7), goddess of the earth, shows a face with two serpent heads set on a thick powerful body. The serpents may represent blood jetting from the heads of ritually sacrificed women. Coatlicue's necklace is made up of human hearts and hands, with a human skull dangling at its base. Her skirt, which consists of writhing snakes, suggests sexual activity and its aftermath, birth.

Coatlicue is said to embody the Aztecs' belief in the creative principle, an attitude reflected in their love of poetry. For the Aztecs, poetic speech, chanted or sung, was a creative force, one that not only conveyed their vision of the world but simultaneously enacted it. This power of the poetic spoken word was further displayed in the Aztec emphasis on systematic memorizing of poems and songs to preserve Aztec cultural traditions. Poetry was called **flower song.** In Aztec painted scrolls, poetry is represented as a flowered scroll emanating from an open mouth. This use of images—of flower and song together—was characteristic of **Nahuatl** metaphor, standing for poetry specifically, and more generally for the symbolic dimension of art.

Aztec Gods.   Among the most important Aztec gods are Huitzilopochtli and Quetzalcoatl. To a considerable degree, the Aztec predilection for human sacrifice derived from their devotion to Huitzilopochtli. Warriors took the god as their patron deity when conquering neighboring peoples. When Aztec wars were successful, the god's priests demanded human sacrificial victims for his appeasement.

Then & Now

MESOAMERICAN BALL GAMES

Ancient Americans played a variety of games using balls of various sizes. In one of them the Hachtli players tried to shoot a rubber ball through a stone ring. The Olmecs left ball courts made around 1500 B.C.E., and colossal Olmec stone heads are sometimes shown wearing helmets presumed to have been used in their ancient ball games.

Much more than a mere sport, in which onlookers sometimes made bets,

Ancient Mesoamerican ball games were rituals of religious significance. They were also a matter of life and death. The Mayan epic *Popol Vub* describes a ball game in which Hero Twins descend into the underworld to defeat the Lords of Death and thereby save humanity.

Unlike modern-day basketball, which tends to be a high-scoring affair, with many baskets made by both teams, ancient ball games were rough defensive contests in which scoring was diffi-

cult, since use of the hands was not allowed.

A more serious difference between contemporary basketball and the ancient version is that modern players, when they fail at a crucial shot at game's end, come back to play another day, whereas members of losing teams in ancient Mesoamerica often found themselves offered as a ritual sacrifice.

FIGURE 10.7 Coatlicue, Aztec, fifteenth century, stone, height 8′ 6″ (2.65 m), Museo Nacional de Antropologia, Mexico City. With her two rattlesnake heads and her skirt of serpents, along with large serpent fangs and necklace of human body parts, this Aztec deity induces awe in some and amazement in others who stand in her presence.

At the dedication of a large temple honoring Huitzilopochtli, the god's priests are reputed to have sacrificed eighty thousand victims, some of whom were Aztec criminals, while others were neighboring peoples who had come under Aztec subjugation.

Quetzalcoatl, the feathered serpent god, was honored under different names by earlier Mesoamerican peoples, including those of Teotihuacán. A more peaceful god than Huitzilopochtli and Coatlicue, Quetzalcoatl was honored as patron of agriculture as well as patron of arts and crafts. Images of Quetzalcoatl can be found in Aztec codices, sheets of parchment that could be folded into long strips in book-like form (fig. 10.8).

The Aztec Language. The primary Aztec language during the time of the Spanish conquest in the sixteenth century was Nahuatl (NA-watl). Nahuatl continues to be spoken by nearly two million Nahua-Mexicans who live in a broad swath of central Mexico. Referred to today as "Mexicano," Nahuatl, which exists in two dozen dialect variants, is among the more than fifty native Indian languages of Mexico that are in danger of disappearing.

Nahuatl is an agglutinative language, one that strings together prefixes, word roots, and suffixes into very long words. Among them is an eighteen-syllable Nahuatl word that reputedly means "you honorable people might have come along banging your noses, so as to make them bleed, but in fact, you didn't." Other words are simple, such as "chocolatl" and "tomatl," from which English has derived "chocolate" and "tomato." Efforts to preserve Nahuatl, along with other Native Mexican Indian languages, are underway with the building of new dictionaries to supplant those made by missionaries centuries ago. Among

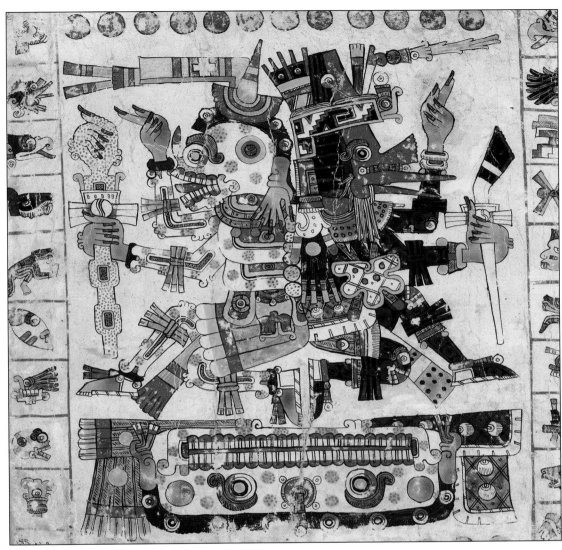

FIGURE 10.8 Aztec peoples, *Mictlantecuhtli and Quetzalcoatl.* Manuscript illumination. Vatican Library, Rome. Biblioteca Apostolica Vaticana.

the techniques being used is having elder Nahuatl native speakers recite traditional stories, which are then scoured for words to include in the dictionary.

THE CULTURES OF PERU

Peru is a land of dramatic geographical contrasts. Along the Pacific coast is one of the driest deserts in the world, where the rivers that descend out of the Andes mountains to the east form strips of oases. The Andes themselves are mammoth mountains, steep and high. Beyond them, to the east, lies the jungle, the tropical rain forest of the Amazon basin. These various terrains were home to a series of cultures, in particular the Moche and the Inca, before the arrival of Spanish colonists.

THE MOCHE

Among the early cultures to develop in Peru was that of the Moche, who controlled the area along the Peruvian north coast from 200 to 700 C.E. They lived around great **huacas,** pyramids made of sun-dried bricks, that rose high above the river floodplains. The largest was Huaca del Sol, the Pyramid of the Sun (fig. 10.9), which is 135 feet high— about two-thirds the height of the Pyramid of the Sun at Teotihuacán. Its truncated summit, however, is much vaster than Teotihuacán's. At least two-thirds of the pyramid was destroyed in the seventeenth century when Spanish colonists, searching for gold, diverted the Moche River into it and used the river's fast current to erode the mound. The colonists did indeed discover many gold artifacts buried with the dead in the sides of the structure. Unfortunately,

FIGURE 10.9   Huaca del Sol (Pyramid of the Sun), Moche culture, Moche Valley, Peru, ca. 500 C.E., height 135′ (41.1 m). Destroyed by Spanish colonizers seeking gold, this giant pyramid was built of more than 143 million sun-dried bricks.

they melted these artifacts down for bullion. What they left, however, is a record of the pyramid's construction. The sliced-away mound reveals at least eight stages of construction, and we can extrapolate to conclude that around 143 million bricks, made in rectangular molds from river silt, were used to build it.

The Moche were gifted metalsmiths, and they employed the same lost-wax technique used by the Romans. They adorned their copper sculptures with gold by binding liquid gold to the copper surface at temperatures reaching as high as 1472°F (800°C). Further decorated with turquoise and shells, the results were often astonishingly beautiful. But the Moche were, above all, the most gifted ceramic artists in the Americas. In addition to working with potter's wheels, they also produced clay objects from molds, allowing them to reproduce the same objects again and again. Their most distinctive designs are found on bottles with stirrup-shaped spouts that curve out from the body of the vessel. Bottles might be decorated with images of anything from the king or high official—as illustrated here (fig. 10.10), in ceremonial headdress and stroking a jaguar cub—to strange part-animal/part-human deities, and to everyday scenes such as a design for a typical Moche house. Warriors do battle on some of the vessels, prisoners are decapitated and dismembered on others, and on another famous example, a ruler in a giant feather headdress looks on as a line of naked prisoners passes before him.

Around 800, Moche society vanished. Evidence suggests that some time between 650 and 700 a great earth-

quake rattled the Andes, causing massive landslides, filling the rivers with debris, and blocking the normal channels to the ocean. As the sand washed ashore, huge dunes were formed, and the coastal plain was suddenly subject to vast, blinding sandstorms. It seems clear as well that **El Niño,** the warm current that slides up and down the Pa-

FIGURE 10.10   *Moche Lord with a Feline,* Moche culture, Moche valley, Peru, ca. 100 B.C.E.–500 C.E., painted ceramic, height $7\frac{1}{2}''$ (19 cm), Buckingham Fund, 1955. 2281. Photograph © 2005, Art Institute of Chicago, All Rights Reserved. Vessels such as this one were buried in large quantities with people of high rank.

cific coast of the Americas, changed the climate, destroying the fisheries and bringing torrential floods to the normally dry desert plain. It was all apparently too much, and the Moche disappeared.

THE INCA

Roughly contemporaneous with the rise of the Aztecs in Tenochtitlán was the emergence of the Inca civilization in Peru around 1300. The Incas inhabited the central Andes in what is today primarily Bolivia and Peru. They became a dominant military force around 1500 and appear also to have developed an organizational capacity to rival the engineering genius of the Romans. The Inca capital was at Cuzco, a city of 100,000 inhabitants at its height, built on a broad open valley between the Andes mountains north of Lake Titicaca. They called their empire *Tawantinsuyu*, "Land of Four Quarters," and, in fact, four highways emanated from Cuzco's central plaza, dividing the kingdom into quadrants. The 19,000 miles of roads and tracks that extended throughout their empire provide some indication of their engineering skill. The Incas understood the need for a functional communications system in a territory as large as theirs. Along these roadways, official runners could carry messages as far as 125 to 150 miles per day. And along them as well llamas carried goods and products for trade.

One of the most impressive of all Inca accomplishments is the fortified town of Machu Picchu (fig. 10.11), built around 1450. Located high in the Andes mountains, Machu Picchu was built perhaps as a refuge for Inca monarchs, perhaps as a place of religious retreat. Terraced fields adorn the slopes of the mountain that rises from the valley thousands of feet below. The stones for the walls and buildings were hoisted without benefit of carts or any wheeled contrivance, because the wheel was not used in either the Andes or Mesoamerica before the arrival of the Spaniards. Tools used for fitting the stones together snugly were primitive—mostly stone hammers, since neither the Andean nor Mesoamerican civilizations had developed metal implements at this time.

Machu Picchu was abandoned shortly after the arrival of Francisco Pizarro and the Spanish conquistadores. The Spaniards destroyed Inca civilization with technologically advanced weapons by enlisting the allied assistance of Inca enemies, and through the agency of contagious diseases, especially smallpox. Just a dozen years after Moctezuma and the Aztecs had been defeated by the Spanish under Hernán Cortés, the Andean Inca civilization suffered an equally ignoble demise. Machu Picchu was overlooked by the Spaniards, perhaps in part because it was a small village of five hundred inhabitants. To this day it remains one of the architectural wonders of the world.

Inca Society and Religion.   Inca society was organized into four main classes: rulers, aristocrats, priests, and peasants. The Incas honored their chief rulers as deities

FIGURE 10.11   Machu Picchu, Inca culture, Peru, ca. 1450. This beautiful mountain habitation escaped destruction when the Spaniards overwhelmed the Inca civilization in 1532, partly because of its remote location high in the Andes mountains, and partly because it was not a large city like the Inca capital of Cuzco.

Connections

THE MYSTERY OF THE NAZCA LINES

Perhaps no phenomenon better underscores the intimate connection between art, archaeology, and science than the mystery of the famous **Nazca lines.** These are giant drawings made on the plains of the south Peruvian coast where the earth is covered by a topsoil of fine sand and pebbles that, when dug away, reveals white alluvium. A culture that traded with the Moche to the north and thrived from 100 B.C.E. to 700 C.E., the Nazca dug away this top soil to create a web of lines, some running straight for as long as five miles, others forming complex geometric designs in the shape, for instance, of a monkey with a coiled tail or, as illustrated here, a hummingbird (fig. 10.12).

Ever since the German-born mathematician and astronomer Maria Reiche became obsessed by the lines in 1932, they have been the center of controversy. Reiche single-handedly surveyed all of the lines over the course of her career and concluded that the straight lines point to celestial activity on the horizon and the animals represent ancient constellations. In 1963, Nazca was visited by Gerald Hawkins of Boston University, whose computer calculations of Stone-

henge had helped reveal its astronomical relations, but he was unable to link many of the lines to the configuration of the heavens in the Nazca period. In the early 1970s, Erich von Däniken theorized that the lines were guidance patterns for alien spacecraft, a proposal that soon gained a wide and vocal following.

More recently, archaeologists have proposed that these **geogylphs,** as they are called, are actually depictions of giant gods whose job it is to guarantee both the availability of water and the fertility of the Nazca valleys. This theory is supported by the fact that in several sites, the straight lines point, not at aspects on the horizon, but directly at natural springs and water sources.

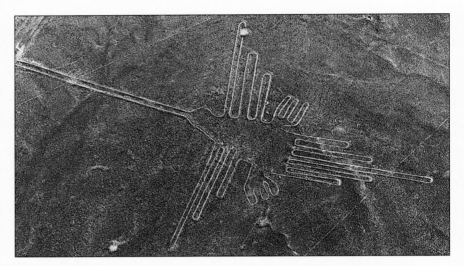

FIGURE 10.12   Earth drawing of a hummingbird, Nazca Plain, southwest Peru, Nazca culture, ca. 200 B.C.E.–200 C.E., length ca. 450′ (138 m), wingspan ca. 200′ (60.5 m). Aerial photographs and satellite images have revealed not only figurative designs such as this one, but over eight hundred miles of straight lines.

descended from the sun. Their rule was absolute, and they retained their exalted position after death. Royal remains, which were mummified, were considered sacred, as dead rulers were believed to serve as intermediaries with the gods. On certain festivals, rulers would dress the remains of their ancestors, adorn them with jewelry, and present them with food and drink both to honor them and to remain on good terms with them.

Inca rulers, who technically owned everything in the realm, including the land, supervised the aristocrats, who allocated land for the peasants to cultivate. Like the priests, aristocrats led privileged lives, including the right to wear large ear spools, which created "big ears." The priests, who descended from royal and aristocratic families, were well educated and influenced Inca society through their over-

Table 10–1 ANCIENT AMERICAN CULTURES AND WORKS		
Olmec	1300 B.C.E.–600 B.C.E.	Colossal heads
Mayan	250 B.C.E.–1000 C.E.	Tikal pyramids/Cyclical calendars
Nazca	200 B.C.E.–200 C.E.	Hummingbird earth drawing
Moche	200 B.C.E.–700 C.E.	Sun-dried brick pyramids
Toltec	900 C.E.–1200 C.E.	Aztec ancestors
Inca	1300 C.E.–1537 C.E.	Machu Picchu
Aztec	1350 C.E.–1521 C.E.	Coatlicue, the "Serpent Skirt"

sight of religious ritual, which included veneration of the sun god, Inti, as well as other astral deities. In Cuzco alone, four thousand priests and attendants served Inti, whose temple attracted pilgrims from the farthest reaches of the Inca empire.

NORTH AMERICA

The Native American populations in North America were far less densely concentrated than those in Meso- and South America. The peoples of the region lived primarily nomadic lives, hunting and fishing, until around 1200 B.C.E., when the production of maize spread from Mexico into the southwest region of the present-day United States, inaugurating agricultural production in the north thousands of years after its introduction in the south. The climate of North America was not, in fact, conducive to raising corn, and the practice was slow to take hold. As a result, the organized and complex civilizations that have usually accompanied agricultural development were also slow to form. Indeed, down to the time of the European colonization of the region at the end of the fifteenth century, many native peoples continued to live as they had since the time of the extinction of the vast herds of mammoth, mastodon, and other species that inhabited the continent at the end of the Ice Age, ca. 6000 B.C.E.

THE NORTHWEST COAST

One of the oldest cultures of the north developed along the northwest coast of the continent, in present-day Oregon, Washington State, British Columbia, and Alaska. Reaching back to approximately 3500 B.C.E., when the world's oceans had more or less stabilized at their current levels, rich fishing grounds developed in the region, with vast quantities of salmon and steelhead migrating inland up the rivers annually to spawn. One of the richest habitats on earth in natural resources, the northwest was home to over three hundred edible animal species.

Here the native peoples—among them the Tlingit, the Haida, and the Kwakiutl—gathered wild berries and nuts, fished the streams and inlets, and hunted game. In the winters, they came together in plank houses, made with wood from the abundant forests, and engaged in a rich ceremonial life. By 450 B.C.E., they had become expert woodworkers, not only building their winter homes out of timber and rough-sawn planks, but also carving out canoes and making elaborate decorative sculpture. The most famous form of this decorative sculpture is the so-called **totem pole** (fig. 10.13). These mortuary poles, erected to memorialize dead chiefs, consist of animal and spirit emblems or totems stacked one upon the other, for which the poles are named.

The kinship ties of the extended family tribe were celebrated at elaborate ceremonies called **potlatches**, hosted

FIGURE 10.13   Haida mortuary poles and house frontal poles at Skedans Village, British Columbia, 1878, National Archives, Canada. Totem poles were traditionally carved to honor the leader of a clan upon his death, and they also stood in front of homes, serving a spiritual function.

by the chief. Guests arrived in ceremonial dress, formal speeches of welcome followed, and gifts were distributed. Then dancing would follow long into the night. The potlatch was intended to confirm the chief's authority and ensure the loyalty of his tribal group.

THE SOUTHWEST

The native populations of the desert southwest faced severe difficulties in adapting to conditions following the end of the Ice Age. Like the Moche in Peru who lived in similar desert conditions, tribes gathered around rivers, streams, and springs that brought precious water from the mountains. However, water in the North American desert was far less abundant than in the South American river oases. Nonetheless, the inhabitants of the region, called the Anasazi (meaning "ancient ones"), slowly learned to recognize good moisture-bearing soil, to plant on north- and east-facing slopes protected from the direct sunlight of late day, and to take advantage of the natural irrigation of floodplains.

Small farming communities developed in the canyons and on the mesas of the region. In the thirty-two square miles of Chaco Canyon, in the northeastern region of present-day Arizona, thirteen separate towns, centered around circular underground ceremonial rooms called **kivas,** had begun to take shape by 700 C.E. In the kiva, the community celebrated its connection to the earth, from which all things were said to emanate and to which all things return—not just humans, but, importantly, water as well. Connected to

Cross Currents

CONQUEST AND DISEASE

The end of the great buffalo herds was not the only devastation the conquering Europeans brought with them. In 1519, in Veracruz, Mexico, one of the invading Spanish soldiers came ashore with smallpox. The Native Americans had no natural immunity. Of the approximately 11 million people living in Mexico before the arrival of the Spaniards, only 6.4 million remained by 1540. By 1607, perhaps 2 million indigenous people remained. When the Spanish arrived in California in 1679, the population was approximately 310,000.

By 1900, there were only 20,000 Native Americans in the region. Along the eastern seaboard of the United States, through the Ohio Valley and the Midwest, entire populations were exterminated by disease. In the matter of a month or two, an entire village might lose 90 percent of its people.

The destruction of Native American peoples, and with them their traditions and cultures, is movingly stated by the Wanapum prophet Smohalla, many of whose people died not long after the 1844 arrival of Marcus Whitman to establish a mission in the Walla Walla Valley of Washington State:

The whites have caused us great suffering. Dr. Whitman many years ago made a journey to the east to get a bottle of poison for us. He was gone about a year, and after he came back, strong and terrible diseases broke out among us. The Indians killed Dr. Whitman, but it was too late. He had uncorked his bottle and all the air was poisoned. Before there was little sickness among us, but since then many of us have died. I have had children and grandchildren, but they are all dead. . . . We are now so few and weak that we can offer no resistance, and their preachers have persuaded them to let a few of us live, so as to claim credit with the Great Spirit for being generous and humane.

---

other sites in the area by a network of wide straight roads, the largest of these towns was Pueblo Benito, which was constructed between 900 and 1250. Shaped like a massive letter "D," its outer perimeter was 1,300 feet long. At the center of the "D" was a giant plaza, built on top of the two largest kivas (there are thirty other kivas at Pueblo Benito).

Perhaps the most famous Anasazi site is Mesa Verde (fig. 10.14) in southwestern Colorado, near the Four Corners where Colorado, Utah, Arizona, and New Mexico all meet. Discovered in 1888 by two cowboys, Richard Wetherill and Richard Morgan, searching for stray cattle, Mesa Verde consists of a series of cliff dwellings built into the cavelike overhangs of the small canyons and arroyos that descend from the mesa top. As many as 30,000 people lived in the Montezuma Valley below, but probably no more than 2,500 people ever lived on the mesa itself. On the mesa these inhabitants developed an elaborate irrigation system consisting of a series of small ditches that filled a mesatop reservoir capable of holding nearly half a million gallons of water.

In about 1150, severe drought struck the Four Corners region, and the Anasazi at both Chaco and Mesa Verde abandoned their communities. They migrated into the Rio Grande Valley of New Mexico, where they were absorbed into the later native societies of the southwest, particularly the Hopi and the Zuni.

THE MOUNDBUILDERS

Throughout the Mississippi and Ohio River basins, beginning in about 1000 B.C.E. with the arrival of **maize** from Mesoamerica, small farming villages began building mon-

FIGURE 10.14   Spruce Tree House, Mesa Verde, Colorado, Anasazi culture, 1200–1300 C.E. Visible in front of the buildings to the right are three round kivas. Originally, these would have been roofed, and the roofs would have formed a common plaza in front of the buildings. The Anasazi farmed on the mesatop above.

umental earthworks in which to bury their dead. By far the largest of these was at Cahokia, in present-day East St. Louis, Illinois, where as many as 30,000 people lived between 1050 and 1250 C.E. The so-called Monk's Mound, the biggest earthwork ever constructed in North America, rises in four stages to a height of nearly one hundred feet and extends over sixteen acres.

The **moundbuilders** had begun by burying their dead in low ridges overlooking river valleys. The sites were apparently sacred, and as more and more burials were added, the mounds became increasingly large, especially as large burial chambers started to be constructed, at about the time of Jesus, to contain important tribal leaders. Sheets of mica, copper ornaments, and carved stone pipes were buried with these chiefs and shamans, and the mounds became increasingly elaborate. One of the most famous is the Great Serpent Mound (fig. 10.15), built by the Adena culture between 600 B.C.E. and 200 C.E. Overlooking a small stream, it rises from its coiled tail as if to strike a giant oval form which its mouth has already encircled. What it symbolizes is as mysterious as the forms of the Nazca lines in Peru.

THE BUFFALO HUNTERS

It remains unclear what led to the extinction of the great game species at the end of the Ice Age—perhaps a combination of over hunting and climatic change. But one large pre-extinction mammal continued to thrive—the bison, commonly known as the buffalo. The species survived because it learned to eat the grasses that soon spread across the Great Plains of North America, where it roamed.

FIGURE 10.15   Great Serpent Mound, Adams County, Ohio, Adena culture, 600 B.C.E.–200 C.E., length ca. 1254′5″ (382.5 m). Although the Great Serpent Mound in Adams County is perhaps the most spectacular example, there are between three and five hundred such mounds in the Ohio Valley alone.

Hunting it became the chief occupation of the peoples who inhabited the region.

Archaeological evidence suggests that as many as 8,500 years ago a group of Native Americans who lived southeast of Kit Carson, Colorado, stampeded an entire herd of buffalo off a cliff. The fall killed about 152 of the animals, and they were butchered where they lay for their hides and meat. The practice of stampeding continued, essentially unchanged, down to the time of the Spanish conquest, when horses were reintroduced to the Americas—the native variety had grown extinct by 600 C.E.—and with the horse, the rifle.

But perhaps the most devastating change as far as the buffalo were concerned was the coming of the Europeans themselves. The great herds that roamed the continent quickly disappeared. Between 1830 and 1870, the buffalo population in the West dropped from around thirty million to an estimated eight million. Between 1872 and 1874, hunters killed an estimated 4,374,000 buffalo on the Great Plains. As the railroad builder Granville Dodge reported in the late summer of 1873: "The vast plain, which only a short twelvemonth before teemed with animal life, was a dead, solitary, putrid desert." The Crow warrior, Two Legs, put it this way: "Nothing happened after that. We just lived. There were no more war parties, no capturing horses from the Piegan and the Sioux, no buffalo to hunt. There is nothing more to tell."

AFRICA

To discuss the diversity of African art and culture in a small space is a great challenge for a variety of reasons. First, Africa is a big place, much bigger than you might think just from looking at a map. Indeed, the continent is more than three times as large as the continental United States. The Sahara desert alone is nearly as large as the United States. Further, Africa is home to a multitude of societies and cultures. Complementing such cultural diversity is also a wide range of economic and political variation. As such, it is difficult to talk about groups as different as the Hausa (a West African people famous for large cities and long-distance trade) and the San (South African hunter-gatherers) in the same breath. Finally, there is the unfortunate reality that most Americans grow up unconsciously accepting a great variety of stereotypes and myths about Africans. For example, despite what we might gather from a host of nature shows, most Africans have never even seen an elephant. Moreover, stereotypes of African so-called primitivism lead many to underestimate the complexity and quality of African achievements.

THE PHYSICAL ENVIRONMENT

The African continent contains a variety of ecological and physical environments. Africa is neither a giant desert nor a huge jungle. Africa has both of these, of course, and a

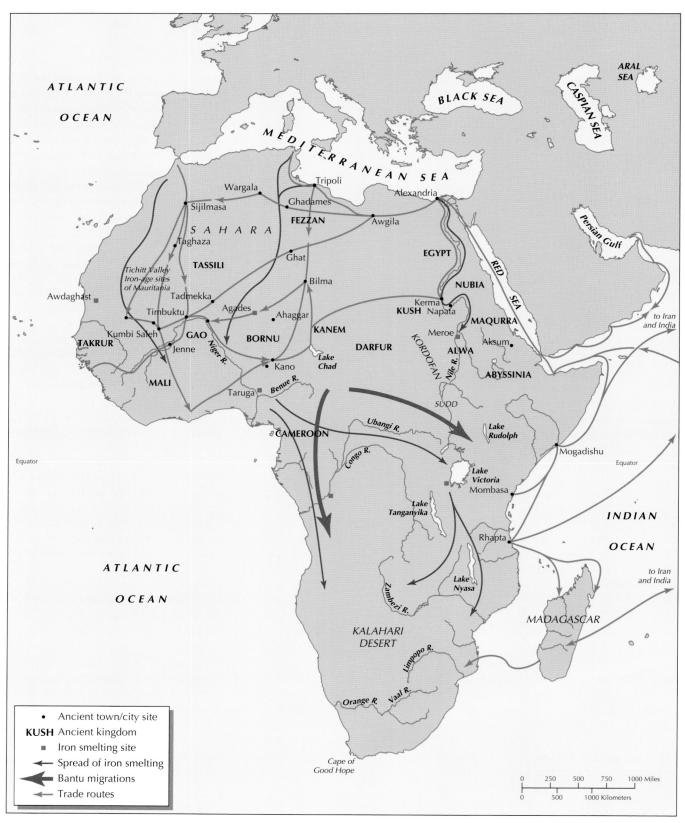

MAP 10.2   Africa before 1300 C.E.

number of other climates as well. The southern tip of Africa, for example, is home to penguins, and Mount Kilimanjaro, in Tanzania, is capped with a permanent glacier. Africa's climates center on the equator, which runs roughly through the middle of the continent. Here, in the region known as the Congo Basin, is found one of the world's largest rain forests. The rain forests also extend along much of the West African coast, stretching westward to Guinea. North and south of these rain forests the weather becomes increasingly dry. The rain forests give way to more typical forests, then to savannah grasslands, and eventually to deserts, with the Sahara in the north and the Kalahari and Namib in the south. The weather in all these regions is determined by what is known as the **Intertropical Convergence Zone (ITCZ),** a climatic border where the cool wet air of the south Atlantic meets the warm dry air from the Sahara Desert. The ITCZ moves north from roughly May to September and south from roughly October to April—taking rain to wherever it goes. Rather than having four seasons, these regions of Africa have only two: wet and dry. In the wet season it may well rain every day, but in the dry season rain is absent for months on end. Such weather patterns have had significant impact on African agricultural practices. However, in the northern and southern extremes of the continent, the weather is what is often described as "Mediterranean," with four distinct seasons and a fairly cool wet winter.

Also important to African history and culture is the nature of the soil itself. Geologically speaking, Africa is what is known as a *shield* surface. It has been exposed to the elements, with very little volcanic, glacial, or otherwise significant geological activity for millions of years. This is critical because it means African soils have had little chance to be renewed or replenished. As a result, most African soils are **lateritic:** high in salt and iron content and notoriously short on nutrients and vulnerable to erosion. Compounding this problem is the general warmth of the regions between the Mediterranean climates of the north and south. It is often thought that warm weather is good for agriculture, but it really is not. The year-round warmth means that decomposition continues even in the dry season when nothing can be grown, resulting in an absence of **humus,** the nutrient-rich decaying matter that enriches the soil. Agriculture in Africa is not impossible, but it is much more difficult than in temperate zones. There is a very good reason that North America and Eurasia are the world's breadbaskets and that Africa, South America, and Australia are not. Notably, the exception to this rule is the **rift valley** of East Africa. Running from Ethiopia to Zimbabwe, this chain of volcanic mountains is one of the world's richest farming areas, producing some of the world's best coffee as a result. The wealth of the Nile, discussed in Chapter 1, is the result of these rich soils being carried from the Ethiopian highlands to the floodplains of ancient Egypt.

EARLY AFRICAN CULTURES AND INNOVATIONS

As indicated in Chapter 1, Africans in Egypt helped found one of the world's most impressive and long-lasting cultures. The remarkable achievements of Egypt, however, are complemented by other impressive developments elsewhere on the continent. Indeed, the fertility provided by the Nile floods made Egypt a fairly easy place to create a state. Hunting and gathering societies (which predated ancient Egypt) not only succeeded in flourishing in the West African savannahs, but also in the forests and southern savannahs (which were for a time geographically isolated from agricultural innovations in the north and east). Hunters and gatherers relied on a complex and thorough understanding of their physical floral and faunal surroundings to survive. Indeed, many today might envy the quality of life of such early societies. Hunters and gatherers, it turns out, have to work only a few hours a day to provide a nutritious diet. Such a situation left them ample free time to undertake crafts such as stone working (for tools) and even artwork. Although artworks of wood or other perishables do not remain, areas of Africa such as the Sahara and southern Africa are home to numerous rock paintings remarkable not only for their artistic qualities, but also for the wealth of information they provide us about the ancient environment. It is how we know that the Sahara was once wet, and what species of plants and animals lived there (fig. 10.16).

Not all Africans remained hunters and gatherers, however. As early as 5000 B.C.E., sedentary agriculture was also being developed in the West African savannahs—built around the farming of millet and sorghum, two grains well adapted to the region's drought-prone climate. Rice also became important along the inland delta of the Niger River. Similarly, agriculture also developed in the

FIGURE 10.16   A rock painting from Tassili, in the central Sahara. Dating to around 10,000 B.C.E., this painting reflects both a keen artistic eye and a remarkable knowledge of the environment.

highlands of Ethiopia, where local crops such as **t'eff** (among the world's smallest grains) allowed early farmers to take advantage of rich soils but also harsh high-elevation weather. Elsewhere in the savannahs and desert fringes, many Africans developed complex pastoralist lifeways around the herding of cattle, goats, and camels. Such animals could feed on plants inedible to humans. By extracting food from the animals in the form of meat, blood, and milk, humans were able to live in the otherwise inhospitable environments.

Beginning from the region of modern-day eastern Nigeria and western Cameroun, perhaps as early as 3000 B.C.E. the Bantu migration occurred. This migration, which was to continue over the next four thousand years, saw the introduction of sedentary agriculture into the forests of central Africa—largely thanks to two forest crops: the oil palm and the yam (*not* the sweet potato). **Bantu** is itself a word that means "the people" in a subfamily of the Niger-Congo language group. Although once the Bantu migrations were thought to be a rapid conquest by superior iron-wielding agriculturalists, who displaced inferior hunters and gatherers, it is increasingly apparent that the process was slow and relatively peaceful. Linguistic and archaeological evidence suggests that Bantu speakers learned many critical skills not only from forest peoples such as the **Batwa** (pygmies), but also from **Cushitic**-speaking savannah agriculturalists millennia later. Ironworking does seem to have been a factor, but it came fairly late in the game (around 500 B.C.E. in West Africa). Similarly, archaeological evidence suggests that ironworking was developed independently in the region of northern Tanzania around 700 B.C.E.

EARLY AFRICAN POLITICAL AND RELIGIOUS CULTURE

Although there are a great variety of African political and religious systems, many African societies, especially in the ancient era, lived in what are often termed *stateless societies.* Such communities, often pastoralists or forest dwellers, had no single individual or group (such as a king or aristocracy) whose job it was to tell other people what to do. This does not mean, however, that such societies lacked *authority.* Rather, institutions of kinship and seniority, and the recognition of knowledge and personal achievement, provided certain individuals with influence. Similarly, the relatively small size of local communities allowed groups to discuss problems and develop solutions through debate and consensus. Such a system is very similar to our modern notion of democracy, in that power rests in the entire community rather than with a few privileged individuals.

Further, such societies were often quite aware of other political alternatives. The Igbo of southeastern Nigeria, for example, have long had a motto that states "the Igbo have no kings." Clearly, the Igbo knew what kings were,

but decided they did not want them. Stateless societies became less common over time, however, as many African societies and states expanded to the point where more centralized systems of authority and bureaucracy became necessary.

Religious authority, too, played an important part in African community life. Although possibly thousands of indigenous African religious systems exist, certain commonalities provide an introduction to these complex systems of cosmology and belief. Perhaps one of the key characteristics of African religions is the concept of **pantheism.** Thus, rather than seeing a single all-powerful God (such as in Judaism or Islam), African religions tend to see divine power as diffuse. There may be a single High God, but that divine being is both too distant and incomprehensible for humans to interact with. Rather, this High God has myriad manifestations (all sharing the single divine spirit) that are more accessible to human needs. For example, among the Yoruba (who have inhabited the southwestern region of what is now Nigeria for at least one thousand years) the High God **OLUDUMARE** (oh-lu-DU-mah-ray) created the world and humanity, but numerous "lesser" gods, known as the **ORISA** (ohr-ISH-ah), interact with humans. For example, **OGUN** (oh-GOON), the orisa of iron, has long served as the patron of soldiers and has more recently become the patron of auto mechanics. Notably, most African traditional religions have little or no notion of the sort of conflict between good and evil that so permeates religions originating from the Middle East. Similarly, African religions generally do not have a concept of an end to time, in the form of a judgment day or apocalypse.

The diffuse nature of political and religious authority in many African societies is also reflected in the nature of artistic expression. Art was not something that belonged only to the rich. Even the most mundane of items could be lavishly decorated. Similarly, African musical traditions make little distinction between performers and audience. Rather than politely sitting and listening, the audience is as much a part of the performance as the musicians themselves, expected to clap, sing, and dance right along with the professionals.

REGIONAL DEVELOPMENTS IN AFRICA BEFORE 1800

North and Northeastern Africa.   From very early on, North and northeastern Africans interacted closely with populations in the Mediterranean and Arabia. This should hardly be a surprise, since it is often easier for long-distance trade to take place across oceans and seas than across land. As such, the ancient Egyptians interacted extensively with populations in Mesopotamia and, later, Greece—just as they carried on extensive relations with Nubia and Ethiopia via the Nile River. Culture is always a two-way street, and these interactions led to mutual influence and exchange. Herodotus, the Greek father of history, for example, credited the Egyptians as the source of mathematics and Greek religion. Contacts with the wider Mediterranean world and Red Sea worlds would be a constant source of influence for North and northeastern Africa. The Phoenician settlement at Carthage intermingled with local Berber-speaking populations to create a unique culture known as **Punic** and grew as a trading power that would dominate the western Mediterranean until the rise of Rome (discussed in Chapter 4). The unification of the circum-Mediterranean world under the Roman empire in the early centuries C.E. encouraged an increased level of interaction around the region (although often unwillingly for those who chafed at Roman rule). Latin and Greek became languages of government and high society.

Following Roman lines of trade and communication, Christianity spread rapidly from the Middle East into North Africa and also into Europe. The new religion spread not only as a unique message of salvation that appealed to the poor and powerless, but also as a rejection of Roman authority. Early Christians drew the ire of the Roman state largely because they refused to make sacrifices to the emperor, who was considered a god. Notably, North Africa and the Nile Valley stretching through Nubia to Ethiopia would become influential parts of the expanding Christian world. Alexandria in Egypt was home to one of the first Christian catechetical schools, called the **Didascalia.** Here early Christian texts were collected, discussed, and translated. Saint Jerome, who first translated the Bible into Latin, is believed to have first studied at the Didascalia. North African Christians would play a central role in debating and defining exactly what it meant to be Christian. Debates over Neo-Platonism and Gnosticism (discussed in Chapter 5) and Arianism and Monophysitism took place among North African Christians. **Arianism,** named for Arius, a priest from Alexandria, argued that Jesus is not the son of God, but rather an angel-like creation sent to provide a new gospel. Arianism would later be spread by missionaries to the Germanic tribes of Europe. Thus the first western European Christians had doctrinal roots in Egyptian Arianism. The Monophysite position, held by the **Coptic** (Egyptian) and Nestorian (Middle Eastern) churches, was that Jesus' divinity outweighed his humanity, which was an anathema to the Roman church's claim that Jesus possesses both human and divine characters in equal measure. In 451, these churches broke with the Roman church. The Coptic church would continue to grow and thrive in the Nile Valley, eventually developing a close relationship with the Ethiopian state. In the twelfth century, King Lalibela of Ethiopia commissioned the creation of churches that were hewn from solid rock, a unique feat in Christian architecture (fig. 10.17). Like the churches themselves, Ethiopian Christianity would prove very durable, weathering chal-

FIGURE 10.17 A rock-hewn church in Ethiopia. Constructed in the twelfth century C.E., these churches are a testimony to the power of the Ethiopian church and state.

lenges from Islam and local religions to survive into the modern era.

The rise of Islam in the seventh century also had a substantial impact in North Africa. The Islamic state spread rapidly across the North African coast, although the defeat of Muslim forces by Christian Nubians at the Battle of Dongala in 651 greatly slowed the expansion of Islam in the upper Nile region. In North Africa, a woman named Al-Kahina (the Soothsayer) led a spirited Berber resistance to Islamic armies until her defeat in 698. Despite such opposition, by the early eighth century, the Islamic state was firmly entrenched in North Africa, although the bulk of the population would not convert to Islam until the tenth and eleventh centuries. Notably, however, North Africa became a refuge for Muslims, particularly **Shi'ites** and KHARIJITES (Car-IH-jites), who were at doctrinal odds with Sunni orthodoxy. In the tenth century, the Shi'ites would found the Fatimid dynasty, expanding from modern Tunisia to a capital in Egypt. This state would dominate the region for over two centuries, and at times challenge the Baghdad-based Abbasid Caliphate for leadership of the Islamic world. Despite such internal conflicts, the expansion of Islam encouraged trade and cultural exchange between North Africa and the Middle East. From poetry to architecture, Islamic artistic elements became deeply entrenched in North Africa.

Savannahs and Forests of Western and Central Africa.
The West African savannahs and forests were home not only to important human innovations in agriculture, such as the domestication of millet and oil palms, respectively, but also to complex urban societies and states. Beginning perhaps as early as the third century B.C.E., cities such as Jenne-Jeno and Gao began to be settled in the fertile inland delta of the Niger River. Several factors encouraged this development. The savannahs themselves were fertile,

and the growing of rice, millet, and sorghum produced a large surplus of grain for trade both into the desert to the north and the forests to the south. In exchange, the savannah cities received forest products, such as ivory, palm oil, kola nuts, and gold, and desert products, such as salt and cloth, from North Africa. The position as intermediaries between the forests and North Africa allowed the residents of the savannah cities to grow wealthy not only from production, but also from the taxation of trade moving across their boundaries. From the early period C.E. to the sixteenth century, this volume of trade continued to increase, and savannah states such as Ghana, Mali, and Songhai grew rich from control over the trade. Close economic ties to North Africa also led to a gradual conversion of these states' rulers and traders to Islam, although rural and agricultural populations would continue to practice traditional African religions well into the nineteenth century. Mali and Songhai were among the richest empires of the era. When MANSA MUSA (MAHN-sah MOO-sah), a Muslim ruler of Mali, performed the Hajj (pilgrimage) to Mecca in 1324 and 1325, he spent so much gold during a stopover in Alexandria that the local economy was temporarily debased by inflation. Such images convinced Europeans of the time that Africa was a land of great wealth and achievement.

Timbuktu has long been a center of the Muslim religion in west Africa. Settled in 1087 by the Tuareg, its fame as a center of trade in gold spread as far as Europe. Under the Songhai emperor Mohammed Askia I (ca. 1494–1527), the Muslim university of Sankore reached its height and preserved an extensive library of native African literature.

The forests of West and Central Africa proved a greater challenge to the creation of cities and states. By the end of the first millennium C.E., Africans in the region had developed technological, social, and political frameworks that allowed for the creation of larger-scale societies in the forests. As early as the ninth century C.E., a state developed in the forest region of what is now southeastern Nigeria. Named Igbo-Ukwu after a nearby modern town, archaeological evidence from the site shows not only a concentration of wealth and authority in the hands of a kinglike figure, but also bronze-working technology. This is significant not only as a sign of metal-working, but also in that it shows Igbo-Ukwu was involved in long-distance trade deep into the Saharan desert, which was the nearest source of copper. Just to the west in south-central Nigeria would develop Benin, one of the largest and longest lived forest states. Growing in power by the thirteenth century, Benin is a testimony to the ability of humans to develop complex economic and political systems despite environmental challenges. Benin not only dominated the region, but also developed a sophisticated state-sponsored art program built around the casting of bronze sculptures. By using a sophisticated system called lost wax casting, full-size models of sculptures were made of beeswax, and then a ceramic mold was built around them. Then molten bronze was poured into the mold, melting away the wax.

Each such sculpture (some of which could be quite large) was unique (fig. 10.18). Similar metalworking techniques would later be adopted in ASANTE (Ah-SHAHN-tay), a state that would rise up in the early eighteenth century in what is modern-day Ghana. Asante grew wealthy in part as a major producer of gold. The Asantehene (king) of Asante and his royal court carried and wore a stunning amount of gold during public appearances. The "throne" of Asante was the Golden Stool, which reputedly appeared from heaven to show the divine support of the first Asantehene, Osei Tutu (fig. 10.19).

East and South Africa. East Africa is in part unique because of its connection to the Indian Ocean. Unlike the Atlantic to the west, the Indian Ocean is friendly to sailing voyages and greatly facilitated long-distance trade. As early as the first century B.C.E. it is clear that traders from the Mediterranean and India were sailing to the East African coast. As such, East Africa was from ancient days very cosmopolitan. In this setting developed a unique culture known as the **Swahili,** (which translates as "people of the coast"). The Swahili language reflects both African and Middle Eastern linguistic elements, and the Swahili

FIGURE 10.18   Head of an Oba, Edo, Court of Benin, Nigeria, eighteenth century, brass, iron, height $13\frac{1}{8}''$ (33 cm), gift of Klaus G. Perls, 1991. Metropolitan Museum of Art, New York. All Oba heads include representations of broad coral-bead necklaces which cover the entire neck—a part of the royal costume to this day.

FIGURE 10.19   This collection of Asante gold weights (used to measure quantities of gold dust), reflects not only the products of lost-wax casting, but also the African tendency to imbue even mundane objects with artistic quality. David Garner/Exeter City Museums & Art Gallery, Royal Albert Memorial Museum.

FIGURE 10.20   A view of the inside wall of the stone enclosure at Great Zimbabwe. Constructed around the thirteenth century, this structure is remarkable in that it was built without the use of mortar in a technique known as drystone architecture.

themselves reflect genetic and cultural ties that are more Indian Ocean than purely African or Arab. As intermediaries in a highly valuable trade, the Swahili grew wealthy, especially as the growth of Islamic states in the Middle East and India fostered even greater demand for trade. Swahili towns featured multistory homes built of coral blocks. Although the outsides were austere, the interiors were lavishly decorated with trade goods from Africa, the Middle East, and Asia. Interestingly, however, as Islam became increasingly influential among the Swahili during the ninth and tenth centuries, it did not spread into the interior of East Africa. Thus, although Islam followed trade routes into West Africa, it did not do so in the east.

One key source of trade goods for the Swahili was Great Zimbabwe. Located in the modern country that shares its name, this state grew to prominence during the thirteenth and fourteenth centuries. Although gold was a major good traded east to the coast, most of Zimbabwe's wealth seems to have been based in a mixed farming and cattle-herding economy. The capital city's huge drystone walls stand even today (fig. 10.20).

AFRICA AND THE TRANSATLANTIC SLAVE TRADE

When advances in European maritime transport first began to facilitate increased interaction between Africans and Europeans, the initial exchanges tended to be peaceful. The Portuguese established trading posts at El Mina (in modern-day Ghana) and with the Kongo Kingdom at Luanda in the fifteenth century, for example. Trade in these early decades focused on items such as ivory, gold, and spices. However, as profits from sugar plantations in the Atlantic islands and Brazil grew in significance, the nature of trade between Africans and Europeans began to change. Africans possessed both a resistance to Old World infectious diseases and tropical parasitic diseases, which allowed them to somewhat better endure the harsh conditions of plantation labor than Native Americans and Europeans. Whereas the life expectancy of European or Native American slaves on sugar plantations was often less than a year, enslaved Africans might live as long as seven. Further, Africans often possessed a knowledge of tropical crops and soils that could enhance the productivity of the plantations. Ironically, for Africans it was strengths, not weaknesses, that made them the victims of the Atlantic slave trade.

Thus, as the value of Africans as slaves increased, so did European demand for slave labor from Africa. Over the course of the next three centuries, the slave trade would grow from a few thousand individuals per year to a peak of nearly 100,000 per year in the latter eighteenth century. Overall, some eleven million enslaved Africans would be exported to the New World, and millions more would die either in wars of conquest fought to acquire captives in Africa or during the torturous continental passage to the coast and middle passage to the Americas. European and African slave traders grew wealthy from this human trade, as did plantation owners and factory owners in the Americas and Europe, who benefited from cheap slave labor. In Africa, wars to capture slaves and the increasing role of slave trading as a source of wealth likely served to disrupt local economies and systems of political legitimacy.

Cultural Impact

Sub-Saharan African societies entered into commercial relationships with Muslim peoples in Southwest Asia and in North Africa. The states that the African peoples established in West Africa and coastal East Africa extended the influence of the sub-Saharan African peoples through extensive trade, particularly in gold, ivory, and slaves. Trade facilitated the introduction of Islam into African society. Mosques were built, as were Islamic schools. By around 1500 C.E., African traditions had blended with Islamic institutions in sub-Saharan African societies.

The original inhabitants of Mesoamerica lived in smaller societies than those in India, China, and Japan. Ancient American peoples lacked an advanced transportation technology that facilitated an extensive trade and communications network among peoples of the Eastern Hemisphere. This, however, did not prevent them from developing complex societies with sophisticated cultural and religious traditions, long before they had contact with European and other peoples. The Aztecs and Incas, in particular, built powerful imperial states organized around agricultural production in widely varying climactic conditions.

Native American peoples of the northwest coast and the midwest and southwest have left legacies of various kinds. The peoples of the northwest have left a respect for the waters and have handed down their skills in canoe building and in fishing. Peoples of the southwest have long had a tradition of outstanding textile weaving, which they share with the Andean peoples. In addition, Native Americans of the southwest remain expert in creating pottery and jewelry, particularly with semi-precious stones and gold and silver. The techniques they developed for hammering, embossing, soldering, welding, casting, and gilding remain in use today.

Africans worked not only as agricultural laborers, but also as mining engineers, cowboys, cooks, and household servants. They often had a far greater degree of cultural influence than they are generally given credit for. In particular, African foods, notions of religion, and styles of music and artwork made deep impressions on the societies of the American South, Latin America, and the Carribean. Gumbo, deep-fried foods, and barbeque are examples of African contributions to the cuisines of the Americas. Similarly, we need only listen to the music of these regions to hear the significant African influence. Finally, African notions of the divine syncretized with Catholicism in many regions to form new religions such as Voudou, Candomble, Santeria, and Macumba. Thus, even what we tend to characterize as "American" or "Latin American" is in many ways African as well. The impact of these African cultural elements in the Americas is discussed in greater detail in Chapter 22.

KEY TERMS

Mesoamerica
Teotihuacán
Wacah Chan
roof comb
Bahlum
daykeepers
mother-fathers
flower song
Nahuatl
huacas
El Niño

Tawantinsuyu
Nazca lines
geoglyphs
totem pole
potlach
kiva
maize
moundbilder
Intertropical Convergence
   Zone (ITCZ)

lateritic
humus
rift valley
rock paintings
t'eff
Bantu
Batwa
Cushitic
pantheism
Oludumare

orisa
Ogun
Punic
Didascalia
Arianism
Coptic
Shi'ites
Swahili

www. WEBSITES FOR FURTHER STUDY

http://www.mesoweb.com/welcome.html
(MesoWeb is a site with several components and can be viewed either in html or with animations using Shockwave Flash plugin. It has many images and descriptions of Mesoamerican cultures.)

http://www.raingod.com/angus/Gallery/Photos/SouthAmerica/Peru/IncaTrail/MachuPicchu1.html
(Several images of Machu Picchu, Inca culture, ca. 1450.)

http://www.civilization.ca/aborig/haida/hvske01e.html
(An extensive discussion of Northwest Native American Indian cultures such as the Skedans.)

http://www-learning.berkeley.edu/wciv/ugis55a/readings/earlyafrica.html
(A good introductory site for early African cultures.)

http://witcombe.sbc.edu/ARTHafrica.html#africa
(Art history resources on the web by Chris Witcombe; a good site for early African art.)

READINGS

Selected Mesoamerican Poems and Songs

The following three selections suggest the range of roles and functions of song and poetry in Mesoamerican civilizations. The first, The midwife addresses the newly delivered woman, is an Aztec poem that describes the valiant heroism of women, whose responsibility is to bear children. Women's endurance of the pains of childbirth is compared to the endurance of male warriors in battle. For the Aztec and for other Mesoamerican peoples, poetic speech was called "flower song," which suggests both its beauty and its creative power. The importance of poetry in everyday life is conveyed in the second work, With flowers you write, a fifteenth-century Nahuatl song. The third selected is a Maya song that testifies to their emphasis on blood sacrifice to ensure fertility and the renewal of life. Oh watcher; watcher from the trees describes the dance of the bowman, who sharpens his arrows and dances around the victims in preparation for the sacrifice.

The Midwife Addresses the Newly Delivered Woman

O my daughter, O valiant woman, you worked, you toiled.
You soared like an eagle, you sprang like a jaguar,
You put all your strength behind the shield, behind the
    buckler;
you endured.
You went forth into battle, you emulated Our Mother,
    Cihuacoatl Quilaztli,   5
and now our lord has seated you on the Eagle Mat, the
    Jaguar Mat.°
You have spent yourself, O my daughter, now be tranquil.
What does our lord Tloque Nahuaque° will?
Shall he bestow his favors upon each of you separately,
    in separate places?
Perhaps you shall go off and leave behind the child that
    has arrived.   10
Perhaps, small as he is the Creator will summon him,
    will call out to him,
or perhaps he shall come to take you.
Do not be boastful of [the child].
Do not consider yourself worthy of it.
Call out humbly to our lord, Tloque Nahuaque.   15

With Flowers You Write

With flowers you write,
Oh Giver of Life!
With songs you give color,
with songs you shade
those who must live on the earth.   5

Later you will destroy
eagles and tigers;
we live only in your painting
here, on the earth.

With black ink you will blot out   10
all that was friendship,
brotherhood, nobility.

You give shading
to those who must live on the earth.

Later you will destroy   15
eagles and tigers;
we live only in your painting
here, on the earth.

Oh Watcher, Watcher from the Trees

Oh watcher, watcher from the trees,
with one, with two,
we go to hunt at the edge of the grove,
in a lively dance up to three.
Raise your head high,   5
do not mistake,
instruct well your eyes
to gather the prize.

Make sharp the tip of your arrow,
make taut the cord   10
of your bow; now you have good
resin of *catsim* on the feathers
at the end of the arrow's rod.
You have rubbed well
the fat of a male deer   15
on your biceps, on your muscles,
on your knees, on your twin muscles,
on your shoulders, on your chest.

Go nimbly three times round
about the painted stone column,   20
where stands that virile lad,
unstained, undefiled, a man.
Go once, on the second round
take up your bow, put in the arrow,
point it at his chest; you need not   25
use all your strength
so as to kill him,
or wound him deeply.
Let him suffer
little by little,   30
as He wishes it,
the magnificent Lord God.

The next time you go round
this stony blue column, the next time
you go round, shoot another arrow.   35
This you must do without
stopping your dance, because
thus it is done by well-bred
men, fighters, those who
are sought after, pleasing   40
in the eyes of the Lord God.
And as the Sun appears
over the forest to the east,
the song of the bowman begins.
These well-bred men, fighters,   45
do their utmost.

°*Jaguar Mat:* Warriors' seat of honor.
°*Tloque Nahuaque:* Ever Present, Ever Near, the supreme spirit.

PABLO NERUDA

from *The Heights of Machu Picchu*

In his poem The Heights of Machu Picchu, the Nobel Prize-win-ning Chilean poet Pablo Neruda (1904–1973) memorialized the settlement as a place where garments for celebration and mourning were woven of the native vicuña wool, where maize, the primary crop that sustained the Inca people, was harvested, where what en-dures is the achievement and the memory of the people who created the city and the civilization it represents.

Then up the ladder of the earth I climbed
through the barbed jungle's thickets
until I reached you Machu Picchu.

Tall city of stepped stone,
home at long last of whatever earth   5
had never hidden in her sleeping clothes.
In you two lineages that had run parallel
met where the cradle both of man and light
rocked in a wind of thorns.

Mother of stone and sperm of condors.   10

High reef of the human dawn.

Spade buried in primordial sand.

This was the habitation, this is the site:
here the fat grains of maize grew high
to fall again like red hail.   15

The fleece of the vicuña was carded here
to clothe men's loves in gold, their tombs and mothers,
the king, the prayers, the warriors.

Up here men's feet found rest at night
near eagles' talons in the high   20
meat-stuffed eyries. And in the dawn
with thunder steps they trod the thinning mists,
touching the earth and stones that they might recognize
that touch come night, come death.

I gaze at clothes and hands,   25
traces of water in the booming cistern,
a wall burnished by the touch of a face,
that witnessed with my eyes the earth's carpet of tapers,
oiled with my hands the vanished wood:
for everything, apparel, skin, pots, words,   30
wine, loaves, has disappeared,
fallen to earth.

And the air came in with lemon blossom fingers
to touch those sleeping faces:
a thousand years of air, months, weeks of air,   35
blue wind and iron cordilleras—
these came with gentle footstep hurricanes
cleansing the lonely precinct of the stone.

POPOL VUH

The Popol Vuh of the sixteenth-century Quiche people of Guatemala has been compared to The Odyssey of the Greeks and the Ma-habharata of India. The work is a compendium of stories that has been and continues to be cherished by the ancient, the colonial, and the modern Mayan peoples. This Quiche work is an epic that is the most significant work of Native American verbal art. The selec-tion that follows is composed of trickster tales, popular in Central America, and a section that describes how two Popol Vuh *heroes conquer the lords of the Maya underworld.*

[The Twins Defeat Seven Macaw]

HERE IS THE BEGINNING OF THE DEFEAT AND DESTRUCTION OF THE DAY OF SEVEN MACAW by the two boys, the first named Hunahpu and the second named Xbalanque.[1] Being gods, the two of them saw evil in his attempt at self-magnification be-fore the Heart of Sky.

* * *

This is the great tree of Seven Macaw, a nance,[2] and this is the food of Seven Macaw. In order to eat the fruit of the nance he goes up the tree every day. Since Hunahpu and Xbal-anque have seen where he feeds, they are now hiding beneath the tree of Seven Macaw, they are keeping quiet here, the two boys are in the leaves of the tree.

And when Seven Macaw arrived, perching over his meal, the nance, it was then that he was shot by Hunahpu. The blowgun shot went right to his jaw, breaking his mouth. Then he went up over the tree and fell flat on the ground. Suddenly Hunahpu appeared, running. He set out to grab him, but ac-tually it was the arm of Hunahpu that was seized by Seven Macaw. He yanked it straight back, he bent it back at the shoulder. Then Seven Macaw tore it right out of Hunahpu. Even so, the boys did well: the first round was not their de-feat by Seven Macaw.

And when Seven Macaw had taken the arm of Hunahpu, he went home. Holding his jaw very carefully, he arrived:

"What have you got there?" said Chimalmat, the wife of Seven Macaw.

"What is it but those two tricksters! They've shot me, they've dislocated my jaw.[3] All my teeth are just loose, now they ache. But once what I've got is over the fire—hanging there, dangling over the fire—then they can just come and get it. They're real tricksters!" said Seven Macaw, then he hung up the arm of Hunahpu.

Meanwhile Hunahpu and Xbalanque were thinking. And then they invoked a grandfather, a truly white-haired grand-father, and a grandmother, a truly humble grandmother—just bent-over, elderly people. Great White Peccary is the name of the grandfather, and Great White Coati is the name of the grandmother.[4] The boys said to the grandmother and grandfather.

---

[1]First mention of the twin hero gods (their origin is recounted in Part 3). Here they confront the false god Seven Macaw, who has arisen during the time of primordial darkness, boasting, "My eyes are of metal; my teeth just glitter with jewels, and turquoise as well. . . . I am like the sun and the moon." Note that all the characters in Parts 1, 2, and 3 are super-natural; humans are not created until Part 4.
[2]A pickle tree (*Byrsonima crassifolia*).
[3]This is the origin of the way a macaw's beak looks, with a huge upper mandible and a small, retreating lower one [translator's note].
[4]Animal names of the divine grandparents, Xpiyacoc and Xmucane, who are also the twins' genealogical grandparents.

"Please travel with us when we go to get our arm from Seven Macaw; we'll just follow right behind you. You'll tell him:

'Do forgive us our grandchildren, who travel with us. Their mother and father are dead, and so they follow along there, behind us. Perhaps we should give them away, since all we do is pull worms out of teeth.' So we'll seem like children to Seven Macaw, even though *we're* giving *you* the instructions," the two boys told them.

"Very well," they replied.

After that they approached the place where Seven Macaw was in front of his home. When the grandmother and grandfather passed by, the two boys were romping along behind them. When they passed below the lord's house, Seven Macaw was yelling his mouth off because of his teeth. And when Seven Macaw saw the grandfather and grandmother traveling with them:

"Where are you headed, our grandfather?" said the lord.

"We're just making our living, your lordship," they replied.

"Why are you working for a living? Aren't those your children traveling with you?"

"No, they're not, your lordship. They're our grandchildren, our descendants, but it is nevertheless *we* who take pity on *them*. The bit of food they get is the portion we give them, your lordship," replied the grandmother and grandfather. Since the lord is getting done in by the pain in his teeth, it is only with great effort that he speaks again:

"I implore you, please take pity on me! What sweets can you make, what poisons[5] can you cure?" said the lord.

"We just pull the worms out of teeth, and we just cure eyes. We just set bones, your lordship," they replied.

"Very well, please cure my teeth. They really ache, every day. It's insufferable! I get no sleep because of them—and my eyes. They just shot me, those two tricksters! Ever since it started I haven't eaten because of it. Therefore take pity on me! Perhaps it's because my teeth are loose now."

"Very well, your lordship. It's a worm, gnawing at the bone.[6] It's merely a matter of putting in a replacement and taking the teeth out, sir."

"But perhaps it's not good for my teeth to come out—since I am, after all, a lord. My finery is in my teeth—and my eyes."

"But then we'll put in a replacement. Ground bone will be put back in." And this is the "ground bone": it's only white corn.

"Very well. Yank them out! Give me some help here!" he replied.

And when the teeth of Seven Macaw came out, it was only white corn that went in as a replacement for his teeth—just a coating shining white, that corn in his mouth. His face fell at once, he no longer looked like a lord. The last of his teeth came out, the jewels that had stood out blue from his mouth.

And when the eyes of Seven Macaw were cured, he was plucked around the eyes, the last of his metal came off.[7] Still he felt no pain; he just looked on while the last of his greatness left him. It was just as Hunahpu and Xbalanque had intended.

And when Seven Macaw died, Hunahpu got back his arm. And Chimalmat, the wife of Seven Macaw, also died.

Such was the loss of the riches of Seven Macaw: only the doctors got the jewels and gems that had made him arrogant, here on the face of the earth. The genius of the grandmother, the genius of the grandfather did its work when they took back their arm: it was implanted and the break got well again; Just as they had wished the death of Seven Macaw, so they brought it about. They had seen evil in his self-magnification.

After this the two boys went on again. What they did was simply the word of the Heart of Sky.

From Part 3

[Victory over the Underworld]

AND NOW WE SHALL NAME THE NAME OF THE FATHER OF HUNAHPU AND XBALANQUE. Let's drink to him, and let's just drink to the telling and accounting of the begetting of Hunahpu and Xbalanque. We shall tell just half of it, just a part of the account of their father. Here follows the account.

These are the names: One Hunahpu and Seven Hunahpu,[8] as they are called.

* * *

AND ONE AND SEVEN HUNAHPU WENT INSIDE DARK HOUSE.[9]

And then their torch was brought, only one torch, already lit, sent by One and Seven Death, along with a cigar for each of them, also already lit, sent by the lords. When these were brought to One and Seven Hunahpu they were cowering, here in the dark. When the bearer of their torch and cigars arrived, the torch was bright as it entered; their torch and both of their cigars were burning. The bearer spoke:

"'They must be sure to return them in the morning—not finished, but just as they look now. They must return them intact,' the lords say to you," they were told, and they were defeated. They finished the torch and they finished the cigars that had been brought to them.

And Xibalba is packed with tests, heaps and piles of tests.

This is the first one: the Dark House, with darkness alone inside.

And the second is named Rattling House, heavy with cold inside, whistling with drafts, clattering with hail. A deep chill comes inside here.

And the third is named Jaguar House, with jaguars alone inside, jostling one another, crowding together, with gnashing teeth. They're scratching around; these jaguars are shut inside the house.

Bat House is the name of the fourth test, with bats alone inside the house, squeaking, shrieking, darting through the house. The bats are shut inside; they can't get out.

---

[5] Play on words as *qui* is translated as both "sweet" and "poison."

[6] The present-day Quiche retain the notion that a toothache is caused by a worm gnawing at the bone [Translator's note].

[7] This is clearly meant to be the origin of the large white and completely featherless eye patches and very small eyes of the scarlet macaw [translator's note].

---

[8] Twin sons of Xpiyacoc and Xmucane; the elder of these twins, One Hunahpu, will become the father of Hunahpu and Xbalanque. "As for Seven Hunahpu," according to the text, "he has no wife. He's just a partner and just secondary; he just remains a boy."

[9] The first of the "test" houses in Yibalba (the underworld) to which One and Seven Hunahpu, avid ballplayers, have been lured by the underworld lords, One and Seven Death; the lords have promised them a challenging ball game. The Mesoamerican ball game, remotely comparable to both basketball and soccer, was played on a rectangular court, using a ball of native rubber.

And the fifth is named Razor House, with blades alone inside. The blades are moving back and forth, ripping, slashing through the house.

These are the first tests of Xibalba, but One and Seven Hunahpu never entered into them, except for the one named earlier, the specified test house.

And when One and Seven Hunahpu went back before One and Seven Death, they were asked:

"Where are my cigars? What of my torch? They were brought to you last night!"

"We finished them, your lordship."

"Very well. This very day, your day is finished, you will die, you will disappear, and we shall break you off. Here you will hide your faces: you are to be sacrificed!" said One and Seven Death.

And then they were sacrificed and buried. They were buried at the Place of Ball Game Sacrifice,[1] as it is called. The head of One Hunahpu was cut off; only his body was buried with his younger brother.

"Put his head in the fork of the tree that stands by the road," said One and Seven Death.

And when his head was put in the fork of the tree, the tree bore fruit. It would not have had any fruit, had not the head of One Hunahpu been put in the fork of the tree.

This is the calabash tree, as we call it today, or "the skull of One Hunahpu," as it is said.

And then One and Seven Death were amazed at the fruit of the tree. The fruit grows out everywhere, and it isn't clear where the head of One Hunahpu is; now it looks just the way the calabashes look. All the Xibalbans see this, when they come to look.

The state of the tree loomed large in their thoughts, because it came about at the same time the head of One Hunahpu was put in the fork. The Xibalbans said among themselves:

"No one is to pick the fruit, nor is anyone to go beneath the tree," they said. They restricted themselves; all of Xibalba held back.

It isn't clear which is the head of One Hunahpu; now it's exactly the same as the fruit of the tree. Calabash came to be its name, and much was said about it. A maiden heard about it, and here we shall tell of her arrival.

AND HERE IS THE ACCOUNT OF A MAIDEN, the daughter of a lord named Blood Gatherer.[2]

And this is when a maiden heard of it, the daughter of a lord. Blood Gatherer is the name of her father, and Blood Moon is the name of the maiden.

And when he heard the account of the fruit of the tree, her father retold it. And she was amazed at the account:

"I'm not acquainted with that tree they talk about. 'Its fruit is truly sweet!' they say,' I hear," she said.

Next, she went all alone and arrived where the tree stood. It stood at the Place of Ball Game Sacrifice:

"What? Well! What's the fruit of this tree? Shouldn't this tree bear something sweet? They shouldn't die, they shouldn't be wasted. Should I pick one?" said the maiden.

And then the bone spoke; it was here in the fork of the tree:

"Why do you want a mere bone, a round thing in the branches of a tree?" said the head of One Hunahpu when it spoke to the maiden. "You don't want it," she was told.

"I do want it," said the maiden.

"Very well. Stretch out your right hand here, so I can see it," said the bone.

"Yes," said the maiden. She stretched out her right hand, up there in front of the bone.

And then the bone spit out its saliva, which landed squarely in the hand of the maiden.

And then she looked in her hand, she inspected it right away, but the bone's saliva wasn't in her hand.

"It is just a sign I have given you, my saliva, my spittle. This, my head, has nothing on it—just bone, nothing of meat. It's just the same with the head of a great lord: it's just the flesh that makes his face look good. And when he dies, people get frightened by his bones. After that, his son is like his saliva, his spittle, in his being, whether it be the son of a lord or the son of a craftsman, an orator. The father does not disappear, but goes on being fulfilled. Neither dimmed nor destroyed is the face of a lord, a warrior, craftsman, orator. Rather, he will leave his daughters and sons. So it is that I have done likewise through you. Now go up there on the face of the earth; you will not die. Keep the word. So be it," said the head of One and Seven Hunahpu—they were of one mind when they did it.

This was the word Hurricane, Newborn Thunderbolt, Sudden Thunderbolt had given them. In the same way, by the time the maiden returned to her home, she had been given many instructions. Right away something was generated in her belly, from the saliva alone, and this was the generation of Hunahpu and Xbalanque.

And when the maiden got home and six months had passed, she was found out by her father. Blood Gatherer is the name of her father.

* * *

AND THEY CAME TO THE LORDS.[3] Feigning great humility, they bowed their heads all the way to the ground when they arrived. They brought themselves low, doubled over, flattened out, down to the rags, to the tatters. They really looked like vagabonds when they arrived.

So then they were asked what their mountain[4] and tribe were, and they were also asked about their mother and father:

"Where do you come from?" they were asked.

"We've never known, lord. We don't know the identity of our mother and father. We must've been small when they died," was all they said. They didn't give any names.

"Very well. Please entertain us, then. What do you want us to give you in payment?" they were asked.

---

[1]Probably not a place name, but rather a name for the altar where losing ball players were sacrificed [translator's note].

[2]Fourth-ranking lord of Xibalba, whose commission is to draw blood from people.

[3]Forced to flee the underworld the maiden (Blood Moon) finds refuge on earth with Xmucane. There she gives birth to the twins, who, like their father and uncle, become ballplayers and are enticed to the underworld. Surviving the Dark House and other tests, they disguise themselves as vagabonds and earn a reputation as clever entertainers among the denizens of Xibalba; as such they are summoned to entertain the high lords.

[4]A metonym for almost any settlement, but especially a fortified town or citadel, located on a defensible elevation [translator's note].

"Well, we don't want anything. To tell the truth, we're afraid," they told the lord.

"Don't be afraid. Don't be ashamed. Just dance this way: first you'll dance to sacrifice yourselves, you'll set fire to my house after that, you'll act out all the things you know. We want to be entertained. This is our heart's desire, the reason you had to be sent for, dear vagabonds. We'll give you payment," they were told.

So then they began their songs and dances, and then all the Xibalbans arrived, the spectators crowded the floor, and they danced everything: they danced the Weasel, they danced the Poorwill,[5] they danced the Armadillo. Then the lord said to them:

"Sacrifice my dog, then bring him back to life again," they were told.

"Yes," they said.

When they sacrificed the dog
he then came back to life.
And that dog was really happy
when he came back to life.
Back and forth he wagged his tail
when he came back to life.

And the lord said to them:

"Well, you have yet to set my home on fire," they were told next, so then they set fire to the home of the lord. The house was packed with all the lords, but they were not burned. They quickly fixed it back again, lest the house of One Death be consumed all at once, and all the lords were amazed, and they went on dancing this way. They were overjoyed.

And then they were asked by the lord:

"You have yet to kill a person! Make a sacrifice without death!" they were told.

"Very well," they said.

And then they took hold of a human sacrifice.

And they held up a human heart on high.

And they showed its roundness to the lords.

And now One and Seven Death admired it, and now that person was brought right back to life. His heart was overjoyed when he came back to life, and the lords were amazed:

"Sacrifice yet again, even do it to yourselves! Let's see it! At heart, that's the dance we really want from you," the lords said now.

"Very well, lord," they replied, and then they sacrificed themselves.

AND THIS IS THE SACRIFICE OF HUNAHPU BY XBALANQUE. One by one his legs, his arms were spread wide. His head came off, rolled far away outside. His heart, dug out, was smothered in a leaf,[6] and all the Xibalbans went crazy at the sight.

So now, only one of them was dancing there: Xbalanque.

"Get up!" he said, and Hunahpu came back to life. The two of them were overjoyed at this—and likewise the lords rejoiced, as if they were doing it themselves. One and Seven Death were as glad at heart as if they themselves were actually doing the dance.

And then the hearts of the lords were filled with longing, with yearning for the dance of little Hunahpu and Xbalanque, so then came these words from One and Seven Death:

"Do it to us! Sacrifice us!" they said. "Sacrifice both of us!" said One and Seven Death to Hunahpu and Xbalanque.

"Very well. You ought to come back to life. What is death to you?[7] And aren't we making you happy, along with the vassals of your domain?" they told the lords.

And this one was the first to be sacrificed: the lord at the very top, the one whose name is One Death, the ruler of Xibalba.

And with One Death dead, the next to be taken was Seven Death. They did not come back to life.

And then the Xibalbans were getting up to leave, those who had seen the lords die. They underwent heart sacrifice there, and the heart sacrifice was performed on the two lords only for the purpose of destroying them.

As soon as they had killed the one lord without bringing him back to life, the other lord had been meek and tearful before the dancers. He didn't consent, he didn't accept it:

"Take pity on me!" he said when he realized. All their vassals took the road to the great canyon, in one single mass they filled up the deep abyss. So they piled up there and gathered together, countless ants, tumbling down into the canyon, as if they were being herded there. And when they arrived, they all bent low in surrender, they arrived meek and tearful.

Such was the defeat of the rulers of Xibalba. The boys accomplished it only through wonders, only through self-transformation.

* * *

Such was the beginning of their disappearance and the denial of their worship.

Their ancient day was not a great one,
these ancient people only wanted conflict,
their ancient names are not really divine,
but fearful is the ancient evil of their faces.

They are makers of enemies, users of owls,[8]

they are inciters to wrongs and violence,
they are masters of bidden intentions as well,
they are black and white,[9]
masters of stupidity, masters of perplexity,

as it is said. By putting on appearances they cause dismay.

Such was the loss of their greatness and brilliance. Their domain did not return to greatness. This was accomplished by little Hunahpu and Xbalanque.

The Epic of Son-Jara

The following selection from the ancient African Epic of Son-Jara *illustrates the oral nature of the poem. The passage also reveals a connection with the Bible in its references to Adam. The footnotes are essential reading for Western readers unfamiliar with ancient African literature. The marginal connects represent the assenting voice of the communal audience.*

---

[5]The goatsucker. The dances apparently were imitations of these animals and birds.
[6]As a tamale is wrapped. In the typical Mesoamerican heart sacrifice, the victim's arms and legs were stretched wide and the heart was excised and offered to a deity.

[7]Evident sarcasm.
[8]The lords had used owls as messengers to lure the ballplayers to Xibalba.
[9]Contradictory, duplicitous.

From Episode I[1]

Prologue in Paradise

Nare Magan Kònatè![2]
Sorcerer-Seizing-Sorcerer![3]
A man of power is hard to find.
And four mastersingers.   (Indeed)
5   O Kala Jula Sangoyi[4]
Sorcerer-Seizing-Sorcerer!   (Mmm)

It is of Adam that I sing.
Of Adam,
Ben Adam.[5]   ('Tis true)
10   As you succeeded some,
So shall you have successors![6]
It is of Adam that I sing, of Adam.   (Indeed)

I sing of Biribiriba![7]   (Indeed)
Of Nare Magan Kònatè!
15   Sorcerer-Seizing Sorcerer!   (True)
From Fatiyataligara
All the way to Sokoto,[8]   (Indeed)
Belonged to Magan Son-Jara.   (Indeed)
Africans call that, my father,[9]
20   The Republic of Mali,[1]   (Indeed)
The Maninka[2] realm: (Mmm, 'tis true)
That's the meaning of Mali.
Magan Son-Jara,
He slayed Bambara-of-the-Border;[3]

25   Settling on the border[4] does not suit the weak. (Indeed)
And slayed Bambara-the-Lizard;[5]
No weak one should call himself lizard.   (Indeed)
And slayed Bambara-of-the-Backwoods;
Settling the backwoods does not suit the weak. (Indeed)
30   All this by the hand of Nare Magan Kònatè.
Sorcerer-Seizing-Sorcerer!
Simbon, Lion-Born-of-the-Cat.[6]   ('Tis true)

I sing of Biribiriba.   (Indeed)
Stump-in-the-Dark-of-Night![7]
35   Should you bump against it,
It will bump against you.   (Indeed)
Granary-Guard-Dog.[8]   (Indeed)
The thing discerning not the stranger,
Nor the familiar.
40   Should it come upon any person,
He will be bitten!   (Indeed)
Kirikara Watita![9]   (Indeed)
Adversity's-True-Place![1]   (Indeed)
Man's reason and a woman's are not the same.[2] (Indeed)
45   Pretty words and truth are not the same.   (Indeed)
Almighty God created Adam,   (Indeed)
Nine Adams.[3]   (Indeed)
The tenth one was Ben Adam.   (True)

Ah, Bèmba![4]   (Indeed)
50   Almighty God created Adam, the forefather, (Indeed)
And caused him to stand upon the earth,
And said that all creation's beings should submit to him.
And all the beings of creation did submit to him, (Indeed)
Save Iblis[5] alone.
55   May God deliver us from Satan!   (Amen, O my Lord)

[Here follows a lengthy account of the Genesis story, in a version that incorporates a cosmological myth and the origin of the races of the world. This provides a background to the epic recall, in the next episode, of the

---

[1]Text by Fa-Digi Sisoko; translated by John William Johnson. The words in parentheses at the right are interjections made by members of the audience, principally by Bèmba.

[2]Son-Jara. This praise name combines a reference to his place of origin (Nare) with his royal title (Magan, "king" or "lord"; the title of the emperor of ancient Ghana was Kaya Magan). Kònatè is Son-Jara's clan.

[3]This praise name refers to Son-Jara's superior magical powers.

[4]A bard reputed to be the originator of the epic; he can thus be considered the equivalent of Homer with respect to the Iliad. He is invoked here in homage to the artistic ancestor of Fa-Digi Sisoko, the bard who is re-creating the epic on this occasion. The exact reference of line 4 is obscure, but its allusion to the bard's professional status is clearly related to the invocation of Kala Jula Sangoyi.

[5]The Adam of Genesis.

[6]A formulaic device employed by the bard at various points in the epic; here it stresses the unbroken continuity of Son-Jara's dynastic line.

[7]This praise name for Son-Jara conveys his immense physical prowess.

[8]An ancient city in northern Nigeria, several hundred miles east of the Manding area. The city was the capital of the Fulani empire which by the early nineteenth century had embraced most of the area in the Niger–Benue basin and was conquered by the British in the early years of the twentieth century. Fatiyataligara can no longer be identified. The bard means the extent of the old Mali empire from west to east.

[9]A term of reverence; here an aside addressed to the older members of the audience.

[1]That is, present-day Mali; the name of the ancient empire was revived in 1960, when the modern republic achieved independence from France.

[2]Manding or Mandenka; the term covers many more ethnic groups than are found in the present Republic of Mali.

[3]That is, Sumamuru, Son-Jara's principal antagonist, who was a Susu, an ethnic group related to the Bambara of present-day Mali.

[4]All areas beyond the safe limits of human settlement. The implication is that it requires an intrepid character, such as that associated with the professional hunter, to venture beyond these limits and confront the dangers of the wilderness.

[5]A derogatory term that alludes to the fact that young boys start to practice hunting with lizards; hence the reptile is associated with the weak and uninitiated.

[6]Compare with "Lion Heart," which became attached to the name of the medieval king of England, Richard. Simbon: hunter; the ideal of manhood in traditional African societies.

[7]This praise name presents Son-Jara as a formidable obstacle to his adversaries.

[8]A praise name that emphasizes the hero's ferocity. A guard dog often does not distinguish between strangers and members of the household.

[9]Ideophone for great strength. An ideophone is an expressive sound employed in African languages to convey an image or idea.

[1]A source of adversity for his enemies.

[2]A reflection on the different dispositions of the sexes in the varied roles played by male and female characters.

[3]Possibly, the succession of founding figures, from the first man in the biblical story of creation down to Son-Jara himself.

[4]The bard's apprentice, who serves as his principal interlocutor throughout the performance.

[5]Satan (Arabic).

original migration of the ancestors of the Manding from the Middle East and their settlement among and interaction with the indigenous peoples in the west African savanna. The reconstruction of the early history of the region serves to trace both the paternal and the maternal lines of Son-Jara's descent.]

From Episode 2

Mecca

I sing of Biribiriba!	(Indeed)
Kirikisa, Spear-of-Access, Spear-of-Service![6]	(Indeed)
170 The Messenger of God, Muhammad, was born,	(Indeed)
On the twelfth day of the month of Dònba.[7]	(Indeed)
On the thirteenth day,	
Tuesday, Bilal was born in Samuda.[8]	(Indeed)
Ask the ones who know of this!	(Mmm)
175 That Bilal,	(Indeed)
His child was Mamadu Kanu.	
That Mamadu Kanu,	(Mmm)
He had three sons:	(Indeed)
Kanu Simbon,	(Indeed)
180 Kanu Nyògòn Simbon,	Indeed)
Lawali Simbon.	(Indeed)
Ah! Bèmba!	(Indeed)
The races of man were ninety in number.	(Indeed)
There were twelve clans of Marakas[9]	(Indeed)
185 Which came from Wagadugu.[1]	(Indeed)
The Sises came from Wagadugu.	(Mmm)
The Janes came from Wagadugu.	(Mmm)
The Tures came from Wagadugu.	(Indeed)
The Beretes came from Wagadugu.	(Indeed)
190 The Sakòs came from Wagadugu.	
The Fulani came from Wagadugu.	(Indeed)
The Jawaras came from Wagadugu.	(Indeed)
The Nyarès came from Wagadugu.	(Indeed)
The Tunkaras came from Wagadugu.[2]	(Mmm)
195 The peoples of Wagadugu thus scattered[3]	(Indeed)
O Bèmba!	(Indeed)
The ancestor of the Jawaras, Damangile,[4]	(Indeed)
And the forefather of the Nyarès,[5] Nyenemba Nyarè,	(Indeed)

Went forth to found a village in Kingi[6]	(Indeed)
200 The name of that village was Bambagile.[7]	(Indeed)
Damangile's tomb is there in Bambagile.	(Indeed)
He had two children:	(Indeed)
Daman and Sila Maan.	(Indeed)
They both went forth to Jala.[8]	(Mmm)
205 Mount Siman and Mount Wala[9] belong to the Jawaras in Jala.	(That's true)
Ah! Bèmba!	(Indeed)
The ancestor of the Tunkaras,[1] Prince Burama,	(Indeed)
He went forth to found the village called Mèma.[2]	(Indeed)
There he had two sons,	(Indeed)
210 Prince Burama[3] and Jasigi.	(Indeed)
Prince Burama and Jasigi,	(Indeed)
'Twas they who joined Son-Jara here,	(Indeed)
And went with him to the Manden.	(Indeed)
They left the Manden later	(Indeed)
215 And came to settle in Kulun.[4]	(Indeed)
They left Kulun,	(Indeed)
And settled in Bangasi,[5]	(Indeed)
And went up on Genu Mountain,[6]	(Indeed)
And founded a village atop the mountain.	(Indeed)
220 That village's name was Kuduguni.[7]	(Mmm, that's true)
'Tis said the Tunkaras of Genu,	(Indeed)
They each had two sons:	(Indeed)
Wali and Gayi,	(Indeed)
Sega and Marama.	(Indeed)
225 The four Tunkara patriarchs	(Indeed)
Who were in Kita[8] country here.	(Indeed)
That is what those people are called.	(True)
I sing of Biribiriba!	
Kirikisa, Spear-of-Access and Spear-of-Service!	(Mmm)
230 Warlord and wailing at his entry, a pile of stone![9]	
Nare Magan Kònatè, Sorcerer-Seizing-Sorcerer!	(Indeed)
Simbon, Lion-Born-of-the-Cat!	(Indeed)
That Kanu Simbon and Kanu Nyògòn Simbon,[1]	(Indeed)

[6]Three praise names for San Jara. *Kirikisa:* denotes great power. *Spear-of-Access:* despite his ferocity in war, the hero remains humane and approachable to his people. *Spear-of-Service:* expands on the idea of approachability in a reference to his generosity.
[7]Or Shawwal in the Muslim calendar; because the calendar is based strictly on the lunar cycle, the month name has no Western equivalent.
[8]The scene of a violent confrontation between Muhammad's disciples and members of a pagan clan that refused to be converted to the new religion of Islam. Bilal bin Rabah was an early companion of Muhammad's.
[9]The Sarakole, the ruling clan of the empire of Ghana, which flourished in the ninth and tenth centuries. Ancient Mali arose as a successor state to Ghana; the Maraka are thus the predecessors of the Manding in the area the latter were later to occupy.
[1]The ancient empire of Ghana; not to be confused with the capital of the present-day Republic of Burkina Faso.
[2]These lines provide a simple but striking example of parallelism. The names listed are clan names, except for *Fulani* and *Jawaras* (one of the major ethnic groups in the Gambia).
[3]Inferring an exodus from a common origin.
[4]A giant of local lore.
[5]A Manding clan.

[6]A region northwest of present-day Mali, on the border with Mauritania.
[7]Known today as Babangede.
[8]Or Jara.
[9]These are actually hills.
[1]A subclan of the Manding.
[2]The exact site of this town in unknown. Son-Jara spends a significant part of his exile here before setting out on his reconquest of the Manding.
[3]Son of the Prince Burama mentioned in line 207. The bard is looking forward here. It should be noted, however, that in the subsequent narration, although the younger Prince Burama gives refuge to Son-Jara in his capital at Mèma, he does not in fact take part in the hero's campaign against Sumamuru.
[4]This site can no longer be identified.
[5]A town in Mali.
[6]Also called Mount Kita.
[7]An early Manding settlement near Mount Kita.
[8]Important town on the railway line linking Dakar, capital of Senegal, to Bamako, capital of the Republic of Mali.
[9]Describes Son-Jara's stern and inflexible aspect. *Wailing at his entry:* because of the sorrow Son-Jara brings to his enemies and their families.
[1]Here the bard picks up the thread of the story suspended (line 181) while he traced the ancestry of the Tunkaras.

Settled in Wagadugu.   (Indeed)
235 They left Wagadugu,   (Indeed)
And they went to Jara.   (Indeed)
They left Jara.   (Mmm)
And went forth to found a farming hamlet,[2]   (Mmm)
Calling that village Farmtown.   (Indeed)
240 That Farmtown is Manden Kiri-kòròni.   (Indeed)
The very first Manden village was Manden
Kiri-koroni.   (Indeed)

Kanu Simbon, Kanu Nyògòn Simbon and   (Indeed)
Lawali Simbon,[3]

Their first village was Manden Kiri-koroni,   (Indeed)

Kiri-koroni!   (Indeed)
245 Kanu Simbon,   (Indeed)
He is the forefather of the Dankòs.   (Indeed)
Lawali Simbon,   (Indeed)
Begat Kòròlen Fabu and Sòkòna Fabu.
The Dugunòs descended from them.   (Indeed)
250 Kanu Nyògòn Simbon   (Indeed)
Begat King Bèrèmu,   (Mmm)
King Bèrèmu begat King Bèrèmu Dana.   (Indeed)
King Bèrèmu Dana begat King Juluku,
the Holy.   (Indeed)
King Juluku, the Holy begat King Belo
Komaan.   (Indeed)
255 Belo Komaan begat Juruni Komaan.
Juruni Komaan begat Fata Magan, the Handsome.
That Fata Magan, the Handsome   (Indeed)
Went forth to found a farm hamlet called
Kakama,   (Indeed)
And they call that place, my father, Bintanya
Kamalen.[4]   (Mmm)
260 O Nare Magan Kònatè!
O Sorcerer-Seizing-Sorcerer!   (Indeed)

That Fata Magan, the Handsome,
He married the daughter of
Tall Magan Berete-of-the-Ruins,
Called Saman Berete, the Pure.   (Mmm)
265 They called her Saman Berete.   (Indeed)
She had not yet borne a child at first.[5]   (Indeed)

---

[2]A temporary settlement in the fields during the sowing or harvesting season, which later forms the nucleus of a new community.
[3]The bard now traces the precise genealogy of the clan's rulers down to Son-Jara's father, Fata Magan the Handsome.
[4]The central region of the Manding area.
[5]Anticipates the confused circumstances in which she later bears a child who will be Son-Jara's half-brother and rival.

[The bard now traces the origins of another clan, the Taraweres, culminating with two brothers, Dan Mansa Wulandin and Dan Mansa Wulanba, who are to play an important role in the next episode of the epic.]

Sundiata: An Epic of Old Mali

Until the introduction of literacy in Arabic during the fourteenth century, the peoples of the West African savannah recorded their knowledge of the past in oral histories. The longer and more complex tales were memorized by individuals known as GRIOTS (GREE-oohs). These were professional historians who could flawlessly recite the equivalent of hundreds or even thousands of pages of text. Sundiata, named for the founder of the Mali empire, tells the story of this hero's rise to power and eventual defeat of his enemy Soumaoro at the Battle of Krina in 1230 C.E. Here follows a short excerpt from the tale, in which Sundiata, who was born crippled, is miraculously healed.

The master of the forges, Farakourou, was the son of the old Nounfairi, and he was a soothsayer like his father. In his workshops there was an enormous iron bar wrought by his father Noufairi. Everybody wondered what this bar was destined to be used for. Farakourou called six of his apprentices and told them to carry the iron bar to Sogolon's [Sundiata's mother] house.

When the smiths put the gigantic iron bar down in front of the hut the noise was so frightening that Sogolon, who was lying down, jumped up with a start. Then Balla Fasseke, son of Gnankouman Doua, spoke.

HERE IS THE GREAT DAY, MARI DJATA [SUNDIATA]. I AM SPEAKING TO YOU, MAGHAN, SON OF SOGOLON. THE WATERS OF THE NIGER CANNOT EFFACE THE STRAIN FROM THE BODY, BUT THEY CANNOT WIPE OUT AN INSULT. ARISE, YOUNG LION, ROAR, AND MAY THE BUSH KNOW THAT FROM HENCEFORTH IT HAS A MASTER.

The apprentice smiths were still there, Sogolon had come out and everyone was watching Mari Djata. He crept on all-fours and came to the iron bar. Supporting himself on his knees and one hand, with the other hand he picked up the iron bar without any effort and stood it up vertically. Now he was resting on nothing but his knees and held the bar with both his hands. A deathly silence had gripped all those present. Sogolon Djata [Sundiata] closed his eyes, held tight, the muscles in his arms tensed. With a violent jerk he threw his weight onto it and his knees left the ground. Sogolon Kedjou was all eyes and watched her son's legs which were trembling as though from an electric shock. Djata was sweating and the sweat ran from his brow. In a great effort he straightened up and was on his feet at one go—but the great bar of iron was twisted and had taken the form of a bow! . . .

After recovering his breath Sogolon's son dropped the bar and the crowd stood to one side. His first steps were those of a giant. Balla Fesseke fell into step and pointing his finger at Djata, he cried:

Room, room, make room!
The lion has walked;
Hide antelopes,
Get out of his way.

CHAPTER 11

HISTORY

6th century	Pope Gregory the Great
768–814	Charlemagne rules as king of the Franks
800	Pope Leo III crowns Charlemagne emperor creating Holy Roman Empire
843	Treaty of Verdun breaks up the Carolingian Empire
987–1328	Capetians rule in France
11th–13th centuries	Crusades
1066	Norman conquest of England
ca. 1140–1170	"Court of Love" established in Poitiers
1200	University of Paris granted royal charter
1215	Magna Carta

ARTS AND ARCHITECTURE

792–805	Palatine Chapel, Aachen
799	Church of Saint-Riquier, Abbeville
ca. 817–20	Plan for ideal monastery
ca. 1025	Guido D'Arezzo, musical notation
ca. 1066–82	Bayeux "tapestry"
begun ca. 1070 or 1077	Saint-Sernin, Toulouse
1120–32	Sainte-Madeleine, Vézelay
1120–32	*Mission of the Apostles,* Sainte-Madeleine, Vézelay
ca. 1120–35	Gislebertus, *Last Judgment,* cathedral, Autun
ca. 1140–70	Hildegard of Bingen, liturgical music
begun 1174	Bonanno Pisano, campanile, Pisa
1181	Nicholas of Verdun, *Klosterneuburg Abbey altarpiece*

LITERATURE AND PHILOSOPHY

700	*Lindisfarne Gospels*
8th century	*Beowulf*
ca. 800–10	*Gospel Book of Charlemagne*
mid-11th century	*Song of Roland*
1170–74	Cappelanus, *Art of Courtly Love*
1405	Christine de Pizan, *Book of the City of Ladies*

Early Middle Ages
and the Romanesque

St. John, ornamental folio from the *Book of Kells*, ca. 800, manuscript illumination,
13 × 19$\frac{1}{2}$″ (33 × 24.1 cm), Trinity College Library, Dublin.

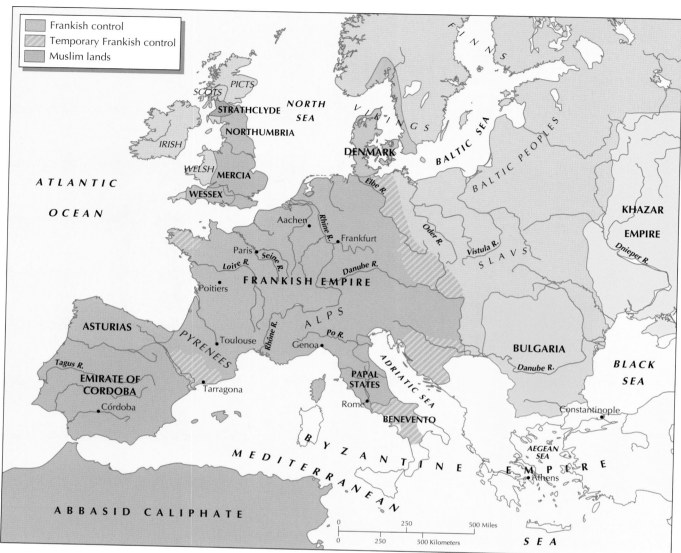

MAP 11.1   The Carolingian world, ca. 814.

CHAPTER OVERVIEW

EARLY MEDIEVAL CULTURE
Charlemagne and Pope Gregory exert their influence on politics and culture

ROMANESQUE CULTURE
The rise of France and England along with their church architecture and sculpture

EARLY MEDIEVAL CULTURE

THE EARLY MIDDLE AGES GENERALLY refers to culture in western Europe from ca. 500 to ca. 1000—that is, the second half of the first millenium C.E. The period referred to as the "Dark Ages" stretched only from the sixth to the eighth century, and can be considered "dark" only in that so few documents survive to shed light on this era. The Early Middle Ages were a period of tremendous cultural accomplishment. The fifteenth-century flowering of Western civilization that we call the Renaissance, or "rebirth," was only possible because of what took place in the thousand years that preceded it. The beginning of this period was marked by the collision of two very different cultural forces: the Christian Church, which gradually spread northward from Rome, and the Germanic tribes and other barbarian groups, who controlled civic and social life in northern Europe. Their mutual cultural assimilation would come to shape early medieval life.

THE MERGING OF CHRISTIAN AND CELTO-GERMANIC TRADITIONS

In the first half of the fifth century C.E., Anglo-Saxons invaded Britain from northeastern Europe as part of the vast migration of Germanic tribes into the former territories of the Roman empire. The Anglo-Saxons were actually three different tribes, the Angles, the Saxons, and the Jutes, who, though distinct, shared the same ancestors, traditions, and language. In Britain, they quickly suppressed the indigenous Christian inhabitants, the Celts. By 550, Christianity had disappeared from all but the most remote corners of Britain, and the culture of the country had become distinctly Germanic. Although by 675 Britain was again predominantly Christian, there is little trace of Christianity in some of the earliest artifacts from this period.

The Animal Style. Some of the finest examples of the art of these Germanic tribes are the exquisite objects discovered in the rich burial ship of an East Anglian king, dated between 625 and 633, at Sutton Hoo in Suffolk, England. As part of the king's funeral rite, the ship was lifted out of the water, dragged some distance inland, and then buried. The site was excavated in 1939. Among the artifacts discovered was a purse cover (fig. 11.1) made of gold, garnet, and enamel (the background has been restored) with a clasp made of enamel on gold. This **animal style** pattern consists of distorted creatures, their bodies twisted and stretched. Some are made up of parts from different animals. Interlaced with these bestial forms are purely abstract patterns. But this is by no means wild, undisciplined design. On the contrary, the symmetrical compositions are meticulously compiled of smaller units that are, in themselves, symmetrical. The unifying aesthetic suggests a preference for vigorous, ornamental patterns. The swirling lines and animal interlace seen here are the two basic forms that later appear in Irish Anglo-Saxon manuscript illumination.

Christian Gospel Books. The only paintings that survive in good condition from the early medieval era are in illuminated manuscripts produced in monasteries in northern England and Ireland after the mid–seventh century. **Illuminated manuscripts** are books written by hand on **parchment** (animal skin; the finest quality is called **vellum**) and elaborately decorated with paintings. Each separate page is referred to as a **folio**. Early examples are usually copies of the four Christian gospels of Matthew,

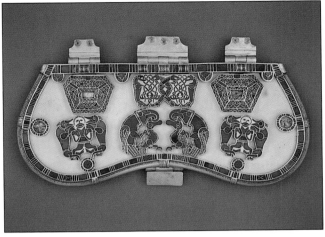

FIGURE 11.1 Purse cover, from the burial ship found at Sutton Hoo, England, 625–33, gold, garnets, and enamel (background restored), length 8″ (20.3 cm), British Museum, London. This and other exquisite objects show how inappropriate it is to call the era during which they were created the "Dark Ages." Working with the highest technical skill, artists created symmetrical patterns from animal shapes.

Mark, Luke, and John. The paintings show the Christian assimilation of the Anglo-Saxon animal style.

A **cross page,** also referred to as a carpet page, in the *Lindisfarne Gospels,* ca. 700 (fig. 11.2), is entirely covered with a symmetrical geometric pattern filled with curvilinear shapes made up of "animal interlace"—birds and animals so elongated and intertwined that they look like ribbons. The page is decorated much as a piece of precious jewelry might be.

The *Book of Kells,* the finest gospel book of the Early Middle Ages still in existence, was written and decorated by Irish monks, probably around 800, but the exact date and place of origin are uncertain. It contains the texts of the four gospels in Latin. As is clear from the ornamental folio depicting St. John (fig. 11.3), perfection is sought on the smallest scale humanly possible. The fine technical execution is accompanied by a lack of concern for the accurate representation of the human body. John is seen from the front yet appears flat, no more three dimensional than the surface on which he is painted. The intentionally stylized human figure is treated as a pattern of lines. The curvilinear drapery falls in impossible folds, forming a two-dimensional decorative design that gives little hint of a solid body beneath. This Celtic style of manuscript illumination, like its Byzantine counterpart (see Chapter 5), takes us far from nature and the Classical tradition's allegiance to portraying the visible world. Such a move from the physical to the spiritual reflects a shift in a patronage from secular to religious and the growing power of the medieval Church.

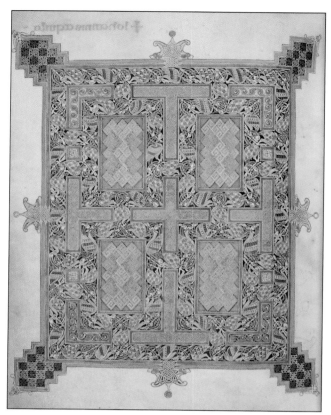

FIGURE 11.2   Cross page from the *Lindisfarne Gospels*, ca. 700, manuscript illumination, $13\frac{1}{2} \times 9\frac{1}{4}''$ (34.3 × 23.5 cm), British Library, London. This dense, intricate work is created by interlacing ribbonlike animals, organized by an underlying cross pattern. The care lavished on the decoration of a manuscript was intended to indicate the importance accorded the words of the text.

FIGURE 11.3   *St. John*, ornamental folio from the *Book of Kells*, ca. 800, manuscript illumination, $13 \times 9\frac{1}{2}''$ (33 × 24.1 cm), Trinity College Library, Dublin. The human body is treated as if it is as flat as the folio's surface and is incorporated into the two-dimensional design. The past Classical tradition of realism and pictorial illusionism is not identifiable here. Do not overlook the "footnotes" at the "foot of the page."

The Beowulf Epic and the Christian Poem.   The greatest of the Anglo-Saxon Germanic epics is *Beowulf*. It was probably composed in the first half of the eighth century, although the only version of it that survives dates from the tenth century, and much of the poem has been lost.

Beowulf is an almost completely Germanic tale. Set in Denmark, its action exemplifies the values of a warrior society. As a good king Beowulf is referred to as "ring giver," or "dispenser of treasure," and his duty is to take care of his loyal thanes or noblemen. Yet the act of giving has a spiritual side as well—out of generosity, unity and brotherhood emerge. This bonding, called *comitatus*, is balanced by the omnipresent threat of death.

There are hints of a Christian perspective in *Beowulf*, though these are submerged and are supplied by the narrator, rather than the characters. Jesus is never mentioned (there are no allusions to the New Testament at all), and Beowulf's funeral, in a burial ship like that found at Sutton Hoo, is entirely pagan. The immortality that is his re-ward is the pagan form of immortality—the celebration of his memory in the poem itself.

In contrast to *Beowulf*, the short *Caedmon's Hymn*, the oldest extant Old English poem, composed between 658 and 680, employs the language of Anglo-Saxon heroic verse in an explicitly Christian context. Like a heroic king, God is referred to as the *Weard*, or Guardian, of his kingdom.

CHARLEMAGNE AND THE CAROLINGIAN ERA

The convergence of Christian and Germanic cultures, which occurred long before the eighth century, culminates in the rule of Charles the Great or CHARLEMAGNE [SHAR-lu-main] (742–814), king of the Franks. His rule is generally considered to have inaugurated a period of cultural reawakening in western Europe. Accordingly, this period is known as the Carolingian era. Often credited with the major achievements of the so-called Carolingian Renaissance, Charlemagne saw himself as a successor to the great Roman emperors, and his court at Aachen was a focal point for the promotion of literacy.

Feudal Society. Charlemagne's government was essentially an early version of **feudalism,** a legal and social system that developed in western Europe in the eighth century. Under feudalism a lord would offer protection and land to his vassals, or servants, in return for an oath of fealty, or loyalty, and military support. Charlemagne divided his enormous empire into approximately three hundred counties, each governed by a count who was given authority to rule over it. Such a land grant was called a *feudum,* a fief, from which the term "feudal" derives. A fiefdom was hereditary, that is, passed on at the death of the vassal to his heir.

Feudalism involved a provision or grant of land for military service. In exchange of the fief or property, a vassal owed his lord a certain number of military service days. The feudal system included other reciprocal obligations of lords and vassals, such as hospitality. Aristocratic vassals were known as chevaliers in France and as knights in Germany and England. Much medieval literature features their exploits, from the French *Song of Roland* to the German *Tristan and Iseult* and the English *Canterbury Tales,* which includes a tale told by a knight.

Architecture. To match his imperial ambitions, Charlemagne created at Aachen in Germany a sumptuous palace and a magnificent royal chapel (fig. 11.4), designed by ODO OF METZ [OH-doh]. Apart from this chapel, little Carolingian architecture has survived. Nonetheless, it is clear that Carolingian ideas influenced later medieval styles. An important example of this is provided by the church of Saint-Riquier in Abbeville, France (fig. 11.5), consecrated in 799, the greatest basilica church of its time.

Literature: The Song of Roland. One of the most famous of all early medieval French literary works is the *Song of Roland,* a **chanson de geste,** or "song of deeds," which dates from the mid–eleventh century in Brittany. It consists of more than four thousand lines, which are given their regularity and shape by the use of **assonance,** or the repetition of vowel and consonantal sounds, rather than by pure rhyme. The poem is based on a historical incident from the year 778, and tells the story of the Christian army of Charlemagne doing battle against the Muslim Saracens.

The poem is noted for its clarity and for the elegance of its language, the simplicity of its narrative, and the masterful precision of its detail. The feudal code of honor serves as a foundation for, and standard against which to measure, the actions of its major characters. Celebrating loyalty over treachery, courage over cowardice, good judgment over foolishness, the *Song of Roland* exemplifies the values of French feudal society. Roland is at once a valiant warrior, an obedient and faithful servant of his king, and

FIGURE 11.4 Odo of Metz, Palatine Chapel, Aachen, Germany, 792–805. © Achim Bednorz, Koln. Charlemagne was determined to make his chapel worthy of his piety, and so had materials brought from Rome and Ravenna to enrich it. The massive proportions and semicircular arches recall the architecture of ancient Rome.

a warm and affectionate friend, whose behavior is governed by a Christian sense of moral rectitude.

MONASTICISM

Monasticism, a term derived from the Greek word *monos,* meaning "alone," had been an integral part of Christian life since the third century. During the Middle Ages, monasticism developed rapidly, resulting in an increasing number of monasteries and religious orders of monks and nuns. However, the observance of rules was anything but strict, and the lifestyle enjoyed in many monasteries was often quite relaxed. Among the earliest monastic guidelines were those provided by St. Benedict (480–543), who established a monastery at Monte Cassino, south of Rome, and created the Benedictine order. Dividing their day into organized periods of prayer, work, and study, the Benedictines had a life that was summed up in the motto "Pray and work." Their lives were based on four vows: They

FIGURE 11.5   Church of Saint-Riquier, Abbeville, consecrated 799, now destroyed, engraving made in 1612 from an eleventh-century manuscript illumination, Bibliothèque Nationale, Paris. Although this church no longer exists, certain features here became standard in church architecture: a massive entryway, two transepts, multiple towers with staircases, and a choir.

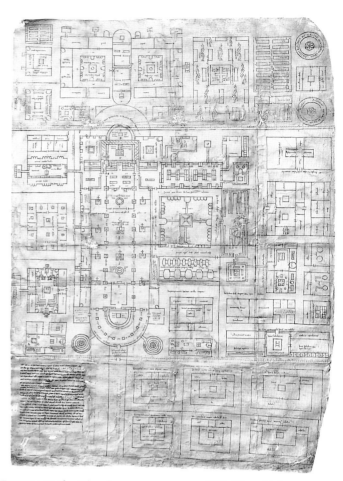

FIGURE 11.6   Plan for a monastery, ca. 817–20, red ink on parchment, $2'4 \times 3'8\frac{1}{8}''$ (71.1 × 112.1 cm), Stiftsbibliothek, St. Gallen, Switzerland. This plan for a prototype monastery was intended to be adopted and adapted to the specific needs of each monastic community—no monastery was ever built that precisely matched its layout. However, the drawing illustrates the basic ideal, which was that the monastery should provide for all the monks' needs.

were to possess nothing (poverty); live in one place their entire life (stability); follow the abbot's direction (obedience); and remain unmarried (chastity).

Another order, established at Cluny, France, instead fostered art and music. The Cluniacs soon spread beyond their original monastery to establish monastic houses throughout Europe. The Cistercian order rebelled against the wealth and luxury of the Cluniacs. Established at Cîteaux in 1098, the Cistercian was a far more ascetic order than the Benedictines. For example, they simplified their religious services, stripping them of elaborate ceremony and complex ritual, as well as removing much religious art from their surroundings. The Cistercians also fasted and prayed longer and more frequently than the Benedictines.

The Monastery.   The original plan for an ideal Carolingian monastery that was never built (fig. 11.6) gives a good idea of what a medieval monastery was like. The monastery was intended to be self-contained and self-sufficient. The largest building is the church. To the south of the church is the cloister, which is a standard part of the medieval monastery. The **cloister** is a square or rectangular space, open to the sky, usually with a source of water such as a fountain or well in the center, surrounded on all four sides by covered walkways. In the cloister garden, or **garth,** the monks might read, study, meditate, talk, and have contact with nature within the confines of the cloistered life. Also on the south side are the **refectory,** where meals were taken, the dormitory, baths, latrines, and var-

EARLY MIDDLE AGES AND THE ROMANESQUE

Cross Currents

THE VIKINGS

The term Viking was used originally for seafarers who raided the British Isles from Vik in southern Norway. Later, Viking referred to Norse raiders of Eastern Europe and the Mediterranean. Still later, Viking came to refer to all medieval Scandinavian seafarers, whether or not they plundered.

The Vikings, who sailed in sleek vessels often decorated with a dragon-headed prow, were the first to establish settlements in Scandinavia, Russia, and Ireland. In 1000 C.E. they established a colony in Newfoundland in modern Canada and others as far south as Maine. Although some of the Viking settlements were short lived, others remained for centuries.

The more peaceful Viking seafarers developed a trade network with other Europeans. The more militant Vikings pushed the British ruler King Alfred (r. 871–899) to establish fortified kingdoms for protection and then merge those kingdoms into a larger realm of England and Scotland. The Vikings also influenced the future history of England and France by creating the duchy of Normandy.

---

ious workshops. To the west are places where animals could be kept. To the north are the guest house, school (monasteries played an important part in the revival of learning, for it was here that education was available), and abbot's house. To the east are the physician's quarters (with bloodletting mentioned on the plan), and the infirmary, a short distance from the cemetery. The plan shows several kitchens, located throughout the monastery. It is worth noting that the plan includes more than one building for servants. However, little if any heating was part of the plan, and winters must have been extremely difficult to endure.

Connections

THE MYSTERY PLAYS AND THE GUILDS

Between the years 1000 and 1300, the population of Europe nearly doubled (to roughly seventy million), and urban areas began to grow as people gathered together in the interest of trade and commerce. The populations of these newly developing towns, which tended to form around old Roman settlements, along trade routes, and near the castles of great landowners, were, at least to a degree, free of feudal control, a fact that made them also free of organized government.

One of the chief means of establishing order in the growing towns and cities was the guild system. **Guilds** were associations of artisans and crafts-people (and soon merchants and bankers too) that regulated the quality of work produced in their own trade and the prices that an individual shopkeeper or tradesperson could charge. The guilds also controlled the training of apprentices and crafts-

people, set wages, supervised contracts, and approved new businesses. They built guild halls around the central square of the town, usually in front of the church. They also provided insurance and burial services for their members.

The guilds actively participated in the presentation of the so-called **mystery plays**—an early English corruption of the Latin word *ministerium*, or "occupation," referring to the guilds—a form of liturgical drama that began to develop in the ninth century. The mystery plays were dramatizations of narratives in the Old and New Testaments, usually composed in cycles containing as many as forty-eight individual plays. Typically, they would begin with the Creation, then recount the Fall of Adam and Eve, the Flood and Noah's Ark, David and Goliath, and so on, through the Old Testament to the Nativity, the events of Jesus's life, the Crucifixion, and the Last Judgment.

Each guild was responsible for an individual play, which was sometimes

connected with its own trade. The shipwrights' guild might present the story of Noah's Ark, for instance, and the bankers the story of Jesus and the moneylenders. These dramas were performed in the open air at different places around the town. In some towns, each guild would have its own wagon that served as a stage, and the wagons would proceed from one location to another, with the actors performing at each stop, so the audience could see the whole cycle without moving. In other towns, the plays were probably acted out on a single stage or platform in the main city square.

The mystery plays were performed every summer, either at Whitsuntide, the week following the seventh Sunday after Easter, or at Corpus Christi, a week later. They served as both entertainment and education for their largely illiterate audience. They also functioned as festive celebrations that brought together every aspect of medieval life—social, political, economic, and religious—for the entire community.

FIGURE 11.7   Cover of the *Lindau Gospels*, ca. 870, gold, pearls, and semiprecious stones, $13\frac{3}{4} \times 10\frac{3}{8}''$ (34.9 × 26.4 cm), Pierpont Morgan Library, New York. This lavish and carefully handcrafted book cover can be contrasted with today's mass-produced paperback books. The stones are treated as cabochons—smoothed and polished rather than cut in facets as is now customary.

Manuscript Illumination.   Much of the work carried out by the monks consisted of revising, copying, and illustrating liturgical books. Medieval manuscripts were more often than not lavishly bound—it was felt the cover enclosing the words of God should be as splendid as possible. Among the most sumptuous of all book covers ever created is that of the *Lindau Gospels* (fig. 11.7), made in about 870, out of gold, pearls, and semiprecious stones. In the Middle Ages, gemstones were smoothed and rounded into what are known as **cabochons,** like the ones on the *Lindau Gospels* cover. The cabochons are not set into the gold, but raised up on little feet, some by almost an inch, so that light can pass through them, enhancing their brilliance. A rich variety of colors, shapes, and patterns is created by the cross, the heavily jeweled border, and the four jeweled medallions between the arms of the cross. Jesus is not depicted here as suffering. He simply appears to be standing. It seems as if he is speaking, in triumph over death. The figure of Jesus, as well as the eight tiny figures, are created in *repoussé* (hammered out from the back), against a plain background.

Due to the classical revival encouraged by Charlemagne, the human figure again became important in the

visual arts. An image of St. John (fig. 11.8) is included in the *Gospel Book of Charlemagne*, also known as the *Coronation Gospels*, dated ca. 800–810. The manuscript is said to have been found in Charlemagne's tomb at his court in Aachen. St. John is portrayed in the Roman tradition—the style is similar to wall paintings found at Pompeii and Herculaneum (see figs. 4.24–4.27). A frame has been painted onto the vellum folio, creating the impression that the viewer is looking through a window to see John outside. The legs of John's footstool overlap the frame, as if the frame were genuinely three dimensional. The proportions of John's body are accurate and he wears a garment much like a Roman toga.

Music: Gregorian Chant.   Music, which in the Middle Ages was largely linked to religion, was a particular passion of Charlemagne's, who brought monks to his kingdom from Rome to standardize ecclesiastical music. In church services for the laity (nonclergy) and in worship in the monasteries, the predominant form of music was **plain-**

FIGURE 11.8   *St. John*, from the *Gospel Book of Charlemagne* (*Coronation Gospels*), ca. 800–810, manuscript illumination, $12\frac{3}{4} \times 9\frac{7}{8}''$ (32.4 × 25.1 cm), Schatzkammer, Kunsthistorisches Museum, Vienna. Emperor Charlemagne encouraged a revival of the antique—in part for political purposes. The impact of the antique is evident in this depiction of St. John, which is more realistic than that in the *Book of Kells* (see fig. 11.3).

chant, in which Latin liturgical texts were sung to a single melody line (**monophony**) without harmonic instrumental accompaniment.

The monks from Rome brought with them a particular tradition of Church music. This was **Gregorian chant,** which took its name from Pope Gregory the Great (540–604), who by legend is connected with the development of this form of music. A distinctly Frankish chant remained popular in Charlemagne's time too. During the centuries that followed, many new types of chant were composed, some of which were elaborated with **tropes,** or turns, in which other texts or melodies were introduced. Chants became more complex as the development of **polyphony** took place, in which two or more voice lines are sung simultaneously.

The basic chants have a serene, otherworldly quality with their flexible rhythms and melodic lines that typically move in tandem within a narrow range of pitch. Part of this quality comes from the use of church modes rather than major-minor scales. It also derives from the lack of harmonic accompaniment, as well as from the large resonating space of the cathedrals or monastery churches in which chants are frequently sung. The free-floating rhythms of the chant, with a lack of a steady beat or pattern of rhythmic accents, contribute to its solemnity, so much so that chant is sometimes described as "prayer on pitch."

During the reign of Charlemagne, Gregorian chants, which had formerly been passed down orally, were codified and written down in a rudimentary form of musical notation that used small curved strokes called **neumes** to indicate the up-and-down movement of the chant melody. This early notation scheme was ill suited to indicate actual melodies of tropes, which were ornamental in structure and often elaborate in their melodic contours. In the eleventh century, an Italian monk, GUIDO D'AREZZO [da-RET-zoh] (ca. 997–1050), created a musical graph, or set of lines, on which to mark the various chanted musical pitches. Guido colored the lines to set a "relative pitch" for each color; eventually the lines and spaces between grew in number as melodies evolved to meet composers' desires for expression. Used primarily for sacred music, this Guidonian graph used colored lines to make the representation of the musical pitches easy to read. It took two more centuries for the musical staff to develop, and until the sixteenth and seventeenth centuries before notes were written in the rounded forms common today.

Problems of rhythmic notation were not solved until Franco of Cologne explained in his treatise, *Ars Cantus Mensurabilis,* that different note shapes could be used to give different rhythmic values to those pitches previously notated in the square-note style of the Gregorian chant. Although there were only four basic shapes, Franco's system gave a definite relationship of time to each note. It was this musical notation that gave both order of performance and freedom of expression to musicians of the Middle Ages.

ROMANESQUE CULTURE

After Charlemagne's death in 814, the personal bonds that held the Holy Roman Empire together weakened. After two centuries of political fragmentation, however, around the year 1000, a few powerful feudal families began to extend their influence, conquering weaker feudal rulers and cementing their gains by intermarriage. These families soon developed into full-fledged monarchies. Two in particular—in France and in England—rose to real and lasting prominence.

THE FEUDAL MONARCHS

The Capetians. When HUGH CAPET [CA-pay] (ca. 938–996) ascended to the French throne, he established a dynasty of kings that would rule for nearly 350 years. Because of the strategic location of his barony—it was the best place to position defenses against invading Viking forces—he was accepted by the feudal lords of France as their king in 987. Throughout the subsequent CAPETIAN [ca-PEA-shun] era, the dukes of Normandy quarreled with their king. Nevertheless, the Capetian monarchs gradually consolidated power around themselves, and Paris became the political and intellectual center of Europe.

The Norman Conquest. Although servants to the Capetian kings in France, the dukes of Normandy claimed England for themselves and ruled as kings in their own right. The story of their conquest of England is recounted in the Bayeux Tapestry, dated ca. 1066–82 (fig. 11.9). The **tapestry** (actually a giant embroidery) tells how William, duke of Normandy (ca. 1027–87), conquered King Harold of England in 1066 and was crowned king of England. William became the first Norman king of England and was known thereafter as William the Conqueror.

William divided England up into fiefs for his Norman barons, ruling as a feudal monarch. And although he maintained some Anglo-Saxon customs and laws, Norman culture proved influential in England. For instance, the Latin-influenced French language spoken by the Norman invaders gradually began to mix with the native Anglo-Saxon, and the English language as we know it today started to emerge.

Magna Carta. Relations between the rulers of England and France remained difficult. In 1199, King Philip Augustus (r. 1180–1223) succeeded in expelling the English from France north of the Loire River. The English barons, outraged at the expense of King John's continued campaign against France, drew up a list of demands that John was forced to sign on June 15, 1215. Called the Magna Carta, or "Great Charter," the document was among the first to set a limit on royal authority. It also gave freemen certain rights, such as trial by jury. The Magna Carta is often seen as a crucial political document that paved the way for constitutional monarchy and the development of democracy in western Europe.

FIGURE 11.9 *King Edward Sends Harold of Wessex to Normandy,* detail of the Bayeux Tapestry, ca. 1066–82, wool embroidery on linen, height approximately $19\frac{1}{2}''$ (49.5 cm), total length ca. 231' (70.41 m), Centre Guillaume le Conquérant, Bayeux, France. The entire story of the invasion of England by William of Normandy, thereafter known as William the Conqueror, is told on this so-called tapestry. A document of military tactics and weaponry, the various parts of the narrative show the soldiers in battle, preparing for combat, traveling, and eating.

The Crusades.   The term **crusade** derived from the Latin word *crux*, meaning cross, refers to a holy war. The crusaders, who organized a series of military expeditions to recover the Holy Land in Palestine from Muslim occupiers, wore strips of cloth in the form of a cross on the backs of their garments. In doing so, they were allying themselves with Jesus, who was executed by the Roman authorities, who had him nailed to a wooden cross.

The first Crusade was launched in 1095 by Pope Urban II, who called for Christian knights to seize from the Turks the holy city of Jerusalem. The response to the Pope's call was enthusiastic, as an army of peasants and knights set out shortly afterward for Palestine, though without adequate planning, weapons, or discipline.

After the first crusade experienced disastrous results with few crusaders reaching the Holy Land and fewer still returning to Europe, French and Norman nobles organized a better planned and armed second crusade, which succeeded in capturing Jerusalem in 1099. This military success, along with others that followed, spurred Turks, Egyptians, and others to settle their differences and expel the Christian invaders. Under the Muslim leader Saladin, the Turks recaptured Jerusalem in 1187.

Other crusades followed, crusades which were largely failures militarily, religiously, and politically. But the crusades did aid in stimulating East–West trade and in accelerating the exchange of ideas. European scholars and missionaries encountered Muslim philosophers and theologians, and Muslim merchants traded with their European counterparts. The extensive exchange of goods, ideas, and technologies greatly influenced European development.

ROMANESQUE ARCHITECTURE

Pilgrimages and the Church. **Pilgrimages** were a social phenomenon of medieval life. Their chief purpose was to worship **relics** (objects believed to be associated with saints and especially with Jesus and Mary, or parts of their bodies), especially relics that were claimed to have miraculous powers. Pilgrimages were an important expression of religious faith, but they also represented a social opportunity to meet people from different cultures, having different customs.

For the many people who traveled great distances along the pilgrimage routes, facilities were available at abbeys, priories, monasteries, and hospices. Some of these were built specifically for pilgrims at intervals of twenty or so miles, not a difficult distance to cover in a day. People slept in big open halls, and there were special chapels for religious services. Charities were set up to aid the sick and the destitute and to take care of the dead.

Churches visited in this way by medieval pilgrims are referred to as "pilgrimage churches." All have the same basic plan and certain similarities of construction. Their

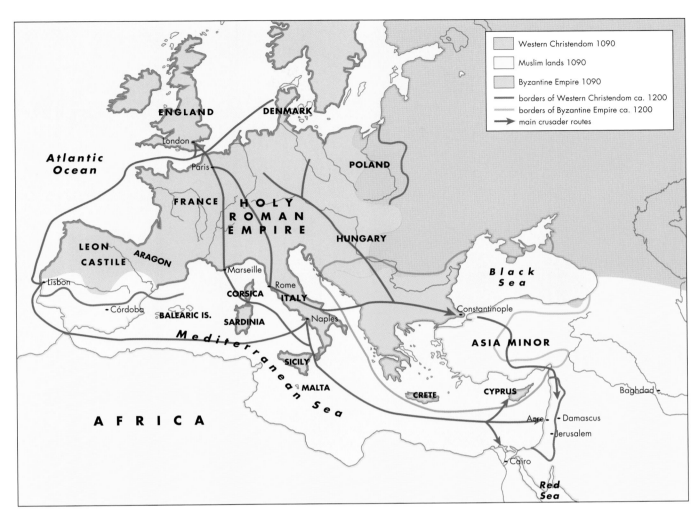

MAP 11.2   The Crusades.

style is called **Romanesque,** and indeed the architecture relies on the basic Roman elements of the **basilica** plan (see fig. 5.4), employing rounded arches, vaulted ceilings, piers and columns for support, and thick, sturdy walls. However, the style is not called Romanesque for this reason but because it was associated with the romance languages. All pilgrimage churches had large naves with flanking aisles, a transept, choir, ambulatory, and radiating chapels on the east end.

Saint-Sernin, Toulouse.   Among the most important buildings constructed in the eleventh century is Saint-Sernin in Toulouse (fig. 11.10), the best known of the great pilgrimage churches. Saint-Sernin was started ca. 1070 or 1077 but never finished. The west **facade,** which underwent restoration in 1855, has been generously described as an "awkward bulk." The builders' original intent (and the Romanesque norm) was to have two facade towers, but they were never completed. The apse end was completed by about 1098, with many different roof levels that reflect

the interior plan. Each chapel is seen as a separate bulge from the outside; above the ambulatory, the apse protrudes; and the levels build up to the crossing tower. Each space is separate, as is typical of Romanesque architecture.

Saint-Sernin, like the other great pilgrimage churches, has a Latin-cross plan (fig. 11.11)—with one long arm—as opposed to the Greek-cross plan, which has four arms of equal length. The proportions of Saint-Sernin are mathematically determined: The aisles are composed of a series of square **bays** that serve as the basic unit; the nave and transept bays are twice as large; the crossing tower is four times the basic unit, as are the bases of the intended facade towers. Certain ancient Greek temples had similar numerical ratios between their different parts.

The nave of Saint-Sernin (fig. 11.12) is typically Romanesque, with thick walls, closely spaced piers, engaged columns on the walls, and a stone vault. The **barrel vault** (also called a **tunnel vault**) covering the nave is a structural system that offers several advantages. Here, the acoustics are superb, with voices reverberating through the vaulted

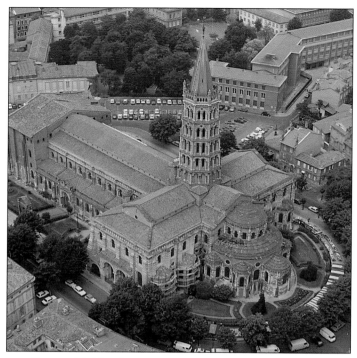

FIGURE 11.10   Saint-Sernin, Toulouse, begun ca. 1070 or
1077, aerial view from the southwest. The exterior of the
building reflects the interior. Each section of space is clearly
defined and neatly separated, unlike the flowing spaces that
will characterize Gothic architecture.

FIGURE 11.11   Saint-Sernin, Toulouse, begun ca. 1070 or
1077, plan. This Latin-cross plan with ambulatory and radiating chapels is typical of churches located along the pilgrimage
route leading to Santiago de Compostela. In the many chapels,
pilgrims venerated relics, especially if a relic were believed to
be able to create miracles.

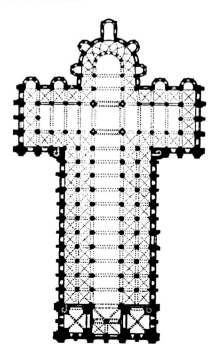

FIGURE 11.12   Saint-Sernin, Toulouse, begun ca. 1070 or 1077,
nave looking toward altar. Romanesque masons experimented
with various vaulting methods, using most frequently the barrel
(tunnel) vault based on the semicircular arch. Advantages of this
stone vault, compared to the wooden ceiling of the Early Christian basilica, include superb acoustics and minimized risk of fire;
disadvantages include lack of direct light into the nave.

space. The threat of fire is reduced—a constant danger in
the Middle Ages, especially to structures with wooden ceilings. The large interior is open, free of the intrusive posts
necessary to the post and lintel system. Yet the barrel vault
also has its disadvantages. An extension of the arch principle, it exerts a constant lateral thrust that must be buttressed. This is accomplished largely by the great thickness
of the walls, which means any opening in the supporting
walls weakens the system. Consequently the windows in

FIGURE 11.13 Sainte-Madeleine, Vézelay, nave looking toward altar, built 1120–32. A solution to the problem of obtaining direct light in the nave is found in the use of cross (groin) vaults, which provide a space for windows on the nave walls.

Romanesque churches are few and small, and the interiors are often very dark.

Sainte-Madeleine, Vézelay.   The pilgrimage church of Sainte-Madeleine in Vézelay was built between 1096 and 1132. At its peak, Vézelay had eight hundred monks and lay brothers living in its monastery.

The nave (fig. 11.13), built between 1120 and 1132, is very light for a Romanesque church. It is also very harmonious, as simple mathematics determine the proportions of the interior. The alternating light and dark **voussoirs** (wedge-shaped blocks of stone that make up the arches) are inconsistent in size, resulting in irregular stripes. The supports are massive. The nave elevation is two stories high, as at Saint-Sernin, which is customary for pilgrimage churches. At Vézelay, however, the upper level is a clerestory with a row of windows. This is made possible because the nave bays are covered by **cross vaults** (also called **groin vaults**)—two tunnel (barrel) vaults intersecting at right angles, which automatically create a flat space on the wall where a window can be constructed. Vézelay's interior therefore offers a solution to the problem of obtaining direct light in the nave. However, the structure was neither well built nor adequately buttressed—problems developed and the walls began to lean. Flying buttresses were added in the Gothic era and then rebuilt in the nineteenth century. The walls now lean outward by about twenty inches.

Cathedral Group, Pisa.   Of all the Romanesque cathedrals constructed outside the pilgrimage routes, perhaps one of the most striking is that in Pisa, Italy. The "cathedral group" in Pisa (fig. 11.14) consists of the cathedral,

FIGURE 11.14 Cathedral group, Pisa: baptistery, begun 1153; cathedral, begun 1063; campanile, begun 1174. In addition to marble incrustation, the architecture of Romanesque Pisa is characterized by tiers of arcades. The "leaning tower of Pisa" owes its fame to foundations that were not made properly.

Cross Currents

THE PISA GRIFFIN

From 1100 until 1828, a three and half-foot-high Islamic bronze griffin (fig. 11.15) (a mythological creature, half eagle, half lion) stood on top of the cathedral in Pisa. This griffin may have originally been a fountain spout, but how it came to Pisa is unknown. Scholars have suggested that its provenance might be Persia, in the east, or perhaps Spain, in the west. But whatever its origins, placed on top of the cathedral that was itself built to celebrate Pisa's 1063 victory over Muslim forces in the western Mediterranean, it soon came to symbolize the city's place at the very center of Mediterranean trade.

The griffin is decorated with incised feathers on its wings, and the carving of its back suggests silk drapery, linking it with Asia. A favorite symbol of both the Assyrians and Persians, the griffin was said to guard the gold of India, and the Greeks believed these creatures watched over the gold of the Scythians. For Muslims, the eaglelike qualities of the beast signified vigilance, and its lionlike qualities, courage. By the time it was placed on Pisa cathedral, Christians had appropriated the beast to their own iconological ends, where it came to signify the dual nature of Jesus, his divinity (the eagle) and his humanity (the lion).

FIGURE 11.15 Griffin, from the Islamic Mediterranean, eleventh century, bronze, height 3'6$\frac{1}{8}$" (1.07 m), Museo dell'Opera del Duomo, Pisa. The griffin, an invention of ancient mytology created by amalgamating a lion and an eagle, has been interpreted symbolically by various cultures. This griffin stood atop Pisa cathedral until it was moved to the cathedral museum in 1828.

---

begun in 1063; the baptistery, begun in 1153; and the **campanile** (the bell tower), of 1174, the famous "leaning tower of Pisa." All three buildings are covered in white marble, inlaid with dark green marble, a technique used by the ancient Romans.

The baptistery is circular and domed. The first two floors are Romanesque, with marble panels and arcades. The pointy gables are fourteenth-century Gothic. The architect of the cathedral was Buscheto, although the facade was designed by Rainaldo. The marble arcades are a Pisan hallmark. **Blind arcades** create a lacy effect, with colorful light and shade patterns. The five stories of arcades on the facade match the interior: The bottom corresponds to the nave arcade; the first open arcade reflects the galleries; the second open arcade the roof of the galleries; the third the clerestory; and the last the roof. Simple mathematical ratios determine the dimensions, for the blind arcade is one-third the height of the facade, whereas each open arcade is one-sixth the height.

Pisa's most famous monument is undoubtedly the "leaning tower." The bell tower is usually a separate building in Italy, whereas in other countries there are normally two bell towers on the facade of a Romanesque church. The designer of the campanile was Bonanno Pisano. The campanile leans because the foundations were poorly laid and offer uneven resistance. Most Italian towers of the Middle Ages leaned, but rarely to this degree. The tower is 179 feet tall and is now approximately sixteen feet out of plumb.

SCULPTURE

The vast majority of people living in western Europe during the Middle Ages were illiterate—a portion of the clergy included. Sermons were therefore, literally, carved in stone, with sculptors creating the equivalent of picture books for those who could not read.

Romanesque architectural sculpture is concentrated on church portals, especially on **tympana** (the **tympanum** is the semicircular section above the doorway, with a horizontal lintel at the bottom, supported by a central **trumeau,** or post) and column capitals. This kind of sculpture was once painted with bright colors.

The typical Romanesque tympanum has a figure of Jesus in the center, in majesty. He is surrounded by a **mandorla,** a glory of light in the shape of a pointed oval. Outside the mandorla, the subjects of different tympana vary.

The Vézelay Mission of the Apostles. An extraordinary tympanum can be found in the narthex of the church of Sainte-Madeleine in Vézelay (fig. 11.16), carved 1120–32. The subject depicted here is the *Mission of the Apostles*, pre-

FIGURE 11.16   *Mission of the Apostles*, tympanum, Sainte-Madeleine, Vézelay, 1120–32. This tympanum (the semicircle above the entry) contains relief sculpture that is simultaneously decorative and didactic. The message is that Jesus's ideas, shown to travel from his fingertips to the heads of the apostles, are to be conveyed to all parts of the world at all times of the year, as represented symbolically around the tympanum by the signs of the zodiac.

sented as an allegory of the congregation's own mission to spread the Christian message continually to all the peoples of the earth. To show Jesus's thoughts passing into the minds of the apostles, rays emanate from Jesus's hands as he touches the head of each of them. To show that the message must be spread at all times, the second **archivolt** (arch above the tympanum) depicts the signs of the zodiac and the labors of the months. The innermost archivolt and the lintel depict the various types of people believed to inhabit the distant regions of the earth. Shown there, as described in fanciful travelers' tales of the time, are people with dog heads, who communicate by barking—the Cynocephali—and a pig-snouted tribe. Such figures continue on the lintel where the different races approach Peter and Paul. Last are the Panotii, whose ears are so large they can be used to envelop the body like a blanket if it is cold, or to fly away if their owner is in danger. The diminutive stature of the pygmies is indicated by their use of ladders to mount their horses. Vézelay's tympanum provides the modern visitor with a revealing insight into the twelfth-century view of the world, which was based largely on ancient literary sources, rather than on contemporary and accurate accounts of actual travel and contact with other peoples.

The Autun Last Judgment.

Closely related in time and style to the sculpture at Vézelay is that at nearby Autun Cathedral. The monumental tympanum on the west facade, carved between 1120 and 1135, is signed *"Gislebertus hoc fecit"* (Gislebertus made it)—a rare example of a signature in medieval art. As in other Romanesque tympana, there is a huge figure of Jesus in the center, surrounded by a mandorla. Flanking Jesus are scenes arranged in different sections. The entire surface is densely covered with figures.

The tympanum at Autun portrays the *Last Judgment* (fig. 11.17), a popular subject in Romanesque art. In medieval depictions of the Last Judgment the soul literally hung in the balance between heaven and hell. On the right side of Autun's tympanum the Weighing of the Souls is represented literally. An angel tugs at the basket and a devil actually hangs from the balance bar. Thus angel and devil both cheat! The angel wins this particular soul; other saved souls already cling to the angel. An angel conducts the saved souls to heaven. But what about the damned? Down on the lintel, these unfortunate souls can be seen rising fearfully from the grave. The wicked cringe in agony. A serpent gnaws at the breasts of Unchastity. Intemperance scrapes an empty dish. The claws of the devil close on the head of a sinner. Such visual intimidation was intended to scare people who might otherwise go astray.

DECORATIVE ARTS

Reliquaries and Enamels.

The relics venerated by pilgrims were kept in containers called **reliquaries.** The reliquary coffer shown in figure 11.18 was made in the French city of Limoges in the twelfth century. Limoges was one of the two major areas in western Europe where enamel work was manufactured, the other being the Mosan area, today part of Belgium. An example of Mosan work is Nicholas of Verdun's masterpiece, the altarpiece at Klosterneuburg Abbey, near Vienna. The original altarpiece had forty-five plaques, each depicting a different scene, the figures engraved and gilded on separate enamel plaques. The *Birth of Jesus* (fig. 11.19) shows the infant on an altar, a reference to his future sacrifice. He is wrapped in swaddling clothes, as babies customarily were in the Middle Ages. The ox and the ass are traditional inclusions, derived from Isaiah, intended to indicate that even these humble animals recognized Jesus's divinity. There is a sense of a three-dimensional body beneath the drapery, a return

FIGURE 11.17   Gislebertus, *Last Judgment*, tympanum, cathedral Saint-Lazare, Autun, ca. 1120–35. Medieval Christians were told, as depicted on the right, that on the day of judgment one's soul literally "hung in the balance." On the left, the Saved ascend to heaven while, on the right, the Damned are consigned to the tortures of hell.

to the classical manner of depicting the relationship between the figure and the fabric that covers it. Artistic representation changed after the mid–twelfth century to accommodate a growing interest in the human figure, in nature, and in the world in general. The art of Nicholas of Verdun, located at this turning point, is moving out of the Romanesque era and into the Gothic.

THE CHIVALRIC TRADITION IN LITERATURE

With their men off fighting in the crusades, medieval women began to play a powerful role in everyday life. Many women of the noble class ran their family estates in their husbands' absence, and, though they had little official or legal status, they promoted a chivalric ideal in which their own position was elevated and the feudal code of

stern courage and valiant warfare was displaced in favor of more genteel and refined patterns of behavior.

The Troubadours.   Among the most influential proponents of this new chivalric code were the **troubadours,** poet-musicians who were active in the area of Provence in southern France. Writing in Occitan, the language of southern France at that time, they wrote words to sing to original melodies (as opposed to church composers, who used chant melodies handed down from the past). Troubadours were especially active in aristocratic circles, and they sometimes had kings and queens as their patrons. Members of the court themselves composed works too.

The chivalric values were promoted especially by Eleanor of Aquitaine, her daughter Marie of Champagne, and her granddaughter Blanche of Castille. Eleanor was

FIGURE 11.18   Reliquary coffer, twelfth century, enamel, French, Limoges, now in Saint-Sernin, Toulouse. Elaborate coffers such as this were used to house precious relics such as a piece of Jesus's cross, a piece of silk worn by his mother Mary, a drop of her milk, or a strand of a saint's hair. Some relics were thought to be endowed with magical powers.

FIGURE 11.19   Nicholas of Verdun, *Birth of Jesus*, detail of the *Klosterneuburg Abbey Altarpiece*, 1181, enamel on gold, height of each plaque $5\frac{1}{2}$" (14 cm), Klosterneuburg Abbey, Austria. By the late twelfth century, the Romanesque was being superseded by the Gothic, and evidence of greater interest in recording the visible world appeared. The drapery now reveals the form beneath, clinging and seemingly wet—unlike the flat folds unrelated to the body found in earlier Romanesque art.

Table 11-1 SYMBOLS IN MEDIEVAL CHRISTIAN ART: ANIMALS	
Medieval art makes extensive use of symbols. Virtually every animal, object, color, or number conveyed a meaning. The interpretation of the symbols may vary depending on the context in which they appear.	
Ape / monkey	Symbol of sin, lust, and the devil. Monkeys are known for their ability to ape human behavior.
Bee	Symbol of industry, as in "busy as a bee."
Cat	Symbol of laziness and lust.
Centaur	A composite creature invented in antiquity, having the head of a man and the body of a horse, thus combining the human's intelligence with the horse's strength and lust; fond of wine and women.
Dog	Symbol of fidelity.
Dragon	In Western art, the dragon symbolizes the devil, sin, and evil in general; in Eastern art, in contrast, the dragon has positive connotations.
Fish	Because the initial letters of "Jesus Christ, God's son, savior" in Greek spell "fish," the fish is a symbol of Jesus.
Lamb	A sacrificial animal and therefore a symbol of Jesus.
Lion	Usually a symbol of Jesus, long regarded as "king of the beasts."
Unicorn	A composite creature invented in antiquity. Unicorns have white fur and the form of a small horse with a single horn in the middle of the forehead. The unicorn can be caught only by a virgin woman and is thus a symbol both of Jesus and of purity.

Critical Thinking

THE ART OF LOVE

In the ancient Rome of the Latin poet Ovid, love and sex were synonymous, and the goal of a man was the seduction of the beloved. As a counter to this pagan emphasis on the physical aspects of love, Christians emphasized spiritual love based on sacrifice for the beloved. In the Middle Ages, a period in which religion governed every aspect of life, court poets had to find ways to come to terms with both the physical and spiritual dimensions of love the following advice in the form of a list is offered by Andreas Capellanus from his medieval book *The Art of Courtly Love.* To what extent do you think that Capellanus has been successful in accommodating love's physical and spiritual dimensions? Does Capellanus introduce any other important aspects of love? To what extent do you think his ideas are relevant today? Explain.

1. The pretext of marriage is no proper excuse against love.
2. No one who is not jealous can love.
3. No one can have two loves at once.
4. Love is always growing or diminishing.
5. There is no savour in anything obtained by the lover against the beloved's will.
6. It is not customary for a man to love before puberty.
7. It is right that the lover should remain unmarried for two years after the death of the beloved.
8. No one should be deprived of his love without very good reason.
9. No one can love unless driven on by the prospect of love.
10. Love is always banished from the home of avarice.
11. It is not right to love women one would be ashamed to take to wife.
12. A love divulged rarely lasts.
13. The true lover desires no embraces from any other than the beloved.
14. An easy conquest makes love worthless; a difficult one gives it value.
15. Every lover grows pale at the sight of the beloved.
16. At the sudden sight of the beloved, the lover's heart quakes.
17. A new love drives out the old.
18. Honesty alone makes a person worthy of love.
19. If love grows less, its decline is swift and it seldom recovers.
20. A man in love is always fearful.
21. True jealousy always increases love's ardour.
22. A suspicion concerning the beloved increases jealousy and love's ardour.
23. A man perturbed by thoughts of love sleeps and eats less.
24. The beloved's every act ends in thoughts of the lover.
25. The true lover esteems nothing good except what he thinks will please the beloved.
26. Love can deny nothing to love.
27. The lover cannot be sated with the solace of the lover alone.
28. A slight presumption forces the lover to suspect the worst of the beloved.
29. He who is fired by too much lust is not likely to love.
30. The true lover is at all times continually absorbed in imagining the beloved.
31. Nothing prevents a woman from being loved by two men or a man from being loved by two women.

herself the granddaughter of one of the first such poets, Duke William IX of Aquitaine, and together with Marie she established a "Court of Love" in Poitiers in 1170. The court was governed by a code of etiquette, which was given written form in *The Art of Courtly Love* (1170–74) by Andreas Cappelanus. Marie commissioned Cappelanus to write, and she clearly intended the book to be an accurate portrayal of life in Eleanor's court.

In fact, the court of love was first developed by Eleanor in England before she left Henry II to live with her daughter in Poitiers. Among the poets who wrote for her in England, evidence suggests, was Marie de France (twelfth century), the first woman to write verse in French. Marie de France is best known for her *lais* (lays), narratives of moderate length, which typically involve one or more miraculous or marvelous incidents and adventures concerning romantic love. A number of her *lais* concern the stories of Arthurian legend, including that of Sir Launfal. Marie's treatment of the action is less heroic than it is romantic, the characters less noble than human, the plot less concerned with grave matters of history and state than with the intimate affairs and feelings of a few people.

One of Eleanor's most gifted troubadour poets was BERNART DE VENTADORN [VEN-tuh-DOR] (d. 1195). The following stanza, from a poem apparently addressed to Eleanor herself, gives the modern reader some idea of the freedom of expression the troubadour poet was given:

Evil she is if she doesn't call me
To come where she undresses alone
So that I can wait her bidding

Then & Now

CHANT

For most of its history, chant was the official music of the Catholic Church, just as Latin was its official language. With the Vatican reforms of 1965, however, both the Church's official language and its official music were changed.

The earliest chants were transmitted orally; they were first written down in the ninth century. One explanation for the consistency of these early melodies is that they were the responsibility of a single individual—St. Gregory, who was often depicted with a dove (symbol of divine inspiration) on his shoulder.

Chant suffered a first challenge to its authority as the dominant liturgical musical form in the Reformation of the sixteenth century. Then it was supplanted in Protestant worship by hymns and cantatas such as those composed by J.S. Bach (see Chapters 14 and 15). Catholic church music during the same time developed a rich tradition of polyphony that coexisted with monophonic chant. In the 1960s, chant gave way, even in Catholic worship, to alternative forms of music, including melodies and hymn tunes in popular styles, such as gospel and folk music.

At the end of the twentieth century, however, chant had a surprising resurgence, less as a form of Catholic liturgy than as a reflection of popular musical taste. In the mid-1990s the CDs *Chant* and *Chant II* exhibited crossover power by heading both the popular and classical music charts. Sung by Spanish monks from the Benedictine abbey of Solesmes, *Chant* inaugurated and reflected a renewed interest in spirituality. The mystical otherworldly character of this early music has brought a bit of the Middle Ages into the contemporary world.

Beside the bed, along the edge,
Where I can pull off her close-fitting shoes
Down on my knees, my head bent down:
If only she'll offer me her foot.

There is no direct reference to sexual consummation, though it is implied. Adultery was strictly forbidden by the chivalric code, and though the passions expressed here are strong, they are carefully controlled. Even if in actual court life nobles succumbed to temptation, in poetry at least the notion of *courtoisie*, "courtesy," was always upheld. In the end, much of the pleasure of the poetry of courtly love is derived from the clever word play. The poetry celebrates, in its purest form, the ennobling power of friendship between man and woman.

Chrétien de Troyes.   An especially popular literary form depicting the chivalric relations between knights and their ladies was the **romance,** a long narrative form taking its subject matter generally from stories surrounding King Arthur and his Knights of the Round Table. Among the very first writers to popularize the romance was CHRÉTIEN DE TROYES [CRE-tee-EN] (ca. 1148–ca. 1190), whose account of the legend of Lancelot and his adulterous affair with King Arthur's wife Guinevere became a particular favorite. Called "the perfect romance," his *Chevalier de la Charette* expresses the doctrines of courtly love in their most refined form. Identifying Lancelot with Jesus, Chrétien goes so far as to equate Lancelot's noble suffering with Jesus's passion.

MUSIC

Hildegard of Bingen.   Only relatively few women, those of the nobility, could enjoy the pleasures of the court of love. Most women worked the fields alongside their husbands. Women who did not marry and thus could not hope to inherit property from their husbands often became nuns and lived in convents.

The head of one such convent was Hildegard of Bingen (1098–1179). Born to noble parents, Hildegard had a mystical vision at the age of five, and when she was eight was put into the care of a small community of nuns attached to the Benedictine monastery outside Bingen, near Frankfurt, Germany. She became a playwright and poet, and composed a cycle of seventy-seven songs in plainchant. She also wrote a book on medicine, and a book of visionary writings.

Hildegard of Bingen's music was written for performance by the nuns of her convent. Her major work, *The Symphony of the Harmony of Celestial Revelations*, which occupied her for much of her creative life, contains some of her finest work. One of her most beautiful compositions, *O Ecclesia*, celebrates St. Ursula who, according to legend, was martyred with eleven thousand virgins at Cologne. Like Hildegard, Ursula had led a company of women and had devoted her life to God. The music for three sopranos is accompanied by an instrumental drone, which serves as a sustained bass over which the voices weave their flowing and undulating chantlike melody.

Cultural Impact

The cross page from the *Lindisfarne Gaspels*, ca. 700, in which an underlying geometric plan organizes the composition (fig. 11.2), exemplifies the emphasis on abstraction and ornamentation in the painting of the early Middle Ages. In the centuries to come, artists emphasized observation and greater realism; but in the twentieth century the pendulum of artistic taste swung back in the direction of abstraction. Thus Piet Mondrian's *Composition in Red, Yellow, and Blue* of 1920 (fig. 21.17) stresses the two dimensionality of the picture plane the pattern created of horizontal and vertical lines is as flat as the surface on which it is painted.

The same history is found in sculpture. During the early Middle Ages and the Romanesque era, the human body is represented symbolically, as in the overtly distorted figures of Jesus at Vézelay and Autun (figs. 11.16 and 11.17). Artists of the Renaissance and for several centuries thereafter preferred a high degree of anatomical accuracy. The twentieth century saw the return to abstraction and distortion in sculptures such as Henry Moore's *Recumbent Figure* of 1938 (fig. 21.20).

Romanesque church architecture emphasizes massive dimensions, thick walls, semicircular arches, and barrel vaults; the barrel vault at Saint-Sernin in Toulouse, begun in the later twelfth century (fig. 11.12), represents the form of nave vaulting most frequently used during the Romanesque era. The same form reappears in the nineteenth century's Crystal Palace (fig. 17.15), designed by Joseph Paxton to display the new architectural materials (cast iron and glass) of the time—the effect very different! The massive stone forms of the Romanesque were used especially by the American architect Henry Hobson Richardson (1838–86), himself a man of comparably generous proportions. Richardson is perhaps best known for Trinity Church in Boston, built 1873–77, which revives the solid dimensions, semicircular arches, and barrel vaults of Romanesque architecture.

KEY TERMS

animal style
illuminated manuscript
parchment
vellum
folio
cross page (carpet page)
feudalism
chanson de geste
assonance
cloister
garth

refectory
guild
mystery play
cabochons
repoussé
plainchant
monophony
Gregorian chant
tropes
polyphony
neumes

tapestry
crusade
pilgrimage
relic
Romanesque
basilica
facade
bay
barrel vault (tunnel vault)
voussoirs
cross vault (groin vault)

campanile
blind arcade
tympanum
trumeau
mandorla
archivolt
reliquaries
troubadours
lais
romance

www. WEBSITES FOR FURTHER STUDY

http://www.uky.edu/%7Ekieman/eBeowulf/guide.htm
(An in-depth discussion on Beowulf, edited by Kevin Kiernan.)

http://www.fordham.edu/halsall/sbook.html
(The Internet Medieval Sourcebook is an excellent site with many links regarding all aspects of medieval society.)

http://www.mayo-ireland.ie/Mayo/Towns/MayAbbey/HistMAbb/Alcuin.htm
(A site focusing on Alcuin of York, the chief architect of educational reform on the continent under Charlemagne.)

http://users.aol.com/butrousch/augustine/gregory.htm
(Visit this site for a biography of Pope Gregory the Great, with relevant websites and his writings.)

http://www.medieval.org/
(The Medieval Music and Arts Foundation has many pertinent links and a wealth of information regarding medieval music.)

READINGS

BEOWULF

Prologue

The heroic cast of the story of the Danish king Beowulf, with its dangerous deeds, its ethical prescriptions, and its legendary monsters, makes it both an engaging work and a didactic one. Like Homer, more than 1,600 years earlier, the Beowulf poet narrates his story with vivacity and vividness.

Hear me! We've heard of Danish heroes,
Ancient kings and the glory they cut
For themselves, swinging mighty swords!
    How Shild° made slaves of soldiers from every
Land, crowds of captives he'd beaten   5
Into terror; he'd traveled to Denmark alone,
An abandoned child, but changed his own fate,
Lived to be rich and much honored. He ruled
Lands on all sides: wherever the sea
Would take them his soldiers sailed, returned   10
With tribute and obedience. There was a brave
King! And he gave them more than his glory,
Conceived a son for the Danes, a new leader
Allowed them by the grace of God. They had lived,
Before his coming, kingless and miserable;   15
Now the Lord of all life, Ruler
Of glory, blessed them with a prince, Beo,
Whose power and fame soon spread through the world.
Shild's strong son was the glory of Denmark;
His father's warriors were wound round his heart   20
With golden rings, bound to their prince
By his father's treasure. So young men build
The future, wisely open-handed in peace,
Protected in war; so warriors earn
Their fame, and wealth is shaped with a sword,   25
    When his time was come the old king died,
Still strong but called to the Lord's hands.
His comrades carried him down to the shore,
Bore him as their leader had asked, their lord
And companion, while words could move on
                    his tongue.   30
Shild's reign had been long; he'd ruled them well.
There in the harbor was a ring-prowed fighting
Ship, its timbers icy, waiting,
And there they brought the beloved body

Of their ring-giving lord, and laid him near   35
The mast. Next to that noble corpse
They heaped up treasures, jeweled helmets,
Hooked swords and coats of mail, armor
Carried from the ends of the earth: no ship
Had ever sailed so brightly fitted,   40
No king sent forth more deeply mourned.
Forced to set him adrift, floating
As far as the tide might run, they refused
To give him less from their hoards of gold
Than those who'd shipped him away, an orphan   45
And a beggar, to cross the waves alone.
High up over his head they flew
His shining banner, then sadly let
The water pull at the ship, watched it
Slowly sliding to where neither rulers   50
Nor heroes nor anyone can say whose hands
Opened to take that motionless cargo.

Then Beo was king in that Danish castle,
Shild's son ruling as long as his father
And as loved, a famous lord of men.   55
And he in turn gave his people a son,
The great Healfdane, a fierce fighter
Who led the Danes to the end of his long
Life and left them four children,
Three princes to guide them in battle, Hergar   60
And Hrothgar and Halga the Good, and one daughter,
Yrs, who was given to Onela, king
Of the Swedes, and became his wife and their queen.
    Then Hrothgar, taking the throne, led
The Danes to such glory that comrades and kinsmen 65
Swore by his sword, and young men swelled
His armies, and he thought of greatness and resolved
To build a hall that would hold his mighty
Band and reach higher toward Heaven than anything
That had ever been known to the sons of men.   70
And in that hall he'd divide the spoils
Of their victories, to old and young what they'd earned
In battle, but leaving the common pastures
Untouched, and taking no lives. The work
Was ordered, the timbers tied and shaped   75
By the hosts that Hrothgar ruled. It was quickly
Ready, that most beautiful of dwellings, built
As he'd wanted, and then he whose word was obeyed
All over the earth named it Herot.
His boast come true he commanded a banquet,   80
Opened out his treasure-full hands.
That towering place, gabled and huge,
Stood waiting for time to pass, for war

°*Shild:* A mythological Danish king; Beo's father, Healfdane's grandfather, and Hrothgar's great-grandfather.

To begin, for flames to leap as high
As the feud that would light them, and for Herot
                                    to burn.   *85*
        A powerful monster, living down
In the darkness, growled in pain, impatient
As day after day the music rang
Loud in that hall, the harp's rejoicing
Call and the poet's clear songs, sung   *90*
Of the ancient beginnings of us all, recalling
The Almighty making the earth, shaping
These beautiful plains marked off by oceans,
Then proudly setting the sun and moon
To glow across the land and light it;   *95*
The corners of the earth were made lovely with trees
And leaves, made quick with life, with each
Of the nations who now move on its face. And then
As now warriors sang of their pleasure:
So Hrothgar's men lived happy in his hall   *100*
Till the monster stirred, that demon, that fiend,
Grendel, who haunted the moors, the wild
Marshes, and made his home in a hell
Not hell but earth. He was spawned in that slime,
Conceived by a pair of those monsters born   *105*
Of Cain, murderous creatures banished
By God, punished forever for the crime
Of Abel's death.° The Almighty drove
Those demons out, and their exile was bitter,
Shut away from men; they split   *110*
Into a thousand forms of evil—spirits
And fiends, goblins, monsters, giants,
A brood forever opposing the Lord's
Will, and again and again defeated.

        Then, when darkness had dropped, Grendel   *115*
Went up to Herot, wondering what the warriors
Would do in that hall when their drinking was done.
He found them sprawled in sleep, suspecting
Nothing, their dreams undisturbed. The monster's
Thoughts were as quick as his greed or his claws: *120*
He slipped through the door and there in the silence
Snatched up thirty men, smashed them
Unknowing in their beds and ran out with their bodies,
The blood dripping behind him, back
To his lair, delighted with his night's slaughter.   *125*

        At daybreak, with the sun's first light, they saw
How well he had worked, and in that gray morning
Broke their long feast with tears and laments
For the dead. Hrothgar, their lord, sat joyless
In Herot, a mighty prince mourning   *130*

The fate of his lost friends and companions,
Knowing by its tracks that some demon had torn
His followers apart. He wept, fearing
The beginning might not be the end. And that night
Grendel came again, so set   *135*
On murder that no crime could ever be enough,
No savage assault quench his lust
For evil. Then each warrior tried
To escape him, searched for rest in different
Beds, as far from Herot as they could find,   *140*
Seeing how Grendel hunted when they slept.
Distance was safety; the only survivors
Were those who fled him. Hate had trimphed.
        So Grendel ruled, fought with the righteous
One against many, and won; so Herot   *145*
Stood empty, and stayed deserted for years,
Twelve winters of grief for Hrothgar, king
Of the Danes, sorrow heaped at his door
By hell-forged hands. His misery leaped
The seas, was told and sung in all   *150*
Men's ears: how Grendel's hatred began,
How the monster relished his savage war
On the Danes, keeping the bloody feud
Alive, seeking no peace, offering
No truce, accepting no settlement, no price   *155*
In gold or land, and paying the living
For one crime only with another. No one
Waited for reparation from his plundering claws:
That shadow of death hunted in the darkness,
Stalked Hrothgar's warriors, old   *160*
And young, lying in waiting, hidden
In mist, invisibly following them from the edge
Of the marsh, always there, unseen.
        So mankind's enemy continued his crimes,
Killing as often as he could, coming   *165*
Alone, bloodthirsty and horrible. Though he lived
In Herot, when the night hid him, he never
Dared to touch king Hrothgar's glorious
Throne, protected by God—God,
Whose love Grendel could not know.
                                But Hrothgar's   *170*
Heart was bent. The best and most noble
Of his council debated remedies, sat
In secret sessions, talking of terror
And wondering what the bravest of warriors could do.
And sometimes they sacrificed to the old
                                    stone gods,   *175*
Made heathen vows, hoping for Hell's
Support, the Devil's guidance in driving
Their affliction off.° That was their way,

---

[108]*Abel's death*: Genesis 4. In some postbiblical traditions Cain was regarded as the ancestor of monsters and evil spirits of various kinds.

[178]*Made heathen . . . off*: As Christianity was regarded as the only true and valid religion, all other religions and gods were ultimately traceable to the enemy of God, the Devil.

And the heathen's only hope, Hell
Always in their hearts, knowing neither God   180
Nor His passing as He walks through our world, the
                                                       Lord
Of Heaven and earth; their ears could not hear
His praise nor know His glory. Let them
Beware, those who are thrust into danger,
Clutched at by trouble, yet can carry no solace   185
In their hearts, cannot hope to be better! Hail
To those who will rise to God, drop off
Their dead bodies and seek our Father's peace!

          So the living sorrow of Healfdane's son
Simmered, bitter and fresh, and no wisdom   190
Or strength could break it: that agony hung
On king and people alike, harsh
And unending, violent and cruel and evil.
          In his far-off home Beowulf, Higlac's°
Follower and the strongest of the Geats—greater   195
And stronger than anyone anywhere in this world—
Heard how Grendel filled nights with horror
And quickly commanded a boat fitted out,
Proclaiming that he'd go to that famous king,
Would sail across the sea to Hrothgar,   200
Now when help was needed. None
Of the wise ones regretted his going, much
As he was loved by the Geats: the omens were good,
And they urged the adventure on. So Beowulf
Chose the mightiest men he could find,   205
The bravest and best of the Geats, fourteen
In all, and led them down to their boat;
He knew the sea, would point the prow
Straight to that distant Danish shore.
          Then they sailed, set their ship   210
Out on the waves, under the cliffs.
Ready for what came they wound through the currents,
The seas beating at the sand, and were borne
In the lap of their shining ship, lined
With gleaming armor, going safely   215
In that oak-hard boat to where their hearts took them.
The wind hurried them over the waves,
The ship foamed through the sea like a bird
Until, in the time they had known it would take,
Standing in the round-curled prow they could see   220
Sparkling hills, high and green,
Jutting up over the shore, and rejoicing
In those rock-steep cliffs they quietly ended
Their voyage. Jumping to the ground, the Geats
Pushed their boat to the sand and tied it   225
In place, mail shirts and armor rattling

As they swiftly moored their ship. And then
They gave thanks to God for their easy crossing.
          High on a wall a Danish watcher
Patrolling along the cliffs saw   230
The travelers crossing to the shore, their shields
Raised and shining; he came riding down,
Hrothgar's lieutenant, spurring his horse,
Needing to know why they'd landed, these men
In armor. Shaking his heavy spear   235
In their faces he spoke:
          "Whose soldiers are you,
You who've been carried in your deep-keeled ship
Across the sea-road to this country of mine?
Listen! I've stood on these cliffs longer
Than you know, keeping our coast free   240
Of pirates, raiders sneaking ashore
From their ships, seeking our lives and our gold.
None have ever come more openly—
And yet you've offered no password, no sign
From my prince, no permission from my people for your
                                                  landing   245
Here. Nor have I ever seen,
Out of all the men on earth, one greater
Than has come with you; no commoner carries
Such weapons, unless his appearance, and his beauty,
Are both lies. You! Tell me your name,   250
And your father's; no spies go further onto Danish
Soil than you've come already. Strangers,
From wherever it was you sailed, tell it,
And tell it quickly, the quicker the better,
I say, for us all. Speak, say   255
Exactly who you are, and from where, and why."

SONG OF ROLAND

The Approach of the Saracens

The following excerpt is from the most famous of medieval French chansons de geste, the Song of Roland. In this section of the poem the narrator describes how the French military leader Roland refuses to sound his ivory born to call for help in fighting against a much larger Saracen army.

80

Oliver climbs to the top of a hill,
looks to his right, across a grassy vale,
sees the pagan army on its way there;
and called down to Roland, his companion:
"That way, toward Spain: the uproar I see coming!   5
All their hauberks, all blazing, helmets like flames!

---

[194]*Higlac:* King of the Geats, a people of southern Sweden. Higlac is both Beowulf's feudal lord and his uncle.

It will be a bitter thing for our French.
Ganelon knew, that criminal, that traitor,
When he marked us out before the Emperor."
"Be still, Oliver," Roland the Count replies.   10
"He is my stepfather—my stepfather.
          I won't have you speak one word against him."

81

Oliver has gone up upon a hill,
sees clearly now: the kingdom of Spain,
and the Saracens assembled in such numbers: 15
helmets blazing, bedecked with gems in gold,
those shields of theirs, those hauberks sewn with brass,
and all their spears, the gonfanons affixed;
cannot begin to count their battle corps,
there are too many, he cannot take their number.   20
And he is deeply troubled by what he sees.
He made his way quickly down from the hill,
came to the French, told them all he had seen.

82

Said Oliver: "I saw the Saracens,
no man on earth ever saw more of them—   25
one hundred thousand, with their shields, up in front,
helmets laced on, hauberks blazing on them,
the shafts straight up, the iron heads like flames—
you'll get a battle, nothing like it before.
My lords, my French, may God give you
          the strength.   30
Hold your ground now! Let them not defeat us!"
And the French say: "God hate the man who runs!
We may die here, but no man will fail you."[1]AOI.

83

Said Oliver: "The pagan force is great;
from what I see, our French here are too few.   35
Roland, my companion, sound your horn then,
Charles will hear it, the army will come back."
Roland replies: "I'd be a fool to do it.
I would lose my good name all through sweet France.
I will strike now, I'll strike with Durendal,   40
the blade will be bloody to the gold from striking!
These pagan traitors came to these passes doomed!
I promise you, they are marked men, they'll die." AOI.

84

"Roland, Companion, now sound the olifant,
Charles will hear it, he will bring the army back,   45
The king will come with all his barons to help us."
Roland replies: "May it never please God
that my kin should be shamed because of me,
or that sweet France should fall into disgrace.
Never! Never! I'll strike with Durendal,   50
I'll strike with this good sword strapped to my side,
you'll see this blade running its whole length with blood.
These pagan traitors have gathered here to die.
I promise you, they are all bound for death." AOI.

85

"Roland, Companion, sound your olifant now,   55
Charles will hear it, marching through those passes.
I promise you, the Franks will come at once."
Roland replies: "May it never please God
that any man alive should come to say
that pagans—pagans!—once made me sound
          this horn: 60
no kin of mine will ever bear that shame.
Once I enter this great battle coming
and strike my thousand seven hundred blows,
you'll see the bloody steel of Durendal.
These French are good—they will strike like
          brave men.   65
Nothing can save the men of Spain from death."

86

Said Oliver: "I see no blame in it—
I watched the Saracens coming from Spain,
the valleys and mountains covered with them,
every hillside and every plain all covered,   70
hosts and hosts everywhere of those strange men—
and here we have a little company."
Roland replies: "That whets my appetite.
May it not please God and his angels and saints
to let France lose its glory because of me—   75
let me not end in shame, let me die first.
The Emperor loves us when we fight well."

87

Roland is good, and Oliver is wise,
both these vassals men of amazing courage:
once they are armed and mounted on their horses,   80
they will not run, though they die for it, from battle.
Good men, these Counts, and their words full of spirit.

[1]These mysterious letters appear 180 times throughout the Song of Roland. Their significance remains a mystery.

Traitor pagans are riding up in fury.
Said Oliver: "Roland, look—the first ones,
on top of us—and Charles is far away.   *85*
You did not think it right to sound your olifant:
if the King were here, we'd come out without losses.
Now look up there, toward the passes of Aspre—
you can see the rear-guard: it will suffer.
No man in that detail will be in another."   *90*
Roland replies: "Don't speak such foolishness—
shame on the heart gone coward in the chest.
We'll hold our ground, we'll stand firm—we're the ones!
We'll fight with spears, we'll fight them hand to hand!"
           AOI.

88

When Roland sees that there will be a battle,   *95*
it makes him fiercer than a lion or leopard;
shouts to the French, calls out to Oliver:
"Lord, companion: friend, do not say such things.
The Emperor, who left us these good French,
had set apart these twenty thousand men: *100*
he knew there was no coward in their ranks.
A man must meet great troubles for his lord,
stand up to the great heat and the great cold,
give up some flesh and blood—it is his duty.
Strike with the lance, I'll strike with Durendal—   *105*
it was the King who gave me this good sword!
If I die here, the man who gets it can say:
it was a noble's, a vassal's, a good man's sword."

89

And now there comes the Archbishop Turpin.
He spurs his horse, goes up into a mountain,   *110*
summons the French; and he preached them a sermon:
"Barons, my lords, Charles left us in this place.
We know our duty: to die like good men for our King.
Fight to defend the holy Christian faith.
Now you will have a battle, you know it now,   *115*
you see the Saracens with your own eyes.
Confess your sins, pray to the Lord for mercy.
I will absolve you all, to save your souls.
If you die here, you will stand up holy martyrs,
you will have seats in highest Paradise."   *120*
The French dismount, cast themselves on the ground;
the Archbishop blesses them in God's name.
He commands them to do one penance: strike.

90

The French arise, stand on their feet again;
they are absolved, released from all their sins: *125*
the Archbishop has blessed them in God's name.
Now they are mounted on their swift battle horses,
bearing their arms like faithful warriors:
and every man stands ready for the battle.
Roland the Count calls out to Oliver: *130*
"Lord, Companion, you knew it, you were right,
Ganelon watched for his chance to betray us,
got gold for it, got goods for it, and money.
The Emperor will have to avenge us now.
King Marsilion made a bargain for our lives,   *135*
but still must pay, and that must be with swords." AOI.

91

Roland went forth into the Spanish passes
on Veillantif, his good swift-running horse.
He bears his arms—how they become this man!—
grips his lance now, hefting it, working it,   *140*
now swings the iron point up toward the sky,
the gonfanon all white laced on above—
the golden streamers beat down upon his hands:
a noble's body, the face aglow and smiling.
Close behind him his good companion follows;   *145*
the men of France hail him: their protector!
He looks wildly toward the Saracens,
and humbly and gently to the men of France;
and spoke a word to them in all courtesy:
"Barons, my lords, easy now, keep at a walk.   *150*
These pagans are searching for martyrdom.
We'll get good spoils before this day is over,
no king of France ever got such treasure!"
And with these words, the hosts are at each other. AOI.

92

Said Oliver: "I will waste no more words.   *155*
You did not think it right to sound your olifant,
there'll be no Charles coming to your aid now.
He knows nothing, brave man, he's done no wrong;
those men down there—they have no blame in this.
Well, then, ride now, and ride with all your might!   *160*
Lords, you brave men, stand your ground, hold the field!
Make up your minds, I beg you in God's name,
to strike some blows, take them and give them back!
Here we must not forget Charlemagne's war cry."
And with that word the men of France cried out.   *165*

A man who heard that shout: Munjoie! Munjoie!
would always remember what manhood is.
Then they ride, God! Look at their pride and spirit!
and they spur hard, to ride with all their speed,
come on to strike—what else would these men do?   *170*
The Saracens kept coming, never fearing them,
Franks and pagans, here they are, at each other.

MARIE DE FRANCE

The Nightingale

*As far as is known, the first woman to write poetry in French was
Marie de France. She is best known for her lais, narratives of moderate length typically involving one or more miraculous or marvelous incidents and other adventures concerning romantic love.
"The Nightingale" reflects a few of the conventions of courtly love,
medieval guidelines for the behavior of lovers outside marriage.*

The story I shall tell today
Was taken from a Breton lay
Called Laustic in Brittany,
Which, in proper French would be
Rossignol. They'd call the tale   *5*
In English lands *The Nightingale*.
There was, near Saint Malo, a town
Of some importance and renown.
Two barons who could well afford
Houses suited to a lord   *10*
Gave the city its good name
By their benevolence and fame.
Only one of them had married.
His wife was beautiful indeed
And courteous as she was fair,   *15*
A lady who was well aware
Of all that custom and rank required.
The younger baron was much admired,
Being, among his peers, foremost
In valor, and a gracious host.   *20*
He never refused a tournament,
And what he owned he gladly spent.
He loved his neighbor's wife. She knew
That all she heard of him was true,
And so she was inclined to be   *25*
Persuaded when she heard his plea.
Soon she had yielded all her heart
To his real merit and, in part,
Because he lived not far away.
Fearful that they might betray   *30*
The love that they had come to share,

They always took the greatest care
Not to let anyone detect
Anything that might be suspect.
And it was easy enough to hide;   *35*
Their houses were almost side by side
With nothing between the two at all
Except a single high stone wall.
The baron's wife need only go
And stand beside her bedroom window   *40*
Whenever she wished to see her friend.
They would talk for hours on end
Across the wall, and often threw
Presents through the window too.
They were much happier than before,   *45*
And would have asked for nothing more;
But lovers can't be satisfied
When love's true pleasure is denied.
The lady was watched too carefully
As soon as her friend was known to be   *50*
At home. But still they had the delight
Of seeing each other day or night
And talking to their heart's content.
The strictest guard could not prevent
The lady from looking out her window;   *55*
What she saw there no one could know.
Nothing came to interfere
With their true love until one year
In the season when the summer grows
Green in all the woods and meadows,   *60*
When birds to show their pleasure cling
To flower tops and sweetly sing.
Then those who were in love before
Do, in love's service, even more.
The baron, in truth, was all intent   *65*
On love; the messages he sent
Across the wall had such replies
From his lady's lips and from her eyes,
He knew that she felt just the same.
Now she very often came   *70*
To her window lighted by the moon,
Leaving her husband's side as soon
As she knew that he was fast asleep.
Wrapped in a cloak, she went to keep
Watch with her lover, sure that he   *75*
Would be waiting for her faithfully.
To see each other was, despite
Their endless longing, great delight.
She went so often and remained
So long, her husband soon complained,   *80*
Insisting that she must reply

To where she went at night and why.
"I'll tell you, my lord," the lady answered;
"Anyone who has ever heard
The nightingale singing will admit   85
No joy on earth compares with it.
That music just outside my window
Gives me such pleasure that I know
I cannot go to sleep until
The sweet voice in the night is still."   90
The baron only answered her
With a malicious raging laughter.
He wrought a plan that could not fail
To overcome the nightingale.
The household servants all were set   95
To making traps of cord or net;
Then, throughout the orchard, these
Were fixed to hazel and chestnut trees,
And all the branches rimmed with glue
So that the bird could not slip through.   100
It was not long before they brought
The nightingale who had been caught
Alive. The baron, well content,
Took the bird to his wife's apartment.
"Where are you, lady? Come talk to me!"   105
He cried, "I've something for you to see!
Look! Here is the bird whose song
Has kept you from your sleep so long.
Your nights will be more peaceful when
He can't awaken you again!"   110
She heard with sorrow and with dread
Everything her husband said,
Then asked him for the bird, and he
Killed it out of cruelty;
Vile, with his two hands he wrung   115
Its neck, and when he finished, flung
The body at his wife. The red
Drops of blood ran down and spread
Over the bodice of her dress.
He left her alone with her distress.   120
Weeping, she held the bird and thought
With bitter rage of those who brought
The nightingale to death, betrayed
By all the hidden traps they laid.
"Alas!" she cried. "They had destroyed   125
The one great pleasure I enjoyed.
Now I can no longer go
And see my love outside my window
At night the way I used to do!
One thing certainly is true: 130
He'll think that I no longer care.

Somehow he must be made aware
Of what has happened. It will be clear
Then why I cannot appear."
And so she began at once to write   135
On a piece of gold-embroidered samite.
When it couldn't hold another word
She wrapped it around the little bird.
Then she called someone in her service
Whom she could entrust with this,   140
Bidding him take without delay
Her message to her chevalier.
Thus he came to understand
Everything, just as she planned.
The servant brought the little bird;   145
And when the chevalier had heard
All that he so grieved to know,
His courteous answer was not slow.
He ordered made a little case,
Not of iron or any base   150
Metal, but fine gold embossed
With jewels—he did not count the cost.
The cover was not too long or wide.
He placed the nightingale inside
And had the casket sealed with care!   155
He carried it with him everywhere.
Stories like this can't be controlled,
And it was very promptly told.

Medieval Lyrics

During the Middle Ages, the lyric was a popular genre. As with the lyric poetry of ancient Greece, medieval lyrics were often written to be sung or performed. The poems that follow represent a tiny sampling of what was a lyric profusion of poems on love, war, nature, and a range of other topics.

WILLIAM IX, DUKE OF AQUITAINE

1071–1127

Spring Song[1]

In the sweetness of new spring
the woods grow leafy, little birds,
each in their own language, sing,
rehearse new stanzas with new words,
and it is good that man should find
the joy that most enchants his mind.

I see no messenger or note
from her, my first source of delight;

---

[1]Translated from the Provençal by Peter Dronke.

my heart can neither sleep nor laugh,
I dare not make a further move,
till I know what the end will be—
is she what I would have her be?

Our love together goes the way
of the branch on the hawthorn-tree,
trembling in the night, a prey
to the hoar-frost and the showers,
till next morning, when the sun
enfolds the green leaves and the boughs.

One morning I remember still
we put an end to skirmishing,
and she gave me so great a gift:
her loving body, and her ring.
May God keep me alive until
my hands again move in her mantle!

For I shun that strange talk which might pull
my Helpmeet and myself apart;
I know that words have their own life,
and swift discourses spread about—
let others vaunt love as they will,
we have love's food, we have the knife!

BEATRICE, COUNTESS OF DIA

ca. 1150–1200

A Lover's Prize[1]

I have been in great distress
for a knight for whom I longed;
I want all future times to know
how I loved him to excess
   Now I see I am betrayed—
he claims I did not give him love—
such was the mistake I made,
   naked in bed, and dressed.

How I'd long to hold him pressed
naked in my arms one night—
if I could be his pillow once,
would he not know the height of bliss?
   Floris was all to Blanchefleur,[2]
yet not so much as I am his:
I am giving my heart, my love,
   my mind, my life, my eyes.

Fair, gentle lover, gracious knight,
if once I held you as my prize
and lay with you a single night
and gave you a love-laden kiss—
   my greatest longing is for you
to lie there in my husband's place,
but only if you promise this:
   to do all I'd want to do.

ARNAUT DANIEL

twelfth century

The Art of Love[1]

To this sweet and pretty air
I set words that I plane and finish;
and every word will fit well,
once I have passed the file there,
for at once Love polishes and aureates
my song, which proceeds from her,
ruler and guardian of merit.

Each day I am a better man and purer,
for I serve the noblest lady in the world,
and I worship her, I tell you this in the open.
I belong to her from my foot to the top of my head;
and let the cold wind blow,
love raining in my heart
keeps me warm when it winters most.

I hear a thousand masses and pay to have them said,
I burn lights of wax and oil,
so may God give me good luck with her,
for no defense against her does me any good.
When I look at her golden hair,
her soft young spirited body,
if someone gave me Luserna,[2] I'd still love her more.

I love her and seek her out with a heart so full,
I think I am stealing her out of my own hands by too
   much wanting,
if a man can lose a thing by loving it well.
For the heart of her submerges
mine and does not abate.
So usurious is her demand,
she gets craftsman and workshop together.

I do not want the empire of Rome,
do not make me pope of it

---

[1]Translated from the Provençal by Peter Dronke.
[2]Lovers in a well-known romance.

[1]Translated from the Provençal by Frederick Goldin.
[2]A city, probably in Spain.

so that I could not turn back to her
for whom the heart in me burns and breaks apart.
If she does not cure me of this torment
with a kiss before new year's,
she murders me and sends herself to hell.

But this torment I endure
could not make me turn away from loving well,
though it holds me fast in loneliness,
for in this desert I cast my words in rhyme.
I labor in loving more than a man who works the earth,

for the Lord of Moncli did not love
N'Audierna an egg's worth more.[3]

I am Arnaut, who hoards the wind,
and chases the hare on an ox,
and swims against the tide.

BERTRAN DE BORN

(ca. 1140–1215)

*Bertran de Born is one of the most famous of the French trouba-
dours. Dante consigned Him to Hell in his Inferno for sowing discord among French political Sauteer. The song below celebrates the
energy and spirit of warfare.*

I love the glad time of Easter[1]

I love the glad time of Easter,
that makes leaves and flowers come out;
and I love when I hear the joy
of the birds, which makes their song
5   resound throughout the woods;
and I love when I see the fields
planted with tents and pavilions;
and I truly rejoice
when I see the countryside ranged
10   with knights and horses armed for war.[2]

And I love it when the runners[3]
make the people flee with their goods;
and I love to see after them
an army's massed ranks on the move;
15   and in my heart I love

to see a strong castle besieged,
the ramparts breached and broken in,
and to see the host on the shore,
closed in, surrounded by ditches,
20   with rows of strong stakes intertwined.

And I love just as much the lord,
when he is first in the assault
astride his horse, armed, unafraid;
thus he emboldens his vassals
25   with valiant and lordly deeds.
And then when battle is joined,
each man must hold himself ready
and follow him with a light heart,
for no man is of any worth,
30   till he's given what he's received.

Maces and swords, bright-colored helms,
shields to slice through and to strip,
we'll see as the melee begins,
vassals all fighting together,
35   wandering, on the loose,
horses of the dead and fallen.
When the battle has been engaged,
any truly noble man
wants only to cleave heads and arms,
40   better off dead than caught, alive.

I tell you nothing is sweeter,
not eating, drinking, or sleeping,
than when I hear the call to "Charge!"
from both sides and I hear neighing
45   horses in the shadows, bare,
and I hear calls "To aid! To aid!"
and I see fall into ditches
the great and small on the grass,
and I see the bodies whose sides
50   the silken streaming lance has pierced.

Barons, mortgage your castles
and your villages and your towns
before you think of stopping war,[4]

Papiols, light-heartedly
55   speed your way to Lord Yes-and-No;
tell him he's been at peace too long.[5]

---

[3]Neither the Lord of Moncli nor his love, N'Audierna, have been identified.
[1]Translated by David L. Pike. The attribution of this song to Bertran is
not certain.
[2]The poem begins with the conventional springtime setting of a pleasure song such as Guillem de Peiteus's "In the sweet time of renewal",
before turning abruptly to the pleasures of war rather than love.
[3]Soldiers who carry messages ahead of the front lines.

---

[4]Feudal barons were often hard put to finance the forces they were expected to raise when lords to whom they owed ties of fealty summoned
them to war.
[5]Papiols is the name of Bertran's *jongleur*, or performer; Lord Yes-and-No
is Richard the Lion-Hearted (1157–99).

Sestina: Altaforte[1]

LOQUITUR[1]: *En*[2] Bertrans de Born.

Dante[3] Alighieri put this man in hell for that he was a
stirrer up of strife.
Eccovi![4]
Judge ye!
Have I dug him up again?

The scene is at his castle, Altaforte. "Papiols" is his jongleur.[5]
"The Leopard," the *device* of Richard Cœur de Lion.

I

Damn it all! all this our South stinks peace.
You whoreson dog, Papiols, come! Let's to music!
I have no life save when the swords clash.
But ah! when I see the standards gold, vair, purple,
    opposing
And the broad fields beneath them turn crimson,
Then howl I my heart nigh mad with rejoicing.

II

In hot summer have I great rejoicing
When the tempests kill the earth's foul peace,
And the lightnings from black heav'n flash crimson,
And the fierce thunders roar me their music
And the winds shriek through the clouds mad, opposing,
And through all the riven skies God's swords clash.

III

Hell grant soon we hear again the swords clash!
And the shrill neighs of destriers[6] in battle rejoicing,

Spiked breast to spiked breast opposing!
Better one hour's stour than a year's peace
With fat boards, bawds, wine and frail music!
Bah! there's no wine like the blood's crimson!

IV

And I love to see the sun rise blood-crimson.
And I watch his spears through the dark clash
And it fills all my heart with rejoicing
And pries wide my mouth with fast music
When I see him so scorn and defy peace,
His lone might 'gainst all darkness opposing.

V

The man who fears war and squats opposing
My words for stour, hath no blood of crimson
But is fit only to rot in womanish peace
Far from where worth's won and the swords clash
For the death of such sluts I go rejoicing;
Yea, I fill all the air with my music.

VI

Papiols, Papiols, to the music!
There's no sound like to swords swords opposing,
No cry like the battle's rejoicing
When our elbows and swords drip the crimson
And our charges 'gainst "The Leopard's" rush clash.
May God damn for ever all who cry "Peace!"

VII

And let the music of the swords make them crimson!
Hell grant soon we hear again the swords clash!
Hell blot black for alway the thought "Peace"!

---

[1]Alternate version translated & adapted by Ezra Pound.
[1]**Loquitur:** Latin, "he speaks."
[2]*En:* Provençal, "Sir" or "Lord."
[3]**Dante:** Dante placed Bertran in the Ninth Circle of Hell in *The Inferno*
as a "Sower of Discord" for setting Prince Henry against his brother
Richard and their father Henry II. Pound translated this passage from
Dante in *SR*, 45.
[4]Eccovi!: Italian, "Here you are."
[5]jongleur: The troubadour's singer, Papiols.
[6]destriers: War horses trained to rear up before the enemy.

CHAPTER 12

HISTORY

1152	Louis VII marries Eleanor of Aquitaine
1180–1223	Philip Augustus reigns
1189–99	Richard the Lionhearted reigns
1215	Magna Carta
1226–70	Louis IX reigns
1285–1314	Philip the Fair reigns
1327–77	Edward III reigns
1337–1453	Hundred Years' War
1348	Worst outbreak of bubonic plague in western Europe
1358	Étienne Marcel revolts against crown
1364–80	Charles V reigns
ca. 1550	Gothic era ends in France, aspects continue in Germany and England

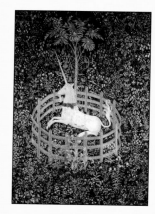

ARTS AND ARCHITECTURE

1140–45	Saint-Denis, choir and ambulatory
1145–55	Column figures of Royal Portals, cathedral, Chartres
1145–1220	Notre-Dame Cathedral, Chartres
begun 1163	Notre-Dame Cathedral, Paris
ca. 1175	Leonin, chant composer active
ca. 1200	Perotin, chant composer active
1220–66/70	Nicholas of Ely et al., cathedral, Salisbury
1243–48	Sainte-Chapelle, Paris
1259–60; 1302–10	Nicholas and Giovanni Pisano depictions of the *Nativity*
ca. 1260	*Psalter of St. Louis,* illuminated manuscript
begun 1296	cathedral, Florence
1300–77	Machaut, *ars nova* composer
1305–06	Giotto, Arena Chapel
1308–11	Duccio, *Madonna and Child Enthroned*
1346	Machaut, *Mass of Notre Dame*
late 14th century	Milan Cathedral
1413–16	Limbourg brothers, *Les Très Riches Heures*
ca. 1500	*Unicorn tapestries*
1503–19	Robert and William Vertue, Chapel of Henry VII, Westminster Abbey, London

LITERATURE AND PHILOSOPHY

1181–1226	Francis of Assisi
1265–74	St. Thomas Aquinas, *Summa Theologica*
1320	Dante, *Divine Comedy*
1349–51	Boccaccio, *Decameron*
1386–1400	Chaucer, *The Canterbury Tales*

Gothic and Late Middle Ages

Cathedral of Notre-Dame, Amiens, begun 1220.

MAP 12.1 Europe during the Hundred Years' War, 1337–1453.

CHAPTER OVERVIEW

THE GOTHIC ERA
The age of the great cathedrals of western Europe, richly embellished

TOWARD THE RENAISSANCE
The trends toward naturalism and realism in painting and sculpture

THE GOTHIC ERA

PARIS IN THE LATER MIDDLE AGES

No city dominated the later middle ages more than Paris. Home to a revival in learning at the newly founded university, Paris was also the seat of the French government, overseen by King Louis IX (later St.

Louis) (r. 1226–70). The monarchy had not enjoyed such power and respect since the time of Charlemagne. Louis made a determined effort to be a king to all his people, sending royal commissioners into the countryside to monitor the administration of local government and to ensure justice for all. He outlawed private warfare and granted his subjects the right to appeal to higher courts. Furthermore, he became something of a peacekeeper among the

Then & Now

THE LOUVRE

The Louvre today is one of the most famous museums in the world. It is also the largest royal palace in the world, a building that has undergone more redevelopment through the ages than any other building in Europe. The first building on the site was a fortress, erected in 1200 by Philip Augustus, with a keep, the symbol of royal power, surrounded by a moat. Today, remnants of the moat and keep can be viewed on the bottom floor of the museum.

Charles V used the building as a royal residence, but over the years its galleries and arcades have also served as a prison, an arsenal, a mint, a granary, a county seat, a publishing house, a ministry, the Institute for Advanced Studies, a telegraph station, a shopping arcade, a tavern, and a hotel for visiting heads of state. The expansive and open plan of the Louvre today, with its two great arms extending from the original building west to the Tuileries gardens, is the result of later additions. In the latter part of the sixteenth century, Henry IV added the Grand Galleries, initially conceived as a covered walkway connecting the palace to the garden. In the seventeenth century, Louis XIV closed off the east end, forming the Cour Carrée.

The result of these additions and alterations is a building that represents almost every architectural style in the history of the West. A Romanesque fortress forms its basis, and outward from it spread two Gothic and two Renaissance wings. Baroque and Rococo ornamentation can be found throughout, and the closed-off end is Neoclassical. In this spirit of heterogeneity and plurality, architect I. M. Pei designed a glass pyramid to serve as the museum's new entrance in 1988. Set above a network of underground rooms and walkways, Pei's pyramid is 61 feet high and 108 feet wide at the base, constructed of 105 tons of glass. Beside it are flat triangular pools that reflect the walls of the surrounding palace.

---

other European powers, and he was in most matters more influential than the pope. In short, he became associated with fairness and justice, and France consolidated itself as a nation around him, with Paris as its focal point. Soon all roads led to Paris, as they had once led to Rome.

GOTHIC ARCHITECTURE

The term **Gothic** refers to the style of visual arts and culture that first developed, beginning about 1140, in the Ile-de-France, and reached its zenith in the thirteenth century. From the mid-thirteenth through the mid-fourteenth century, Paris was an important source of artistic inspiration for the rest of France, Germany, and England; Italy remained quite separate aesthetically. By the middle of the sixteenth century, the Gothic style was at an end in France, although aspects of it continued to influence artists in Germany and England until the seventeenth century.

What is now called "Gothic art" was originally called the "French style," and referred to architecture. Architecture, in fact, dominates the era for this is the age of the great **cathedrals** of northern Europe. However, it was the Italians who gave the style its name; preferring the classical style, the Italians thought the Gothic barbaric and identified it with the most notorious of the barbarian tribes, the Goths. Thus the style was labeled "Gothic," with a decidedly derogatory intent.

The Gothic style developed out of the Romanesque. Romanesque buildings are broad and massive, characterized by semicircular arches, thick walls, and closely spaced supports that create a feeling of security. Solid and heavy, Romanesque buildings seem to be bound to the earth. In contrast, Gothic buildings have a soaring quality, for the vertical is constantly emphasized and the walls are thin. Small Romanesque windows give way in Gothic architecture to vast windows of stained glass.

Gothic architecture was confident and daring. The tremendous height of the buildings was a reflection of religious ideals and enthusiasm, of inspiration and aspiration. The vast naves of the Gothic cathedrals create an extraordinary atmosphere of spirituality. The chants sung here reverberated from the high vaults.

The structural innovations (fig. 12.1) that characterized this new style include the following:

1. **Pointed arches and vaults** that exert less lateral thrust than the semicircular Romanesque arches and vaults. The pointed ribbed vault can be constructed in a variety of floor plans and, in theory, built to any height.
2. **Ribs** that serve to concentrate the weight of the vault at certain points, making it possible to eliminate the wall between these points.
3. **Flying buttresses** that were introduced in response to the problem created by the lateral thrust exerted by a true vault. The idea of a buttress, a solid mass of masonry used to reinforce a wall, was an old one. But the "flying" part, the exterior arch, was an invention of the Gothic era. Flying buttresses project outward on the exterior of the building and cannot be seen from the inside through the stained glass windows.

Royal Abbey, Saint-Denis. The Gothic style began at the royal abbey of Saint-Denis, located just north of Paris.

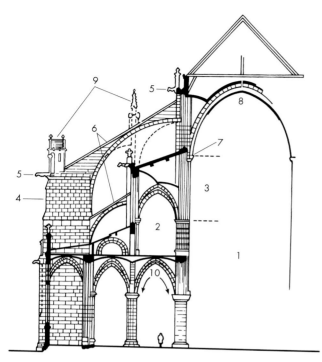

FIGURE 12.1   The principal features of a Gothic church include (1) the nave; (2) gallery/triforium; (3) clerestory window; (4) buttress; (5) gargoyle; (6) flying buttresses; (7) architectural rib; (8) vault; (9) pinnacles; and (10) pointed arch.

The first church on the site was erected in 475 in honor of St. Denis, who went to Paris around 250 C.E. to convert the Gauls and was rewarded for his efforts by being tortured on a hot grill and then decapitated. St. Denis is said to have picked up his head and walked north to the site where the abbey was subsequently built.

The parts of the abbey of Saint-Denis that herald the beginning of the Gothic were built under Abbot SUGER [SOO-zjay] (1081–1151) around 1140. A Benedictine monk, Suger advised successive kings of France and was even regent of the country during the Second Crusade. He regarded the church as symbolic of the kingdom of God on earth and was intent on making Saint-Denis as magnificent as possible. Suger rebuilt the facade, the narthex, and the east end of Saint-Denis. He commissioned a golden altar, jeweled crosses, chalices, vases, and ewers made of precious materials. This richness was in honor of God, France, and possibly also Suger. At a time when humble anonymity was the norm, Suger had himself depicted in stained glass and sculpture and his name included in inscriptions.

The first large and truly Gothic building, Saint-Denis served as the prototype for other Gothic structures. The facade of Saint-Denis was the first to synthesize monumental sculpture and architecture. Its two towers, **rose**

FIGURE 12.2   Royal Abbey, Saint-Denis. Ambulatory, 1140–44. The eccentric and egocentric Abbot Suger initiated the Gothic style of architecture, characterized by a new lightness of proportion and sense of flowing space. The pointed Gothic arches exert less lateral thrust than the Romanesque semicircular arches, and the ribs reinforce the vaults.

window (a circular window with tracery radiating from its center to form a roselike symmetrical pattern), rows of figures representing Jesus's biblical ancestors, and column figures on the jambs all became standard features of later Gothic cathedrals. Today, the ambulatory and the seven chapels of the ambulatory remain as they were in Suger's day (fig. 12.2).

In Suger's plan, the divisions between the chapels are almost eliminated. Each chapel has two large windows. This introduction of light was a new concept. The space is not divided into distinct units, as in Romanesque architecture. Instead, without the solid walls and massive supports of the Romanesque, Gothic space flows freely and areas merge with each other.

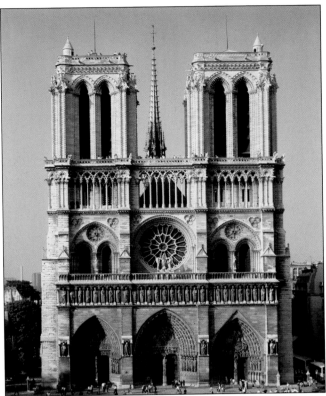

FIGURE 12.3   Cathedral of Notre-Dame, Paris, west facade, 1163–ca. 1250, mostly first half of thirteenth century. This celebrated cathedral is an example of the first phase of the Gothic, referred to as Early Gothic. In Romanesque architecture horizontals dominated; here horizontals and verticals balance; soon the verticals will dominate.

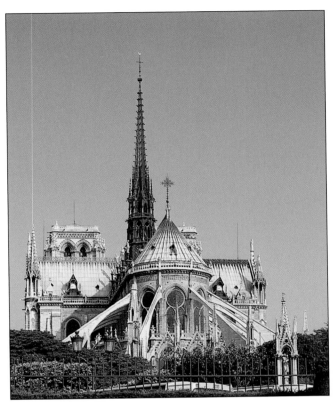

FIGURE 12.4   Cathedral of Notre-Dame, Paris, 1163–ca. 1250, apse, flying buttresses added in the 1180s. Exterior wall buttresses have a long history; innovative are the arch-shaped flying buttresses, used especially on large multistoried buildings to absorb the lateral thrust exerted by the vaulting. The solid walls of Romanesque architecture were replaced by the characteristically Gothic flying buttresses.

Notre-Dame, Paris.   The cathedral of Notre-Dame-de-Paris (Our Lady of Paris) (fig. 12.3), is located in the heart of Paris on the Ile-de-la-Cité, an island in the Seine river. The historical center of the city, Gallo-Roman ramparts once fortified the site, and earlier churches had been built there as well. Bishop Maurice of Sully, founder of the cathedral, had these removed, however.

Construction of Notre-Dame started in 1163. Work began with the choir—the construction of a church or cathedral usually commences at the choir end. With few exceptions the Christian altar is oriented to the east, the church entrance toward the west. Notre-Dame was first finished in 1235. Reconstruction began almost immediately. The vaulting of the choir was redone; almost all the clerestory windows were enlarged; the flying buttresses were doubled; the transepts were rebuilt; and work was carried out on over forty chapels. All this remodeling took several decades.

The facade (fig. 12.3) dates, for the most part, from the first half of the thirteenth century. Large amounts of wall are still evident, a holdover from the Romanesque period.

The facade's equilibrium of horizontals and verticals creates a masterpiece of balance. Based on a sequence of squares, one inside another, the entire facade is one large square, 142 feet on each side. The towers are one-half the height of the whole solid area—a simple, satisfying geometry.

In the 1180s, the first flying buttresses (see fig. 12.4) were added at Notre-Dame to stabilize its great height. The buttresses are in two parts: The outer buttress is exposed; the inner buttress is hidden under the roof of the inner aisle. From this time forward, flying buttresses would play an important structural and visual role in Gothic architecture.

Notre-Dame, Chartres.   The cathedral of Notre-Dame in Chartres (fig. 12.5), a spectacular structure with splendid sculpture and sparkling stained glass, begins the **High Gothic.**

Chartres cathedral was intended to be a "terrestrial palace" for Jesus's mother Mary, built on the highest part of the city in order to bring it closer to heaven. This cathedral possesses an important relic of Mary. Known as the

FIGURE 12.5   Cathedral of Notre-Dame, Chartres, rebuilding 1145–1220; north spire 1507–13. This cathedral dominates the surrounding landscape and is visible for miles around; Gothic cathedrals were routinely built on the highest site available. The typical French Gothic facade has one rose (wheel) window, two towers, and three entry portals.

sancta camisia, it is a piece of cloth, said to have been worn by Mary when Jesus was born. Chartres was believed to be protected by Mary and became an extremely popular pilgrimage site. Although it was believed to have produced many miracles, the relic could not fend off fire, constant enemy of churches during the Middle Ages and the cause of the cathedral's destruction in 1020. Rebuilding began

immediately and, by 1024, a new crypt was finished. Known as "Fulbert's Crypt," it is still the largest crypt in France. A Romanesque cathedral was then constructed on the site, but in 1134 fire destroyed the town, and the building was damaged. The Royal Portals and the stained glass windows on the west facade were made 1145–55. In 1194, there was yet another fire in which the cathedral suffered

Connections

NUMEROLOGY AT CHARTRES

At the cathedral school at Chartres, Plato's theory of the correspondence between visual and musical proportions and the beauty of the cosmos was carefully studied. The number three, also important in Christian theology, assumed special importance for the builders at Chartres. It symbolized the Holy Trinity and Plato's secular trinity of truth, beauty, and goodness.

The architecture of Chartres is replete with threes—on the exterior a three-story facade is matched by three corresponding interior levels, culminating in the colored light of the clerestory. There are three semicircular chapels off the apse, and each clerestory window consists of one rose and two lancet windows. The six-petaled rose in the mosaic in the center of the nave represents the sum of one, two, and three.

The number nine, associated with Jesus's mother Mary, is also of special importance. The cathedral, which houses fabric said to be part of her veil from the Nativity, celebrates her number. Mary is, as Dante said, "the square of the Trinity." Chartres has nine entrance portals—three times three—and in its original plan it was to have nine towers, two on the facade, two on each of the transepts, two flanking the apse, and one rising over the crossing.

---

great damage. Little more than Fulbert's Crypt and the Royal Portals and windows survived.

Mary's cloth, safe in the crypt, did survive the fire of 1194. Taken as a sign to build a yet more magnificent monument, the people of Chartres gave money, labor, and time, all social classes participating, from the high nobility to the humble peasantry. Rough limestone was brought from five miles away in carts, an activity referred to as the "cult of the carts." By 1220, the main structure and the vaults were finished, built with great speed and in a consistent style. In 1260, the cathedral was dedicated. Like the facade of Notre-Dame in Paris, Chartres has four buttresses, three portals, two towers, and one rose window. Yet, at Chartres, the two facade towers are strikingly dissimilar. The south spire is 344 feet high, built at the same time as the rest of the upper facade. But the north steeple of the early sixteenth century, built in a much more **Flamboyant Gothic** style, rises 377 feet. Each tower was constructed in the style popular at the time of its construction.

Chartres is the first masterpiece of the High Gothic, the first cathedral to be planned with flying buttresses (at Notre-Dame in Paris they are later additions), and to use them for the entire cathedral. The buttresses at Chartres are designed as an integral part of the structure. They join the wall at the critical point of thrust, between the clerestory windows, where there is a minimum of stone and a maximum of glass.

The nave (fig. 12.6) is soaring, open, and airy. Whereas the nave at Notre-Dame in Paris is just over 108 feet high, Chartres's is 121 feet high and 422 feet long. The three-story elevation consists of the arcade, the triforium, and the clerestory. The clerestory windows are tall and narrow, emphasizing the vertical rather than the horizontal. A vast amount of window area is permitted by the exterior buttressing, yet this does not produce a brightly lit interior. Instead, stained glass provides colored and changing light

FIGURE 12.6 Cathedral of Notre-Dame, Chartres, nave looking toward altar, rebuilding begun 1145, vault finished by 1220. The first architectural masterpiece of the second phase of the Gothic, known as the High Gothic, Chartres Cathedral was designed from the start to have flying buttresses. In this three-story nave elevation, large clerestory windows allow light to enter directly into the nave, the deep colors of stained glass creating an atmosphere of multicolored light.

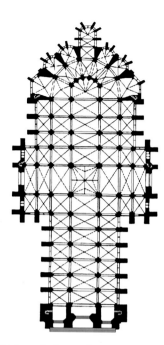

FIGURE 12.7   Robert de Luzarches, Thomas de Cormont, and Renaud de Cormont, Cathedral of Notre-Dame, Amiens, 1220–70, plan. When building with pointed arches, ribbed vaulting, and flying buttresses, in theory, there is no limit to the height attainable. Soaring heavenward, the nave of Notre-Dame at Paris rises over 108 feet; at Chartres 121 feet; and at Amiens 139 feet. Yet Beauvais Cathedral, at 158 feet, after it collapsed and was rebuilt, demonstrated the practical limits of the structural system.

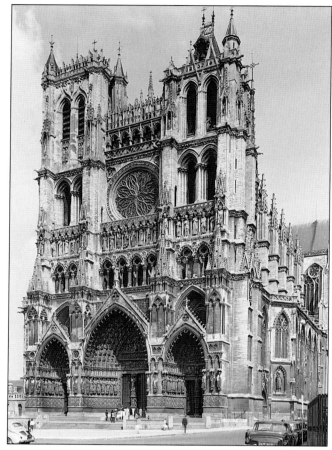

FIGURE 12.8   Robert de Luzarches, Thomas de Cormont, and Renaud de Cormont, Cathedral of Notre-Dame, Amiens, west facade, begun 1220. Buildings became ever more delicate during the Gothic era, stone seemingly turned into lace. The height of a city's cathedral was a matter of civic pride—similar to the twentieth-century battle in Manhattan between the architects of the Chrysler Building and those of the Empire State Building to erect "the tallest building in the world."

in the windows themselves and flickering light over the stone interior.

Notre-Dame, Amiens.   The cathedral of Notre-Dame in Amiens (fig. 12.7) represents the climax of the High Gothic style. Building began in 1220 and was almost finished by 1270; only the tops of the towers above the rose window date from the fourteenth and fifteenth centuries. The facade (fig. 12.8) has five parts: (1) the usual three portals on the ground floor, which are exceptionally deep; (2) the gallery; (3) the gallery of kings—twenty-two figures, each fifteen feet high, representing the Kings of Judah, each holding a rod of the Tree of Jesse; (4) the rose window, with sixteenth-century glass; and (5) above this, the fourteenth- and fifteenth-century work. The great height achieved by medieval masons was a matter of civic pride and a symbol of strength. Each town tried to outdo the others in terms of height. When a conquering army took a defeated city, they destroyed its church or cathedral spire; to lop off the top of the tower was the sign of the city's submission.

Sainte-Chapelle, Paris.   By the middle of the thirteenth century, a new **Rayonnant** style of Gothic architecture had begun to emerge. The name "Rayonnant" comes from the French *rayonner*, which means "to shine" or "to radiate." The move to this new phase was the result of a chang-

ing sense of harmony and the gradual substitution of window for wall. In this Rayonnant style, stone tracery divisions between the areas of glass in rose windows were made thinner and ever more intricate.

Paris under King Louis IX was the center for the Rayonnant style. Louis acquired a portion of Jesus's crown of thorns and many other relics, including a piece of Jesus's cross, iron fragments of the holy spear that pierced his side, the holy sponge, the robe, the shroud of Jesus, a nail from the crucifixion, and part of the skull of St. John the Baptist. Louis had these relics placed in an ornate shrine in the Sainte-Chapelle.

Rich and refined, the Sainte-Chapelle looks like an enormous reliquary. Its architectural importance is not due to great scale; when compared to other Gothic buildings, the Sainte-Chapelle is extremely small—the interior is a mere 108 feet long, and 35 feet wide. Divided into a lower and an upper chapel, the lower is only a little under 22 feet high, and the upper only just over 67 feet. The upper chapel (fig. 12.9) was dedicated to the Holy Crown of

FIGURE 12.9   Pierre de Montreuil (?), Sainte-Chapelle, Paris, upper chapel, looking toward apse, 1243–48. In this example of the third phase, the Rayonnant Gothic, the amount of masonry is reduced and the building becomes a cage of glass. Standing inside the upper chapel, when sunlight streams through the stained-glass windows, it is as if one is standing inside a sparkling, multicolored, multifaceted jewel.

FIGURE 12.10   Pierre Robin, Saint-Maclou, Rouen, designed 1434, west facade designed by Ambroise Havel (?) 1500–21. The finest example of the fourth and final phase of the Gothic, the Flamboyant or Late Gothic, this small building has enough decoration to equal that of a huge cathedral. The lacy stone tracery is "flamboyant"—flamelike—with its undulating curves.

Thorns and the Holy Cross. The plan is simple, consisting of only the nave of four rectangular bays and a seven-sided apse. The walls disappear. The lines soar. The windows are shafts of light. A cage of glass and stone, the Sainte-Chapelle appears to defy the laws of gravity. All the space between the piers is given over to huge windows, with more than three-quarters of the walls actually stained glass. The piers project inward over three feet, but their bulk is masked by groups of nine colonettes. All other supports are placed outside, leaving the interior a continuous uninterrupted space. In 1323, Master Jean de Jandun described his experience of the chapel in the following way: "On entering, one would think oneself transported to heaven and one might with reason imagine oneself taken into one of the most beautiful mansions of paradise."

The program of the upper chapel glass relates to the relics kept there. The central apse window shows Jesus's passion, introduced by the Old Testament stories in the nave. The cycle begins on the north side with the Book of Genesis and concludes on the south side with the story of the relics of the passion, especially the crown of thorns, and their arrival in Paris. The French king is depicted alongside kings David and Solomon. The windows of the Sainte-Chapelle include a great number of coronation scenes—twenty plus that of Jesus, seemingly linking French royalty and biblical royalty.

Saint-Maclou, Rouen.   Saint-Maclou in Rouen (fig. 12.10), a small parish church, is the paradigm of the **Flamboyant** Gothic style, the final phase in the development of Gothic architecture. The church was designed in 1434 by

Pierre Robin, although the facade was probably designed by Ambroise Havel. Its most striking feature is the porch, which is faceted into three planes and thus bows outward.

Called Flamboyant because of the flamelike curving stone tracery (*flamboyant* is the French for "flaming"), this style is characterized more by ornament than by structure. Delighting in delicacy and complexity, the masons covered the church in lace-like fantasy. Indeed, the ornament obscures the structure beneath it. Exuberant and interlacing, the steeply pitched openwork gables form a surface tangle that is animated by light and shadow as the sun moves.

GOTHIC ARCHITECTURE OUTSIDE FRANCE

Salisbury Cathedral.   The French Gothic spread outside France, each country modifying it to its own tastes. In England, the Early Gothic was relatively understated, but the Late Gothic reached extremes of eccentricity beyond anything found in France.

Early English Gothic is represented by Salisbury Cathedral (fig. 12.11). The choir, Lady Chapel, transepts, and nave were built between 1220 and 1258 by Nicholas of Ely and work was finally completed by 1270. The expansive structure, which measures 473 by 230 feet, lacks a rounded apse, ambulatory, and radiating chapels found in France, having instead, as is typical of English Gothic, a square east end. The nave has ten bays instead of the seven usually found in France.

The facade of Salisbury Cathedral, although begun in the same year as Amiens Cathedral, has very different proportions. Salisbury is low and wide, as if stretched horizontally, with no particular emphasis on height. The facade is wider, in fact, than the church and is treated as a screen, divided into horizontal bands with emphasis placed on the sculpture, not on the portals. English cathedrals are usually entered by a porch on the side of the nave or on the transept. Flying buttresses, so characteristic of French Gothic, were used only sparingly in England.

Westminster Abbey, London.   After English Gothic architects had thoroughly mastered initial structural problems, they refined and enriched their forms. Vaulting became progressively more adventurous. The ultimate example of English vaulting is in Westminster Abbey, London, culminating in the fantastic chapel of Henry VII (fig. 12.12), by the architects Robert and William Vertue. The tomb of Henry VII is behind a grill at the back of the altar. William Vertue replaced the axial chapel, originally built in 1220, with this one, built 1503–19. The most remarkable feature is the ceiling, an example of **fan vaulting,** thus called because the ribs radiate in a manner similar to those on a fan. But here the idea is carried to an extreme, to become pendant vaults hanging down in knobs, apparently denying both logic and gravity. Describing the chapel, one historian noted, "Its extraordinary, petrified foliage gives

FIGURE 12.11   Nicholas of Ely, Cathedral, Salisbury, west facade, 1220–70. Typical of early English Gothic, Salisbury is sprawling in plan, surrounded by a green lawn, and makes little use of flying buttresses—as opposed to French Gothic cathedrals, which are typically compact in plan, located in the city center, and rely on flying buttresses for structural support.

the impression of some fantastic, luminous grotto encrusted with stalactites." Elaborate designs cover the entire surface, an indication of the English inclination toward the architectural extreme, the eccentric, the intricate, and the opulent.

Florence Cathedral.   Italy was little affected by the Gothic style. Instead of the elaborate buttress systems and large windows popular in the north, Italian architects favored large wall surfaces with emphasis on the horizontal, as is evident in the landmarks of the city of Florence—its cathedral (*duomo*), bell tower (*campanile*), and baptistery (fig. 12.13).

The single most important construction work carried out during the Gothic era in Florence was that done on the cathedral. There had been an older church on the site, but in 1296, Arnolfo di Cambio began to build a new cathedral. Work started atypically at the west (entrance) end and proceeded quickly, until Arnolfo's death in 1302. Work

FIGURE 12.12   Robert and William Vertue, Chapel of Henry VII, Westminster Abbey, London, 1503–19, interior. The radiating ribs of fan vaulting are taken to an extreme here, becoming pendant vaults that actually hang down into the space of the chapel. The surface dissolves in this late and extreme example of English architectural eccentricity.

FIGURE 12.13   Arnolfo di Cambio, Francesco Talenti, Andrea Pisano, and others, Cathedral, Florence, begun 1296; redesigned 1357 and 1366, drum and dome 1420–36; campanile designed by Giotto, built ca. 1334–50. The dome of the cathedral could not be built as originally designed. It was only in the early part of the Renaissance that Filippo Brunelleschi would solve the engineering problems that had prevented its earlier construction (see Chapter 13).

gradually continued over a long period of time, with various architects involved. The cathedral is distinctive for its flat, colorful marble incrustation.

In 1334, Giotto was appointed architect-in-chief of the building of Florence Cathedral. Giotto, however, was a painter who knew little about architectural structure and was to design only the campanile. His original drawing of it survives, from which it is known that he intended the tower to be topped by a spire. When Giotto died in 1337,

only the first floor of the tower was finished. Work was continued by Andrea Pisano among others, and finished by Francesco Talenti in a somewhat different design around 1350–60. The interior of the tower consists of a series of rooms connected by staircases.

The campanile is referred to as "Giotto's Tower." Although the freestanding campanile is typically Italian, it is not an invention of the Italian Gothic; the campanile of Pisa, the famous "leaning tower," was built in the

FIGURE 12.14   Cathedral, Milan, east end, begun 1386. With its plethora of pinnacles and delicate decoration, Milan Cathedral is the most Gothic example—in the French sense—of cathedral architecture in Italy. Architects came from northern Europe to work on this northern Italian cathedral.

FIGURE 12.15   Column figures, flanking the Royal Portals, west facade, Cathedral of Notre-Dame, Chartres, ca. 1145–55, stone. Early Gothic figures perpetuate the distortion seen in Romanesque figures, but no longer have their agitated animation. Instead, these stiff elongated figures maintain the shape of the column to which they are attached, emphasizing their architectural function.

Romanesque era (see fig. 11.14). The richly ornamented Gothic campanile of Florence, with its multicolored marble incrustation and sculpture, served not only as the bell tower but also as a symbol of the sovereignty of the Florence commune.

Milan Cathedral.   The most Gothic of Italian cathedrals is Milan Cathedral (fig. 12.14), consecrated in 1386 by the ruler of Milan, Gian Galeazzo Visconti. Occupying an impressive site before an enormous piazza, the cathedral was built with the support of all classes of Milanese society. Different guilds performed different tasks, each one trying to outdo the others in their contributions. The exterior is covered in Rayonnant ornament, the result of architects from the north coming to Milan to give advice on the cathedral's construction. The building has been said to have an "overabundance" of ornament, all of which seems to compete for the visitor's attention.

SCULPTURE

Notre-Dame, Chartres.   The logical place to find the earliest Gothic sculpture would be Saint-Denis, but the work there has been badly damaged. Fortunately, the sculpture at Chartres Cathedral has fared better. The cathedral has

three triple portals, on the west facade and the north and south transepts, all richly adorned with sculpture. On the west are the Royal Portals (fig. 12.15), from the early Gothic era, dated ca. 1145–55. All the sculpture was once painted and gilded, but now only beige stone remains.

Each of the three entrances of the Royal Portal is flanked by statues. Symmetrical, ordered, and clear, Gothic compositions can typically be grasped at a glance, whereas the Romanesque preferred greater complexity. These **jamb** figures form what is known as a "precursor portal," of a type first seen at Saint-Denis and perhaps started by Abbot Suger. The visitor passes by Old Testament figures to enter the church. Those without crowns are the prophets, priests, and patriarchs of the Old Testament, Jesus's spiritual precursors. Those with crowns are the kings and queens of Judah—Jesus and Mary's physical ancestors. Medieval iconography is complex, with layered meanings, permitting multiple interpretations. Thus, in addition to being the royal ancestors of Mary and Jesus, the kings and queens of Judah are

FIGURE 12.16   *Annunciation* and *Visitation*, west facade, Cathedral of Notre-Dame, Reims, ca. 1230–45, stone. Descendants of column figures, these High Gothic sculptures dominate their architectural setting and have little to do with the columns behind. Characteristic of the increased realism and idealism of the Gothic era, the proportions and movements of these figures are now normal, and they even turn toward one another as if conversing.

also associated with the kings and queens of France, joining together religious and secular authority. Further, the church was an earthly version of the heavenly Jerusalem, and these portals were regarded as the "gates of heaven," through which Christians could enter a symbolic journey through biblical history to arrive at Jesus in the present.

Such jamb figures are also called "column figures," as the shape of the figure follows that of the column. Sculpture here is very closely tied to architecture. Unlike their energetic Romanesque forerunners, these figures are calm and serene, with a noble dignity. There is no twisting, turning, or bending; they do not interact with one another or with the viewer. The drapery, of many linear folds that fall to perfect zigzag hems, looks much like the fluting of a column, stressing the architectural role of these figures. Only slightly wider than their columns, the figures are not bodies with weight, but immaterial beings, seemingly hovering as their feet dangle.

Notre-Dame, Reims.   The High Gothic figures who act out the *Annunciation and Visitation* (fig. 12.16) on the west facade of Reims Cathedral, dated to the 1230s or early 1240s, are descendants of the column figures at Chartres. Yet at Reims, rather than standing unaware of the next figure's presence, they interact. Moreover, the columns from which they extend are less noticeable.

The *Annunciation* depicts the moment when the angel Gabriel tells Mary that she will give birth to Jesus. In view of the extraordinary news she has just received, Mary shows little response. She is severe, standing erect, her heavy drapery falling in broad sharp folds to completely obscure her legs. But Gabriel is different. He holds his drapery so it falls diagonally, his slender body forms an S curve and he moves gracefully, with a relaxed elegance. And he gives a Gothic grin! The new interest in emotion is a characteristic of the Gothic era.

The *Visitation* shows the meeting of Mary, now pregnant with Jesus, and her cousin Elizabeth, pregnant with John the Baptist, as they exchange their happy news. According to the story, Elizabeth is older, and this is shown by the sculptor. Both figures form an S curve—a revival of the *contrapposto* pose of antiquity—so that they seem to move in space. Many small drapery folds run on diagonals and horizontals, the creases following the outlines of the body.

Notre-Dame-de-Paris.   Medieval art includes many images of Mary and the infant Jesus. From the late eleventh century on, popular devotion to the Virgin Mary was great; many churches, cathedrals, religious orders, and brotherhoods were dedicated to Mary. She was portrayed as the ideal woman, the second Eve. As religion became more humanized, the Church intentionally appealed to the tenderer emotions. Additionally, Mary was seen as able to intercede on behalf of sinners on Judgment Day. People appealed to Mary for help as the Madonna of Mercy. Members of all levels of

FIGURE 12.17 *Notre-Dame-de-Paris*, French, in the crossing of the Cathedral of Notre-Dame, Paris, early fourteenth century, marble. Gracefully swaying in space, with Jesus on her hip, this image of Mary is very different from the stiff images of her created during the Romanesque era. Mary is now shown as an elegant French princess.

FIGURE 12.18 Gargoyle, west facade, Cathedral of Saint-Pierre, Poitiers, thirteenth century, stone. Gargoyles, which reached their peak of popularity during the Gothic era, are glorified gutters, typically carved to look like monstrous creatures, the water usually issuing from the mouth. When carving for the gargoyles' aerial realm, sculptors seem to have been exempt from the usual iconographic restraints of medieval art.

society participated in the Cult of the Virgin. Images of Mary were commissioned by those who could barely afford a humble work, and by those who could have a work made in gold by the finest metalworkers and set with glittering gems. By the fourteenth century, Mary was often shown being crowned by Jesus and was given comparable status.

A devotional image of Mary known as *Notre-Dame-de-Paris* (Our Lady of Paris) (fig. 12.17), a marble statue that dates from the early fourteenth century, stands in the crossing of the Cathedral of Notre-Dame in Paris. Graceful and elegant, Mary pulls a garment across her body, indi-cating the form beneath. Rather than a pattern of parallel pleats, the drapery now has broader sweeping folds. The silhouette is broken and animated. The infant Jesus plays with his mother's clothing and is portrayed with the bodily proportions of a baby, looking quite different from his portrayal as a little man in the Romanesque era.

Gargoyles. A multitude of gargoyles (fig. 12.18) glower from the roof lines of medieval buildings. The true **gargoyle,** a characteristic feature of Romanesque and especially Gothic buildings, is a waterspout, a functional necessity turned into a decorative fantasy.

Often located on churches and cathedrals, gargoyles are surprisingly irreverent. The rainwater may issue from a barrel held by a gargoyle in the form of a person, but more often the figure appears to vomit, and some even defecate. Animals, such as dogs or pigs, and more exotic ones like lions or monkeys, as well as human figures, serve as gargoyles, grotesque inventions of the fertile medieval imagination.

FIGURE 12.19 *Joshua Bidding the Sun to Stand Still*, from the *Psalter of St. Louis*, French, ca. 1260, manuscript illumination, $5 \times 3\frac{1}{2}''$ (13.6 × 8.7 cm), Bibliothèque Nationale, Paris. Manuscript illumination reached a high point during the Gothic era, with the finest manuscripts produced in Paris. The elegant, animated, modeled figures are not in scale with the building they enter, and contrast with the flat patterned background, which is based on contemporary architecture.

FIGURE 12.20 Limbourg brothers, *January*, from *Les Très Riches Heures* of the duke of Berry, French, 1413–16, manuscript illumination, $11\frac{1}{2} \times 8\frac{1}{4}''$ (29.2 × 21 cm), Musée Condé, Château of Chantilly. This manuscript includes twelve folios, one for each month of the year, that record how the upper and the lower classes lived, including pleasures and hardships.

PAINTING AND DECORATIVE ARTS

Manuscript Illumination. Manuscript illumination reached a peak in the Gothic period. Books were written in finer lettering than ever before, and the size of the books was reduced. Stained glass affected painting after the mid-thirteenth century, for reds and blues dominate, the figures are outlined in black, and the effect is ornamental and flat. A good example is *Joshua Bidding the Sun to Stand Still* (fig. 12.19), a folio in the *Psalter of St. Louis*, made ca. 1260 for King Louis IX of France. Gothic architecture, including rose windows and pinnacles, forms the background in this miniature. The two-dimensional buildings contrast with the long, thin, three-dimensional, modeled figures.

In the years just before and following 1400, a single style of painting was popular throughout Europe. Typical of this **International Style** are bright contrasting colors, decorative flowing lines, elongated figures, surface patterns, a crowded quality, and opulent elegance. A prime example is the manuscript known as *Les Très Riches Heures*

(*The Very Rich Hours*) of the duke of Berry, which dates from 1413–16. It is the work of the Limbourg brothers, Pol, Herman, and Jean, who were probably German or Flemish but worked in France for the duke of Berry, brother of the French king Charles V, and a patron of the arts. *Les Très Riches Heures* is a book of hours or private prayer book. It contains a series of illuminations, one for each calendar month. *June* includes a depiction of the Sainte-Chapelle in Paris, and *October* shows the Louvre. In both, women and men are shown working in the fields. A different level of society is portrayed in *January* (fig. 12.20), one of several scenes of aristocratic life. The duke of Berry is hosting a banquet, perhaps in celebration of the Twelfth Night, the day the magi, following the star of Bethlehem, arrived to present gifts to the infant Jesus. The duke sits in front of a large fireplace that creates a halo around him. Above the head of the man behind him—some think this is a portrait of Pol de Limbourg—are the words *aproche*, *aproche*, "come in, come in," signifying the duke's hospitality. The manuscript is an extraordinary record detailing the customs, costumes, and consumption that characterized medieval life.

Stained Glass. Gothic architecture offered new possibilities for glass. The solid walls of the Romanesque period were covered with murals simultaneously decorative and instructive. In the Gothic period the dual functions passed to stained-glass windows. To create colored glass, various metallic oxides are added while the glass is still in a molten state. A stained-glass window is made of many small pieces of colored glass held together by lead strips. From the exterior of the building there is little to see in a stained-glass window, for stained glass is interior decoration, intended to be seen illuminated from behind by sunlight.

The colored light that floods the interior of Gothic buildings through their stained-glass windows had special importance in the Middle Ages. Light was believed to have mystical qualities as an attribute of divinity. John the Evangelist saw Jesus as "the true light" and as "the light of the world who came into the darkness." St. Augustine called God "light" and distinguished between types of physical and spiritual light.

In addition to the twelfth-century rose window and three lancets on the west facade (fig. 12.21), Chartres Cathedral has over 150 early thirteenth-century stained-glass windows. Local merchants donated forty-two windows, which include over a hundred depictions of their occupations. These windows document medieval tools, materials, and working methods. The masons, for instance,

are depicted carving royal figures and show us just how Chartres's sculptures themselves were created.

Tapestry. Also characteristic of the Gothic era, tapestries were a form of insulation as well as decoration, for these woven wall hangings helped keep the cold air from seeping through the stone walls to the interior living space. Tapestries were luxury items, to be coveted and collected.

To produce a tapestry, the artist first makes a small-scale color drawing. This is then copied and enlarged on paper to the dimensions intended for the tapestry. This enlarged design is called the **cartoon**. Next, the weavers translate the cartoon into tapestry. A tapestry is woven on a loom, which is worked by several people sitting side by side. If a set of tapestries was to be produced, as was often the case, several looms were employed. The loom is strung with warp threads of tightly twisted wool. The number of warp threads per inch determines how fine the tapestry will be. The warp threads will be hidden by the weft threads of wool, silk, and even silver and gold. Tapestries are woven from the back; the finished image is an inversion of the artist's original design. When the design is woven, every change of color requires a change of thread; the weaving of a tapestry is a slow tedious process.

The *Unicorn Tapestries*, made in Brussels around 1500, tell the story of the hunt, capture, and murder of the unicorn. The first and the last tapestry (fig. 12.22) are in the *millefleurs* ("thousands of flowers") style, which is characterized by dense backgrounds of plants. These plants are meticulously observed and many can be identified, yet they represent an unreal realm, in which plants from different

Table 12–1	SYMBOLS USED IN MEDIEVAL CHRISTIAN ART: COLORS AND OBJECTS
Colors	
Black	symbol of mourning, death
Blue	symbol of heaven, truth, fidelity—"true blue"
Green	symbol of fertility, springtime growth
Red	symbol of passion, of both love and hate
White	symbol of purity, innocence
Yellow/gold	symbol of God, of the sun, of truth, yet also of deceit and cowardice
Objects	
Globe/orb	symbol of the world
Grapes	used to make wine, a symbol of Jesus's blood
Hourglass	symbol of the shortness of life
Keys	identifying attribute of St. Peter because Jesus is said to have given him the keys to heaven
Lamp	symbol of intelligence
Pomegranate	due to the fruit's many seeds, a symbol of the unity of the church; hope for resurrection
Scallop shell	worn by pilgrims to Santiago de Compostela, Spain
Ship	symbol of the Christian church

FIGURE 12.22   *The Unicorn in Captivity*, from the *Unicorn Tapestries*, Franco-Flemish, made in Brussels, ca. 1500, wool and silk tapestry, 12′ 1″ × 8′ 3″ (3.68 × 2.51 m). Gift of John D. Rockefeller, Jr., 1937. Cloisters Collection, Metropolitan Museum of Art, New York. During the Middle Ages, people believed in the existence of the unicorn, a fabulous animal said to have a single horn in the center of its forehead. When a tapestry is made, the picture is formed as the fabric is woven from colored threads. This type of tapestry is known as *millefleurs*—"thousands of flowers," shown scattered over the background.

FIGURE 12.21   *Life of Jesus*, west facade, Cathedral of Notre-Dame, Chartres, ca. 1150, stained glass, central lancet window. Stained glass reached its peak during the Gothic era, filling the huge windows permitted by the skeletal architectural system, creating constantly changing patterns of colored light flickering over the interiors. Narratives that had been told in paintings on walls and vaults were now told in stained-glass windows.

geographic areas and climates all bloom simultaneously, the weavers accomplishing what nature could not.

These tapestries may have been made as a wedding gift. According to religious interpretation, the unicorn represents Jesus at the Resurrection, in a heavenly garden. According to secular interpretation, the unicorn represents the lover, now wearing the *chaîne d'amour* (chain of love) around his neck and surrounded by a fence, perhaps tamed and domesticated by obtaining his lady's affection. Red juice falls on the unicorn's white fur from the pomegranates above. Like the unicorn, the pomegranate can be read in both religious and secular terms. Taken from a religious point of view, the many seeds of the pomegranate represent

Cross Currents

MUSLIM SPAIN

The Gothic cathedrals of northern Europe are contemporaneous with one of Spain's most beautiful Islamic buildings, the Alhambra in Granada (see fig. 6.8). Spain was the most multicultural country in Europe, a legacy of the arrival of the first Muslim conquerors in Spain in 711. Spain had been controlled since 589 by Visigoth kings, but by the turn of the eighth century most Spaniards were unwilling to serve in the Visigoth army, a duty required of all free men. Furthermore, until 650, Jews had controlled most of the commerce in Spain, but in 694, the Visigoth kings, who had become Christian, enslaved Jews who would not accept Christian baptism. Thus Spaniards greeted the Muslim army in 711 as liberators.

And liberators they were. Both the Jews and the Christians were tolerated as "protected" groups. They paid taxes to the Muslim lords, but they were free to practice their own religion and to engage in business as they pleased. Thus Spain became a multicultural country like no other, with Jews, Islamic Moors, and Christians working together in a spirit of *convivencia*, "coexistence." The population consisted of six groups: (1) *Mozárabes*, Christians who had adopted Muslim culture; (2) *Mudéjares*, Moors who were vassals of Christians; (3) *Muladíes*, Christians who had adopted the Islamic faith; (4) *Tornadizos*, Moors who had turned Christian; (5) *Enaciados*, those who sat on the fence between both Islam and Christianity, and who pretended to be one or the other as the occasion warranted; and (6) the large Jewish community.

The cultures invigorated each other. An older Christian man, writing in 854, lamented the acceptance of Muslim ways by the Christian youth, but his protest reveals much of the culture's vitality:

Our Christian young men, with their elegant airs and fluent speech, are showy in their dress and carriage, and are famed for the learning of the Gentiles; intoxicated with Arab eloquence, they greedily handle, eagerly devour and zealously discuss the books of the Mohammadans. . . . They can even make poems, every line ending with the same letter, which display high flights of beauty and more skill in handling meter than the Gentiles themselves possess.

The odes of the Islamic poets that the Christian youth were imitating began with an erotic prelude, then moved through a series of conventional themes such as descriptions of camels and horses, hunting scenes, and battles, and then culminated in the praise of a valiant chieftain. The odes soon developed into independent love songs and drinking songs, and it was out of this tradition that the troubadour poets sprang.

Moorish influence on medieval and Renaissance Europe extended beyond this. For instance, Arab scholars passed back much classical learning into Europe (see Chapter 6). Nonetheless, by 1492, the last traces of this happy cohabitation were erased when Ferdinand and Isabella of Aragon reclaimed Granada for Christianity and expelled the Moors and Jews.

---

the unity of the church and hope for the resurrection. In a secular light, the crownlike finial represents royalty, and the many seeds, fertility. The iconography of medieval art is often multi-layered in meaning.

SCHOLASTICISM

As the Middle Ages progressed, the attitude of the Roman Catholic Church toward secular learning and the wisdom of ancient writers began to change. More often than not, the church incorporated into its own teaching the learning it acquired from other cultures, including the literature and philosophy of ancient Greece and Rome, along with the Byzantine and Islamic religious and philosophical traditions. In this intellectual climate, forms of learning that derived from observation of the natural world rather than the written word of scripture were no longer at odds with a Christian perspective. Such natural knowledge was seen as a foundation for the more advanced states of religious contemplation.

The Growth of the University. The shift in the church's intellectual perspective was stimulated by the preservation and translation by Muslim scholars of Aristotle's writings, which passed back into Christian Europe in the twelfth and thirteenth centuries. This new perspective was complemented by the rise of the universities, which were evolving into major centers of learning. The University of Paris was the result of the expansion of the cathedral school at Notre-Dame. In turn, the University of Paris gave rise to institutions like Oxford and Cambridge in England, the former founded by teachers and students who had left Paris, the latter created by a group disenchanted with the Oxford curriculum. Debate about what should be studied led to the foundation of more and more universities. Soon universities in Spain, Portugal, and Germany joined the approximately eighty institutions of higher learning that existed by the end of the Middle Ages.

The university curriculum consisted of seven "liberal arts": the *trivium* (grammar, logic, and rhetoric) and the *quadrivium* (arithmetic, astronomy, geometry, and music). Soon degrees were awarded in both civil and canonical law, in medicine, and in theology.

Prior to the thirteenth century, medieval philosophy had centered on demonstrating the truths of religious faith through reason. But now a focus on the empirical obser-

Connections

Scholasticism and Gothic Architecture

During the Middle Ages, from about 1130 to 1270 the philosophy of Scholasticism reached its culmination in the grand *Summa Theologica* of St. Thomas Aquinas, and Gothic architecture reached its zenith in the cathedrals in and around Paris.

Scholastic philosophy and Gothic architecture both embody the aspiration toward a unity of truth. The grandness of both enterprises, their vastness and inclusivity manifest an all-encompassing belief centered on the divine creation of the world, the Incarnation and divinity of Jesus, the mystery of the trinity, and the role of faith in achieving salvation.

In Aquinas and in the cathedrals, the sacred doctrine was clarified through the use of human reason. Aquinas's *Summa* manifested reason in the careful ordering of its parts in their comprehensiveness and distinctness. Analogously, in their overall structure and design, the cathedrals revealed a rational order. The Gothic cathedral—in every element of its construction, from its portals to its apse, its sculpture to its architectural design, its stained glass windows to its gargoyles—collectively embodied the whole of Christian knowledge. The cathedral exemplified a visual structure analogous to the logical organization of Scholastic thought.

---

vation of the natural world began to emerge, divorced from the service of Christian belief. Tensions between faith and reason resulted.

Peter Abelard. Peter Abelard (1079–1144) was one of the first to wield the twin powers of logic and language in a philosophical approach called *dialectic*, a razor sharp form of logic. The most able student of the renowned William of Champeaux (Sham POE) of the Cathedral school of Paris, Abelard renounced Champeaux's philosophical approach as he challenged church authorities in his *Sic et Non (Yes and No)* by calling attention to apparently contradictory statements they made. Abelard suggested that such conflicting statements could be resolved by analyzing their language to see if the same words were being used in differing ways. Believing that most theological and philosophical confusion resulted from confusion about language, Abelard argued that words signify or refer only to individual things rather than to general concepts.

At stake for Abelard and for many medieval philosophers was a debate about "universals" that had its origin in the Greek philosophy of Aristotle and Plato. The issue debated was whether general concepts, or universals, actually exist. The realists believed that they do—and that, for example, goodness actually exists irrespective of its manifestation in particular good individuals. The nominalists, led by Abelard, denied the existence of such concepts as real entities, arguing that no such thing as goodness, redness, or catness actually exists, but only particular examples of good men, red objects, or of actual cats. Abelard did not deny that the concepts existed; he argued that they exist only as mental words signifying an abstract concept, which itself has none other than mental existence.

Although Abelard is known in philosophical circles as a gifted logician who exerted an influence on subsequent philosophical thought, including that of Thomas Aquinas, he is better known as the teacher and then lover of his brilliant student Heloise. Abelard was hired by Heloise's uncle as a guardian and tutor. He fell in love with Heloise and secretly married her. Her uncle hired a group of thugs to attach and punish Abelard by castrating him. He became a monk, and Heloise entered a convent. The letters they wrote during their years of solitude are among the richest reflections on love ever written.

The Synthesis of St. Thomas Aquinas. Using Aristotle's focus on the natural world to explain how God's wisdom is revealed, the Dominican friar ST. THOMAS AQUINAS [a-KWHY-ness] (1225–74) effected a synthesis of Aristotelian philosophy and Catholic religious thought. Aquinas, like Aristotle, began with empirical knowledge. Unlike Aristotle, however, Aquinas then moved from the physical, rational, and intelligible to the divine. Aquinas claimed that the order of nature, a beautiful harmonious structure in its own right, reflected the mind of God.

Aquinas saw no conflict between the demands of reason and the claims of faith. Nor did he see a conflict between the requirements of belief and the inducements of independent thought. For Aquinas, the exercise of intellectual freedom was granted by God according to the divine plan. This freedom not only makes a person human, but also presents the opportunity for every individual to choose or deny God by using the tools of reason.

Unlike his forebears Plato and Augustine, for whom physical reality and material circumstance were not as real or important as spiritual essences or qualities, Aquinas argued, much like Aristotle, that the soul and body are inextricable. The body needs the soul to live; the soul needs the body's experience. Each completes the other in a unity. According to Aquinas, spiritual knowledge and theological understanding require a grounding in the body's experience and observation of the world.

In this integration, Aquinas showed that philosophy and theology need not conflict, that they could coexist. Nevertheless, with the introduction of rational analysis into theological speculation, and the acceptance of empirical evidence as elements of philosophical truth, critics of Aquinas began to question the validity of his unification of faith and reason.

Duns Scotus and William of Ockham.

Two who refused to accept Aquinas's grand synthesis were Duns Scotus (1265–1308) and William of Ockham (1285–1349), both of whom were Franciscan friars. Scotus was a Scotsman who had studied at Oxford and Paris; Ockham was an Englishman, who had also studied at Oxford, and who wound up vilified and excommunicated for what were perceived as heretical views. Duns Scotus, known as "the subtle doctor," reacted against the theological views of both Aquinas and Augustine. In place of Augustine's divine illumination and Aquinas's integration of faith and reason, Scotus posited the central importance of will, emphasizing the freedom of individuals in their actions. Scotus believed that a person's will is guided on the one hand by what is good for the individual, and on the other by what is good for all, the two being modulated according to a sense of justice.

Scotus also rejected Aquinas's notion that the identity of an individual thing depends on its matter, while sharing its form with all other things of the same kind. For Scotus, the individual identity of a thing is part of its form, as distinguished between a thing's "common nature" (its *quiddity* or whatness) and its individualizing difference, a notion that inspired the Jesuit priest-poet Gerard Manley Hopkins who celebrated Scotus in his poem *Duns Scotus at Oxford*. Such philosophical hairsplitting among scholastic philosophers gave rise to the criticism that such subtleties had little, if anything, to do with faith and everyday living. Ironically, though, Scotus came to emphasize faith as superior to reason and to argue that philosophy and religion should be separated because they have different tasks.

William of Ockham went beyond Scotus by denying the existence of any correspondence between concrete individual beings or things. Like Peter Abelnd, he eschewed the notion of universals except as mental concepts. Similarities among individual human beings, or, say, particular dogs or trees, exist strictly in the mind as mental abstractions, as ideas rather than as real things. For Ockham, the issue of the universal existing beyond the physical was a matter for theology or for logic rather than a concern of philosophy. Thus he rejected Aquinas's notion that the human mind possessed a divine light that guided the intellect toward a proper understanding of reality, and he severed the link between faith and reason that Aquinas had so carefully established. With "Ockham's razor," his principle that the best explanation is the simplest and most direct, Ockham also broke away from the elaborate and subtle explanations of the scholastic philosophers or "schoolmen," whose ideas had dominated medieval philosophical thinking. In doing so, Ockham helped prepare the ground for the developments of Cartesian rationalism and Baconian empiricism.

Francis of Assisi.

The intellectualism of scholars was challenged by the life and teachings of Giovanni Bernadone (1181–1226), nicknamed "Francesco" by his father, who was born in the Italian town of Assisi. Captured as a youth in a battle against the neighboring town of Perugia and held in solitary confinement, Francis of Assisi (fig. 12.23), decided in prison that real freedom demanded complete poverty. On his release, he gave up all worldly goods and, identifying closely with Jesus, began to lead the life of a wandering preacher. St. Francis's identification with the passion was so strong that his body was said to bear the crucifixion marks, or *stigmata*, of Jesus. Best known for his love of birds and animals, Francis's lifestyle made him wholly dependent on the generosity of others. His many followers, who came to be known as Franciscans, were already a powerful monastic order of the church by the time of his death in 1226.

LITERATURE

Dante's Divine Comedy.

The most celebrated literary work of the Middle Ages is the epic poem *The Divine Comedy* by the Italian poet DANTE ALIGHIERI [DAHN-tay] (1265–1321) (fig. 12.24). Born in Florence in 1265, Dante was involved in politics as well as literature. When a rival party seized power in 1302, Dante was exiled from his home city, never to return. *The Divine Comedy* was completed in Ravenna shortly before Dante's death. In the poem, Dante makes numerous references to the politics of his day, especially to the rivalry between the Guelphs and the Ghibellines, two opposing Florentine political parties.

The Divine Comedy is divided into three parts: *Inferno* (Hell), *Purgatorio* (Purgatory), and *Paradiso* (Heaven). These are the three different places in medieval theology to which the soul can be sent after death. In the poem Dante ascends through Hell and Purgatory to Heaven, guided in the first stages by the pagan poet Virgil, who represents human reason, and at the end by his beloved, Beatrice, who represents divine revelation. Though indebted to the classical poetic tradition, *The Divine Comedy* is an explicitly Christian poem.

The poem contains one hundred cantos equally divided among the three sections, with the opening canto of the prologue prefacing the *Inferno*. Dante's attention to organization, especially structural symmetry, is apparent in every aspect, particularly in the use of *terza rima*, a succession of three-line stanzas that rhyme ABA, BCB, CDC, and so on, in which the unrhymed line ending in each

FIGURE 12.23 *St. Francis of Assisi*, thirteenth century, fresco, Sacro Speco, Subiaco, Italy. The earliest known portrait of St. Francis, this fresco may have been executed during his lifetime. St. Francis founded his own monastic order, the Franciscan order, in 1209, and it had already grown to be a powerful movement within the medieval church by the time of his death in 1226. One of the most important features of the order was its imposition of poverty on its members.

stanza is picked up in the following stanza, where it becomes the principal rhyme. Dante employs this pattern of interlocked rhyme through the entire work.

One of the most notable features of Dante's *Inferno* is the law of symbolic retribution, which suggests how a punishment should fit a sin. In depicting opportunists, for example, Dante positions them outside of Hell proper, in a kind of vestibule. Because they were unwilling to take firm positions in life, they are not completely in or out of Hell after death. And as they were swayed by winds of change and fashion, their eternal punishment is to follow a waving banner that continually changes direction.

Other punishments that seem particularly well suited to their corresponding sins include those who have committed carnal offenses, who in life were swayed by sexual passion and in death are swept up in a fiercely swirling wind. Murderers are punished by being immersed in a river of boiling blood, the degree of their immersion determined by the degree of their bloodlust in life. Gluttons are punished by being made to lie in the filthy slush of a garbage dump while the giant three-headed dog, Cerberus, tears at their flesh with claws and teeth. The souls of those who committed suicide are imprisoned in trees, whose limbs are torn and eaten by giant ugly birds, the fearful Harpies.

This law of symbolic retribution is complemented by another—that the most grievous and heinous of sinners are punished more severely than those who committed less odious crimes in life. Dante's poem is a synthesis of all the learning of his day—astronomy, history, natural science, philosophy—and this differentiation among sinners is indebted to the theology of Thomas Aquinas. Dante follows Aquinas, for example, in suggesting that sins of the flesh, such as lust, are not as serious as those of malice or fraud. Thus lust, gluttony, and anger are punished in the upper portion of Hell, where the punishments are less painful; sins of violence and fraud are punished in the deeper recesses of the Inferno.

Because deceit and treachery are, for Dante, the most pernicious of sins, these are punished at the very bottom of hell. Dante's scheme is so carefully worked out that he even divides the betrayers into categories—betrayers of their kin, of their country, of their guests and hosts, and, finally, those who betrayed their masters. This last and worst kind of sin Dante represents by the crimes of Brutus and Cassius, who betrayed Julius Caesar; by Judas Iscariot, the betrayer of Jesus; and, worst of all, by Satan, who betrayed God. These sinners are the furthest from God, deep in the cold dark center of Hell. Satan, a three-headed monster, lies encased in ice; in his three mouths he chews incessantly on the bodies of Brutus, Cassius, and Judas. Many of Dante's political enemies in Florence are discovered by the poet suffering the torments of Hell.

Just as Dante's *Inferno* reflects the type and degree of sinners' guilt, so his *Purgatorio* reflects a concern for justice.

Critical Thinking

SIN AND ERROR

In his Inferno, Dante punishes sinners according to the type of sin they committed during life and according to the degree of their guilt, making the punishment fit the crime. Although this idea reflects medieval religious thought, especially that of Thomas Aquinas, in some attenuated sense, perhaps, it remains alive today in the criminal justice system, in which "crimes" rather than "sins" are prosecuted and punished. To what extent do you think that punishment—of whatever type—is the appropriate response to "sin" and to "crime"? To what extent are contemporary attitudes toward punishment for crimes similar to medieval ideas regarding punishment for "sin"? How do they differ?

Dante's Purgatory is a mountain that is also an island. The mountain is arranged in tiers, with the worst sins punished at the bottom, since the sinners punished there are furthest from the Garden of Eden and from the heavens. In ascending order, the sins punished on the mountain of Purgatory are pride, envy, anger, sloth, avarice, gluttony, and lust—roughly the reverse of their positions in the *Inferno*.

Dante's *Paradiso* is based on the seven planets of medieval astronomy—the Moon, Mercury, Venus, the Sun, Mars, Jupiter, and Saturn. Just as the *Inferno* and the *Purgatorio* describe the subject's movement through hell and the purgatorial mountain, Dante's *Paradiso* also describes a journey, this one celestial, from planet to planet and beyond, to the Empyrean, the heavenly abode of God and his saints.

FIGURE 12.24   Domenico di Michelino, *Dante and His Poem*, 1465, fresco, Cathedral, Florence. Dante stands holding his poem. To his right is the Inferno, behind him Mount Purgatory, and to his left, representing Paradise, is Florence Cathedral itself, with its newly finished dome by Brunelleschi.

Table 12-2 THE STRUCTURE OF DANTE'S COMEDY

Hell

The Anteroom of the Neutrals

Circle 1: The Virtuous Pagans (Limbo)

Circle 2: The Lascivious

Circle 3: The Gluttonous

Circle 4: The Greedy and the Wasteful

Circle 5: The Wrathful

Circle 6: The Heretics

Circle 7: The Violent Against Others, Self, God/Nature/ and Art

Circle 8: The Fraudulent (subdivided into ten classes, each of which dwells in a separate ditch)

Circle 9: The Lake of the Treacherous against kindred, country, guests, lords and benefactors. Satan is imprisoned at the center of this frozen lake.

Purgatory

Ante-Purgatory: The Excommunicated/The Lazy/The Unabsolved/Negligent Rulers

The Terraces of the Mount of Purgatory

1. The Proud

2. The Envious

3. The Wrathful

4. The Slothful

5. The Avaricious

6. The Gluttonous

7. The Lascivious

The Earthly Paradise

Paradise

1. The Moon: The Faithful who were inconstant

2. Mercury: Service marred by ambition

3. Venus: Love marred by lust

4. The Sun: Wisdom; the theologians

5. Mars: Courage; the just warriors

6. Jupiter: Justice; the great rulers

7. Saturn: Temperance; the contemplatives and mystics

8. The Fixed Stars: The Church Triumphant

9. The Primum Mobile: The Order of Angels

10. The Empyrean Heavens: Angels, Saints, the Virgin, and the Holy Trinity

MUSIC

The Notre-Dame School. One of the more elegant features of Gregorian plainchant is the way its single melodic line molds itself to the words of the Latin text. The rounded shape of its vocal melody and the concentrated focus of its single melodic line suit the devotional quality of the liturgy. In the ninth and tenth centuries, however, chants began to be composed with multiple voice lines. Those with two voice lines an interval of a fourth, fifth, or octave apart were known as a parallel **organum,** the simplest kind of polyphonic, or multivoiced, musical practice. In parallel organum, the two melodic lines move together, note for note, parallel, and with identical rhythmic patterns. The lower, or bottom, line is the main melody, or **cantus firmus,** above which the second line is composed. By the eleventh century, the organum developed from the entrance of a second voice into music moving in parallel, oblique, and contrary motion. The harmonies were random and, although the two singers were on the same note when starting, intervals between the notes would sound to our modern ears dissonant and hollow. The original chant, which was sung as the bottom line of the organum, could not be varied and provided the polyphonic basis to the upper voice, which began to expand movement and range.

As polyphonic music became standard in church ritual, the organum grew to three, four, or as many as five separate voice parts. Moreover, the melodies above the cantus firmus began to change with each of the voice lines, thus imparting an independent quality absent in simpler forms of parallel-voiced polyphony.

The two most prominent chant composers of the twelfth century, LEONIN [LAY-oh-nan] (ca. 1135–ca. 1200) and PEROTIN [PEAR-oh-tan] (ca. 1170–ca. 1236), were associated with the cathedral of Notre-Dame in Paris. Though the church was not completed until the 1220s, during the 1180s an altar was consecrated and services were held. Léonin, who was active around 1175, favored a chant for two voices called *organum duplum,* in which the lower cantus firmus spread slowly over long held notes while a second voice, scored higher, moved more quickly and with many more notes through the text. This top line was called the *duplum* and the bottom cantus firmus line the **tenor,** from the Latin *tenere,* which means "to hold." (This "tenor" has nothing to do with the later development of "tenor," referring to one of the voice ranges, as in soprano, alto, tenor, and bass.)

Working a generation later, at the turn of the thirteenth century, Pérotin was Léonin's most notable successor in composing polyphonic chants. Pérotin wrote mostly three- or four-voiced chants called respectively *organum triplum* and *organum quadruplum.* Pérotin's more complex polyphony still used the cantus firmus tenor voice, but over it were placed two or three lively voice parts, which the tenor imitated from time to time. An additional distinguishing feature of the polyphonic chants of Léonin and Pérotin was their use of measured rhythm. Unlike the free unmeasured rhythms of plainchant, the polyphonic chants of Léonin and Pérotin had a clearly defined meter with precise time values for each note. Initially, the rhythmic notations for the music were restricted to only certain patterns of notes, with the beat subdivided into threes to acknowledge the Trinity. Later, however, these rules were loosened, and polyphonic chant became even freer in structure and more richly textured.

Probably the most viable result from the addition of rhythm by the Notre Dame school was that music fit melody to the rhythm of words. The result was more form in music, liturgy became easier to memorize and the rhythmic flow lent a steady pulse to the movement of clerics in procession. The extemporaneous lines of the upper voice, which was sometimes left to the improvisation of the performer, provided the basis for new musical forms—both sacred and secular.

It has been suggested that the metrical regularity of Léonin's and Pérotin's chants are especially suited to the Gothic cathedral. The repeating and answering patterns of polyphonic chant music have their architectural counterpart in the Gothic cathedral's repetitive patterns of arches, windows, columns, and buttresses, and its visual rhythms.

MEDIEVAL CALAMITIES

THE BLACK DEATH

Among the most devastating calamities to befall Europe during the Middle Ages was the plague, which caused the deaths of more than a third of Europe's seventy million people. There were many outbreaks of the plague, which was carried over sea and land trade routes to most parts of Europe. The carriers of the plague bacillus were fleas that had bitten infected rats, and which then bit other rats and humans. Three forms of the plague existed: bubonic, or infected lymph nodes; pneumonic, or infected lungs; and septicemic, or infected blood. These forms of the plague were so virulent that death would result within a few days and sometimes within hours. The symptoms of those afflicted were painful and horrifying. Abscesses, or *buboes*, appeared in the armpits or groin lymph nodes, filling them with pus and turning the body black—hence the term by which the disease is best known, the "Black Death."

References to the Black Death appear in the *Decameron*, a collection of linked short stories, by Giovanni Boccaccio, who lived through the plague. Boccaccio set his collection of stories in the hills around Florence, to which the stories' narrators flee to escape the ravages of the disease. In the introduction to the *Decameron*, Boccaccio noted both the physical and psychological consequences of the pestilence, as he describes the despair of the citizens of Florence.

The plague disrupted societies and economies throughout Europe and into Asia and North Africa, where the plague had spread by travelers and merchants plying land and sea trade routes. The disease caused massive labor shortages, which fed social unrest exacerbated by the conflicting interests of landlords and workers. In addition to the social and economic consequences there were religious effects. Boccaccio describes how many Florentines abandoned funeral rites and burial rituals, as they feared contagion from infected victims. People also wondered about a world that could include such a horrifying form of death for so many people and a God who allowed such a calamity to occur. Lack of understanding of the causes of the Black Death and absence of information about its transmission created fear and confusion. This, in turn, gave rise to a greater preoccupation with death, which resulted in various artistic renderings, such as the *danse macabre*, or the Dance of Death, portrayed by skeletons and by cadavers leading the living to their graves.

THE HUNDRED YEARS' WAR

To the horrors of the Black Death, which raged throughout the second half of the fourteenth century, were added the blood and gore of more than a hundred years of war between France and England. The Hundred Years' War, which lasted from 1337 to 1453, was fought completely on French soil. Although the proximate cause of the war was the English claim to the French throne upon the death of Charles IV in 1328, the major and longer contributing cause was the English claim to French lands, a claim dating from the time of the Norman Conquest, when English kings held land in France.

Although French soldiers greatly outnumbered the English invaders, the English won most of the battles, including those of Poitiers and Agincourt, which Shakespeare immortalized in his play *Henry V.* Although the battles themselves were deadly, with foot soldiers and archers slaughtering one another with improved weapons such as the English longbow, the time between battles also brought destruction, as mercenaries roamed the countryside pillaging and killing. And even though the English were consistently victorious in the battles of the Hundred Years' War, they suffered serious financial losses due to the cost of waging war abroad and maintaining garrisons there. The war depleted the French aristocracy and rendered obsolete the institution of knighthood and feudal vassalage.

TOWARD THE RENAISSANCE

We begin to detect the seeds of scientific inquiry, an increasing urge to know the world in its every detail. Life, more and more people believed, should be a quest for "truth." And the realization of visual and literary truth—the depiction of things in a manner "true to nature"—began to seem more urgent. Scholars increasingly found what seemed to be the "truth" in the writings of antiquity and artifacts of the classical past.

NATURALISM IN ART

The Pisanos. Sculpture in Italy differs from that of the rest of Gothic Europe. NICOLA PISANO [pea-SAH-noh] (ca. 1220/25 or before–1284) reintroduced a classical style, as demonstrated by the marble pulpit he made for the baptistery in Pisa, 1259–60. He may have studied the ancient Roman sarcophagi preserved in Pisa, for in the panel that portrays the *Nativity* (fig. 12.25) he has carved classical figures and faces. Included are three separate events: the Annunciation on the left; the Nativity itself in the middle; and the Adoration at the top right. Mary appears twice in the center of the composition, once with the angel Gabriel at the Annunciation, and directly below, lying prostrate at the Nativity. She is recognizably the same individual in each instance, although her expression changes. Deeply undercut, solid and massive, the forms bulge outward from the background. The crowding is typically Gothic, but the **naturalism** and classicism of the figures looks forward to the Renaissance.

Nicola's son Giovanni Pisano (ca. 1240/45–after 1314) also carved a *Nativity* for Pisa, this time for the cathedral (fig. 12.26). Executed between 1302 and 1310, the figures are slimmer than his father's, and the Mary seems more a young woman than the matronly figure in the earlier work. Her drapery is more flowing, her body almost substantial beneath its folds. The composition is not as crowded as Nicola's, the effect more energetic than serene. Each figure now has a logical amount of space, and the viewer seems to look down from above, thereby making the composition clearer. Giovanni includes more landscape and setting in his depiction than his father, creating a greater sense of depth, and in his sculpting uses even deeper undercutting for a greater play of light and shade.

Cimabue, Duccio, and Giotto. Cenni di Pepi (ca. 1250–ca. 1302), known as CIMABUE [chee-muh-BU-ee], painted the unusually large *Madonna and Child Enthroned* (fig. 12.27) for the altar of the church of Santa Trinita in Florence. Cimabue is a link between the older Byzantine Greek style and the new progressive style soon to develop in Florence. Looking back to the Byzantine style are the linear gold highlights on Mary's drapery, her abnormally elongated proportions, and the disparity in scale between enormous Mary and the notably smaller prophets below. Looking forward are the large size of the panel, the implication of space created by the overlapping angels, and the individualized faces and varied poses of the prophets. Cimabue is believed to have been the teacher of the highly innovative Florentine artist Giotto.

At the end of the thirteenth and beginning of the fourteenth century, two trends emerged in Italian painting, associated with the rival cities of Siena and Florence. Conservative Siena, represented by the artist Duccio, clung to the medieval and Byzantine traditions, favoring abstract patterns, gold backgrounds, and emphasis on line. Progressive Florence, however, represented by the artist Giotto, displayed a greater concern for depiction of the physical world and three-dimensional space and mass. This is the more naturalistic style that Europe would follow for the next several centuries.

DUCCIO [DOOCH-chee-OH] (ca. 1255–before 1319) is frequently mentioned in the Sienese archives, not only for his art but also for disturbing the peace, for his many wine bills, and for having debts. His most famous work, the *Maestà Altarpiece*, 1308–11, on the front of which is the *Madonna and Child Enthroned* (fig. 12.28) (the Italian word *maestà* refers to the "majesty" of the Madonna), was made for the high altar of the cathedral of Siena. It was painted entirely by Duccio (the contract has survived), although the usual practice at this time was for the artist to employ assistants. When the painting was finished a feast day was proclaimed in Siena.

In this rigidly symmetrical composition, Mary and the infant Jesus are enthroned, surrounded by tiers of saints and angels. Still in the medieval manner, much larger than any of the other figures, Mary is elongated, ethereal, and immaterial. Her drapery has a linear quality emphasized by the gold edging. Outline and silhouette play a major role; the effect of shading is minor. The faces are wistful and melancholic, and the angels look tenderly at Mary. The throne appears to splay outwards, is not rendered with scientific perspective, and does not suggest depth. Duccio represents the culmination of the old Byzantine style rather than the start of a new one.

GIOTTO [JOT-toh] (1267?–1336/7) was Duccio's contemporary. Giotto's naturalism is apparent if we compare his *Madonna and Child Enthroned* (fig. 12.29) to Duccio's. Although Duccio's Madonna seems like an icon, insubstantial and elongated, Giotto's Mary appears more realistic. Not only does she appear to sit in actual physical space, but it is as if real bones lie beneath her skin.

Giotto's most famous work is the extensive fresco cycle portraying the lives of Mary and Jesus in the Arena Chapel (Scrovegni Chapel) in Padua, painted 1305–06. In the scene of the *Lamentation over the Body of Jesus* (fig. 12.30), the composition is used to emphasize the sadness of the subject. Here, the focus of attention is low and off center. Figures bend down to the dead Jesus. The diagonal of the hill leads down to the heads of Mary and Jesus. The figures form a circle around Jesus, leaving a space for one more person—the viewer, who thereby joins in their grieving. Emphasis is on mass rather than line, figures are three-dimensional, solid, and bulky, and seen to occupy the actual space of the landscape. Most important of all, the mourners convey emotion, a tangible sense of grief and loss.

REALISM IN LITERATURE

Boccaccio's Decameron. If the visual arts were becoming more and more naturalistic by the end of the fourteenth century, literature achieved something of the same effect

FIGURE 12.25   Nicola Pisano, *Nativity*, panel on pulpit, Baptistery, Pisa, Italy, 1259–60, marble, $33\frac{1}{2} \times 44\frac{1}{2}''$ (85.1 × 113 cm). Important interests in antiquity and in reviving Italy's cultural past, which were to lead to the Renaissance, are already evident in the sculpture of Nicola Pisano. Ancient Roman sarcophagi reliefs provided inspiration for the classical type of figures.

FIGURE 12.26   Giovanni Pisano, *Nativity*, panel on pulpit, Cathedral, Pisa, Italy, 1302–10, marble, $34\frac{3}{8} \times 43''$ (87.2 × 109.2 cm). The greater naturalism of Nicola Pisano's son, Giovanni, when carving the same subject half a century later, is evidenced in his work by less crowding, a greater sense of space, and increased attention to the setting.

FIGURE 12.27   Cimabue, *Madonna and Child Enthroned*, ca. 1280, egg tempera and gold on wooden panel, 12′ 7 1/2″ × 7′ 4″ (3.9 × 2.2 cm), Galleria degli Uffizi, Florence. Cimabue's painting is transitional between the old Byzantine style and the progressive Florentine style of painting represented by Giotto.

FIGURE 12.28 Duccio, *Madonna and Child Enthroned*, main panel of the *Maestà Altarpiece*, 1308–11, egg tempera and gold on wooden panel, 7′ × 13′6¼″ (2.13 × 4.12 m), Museo dell'-Opera del Duomo, Siena. The paintings by Duccio were the final flowering of the medieval Byzantine tradition in Italy. The *Maestà*, which means "majesty" of the Madonna, portrays Mary as extremely elongated, enormous in size, flanked by angels and saints, as if she were a feudal queen holding court. Bright color and flowing outline are stressed rather than three-dimensionality of solid forms in space.

by forsaking Latin for the spoken language, the **vernacular,** of the day. This is especially true of the work of GIO-VANNI BOCCACCIO [bo-CAH-choh] (1313–75). His most famous prose work, the *Decameron*, has similarities with Dante's *Divine Comedy*, on which Boccaccio wrote a commentary. Furthermore, his interest in classical antiquity, his translations of ancient Greek texts, his Latin writings, and his search for lost Roman works make him an early Italian Renaissance figure.

Boccaccio spent much of his youth in Naples, where his father was a merchant and attorney. Trained in banking himself, Boccaccio nonetheless preferred literature, and spent most of his adult life in Florence pursuing a literary career. *The Decameron* is a collection of a hundred ***novelle,*** or short stories, told by ten Florentines, seven women and three men, who leave plague-infested Florence for the neighboring hill town of Fiesole. Written in the vernacular Tuscan, their tales center on the lives and fortunes of ordinary people, who are given a voice for the first time in Western literature. An eye for detail, convincing characters, wit, frankness, and worldly cynicism make Boccacio a lively read.

Chaucer's Canterbury Tales. As a well-educated medieval intellectual, the English poet GEOFFREY CHAUCER [CHAW-ser] (ca. 1342–1400) was, like Boccaccio, familiar with Latin literature, history, and philosophy. He read Ovid and Virgil in their original language, and was familiar with Greek myth, literature, and history through his knowledge of the Latin writers.

The most important influence on Chaucer's work, however, was not Latin but Italian. Chaucer's trip to Italy in 1372 immersed him in Italian literature, especially the works of Dante and Boccaccio. A number of Chaucer's *Canterbury Tales*, as well as the basic narrative structure, derive from Boccaccio's *Decameron*.

Unfinished at the time of his death in 1400, Chaucer had been working on *The Canterbury Tales*, a collection of stories told by a group of pilgrims traveling from London to Canterbury, for nearly fifteen years. The tales depict medieval figures from the highest to the lowest social classes.

Chaucer had originally planned to write 120 tales (or so the Host of the tavern where the pilgrims all first gather tells us in the General Prologue), two for each of his thirty

FIGURE 12.29   Giotto, *Madonna and Child Enthroned*, 1310, egg tempera and gold on wooden panel, $10'8'' \times 6'8\frac{1}{4}''$ (3.53 × 2.05 m), Galleria degli Uffizi, Florence. In contrast to Duccio's slender Mary, Giotto's is solid and appears to sit within the space implied by her throne.

FIGURE 12.30   Giotto, *Lamentation over the Body of Jesus*, Arena (Scrovegni) Chapel, Padua, 1305–06, fresco, 6′6¾″ × 6′7⅞″ (2.00 × 1.85 m). The profound grief of this subject is magnified by the way in which it is depicted by Giotto. The center of attention, usually in the physical center of the composition, is instead low on the left, emotionally "down," and the barren background leads the viewer's eyes down to the heads of Jesus and his mother Mary.

pilgrims to tell on the pilgrimage to Canterbury, and two on the return trip. However, Chaucer only completed twenty-two tales and composed fragments of two others. He also composed a General Prologue, which provides a pretext for the tales—the pilgrimage to the shrine of St. Thomas à Becket at Canterbury introduces the characters, who later narrate their own tales. Chaucer further reveals the characterizations of these narrators through the tales they tell and the manner in which they tell them.

Chaucer's attitude toward the characters in the General Prologue varies. Some, such as the Clerk and the Knight, he depicts as models, whose behavior is to be emulated; others, such as the Monk and the Pardoner, he portrays negatively, with their warts (both literal and figurative) showing. The ironic and satiric portraits of the other pilgrims are constructed through the voice of Chaucer's narrator. Yet this narrator himself is slightly naïve. The "naïve" narrator sometimes fails to discriminate between good and evil manifestations of human behavior or to distinguish be-

tween the supposed ideals of certain characters and the less admirable qualities they embody.

Chaucer employs irony as an instrument of satire. His wit and observation—evident throughout the work, though perhaps most clearly in the General Prologue— reveal a zest for life from its lowest and bawdiest to its most elegant and spiritual manifestations.

Christine de Pizan.   One of the outstanding writers of the later Middle Ages, CHRISTINE DE PIZAN [PEA-zan] (1364–ca. 1431) was a scholar and court adviser, as well as a poet and writer of prose pieces (fig. 12.31). Born in Venice, Christine de Pizan moved with her father to France, where he served as court astrologer to the French monarch Charles V. There she learned to write French and Italian as well as to read Latin, an unusual accomplishment for a woman at the time.

At the age of fifteen, she married a court notary, Eugène of Castal, who died four years later in an epidemic.

FIGURE 12.31   *Christine de Pizan Presenting Her Poems to Isabel of Bavaria,* manuscript illumination, British Library, London. The illumination shows the world of women that Christine celebrates in her writing.

As a widow with three young children, she began writing to support her family. Before long she was a recognized literary luminary, an accomplished poet and the officially sanctioned biographer of Charles V. In her works, she consistently argued for the recognition of women's status and abilities.

Among her many works are a poem about Joan of Arc; a set of letters challenging the depiction of women in the influential medieval poem *The Romance of the Rose;* a book of moral proverbs; a dream vision; a collection of a hundred brief narratives accompanied by their own commentary; a manual of instruction for knights; an admonitory essay on the art of prudence, *The Book of Feats of Arms and Chivalry;* and her best known work, *The Book of the City of Ladies.* A universal history of women, *The Book of the City of Ladies* includes discussion of pagan as well as Christian women, of those long deceased as well as those of her own time, and of fictional characters as well as actual people. Throughout the book, she attempts to alter the reader's perceptions of women. It is this desire to represent women from a woman's point of view that makes the writing of Christine de Pizan unique. Her book is a refutation of misogynistic images of women constructed by male writers of the past. In particular, she rebuts the images of women portrayed in Giovanni Boccaccio's *De mulieribus*

claris (Concerning Famous Women). For example, in response to the charge that women are greedy, she states that what appears as greed in women is a prudent and sensible response to male profligacy. Because men squander, women have to protect themselves against such destructive behavior. She counterattacks by arguing that women are fundamentally generous.

Even as she argued for opportunities for women, Christine de Pizan echoed the ideals of Christian life as espoused in church teaching. She supported the goals of Christian marriage, in which a commitment between spouses enables them to advance in grace and spirituality while fulfilling their roles as husband and wife. To a large extent, she appears to have been an idealist, one who aspired to achieve the highest values articulated in her religious tradition while ridding it of its entrenched bias against women.

While urging women to accept their place in the hierarchy of the time, she also encouraged them to fulfill their potential—intellectually, socially, and spiritually—by developing nobility of soul, whatever their particular social status or individual circumstances. Nobility, for Christine de Pizan, was a matter of mind, heart, and spirit, rather than of birthright. She believed that through patient and persistent striving, women of her time could become embodiments of the highest ideals of heart and mind.

Cultural Impact

Fundamental structural and aesthetic changes occurred in architecture during the Gothic period. The supporting role of the thick walls and the small windows of Romanesque architecture were superceded by exterior flying buttresses and vast stained-glass windows in Gothic architecture (Chartres Cathedral, figs. 12.5, 12.6, 12.21).

In modern times, rather than flying buttresses of hand-hewn stone, architecture employs modern materials and techniques, such as skeletal steel supports, reinforced concrete, and cantilevered construction. Rather than windows of meticulously assembled stained glass, modern windows are mass produced in great volume in factories. Slender skeletal constructions with glass walls are a characteristic of modern urban life, as seen in Mies van der Rohe's Lake Shore Drive Apartment Houses, Chicago, 1950–52 (fig. 23.8), and the sweeping space and colored glass of Gothic churches reappear occasionally in modern variation, such as Corbusier's Notre-Dame-du-Haut, Ronchamp, France, 1950–55 (fig. 23.9).

The interest in human emotions and everyday life increased in the art of the Gothic period, as evidenced in numerous images of Mary and the infant Jesus. *Notre-Dame-de-Paris*, sculpted in the early fourteenth century (fig. 12.17), portrays a fashionable young French mother and her endearing child. In the same years, the painter Giotto portrayed Mary as a real Italian mother holding her son.

In more recent years, images of maternal love and devotion may be created for reasons connected with political/social problems rather than with religion. Thus Käthe Kollwitz's *The Mothers*, a lithograph of 1919, refers to the plight of widowed German mothers in the aftermath of World War I, and Dorothea Lange's photograph of 1936 of a widowed *Migrant Mother* with several of her children comments on the Great Depression in the United States.

SECULAR SONG

Guillaume de Machaut.   In the fourteenth century, medieval music underwent significant changes, including the rise of secular music along with church music. Drinking songs and music that drew on the everyday began to be composed and performed as often as devotional music inspired by religious faith. In addition, a new system of musical notation had developed by the fourteenth century so composers were now able to spell out the rhythmic values as well as the melodic pitches of notes. Other changes in musical style, such as the use of syncopation (which emphasizes notes off the regular beat), became so significant that theorists referred to the new music as ***ars nova*** (new art) to distinguish it from the *ars antiqua* (ancient or old art) of previous centuries.

One composer who wrote both sacred and secular music in the *ars nova* style was GUILLAUME DE MACHAUT [ghee-OHM duh mash-OH] (1300–77), the foremost French composer of the time and one of France's leading poets. Like Giotto in painting, Machaut helped usher in the Renaissance by breaking away from the older medieval style. Machaut wrote the first complete polyphonic setting of a mass, called *La Messe de Nostre Dame* (Our Lady's Mass). Until this time, the mass was a collection of Gregorian chants by anonymous composers; Machaut's was the first by an identified composer. As the liturgy's most important musical form, the mass, which reenacts the last supper of Christ, became a foundation for many other multimovement musical forms that followed.

Machaut spent most of his life at court. Born in the French province of Champagne, he traveled throughout Europe and spent his later years in Reims. During his many travels, he presented carefully written and decorated copies of his music and poems to court patrons and foreign nobility. The great care he took in making these copies has ensured their survival.

English Song.   The English song "Sumer Is Icumen In" is unlike anything else that has survived from the thirteenth century in providing a foretaste of musical tendencies and techniques that were to emerge over a century and a half later, in the works of Renaissance madrigalists such as Thomas Weelkes and Thomas Morley (see Chapter 1,4). The words of the text were composed in English, not Latin, and they celebrate nature rather than religion, the physical life of earth rather than the spiritual joys of heaven. The composer set the words to a lively tune, which is sung by all four voice parts in a canon, or round. Each voice enters before the others have finished so all four sing simultaneously, although they are at different places in the music at any given time.

KEY TERMS

Gothic	Flamboyant Gothic	International Style	naturalism
cathedral	Rayonnant Gothic	cartoon	vernacular
flying buttress	fan vaulting	organum	*novelle*
rose window	jamb	*cantus firmus*	*ars nova*
High Gothic	gargoyle	tenor	

www. WEBSITES FOR FURTHER STUDY

http://www.elore.com/Gothic/Glossary/components.htm
(A good site on Gothic architecture, with a glossary and links.)

http://web.kyoto-inet.or.jp/org/orion/eng/hst/gothic.html
(Visit many of the greatest Gothic cathedrals on this site.)

http://www.metmuseum.org/works_of_art/collection.asp
(This site discusses the seven individual tapestries known as the "Unicorn Tapestries," some of the most beautiful and complex works of the late Middle Ages.)

http://w3.rz-berlin.mpg.de/cmp/machaut.html
(This site has a brief but thorough discussion on Machaut, one of the most important Gothic composers.)

http://worldart.sjsu.edu/prt31*1$596
(This site covers select sculptural works of the Gothic era found on and in French cathedrals.)

READINGS

ST. FRANCIS OF ASSISI

The Canticle of the Creatures

Francis of Assisi's poem "The Canticle of the Creatures" is among the earliest poems written in the Italian vernacular. It conveys St. Francis's prayerful thanksgiving for the wonders God has provided. His poem reflects the ancient Hebrew tradition of poetic prayer, a psalm of praise that derives from the biblical book of Psalms. Francis's canticle also reflects the humility for which he is famous.

Most High, All-powerful, All-Good, Lord!
All praise is Yours,
all glory, all honor
And all blessing.

To You alone, Most High, do they belong.
No mortal lips are worthy
To pronounce your name.

All praise be Yours, my Lord, through all that You have
   made,
And first my lord Brother Sun,
Who brings the day; and light you give to us through him.
How beautiful is he, how radiant in all his splendor!
Of You, Most High, he bears the likeness.

All praise be Yours, my Lord, through Sister Moon and
   Stars;
In the heavens You have made them, bright
And precious and fair.

All praise be Yours, my Lord, through Brothers Wind
   and Air,
And fair and stormy, all the weather's moods,
By which You cherish all that You have made.

All praise be Yours, my Lord, through Sister Water,
So useful, lowly,
precious, and pure.

All praise be Yours, my Lord, through Brother Fire,
Through whom You brighten up the night
How beautiful he is, how gay!
Full of power and strength.

All praise be Yours, my Lord, through Sister Earth, our
   mother,
Who feeds us in her sovereignty and produces
Various fruits and colored flowers and herbs.

All praise be Yours, my Lord,
through those who grant pardon
For love and You;
through those who endure
Sickness and trial.

Happy those who endure in peace,
By You, Most High,
they will be crowned.

All praise be Yours, my Lord,
through Sister Death-of-the-Body,
From whose embrace

no mortal can escape.
Woe to those who die
in mortal sin,
Happy those She finds
doing Your holy will!
The second death can do
no harm to them.

Praise and bless my Lord,
and give Him thanks,
And serve Him with great humility.

ST. THOMAS AQUINAS

from the *Summa Theologica*

In the Summa Theologica, *Aquinas's summation of what can be known about God and human beings, the scholastic philosopher presents his arguments in the form of assertions, objections, and replies to those objections. In the following passage Aquinas analyzes the question of whether people can believe the things they know and know the things they believe, whether, that is, faith and science are about the same things.*

QUESTION I—OF FAITH

Fifth Article

Whether Those Things That Are of Faith Can Be an Object of Science?

We proceed thus to the Fifth Article:—Objection 1.   It would seem that those things that are of faith can be an object of science. For where science is lacking there is ignorance, since ignorance is the opposite of science. Now we are not in ignorance of those things we have to believe, since ignorance of such things savors of unbelief, according to 1 Tim. i. 13: *I did it ignorantly in unbelief.* Therefore things that are of faith can be an object of science.

Obj. 2.   Further, science is acquired by reasons. Now sacred writers employ reasons to inculcate things that are of faith. Therefore such things can be an object of science.

Obj. 3.   Further, things which are demonstrated are an object of science, since a *demonstration is a syllogism that produces science.* Now certain matters of faith have been demonstrated by the philosophers, such as the Existence and Unity of God, and so forth. Therefore things that are of faith can be an object of science.

Obj. 4.   Further, opinion is further from science than faith is, since faith is said to stand between opinion and science. Now opinion and science can, in a way, be about the same object, as stated in *Poster.* i. Therefore faith and science can be about the same object also.

On the contrary, Gregory says (*Hom.* xxvi *in Ev.*) that *when a thing is manifest, it is the object, not of faith, but of perception.* Therefore things that are of faith are not the object of perception, whereas what is an object of science is the object of perception. Therefore there can be no faith about things which are an object of science.

I answer that, All science is derived from self-evident and therefore *seen* principles; wherefore all objects of science must needs be, in a fashion, seen.

Now as stated above (A. 4) it is impossible that one and the same thing should be believed and seen by the same person. Hence it is equally impossible for one and the same thing to be an object of science and of belief for the same person. It may happen, however, that a thing which is an object of vision or science for one, is believed by another: since we hope to see some day what we now believe about the Trinity, according to 1 Cor.xiii. 12: *We see now through a glass in a dark manner; but then face to face:* which vision the angels possess already; so that what we believe, they see. In like manner it may happen that what is an object of vision or scientific knowledge for one man, even in the state of a wayfarer, is, for another man, an object of faith, because he does not know it by demonstration.

Nevertheless that which is proposed to be believed equally by all, is equally unknown by all as an object of science; such are the things which are of faith simply. Consequently faith and science are not about the same things.

Reply Obj. 1.   Unbelievers are in ignorance of things that are of faith, for neither do they see or know them in themselves, nor do they know them to be credible. The faithful, on the other hand, know them, not as by demonstration, but by the light of faith which makes them see that they ought to believe them, as stated above (A. 4, *ad* 2, 3).

Reply Obj. 2.   The reasons employed by holy men to prove things that are of faith, are not demonstrations; they are either persuasive arguments showing that what is proposed to our faith is not impossible, or else they are proofs drawn from the principles of faith, i.e. from the authority of Holy Writ, as Dionysius declares (*Div. Nom.* ii). Whatever is based on these principles is as well proved in the eyes of the faithful, as a conclusion drawn from self-evident principles is in the eyes of all. Hence again, theology is a science, as we stated at the outset of this work (P. I, Q. 1, A. 2).

Reply Obj. 3.   Things which can be proved by demonstration are reckoned among the articles of faith, not because they are believed simply by all, but because they are a necessary presupposition to matters of faith, so that those who do not know them by demonstration must know them first of all by faith.

Reply Obj. 4.   As the Philosopher says (*loc. cit.*), *science and opinion about the same object can certainly be in different men,* as we have stated above about science and faith; yet it is possible for one and the same man to have science and faith about the same thing relatively, i.e. in relation to the object, but not in the same respect. For it is possible for the same person, about one and the same object, to know one thing and to think another: and, in like manner, one may know by demonstration the unity of the Godhead, and, by faith, the Trinity. On the other hand, in one and the same man, about the same object, and in the same respect, science is incompatible with either opinion or faith, yet for different reasons. Because science is incompatible with opinion about the same object simply, for the reason that science demands that its object should be deemed impossible to be otherwise, whereas it is essential to opinion, that its object should be deemed possible to be otherwise. Yet that which is the object of faith, on account of the certainty of faith, is also deemed impossible to be otherwise: and the reason why science and faith cannot be about the same object and in the same respect is because the object of science is something seen, whereas the object of faith is the unseen, as stated above.

from *The Divine Comedy*

Throughout The Divine Comedy *Dante creates dramatic scenes, provides numerous comments on the political history of medieval Florence, and describes hundreds of characters—from history, mythology, and religion, as well as from Dante's own world. Saints and sinners, philosophers and heroes, popes and clerics, along with people from all walks of life, make an appearance. In the* Inferno, *Dante selects individual sinners for close-up portrayal. Among the most memorable are the illicit lovers Paolo and Francesca, who are swirled around together in a maelstrom, which represents their passion. Dante the pilgrim pauses to hear Francesca tell their sad story, as Dante the poet characterizes her as she tells it. The introductions to each canto summarize the action described therein, while the notes gloss historical, biblical, and literary allusions. These aids to reading* The Divine Comedy *make the reader's challenge easier and the poem's rewards even greater.*

INFERNO

Canto I

The Dark Wood of Error

Midway in his allotted threescore years and ten, Dante comes to himself with a start and realizes that he has strayed from the True Way into the Dark Wood of Error (Worldliness). As soon as he has realized his loss, Dante lifts his eyes and sees the first light of the sunrise (the Sun is the Symbol of Divine Illumination) lighting the shoulders of a little hill (The Mount of Joy). It is the Easter Season, the time of resurrection, and the sun is in its equinoctial rebirth. This juxtaposition of joyous symbols fills Dante with hope and he sets out at once to climb directly up the Mount of Joy, but almost immediately his way is blocked by the Three Beasts of Worldliness: The Leopard of Malice and Fraud, The Lion of Violence and Ambition, and the She-Wolf of Incontinence. These beasts, and especially the She-Wolf, drive him back despairing into the darkness of error. But just as all seems lost, a figure appears to him. It is the shade of Virgil, Dante's symbol of Human Reason.

Virgil explains that he has been sent to lead Dante from error. There can, however, be no direct ascent past the beasts: The man who would escape them must go a longer and harder way. First he must descend through Hell (The Recognition of Sin), then he must ascend through Purgatory (The Renunciation of Sin), and only then may he reach the pinnacle of joy and come to the Light of God. Virgil offers to guide Dante, but only as far as Human Reason can go. Another guide (Beatrice, symbol of Divine Love) must take over for the final ascent, for Human Reason is self-limited. Dante submits himself joyously to Virgil's guidance and they move off.

Midway in our life's journey,° I went astray
    from the straight road and woke to find myself
    alone in a dark wood. How shall I say
what wood that was! I never saw so drear,
    so rank, so arduous a wilderness!   5
    Its very memory gives a shape to fear.
Death could scarce be more bitter than that place!
    But since it came to good, I will recount
    all that I found revealed there by God's grace.

---

[1] *Midway . . . journey:* The biblical life span is three-score years and ten (seventy years). The action opens in Dante's thirty-fifth year, i.e., 1300 C.E.

How I came to it I cannot rightly say,   10
    so drugged and loose with sleep had I become
    when I first wandered there from the True Way.
But at the far end of that valley of evil
    whose maze had sapped my very heart with fear,
    I found myself before a little hill   15
and lifted up my eyes. Its shoulders glowed
    already with the sweet rays of that planet°
    whose virtue leads men straight on every road,
and the shining strengthened me against the fright
    whose agony had wracked the lake of my heart   20
    through all the errors of that piteous night.
Just as a swimmer, who with his last breath
    flounders ashore from perilous seas, might turn
    to memorize the wide water of his death—
so did I turn, my soul still fugitive   25
    from death's surviving image, to stare down
    that pass that none had ever left alive.
And there I lay to rest from my heart's race
    till calm and breath returned to me. Then rose
    and pushed up that dead slope at such a pace   30
each footfall rose above the last.° And lo!
    almost at the beginning of the rise
    I faced a spotted Leopard, all tremor and flow
and gaudy pelt. And it would not pass, but stood
    so blocking my every turn that time and again   35
    I was on the verge of turning back to the wood.
This fell at the first widening of the dawn
    as the sun was climbing Aries with those stars
    that rode with him to light the new creation.°
Thus the holy hour and the sweet season   40
    of commemoration did much to arm my fear
    of that bright murderous beast with their good omen.
Yet not so much but what I shook with dread
    at sight of a great Lion that broke upon me
    raging with hunger, its enormous head   45
held high as if to strike a mortal terror
    into the very air. And down his track,
    a She-Wolf drove upon me, a starved horror
ravening and wasted beyond belief.°

She seemed a rack for avarice, gaunt and craving.   50
    Oh many the souls she has brought to endless grief!
She brought such heaviness upon my spirit
    at sight of her savagery and desperation,
    I died from every hope of that high summit.
And like a miser—eager in acquisition   55
    but desperate in self-reproach when Fortune's wheel
    turns to the hour of his loss—all tears and attrition
I wavered back; and still the beast pursued,
    forcing herself against me bit by bit
    till I slid back into the sunless wood.   60
And as I fell to my soul's ruin, a presence
    gathered before me on the discoloured air,
    the figure of one who seemed hoarse from long silence.
At sight of him in that friendless waste I cried:
    "Have pity on me, whatever thing you are,   65
    whether shade or living man." And it replied:
"Not man, though man I once was, and my blood
    was Lombard, both my parents Mantuan.
    I was born, though late, *sub Julio,*° and bred
in Rome under Augustus in the noon   70
    of the false and lying gods. I was a poet
    and sang of old Anchises' noble son°
who came to Rome after the burning of Troy.
    But you—why do *you* return to these distresses
    instead of climbing that shining Mount of Joy   75
which is the seat and first cause of man's bliss?"
    "And are you then that Virgil and that fountain
    of purest speech?" My voice grew tremulous:
"Glory and light of poets! now may that zeal
    and love's apprenticeship that I poured out   80
    on your heroic verses serve me well!
For you are my true master and first author,
    the sole maker from whom I drew the breath
    of that sweet style whose measures have brought me
        honor.
See there, immortal sage, the beast I flee.   85
    For my soul's salvation, I beg you, guard me from her,
    for she has struck a mortal tremor through me."
And he replied, seeing my soul in tears:
    "He must go by another way who would escape
    this wilderness, for that mad beast that fleers   90
before you there, suffers no man to pass.
    She tracks down all, kills all, and knows no glut,
    but, feeding, she grows hungrier than she was.
She mates with any beast, and will mate with more
    before the Greyhound° comes to hunt her down.   95
    He will not feed on lands nor loot, but honor
and love and wisdom will make straight his way.
    He will rise between Feltro and Feltro, and in him
    shall be the resurrection and new day

---

[17] *planet:* The sun. Ptolemaic astronomers considered it a planet. It is also symbolic of God as He who lights the way.

[31] *each . . . last:* The literal rendering would be: "So that the fixed foot was ever the lower." "Fixed" has often been translated "right" and an ingenious reasoning can support that reading, but a simpler explanation offers itself and seems more competent: Dante is saying that he climbed with such zeal and haste that every footfall carried him above the last despite the steepness of the climb. At a slow pace, on the other hand, the rear foot might be brought up only as far as the forward foot.

[39] *creation:* The medieval tradition had it that the sun was in Aries at the time of the creation. The significance of the astronomical and religious conjunction is an important part of Dante's intended allegory. It is just before dawn of Good Friday 1300 C.E. when he awakens in the Dark Wood. Thus his new life begins under Aries, the sign of creation, at dawn (rebirth) and in the Easter season (resurrection). Moreover the moon is full and the sun is in the equinox, conditions that did not fall together on any Friday of 1300. Dante is obviously constructing poetically the perfect Easter as a symbol of his new awakening.

[33–49] *Leopard . . . him . . . She-wolf:* These three beasts undoubtedly are taken from Jeremiah v, 6. Many additional and incidental interpretations have been advanced for them but the central interpretation must remain as noted. They foreshadow the three divisions of Hell (incontinence, violence, and fraud) which Virgil explains at length in Canto XI, 16–111.

[69] *sub Julio:* In the reign of Julius Caesar.

[72] *Anchises' noble son:* Aeneas.

[95] *The Greyhound . . . Feltro and Feltro:* Almost certainly refers to Can Grande della Scala (1290–1329), great Italian leader born to Verona, which lies between the towns of Feltre and Montefeltro.

of that sad Italy for which Nisus died,   *100*
　　and Turnus, and Euryalus, and the maid Camilla.°
　　He shall hunt her through every nation of sick pride
till she is driven back forever to Hell
　　whence Envy first released her on the world.
　　Therefore, for your own good, I think it well   *105*
you follow me and I will be your guide
　　and lead you forth through an eternal place.
　　There you shall see the ancient spirits tried
in endless pain, and hear their lamentation
　　as each bemoans the second death° of souls.   *110*
　　Next you shall see upon a burning mountain
souls in fire and yet content in fire,
　　knowing that whensoever it may be
　　they yet will mount into the blessed choir.
To which, if it is still your wish to climb,   *115*
　　a worthier spirit shall be sent to guide you.
　　With her shall I leave you, for the King of Time,
who reigns on high, forbids me to come there
　　since, living, I rebelled against his law.°
　　He rules the waters and the land and air   *120*
and there holds court, his city and his throne.
　　Oh blessed are they he chooses!" And I to him:
　　"Poet, by that God to you unknown,
lead me this way. Beyond this present ill
　　and worse to dread, lead me to Peter's gate°   *125*
　　and be my guide through the sad halls of Hell."
And he then: "Follow." And he moved ahead
in silence, and I followed where he led.

Canto III

The Vestibule of Hell   The Opportunists

*The Poets pass the Gate of Hell and are immediately assailed by
cries of anguish. Dante sees the first of the souls in torment. They
are The Opportunists, those souls who in life were neither for good
nor evil but only for themselves. Mixed with them are those outcasts
who took no sides in the Rebellion of the Angels. They are neither
in Hell nor out of it. Eternally unclassified, they race round and*

*round pursuing a wavering banner that runs forever before them
through the dirty air; and as they run they are pursued by swarms
of wasps and hornets, who sting them and produce a constant flow
of blood and putrid matter which trickles down the bodies of the sinners and is feasted upon by loathsome worms and maggots who coat
the ground.*

*The law of Dante's Hell is the law of symbolic retribution. As
they sinned so are they punished. They took no sides, therefore they
are given no place. As they pursued the ever-shifting illusion of their
own advantage, changing their courses with every changing wind,
so they pursue eternally an elusive, ever-shifting banner. As their
sin was a darkness, so they move in darkness. As their own guilty
conscience pursued them, so they are pursued by swarms of wasps and
hornets. And as their actions were a moral filth, so they run eternally through the filth of worms and maggots which they themselves feed.*

*Dante recognizes several, among them Pope Celestine V, but
without delaying to speak to any of these souls, the Poets move on to
Acheron, the first of the rivers of Hell. Here the newly-arrived souls
of the damned gather and wait for monstrous Charon to ferry them
over to punishment. Charon recognizes Dante as a living man and
angrily refuses him passage. Virgil forces Charon to serve them,
but Dante swoons with terror, and does not reawaken until he is on
the other side.*

I AM THE WAY INTO THE CITY OF WOE.
　　I AM THE WAY TO A FORSAKEN PEOPLE.
　　I AM THE WAY INTO ETERNAL SORROW.
SACRED JUSTICE MOVED MY ARCHITECT.
　　I WAS RAISED HERE BY DIVINE OMNIPOTENCE,   *5*
　　PRIMORDIAL LOVE AND ULTIMATE INTELLECT.
ONLY THOSE ELEMENTS TIME CANNOT WEAR.°
　　WERE MADE BEFORE ME, AND BEYOND TIME I
　　　　STAND.°
　　ABANDON ALL HOPE YE WHO ENTER HERE.°
These mysteries I read cut into stone   *10*
　　above a gate. And turning I said: "Master,
　　what is the meaning of this harsh inscription?"
And he then as initiate to novice:
　　"Here must you put by all division of spirit
　　and gather your soul against all cowardice.   *15*
This is the place I told you to expect.
　　Here you shall pass among the fallen people,
　　souls who have lost the good of intellect."
So saying, he put forth his hand to me,
　　and with a gentle and encouraging smile   *20*
　　he led me through the gate of mystery.
Here sighs and cries and wails coiled and recoiled
　　on the starless air, spilling my soul to tears.
　　A confusion of tongues and monstrous accents toiled

[100-101] *Nisus, Turnus, Euryalus, Camilla:* All were killed in the war between
the Trojans and the Latins when, according to legend, Aeneas led the
survivors of Troy into Italy. Nisus and Euryalus (*Aeneid* IX) were Trojan
comrades-in-arms who died together. Camilla (*Aeneid* XI) was the daughter of the Latin king and one of the warrior women. She was killed in a
horse charge against the Trojans after displaying great gallantry. Turnus
(*Aeneid* XII) was killed by Aeneas in a dual.
[110] *The second death:* Damnation. "This is the second death, even the lake
of fire." (*Revelation* xx, 14).
[119] *forbids me to come there since, living, etc.:* Salvation is only through Christ
in Dante's theology. Virgil lived and died before the establishment of
Christ's teachings in Rome, and cannot therefore enter Heaven.
[125] *Peter's gate:* The gate of Purgatory. The gate is guarded by an angel
with a gleaming sword. The angel is Peter's vicar (Peter, the first Pope,
symbolized all Popes; i.e., Christ's vicar on earth) and is entrusted with
the two great keys. Some commentators argue that this is the gate of
Paradise, but Dante mentions no gate beyond this one in his ascent to
Heaven. It should be remembered, too, that those who pass the gate of
Purgatory have effectively entered Heaven.

---

[7] *ELEMENTS:* The angels, the Empyrean, and the First Matter are the elements time cannot wear, for they will last to all time. Man, however, in
his mortal state, is not eternal. The Gate of Hell, therefore, was created
before man.
[8] *BEYOND TIME:* So odious is sin to God that there can be no end to its
just punishment.
[9] *ABANDON . . . HERE:* The admonition, of course, is to the damned and
not to those who come on Heaven-sent errands.

in pain and anger. Voices harsh and shrill   25
  and sounds of blows, all intermingled, raised
  tumult and pandemonium that still

whirls on the air forever dirty with it
  as if a whirlwind sucked at sand. And I,
  holding my head in horror, cried: "Sweet Spirit,   30

What souls are these who run through this black haze?"
  And he to me: "These are the nearly soulless
  whose lives concluded neither blame nor praise.

They are mixed here with that despicable corps
  of angels who were neither for God nor Satan,   35
  but only for themselves. The High Creator

scourged them from Heaven for its perfect beauty,
  and Hell will not receive them since the wicked
  might feel some glory over them." And I:

"Master, what gnaws at them so hideously   40
  their lamentation stuns the very air?"
  "They have no hope of death," he answered me,

"and in their blind and unattaining state
  their miserable lives have sunk so low
  that they must envy every other fate.   45

No word of them survives their living season.
  Mercy and Justice deny them even a name.
  Let us not speak of them: look, and pass on."

I saw a banner there upon the mist.
  Circling and circling, it seemed to scorn all pause.   50
  So it ran on, and still behind it pressed

a never-ending rout of souls in pain.
  I had not thought death had undone so many
  as passed before me in that mournful train.

And some I knew among them; last of all   55
  I recognized the shadow of that soul
  who, in his cowardice, made that Great Denial.°

At once I understood for certain: these
  were of that retrograde and faithless crew
  hateful to God and to His enemies.   60

These wretches never born and never dead
  ran naked in a swarm of wasps and hornets
  that goaded them the more the more they fled,

and made their faces stream with bloody gouts
  of pus and tears that dribbled to their feet   65
  to be swallowed there by loathsome worms and
    maggots

Then looking onward I made out a throng
  assembled on the beach of a wide river,
  whereupon I turned to him: "Master, I long

to know what souls these are, and what strange usage   70
  makes them as eager to cross as they seem to be
  in this infected light." At which the Sage:

"All this shall be made known to you when we stand
  on the joyless beach of Acheron." And I
  cast down my eyes, sensing a reprimand   75

in what he said, and so walked at his side
  in silence and ashamed until we came
  through the dead cavern to that sunless tide.

There, steering toward us in an ancient ferry
  came an old man° with a white bush of hair,   80
  bellowing: "Woe to you depraved souls! Bury

here and forever all hope of Paradise:
  I come to lead you to the other shore,
  into eternal dark, into fire and ice.

And you who are living yet, I say begone   85
  from these who are dead." But when he saw me stand
  against his violence he began again:

"By other windings and by other steerage
  shall you cross to that other shore. Not here! Not here!
  A lighter craft than mine must give you passage."°   90

And my Guide to him: "Charon, bite back your spleen:
  this has been willed where what is willed must be,
  and is not yours to ask what it may mean."

The steersman of that marsh of ruined souls,
  who wore a wheel of flame around each eye,   95
  stifled the rage that shook his woolly jowls.

But those unmanned and naked spirits there
  turned pale with fear and their teeth began to chatter
  at sound of his crude bellow. In despair

they blasphemed God,° their parents, their time on earth
  the race of Adam, and the day and the hour   101
  and the place and the seed and the womb that gave
    them birth.

But all together they drew to that grim shore
  where all must come who lose the fear of God.
  Weeping and cursing they come for evermore,   105

and demon Charon with eyes like burning coals
  herds them in, and with a whistling oar
  flails on the stragglers to his wake of souls.

As leaves in autumn loosen and stream down
  until the branch stands bare above its tatters   110
  spread on the rustling ground, so one by one

the evil seed of Adam in its Fall
  cast themselves, at his signal, from the shore
  and streamed away like birds who hear their call.

So they are gone over that shadowy water,   115
  and always before they reach the other shore
  a new noise stirs on this, and new throngs gather.

---

⁵⁷ *soul . . . Denial:* This is almost certainly intended to be Celestine V, who became Pope in 1294. He was a man of saintly life, but allowed himself to be convinced by a priest named Benedetto that his soul was in danger since no man could live in the world without being damned. In fear for his soul he withdrew from all worldly affairs and renounced the papacy. Benedetto promptly assumed the mantle himself and became Boniface VIII, a Pope who became for Dante a symbol of all the worst corruptions of the Church. Dante also blamed Boniface and his intrigues for many of the evils that befell Florence. We shall learn in Canto XIX that the fires of Hell are waiting for Boniface in the pit of the Simoniacs, and we shall be given further evidence of his corruption in Canto XXVII. Celestine's great guilt is that his cowardice (in selfish terror for his own welfare) served as the door through which so much evil entered the Church.

---

⁸⁰ *old man:* Charon. He is the ferryman of dead souls across the Acheron in all classical mythology.

⁹⁰ *A lighter craft:* Charon recognizes Dante not only as a living man but as a soul in grace, and knows, therefore, that the Infernal Ferry was not intended for him. He is probably referring to the fact that souls destined for Purgatory and Heaven assemble not at his ferry point, but on the banks of the Tiber, from which they are transported by an angel.

¹⁰⁰ *blasphemed God:* The souls of the damned are not permitted to repent, for repentance is a divine grace.

"My son," the courteous Master said to me,
   "all who die in the shadow of God's wrath
   converge to this from every clime and country.   *120*
And all pass over eagerly, for here
   Divine Justice transforms and spurs them so
   their dread turns wish: they yearn for what they fear.°
No soul in Grace comes ever to this crossing;
   therefore if Charon rages at your presence   *125*
   you will understand the reason for his cursing."
When he had spoken, all the twilight country
   shook so violently, the terror of it
   bathes me with sweat even in memory:
the tear-soaked ground gave out a sigh of wind   *130*
   that spewed itself in flame on a red sky,
   and all my shuttered senses left me. Blind,
like one whom sleep comes over in a swoon,
   I stumbled into darkness and went down.°

Canto V

Circle Two   The Carnal

The Poets leave Limbo and enter the Second Circle. Here begin the torments of Hell proper, and here, blocking the way, sits Minos, the dread and semi-bestial judge of the damned who assigns to each soul its eternal torment. He orders the Poets back; but Virgil silences him as he earlier silenced Charon, and the Poets move on.

They find themselves on a dark ledge swept by a great whirlwind, which spins within it the souls of the Carnal, those who betrayed reason to their appetites. Their sin was to abandon themselves to the tempest of their passions: so they are swept forever in the tempest of Hell, forever denied the light of reason and of God. Virgil identifies many among them. Semiramis is there, and Dido, Cleopatra, Helen, Achilles, Paris, and Tristan. Dante sees Paolo and Francesca swept together, and in the name of love he calls to them to tell their sad story. They pause from their eternal flight to come to him, and Francesca tells their history while Paolo weeps at her side. Dante is so stricken by compassion at their tragic tale that he swoons once again.

So we went down to the second ledge alone;
   a smaller circle° of so much greater pain
   the voice of the damned rose in a bestial moan.

There Minos° sits, grinning, grotesque, and hale.
   He examines each lost soul as it arrives   *5*
   and delivers his verdict with his coiling tail.
That is to say, when the ill-fated soul
   appears before him it confesses all,
   and that grim sorter of the dark and foul
decides which place in Hell shall be its end,   *10*
   then wraps his twitching tail about himself
   one coil for each degree it must descend.
The soul descends and others take its place:
   each crowds in its turn to judgement, each confesses,
   each hears its doom and falls away through space.   *15*
"O you who come into this camp of woe,"
   cried Minos when he saw me turn away
   without awaiting his judgement, "watch where you go
once you have entered here, and to whom you turn!
   Do not be misled by that wide and easy passage!"   *20*
   And my Guide to him: "That is not your concern;
it is his fate to enter every door.
   This has been willed where what is willed must be,
   and is not yours to question. Say no more."
Now the choir of anguish, like a wound,   *25*
   strikes through the tortured air. Now I have come
   to Hell's full lamentation, sound beyond sound.
I came to a place stripped bare of every light
   and roaring on the naked dark like seas
   wracked by a war of winds. Their hellish flight   *30*
of storm and counterstorm through time foregone,
   sweeps the souls of the damned before its charge.
   Whirling and battering it drives them on.
and when they pass the ruined gap of Hell°   *34*
   through which we had come, their shrieks begin anew.
   There they blaspheme the power of God eternal.
And this, I learned, was the never ending flight
   of those who sinned in the flesh, the carnal and lusty
   who betrayed reason to their appetite.
As the wings of wintering starlings bear them on   *40*
   in their great wheeling flights, just so the blast
   wherries these evil souls through time foregone.
Here, there, up, down, they whirl and, whirling, strain
   with never a hope of hope to comfort them,
   not of release, but even of less pain.   *45*

---

¹²³ *their dread . . . fear:* Hell (allegorically, Sin) is what the souls of the damned really wish for. Hell is their actual and deliberate choice, for divine grace is denied to none who wish for it in their hearts. The damned must, in fact, deliberately harden their hearts to God in order to become damned. Christ's grace is sufficient to save all who wish for it.

¹³⁴ *went down:* This device (repeated at the end of Canto V) serves a double purpose. The first is technical: Dante uses it to cover a transition. We are never told how he crossed Acheron, for that would involve certain narrative matters he can better deal with when he crosses Styx in Canto VII. The second is to provide a point of departure for a theme that is carried through the entire descent: the theme of Dante's emotional reaction to Hell. These two swoons early in the descent show him most susceptible to the grief about him. As he descends, pity leaves him, and he even goes so far as to add to the torments of one sinner. The allegory is clear; we must harden ourselves against every sympathy for sin.

² *smaller circle:* The pit of Hell tapers like a funnel. The circles of ledges accordingly grow smaller as they descend.

---

⁴ *Minos:* The son of Europa and Zeus, who descended to her in the form of a bull. Minos became a mythological king of Crete, so famous for his wisdom and justice that after death his soul was made judge of the dead. Virgil presents him fulfilling the same office at Aeneas' descent to the underworld. Dante, however, transforms him into an irate and hideous monster with a tail. The transformation may have been suggested by the form Zeus assumed for the rape of Europa—the monster is certainly bullish enough here—but the obvious purpose of the brutalization is to present a figure symbolic of the guilty conscience of the wretches who come before it to make their confessions.

³⁴ *ruined gap:* . . . At the time of the Harrowing of Hell a great earthquake shook the underworld shattering rocks and cliffs. Ruins resulting from the same shock are noted in Canto XII, 34, and Canto XXI, 112 ff. At the beginning of Canto XXIV, the Poets leave the *bolgia* of the Hypocrites by climbing the ruined slabs of a bridge that was shattered by this earthquake.

As cranes go over sounding their harsh cry,
    leaving the long streak of their flight in air,
    so come these spirits, wailing as they fly.
And watching their shadows lashed by wind, I cried:
    "Master, what souls are these the very air   50
    lashes with its black whips from side to side?"
"The first of these whose history you would know,"
    he answered me, "was Empress of many tongues.°
    Mad sensuality corrupted her so
that to hide the guilt of her debauchery   55
    she licensed all depravity alike,
    and lust and law were one in her decree.
She is Semiramis of whom the tale is told
    how she married Ninus and succeeded him
    to the throne of that wide land the Sultans hold.   60
The other is Dido;° faithless to the ashes
    of Sichaeus, she killed herself for love.
    The next whom the eternal tempest lashes
is sense-drugged Cleopatra. See Helen° there,
    from whom such ill arose. And great Achilles;°   65
    who fought at last with love in the house of prayer.
And Paris. And Tristan." As they whirled above
    he pointed out more than a thousand shades
    of those torn from the mortal life by love.
I stood there while my Teacher one by one   70
    named the great knights and ladies of dim time;
    and I was swept by pity and confusion.
At last I spoke: "Poet, I should be glad
    to speak a word with those two swept together
    so lightly on the wind and still so sad."°   75

And he to me: "Watch them. When next they pass,
    call to them in the name of love that drives
    and damns them here. In that name they will pause."
Thus, as soon as the wind in its wild course
    brought them around, I called: "O wearied souls!   80
    if none forbid it, pause and speak to us."
As mating doves that love calls to their nest
    glide through the air with motionless raised wings,
    borne by the sweet desire that fills each breast—
Just so those spirits turned on the torn sky   85
    from the band where Dido whirls across the air;
    such was the power of pity in my cry.
"O living creature, gracious, kind, and good,
    going this pilgrimage through the sick night,
    visiting us who stained the earth with blood,   90
were the King of Time our friend, we would pray His peace
    on you who have pitied us. As long as the wind
    will let us pause, ask of us what you please.
The town where I was born lies by the shore
    where the Po descends into its ocean rest   95
    with its attendant streams in one long murmur.
Love, which in gentlest hearts will soonest bloom
    seized my lover with passion for that sweet body
    from which I was torn unshriven to my doom.
Love, which permits no loved one not to love,   100
    took me so strongly with delight in him
    that we are one in Hell, as we were above.°
Love led us to one death. In the depths of Hell
    Caïna waits for him° who took our lives."
    This was the piteous tale they stopped to tell.   105
And when I had heard those world-offended lovers
    I bowed my head. At last the Poet spoke:
    "What painful thoughts are these your lowered brow covers?"
When at length I answered, I began: "Alas!
    What sweetest thoughts, what green and young desire
    led these two lovers to this sorry pass."   111
Then turning to those spirits once again,
    I said: "Francesca, what you suffer here
    melts me to tears of pity and of pain.
But tell me: in the time of your sweet sighs   115
    by what appearances found love the way
    to lure you to his perilous paradise?"

---

[53] *Empress:* Semiramis, a legendary queen of Assyria who assumed full power at the death of her husband, Ninus.

[61] *Dido:* Queen and founder of Carthage. She had vowed to remain faithful to her husband, Sichaeus, but she fell in love with Aeneas. When Aeneas abandoned her she stabbed herself on a funeral pyre she had had prepared. According to Dante's own system of punishments, she should be in the Seventh Circle (Canto XIII) with the suicides. The only clue Dante gives to the tempering of her punishment is his statement that "she killed herself for love." Dante always seems readiest to forgive in that name.

[64] *Helen:* She was held responsible for the Trojan War; the wife of King Menelaus of Sparta, she ran away with the visiting Prince Paris from Troy.

[65] *Achilles:* He is placed among this company because of his passion for Polyxena, the daughter of Priam. For love of her, he agreed to desert the Greeks and to join the Trojans, but when he went to the temple for the wedding (according to the legend Dante has followed) he was killed by Paris.

[74-75] *those two . . . sad:* Paolo and Francesca. In 1275 Giovanni Malatesta of Rimini, called Giovanni the Lame, a somewhat deformed but brave and powerful warrior, made a political marriage with Francesca, daughter of Guido da Polenta of Ravenna. Francesca came to Rimini and there an amour grew between her and Giovanni's younger brother Paolo. Despite the fact that Paolo had married in 1269 and had become the father of two daughters by 1275, his affair with Francesca continued for many years. It was sometime between 1283 and 1286 that Giovanni surprised them in Francesca's bedroom and killed both of them. Around these facts the legend has grown that Paolo was sent by Giovanni as his proxy to the marriage, that Francesca thought he was her real bridegroom and accordingly gave him her heart irrevocably at first sight. The legend obviously increases the pathos, but nothing in Dante gives it support.

[102] *we are . . . above:* At many points of *The Inferno* Dante makes clear the principle that the souls of the damned are locked so blindly into their own guilt that none can feel sympathy for another, or find any pleasure in the presence of another. The temptation of many readers is to interpret this line romantically: *i.e.*, that the love of Paolo and Francesca survives Hell itself. The more Dantean interpretation, however, is that they add to one another's anguish (a) as mutual reminders of their sin, and (b) as insubstantial shades of the bodies for which they once felt such great passion.

[104] *him:* Giovanni Malatesta was still alive at the writing. His fate is already decided, however, and upon his death, his soul will fall to Caïna, the first ring of the last circle (Canto XXXII), where lie those who performed acts of treachery against their kin.

And she: "The double grief of a lost bliss
 is to recall its happy hour in pain.
  Your Guide and Teacher knows the truth of this. *120*
But if there is indeed a soul in Hell
 to ask of the beginning of our love
 out of his pity, I will weep and tell:
On a day for dalliance we read the rhyme
 of Lancelot,° now love had mastered him. *125*
  We were alone with innocence and dim time.°
Pause after pause that high old story drew
 our eyes together while we blushed and paled;
 but it was one soft passage overthrew
our caution and our hearts. For when we read *130*
 how her fond smile was kissed by such a lover,
 he who is one with me alive and dead
breathed on my lips the tremor of his kiss.
  That book, and he who wrote it, was a pander.°
  That day we read no further." As she said this, *135*
the other spirit, who stood by her, wept
 so piteously, I felt my senses reel
 and faint away with anguish. I was swept
by such a swoon as death is, and I fell,
as a corpse might fall, to the dead floor of Hell.

BOCCACCIO

from *The Decameron*

The two tales that follow reveal Boccaccio's interest in social mores, legal obligation, and human interaction. In the first tale a woman is at the center of the action in and out of bed. The story reflects fourteenth-century Italian customs, including the importance of duty and law, and the legal subservience of women to men. The tale also emphasizes the courage and intelligence of women in the person of the aristocratic protagonist, who not only confesses to her crime of committing adultery, but who also questions the law under which she is to be sentenced. In the second tale, Boccaccio satirizes the behavior of Catholic monks while portraying the subordinate monk's ingenuity in outsmarting his superior. Like the other tales of the Decameron, these position their author on the brink of new ways of looking at old realities.

FIRST DAY, FOURTH TALE

. . . Having completed her story, Filomena fell silent and Dioneo, who was sitting close to her, without awaiting any further order from the Queen (for he realized by the order

already begun that he was the next to speak), started speaking in the following manner:

Lovely ladies, if I have understood your intention correctly, we are here in order to amuse ourselves by telling stories, and therefore, as long as we do nothing contrary to this, I think that each one of us ought to be permitted (and just a moment ago our Queen said that we might) to tell whatever story he thinks is likely to be the most amusing. Therefore, having heard how the good advice of Giannotto di Civignì saved Abraham's soul and how Melchisdech defended his riches against the schemes of Saladin, I am going to tell you briefly, without fear of disapproval, how cleverly a monk saved his body from a most severe punishment.

In Lunigiana, a town not too far from here, there was a monastery (once more saintly and full of monks than it now is), in which there lived a young monk whose virility and youth could not be diminished by fasts or by vigils. One day around noon while the other monks were sleeping, he happened to be taking a solitary walk around the church—which was somewhat isolated—when he spotted a very beautiful young girl (perhaps the daughter of one of the local workers) who was going through the fields gathering various kinds of herbs. The moment he saw her, he was passionately attacked by carnal desire.

He went up to her and began a conversation. One subject led to another, and finally, they came to an understanding; he took the girl to his cell without anyone's noticing them. His excessive desire got the better of him while he was playing with the girl, and it happened that the Abbot, who had just got up from his nap, was passing quietly by the monk's cell when he heard the commotion the pair was making. So that he might better recognize the voices, he silently edged up to the entrance of the cell to listen, and it was clear to him that there was a woman inside. At first he was tempted to have them open the door, but then he thought of using a different tactic; so he returned to his room and waited for the monk to come out.

Although the monk was, to his great pleasure and delight, quite occupied with this young lady, he nevertheless suspected something, for he thought he had heard some footsteps in the corridor. In fact, he had peeked out a small opening and had clearly seen the Abbot standing there and listening: he was well aware the Abbot must have realized that the young girl was in his cell, and knowing that he would be severely punished, he was very worried; but without revealing his anxiety to the girl, he immediately began to think of a number of alternative plans, in an attempt to come up with one which might save him. But then he thought of an original scheme which would achieve the exact end he had in mind, and pretending that he felt they had stayed together long enough, he said to the girl:

"I have to go and find a way for you to leave without being seen, so stay here until I come back."

Having left his cell and locked it with his key, he went immediately to the Abbot's room (as every monk must do before leaving the monastery) and with a straight face he said:

"Sir, this morning I could not bring in all of the firewood that was cut for me; with your permission, I should like to go to the forest to have it carried in."

The Abbot, thinking that the monk did not know he had been observed by him, was happy at this turn of events, and

---

124–25 the rhyme of Lancelot: The story exists in many forms. The details Dante make use of are from an Old French version.

126 dim time: The original simply reads "We were alone, suspecting nothing." "Dim time" is rhyme-forced, but not wholly outside the legitimate implications of the original, I hope. The old courtly romance may well be thought of as happening in the dim ancient days. The apology, of course, comes after the fact: one does the possible, then argues for justification, and there probably is none.

134 that book, and he who wrote it, was a pander: "Galeotto," the Italian word for "pander," is also the Italian rendering of the name of Gallehault, who in the French Romance Dante refers to here, urged Lancelot and Guinevere on to love.

since this offered him the opportunity to get more firsthand information on the sin committed by the monk, he gladly took the monk's key and gave him permission to leave. And when he saw him go off, he began to plan what he would do first: either to open the monk's cell in the presence of all the monks in order to have them see what the sin was—and in doing so prevent any grumbling when he punished the monk—or to hear first from the girl how the affair had started. But then thinking that she might very well be the wife or the daughter of some person of importance and not wanting to shame such a person in front of all his monks, he decided first to see who the girl was and then to make his decision. And so he quietly went to the cell, opened it, entered the room and closed the door.

When the young girl saw the Abbot come in, she became frightened and began to cry out of shame. Master Abbot gave her a quick look and found her to be beautiful and fresh, and although he was old, he immediately felt the warm desires of the flesh, which were no less demanding than those the young monk had felt, and he thought to himself:

"Well, now! Why shouldn't I have a little fun when I can get it? Troubles and worries I can get every day! This is a pretty young girl, and no one knows she's here. If I can persuade her to serve my pleasure, I don't see any reason why I shouldn't! Who will be the wiser? No one will ever know, and a sin that's hidden is half forgiven! This opportunity may never present itself again. I believe it is a sign of great wisdom for a man to profit from what God sends others."

Having thought all this and having completely changed the purpose of his visit, he drew nearer to the girl and gently began to comfort her, begging her not to cry; and, as one thing will lead to another, he eventually explained to her what he wanted.

The young girl, who was by no means as hard as iron or diamond, most willingly agreed to the Abbot's wishes. He took her in his arms and kissed her many times, then lay down on the monk's bed. And perhaps out of concern for the heavy weight of his dignified person and the tender age of the young girl (or perhaps just because he was afraid to lay too much weight on her) he did not lie on top of her but rather placed her on top of him, and there he amused himself with her for quite a while.

Meanwhile, pretending to have gone into the woods, the monk had concealed himself in the dormitory; when he saw the Abbot enter his cell alone, he was reassured that his plan would be successful. And when he saw the Abbot lock himself inside, he knew it for certain. Leaving his hiding place, he quietly crept up to an opening through which he could see and hear everything the Abbot did and said.

When the Abbot decided that he had stayed long enough with the girl, he locked her in the cell and returned to his own room. And after a while, having heard the monk return and believing that he had come back from the woods, he decided that it was time to give him a sound talking to—he would have him locked up in prison in order to enjoy by himself the spoils they had both gained. He had him summoned, and he reprimanded him very severely, and with a stern face he ordered that he be put into prison.

The monk promptly replied:

"But sir, I have not been a member of the Order of Saint Benedict long enough to have had the opportunity to learn every detail of the order's rules. And up until just a moment ago, you never showed me how monks were supposed to support the weight of women as well as fasts and vigils. But now that you have shown me how, I promise you that if you forgive me this time, I shall sin no more in this respect; on the contrary, I shall always behave as I have seen you behave."

The Abbot, who was a clever man, realized immediately that the monk had outsmarted him: he had been witness to what he had done; because of this, and feeling remorse for his own sin, he was ashamed of inflicting upon the monk the same punishment that he himself deserved. And so he pardoned him and made him promise never to reveal what he had seen. They quickly got the young girl out of the monastery, and as one might well imagine, they often had her brought back in again.

SIXTH DAY, SEVENTH TALE

In the city of Prato, there was once a statute—in truth, no less harsh than it was worthy of criticism—which, without any extenuating circumstances whatsoever, required that any woman caught by her husband committing adultery with a lover should be burned alive, just the way a woman who goes with a man for money would be. And while this statute was in effect, it happened that a noble lady named Madonna Filippa, who was beautiful and more in love than any woman could be, was discovered in her own bedroom by her husband, Rinaldo de'Pugliesi, in the arms of Lazzarino de' Guazzagliotri, a noble and handsome young man from that city, whom she loved more than herself. When Rinaldo discovered this, he was extremely angry and could hardly restrain himself from rushing at them and murdering them, and had he not been so concerned over what might happen to him if he were to follow the impulse of his anger, he would have done so. While able to restrain himself from doing this, he was, however, unable to refrain from claiming the sentence of Prato's statute, which he was not permitted to carry out by his own hand, that is, the death of his wife.

And so, in possession of very convincing evidence of his wife's transgression, when day broke, without thinking further about the matter, he denounced the lady and had her summoned to the court. The lady, who was very courageous, as women truly in love usually are, was determined to appear in court, and in spite of the fact that she was advised against this by many of her friends and relatives, she decided that she would rather confess the truth and die with a courageous heart than, fleeing like a coward, live in exile condemned *in absentia* and show herself unworthy of such a lover as the man in whose arms she had rested the night before. Escorted by a large group of women and men, all of whom were urging her to deny the charges, she came before the *podestà* and, with a steady gaze and a firm voice, demanded to know what he wanted of her. Gazing at the lady and finding her to be most beautiful and very well-bred as well as most courageous, indeed, as her own words bore witness, the *podestà* took pity on her and was afraid she might confess to something which would force him, in order to fulfill his duty, to condemn her to death

But since he could not avoid questioning her about what she had been accused of doing, he said to her:

"Madam, as you can see, your husband Rinaldo is here and has lodged a complaint against you, in which he states that he has found you in adultery with another man; and because of this he demands that I punish you by putting you to death in accordance with the statute which requires such sentence here in Prato. But since I cannot do this if you do not confess, I suggest you be very careful how you answer this charge; now, tell me if what your husband accuses you of is true."

Without the slightest trace of fear, the lady, in a lovely tone of voice replied:

"Sir, it is true that Rinaldo is my husband and that this past night he found me in Lazzarino's arms, where, because of the deep and perfect love I bear for him, I have many times lain; nor would I ever deny this; but, as I am sure you know, the laws should be equal for all and should be passed with the consent of the people they affect. In this case these conditions are not fulfilled, for this law applies only to us poor women, who are much better able than men to satisfy a larger number; furthermore, when this law was put into effect, not a single woman gave her consent, nor was any one of them ever consulted about it; therefore, it may quite rightly be called a bad law. And if, however, you wish, to the detriment of my body and your own soul, to put this law into effect, that is your concern; but, before you proceed to any judgment, I beg you to grant me a small favor: that is, to ask my husband whether or not I have ever refused, whenever and however many times he wished, to yield my entire body to him."

To this question, without waiting for the *podestà* to pose it, Rinaldo immediately replied that without any doubt, the lady had yielded to his every pleasure whenever he required it.

"So then," the lady promptly continued, "I ask you, *Messer Podestà*, if he has always taken of me whatever he needed and however much pleased him, what was I supposed to do then, and what am I to do now, with what is left over? Should I throw it to the dogs? Is it not much better to give it to a gentleman who loves me more than himself, rather than let it go to waste or spoil?"

The nature of the case and the fact that the lady was so well known brought almost all of Prato's citizens flocking to court, and when they heard such an amusing question posed by the lady, after much laughter, all of a sudden and almost in a single voice, they cried out that the lady was right and had spoken well; and before they left the court, with the *podestà's* consent, they changed the cruel statute, modifying it so that it applied only to those women who were unfaithful to their husbands for money. And Rinaldo, confused by the whole mad affair, left the courtroom, and the lady, now free and happy, and resurrected from the flames, so to speak, returned to her home in triumph.

CHAUCER

from *The Canterbury Tales*

The Canterbury Tales *is essentially a collection of stories told in rhymed couplets by a group of pilgrims traveling to Canterbury. In the General Prologue, Chaucer includes both generalized and particularized character portrayals of his travelers. Chaucer's type of portrayals generalize the qualities of a particular group, usually idealizing it, as in his portrayal of the Clerk and the Knight. Chaucer's individualized portraits, such as those of the Prioress, the Monk, and the Wife of Bath, blend attractive and less appealing qualities. The process of characterization is continued in the tales that follow, for the reader learns a good deal about the teller from her or his tale. Moreover, the poet does not neglect the relationships between the pilgrims. These subtle and complex relationships emerge, for example, in the exchange of words between the Host and the Pardoner that precede and follow the Pardoner's Prologue and Tale. Chaucer's presentation of the Host's comments on the tale that precedes the Pardoner's, and Chaucer's description of the Host inviting the next pilgrim to begin his tale, reveal the writer's concern for the thematic and dramatic unity of his work.*

THE GENERAL PROLOGUE

When in April the sweet showers fall
And pierce the drought of March to the root, and all
The veins are bathed in liquor of such power
As brings about the engendering of the flower,
When also Zephyrus with his sweet breath   *5*
Exhales an air in every grove and heath
Upon the tender shoots, and the young sun
His half-course in the sign of the *Ram* has run,
And the small fowl are making melody
That sleep away the night with open eye   *10*
(So nature pricks them and their heart engages)
Then people long to go on pilgrimages
And palmers long to seek the stranger strands
Of far-off saints, hallowed in sundry lands,
And specially, from every shire's end   *15*
Of England, down to Canterbury they wend
To see the holy blissful martyr, quick
To give his help to them when they were sick.
    It happened in that season that one day
In Southwark, at *The Tabard*, as I lay   *20*
Ready to go on pilgrimage and start
For Canterbury, most devout at heart,
At night there came into that hostelry
Some nine and twenty in a company
Of sundry folk happening then to fall   *25*
In fellowship, and they were pilgrims all
That towards Canterbury meant to ride.
The rooms and stables of the inn were wide;
They made us easy, all was of the best.
And, briefly, when the sun had gone to rest,   *30*
I'd spoken to them all upon the trip
And was soon one with them in fellowship,
Pledged to rise early and to take the way
To Canterbury, as you heard me say.
    But none the less, while I have time and space,   *35*
Before my story takes a further pace,
It seems a reasonable thing to say
What their condition was, the full array
Of each of them, as it appeared to me,
According to profession and degree,   *40*
And what apparel they were riding in;
And at a Knight I therefore will begin.
There was a *Knight*, a most distinguished man,
Who from the day on which he first began
To ride abroad had followed chivalry,   *45*
Truth, honour, generousness and courtesy.
He had done nobly in his sovereign's war

And ridden into battle, no man more,
As well in Christian as in heathen places,
And ever honoured for his noble graces.   *50*
    When we took Alexandra, he was there.
He often sat at table in the chair
Of honour, above all nations, when in Prussia.
In Lithuania he had ridden, and Russia,
No Christian man so often, of his rank.   *55*
When, in Granada, Algeciras sank
Under assault, he had been there, and in
North Africa, raiding Benamarin;
In Antolia he had been as well
And fought when Ayas and Attalia fell,   *60*
For all along the Mediterranean coast
He had embarked with many a noble host.
In fifteen mortal battles he had been
And jousted for our faith at Tramissene
Thrice in the lists, and always killed his man.   *65*
This same distinguished knight had led the van
Once with the Bey of Balat, doing work
For him against another heathen Turk;
He was of sovereign value in all eyes.
And though so much distinguished, he was wise   *70*
And in his bearing modest as a maid.
He never yet a boorish thing had said
In all his life to any, come what might;
He was a true, a perfect gentle-knight.
    Speaking of his equipment, he possessed   *75*
Fine horses, but he was not gaily dressed.
He wore a fustian tunic stained and dark
With smudges where his armour had left mark;
Just home from service, he had joined our ranks
To do his pilgrimage and render thanks.   *80*
    He had his son with him, a fine young *Squire*,
A lover and cadet, a lad of fire
With locks as curly as if they had been pressed.
He was some twenty years of age, I guessed.
In stature he was of a moderate length,   *85*
With wonderful agility and strength.
He'd seen some service with the cavalry
In Flanders and Artois and Picardy
And had done valiantly in little space
Of time, in hope to win his lady's grace.   *90*
He was embroidered like a meadow bright
And full of freshest flowers, red and white.
Singing he was, or fluting all the day;
He was as fresh as is the month of May.
Short was his gown, the sleeves were long and wide;   *95*
He knew the way to sit a horse and ride.
He could make songs and poems and recite,
Knew how to joust and dance, to draw and write.
He loved so hotly that till dawn grew pale
He slept as little as a nightingale.   *100*
Courteous he was, lowly and serviceable,
And carved to serve his father at the table.
    There was a *Yeoman* with him at his side,
No other servant; so he chose to ride.
This Yeoman wore a coat and hood of green,   *105*
And peacock-feathered arrows, bright and keen
And neatly sheathed, hung at his belt the while

—For he could dress his gear in yeoman style,
His arrows never drooped their feathers low—
And in his hand he bore a mighty bow.   *110*
His head was like a nut, his face was brown.
He knew the whole of woodcraft up and down.
A saucy brace was on his arm to ward
It from the bow-string, and a shield and sword
Hung at one side, and at the other slipped   *115*
A jaunty dirk, spear-sharp and well-equipped.
A medal of St Christopher he wore
Of shining silver on his breast, and bore
A hunting-horn, well slung and burnished clean,
That dangled from a baldrick of bright green.   *120*
He was a proper forester, I guess.
    There also was a *Nun*, a Prioress,
Her way of smiling very simple and coy.
Her greatest oath was only 'By St Loy!'
And she was known as Madam Eglantyne.   *125*
And well she sang a service, with a fine
Intoning through her nose, as was most seemly,
And she spoke daintily in French, extremely,
After the school of Stratford-atte-Bowe;
French in the Paris style she did not know.   *130*
At meat her manners were well taught withal;
No morsel from her lips did she let fall,
Nor dipped her fingers in the sauce too deep;
But she could carry a morsel up and keep
The smallest drop from falling on her breast.   *135*
For courtliness she had a special zest,
And she would wipe her upper lip so clean
That not a trace of grease was to be seen
Upon the cup when she had drunk; to eat,
She reached a hand sedately for the meat.   *140*
She certainly was very entertaining,
Pleasant and friendly in her ways, and straining
To counterfeit a courtly kind of grace,
A stately bearing fitting to her place,
And to seem dignified in all her dealings.   *145*
As for her sympathies and tender feelings,
She was so charitably solicitous
She used to weep if she but saw a mouse
Caught in a trap, if it were dead or bleeding.
And she had little dogs she would be feeding   *150*
With roasted flesh, or milk, or fine white bread.
And bitterly she wept if one were dead
Or someone took a stick and made it smart;
She was all sentiment and tender heart.
Her veil was gathered in a seemly way,   *155*
Her nose was elegant, her eyes glass-grey;
Her mouth was very small, but soft and red,
Her forehead, certainly, was fair of spread,
Almost a span across the brows, I own;
She was indeed by no means undergrown.   *160*
Her cloak, I noticed, had a graceful charm.
She wore a coral trinket on her arm,
A set of beads, the gaudies tricked in green,
Whence hung a golden brooch of brightest sheen
On which there first was graven a crowned A,   *165*
And lower, *Amor vincit omnia.*
    Another *Nun*, the secretary at her cell,

Was riding with her, and *three Priests* as well.
A *Monk* there was, one of the finest sort
Who rode the country; hunting was his sport. *170*
A manly man, to be an Abbot able;
Many a dainty horse he had in stable.
His bridle, when he rode, a man might hear
Jingling in a whistling wind as clear,
Aye, and as loud as does the chapel bell *175*
Where my lord Monk was Prior of the cell.
The Rule of good St Benet or St Maur
As old and strict he tended to ignore;
He let go by the things of yesterday
And took the modern world's more spacious way. *180*
He did not rate that text at a plucked hen
Which says that hunters are not holy men
And that a monk uncloistered is a mere
Fish out of water, flapping on the pier,
That is to say a monk out of his cloister. *185*
That was a text he held not worth an oyster;
And I agreed and said his views were sound;
Was he to study till his head went round
Poring over books in cloisters? Must he toil
As Austin bade and till the very soil? *190*
Was he to leave the world upon the shelf?
Let Austin have his labour to himself.
 This Monk was therefore a good man to horse;
Greyhounds he had, as swift as birds, to course.
Hunting a hare or riding at a fence *195*
Was all his fun, he spared for no expense.
I saw his sleeves were garnished at the hand
With fine grey fur, the finest in the land,
And on his hood, to fasten it at his chin
He had a wrought-gold cunningly fashioned pin; *200*
Into a lover's knot it seemed to pass.
His head was bald and shone like looking-glass;
So did his face, as if it had been greased.
He was a fat and personable priest;
His prominent eyeballs never seemed to settle. *205*
They glittered like the flames beneath a kettle;
Supple his boots, his horse in fine condition.
He was a prelate fit for exhibition,
He was not pale like a tormented soul.
He liked a fat swan best, and roasted whole. *210*
His palfrey was as brown as is a berry.
 There was a *Friar*, a wanton one and merry,
A Limiter, a very festive fellow.
In all Four Orders there was none so mellow,
So glib with gallant phrase and well-turned speech. *215*
He'd fixed up many a marriage, giving each
Of his young women what he could afford her.
He was a noble pillar to his Order.
Highly beloved and intimate was he
With County folk within his boundary, *220*
And city dames of honour and possessions;
For he was qualified to hear confessions,
Or so he said, with more than priestly scope;
He had a special licence from the Pope.
Sweetly he heard his penitents at shrift *225*
With pleasant absolution, for a gift.
He was an easy man in penance-giving

Where he could hope to make a decent living;
It's a sure sign whenever gifts are given
To a poor Order that a man's well shriven, *230*
And should he give enough he knew in verity
The penitent repented in sincerity.
For many a fellow is so hard of heart
He cannot weep, for all his inward smart.
Therefore instead of weeping and of prayer *235*
One should give silver for a poor Friar's care.
He kept his tippet stuffed with pins for curls,
And pocket-knives, to give to pretty girls.
And certainly his voice was gay and sturdy,
For he sang well and played the hurdy-gurdy. *240*
At sing-songs he was champion of the hour.
His neck was whiter than a lily-flower
But strong enough to butt a bruiser down.
He knew the taverns well in every town
And every innkeeper and barmaid too *245*
Better than lepers, beggars and that crew,
For in so eminent a man as he
It was not fitting with the dignity
Of his position, dealing with a scum
Of wretched lepers; nothing good can come *250*
Of commerce with such slum-and-gutter dwellers,
But only with the rich and victual-sellers.
But anywhere a profit might accrue
Courteous he was and lowly of service too.
Natural gifts like his were hard to match. *255*
He was the finest beggar of his batch,
And, for his begging-district, paid a rent;
His brethren did no poaching where he went.
For though a widow mightn't have a shoe,
So pleasant was his holy how-d'ye-do *260*
He got his farthing from her just the same
Before he left, and so his income came
To more than he laid out. And how he romped,
Just like a puppy! He was ever prompt
To arbitrate disputes on settling days *265*
(For a small fee) in many helpful ways,
Not then appearing as your cloistered scholar
With threadbare habit hardly worth a dollar,
But much more like a Doctor or a Pope.
Of double-worsted was the semi-cope *270*
Upon his shoulders, and the swelling fold
About him, like a bell about its mould
When it is casting, rounded out his dress.
He lisped a little out of wantonness
To make his English sweet upon his tongue. *275*
When he had played his harp, or having sung,
His eyes would twinkle in his head as bright
As any star upon a frosty night.
This worthy's name was Hubert, it appeared. . . .

The Wife of Bath's Prologue

"Experience, though no authority
Were in this world, were° good enough for   *would be*
 me,
To speak of woe that is in all marriage;
For, masters, since I was twelve years of age,

5   Thanks be to God Who is for aye° alive,   *ever*
       Of husbands at church door have I had five;
       For men so many times have wedded me;
       And all were worthy men in their degree.°   *rank*
       But someone told me not so long ago
10   That since Our Lord, save once, would never go
       To wedding (that at Cana in Galilee),[1]
       Thus, by this same example, showed He me
       I never should have married more than once.
       Lo and behold! What sharp words, for the nonce,
15   Beside a well Lord Jesus, God and man,
       Spoke in reproving the Samaritan:
       'For thou hast had five husbands,' thus said He,
       'And he whom thou hast now to be with thee
       Is not thine husband,'[2] Thus He said that day,
20   But what He meant thereby I cannot say;
       And I would ask now why that same fifth man
       Was not husband to the Samaritan?
       How many might she have, then, in marriage?
       For I have never heard, in all my age,
25   Clear exposition of this number shown,
       Though men may guess and argue up and down.[3]
       But well I know and say, and do not lie,
       God bade us to increase and multiply;
       That worthy text can I well understand.
30   And well I know He said, too, my husband
       Should father leave, and mother, and cleave to me;[4]
       But no specific number mentioned He,
       Whether of bigamy or octogamy;°   *eight marriages*
       Why should men speak of it reproachfully?
35   "Lo, there's the wise old king Dan Solomon;
       I understand he had more wives than one;[5]
       And now would God it were permitted me
       To be refreshed one half as oft as he!
       Which gift of God he had for all his wives!
40   No man has such that in this world now lives.
       God knows, this noble king, it strikes my wit,
       The first night he had many a merry fit
       With each of them, so much he was alive!
       Praise be to God that I have wedded five!
45   Welcome the sixth whenever come he shall.
       Forsooth,° I'll not keep chaste for good and
           all;   *truly*

       When my good husband from the world is gone,
       Some Christian man shall marry me anon;
       Of whom I did pick out and choose the best
50   Both for their nether° purse and for their
           chest.   *lower*
       Different schools make divers perfect clerks,
       Different methods learned in sundry works
       Make the good workman perfect, certainly.
       Of full five husbands tutoring am I.
55   For then, the apostle° says that I am free   *Paul*
       To wed, in God's name, where it pleases me.
       He says that to be wedded is no sin;
       Better to marry than to burn within[6]
       What care I though folk speak reproachfully
60   Of wicked Lamech and his bigamy?
       I know well Abraham was holy man,
       And Jacob, too, as far as know I can;
       And each of them had spouses more than two;
       And many another holy man also.[7]
65   Or can you say that you have ever heard
       That God has ever by His express word
       Marriage forbidden? Pray you, now, tell me;
       Or where commanded He virginity?
       I read as well as you no doubt have read
70   The apostle when he speaks of maidenhead;
       He said, commandment of the Lord he'd none.
       Men may advise a woman to be one,
       But such advice is not commandment, no;
       He left the thing to our own judgment so.[8]
75   For had Lord God commanded maidenhood,
       He'd have condemned all marriage as not good;
       And certainly, if there were no seed sown,
       Virginity—where then should it be grown?[9]
       Paul dared not to forbid us, at the least,
80   A thing whereof his Master'd no behest.°   *injunction*
       The dart° is set up for virginity;   *prize*
       Catch it who can; who runs best let us see.
       "But this word is not meant for every wight,
       But where God wills to give it, of His might.
85   I know well that the apostle was a maid;°   *virgin*
       Nevertheless, and though he wrote and said
       He would that everyone were such as he,
       All is not counsel to virginity;
       And so to be a wife he gave me leave
       Out of permission; there's no shame should grieve 90
       In marrying me, if that my mate should die,

---

[1]Site of Jesus's first miracle (John 2:1–10). This was a standard passage for arguments in favor of monogamy, dating back to St. Jerome, from whose treatise *Adversus Jovinianum* (393) the bulk of the scriptural argument that follows was drawn.
[2]John 4:5–30.
[3]The Wife of Bath avoids the plain sense of the passage by claiming it must have some obscure mystical meaning.
[4]Following standard practice in biblical interpretation, she counters one biblical precept with several others that seem to give the opposite instructions: God's instruction to Adam and Eve to "increase and multiply" (Genesis 1:28) and Jesus's words in Matthew 19:5–6 (in fact arguing against divorce), citing Adam and Eve.
[5]King Solomon had a thousand wives and concubines (1 Kings 11:3).

[6]Quoting 1 Corinthians 7:9 and 7:28.
[7]Lamech was a descendant of the accursed Cain who was considered to have been the first bigamist (Genesis 4:19–24). By contrast, Abraham and Jacob were biblical patriarchs who also had several wives.
[8]According to Paul, "if a virgin marry, she hath not sinned," since there was no commandment against marriage (1 Corinthians 7:25 and 28), but he did advise even those who had wives to remain celibate (7:29).
[9]How would virgins be born unless people have sex?

Without exception,° too, of bigamy.   *objection*
And though 'twere good no woman's flesh to touch,
He meant, in his own bed or on his couch;
95   For peril 'tis fire and tow to assemble;
You know what this example may resemble.[1]
This is the sum: he held virginity
Nearer perfection than marriage for° frailty.   *out of*
And frailty's all, I say, save° he and she   *unless*
100 Would lead their lives throughout in chastity.
       "I grant this well, I have no great envy
Though maidenhood's preferred to bigamy;
Let those who will be clean, body and ghost,°   *soul*
Of my condition I will make no boast.
105 For well you know, a lord in his household,
He has not every vessel all of gold;
Some are of wood and serve well all their days.
God calls folk unto Him in sundry° ways,   *diverse*
And each one has from God a proper gift,
110 Some this, some that, as pleases Him to shift.
"Virginity is great perfection known,
And continence e'en° with devotion shown.   *equally*
But Christ, Who of perfection is the well,
Bade not each separate man he should go sell
115 All that he had and give it to the poor
And follow Him in such wise going before.[2]
He spoke to those that would live perfectly;
And, masters, by your leave, such am not I.
I will devote the flower of all my age
120 To all the acts and harvests of marriage.
       "Tell me also, to what purpose or end
The genitals were made, that I defend,
And for what benefit was man first wrought?[3]
Trust you right well, they were not made for
       naught°   *nothing*
125 Explain who will and argue up and down
That they were made for passing out, as known,
Of urine, and our two belongings small
Were just to tell a female from a male,
And for no other cause—ah, say you no?
130 Experience knows well it is not so;
And, so the clerics be not with me wroth,°   *angry*
I say now that they have been made for both,
That is to say, for duty and for ease
In getting,° when we do not God displease.   *procreation*
135 Why should men otherwise in their books set

That man shall pay unto his wife his
       debt?°   *marital duty*
Now wherewith should he ever make payment,
Except he used his blessed instrument?
Then on a creature were devised these things
140 For urination and engenderings.
       "But I say not that every one is bound,
Who's fitted out and furnished as I've found,
To go and use it to beget an heir;
Then men would have for chastity no care.
145 Christ was a maid, and yet shaped like a man,
And many a saint, since this old world began,
Yet has lived ever in perfect chastity.
I bear no malice to virginity;
Let such be bread of purest white wheat-seed,
150 And let us wives be called but barley bread;
And yet with barley bread (if Mark you scan)
Jesus Our Lord refreshed full many a man.[4]
In such condition as God places us
I'll persevere, I'm not fastidious.
155 In wifehood I will use my instrument
As freely as my Maker has it sent.
If I be niggardly,° God give me sorrow!   *stingy*
My husband he shall have it, eve and morrow,
When he's pleased to come forth and pay his debt.
160 I'll not delay, a husband I will get
Who shall be both my debtor and my thrall°   *slave*
And have his tribulations therewithal
Upon his flesh, the while I am his wife.
I have the power during all my life
165 Over his own good body, and not he.
For thus the apostle told it unto me;
And bade our husbands that they love us well.[5]
And all this pleases me wherof I tell." . . .

The Pardoner's Tale

The Pardoner's Prologue

'My lords,' he said, 'in churches where I preach
I cultivate a haughty kind of speech
And ring it out as roundly as a bell;
I've got it all by heart, the tale I tell:
I have a text, it always is the same   5
And always has been, since I learnt the game,
Old as the hills and fresher than the grass,
Radix malorum est cupiditas.
       'But first I make pronouncement whence I come,
Show them my bulls in detail and in sum.   10

---

[1] 1 Corinthians 7:1: "It is good for a man not to touch a woman"; Alisoun adds a proverb ("example") that fire and tow (flax or hemp) placed too closely together will burn.
[2] Matthew 19:21: "If thou wilt be perfect, go and sell what thou hast, and give to the poor, and thou shalt have treasure in heaven: and come and follow me."
[3] Here, as most of her other arguments in favor of sexual activity, the Wife of Bath closely echoes Jean de Meun's continuation of *The Romance of the Rose* (pages 993–995), which Chaucer had translated from the French.

---

[4] Jesus made enough food to feed five thousand out of five barley loaves and two small fishes. Bread made from barley was considered very low fare.
[5] This is not exactly what Paul intended by his metaphors of debt and subordination (1 Corinthians 7:3–5), which advised husband and wife rather to be sparing in their possession of each other.

And flaunt the papal seal for their inspection
As warrant for my bodily protection,
That none may have the impudence to irk
Or hinder me in Christ's most holy work.
Then I tell stories, as occasion calls,   15
Showing forth bulls from popes and cardinals,
From patriarchs and bishops; as I do,
I speak some words in Latin—just a few—
To put a saffron tinge upon my preaching
And stir devotion with a spice of teaching.   20
Then I bring all my long glass bottles out
Cram-full of bones and ragged bits of clout,
Relics they are, at least for such are known.
Then, cased in metal, I've a shoulder-bone,
Belonging to a sheep, a holy Jew's.   25
"Good men," I say, "take heed, for here is news.
Take but this bone and dip it in a well;
If cow or calf, if sheep or ox should swell
From eating snakes or that a snake has stung,
Take water from that well and wash its tongue,   30
And it will then recover. Furthermore,
Where there is pox or scab or other sore,
All animals that water at that well
Are cured at once. Take note of what I tell.
If the good man—the owner of the stock—   35
Goes once a week, before the crow of cock,
Fasting, and takes a draught of water too,
Why then, according to that holy Jew,
He'll find his cattle multiply and sell.
    "And it's a cure for jealousy as well;   40
For though a man be given to jealous wrath,
Use but this water when you make his broth,
And never again will he mistrust his wife,
Though he knew all about her sinful life,
Though two or three clergy had enjoyed her love.   45
    "Now look; I have a mitten here, a glove.
Whoever wears this mitten on his hand
Will multiply his grain. He sows his land
And up will come abundant wheat or oats,
Providing that he offers pence or groats.   50
    "Good men and women, here's a word of warning;
If there is anyone in church this morning
Guilty of sin, so far beyond expression
Horrible, that he dare not make confession,
Or any woman, whether young or old,   55
That's cuckolded her husband, be she told
That such as she shall have no power or grace
To offer to my relics in this place.
But those who can acquit themselves of blame
Can all come up and offer in God's name,   60
And I will shrive them by the authority
Committed in this papal bull to me."
    'That trick's been worth a hundred marks a year
Since I became a Pardoner, never fear.
Then, priestlike in my pulpit, with a frown,   65
I stand, and when the yokels have sat down,
I preach, as you have heard me say before,
And tell a hundred lying mockeries more.
I take great pains, and stretching out my neck
To east and west I crane about and peck   70
Just like a pigeon sitting on a barn.

My hands and tongue together spin the yarn
And all my antics are a joy to see.
The curse of avarice and cupidity
Is all my sermon, for it frees the pelf.   75
Out come the pence, and specially for myself,
For my exclusive purpose is to win
And not at all to castigate their sin.
Once dead what matter how their souls may fare?
They can go blackberrying, for all I care!   80
    'Believe me, many a sermon or devotive
Exordium issues from an evil motive.
Some to give pleasure by their flattery
And gain promotion through hypocrisy,
Some out of vanity, some out of hate;   85
Or when I dare not otherwise debate
I'll put my discourse into such a shape,
My tongue will be a dagger; no escape
For him from slandering falsehood shall there be.
If he has hurt my brethren or me.   90
For though I never mention him by name
The congregation guesses all the same
From certain hints that everybody knows,
and so I take revenge upon our foes
And spit my venom forth, while I profess   95
Holy and true—or seeming holiness.
    'But let me briefly make my purpose plain;
I preach for nothing but for greed of gain
And use the same old text, as bold as brass,
Radix malorum est cupiditas.   100
And thus I preach against the very vice
I make my living out of—avarice.
And yet however guilty of that sin
Myself, with others I have power to win
Them from it, I can bring them to repent;   105
But that is not my principal intent.
Covetousness is both the root and stuff
Of all I preach. That ought to be enough.
    'Well, then I give examples thick and fast
From bygone times, old stories from the past.   110
A yokel mind loves stories from of old,
Being the kind it can repeat and hold.
What! Do you think, as long as I can preach
And get their silver for the things I teach,
That I will live in poverty, from choice?   115
That's not the counsel of my inner voice!
No! Let me preach and beg from kirk to kirk
And never do an honest job of work,
No, nor make baskets, like St Paul, to gain
A livelihood. I do not preach in vain.   120
There's no apostle I would counterfeit;
I mean to have money, wool and cheese and wheat
Though it were given me by the poorest lad
Or poorest village widow, though she had
A string of starving children, all agape.   125
No, let me drink the liquor of the grape
And keep a jolly wench in every town!
    'But listen, gentlemen; to bring things down
To a conclusion, would you like a tale?
Now as I've drunk a draught of corn-ripe ale,   130
By God it stands to reason I can strike
On some good story that you all will like.

For though I am a wholly vicious man
Don't think I can't tell moral tales. I can!
Here's one I often preach when out for winning;   *135*
Now please be quiet. Here is the beginning.'

The Pardoner's Tale

In Flanders once there was a company
Of youngsters haunting vice and ribaldry,
Riot and gambling, stews and public-houses
Where each with harp, guitar or lute carouses,   *140*
Dancing and dicing day and night, and bold
To eat and drink far more than they can hold,
Doing thereby the devil sacrifice
Within that devil's temple of cursed vice,
Abominable in superfluity,   *145*
With oaths so damnable in blasphemy
That it's a grisly thing to hear them swear.
Our dear Lord's body they will rend and tear
As if the Jews had rent Him not enough;
And at the sin of others every tough   *150*
Will laugh, and presently the dancing-girls,
Small pretty ones, come in and shake their curls,
With youngsters selling fruit, and ancient bawds,
And girls with cakes and music, devil's gauds
To kindle and blow the fires of lechery   *155*
That are so close annexed to gluttony.
Witness the Bible, which is most express
That lust is bred of wine and drunkenness.
    Look how the drunken and unnatural Lot
Lay with his daughters, though he knew it not;   *160*
He was too drunk to know what he was doing.
    Take Herod, too, his tale is work pursuing.
Replete with wine and feasting, he was able
To give the order at his very table
To kill the innocent Baptist, good St John.   *165*
    Seneca has a thought worth pondering on;
No difference, he says, that he can find
Between a madman who has lost his mind
And one who is habitually mellow
Except that madness when it takes a fellow   *170*
Lasts longer, on the whole, than drunkenness.
O cursed gluttony, our first distress!
Cause of our first confusion, first temptation,
The very origin of our damnation,
Till Christ redeemed us with his blood again!   *175*
O infamous indulgence! Cursed stain
So dearly bought! And what has it been worth?
Gluttony has corrupted all the earth.
    Adam, our father, and his wife as well,
From Paradise to labour and to Hell   *180*
Were driven for that vice, they were indeed.
While she and Adam fasted, so I read,
They were in Paradise; when he and she
Ate of the fruit of that forbidden tree
They were at once cast forth in pain and woe.   *185*
O gluttony, it is to thee we owe
Our griefs! O if we knew the maladies
That follow on excess and gluttonies,
Sure we would diet, we would temper pleasure
In sitting down at table, show some measure!   *190*

Alas the narrow throat, the tender mouth!
Men labour east and west and north and south
In earth, in air, in water—Why, d'you think?
To get a glutton dainty meat and drink!
How well of this St Paul's Epistle treats!   *195*
'Meats for the belly, belly for the meats,
But God shall yet destroy both it and them.'
Alas, the filth of it! If we contemn
The name, how far more filthy is the act!
A man who swills down vintages in fact   *200*
Makes a mere privy of his throat, a sink
For cursed superfluities of drink!
    So the Apostle said, whom tears could soften:
'Many there are, as I have told you often,
And weep to tell, whose gluttony sufficed   *205*
To make them enemies of the cross of Christ,
Whose ending is destruction and whose God
Their belly!' O thou belly! stinking pod
Of dung and foul corruption, that canst send
Thy filthy music forth at either end,   *210*
What labour and expense it is to find
Thy sustenance! These cooks that strain and grind
And bray in mortars, transubstantiate
God's gifts into a flavour on a plate,
To please a lecherous palate. How they batter   *215*
Hard bones to put some marrow on your platter,
Spicery, root, bark, leaf—they search and cull it
In the sweet hope of flattering a gullet!
Nothing is thrown away that could delight
Or whet anew lascivious appetite.   *220*
Be sure a man whom such a fare entices
Is dead indeed, though living in his vices.
    Wine is a lecherous thing and drunkenness
A squalor of contention and distress.
O drunkard, how disfigured is thy face,   *225*
How foul thy breath, how filthy thy embrace!
And through thy drunken nose a stertorous snort
Like 'samson-samson'—something of the sort.
Yet Samson never was a man to swig.
You totter, lurch and fall like a stuck pig,   *230*
Your manhood's lost, your tongue is in a burr.
Drunkenness is the very sepulchre
Of human judgment and articulation.
He that is subject to the domination
Of drink can keep no secrets, be it said.   *235*
Keep clear of wine, I tell you, white or red,
Especially Spanish wines which they provide
And have on sale in Fish Street and Cheapside.
That wine mysteriously finds its way
To mix itself with others—shall we say   *240*
Spontaneously!—that grow in neighbouring regions.
Out of the mixture fumes arise in legions,
So when a man has had a drink or two
Though he may think he is at home with you
In Cheapside, I assure you he's in Spain   *245*
Where it was made, at Lepé I maintain,
Not even at Bordeaux. He's soon elate
And very near the 'samson-samson' state.
    But seriously my lords, attention, pray!
All the most notable acts, I dare to say,   *250*
And victories in the Old Testament,

Won under God who is omnipotent,
Were won in abstinence, were won in prayer.
Look in the Bible, you will find it there.
　　Or else take Attila the Conqueror;　　　　255
Died in his sleep, a manner to abhor,
In drunken shame and bleeding at the nose.
A general should live sober, I suppose.
Moreover call to mind and ponder well
What was commanded unto Lemuel　　　　260
—Not Samuel, but Lemuel I said—
Read in the Bible, that's the fountain-head,
And see what comes of giving judges drink.
No more of that. I've said enough, I think.
　　Having put gluttony in its proper setting　　265
I wish to warn you against dice and betting,
Gambling's the very mother of robbed purses,
Lies, double-dealing, perjury, and curses,
Manslaughter, blasphemy of Christ, and waste
Of time and money. Worse, you are debased　　270
In public reputation, put to shame.
'A common gambler' is a nasty name.
　　The more exalted such a man may be
So much the more contemptible is he.
A gambling prince would be incompetent　　　275
To frame a policy of government,
And he will sink in general opinion
As one unfit to exercise dominion.
　　Stilbon, that wise ambassador whose mission
Took him to Corinth, was of high position;　　280
Sparta had sent him with intent to frame
A treaty of alliance. When he came,
Hoping for reinforcement and advice,
It happened that he found them all at dice,
Their very nobles; so he quickly planned　　　285
To steal away, home to his native land.
He said, 'I will not lose my reputation,
Or compromise the honour of my nation,
By asking dicers to negotiate.
Send other wise ambassadors of state,　　　　290
For on my honour I would rather die
Than be a means for Sparta to ally
With gamblers; Sparta, glorious in honour,
Shall take no such alliances upon her
As dicers make, by any act of mine!'　　　　295
He showed his sense in taking such a line.
　　Again, consider King Demetrius;
The King of Parthia—history has it thus—
Sent him a pair of golden dice in scorn,
To show he reckoned him a gambler born　　　300
Whose honour, if unable to surmount
The vice of gambling, was of no account.
Lords can amuse themselves in other ways
Honest enough, to occupy their days.
　　Now let me speak a word or two of swearing　305
And perjury; the Bible is unsparing.
It's an abominable thing to curse
And swear, it says; but perjury is worse.
Almightly God has said, 'Swear not at all,'
Witness St Matthew, and you may recall　　　310
The words of Jeremiah, having care
To what he says of lying: 'Thou shalt swear

In truth, in judgement and in righteousness.'
But idle swearing is a sin, no less.
Behold and see the tables of the Law　　　　315
Of God's Commandments, to be held in awe;
Look at the third where it is written plain,
'Thou shalt not take the name of God in vain.'
You see He has forbidden swearing first;
Not murder, no, nor other thing accurst　　　320
Comes before that, I say, in God's commands.
That is the order; he who understands
Knows that the third commandment is just that.
And in addition, let me tell you flat,
Vengeance on him and all his house shall fall　325
That swears outrageously, or swears at all.
'God's precious heart and passion, by God's nails
And by the blood of Christ that is at Hailes,
Seven's my luck, and yours is five and three;
God's blessed arms! If you play false with me　330
I'll stab you with my dagger!' Overthrown
By two small dice, two bitching bits of bone,
Their fruit is perjury, rage and homicide.
O for the love of Jesus Christ who died
For us, abandon curses, small or great!　　　335
But, sirs, I have a story to relate.
　　It's of three rioters I have to tell
Who, long before the morning service bell,
Were sitting in a tavern for a drink.
And as they sat, they heard the hand-bell clink　340
Before a coffin going to the grave;
One of them called the little tavern-knave
And said 'Go and find out at once—look spry!—
Whose corpse is in that coffin passing by;
And see you get the name correctly too.'　　　345
'Sir,' said the boy, 'no need, I promise you;
Two hours before you came here I was told.
He was a friend of yours in days of old,
And suddenly, last night, the man was slain,
Upon his bench, face up, dead drunk again.　　350
There came a privy thief, they call him Death,
Who kills us all round here, and in a breath
He speared him through the heart, he never stirred.
And then Death went his way without a word.
He's killed a thousand in the present plague,　355
And, sir, it doesn't do to be too vague
If you should meet him; you had best be wary.
Be on your guard with such an adversary,
Be primed to meet him everywhere you go,
That's what my mother said. It's all I know.'　360
　　The publican joined in with, 'By St Mary,
What the child says is right; you'd best be wary,
This very year he killed, in a large village
A mile away, man, woman, serf at tillage,
Page in the household, children—all there were.　365
Yes, I imagine that he lives round there.
It's well to be prepared in these alarms,
He might do you dishonour.' 'Huh, God's arms!'
The rioter said, 'Is he so fierce to meet?
I'll search for him, by Jesus, street by street.　370
God's blessed bones! I'll register a vow!
Here, chaps! The three of us together now,
Hold up your hands, like me, and we'll be brothers

In this affair, and each defend the others,
And we will kill this traitor Death, I say!   375
Away with him as he has made away
With all our friends. God's dignity! Tonight!'
     They made their bargain, swore with appetite,
These three, to live and die for one another
As brother-born might swear to his born brother.   380
And up they started in their drunken rage
And made towards this village which the page
And publican had spoken of before.
Many and grisly were the oaths they swore,
Tearing Christ's blessed body to a shred;   385
'If we can only catch him, Death is dead!'
     When they had gone not fully half a mile,
Just as they were about to cross a stile,
They came upon a very poor old man
Who humbly greeted them and thus began,   390
'God look to you, my lords, and give you quiet!'
To which the proudest of these men of riot
Gave back the answer, 'What, old fool? Give place!
Why are you all wrapped up except your face?
Why live so long? Isn't it time to die?'   395
     The old, old fellow looked him in the eye
And said, 'Because I never yet have found,
Though I have walked to India, searching round
Village and city on my pilgrimage,
One who would change his youth to have my age.   400
And so my age is mine and must be still
Upon me, for such time as God may will.
     'Not even Death, alas, will take my life;
So, like a wretched prisoner at strife
Within himself, I walk alone and wait   405
About the earth, which is my mother's gate,
Knock-knocking with my staff from night to noon
And crying, "Mother, open to me soon!
Look at me, mother, won't you let me in?
See how I wither, flesh and blood and skin!   410
Alas! When will these bones be laid to rest?
Mother, I would exchange—for that were best—
The wardrobe in my chamber, standing there
So long, for yours! Aye, for a shirt of hair
To wrap me in!" She has refused her grace,   415
Whence comes the pallor of my withered face.
     'But it dishonoured you when you began
To speak so roughly, sir, to an old man,
Unless he had injured you in word or deed.
It says in holy writ, as you may read,   420
"Thou shalt rise up before the hoary head
And honour it." And therefore be it said
"Do no more harm to an old man than you,
Being now young, would have another do
When you are old"—if you should live till then.   425
And so may God be with you, gentlemen,
For I must go whither I have to go.'
     'By God,' the gambler said, 'you shan't do so,
You don't get off so easy, by St John!
I heard you mention, just a moment gone,   430
A certain traitor Death who singles out
And kills the fine young fellows hereabout.
And you're his spy, by God! You wait a bit.
Say where he is or you shall pay for it,

By God and by the Holy Sacrament!   435
I say you've joined together by consent
To kill us younger folk, you thieving swine!'
     'Well, sirs,' he said, 'if it be your design
To find out Death, turn up this crooked way
Towards that grove, I left him there today   440
Under a tree, and there you'll find him waiting.
He isn't one to hide for all your prating.
You see that oak? He won't be far to find.
And God protect you that redeemed mankind,
Aye, and amend you!' Thus that ancient man.   445
     At once the three young rioters began
To run, and reached the tree, and there they found
A pile of golden florins on the ground,
New-coined, eight bushels of them as they thought.
No longer was it Death those fellows sought,   450
For they were all so thrilled to see the sight,
The florins were so beautiful and bright,
That down they sat beside the precious pile.
The wickedest spoke first after a while.
'Brothers,' he said, 'you listen to what I say.   455
I'm pretty sharp although I joke away.
It's clear that Fortune has bestowed this treasure
To let us live in jollity and pleasure.
Light come, light go! We'll spend it as we ought.
God's precious dignity! Who would have thought   460
This morning was to be our lucky day?
     'If one could only get the gold away,
Back to my house, or else to yours, perhaps—
For as you know, the gold is ours, chaps—
We'd all be at the top of fortune, hey?   465
But certainly it can't be done by day.
People would call us robbers—a strong gang,
So our own property would make us hang.
No, we must bring this treasure back by night
Some prudent way, and keep it out of sight.   470
And so as a solution I propose
We draw for lots and see the way it goes;
The one who draws the longest, lucky man,
Shall run to town as quickly as he can
To fetch us bread and wine—but keep things dark—   475
While two remain in hiding here to mark
Our heap of treasure. If there's no delay,
When night comes down we'll carry it away,
All three of us, wherever we have planned.'
     He gathered lots and hid them in his hand   480
Bidding them draw for where the luck should fall.
It fell upon the youngest of them all,
And off he ran at once towards the town.
     As soon as he had gone the first sat down
And thus began a parley with the other: 485
'You know that you can trust me as a brother;
Now let me tell you where your profit lies;
You know our friend has gone to get supplies
And here's a lot of gold that is to be
Divided equally amongst us three.   490
Nevertheless, if I could shape things thus
So that we shared it out—the two of us—
Wouldn't you take it as a friendly act?'
     'But how?' the other said. 'He knows the fact
That all the gold was left with me and you;   495

What can we tell him? What are we to do?'
   'Is it a bargain,' said the first, 'or no?
For I can tell you in a word or so
What's to be done to bring the thing about.'
'Trust me,' the other said, 'you needn't doubt   *500*
My word. I won't betray you, I'll be true.'
   'Well,' said his friend, 'you see that we are two,
And two are twice as powerful as one.
Now look; when he comes back, get up in fun
To have a wrestle; then, as you attack,   *505*
I'll up and put my dagger through his back
While you and he are struggling, as in game;
Then draw your dagger too and do the same.
Then all this money will be ours to spend,
Divided equally of course, dear friend.   *510*
Then we can gratify our lusts and fill
The day with dicing at our own sweet will.'
Thus these two miscreants agreed to slay
The third and youngest, as you heard me say.
   The youngest, as he ran towards the town,   *515*
Kept turning over, rolling up and down
Within his heart the beauty of those bright
New florins, saying, 'Lord, to think I might
Have all that treasure to myself alone!
Could there be anyone beneath the throne   *520*
Of God so happy as I then should be?'
   And so the Fiend, our common enemy,
Was given power to put it in his thought
That there was always poison to be bought,
And that with poison he could kill his friends.   *525*
To men in such a state the Devil sends
Thoughts of this kind, and has a full permission
To lure them on to sorrow and perdition;
For this young man was utterly content
To kill them both and never to repent.   *530*
   And on he ran, he had no thought to tarry,
Came to the town, found an apothecary
And said, 'Sell me some poison if you will,
I have a lot of rats I want to kill
And there's a polecat too about my yard   *535*
That takes my chickens and it hits me hard;
But I'll get even, as is only right,
With vermin that destroy a man by night.'
   The chemist answered, 'I've a preparation
Which you shall have, and by my soul's salvation   *540*
If any living creature eat or drink
A mouthful, ere he has the time to think,
Though he took less than makes a grain of wheat,
You'll see him fall down dying at your feet;
Yes, die he must, and in so short a while   *545*
You'd hardly have the time to walk a mile,
The poison is so strong, you understand.'
   This cursed fellow grabbed into his hand
The box of poison and away he ran
Into a neighbouring street, and found a man   *550*
Who lent him three large bottles. He withdrew
And deftly poured the poison into two.
He kept the third one clean, as well he might,
For his own drink, meaning to work all night
Stacking the gold and carrying it away.   *555*
And when this rioter, this devil's clay,

Had filled his bottles up with wine, all three,
Back to rejoin his comrades sauntered he.
   Why make a sermon of it? Why waste breath?
Exactly in the way they'd planned his death   *560*
They fell on him and slew him, two to one.
Then said the first of them when this was done,
'Now for a drink. Sit down and let's be merry,
For later on there'll be the corpse to bury.'
And, as it happened, reaching for a sup,   *565*
He took a bottle full of poison up
And drank; and his companion, nothing loth,
Drank from it also, and they perished both.
   There is, in Avicenna's long relation
Concerning poison and its operation,   *570*
Trust me, no ghastlier section to transcend
What these two wretches suffered at their end.
Thus these two murderers received their due,
So did the treacherous young poisoner too.
   O cursed sin! O blackguardly excess!   *575*
O treacherous homicide! O wickedness!
O gluttony that lusted on and diced!
O blasphemy that took the name of Christ
With habit-hardened oaths that pride began!
Alas, how comes it that a mortal man,   *580*
That thou, to thy Creator, Him that wrought thee,
That paid His precious blood for thee and bought thee,
Art so unnatural and false within?
   Dearly beloved, God forgive your sin
And keep you from the vice of avarice!   *585*
My holy pardon frees you all of this,
Provided that you make the right approaches,
That is with sterling, rings, or silver brooches.
Bow down your heads under this holy bull!
Come on, you women, offer up your wool!   *590*
I'll write your name into my ledger; so!
Into the bliss of Heaven you shall go.
For I'll absolve you by my holy power,
You that make offering, clean as at the hour
When you were born . . . That, sirs, is how I preach.   *595*
And Jesus Christ, soul's healer, aye, the leech
Of every soul, grant pardon and relieve you
Of sin, for that is best, I won't deceive you.
   One thing I should have mentioned in my tale,
Dear people. I've some relics in my bale   *600*
And pardons too, as full and fine, I hope,
As any in England, given me by the Pope.
If there be one among you that is willing
To have my absolution for a shilling
Devoutly given, come! and do not harden   *605*
Your hearts but kneel in humbleness for pardon;
Or else, receive my pardon as we go.
You can renew it every town or so
Always provided that you still renew
Each time, and in good money, what is due.   *610*
It is an honour to you to have found
A pardoner with his credentials sound
Who can absolve you as you ply the spur
In any accident that may occur.
For instance—we are all at Fortune's beck—   *615*
Your horse may throw you down and break your neck.
What a security it is to all

To have me here among you and at call
With pardon for the lowly and the great
When soul leaves body for the future state!   *620*
And I advise our Host here to begin,
The most enveloped of you all in sin.
Come forward, Host, you shall be the first to pay,
And kiss my holy relics right away.
Only a groat. Come on, unbuckle your purse!'   *625*
    'No, no,' said he, 'not I, and may the curse
Of Christ descend upon me if I do!
You'll have me kissing your old breeches too
And swear they were the relic of a saint
Although your fundament supplied the paint!   *630*
Now by St Helen and the Holy Land
I wish I had your ballocks in my hand
Instead of relics in a reliquarium;
Have them cut off and I will help to carry 'em.
We'll have them shrined for you in a hog's turd.'   *635*
    The Pardoner said nothing, not a word;
He was so angry that he couldn't speak.
'Well,' said our Host, 'if you're for showing pique,
I'll joke no more, not with an angry man.'
    The worthy Knight immediately began,   *640*
Seeing the fun was getting rather rough,
And said, 'No more, we've all had quite enough.
Now, Master Pardoner, perk up, look cheerly!
And you, Sir Host, whom I esteem so dearly,
I beg of you to kiss the Pardoner.   *645*
    'Come, Pardoner, draw nearer, my dear sir.
Let's laugh again and keep the ball in play.'
They kissed, and we continued on our way.

CHRISTINE DE PIZAN

from *The Book of the City of Ladies*

One of the most important aspects of The Book of the City of Ladies *is its celebration of learning, particularly its contention that women are as intellectually able as men. Arguing that the education of women had long been woefully neglected, Christine de Pizan was the first woman to insist in writing that women need and deserve to be educated. Citing examples from history and mythology, including the Greek poet Sappho and the Roman goddess of wisdom, Minerva, she illustrates the accomplishments of women and celebrates their achievements. Her arguments in support of women provide one of the earliest and strongest counters to the deep male bias against women because she is the first professional woman writer to write from the point of view of women.*

Christine asks Reason whether God has ever wished to ennoble the mind of woman with the loftiness of the sciences; and Reason's answer

After hearing these things, I replied to the lady who spoke infallibly: "My lady, truly has God revealed great wonders in the strength of these women whom you describe. But please enlighten me again, whether it has ever pleased this God, who has bestowed so many favors on women, to honor the feminine sex with the privilege of the virtue of high understanding and great learning, and whether women ever have a clever enough mind for this. I wish very much to know this because men maintain that the mind of women can learn only a little."

She answered, "My daughter, since I told you before, you know quite well that the opposite of their opinion is true, and to show you this even more clearly, I will give you proof through examples. I tell you again—and don't doubt the contrary—if it were customary to send daughters to school like sons, and if they were then taught the natural sciences, they would learn as thoroughly and understand the subtleties of all the arts and sciences as well as sons. And by chance there happen to be such women, for, as I touched on before, just as women have more delicate bodies than men, weaker and less able to perform many tasks, so do they have minds that are freer and sharper whenever they apply themselves."

"My lady, what are you saying? With all due respect, could you dwell longer on this point, please. Certainly men would never admit this answer is true, unless it is explained more plainly, for they believe that one normally sees that men know more than women do."

She answered, "Do you know why women know less?"

"Not unless you tell me, my lady."

"Without the slightest doubt, it is because they are not involved in many different things, but stay at home, where it is enough for them to run the household, and there is nothing which so instructs a reasonable creature as the exercise and experience of many different things."

"My lady, since they have minds skilled in conceptualizing and learning, just like men, why don't women learn more?"

She replied, "Because, my daughter, the public does not require them to get involved in the affairs which men are commissioned to execute, just as I told you before. It is enough for women to perform the usual duties to which they are ordained. As for judging from experience, since one sees that women usually know less than men, that therefore their capacity for understanding is less, look at men who farm the flatlands or who live in the mountains. You will find that in many countries they seem completely savage because they are so simple-minded. All the same, there is no doubt that Nature provided them with the qualities of body and mind found in the wisest and most learned men. All of this stems from a failure to learn, though, just as I told you, among men and women, some possess better minds than others. Let me tell you about women who have possessed great learning and profound understanding and treat the question of the similarity of women's minds to men's."

She begins to discuss several ladies who were enlightened with great learning, and first speaks about the noble maiden Cornificia

"Cornificia, the noble maiden, was sent to school by her parents along with her brother Cornificius when they were both children, thanks to deception and trickery. This little girl so devoted herself to study and with such marvelous intelligence that she began to savor the sweet taste of knowledge acquired through study. Nor was it easy to take her away from this joy to which she more and more applied herself, neglecting all other feminine activities. She occupied herself with this for such a long period of time that she became a consummate poet, and she was not only extremely brilliant and expert in the learnedness and craft of poetry but also seemed to have been nourished with the very milk and teaching of perfect philosophy, for she wanted to hear and know about every branch of learning, which she then mastered so thoroughly that she surpassed her brother, who was also a very great poet, and excelled in every field of learning. Knowledge was not enough for her unless she could put her mind to work and her pen to paper in the compilation of several very famous books. These works, as well as her poems, were much prized during the time of Saint Gregory and he himself mentions them. The Italian, Boccaccio, who was a great poet, discusses this fact in his work and at the same time praises this woman: 'O most great honor for a woman who abandoned all feminine activities and applied and devoted her mind to the study of the greatest scholars!' As further proof of what I am telling you, Boccaccio also talks about the attitude of women who despise themselves and their own minds, and who, as though they were born in the mountains totally ignorant of virtue and honor, turn disconsolate and say that they are good and useful only for embracing men and carrying and feeding children. God has given them such beautiful minds to apply themselves, if they want to, in any of the fields where glorious and excellent men are active, which are neither more nor less accessible to them as compared to men if they wished to study them, and they can thereby acquire a lasting name, whose possession is fitting for most excellent men. My dear daughter, you can see how this author Boccaccio testifies to what I have told you and how he praises and approved learning in women.''

Here she tells of Proba the Roman

"The Roman woman, Proba, wife of Adelphus, was equally outstanding and was a Christian. She had such a noble mind and so loved and devoted herself to study that she mastered all seven liberal arts and was an excellent poet and delved so deeply into the books of the poets, particularly Vergil's poems, that she knew them all by heart. After she had read these books and poems with profound insight and intelligence and had taken pains in her mind to understand them, it occurred to her that one could describe the Scriptures and the stories found in the Old and New Testament with pleasant verses filled with substance taken from these same works. 'Which in itself,' Boccaccio remarked, 'is not just admirable, that such a noble idea would come into a woman's brain, but it is even more marvelous that she could actually execute it.' For then this woman, quite eager to bring her thinking to fruition, set to work: now she would run through the *Eclogues*, then the *Georgics*, and the *Aeneid* of Vergil—that is, she would skim as she read—and in one part she would take several entire verses unchanged and in another borrow small snatches of verse and, through marvelous craftsmanship and conceptual subtlety, she was able to construct entire lines of orderly verse. She would put small pieces together, coupling and joining them, all the while respecting the metrical rules, art and measure in the individual feet, as well as in the conjoining of verses, and without making any mistakes she arranged her verses so masterfully that no man could do better. In this way, starting from the creation of the world, she composed the opening of her book, and following all the stories of the Old and New Testament she came as far as the sending of the Holy Spirit to the Apostles, adapting Vergil's works to fit all this in so orderly a way that someone who only knew this work would have thought that Vergil had been both a prophet and evangelist.

For these reasons, Boccaccio himself says that this woman merits great recognition and praise, for it is obvious that she possessed a sound and exhaustive knowledge of the sacred books and volumes of Holy Scripture, as do many great scholars and theologians of our time. This most noble lady wished that this said work, drawn up and composed through her labor, be called the *Cento*. Although the labor demanded by this work, because of its grandeur, would have been enough for one man's life-time, she spent much less time in devoting herself to its execution, and was also able to compose several other excellent books. One, among others, she composed in verse, also called *Cento* because it contained one hundred lines of verse. She also made use of the poems and verses of the poet Homer, so that in praising her one can conclude that she knew not only Latin literature but also Greek literature perfectly. Boccaccio observes that it should be a great pleasure for women to hear about her and these things.''

Here she speaks of Sappho, that most subtle woman, poet, and philosopher

"The wise Sappho, who was from the city of Mytilene, was no less learned than Proba. This Sappho had a beautiful body and face and was agreeable and pleasant in appearance, conduct, and speech. But the charm of her profound understanding surpassed all the other charms with which she was endowed, for she was expert and learned in several arts and sciences, and she was not only well-educated in the works and writings composed by others but also discovered many new things herself and wrote many books and poems. Concerning her, Boccaccio has offered these fair words couched in the sweetness of poetic language: 'Sappho, possessed of sharp wit and burning desire for constant study in the midst of bestial and ignorant men, frequented the heights of Mount Parnassus, that is, of perfect study. Thanks to her fortunate boldness and daring, she kept company with the Muses, that is, the arts and sciences, without being turned away. She entered the forest of laurel trees filled with may boughs, greenery, and different colored flowers, soft fragrances and various aromatic spices, where Grammar, Logic, noble Rhetoric, Geometry, and Arithmetic live and take their leisure. She went on her way until she came to the deep grotto of Apollo, god of learning, and found the brook and conduit of the fountain of Castalia, and took up the plectrum and quill of the harp and played sweet melodies, with the nymphs all the while leading the dance, that is, following the rules of harmony and musical accord.' From what Boccaccio says about her, it should be inferred that the profundity of both her understanding and of her learned books can only be known and understood by men of great perception and learning, according to the testimony of the ancients. Her writings and poems have survived to this day, most remarkably constructed and composed, and they serve as illumination and models of consummate poetic craft and composition to those who have come afterward. She invented different genres of lyric and poetry, short narratives, tearful laments and strange lamentations about love and other emotions, and these were so well made and so well ordered that they were named 'Sapphic' after her. Horace recounts, concerning her poems, that when Plato, the great philosopher who was Aristotle's teacher, died, a book of Sappho's poems was found under his pillow.

"In brief this lady was so outstanding in learning that in the city where she resided a statue of bronze in her image was dedicated in her name and erected in a prominent place so that she would be honored by all and be remembered forever. This lady was placed and counted among the greatest and most famous poets, and, according to Boccaccio, the honors of the diadems and crowns of kings and the miters of bishops are not any greater, nor are the crowns of laurel and victor's palm.

"I could tell you a great deal about women of great learning. Leontium was a Greek woman and also such a great philosopher that she dared, for impartial and serious reasons, to correct and attack the philosopher Theophrastus, who was quite famous in her time."

CHAPTER 13

HISTORY

1494	First French invasion of Italy
ca. 1495	Savonarola takes control of Florence
1494–1512	Medici exiled from Florence
1516–23	Leo X controls Florence
1519	Charles V becomes Holy Roman Emperor
1523–27	Clement VII controls Florence
1527	Sack of Rome
1553–63	Council of Trent

ARTS AND ARCHITECTURE

ca. 1425–30s	Donatello, *David*
1427–28	Masaccio, *Trinity*
1425–52	Ghiberti, *Gates of Paradise*
1430	Dufay Alma Redemptoris Mater
1436	Brunelleschi finishes dome for Florence Cathedral; Dufay, "Il Duomo"
1453–55	Donatello, *Mary Magdalene*
1438–45	Fra Angelico, *Annunciation*
1445–ca. 1452	Michelozzo, Palazzo Medici-Riccardi
ca. 1484–86	Botticelli, *Birth of Venus*
ca. 1499	Michelangelo, *Pietà*
1502	Josquin des Près, "Ave Maria . . . virgo serena"
ca. 1503	Leonardo da Vinci, *Mona Lisa*
1508–12	Michelangelo, ceiling of Sistine Chapel
1510–11	Raphael, *School of Athens*
ca. 1520	Properzia de Rossi, *Joseph and Potiphar's Wife*
1524–59	Laurentian Library
1534–40	Parmigianino, *Madonna with the Long Neck*
1543–54	Cellini, *Perseus*
ca. 1559	Sofonisba Anguissola, *Portrait of the Artist's Sister Minerva*
1565	Palestrina, *Pope Marcellus Mass*

LITERATURE AND PHILOSOPHY

1327–72	Petrarch, *Canzonieri*
1429	Bruni finishes *History of Florence*
1435–50	Alberti, *De pictura/De re aedificatoria*
ca. 1455	Gutenberg and the printing press
1462	Platonic Academy of Philosophy
ca. 1484–86	Ficino, *Theologia Platonica*
1486	Pico, *Oration on the Dignity of Man*
1524–59	Castiglione, *Book of the Courtier*
1534–40	Machiavelli, *The Prince*
1550	Vasari, *Lives*
1553–63	Cellini, *Autobiography*

The Renaissance
and Mannerism in Italy

Leonardo da Vinci, *The Last Supper*, refectory, Santa Maria delle Grazie, Milan, 1495–98, tempera and oil on plaster, 15′2″ × 28′10″ (4.60 × 8.80 m). Superstock.

MAP 13.1   The division of Italy into city-states at the end of the fifteenth century.

CHAPTER OVERVIEW

THE EARLY RENAISSANCE
Rebirth of interest in antiquity, the individual, and nature

THE HIGH RENAISSANCE
The maturation of the arts

MANNERISM
Moving away from the classical ideal

THE EARLY RENAISSANCE

The transition from the Middle Ages to the Renaissance was gradual. The intense religiosity of the Middle Ages persisted into the Renaissance, though it came to coexist with a more worldly philosophy and a more secular outlook. A number of important broad changes developed during the Renaissance, such as the development of nation states, the advent of commercial capitalism, the emergence of the middle class, and the rise of rationalist thought. European exploration of the Americas was abetted by scientific and technological developments, especially in navigation. And the invention of movable type, which allowed for printing, expanded the world of learning.

Of particular importance in Europe, originally in Italy, was a reinvigoration of classical learning based on the literary and philosophical writings of the Greeks and Romans. This development, called "classical humanism," was a defining Renaissance intellectual preoccupation. The influence of Greco-Roman antiquity on Renaissance Europe was pervasive, and included an impact on social, political, and diplomatic life, as well as upon education and the arts. Of great importance is the part played by Arab scholars in preserving ancient Greek scholarship, which enabled European scholars like Petrarch and Boccaccio to benefit from their labors.

In Italy, changes were developing across the social, political, and economic spectrums. Italy underwent significant urbanization, increased political stability, and economic expansion, along with increasing contact with other societies. Venice, for example, was a crossroads for East–West commercial exchanges, and also for exchange of customs and ideas.

The French word **Renaissance,** meaning "rebirth," was first employed in the nineteenth century to describe the period from the early fifteenth century to the middle of the next. The Italians of the time believed this period marked a radical break from the past and a reinvention of the civilization and ideals of classical Greece and Rome.

The Renaissance was characterized by—in addition to this interest in classical art, literature, law, and ideals—an interest in the individual person, now emerging from the anonimity of the Middle Ages, as well as a new fascination with nature and the physical world. A number of Italian city-states had grown powerful in Italy—the kingdom of Naples in the south, the church states around Rome, and in the north, the duchy of Milan and the republics of Venice and Florence. Located on the main road connecting Rome with the north, Florence had become the center of trade, and European banking had been established with credit operations available to support and spur on an increase in trade (fig. 13.1).

Florence itself was ruled by its guilds, or *arti.* The seven major guilds, which were controlled by bankers, lawyers, and exporters, originally ran the civic government, but by the middle of the fourteenth century all the guilds, even the lesser guilds of middle-ranking tradesmen, had achieved some measure of political voice, and the city prided itself on its "representative" government and its status as a republic. Still, the long-standing division between those who favored the Holy Roman Emperor and those who favored the popes continued unabated. Such civil strife, sometimes marked by street battles, had one inevitable result. By the fifteenth century, what Florence needed most was a leader with enough political skill, power, and wealth to stop the feuding.

FIGURE 13.1   A map of Florence in 1490.

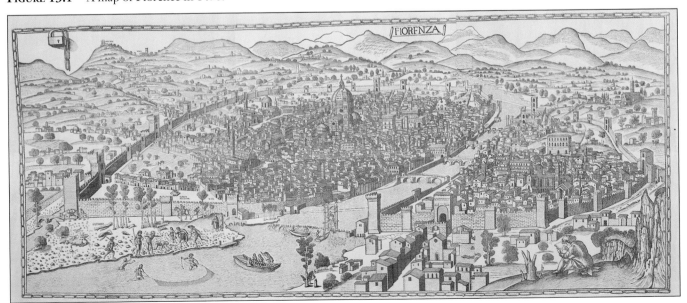

THE MEDICIS' FLORENCE

A single family, the Medici, led Florence to its unrivaled position as the cultural center of Renaissance Europe in the fifteenth century. The family had begun to accumulate its fortune by lending money to other Florentines out of income derived from its two wool workshops. GIO-VANNI DI BICCI DE' MEDICI [geo-VAHN-nee dee BEE-chee deh MED-uh-chee] (1360–1429) multiplied this fortune by setting up branch banks in major Italian cities and creating close financial allegiances with the papacy in Rome, allegiances that tended to switch the balance of power, making secular concerns more important than religious ones to the Vatican.

Cosimo de' Medici.   COSIMO [CAH-zee-moh] (1389–1464), the son of Giovanni Di Bicci, led the family to a position of unquestioned preeminence, not only in Florence but, as branches of the Medici banks opened elsewhere, throughout Europe. Although never the official leader of the city, Cosimo ruled from behind the scenes. By 1458, Pope Pius II said of Cosimo that "He is King in everything but name."

Cosimo's power was based on calculated acts of discretion and benevolence. Cosimo built the first public library since ancient times and stocked it with ancient manuscripts and books, chiefly Greek and Roman, with a special eye toward the works of Plato and Aristotle. At some point, Cosimo employed virtually every major Italian artist, architect, writer, philosopher, or scholar of the day.

In many ways, Cosimo's largesse simply solidified what was already fact—Florence had been a cultural center since the middle of the fourteenth century (see Chapter 12). The growing wealth of the city itself, together with the peace brought by Cosimo's leadership, created an atmosphere in which the arts could prosper, and this in turn contributed to the increasing sophistication of its citizenry.

Lorenzo the Magnificent.   The city's dream of achieving the status of the Golden Age of Athens was fully realized by LORENZO [LOR-enn-zoh] (1449–1492), Cosimo's grandson, who assumed his place as head of the

FIGURE 13.2   Giorgio Vasari, *Posthumous Portrait of Lorenzo the Magnificent*, oil on canvas, Galleria degli Uffizi, Florence. SCALA/Art Resource, NY. The impressive presence of Lorenzo, as well as his broken nose, are recorded in this painting by Vasari, author of the *Lives of the Most Eminent Sculptors, Painters, and Architects.*

Medici family at the age of twenty in 1469, inaugurating twenty-three years of influence. Lorenzo's father, PIERO [pea-AIR-oh] (1416–1469), cursed with ill health, had ruled for only five years after Cosimo before his own death, but he had raised Lorenzo in Cosimo's image, and Lorenzo quickly established himself as a force to be reckoned with. "Lorenzo the Magnificent" he was called (fig. 13.2), and he lived with a sense of grandeur. He was one of the leading

Table 13–1 POPES DURING THE RENAISSANCE AND MANNERIST PERIODS					
The Catholic popes of the fifteenth and sixteenth centuries and the dates they reigned:					
Boniface IX	1389–1404	Innocent VIII	1484–1492	Paul IV	1555–1559
Innocent VII	1404–1406	Alexander VI	1492–1503	Pius IV	1559–1565
Gregory XII	1406–1415	Pius III	1503	St. Pius V	1566–1572
Martin V	1417–1431	Julius II	1503–1513	Gregory XIII	1572–1585
Eugene IV	1431–1447	Leo X	1513–1521	Sixtus V	1585–1590
Nicholas V	1447–1455	Adrian VI	1522–1523	Urban VII	1590
Callistus III	1455–1458	Clement VII	1523–1534	Gregory XIV	1590–1591
Pius II	1458–1464	Paul III	1534–1549	Innocent IX	1591
Paul II	1464–1471	Julius III	1550–1555	Clement VIII	1592–1605
Sixtus IV	1471–1484	Marcellus II	1555		

Cross Currents

MONTEZUMA'S TENOCHTITLAN

While Florence stood as the center of the Early Renaissance world, in the other hemisphere stood a city of equal grandeur, one that the Europeans did not know existed until Hernán Cortés invaded Mexico in 1519. It was called Tenochtitlan, and it was the capital of Montezuma's Aztec empire.

The Aztecs, who founded the city, believed they had been ordered by their god Huitzilopochtli to wander until they saw an eagle perched upon a prickly pear, or *tenochtli*. They finally encountered such a vision in 1325 on an island in the marshes of Lake Texcoco in the Valley of Mexico. There they built their city, connecting it to the mainland by four causeways. By the end of the fifteenth century, it was a metropolis inhabited by 150,000 to 200,000 people and ruled by a priest and emperor, Montezuma.

The *Codex Mendoza* (fig. 13.3) is the fullest account that we have of early sixteenth-century Aztec life. It consists of seventy-two annotated pictorial pages together with sixty-three more pages of re-lated Spanish commentary. It was compiled under the supervision of Spanish friars and at the request of the Spanish crown in about 1541 to aid in their colonial expansion.

As depicted by Aztec scribes, the city is represented by the eagle on the cactus, the shield and arrows symbolizing war, and the waterways dividing the city into equal quadrants. At the heart of the city was the Great Pyramid, imaged by the scribes in the temple at the top. Here, the Aztecs worshiped both Huitzilopochtli, god of the sun and of warfare, and Tlaloc, god of rain and fertility, and here they engaged in ritual human sacrifice to both gods by cutting out the still-beating hearts of their victims, then decapitating them.

As the cultural center of the Aztec civilization, Tenochtitlan was magnificent, grander in fact than anything in Europe at the time. In the words of one of Cortés's soldiers: "When we saw . . . that straight and level causeway going towards Tenochtitlan, we were amazed. . . . Some of our soldiers even asked whether the things that we saw were not a dream."

FIGURE 13.3   *The Founding of Tenochtitlan*, page from the *Codex Mendoza*, Aztec, sixteenth century, ink and color on paper, $81\frac{7}{10} \times 12\frac{3}{8}$″ (21.5 × 31.5 cm), The Bodleian Library, Oxford. The skull rack just to the right of center is one of the very few images in the Codex that openly acknowledges the practice of human sacrifice in Aztec life.

---

poets of his day, as well as an accomplished musician, playing the lute and composing dances. He surrounded himself with scholars, built palaces and parks, sponsored festivals and pageants, all the while dipping deeply into the city's coffers, which he controlled, as well as his own. He commissioned little in the way of painting, preferring instead to spend money on gemstones and ancient vases, which he believed to be better investments. Many of the precious stones in his collection, for example, were valued at over a thousand florins (the coin of the day), whereas a painting by Botticelli might be bought for as little as a hundred florins. Spend Lorenzo did, and by the time of his death in 1492, the Medici bank was in financial trouble and Florence itself was verging on bankruptcy.

Although the Medici ruled Florence with minor interruptions until 1737, they never again held the same power and authority as Cosimo and Lorenzo. Outside Florence, the most important patron of the Renaissance in Rome would be Lorenzo's son, Pope Leo X. In generations to come, several female Medici descendants would marry the most powerful figures in Europe—Catherine de' Medici (1519–89) was queen to Henry II of France, and Marie de'

Medici (1573–1642) was queen consort to Henry IV of France.

THE HUMANIST SPIRIT

Cosimo, Piero, and Lorenzo de' Medici were all **humanists**—they believed in the worth and dignity of the individual. Celebrating human reason, spirit, and physical beauty, the humanists echoed the Greek philosopher Protagorus in seeing human beings as the measure of all things. Seeking to discover what was best about humanity, they turned to the culture of classical antiquity. In the literature, history, rhetoric, and philosophy of ancient Greece and Rome, they discovered what the Latin scholar and poet PETRARCH [PEH-trark] (1304–72) a century before had called a "golden wisdom." Cosimo and Lorenzo worked to make Florence the humanist capital of the world, a place where the golden wisdom of the ancients might flourish.

Petrarch is often called the father of humanism, and in many ways he determined its high moral tone. He believed that learning was the key to living a virtuous life, and that life should be an eternal quest for truth. Every individual leading a virtuous life in the pursuit of knowledge and truth would provide a basis for improving humanity's lot. He encouraged an appreciation of beauty, in nature and in human endeavor, which he thought to be a manifestation of the divine. For Petrarch, reading the ancients was like having conversations with them, and he took to writing letters to the ancients as if they were personal friends, even family. He called the poet Virgil his brother and Cicero his father. In the writings of the ancients, Petrarch sensed their uniquely human (noble and ignoble) qualities.

In the middle of the fourteenth century, Petrarch's friend, the writer Boccaccio, was one of the first men to study Greek since the classical age itself. During the next fifty years, humanist scholars combed monastery libraries for long-ignored ancient Greek texts and translated them into Latin and Italian. By 1400, the works of Homer, Aeschylus, Sophocles, Euripides, Aristophanes, Herodotus, Thucydides, and all of Plato's dialogues were available. In addition, after the fall of Constantinople to the Muslim forces of the Ottoman Turks in 1453, ending the already weakening Byzantine Empire, Greek scholars flooded into Italy. Greek learning spread with the rapid rise of printing in Italy following Johann Gutenberg's invention of printing with movable type in 1455. Between 1456 and 1500, more books were published than had been copied by manuscript scribes in the previous thousand years. Many of these were in vernacular (or native) Italian, which contributed to the growing literacy of the middle class. By the sixteenth century, many educated persons owned the complete works of Plato.

THE PLATONIC ACADEMY OF PHILOSOPHY

The center of humanist study was the Platonic Academy of Philosophy in Florence, founded by Cosimo de' Medici in 1462 and supported with special enthusiasm by Lorenzo the Magnificent. The academy sponsored **Neoplatonism,** or a "new Platonism," which sought to revive Platonic ideals in contemporary culture, especially as espoused by the Roman philosopher PLOTINUS [Ploh-TINE-us] (205–270 C.E.). The Platonic Academy was an important example of the shift of interest from Aristotle during the Middle Ages to Plato during the Renaissance.

Marsilio Ficino.   At the head of the academy was MARSILIO FICINO [fi-CHEE-noh] (1433–99), who translated both Plato and Plotinus into Latin and wrote the *Theologia Platonica* (1482). Ficino's Neoplatonism was a conscious rereading of Plato (see Chapter 3), particularly his dualistic vision of the psyche (roughly equivalent to the soul or spirit) trapped in the body, but Ficino thought we could glimpse the higher world of forms or ideas through study and learning, and so he looked to Plotinus. Plotinus argued that the material and spiritual worlds could be united through ecstatic, or mystical, vision. Following Plotinus, Ficino conceived of beauty in the things of this world as God's means of making himself manifest to humankind. The contemplation and study of beauty in nature—and in all things—was a form of worship, a manifestation of divine or spiritual love, and Plato's ideas about love were central to Ficino's philosophy. Like erotic love, spiritual love is inspired by physical beauty, but spiritual love moves beyond the physical to an intellectual plane and, eventually, to such an elevated spiritual level that it results in the soul's union with God. Thus, in Neoplatonic terms, Lorenzo's fondness for gems was a type of spiritual love, as was Petrarch's love for Laura, celebrated in his sonnets, and so was the painter Botticelli's love of the human form (both discussed later in this chapter). If in real things one could discover the divine, realism became, in Neoplatonic terms, a form of idealism. In fact, Ficino saw "Platonic love," the love of beauty, as a kind of spiritual bond on which the strongest kind of community could be constructed. In this way, Neoplatonism even had political implications. The Neoplatonists even had political implications. The Neoplatonists envisioned Florence as a city whose citizenry was spiritually bound together in a common love of the beautiful.

Pico della Mirandola.   Another great Neoplatonic philosopher at the academy was PICO DELLA MIRANDOLA [PEA-coh DELL-ah mee-RAN-doh-lah] (1463–94), whose religious devotion, intense scholarship, and boundless optimism attracted many followers. His *Oration on the Dignity of Man* (1486) encapsulates one of the central impulses of the Renaissance: humankind serving as a link between the lower orders of nature, including animals, and the higher spiritual orders, of which angels are a part. For Pico, human beings possess free will; they can make of themselves what they wish. Though linked with the lower order of matter, they are capable of rising to the higher realm of spirit and ultimately being united with God. Each person's destiny is thus a matter of individual choice.

In the *Oration*, Pico presents God speaking to Adam, telling him that "in conformity with thy free judgment in whose hands I have placed thee, thou art confined by no bonds, and constrained by no limits." God also tells Adam directly that he is "the molder and maker" of himself, who "canst grow downward into the lower natures which are brutes" or "upward from the mind's reason into the higher natures which are divine." This central tenet of humanist philosophy is often misunderstood to mean that an emphasis on the individual results in or implies a rejection of God. Although Pico, and humanists in general, place the responsibility for human action squarely on humans and not on the Almighty, Pico also believed the human mind—with its ability to reason and imagine—could conceive of and move toward the divine. It follows that individual genius, which was allowed to flower in Renaissance Italy as never before in Western culture, is the worldly manifestation of divine truth.

ARCHITECTURE

Renaissance architecture reflects a renewed interest in ancient Roman models for mathematically derived proportions as well as logic of construction.

Filippo Brunelleschi.   The greatest architect of the Early Renaissance was FILIPPO BRUNELLESCHI [brew-nuh-LESS-key] (1377–1446), whose triumph is the dome of Florence Cathedral (fig. 13.4). Measuring $138\frac{1}{2}$ feet wide and 367 feet high, it was the largest dome since the Pantheon built in 125 C.E. (see Chapter 4). Although influenced by antique architecture, the octagonal dome of Florence Cathedral does not look like the hemispherical dome of the ancient Roman Pantheon. Using the basic structural principles perfected in the pointed arches of Gothic cathedrals, Brunelleschi produced a dome with less outward thrust than a hemispherical one. Because his predecessor, Arnolfo di Cambio, had designed the base of the dome to be extraordinarily wide, Brunelleschi flanked his octagonal dome with three half domes to buttress it.

Brunelleschi used stone at the bottom of the dome; for the upper portion, he used brick. The heavier material at the bottom produced a self-buttressing system, an idea seen in the Pantheon. Brunelleschi's innovation was to build a double dome with an inner and an outer shell—a

FIGURE 13.4   Filippo Brunelleschi, Florence Cathedral, dome, 1420–36; lantern completed 1471. Brunelleschi managed to erect this enormous double-shell pointed dome without the use of temporary scaffolding. It is the major landmark of Florence.

dome within a dome that was much lighter than the solid concrete dome of the Pantheon. The octagonal dome is reinforced by eight major ribs, visible on the exterior, plus three minor ribs between every two major ribs (fig. 13.5). Finally, Michelozzo added an open structure to crown the roof, a **lantern.** The metal lantern's weight stabilized the whole, its downward pressure keeping the ribs from spreading apart at the top.

Leon Battista Alberti.   The other great architect of the day, LEON BATTISTA ALBERTI [al-BEAR-tee] (1404–72), was celebrated both as an architect and as an author. He was the first to detail the principles of linear perspective in his treatise *De pictura (On Painting)*, written in 1434–35. His ten books on architecture, *De re aedificatoria*, completed about 1450, were inspired by the late-first-century B.C.E. Roman writer Vitruvius, who had himself written an encyclopedic ten-volume survey of classical architecture.

Alberti worked to create beauty in architecture that derived from harmony among all parts, using mathematics to determine the proportions of his buildings. A prime example is the church of Sant' Andrea in Mantua (fig. 13.6), designed in 1470 and completed after his death. Hampered by an older building on the site, Alberti had to adapt his ideal design for the church to the preexisting surroundings. His solution exemplifies Renaissance theory. For the facade he combined the triangular pediment of a classical temple with the arches characteristic of ancient Roman triumphal arches—one large central arch flanked by two smaller arches. The facade balances horizontals and verticals, with the height of the facade equaling the

FIGURE 13.6   Leon Battista Alberti, Sant' Andrea, Mantua, facade, designed 1470. An ideal demonstration of the Early Renaissance devotion to the antique, the design of this facade combines the form of an ancient temple with that of an ancient triumphal arch.

FIGURE 13.5   Line drawing of Brunelleschi's dome for Florence Cathedral, indicating the double-shell construction.

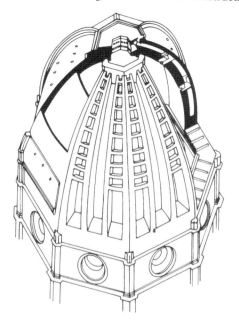

width. Four colossal Corinthian pilasters paired with small pilasters visually unite the stories of the facade. Large and small pilasters of the same dimensions appear in the nave, linking the exterior and interior in a harmonious whole.

Michelozzo di Bartolommeo.   In fifteenth-century Florence, wealthy families customarily hired architects to build fortresslike palaces, emblematic of their power. The Palazzo Medici-Riccardi (fig. 13.7), designed by MICHELOZZO DI BARTOLOMMEO [MEE-kel-LOTZ-oh] (1396–1472), was begun in 1445 and probably completed by 1452. Although built for Cosimo de' Medici, the Riccardi family acquired the palazzo in the seventeenth century. Located on a corner of the Via Larga, the widest street in Florence, it is an imposing residence, dignified yet grand, that heralded its resident—the city's most powerful person—literally and metaphorically at the center of the city's cultural and political life.

Michelozzo created an austere three-story stone building. The stonework, beginning with a ground level of rusticated stone (the same rough-hewn masonry used in fortifications), becomes increasingly smoother from bottom story to top. Michelozzo further differentiated the

FIGURE 13.7   Michelozzo di Bartolommeo, Palazzo Medici-Riccardi, Florence, exterior, begun 1445, probably completed by 1452; ground-floor windows by Michelangelo, ca. 1517. Typical of Early Renaissance palazzi, the facades of this massive city residence, built for Cosimo de' Medici the Elder, are neatly divided into three stories with evenly spaced windows.

levels visually by successively diminishing the height of each, although they all remain over twenty feet high. Typical of the Renaissance, the division of the stories is neat and clear, and the divisions are formed by classical moldings.

The Renaissance interest in orderliness is seen also in the even spacing of the windows. The form of window used—two arched openings within an overriding arch—was already popular in the Middle Ages. At the top of the palazzo, a heavy projecting cornice fulfills both aesthetic and architectural roles. The cornice serves visually to frame and conclude the architectural composition; it also sent the rainwater wide of the wall. The Medici coat of arms with its seven balls appears on the corners of the second story. What are now its ground-level windows were originally arches that opened onto the street creating a *loggia*, or covered gallery. (The arches were filled and the windows added in the sixteenth century by Michelangelo.)

The first story provided offices and storage rooms for the Medici business; the family's living quarters were on the second level.

The rooms of the Palazzo Medici-Riccardi are arranged around a central colonnaded courtyard, a typical Florentine system in which the palace is turned in on itself, ostensibly for protection but also for privacy and quiet. Whereas the plain exterior reflected the original owner's public posture as a careful, even conservative man, the inside, especially the second floor, or *piano nobile* (the grand and "noble" family rooms of the palace), displayed ostentatious grandeur.

SCULPTURE

Renaissance culture promoted the notion of individual genius by encouraging competitions among artists for prestigious public and religious commissions. In 1401, the Florentine humanist historian Leonardo Bruni sponsored a competition to determine who would make the doors of Florence Cathedral's octagonal **baptistery,** the small structure seen in the left foreground in fig 12.13, separate from the main church, where baptisms are performed. Seven sculptors were asked to submit depictions of the sacrifice of Isaac.

Lorenzo Ghiberti.   The winner of the competition was the young sculptor LORENZO GHIBERTI [ghee-BAIR-tee] (1378–1455), and his reaction typifies the heightened sense of self-worth that Renaissance artists felt about their artistic abilities and accomplishments: "To me was conceded the palm of victory by all the experts. . . . To me the honor was conceded universally and with no exception. To all it seemed that I had at that time surpassed the others."

So well were these doors received that as soon as they were completed Ghiberti was commissioned to make a second set for the east side of the baptistery. These, depicting ten stories from the Old Testament, were completed in 1452. Impressed by their beauty, Michelangelo called them the "gates of paradise," and the name stuck. *The Gates of Paradise* face the cathedral facade, occupying the most prominent position on the baptistery.

The panels are fewer in number and larger in size; scenes are set in simple square formats, and this time the whole square is gilded rather than just the raised areas. Each panel includes several scenes. The first, *The Creation* (fig. 13.8), portrays five scenes from Genesis. At the top, God creates the heavens and earth. At the bottom left, Adam is created from the earth. The central scene depicts Eve being created from Adam's rib. To the left and behind, Adam and Eve are tempted by Satan in the guise of a serpent. And to the right, Adam and Eve are expelled from the Garden of Eden. This is simultaneous presentation of events that took place sequentially, a technique called continuous narration.

FIGURE 13.8   Lorenzo Ghiberti, *The Creation of Adam and Eve*, relief panel from the *Gates of Paradise*, east doors, Baptistery, Florence, 1425–52, gilt bronze, $31\frac{1}{4} \times 31\frac{1}{4}''$ (79.4 × 79.4 cm), now in the Museo dell'Opera del Duomo, Florence. Because of their beauty, Michelangelo referred to these doors as the "Gates of Paradise."

Donatello.   Ghiberti's interest in correct perspective, proper proportions, and the accurate representation of nature was shared by DONATELLO [don-ah-TELL-oh] (1386–1466). His *Feast of Herod* (fig. 13.9), a gilded bronze relief made ca. 1423–27 for the font in the baptistery of Siena Cathedral, is a triumph in the creation of perspectival space. Although perspective had been employed by the ancient Romans in their murals, the principles of Renaissance **linear perspective** are believed to have been developed by Filippo Brunelleschi, whom Ghiberti had defeated in the original competition for the Florentine baptistery doors. These principles were later codified by the architect Leon Battista Alberti in his *De pictura (On Painting)*. In the simplest terms, perspective allows the picture plane (or surface of the picture) to function as a window through which a scene is presented to the viewer.

The effectiveness of linear perspective in organizing a composition and in creating the illusion of pictorial space cannot be overstated. The actual physical space of Donatello's *Feast of Herod* is shallow, but perspective creates the illusion of a deep space, with two courtyards behind the foreground action. In each courtyard the people are progressively smaller. The floor pattern, drawn in linear perspective, enhances the illusion of recession. Donatello's emphasis on the mathematical discipline of his design and his rigorous application of the laws of perspective are balanced by the dramatic and emotional content of the scene.

FIGURE 13.9   Donatello, *Feast of Herod*, relief panel from baptismal font, Baptistery, Siena, ca. 1423–27, gilt bronze, $23\frac{1}{2}'' \times 23\frac{1}{2}''$ (59.7 × 59.7 cm). Donatello's harsh drama contrasts with Ghiberti's fluid charm.

Indeed, the *Feast of Herod* possesses a dramatic force never before seen in Italian sculpture. The composition is split down the middle so there are two competing centers of attention, an unusual device. John the Baptist's head is brought on a platter to Herod on the left, and Salome dances seductively on the right. This split adds to the emotional impact and tension of the composition.

Donatello depicted a very different subject, one popular in the Early Renaissance, the shepherd boy David (fig. 13.10) who slew the giant, Goliath, with a stone from his slingshot. In Donatello's *David* (ca. 1425–30s), the stone is still in David's sling, although Goliath's head lies beneath David's foot. By depicting David both before and after the conflict, Donatello provides a condensed version of the story. With the first large-scale nude created since Roman antiquity, Donatello portrays his hero as an adolescent male wearing only a hat and boots. According to the Bible, David casts off only his armor as too cumbersome for battle. To depict David in the nude is to link him to heroic nudes of antiquity. In addition, David adopts the antique *contrapposto* posture, in which the weight of the body rests on one leg, elevating the hip and the opposite shoulder, putting the spine into an S curve.

Between 1453 and 1455, Donatello carved his polychromed wooden figure of *Mary Magdalene* (fig. 13.11), which stands over six feet high. After a sermon by Pope Gregory the Great in 594, in which he made a suggestive comparison to Mary Magdalene's sinfulness, she came to be identified as a prostitute. She remained among the followers of Jesus, is said to have annointed him with oil after his crucifixion, to have attended to his burial, and discov-

FIGURE 13.10   Donatello, *David*, ca. 1425–30, bronze, height 5′2¼″ (1.58 m), Museo Nazionale del Bargello, Florence. Scala/Art Resource, NY. The Early Renaissance interest in antiquity and the accurate portrayal of the nude are evidenced in Donatello's work.

FIGURE 13.11   Donatello, *Mary Magdalene*, 1453–55, wood, painted and gilded, height 6′2″ (1.88 m), Museo dell'Opera del Duomo, Florence. Scala/Art Resource, NY. Not only beauty, but also its absence can be used to create emotionally moving art, as in this portrayal of the repentant sinner.

ered his resurrection. Donatello depicts her after years of living in the desert, rejecting the life of the body in anticipation of the immortal life of the soul after a spiritual resurrection. Her body now gaunt, her arms and legs withered, she prays. Donatello's figure is intentionally unnerving, even repulsive. It is the striking absence of beauty that makes her both powerful and memorable.

PAINTING

Masaccio.   Of all the Early Renaissance painters, it was MASACCIO [mah-SAH-chee-oh] (1401–29), in his short life, who carried the naturalistic impulse in painting furthest. In the 1436 Italian edition of *On Painting*, Alberti named Masaccio, along with Brunelleschi, Donatello, and Ghiberti, as a leading artist of the day.

Masaccio's extraordinary inventiveness is evident in the frescoes painted on the walls of the Brancacci Chapel in Santa Maria del Carmine, Florence, completed in 1428. In one, *The Tribute Money* (fig. 13.12), Masaccio depicts the scene from the Bible in which Jesus orders his disciples to "render unto Caesar that which is Caesar's, and unto God the things that are God's." In the center, Jesus, in response to the arrival of a Roman tax collector, tells his disciple Peter to look for money in the mouth of a fish. On the left, having removed his cloak, Peter takes the money from the fish. On the right, he gives the money to the tax collector. It is an example of continuous narration.

Masaccio's figures are harmoniously arranged, the main figure group placed to the left of center, balancing the

FIGURE 13.12   Masaccio, *The Tribute Money*, Brancacci Chapel, Santa Maria del Carmine,
Florence, finished 1428, fresco, 8′1″ × 19′7″ (2.3 × 6.0 m). A narrative based on Matthew
17:24–27 is related in a three-part perfectly balanced composition, seemingly illuminated by
light coming from the chapel windows. Perspective converges to a point behind Jesus' head,
thereby directing the viewer's eyes to Jesus.

visually heavier group on the far right. The entire space is
carefully composed by the one-point perspective of the architecture, the vanishing point behind Jesus's head. The
depth of the whole scene is further enhanced by means of
atmospheric (aerial) perspective, duplicating in point
the optical phenomenon of the atmosphere's ability to
modify the clarity and color of objects at a distance.

The figures seem to stand in a three-dimensional space.
The tax collector, wearing the short tunic, has turned his
back to us, and stands in a *contrapposto* pose, balanced, relaxed, and natural. When Vasari later wrote that "Masaccio made his figures stand upon their feet," he was praising
the naturalism of such poses. The tax collector also echoes
our own relationship to the space; real viewers and painted
figures alike look at Jesus. All the faces are individualized,
not idealized, and reflect Masaccio's models, real people
of the peasant class of Florence. Masaccio's use of strong
contrast between light and shadow creates an illusion of
three-dimensional, almost sculptural, figures moving in
space. They are lit from the right in imitation of physical
reality, since the windows in the Brancacci Chapel are to
the right of the fresco.

Masaccio's fresco of the *Trinity with the Virgin, St. John
the Evangelist, and Donors* (fig. 13.13), in Santa Maria
Novella in Florence, of ca. 1427–28, summarizes several
characteristics of the Renaissance. The Renaissance interest in lifelike portraiture can be seen in the life-size de-

pictions of two members of the Lenzi family who commissioned the work. Unlike the anonymous marginal figures of donors seen in medieval paintings, these donors
have a real presence in the scene. So successful was Masaccio in his use of linear perspective that the chapel appears
to recede into the wall; the vanishing point is just below
the bottom of the cross, five feet from the floor, approximately eye level for the adult viewer. Situated deeper in
the space and therefore drawn smaller than the Lenzis,
Mary and John the Evangelist plead with Jesus on behalf
of humankind. The only figure to defy natural logic is
God, for his feet are on the back wall, yet he holds the
cross in the foreground. The Renaissance interest in the
antique is seen in the coffered barrel vault, Ionic and
Corinthian capitals, and the moldings—all based upon
ancient Roman models.

Piero della Francesca.   PIERO DELLA FRANCESCA
[pea-AIR-oh del-uh-fran-CHES-kah] (ca. 1406/12–1492)
was also deeply interested in portraiture, a reflection of
the Renaissance concern for the individual. His double depiction of Battista Sforza and Federico da Montefeltro
(figs. 13.14 and 13.15) shows wife and husband holding
their heads motionless, high above the landscape behind
them. They are noble, elevated, grand. The profile presentation was especially popular in the Early Renaissance,
revealing the sitter's most distinctive features.

FIGURE 13.14 Piero della Francesca, *Battista Sforza*, 1472–73, oil on panel, $18\frac{1}{2}'' \times 13''$ (47 × 33 cm), Galleria degli Uffizi, Florence. SCALA/Art Resource, NY. The profile portrait was favored in the Early Renaissance; later the three-quarter view became popular.

Piero began the portraits in 1472, the year the countess died, suggesting her portrait was made from her death mask. She is shown in the fashion of the times, with her plucked and shaved forehead, her elaborate hairstyle, and sparkling jewels. The count was ruler of Urbino, which had begun to compete with Florence as an intellectual center. He was a gentleman, scholar, bibliophile, and warrior, whose court included humanists, philosophers, poets, and artists. A left profile view was chosen because the count had lost his right eye and the bridge of his nose to a sword in a tournament. It is nonetheless with unsparing realism that Piero presents him "warts and all." We can assume the countess and count looked exactly like this, and that Piero faithfully recorded all the crannies and crevices of their facial terrain.

Fra Angelico. FRA ANGELICO [FRAH an-JELL-ee-coh] (ca. 1400–55), nicknamed "Angelic Brother" by his brother Dominican monks, was the most popular painter in Florence in the first half of the fifteenth century. His

FIGURE 13.13 Masaccio, *Trinity with the Virgin, St. John the Evangelist, and Donors*, Santa Maria Novella, Florence, probably 1427 or 1428, fresco, 21′ × 10′5″ (6.5 × 3.2 m). The architectural setting demonstrates the Early Renaissance interest in the antique and in spatial illusion; the naturalistic portrayal of the life-size donors indicates the new concern for the individual.

FIGURE 13.15   Piero della Francesca, *Federico da Montefeltro*, 1472–73, oil on panel, $18\frac{1}{2} \times 13''$ (47 × 33 cm), Galleria degli Uffizi, Florence. Scala/Art Resource, NY. In this pair of portraits, wife and husband are recorded with unsparing realism. An accident in combat accounts for the count's curious profile.

Annunciation (fig. 13.16), painted between 1438 and 1445 in the monastery of San Marco in Florence, was part of a vast project in which Fra Angelico painted on the walls in one of the cloisters, the chapter house, upstairs in the corridors, and especially in the monks' dormitory cells with the help of assistants. It would be difficult to create gentler, more graceful gestures than those of Mary and Gabriel in this scene. Their crossed arms are a sign of respect as well as a reference to Jesus's cross and prefiguration of his crucifixion. In the garden to the left are accurate depictions of real plants, but Fra Angelico, in medieval fashion, has spaced them evenly across the ground so each maintains its separate identity. The architecture of the space is rendered with typical Early Renaissance respect for the laws of perspective, but Fra Angelico has placed his figures in the architectural setting without regard to proper relative scale. The scene is accurately set within the architecture of San Marco, newly finished by the architect Michelozzo; thus the Annunciation is shown to take place in a specific and contemporary building. The immediacy and conviction of the event were enhanced for the monks

who saw the angel Gabriel addressing Mary in their own monastery.

Sandro Botticelli.   SANDRO BOTTICELLI [bott-tee-CHEL-lee] (1445–1510) received his artistic training as an assistant to Fra Filippo Lippi, a painter who had worked with Fra Angelico.

His *Primavera* (fig. 13.17), painted about 1482, is a complex allegory of spring taken from the Latin writers Horace and Lucretius. It embodies the growing interest in classical literature and pagan mythology of the Neoplatonists of the Florentine Academy. Botticelli was himself a member of this Neoplatonist circle, which also included Lorenzo de' Medici. *Primavera* was commissioned by Lorenzo di Pierfrancesco de' Medici, a cousin of Lorenzo's, for a chamber next to his bedroom.

Botticelli was unconcerned with the representation of deep space; his orange grove behind functions more like a stage backdrop than an actual landscape. However, Botticelli is, above all, a master of line, and the emphasis of his work is on surface pattern. Neither solid nor three dimensional, his figures are clearly outlined, and they seem to flow along the rhythmic lines of a dance or procession. The painting moves from right to left, as if blown on the breath of Zephyrus, god of the west wind, shown with his cheeks puffed out on the far right. Next is Chloris, the spring nymph, with a leafy vine coming from her mouth. Beside her is Flora, the goddess of flowers, strewing their path with petals. In the middle stands Venus, goddess of love, shown pregnant as a symbol of her fruitfulness in spring. With her, the movement of the scene almost comes to a halt, but she gestures toward the three Graces as Cupid, above her, shoots an arrow in their direction. The three Graces themselves, daughters of Zeus and the personifications of beauty and charm, twirl and whirl us around, but they too seem to spin to the left where finally Mercury, messenger of the gods, holds up his caduceus, or staff, as if to halt the entire procession.

Botticelli's *Birth of Venus* (fig. 13.18), of ca. 1484–86, was also painted for Lorenzo di Pierfrancesco de' Medici, and also depicts a subject from antique pagan mythology, made acceptable to the Christian church by equating Venus with Jesus's mother Mary on the grounds that both were sources of love. According to Neoplatonic interpretation, the birth of Venus is equivalent to the birth of the human soul, as yet uncorrupted by the matter of the world. In Neoplatonic terms, the soul is free to choose for itself whether to follow a path toward sin and degradation or to attempt to regain, through the use of reason, a spiritual perfection manifested in the beauty of creation and felt in the love of God. To love beauty is to love not the material world of sensual things, but rather the world's abstract and spiritual essence.

In 1494, a Dominican friar, Girolamo Savonarola, who had lived in the same monastery of San Marco in Florence that Fra Angelico had painted, took control of the city.

FIGURE 13.16   Fra Angelico, *Annunciation*, monastery of San Marco, Florence, 1438–45, fresco, 7′6″ × 10′5″ (2.29 × 3.18 m). Fra Angelico cleverly painted the Annunciation as if it were taking place within the actual architecture of the monastery of San Marco.

Savonarola proclaimed that Florence had condemned itself to perdition, saying that its painters—artists such as Botticelli—"make the Virgin look like a harlot." A bonfire was built in the Piazza della Signoria, the main square of the city, and on it signs of vanity—clothing, wigs, false beards, make-up, and mirrors—as well as books, board games, and paintings were burned.

EARLY RENAISSANCE MUSIC

March 15, 1436, was a day of dedication for the completed Florence Cathedral, now crowned by Brunelleschi's extraordinary dome. A procession wound its way through the city's streets and entered the cathedral, led by Pope Eugene IV and seven cardinals, thirty-six bishops, and untold numbers of church officials, civic leaders, artists, scholars, and musicians. The papal choir included one of the greatest figures in Renaissance music, the composer Guillaume Dufay. The choir performed a motet called informally "Il Duomo" composed by Dufay especially for the occasion. As one eyewitness recalled, "The whole space of the temple was filled with such choruses of harmony, and such a concert of diverse instruments, that it seemed (not without reason) as though the symphonies and songs of the angels and of divine paradise had been sent forth from Heaven to whisper in our ears an unbelievable celestial sweetness."

Guillaume Dufay.   More than any other composer, GUILLAUME DUFAY [dew-FAY] (1400–74) shaped the musical language of the Early Renaissance. Born in northern France, Dufay served first as a music teacher for the French court of Burgundy, then as a court composer in Italy, working at various times in Bologna, Florence, and Rome. A musical celebrity, he was often solicited to compose music for solemn occasions, such as the dedication of "Il Duomo."

The English had developed pleasing harmonies using a three-note interval (rather than the four-, five-, or eight-note intervals of the Middle Ages), but it was Dufay who used this triadic harmony in polyphonic and imitative style. Dufay was a composer of the increasingly popular "parody mass," where a popular song of the day was inserted into a liturgical mass. Congregations loved the familiar secular tune used in their daily worship. However, com-

FIGURE 13.17   Sandro Botticelli, *Primavera*, ca. 1482 (?), tempera on panel, 6'8" × 10'4" (2.03 × 3.15 m), Galleria degli Uffizi, Florence. Neoplatonic theory is given visual form in this allegory, perhaps a depiction of the Floralia, an ancient Roman celebration of spring. It was made for a cousin of Lorenzo de' Medici, ruler of Florence.

posers of parody masses were careful to hide the pop tune in a slow-moving tenor line to escape criticism from the clergy.

Dufay wrote music in all the popular genres of his time: masses for liturgies, Latin motets, or compositions for multiple voices; music for ceremonies; and French and Italian *chansons*, or songs, for the pleasure of his patrons and friends. In each genre, Dufay's melodies and rhythms were more easily identifiable than those of earlier composers.

Motets.   Dufay wrote many **motets:** one-movement compositions that set a sacred text to polyphonic choral music, usually with no instrumental accompaniment. Dufay's motet *Alma Redemptoris Mater,* composed in about 1430, fuses medieval *polyphony*—that is, the simultaneous singing of several voices each independent of the others—with a newer Early Renaissance form. The result was a multimelodic, rather than merely a multivoiced, musical style, with more lyrical, less chantlike melodies and a more sensuous sound. Earlier composers typically put the *plainchant* melody, or main melody, in the lowest voice, but Dufay puts the main melody in the highest or uppermost voice, where it can be better heard. He also avoids the

rhythmic distortion of medieval composition. The three voices of Dufay's *Alma Redemptoris Mater*—bass, tenor, and soprano—maintain rhythmic independence (also a late medieval characteristic) until the third and last section of the motet. Then Dufay blocks them together in chords to emphasize the text's closing words, which ask Mary to be merciful to sinners; the chords, arranged in graceful harmonies, soothe the listener's ears more than those of the traditional medieval motet. In this last part Dufay adds an additional voice by giving the sopranos two different parts to sing. In doing so, he moves toward the four-part texture of soprano, alto, tenor, and bass that was to become the norm for later Renaissance vocal music.

Word Painting.   Dufay's emphasis on lyrics is an early example of **word painting,** in which the meaning of words is underscored and emphasized through the music that accompanies them. One sixteenth-century musical theorist offered composers this suggestion: "When one of the words expresses weeping, pain, heartbreak, sighs, tears, and other similar things, let the harmony be full of sadness." A composer might also employ a descending melodic line (going from high to low), or a bass line, to

FIGURE 13.18   Sandro Botticelli, *Birth of Venus*, ca. 1484–86, tempera on canvas, 6′7″ × 9′2″ (2.01 × 2.79 m), Galleria degli Uffizi, Florence. SCALA/Art Resource, NY. Botticelli painted this important revival of the nude based upon antique prototypes.

express anguish; conversely, an ascending line (going from low to high), utilizing soprano voices, might express joy and hope. This increasing sense of the drama of language, comparable to the Renaissance artists' attention to the drama of the stories they chose to depict—Donatello's *Mary Magdalene* (see fig. 13.11), for example—led Renaissance composers to use music to enrich the feelings their music expressed, and to support the meaning of a song's text, whether sacred or secular. Though little music had survived from ancient Greece, humanist philosophers like Ficino understood that Aristotle had considered music the highest form of art and the rhythms of Greek music imitated the rhythms of Greek poetry, for which it served as a setting. Thus word painting as the intimate relation of sound and sense has classical roots.

As in the Middle Ages, musicians like Dufay were employed by the churches, towns, and courts. However, unlike music in the Middle Ages, which served mostly religious ends, music in the Renaissance became increasingly secularized. Musicians still depended on such patronage, but commissions came from wealthy burghers and aristocrats such as the Medici family, as well as from the church, which remained the staunchest of musical patrons. The nobility commissioned secular works to accompany formal occasions such as coronations, weddings, processions, and even political events. However, before long secular music also found its way into sacred settings. Dufay, for instance, introduced the popular French folksong "*L'Homme arme*" ("The Man in Armor") into a mass, and other composers soon followed suit, creating an entire musical genre known as *chanson masses*, or "song masses."

Musical accomplishment was one of the marks of an educated person in the Renaissance, and most people among the nobility both played an instrument and sang. Moreover, many uneducated people were accomplished musicians; in fact, the music of the uneducated masses— their songs and dances—was most influenced by the secular music of the age. Music was an integral part of an evening's entertainment. Although it was common for professionals to provide this entertainment, increasingly individuals at a party might entertain the group. Dance, too, became the focus of social gatherings, and much of the instrumental music of the day was composed to accompany dances. By the Early Renaissance, instruments had evolved

Connections

MATHEMATICAL PROPORTIONS: BRUNELLESCHI AND DUFAY

Mathematics played an important part in all the arts of the Renaissance. Architects designed buildings guided by mathematical ratios and proportions. Painters employed the mathematical proportions governed by linear perspective. Composers wrote music that reflected mathematical ratios between the notes of a melody and in the intervals between notes sounded together in harmony. Poets structured their poems according to mathematical proportions.

One especially striking set of relationships exists between the proportions of the dome built by Filippo Brunelleschi for Florence Cathedral and "Il Duomo," the motet for four voices that Guillaume Dufay wrote for its dedication in 1436. Its formal title is *Nuper Rosarum Flores (Flowers of Roses)*, the word *flores* referring to Florence itself. The mathematical ratios in Dufay's motet are evident in its rhythm rather than its melody. The slower-moving lower voices of the two tenors proceed in strict rhythmic progressions that reflect the ratio of 6:4:2:3. The initial ratio of 6:4 is reducible to 3:2; thus it is a mirror reverse ratio of 3:2:2:3, which appears in the number of beats in each of the work's four sections: 6, 4, 4, and 6. In addition, Dufay's motet contains a total of 168 measures, proportionally divided into four harmonious parts of 56, 56, 28, and 28 measures each. The last two parts contain exactly half the number of measures of the first two, creating a mathematically harmonious and intellectually pleasing structure.

Brunelleschi's dome's proportions exhibit mathematical ratios that are 6:4:2:3, just as in Dufay's motet. This is the ratio of the internal dimensions to the external ones. And motet and dome both have a doubling. Dufay's motet employs a doubling of the tenor voices, which sing the lower melody five notes apart. Brunelleschi's dome is a double shell, having an internal and an external structure.

The structure of a Petrarchan sonnet also employs a harmonious mathematical ratio for its basic structure. The Petrarchan sonnet is composed of fourteen lines, which typically break into two parts: an octave of eight lines and a sestet of six that yield a ratio of 8:6, which reduces to 4:3. Moreover, both the octave and the sestet usually split evenly into two equal parts: 4 + 4 and 3 + 3, yielding a further neatly symmetrical balanced pair of proportions in both octave and sestet of 1:1.

In these and numerous other instances of Renaissance architecture and music, as well as perspectivist painting, sculptural proportions, and poetry, mathematics lies at the heart of the harmonious nature of the works. This concern with geometric symmetry and mathematical proportions illustrates one more way in which the arts of the Renaissance were a legacy of the golden age of Greece.

---

to look much as they do today. The lute was used both as a solo instrument and to accompany singers. Bowed instruments came in all sizes; wind instruments with brass mouthpieces and single and double reeds were used in festivals and in church. Instruments were classified as either loud (*haut*) or soft (*bas*), which also designated the activity for which the instrument was intended. Before this time, instruments had always performed vocal parts. During the Renaissance, music was written specifically for particular instruments without regard for the capability of the human voice.

Movable type contributed to the growth and popularity of music during the Renaissance. The first collection of music printed in movable type, *One Hundred Songs*, was published in 1501 in Venice by Ottaviano de' Petrucci. Half a century later, printed music was widely available to scholars and amateurs alike. With the greater availability of printed scores, Renaissance composers became more familiar with each other's works and began to influence one another. Amateurs were able to buy and study the same music, and soon songs and dances in particular achieved the kind of widespread popularity that today might put a song into the "Top Ten."

LITERATURE

Petrarch.   The first great figure of Italian Renaissance letters, and the first important representative of Italian Renaissance humanism, was Petrarch, a scholar and prolific writer, whose work simultaneously reflects the philosophy of Greek antiquity and the new ideas of the Renaissance. Born Francesco Petrarca in Arezzo and taken, at the age of eight, to Avignon, where the papal courts had moved in 1309, Petrarch studied law in Bologna and Montpelier, then returned in 1326 to Avignon. Petrarch once said of himself, "I am a pilgrim everywhere," for he also traveled widely in France and Italy, hunting down classical manuscripts.

Unlike his Florentine predecessor, Dante Alighieri, whose *Divine Comedy* (see Chapter 12) summed up the sensibility of late medieval culture, Petrarch positioned himself at the beginning of a new literary and artistic era, one that placed greater emphasis on human achievement. Without rejecting the importance of spirituality and religious faith, Petrarch celebrated human accomplishment as the crowning glory of God's creation but praised human beings for their achievements as well.

Petrarch's work is poised between two powerful, inter-twined impulses: the religious and moral impulse of the early medieval thinkers, such as St. Augustine, and the humanist dedication to the disciplined study of ancient writers, coupled with a desire for artistic excellence.

Petrarch was especially affected by the elegance and beauty of early Latin literature. However, he disliked the Latin of the Middle Ages, seeing in it a barbarous falling off from the heights of eloquence exemplified by ancient Roman writers such as Virgil, Horace, Ovid, Seneca, and Cicero. Petrarch strove to revive classical literature rather than absorb its elements into contemporary Italian civilization. He considered classical culture a model to be emulated and an ideal against which to measure the achievements of other civilizations. For Petrarch, ancient culture was not merely a source of scientific information, philosophical knowledge, or rhetorical rules; it was also a spiritual and intellectual resource for enriching the human experience. Petrarch would help first Italy, and then Europe, recollect its noble classical past. And although Petrarch did not invent humanism, he breathed life into it and was its tireless advocate.

Soon after his return to Avignon in 1326, Petrarch fell in love with a woman whose identity is unknown, but whom he called Laura in his *Canzoniere (Songbook).* This collection of 366 poems—**sonnets, ballads, sestinas,** madrigals, and **canzoni** (songs)—was written and re-worked over more than forty years. Many of the poems are about love, and they are notable for their stylistic elegance and formal perfection. The poems about Laura are the most famous and the most beautiful.

The Petrarchan Sonnet.   Thematically, Petrarch's sonnets introduced what was to become a predominant subject of Renaissance lyric poetry: the expression of a speaker's love for a woman and his experience of the joy and pain of love's complex and shifting emotions. Laura's beauty and behavior cause the poet/speaker to sway between hope and despair, pleasure and pain, joy and anguish. Throughout the sequence of poems, Laura remains unattainable. Like so many figures in Renaissance painting, she is at once a real person and an ideal form, a contradiction expressed in the ambivalent feelings the poet/speaker has about her. Petrarch's popularity spawned a profusion of imitators, who borrowed from his situations, psychological descriptions, figurative language, and particularly his sonnet form. Petrarch's sonnets also inspired poets throughout Europe to write their own sonnet sequences. The most famous examples in English are Philip Sidney's *Astrophel and Stella* (1591), Edmund Spenser's *Amoretti* (1595), and William Shakespeare's 154 sonnets. Petrarch's sonnet structure established itself as one of the two dominant sonnet patterns used by poets.

The Petrarchan (sometimes called the Italian) sonnet is organized in two parts: an octave of eight lines and a ses-tet of six. The octave typically identifies a problem or situation, and the sestet proposes a solution; or the octave introduces a scene, and the sestet comments on or complicates it. The rhyme scheme of the Petrarchan sonnet reinforces its logical structure, with different rhymes occurring in octave and sestet. The octave rhymes *abba abba* (or *abab abab*), and the sestet rhymes *cde cde* (or *cde ced; cde dce;* or *cd, cd, cd*).

The following sonnet was the most popular poem in the European Renaissance; it depicts the lover's ambivalence in a series of paradoxes.

> I find no peace and all my war is done,
> I fear and hope, I burn and freeze like ice;
> I fly above the wind yet can I not arise,
> And nought I have and all the world I sesan.
> That loseth nor locketh holdeth me in prison   *5*
> And holdeth me not, yet can I escape nowise;
> Nor letteth me live nor die at my devise,
> And yet of death it giveth me occasion.
> Without eyes, I see, and without tongue I plain,
> I desire to perish, and yet I ask health,   *10*
> I love an other, and thus I hate my self,
> I feed me in sorrow and laugh in all my pain,
> Likewise displeaseth me both death and life,
> And my delight is cause of this strife.

THE HIGH RENAISSANCE

In the High Renaissance, focus shifted from Florence to Rome due to the wealth and power of the popes. Lavish artistic patronage was provided especially by Pope Julius II (1503–13), patron of Bramante, Raphael, and Michelangelo, and Pope Leo X (1513–21), who also patronized Michelangelo (and excommunicated Martin Luther). Rome had now become a city in which the two major national traditions of Italy converged—Classicism and Christianity.

The High Renaissance begins around 1485 or 1490 in Italy. Only one generation long, the High Renaissance was a short yet extremely important period that was to prove enormously influential on future art. Although there is no precise conclusion to the High Renaissance, the period may be said to come to a close at the death of Raphael in 1520, because this artist's paintings are widely held to epitomize the Renaissance style. Alternatively, the Renaissance may be said to have ended when Rome was sacked and burned by troops serving the Holy Roman Emperor Charles V (in Germany) in 1527. Many artists fled the city, thereby further spreading the ideas of Italy over western Europe.

The High Renaissance continued Early Renaissance interests in humanism, classicism, and individualism, artists and authors perfecting some of the ideas of their Early Renaissance predecessors and developing ideas of their own.

PAINTING

Leonardo da Vinci.   Born in Vinci, about twenty miles
west of Florence, LEONARDO DA VINCI [lay-o-NAR-
doh dah VIN-chee] (1452–1519) was the illegitimate son
of a peasant named Caterina and Ser Piero, a Florentine
lawyer, or notary. Leonardo later joined his father in Florence, and in 1469 he entered the workshop of Andrea del
Verrocchio, whose other apprentices included Sandro Botticelli. Giorgio Vasari wrote of Leonardo's "beauty as a
person," describing him as "divinely endowed" and "so
pleasing in conversation that he won all hearts." But he
was, Vasari noted, unstable in temperament, often abandoning projects, constantly searching and restless.

Leonardo was sent to Milan by Lorenzo the Magnificent
in 1481 or 1482 as an ambassador, charged with presenting
an ornate lyre to the duke, Ludovico Sforza, as a gesture of
peace. Leonardo chose to remain in Milan. In Florence,
Leonardo had been known as a painter and sculptor, but he
was, he told the duke, primarily a designer of military and
naval weaponry and only secondarily an architect, painter,
drainage engineer, and sculptor. He was, in short, the epitome of what we have come to call the "Renaissance" or
"universal man," a person not merely capable but talented
in an extraordinarily wide range of endeavors.

Leonardo was fascinated by all aspects of nature, as is
amply evidenced in his *Madonna of the Rocks* (fig. 13.19),
begun in 1483, soon after his arrival in Milan. This is the
first time Mary has been depicted in a grotto. The geol-
ogy—cliffs, mountains, and a grotto filled with stalactites
and stalagmites—comes out of his lifelong fascination with
the effects of wind and water on the environment. Hurricanes and deluges, eddies and currents of moving water,
particularly intrigued him. The *Madonna of the Rocks*
demonstrates Leonardo's preoccupation with the interre-
lated effects of perspective, light, color, and optics. Naturalistic lighting and atmospheric perspective are taken to
new heights.

Leonardo developed a technique for modeling forms
called **chiaroscuro.** In Italian, *chiaro* means "clear" or
"light," and *oscuro* means "obscure" or "dark." Chiaroscuro
describes Leonardo's technique of working in areas of light
and dark in space. Leonardo also developed a painting
technique called **sfumato** (in Italian, "smoky"), which is
the intentional suppression of the outline of a figure in a
hazy, almost smoky atmosphere. Leonardo's figures do not
so much emerge from the darkness of the grotto as they are
immersed in it, surrounded by it, even protected by it, as
if the grotto were the womb of the earth itself and Mary
the site's resident mother goddess. In the *Madonna of the
Rocks*, the child Jesus blesses his cousin John, the infant
John the Baptist, who represents the congregation of
Christians, literally protected by Mary's cloak but figura-
tively taken under her wing. The figures form a triangular or pyramid grouping, a favorite Renaissance
compositional device.

FIGURE 13.19   Leonardo da Vinci, *Madonna of the Rocks*,
ca. 1483, oil on panel, 6′6½″ × 4′ (2.0 × 1.2 m), Musée du
Louvre, Paris. SCALA/Art Resource, NY. Leonardo, both
artist and scientist, created a grotto setting with stalactites,
stalagmites, and identifiable foliage, an unusual environment
for these religious figures.

Leonardo's greatest achievement in Milan was *The Last
Supper* (fig. 13.20), painted between 1495 and 1499. The
orderly composition of *The Last Supper* clarifies the painting's meaning. The largest of the three windows on the
back wall is directly behind Jesus, thereby emphasizing
him. The curved pediment, which arches above his head,
serves as a halo. He is perfectly centered in the mural, and
all perspective lines converge toward a vanishing point directly behind his head, leading the viewer's eyes to him.
The twelve apostles are arranged six on each side, divided
into four equal groups of three figures. The result is a composition that is symmetrically balanced on either side
around the central figure of Jesus, whose arms are extended
diagonally so that he forms an equilateral triangle in the
center. The arrangement of the five segments is somewhat
theatrical—action building from the wings, leading to the
central calm figure of Jesus.

FIGURE 13.20   Leonardo da Vinci, *The Last Supper*, refectory, Santa Maria delle Grazie, Milan, 1495–98, tempera and oil on plaster, 15′ 2″ × 28′10″(4.60 × 8.80 m). Superstock. The mural's poor condition is due to the experimental media in which Leonardo painted. Nevertheless, his ability to merge form and content, using perspective to create simultaneously an illusion of a cubic space and focus the viewer's attention on Jesus, can still be appreciated.

Leonardo chose the most psychologically powerful moment in the story: Jesus has just announced that one of his apostles will betray him, and they respond with dismay. Judas, his betrayer, sits with John and Peter directly to the left of Jesus, his face lost in shadow as he leans away, clutching a money bag in his right hand. We know from preparatory sketches that Leonardo wanted to depict a different emotion on each of the apostles' faces. The most difficult thing to paint, Leonardo said, was "the intention of Man's soul." It could only be shown by pose, facial expression, and surrounding events and figures. Painting Judas and Jesus, apparently, gave Leonardo the most difficulty. Vasari tells the story:

> The prior [of Santa Maria delle Grazie] was in a great hurry to see the picture done. He could not understand why Leonardo would sometimes remain before his work half a day together, absorbed in thought. . . . [Leonardo] made it clear that men of genius are sometimes producing most when they seem least to labor, for their minds are then occupied in the shaping of those conceptions to which they afterward give form. He told the duke [Sforza, under whose protection the monastery was] that two heads were yet to be done: that of the Savior, the likeness of which he could not hope to find on earth and . . . the other, of Judas. . . . As a last resort he could always use the head of that troublesome and impertinent prior.

Leonardo solved his problem with Judas by grouping him with Peter and John. "I say," Leonardo explained in his

Notebooks, "that in narratives it is necessary to mix closely together direct contraries, because they provide a great contrast with each other, and so much more if they are adjacent, that is to say the ugly to the beautiful."

Sometime in 1503, after Leonardo had been forced to return to Florence, he painted the *Mona Lisa* (fig. 13.21), a portrait of Lisa di Antonio Maria Gherardini, the twenty-four-year-old wife of a Florentine official, Francesco del Gioconda—hence the painting is sometimes called *La Gioconda.* Mona Lisa appears relaxed and natural. Leonardo presents his sitter in a half-length, three-quarter view, the hands showing. With this pose, set against a landscape background, Leonardo established a type. In accordance with the fashion of the time, her high forehead indicates Mona Lisa's nobility—the effect achieved by her shaved hairline and absence of eyebrows. The sitter's lofty mind is indicated by the stormy weather shown in the background. The fame of this painting rests on the sitter's facial expression. Leonardo was concerned with not only the exterior, but also with the interior, with the psychological subtleties of individual personality.

THE REINVENTION OF ROME

In the middle of the fifteenth century, Pope Nicholas V had close ties to the Florentine humanists, especially to Leon Battista Alberti, who made a massive survey of classical architecture, *De re aedificatoria.* With Alberti as his

FIGURE 13.21 Leonardo da Vinci, *Mona Lisa*, ca. 1503, oil on panel, 2′6¼″ × 1′9″ (76.8 × 53.3 cm), © Musée du Louvre, Paris/Reunion des Musées National/Art Resource, NY. Probably the most famous painting in the world, Mona Lisa's mysterious smile continues to intrigue viewers today.

FIGURE 13.22 Melozzo da Forlì, *Sixtus IV Appoints Platina Head of the Vatican Library*, 1480–81, fresco, 13′1″ × 10′4″ (3.99 × 3.15 m), Pinacoteca Vaticana, Rome. Platina kneels before Pope Sixtus IV while the Pope's nephews stand behind. In the middle is Cardinal Giuliano della Rovere, later Pope Julius II.

chief consultant, Nicholas V began to rebuild Rome's ancient churches and initiated plans to remake the Vatican as a new sacred city. Nicholas V also began to assemble a massive classical library, paying humanist scholars to translate ancient Greek texts into Latin and Italian.

The New Vatican. The Vatican library became one of the chief preoccupations of Pope Sixtus IV (reigned 1471–84). With Platina as its head, the library became a true "Vatican," or "public," library, with rules for usage, a permanent location, and an effective, permanent administration. Platina's appointment is celebrated in a fresco painted by Melozzo da Forlì for the library (fig. 13.22). The Latin couplets below the scene, written by Platina himself, outline Sixtus's campaign to restore the city of Rome, rebuilding churches, streets, walls, bridges, and aqueducts, but praise Sixtus IV most of all for the creation of the library. By 1508, the Vatican Library was said to be the "image" of Plato's Academy. Athens had been reborn in Rome.

Archaeological discoveries led to Rome's reinvention as the classical center of learning and art. Sixtus established a museum in 1474 to house the recently uncovered Etruscan bronze statue of the she-wolf that had nourished Romulus and Remus, the mythical twin founders of the city (see Chapter 4). Other discoveries followed: *Spinario*, a Hellenistic bronze of a youth pulling a thorn from his foot; *Hercules*, the life-size bronze discovered in the ruined temple of Hercules in the Forum Boarium; and two antique marble river gods that came from the ruins of the Constantinian baths.

To execute Pope Nicholas's plans for a new Vatican palace, Sixtus IV commissioned the Sistine Chapel, which he named after himself, and inaugurated plans for its decoration. Perugino and Botticelli, among others, painted frescoes for the chapel's walls, which were completed in 1482. Sixtus's nephew, Pope Julius II (reigned 1503–13), continued Sixtus's plans. Classical sculpture was placed in the Vatican's sloping gardens: the *Apollo Belvedere*, which had been discovered during excavations, and the *Laocoön* (see Chapter 3), found buried in the ruins of some Roman baths. Composers were hired to write new hymns. Josquin des Près served in the sixteen- to twenty-four-member *Sistina Cappella*, or Sistine Choir, from 1476 to 1484. Soon the rough rhythms of medieval poetry were supplanted by the softer, finer meter of the Horatian odes. To add to the pomp of the liturgical processions, Julius established a large chorus to perform exclusively in St. Peter's, the *Cappella Giulia*, or Julian Choir, which remains active to this day. And, most important, Julius invited Raphael and Michelangelo to work in Rome.

PAINTING AND SCULPTURE

Raphael.   When RAPHAEL [RAFF-ay-el], born Raffaello Santi of Urbino (1483–1520), was invited to Rome in 1508, he was not yet twenty-five years old, but his renown as a painter was well established. He had grown up surrounded by culture and beauty. He studied painting under his father, Giovanni Santi, a painter for the dukes of Urbino. In Perugia he studied with Perugino.

One of Raphael's first major works is directly indebted to Perugino's *Jesus Delivering the Keys*. It is the *Marriage of the Virgin* (fig. 13.23), signed and dated 1504, the year he came to Florence. As in Perugino's work, the composition is divided into a foreground with large figures, a middle ground of open space with smaller figures, and a background with a temple and tiny figures. In the foreground, Mary and Joseph wed. The story says that Joseph, although older than the many other suitors, was selected because, among all the symbolic rods presented to Mary, his alone flowered. Beside him a disgruntled suitor snaps his own rod in half over his knee. The absence of facial expression is a stylistic habit derived from Perugino, which Raphael would soon discard under the influence of Leonardo and Michelangelo. Everything in Raphael's painting is measured and rendered in careful perspective, as is emphasized by the pattern of rectangles that cross the square. In fact, so powerful is the perspective grid that the viewer's eyes are led away from the marriage in the foreground to the temple behind, creating a competing focal point, in contrast to Leonardo da Vinci's use of perspective to focus the viewer's attention on the most important person in a scene (fig. 13.20).

Raphael became famous for his paintings of the Madonna and Child. His *Madonna of the Meadows* (fig. 13.24), painted in 1505, is typical of his style: pale, sweet, and serious. She is maternal and meditative, thinking ahead to Jesus's passion, prefigured by the cross offered by the infant St. John, who in turn is identified by the camel-hair garment he would wear as an adult. In most Early Renaissance depictions of this subject, the Madonna is elevated on a throne. Raphael's Madonna has descended to our earthly level; she even sits upon the ground—in this pose she is referred to as the "Madonna of Humility." The

FIGURE 13.23   Raphael, *Marriage of the Virgin*, 1504, oil on panel, 5′7″ × 3′10½″ (1.70 × 1.18 m), Giancarlo Costa/Brera Gallery, Milan. Raphael's carefully composed scene includes figures in the foreground, middleground, and background. The lines of perspective lead to a central plan building (the type favored by Bramante); the marriage is shown taking place in the foreground, dividing the composition.

differences between the sacred and the secular are minimized—even the figures' halos have become thin gold bands.

A master of composition, with ease and grace, Raphael contrasts the curved and rounded shapes of his substantial figures with their triangular and pyramidal positions in space. The triangular format recalls that of Leonardo's *Madonna of the Rocks* (fig. 13.19), but the difference between the dark grotto setting of Leonardo's painting and Raphael's pastoral countryside is instructive. Raphael's composition is simpler, possessing far less contrast between light and dark. His figures are more tightly grouped. Leonardo's children have serious facial expressions, lending them the emotional complexity of adults; Raphael's are far more playful.

Beginning in 1508, Julius II commissioned Raphael to paint frescoes in several rooms in the Vatican Palace, including the Stanza della Segnatura, the room where papal

FIGURE 13.24   Raphael, *Madonna of the Meadows*, 1505, oil on panel, $44\frac{1}{2}'' \times 34\frac{1}{4}''$ (113 × 87 cm), Kunsthistorisches Museum, Vienna. Erich Lessing/Art Resource, NY. Often considered the epitome of High Renaissance painters, Raphael was celebrated for his ability to arrange several figures into compact units. Mary, Jesus, and John the Baptist form a pyramid, a favorite Renaissance compositional device.

documents were signed. The *School of Athens* (fig. 13.25) embodies the Renaissance humanist's quest for classical learning and truth. In the center of this bilaterally symmetrical composition are the ancient Greek philosophers, Plato and Aristotle. The figure of the older Plato, which might be a portrait of Leonardo da Vinci, holds Plato's *Timaeus* and points upward, indicating the realm of his ideal Forms. The younger Aristotle holds his *Ethics* and points toward earth, indicating the philosopher's emphasis on material reality. The scene includes representations of Diogenes or Socrates, sprawling on the steps in front of the philosophers; Pythagoras, calculating on a slate at the lower left; Ptolemy, holding a globe at the right; and Euclid in front of him, inscribing a slate with a compass. Michelangelo is shown as the philosopher Heraclitus in the foreground leaning on a block of marble while sketching. Raphael painted his own portrait, the second figure from the right, looking at us. Pope Julius had made Raphael "prefect of antiquities," in charge of the papal ex-

cavation and preservation of antiques. Perhaps because of this, the setting is based on the ancient Roman baths and has the classical statues of Apollo (god of sunlight, rationality, and poetry) and Minerva (goddess of wisdom).

Michelangelo.   MICHELANGELO BUONARROTI [my-kuhl-AN-gel-oh] (1475–1564), born near Florence, lived as a child in the Palazzo Medici there, which served not only as Lorenzo the Magnificent's home but also as an art school, and there he studied sculpture under Giovanni Bertoldo, once a student of Donatello. In Lorenzo's palace, bursting with Neoplatonic and humanist ideas, Michelangelo was nurtured on the virtues of antique classical sculpture. As a boy, in Florence, he studied fresco painting under Domenico del Ghirlandaio and routinely copied the frescoes by Giotto in Santa Croce and those by Masaccio in Santa Maria del Carmine. He was, like so many Renaissance artists, skilled in many areas—painting, architecture, poetry—but in his own mind he was a sculptor.

Michelangelo believed the figure is imprisoned within the block of marble in the same way the soul is trapped within the body. In fact, to release the figure from the marble was a matter of subtraction, as the sculptor chiseled away the shell of stone that hid the figure within. Michelangelo's approach to sculpture was, in short, profoundly Neoplatonic; sculpture, from his point of view, both revealed and liberated the human ideal, as the first stanza of the following poem by him suggests:

Even the best of artists can conceive no idea
That a single block of marble will not contain
In its excess, and such a goal is achieved
Only by the hand that obeys the intellect.
    The evil which I flee and the good I promise myself   5
Hides in you, my fair, proud, and divine lady;
And working against my very life,
My skill is contrary to my purpose.
My ill cannot be blamed upon your beauty,
    Your harshness, bad fortune, or your disdain,   10
Nor upon my destiny or my fate,
If in your heart you bear both death and mercy
At the same time, and if my lowly talent
Ardently burning, can draw forth only death.

Unlike Leonardo, who believed beauty was found in nature, Michelangelo believed beauty was found in the imagination. One of his earliest sculptures is a *Pietà* (fig. 13.26), meaning "pity." The term refers to depictions of Mary mourning over the dead Jesus in her lap. Commissioned by a French cardinal, Michelangelo bragged his *Pietà* would be "the most beautiful work in marble that exists today in Rome." In order to heighten the viewer's feelings of pity and sorrow, Michelangelo made the figure of Jesus disproportionately small in comparison to the monumental figure of Mary. Despite the fact that Jesus died as a grown man of thirty-three, Mary is portrayed as a very young woman; the poignant implication is that Mary thinks back to when Jesus was an infant in her lap.

FIGURE 13.25   Raphael, *School of Athens*, 1510–11, fresco, 19 × 27′ (5.79 × 8.24 m), Stanza della Segnatura, Vatican Museums, Rome. Raphael painted several rooms in the Vatican for Pope Julius II, a great patron of the arts. Statues of Apollo and Minerva flank Plato and Aristotle, shown surrounded by scientists and philosophers of antiquity, some of whom have been given the facial features of Raphael's contemporaries.

Michelangelo carved the enormous *David* (fig. 13.27) between 1501 and 1504. The statue, which is over 13 feet tall, was intended to stand 40 feet above the ground on a buttress on Florence Cathedral. However, when it was finished, the city officials designated it a "masterpiece," too good to be placed so high on the cathedral; instead it was placed in front of the Palazzo Vecchio in the Piazza della Signoria. There, in the square where political meetings took place, it would symbolize not only freedom of speech, but the Republic of Florence itself, free from foreigners, papal domination, and Medici rule. (The Medici had been exiled in 1494.)

The *David*'s pose is taken from antiquity, with the weight on one leg in the *contrapposto* position. The sculptor's virtuosity is most evidenced in David's tightly muscled form, his tendons and veins recorded. A sense of enormous pent-up energy emerges, of latent power about to

explode, and the question seems to be less *if* he will move than *when*. The absence of attire recalls the heroic nudes of antiquity and avoids linking the *David* to a specific time period; instead *David* has universal meaning. He represents the battle between good and evil, as well as every person who must face their foe.

Michelangelo was called to Rome in 1505 to create the monumental tomb of Pope Julius II. The project was halted by Julius II himself soon after Michelangelo's arrival when the pope decided that finishing the painting of the Sistine Chapel, a project initiated by his predecessor Sixtus IV, should take priority. Michelangelo is reputed to have said, "Painting is for women, sculpture for men." Reluctantly, he began to paint. The ceiling, which covers more than 5,800 square feet, is nearly seventy feet high. Michelangelo would have to work long hours on scaffolding, paint dripping on him. The center of the ceiling features the story of

FIGURE 13.26   Michelangelo, *Pietà*, 1498/99–1500, marble, height 5′8½″ (1.70 m), St. Peter's, Vatican, Rome. Araldo de Luca, Roma/Vatican Museums, Rome, Italy/Fabbrica di San Pietro. "Pietà" refers to the depiction of Mary mourning over Jesus, lying across her lap. Although the subject was developed in Gothic Germany, the most famous *Pietà* is surely Michelangelo's version.

Creation—nine scenes from Genesis. Four further scenes from the Old Testament appear in the corners. Old Testament prophets and ancient pagan sibyls (female prophets) are included, along with Jesus's ancestors, and assorted medallions, *putti* (cherubs), and male nudes. There are over three hundred figures in all, many of which have no known meaning. Michelangelo claimed that Julius II let him paint what he pleased, but the complexity of the program suggests he had advisers. Neoplatonist numerology, symbolism, and philosophy inform many of the subjects and pagan stories and motifs are also evident. Old Testament stories are used to prefigure those in the New Testament.

In the scene of the *Creation of Adam* (fig. 13.28), God, noble and powerful, flies in swiftly, bringing Eve with him under his arm. Compare this scene with Ghiberti's depiction in the *Gates of Paradise* (see fig. 13.8). Michelangelo's dynamic God contrasts with a listless Adam, whose figure Michelangelo derived from an ancient Roman coin. Momentarily, God will give Adam his soul and bring him fully to life, for their fingers are about to touch. Note the masculine musculature of the figures; even the female figures on the Sistine ceiling are based on male models. Michelangelo's figures are heroic and powerful, yet they have a grace and beauty.

FIGURE 13.27   Michelangelo, *David*, 1501–04, marble, height 13′5″ (4.09 m), Galleria dell'Accademia, Florence. A magnificent marble man, akin to the heroic nudes of antiquity and undated by costume, David becomes a universal symbol of the individual facing unseen conflict.

FIGURE 13.28   Michelangelo, *Creation of Adam*, detail of Sistine Chapel ceiling, 1511–12, fresco, 9′2″ × 18′ 8″ (2.79 × 5.69 m), Vatican, Rome. Adam's enormous latent power will be released in the next instant when swift-moving God, with Eve already under his arm, brings him to life.

In both the tenseness of its mood and its distortion of human anatomy, Michelangelo's fresco of *The Last Judgment* (fig. 13.29) reflects the Mannerist style. Although his plan for St. Peter's, built in 1546, embodies the ideals of the High Renaissance, much of Michelangelo's late work leaves those ideals far behind. A new spirit entered his art in *The Last Judgment*, commissioned for the altar wall of the Sistine Chapel in 1534 by a dying Pope Clement VII. Painted between 1536 and 1541, it lacks the optimism and sense of beauty that define Michelangelo's work on the ceiling. His figures, no longer beautifully proportioned, now look twisted and grotesque, with heads too small for their giant, inflated bodies. The space is filled with bodies that are larger at the top of the picture than the bottom; no illusion of realistic depth is even intended here.

However, this style befits Michelangelo's subject. The dead are dragged from their graves and pulled upward to be judged by Jesus. Mary, at his side, cringes at the vision. At his feet, to his right, is St. Bartholomew. Legend states that Bartholomew was martyred by being skinned alive, and he holds his skin in his hand. But the face is a self-portrait of Michelangelo, and such grimness extends to the whole painting. The hands of Bartholomew's flayed skin seem to reach downward, to the chasm of hell that opens at the bottom of the painting, where a monstrous Charon (the ferryman of the dead) guides his boat across the River Styx, driving the damned before him into perpetual torment.

Properzia de' Rossi.   PROPERZIA DE' ROSSI [Pro-PEHR-tzee-ah deh RAW-see] (ca. 1490–1530), from Bologna, is known for her work in miniature, carving entire scenes on the pit of an apricot or a peach! Yet she also sculpted on a huge scale, for de' Rossi won a competition to create sculpture for the facade of the church of San Petronio in Bologna, from which the scene of *Joseph and Potiphar's Wife* (fig. 13.30) is believed to come. The semiclad wife of the Egyptian officer Potiphar has failed to seduce Joseph; she reaches quickly to grab for his cloak as he flees her bed. The sense of animation achieved is notable, the draperies and hair of Joseph and of Potiphar's wife shown to respond to the speed of their movements. Properzia de' Rossi died at the age of 39—one can only wonder what she would have achieved had her productive years been extended.

FIGURE 13.29 Michelangelo, *The Last Judgment*, Sistine Chapel, 1536–41, fresco, 48 × 44′ (14.63 × 13.41 m), Vatican Museums, Rome. Michelangelo's optimism and the idealized beauty of the ceiling of this chapel are now replaced with a pessimistic view and anatomical anomalies.

Critical Thinking

THE QUESTION OF ART RESTORATION

Among questions debated strongly in recent years is the extent to which works of art that have deteriorated over the centuries should be restored, or even cleaned. Cleaning refers to removing grime and soot, or layers of varnish from works. Restoration involves repairing elements that have become damaged and replacing missing elements. One major example that occasioned strenuous debate was the cleaning of the Sistine Chapel frescoes painted by Michelangelo, and which had, over the centuries, become darkened with dirt. Another ex-ample is the restoration of Leonardo da Vinci's *Last Supper*, which took twenty years, and involved not only cleaning, but also filling in some missing sections of the image with new paint.

Among the arguments against clean-ing Michelangelo's work was that the cleaning agents might also remove some of the original pigment, and could dam-age the painting irretrievably by remov-ing the darkened colors that over many generations people had become accus-tomed to seeing and revealing a brighter set of hues that some considered garish. Against adding newly painted sections to Leonardo's work were those who said the great painting would effectively no longer be Leonardo's. Countering these arguments were those who claimed that cleaning the Sistine frescoes would re-store them to how Michelangelo origi-nally painted them. Similarly, those who favored restoring Leonardo's *Last Supper* believe that the painting has now been restored to its former glory.

Which point of view do you find more convincing, and why? What other issues do you think should be evaluated when a major art masterpiece is being considered for cleaning and/or restora-tion? What do you think should be done with Leonardo's *Mona Lisa*, which is the most famous prime candidate for clean-ing today?

FIGURE 13.30 Properzia de' Rossi, *Joseph and Potiphar's Wife*, ca. 1520, marble bas-relief, $19'\frac{1}{4}'' \times 18'\frac{1}{8}''$ (49 × 46 cm), Museo di San Petronio, Bologna. Photographer: Alinari, Art Resource, NY. Powerful full figures, so admired during the High Renais-sance, move rapidly through space in this compact composition, the garments reveal-ing the bodies beneath as well as enhancing the action.

ARCHITECTURE

Donato Bramante.   DONATO BRAMANTE's [bra-MAHN-tay] (1444–1514) reputation was based largely on a building called the Tempietto, or "little temple" (fig. 13.31) constructed from 1502 on the site where St. Peter was believed to have been crucified. Commissioned by Ferdinand and Isabella of Spain (patrons of the explorer Christopher Columbus), the Tempietto is an adaptation of a classical temple of the Doric order (see Chapter 2), including a complete entablature.

The building itself is set on a stepped base and surrounded by a **peristyle,** or continuous row of columns. The first story is topped by a balustrade, or carved railing, inside of which is a **drum,** or circular wall, on which Bramante set a classically hemispheric dome. The plan, with its deeply recessed spaces, creates a dramatic play of light and dark, despite the relatively small scale of the building itself.

THE NEW ST. PETER'S BASILICA

In 1506, Pope Julius II decided to tear down the old St. Peter's Basilica, which had stood at the Vatican since the time of Constantine in the early fourth century, and re-

FIGURE 13.31   Donato Bramante, Tempietto, San Pietro in Montorio, Rome, 1502–after 1511. Small in size but of great importance, the Tempietto demonstrates the reuse of ancient pagan architecture for Renaissance Christian purposes.

(a)

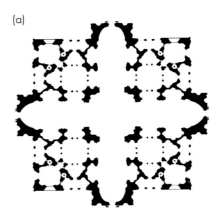

(b)

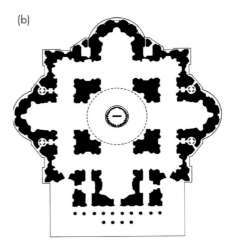

(c)

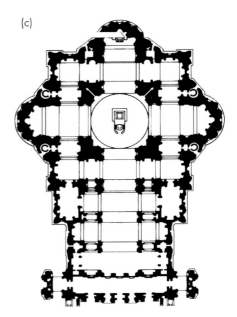

FIGURE 13.32   Floor plans for St. Peter's, Rome, by (a) Bramante, (b) Michelangelo, and (c) Carlo Maderno. Although Bramante and Michelangelo intended Greek-cross plans, the long nave of the Latin-cross plan was added by Maderno to accommodate the crowds of people.

place it with a new church more befitting the dignity and prestige of the papacy. To this end he appointed Donato Bramante as architect.

Bramante's plan for St. Peter's Basilica (fig. 13.32) is, essentially, a grander version of the Tempietto, over 450 feet in diameter instead of 15. Instead of basing his plan on the traditional longitudinal Latin cross (three short arms and one long one), Bramante chose to utilize a Greek cross (four arms of equal length) with a central dome. The plan is symmetrical and harmonious, symbolizing the perfection of God, topped by an enormous dome modeled after the Pantheon's.

Michelangelo's St. Peter's.   With the deaths of Julius II in 1513 and of Bramante in 1514, work ceased temporarily. After several other architects, including Raphael, attempted to revise Bramante's plan, Michelangelo was appointed architect in 1546. He described Bramante's original design as "clear and straightforward." He wrote, "Indeed, every architect who has departed from Bramante's plan . . . has departed from the right way." Nevertheless, Michelangelo modified the original (fig. 13.32). Instead of an interior of interlocking Greek crosses, Michelangelo simplified the scheme, in part, due to structural necessity. The four main piers had to be massively enlarged to support the dome, causing Michelangelo to simplify the remaining interior space. Michelangelo also intended a double-columned portico across the front.

Michelangelo did not live to see the completion of his plan. The dome was finished in 1590 (fig. 13.33), with a somewhat higher and more pointed profile than Michelangelo had intended, in part because of engineering requirements, the vertical shape minimizing the lateral thrust exerted by the dome. In 1606, Pope Paul V appointed the architect Carlo Maderno to restore the church to a Latin-cross plan (fig. 13.32).

FIGURE 13.33   View of St. Peter's, Rome. St. Peter's underwent so many changes that only a hint of the simplicity of Bramantés and Michelangelo's original Greek cross plans remains.

VENICE

Throughout the fifteenth century and into the sixteenth, Venice was one of the most powerful city-states in all of Europe, exercising control over the entire Adriatic and much of the eastern Mediterranean. It was celebrated in Vittore Carpaccio's *Lion of St. Mark* (fig. 13.34), painted in 1516 for a government office in the city's Ducal Palace.

FIGURE 13.34   Vittore Carpaccio, *Lion of St. Mark*, 1516, oil on canvas, $4'6\frac{3}{4}'' \times 12'1''$ (1.40 × 3.70 m), Ducal Palace, Venice. The winged lion was a symbol of the Evangelist Mark and of Venice. This painting documents the early sixteenth-century appearance of the city, with its campanile, Ducal Palace, and the domes of St. Mark's Cathedral.

The lion is the symbol of the city's patron saint, Mark the Evangelist, whom God was said to have visited on the Evangelist's arrival at the Venice lagoon, thereby designating Venice as the saint's final resting place. Greeting St. Mark, God's angel is said to have announced, "Peace unto you, Mark, my evangelist," the Latin words inscribed on the tablet held in the lion's paws. The lion stands with its front paws on land and its hind paws in the water, signifying Venice's dominion over land and sea. Behind the lion, to the left, is the Ducal Palace, the seat of government and law and the source of the city's order and harmony. The Byzantine domes of St. Mark's Cathedral rise behind it, the basis of the city's moral fabric, and the giant campanile (bell tower) that dominates St. Mark's Square stands on the far left housing the five bells of St. Mark's, one of which chimed to announce the beginning and end of each working day. Behind the lion to the right is a fleet of Venetian merchant ships, the source of the city's wealth and prosperity.

Venetian Oil Painting.   Surrounded by water and built over a lagoon, humidity made fresco painting, so popular elsewhere in Europe, virtually impossible in Venice. From 1475, after **oil painting** (pigments mixed with linseed oil) was developed in The Netherlands, fresco painting in Venice gradually ceased. The use of oil on canvas led in turn to a new kind of painting. Applying colors in glazes—that is, in layers of transparent color—created by mixing a little pigment with a lot of linseed oil, painters were able to create a light that seemed to emanate from the depths of the painting itself. Furthermore, the texture of the canvas itself was exploited. Stroked over a woven surface, the brush deposits more paint on the top of the weave and less in the crevices. This textured surface in turn "catches" actual light, lending an almost shimmering vibrancy.

Titian.   Tiziano Vecelli of Venice, known as TITIAN [TISH-un] (ca. 1488/90-1576) favored paintings with complex iconography—in fact, Titian classified his paintings as poetry. Characteristic of the Renaissance interest in antiquity, the subject of Titian's festive *Bacchanal* (fig. 13.35), painted ca. 1518, derives from Classical mythology; Bacchus is the ancient Roman god of wine. Titian popularized the type of strawberry blond female seen here, portrayed with his characteristically sensuous handling of

FIGURE 13.35   Titian, *Bacchanal*, ca. 1518, oil on canvas, 5′8$\frac{7}{8}$″ × 6′4″ (1.75 × 1.93 m), Museo del Prado Madrid. Botticelli's slender Early Renaissance figure type (figs. 13.17–18) matured in the work of High Renaissance painters such as Titian to a full-bodied ideal of beauty.

flesh. The richness of Titian's paintings is due in part to his use of an underpainting of red bolus (an earth pigment) in many of his works, rather than the usual green-black underpainting. He also used **impasto**—thick paint made by mixing the pigment with beeswax. Titian is associated with the so-called "golden glow" of Venetian painting, achieved, in part, by adding a bit of yellow pigment to the final protective glaze applied to the painting.

MUSIC

The reinvention of Rome required the reinvention of music—a new St. Peter's needed a new mass to fill its vast space with sound.

Josquin des Près. The most important composer of the new Rome took on the job: JOSQUIN DES PRÈS [JOZ-skanh de-PRAY] (1440–1521), from Flanders. It was Josquin who led the Sistine Choir as Michelangelo painted the ceiling and Raphael worked in the papal suites. Like Dufay, Josquin spent many years in Italy, serving the Sforza family in Milan, the Estes at their court in Ferrara, and finally several Roman popes, including Sixtus IV (for whom he directed the Sistine Choir), Julius II, and Leo X. So highly regarded was Josquin that the French king Louis XII and the Austrian queen Margaret both bid for his services. His contemporaries extolled him as "the Father of Musicians" and "the best of composers." An enchanted Martin Luther remarked that Josquin was "the master of the notes; they must do as he wills."

Josquin composed approximately two hundred works— motets, **masses,** and **chansons** (songs). His many motets and chansons attest to his interest in exploring new trends in setting words to music. His motet "Ave Maria . . . virgo serena" ("Hail, Mary . . . Serene Virgin") (1502) exemplifies his style. The opening employs imitative counterpoint with the melody for the words "Ave Maria" first heard in the soprano, then repeated in succession by the alto, the tenor, and the bass while the original parts continue, as in a round. On the words *gratia plena* ("full of grace") Josquin introduces a new, second melody, again in the soprano, which is again passed from one voice to the next. Josquin overlaps the voices in both melodies, allowing the altos to enter, for example, before the sopranos have sung the complete melody. This overlapping of voices enriches the music's texture, giving it body and providing it with a continuous and fluid motion. Josquin also allows two voices, and sometimes three or four, to sing the same melody simultaneously—a duet between the two lower voice parts (tenor and bass), for instance, will imitate a duet between alto and soprano. The motet concludes serenely with emphatic slow chords on the words *O mater Dei, memento mei* ("O mother of God, remember me"). Just before this ending, Josquin introduces a significant silence that sounds at first like an ending. He uses this silence to focus the listener's attention on the true ending, which comes imme-

diately after. The dignified serenity and graceful restraint of Josquin's "Ave Maria . . . virgo serena" can be compared with the quiet beauty and restrained elegance of Raphael's madonnas.

Palestrina. The music of the Italian GIOVANNI PIERLUIGI DA PALESTRINA [pal-uh-STREE-nah] (1525–94) came to dominate the church throughout most of the sixteenth century. As the church came under attack from the north for its excessive spending and ornate lavishness, it responded by simplifying the mass and the music designed to accompany it. Although it considered banning polyphony altogether, thinking it too elaborate to be easily understood by laypeople, in the end the church endorsed the controlled and precise style of Palestrina.

Palestrina held a number of important church positions. He was organist and choirmaster of the large chorus that performed exclusively in St. Peter's, the *Cappella Giulia* (Julian Choir), and he was music director for the Vatican. His music evokes the Gregorian roots of traditional church music and relies directly on the emotional appeal of the listener's potential union with God. He wrote nearly a thousand compositions, including over a hundred masses. Among the most beautiful of all Palestrina's works is his *Pope Marcellus Mass*, written in honor of the pope and set for an **a cappella**—or unaccompanied—choir in six voice parts: soprano, alto, two tenors, and two basses. It contains music for the Kyrie, Gloria, Credo, Sanctus, Benedictus, and Agnus Dei, as did the Gregorian Mass before it, and Palestrina utilizes the traditional Gregorian melodies connected with each of these parts of the mass. Still, it is clearly Renaissance in its style, utilizing an orderly and clear imitative polyphony that allows the listener to follow each of the voices in the mass as they weave together with precision.

LITERATURE

Baldassare Castiglione. BALDASSARE CASTIGLIONE [KAS-till-YOH-nay] (1478–1529) was a courtier to the Italian ducal courts, first at the court of Francesco Gonzaga, the ruler of Mantua in the early sixteenth century, and then at the court of Urbino, established by Federico da Montefeltro, the father of Guidobaldo da Montefeltro, in whose service Castiglione prospered. Later unrest caused him to return to service in Duke Francesco's court. After serving as ambassador to Rome, Castiglione was appointed by Pope Clement VII as papal ambassador to Spain, where he lived out the remaining years of his life.

While at Urbino, Castiglione wrote the *Book of the Courtier,* which memorializes, celebrates, and idealizes life at court, especially Urbino. It is cast in the form of a series of dialogues spread out over four evenings at the court of Urbino. The central topic is the manners, education, and behavior of the ideal courtier, whose virtues Castiglione extols. The courtier must be a man of courage with experience in war; he must be learned in the classics and in classical languages; he must be able to serve his prince with generosity. Castiglione's ideal courtier had to be physically and emotionally strong, able to perform feats requiring agility, skill, courage, and daring. His physical prowess was measured by his grace as a dancer and elegance as a singer and musician. He was also expected to be an engaging and witty conversationalist, a good companion, an elegant writer, even a bit of a poet. In short, Castiglione's courtier was the ideal Renaissance gentleman—of sound mind, body, and character, and learned in the ideas of Renaissance humanism.

Castiglione's blending of the soldier and the scholar, his merging of the ideals of medieval chivalry with those of Renaissance humanism, made his *Book of the Courtier* popular both in its own time and afterward. Castiglione himself was no exception and embodied the ideals his book celebrated. Raphael's portrait of Castiglione (fig. 13.36) displays many of the qualities Castiglione extols, from the

FIGURE 13.36 Raphael, *Baldassare Castiglione*, ca. 1515, oil on panel, transferred to canvas, $32\frac{1}{4}'' \times 26\frac{1}{2}''$ (81.9 × 67.3 cm), Musée du Louvre, Paris. J.G. Berizzi/Reunion des Musées National, France/Art Resource, NY. Castiglione wrote about the qualities of the ideal courtier; it is not surprising that Raphael, a refined gentleman, was a personal friend of his. Perhaps some of the calm restraint recommended by Castiglione is seen in Raphael's portrait with its restricted range of color.

nobility of the graceful head to the intelligence of the shining eyes, complemented by the elegant refinement of the attire.

Niccolò Machiavelli.   A contemporary of Castiglione, NICCOLO MACHIAVELLI [mak-ee-ah-VEL-ee] (1469–1527), also wrote a guidebook on behavior—*The Prince*, a manual for princes and rulers.

Like Castiglione, Machiavelli was well educated in the Renaissance humanist tradition. Like Castiglione's courtier, Machiavelli's prince is a model of an ideal. The difference between the two writers' "ideals," however, is dramatic: Castiglione supported the tenets of Renaissance humanism, but Machiavelli challenged them by introducing a radically different set of standards, standards that inform, among other things, Mannerist art.

Young Machiavelli was employed as a clerk and secretary to the Florentine magistrates responsible for war and internal affairs. From 1498 to 1512, he also served as an ambassador to, among others, the Holy Roman Emperor Maximilian, the king of France, and Pope Julius II. During his lifetime, the Italian city-states were almost continually at war either with one another or with other countries, such as France and Spain. Machiavelli himself suffered from the changing fortunes of the ruling families: When the Medici came to power in Florence, for instance, he was accused of conspiracy, tortured, and imprisoned. Later, when the Medici government collapsed, he was accused of being a Medici sympathizer.

The Prince was written in 1513 and published in 1532 after Machiavelli's death. It quickly acquired fame or, as some would have it, notoriety. Based on a series of premises about human nature—none favorable—*The Prince* asserts that people are basically selfish, deceitful, greedy, and gullible. Accordingly, Machiavelli advises princes to rule in ways that play on these fundamental human characteristics. A prince can be—indeed, should be—hypocritical, cruel, and deceitful when necessary. He should keep faith with no one but himself and employ ruthlessness and cunning to maintain his power over the people. As Machiavelli writes, "it is far better to be feared than loved," although he notes, "the prince must nonetheless make himself feared in such a way that, if he is not loved, he will at least avoid being hated."

The view of human beings that forms the foundation of Machiavelli's arguments in *The Prince* reflects political expediency, based on Machiavelli's observation of Florentine politics and the politics of other city-states and countries he visited as a Florentine ambassador. Having witnessed the instability of power in Italy, particularly the surrender of parts of Italy to France and Spain, Machiavelli wrote that a ruler must be strong enough to keep himself in power, for only with the strength of absolute power could he rule effectively.

Machiavelli's *The Prince* was the most widely read book of its time, after the Bible. The questions it raises about the relationship between politics and morality, the starkly realistic depiction of power it presents, and the authority, immediacy, and directness with which it is written, ensured its success. Whatever we may think of its vision of human nature or of the advice it offers rulers, it is hard to deny the power of its language, the strength of its convictions, and force of its arguments.

MANNERISM

Mannerism was defined as a style in 1914 by Walter Friedländer; the term **Mannerism** derived from the Italian *manièra* (manner of style, suggesting affectation). The style is also referred to as the Manièra as well as the anti-Classical style, although the artists today labeled as Mannerists considered themselves classical. Mannerism originally referred only to painting, and meant that one painted "in the manner of . . ." Later, it came to have a negative connotation, one associated with affectation, academicism, and decadence: Mannerism became a derogatory term connoting artificiality and artistic decline on the grounds that artists did not assimilate the style of a master, but only affected it. Today, Mannerism is no longer considered a decline, for it is felt the distorted elements that characterize the style give spiritual feeling and convey emotion. The Mannerist period dates from approximately 1520 to 1600, the style seen especially in Italy, centering in Rome and Florence, although it was also fashionable in France and elsewhere.

Mannerism coincides with a period of political and religious unrest. The sack of Rome in 1527 by the troops of Charles V, six months of murder and destruction, undermined the confidence of the Renaissance humanists. Religious feelings were strong in the time of the Reformation and Counter-Reformation. In an age of anxiety, an era of crisis, the clarity and confidence of the High Renaissance was lost, replaced by ambiguity and despair. The emotional impact of Mannerist art is likely to be tense and disturbing.

Never intended to have broad public appeal, Mannerism was a court style oriented to the tastes of the upper class. It was formulated to appeal to the sophisticated, elegant, aristocratic sensibilities of the sixteenth century. Thus, although the style was in vogue for a long period of time, its audience was restricted and it was not to have significant impact on future artistic trends. Mannerism, therefore, is not considered as important in the history of culture as the preceding Renaissance style or the succeeding Baroque style.

PAINTING

Mannerism was a departure from Renaissance ideals. Whereas Renaissance painting was characterized by clear presentations of subject matter, balanced compositions, normal body proportions, scientific spatial constructions, and preference for primary colors, Mannerist painting, in contrast, was characterized by intentionally obscure subject matter, unbalanced compositions, bodies with distorted proportions and contorted poses, confusing spatial constructions, and a preference for secondary and acidic colors. Facial expressions may be strained or inappropriate for the subject. Aesthetic forms became of greater concern than content.

Parmigianino. Among the most characteristic examples of the Mannerist departure from the Renaissance norm is the *Madonna with the Long Neck* (fig. 13.37), painted 1534–40 by PARMIGIANINO [par-mee-jah-NEE-noh]

FIGURE 13.37 Parmigianino, *Madonna with the Long Neck*, 1534–40, oil on panel, 7′1″ × 4′4″ (2.16 × 1.32 m), Galleria degli Uffizi, Florence. Scala/Art Resource, NY. Comparison with Raphael's High Renaissance *Madonna of the Meadows* (see fig. 13.24) makes obvious the Mannerist preference for distorted figures and spatial ambiguity.

(1503–40) of Parma. The figures are perfect, but, in contrast to the classical canon of proportions admired in the Renaissance, they have become unreal, other worldly, elongated and ethereal, artificial and affected, graceful and refined beyond nature's capabilities. Mary is especially large, with an almost balloonlike inflation through the hips and thighs. Only a complete absence of bones and joints would explain the curving contours of Mary's right hand.

The composition is unbalanced and spatially ambiguous. The figures are crowded on the left side, yet the open area on the right side is almost empty. The column in the background is a symbol of the torture of Jesus, because he was bound to a column and flagellated. The tiny prophet emphasizes the odd and unclear spatial arrangement—the viewer looks up to the foreground figures but down to the prophet.

Bronzino. Another representative of the Mannerist or anti-Classical style is Bronzino (1503–72), court painter to Cosimo de' Medici. Mannerism was noted to be the style of the courts and was not intended to appeal to the general public. Bronzino's painting of the *Allegory of Venus* (figure 13.38), ca. 1546, demonstrates the intentional ambiguity of Mannerist iconography. The two main figures are Venus and Cupid, their relationship shown to be uncomfortably erotic. On the right, Folly throws roses. In the upper right, Father Time uncovers the follies of love—or perhaps he tries to hide them! The figure in the right background, with the body of a snake and the left and right hands reversed, is Deceit—the masks suggest falseness. The figures in the left background are probably Hatred and Inconstancy. Typically Mannerist is the complexity and obscurity of the **allegory,** which has been interpreted in various ways by historians.

Like the subject, the composition is also unclear. Characteristic of Mannerism is the absence of a single center of focus—the figures seem to compete with each other for the viewer's attention. The figures completely fill the composition, choking the space. Still and tense, their poses are elegant but affected, agitated, and exaggerated—and certainly difficult for a person to actually assume. Relative scale of the figures is inconsistent. Their uneasy expressions cause them to appear disturbed, and they are intended to disturb the viewer in this style that is distorted psychologically and physically. The colors are acid and metallic, the style of painting linear and hard with harsh lighting. Figures weave in and out in a paper-thin space, crowded, limited, and confined, set against a heavy and impenetrable background. Spatial contradictions abound—a floor plan of this space and its inhabitants cannot be drawn, for neither linear nor aerial perspective is used.

Tintoretto. The leader of the Mannerists in Venice was Tintoretto (1518–94), whose real name was Jacopo Robusti, painter of the *Last Supper* (fig. 13.39) of 1592–94. The coveted Renaissance iconographic clarity, seen in Leonardo da Vinci's depiction of this subject (fig. 13.20),

FIGURE 13.38 Agnolo Bronzino, *Allegory with Venus and Cupid,* ca. 1546, oil on panel, 4′9½″ × 3′9¼″ (1.46 × 1.16 m), National Gallery, London. Typically Mannerist are the intentionally complex iconography (including an oddly erotic encounter between Venus and Cupid) and the pictorial space choked with figures.

is gone. In fact, the viewer may need some time to find Jesus in this scene, for the perspective leads the viewer's eyes away from Jesus and out of the composition, many figures compete with Jesus for the viewer's attention, and Jesus is pushed back into the space. He is singled out only by his central position and aureole of light. The lighting is unnatural, radiating from Jesus and the hanging lamp, from which the smoke turns into floating transparent angels. Judas is singled out from the apostles as the only figure on the opposite side of the table. The table is not parallel to the picture plane, as in Renaissance portrayals of the Last Supper, but placed on a strong diagonal into depth—the rapid recession is characteristic of Tintoretto. This Mannerist portrayal of the Last Supper is set in a tavern, an unusually commonplace location for a religious event.

Yet there is no possibility of mistaking this for a genre scene. Religious drama and emotion derive from Tintoretto's striking composition and lighting. Far from a calm, stable, static depiction, Tintoretto's verve changed Leonardo da Vinci's format for the Last Supper and broke Leonardo's hold on this subject. But Tintoretto's presen-

FIGURE 13.39   Tintoretto, *The Last Supper*, 1592–94, oil on canvas, 12′ × 18′8″ (3.66 × 5.69 m), San Giorgio Maggiore, Venice. SCALA/Art Resouce, NY. In striking contrast to the compositional clarity of Leonardo da Vinci's High Renaissance depiction (see fig. 13.20), the viewer may have some difficulty in locating Jesus in Tintoretto's Mannerist version of this subject, for the perspective leads away from, rather than toward, Jesus.

tation has been criticized for losing sight of the spirituality of the subject, with too much stress placed on the incidental activity in the foreground. Instead, Tintoretto's greatest concern was the aesthetic problem and the potential of light, movement, and drama.

El Greco.   One of the most interesting artists whose work displays Mannerist qualities is known as EL GRECO [el GRECK-oh] (1541–1614), or "the Greek." Domenikos Theotokopoulos was born on the island of Crete. He studied in Venice from about 1566, where he was deeply influenced by Titian, and then for seven years in Rome. In 1577, he emigrated to Spain, going first to Madrid and then to Toledo.

The most important of his major commissions is *The Burial of Count Orgaz* (fig. 13.40) of 1586. Legend held that at the count's burial in 1323, Saints Augustine and Stephen appeared and lowered him into his grave even as his soul was seen ascending to heaven. In the painting, the

burial and the ascension occur in two separate realms, neither of which fits spatially with the other, and both of which are packed with figures. On the lower portion, El Greco has painted the local contemporary aristocracy—people he knew—in attendance at the funeral, not the aristocracy of the count's day. In fact, El Greco's eight-year-old son stands at the lower left next to St. Stephen, and above him, looking out at the viewer from the back row, is quite possibly El Greco himself.

The top half of the scene is as spatially ambiguous as any example of Mannerist painting. A crowd of saints enters from a deep space at the top right. A chorus of angels playing instruments occupies a sort of middle space on the left. In the foreground, St. John and the Virgin Mary greet the angel who arrives with the soul of the count, shown about the size of a baby, as if to emphasize its innocence. John and Mary plead the count's case with Jesus, who is peculiarly small and seated far enough in the distance almost to occupy the vanishing point to the heavens. The most no-

generous dowry the Spanish monarchy provided for her first marriage in 1570.

Sofonisba Anguissola frequently painted self-portraits, which were much in demand due to her fame, as well as portraits of her family, such as fig. 13.41 of one of her sisters, Minerva. Her sitters appear relaxed, almost alive; Giorgio Vasari noted that she created "breathing likenesses." Minerva wears a large gold medallion of the ancient Minerva, goddess of wisdom and the arts.

Lavinia Fontana.   LAVINIA FONTANA [La-VEEN-nee-eh Fohn-THAN-nah] (1552–1614) grew up in Bologna, where she was instructed by her father, the artist Prospero Fontana. She is believed to be the first woman in western Europe to establish herself as a professional artist equal to her male contemporaries in fame. Her *Portrait of a Noblewoman* (fig. 13.42) is representative of her work; although women artists were likely to specialize in portraiture, Fontana's repertoire included religious and mythological subjects as well. Her husband and fellow

FIGURE 13.40   El Greco, *The Burial of Count Orgaz*, 1586, oil on canvas, 16′ × 11′10″ (4.88 × 3.61 m), Church of San Tomé, Toledo. Although El Greco's distorted figures were once attributed to astigmatism, they are now recognized as part of the Mannerist preference for elongated bodily proportions.

FIGURE 13.41   Sofonisba Anguissola, *Portrait of the Artist's Sister Minerva*, ca. 1564, oil on canvas, 33½ × 26″, Milwaukee Art Museum. Gift of the family of Mrs. Fred Vogel, Jr. As was customary for women artists of this era, Anguissola specialized in portraits. Such realistic records are one of the manifestations of the interest accorded the individual that began during the Renaissance.

table aspect of El Greco's style is exemplified by Jesus' right arm, which stretches far forward into the space above Mary's head. The elongated hands and arms are the most "mannered" feature of El Greco's art, and yet it is difficult to label his work "Mannerist." His aim is to move his audience by conveying a sense of the spiritual, almost mystical power of deeply religious faith and conviction. In this, his painting anticipates that of the Baroque age, and captures something of the power of the great Spanish mystics of his own day, Teresa of Avila and Ignatius Loyola, both of whom would be made saints in Rome in 1622.

Sofonisba Anguissola.   Castiglione's *Book of the Courtier* advocated that aristocrats, be they male or female, be educated in social arts, and that women, specifically, should learn to paint, not as a career, but as part of training for aristocratic life. SOFONISBA ANGUISSOLA [So-fo-NEES-bah Ahn-gwee-SO-lah] (1528/35– 1625), from Cremona, and her five younger sisters studied painting and all became painters; only the youngest sibling, a boy, did not. In 1560, Anguissola became a painter at the court of Philip II in Madrid, indicating her international fame. The high regard in which she was held is made clear by the

FIGURE 13.42 Lavinia Fontana, *Portrait of a Noblewoman*, ca. 1580, oil on canvas, $45\frac{1}{4}'' \times 35\frac{1}{4}''$ (114.9 × 89.5 cm), National Museum of Women in the Arts, Washington, DC. Gift of Wallace and Wilhelmina Holladay. This portrait of an unknown Bolognese lady is believed to be a marriage portrait because red was the customary color of a wedding gown in Bologna; she is shown wearing one of the garments, and some of the gems, in her trousseau. The dog is a standard symbol of marital fidelity.

FIGURE 13.43 Benvenuto Cellini, *Saltcellar of Francis I*, 1539–43, gold with enamel, $10\frac{1}{4}'' \times 13\frac{1}{8}''$ (26 × 33.3 cm), Kunsthistorisches Museum, Vienna, Austria. An example of extreme elegance and opulence, this table ornament contained salt and pepper.

painter Gian Paolo Zappi worked as her assistant. She was the mother of eleven children, although was survived by only three of them. In 1604 she moved to Rome to work as a portrait painter for Pope Paul V. The appeal of Fontana's style lies in the meticulously painted details of the costume, her superb technical skill in depicting various textures, and the absence of a distracting background, thereby placing all attention on the subject.

SCULPTURE

By the mid-sixteenth century, Mannerism was the dominant style in France, largely as a result of the influence of Italian artists who moved there after the sack of Rome in 1527. Benvenuto Cellini's sculpture and writings reflected the full flowering of the style.

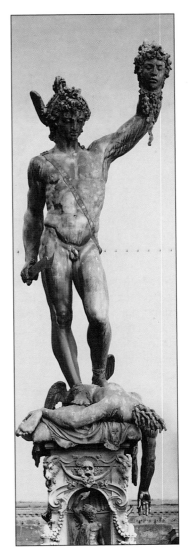

FIGURE 13.44 Benvenuto Cellini, *Perseus*, 1545–54, bronze, height 18′ (5.4 m), Loggia dei Lanzi, Florence. Even the depiction of the decapitation of the ancient mythological gorgon Medusa, blood gushing, attains elegance in the Mannerist style.

Then & Now

THE VENICE GHETTO

One of the most horrifying events in twentieth-century history is the Holocaust, the anti-Semitism movement in Hitler's Germany that led to the murder of more than six million Jews. One of the reasons Hitler could so easily control the Jewish population in Europe was that he created ghettos for the vast majority of Jews in the major European capitals. The earliest known segregation of Jews into their own distinct neighborhoods occurred in Spain and Portugal in the fourteenth century, but a large ghetto was established in Frankfurt in 1460. Ghettos in Venice appeared early in the sixteenth century.

A Jewish presence in Venice dates to the early fourteenth century, and by 1381 the city had authorized Jews to live in the city, practice usury—the lending of money with interest—and sell secondhand clothes and objects, which led to the profession of pawnbroking. In 1397, all Jews were expelled, ostensibly because of irregularities that had been discovered in the monetary practices of Jewish bankers and merchants. They were permitted to visit the city for no more than fifteen consecutive days and forced to wear an emblem identifying their religion. But this order became more and more laxly enforced, and the Venetian Jewish community flourished until 1496, when they were once again banished, and this time only permitted to stay in Venice for two weeks a year.

In 1508, Julius II formed an alliance with the rest of Italy and Europe against Venice, and when his army approached the city in the spring of 1509, the large Jewish community that lived on the mainland at the lagoon's edge fled to Venice proper. Many Jewish leaders offered much-needed financial support, and the city found itself in a quandary about where they should be allowed to live. The issue was hotly debated for seven years. Franciscan sermons routinely warned that God would punish the city if Jews were admitted. Finally, on March 29, 1516, a substantial majority of the Senate approved a proposal to move the Jews en masse to an islet linked to the rest of the city by two points of access that could be closed at night. In this way, Venice could make use of the skills—and money—of the Jewish community and still segregate them.

The island to which they were banished was the site of a new foundry. The Venetian word for the smelting process is *gettare*, and the new foundry built on the island was named *getto nuovo*. Soon the island itself was called Ghetto Nuovo, and the word "ghetto" entered the language, and came to be used throughout Europe to describe the areas in cities where Jewish communities were to be found.

Benvenuto Cellini. BENVENUTO CELLINI [che-LEE-nee] (1500–71) was a Florentine who worked in France for King Francis I (reigned 1515–47). Cellini made an extraordinary gold and enamel *Saltcellar of Francis I* (fig. 13.43), between 1539 and 1543. It is functional, yet elegant and fantastic. Salt is represented by the male figure Neptune, because salt comes from the sea (the salt is actually in a little boat), and pepper is represented by the female figure Earth, because pepper comes from the earth (the pepper is actually in a little triumphal arch). On the base are complex allegorical figures of the four seasons and four parts of the day, meant to evoke both festive seasonal celebrations and the daily meal schedule. Cellini wrote that figures should be elongated; these with small heads and boneless limbs are graceful and charming.

The Autobiography of Benvenuto Cellini. Among the most widely read of Renaissance works, Cellini's *Autobiography* is notable for the way in which it portrays the Italian Mannerist sculptor and goldsmith. His response to his patron, the duke of Florence, Cosimo de' Medici, who had just commissioned a new sculpture, *Perseus* (fig. 13.44), shows his Mannerist extravagance. When the duke questioned Cellini's ability to complete a sculpture in bronze, the artist responded with supreme confidence. In Cellini's account of the incident, the artist is portrayed as heroic, brave, violent, passionate, promiscuous, and entirely committed to his art.

Like the elongated figures in Parmigianino's paintings, Cellini's exaggerated portrayal of himself and others, in his *Autobiography*, typifies the Mannerist tendency. Unlike Parmigianino's delicacy and grace, however, Cellini is all drama and vigor. Cellini's *Autobiography*, in the end, is akin to his *Saltcellar of Francis I*. His sculpture extends the Mannerist style to its limits—the decorous Classical ideal of his Renaissance predecessors is gone.

ARCHITECTURE

Mannerist architects responded to the revival of the antique in unorthodox ways. The vestibule of the Laurentian Library in Florence (fig. 13.45) was built as the Medici family library above the monastery of the church of San Lorenzo. Begun by Michelangelo in 1524, the staircase was designed between 1558 and 1559, and the room was completed by GIORGIO VASARI [va-SAH-ree] (1511–74) and AMMANATI [ah-mahn-AH-tee] (1511–92). One of the most peculiar rooms ever built, the foyer has among its oddities that it is two stories high and thus higher than it is long or wide. The niches (wall recesses) are smaller at the bottom than at the top, and the same inversion of the norm is true of the pilasters that flank the niches. The columns are set into the wall, not in front of it, reversing the usual column and wall relationship. Scroll brackets, usually supporting elements, are rendered nonfunctional by their placement. The impression is one of walls pushing in, crushing the visitor. Finally, the staircase has three separate flights at the bottom but only one into the doorway at the top—a guaranteed traffic problem. This intriguing and uncomfortable room, in which everything is contrary to the classical rules of architecture, may be regarded as an ingenious Mannerist interpretation of the antique vocabulary.

The architect ANDREA PALLADIO (1508–80), from Vicenza in northern Italy, created a building in the Mannerist style that was to be highly influential—the Villa Rotunda (fig. 13.46), ca. 1567–70, one of many villas he built in and around Vicenza. The Villa Rotunda demonstrates the extreme to which Palladio carried his passion for symmetry and ancient architecture, since all four sides are identical, each mimicking an ancient temple facade with a triangular pediment supported on columns. The central dome recalls that of the ancient Roman Pantheon (Chapter 4, fig. 4.13). Certainly the result is harmonious, dignified, majestic, with an impressive grandeur. Yet the idea of a home as inviting and welcoming has been transformed into something intimidating: The visitor is humbled by the ascent of many steps required to gain entry, and, although the spacious main floor was used for entertaining, the bedrooms upstairs have low ceilings.

Palladio was not only an architect but also an author: His *Four Books on Architecture*, published in 1570, became the handbook of architects. An admirer of classical architecture, as the Villa Rotunda demonstrates, the ancient architect's logic is replaced by impracticality in the Mannerist's reinterpretation.

FIGURE 13.45   Michelangelo, Vasari, and Ammanati, vestibule of Laurentian Library, begun 1524, staircase completed 1559, monastery of San Lorenzo, Florence. The antique architectural vocabulary has been used to create a space in which the visitor is unlikely to feel comfortable. The stairs, which seem to flow downward, fill most of the floor space and, because three flights lead to a single doorway at the top, a traffic jam is likely.

Cultural Impact

The Renaissance changed the way human beings thought of themselves. People were no longer content to see themselves simply as a part of a larger social or religious group. With the Italian Renaissance emerged the notion of the individual self, an idea that would be celebrated two centuries later in the age of Romanticism.

One legacy of the Italian Renaissance was a restless intellectual energy. The independent thought and critical scrutiny encouraged during the Renaissance would result in the scientific revolution of the seventeenth century, as thinkers like Copernicus and Galileo built on the advances of that earlier time.

The power of individual artistic genius is most evident perhaps, among Italy's painters and sculptors. Who better than Raphael, Leonardo, and Michelangelo epitomize the genius of the Renaissance and its cultural influence? The very concept of the "Renaissance man," a multitalented individual who operates at the peak of perfection in many areas, is synonymous with these splendid artists, whose achievements have never been surpassed.

Outside the arts proper, the political ideas of Macchiavelli have been profoundly influential. Machiavelli's realistic approach to governing established principles by which rulers not only of his own day, but also of future eras, would rule. More quiet but no less influential were the social ideals of Renaissance court etiquette, especially those set down by Castiglione. His ideals of behavior established a standard for educated people of his own and future centuries to emulate.

FIGURE 13.46   Andrea Palladio, Villa Rotunda, Vicenza, ca. 1567–70. This home takes the idea of symmetry and repetition beyond the limits of practicality, for all four sides look exactly the same. Palladio's passion for his antique prototype—the Roman Pantheon (see Chapter 4)—led him to create this Mannerist example.

KEY TERMS

Renaissance	motet	chiaroscuro	mass
humanist	word painting	sfumato	chanson
Neoplatonism	sonnet	peristyle	a cappella
lantern	ballad	drum	Mannerism
baptistery	sestina	oil painting	allegory
linear perspective	canzoni	impasto	
atmospheric (aerial)			

WWW. WEBSITES FOR FURTHER STUDY

http://www.nga.gov/collection/gallery/gg4/gg4-main2.html
(A virtual tour of the early Renaissance in Florence, with many excellent images from the period.)

http://www.artchive.com/artchive/D/donatello.html
(This is the Artchive, a website with virtually every major artist in every style from every era in art history. It is an excellent resource.)

http://www.michelangelo.com/buon/bio-index2.html
(This site is a comprehensive resource for the life and career of Michelangelo.)

http://www.GreatBuildings.com/buildings/St Peters of Rome.html
(The Great Buildings site is an excellent tool for architecture of all eras.)

READINGS

PICO DELLA MIRANDOLA

ORATION ON THE DIGNITY OF MAN

Pico della Mirandola's Oration on the Dignity of Man *is a preface to a disputation he prepared to debate the Roman Church on theological and phisophical questions. His oration focuses on the centrality and importance of the individual human being, including the potential for perfectibility. A kind of humanist manifesto, Pico's oration celebrates human potentiality and demonstrates his skill at argumentation.*

Most esteemed Fathers,[1] I have read in the ancient writings of the Arabians that Abdala the Saracen[2]" on being asked what, on this stage, so to say, of the world, seemed to him most evocative of wonder, replied that there was nothing to be seen more marvelous than man. And that celebrated exclamation of Hermes Trismegistus,[3] "What a great miracle
is man, Asclepius"[4] confirms this opinion.
And still, as I reflected upon the basis assigned for these estimations, I was not fully persuaded by the diverse reasons advanced by a variety of persons for the preeminence of human nature; for example: that man is the intermediary between creatures, that he is the familiar of the gods above him as he is lord of the beings beneath him; that, by the acuteness of his senses, the inquiry of his reason and the light of his intelligence, he is the interpreter
of nature, set midway beween the timeless unchanging and the flux of time; the living union (as the Persians say), the very marriage hymn of the world, and, by David's testimony[5]
but little lower than the angels. These reasons are all, without question, of great weight; nevertheless, they do not touch the principal reasons, those, that is to say, which justify man's unique right to such unbounded admiration.
Why, I asked, should we not admire the angels themselves and the beatific choirs more?
At long last, however, I feel that I have come to some understanding of why man is the most fortunate of living things and, consequently, deserving of all admiration; of what may be the condition in the hierarchy of beings assigned to him, which draws upon him the envy, not of the brutes alone, but of the astral beings and of the very intelligences which dwell beyond the confines of the world. A thing surpassing belief and smiting the soul with

wonder. Still, how could it be otherwise? For it is on this ground that man is, with complete justice, considered and called a great miracle and a being worthy of all admiration.
Hear then, oh Fathers, precisely what this condition of man is; and in the name of your humanity, grant me your benign audition as I pursue this theme.
God the Father, the Mightiest Architect, had already raised, according to the precepts of His hidden wisdom, this world we see, the cosmic dwelling of divinity, a temple most august. He had already adorned the supercelestial region with Intelligences, infused the heavenly globes with the life of immortal souls and set the fermenting dungheap of
the inferior world teeming with every form of animal life. But when this work was done, the Divine Artificer still longed for some creature which might comprehend the meaning of so vast an achievement, which might be moved with love at its beauty and smitten with awe at its grandeur. When, consequently, all else had been completed, ... in the very last place, He bethought Himself
of bringing forth man. Truth was, however, that there remained no archetype according to which He might fashion a new offspring, nor in His treasure-houses the wherewithal to endow a new son with a fitting inheritance, nor any place, among the seats of the universe, where this new creature might dispose himself to contemplate the world. All space was already filled; all things had been distributed in the highest, the middle and the lowest orders. Still, it was not in the nature of the power of the Father to fail in this last creative élan; nor was it in the nature of that supreme Wisdom to hesitate through lack of counsel in so crucial a matter; nor, finally, in the nature of His beneficent love to compel the creature destined to praise the divine generosity in all other things to find it wanting in himself.
At last, the Supreme Maker decreed that this creature, to whom He could give nothing wholly his own, should have a
share in the particular endowment of every other creature. Taking man, therefore, this creature of indeterminate image,   *70*
He set him in the middle of the world and thus spoke to him:
"We have given you, Oh Adam, no visage proper to yourself,
nor any endowment properly your own, in order that whatever
place, whatever form, whatever gifts you may, with premeditation, select, these same you may have and possess through your own judgment and decision. The nature of all other creatures is defined and restricted within laws which We have laid down; you, by contrast, impeded by no such restrictions, may, by your own free will, to whose custody We
have assigned you, trace for yourself the lineaments of your   *80*
own nature. I have placed you at the very center of the world,
so that from that vantage point you may with greater ease glance round about you on all that the world contains. We

[1]The assembly of clergymen to whom the oration was to be addressed.
[2]The Arabic philosopher and translator Abd-Allah Ibn al Muqaffa (718–775).
[3]The Greek name (Hermes Thrice-Great) for the Greek god Thoth, the presumed author of a body of occult philosophy that mingled Neoplatonism, alchemy, and mystical interpretations of the Scriptures.
[4]The Greek god of healing and medicine.
[5]In Psalms 8.6.

have made you a creature neither of heaven nor of earth, neither mortal nor immortal, in order that you may, as the free and proud shaper of your own being, fashion yourself in the form you may prefer. It will be in your power to descend to the lower, brutish forms of life; [or] you will be able, through your own decision, to rise again to the superior orders whose life is divine."   *90*

Oh unsurpassed generosity of God the Father, Oh wondrous and unsurpassable felicity of man, to whom it is granted to have what he chooses, to be what he wills to be! The brutes, from the moment of their birth, bring with them, as Lucilius[6] says, "from their mother's womb" all that they will ever posses. The highest spiritual beings were, from the very moment of creation, or soon thereafter, fixed in the mode of being which would be theirs through measureless eternities. But upon man, at the moment of his creation, God bestowed seeds pregnant with all possibilities, the germs of every form of life. Whichever of these a man shall cultivate, the same will mature and bear fruit in him. If vegetative, he will become a plant; if sensual, he will become brutish; if rational, he will reveal himself a heavenly being; if intellectual, he will be an angel and the son of God. And if, dissatisfied with the lot of all creatures, he should recollect himself into the center of his own unity, he will there, become one spirit with God, in the solitary darkness of the Father, Who is set above all things, himself transcend all creatures. Who then will not look with awe upon this our chameleon,   *110* or who, at least, will look with greater admiration on any other being? This creature, man, whom Asclepius the Athenian, by reason of this very mutability, this nature capable of transforming itself, quite rightly said was symbolized in the mysteries by the figure of Proteus. This is the source of those metamorphoses, or transformations, so celebrated among the Hebrews and among the Pythagoreans;[7] . . . . . . while the Pythagoreans transform men guilty of crimes into brutes or even, if we are to believe Empedocles,[8] into plants; and Mohamet,[9] imitating them, was

known frequently to say that the man who deserts the divine law becomes a brute. And he was right; for it is not the bark that makes the tree, but its insensitive and unresponsive nature; nor the hide which makes the beast of burden, but its brute and sensual soul; nor the orbicular form which makes the heavens, but their harmonious order. Finally, it is not freedom from a body, but its spiritual intelligence, which makes the angel. If you see a man dedicated to his stomach, crawling on the ground, you see a plant and not a man; or if you see a man bedazzled by the empty forms of the imagination, as by the wiles of Calypso,[10] and through their alluring solicitations made a slave to his own senses, you see a brute and not a man. If, however, you see a philosopher, judging and distinguishing all things according to the rule of reason, him shall you hold in veneration, for he is a creature of heaven and not of earth; if, finally, a pure contemplator, unmindful of the body, wholly withdrawn into the inner chambers of the mind, here indeed is neither a creature of earth nor a heavenly creature, but some higher divinity, clothed with human flesh:

PETRARCH

SONNET 159

The following poem is just one of the many in which Petrarch celebrated his beloved Laura. Consider how the poet refers to Neoplatonic and humanist ideas. Petrarch was master of the extended metaphor; here it comprises the entire sonnet.

From what part of the Heavens, from what Idea
did Nature take the model to derive
that lovely face of charm by which she chose
to show down here her power up above?

What fountain nymph, what woodland goddess ever   *5*
let such fine hair of gold flow in the breeze?
How did a heart collect so many virtues
the sum of which is guilty of my death?

Who seeks for divine beauty seeks in vain,
if he has not yet looked upon those eyes   *10*
and seen how tenderly she makes them move;

he does not know how love can heal and kill,
who does not know the sweetness of her sighs,
the sweetness of her speech, how sweet her smile.

FRANCOIS VILLON

Francois Villon (1431–ca. 1474), was a poet and a vagabond and, some claim, a thief. He is as well known for his life as for his poems. The following ballads with their repeating refrains memorably evoke certain realities about life and death.

---

[6]A Roman writer of satires (180–102 B.C.E.).
[7]Followers of the Greek philosopher and mathematician Pythagoras (fl. 530 B.C.E.).
[8]A Greek philosopher and poet (495–435 B.C.E.).
[9]The prophet Muhammad (570–632).

---

[10]In Greek mythology, a sea nymph who lured Odysseus to remain with her for seven years.

THE BALLAD OF DEAD LADIES[1]

Tell me now in what hidden way is
Lady Flora the lovely Roman?
Where's Hipparchia, and where is Thais,
Neither of them the fairer woman?
Where is *Echo*, beheld of no man,
Only heard on river and mere,—
She whose beauty was more than human? . . .
But where are the snows of yester-year?

Where's Héloise, the learned nun,
For whose sake Abeillard, I ween,
Lost manhood and put priesthood on?
(From Love he won such dule and teen!)
And where, I pray you, is the Queen
Who willed that Buridan should steer
Sewed in a sack's mouth down the Seine? . . .
But where are the snows of yester-year?

White Queen Blanche, like a queen of lilies,
With a voice like any mermaiden,—
Bertha Broadfoot, Beatrice, Alice,
And Ermengarde the lady of Maine,—
And that good Joan whom Englishmen
At Rouen doomed and burned her there,—
Mother of God, where are they then? . . .
But where are the snows of yester-year?

Nay, never ask this week, fair lord,
Where they are gone, nor yet this year,
Save with this much for an overword,—
But where are the snows of yester-year?

BALLADE OF FORGIVENESS[1]

Brothers and sisters, Celestine,
Carthusian, or Carmelite,
Street-loafers, fops whose buckles shine,
Lackeys, and courtesans whose tight
Apparel gratifies the sight,
And little ladies'-men who trot
In tawny boots of dreadful height:
I beg forgiveness of the lot.

Young whores who flash their teats in sign
Of what they hawk for men's delight,
Ape-handlers, thieves and, soused with wine,
Wild bullies looking for a fight,
And Jacks and Jills whose hearts are light,
Whistling and joking, talking rot,
Street-urchins dodging left and right:
I beg forgiveness of the lot.

Excepting for those bloody swine
Who gave me, many a morn and night,
The hardest crusts on which to dine;
Henceforth I'll fear them not a mite.
I'd belch and fart in their despite,
Were I not sitting on my cot.

Well, to be peaceful and polite,
I beg forgiveness of the lot.

May hammers, huge and heavy, smite
Their ribs, and likewise cannon-shot.
May cudgels pulverize them quite.
I beg forgiveness of the lot.

VITTORIA DA COLONNA

I LIVE ON THIS DEPRAVED AND LONELY CLIFF

Vittoria da Colonna (1490–1547), one of the most celebrated women of the Italian Renaissance, was a member of the nobility and a friend to prominent artists and writers. She is generally recognized as the inspiration for a number of Michelangelo's poems. In all her own poems, exclusively written in sonnet form, Vittoria da Colonna describes her relationship with and love for her husband. The following poem contains Neoplatonic light imagery, popular in Renaissance lyric poetry.

I live on this depraved and lonely cliff
like a sad bird abhorring a green tree
or plashing water; I move forcefully
away from those I love, and I am stiff
even before myself, so that my thoughts   5
may rise and fly to him: sun I adore
and worship. Though their wings could hurry more,
they race only to him; the forest rots
until the instant when they reach that place.
Then deep in ecstasy, though brief, they feel   10
a joy beyond all earthly joy. I reel,
and yet if they could recreate his face
as my mind, craving and consuming, would,
then here perhaps I'd own the perfect good.

BALDASSARE CASTIGLIONE

from the *Book of the Courtier*

The Book of the Courtier *was not published until 1528, but it is one of the most representative books of the Italian High Renaissance. It is also one of the most highly regarded. The English scholar Roger Ascham (1515–68) claimed that, when diligently read, Castiglione's book was more instructive than a three-year sojourn in Italy. Among other things, it offered practical advice to the Renaissance gentleman on how to get ahead. However, it was in some respects a bit naive, as Machiavelli's* The Prince *would show.*

"Then, as for the physical appearance of the courtier, I would say that all that is necessary is that he should be neither too small nor too big, since either of these two conditions causes a certain contemptuous wonder and men built in this way are stared at as if they were monsters. However, if one is forced to choose between the two evils, then it is better to be on the small side than unduly large; for men who are so huge are often found to be rather thick-headed, and moreover, they are also unsuited for sport and recreation, which I think most important for the courtier. So I wish our courtier to be well built, with finely proportioned members, and I would have him demonstrate strength and lightness and suppleness and be good at all the physical exercises befitting a warrior. Here, I believe, his first duty is to know how to handle expertly every

---

[1]Translated by Dante Gabriel Rossetti.
[1]Translated by Richard Wilbur.

kind of weapon, either on foot or mounted, to understand all their finer points, and to be especially well informed about all those weapons commonly used among gentlemen. For apart from their use in war, when perhaps the finer points may be neglected, often differences arise between one gentleman and another and lead to duels, and very often the weapons used are those that come immediately to hand. So, for safety's sake, it is important to know about them. And I am not one of those who assert that all skill is forgotten in a fight; because anyone who loses his skill at such a time shows that he has allowed his fear to rob him of his courage and his wits.

"I also believe that it is of the highest importance to know how to wrestle, since this often accompanies combat on foot. Next, both for his own sake and for his friends, the courtier should understand about seeking restitution and the conduct of disputes, and he should be skilled in seizing the advantage, and in all this he must show both courage and prudence. Nor should he be too anxious for these engagements, save when his honour demands it; for, as well as the considerable danger that an uncertain outcome brings with it, whoever rushes into these things precipitately and without urgent cause deserves to be gravely censured, even if he is successful. However, when a man has committed himself so far that he cannot withdraw without reproach then both in the preliminaries and in the duel itself he should be very deliberate. He should always show readiness and courage; and he should not behave like those who are always quibbling and arguing over points of honour, and when they have the choice of weapons, select those which can neither cut nor prick, arm themselves as if they had to face a cannonade, and, thinking it enough if they are not defeated, retreat all the time and keep on the defensive, giving proof of utter cowardice, and in this way making themselves the sport of children, like those two men from Ancona who fought at Perugia a little while ago, and made everyone who saw them burst out laughing."

"And who were they?" asked Gaspare Pallavicino.

"Two cousins," answered Cesare.

"And in their fighting, more like two dear brothers," said the Count. Then he continued:

"Weapons are also often used in various sports during peace-time, and gentlemen often perform in public spectacles before the people and before ladies and great lords. So I wish our courtier to be an accomplished and versatile horseman and, as well as having a knowledge of horses and all the matters to do with riding, he should put every effort and diligence into surpassing the rest just a little in everything, so that he may always be recognized as superior. And as we read of Alcibiades, that he surpassed all those peoples among whom he lived, and each time in regard to what they claimed to be best at, so this courtier of ours should outstrip all others, and in regard to the things they know well. Thus it is the peculiar excellence of the Italians to ride well with the rein, to handle spirited horses very skilfully, and to tilt and joust; so in all this the courtier should compare with the best of them. In tourneys, in holding his ground, in forcing his way forward, he should compare with the best of the French; in volleying, in running bulls, in casting spears and darts, he should be outstanding among the Spaniards. But, above all, he should accompany his every act with a certain grace and fine judgement if he wishes to earn that universal regard which everyone covets." . . .

"If I remember rightly, my dear Count, it seems to me that you have repeated several times this evening that the courtier has to imbue with grace his movements, his gestures, his way of doing things and in short, his every action. And it appears to me that you require this in everything as the seasoning without which all other attributes and good qualities would be almost worthless. Now I admit that everyone should easily be persuaded of this, seeing that, by the very meaning of the word, it can be said that a man who behaves with grace finds it with others. You have said that this is very often a natural, God-given gift, and that even if it is not quite perfect it can be greatly enhanced by application and effort. It seems to me that those who are born as fortunate and as rich in such treasures as some we know have little need of any further instruction, since the gracious favour they have received from heaven raises them, almost despite themselves, higher than they might have desired, and makes everyone both like and admire them. I do not argue about this, since it is not in our power to acquire it of ourselves. But regarding those who receive from Nature only so much as to make it possible for them to acquire grace through enterprise, application and effort, I should like to know by what art, teaching and method they can gain this grace, both in sport and recreation which you believe are so important, and in everything else they say or do. Now since by praising this quality so highly you have, I believe, aroused in all of us a strong desire to obtain it, because of the task given you by signora Emilia, you are also obliged to satisfy us by teaching the way to do so." . . .

"Therefore anyone who wants to be a good pupil must not only do things well but must also make a constant effort to imitate and, if possible, exactly reproduce his master. And when he feels he has made some progress it is very profitable for him to observe different kinds of courtiers and, ruled by the good judgement that must always be his guide, take various qualities now from one man and now from another. Just as in the summer fields the bees wing their way among the plants from one flower to the next, so the courtier must acquire this grace from those who appear to possess it and take from each one the quality that seems most commendable. And he should certainly not act like a friend of ours, whom you all know, who thought that he greatly resembled King Ferdinand the Younger of Aragon, but had not tried to imitate him except in the way he raised his head and twisted a corner of his mouth, a habit which the King had acquired through illness. There are many like this, who think they are marvellous if they can simply resemble a great man in some one thing; and often they seize on the only defect he has. However, having already thought a great deal about how this grace is acquired, and leaving aside those who are endowed with it by their stars, I have discovered a universal rule which seems to apply more than any other in all human actions or words: namely, to steer away from affectation at all costs, as if it were a rough and dangerous reef, and (to use perhaps a novel word for it) to practise in all things a certain nonchalance which conceals all artistry and makes whatever one says or does seem uncontrived and effortless. I am sure that grace springs especially from this, since everyone knows how difficult it is to accomplish some unusual feat perfectly, and so facility in such things excites the greatest wonder; whereas, in contrast, to labour at what one is doing and, as we say, to make bones over it, shows an extreme lack of grace and causes everything, whatever its worth, to be discounted. So we can truthfully say that true art is what does not seem to be art; and the most important thing is to conceal it, because if it is revealed this discredits a man completely and ruins his reputation. I remember once having read of certain outstanding orators of the ancient world who, among the other things they did, tried hard to make everyone believe that they were ignorant of letters; and, dissembling their knowledge, they made their speeches appear to have been composed very simply and according to the promptings of Nature and truth rather than effort and artifice. For if the people had known of their skills, they would have been frightened of being deceived. So you see that to reveal intense application and skill robs everything of grace. Who is there among you who doesn't laugh when our Pierpaolo dances in that way of his, with those little jumps and with his legs stretched on tiptoe, keeping his head motionless as if he were made of wood, and all so laboured that he seems to be counting every step? Who is so blind that he doesn't see in this the clumsiness of affectation? And in contrast we see in many of the men and women who are with us now, that graceful and nonchalant spontaneity (as it is often called) because of which they seem to be paying little, if any, attention to the way they speak or laugh or hold themselves, so that those who are watching them imagine that they couldn't and wouldn't ever know how to make a mistake."

Then, without waiting, Bernardo Bibbiena said:

"Well, it seems that our Roberto has now found someone who will praise his style of dancing, which you all despise. For if the excellence we are discussing consists in being nonchalant, and displaying indifference, and thinking of anything except what one is actually doing, then when it comes to dancing Roberto is without equal, because to demonstrate that he isn't thinking what he is doing he lets his clothes fall from his back and his slippers from his feet, and he dances away without bothering to pick them up."

The Count went on: "Since you wish me to continue with the discussion, I shall now say something about our faults. Do you not realize that what you are calling nonchalance in Roberto is in fact affectation, since he evidently goes to great pains to show that he is not thinking about what he is doing? He is really taking too much thought, and by passing the bounds of moderation his nonchalance is affected and inappropriate, and it has exactly the opposite effect of what is intended, namely the concealment of art. So although nonchalance is praiseworthy as such, when it leads to someone letting the clothes fall off his back it degenerates as easily into affectation as does a meticulous regard for one's personal appearance (also praiseworthy as such), when it means holding one's head rigid for fear of spoiling one's coiffure, or carrying a mirror in the fold of one's cap and a comb in one's sleeve, and walking through the streets always followed by a page with a brush and sponge. For this kind of self-regard and nonchalance goes too much to extremes, which is always a fault and the opposite of the pure and agreeable simplicity which appeals to everyone. Notice how ungraceful a rider is when he forces himself to sit bolt upright in the saddle, as is said, in the Venetian way, in comparison with another who sits on his horse as free and relaxed as if he were on the ground. How much more agreeable and admired is a warrior when he is modest, saying little and boasting hardly ever, than one who is forever singing his own praises

and threatening all and sundry with his swearing and bragging! And this is simply the affectation of wanting to appear a bold fellow. The same applies whatever one's profession; indeed, it holds good for every single thing we do or say."

At this, the Magnifico Giuliano remarked: "It certainly holds true in music, in which it is very wrong to have two perfect consonances one after the other; for our sense of hearing abhors this, whereas it often likes a second or a seventh, which in itself is a harsh and unbearable discord. This is because to continue in perfect consonances produces satiety and offers a harmony which is too affected; but this disappears when imperfect consonances are introduced to establish the contrast which keeps the listener in a state of expectancy, waiting for and enjoying the perfect consonances more eagerly and delighting in the discord of the second or seventh, as in a display of nonchalance."

"So you see," answered the Count, "that affectation is as dangerous in music as in other things. Moreover, it is said to have been proverbial among certain great painters of the ancient world that excessive diligence is harmful; and Protogenes is said to have been censured by Apelles for not knowing when to take his hands from the board."

Then Cesare added: "It seems to me that our Fra Serafino shares this same fault of not being able to take his hands from the board, at least not before all the food has been taken away as well."[1]

The Count laughed and continued: "What Apelles meant was that when painting Protogenes did not know when he had done enough; in other words, he was blaming him for finishing his work too thoroughly. So this quality which is the opposite of affectation and which we are now calling nonchalance, apart from being the real source of grace, brings with it another advantage; for whatever action it accompanies, no matter how trivial it is, it not only reveals the skill of the person doing it but also very often causes it to be considered far greater than it really is. This is because it makes the onlookers believe that a man who performs well with so much facility must possess even greater skill than he does, and that if he took great pains and effort he would perform even better. To give other examples, consider a man using weapons, and about to throw a dart or handle a sword or some other weapon. If, without thinking about it, he casually takes up a position at the ready, so naturally that it seems as if his whole body assumes the right posture without any strain, then even if he does nothing more he demonstrates that he is in complete command of what he is doing. Similarly in dancing, a single step, a single unforced and graceful movement of the body, at once demonstrates the skill of the dancer. When a musician is singing and utters a single word ending in a group of notes with a sweet cadence, and with such ease that it seems effortless, that touch alone proves that he is capable of far more than he is doing. Then again, in painting, a single line which is not laboured, a single brush stroke made with ease, in such a way that it seems that the hand is completing the line by itself without any effort or guidance, clearly reveals the excellence of the artist, about whose competence everyone will then make his own judgement. The same happens in al-

---

[1]The pun, untranslatable into English, relies on the use of the same word *tavola* for both table and board or panel.

most every other thing. Our courtier, therefore, will be judged to be perfect and will show grace in everything, and especially in his speech, if he shuns affectation. However, affectation is a vice of which only too many people are guilty, and sometimes our Lombards more than others, who, if they have been away from home for a year, on their return immediately start speaking Roman or Spanish or French, and God knows what. And all this springs from the over-anxiety to show how much they know; so that they put care and effort into acquiring a detestable vice. Certainly it would require a great deal of effort on my part if in these discussions of ours I wished to use those old Tuscan words which the Tuscans of today have discarded; and what's more I'm sure you would all laugh at me."

At this, Federico remarked: "It is true that in talking among ourselves as we are doing now it would perhaps be wrong to use those old Tuscan words; because, as you say, they would prove tedious both for the speaker and his listeners, and many of us would have difficulty in understanding them. But for myself I believe that it would be wrong not to make use of them in writing, because they impart considerable grace and authority to what is written, and they produce a style which is more dignified and sonorous than can be achieved with modern words."

To this, the Count replied: "I can hardly think how grace and authority may be conferred by words which should be eschewed not only (as you yourself admit) in the kind of conversation we are enjoying at the moment but also in any conceivable circumstance. For if any man of good judgement had to make a speech on a serious subject before the very senate of Florence, which is the capital of Tuscany, or had to discuss important business in private with a highranking Florentine, or even amusing things with a close friend, or romantic affairs with ladies or gentlemen, or had to join in the jesting and joking at feasts, games or anywhere else, whatever the time, place or subject, I am certain that he would go out of his way to avoid using those old Tuscan words. And if he did use them, as well as making a fool of himself he would give no little annoyance to anyone listening. So it seems to me very curious to accept as good in writing those very words which are shunned as wrong in all kinds of conversation, and to insist that what is never appropriate in speech should be highly appropriate when it comes to writing. For it is my belief that writing is nothing other than a kind of speech which remains in being after it has been uttered, the representation, as it were, or rather the very life of our words. And so in speech, which ceases to exist as soon as it is uttered, some things are perhaps tolerable which are not so in writing; because writing preserves the words and submits them to the judgement of the reader, who has the time to give them his considered attention. Therefore it is right that greater pains should be taken to make what is written more polished and correct; not, however, that the written words should be different from those which are spoken, but they should be chosen from the most beautiful of those employed in speech. If we were to allow in writing what is not allowed in speech, in my opinion there would be one very unfortunate result: namely, more liberties could be taken in an area demanding the strictest discipline, and all the endeavour that goes into writing would be harmful instead of beneficial. So surely the rule is that what is proper in writing is also proper in speaking; and the finest speech resembles the finest writing. Moreover, I believe that it is more important to make one's meaning clear in writing than in speaking; because unlike someone listening, the reader is not always present when the author is writing. However, I would praise any man who, as well as shunning the use of many old Tuscan words, also makes certain, whether he is writing or speaking, that he employs words in current usage in Tuscany or elsewhere in Italy which possess a certain grace when they are pronounced. It seems to me that anyone who follows some other practice runs the risk of that affectation which attracts so much censure and about which we were talking a moment ago."

Then Federico said: "I cannot deny, Count, that writing is a kind of speech. I would say, however, that if the spoken word is at all obscure what is said will fail to penetrate the mind of the listener and, since it will not be understood, will be useless. And this is not the case with writing, for if the words used by the writer carry with them a certain, I will not say difficulty but veiled subtlety, and so are not as familiar as those commonly used in speech, they give what is written greater authority and cause the reader to be more attentive and aware, and so reflect more deeply and enjoy the skill and message of the author; and by judiciously exerting himself a little he experiences the pleasure that is to be had from accomplishing difficult tasks. If the reader is so ignorant that he cannot overcome these difficulties, that is not the fault of the writer and his language should not, on this account, be judged to lack beauty. Therefore in writing I believe that it is right to use Tuscan words, and only those employed by the ancient Tuscans, because that is a convincing proof, tested by time, that they are sound and effective in conveying what they mean. Furthermore, they possess the grace and dignity which great age imparts not only to words but also to buildings, statues, pictures and to everything that is able to endure. And often simply by such splendour and dignity they beautify one's diction, through whose force and eloquence everything, no matter how mean, can be so embellished that it deserves the highest praise. But this matter of contemporary usage, on which you put so much stress, seems to me highly dangerous and very often wrong. If some solecism or other is adopted by many ignorant people, this, in my opinion, hardly means that it should be accepted as a rule and followed by others. What is more, current practice varies a great deal, and there's not a city in Italy where the mode of speech is not different from everywhere else. However, since you have not felt obliged to declare which of them is the best, a man might just as well take up Bergamasque as Florentine and, according to you, this would be perfectly correct. It seems to me, therefore, that if one wants to avoid all misgivings and be absolutely certain, one has to decide to imitate someone who by common consent is accepted as sound, and to employ him continuously as a guide and protection against hostile critics. And this model (I mean in the vernacular) should be none other, I think, than Petrarch or Boccaccio; and whoever strays from these two has to grope his way, like a man walking through the darkness without a light, and will frequently take the wrong path. But nowadays we are so headstrong that we are contemptuous of doing what the best men did in the ancient world, namely, of practising imitation. But unless we do I believe it is impossible to write well. It seems to me that there is convincing proof of this in Virgil who, although his inspired judgement and genius were such that he made it impossible for anyone afterwards to hope to imitate him successfully, yet himself wished to imitate Homer."

NICCOLO MACHIAVELLI

from *The Prince*

Fundamentally, Machiavelli's The Prince *is a book about power, especially how power is seized and administered. The political arena is a jungle in which the strongest prevail, a relentlessly competitive world in which maintaining moral standards and ethical behavior is merely naive. For the prince who wants to retain his power, the end justifies the means. To gain and hold power, Machiavelli notes, the prince requires the cunning of the fox and the strength of the lion. The heart of Machiavelli's advice appears in the chapters extolling the "virtues" of a prince; an excerpt follows.*

XV. THE THINGS FOR WHICH MEN, AND ESPECIALLY PRINCES, ARE PRAISED OR BLAMED

It now remains for us to see how a prince must govern his conduct towards his subjects or his friends. I know that this has often been written about before, and so I hope it will not be thought presumptuous for me to do so, as, especially in discussing this subject, I draw up an original set of rules. But since my intention is to say something that will prove of practical use to the inquirer, I have thought it proper to represent things as they are in real truth, rather than as they are imagined. Many have dreamed up republics and principalities which have never in truth been known to exist; the gulf between how one should live and how one does live is so wide that a man who neglects what is actually done for what should be done learns the way to self-destruction rather than self-preservation. The fact is that a man who wants to act virtuously in every way necessarily comes to grief among so many who are not virtuous. Therefore if a prince wants to maintain his rule he must learn how not to be virtuous, and to make use of this or not according to need.

So leaving aside imaginary things, and referring only to those which truly exist, I say that whenever men are discussed (and especially princes, who are more exposed to view), they are noted for various qualities which earn them either praise or condemnation. Some, for example, are held to be generous, and others miserly (I use the Tuscan word rather than the word avaricious: we call a man who is mean with what he possesses, miserly, and a man who wants to plunder others, avaricious).[1] Some are held to be benefactors, others are called grasping; some cruel, some compassionate; one man faithless, another faithful; one man effeminate and cowardly, another fierce and courageous; one man courteous, another proud; one man lascivious, another pure; one guileless, another crafty; one stubborn, another flexible; one grave, another frivolous; one religious, another sceptical; and so forth. I know everyone will agree that it would be most laudable if a prince possessed all the qualities deemed to be good among those I have enumerated. But, because of conditions in the world, princes cannot have those qualities, or observe them completely. So a prince has of necessity to be so prudent that

[1]The two words Machiavelli uses are *misero* and *avaro*.

he knows how to escape the evil reputation attached to those vices which could lose him his state, and how to avoid those vices which are not so dangerous, if he possibly can; but, if he cannot, he need not worry so much about the latter. And then, he must not flinch from being blamed for vices which are necessary for safeguarding the state. This is because, taking everything into account, he will find that some of the things that appear to be virtues will, if he practises them, ruin him, and some of the things that appear to be vices will bring him security and prosperity.

XVI. GENEROSITY AND PARSIMONY

So, starting with the first of the qualities I enumerated above, I say it would be splendid if one had a reputation for generosity; nonetheless if you do in fact earn a reputation for generosity you will come to grief. This is because if your generosity is good and sincere it may pass unnoticed and it will not save you from being reproached for its opposite. If you want to acquire a reputation for generosity, therefore, you have to be ostentatiously lavish; and a prince acting in that fashion will soon squander all his resources, only to be forced in the end, if he wants to maintain his reputation, to lay excessive burdens on the people, to impose extortionate taxes, and to do everything else he can to raise money. This will start to make his subjects hate him, and, since he will have impoverished himself, he will be generally despised. As a result, because of this generosity of his, having injured many and rewarded few, he will be vulnerable to the first minor setback, and the first real danger he encounters will bring him to grief. When he realizes this and tries to retrace his path he will immediately be reputed a miser.

So as a prince cannot practise the virtue of generosity in such a way that he is noted for it, except to his cost, he should if he is prudent not mind being called a miser. In time he will be recognized as being essentially a generous man, seeing that because of his parsimony his existing revenues are enough for him, he can defend himself against an aggressor, and he can embark on enterprises without burdening the people. So he proves himself generous to all those from whom he takes nothing, and they are innumerable, and miserly towards all those to whom he gives nothing, and they are few. In our own times great things have been accomplished only by those who have been held miserly, and the others have met disaster. Pope Julius II made use of a reputation for generosity to win the papacy but subsequently he made no effort to maintain this reputation, because he wanted to be able to finance his wars. The present king of France has been able to wage so many wars without taxing his subjects excessively only because his long-standing parsimony enabled him to meet the additional expenses involved. Were the present king of Spain renowned for his generosity he would not have started and successfully concluded so many enterprises.

So a prince must think little of it, if he incurs the name of miser, so as not to rob his subjects, to be able to defend himself, not to become poor and despicable, not to be forced to grow rapacious. Miserliness is one of those vices which sustain his rule. Someone may object: Caesar came to power by virtue of his generosity, and many others, because they practised and were known for their generosity, have risen to the very highest positions. My answer to this is as follows. Either you are already a prince, or you are on the way to becoming one. In the first case, your generosity will be to your cost; in the second, it is certainly necessary to have a reputation for generosity. Caesar was one of those who wanted to establish his own rule over Rome; but if, after he had established it, he had remained alive and not moderated his expenditure he would have fallen from power.

Again, someone may retort: there have been many princes who have won great successes with their armies, and who have had the reputation of being extremely generous. My reply to this is: the prince gives away what is his own or his subjects', or else what belongs to others. In the first case he should be frugal; in the second, he should indulge his generosity to the full. The prince who campaigns with his armies, who lives by pillaging, sacking, and extortion, disposes of what belongs to aliens; and he must be openhanded, otherwise the soldiers would refuse to follow him. And you can be more liberal with what does not belong to you or your subjects, as Caesar, Cyrus, and Alexander were. Giving away what belongs to strangers in no way affects your standing at home; rather it increases it. You hurt yourself only when you give away what is your own. There is nothing so self-defeating as generosity: in the act of practising it, you lose the ability to do so, and you become either poor and despised or, seeking to escape poverty, rapacious and hated. A prince must try to avoid, above all else, being despised and hated; and generosity results in your being both. Therefore it is wiser to incur the reputation of being a miser, which invites ignominy but not hatred, than to be forced by seeking a name for generosity to incur a reputation for rapacity, which brings you hatred as well as ignominy.

XVII. CRUELTY AND COMPASSION; AND WHETHER IT IS BETTER TO BE LOVED THAN FEARED, OR THE REVERSE

Taking others of the qualities I enumerated above, I say that a prince must want to have a reputation for compassion rather than for cruelty: nonetheless, he must be careful that he does not make bad use of compassion. Cesare Borgia was accounted cruel; nevertheless, this cruelty of his reformed the Romagna, brought it unity, and restored order and obedience. On reflection, it will be seen that there was more compassion in Cesare than in the Florentine people, who, to escape being called cruel, allowed Pistoia to be devastated.[2] So a prince must not worry if he incurs reproach for his cruelty so long as he keeps his subjects united and loyal. By making an example or two he will prove more compassionate than those who, being too compassionate, allow disorders which lead to murder and rapine. These nearly always harm the whole community, whereas executions ordered by a prince only affect individuals. A new prince, of all rulers, finds it impossible to avoid a reputation for cruelty, because of the abundant dangers inherent in a newly won state. Vergil, through the mouth of Dido, says:

Res dura, et regni novitas me talia cogunt
Moliri, et late fines custode tueri.[3]

Nonetheless, a prince must be slow to take action, and must watch that he does not come to be afraid of his own shadow; his behaviour must be tempered by humanity and prudence so that over-confidence does not make him rash or excessive distrust make him unbearable.

From this arises the following question: whether it is better to be loved than feared, or the reverse. The answer is that one would like to be both the one and the other; but because it is difficult to combine them, it is far better to be feared than loved if you cannot be both. One can make this generalization about men: they are ungrateful, fickle, liars, and deceivers, they shun danger and are greedy for profit; while you treat them well, they are yours. They would shed their blood for you, risk their property, their lives, their children, so long, as I said above, as danger is remote; but when you are in danger they turn against you. Any prince who has come to depend entirely on promises and has taken no other precautions ensures his own ruin; friendship which is bought with money and not with greatness and nobility of mind is paid for, but it does not last and it yields nothing. Men worry less about doing an injury to one who makes himself loved than to one who makes himself feared. The bond of love is one which men, wretched creatures that they are, break when it is to their advantage to do so; but fear is strengthened by a dread of punishment which is always effective.

The prince must nonetheless make himself feared in such a way that, if he is not loved, at least he escapes being hated. For fear is quite compatible with an absence of hatred; and the prince can always avoid hatred if he abstains from the property of his subjects and citizens and from their women. If, even so, it proves necessary to execute someone, this is to be done only when there is proper justification and manifest reason for it. But above all a prince must abstain from the property of others; because men sooner forget the death of their father than the loss of their patrimony. It is always possible to find pretexts for confiscating someone's property; and a prince who starts to live by rapine always finds pretexts for seizing what belongs to others. On the other hand, pretexts for executing someone are harder to find and they are less easily sustained.

However, when a prince is campaigning with his soldiers and is in command of a large army then he need not worry about having a reputation for cruelty; because, without such a reputation, no army was ever kept united and disciplined. Among the admirable achievements of Hannibal is included this: that although he led a huge army, made up of countless different races, on foreign campaigns, there was never any dissension, either among the troops themselves or against their leader, whether things were going well or badly. For this, his inhuman cruelty was wholly responsible. It was this, along with his countless other qualities, which made him feared and respected by his soldiers. If it had not been for his

---

[2]Pistoia was a subject-city of Florence, which forcibly restored order there when conflict broke out between two rival factions in 1501–02. Machiavelli was concerned with this business at first hand.

[3]"Harsh necessity, and the newness of my kingdom, force me to do such things and to guard my frontiers everywhere." *Aeneid* i, 563

cruelty, his other qualities would not have been enough. The historians, having given little thought to this, on the one hand admire what Hannibal achieved, and on the other condemn what made his achievements possible.

That his other qualities would not have been enough by themselves can be proved by looking at Scipio, a man unique in his own time and through all recorded history. His armies mutinied against him in Spain, and the only reason for this was his excessive leniency, which allowed his soldiers more licence than was good for military discipline. Fabius Maximus reproached him for this in the Senate and called him a corrupter of the Roman legions. Again, when the Locri were plundered by one of Scipio's officers, he neither gave them satisfaction nor punished his officer's insubordination; and this was all because of his having too lenient a nature. By way of excuse for him some senators argued that many men were better at not making mistakes themselves than at correcting them in others. But in time Scipio's lenient nature would have spoilt his fame and glory had he continued to indulge it during his command; when he lived under orders from the Senate, however, this fatal characteristic of his was not only concealed but even brought him glory.

So, on this question of being loved or feared, I conclude that since some men love as they please but fear when the prince pleases, a wise prince should rely on what he controls, not on what he cannot control. He must only endeavour, as I said, to escape being hated.

XVIII. HOW PRINCES SHOULD HONOUR THEIR WORD

Everyone realizes how praiseworthy it is for a prince to honour his word and to be straightforward rather than crafty in his dealings; nonetheless contemporary experience shows that princes who have achieved great things have been those who have given their word lightly, who have known how to trick men with their cunning, and who, in the end, have overcome those abiding by honest principles.

You must understand, therefore, that there are two ways of fighting: by law or by force. The first way is natural to men, and the second to beasts. But as the first way often proves inadequate one must needs have recourse to the second. So a prince must understand how to make a nice use of the beast and the man. The ancient writers taught princes about this by an allegory, when they described how Achilles and many other princes of the ancient world were sent to be brought up by Chiron, the centaur, so that he might train them his way. All the allegory means, in making the teacher half beast and half man, is that a prince must know how to act according to the nature of both, and that he cannot survive otherwise.

So, as a prince is forced to know how to act like a beast, he must learn from the fox and the lion; because the lion is defenceless against traps and a fox is defenceless against wolves. Therefore one must be a fox in order to recognize traps, and a lion to frighten off wolves. Those who simply act like lions are stupid. So it follows that a prudent ruler cannot, and must not honour his word when it places him at a disadvantage and when the reasons for which he made his promise no longer exist. If all men were good, this precept would not be good; but because men are wretched creatures who would not keep their word to you, you need not keep your word to them. And no prince ever lacked good excuses to colour his bad faith. One could give innumerable modern instances of this, showing how many pacts and promises have been made null and void by the bad faith of princes: those who have known best how to imitate the fox have come off best. But one must know how to colour one's actions and to be a great liar and deceiver. Men are so simple, and so much creatures of circumstance, that the deceiver will always find someone ready to be deceived.

There is one fresh example I do not want to omit. Alexander VI never did anything, or thought of anything, other than deceiving men; and he always found victims for his deceptions. There never was a man capable of such convincing asseverations, or so ready to swear to the truth of something, who would honour his word less. Nonetheless his deceptions always had the result he intended, because he was a past master in the art.

A prince, therefore, need not necessarily have all the good qualities I mentioned above, but he should certainly appear to have them. I would even go so far as to say that if he has these qualities and always behaves accordingly he will find them harmful; if he only appears to have them they will render him service. He should appear to be compassionate, faithful to his word, kind, guileless, and devout. And indeed he should be so. But his disposition should be such that, if he needs to be the opposite, he knows how. You must realize this: that a prince, and especially a new prince, cannot observe all those things which give men a reputation for virtue, because in order to maintain his state he is often forced to act in defiance of good faith, of charity, of kindness, of religion. And so he should have a flexible disposition, varying as fortune and circumstances dictate. As I said above, he should not deviate from what is good, if that is possible, but he should know how to do evil, if that is necessary.

A prince, then, must be very careful not to say a word which does not seem inspired by the five qualities I mentioned earlier. To those seeing and hearing him, he should appear a man of compassion, a man of good faith, a man of integrity, a kind and a religious man. And there is nothing so important as to seem to have this last quality. Men in general judge by their eyes rather than by their hands; because everyone is in a position to watch, few are in a position to come in close touch with you. Everyone sees what you appear to be, few experience what you really are. And those few dare not gainsay the many who are backed by the majesty of the state. In the actions of all men, and especially of princes, where there is no court of appeal, one judges by the result. So let a prince set about the task of conquering and maintaining his state: his methods will always be judged honourable and will be universally praised. The common people are always impressed by appearances and results. In this context, there are only common people, and there is no room for the few when the many are supported by the state. A certain contemporary ruler, whom it is better not to name, never preaches anything except peace and good faith;[4] and he is an enemy of both one and the

---

[4]Ferdinand of Aragon.

other, and if he had ever honoured either of them he would have lost either his standing or his state many times over.

BENVENUTO CELLINI

from *The Autobiography*

Cellini displays self-pride and self-confidence in the following lively description of his problems in casting his sculpture, Perseus, *boasting how he overcame enormous obstacles and performed near-superhuman feats, all in heightened drama. Cellini casts himself as the hero, of course, and the plot begins with an exposition on the difficult technical requirements, proceeding to a dramatic climax when Cellini frantically tries to undo the near-disastrous work his assistant has done. It concludes in a quiet denouement, as everyone celebrates the completion; even here, Cellini continues his unabashed self-promotion.*

Having succeeded so well with the cast of the Medusa, I had great hope of bringing my Perseus through; for I had laid the wax on, and felt confident that it would come out in bronze as perfectly as the Medusa. The waxen model produced so fine an effect, that when the Duke saw it and was struck with its beauty—whether somebody had persuaded him it could not be carried out with the same finish in metal, or whether he thought so for himself—he came to visit me more frequently than usual, and on one occasion said: "Benvenuto, this figure cannot succeed in bronze: the laws of art do not admit of it." These words of his Excellency stung me so sharply that I answered: "My lord, I know how very little confidence you have in me; and I believe the reason of this is that your most illustrious Excellency lends too ready an ear to my calumniators, or else indeed that you do not understand my art." He hardly let me close the sentence when he broke in: "I profess myself a connoisseur, and understand it very well indeed." I replied: "Yes, like a prince, not like an artist; for if your Excellency understood my trade as well as you imagine, you would trust me on the proofs I have already given. These are, first, the colossal bronze bust of your Excellency, which is now in Elba; secondly, the restoration of the Ganymede in marble, which offered so many difficulties and cost me so much trouble, that I would rather have made the whole statue new from the beginning; thirdly, the Medusa, cast by me in bronze, here now before your Excellency's eyes, the execution of which was a greater triumph of strength and skill than any of my predecessors in this fiendish art have yet achieved. Look you, my lord! I constructed that furnace anew on principles quite different from those of other founders; in addition to many technical improvements and ingenious devices, I supplied it with two issues for the metal, because this difficult and twisted figure could not otherwise have come out perfect. It is only owing to my intelligent insight into means and appliances that the statue turned out as it did; a triumph judged impossible by all the practitioners of this art."

With all the forces of my body and my purse, employing what little money still remained to me, I set to work. First I provided myself with several loads of pinewood from the forests of Serristori, in the neighbourhood of Montelupo. While these were on their way, I clothed my Perseus with the clay which I had prepared many months beforehand, in order

that it might be duly seasoned. After making its clay tunic (for that is the term used in this art) and properly arming it and fencing it with iron girders, I began to draw the wax out by means of a slow fire. This melted and issued through numerous air-vents I had made; for the more there are of these, the better will the mould fill. When I had finished drawing off the wax, I constructed a funnel-shaped furnace all round the model of my Perseus. It was built of bricks, so interlaced, the one above the other, that numerous apertures were left for the fire to exhale at. Then I began to lay on wood by degrees, and kept it burning two whole days and nights. At length, when all the wax was gone, and the mould was well baked, I set to work at digging the pit in which to sink it. This I performed with scrupulous regard to all the rules of art. When I had finished that part of my work, I raised the mould by windlasses and stout ropes to a perpendicular position, and suspending it with the greatest care one cubit above the level of the furnace, so that it hung exactly above the middle of the pit, I next lowered it gently down into the very bottom of the furnace, and had it firmly placed with every possible precaution for its safety. When this delicate operation was accomplished, I began to bank it up with the earth I had excavated; and, ever as the earth grew higher, I introduced its proper air-vents, which were little tubes of earthenware, such as folk use for drains and such-like purposes. At length, I felt sure that it was admirably fixed, and that the filling-in of the pit and the placing of the air-vents had been properly performed. I also could see that my workpeople understood my method, which differed very considerably from that of all the other masters in the trade. Feeling confident, then, that I could rely upon them, I next turned to my furnace, which I had filled with numerous pigs of copper and other bronze stuff. The pieces were piled according to the laws of art, that is to say, so resting one upon the other that the flames could play freely through them, in order that the metal might heat and liquefy the sooner. At last I called out heartily to set the furnace going. The logs of pine were heaped in, and, what with the unctuous resin of the wood and the good draught I had given, my furnace worked so well that I was obliged to rush from side to side to keep it going. The labour was more than I could stand; yet I forced myself to strain every nerve and muscle. To increase my anxieties, the workshop took fire, and we were afraid lest the roof should fall upon our heads; while, from the garden, such a storm of wind and rain kept blowing in, that it perceptibly cooled the furnace.

Battling thus with all these untoward circumstances for several hours, and exerting myself beyond even the measure of my powerful constitution, I could at last bear up no longer, and a sudden fever, of the utmost possible intensity, attacked me. I felt absolutely obliged to go and fling myself upon my bed. Sorely against my will having to drag myself away from the spot, I turned to my assistants, about ten or more in all, what with master-founders, hand-workers, country-fellows, and my own special journeymen, among whom was Bernardino Mannellini of Mugello, my apprentice through several years. To him in particular I spoke: "Look, my dear Bernardino, that you observe the rules which I have taught you; do your best with all despatch, for the metal will soon be fused. You cannot go wrong; these honest men will get the channels ready; you will easily be able to drive back the two plugs with this pair of iron crooks; and I am sure that my mould will fill miraculously. I feel more ill than I ever did in all my life, and verily believe that it will kill me before a few hours are over." Thus, with despair at heart, I left them, and betook myself to bed.

No sooner had I got to bed, than I ordered my serving-maids to carry food and wine for all the men into the work-shop; at the same time I cried: "I shall not be alive to-morrow." They tried to encourage me, arguing that my illness would pass over, since it came from excessive fatigue. In this way I spent two hours battling with the fever, which steadily increased, and calling out continually: "I feel that I am dying." My housekeeper, who was named Mona Fiore da Castel del Rio, a very notable manager and no less warmhearted, kept childing me for my discouragement; but, on the other hand, she paid me every kind attention which was possible. However, the sight of my physical pain and moral dejection so affected her, that, in spite of that brave heart of hers, she could not refrain from shedding tears; and yet, so far as she was able, she took good care I should not see them. While I was thus terribly afflicted, I beheld the figure of a man enter my chamber, twisted in his body into the form of a capital S. He raised a lamentable, doleful voice, like one who announces their last hour to men condemned to die upon the scaffold, and spoke these words: "O Benvenuto! your statue is spoiled, and there is no hope whatever of saving it." No sooner had I heard the shriek of that wretch than I gave a howl which might have been heard from the sphere of flame. Jumping from my bed, I seized my clothes and began to dress. The maids, and my lad, and every one who came around to help me, got kicks or blows of the fist, while I kept crying out in lamentation: "Ah! traitors! enviers! This is an act of treason, done by malice prepense! But I swear by God that I will sift it to the bottom, and before I die will leave such witness to the world of what I can do as shall make a score of mortals marvel."

When I had got my clothes on, I strode with soul bent on mischief toward the workshop; there I beheld the men, whom I had left erewhile in such high spirits, standing stupefied and downcast. I began at once and spoke: "Up with you! Attend to me! Since you have not been able or willing to obey the directions I gave you, obey me now that I am with you to conduct my work in person. Let no one contradict me, for in cases like this we need the aid of hand and hearing, not of advice." When I had uttered these words, a certain Maestro Alessandro Lastricati broke silence and said: "Look you, Benvenuto, you are going to attempt an enterprise which the laws of art do not sanction, and which cannot succeed." I turned upon him with such fury and so full of mischief, that he and all the rest of them exclaimed with one voice: "On then! Give orders! We will obey your least commands, so long as life is left in us." I believe they spoke thus feelingly because they thought I must fall shortly dead upon the ground. I went immediately to inspect the furnace, and found that the metal was all curdled; an accident which we express by "being caked." I told two of the hands to cross the road, and fetch from the house of the butcher Capretta a load of young oak-wood, which had lain dry for above a year; this wood had been previously offered me by Madame Ginevra, wife of the said Capretta. So soon as the first armfuls arrived, I began to fill the grate beneath the furnace. Now oak-wood of that kind

heats more powerfully than any other sort of tree; and for this reason, where a slow fire is wanted, as in the case of gun-foundry, alder or pine is preferred. Accordingly, when the logs took fire, oh! how the cake began to stir beneath that awful heat, to glow and sparkle in a blaze! At the same time I kept stirring up the channels, and sent men upon the roof to stop the conflagration, which had gathered force from the increased combustion in the furnace; also I caused boards, carpets, and other hangings to be set up against the garden, in order to protect us from the violence of the rain.

When I had thus provided against these several disasters, I roared out first to one man and then to another: "Bring this thing here! Take that thing there!" At this crisis, when the whole gang saw the cake was on the point of melting, they did my bidding, each fellow working with the strength of three. I then ordered half a pig of pewter to be brought, which weighed about sixty pounds, and flung it into the middle of the cake inside the furnace. By this means, and by piling on wood and stirring now with pokers and now with iron rods, the curdled mass rapidly began to liquefy. Then, knowing I had brought the dead to life again, against the firm opinion of those ignoramuses, I felt such vigour fill my veins, that all those pains of fever, all those fears of death, were quite forgotten.

All of a sudden an explosion took place attended by a tremendous flash of flame, as though a thunderbolt had formed and been discharged amongst us. Unwonted and appalling terror astonished every one, and me more even than the rest. When the din was over and the dazzling light extinguished, we began to look each other in the face. Then I discovered that the cap of the furnace had blown up, and the bronze was bubbling over from its source beneath. So I had the mouths of my mould immediately opened, and at the same time drove in the two plugs which kept back the molten metal. But I noticed that it did not flow as rapidly as usual, the reason being probably that the fierce heat of the fire we kindled had consumed its base alloy. Accordingly I sent for all my pewter platters, porringers, and dishes, to the number of some two hundred pieces, and had a portion of them cast, one by one, into the channels, the rest into the furnace. This expedient succeeded, and every one could now perceive that my bronze was in most perfect liquefaction and my mould was filling; whereupon they all with heartiness and happy cheer assisted and obeyed my bidding, while I now here, now there, gave orders, helped with my own hands, and cried aloud: "O God! Thou that by Thy immeasurable power didst rise from the dead, and in Thy glory didst ascend to heaven!" . . . even thus in a moment my mould was filled; and seeing my work finished, I fell upon my knees, and with all my heart gave thanks to God.

After all was over, I turned to a plate of salad on a bench there, and ate with hearty appetite, and drank together with the whole crew. Afterwards I retired to bed, healthy and happy, for it was now two hours before morning, and slept as sweetly as though I had never felt a touch of illness. My good house-keeper, without my giving any orders, had prepared a fat capon for my repast. So that, when I rose, about the hour for break-ing fast, she presented herself with a smiling countenance, and said: "Oh! is that the man who felt that he was dying? Upon my word, I think the blows and kicks you dealt us last night, when you were so enraged, and had that demon in your body as it seemed, must have frightened away your mortal fever! The fever feared that it might catch it too, as we did!" All my poor household relieved in like measure from anxiety and overwhelming labour, went at once to buy earthen vessels in order to replace the pewter I had cast away. Then we dined together joyfully; nay, I cannot remember a day in my whole life when I dined with greater gladness or a better appetite.

After I had let my statue cool for two whole days, I began to uncover it by slow degrees. The first thing I found was that the head of Medusa had come out most admirably, thanks to the air-vents; for, as I had told the Duke, it is the nature of fire to ascend. Upon advancing farther, I discovered that the other head, that, namely, of Perseus, had succeeded no less admirably; and this astonished me far more, because it is at a considerably lower level than that of the Medusa. Now the mouths of the mould were placed above the head of Perseus and behind his shoulders; and I found that all the bronze my furnace contained had been exhausted in the head of this figure. It was a miracle to observe that not one fragment remained in the orifice of the channel, and that nothing was wanting to the statue. In my great astonishment I seemed to see in this the hand of God arranging and controlling all.

I went on uncovering the statue with success, and ascertained that everything had come out in perfect order, until I reached the foot of the right leg on which the statue rests. There the heel itself was formed, and going farther, I found the foot apparently complete. This gave me great joy on the one side, but was half unwelcome to me on the other, merely because I had told the Duke that it could not come out. However, when I reached the end, it appeared that the toes and a little piece above them were unfinished, so that about half the foot was wanting. Although I knew that this would add a trifle to my labour, I was very well pleased because I could now prove to the Duke how well I understood my business. It is true that far more of the foot than I expected had been perfectly formed; the reason of this was that from causes I have recently described, the bronze was hotter than our rules of art prescribe; also that I had been obliged to supplement the alloy with my pewter cups and platters, which no one else, I think, had ever done before.

Having now ascertained how successfully my work had been accomplished, I lost no time in hurrying to Pisa, where I found the Duke. He gave me a most gracious reception, as did also the Duchess; and although the major-domo had informed them of the whole proceedings, their Excellencies deemed my performance far more stupendous and astonishing when they heard the tale from my own mouth. When I arrived at the foot of Perseus, and said it had not come out perfect just as I previously warned his Excellency, I saw an expression of wonder pass over his face, while he related to the Duchess how I had predicted this beforehand. Observing the princes to be so well disposed towards me, I begged leave from the Duke to go to Rome. He granted it in most obliging terms, and bade me return as soon as possible to complete his Perseus; giving me letters of recommendation meanwhile to his ambassador, Averardo Serristori.

Glossary

Note: Words in **boldface** indicate terms defined elsewhere in the glossary.

a cappella (ah kuh-PELL-uh) Italian for "chapel style." In music, a composition for voices only, not accompanied by any other instruments.

abstraction Art that does not portray the visual reality of a subject but reflects an artist's nonrepresentational conception of it.

academy Generally, a society of artists or scholars. The Academy was Plato's school for the study of philosophy.

acanthus Mediterranean plant whose leaves were copied as decoration on the **capitals** of **Corinthian** columns.

acropolis Literally meaning "high city," this was the fortified, elevated point in an ancient Greek city. The Acropolis is the specific site in Athens where the Parthenon was built.

aesthetic Related to the appreciation of beauty in the arts.

agora Meeting place in ancient Greece, especially a marketplace.

aisle Long side passageway of a church. Aisles run parallel to the central **nave.**

alap In music, an improvised prelude to an Indian **raga** composition.

allegory A symbolic narrative in which a deeper, often moral meaning exists beyond the literal level of a work.

altar Raised platform or table at which religious ceremonies take place. It is where the Eucharist is celebrated in Christian churches.

altarpiece Painted or carved panel behind or above the **altar** of a church.

alto In music, the range of the lowest female voice.

ambulatory Passageway or aisle around the interior of a church or cathedral.

amphitheater Oval or round theater with tiers of seats gradually rising from a central arena.

amphora (AM-fur-uh) Two-handled jar with a narrow neck, used by ancient Greeks and Romans to carry wine or oil.

anagnorisis In drama, the point at which a character experiences recognition or increased self-knowledge.

animal style An artistic design popular in ancient and medieval times, characterized by decorative patterns of intricate animal motifs.

anthropomorphism The act of attributing human characteristics to non-human entities, such as gods or animals.

antiphony Vocal or instrumental music in which two or more groups sing or play in alternation.

apse Semicircular space at the end of a church sanctuary, often highly decorated; usually the location of the **altar.**

aqueduct Literally "water tube." A structure using gravity to bring water from higher sources into cities and towns below.

arcade Series of connected **arches,** supported by columns or **piers.**

arch In architecture, the curved or pointed structure spanning the top of an open space, such as a doorway, and supporting the weight above it.

Archaic period Greek cultural and artistic style of about 600–480 B.C.E.

Archaic smile An enigmatic facial expression, almost a half-smile, typical of early ancient Greek sculpture.

architrave Lowest horizontal portion of the **entablature,** supported by column **capitals.**

archivolt Semicircular molding outlining an **arch.**

Arianism Theological doctrine denying the divinity of Jesus, proclaimed by Arius (256–336 C.E.), condemned as heresy by the Roman Catholic Church.

Ars Nova Latin for New Art. Musical style of the fourteenth century that used more secular themes and more complex rhythms and harmonies than the old music of previous centuries.

ashlar masonry Masonry of square-cut stones with right angle corners.

assonance Similarity of sound, especially the half rhyme of words with the same vowel sounds but different consonants, as in *heap* and *leak.*

atlas (plural, atlantes) Sculpted male figure that serves as an architectural support.

atmospheric (aerial) perspective See **perspective.**

atrium Room in the center of an ancient Roman house.

avatar In **Hinduism,** an **incarnation** of a deity in human or animal form.

ballad In poetry, a narrative poem, often of folk origin, written in four-line stanzas. In music, a song that tells a story, often about love and loss.

Bantu Member of any of a large number of linguistically related peoples of central and southern Africa. The word means "people" in the Bantu language.

baptistery Small building or room where baptisms are performed.

barrel vault (tunnel vault) See drawing in Starter Kit, page xxvi.

bas relief French for "low" relief. In sculpture, relief that projects only slightly from its background.

basilica Large rectangular building with a central **nave** and an **apse** at one or both ends, originally used in Rome for business and legal meetings, later adapted for early Christian churches.

bass In music, the range of the lowest male voice.

battered In architecture, sloping inward toward the top, as in a wall.

bay In architecture, a spatial unit that is repeated.

Benedictines Members of the religious order founded by St. Benedict in 529.

bhakti (BUCK-tee) In Hinduism, the expression of personal devotion to a particular deity, especially in the form of poetry.

black-figure style Greek vase painting style featuring black figures painted on a red clay background with details incised to reveal the red clay below.

blind arcade Decorative **arcade** in which the **arches** and **columns** are attached to the background wall.

Bodhi In Buddhism, perfect knowledge.

bodhisattva (boe-di-SUTT-vuh) In Buddhism, an enlightened being on the brink of buddhahood who forgoes **nirvana** to help others attain salvation.

Brahmanism In Hinduism, the religious practices of ancient India as embodied in the **Vedas.**

Buddhism Religious response to **Hinduism** in East Asia that adheres to the doctrines of the Buddha, including the Four Noble Truths and the Eightfold Path.

buttress In architecture, a projecting support or reinforcement.

Byzantine (BIZ-un-teen) Artistic style of Eastern Europe in the fourth through fifteenth centuries that featured rich colors, Christian imagery, domed churches, and mosaics.

cabochon (CAB-uh-shawn) Gem that is not cut in facets but is smoothed and rounded.

caliph One of a succession of leaders who assumed religious and secular control of Islam after Muhammad's death.

calligraphy Beautiful handwriting.

campanile Italian word for bell tower.

canon In religion, the books of the Bible officially sanctioned by a church as inspired by God.

canto Main division of a poem.

cantus firmus (CAN-tuss FURR-muss) Preexisting melody line around which a new polyphonic composition is constructed.

canzone; canzoni (can-TSOE-neh; can-TSOE-nee) A song, especially one performed by troubadours in the eleventh through thirteenth centuries and using a love poem as text.

capital Decorative top part of a column that supports the **entablature.**

capstone Topmost stone in a **corbeled** arch or **dome.**

cartoon Full-scale preparatory drawing made on heavy paper for a large work such as a **tapestry** or **mural.**

caryatid Sculpted female figure used in place of an architectural support.

catacomb Underground burial area of early Christians.

catharsis Purging of emotional tension, especially by art; originally described by Aristotle as the effect of tragic drama on the audience.

cella (SELL-uh) Inner room of a Greek or Roman temple, where the temple's cult statue was kept.

centering In architecture, a temporary wooden semicircular device used for support during construction of an **arch, vault,** or **dome.**

central plan Building having no longitudinal **axis,** such as one with a polygonal or circular floor plan.

cha-no-yu Japanese ritualistic tea ceremony.

chanson (shawn-SAWN) French for "song." A general term for a song with French lyrics, especially one performed by troubadours in the eleventh through sixteenth centuries.

chanson de geste (shawn-SAWN duh JZEST) French for "song of deeds." A medieval **epic** poem that celebrates the actions of historical figures or heroes.

chapel Small area for worship, usually found as part of a larger church or within a secular building.

chiaroscuro (key-are-oh-SKOO-roe) From the Italian *chiaro,* "clear" or "light," and *oscuro,* "obscure" or "dark." In painting, a method of modeling that combines subtle shifts of light and dark to give the impression of depth.

chiton Soft clinging outer garment worn by women in ancient Greece.

chivalry System of ethical conduct of the Middle Ages based on a blend of Christian and military morals.

choir In architecture, the part of a church where the singers perform, usually between the **transept** and the **apse.**

choka A long Japanese poem.

chorale Simple Protestant hymn sung in unison by a church congregation.

chorus In ancient Greek drama, the group of actors who spoke or chanted in unison, often while moving in a stylized dance; the chorus provided a commentary on the action. Later, the term was generalized to mean a company of singers.

Cistercians Members of the austere order of monks established at Cîteaux in 1098.

Classical Artistic style of ancient Greece or Rome that emphasized balance, restraint, and quest for perfection. In music, the eighteenth-century style characterized by accessibility, balance, and clarity.

classicism Any later artistic style reminiscent of the ancient Greek or Roman **Classical** style and its values of balance, restraint, and quest for perfection.

clerestory/clearstory Story of a building with windows.

cloister Room in a monastery, square or rectangular in plan, open to the sky and containing a **garth.**

coffers Square indentations of the underside of an **arch, vault,** or **dome.**

colonette Small column, usually attached to a **pier** in **Gothic** cathedrals.

colonnade Row of columns placed side by side, usually to support a roof or series of **arches.**

column A vertical architectural support, usually consisting of a base, **shaft,** and decorative **capital.**

comedy Amusing play or novel with a happy ending, usually including a marriage.

composite order Combination of the volute scroll of the **Ionic** order with the acanthus leaves of the **Corinthian** order.

concrete A hard building material made of cement, sand, and gravel; popularized by the ancient Romans.

Confucianism Chinese philosophical perspective based on the teachings of Confucius that emphasized morality, tradition, and ethical behavior.

contrapposto (CONE-truh-POSE-toe) In sculpture and painting, an asymmetrical positioning of the human body in which the weight rests on one leg, elevating the hip and opposite shoulder.

corbel In architecture, a bracket of metal, wood, or stone.

corbeled dome Dome constructed of courses of stone laid horizontally.

Corinthian Ancient Greek order of architecture characterized by a capital ornamented with acanthus leaves.

cornice In architecture, a horizontal molding that forms the uppermost, projecting part of an **entablature.**

cosmology Philosophical study of the evolution of the universe.

couplet Unit of poetry consisting of two successive rhyming lines.

covenant In theology, an agreement or contract between God and humans.

crepidoma; crepis The three visible steps of a **column's platform.**

cromlech (CROM-leck) A prehistoric monument of huge stones arranged in a circle.

cross vault (groin vault) See drawing in Starter Kit, page xxvi.

crossing The intersection of the **nave** and the **transept** in a cross-shaped church.

cruciform Cross shaped.

crusades Military expeditions undertaken by European Christians in the eleventh through thirteenth centuries to recover the Holy Land from Muslims.

cult A community that follows special religious practices.

culture A group's way of living, including its beliefs, art, and social organization, that is transmitted from one generation to the next.

cuneiform (KYOO-nee-ah-form) Ancient Mesopotamian system of writing that uses wedge-shaped characters.

Cynicism Ancient Greek philosophy that held virtue is the highest good and self-control is the way to achieve it.

demes Local townships in ancient Attica in Greece.

dharma Hindu concept of duty or moral responsibility.

diptych Work of art consisting of two hinged panels.

dome A hemispherical **vault.**

Doric Ancient Greek order of architecture characterized by a **capital** consisting of a square block supported by a cushion shape.

dramatic irony Type of irony in which the audience is aware of things about which a character in a play or novel is unaware.

dromos Entryway to a **tholos.**

drum In architecture, a circular wall, usually topped by a **dome.** Also the individual cylindrical stones that make up the shaft of a column.

dualism (or dualistic religion) Religious system that divides the universe into two opposing forces, good and evil (e.g., Zoroastrianism).

duplum Higher pitched of two voice parts in medieval **organum.**

earthenware Pottery made of porous clay fired at a relatively low temperature.

earthwork Large-scale artwork created by altering the land or a natural geographic area.

echinus (ee-KYE-nuhs) The cushion-shaped stone below the abacus of a **Doric capital.**

enamel Artistic technique of fusing powdered colored glass to a metal surface in a decorative pattern, or the object created by this method.

engaged column Column attached to a wall.

engraving Type of print made by cutting an image onto metal and inking the recesses.

entablature In architecture, the horizontal structure above the columns and **capitals** and below the roof.

entasis Slight bulge in the middle of a column.

epic Extended narrative poem written in a dignified style about a heroic character or characters.

Epicureanism Greek philosophy founded by Epicurus that held that pleasure, or the avoidance of pain, was the ultimate good.

epistle Book of the New Testament originally written as a letter.

etiological stories Religious myths that account for the origins of things.

evangelists From the Greek term for "bearer of good news." The name given to Matthew, Mark, Luke, and John, who wrote the gospel books of the New Testament; generally, one who preaches or attempts to spread the gospel.

facade Front face of a building.

faience High-quality glazed ceramics.

fan vaulting A decorative style of **vaulting** with **ribs** radiating like those of a fan.

fang ding Square bronze vessel with four legs, used for storing ceremonial offerings during the Chinese Shang dynasty.

feudalism A medieval European political and economic system based on the holding of land and the rights and obligations of lords and vassals, respectively.

Flamboyant Late stage of Gothic architectural style of the fifteenth and sixteenth centuries, characterized by wavy, flame-like tracery and elaborate decoration.

fluting Vertical grooves on the surface of a column.

flying buttress Characteristic of **Gothic** architecture, an arch-shaped buttress.

folio Manuscript page.

foreshortening In painting and relief sculpture, to reduce a form that is not parallel to the picture plane, thereby creating an illusion of three dimensionality.

Franciscans Members of a Christian order of monks founded by St. Francis of Assisi in 1209; noted for their emphasis on poverty and humility.

fresco Painting technique in which ground pigment mixed with water is applied to wet lime plaster.

fret Ridge on the fingerboard of a stringed instrument.

friar Male member of certain Christian monastic orders.

frieze A band of ornamental carving or painting, especially the middle section of an **entablature,** between the **architrave** and **cornice.**

gable In architecture, the triangular section at the end of a pitched roof, between the two sloping sides.

gallery In architecture, a long narrow passageway, especially found above the side aisles of a church, overlooking the **nave.**

gargoyle Gutter, carved usually in the form of a fantastic creature, the mouth serving as a waterspout. Found especially on **Gothic** churches and cathedrals.

garth The garden in a **cloister.**

genre (JON-ruh) Category of art, music, or literature, such as portrait bust, symphony, and novel.

genre painting Scene in which the subject is taken from everyday life.

geoglyph Huge earthen design, such as the Nazca lines.

Geometric period (or Geometric style) The Greek cultural and artistic style of about 1000–700 B.C.E., noted for abstract geometric designs, especially on pottery.

glaze Thin, transparent layer of oil paint, usually applied on top of another layer or over a painted surface to achieve a glowing or glossy look. In ceramics, a glasslike surface coating.

glissando (plural, glissandi) (gli-SAHN-doe) In music, a rapid slide of a succession of adjacent tones.

Gnosticism (NOHS-tih-sizm) Dualistic doctrine of certain pagan, Jewish, and early Christian sects that redemption is achieved through an occult knowledge of God, revealed to their believers alone.

Golden Section A mathematical formula, developed in ancient Greece, for ideal proportions in fine art. The smaller of two dimensions is the same proportion to the larger as the larger is to the whole work, a ratio of about five to eight.

gospels First four books of the New Testament (Matthew, Mark, Luke, John), which describe the life and teachings of Jesus.

Gothic Style of architecture and art of the twelfth through sixteenth centuries in Western Europe and revived during the Romantic era. Characterized, especially in churches, by ribbed **vaults,**

pointed **arches, flying buttresses, stained glass,** and high steep roofs.

Greek cross In architecture, a floor plan of four arms of equal length. Compare to **Latin cross.**

Gregorian chant Monophonic liturgical chant, usually sung with no accompaniment; named after St. Gregory, who was pope from 590 to 604. Also called plainchant; plainsong.

ground bass In music, a phrase in the bass that is repeated continually throughout the composition or musical section.

guild Association of people in the same craft or trade, formed during the Middle Ages or Renaissance to give economic and political power to its members and to control the trade's standards.

hadith Islamic document containing the sayings of Muhammad and anecdotes about him.

half step In music, the distance between two adjacent keys on a piano or between two adjacent frets on a guitar.

harmony In music, playing or singing two or more tones at the same time, especially when the resulting sound is pleasing to the ear; generally, the arrangement of chords.

Hellenic Relating to the culture of **Classical** Greece (480–323 B.C.E.).

Hellenistic Relating to the post-**Classical** period in Greek history (after 323 B.C.E.), during which basic tenets of Classical Greek culture and thought spread throughout the Mediterranean, Middle East, and Asia.

henge A prehistoric circle of stones or posts.

hieroglyphics Writing system, such as that of the ancient Egyptians, that uses pictorial characters to convey sounds or meanings.

Hijrah (or Hegira) (hi-JYE-ruh) Muhammad's flight from Mecca to Medina in 622 C.E. that marks the beginning of the Muslim era.

himation Rectangular piece of fabric draped over one shoulder as a garment in ancient Greece.

Hinduism Ancient religion of India characterized by a belief in reincarnation, the search for union with the divine, and liberation from earthly evils.

huaca (WAH-cah) Pyramid made of sun-dried bricks, around which the Moche lived in Peru.

humanism Belief system, especially during the Renaissance, that stressed the worth, dignity, and accomplishments of the individual. Stemmed from renewed interest in **Classical** values of ancient Greece and Rome.

icon Religious image, such as a figure from the Bible, painted on wood and used as a sacred reminder of important elements of Christianity.

iconoclasm; iconoclastic controversy (eye-KON-o-KLAZ-em) Opposition to the use of religious images; the systematic destruction of religious **icons.**

iconography In visual arts, the symbols used to communicate meaning.

iconophile A lover of artistic images, at odds with iconoclasts in the **iconoclastic controversy** of the Byzantine era.

ideogram Symbol that represents an idea, not just a word or its pronunciation.

illuminated manuscript A manuscript illustrated with richly colored, gilded paintings, and ornamental lettering and borders.

imago Roman death mask.

impost block In architecture, a block placed between the **capital** and the **arch,** used to channel the weight of the arch down onto the column.

Impressionism Late-nineteenth-century artistic style that sought to portray a fleeting view of the world, usually by applying paint in short strokes of pure color. In music, a style that suggested moods and places through lush and shifting harmonies and vague rhythms.

incarnation Generally, the act of assuming a human body, especially by a god or spirit. In Christian theology, the doctrine of the birth of God in human form as Jesus Christ.

International style Twentieth-century architectural style focusing primarily on modern materials, especially steel and concrete, and boxlike shapes.

Intertropical Convergence Zone Climatic border zone where the cool wet air of the south Atlantic meets the warm dry air of the Sahara desert.

Ionic Ancient Greek order of architecture characterized by a capital in the shape of a curling volute scroll.

irony Language that states something different from or opposite to what is intended; **dramatic irony** puts characters in a position of ignorance about such an incongruity while keeping the audience aware of the situation.

Isis Egyptian goddess of fertility, whose cultlike worship gradually extended throughout the Roman empire.

Jainism Ascetic religion founded in sixth century B.C.E. India that affirms the immortality and the transmigration of the soul and denies the existence of a perfect or supreme being.

jamb The sides of a doorway or window.

jazz Category of music, first developed by African Americans in the early twentieth century, that usually features **syncopated** rhythms and improvisation of the melody or a phrase.

ka Ancient Egyptian concept of the human soul or spirit, believed to live on after death.

Kamares ware Type of Minoan ceramics characterized by curving motifs, often aquatic, painted in white and orange on a dark ground.

kami Local deities in the Japanese **Shinto** system of belief.

kana Japanese writing system.

karma Hindu and **Buddhist** doctrine that one's moral actions have a future consequence in determining personal destiny.

kiva (KEE-vah) Large underground ceremonial room in a Pueblo village.

koan Riddle in the form of a paradox used in **Zen** as an aid to meditation and intuitive understanding.

Kojiki Japanese ancient historical records.

Koran See **Quran.**

kore Ancient Greek statue of a standing clothed woman.

kouros Ancient Greek statue of a standing nude man.

krater Ancient Greek vase with a large opening and two handles.

Krishna Hindu god, an **avatar** of **Vishnu,** often depicted as a handsome young man playing the flute.

lais French medieval narrative poems.

Lakshmi In **Hinduism,** a female goddess, consort of **Vishnu.**

lancet Window with a narrow **arch** shape, used frequently in **Gothic** architecture.

landscape Painting, photograph, or other visual art form that uses a natural outdoor scene as its main subject.

lantern In architecture, a open or windowed structure placed on top of a roof to allow light to enter below.

Latin cross In architecture, a floor plan of three short arms and one long one. Compare to **Greek cross.**

leitmotif (LIGHT-moe-teef) German for "leading motive." In Wagnerian opera, brief fragments of melody or rhythm that trigger the audience to think of particular characters, actions, or objects.

lekythos Ancient Greek vase, small, cylindrical in shape, with a single handle.

linear perspective See **perspective.**

lintel In architecture, a horizontal beam, as above a doorway.

liturgy Religious rite used in public organized worship.

loggia (LOH-juh) In architecture, a covered open-air gallery.

logic Study of reasoning, or a particular system of reasoning.

lost-wax process (also known as the "cire-perdu" process) A method of metal casting in which a wax mold is coated with plaster or clay, then heated so the wax melts and runs out of vents. Molten metal is then poured into the hollow space and, when cooled, the clay or plaster mold is broken, leaving a metal core.

lozenge Ornamental diamond-shaped motif.

lyre A stringed instrument of the harp family used to accompany a singer or chanter of ancient poetry, common among the Egyptians, Assyrians, and Greeks.

lyric poetry Poems that have a songlike quality; usually emotional in nature.

mandorla In religious art, an almond-shaped glory of light surrounding a sacred figure, such as Jesus.

Manicheism (MAN-i-key-izm) The religious philosophy, founded by the Persian prophet Manes in the third century C.E. and synthesized from elements of Christianity, Gnosticism, and Zoroastrianism, that divided the world between good and evil forces.

Mannerism Artistic style of the sixteenth century that rejected Renaissance aesthetic principles; noted for its obscure subject matter, unbalanced compositions, distorted bodies and poses, strange facial expressions, confusing spatial constructions, and harsh colors.

manuscript Handwritten book or document.

mass Central religious ritual, principally in the Roman Catholic Church; a musical setting of this ritual.

Manyoshu Eighth-century collection of Japanese poems.

mastaba Type of ancient Egyptian tomb, rectangular in shape with sloping walls and flat roof.

mausoleum Monumental tomb, or the building used to store one or more such tombs.

maya In **Hinduism,** the transitory, manifold appearance of the sensory world that obscures the true spiritual reality.

mazurka Lively Polish dance in triple meter.

meander Ornamental maze pattern common in Greek art.

megalith Huge stone, especially used as part of a prehistoric monument.

menhir (MEN-hear) Prehistoric monument of a single huge slab of stone, set in an upright position.

Mesoamerica Region extending south and east from central Mexico to include parts of Guatemala, Belize, Honduras, and Nicaragua. In pre-Columbian times, home to the Mayan and Olmec civilizations.

metope Part of the **entablature** of the Doric order. Metopes, squarish in shape and painted or carved, alternate with **triglyphs.**

mihrab (ME-rahb) Prayer niche in the interior wall of a mosque indicating the direction of Mecca.

mille-fleurs (meel-FLUHR) French for "thousand flowers." A background pattern consisting of many flowers and plants, particularly in **tapestry** designs.

minaret (min-uh-RET) In Islamic architecture, a tall slender tower attached to a **mosque,** from which a **muezzin** calls the faithful to prayer.

miniature Detailed small-scale painting, often on an **illuminated manuscript.**

minstrel Traveling entertainer of the Middle Ages, especially one who performed secular music.

Mithras Persian god of light and wisdom, whose cultlike worship spread throughout the Roman empire, eventually rivaling Christianity.

mode Organization of musical intervals into **scales,** used in ancient and medieval music; later limited to just the major and minor scales.

model In painting, to create the illusion of depth by using light and shadow. In sculpture, to shape a pliable substance into a three-dimensional object.

monastery Residence for monks.

monasticism Life of organized religious seclusion, as in a **monastery** or convent.

monolith Single slab of stone.

monophony Musical texture with a single melody and no accompaniment. Compare **polyphony.**

monotheism Belief in and worship of a single god.

mosaic Design or picture created by inlaying small pieces of colored glass, stone, or tile in mortar; mosaics are usually placed on walls, floors, or ceilings.

mosque Islamic house of worship.

motet In Renaissance music, a multi-voiced composition, usually based on a sacred Latin text and sung **a cappella.**

moundbuilders Early Native American cultures in the Mississippi or Ohio river valley noted for their construction of monumental burial mounds.

mudra (moo-DRAH) Symbolic, stylized position of the body or hand in Indian art.

muezzin (myoo-EZ-in) Crier who calls the Muslim faithful to prayer five times a day.

mural A large wall painting.

music drama Musical term first used by Wagner to describe his **operas** that combined song, instrumental music, dance, drama, and poetry with no interruptions and without breaking the opera up into conventional arias or recitatives.

mystery play Medieval drama form based on biblical narratives.

myth A traditional story, usually featuring heroes, gods, or ancestors, that explains important cultural practices or beliefs.

mythology A system or collection of myths belonging to a people and expressing their origin, history, deities, ancestors, and beliefs.

Nahuatl Ancient language of the Aztecs. Also, a member of the various ancient Indian peoples of central Mexico, including the Aztecs.

narthex Entrance hall or vestibule of a church.

natural law Set of rights derived from nature and therefore superior to those established in the civil code.

naturalism Late nineteenth-century literary movement that strove to depict characters in naturalistic, objective detail, focusing on the authenticity of characters, setting, and situations; emphasized biological and cultural determinants for the behavior and fate of literary characters.

nave Long central space of a church, flanked on both sides by narrower aisles.

Neolithic The New Stone Age, about 8000 B.C.E. to 2000 B.C.E., a period characterized by the use of pottery, agriculture, development of early writing, and construction of **megalithic** structures.

Neoplatonism Revival of the philosophy of Plato, developed by Plotinus in the third century C.E. and prevalent during the Renaissance; based on the belief that the psyche is trapped within the body and philosophical thought is the only way to ascend from the material world to union with the single, higher source of existence.

neume Basic musical notation symbol used in **Gregorian chants.**

niche In architecture, a hollow recess in a wall, often used to hold a statue or vase.

Nihongi Chronicles of Japan that continue the Kojiki.

nirvana In **Buddhism, Hinduism,** and **Jainism,** the state of ultimate bliss.

notation In music, a symbolic method of representing tones.

novella (plural, novelle) Short story, usually satirical and with a moral.

octave Eight-line section of a poem, particularly the first section in a **Petrarchan sonnet;** in music, an eight-note interval.

oculus Circular window.

ode Lyric poem, usually addressed to a person or object and written in a dignified style.

Oedipus complex In psychoanalysis, a subconscious sexual desire in a male child for the female parent and a sense of hostility toward the male parent.

Ogun One of the African orisa, or lesser gods who interact with humans; the god of iron.

oil paint Paint consisting of ground pigment and oil (usually linseed oil).

oinochoe A Greek wine jug with a pinched lip and curved handle.

oligarchy Form of government in which a few people rule.

olpe A Greek vase or jug with a broad lip.

Oludumare Major African god of the Yoruba, who created the world and humanity.

oracle A prophet who interprets the will of the gods.

orans In early Christian art, the pose of a person in prayer, with hands raised to heaven.

order In architecture, a style determined by the type of column used. See also **Doric; Ionic; Corinthian.**

organum (ORE-guh-num) Early polyphonic music with the voices a fourth, a fifth, or an **octave** apart. The **organum duplum** is such a chant with two voices, with the lower voice holding long notes and the higher voice moving more quickly. Such a chant with three voices is an **organum triplum;** such a chant with four voices is an **organum quadruplum.**

Orientalizing period The Greek cultural and artistic style of about 700–600 B.C.E. that was influenced greatly by the Near East.

orthogonal In visual arts, a receding line perpendicular to the picture plane. In linear perspective, orthogonals converge and disappear at a **vanishing point.**

pagoda **Buddhist** temple in the shape of a tower, with many stories that each have an upward-curving roof.

Palace Style Type of Minoan ceramics characterized by plant forms painted on a pale beige background.

palaestra (plural, palaestrae) Public place in ancient Greece where young men learned to wrestle and box under the guidance of a master.

Paleolithic The Old Stone Age, about 2,000,000–10,000 B.C.E., a period characterized by hunting, fishing, the use of stone tools, the increasing dominance of *homo sapiens*, and the creation of the earliest works of art.

palette Artist's choice of colors for a particular work of art, or the surface on which such colors are placed and mixed.

pallium Ancient Roman garment made of a rectangular piece of fabric.

palmette Stylized palm leaf ornament.

Pancatantra Collection of **Sanskrit** animal fables that convey the religious principles of **Hinduism.**

pantheism Doctrine that identifies deity with the phenomena of the universe, including both animate beings and inanimate objects.

pantheon All the gods of a people, or a temple dedicated to all the gods; the Pantheon is the specific circular temple in Rome dedicated to all gods.

parables Brief stories that reveal a religious teaching, like the parables of Jesus and those of Asian traditions, including **Confucianism** and **Zen Buddhism.**

parchment Animal skin used to make manuscripts.

patrician Member of the noble family class in ancient Rome who was originally granted special civil and religious rights.

patronage Originally, a system of **patrician** support and protection of a **plebeian** in ancient Rome; later, a system of financially sponsoring art or artists.

pediment In **Classical** architecture, a triangular space at the end of a building, formed by the **cornice** and the ends of the sloping roof.

pendentive In architecture, triangular shape used to make the transition from a square base to a circular dome.

peplos Loose outer garment worn by women in ancient Greece, hanging from the shoulders and belted at the waist.

percussion instrument Musical instrument, such as a timpanum or bass drum, played by hitting or shaking.

peripteral In architecture, the adjective describing a building that is surrounded by a **peristyle.**

peristyle In architecture, a continuous row of columns, forming an enclosure around a building or courtyard.

perspective A method of creating the illusion of three-dimensional space on a two-dimensional surface. Achieved by methods such as *atmospheric perspective*, using slight variations in color and sharpness of the subject, or *linear perspective*, creating a horizon line and - **orthogonals,** which meet at **vanishing points.**

piazza (pee-AHT-zuh) A public square in Italy.

pictograph Picture used to represent a word or idea.

pier In architecture, a vertical support structure similar to a column, but usually square or rectangular in shape, rather than cylindrical.

pillar Freestanding vertical element, usually used as an architectural support.

plainchant; plainsong In music, the **monophonic,** unmetered vocal music of the early Christian church, as in **Gregorian chant.**

platform A raised horizontal surface, especially one on which **columns** sit.

Platonism Philosophy of Plato, focusing on the notion that Ideal Forms are an absolute and eternal model that all worldly phenomena strive toward.

plebeian Member of the common lower class in ancient Rome who at first lacked many of the rights **patricians** enjoyed.

plinth Slab that supports a sculpture or column.

podium In architecture, an elevated platform; often the foundation of a building, especially an ancient temple.

polis (plural, poleis) An independent city-state in ancient Greece.

polyphony Simultaneous playing or singing of several independent musical lines. Compare **monophony.**

polytheism Belief in or worship of more than one god. Compare **monotheism.**

portal In architecture, a grand entrance or doorway.

portico In architecture, a porch or walkway covered by a roof supported by **columns.** It often marks an entrance to the main building.

post and lintel In architecture, vertical posts supporting a horizontal **lintel.**

potlatch Lavish ceremony among some Native Americans of northwest North America at which the host distributes gifts to guests according to their rank or status.

prelude (PRELL-yood) Short instrumental composition that usually precedes a larger musical work.

primary colors The colors red, yellow, and blue. See also **secondary colors.**

pronaos Enclosed vestibule of a Greek or Roman temple, supported by **columns.**

propylon (plural, propylaia) Gateway to a temple or a group of buildings.

pseudo-peripteral Having a single row of **engaged columns** on all sides.

Punic Relating to ancient Carthage, its inhabitants, or their language or history.

pylon Massive gateway, especially to an Egyptian temple.

qasidah Highly formalized Arabic **ode** of 30 to 120 lines, each line ending with the same rhyme. It focuses on the poet's attempt to find his beloved.

qibla (KIB-luh) Direction facing Mecca, to which a Muslim turns when praying.

quadrivium Program of arithmetic, astronomy, geometry, and music in medieval universities.

quatrain Four-line unit of poetry.

Quran; Koran Sacred text of Islam.

radiating chapels Several chapels arranged around the **ambulatory** or **apse** of a church.

raga Indian musical composition, usually partly improvised, that attempts to convey a mood or feeling.

Ramadan Holy ninth month of the Islamic lunar calendar, during which Muslims must fast from sunrise to sunset.

Rayonnant (ray-on-NANT) From the French term for "to radiate." The High **Gothic** architectural style of the mid-thirteenth century, noted for its radiating **tracery** patterns and liberal use of **stained glass.**

red-figure style Greek vase painting style featuring red figures surrounded by a black background, with details painted on the surface.

refectory Room in a monastery where meals are taken.

register system Method of organizing an artistic composition in horizontal bands or rows, each of which depicts a different event or idea.

regular temple Architectural plan for a temple in which the number of columns along the sides of the temple is double the number of columns on the ends plus one (e.g., an eight-by-seventeen proportion).

relic Venerated object associated with, or portion of the body of, a saint or martyr.

relief Sculpture attached to a solid background, rather than freestanding.

relieving triangle Triangular opening above a lintel, intended to relieve pressure on the **lintel.**

reliquary Decorative container for **relic.**

repoussé Metalworking technique in which the design is hammered in relief by working on the back of the metal plate.

representational Art that portrays the visual reality of an object.

responsorial Chant or anthem sung after a reading in a church service.

rhyton An ancient Greek drinking horn which may be shaped like an animal head.

rib In architecture, a curved, projecting **arch** used for support or decoration in a **vault.**

ritornello (rit-or-NELL-low) Musical passage that will recur several times throughout a **concerto** movement.

romance Long medieval narrative form that related **chivalric** Celtic stories, especially the exploits of King Arthur and his Knights of the Round Table.

Romanesque The style of architecture and art of the eleventh and twelfth centuries in Western Europe. Characterized, especially in churches, by semi-circular **arches,** barrel **vaults,** thick walls, and small windows.

rondo form Organizing structure for a musical work in which the main theme repeats itself frequently, with new, contrasting material added between each repetition. Often the form of the second or last movements of a **concerto.**

roof comb A crestlike extension along the roof of a Mayan temple that resembles the comb of a rooster.

rose window Circular "wheel" window, characteristic especially of **Gothic** architecture.

rosette A roselike ornament that is painted or sculpted.

rotunda Circular building, usually topped by a dome.

ruba'i (plural, ruba'iyat) Persian poetry form of four lines with a rhyming pattern of AABA.

sacramentary **Liturgical** book of prayers and rites of the sacraments of the Roman Catholic Church.

samsara Hindu concept of the eternal cycle of birth and death.

samurai Ruler-warriors of Japan, especially during the feudal era.

Sanskrit Ancient Indic language; the classic language of ancient India, including Hinduism and the Vedas.

sarcophagus A stone coffin.

satire Literary or dramatic work that exposes vice or follies with ridicule or sarcasm, often in a humorous way.

satori Zen Buddhist state of enlightenment.

scale In music, an ascending or descending series of notes.

schism Break or split among factions, often religious and involving a formal breach in a church.

scroll In Chinese and Japanese art, a painting or text drawn on paper or silk. The scroll is conventionally kept rolled and tied except on special occasions. Some are vertical *hanging scrolls;* others are horizontal *band scrolls.* Japanese narrative scrolls are called *emaki-mano.*

secondary colors The colors orange, green, and purple, formed when two primary colors (red, yellow, or blue) are mixed. See also **primary colors.**

secular Not sacred or religious.

serdab The cellar of an Egyptian **mastaba,** containing the **ka** statue.

sestina Verse form developed by Renaissance troubadours that employs six-line stanzas and a three-line concluding envoy, with the six end words of the first **stanza** repeated throughout the other five stanzas and envoy.

sfumato (sfoo-MA-toe) Italian for "smoky." In painting, the intentional blurring of the outline of a figure in a hazy, almost smoky atmosphere.

shaft The vertical section of a **column** between the **capital** and the base.

shastras Ancient Hindu texts that describe instructions for various activities, including temple building, cooking, warfare, and music.

Shi'ites Muslim sect that, along with the Sunnis, share basic theological convictions but differ strongly over the line of legitimate succession from Muhammad.

Shinto Principal and former state religion of Japan characterized by rituals and venerations for local deities and strong patriotism.

Shiva One of the principal Hindu deities, worshipped as destroyer and restorer of worlds, and often associated with two other central Hindu gods, Brahma and **Vishnu.** Shiva is often represented as a dancing figure, the Shiva Nataraja.

shogun Hereditary military dictator of Japan; originally, commander-in-chief of the **samurai.**

sitar Long-necked lute-shaped instrument from India.

skene (SKAY-nuh) In Greek theater, a building behind the acting area that functioned as a dressing room and as scenic background.

Skepticism Greek philosophical doctrine that absolute knowledge is not usually possible and inquiry must therefore be a process of doubt.

sonnet Renaissance lyric poetic form invented by Petrarch in Italy and imitated by English Renaissance poets, including Shakespeare. A sonnet includes fourteen lines in iambic pentameter with one of two predominant structural and rhyming patterns: (1) the Italian or Petrarchan sonnet comprised of an eight-line octave and six-line sestet, with a rhyme pattern of abba abba cde cde cde, or cd cd cd (or a variation on these); (2) the English or Shakespearean sonnet comprised of three quatrains and a concluding couplet—typically rhyming aab cdcd efef gg.

Sophists Ancient Greek philosophers and teachers, less interested in the pursuit of truth than in the use of clever rhetoric and argumentation.

soprano In music, the range of the highest voice of females or young boys.

staff In music, the five horizontal lines and four spaces used in **notation.**

stained glass Artistic technique in which many small pieces of glass are colored with internal pigment or surface paint and then held together with lead strips; used extensively in **Gothic** cathedrals.

statue in the round Sculpture that stands free of a background and is fully formed to be seen from all sides.

stele Slab of stone, set vertically.

stigmata Physical marks or scars on humans that resemble the crucifixion marks of Jesus; said to appear during states of religious ecstasy.

stoa In ancient Greek architecture, a long, freestanding **portico.**

Stoicism Greek and a Roman philosophy characterized by indifference to pleasure and pain and a willingness to accept what life brings with impassive equanimity.

stupa Buddhist memorial monument in the shape of a mound.

Sufi Islamic mystic.

Surah Chapter in the **Quran.**

Swahili People inhabiting the coast and islands of East Africa, and their language, which is widely used as a common language in that part of the continent.

syllogism Form of deductive reasoning consisting of a major premise, a minor premise, and a conclusion. For example, *All philosophers are mortal; Aristotle was a philosopher; Aristotle was mortal.*

synoptic gospels The **gospels** of Matthew, Mark, and Luke, which are similar. The gospel of John is unique.

tambura Unfretted lute used to sustain the drone chord in Indian music.

tanka A short Japanese poem.

tapestry Heavy textile, the design created as the fabric is woven; a specialty of medieval and Renaissance northern Europe.

teleology In philosophy, the study of an end and how it relates to the natural processes leading up to it.

tempera (TEM-purr-uh) Paint made of egg yolk and pigment.

tenor In music, the range of the highest male voice, which usually carries the melody; also, the bottom, slower line of an **organum duplum.**

Teotihuacan Major Aztec city of central Mexico, just north of present-day Mexico City.

terra cotta Italian for "baked earth." An orange-red baked clay used for pottery or sculpture.

terza rima (turr-tsah-REE-ma) Poetry form consisting of three-line stanzas in which each stanza's middle line rhymes with the first and third lines of the subsequent stanza (aba, bcb, cdc, etc.).

tessera (plural, tesserae) (TESS-ur-ah) Small cubes of stone or other material used in making a **mosaic.**

tetrarchy Area ruled by one of four rulers, or tetrarchs.

tholos Circular domed room built by **corbelled** construction.

thrust In architecture, outward or lateral pressure in a structure.

toga Ancient Roman garment.

tonal center Home key of a musical composition.

tonality In music, the arrangement of all tones of a composition in relation to the central key, or tonic.

Torah Hebrew for "instruction." The first five books of Hebrew scripture.

totem pole Post carved with animal and spirit images and erected by some Native Americans of northwest North America to memorialize the dead.

tracery Elaborate pattern of interlacing stone lines, especially in **Gothic** windows.

tragedy Serious literary or theatrical work about a central character's problems, with an unhappy ending.

transept In architecture, the portion of the church at a right angle to the **nave,** between the nave and the **choir,** or **apse.**

treasury Building, room, or box for storing valuables or offerings.

triclinium Dining room in an ancient Roman home, named for the three couches on which the diners reclined.

triforium In architecture, the elevated galleries above the aisles of a chuch or cathedral.

triglyphs Part of the **entablature** of **Doric** order. Triglyphs have three (tri) sections and alternate with **metopes.**

triumphal arch Grand freestanding gateway with a large **arch.**

trivium Program of grammar, logic, and rhetoric in medieval universities.

trope In music, a new word or phrase added to an existing chant as an embellishment.

troubadour (TRUE-buh-door) Poet-musician of medieval southern France.

trumeau In architecture, the vertical post supporting a **lintel** and between two doors.

tufa A porous whitish stone that is soft when cut but hardens after exposure to air.

Tuscan order Ancient Roman order, much like the Greek **Doric** order, with the addition of a base.

tympanum Semicircular area above a window or door.

vanishing point In linear perspective, a point on the horizon line at which the **orthogonals** appear to converge. See drawing in Starter Kit on p. xxii.

vault Arched masonry roof or ceiling. A **barrel** (or tunnel) **vault** is an uninterrupted semicircular vault made of a series of **arches**. A **cross** or **groin vault** is created by the intersection of two barrel vaults set at right angles. A **ribbed vault** is a form of groin vault in which the groins formed by the intersection of curved sides are reinforced with raised **ribs**. See drawing in Starter Kit on p. xxvi.

Vedas The oldest sacred Hindu writings, composed 1500–1000 B.C.E. by the Aryans in present-day India.

vellum Thinnest, finest **parchment.**

veneer In architecture, a thin layer of high-quality material used as a surface, often covering inferior materials.

vernacular Common language spoken in a particular country or region.

vibrato (vi-BRAHT-oh) In vocal or instrumental music, a pulsing effect achieved by slight, rapid variations in pitch.

Vishnu One of the central Hindu gods, worshipped as the protector and preserver of worlds.

volute Spiral scroll ornament, as on an **Ionic capital.**

voussoirs Wedge-shaped stones that makes up a true arch.

warp Thick threads that run vertically on a loom and provide the structure for a piece of fabric woven of the **weft** threads.

weft Threads that run horizontally on a loom and usually form the visible pattern on a piece of woven fabric.

westwork Monumental western entryway in a Carolingian, Ottonian, or Romanesque church.

white-ground ceramics (or white-ground technique) Ancient Greek pottery ware in which a white matte slip is painted over the surface of a reddish clay vessel, with details painted on the surface with a fine brush.

whole tone; whole step In music, the **interval** between any two consecutive white keys on the piano, when a black key intervenes. A whole step is made up of two half steps.

word painting In Renaissance music, a composition style that emphasizes the meaning of words through the accompanying music. For example, the word "weep" might be expressed by a descending melodic line.

yakshis In **Hinduism**, local nature spirits represented on temple gates in the form of shapely females.

yin and yang The Chinese **dualistic** philosophical image that represents simultaneous contrast and complement. The yin form represents the passive, negative, feminine, dark, and earthly; the yang form represents the light, masculine, positive, constructive, and heavenly. The two are in perpetual interplay.

Zen Buddhism Chinese and Japanese form of **Buddhism** that emphasizes enlightenment achieved by self-awareness and meditation instead of by adherence to a set religious doctrine.

ziggurat In ancient Near Eastern architecture, a monumental stepped base made of brick, to support a temple.

Picture Credits and Further Information

Introduction

0.1 Nasjonalmuseet for Kunst/Nasjonalgalleriet, Oslo. © 2003 The Munch Museum/The Munch-Ellingsen Group/ Artists Rights Society (ARS), NY/ADAGP, Paris. J. Lathion/© Nasjonalgalleriet; 0.3 Robert Harding World Imagery

Chapter One

1.1 AKG London Ltd.; 1.2 © Archivo Iconografico, S.A./Corbis/Bettmann; 1.3 Berna Villiers/Douglas Mazonowicz; 1.4 Aerofilms; 1.5 Hirmer Fotoarchiv, Munich, Germany; 1.6 Fletcher Fund, 1940, The Metropolitan Museum of Modern Art, NY; 1.7 The British Museum; 1.8 Herve Lewandowski/Musée du Louvre/Reunion Des Musées Nationaux/Art Resource, NY; 1.9 Herve Lewandowski/Musée du Louvre/Reunion Des Musées Nationaux/Art Resource, NY; 1.10 The Metropolitan Museum of Art, NY; 1.11 The British Museum; 1.12 The British Museum; 1.13 Reinhard Saczewski/Vorderasiatisches Museum/Staatliche Museen zu Berlin, Preussischer Kulturbesitz, Vorderasiatiches Museum, Berlin, Germany/Art Resource, NY; 1.14 Comstock Images; 1.15 Musée du Louvre/Reunion de Musées Nationaux/Art Resource, NY; 1.16 Courtesy of the Oriental Institute Museum/University of Chicago; 1.17 Egyptian Museum, Cairo/Hirmer Fotoarchiv, Munich, Germany; 1.18 The British Museum; 1.19 Picture Desk, Inc./Kobal Collection/The Art Archive/Dagli Orti; 1.20 Peter Wilson © Dorling Kindersley; 1.21 Petera A. Clayton; 1.22 Harvard University–Boston Museum of Fine Arts; 1.23 Egyptian Museum, Cairo/Hirmer Fotoarchiv, Munich, Germany; 1.24 A. F. Kersting; 1.25 Egyptian Tourist Authority; 1.26 The British Museum; 1.27 Robert Harding World Imagery; 1.28 The British Museum; 1.29 The British Museum; 1.30 Art Resource/Bildarchiv Preussischer Kulturbesitz, Berlin, Germany; 1.31 Art Resource/Bildarchiv Preussischer Kulturbesitz, Berlin, Germany; 1.32 Egyptian Museum, Cairo/Hirmer Fotoarchiv, Munich, Germany; 1.33 Stephan Petegorsky/Smith College Museum of Art

Chapter Two

2.1 Gift of Christas–G. Bastis. The Metropolitan Museum of Art, NY; 2.2 Archaeological Museum of Herakleion/ Museum of Prehistoric Thera, Crete, Greece; 2.3 The Ancient Art & Architecture Collection Ltd.; 2.4 Egyptian Tourist Authority; 2.5 The Ancient Art & Architecture Collection Ltd.; 2.6 Archeological Museum, Iraklion, Crete, Greece/Studio Kontos Photostock; 2.7 Archaeological Museum of Herakleion, Crete, Greece; 2.8 Archaeological Museum of Herakleion, Crete, Greece; 2.9 C. M. Dixon/Archaeological Museum of Herakleion, Crete, Greece, 2.10 A. F. Kersting; 2.11 Dagli Orti/ Picture Desk, Inc./Kobal Collection; 2.12 National Archeological Museum, Athens/Hirmer Fotoarchiv, Munich, Germany; 2.13 Studio Kontos Photostock; 2.14 The Metropolitan Museum of Art, Rogers Fund, 1914. Photograph © 1996 The Metropolitan Museum of Art, NY; 2.15 Staatliche Museum, Berlin, Germany/Art Resource/Bildarchiv Preussischer Kulturbesitz; 2.16 Herve Lewandowski/Musée du Louvre, Paris. Reunion des Musées Nationaux/Art Resource, NY; 2.17 The British Museum; 2.18 © SCALA/Art Resource, NY, Museo Gregoriano Etrusco, Vatican Museums, Vatican State; 2.19 Purchase Fund 1978. The Metropolitan Museum of Art, NY; 2.20 Purchase, Bequest of Joseph H. Durkee, Gift of Darius Ogden Mills and Gift of C. Ruston Love, by exchange, 1972. The Metropolitan Museum of Art, NY; 2.21 American Academy in Rome; 2.22 Fletcher Fund, 1932. The Metropolitan Museum of Art, NY; 2.23 Alison Frantz Photographic Collection, American School of Classical Studies at Athens

Chapter Three

3.1 Spectrum Pictures; 3.3 Bill Bachmann/PhotoEdit, Inc.; 3.4 The British Museum; 3.5 Hirmer Fotoarchiv, Munich, Germany; 3.6 Herve Lewandowski/Musée du Louvre, Paris/Reunion des Musées Nationaux/Art Resource, NY; 3.7 A. F. Kersting; 3.8 A. F. Kersting; 3.9 Alison Frantz Photographic Collection, American School of Classical Studies at Athens; 3.10 Acropolis Museum/ Hirmer Fotoarchiv, Munich, Germany; 3.11 Museo Archelogico Nazionale, Naples, Italy. SCALA/Art Resource, NY; 3.12 Musei Vaticani, Rome/SCALA/Art Resource, NY; 3.13 Museo Nazionale Romano delle Terme, Rome, Italy. SCALA/Art Resource, NY; 3.14 Anderson-Roma/ Art Resource, NY; 3.15 ALINARI/Art Resource, NY; 3.16 ALINARI/Art Resource, NY; 3.17 Museo Nacionale Romano, Rome/Hirmer Fotoarchiv, Munich, Germany; 3.18 Staatliche Antikensammlungen und Glyptothek, Munich, Germany; 3.19 Staatliche Kunstsammlungen Dresden Museum, Germany; 3.20 A. F. Kersting; 3.21 Johannes Laurentius/Antiken, Staat Museen zu Berlin, Germany/ Art Rerource/Bildarchiv Preussischer Kulturbesitz; 3.22 Antikensammlung, Staatliche Museen zu Berlin, Germany, Art Resource/Bildarchiv Preussischer Kulturbesitz; 3.23 Art Resource/Bildarchiv Preussischer Kulturbesitz; 3.24 Musée du Louvre/Reunion des Musées Nationaux/ Eric Lessing/Art Resource, NY; 3.25 Museo Pio Clementino, Musei Vaticani, Rome. Reunion des Musées Nationaux (RMN)/Art Resource, NY

Chapter Four

4.1 Tourist Organization of Greece; 4.2 SCALA/Art Resource, NY; 4.3 Robert Harding World Imagery; 4.4 Hirmer Fotoarchiv, Munich, Germany; 4.5 ALINARI/Art Resource, NY; 4.6 SCALA/Art Resource, NY; 4.7 A. F. Kersting; 4.8 A. F. Kersting; 4.9 A. F. Kersting; 4.10 Musei Capitolini, Rome, Italy. Photograph © SCALA/Art Resource NY; 4.11 Bernard Regent/Hutchison Picture Library; 4.12 Mike Dunning © Dorling Kindersley; 4.13 © SCALA/Art Resource, NY; 4.14 Richard Carafelli. Samuel H. Kress Collection. Photograph © 2001 Board of Trustees, National Gallery of Art, Washington, DC; 4.15 Vatican Museums, Rome, Italy; 4.17 ALINARI/Art Resource, NY; 4.19 ALINARI/Art Resource, NY; 4.20 Samuel D. Lee Fund. Metropolitan Museum of Art, NY; 4.21 Janetta Rebold Benton, Prof. of Fine Arts, Pace University; 4.22 Araldo de Luca Archives/Index Ricerca Iconografica; 4.23 ALINARI/Art Resource, NY; 4.24 SCALA/Art Resource, NY; 4.25 C. M. Dixon; 4.26 Rogers Fund, 1903. Metropolitan Museum of Art, NY; 4.27 SCALA/Art Resource, NY; 4.28 Fotografica Foglia

Chapter Five

5.1 Canali PhotoBank; 5.2 Israel Ministry of Tourism, North America; 5.5 Canali PhotoBank, Milan/SuperStock, Inc.; 5.7 Kim Sayer © Dorling Kindersley; 5.8 C. M. Dixon; 5.9 SCALA/Art Resource, NY; 5.10 ALINARI/Art Resource, NY; 5.11 ALINARI/Art Resource, NY; 5.12 Dagli Orti. Picture Desk, Inc./Kobal Collection; 5.13 SCALA/Art Resource, NY; 5.14 SCALA/Art Resource, NY; 5.15 Cameraphoto Arte, Venice/SCALA/Art Resource, NY; 5.16 Sonia Halliday Photographs; 5.18 Walter B. Denny; 5.19 Gavin Hellier/Nature Picture Library; 5.20 SuperStock, Inc.; 5.21 Cameraphoto Arte di Codato G. P. & C.snc; 5.22 Samuel H. Kress Collection. Margarite d'Arezzo. Photograph © Board of Trustees, National Gallery of Art, Washington, DC

Chapter Six

6.1 Courtesy of Edinburgh University Library; 6.2 Robert Frerck/Robert Harding World Imagery; 6.4 Spectrum Pictures; 6.5 A. F. Kersting; 6.6 Dagli Orti (A)/Picture Desk, Inc./Kobal Collection; 6.7 Walter Bibikow. Getty Images, Inc.–Taxi; 6.8 Patricio Goycoolea/Hutchison Picture Library; 6.9 The Nasser D. Khalili Collection of Islamic Art. Photographer © NOUR Foundation © Copyright The British Museum; 6.10 Courtesy of the Freer Gallery of Art, Smithsonian Institution, Washington, DC; 6.11 Francis Bartlett Donation and Picture Fund. Reproduced with Permission © 2005 Museum of Fine Arts, Boston. All Rights Reserved; 6.12 Bodleian Library, University of Oxford

Chapter Seven

7.1 The Cleveland Museum of Art, Purchase from the J. H. Wade Fund; 7.2 The Nasli and Alice Heeramaneck Collection, Gift of Paul Mellon. Katherine Wetzel/Virginia Museum of Fine Arts, Richmond; 7.3 A. F. Kersting; 7.4 Dale Williams; 7.5 A. F. Kersting; 7.6 The Adolph D. and Wilkins C. Williams Fund. Katherine Wetzel/Virginia Museum of Fine Arts, Richmond; 7.7 A. F. Kersting; 7.8 Dinodia Picture Agency; 7.9 A. F. Kersting; 7.10 Dinesh Khanna © Dorling Kindersley; 7.11 Von der Heydt Collection/Museum Rietberg, Zurich; 7.12 Redferns Music Picture Library

Chapter Eight

8.1 Copyright © The British Museum Great Court, Ltd.; 8.2 Hubei Provincial Museum, Wuhan/China Pictorial Photo Service, Beijing; 8.4 National Geographic Image Collection; 8.5 Werner Forman Archive Ltd.; 8.6 Tokyo National Museum DNP Archives.com Co., Ltd.; 8.7 © National Palace Museum, Taiwan, Republic of China; 8.8 The National Palace Museum; 8.9 The National Palace Museum; 8.10 Robert Newcombe/The Nelson-Atkins Museum of Art, Kansas City, MO; 8.11 Dorling Kindersley Media Library. © Judith Miller & Dorling Kindersley & Cheffins; 8.12 The National Palace Museum, Taiwan, Republic of China

Chapter Nine

9.1 The Cleveland Museum of Art, John L. Severenance Fund; 9.2 Tokyo National Museum/DNP Archives.com Co., Ltd/http://TnmArchives.jp/; 9.3 Courtesy of JICC Japan Information & Cultural Center/Embassy of Japan, London; 9.4 Courtesy of JICC Japan Information & Cultural Center/Embassy of Japan, London; 9.5 The Tokugawa Reimeikai Foundation; 9.6 Werner Forman/Art Resource, NY; 9.7 The Art Archive/Laurie Platt Winfrey. Picture Desk, Inc./Kobal Collection; 9.8 Bill Tingrey/ Arcaid

Chapter Ten

10.1 South American Pictures; 10.2 © Danny Lehman/CORBIS, NY. All Rights Reserved; 10.3 George Gerster/Photo Researchers, Inc.; 10.4 University of Pennsylvania Museum of Archaeology and Anthropology; 10.5 South American Pictures; 10.6 © Merle Green Robertson, 1976/Howard Tilton Memorial Library; 10.7 South American Pictures; 10.8 Biblioteca Apostolica Vaticana; 10.9 George Gerster/Photo Researchers, Inc.; 10.10 Buckingham Fund. Photograph © 2005, The Art Institute of Chicago. All Rights Reserved; 10.11 Dagli Orti. Picture Desk, Inc./Kobal Collection; 10.12 South American Pictures; 10.13 National Archives of Canada; 10.14 Robert Harding World Imagery; 10.15 George Gerster/Photo Researchers, Inc.; 10.16 Jack Jackson/Robert Harding World Imagery; 10.17 Kal Muller/Woodfin Camp & Associates; 10.18 Gift of Klaus G. Perls. Metropolitan Museum of Art, NY; 10.19 David Garner/Dorling Kindersley. © Exeter City Museums & Art Gallery, Royal Albert Memorial Museum; 10.20 Robert Aberman/Barbara Heller. Werner Forman/Art Resource, NY

Chapter Eleven

11.1 The British Museum; 11.2 By permission of The British Library; 11.3 The Bridgeman Art Library International; 11.4 © Achim Bednorz, Koln; 11.5 Bibliotheque Nationale de France; 11.6 Stiftsbibliothek, St. Gallen, Switzerland; 11.7 The Pierpont Morgan Library/Art Resource, NY; 11.8 Kunsthistorisches Museum, Vienna, Austria; 11.9 Centre Guillaume Le Conquerant/By special permission of the City of Bayeux; 11.10 YAN/Jean Dieuzaide; 11.12 CAISSE/Societe des Auteurs des Arts Visuels; 11.13 SCALA/Art Resource, NY; 11.14 David Jacobs/Robert Harding World Imagery; 11.15 SCALA/Art Resource, NY; 11.16 © Achim Bednorz, Koln; 11.17 Paul M. R. Maeyaert, Photographie; 11.18 The Ancient Art & Architecture Collection, Ltd.; 11.19 Vienna Tourist Information Bureau. Courtesy of Foto Ritter, Vienna/ Klosterneuburg Abbey, Austria

Chapter Twelve

12.2 Hirmer Fotoarchiv, Munich, Germany; 12.3 © SCALA/Art Resource, NY; 12.4 Spectrum Pictures; 12.5 © Angelo Hornak, London/A. F. Kersting; 12.6 A. F. Kersting; 12.8 De Agostina Editore Picture Library; 12.9 Sonia Halliday Photographs; 12.10 Giraudon/The Bridgeman Art Library International; 12.11 A. F. Kersting; 12.12 British Tourist Authority; 12.13 © Guido Alberto Rossi/TIPS Images North America; 12.14 Janetta Rebold Benton, Prof. of Fine Arts, Pace University; 12.15 Spectrum Pictures; 12.16 A. F. Kersting; 12.17 Janetta Rebold Benton, Prof. of Fine Arts, Pace University; 12.18 Janetta Rebold Benton, Prof. of Fine Arts, Pace University; 12.19 Giraudon/Bibliotheque Nationale de France; 12.20 Janetta Rebold Benton, Prof. of Fine Arts, Pace University; 12.21 Sonia Halliday Photographs; 12.22 Gift of John D. Rockefeller, Jr., 1937. Cloisters Collection, Metropolitan Museum of Art, NY; 12.23 SCALA/Art Resource, NY; 12.24 SCALA/Art Resource, NY; 12.25 SCALA/Art Resource, NY; 12.26 SCALA/Art Resource, NY; 12.27 Index Ricerca Iconografica; 12.28 SCALA/Art Resource, NY; 12.29 SCALA/Art Resource, NY; 12.30 SCALA/Art Resource, NY; 12.31 By permission of The British Library, London

Chapter Thirteen

13.1 SCALA/Art Resource, NY; 13.2 Galleria degli Uffizi, Florence. SCALA/Art Resource, NY; 13.3 Bodleian Library, University of Oxford; 13.4 SCALA/Art Resource,

Literature Credits

Chapter One
From *The Epic of Gilgamesh*, translated by N. K. Sandars (Penguin Classics 1960, Third edition 1972) Copyright © N. K. Sandars, 1960, 1964, 1972, Penguin UK; *Enheduanna*, excerpt from *The Hymn to Inanna*, based on a translation by William W. Hallo and J. J. A. Van Dijk, *The Exaltation of Inanna.* Copyright © 1968 by Yale University Press. All rights reserved. Reprinted with permission; *The Egyptian Book of the Dead*, ed. E.A. Wallis Budge, University Books, by permission of Kensington Publishing; *Declaration of Innocence Before the Gods of the Tribunal*, translated by John L. Foster, *The Egyptian Book of the Dead*, ed. E.A. Wallis Budge, University Books, by permission of Kensington Publishing; *The Harper's Song for Inherkhawy*, from *Ancient Egyptian Literature: An Anthology*, translated by John L. Foster, Copyright © 2001. By permission of University of Texas Press; *Love of You is Mixed Deep in My Vitals, My Love is One and Only, Without Peer, Why, Just Now, Must You Question Your Heart?, I Love You Through the Daytimes*, and *Spell for Causing the Beloved to Follow After* from *Love Songs of the New Kingdom*, translated from Ancient Egyptian Literature by John L. Foster. By permission of the University of Texas Press. Copyright © 1969, 1970, 1971, 1972, 1973, 1974 by John L. Foster; *The Rage of Achilles, The Death of Hector,* and *Funeral Games for Patroclus* by Homer, from *The Illiad* by Homer, translated by Robert Fagles, copyright © 1990 by Robert Fagles. Used by permission of Viking Penguin, a division of Penguin Group (USA), Inc.; *Akhenaten: Hymn to the Sun*, translated by John L. Foster, University of Texas Press

Chapter Two
From Hesiod, *Theogony*, and *Works and Days* (1978), translated by M. L. West, by permission of Oxford University Press; *Alone* and *Seizure* from *Sappho and the Greek Lyric Poets*, translated by Willis Barnstone, Copyright © 1962, 1967, 1988 by Willis Barnstone. Used by permission of Schocken Books, a division of Random House, Inc.; Arkhilokhos, *The Fox and the Hedgehog* and *Elegies*, and Alkaios, *And Fluttered Argive Helen's Heart* translated by M. L. West, Greek Lyric Poetry, Oxford University Press; *Maxims and Sayings*, from *Herakleitos*, translated by Guy Davenport. Bolinas, Grey Fox Press, 1979

Chapter Three
Herodotus, *History of the Persian Wars* from *The Histories*, translated by Aubrey De Selincourt (Penguin, 1954). Translation Copyright © Aubrey De Selincourt, 1954; Thucydides, *History of the Peloponnesian War*, from *History II*, translated by P. J. Rhodes, by permission of Aris & Phillips; Sophocles, *Oedipus the King*, scene 1 and ode 1, from *Oedipus Rex of Sophocles: An English Version* by Dudley Fitts and Robert Fitzgerald, Copyright © 1949 by Harcourt, Inc. and renewed 1977 by Cornelia Fitts and Robert Fitzgerald, reprinted by permission of Harcourt; *Agamemnon* from *Oresteia* by Aeschylus. Translated by Robert Fagles, Copyright © 1966, 1967, 1975 by Robert Fagles. Used by permission of Viking Penguin, a division of Penguin group (USA), Inc.; Plato, excerpt from *The Apology*, translated by Hugh Tarrant. *The Last Days of Socrates*, Penguin; Aristotle, from *Nicomachean Ethics*, translated by Martin Ostwald © 1962 by Martin Ostwald by permission of Prentice-Hall, Inc. Upper Saddle River, NJ

Chapter Four
The Aenid by Virgil, translated by Robert Fitzgerald, Copyright © 1980, 1982, 1983 by Robert Fitzgerald.

Used by permission of Random House, Inc.; Catullus: *We Should Live, My Lesbia, and Love, That Man is Seen by Me as a God's Equal*, and *I Hate and Love* from *The Poems of Catullus*, translated by Guy Lee, by permission of Oxford University Press; Ovid, *Siesta Time in Sultry Summer*, from *Amores*, translated by Guy Lee, John Murray Publishers, Ltd.; Ovid, *The Story of Daedalus and Icarus*, from *Metamorphoses*, translated by Rolfe Humphries, Indiana University Press; Horace, *Ah God how They Race*, from *The Odes of Horace*, translated by Helen Rowe Henze. Copyright © 1961 by The University of Oklahoma Press. Reprinted by permission of the publisher; Juvenal, excerpts from *"Against the City of Rome"* and *"Against Women,"* translated by Rolfe Humphries from *The Satires of Juvenal*, Indiana University Press; Marcus Aurelius, from *The Meditations*, translated by G. M. A. Grube © 1983, Hackett Publishing Company, Inc., reprinted by permission of Hackett; Suetonius, excerpts from *The Lives of the Caesars* from *The Twelve Caesars*, translated by Robert Graves, revised with an introduction by Michael Grant (first printed Penguin Books 1957, revised edition 1979) Copyright © Robert Graves 1957, Introduction, editorial matter and revisions to the translation Copyright © Michael Grant Publications Limited, 1979

Chapter Five
Excerpts from *Rabbinic Stories*, translated and introduced by Jeffrey L. Rubenstein, from *The Classics of Western Spirituality*, Copyright © 2002 by Jeffrey L. Rubenstein, Paulist Press, Inc. New York/Mahwah, NJ. Used with permission of the Paulist Press. www.paulistpress.com

Chapter Six
Women, Man, and *Muhammed* from *The Koran: With a Parallel Arabic Text*, translated with notes by N. J. Dawood (Penguin Classics 1956, Fifth revised edition 1990). Copyright © N. J. Dawood, 1956, 1959, 1966, 1968, 1974, 1990, 1993, 1997, 1999, 2003; *The Story of the Merchant and the Demon* from the *The Arabian Nights: The Thousand and One Nights*, translated by Husain Haddawy. Copyright © 1990 by W. W. Norton & Company, Inc. Used by permission of W. W. Norton & Company, Inc.; Jalaloddin Rumi, *The Question*, from *Open Secret*, translated by Coleman Barks and John Moyne, by permission of Threshold Books; *The Tale of the Sands, The Blind Ones & the Matter of the Elephant*, and *The Ancient Coffer of Nuri Bey*, from *Tales of the Dervishes* by Idries Shah, Copyright © 1967 by Idries Shah. Used by permission of Dutton, a division of Penguin Group (USA), Inc., Courtesy Octagon Press Ltd.; *O My Lord If I Worship You from Fear of Hell* and *O My Lord, the Stars Glitter and the Eyes of Men are Closed* by Rabi'a the Mystic, translated by Willis Barnstone, from *A Book of Women Poets from Antiquity to Now* by Aliki Barnstone and Willis Barnstone, Copyright © 1980 by Schocken Books, a division of Random House, Inc.; *On Her Brother Sakhr*, by Al-Khansa, translated by Willis Barnstone, from *A Book of Women Poets from Antiquity to Now* by Aliki Barnstone and Willis Barnstone, Copyright © 1980 by Schocken Books, a division of Random House, Inc.

Chapter Seven
Selections from *Bhagavad-Gita*, translated by Barbara Stoler Miller, Copyright © 1986 by Barbara Stoler Miller. Used by permission of Bantam Books; Buddhist Texts: *Setting in Motion the Wheel of Truth, The Fire Sermon*, and *Universal Love*, from *What the Buddha Taught*, ed. Walpola Sri Rahula, Grove Press, NY, Copyright © 1959 by W.

Rahula. Used by permission of Grove/Atlantic; *The Ramayana* by Valmiki, *The Monk Who Left His Body Behind, The Girl Who Married a Snake*, and *Poor Blossom* from *Panchatantra*, translated by Arthur W. Ryder, (1964) by permission of The University of Chicago Press; Bhartrihari, selections from *Satakatrayam*, translated by Barbara Stoler Miller. Columbia University Press; Amaru, selections from *Amarusataka*, translated by Martha Ann Selby, University of Texas-Austin; from Mahadeviyakka, *What's Come Tomorrow, You Can Confiscate*, and *I Love the Handsome One* from *Speaking of Siva* translated by A. K. Ramanujan (Penguin Classics, 1973) Copyright © A. K. Ramanujan, 1973; Kalidasa, from Act I of *Sakuntala and the Ring of Recollection*, translated by Barbara Stoler Miller. *Theater of Memory: The Plays of Kalidasa*, Columbia University Press

Chapter Eight
Selected poems from the *Book of Songs*, translated by Arthur Waley (George Allen & Unwin, 1937 Harper Collins) © by permission of The Arthur Waley Estate; *Midnight Songs* from *The Book of Songs*, translated by Jeanne Larsen in Brocade River Poems, edited by Kang-I, Sun Chang, and Haun Saussy. © 1987 Princeton University Press. Reprinted by permission of Princeton University Press; From *The Analects* by Confucius, translated by D. C. Lau (Penguin Classics, 1979) Copyright © D. C. Lau, 1979; *The Tao Te Ching*, translated by Stephen Addiss; *The Return* by Tao Qian, translated by James Robert Hightower, *The Poetry of Tao Qian*, Oxford University Press; Wang Wei, *Villa on Chung-nan Mountain* and *Answering Magistrate Chang* from *An Anthology of Chinese Literature: Beginnings to 1911*, by Stephen Owen, editor and translator. Copyright © 1996 by Stephen Owen and the Council for Cultural Planning and Development of the Executive Yuan of the Republic of China, used by permission of W. W. Norton and Co.; Li Bai, *Dialogue in the Mountains*, and *Drinking Alone by Moonlight* from *The Great Age of Chinese Poetry: The High T'Ang*, translated by Stephen Owen, Yale University Press; Li Bai, *The Jewel Stairs' Grievance* and *The River Merchant's Wife: A Letter* by Li Po, translated by Ezra Pound from *The Translations of Ezra Pound*, Copyright © 1963 by Ezra Pound. Reprinted by permission of New Directions Publishing Corp.; Du Fu, *Spending the Night in a Tower by the River* and *A Guest Comes*, from *The Great Age of Chinese Poetry: The High T'Ang*, translated by Stephen Owen, Yale University Press; Du Fu, *Ballad of the Army Carts* and *Moonlit Night* translated by Vikram Seth in *Three Chinese Poets*. Translation © 1992. Reprinted by permission of Harper Collins Publishers; Li Ch'ing Chao (Li Qingzhao), *Southern Song*, translated by Burton Watson, from *The Columbia Book of Chinese Poetry: From Early Times to the Thirteenth Century*, Columbia University Press; Li Ch'ing Chao, *To the Tune Wulung Chun*, and *To the Tune Sheng sheng man*, translated by Pauline Yu. Comparative Literature Studies, Vol. 20, No. 1, © 1983 by The Pennsylvania State University. Reproduced by permission of the publisher

Chapter Nine
Kakinoto no Hitomaro, *After the Death of His Wife*, translated by Ian Levy from *The Ten Thousand Leaves: A translation of the Man'yoshu, Japan's Premier Anthology of Classical Poetry*, Vol. 1 (paperback) by Ian Hideo Levy. Reprinted with permission of University of Tokyo Press; Selected poems from Ono no Komachi from *The First Im-*

perial Anthology of Japanese Poetry, translated by Helen Craig McCullough, Copyright © 1985 by the board of trustees of the Leland Stanford, Jr. University; *Hateful Things* by Sei Shonagan from *The Pillow Book*, translated by Ivan Morris, Columbia University Press; Murasaki Shikibu, *The Shell of the Locust*, from the *Tale of the Genji*, translated by Edward G. Seidensticker © 1976 by Edward G. Seidensticker. Used by Permission of Random House, Inc.; *Essays in Idleness* by Yoshido Kenko, translated by Donald Keene. Published 1968 by Columbia University Press. Used with permission

Chapter Ten
Selected Mesoamerican Poems and Songs from *Precolumbian Literatures of Mexico*, by Miguel Leon-Portilla. Translated from the Spanish by Grace Lobanov and Miguel Leon-Portilla. Copyright © 1969 by the University of Oklahoma Press, Norman. Reprinted by permission; Part VI from *The Heights of Machu Picchu* by Pablo Neruda, translated by Nathaniel Tarn. Translation Copyright © 1966, renewed © 1994 by Nathaniel Tarn. Reprinted by permission of Farrar, Straus & Giroux, LLC.; *The Twins Defeat the Seven Macaw* and *Victory Over the Underworld* from *Popol Vuh: Selections*, translated by Dennis Tedlock, Copyright © 1985, 1996 by Dennis Tedlock. Reprinted with permission from Simon & Schuster Adult Publishing Group; *The Epic of Son-Jara: Fra-Digi Sisoko*, translated by John William Johnson, Indiana University Press

Chapter Eleven
From *Beowulf*, translated by Burton Raffel. Translation Copyright © 1963 by Burton Raffel. Used by permission of Viking Penguin, a division of Penguin Group (USA) Inc.; *The Approach of the Saracens* from *The Song of Roland*, translated by Frederick Goldin. Copyright © 1978 by

W. W. Norton & Company, Inc. Used by permission of W. W. Norton & Company, Inc.; Excerpt from Marie de France, *Bisclavret (the werewolf)* translation by Robert Hanning and Joan Ferrante from *The lais of Marie de France*. Baker Academic, a division of Baker Publishing Group; William IX, Duke of Auquitane, *Spring Song*, from *The Medieval Lyric*, translated by Peter Dronke, published by D. S. Brewer, Cambridge and Rochester, NY; Beatrice, Countess of Dia, *A Lover's Prize* from *The Medieval Lyric*, translated by Peter Dronke, published by D. S. Brewer, Cambridge and Rochester, NY; *The Art of Love*, by Daniel Amaut, from *The Lyrics of the Troubadour, Trouveres*, translated by Frederick Goldin, Copyright © 1973 by Frederick Goldin. Used by permission of Doubleday, a division of Random House, Inc.; Bertran de Born, *I Love the Glad Time of Easter*, translated by David Pike, Permission of David L. Pike; Bertran de Born, *Sestina: Altaforte*, translated by Ezra Pound, from *Personnae*. Copyright © 1926 by Ezra Pound. Reprinted by permission of New Directions Publishing Corp.

Chapter Twelve
St. Francis of Assisi, *The Canticle of the Creatures*, from *Lyric Poetry of the Italian Renaissance*, translated by Eleanor Turnbull. Copyright © 1954, Yale University Press; From the *Summa Theologica* by St. Thomas Aquinas, Benziger Brother Edition © 1947, McGraw Hill. Now defunct; From *The Divine Comedy* by Dante Alighieri, translated by John Ciardi, Copyright © 1954, 1957, 1959, 1960, 1961, 1965, 1967, 1970 by the Ciardi Family Publishing Trust, reprinted with permission of W. W. Norton & Co., Inc.; Bocaccio, from *The Decameron: First Day, Fourth Story*, and *Sixth Day, Seventh Story*, from *The Italian Renaissance Reader*, edited by Julia Conaway Bondanella & Mark Musa, translated by Julia Conaway Bondanella & Mark Musa, Copyright ©

1987 by Julia Conaway Bondanella & Mark Musa. Used by permission of Dutton Signet, a division of Penguin Group (USA) Inc.; *The Canterbury Tales: The General Prologue, Prologue to The Wife of Bath, Prologue to The Pardoner's Tale*, and *The Pardoner's Tale*, by Geoffrey Chaucer, translated by Nevill Coghill (Penguin Classics 1951, fourth revised edition 1977), Copyright © 1951 by Nevill Coghill, Copyright © the Estate of Nevill Coghill, 1958,1960, 1975, 1977; *The Books of the City of Ladies* by Christine de Pizan translated by Earl Jeffrey Richards. Copyright © 1982 by Persea Books, Inc. Reprinted by permission of Persea Books, Inc. (New York)

Chapter Thirteen
Pico della Mirandola, *Oration on the Dignity of Man*, Regnery Publishing; Petrarch: *Sonnet*, from *The Italian Renaissance Reader*, edited by Julia Conaway Bondanella & Mark Musa, translated by Julia Conaway Bondanella & Mark Musa, Copyright © 1987 by Julia Conaway Bondanella & Mark Musa. Used by permission of Dutton Signet, a division of Penguin Group (USA) Inc.; Francois Villon *Ballade of Forgiveness* from *The Mindreader*, English translation Copyright © by Richard Wilber, reprinted by permission of Harcourt; *I Live on This Depraved and Lonely Cliff* by Vittoria da Colonna, from *A Book of Women Poets from Antiquity to Now* by Aliki Barnstone and Willis Barnstone, Copyright © 1980 by Schocken Books, a division of Random House, Inc.; From *The Book of the Courtier* by Baldesar Castiglione, translated by George Bull, Penguin, 1967, Copyright © George Bull, 1967; From *The Prince* by Niccolo Machiavelli, translated by George Bull (Penguin Classics 1961, Third revised edition 1983) Copyright © George Bull, 1961, 1975, 1981, 1983; From *The Autobiography of Benvenuto Cellini* by Benvenuto Cellini, translated by George Bull (Penguin, 1956), translation © George Bull, 1956

Index